Observability For Legacy Systems

Methods and Solutions with OpenTelemetry and AIOps

Hyen Seuk Jeong

Apress®

Observability For Legacy Systems: Methods and Solutions with OpenTelemetry and AIOps

Hyen Seuk Jeong
Goyang-si, Gyeonggi-do, Republic of Korea

ISBN-13 (pbk): 979-8-8688-1687-1   ISBN-13 (electronic): 979-8-8688-1688-8
https://doi.org/10.1007/979-8-8688-1688-8

Copyright © 2025 by Hyen Seuk Jeong

This work is subject to copyright. All rights are reserved by the Publisher, whether the whole or part of the material is concerned, specifically the rights of translation, reprinting, reuse of illustrations, recitation, broadcasting, reproduction on microfilms or in any other physical way, and transmission or information storage and retrieval, electronic adaptation, computer software, or by similar or dissimilar methodology now known or hereafter developed.

Trademarked names, logos, and images may appear in this book. Rather than use a trademark symbol with every occurrence of a trademarked name, logo, or image we use the names, logos, and images only in an editorial fashion and to the benefit of the trademark owner, with no intention of infringement of the trademark.

The use in this publication of trade names, trademarks, service marks, and similar terms, even if they are not identified as such, is not to be taken as an expression of opinion as to whether or not they are subject to proprietary rights.

While the advice and information in this book are believed to be true and accurate at the date of publication, neither the authors nor the editors nor the publisher can accept any legal responsibility for any errors or omissions that may be made. The publisher makes no warranty, express or implied, with respect to the material contained herein.

    Managing Director, Apress Media LLC: Welmoed Spahr
    Acquisitions Editor: Anandadeep Roy
    Editorial Project Manager: Jessica Vakili
    Copy Editor: Kezia Endsley

Distributed to the book trade worldwide by Springer Science+Business Media New York, 1 New York Plaza, New York, NY 10004. Phone 1-800-SPRINGER, fax (201) 348-4505, e-mail orders-ny@springer-sbm.com, or visit www.springeronline.com. Apress Media, LLC is a Delaware LLC and the sole member (owner) is Springer Science + Business Media Finance Inc (SSBM Finance Inc). SSBM Finance Inc is a **Delaware** corporation.

For information on translations, please e-mail booktranslations@springernature.com; for reprint, paperback, or audio rights, please e-mail bookpermissions@springernature.com.

Apress titles may be purchased in bulk for academic, corporate, or promotional use. eBook versions and licenses are also available for most titles. For more information, reference our Print and eBook Bulk Sales web page at http://www.apress.com/bulk-sales.

Any source code or other supplementary material referenced by the author in this book is available to readers on GitHub. For more detailed information, please visit https://www.apress.com/gp/services/source-code.

If disposing of this product, please recycle the paper

To my most cherished and respected family

Table of Contents

About the Author xiii

Introduction xv

Chapter 1: RCA Essentials 1

    1.1. Introduction 1

    1.2. Root Cause Analysis (RCA) Process 19

        1.2.1. Identify the Problem Area 20

        1.2.2. Analyze Individual Requests 29

        1.2.3. Understand Low-Level Methods 36

    1.3. Observability Signals 46

        1.3.1. Logs 47

        1.3.2. RUM (Real User Monitoring) 55

        1.3.3. Profiles 69

        1.3.4. Debugging 77

        1.3.5. Events 78

        1.3.6. Root Cause Analysis Data Model 87

    1.4. Summary 92

Chapter 2: The RCA Approach 95

    2.1. Introduction 95

    2.2. Using Correlations 96

        2.2.1. From Distributed to System Traces 96

        2.2.2. From Events to Traces 98

        2.2.3. From Traces to Logs 99

        2.2.4. From Traces to Profiles 100

        2.2.5. From Logs to Profiles 101

        2.2.6. From Metrics to Traces 102

        2.2.7. From RUMs to Traces 102

        2.2.8. From Events to Anomalies 103

        2.2.9. From Logs to Traces 104

TABLE OF CONTENTS

    2.2.10. From Networks to Traces 105

    2.2.11. From Traces to Metrics 106

    2.2.12. From Traces to Service Maps 106

    2.2.13. From Service Maps to Metrics 107

    2.2.14. From Metrics to Logs 107

2.3. Grafana Correlations 108

    2.3.1. From Metrics to Traces 108

    2.3.2. From Traces to Metrics 110

    2.3.3. From Logs to Traces 114

    2.3.4. From Traces to Logs 115

2.4. Using a New Stack 116

    2.4.1. Introducing The New Stack (TNS) 117

    2.4.2. Configure TNS 120

    2.4.3. TNS Correlation 122

2.5. Grafana Observability 131

    2.5.1. Code Description 134

    2.5.2. System Configuration 136

    2.5.3. Setting Up Grafana 139

2.6. Running the o11y Shop Demo 141

    2.6.1. Demo Architecture 141

    2.6.2. Demo Process 142

    2.6.3. Code Description 143

    2.6.4. Install the Demo 146

    2.6.5. Checking Results in OpenSearch 148

    2.6.6. Summary 152

2.7. Dashboard Visualizations 152

    2.7.1. Polystats 153

    2.7.2. Service maps 155

    2.7.3. Histograms 156

    2.7.4. Heatmaps 156

    2.7.5. Time Series 157

    2.7.6. Flame graphs 158

    2.7.7. State Timelines 158

    2.7.8. Stats 160

TABLE OF CONTENTS

2.7.9. Traces 160

2.7.10. Annotations 160

2.7.11. Dashboard Development 161

2.8. Summary 169

Chapter 3: Trace-Centric RCA 171

3.1. Introduction 171

3.2. How Trace Works 173

    3.2.1. Context 180

    3.2.2. Propagators 182

    3.2.3. Propagating Trace 187

    3.2.4. Propagating Baggage 192

    3.2.5. OpenTracing Shim 194

3.3. Propagating Managed Services 196

    3.3.1. AWS CloudFront Demo 199

    3.3.2. GCP PubSub Demo 202

    3.3.3. Azure SQS Demo 211

3.4. Propagating Message Services 217

    3.4.1. Solace JMS Demo 219

    3.4.2. TIBCO JMS Demo 223

    3.4.3. MQTT Demo 225

    3.4.4. Kafka Demo 226

    3.4.5. Spring Cloud Stream Demo 229

3.5. Propagating an EAI Server 233

3.6. Propagation a Black Box System 237

3.7. Propagating Server Frameworks 239

    3.7.1. Commercial Observability SDK Trace Demo 241

    3.7.2. Micrometer Trace Demo 243

    3.7.3. Commercial Observability Demo 245

    3.7.4. WebSocket Demo 247

3.8. Using OpenTelemetry Extensions 252

    3.8.1. Bytecode Instrumentation Demo 254

    3.8.2. Extension Demo 257

    3.8.3. Debugging Extensions 263

vii

TABLE OF CONTENTS

- 3.9. Propagating Commercial Observability 264
  - 3.9.1. Automating Commercial Observability 266
  - 3.9.2. Agent Chaos 272
- 3.10. Summary 277

Chapter 4: Observability Practices by the Industry 279
- 4.1. Introduction 279
- 4.2. Observability in Banking 284
  - 4.2.1. The Bank Process 284
  - 4.2.2. Bank Legacy Systems 290
  - 4.2.3. Banking Demo Overview 316
  - 4.2.4. From RUM to API Server 323
  - 4.2.5. From API Server to Kafka 324
  - 4.2.6. From API Server to Microservices 325
  - 4.2.7. From API Server to EAI Server 328
  - 4.2.8. From EAI Server to Legacy System 328
  - 4.2.9. Transfer to Jaeger 330
- 4.3. Observability in Telecom 334
  - 4.3.1. Telecom Architecture 341
  - 4.3.2. Order Orchestration 352
  - 4.3.3. Network Provisioning 359
- 4.4. Observability in Online Games 364
  - 4.4.1. Game Operation 365
  - 4.4.2. Game Observability 370
- 4.5. Trading Observability 374
  - 4.5.1. Designing Ultra-Low Latency 375
  - 4.5.2. Ultra-Low Latency Reference 389
- 4.6. Summary 392

Chapter 5: OpenTelemetry Demo 393
- 5.1. Introduction 393
- 5.2. Overview 394
- 5.3. Observability Demo 398
  - 5.3.1. Profile Support 399
  - 5.3.2. OpenTelemetry Agent 405
  - 5.3.3. SLOs 405

- 5.3.4. OpenTelemetry Collector 414
- 5.3.5. RUM 415
- 5.3.6. Automated Instrumentation 418
- 5.3.7. Commercial Observability Demo 419
- 5.3.8. Live Debugging 421
- 5.3.9. Baggage Context 423
- 5.3.10. Span Attributes 424
- 5.3.11. Span Annotations 429
- 5.3.12. Promscale Kubernetes 432
- 5.3.13. Promscale SQL 439
- 5.4. Summary 441

Chapter 6: Infrastructure RCA 443

- 6.1. Introduction 443
- 6.2. System Traces 448
  - 6.2.1. KUtrace 452
  - 6.2.2. ftrace 471
  - 6.2.3. Kubeshark 476
  - 6.2.4. System Utilities 476
  - 6.2.5. How the Kernel Works 479
  - 6.2.6. Kernel Development 499
- 6.3. eBPF 504
  - 6.3.1. BCC and bpftrace 505
  - 6.3.2. PCP 521
- 6.4. Chaos Engineering 528
  - 6.4.1. Overview 528
  - 6.4.2. Demo 532
- 6.5. Network Observability 541
  - 6.5.1. Introduction 543
  - 6.5.2. Metrics 543
  - 6.5.3. Hubble 545
  - 6.5.4. The Grafana Plugin 548
- 6.6. The Cilium L7 Network 549
  - 6.6.1. Introduction 549
  - 6.6.2. Cilium Architecture 551
  - 6.6.3. Demo 552

TABLE OF CONTENTS

- 6.7. Cilium Add-ons 560
    - 6.7.1. Network Policies 561
    - 6.7.2. Multi-Cluster 566
    - 6.7.3. Service Meshes 567
    - 6.7.4. Ingress 568
- 6.8. Summary 569

Chapter 7: Anomaly Detection **571**
- 7.1. SQL Anomaly Detection 574
    - 7.1.1. Anomaly Detection Method 575
    - 7.1.2. Anomaly Types 577
- 7.2. Machine Learning Anomaly Detection 578
    - 7.2.1. Example 1: Internet of Things 581
    - 7.2.2. Example 2: Security 581
    - 7.2.3. Example 3: IT Operations 581
    - 7.2.4. Ratio Analysis 585
    - 7.2.5. Category Analysis 587
    - 7.2.6. Analyzing Populations 588
    - 7.2.7. Pattern Analytics 590
    - 7.2.8. Bucket Analysis 591
- 7.3. Analyzing the Results 592
    - 7.3.1. How to Analyze Your Results 593
    - 7.3.2. Results Analytics API 594
- 7.4. Configuring Anomaly Detection 599
    - 7.4.1. Configuring OpenSearch Anomaly Detection 599
    - 7.4.2. Detector Considerations 603
- 7.5. Summary 604

Chapter 8: Analyze RCA Data **607**
- 8.1. Analyzing SQL Data 611
    - 8.1.1. Time Windows 612
    - 8.1.2. Cumulative Values 613
    - 8.1.3. Seasonality Analysis 613
- 8.2. Using Promscale 614
    - 8.2.1. Promscale Features 616
    - 8.2.2. The Promscale Method 617

8.3. Promscale Demo	618
8.3.1. Metric SQL	619
8.3.2. Metric SQL Demo	620
8.3.3. Trace SQL	625
8.3.4. Trace SQL Demo	626
8.4. Summary	633
Chapter 9: Aggregate RCA Data	**635**
9.1. The Presto Case Study	635
9.1.1. Analytics Frameworks	638
9.1.2. OpenTelemetry Data Model	639
9.1.3. Presto's Features	643
9.1.4. Presto's Configuration	646
9.2. The Apache Druid Case Study	650
9.2.1. Schema-Less Searches	652
9.2.2. Index Methods	652
9.2.3. Rollups	652
9.2.4. Druid Components	652
9.2.5. Performance Improvements	656
9.2.6. Druid Observability	663
9.3. Java Observability	670
9.3.1. Java CPU Profile	671
9.3.2. The Java Virtual Machine	683
9.3.3. Coroutines	684
9.3.4. Implementing Threads	687
9.3.5. The Virtual Thread Demo	689
9.3.6. Spring WebFlux Demo	703
9.3.7. Non-Blocking Reactor Demo	704
9.4. Summary	711
Chapter 10: AIOps RCA	**713**
10.1. AIOps Limitations	714
10.1.1. Example 1	714
10.1.2. Example 2	715
10.1.3. Example 3	716

TABLE OF CONTENTS

- 10.2. AIOps Correlation 720
  - 10.2.1. AIOps Correlation Demo 724
- 10.3. IT Operation Data 729
  - 10.3.1. Using CMDB 737
  - 10.3.2. Autoscaling 742
- 10.4. The Failure List Data Model 755
  - 10.4.1. System Resource Failures 759
  - 10.4.2. Cluster Failures 763
  - 10.4.3. Server Framework Failures 765
  - 10.4.4. Legacy Middleware Failures 767
  - 10.4.5. Data Pipeline Failures 773
  - 10.4.6. Data Consistency Failures 774
  - 10.4.7. Microservices Failures 776
- 10.5. The Observability Failure Case 777
- 10.6. Retrieval-Augmented Generation (RAG) 782
  - 10.6.1. LangChain 783
  - 10.6.2. Searching Observability Data 788
  - 10.6.3. OpenSearch AIOps 797
  - 10.6.4. RAG's Advanced Features 833
  - 10.6.5. RCA Agents 844
- 10.7. Summary 887

Index 889

About the Author

Hyen Seuk Jeong has worked as a systems engineer at IBM, Accenture, and Oracle. He is an engineer who enjoys solving complex problems and developing solutions. As an SRE in complex banking and telecommunications, he has experienced many failures with observability. He recently began working on root cause analysis and automation through AI using agents and RAG.

Introduction

Writing this book was a challenge. The banking and telecom industries are technically constrained and demanding in terms of compliance and security. Rerunning many legacy applications and preparing demos from long ago is a challenge. I initially thought that E2E trace would not be technically possible, but the process of solving it provided a great opportunity to learn new skills. I believe that this book will be helpful to someone in a position similar to mine.

Although observability has matured and a variety of technologies are available, many observability and AI projects still fail.

- The banking and telecom industries have a lot of legacy, black box, and complicated processes that make it difficult for them to implement E2E observability. They often spend a lot, yet don't get the results they expect.

- The banking and telecom industries use AI technology to configure anomaly detection and AIOps, but the results are inaccurate and noisy, making them impractical.

- The data required for IT operations is missing, broken, or lacking relationships and structure, making it impossible to analyze and automate.

- There is a lot of unnecessary work for IT operations, including unnecessary data pipelines, API interfaces, and manual tagging, and technical debt continues to grow.

- AI agents and RAG are being applied to observability and IT operations, but no one has successfully implemented them yet.

If my project hadn't failed, I wouldn't have had the opportunity to publish this book. However, the reality is that most projects don't work out.

What This Book Covers

This book explains how to successfully configure complex E2E trace, minimize MTTR, analyze root cause in nanoseconds, and automate IT operations with AI agents and RAG.

- Using OpenTelemetry and commercial observability, the book provides a variety of demos. The demos run on Kubernetes to give readers a better understanding of observability.

INTRODUCTION

- This book explains the limitations of entities such as resources, and covers service and signals, such as traces, events, and logs. It describes 14 correlations between signals and entities to overcome limitations.

- The book explains the data models needed for observability and IT operations, including CMDB, to guide cost savings and build successful IT operations.

- It analyzes nearly 40 legacy systems, including IBM CICS, SAP, Siebel, and Tuxedo, and develops an OpenTelemetry agent and extension to apply E2E trace.

- It designs a data model for root cause analysis by correlating 12 signals. It analyzes approximately 400 failure cases and uses RAG to analyze root causes with AI.

- It identifies nanosecond-level waiting, interference, contention, and saturation in the CPU, network, and kernel, and quickly analyzes the root cause. It also creates 5,000 spans on a single transaction and visualizes them in a dashboard. It describes bytecode instrumentation and various kernel instrumentation methods.

- It demonstrates how to apply observability to diverse legacy and complex processes and automate operations using the AI agents and RAG technology.

Who This Book Is For

This book is ideal for developers, data engineers, SREs, architects, operators, and DevOps engineers.

It's also appropriate for system developers, infrastructure engineers, system architects, and Java developers who are enthusiastic about observability and want to implement it with legacy technology.

Potential readers include the following.

Developers

Developers who want to understand the internal operation of their systems and the root cause of a problem.

It often happens that something fails, but you don't understand why. Due to time and manpower constraints, the application is restarted and they move on without understanding the root cause. Willing or unwilling, developers and engineers cannot analyze root causes if they do not have knowledge of how internal systems process, or if the signals within their observability are not accurately collected.

The purpose of this book is to help engineers understand the internal operation of their systems, collect signals, and analyze root causes. That's why I go into great detail about kernel, VM, instrumentation, CPU, IO, trace, stack trace, and more.

This book is also for developers who are curious about observability best practices at tech companies and large enterprises.

INTRODUCTION

Developers love Google's SRE culture and practices and have a certain amount of admiration for SRE at tech companies. At my current job, my manager, team leader, and teammates are from Google SRE, so I have a great opportunity to understand and learn about SRE from the perspective of people from tech companies.

What I've learned from working with them is that, like everything, there are pros and cons. It's true that legacy is the most important core system, so there are many constraints to implementing observability. The difference is the complexity of the domain and business processes that we don't have in tech companies.

Data Engineers

Data engineers who want to automate observability and understand AIOps.

From a data perspective, observability is big data, and it's a great place to apply AI. It's a transitional time, and both open source and commercial observability offerings have limited capabilities in terms of data utilization. At the same time, companies are investing heavily in emerging technologies like AIOps. My experience with commercial AIOps deployments is that they are not effective in terms of analyzing root causes and reducing noise in operations. AI, as it is currently evolving, is still far from being cost-effective, but given the evolution of the technology, it is worth staying interested and learning.

Analyzing and aggregating observability data is something developers need to understand. The RAG, AI agents, and ML described in this book are highly accurate and successfully produce results.

SREs

Site reliability engineers (SREs) who want to quickly identify root causes and understand solutions.

An important part of operations is automating systems and resolving issues quickly. The ability to identify and resolve problems is especially important for SREs. It is not easy to recognize failures quickly and come up with solutions in a situation where development languages and types of problems vary and propagate.

Recently published SRE books have focused more on the macro view than on the practical details that help solve problems, and it would be helpful for many SREs to have a book that explains approaches and solutions to the various errors encountered in practice. To understand and solve the problem, traces are discussed in detail. Traces consist of two types: distributed traces and system traces. My approach is to start with traces, as they are the most basic signals and the starting point for observability, and then gradually expand to other signals. Despite the complexity and difficulty of traces, it is necessary to configure distributed traces across the board and system traces at the system-lease level to troubleshoot.

Operators in Banking and Telecom

Operators in banking, telecom, and other organizations with a lot of legacy who want to bring in new observability.

It's true that SRE cultures are often introduced in the context of tech companies, but tech companies are the minority of organizations, with more observability examples coming from traditional banking, telecom, and manufacturing companies. It's important to consider whether the SRE culture of tech companies is applicable to larger organizations and industries with more legacy.

Organizing observability as a cross-cutting concern is difficult and progress is slow. This is because legacy breaks the propagation of traces, and agents are often difficult to configure and not technically supported. This book describes a variety of middleware. Since legacy is often connected through EAI servers and message servers, this book shows you how to instrument this middleware to configure E2E observability. It describes various legacy applications, such as SAP ERP and Tuxedo, and explains how to configure observability in legacy.

Architects

Architects who want to technically advance observability and understand its business value.

In this book, I divided observability into three phases:

- Configure application and infrastructure observability and leverage it for root cause analysis.

- Automate the analysis and aggregation of observability data and use AIOps to analyze root causes and predict failures.

- Deliver reliable services to customers to minimize losses from failures and use observability to improve the business and create opportunities.

Looking at observability as a tool for business improvement and opportunity is new. This is because observability has only been considered in the realm of systems—applications, kernels, and VM. Gone are the days when observability was viewed solely from a technical and cost perspective. In the future, observability can be utilized as a tool to further support and align with the business and increase revenue.

I explain how to move beyond root cause analysis and operational automation to observability that can lead the business and deliver value to product owners and executives. In the future, expect observability to expand, supporting both business and technology. This book will help you see what's possible.

DevOps Engineers

DevOps engineers torn between open source and commercial observability.

While I personally prefer open source, many companies are paying tens of billions of dollars for commercial observability. They want to minimize failures and resolve issues quickly, even at a high cost, because failures can be costly to their business. They're paying a lot of money, so they need to prove value. Observability is not just a tool for SRE, it's a tool used across the organization with developers, and they are looking for ways to reduce costs and increase developer productivity.

Open source is difficult to support productively and externally, so internal SRE capabilities are critical. The main disadvantage is that it is difficult to support the rapid growth of the business and the time-to-market schedule. It takes time and patience from many people to develop internal technical capabilities, know-how, and trial and error. It's a mistake to choose open source observability just to save money. There are pros and cons.

CHAPTER 1

RCA Essentials

1.1. Introduction

This book explains how to analyze root causes and uses observability and AIOps. There are differences in terminology:

- *Root cause analysis* is the process of identifying problems, understanding their causes, and proposing solutions. It focuses on the problem.
- *Observability* is the process of correctly defining signals, collecting, transforming, storing, and analyzing signals, and the series of processes used by the SRE (site reliability engineer). It focuses on signals.
- AIOps refers to the use of AI based on data to automate IT operations. It focus on automation.

Although there are some terminological differences, the goal is the same—to improve the reliability of services and reduce costs. More specifically, to:

- Reduce losses from failures with observability.
- Improve and tune performance to reduce costs.
- Optimize observability to reduce costs.
- Automate IT operations to reduce operational costs.
- Improve reliability to provide stable services.
- Leverage collected events for marketing and increased sales.

This book describes the various errors and failures you will encounter in IT operations, including commercial legacy, Linux kernel, system resources, and large cluster issues.

You will learn to accurately match the relationships between business processes, applications, and system resources and clearly identify any problems.

For example, a one-second delay experienced by a user is composed of multiple microsecond delays occurring in the application. What are multiple microsecond delays?

CHAPTER 1   RCA ESSENTIALS

Microsecond delays in an application are composed of multiple nanosecond delays occurring in the system resources. Multiple nanosecond delays can be clearly identified.

The book is organized into four topics: observability theory, application observability, infrastructure observability, and utilizing observability data.

Part 1, "RCA theory," includes the following:

- Chapter 1, RCA Essentials: This chapter analyzes the limitations and problems of existing observability and the root cause analysis methods. It explains a successful root cause analysis definition.

- Chapter 2, RCA Approach: Most of the observability dashboards and alerts are inaccurate and fail. This chapter explains the causes of failure and solutions.

Part 2, "Application RCA," includes the following:

- Chapter 3, Trace-Centric RCA: When building observability, there is a problem where the trace is broken or logs are conflicted in the server framework and message server. This chapter analyzes a practical correlation example in Grafana and OpenSearch.

- Chapter 4, Observability Practices in the Industry: This chapter explains complex trace reference in banking, telecom, trading, and gaming. Through practical examples, you learn about the advantages and direction of observability.

- Chapter 5, OpenTelemetry Demo: This chapter introduces new techniques and augments the observability described so far.

Part 3, "Infrastructure RCA," includes the following:

- Chapter 6, Infrastructure RCA: Traditional infrastructure observability cannot analyze the root cause. This chapter explains how to understand the existing problem and configure new system traces and profiles for successful root cause analysis.

- Chapter 7, Anomaly Detection: Traditional anomaly detection is mostly unsuccessful because it has low accuracy and includes a lot of noise. The chapter explains the existing anomaly detection problem and explains how to configure successful anomaly detection.

This book focuses more on infrastructure than on applications.

Part 4, "Leveraging Observability Data," includes the following:

- Chapter 8, Analyze RCA Data: The advantage of commercial observability is that observability data can be analyzed in detail. This chapter explains how to analyze observability data.

CHAPTER 1　RCA ESSENTIALS

- Chapter 9, Aggregate RCA Data: Commercial observability cannot analyze the root causes of complex clusters. This chapter explains how to successfully analyze the root cause in large clusters through Java observability.

- Chapter 10, AIOps Data: This chapter analyzes why AIOps for commercial observability fails to perform root cause analysis. It proposes a procedure and process for successful AIOps implementation.

This book does root cause analysis using an approach that hasn't been described in any book. If you understand the concepts in this book, you will be able to get a clear answer to the cases outlined in Table 1-1.

Table 1-1. Three Goals Covered in This Book

Goal	Description
Configure E2E trace for applications and infrastructure.	New wireline activation in telecom, ultra-low latency in online games, and fund transfers to a bank are complicated processes. For example, when you click the fund transfer button in the mobile bank app. • 30 legacy servers are connected • Over 500 requests and responses processed • Fund transfer transactions are completed in less than one second
	I denote 500 requests as a span, which I refer to as an E2E distributed trace. When analyzed at the system resource level, each span is subdivided into 100 system traces. I subdivide the fund transfer transaction into 5,000 (500 x 100) spans and analyze the nanosecond delay for each of the 5,000 spans within the total process time of 1 second.
	This book will help you understand how to visualize 5,000 spans, measure delay, and perform root cause analysis.
	You can configure traces that never break.
Quickly identify failures and reduce problem resolution time.	A new activation order for a bundled product in telecom is more complex and difficult than a fund transfer in a bank. It has roughly 40+ legacy servers and over 5,000 spans are generated in the system trace. If there is a delay, is it possible to clearly identify where the delay is occurring? How long does it take to identify the delay? The distributed and system traces from single button clicks can be collected in the thousands to accurately identify where the delays occur.
	Due to black boxes and technical limitations in legacy, the traces can be interrupted. The SRE has to come up with a number of solutions.

(*continued*)

3

CHAPTER 1 RCA ESSENTIALS

Table 1-1. (*continued*)

Goal	Description
Configure AI-based automated observability.	The kernel has more than 1,000 events and more than 10,000 methods. For example, the 5,000 spans described by the telecom order process contain a large number of events and methods, and you need to use a system trace to accurately identify the event and method in the sections where the delay occurred and measure the 99th percentile.
	By connecting events in your business, distributed traces in your applications, and system traces in your infrastructure, you can dramatically reduce the time it takes to identify and resolve failures.
	It provides eight signals, 14 correlations, 300 failure cases, 40 observability failures, and 40 legacies. To automate this, AIOps will enable root cause analysis and automation using ML and LLM.

This book describes new observability and approaches that do not exist in traditional monitoring:

- Traditionally, we use metrics and logs, but now we can use events, traces, and profiles to organize observability.

- The business is more complex than technology and applications. I explain how to easily integrate your business with observability.

- Weaknesses in observability include black boxes and various legacies that are difficult to instrument.

- You'll learn about the internal behavior of the agent and how to debug it, as well as develop an agent.

- You'll learn about system traces and relate them to distributed traces. Observability is divided into two types—application and infrastructure. You'll learn about the correlation between the two.

- You'll also learn why root cause analysis, anomaly detection, and AIOps fail, and I'll suggest successful solutions. This book analyzes and aggregates observability data and uses AIOps to automate and optimize observability.

The process of troubleshooting a problem can be summarized in three steps. If you don't understand the root cause, you can't come up with a solution, which could lead to similar problems in the future.

1. Identify the problem.

2. Understand the cause.

3. Provide the solution.

The term *kernel* is specific to Linux, but I use it as a universal term for OS, including Windows, UNIX, and Linux.

This book does not detail specific technology solutions. Solutions vary by language, OS, application, and infrastructure. It is important to find problems quickly and understand what is causing them. To do this, I focus on the observability of infrastructure and applications.

Observability in a tech company is a more comprehensive and realistic and many books have been written in this vein. However, they lack practical demos and examples, or they focus on tech companies like Google, Facebook, and Netflix. They are not suitable for general domains. Many organizations have the following problems:

1. They are hard to collaborate and have a manual organizational culture.
2. Their processes are complex and poorly documented.
3. They avoid risk and reduce costs.
4. They are hard to change, and they have to consider legacy maintenance.

It's not appropriate to describe observability in technical theory only, ignoring the real-world challenges.

There's been a lot of interest in agents lately. Agents will be a key technology in the future. Most of the time, you can use agents that are already developed, but you can also develop them if necessary. This book describes two types of agents:

- Agents that automate OpenTelemetry instruments. If the instrument fails, additional spans can be generated using the OpenTelemetry API and bytecode instrument.
- For RAG implementations, this is the agent that automates the interface for the Vector database and the LLM. The agent contains a variety of tools to be developed.

Just as Kubernetes operators automate resource provisioning, agents are useful for automation. There will be a lot of demand for agent development in the future.

Focus more on the problem, cause, error, and failure than on building a large-scale system. There is no dependency on a specific observability solution. In the past, performance tuning for WAS (Web Application Server), Oracle databases, and Java was a popular and interesting topic. The recent development trend is no longer dependent on a small number of commercial software programs, but on various open source products. This book differs from existing approaches in the following ways:

- Uses a message server, an EAI server, and various legacies other than the WAS and Oracle databases.
- Develops in a variety of development languages, (e.g., Java, Golang, and Python).
- Configures observability in the new cloud and Kubernetes infrastructure.
- Describes non-blocking, coroutine, and asynchronous workloads in microservices.

CHAPTER 1   RCA ESSENTIALS

Observability is different from past performance tuning methods. It assumes that the expected number of users and the deployed system resources are fixed. TPS is a basic performance metric. This book does not discuss these SLOs in detail. What is clear is that TPS is not measured as critically as it once was. From an operational perspective, it is more important to minimize MTTR by reducing cost, minimizing overhead on system resources, and improving service reliability.

This book helps you think differently and present an alternative approach:

- It's natural to deploy dozens of times a day, but this book doesn't encourage that fantasy. It is appropriate for services to run on a set schedule and procedure and for applications and infrastructure to run reliably with as little variability as possible. Minimizing MTTR is the latest trend, but you need to minimize failures through robust testing and deployment.

- There isn't a lot of emphasis on SLO. The one root cause analysis dashboard, as described in this book, is sufficient. If you can complete one dashboard, it is enough to answer your SLO. The book provides clear guidelines for SLO and the dashboard.

- While it's important to get experience with high-volume traffic and large-scale clusters, I think the fundamentals of kernel, CPU, IO, and other topics you learn in computer science are more important. If you don't understand the basics, it's hard to properly control the complexity of your environment.

SREs must improve the reliability of the various middleware, database, legacy, and system resources used in production. More than 300 failure cases are described in this book. Observability signal data is often inaccurate. Failures can be caused by misconfigurations, delays in processing high volumes of traffic, or lack of resources. This book describes various practices to improve observability. It also provides best practices to ensure that observability is successfully configured within your organization.

Backend developers value a high traffic experience, but as an SRE, high traffic should not be a high priority. There is easy provisioning of the resources using the cloud and elasticity for growing loads using Kubernetes autoscale. System resources are always changing and dynamic. This requires a different way of operating; it's hard to respond effectively with traditional monitoring.

1. There are over 10,000 microservices developed in multiple languages.

2. The number of resources registered in the multi-cloud is hundreds of thousands.

3. Mainframe, SAP, and dozens of other legacy and black boxes exist in the backend.

While performance degradation and issues with individual microservices are important, it's more important to manage critical failures and errors before individual performance problems. There are easy and flexible ways to respond to performance degradation or increased traffic, such as increasing resources or scaling out with autoscale. This is also why traditional performance methodologies are not suitable for production today. Even if traffic is unpredictable, the goal of observability is to ensure that services are delivered reliably, not to focus on performance problems, as in the past. While I agree with the theoretical and deep academic achievements of traditional monitoring, I explain the differences between observability and traditional monitoring and elaborate on the future direction of observability and SRE.

As services become more distributed and dynamic, rather than static systems like in the past, it is less a problem of performance and more a requirement of how stable and reliable systems are built and operated. This includes the potential risks of having a system that is distributed like microservices, dynamic like clouds and Kubernetes, or open source, where bugs and exceptions are likely to occur at any time. Legacy and rapidly changing, old technologies have created a complex situation with increasing technical debt.

You need to understand the difference between traditional monitoring and new observability. You need to be willing to improve on the old ways and embrace new technologies and methods. This is not to say that the performance theory and monitoring approaches of the past are wrong, but they need to be improved for today's observability. And beyond observability, the goal should be advanced and automated operations.

There are many tools to analyze performance or understand problems, but it is difficult to configure observability in complex productions with specific CLIs and utility tools alone. It's not a tool that one person uses. It's a tool that everyone uses together, and it's a collaborative process to find improvements and continuously evolve. A few good SREs can't solve all the problems, but together with the developer architect, everyone needs to understand and work together to improve reliability.

The purpose of observability is not a specific solution such as Grafana or OpenSearch but a root cause analysis performed by the SRE. The main purpose is to find problems quickly and understand the exact root cause.

This book focuses less on building observability and more on the failure you'll encounter when operating production and approaches for root cause analysis.

This book also analyzes observability in detail at a low level using eBPF and Java Agent and applies AI technologies such as anomaly detection, AIOps, and generative AI to automate. By using multiple technologies, you can learn various root cause analysis methods according to your environment and preferences.

After reading this book, you will understand how AI can be used to advance RCA. The process of discovering a problem, understanding the problem, and solving the problem is explained with detailed demonstrations in each chapter.

I organize application observability, and then root cause analysis in infrastructure observability. In Figure 1-1, the horizontal line represents application observability. The vertical line represents infrastructure observability. The horizontal shouldn't break in the middle, and the vertical should go down deep.

- **Horizontal:** This refers to the application and means that the trace can be broken in the middle or connected by correlation with event or log. You construct an E2E trace to understand the process and the 99th percentile latency for each section. Then you identify the method causing the latency with the profile where the latency is identified.

- **Vertical:** This refers to infrastructure and means that it should be able to identify lower-level latency such as the kernel or system resources. You configure a system trace to understand the process of system resources and the 99th percentile latency of each section. You then check the eBPF profile of the section where the latency is identified to find the method that causes the latency.

For example, if you look at the arrow on the left in Figure 1-1, the failure occurs on the API server. Analyzing the cause, you will find that the file descriptor and epoll configuration are incorrect in the kernel parameter.

Looking at the right-most down arrow, you can see that the latency is caused by the message server. After analyzing the cause, it's determined that there's a bug in the kernel's timer interrupt.

Application observability organizes distributed trace across E2E; infrastructure observability organizes system traces across various system resources. Note the correlation between application observability and infrastructure observability.

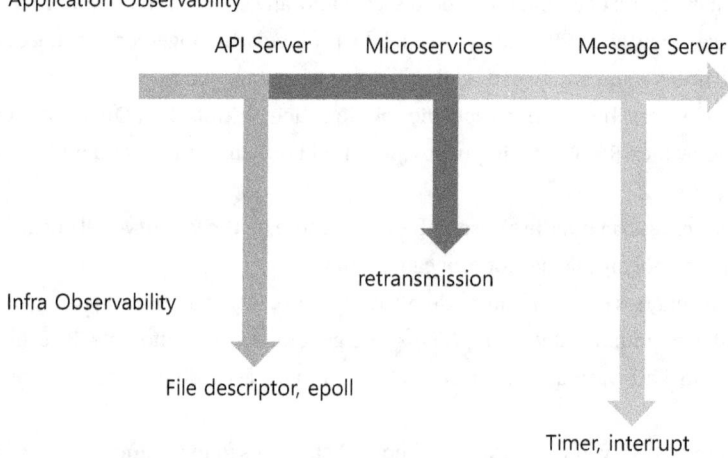

Figure 1-1. Process for application and infrastructure observability

The goal of this book is to get you to a point where observability is not just a technology to monitor but a tool used to collaborate, improve IT reliability, and eventually increase revenue.

First of all, configure application and infrastructure observability, and finally configure AIOps. A rough data flow of observability data using AIOps is shown in Figure 1-2.

There are many different pipelines in commercial observability:

- Observability, which primarily uses a time series, has the advantage of real time, but it is difficult to construct complex queries.

- Pipelines that ingest various data and load it into a data lake are not real time and have a delay, but it is possible to configure complex queries.

CHAPTER 1 RCA ESSENTIALS

- There is also a separate AIOps pipeline for failure determination and root cause analysis. In order to determine the root cause of an error, algorithms and various data must be comprehensively analyzed. This is one of the fundamental features of AIOps. When failure occurs, the AIOps pipeline analyzes the root cause and generates a result.

Figure 1-2 includes three types of pipelines, with minor differences from the commercial observability option:

- **Observability:** Saves any unstructured data whose internal data type is unknown. Grafana LGTM loads signals into object storage, which is difficult to process with ETL.

- **Data analysis:** This second pipeline handles metrics and traces and uses Promscale and Druid. Analytics and aggregation pipelines are structured data.

- **ML, LLM:** This third pipeline handles searching, anomaly detection, and AIOps. It processes logs using OpenSearch.

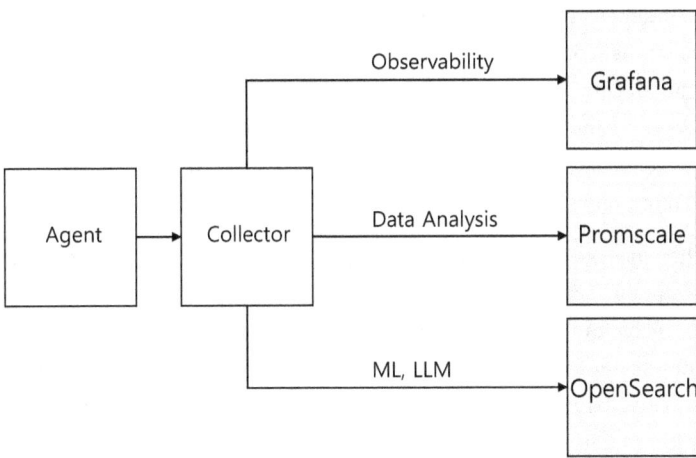

Figure 1-2. Aligning observability with AIOps

To implement the architecture shown in Figure 1-2, you need to build a pipeline of observability and AIOps systems.

1. Think about how to identify problems and understand their causes, as well as how to understand the signals generated by the system. This direction is consistent with the OpenTelemetry roadmap. Currently, OpenTelemetry has also defined traces and metrics, is enhancing the logs, and has a roadmap to implement RUM (real user monitoring) and profiles. While I describe various correlations, it is inefficient to use all of them, and you need to design your root cause analysis process to fit your requirements.

2. Analyze observability data using SQL. There are several ways to perform root cause analysis. The most basic way is to visualize the data on a screen, such as using a dashboard. Readers who are familiar with SQL data can write their own query to understand and solve problems. Senior SREs are familiar with root cause analysis using SQL to develop procedure for various automation and operational needs. The various signals that are collected are observability data. It is important to understand the process of searching (regular expression and algorithmic search, semantic search), analyzing (using GROUP BY, look up, join, and filter), and aggregating (multi-dimensional OLAP) various signals. Queries allow you to retrieve the metrics and traces data you want using standard SQL without complex preprocessing. Anomaly detection and AIOps are modern methods of root cause analysis. AIOps is applied to the collected log, metric, and trace data to automate root cause analysis.

3. As cloud systems become mainstream, Linux has become the most common and popular OS. While Golang and Python are utilized for specific purposes, Java is popular in enterprise applications. It is important to have an accurate understanding of the Linux kernel and Java virtual machine, including how to instrument them. Without a deep understanding of the Java virtual machine, it is difficult to identify problems in enterprise application and understand their cause. A promising recent Linux observability technology is eBPF, which can analyze events in the Linux kernel and has been actively applied to networking, observability, and security.

4. Since there has been no case study until now, this book presents an architecture with a concrete demonstration of how to implement E2E observability. It explains realistic observability solutions for the bank, trading, and telecom industries, including legacy, and for online games without legacy. You'll use microservices to implement complex two PC, Saga pattern, event sourcing, and integration with legacy systems.

5. This book describes various microservices patterns in practice and explains how observability is being applied. It includes various demos of API servers, message servers, EAI servers, batch processing systems, and legacy solutions.

Banking, telecom, and legacy organizations are adopting commercial observability and working to consolidate various observability systems around commercial observability. By operating various observability systems, SREs lack expertise, and it becomes difficult to organize E2E trace. It is difficult to instrument due to legacy issues, and even if you use commercial observability, you will experience various constraints. It is important to find a proven commercial observability that is suitable for your environment, and even more important to get support from a commercial observability consultant to solve problems together.

Over time, the scope and scale of observability are growing. A handful of talented engineers and open source solutions alone are not enough to run a complex and massive system that includes cloud, Kubernetes, and legacy systems. It requires a high degree of automation, shared experience, and a level of service and consulting to back it all up. While all of this may be possible with open source alone, it is not easy to provide reliable service with minimal failures in a rapidly changing business environment. If you don't achieve a high level of reliability in a short period of time with open source, commercial observability is a good way to achieve your goals in the short term.

Data analysts say that the value of data only increases when disparate data is correctly combined. Logs, metrics, and traces are simply disparate data that has not yet been combined. They need to be combined in order to better utilize observability and discover new value. This book explains the various correlations.

- You'll implement a static correlation using the ID of each signal, such as trace and session IDs.

- Later in this book, you'll learn about the dynamic correlation in AIOps implementations, which means that you can use machine learning to implement correlations between variables based on statistics.

The role of the SRE is to respond to failures. Improving architecture and tuning performance are important, but it's especially important to identify failures and resolve them. Improving reliability requires a variety of improvements and requires thinking about architecture, processes, and more. Even if there are problems with the code due to poor development, the goal should be to improve reliability and reduce MTTR. While it's important to prevent a few microservices from going wrong and causing problems for a particular service, it's more important to prevent an API server and database from going down, causing all the services to stop working. SREs should strive to improve reliability.

There are many ways to reduce the cost of observability.

Logs:

- Change the log level.

- Reduce indexing.

- Optimize the use of buckets, tiering, and partitions.

- Avoid full scans and apply multi-tenant instead.

Metrics:

- Increase the scraping interval.

- Add a filter to the pipeline.

- Reduce resolution.

- Reduce retention.

CHAPTER 1 RCA ESSENTIALS

Profiles:

- Reduce sampling.
- Choose methods that are executed less often.
- Minimize dependency.

Traces:

- Reduce sampling.
- Filter out specific spans, so they don't collect.

It's not a good practice to collect all signals, but it's never too late to collect them when you need them. For example, you might experience unexpected delays in your test environment, and it's hard to analyze the cause. You can enable system trace for a while, analyze all the signals in detail, come up with a solution, and then disable it again.

Productions can be used similarly. If you can't find the root cause and it's likely to recur, you should enable system trace to monitor the issue around the clock. If you don't operate elastically, you'll spend too much, so be careful.

You can use open source to build observability, but it requires a long-term investment to hire and train people. With commercial observability, you can build observability in a short period of time. If observability is not just a means of solving a problem but will be extended to collaboration, business, AI automation, and other aspects, it is worth paying more and investing in commercial observability. This book also aims to explain how to use observability for more than just solving problems. If the current system is unstable, failures are frequent, and the financial losses are high, it is not easy to plan for the future and make incremental and continuous observability improvements. Management wants immediate results, and they don't know how long they'll be able to work. In these situations, it's better to invest in commercial observability that can deliver results now rather than using open source.

If your goal is to achieve a high level of observability, it is difficult and time-consuming to reach a high level with open source alone. On an observability maturity stage of 0 to 10, it takes more than two years to reach stage 3 with open source. With Datadog and Dynatrace commercial observability, you can start at stage 5, saving time and money. I recommend trying a mature solution. Observability is not as simple as it sounds.

Root cause analysis is the process of minimizing MTTR, narrowing the scope of the problem, and finding the original or initial cause of the problem. Once the root cause is analyzed and understood, solutions, improvements, and tuning can be applied. Root cause analysis is not only necessary when an application is slowing down or failing. The scope of root cause analysis is not limited to infrastructure and application.

It's common for observability systems to be built separately. However, to be efficient and successful, they all need to be connected into one unified platform. Once integrated, correlations between observability signals need to be defined.

CHAPTER 1 RCA ESSENTIALS

To quickly understand signals and apply them to the dashboard, alerts, SLOs, and more, you need to organize the following relationships:

- Correlations between signals
- Relationships between businesses, applications, and infrastructures
- Structures and relationships between IDs

The correlation between the eight signals can be represented as shown in Figure 1-3. Note the 14 correlations between the signals.

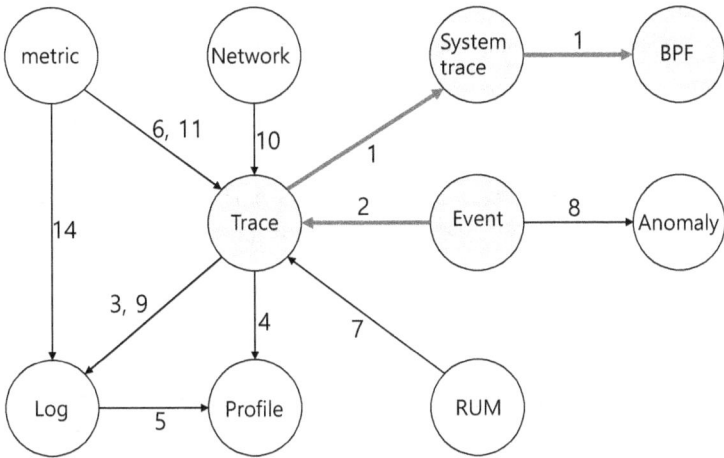

Figure 1-3. *The correlation between application observability signals*

At the center of the various signals is the trace. A *trace* is an individual transaction, and a trace is associated with a log, a profile, a metric, and RUM (real user monitoring). It is important to continuously improve traces to correlate other signals.

Although there are complex and diverse correlations, I explain how to improve reliability and reduce MTTR using events, distributed traces, and system traces.

Figure 1-3 shows the correlation between the signals used in application observability, to which signals from infrastructure observability can be added.

In general, a trace refers to a distributed trace. This book categorizes traces into distributed traces and system traces. Distributed traces are used for application observability, and system traces are used for infrastructure observability.

Figure 1-3 does not include infrastructure observability. Signals for infrastructure observability are different from application observability signals.

There are many correlations, but two signals are critical:

- Events and distributed traces work together to correlate business and IT.
- You correlate applications and infrastructure by correlating distributed traces and system traces.

13

CHAPTER 1 RCA ESSENTIALS

When correlations are well organized, even complex trace with thousands of spans can be easily identified for root cause analysis. For example, there are a few failures, starting with the event, then a distributed trace, system trace, and eBPF, and correlation should be used to reduce MTTR. Configuring correlation does not require any modifications to the code, just a configuration.

The S in SRE stands for service, and service refers to applications and microservices. System resources are infrastructure, and SREs should manage services first. If there are 200 microservices, there is no problem, but if there are more than 10,000 microservices, 100 legacy systems, and the business is complex, such as in bank and telecom, it is not easy to resolve failures at the service level. Although the problem can be identified by a distributed trace, it is difficult to distinguish whether it is a business error or a technical error, and it is impossible to determine the loss and impact of a failure without understanding the business. To solve this problem, you need to use events. The dashboard should be configured to include multiple traces within each event.

To elaborate on this correlation, events are used to correlate business and IT and traces are used to correlate application and infrastructure. The SRE must understand not only applications and microservices but also the business and system resources, define the relationship between them, and explain them in some way to the developers and stakeholders. Figure 1-4 shows how to analyze the root cause in this way.

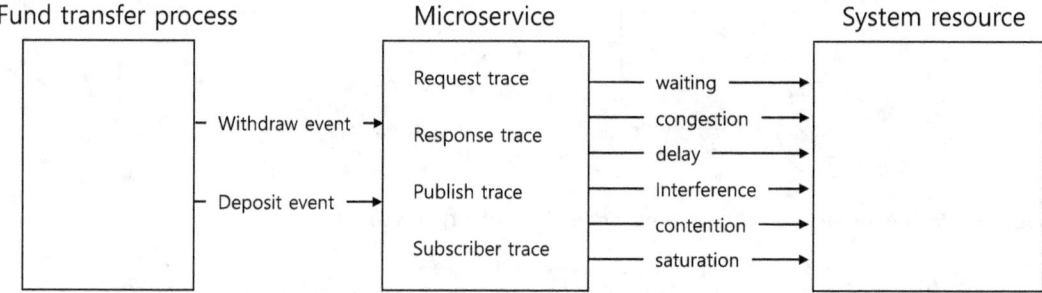

Figure 1-4. Aligning businesses, applications, and infrastructures

You need to develop dashboards to understand the business and improve observability. But before developing a dashboard, you need to understand the structure and relationship using IDs.

For example, consider this fund transfer process:

- The payment ID captured by an event within a single transaction are the same. A single payment ID contains multiple trace IDs.

- The trace ID contains multiple span IDs. The span ID contains thread IDs, which contain multiple system traces, with the exception of non-blocking and virtual threads.

- Define the filter on the dashboard in the following order: user journey name (fund transfer), payment ID, trace ID, span ID, thread ID, and system trace ID. The dashboard displays the latency and errors of the distributed and system trace in chronological order. You can further configure the eBPF dashboard.

- If the system trace has large latency or failures, use `ftrace` and `strace` to check the method and eBPF to measure the 99th percentile. Use PCP to configure the 99th percentile dashboard.

It is possible to have 5,000 or more traces in a system and present them in a dashboard without interruption. This book explains how to organize these systems and visualize them in a dashboard. Once the data is organized and visualized in this way, the next step is to automate it using AI.

A number of identifiers are created: session ID, order ID, request ID, and trace ID. The relationship between these identities is shown in Figure 1-5.

Understanding the ID structure is important. SREs need to understand the approximate ID structure of a user's journey and be able to structure them as shown in Figure 1-5. This is because this is how signals will be collected, data will be stored, and data will be retrieved and analyzed. This is necessary to create deep insights and analytics. Starting with the business context and ID you have identified, you will define the correlations between application services and system resources.

Figure 1-5 displays the structure and relationship between IDs. Once you understand the ID structure, you don't need to modify the code to develop the dashboard. Time-consuming preprocessing is also unnecessary. You can avoid a lot of time developing new code and preprocessing when you understand the ID structure.

- Commercial observability options have sophisticated data modeling of the signal. These include multiple distributed traces within an event. This configuration makes it easy to measure service reliability and improve MTTR.

- Open source configurations include system trace within distributed trace. With this configuration, you can quickly perform root cause analysis.

- Commercial offerings have their limitations, and it's important to use open source to fill in the gaps.

CHAPTER 1 RCA ESSENTIALS

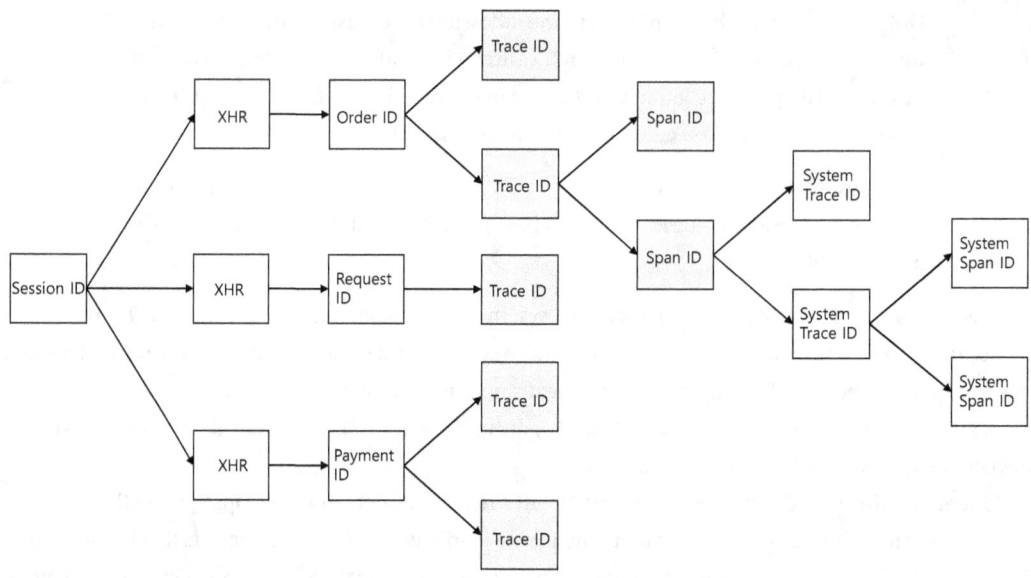

Figure 1-5. *Structure and relationships between IDs*

Browsing a catalog is a simple task. A single trace ID is all that's needed. But placing an order is more complicated. When placing an order, multiple buttons are clicked and multiple trace IDs are created. To combine multiple trace IDs, you use events.

Figure 1-5 illustrates the drawbacks of trace. The trace ID is in the middle, so without clear context before and after the trace, it is impossible to understand the root cause from the trace alone.

I tried to match the internal structure of the eight signals with the important ID. This means that observability can integrate technology and business processes. This is consistent with the direction of this book. The eight signals and 14 correlations are complex and overwhelming. In practice, you'll refine your signals and architecture over a long period of time.

It is important to understand the overall scope. There is no need to rush, just take it one step at a time.

Data is stored according to the following structure. Once you understand the structure of your data, you need to implement aggregation and filtering.

- The session ID contains multiple request IDs (e.g., change personal information), order IDs, and payment IDs. Once you access the web or app and start a session, you use the session ID to request a specific transaction.

- It is possible to aggregate request IDs and order IDs based on a specific session ID.

- Events can capture the message header and body in any section of business process.

- Order IDs contain multiple trace IDs, and it is possible to aggregate a trace ID by its order ID.

- Trace IDs contain span IDs, and aggregating the span ID within a trace ID is possible.

You build queries with join and lookup, then filter and apply them to dashboards and alerts using this structure.

You can search for order in a session and print out traces within order. You can configure the dashboard by implementing filtering to make it easier for users to choose. The observability data stored in the data lake is displayed in this structure and is modeled as a non-denormalized big data-style table structure. Unnecessary join and lookup are minimized, and various results can be generated by querying a single table. Developing a dashboard with this structure allows you to structure your process and easily drill down to the desired trace.

If you're developing a dashboard for the first time, you may not know what to do. Unless you're developing a pure infrastructure dashboard, listing a bunch of SLOs is not a good idea. The dashboard needs to be relevant to your business processes and tell a story. Once you understand the structure of your IDs and relate them to your business processes, you'll naturally find the story. You need to understand the request ID, the order ID that starts the order process, the payment ID that starts the payment process, and the trace ID that starts the E2E trace.

The technology stack is divided into three main areas: infrastructure observability, application observability, and AIOps, as shown in Figure 1-6.

There are two broad categories: observability and AIOps. In detail, observability is divided into three areas—infrastructure, application, and database observability. This book focuses on infrastructure and application observability and does not include database observability. I also encourage you to take an interest in database reliability engineering, which is similar to data observability.

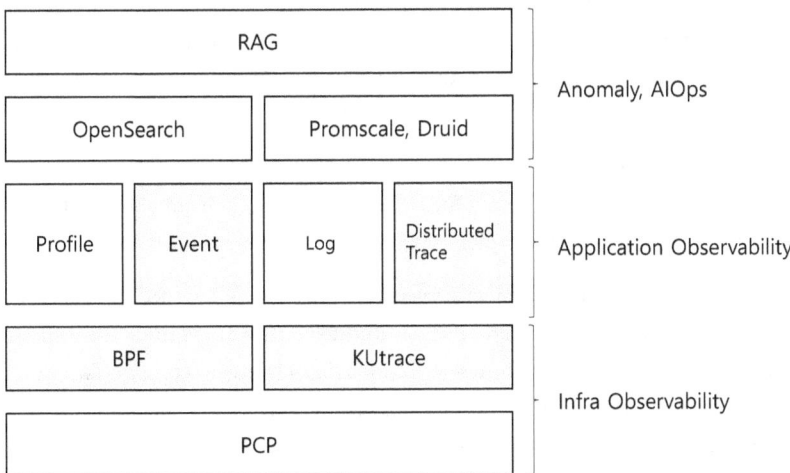

Figure 1-6. Technology stack

In this book, you build observability and AIOps using Grafana Pyroscope and a variety of open sources, including Grafana Faro, Promscale, OpenSearch, Performance Copilot, and Cilium.

CHAPTER 1   RCA ESSENTIALS

- Pyroscope is Grafana's continuous profile open source. It supports various languages and outputs profile results via a flame graph. It supports correlation with other signals and allows you to compare and analyze differences in stack trace.

- Faro is a Grafana RUM open source. It is a JavaScript library, instrumentation for web applications, and trace support.

- Promscale is an open source metric and trace backend storage system. It is based on PostgreSQL.

- Presto and Druid are open source for large data aggregation.

- eBPF provides the ability to profile system resources with a small overhead. Performance Copilot (PCP) is an open source observability system for eBPF visualization. It helps you develop eBPF dashboard quickly and easily.

- OpenSearch is open source and supports observability, SIEM, anomaly detection, and the Vector database.

- KUtrace is open source and supports system trace. It generates and visualizes event and latency occurring in the system resource as a span.

Traditional root cause analysis methods use screens. The root cause analysis described by commercial observability solutions tends to focus on the screen. This means that various charts of infrastructure, business processes, and applications are displayed on a single dashboard and compared and analyzed over time.

We use the trace, metric, log, profile, and RUM signals to define correlations and refine data search, analysis, and aggregation. You need to understand the signals and apply AIOps to automate forecasting and inference.

- Instead of doing root cause analysis with dashboards and charts, I introduce you to automating it using SQL. It's a difficult, complex, and interesting topic. SQL is a fundamental technology for implementing anomaly detection and AIOps.

- If you process queries on S3 object storage every time, you'll pay for expensive full scan and processing. As an alternative, I introduce Promscale. Promscale is based on PostgreSQL and supports time series data. It is 100 percent compatible with Prometheus and serves as the backend storage for metrics and Jaeger traces. These are useful features that are hard to find in commercial observability options.

- You should strive to become more familiar with SQL and make better use of it, rather than analyze it on the screen. This is because SQL can be used to analyze detailed data that cannot be seen on the screen and can be automated. An experienced SRE should be able to process multiple SQL queries in sequence to automate and sort the results by time stamp for root cause analysis.

This book is for SREs and data engineers. You will ingest signals into Promscale and use OpenSearch to implement anomaly detection and AIOps.

1.2. Root Cause Analysis (RCA) Process

The goal of this section is to explain the various obstacles that occur during operation and roughly explain the RCA of this book.

This book explains the several types of root cause analysis. The signals used to troubleshoot them are different. Errors in the kernel and virtual machines are different from errors in a distributed environment like microservices. Errors in large clusters are different from errors in networks or system resources. Although failures propagate and overlap, it is important to correctly identify the problem based on the technology area.

I discuss various problems that occur in applications, system resources, networks, kernels, and virtual machines. A three-step approach to root cause analysis is the direction taken in this book:

1. **Identify problem areas:** Metrics are time series data points and represent aggregation. They help you understand the problem area. The dashboard uses metrics to express the degree of change over time. Despite the large number and scope of the system, metrics can help you narrow down the scope of the problem and configure alerts to reduce MTTD. The custom metric provided by each solution is useful. Issues such as misconfigured resources can be resolved with metrics alone.

2. **Understand individual requests:** If metrics and dashboards aren't enough to identify the problem, using traces and profiles is a good way to go. Traces output latency and error for specific microservices and SQL, whereas profiles can help you understand CPU and memory performance and latency at the method level. In other words, traces can help you understand issues at the individual request level. Traces and profiles in Step 2 are more detailed than metrics and dashboards in Step 1 and can help you get to the root cause more quickly and easily than system traces and eBPF profiles in Step 3. You need to reduce MTTR by accurately and quickly understanding the problem and providing solutions with less labor. I believe that by efficiently organizing Step 2, you can maximize the technical benefit of observability and make it business-scalable.

3. **Analyze lower levels:** There is no metric to measure the time spent on lower-level root cause analysis. The reason why Step 3 is important is related to root cause analysis. If you don't address the root cause, the same issue is likely to recur in the future. Step 3 is about finding and fixing the cause, even if it takes a lot of time and labor. Metrics, traces, and profiles are useful signals provided by observability. But if they don't help you understand the root cause, you need to analyze lower-level methods and signals. With knowledge of the kernel and system resources, system trace and eBPF profile are used to identify and resolve issue.

The type of problems are more varied and complex in the modern era of open source than they were in the past, when we were operating on a specific legacy vendor. This chapter explains the problems and then discusses the right approach.

This book explains the theory first and then proceeds in a way that organizes the demonstration. For demonstrations that require complex configurations, you can ask questions through the author's Git.

1.2.1. Identify the Problem Area

Poor performance can be a symptom of other problems. Long latency or spike-like loads can be a symptom of problems that exceed threshold and SLO. These problems can propagate and affect all services and API, even if they are initially limited to specific scenarios.

For example, if a downstream service has a problem, the throughput of all APIs in the downstream service can drop significantly. High or low resource consumption alone does not indicate a performance problem. High CPU or memory utilization can be valid if users are not affected.

You can detect performance problems by monitoring SLO and raise latency alerts. If the problem is widespread and not limited to a specific scenario, you should look at the overall resource utilization and saturation, including CPU, memory, and number of threads to find the bottleneck. You may need to collect and analyze various signals. Metrics alone are often not enough to solve the problem. The next section explains how to apply traces and profiles to solve problems.

1.2.1.1. Incorrect Resource Settings

You need to understand the internal operation of microservices and clusters and make capacity calculations and allocate resources based on expected traffic. For example, you should maintain a reasonable number of threads and connection pools in Spring Boot. Individual threads use memory, so you need to make sure you have the right amount of memory set aside that is proportional to the number of threads.

To understand the thread problem, it is useful to show a metric time series, but you can also use a trace. If the thread pool, connection pool, and resource pool are set incorrectly, you may see multiple span cascading. In Figure 1-7, you can see multiple span timeouts at the same time.

The answer is not always to set the resource to a higher value. Increasing the number of autoscales and pools can have other unexpected side effects, and sometimes reducing the number of allowed resource can help keep the system running reliably.

CHAPTER 1   RCA ESSENTIALS

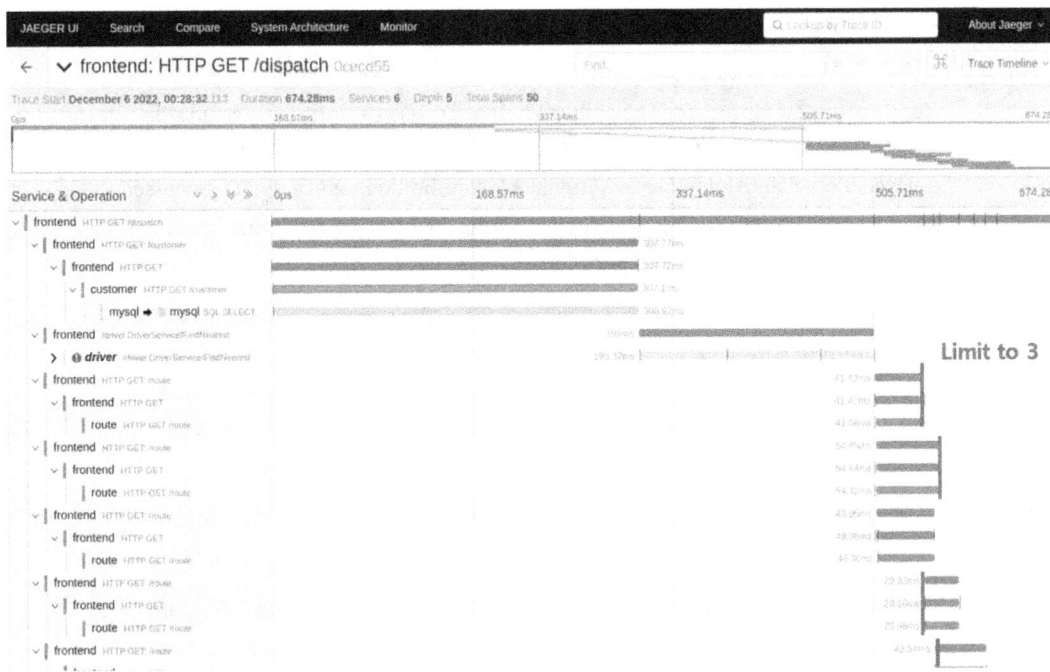

Figure 1-7. *Resource limitation in trace*

The variety of problems and failures makes it difficult to reduce MTTR, but the complexity of overlap and propagation makes root cause analysis difficult. Kernel and virtual machine errors can be analyzed using system traces and profiles, and cluster-level errors are often not supported by observability.

Failures of the resources that manage the cluster are very different from failures of the kernel and virtual machine. Changes in the number of nodes, restarts, and backups are considered failures by the cluster. Even backups and scheduled restarts of configured shards can cause service failures. It is normal maintenance without operator failure, but from the cluster's point of view, the operator's change of normal cluster configuration is no different from the recovery procedure. From the cluster's perspective, there is no difference between the operator's normal reduction of the number of nodes and the sudden death of a node due to failure.

In the process of operating a cluster, you need to understand the principles of data consistency, consensus, rebalancing, partitioning and sharding, and replication.

Whereas microservices are stateless, clusters are stateful, so their internal behavior and operations are quite different.

CHAPTER 1   RCA ESSENTIALS

The management tasks that occur in the cluster are technically normal, but they can be a major failure in production.

- **Replication:** This improves availability, but it can cause various unexpected side effects. As the number of replicas increases in Kafka, subscriber performance may be delayed. Replication generates additional IO. You should monitor the IO processed by the partition in the broker. Simply monitoring the broker is not enough to understand an IO problem in a partition.

- **Data consistency:** Elasticsearch can take a considerable amount of time to scale out. The write path is difficult to change, and the read path can be changed at runtime, but this negatively affects the runtime service. The cluster requires a lot of work when restarting, including bootstrapping, checking the status of nodes with the gossip protocol, and synchronizing the cache.

- **Fault tolerance:** HDFS and Presto are designed to be reprocessed if they fail or timeout during processing. This prevents data loss, but causes delays in service.

- **Consensus:** Traditional replication methods are heavy and inflexible, so quorum consensus protocols like Loki give you the flexibility to manage replication. Rather than always having the right number of replicas, introduce a gossip protocol that is lighter than the Bootstrap health check. While these technologies make clusters lighter to run, clusters are still heavy. To prevent data loss due to sudden failures, write WAL log files and use a quorum that maintains a consistent number of replicas.

- **Rebalancing:** Adding and deleting nodes takes a lot of time, and rebalancing can also affect network bandwidth. This is not a problem if it is not real time like HDFS, but it can be a problem if it is real time like Redis.

- **Large resources:** Clusters often go down due to insufficient memory rather than lack of CPU. If more data is ingested than the allocated memory handles, problems can occur. Set up WAL to prevent data in memory from being lost and set up replication, buffering, and flushing.

- **Additional IO:** Compression, merging, compaction, and tiering are always processed in large-capacity clusters. High availability is supported, but minor failures are always present. Retry may occur due to a lack of resource, or timeout may occur due to priority levels.

- **Partitioning:** Data is not distributed fairly, and skew can occur. You should consider skew when partitioning and sharding.

Cluster failures are a different type of failure than microservices. There may be cases where cluster delays and failures have a negative impact on microservices.

These are important topics in cluster management. Clusters that process large volumes are often developed in Java, so Java observability is important. Most commercial observability is not sufficient for cluster operation. A common error in cluster operation is related to memory.

- The Prometheus write path requires a sufficient memory setup. It holds incoming data in memory and flushes it to disk at regular intervals. Since the disk is slower than the CPU, keep data in memory instead of writing it to disk each time, creating blocks of a certain size and then flushing them to disk. If the incoming data is larger than the allocated memory, it is likely to cause an OOM problem.

- Presto and Spark require a lot of memory compared to other clusters. This is because they internally load data into memory before they start processing it. This can cause threads to stop processing due to insufficient memory.

- Elasticsearch offers three type of caches. Many customers use Elasticsearch caches to save on cost and improve performance. While caches are useful, they are prone to failure and should be used with caution. In addition to Redis, there are many other uses of cache internally in the cluster.

- Druid's cache is allocated in the Java non-heap area. The heap area is processed by the garbage collector and should not be used as a cache. Druid stores its cache in the JVM's non-heap memory so that it is not deleted when garbage collection occurs. It is important to calculate the size of the heap and non-heap memory. If the memory settings are incorrect, the pod will restart every time.

- When configuring a pipeline with the OpenTelemetry collector, configure batches, compressions, and buffers. If the pipeline processes ingestion into Elasticsearch, it does not transfer data to Elasticsearch immediately whenever it is ingested. Pipelines can buffer incoming data, and then will compress and flush it to improve performance. The number of replicas should be based on availability and performance. HDFS, the zookeeper, has three replicas. Many clusters default to three nodes.

- The number of replicas is important when configuring a cluster in Kafka and Elasticsearch. Having more replicas than necessary increases IO and degrades performance.

- Design for consistency and load. Frequent flushing can improve data consistency and increases the load on Elasticsearch.

Applications are directly tied to hosts, clusters, VMs, and frameworks, which are complex and consume many resources. If the resources are not set up correctly, you will experience unexpected errors.

CHAPTER 1   RCA ESSENTIALS

The failures that occur due to the maintenance of external cloud and SaaS services are as follows:

- Restart broker during the maintenance of a Kafka cluster. All brokers are not restarted at once. Brokers in the cluster are restarted sequentially and rebalancing occurs within the cluster. If your application is in the middle of processing a transaction, there is a chance that the transaction will have a problem and an error will occur. In this case, the application needs to retry, but if no retry logic is implemented, the user's transaction will fail.

- If you are building a cluster with virtual machine in the cloud, you may encounter problems with shards. A problem occurs with a particular shard in the cluster due to the maintenance of the virtual machine, and the shard suddenly goes down. Recovery is then performed. The root cause is that the host is down due to VM maintenance, so the shard on the host are also down. The shard in the cluster recognizes the failure and proceeds to recover the shard. A new shard is created, and the recovery process is completed. If you use external cloud services, they are often affected by external maintenance.

- Cloud instability can occur for a variety of reasons. Kubernetes clusters disappear, there aren't enough resources available in the data center for spark processing, or managed service in the region is unavailable so it uses another region, causing interference that reduces disk and network bandwidth.

Since failures can occur for a variety of reasons, improving the reliability of services is a high priority. While it's important to fix problems that cause slow performance and latency, SREs should also work to prevent service outages and improve reliability.

While metrics and dashboards can help identify the scope of the problem, they are not enough to determine the detailed root cause.

1.2.1.2. Java Troubleshooting

Java is a popular programming language. Memory leaks and thread issues are common problems encountered in Java environments. It is important to understand the internal operation of the JVM so that you can improve the performance and efficiency of Java applications running within the JVM. The following topics are discussed:

- Threads
- JVM parameters
- Garbage collection

Optimal performance and scalability can be realized by using threads efficiently.

- **Minimize thread race conditions:** Thread race conditions occur when multiple threads race over a shared resource. To avoid these race conditions, it is important to design thread-safe data structures and synchronization mechanisms that minimize the need for locks and reduce their duration. High-level synchronization, such as the Lock and Condition object, can be utilized to provide flexibility and control over thread interaction.

- **Utilize a thread pool:** It's usually more efficient to use a thread pool instead of explicitly creating threads for each task. A thread pool creates a fixed number of threads and reuses them to process jobs. This avoids the overhead of creating and destroying threads and gives you more control over resource consumption.

- **Avoid excessive context switches:** A context switch refers to the process of switching from thread A to thread B. However, excessive context switching causes overhead problems and degrades performance. Using an appropriate thread pool size for the available CPU cores helps avoid excessive context switching.

- **Use asynchronous and non-blocking IO:** Instead of blocking a thread while waiting for an IO operation to complete, asynchronous IO allows the thread to continue processing other tasks. This allows a single thread to process multiple IO operations simultaneously, resulting in better resource utilization and increased application throughput.

You'll encounter a variety of thread problems in production: race conditions, non-blocking IO, context switching, and thread pooling are common failures, and you'll need to learn about their solutions. In this chapter, I explain the basic ones, but I also explain the advanced tuning required for ultra-low latency servers in detail in a later chapter.

It is essential to optimize the performance and behavior of Java applications running on the Java Virtual Machine. The JVM parameters that can be optimized include:

- **Heap size (-Xmx and -Xms):** The heap is the area of memory allocated and managed by a Java object. The -Xmx parameter is the maximum heap size, and -Xms is the initial heap size. Setting the maximum heap size too low can cause frequent garbage collection and out-of-memory errors. Setting it too high will consume excessive memory and make garbage collection take longer. Setting the initial heap size too low can cause frequent resizing operations, which can degrade performance.

- **Thread stack size:** The -Xss parameter defines the thread stack size. Adjusting the thread stack size affects the number of threads that can be created and the memory consumption of the application. Setting it too low can cause a StackOverflowError error while setting it too high limits the number of threads that can be created.

CHAPTER 1　RCA ESSENTIALS

- **IO buffer size:** The JVM uses a default buffer size for IO operations. For applications with heavy IO operation, adjusting the buffer size using the `Dsun.nio.ch.maxUpdateArrayLength` parameter improves IO performance.

- **Parallel processing and concurrency:** The JVM provides parameters for controlling the level of parallel processing and concurrency in an application. For example, the `XX:ParallelGCThreads` parameter sets the number of threads used for parallel garbage collection.

- **JIT compilation:** The JVM's JIT compiler translates frequently executed bytecode into native machine code to increase performance. You can fine-tune JIT compilation parameters such as `-XX:CompileThreshold` and `-XX:MaxInlineSize` to control compilation behavior.

This helps you analyze metrics and determine where you can benefit from tuning JVM parameter. This book does not discuss Java Virtual Machine and garbage collection in detail. However, they are important and should be studied further.

Java garbage collector optimization is an essential part of JVM optimization, and it focuses on improving memory management and minimizing the impact of garbage collection on Java application performance. The garbage collector reclaims memory occupied by unused objects.

- **Garbage collector:** Simply choosing the right garbage collector for your application can significantly improve performance. For example, Concurrent Mark Sweep (CMS) collectors are ideal for applications with low downtime requirements, while the Garbage First (G1) collector is designed with a balance between throughput and downtime.

- **Choosing the right garbage collector:** The JVM provides a variety of garbage collectors that implement different garbage collection algorithms. There are serial, parallel, and concurrent mark-sweep (CMS), as well as newer variants such as G1 and ZGC. Understanding the characteristics of your application, such as its requirements, including memory usage patterns, will help you choose the most effective garbage collector.

- **Adjusting garbage collector parameters:** The JVM supports configuration parameters that can be adjusted to optimize the behavior of the garbage collector. The parameters include the heap size, the threshold that triggers garbage collection, and the generation memory management ratio. Adjusting JVM parameters helps balance memory utilization with garbage collection overhead.

- **Generational memory management:** Most garbage collectors in the JVM are generational garbage collectors that divide the heap into new and old generations. Ways to optimize generational memory management include sizing each generation, setting the ratio between each generation, and optimizing the garbage collection cycle frequency and strategy for each generation.

- **Minimize object creation and retention:** Excessive object creation and unnecessary object retention increases memory usage, which leads to more frequent garbage collection. This is where object creation optimization comes in. This includes reusing objects, introducing object pooling techniques, and minimizing unnecessary allocations. To reduce object retention, you need to find and eliminate memory leaks, such as unreferenced objects that are unintentionally retained.

- **Concurrent and parallel collection:** Some garbage collectors, such as CMS and G1, support concurrent and parallel garbage collection. When you enable the concurrent garbage collector rule, your application runs concurrently with the garbage collection, which improves response time.

- **Garbage collector logging:** Monitoring and analyzing garbage collection logs and statistics can give you in-depth information about the behavior and performance of the garbage collector. It can also help you identify potential bottlenecks, prolonged stalls, or excessive memory usage. Using this information, you can fine-tune your garbage collection parameters and the optimization strategy.

Optimizing garbage collection can improve memory management, reduce garbage collection overhead, and improve application performance. It is important to note that much of this depends on the characteristics and requirements of your application.

In production, errors in the JVM garbage collection are common, so it is necessary to learn about them in detail. A detailed understanding of older generations of OOM errors and how to resolve them with memory and thread dumps is necessary in practice.

As an example, memory leaks are common errors. If you continue to ignore a memory leak, you may one day encounter an `OutOfMemoryError` (OOM). In Java, an error is more serious than an exception. When do OOM errors occur?

- When the garbage collector has run out of space to create new objects and the memory in the heap area can no longer be increased.

- If you set the memory size too low, or if you didn't specify a memory size.

- An old object is still being referenced, and no has been garbage collected.

Memory leaks occur when an application consumes more memory over time. For example, if you cache objects in memory without proper expiration, your application will consume more memory over time. Increased memory consumption triggers garbage collection, but the garbage collector cannot release it because it maintains references to all objects.

Memory leaks can be seen to increase over time with virtual memory. The physical memory used by processes increases, which means that the OS is starting to use disk space in addition to RAM. This process is called *paging* or *swapping*, and it can be enabled at the OS level. When this process is enabled, it can have a significant impact on performance because RAM is typically much faster than disk saving. Eventually, the system will run out of physical memory, and the process will crash with an `OutOfMemoryException` error

CHAPTER 1 RCA ESSENTIALS

when the page file reaches its size limit. This can happen earlier depending on the heap size configuration. For example, for 32-bit processes, OOM occurs when the virtual memory size reaches 4GB due to insufficient address space.

If memory usage grows quickly, garbage collection will aggressively try to free up memory and may consume CPU and suspend managed threads.

For example, if you have frequent garbage collection, you may suspect that you have a memory leak based on the consistent memory growth and frequency of garbage collection.

If OOM occurs, there may be insufficient resources for the processing or a memory leak. Garbage collection in Java VM has a pattern:

- If memory leaks continue to increase memory occupancy, the JVM will call full garbage collection frequently. As the number of calls increases, the CPU spikes to 100 percent utilization.

- If you notice that after a full garbage collection is called, the memory drops to a small amount and then rises again, you can suspect a memory leak.

You've learned why garbage collection is important and why OOMs occur. Since OOMs indicate a failure, you can define anomaly detection to recognize them in advance.

- You need to distinguish between basic garbage collection and full garbage collection. You also want to see if the frequency and number of full garbage collections per hour increases dramatically. Measure the frequency of full garbage collections.

- If a full garbage collection occurs frequently, you'll experience rapid CPU spikes.

- Measure the number of CPU spikes and full garbage collections occurring at the same time.

As garbage collection frequency increases, CPU spikes at 100 percent usage. If memory leaks occur, full garbage collection will eventually occur. User will experience latency and have a negative experience. There is less memory available in the heap. Non-heap areas that are not processed by garbage collection are irrelevant to garbage collection.

You may notice that there are periods when CPU utilization goes up. You can collect a memory dump to see what's in it. Assuming you can reproduce the problem on your local machine, you can capture and analyze the memory dump.

If your application crashes frequently, you may notice that there are certain time periods when user resource utilization goes up. You can capture a number of memory dump before it crashes to see what's inside.

Once the dumps are collected, you can analyze them using other tools that automate and simplify this process. Memory leaks can also be understood by using metrics. However, for other errors, metrics alone are often insufficient. You use memory dumps simply to identify which objects and methods are leaking.

1.2.2. Analyze Individual Requests

Analyzing individual transactions for memory leaks won't reveal anything special. It's important to understand that different problems require different approaches. While the aggregation of metrics may be enough to understand the problem, certain errors can only be understood by analyzing individual transactions. This section looks at how to investigate performance problems related to a specific APIs or individual requests.

To analyze individual requests, you should check the trace. The trace matches individual transactions and outputs latency and errors for each section processed. With trace, you can quickly and accurately understand the latency and error that occur in a specific section for each individual request. Understanding the latency of a specific section per transaction was a complex and time-consuming task before distributed trace was introduced.

If you suspect an inefficient method in your code, which signals should you analyze first?

Even when you use metrics, traces, and logs, which are the main signals of observability, it is not uncommon to find inefficient methods in your code. You can identify inefficient methods if you have a stack trace, a call tree, and a dump. You should use profiles if you're worried about overhead. You can minimize the performance impact of profile collection by running the profile for a short period of time and transferring it to backend storage. Use a profile to identify the inefficient method.

- At the method level of the code, the profile contains the duration of the method, which is the number of times the method is called.

- The thread dump provides thread state information and latency. This allows you to understand locks and contentions.

- Understand the call relationship between object in the call tree.

- Compare the improvement before and after the code change from a CPU and memory perspective using a flame graph.

A profile provides details so that you can see what's happening under the hood of your application or third-party library code. By capturing a profile, you can see a detailed stack trace, get statistics on CPU usage, and more accurately monitor internal operations. This is a great tool not only for investigating lower-level problems but also for optimizing your code.

Profiles are useful if you run into problems with your dependency. Additionally, profiles provide live debugging.

You can use profiles to measure performance and identify areas in your code where problems are occurring, but profiles also have a number of limitations.

For example, a transaction like a fund transfer in banking creates hundreds of spans internally. It's not uncommon for a user to click a button to transfer funds, after which the transaction traverses dozens of microservices, multiple databases, and legacy systems before it reaches the external financial organization. It would be inefficient and time-consuming to find and remediate latency using only profiles. Profiles have less context. In the end, the developer is unlikely to be able to find the root cause and location of the latency.

You should configure trace and correlation and use them together rather than using profiles alone.

A profile is inadequate for analyzing individual requests. Profiles do not provide information from a business process and transaction perspective. Profiles are useful when you need a detailed analysis of CPU, memory, and other resources at the method level. Deadlocks, starvations, hotspots, OOM memory issues, and infrastructure issues can all be identified with profiles. Profiles have the following limitations:

- The charts used for visualizing profiles are flame graphs and histograms, which are limited in visualization compared to other signals.

- Different languages have different profiles, so profiles for certain languages are not as useful as you might expect.

- While the eBPF profile can accurately measure the latency of the 99th percentile as a histogram, the values that a typical profile outputs are only averages. This makes it difficult to identify the distribution of the problem and the individual transaction where the problem occurred.

When an error occurs during the transaction processing, you need to analyze the error in the span. In many cases, trace is not technically capable of instrumenting the API server. In this case, you can use logs to calculate the user's failure.

While it's important to understand specific signals in detail, there are limits to understanding a problem using only one signal. You need to be able to analyze a problem from multiple perspectives using a variety of signals. Given the specific signal that SREs prefer and the fact that no single signal can solve all problems, and given the large-scale observability that needs to be used with thousands of developers, not just individual, it is the role of the SRE to provide a variety of signals and guide developers to use them easily.

1.2.2.1. Incorrect Process Order

Retries can occur due to poor thread management or lack of control over the order of the call. Constant retries mean increased latency.

It's important to set retries and timeouts correctly. Retry is useful for technical errors and should not be used for business errors. Unnecessary retries increase latency and should be avoided. You should also be careful with redeliveries and timeouts.

You shouldn't set long timeouts without principles, and you should understand the nature of your work and define the timeouts accordingly. If your code is managing connections incorrectly or not closing them properly, increasing the resources of the pod and increasing the number of connections and timeouts will not help. In asynchronous processes, you should define retries and timeouts, assuming that the appropriate latency is acceptable. Setting the offset, confirm, checkpoint, and redelivery flag on the message server is important.

It's common to call multiple APIs from a single screen, and the processing between them is sequential, not parallel. To be sequential, it must be more carefully designed.

CHAPTER 1 RCA ESSENTIALS

In some cases, the order of the XHR call can change during the thread process, causing the backend microservices to fail and retry from the beginning. Not surprisingly, this has a negative impact on the user experience.

Latency should be more important than throughput, concurrent use, and large volumes of traffic, and the goal should be to reduce any errors and improve reliability.

As shown in Figure 1-8, the trace shows what the process is doing when the retry occurs.

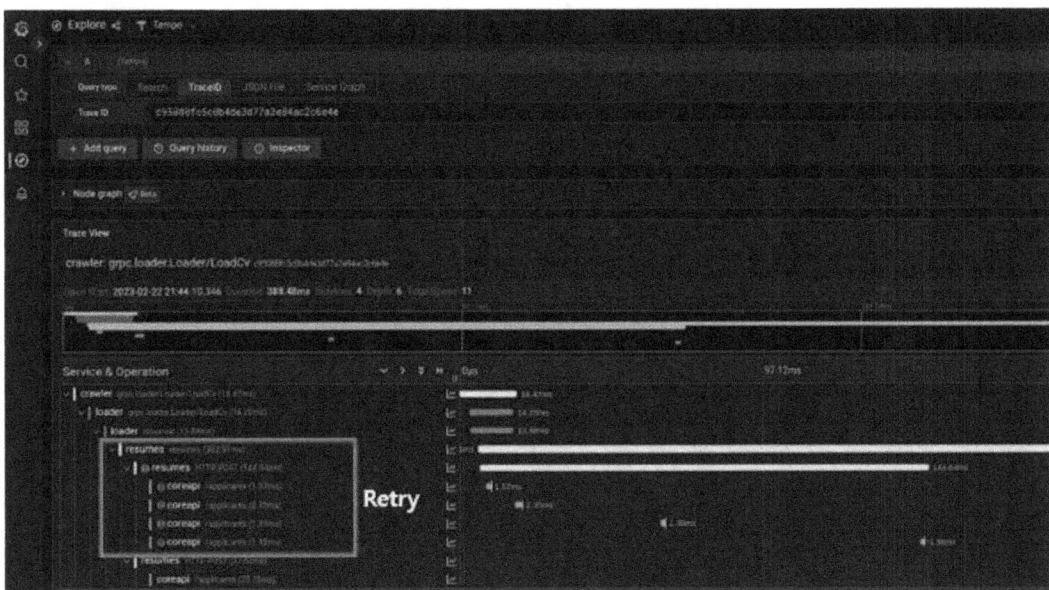

Figure 1-8. *Retry in a trace*

The retry setting is not configured in microservices, but on the service mesh and API server. It sets the number of retries and the reconnection interval. Since retries are not related to business logic and need to be managed policy-wise, it makes sense to set them on the API server. However, if the API server is not instrumented with trace, it does not generate a span when a retry occurs, as shown in Figure 1-8. Therefore, the SRE does not know when a retry has occurred. You need to accurately instrument the API server and set the number of retries, the retry interval, and the timeout correctly. And you need to visualize it with a span so that you can respond to problems when they occur.

Indiscriminate retries can be confusing and can lead to problems with data consistency. It is possible to configure the API server to not retry, and only allow retry on the frontend.

Generally it is useful to organize retries using queues in the message server.

The problems with sequential and parallel processes are as follows:

- For parallel processing. However, by setting up and allocating the wrong resources, you get less parallel processing, even though you could get more parallel processing. For example, the number of thread pools could be 10, but if you configure it to be 2 and experience delays, the span will output exactly this misconfiguration.

31

CHAPTER 1   RCA ESSENTIALS

- Despite being able to process in parallel, there are times when sequential processing increases latency.

- For sequential processing, you configure only one subscriber corresponding to one queue, but the order could be reversed during the process. For sequential processing, you must also configure only one subscriber. However, it performs fewer parallel processes, even though more parallel processing could be achieved by allocating constrained resources.

- Failures can be caused by incorrect retries and timeout settings.

Sequential processing cascades individual spans, as shown in Figure 1-9.

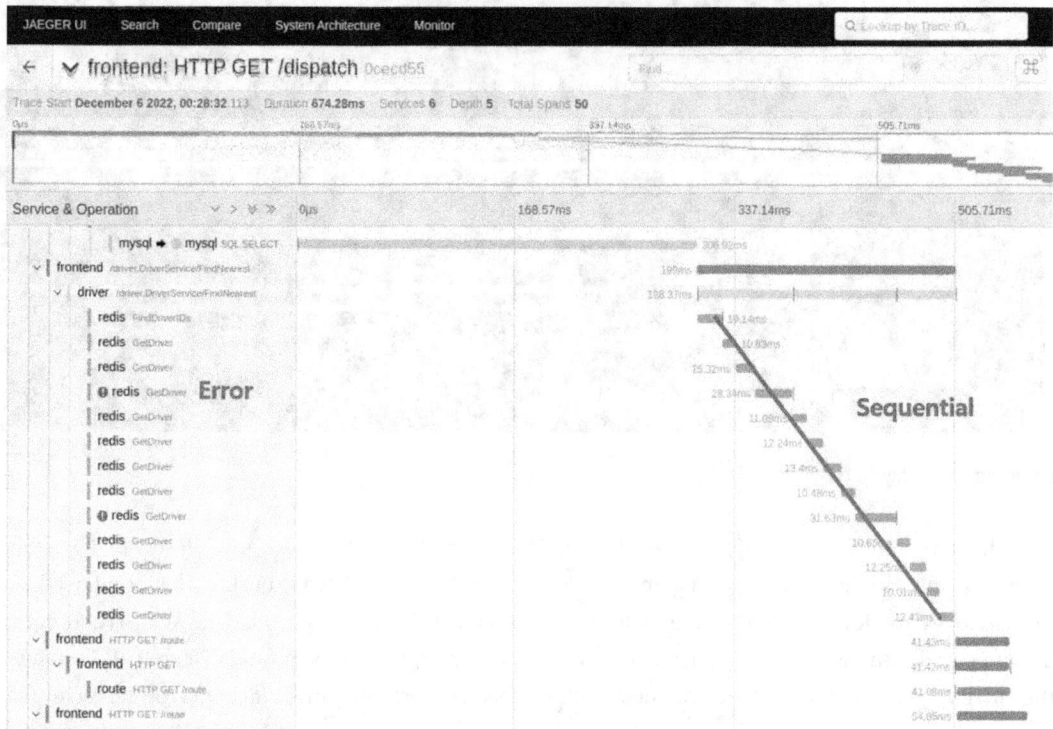

Figure 1-9. *Sequential process in a trace*

In the example shown in Figure 1-9, you can see that the process should be processed in parallel instead of being processed sequentially, causing unnecessary delay. Implementing effective parallel processing is difficult, and you will encounter various problems while doing so.

In summary, you can identify sequential processing, parallel processing, retries, timeouts, incorrect resource constraints, and more, all using traces.

1.2.2.2. Parallel Processing

Synchronization

Thread synchronization is when you ensure that resources are accessed sequentially to prevent problems that can occur when multiple threads are running simultaneously. Synchronization is a process-management technique that keeps multiple processes in line with each other's progress in a multitasking environment and controls the processing of two or more independent processes.

The delay for CPU and IO are not exactly different. This book is limited in explaining the various types of IO, so it focuses on the system resources that are common to CPU and explain root cause analysis. Compared to IO, CPU have fewer types and their failures can be forecast.

The types of IO processed by various open sources are also varied and complex.

Most clusters have implemented IO for block merging, offsets, gossip protocols, rebalancing, quorums, replication, WAL, and cache LRUs, They use IO in a complex way at the cluster level. While individual IO is not difficult to understand, troubleshooting is complicated by multiple IOs competing for the same resources. It is harder to isolate failures in cluster environments than in microservices.

It is beyond the scope of this book to describe the unique IO implementations of clusters such as Kafka, Redis, and Elasticsearch. Because they are open source specific, I describe IO at the resource level. It is useful to have an SRE with experience in system resources and an expert who understands your specific cluster to troubleshoot failures in your cluster.

IO that you don't understand is no different than a black box, even if it's open source. Most open source implementations of clusters are implemented in Java, and Java uses NIO. Java's IO can be analyzed using profiles and various system utilities.

Due to the nature of threads, they appear to be executing simultaneously. They are not actually simultaneous, but for that reason, when more than one thread is being performed, synchronization between threads is required. If their work is unrelated, they don't need to be synchronized, but if it is, they need to sync. The other aspect of synchronization is controlling access to shared resources. If you try to access and control them at the same time, you may end up with something other than the desired result. For example, if one side is writing data and the other side is reading the value, the value becomes unreliable.

Inside a process, resources are shared among threads, and there will always be problems with synchronization: multiple threads accessing a shared resource at the same time.

Mutexes and semaphores are essential synchronization mechanisms.

Mutexes are used to control exclusive access to resources, primarily through mutual exclusion. Semaphores are used to allow limited access to a resource by multiple threads at the same time.

The main difference is the number of synchronization targets:

- Mutexes are used when there is only one synchronization target, and semaphores are used when there is more than one synchronization target.
- Mutexes can own resources and are responsible for them, while semaphores do not.

- Mutexes can have locks because they only have 0 and 1 states, and only the thread that owns a mutex can release a mutex. A semaphore, on the other hand, can be freed by a thread that does not own the semaphore. Semaphores scope the system scope and exist as files on the file system. Mutexes, on the other hand, have the scope of the process and are automatically cleaned up when the process terminates.

A common problem with threads is locking. Temporarily locking to process shared data is not a problem. However, if the lock is not released, or if multiple threads are waiting for it to be released, it can cause not only a performance problem but also a service failure.

Race Conditions

When processing one or more pieces of shared data in a multi-threaded environment, it is possible for multiple threads to change the data at the same time if a lock is not handled. In some cases, threads can get stuck in an infinite wait when they come in to process at the same time. This is called a *race condition*.

Using account balances as an example, suppose there are two threads and a shared resource called *balance*:

- You can't make a withdrawal if your balance is less than the withdrawal amount. You currently have 50,000 USD in your balance.

- If thread 1 wanted to withdraw 50,000 USD, it first checks the balance and finds that there is 50,000 USD.

- However, a context switch occurred, and it was replaced by Thread 2.

- Thread 2 does the same thing. In Thread 2, the context switch did not occur before the withdrawal, so the withdrawal is completed, and the balance becomes zero.

- A context switch occurs and Thread 1 is replaced by Thread 2. Thread 1 has finished checking the balance, so it tries to withdraw the money, but the balance is zeroed out by Thread 2's work, so the withdrawal will result in a number less than zero.

Concurrency

Languages such as Java and Golang provide a variety of features for handling concurrency and ensure data consistency for transactional processing in enterprise applications.

The problem with concurrency has a lot to do with parallel processing and threads. In situations where multiple threads are running simultaneously, conflicts or errors over resources can occur. These errors can lead to fatal conditions, such as deadlocks, which can prevent the system from progressing further.

Locking

I recommend using profiles to identify locks, but they can also be identified from distributed traces. Figure 1-10 assumes that your code has implemented exception handling for locks. If you have a problem with a lock, check the log in the trace. If a lock occurs, you can see the longer-than-normal latency in the span. It is difficult to judge concurrency problems by individual call, and latency or timeout occur when multiple transactions are processed simultaneously. This can be easily seen by comparing the duration of the span in a normal state with the duration of the span in an abnormal state.

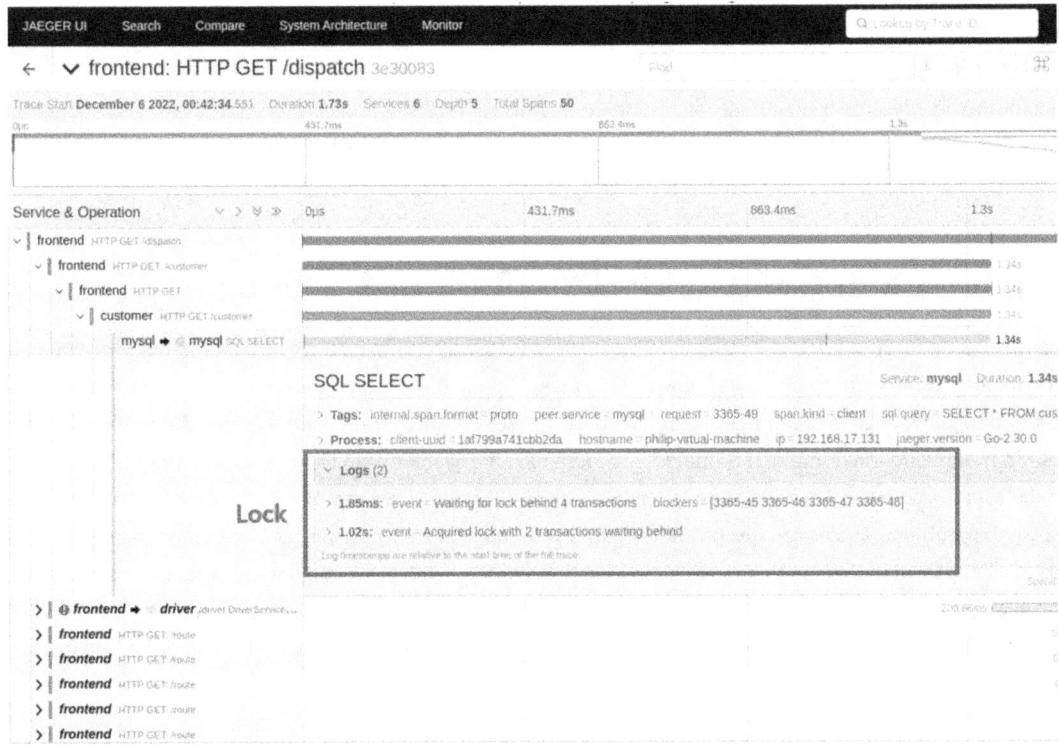

Figure 1-10. *Error messages in a trace*

With trace, you can suspect problems with lock and critical sections. You need more detailed analysis. This is where profiles and system traces come in. For locks and critical sections, system trace and stack trace are more accurate.

It is a great advantage to be able to quickly identify problems using trace and flame graphs instead of analyzing complex thread dumps, which takes a long time. Complex stack traces are difficult to analyze, so you can use flame graphs for visualization. However, it is often difficult to determine the root cause from the flame graph alone. You need to learn how to understand stack traces and thread dumps. It's hard at first, but you'll get used to it.

When a lock occurs, you can understand it by looking at the latency in the distributed trace and the log in the trace. If these signs are not enough, you can analyze the profile in more detail.

For example, if you check the CPU and memory usage, you might see that the CPU and memory usage are low and not increasing significantly, the number of threads is not changing much, the thread queue is empty, and the race condition rate is low. However, at the same time, the throughput is low and the latency is high. So, the application is doing nothing and cannot get faster. If you check the trace, you can see a large gap, but there is no data to analyze further.

Since this issue is limited to the API that is causing the lock, calls to other APIs and health check APIs that are not related to the lock will respond immediately. This helps narrow down the search for the API that is causing the lock.

If you get the topN stack, assuming you don't know there are locks, you will only see threads waiting for work. A lock is fast, but waiting for a locked resource to become available takes much longer.

You can see that the CPU is low, memory usage is low, and the thread count is fine. In a real-world scenario, this problem is not apparent among other calls.

The problem is obvious in the code, but in the actual code, it may be hidden behind a feature flag or a third-party library. Profiles are useful for issues that traces and logs can't identify.

1.2.3. Understand Low-Level Methods

Failures in operations are highly related to business processes. It is not easy to understand the problem using technology alone without understanding the business. Application observability is successful when there is a working knowledge of the domain, along with the processes for the microservices that do the work. If SREs don't understand the domain, it is difficult for them to solve problems on their own, and they will request help from developer. Even if they don't understand the domain, traces can often provide important clues to solve the problem. Traces can identify latency and problems on a section-by-section basis and provide clues as to what part of the business process is causing the problem. Once you understand what is causing the problem, you can reach out to the right person in your organization and work together to resolve it.

Large infrastructure failures are infrequent. As a percentage of all failures, they are divided into business and technical failures.

Business errors:

- Data consistency: 10%

- Lack of deployment, testing: 20%

- Other: 20%

Technical errors:

- Vendor bug: 5%

- Cluster, security, network: 15%

- Operator mistakes: 10 %

- Microservices and legacy: 15%

- Other: 5%

While there are many different types of failures, this book focuses on failures in data integrity, clusters, microservices, and legacy services.

Building observability using open source is a difficult and complex task—the internal processing of open source observability is read and write separated, like microservices, and the scale of the data it processes is big data.

Various failures also occur within observability.

- Delays in write and read paths
- Pipeline is down
- Data duplication and loss
- Agent is down
- Disk errors
- Interruption when scale-out write paths
- Redis cache cluster is down

Collecting lower-level data in a multi-instance environment is not easy. It is not uncommon to use agents and Prometheus to restart due to OOM errors.

For example, if a problem, such as a slow memory leak or a rare deadlock, affects only a few instances, it can be difficult to detect. Even if you do detect it, the instances may have already shut down, and the problem will no longer be visible. It is difficult to reproduce the problem on a specific instance of a running process and to collect a profile or dump from the application. If a thread deadlock occurs, a CPU profile is no longer available, and if an OOM error occurs, a memory profile is not possible. In this case, the profile is not working and you need to capture a dump.

Profiles can collect profile data on demand, in batches, or by specific triggers, and they must be configured so that signals are not missed when collected.

Unlike application observability from a user service perspective, infrastructure observability is based on system resources and involves complex interactions between the CPU, the kernel, and the IO. It is difficult to identify procedures and people in charge like a business process or distributed trace. Metrics, profiles, and logs are not enough to visualize the process that occurs in the infrastructure. eBPF, a type of profile, is not yet popular, infrastructure operators are familiar with system utilities, and most infrastructure observability is centered on metrics and logs. Therefore, it takes a lot of time and cost to identify and resolve problems in the infrastructure.

- **Metrics:** Count the number of events such as disk access, interrupts, memory errors, L1 cache misses, and the number of bytes of network data transferred. They do not provide detailed information but give a general overview of system activity. They help you understand overall load or speed, such as bytes transferred per second, error per disk access, or context switch per second. Abnormally high or low numbers

CHAPTER 1 RCA ESSENTIALS

compared to the average value can indicate a variety of problems, such as a sharp increase in error rate or a disk activity suddenly becoming unavailable. Metrics can include not only CPU events but also memory, disk, and network issues, locks and waits, and idle time.

- **Profiles:** Collect a certain amount of samples periodically. A profile is not aware of the time spent waiting for a program not to run. Typically, the program counter value is PC, which represents the CPU core program counter value while an individual program is running. While profiles can help you understand average CPU performance, they can also hide abnormal behavior by mixing normal and abnormal execution. Profiles do not show latency or program start and end times. It is clear that eBPF is not a trace. eBPF has the characteristics of a profile, and the output format is metrics, such as counters and histograms.

- **Logs:** A type of trace. Messages are usually written with a timestamp in usec. Log files are useful for recording program startups, shutdowns, and restart events, errors, and abnormal situations, as well as for finding slow transactions. Log can be used to record the arguments and start and end times of all transactions. Logs are of limited use for infrastructure observability. They are more useful for application developers.

You need a tool that allows you to visualize the internal processes of your infrastructure and quickly identify where problems are occurring. Similar to the distributed trace used for application observability, it would be helpful to have a trace for infrastructure observability. System traces collect events from system resources and output them to spans. KUtrace, `strace`, and `ftrace` are tools that enable trace in infrastructure observability. Similar to distributed traces in application observability, KUtrace allows you to identify latency in system resources on a per-span basis and understand the root cause in infrastructure observability.

A system trace is a record of all system calls in a program or a chronological event, such as disk access or packet transmission.

Any process that occurs on disk or CPU, including system libraries, filesystem accesses, kernel code, and processing that is not externally visible, identify through a system trace. A well-designed system trace will not miss problems and latency in system resource.

With a trace, you can distinguish between abnormal transactions and normal behavior, and you can see the path that abnormal transactions take. By using trace CPU, disk, network, and other events, you can determine why a program is waiting instead of running. Simple counters and CPU profiles can't measure CPU-free latency. They can't determine the cause and effect of interactions between events that happen at nearly the same time, including their chronological order. Therefore, system trace is the only way to understand the dynamic behavior of running programs and unusual transactions.

- CPU traces can trace and timestamp all method calls. You can trace switches between kernel space and user space, and context switches between threads.

- Memory traces can record a program's dynamic allocation and the freeing of memory.

CHAPTER 1   RCA ESSENTIALS

- Disk traces can record every read and write to a disk with a timestamp. Disks are buffered and flushed, so you can capture traffic to any disk with no overhead.

- Network traces can capture packets sent and received, as well as time and nodes. All messages sent and received can be logged with a timestamp.

- Critical section traces can record the acquisition and release of locks.

Just as distributed trace is the starting point for application observability, system trace can be a starting point for infrastructure observability. However, system trace alone is not enough for infrastructure observability to be successful. They must be used in conjunction with other signals: metrics and profiles.

Metrics get the utilization of the system resources and saturation rates and configure the USE dashboard. For this, the Prometheus exporter is a good choice. USE dashboards are useful for understanding the context of high-level infrastructure. You should collect infrastructure metrics while keeping costs down.

Using the KUtrace system trace, it is possible to identify the areas where latency is occurring. Once you've identified the areas, what's next?

- You use profile to analyze the method that caused latency in the code. By using BCC and bpftrace provided by eBPF, you can select the method that may cause problem and analyze the number of calls per method, the latency per method, and the stack trace of the kernel.

- Use ftrace and strace to get a detailed method-level RCA of the processing of that section.

- Infrastructure observability proceeds in the following order: metric, KUtrace, ftrace, eBPF.

PCP is useful as a tool for the visualization of eBPF results as histograms and flame graphs. With PCP, you can quickly develop bpftrace one-liners and measure the performance and latency of method in the kernel. PCP is used for infrastructure observability and is useful in conjunction with system trace.

- Just like understanding the distribution of problematic transactions at the 99th percentile in application observability, it is important to understand the 99th percentile in infrastructure observability and find the point and method where latency is occurring. However, identifying and fixing the problem is more difficult because it's not a user-facing service like application observability, and it could be an internal bug operating with latencies as small as nanoseconds.

- Use the Linux kernel's instrumentation, trace point, and eBPF to identify the latency of a method in the kernel. Understand how to use PCP to understand kernel latency, measure performance, and visualize in PCP. Configure eBPF to overcome the shortcomings of system trace. PCP and eBPF are necessary because it is difficult to identify methods in the kernel code with the information provided by the system trace.

- Understand network observability and Cilium. You need to improve Kubernetes monitoring by addressing the shortcomings of application-centric distributed trace.

CHAPTER 1   RCA ESSENTIALS

After the system trace and eBPF are complete, the next step is to establish a correlation between application observability and infrastructure observability. Infrastructure signals are not independent. They are closer to the root cause than application signals.

It is difficult to identify problems based on application observability alone. If the problem is in the infrastructure, it is necessary to narrow the scope of the problem based on the analysis results identified in the application and continue the root cause analysis using the infrastructure signals.

1. There are three types of spans for distributed trace. They are server, client, and network spans. If you see latency on a network span, use `kubeshark` to filter packets by session. View the detailed latency within the network span.

2. If latency is checked on the server and client spans, check the span attributes that correlate to profiles and stack traces. Also check the log for trace and thread IDs.

3. When searching for observability logs by trace ID, it is likely that many records are excluded. Different agents output different trace contexts in their logs. OpenTelemetry and commercial observability output different trace contexts to logs, so be careful when searching logs. Developers should check thread IDs, thread names, and trace context to be written to logs correctly. Although logs are best used to fill in the gaps of distributed traces, in practice, you'll experience a number of technical constraints and system limitations: trace and log correlation is not always as complete as we would like. Depending on the type of problem, profiles are needed, and due to these limitations, system traces are recommended.

4. If you suspect that the problem is in the infrastructure area, first get a general understanding of the infrastructure metrics and then perform a detailed root cause analysis using system traces. Identify the section where latency occurs through system traces.

5. Given the large overhead, `strace` and `ftrace` are difficult to use in production. Check the thread ID output from system calls, `ftrace`, and `strace`. Identify the method name of the kernel space that is processed in the interval in the `ftrace` log.

6. Use eBPF and trace point to understand the 99th percentile, latency, stack trace, and frequency of method call in your code. Then analyze the problem.

7. Use PCP to create histograms, heatmaps, and flame graphs and align application observability with infrastructure observability.

The system traces and eBPF are discussed in more detail later.

1.2.3.1. Propagated and Overlapping Failures

It's important to understand the latency experienced by your system resources. It is important to analyze even small latencies in advance to prevent failures from propagating to SPOF, such as core services like user authentication and API servers. This is because even negligible latency can propagate to the application and cause a major failure. I introduce a real-world example to illustrate how the latency of a system resource can lead to failure.

Although SOA and microservices look similar, SOA is centralized. SOA aims to reuse services, but if the load is concentrated on a specific service or the delay increases, the entire service is likely to be affected. Microservices, on the other hand, are fully distributed. Microservices were introduced to avoid becoming an SOPF like SOA, but the downside of microservices is that they are so distributed that failures easily propagate.

However, the system is decomposed and distributed in the same way as microservices, the following unexpected propagation problems can occur. I also share examples of failures where a failure in the downstream propagates to the upstream.

Example 1

Situation	The problems are as follows: • The system was processing more traffic than usual and the downstream was down. • There's a failure downstream, and it doesn't respond upstream. • The upstream is set to a nine-second timeout and processes retries. • The upstream has created the maximum number of threads allowed by the thread pool. Most of the threads are communicating with the downstream, and the state of the upstream's request thread is RUNNABLE, waiting for a response from the downstream. • The upstream receives a new request. It needs to create a new thread, but it can't create any more threads.
Solution	A nine-second timeout is inadequate, and retry can create an 18-second latency. The service is unavailable to users for a long period of time. Due to the long timeout, the failure propagated upstream. If there is a failure of a critical upstream service, such as the ones shown here, the entire site will be unavailable. • API server • Common security services To identify the cause, you need to analyze the thread state in profiles and dumps. Observability does not provide thread state information, so you need to understand thread state through multiple thread dumps.

CHAPTER 1   RCA ESSENTIALS

Example 2

Situation	The problems are as follows: • Downstream response times suffer. • Upstream, if the response does not arrive within three seconds, is processed as a timeout. • There are repeated failures downstream and frequent timeout errors upstream.
Solution	The developer may think that the three-second timeout process protects the upstream and prevents the failure from propagating. What they don't understand is that a large number of timeouts can have side-effects. Failures occur irregularly downstream, and it is difficult to identify the cause based on application-level observability alone. To identify the cause, it is necessary to analyze network system utilities and kernel parameters. The side that terminated the connection creates the `TIME-WAIT` socket, so it creates multiple `TIME-WAIT` sockets upstream. The `TIME-WAIT` sockets automatically disappear over time, so the failure is recovered. If the process flow is a load balancer, API server, or a microservice, then from the load balancer's perspective, the API server is downstream. The API server establishes a session with the load balancer and sets a timeout. From the microservice's perspective, the API server is upstream. For each section, you need to configure the `TIME_WAIT`, `CLOSE_WAIT`, keepalive, file descriptor, number of threads, number of sessions, various timeouts, retransmission, asynchronous, non-blocking, and epoll. Through chaos engineering, it is necessary to understand failures, consider possible failures, and set them up so that they do not propagate. Each server has different settings, so when introducing the message server and server framework, you should test a lot to select the appropriate values.

If a specific microservice goes down, only a small portion of the service is unavailable. However, if the API server and common services fail, it becomes a major failure. For example, if the security service fails, all users cannot log in. If a common service fails, restarting it does not solve the problem. Even if the common service restarts and works normally, the failure has already propagated to other services, and other services may continue to fail. This is because the configuration conditions propagate.

- `TIME-WAIT` occurs on the side that disconnects the socket. Even though hardware has become much more powerful, a large number of socket disconnects at once can cause local ports to run out of space. It is also possible that excessive resource usage can cause memory to run out.

- The `CLOSE-WAIT` setting occurs when a client fails to `CLOSE`, or a misconfiguration results in a zombie connection.

- HTTP keepalive and TCP keepalive timeouts allow connections to be reused as much as possible. This reduces latency by eliminating unnecessary connection openings and closings.

- A file descriptor is created for each socket. The number of file descriptors is also important.

- There are two timeout settings at the application level: connection timeout and read timeout. The connection timeout should be set to at least three seconds, and the read timeout should be set to at least 300 milliseconds.

- Message servers set up redelivery to ensure the delivery of messages, and you can only prevent reprocess by processing checkpoints.

- Too many thread pools cause you to run out of resources, and context switches increase latency. An insufficient number of threads processing new requests can cause latency. If there are too few, you'll have problems with throughput, causing queuing and increased latency. Threads aren't the only resource that can be depleted: sockets, file descriptors, and more can also be.

- Newly configured network switches, routers, and load balancers require a lot of testing. I have experienced several major failures with the introduction of new equipment.

There are differences between CPU and IO latency. This book is limited in its ability to explain the different types of IO, so I focus on CPU and system resources to explain root cause analysis. Compared to IO, CPU has fewer types, and errors are more predictable.

The types of IO handled by various open sources are also varied and complex.

Most clusters have implemented IO for block merges, offsets, gossip protocols, rebalancing, quorum, replication, WALs, cache LRUs, and more, and they use IO in complex ways at the cluster level. While individual IOs are not difficult to understand, troubleshooting becomes complicated when multiple IOs are competing for the same resources. It's harder to isolate failures in cluster environments than in microservices. I don't discuss the unique IO implementations of clusters like Kafka, Redis, and Elasticsearch because they are beyond the scope of this book. I describe IO at the system resource level because there are many commonalities among the various open sources. Having an SRE with experience with system resources and an expert who understands your specific cluster will help you troubleshoot your cluster.

Examples 1 and 2 occur in blocking calls, like spring MVC. Non-blocking calls are harder to develop and manage than blocking ones. Non-blocking calls make it easy to increase the number of threads and often run out of resources. There are also more requests to process downstream, increasing the risk of failure downstream. It is difficult to understand the cause of non-blocking issues using only metrics and traces, and it requires more observability of system resources using logs and profiles.

Incorrect timeout settings can have unexpected and adverse effects and can bring down the entire system. Short timeouts can weaken resiliency, while long timeouts can add unnecessary latency to customer service. Setting accurate and consistent timeouts is difficult.

CHAPTER 1 RCA ESSENTIALS

Example 3

Situation	It processes tasks such as periodically flushing from memory to disk and merging file blocks. These operations are more IO-intensive than CPU-intensive and are fundamental to applications and kernels that process large amounts of data.
	Pay attention to the frequency and throughput of IO operations. Low frequency means that flush IO threads don't run as often but can lead to high IO utilization. High frequency results in low IO usage but adds overhead to scheduling. Performance degradation can occur because too many frequent flush IO threads can eat up CPU resources. As IO utilization increases, you should be able to accurately diagnose latency through system calls and system monitoring. Application and kernel parameters that can configure frequency and throughput should be tested and assigned the appropriate values. Monitor IO at the kernel level, not just at the application IO level.
Solution	Use the compaction processes merge, compress, and sort to improve disk throughput. If the compaction tasks are not processed properly and are pushed back, or if large blocks are processed at a later time, IO utilization increases dramatically, and CPU utilization increases as well. This can lead to unexpected interrupts and latency in your application. Kernel parameters for the IO scheduler are provided, so you need to understand your workload and configure the kernel parameters accordingly.
	IO WAIT utilization is high, USER utilization is not allocated as much as needed, or SYSTEM utilization is abnormally high, which often negatively impacts other tasks.

Commercial observability and the automated instrumentation provided by OpenTelemetry may not generate spans at the thread level. For example, suppose you create a thread pool, make external calls from the threads, and spawn multiple threads through the scheduler. In these cases, you create a single span for the external calls but not for the span processed by the scheduler. Assuming that multiple threads created by the scheduler fail with a timeout error at the same time, the timeout error of the scheduler thread will not be identified in the trace. Since you do not generate span at the fine-grained thread level in most cases, you need an alternative solution.

In this case, you can use logs. Depending on the agent, they will output different results.

1. The log shows the new span ID of ten threads.

2. The log prints the span ID of only the first thread.

3. No new span ID is printed in the log, only the existing span IDs.

4. Generate a thread's span ID in the log but only support HTTP.

5. Print nothing.

Each agent can output five different results for the same thread. This is quite confusing.

Example 4

Situation	Latency can also occur in memory. The memory space that is reserved for emergency use so that the system can operate stably is the swap area. Since the swap is not physical memory, but a part of the disk that is set aside to be used as memory, it can be used when memory is low, but access and response time is low compared to memory. Therefore, using the swap will cause the system's performance to decrease.
Solution	Memory reallocation in the kernel is processed by two pieces of logic.
	This is the reallocation of cache memory used by the kernel. Free memory that is not being used by a process is primarily used by the kernel for cache purposes. By freeing up unused memory for cache, the overall performance of the system improves. However, when a process needs memory again, it may run out of memory. In this case, memory reallocation occurs.
	What if you have freed up enough memory for cache, but there is no more memory to allocate to processes? This is where swapping comes in. Writing or reading memory to and from the swap area happens on disk, causing IO and slowing down the system in the process.

Example 5

The following are the additional considerations for microservices failures:

- **Proper timeout settings:** Communication with external services is not always successful. There is a possibility of failure. If a timeout is not set or is too long, it may take a long time to process the server's request when the external service fails to return a response. You can see unnecessary latency in system traces and profiles. If that happens, the requests being processed by the server can pile up in large numbers, resulting in a high load. Therefore, you should set an appropriate timeout. It is effective to separate the timeout values according to the characteristics of the request. For example, a GET request sets a short timeout, and a POST request sets a long timeout. This allows for quick responses to requests that do not update data and sufficient time to complete requests that do update data.

- **Limiting the number of connections:** To minimize the load on external services, the number of connections to the target host can be limited. If you send a large number of requests to the same host, you should check the number of connections that are limited per host. Both the requesting and receiving services should investigate the load that they can withstand and make appropriate settings.

- **Reuse of connections:** If an HTTP client does not reuse the TCP connection of the target host for each request, it must repeat the TCP handshake, which increases the number of communications between servers and consumes a large number of local ports. Therefore, reusing TCP connections helps improve performance. In this handshake, multiple communications are made between the server and the client. Since TLS handshakes require a lot of CPU, once a TLS session is set up, it should be reused as much as possible.

Examples 1, 2, 3, 4 and 5 are failures that commercial observability options do not detect. Monitoring kernel and system resources is not supported by observability. Observability does not support monitoring of system calls between the user space and kernel space. An alternative is needed to fill the gap for these issues.

1.3. Observability Signals

The goal of this section is to explain the limitations of various signals and solutions.

If signals are configured incorrectly, the correlation is broken and the data join and lookup between signals cannot be configured. Developers can't retrieve the data they need, dashboards can't be created, and inaccurate alerts are generated.

It's not easy to notice when SRE misconfigure signals, leading to increased noise.

Be sure to describe the signals in detail and understand the problem. In the case of traces, there is an issue with span breaks. There can be constraints and issues with traces as well as the other signals: log, event, real user monitoring, and anomaly. Describing a real-world failure is the best way to understand each signal.

- **Anomalies:** It is difficult to use a metric as a data source for an anomaly. The metric structure of the histogram is too complex to be a good data source. Experience has shown that anomaly detection is difficult to operate successfully. Most anomaly detection systems built on observability fail because they are inaccurate and noisy. I describe the reasons for these failures, suggest methods and procedures, and explain how to configure them correctly. Anomaly detection is also closely related to AIOps, so it is important to configure it successfully.

- **Events:** Events don't support many protocols, only a few. This limitation is not a big deal. Events are important signals and should be considered before other signals, but many developers don't know how to use them. In production, there are many technical limitations, so there are many problems that cannot be solved by technology alone. When they are used well, events can overcome observability limitations and improve root cause analysis by event sourcing.

- **Logs:** If you can't automate the instrumentation of critical threads in your agent, you'll need to develop instrumentation manually. If you ask which is more complex, logs or traces, logs are more complex in terms of observability. Especially in older and larger companies, misconfiguration of logs sometimes leads to broken correlations and increased noise. I describe several examples and provide solutions.

- **Real user monitoring:** If you cannot instrument critical middleware such as API servers, CDNs, and load balancers, you should use real user monitoring to measure user experiences and failures. The architecture of real user monitoring can vary across vendor solutions. For example, real user monitoring can be trace- or event-based. You need to understand your commercial real-time monitoring capabilities and correlate them with other signals.

- **Debugging:** You need live debugging, which most observability systems don't yet support. This section describes how to configure remote debugging using development tools and live debugging using profiles.

- **Profiles:** Profiles lack functionality or are implemented differently for different languages. They don't support specific Java VM versions, don't come with infrastructure profiles, and have other limitations. Be careful using profiles with agents, as they can be heavy and have a high overhead because their internal operation are unknown. Profiles can be used in a variety of ways. This book describes three types of profiles. At the end of root cause analysis, it's not traces and logs that identify the cause and fix the problem. It's profiles and debugging.

The different types of profiles vary by language and product, which can be confusing for readers. To make things easier, I have unified the terminology. I don't use call stacks. Instead I use call trees, stack traces, and thread dumps. These concepts belong to profiles.

Rather than trying to fix the problem right away, being aware of the problem in advance allows you to consider other solutions and saves you time. Even if you're using an off-the-shelf product, there are still gaps, and you need to think about how to fill them.

As observability is a nascent technology, it is not yet technically mature and needs to be improved. This is not a problem when implementing simple technologies, but when implementing complex requirements, I often encounter situations where the functionality is not available and it is difficult to implement in time.

1.3.1. Logs

The limitations of the traces can be enhanced by using a log. With automated instrumentation, developers are limited to adding customized messages in trace and alternative solutions by appending the message and attributes to the log. While automated instrumentation provides convenience, it doesn't always output as much detail as intended, and black boxes and legacy systems don't support other signals, so you have to configure observability with logs only. It's important to understand that, while logs are a lower priority than other signals in observability, there are some things that only logs can do.

In observability, the log requirements are as follows:

- When outputting logs, you should output the trace context of OpenTelemetry and the trace context of commercial observability together. Because each agent has different instrumentation logic, the results printed in the log may differ between agents.

CHAPTER 1   RCA ESSENTIALS

- Logs can enhance other signals and provide additional context. However, there are bugs and problems with agents, MDCs, and threads that can cause the output of logs to be incorrect or missing.

This is where things get complicated. If you don't understand, you should reread it several times. Logs are not simple when it comes to observability. They have more problems and limitations than traces. Logs play an important role in the root cause analysis data model.

Logs from observability are not as simple as you might think. It is important to understand that commercial observability and OpenTelemetry agent log results are different. Problems can occur, as shown in Figure 1-11 with the bold line. Problems often occur between the agent and the JVM thread. For example, searching for logs with just the commercial observability trace ID returns 70 percent of the records, while searching for logs with the OpenTelemetry trace ID returns 90 percent of the records. Because each agent has different instrumentation, the logs that contain the trace context will be different. Therefore, when searching for logs, you should use a combination of commercial observability and OpenTelemetry trace ID. If you don't enter the log query correctly, you won't get the results you want.

OpenTelemetry agents use `trace_id`, micrometer traces use `traceId`, and commercial observability agents use `dt.trace_id`. These are reserved words and are the trace contexts that are written to the log. If you use reserved words for other purposes, this may cause unexpected side-effects. For example, trace IDs may not be printed to the log or may cause conflicts. This is why naming conventions and standardization of IDs is necessary. Arbitrarily replacing or interfering with them can lead to a loss of correlation between logs and other signals.

By default, Spring Boot processes logs in four steps:

1. Create a context.
2. The context from the individual threads is stored in `ThreadLocal`.
3. It is then copied from `ThreadLocal` to the MDC.
4. The log library outputs to the MDC.

The agent doesn't use `ThreadLocal`, and the rest of the process is the same.

1. Create a context.
2. The agent obtains trace context information from individual threads using automatic instrumentation; for manual instrumentation, you must use an API to obtain trace context.
3. The agent copies the acquired trace context to the MDC.
4. The log library outputs to the MDC.

The OpenTelemetry Java agent reads the trace context, then injects several pieces of information about the current span into the MDC.

CHAPTER 1 RCA ESSENTIALS

If you encounter problems with the traces, investigate whether you are creating the context correctly. Context is important in agents. If an external call is made, the next step is to investigate the propagator. OpenTelemetry logs and traces are handled differently.

If a problem occurs in the logs while using the agent, you should investigate the context, ThreadLocal, MDC, and log libraries in that order. You need to debug whether a variable is defined at a certain stage or whether its value is null.

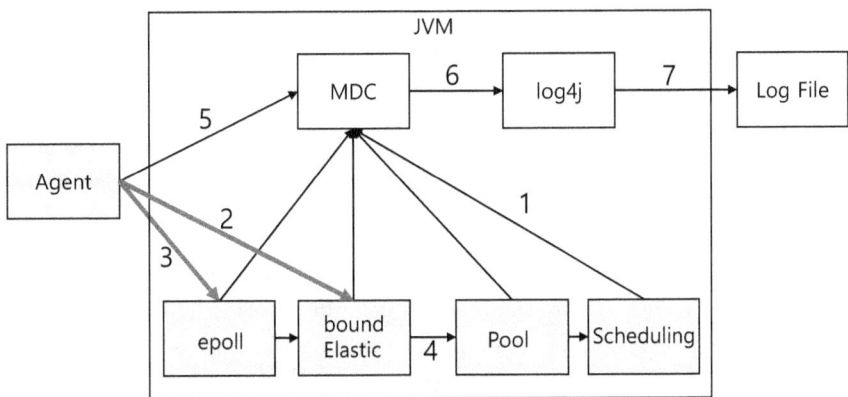

Figure 1-11. *Relationship between log and trace contexts*

Figure 1-11 shows the flow of an OpenTelemetry log:

1. JVM threads store data in the MDC using ThreadLocal. It is a good idea to add data, such as the transaction ID, to the MDC that is used throughout. If you pass the thread ID, you can see that the MDC outputs a single thread ID. There's nothing wrong with one thread doing everything, like blocking. The problem is non-blocking.

2. The OpenTelemetry agent instruments the thread and gets context. It uses two APIs internally—Span.current().getSpanContext().gettraceId() and Span.current().getSpanContext().getSpanId(). If the instrumentation fails and the trace context is not obtained, it becomes empty. The API returns a null value. The agent must correctly create and read the thread's context.

3. The agent attempts to read the context. The problem is that the agent might not support the trace context on a particular thread, or might only partially support it.

4. OpenTelemetry may not create spans during internal thread processing. Developers must manage the many actions and states generated inside threads and the passing of context between threads.

5. The OpenTelemetry agent injects the trace context into the MDC.

49

CHAPTER 1 RCA ESSENTIALS

6. The code uses the logger in the log4j API to store the data you want to output in the internal memory.

7. log4j writes the data stored in the internal memory to the log files.

Commercial observability agents can automatically inject trace context into logs. This is done by extracting the context from the thread and injecting the trace context into the MDC.

Three problems can arise during this process:

- Automated instrumentation does not generate spans of internal threads.

- Since `ThreadLocal` cannot be used in non-blocking processing, MDC context handling is complicated. In blocking, only one thread ID is stored in MDC, but in non-blocking, order IDs and request IDs must be stored in MDC. Developers need to implement the context management logic.

- It may be a commercial observability bug, but it does not print the trace context of some threads in the log. Commercial observability does not instrument internal threads, but OpenTelemetry does in some cases. Therefore, OpenTelemetry writes more trace context to the log than commercial observability.

Trace only generates spans for remote calls; inter-threaded calls do not generate spans.

For example, when using the agent, WebFlux creates a single span. Since it uses multiple threads internally, it might assume that it is normal to generate multiple spans. In terms of reactors, the trace will only generate a span for Netty and not for any subsequent threads. Reactors use multiple threads for a single request, which makes debugging difficult when using a trace. Coroutine, elastic, and parallel threads called by event loops and callbacks do not create spans, making them difficult to troubleshoot.

Non-blocking creates problems for the MDC.

When requests and responses are processed by a single thread, the context contained in the MDC remains consistent. This is because a single thread uses a `ThreadLocal`. However, non-blocking, asynchronous batches create multiple threads, and each thread creates a separate `ThreadLocal`. Using multiple threads creates different thread IDs for MDC. For example, Spring MVC is processed with a single thread that is blocked, so there is no problem with MDC processing. Since only one thread is used, there is no problem maintaining context.

Blocking printed the thread ID to the log, and non-blocking no longer uses the thread ID. Trace IDs may not be logged due to internal issues with the agent. Therefore, transactions and order IDs are used throughout the E2E process.

Transactions processed by Reactor and WebFlux go through an event loop and are processed asynchronously, non-blocking, by multiple threads instead of a single thread. As they are processed by multiple threads, they lose context. `ThreadLocal` cannot be used.

Context uses the term passing, not propagation. Between threads, it's called *passing*. It is important to understand that the terms propagate, pass, and transfer are used differently in different use cases.

The context is not passed automatically by agents between threads, and this breaks the context that should be passed between threads. When a new thread is created and a context switch occurs, the MDC needs to be copied manually by the developer so that the context can maintain consistency. This requires additional work for developers.

If you are trying to use a thread ID in observability to understand context from logs, you may run into problems.

You cannot use a thread ID alone, but must use it in combination with other IDs (trace context, transaction IDs, payment IDs). Use a combination of different trace contexts and global identifiers. Given that the thread ID is an important identifier for infrastructure observability, the non-blocking approach makes it difficult for SREs and developers to understand the context.

Tracing alone is not enough for a non-blocking approach; observability must be augmented in a variety of ways.

Different frameworks have different APIs for propagating the MDC.

Depending on the agent, it fails to instrument the thread, and it fails to write to the log.

The developer is responsible for maintaining the consistency of the MDC if there are problems with the MDC as it goes through multiple threads in non-blocking. However, if a problem occurs with a value that OpenTelemetry uses and injects, such as `trace_id`, the SRE should be able to answer the question. Propagating between internal threads, such as non-blocking, is best done using logs.

The trace results between OpenTelemetry and commercial observability traces show differences. There are differences in the results of traces as well as the logs. It is important to understand the differences and limitations between these two agents.

Any differences in the MDC results between the OpenTelemetry agent and the commercial observability agent should be resolved by the SRE. For example, if the MDC results from OpenTelemetry are different from the MDC results from the commercial observability agent, the SRE should explain these differences to the developer. The developer has developed the MDC to propagate across multiple threads, but sometimes the trace context of the agent (e.g., trace context `trace_id` in OpenTelemetry and trace context `dt.trace_id` in the commercial observability agent) is not written to the log.

The agent injects an empty value into the MDC. This is because the agent's instrumentation of the thread fails and returns an empty value. The OpenTelemetry agent officially supports Spring Scheduling, Spring WebFlux, Reactor, Netty HTTP codec, Reactor Netty, and Kotlin Coroutines and shows satisfactory results. However, in commercial observability, the Spring framework instrumentation may fail.

When configuring traces and logs based on observability, you will experience cases where context propagation fails and breaks. The problem is that OpenTelemetry succeeds, but commercial observability agents fail. Since propagation only fails with expensive commercial observability agents, many developers will question why. SREs need to respond to these problems carefully. When introducing new observability, SREs sometimes hear complaints from developers who are used to logs.

Here's how to use logs in observability:

- Understand the difference between traditional log-centric monitoring and observability, and be able to utilize logs differently. In observability, logs should not be the centerpiece but rather augment other signals.

CHAPTER 1 RCA ESSENTIALS

- There are many systems where it is difficult to configure observability using traces, such as black boxes and legacy. In these cases, using logs to configure observability is more effective.

- Make sure to include detailed error and debugging messages when configuring automated instrumentation, as this adds context to the logs and helps in troubleshooting problems.

- For complex non-blocking processes, such as WebFlux and virtual threads, you should use logs to analyze the problem and fill any gaps.

- While metrics and traces are restricted when adding attributes, logs are relatively flexible when adding attributes. This allows you to utilize it for alerts and dashboards.

1.3.1.1. Case 1

The problem with outputting the trace context to the log is as follows.

If service A's scheduling-1 is doing critical processes, it is important to monitor it. Since tracing does not support scheduling-1 threads, you must use a log. You can search for scheduling-1 threads in the logs by their OpenTelemetry span IDs. The problem is that you cannot search for scheduling-1 threads with commercial observability trace IDs and span IDs. Table 1-2 shows that the results instrumented with commercial observability agents and OpenTelemetry are output to the trace differently.

Table 1-2. *Trace Comparison in a Log*

	OpenTelemetry Trace ID	OpenTelemetry Span ID	Commercial Observability Trace ID	Commercial Observability Span ID	Thread Name
Service A	1	1-1	A	A-1	pool-4-thread-10
Service A	1	1-1			scheduling-1
Service A	1	1-1			scheduling-1
Service A	1	1-1			scheduling-1
Service B	1	1-2	A	A-2	reactor-http-epoll-4

As the agent is being enhanced, the instrumentation results may change in the future, but the current results are shown in Table 1-3.

Table 1-3. Java Thread Type

Thread Name	OpenTelemetry	Commercial Observability
pool-4-thread-10	Unsupported	Unsupported
boundedElastic-439	Unsupported	Unsupported
reactor-http-epoll-4	Partial support; some threads have no span	Partial support; fewer spans output than OpenTelemetry
scheduling-1	Partial support; span output on all threads; no new span creation	Partial support; span output for first thread only

If you need to monitor scheduling-1, you are always under pressure to use OpenTelemetry. Commercial observability agents have problems processing MDC for certain threads.

1.3.1.2. Case 2

Logs are used for various purposes and must be recorded accurately. You should avoid cases where the search does not work or is missing from the log.

Before the introduction of OpenTelemetry, there was often no naming convention in the logs, or the naming convention was not followed. For example, trace_id is a reserved word used by the OpenTelemetry agent, and developers can use trace_id, causing a conflict. If multiple agents are used together, you must be able to debug the context, ThreadLocal, and the MDC. The behavior of each agent is different, and there may be bugs. Eventually, the trace context may not be searched in the log, or it may not be recorded correctly and omitted.

You can either change the log settings for all microservices and redeploy them, or find and change the code that handles OpenTelemetry's logs.

It is difficult to find the right method in code that has over hundreds of thousands of lines, when only the key of the trace context needs to be changed. It was difficult to find the method by just loading the class, but I was able to identify the following method while understanding the process that the logback library handles in the profile's call tree.

```
opentelemetry-java-instrumentation/instrumentation/logback/logback-mdc-1.0/library/src/main/
java/io/opentelemetry/instrumentation/logback/mdc/v1_0/OpenTelemetryAppender.java
private String traceIdKey = LoggingContextConstants.TRACE_ID;

  /** Customize MDC key name for the trace id. */
  public void setTraceIdKey(String traceIdKey) {
    this.traceIdKey = traceIdKey;
  }
```

CHAPTER 1 RCA ESSENTIALS

As explained, instead of using ThreadLocal, the OpenTelemetry agent injects trace context into the MDC, intercepting it in the middle and changing the MDC key of the trace ID.

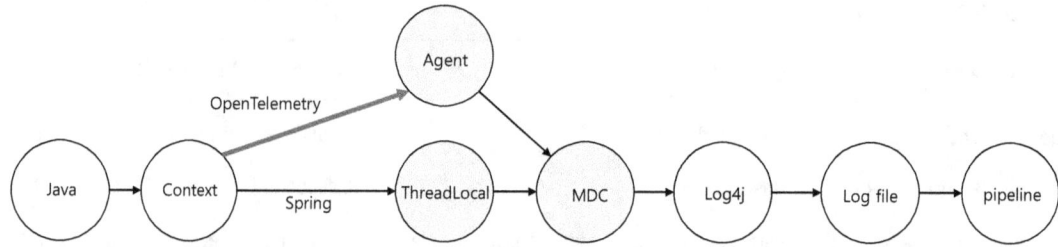

Figure 1-12. *Processing order of the agent*

Figure 1-12 shows the processing order of agent, an OpenTelemetry agent requires context injection for tracing. The log is processed through the following five-step process:

1. Context is created.

2. The Java agent reads the context.

3. The Java agent copies the context to the MDC.

4. The log library reads from the MDC.

5. The log library is used in the runtime code to output the log.

In Step 3, the agent copies the context to the MDC. The issue was resolved by finding the code, modifying the MDC key of the trace context to prevent conflicts, and redeploying it.

It is easy for a developer to set the standard of the log, modify the code according to the guidelines, redeploy it, and correctly output it to the log. However, with thousands of microservices already in production, it is difficult to accurately output logs without modifying the code.

There are situations where SREs need to analyze hundreds of thousands of lines of agent code and accurately output logs without requiring developers to change their code.

You will most likely experience these problems if you use a commercial observability agent or multiple agents. It was impossible to solve the problem with the log pipeline after it was ingested. Log modification is led by the SRE, but collaboration with developers is required.

- The previous code is managed by the SRE because it is the code of the OpenTelemetry agent. If it is a library managed by developers like Spring Boot, the SRE will not be able to change the code.

- OpenTelemetry extensions can be used to instrument bytecode, but developers may not allow it.

It is necessary to establish a standard for logs and provide developers with accurate guidance. However, as organizations, platforms, and technologies continue to change, it is difficult to accurately output logs according to a set log standard. It is almost impossible to change the log settings of a microservice with a million instances and redeploy it in production.

1.3.1.3. Case 3

In Figure 1-13, after receiving a request from WebFlux, you can process the coroutine and the virtual thread. Even if it is blocked by being processed by JPA downstream, there is no problem because the reactor is non-blocking.

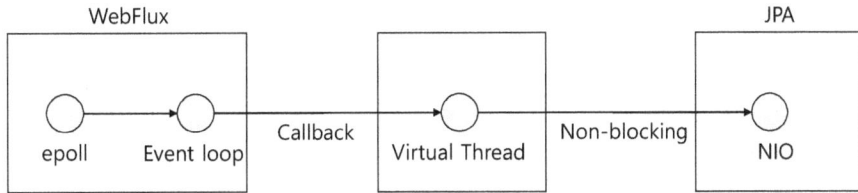

Figure 1-13. *Spring processing*

Without non-blocking, a reactor meltdown will occur. If you are using the reactor scheduler with WebFlux, parallel threads may not create spans. In commercial observability, the span may not be created. Through technical verification, you should check whether a trace is being performed.

When using Project Reactor or the Reactor Scheduler, it is necessary to configure the logs correctly.

1.3.2. RUM (Real User Monitoring)

Distributed traces are specialized for backend applications, while RUM is specialized for frontend applications such as web and apps.

There are two ways to monitor from a frontend user perspective—synthetic testing and RUM. Synthetic testing is an automated testing method and is used primarily to measure the availability of endpoints, while RUM (real user monitoring) measures actual user sessions, actions, events, and errors. In practice, you should be able to utilize both appropriately.

Synthetic tests are useful for health checks on a variety of services:

- Health checks for various protocols and endpoints, including HTTP and TCP.
- Kubernetes Liveness checks the health of the service.
- Health checks with lookup queries in the database.
- Message servers (Kafka, JMS, GCP PubSub) do not provide endpoints, making health checks difficult. Develop an application that measures the number of messages pending in topics and queues and outputs them as logs and metrics for health checks.

CHAPTER 1 RCA ESSENTIALS

CNCF is adding support for RUM to the OpenTelemetry standard. It supports client development languages (JavaScript, SWIFT, and Kotlin) to support a variety of apps in addition to the JavaScript used by web browsers.

The RUM demo uses Grafana Faro to implement RUM and span the network latency between the frontend and backend. Grafana Faro provides an API for RUM. For example, it automates instruments for the frontend JavaScript and generates various logs and traces.

To explain the terminology, images and documents are loaded, and XHR uses fetch.

There are two cases where traces are generated on the frontend:

- When an XHR event occurs on the frontend
- When image resources and documents are loaded.

Interact CDN is similar to the screen in the Google Chrome developer tool and helps developers understand the latency and order in which documents and images are loaded. The XHR method is responsible for calling the backend.

By connecting RUM and trace, you can monitor the session that the user connects to the mobile app or web browser through the frontend, to the backend, and finally to the E2E. This monitoring approach is very helpful for root cause analysis.

With the addition of RUM, the scope of instrumentation has changed. As shown in Figure 1-14, you instrument events in the mobile app and for the web, and create a new trace for the frontend. Previously, the backend microservices or API server was the point where the trace ID started, but with the addition of RUM, the frontend becomes the point where the trace ID is generated.

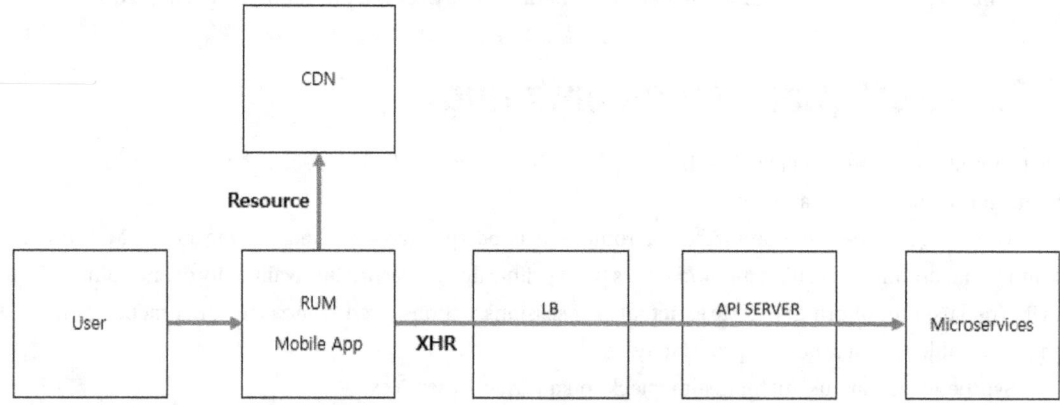

Figure 1-14. *RUM's trace process flow*

With RUM, you can monitor from the user's perspective. For example, you can analyze the cause of problems across the E2E, including areas that the SRE doesn't consider, such as location and the user's device.

CHAPTER 1   RCA ESSENTIALS

Grafana Faro consists of frontend instrumentation and trace instrumentation. I start with frontend instrumentation. The Grafana Faro library collects data from the frontend using the tools described here. Once the required data is collected, the Grafana Faro web SDK sends it to the Grafana agent. Here, the data is categorized into logs, exceptions, events, and measurements. To observe the frontend, you can use the following instrumentation:

- Console instrumentation collects logs based on the enabled log-level filters (debug, error, and log).

- Error instrumentation collects errors, extracts the corresponding stack traces, and reports any errors to the server.

- Web Vitals instrumentation measures the actual performance of your site in the browser so that you can improve the user experience.

- Session trace instrumentation helps you correlate errors, logs, and events that occur for a specific end user during a single session of your application.

- View trace instrumentation helps you correlate errors, logs, and events that occur in specific sections of your application.

Trace instrumentation occurs after frontend instrumentation. When a user interacts with frontend, trace instrumentation measures the duration and collects metadata of the events that are called in the browser. The instrumentation for the trace is as follows:

- User interaction instrumentation records the duration of triggered events and the kinds of user interactions that occurred.

- Load instrumentation measures the time it takes for a web page to initially load static resources.

- Fetch instrumentation uses the Fetch API. It measures the time it takes for a request to be delivered.

- `XMLHttpRequest` is an older version of the Fetch API. A distributed trace is generated and associated with the backend.

The OpenTelemetry RUM procedure is as follows:

1. You see the errors in the log and recognize the problem.

2. The session ID is printed in the log with an error message.

3. The event of clicking the button calls XHR and generates a trace ID. XHR adds the trace ID to the header, and the frontend can be propagated.

4. The session ID is injected into the header or cookie.

5. You then identify, troubleshoot, and tune the user experience.

For example, if you experience slow service in certain regions or if certain users have problems with the quality of service, you need to address them. RUM is useful in these cases and can provide a solution.

OpenTelemetry JavaScript can generate traces from requests called from the web screen. At this time, OpenTelemetry RUM simply generates traces, but does not provide full observability of the frontend. The data collected by RUM can be very valuable and useful for analytics, but the technology still has a lot of room for improvement.

1.3.2.1. RUM Demo

Correlation between traces and other signals is one of the keys to implementing observability. This demo explains the correlation between RUM and distributed traces. The traces described in RUM are more complex than distributed traces. This is because there is additional instrumentation on the frontend.

Currently, OpenTelemetry provides some API for RUM and profiles, but it does not satisfy the functional requirements. In particular, OpenTelemetry RUM cannot be built using the API alone, but requires a variety of additional features and backend storage.

There are many different events in RUM. For example, there are a number of events that load images and documents, click buttons, and output results. There are resources that are loaded when a page is loaded, when requests are fetched, and when users interact with the program. Faro provides automated instrumentation for events and generates spans of traces from events:

- When the initial document is loaded, the OpenTelemetry instrumentation generates a span for the client-side event. The trace instrumentation provided by Faro automatically creates a trace parent and generates a span when instrumenting loading for the document.

- When you run the fetch request, the trace parent header is injected into the request. The OpenTelemetry API extracts this header and processes the propagation.

- In addition to automated instrumentation, Faro also provides an API called push traces for manual generation of spans.

Here's how to set up the demo:

```
docker-compose --profile demo up -d
```

Run it according to your package manager. This command installs the library in your project:

```
npm i -S @grafana/faro-web-sdk
```

```
yarn add @grafana/faro-web-sdk
```

CHAPTER 1 RCA ESSENTIALS

You can use OpenTelemetry traces with instrumentation. OpenTelemetry tracing is available in the @grafana/faro-web-tracing package.

The provided OpenTelemetry setup includes trace tools for user interactions, document loading, and propagating W3C trace contexts via fetch and XHR.

```
import { getWebInstrumentations, initializeFaro } from '@grafana/faro-web-sdk';
import { TracingInstrumentation } from '@grafana/faro-web-tracing';

const faro = initializeFaro({
  url: 'http://localhost:12345/collect',
  apiKey: 'secret',
  instrumentations: [...getWebInstrumentations(), new TracingInstrumentation()],
  app: {
    name: 'frontend',
    version: '1.0.0',
  },
});

const { trace, context } = faro.api.getOTEL();

const tracer = trace.getTracer('default');
const span = tracer.startSpan('click');
context.with(trace.setSpan(context.active(), span), () => {
  doSomething();
  span.end();
});
```

The demo outputs the session ID and trace ID in the log (i.e., it checks the session ID in the log in Grafana Loki, and goes from the log to the trace in Grafana Tempo).

As shown in Figure 1-15, RUM creates a session ID, a span ID, and a trace ID to associate with trace. The test scenario is explained here:

1. Go to the Seed page and click the Seed button. Check the trace and span IDs, and check for errors in Grafana.

2. Go to the article page, add an article, check the trace and span IDs, and check the results in Grafana.

3. Write a comment on the article you created. Check the trace and span IDs.

CHAPTER 1 RCA ESSENTIALS

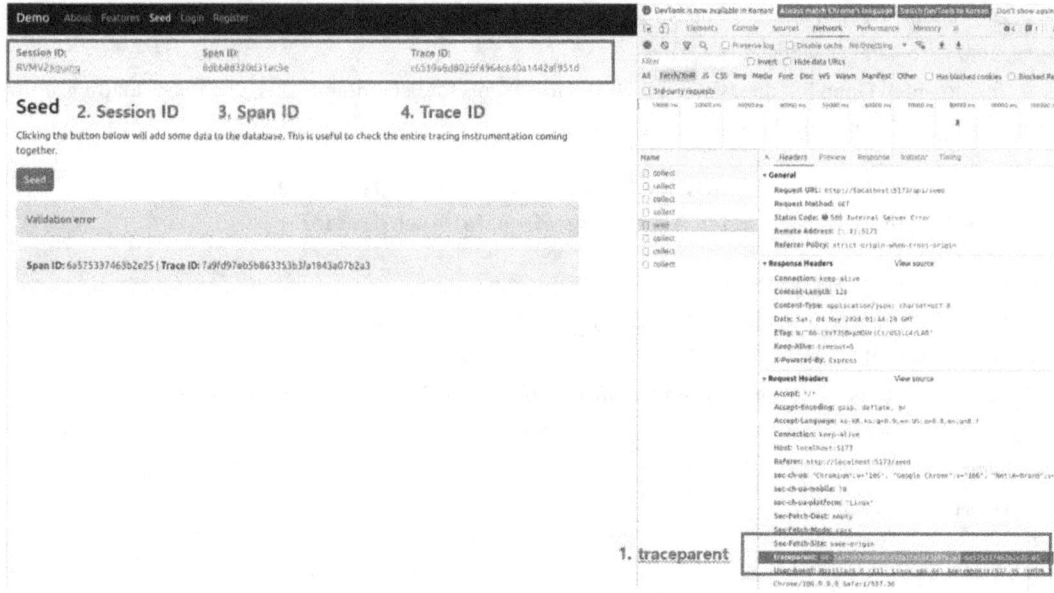

Figure 1-15. *Checking the trace ID in RUM*

Figure 1-15 shows the trace header being generated by RUM. Without any monitoring tools, Chrome developers can see the trace ID in the header.

You can see that errors are thrown, as shown in Figure 1-16. To check these errors, enter the trace ID into Tempo. You can check the span of the client and server sides, and you can see that the error occurred in the server. This is useful for checking detailed errors on the backend server and troubleshooting errors.

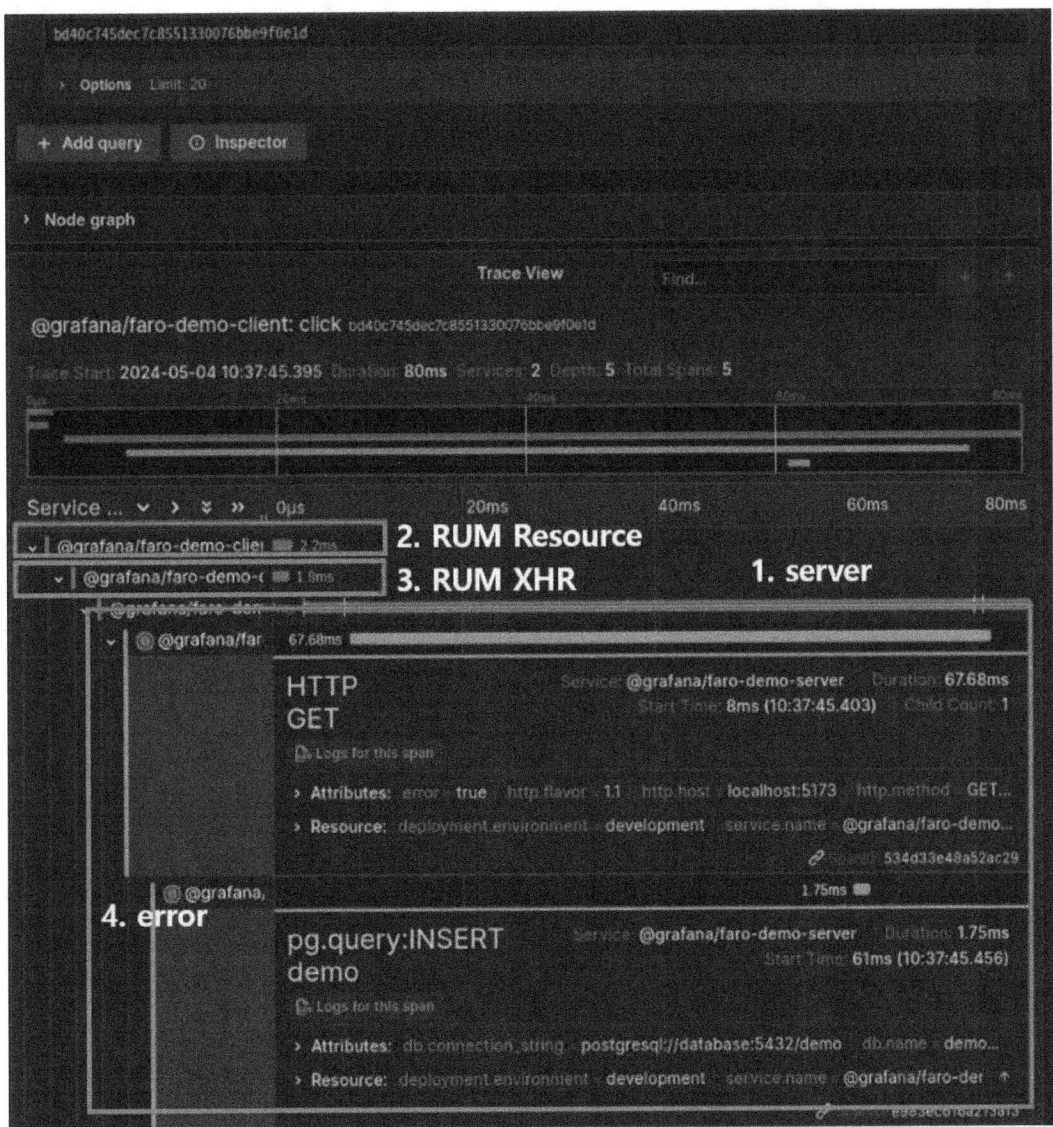

Figure 1-16. Propagate between RUM and distributed traces

As mentioned earlier, you can check the trace ID directly in the browser and search for the trace ID in Tempo to understand the problem. I've created a trace context from the frontend and connected it to the backend with a distributed trace. Traces are configured from the frontend to the backend, and you can easily identify errors when problems occur in the frontend.

The log outputs the session ID. It is common for the session ID to be associated with the trace ID.

The data visualization is shown here:

1. Select a Loki data source.

2. In the filter, select `kind=event`.

3. Some events are added to a span or to multiple spans. When you expand such an event, you can access the corresponding span by clicking the Tempo button.

The frontend application generates logs and navigates to the trace via the trace ID contained in the logs. To summarize, there are two ways to identify failures in the frontend:

- The frontend creates a trace context so you can identify the error via the trace ID.

- The frontend writes the trace context to the log so you can identify the trace ID where the error occurred in the log.

You can see that the trace ID has the Tempo connection enabled.

The frontend of the demo fetches resources and documents and then generates spans when a button click event occurs. It then propagates the trace to a distributed trace on the backend.

Microservices are affected by requests from the frontend. There are many types of errors that can occur, such as retrying an incorrect XHR, which increases latency, or the XHR failing to reach the backend and causing an error.

The client does not control the order of parallel XHR calls, or latency increases due to sequential XHR calls. Even if the backend is analyzed in detail using distributed traces, it is difficult to solve the problem if the frontend continues to make calls in the wrong way. This is why it is difficult to analyze the problem from the backend alone and why it is necessary to configure E2E observability in combination with RUM. To understand and solve problems, you need to analyze the frontend and backend at the same time. RUM enables this analysis.

1.3.2.2. RUM Metrics

If you are using a commercial observability RUM, metrics are automatically created or provided. If you're using open source, you may only have the RUM API, so you'll need to create your own metrics, as shown in Figure 1-17.

CHAPTER 1   RCA ESSENTIALS

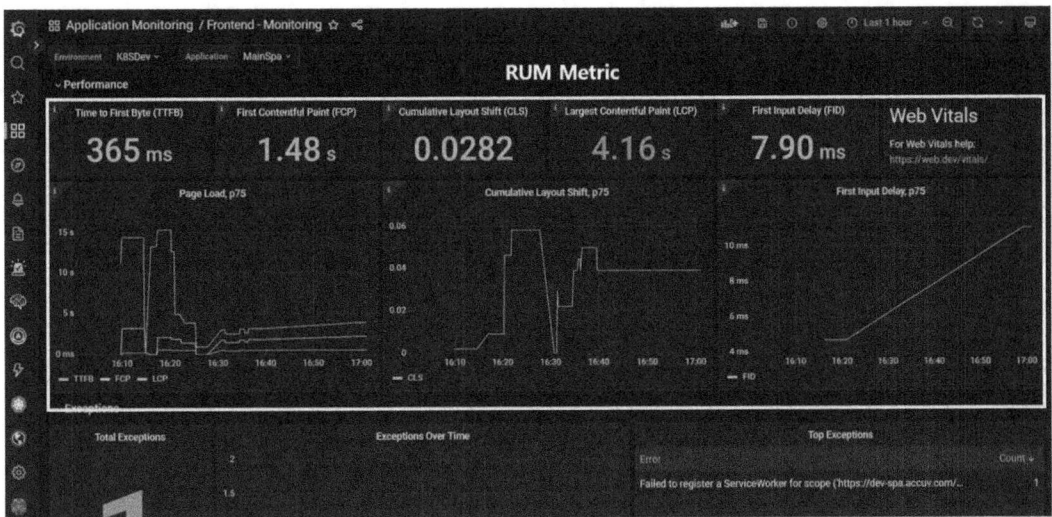

Figure 1-17. RUM dashboard layout

Grafana Faro outputs the RUM metric in the log. If you look at the data source of the Faro RUM dashboard, some charts use metrics, but most of them use logs. While it's good to output logs to the dashboard, I recommend changing logs to metrics.

TTFB, FCP, CLS, LCP, FID Vitals, and Apdex are frequently used metrics in RUM. Most of them are related to response time:

- FCP is an important user-centered metric that measures perceived load speed. It shows the first point in the page load timeline, where the user can see everything on the screen. FCP measures the time between when a user first navigates to a page and when some of the page's content is rendered on the screen. In this metric, "content" means document and images.

- TTFB is a metric that measures the time between a request for a resource and when the first byte of the response begins to arrive. TTFB takes precedence over user-centric metrics like FCP and LCP, so you want your server to respond to navigation requests fast enough so that the 75th percentile of users experience an FCP within the "good" standard. As a rough guide, most sites should strive for a duration to the first byte of 0.8 seconds or less.

- Web Vitals is a Google initiative that provides a unified guide to the web page quality signals that are essential to delivering a great user experience on the web. It aims to simplify the various performance measurement tools available and help site owners focus on the metrics that matter most.

CHAPTER 1 RCA ESSENTIALS

- The maximum content render time (LCP) measures load performance. To provide a good user experience, the LCP should occur within 2.5 seconds after the page first starts to load.

- First-input response time (FID) measures interactions. To provide a good user experience, your page should have an FID of 100 milliseconds or less.

- Cumulative layout change (CLS) is a measure of visual stability. To provide a good user experience, you should keep CLS below 0.1.

Frontend applications generate logs during operation. By reading and processing the logs, you can generate RUM metrics. Given the nature of frontend applications, it is useful to collect logs. The way to convert logs to metrics is to use the Prometheus recording rules.

In order to develop recording and alert rules in Grafana Mimir, you need to configure the following:

```
ruler_storage:
  backend: filesystem
  filesystem:
    dir: /tmp/mimir/rules
```

Alerts are based on metrics. Traces, profiles, and logs are not suitable for developing complex rules. Therefore, it is useful to convert signals to metrics and develop rules.

Loki uses a Prometheus recording rule. Using the recording rule, you can create a metric for Loki and use that metric in the alert rule, as shown here:

```
groups:
    - name: Loki logs disk usage
      interval: 1m
      rules:
        - record: logs_bytes_over_time_1m
          expr: |
            bytes_over_time({job="hotrod"} [1m])
```

The Loki configuration file is shown here:

```
auth_enabled: false

server:
  http_listen_port: 3100

ingester:
  lifecycler:
    address: 127.0.0.1
    ring:
      kvstore:
```

```
        store: inmemory
      replication_factor: 1
    final_sleep: 0s
  chunk_idle_period: 5m
  chunk_retain_period: 30s
  max_transfer_retries: 0

ruler:
  storage:
    type: local
    local:
      directory: /rules
  remote_write:
    enabled: true
    client:
      url: http://localhost:9090/api/v1/write

storage_config:
  boltdb:
    directory: /data/loki/index

table_manager:
  retention_deletes_enabled: false
  retention_period: 0s
```

If you are not enforcing multitenancy, use the /fake directory.

```
$ pwd
/rules/fake
```

In a multitenant environment, recording and alert rules should be developed on a per-tenant basis. Logs, traces, and metrics should be isolated per tenant. Despite the fact that multitenancy can make your system more reliable, it is not always easy to configure. If you have a difficult organizational structure, you don't need to force multitenancy.

1.3.2.3. RUM in Commercial Observability Agents

Dynatrace provides a number of features for monitoring your frontend.

You need to associate user sessions and user actions that happen on the frontend with backend traces. However, there is no clear standard for how to propagate from RUM to traces. OpenTelemetry provides APIs to develop traces in web and developed in JavaScript, Swift, and Kotlin, but it is common for different solutions to propagate in various ways.

CHAPTER 1   RCA ESSENTIALS

Before you decide to adopt observability, make sure that your RUM can be configured with OpenTelemetry distributed traces. Commercial observability RUM does not support distributed traces and configures RUM with OpenTelemetry-incompatible technology. Rather than propagating traces to microservices, RUM and distributed traces are coupled by passing user sessions and actions via cookies. You need to understand why this is appropriate and configure a commercial observability RUM.

With open source agents, RUM is part of the trace. In commercial observability agents, RUM is separate from traces and propagates directly to the microservices:

- Some API servers do not support distributed traces. Even if you propagate distributed traces in RUM, they may not be propagated in the API server. They bypass the API server.

- Managed API servers do not allow for instrumentation and cannot generate traces because the agents are not configurable. For example, Spring Cloud Gateway allows you to configure agents so you can generate traces. Managed API servers do not allow agent instrumentation.

- API servers often use the B3 zipkin and do not use OpenTelemetry. If the API server propagates to the microservice with B3, the microservice must be configured as a B3 propagator. B3 propagators for hundreds of microservices are architecturally inefficient and difficult to configure.

Configuring traces on the API server is important for traffic flow. If you experience frequent failures on your API server, it is important to configure traces on your API server and respond to failures. For the reasons described here, it may be difficult to configure traces on the API server.

In RUM, the principle is to automate the instrument in the frontend to generate spans. As a result, context is propagated between the frontend span and the backend span. However, this can vary depending on the implementation of the RUM solution. If the frontend does not generate traces, the API server is the starting point for generating traces. Depending on the RUM solution, traces may be generated on the frontend or on the API server. It's important to understand the solution and configure the E2E trace architecture. If your API server doesn't support distributed trace, you'll need to create traces in the microservices on the backend. If your CDN, load balancer, and API server don't support traces, it will be difficult to perform root cause analysis on transactions coming from the frontend.

Figure 1-18 shows the relationship between RUM and traces. It is important to understand the concepts of sessions and actions that make up a RUM and map them to distributed traces:

- A session records the time when a user accesses and exits the frontend. As an example of a session, if a user accesses the site with a browser, a session has been created, such as "The user accessed online banking at 9:00 on the iPhone."

- Users perform various actions within a web application. An example of a user action is "The user transferred funds to another banking." If the user clicks the transfer button, an action has occurred.

CHAPTER 1 RCA ESSENTIALS

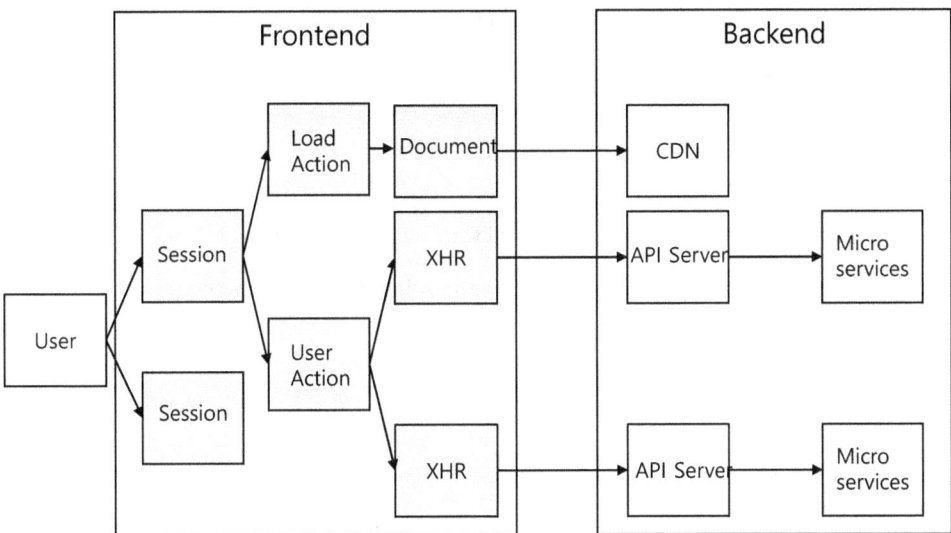

Figure 1-18. *RUM object relationships*

In commercial observability use, user sessions, load actions, and XHR are not included in traces but are stored in events. The correlation between RUM and traces is processed as a cookie, and the data can be joined between events and traces. Commercial RUMs are stored in events, not traces.

There are three types of events, listed here. Events can be created in a variety of ways:

- Capture the headers and bodies of requests and responses for specific sections, as requested.

- Generate an event with an external hook.

- Generate them when RUMs are processed.

You need a separate database to store this structure.

User sessions, load actions, and user action XHRs are instrumented by RUM, while the backend uses distributed traces. In RUM, user actions are associated with a trace ID. XHR is the starting point for generating traces. When a user accesses your web and app, it creates a user session, structures all user experiences, and records them in the RUM database.

When a user connects to your web or app, they create a session. When you measure sessions, you can measure a lot more than just access and user traffic. The web is made up of many web pages, so you can measure user traffic to a specific page on the website. A web page may have multiple buttons, and when a button is clicked, it generates an event, which makes a request to the backend. In addition to the XHR event of a button click, the web page automatically calls a number of API when it loads, all of which need to be measured.

In RUM, you can use these IDs to build queries. In dashboards and alerts, you can use RUM queries to perform root cause analysis and generate business reports.

RUM has many different IDs. To retrieve data, various IDs are required:

- If the user is using a web browser, a session ID can be used. The session ID contains multiple trace IDs. When the session expires, a session ID is generated for a new RUM.

- The session ID contains a load action and a user action. The user action contains multiple XHRs. The XHRs are associated with a distributed trace.

- Resources such as images are load actions and should be processed on the CDN, while user actions are processed on the API server through XHR. You can identify whether a failure occurred on the CDN through the load action or on the API server through the user action. By joining the session ID and user ID, you can analyze the impact of a failure on the user. Even if the CDN and API server are not instrumented, RUM can act as a client to the CDN and API server to fill in the gaps.

You may want to monitor whether XHR is being processed in parallel or sequentially, whether unnecessary retries are occurring, and whether errors are occurring on certain pages in your frontend.

You can configure dashboards and with queries that look for errors in your CDN, API server, and frontend.

RUM doesn't just provide an API; it also provides a RUM backend to manage all user experiences and a query language to query RUM data, as shown in Figure 1-19. RUM delivers high value from a business perspective, so you should build a RUM backend and make the data available to the entire organization to make good use of it.

Sometimes, the backend storage for RUM is separate from the distributed traces, as shown in Figure 1-19, and should be consolidated in distributed traces whenever possible.

It is important to monitor the response time and errors of multiple actions within a session. To analyze multiple actions in a session, a session ID is used.

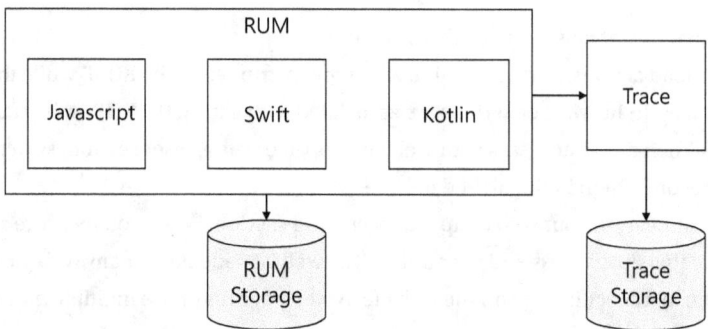

Figure 1-19. *Backend storage in RUM*

RUM collects two types of data:

- Manage resources and documents

- Fetch and XHR API calls

In OpenTelemetry RUM, these features are created as spans and stored in backend storage. In OpenTelemetry, RUM's backend storage is the same as trace's backend storage. However, in commercial observability, the RUM backend storage is built separately.

OpenTelemetry supports Kotlin and Swift, so RUM of apps is possible, but automated instrumentation is difficult and features are lacking compared to commercial observability. Commercial observability offers additional features such as session replays.

1.3.3. Profiles

To be precise, logs and traces are not suitable for root cause analysis. Profiles and debugging are more suitable signals for root cause analysis.

The term *profile* is used in a variety of ways, which can be confusing. The profile I am talking about is the profile of an application running in a user space.

This book discusses three types of profiles:

- Traditional profile VisualVM, there are profiles that allow you to drill down into CPU, memory, locks, IO, garbage collection, queries, and samples for a specific language. You can visualize the process through stack traces and call trees.

- Grafana Pyroscope is called a continuous profile, and it is suitable for observability and collaboration. Correlations can be constructed between other signals and profiles. The visualization method is a flame graph, histogram, or heatmap. It can output duration, utilization, and the number of calls.

- You can profile using eBPF and system utilities at the infrastructure level. It can be confusing because eBPF provides a lot of functionality, but it supports profile and outputs data as metrics. eBPF supports profiles, not traces.

For now, I discuss the continuous profile.

If you don't understand the low-level systems, you can't interpret the profiles. The results of the profile do not directly indicate issues or errors. They only describe time, frequency, distribution, counts, relationships, and order, making it difficult to interpret the results. It's hard to understand traces if you don't understand business processes, but understanding profiles requires different knowledge.

Traditional profiles, such as VisualVM, are not well suited for observability but are technically mature and require a large learning curve.

Pyroscope is good for observability and supports many languages, but it is still lacking in functionality. eBPF has less overhead than system utilities and allows for more detailed profiles, but the user interface is poor and disorganized, and the learning curve is high. There are clear differences between the profiles, and you should choose the one that's right for your situation and goals.

A profile captures an application's characteristics while it is running and uses this information to make the application faster and more efficient. The problems with metrics and traces are as follows:

- Metrics often don't allow for detailed analysis. It is possible to recognize a problem through metrics, but it is difficult to provide a solution to the problem. Metrics are suitable for high-level aggregations, not method-level.

- While tracing is useful for understanding latency, it doesn't provide much detail about resource usage, such as CPU memory and problems with methods and threads.

Traditional profiles were primarily utilized during application development, requiring the ability to develop separate load tests and benchmarks that could accurately forecast production environments.

Continuous profiling refers to profiling an application while it is running in production. This approach eliminates the need to develop accurate forecast load tests and benchmarks of your production environment. It has low overhead and allows for statistical or sampling profiles that are appropriate for production environments.

I prioritize profiles for the following reasons:

- **Support for multiple development languages:** Rather than supporting only one language, profiling supports multiple development languages to fit modern development environments. The downside is that there may be differences in the features supported by various languages.

- **Correlates with other signals:** A continuous profile fills important gaps left by metrics, logs, and traces and creates a more comprehensive observability strategy.

- **Low overhead:** Profiles operate with low overhead. Continuous profiling allows teams to proactively identify and resolve performance bottlenecks, resulting in more efficient and reliable applications.

1.3.3.1. Profile Architecture

The existing profile helps you understand how the program utilizes limited resources.

- **Sample-based profiles:** Like thread dumps and memory dumps, a profile interrupts the program at regular intervals and captures the state of the program each time. By analyzing these snapshots, developers can make inferences about how often parts of the code are executed.

- **Instrumentation-based profiles:** Developers inject additional code into the program that records information about execution. This approach provides detailed insights, such as whether the added code is optimized, and whether the added code overhead is a burden.

It is important to perform a thread dump at the time the error occurs. This is not an easy task, as it requires multiple thread dumps, which can cause problems with traffic in production. Profiles are not intended to replace thread dumps but are more useful when used in conjunction with thread dumps to enhance for their shortcomings. A profile provides detailed information about whether there are any problems after a code change, including hotspots, thread status, duration, and number of threads at the thread level.

Once you've modified and deployed code based on your analysis of thread dumps, you'll need observability to compare the changes in production. Profiles can play a role. Profiles provide more detail at the method level than traces can provide, so when combined with traces, they allow for quick and accurate analysis. It's also a good idea to associate logs with profiles.

The disadvantages of traditional profiles include:

- Difficult to integrate with observability.

- Difficult to configure correlation.

- Difficult to analyze using Grafana dashboards or SQL.

- Since they are utilized during development, it is difficult to implement additional rules, such as alerts.

- Different profiles use different methods and output different results, requiring a high learning curve.

Profiles do not replace thread dumps. They are useful together but they reduce the need to try thread dumps. Running multiple thread dumps multiple times is not a good idea.

Profiles use flame graphs to represent various resources at a glance. Basic usage and duration can be seen, but complex functionality is not yet supported. Profiles support common and basic language-specific technologies but are not capable of expressing the level of granularity of eBPF and many programming languages. Different languages have different capabilities for profiles. For example, certain profiles can identify race conditions in Golang but not in Java.

Continuous profiles lack functionality. Traditional profiles provide detailed profile information specific to the development language, but standardization is difficult, and the learning curve is high in microservice environments. However, they are feature-rich and allow for more detailed profiles than continuous profiles do.

Managing different profiles for different languages is time-consuming and inefficient. A typical profile outputs frequency, count, usage, and duration at method level. This allows you to understand the problems that cause latency, slowdowns, or excessive resource usage. CPU duration and memory usage are discussed in more detail in the following example.

CPU duration:

- CPU time is the amount of time the CPU spends executing the block of code. It's also important to measure how long the CPU is waiting.

CHAPTER 1 RCA ESSENTIALS

- The actual duration of a method is a measure of the duration from entry method to exit method. The actual duration includes all latency, including locks and thread synchronization. The actual duration of a block of code cannot be shorter than the CPU duration.

- If the actual duration is longer than the CPU time, it means that the code is taking time to wait. If the difference is large, it can cause a resource bottleneck in your application.

- If the CPU time is close to the actual duration, this means that the code is CPU intensive. Most of the time spent executing the code is spent on the CPU. You should optimize CPU-intensive methods in your code that run for a long time.

It is important to distinguish between actual duration and the CPU time.

Memory usage:

- Heap usage is the amount of memory allocated to a program's heap at the moment the profile is collected. With profile types where data is collected over a specific interval, the profile collects heap usage at a single point in time.

- Heap usage includes all memory that was allocated and is now released and no longer in use. For example, suppose you allocate 1M, wait 500 milliseconds, free that 1M, wait 500 milliseconds, and repeat the sequence. There are ten allocations and ten releases in the ten seconds that the allocated heap profile is collected. The profile shows an allocated heap of 10M because the released memory is not considered. The average rate of allocations is 10M/10 seconds, or 1M per second.

By profiling heap usage, you can identify potential inefficiencies and memory leaks in your program. You can see which allocations are causing the most workload for the garbage collector.

In the case of Java profiles, they allow not only latency measurements but also indicate complex concurrency problems in detail.

1.3.3.2. Flame Graphs

A chart that visualizes the profile is a flame graph. The best way to understand your application's processes and problems is to analyze the stack trace. Flame graphs are a great way to visualize stack traces. A stack trace is a sequence of methods that shows the flow of code. Stack traces collect thousands of stacks, and the flame graph samples the stack, each of which can be a few hundred lines long.

- The y-axis shows the depth of the stack. If you look up, you can understand the flow of the code, and if you look down, you can see the lineage of the methods.

- The x-axis represents the frequency of samples.

- The width of the box indicates the presence of the method in the profile.

CHAPTER 1 RCA ESSENTIALS

To read the flame graph, you need to find the widest tower and understand it first.

A large profile with thousands of samples will be displayed so narrowly that there is no room to include the method names, so your attention will naturally be drawn to the wider towers where the method names are easily readable, which will help you understand the profile.

To summarize, here's how to use flame graphs:

1. Starting with the top methods in the table on the left, analyze why the values are high.

2. If the x-axis is unusually long, it needs to be analyzed carefully.

3. Moving down the y-axis, analyze the relatively long x-axis.

4. Check the methods on the long x-axis and compare the length as you modify the code.

Flame graphs are used to display profile data. Unlike trees and graphs, flame graphs display large amounts of information in a small, easy-to-read format, making efficient use of screen space. These steps are illustrated in Figure 1-20.

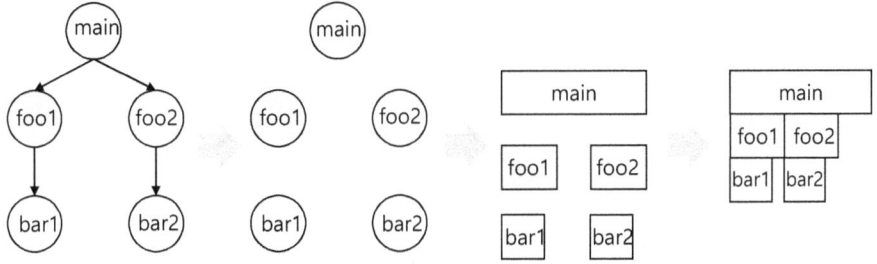

Figure 1-20. *The process of creating a flame graph*

To illustrate flame graphs, I show you how to convert a tree into a flame graph and briefly describe the main features of flame graphs.

- Delete the arrow representing the method call from the tree.

- Replace each tree node with a flame.

Remove whitespace and color the flames by their self CPU time. The flame shape is rectangular, and all flames are the same height. The total CPU time used by the methods named in the flame determines the width of the flame.

Table 1-4 compares self CPU time and total CPU time.

CHAPTER 1   RCA ESSENTIALS

Table 1-4. Self CPU Time and Total CPU Time

Pseudocode	Self CPU Time	Total CPU Time
main(): foo1() foo2()	2	4+3+2=9
foo1(): bar()	1.5	2.5+1.5=4
foo2(): bar()	0.5	2.5+0.5=3
bar():	2.5	2.5

Now notice that the call stack starting with foo2 is preserved. Even though it is next to the foo1 flame, the call stacks of foo1 and foo2 are preserved.

Except for bar, you can see the 1.5-second CPU time of foo1 in Figure 1-21. The profile displays the average, so the problem of the 99th percentile can't be identified. This is why you should refer to metrics for information that the flame graph cannot output.

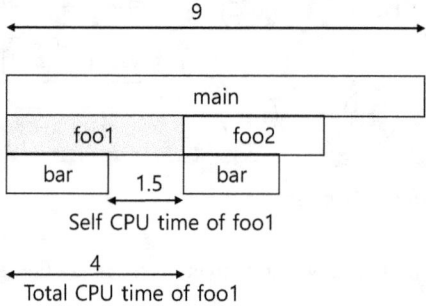

Figure 1-21. CPU time in the flame graph

Profiles are useful for finding and improving inefficient code by comparing the resource released and usage of CPU and memory, unoptimized duration, latency due to IO other than CPU, latency due to locks, and the number of calls per method. You need to compare and iterate as you modify your code:

- Identify CPU-intensive methods and optimize their implementation using CPU time profiles.

- Using memory profiles, identify methods in your application that use a lot of allocation.

- It is common to use profiles in flame graphs, comparing the results of an application before and after a change. It is important to understand the process of changing versions and making comparisons.

1.3.3.3. HotROD Profiles

So far, I have only described profiles and have not explained how to use them in terms of correlation with traces and overall root cause analysis. With thousands of microservices and lots of legacy, understanding the full context and pinpointing exactly what to profile is a difficult process.

HotROD has some problems:

- Sequential processes
- Managing thread pools

I identified these problems with traces from HotROD. I looked at how to reduce latency and improve performance by changing from sequential to parallel processing, changing the thread pool set in the configuration parameters, and fixing concurrency problems.

You need to understand the sequential processes, the limited number of thread pools, the connection timeouts, and the retries. With the visualization of spans in tracing, it is limited for root cause analysis because it is difficult to analyze resources such as threads and memory. If you suspect inefficient code, or if the problem is resource-related, you should use profiles.

Let's configure the demo.

The Pyroscope Helm chart deploys the Pyroscope server and creates the appropriate RBAC roles.

```
helm repo add pyroscope-io https://pyroscope-io.github.io/helm-chart
helm install demo pyroscope-io/pyroscope -f values.yaml
```

It applies the configuration defined in `values.yaml`. Pyroscope uses the same search mechanism as Prometheus and supports Kubernetes service discovery.

As a sample application, I use Jaeger HotROD. I enable the built-in Go `pprof` endpoint. Pyroscope can pull profiles from the endpoint.

Kubernetes resources are defined in `manifests.yaml` and pod labels are defined. This tells it to collect CPU and memory profiles.

```
pyroscope.io/scrape: "true"
pyroscope.io/application-name: "hotrod"
pyroscope.io/profile-cpu-enabled: "true"
pyroscope.io/profile-mem-enabled: "true"
pyroscope.io/port: "6060"
```

Then I created an application using this command:

```
kubectl apply -f manifests.yaml
```

CHAPTER 1 RCA ESSENTIALS

When HotROD started successfully, the profile started ingesting. Next, I created a transaction in HotROD:

```
$ kubectl get pod
NAME                              READY   STATUS    RESTARTS   AGE
demo-pyroscope-8598bbd875-5h29w   1/1     Running   0          2m2s
hotrod-golang-79f4976d9-5ctpz     1/1     Running   0          99s
jaeger-69f49ff949-2rj7m           1/1     Running   0          99s
```

The only change is to enable the pprof endpoint.

```go
func main() {
    mux := http.NewServeMux()
    mux.HandleFunc("/debug/pprof/", pprof.Index)
    mux.HandleFunc("/debug/pprof/cmdline", pprof.Cmdline)
    mux.HandleFunc("/debug/pprof/profile", pprof.Profile)
    mux.HandleFunc("/debug/pprof/symbol", pprof.Symbol)
    mux.HandleFunc("/debug/pprof/trace", pprof.Trace)
    go func() {
        log.Println(http.ListenAndServe(":6060", mux))
    }()

    cmd.Execute()
}
```

The pprof package can also register endpoints.

```go
package main

import (
    "fmt"
    "net/http"
    _ "net/http/pprof"
)

func main() {
    // Server for pprof.
    go func() {
        fmt.Println(http.ListenAndServe(":6060", nil))
    }()

}
```

1.3.4. Debugging

Remote debugging generally describes troubleshooting or debugging code from a distance.

Metrics are aggregations. Tracing can analyze remote calls, profiles can analyze methods, and debugging can analyze variables. Debugging allows for the most granular level of analysis.

It's best to access the code with an IDE and start a remote debug session.

VSCode and IntelliJ provide remote debugging and work in conjunction with the debuggers provided by the language, such as `jdwp` in Java and `dlv` in Golang. Containers can be remotely debugged in a variety of ways, including Docker and Kubernetes pods.

Using agents sometimes causes instrumentation to fail, and debugging is necessary to understand why this happens. Understanding the internal operation of the agent is not straightforward, but you can create breakpoints in many of its methods and compare when the span is created to ensure that the instrumentation is being processed correctly. Problems can arise when using OpenTelemetry and commercial observability agents simultaneously, and remote debugging is useful for analyzing and debugging differences in instrumentation between agents.

Suppose two agents are being instrumented at the same time, and the OpenTelemetry agent generates a span on method A, but the commercial observability agent does not. With remote debugging, you can verify that the instrumentation of a particular method is failing.

Debugging is a recommended signal for customizing open source agents or to understand the core internal functionality of open source agents. Because open source agents are bug-prone and difficult to support, you'll often need to debug and modify the code yourself to fix bugs. This includes setting breakpoints, looking at the values of variables, and understanding whether the code is correct.

You can debug open source agents in a variety of ways:

- Java is remotely debuggable through JDWP, which means you can connect to the Java server process running in your IDE.

- VSCode provides remote debugging capabilities via SSH. You can SSH into a server and run the code on the server with your local VSCode.

- Go provides Delve remote debugging capabilities.

- JetBrains provides great remote debugging capabilities.

For remote debugging of Apache Atlas with JDWP, add the settings to the `httpd` configuration file as shown here:

```
DEFAULT_JVM_OPTS="-Xdebug -agentlib:jdwp=transport=dt_socket,address=9999,server=y,suspend=n -Dlog4j.configuration=atlas-log4j.xml -Djava.net.preferIPv4Stack=true -server"
```

Add the following configuration to the IDE:

```
-agentlib:jdwp=transport=dt_socket,server=y,suspend=n,address=9999
```

Remote debugging is disadvantageous in a few ways.

Live debugging uses more dynamic bytecode injection, which runs alongside your application, so you don't have to redeploy your application every time you want to debug. Profiles also use bytecode injection to provide similar functionality to live debugging.

Breakpoints in remote debugging can interrupt execution. The ability to debug variables in production without interruption from breakpoints is called live debugging. Live debugging also uses bytecode instrumentation internally:

- **Administrator-only access:** Applying proper remote debugging settings requires administrator access to the relevant server, which limits who can initiate a debug session in production.

- **Data exposure:** Data exposure is a risk in remote debug sessions. Depending on how traffic flows between the server and your environment and how data is requested, tokens and passwords can be exposed during the debugging process.

- **Latency:** Your location relative to the cloud server can slow down the debugging process and even lead to timeouts, further delaying the resolution of the problem.

- **Kubernetes debugging:** Remote debugging is likely only available for certain environments, excluding Kubernetes production. It's not efficient because it's limited in scope and target.

Live debugging incorporates cloud-native requirements from the design phase. Using more dynamic instrumentation, it provides log, metric, and distributed trace data as part of the overall debugging process. It runs alongside the application, eliminating the need to redeploy the application every time you want to debug.

1.3.5. Events

While RUM and tracing only manage headers and have no visibility into the body, events help solve the limitations of trace. Events capture both the header and body of a message and help you utilize it from a business perspective.

It's useful to connect, extend, and make good use of different observables, such as deployment, to add context to a lacking trace.

In a commercial observability agent, RUM is organized as events, not traces. In my experience, it's more useful to store RUM in events than in traces. When RUM is organized in traces, it becomes difficult to express business processes. If you store RUM in events, use events to combine multiple RUMs and display your business processes quickly.

Events can be used to augment observability data with business data, for example, tracing complex business processes such as order management and fulfillment, extracting and segmenting financial details from payment gateways, or getting user feedback derived from the voice of the customer (VOC) solutions.

The event data flow consists of three phases:

- **Capture:** Business event data can be collected from the API and the external code.

- **Process:** Data processing pipelines process incoming business events to improve analytics and reporting. You can create rules to filter, parse, enrich, and transform data.

- **Analytics:** Stored data can be analyzed using DQL, a query language, to explore patterns, identify anomalies, and report on trends.

Events are not used alone but in conjunction with traces. They are used in conjunction with trace. For most of the work done in observability, such as dashboards, alerts, and SLOs, this book does not use signals in isolation but rather joins multiple signals together. When events used with trace, the following advantages are provided:

- Solves the problem of trace breaking.

- Improves alerts and dashboards.

- Organizes all your business processes.

- Complex data analysis requirements such as deployments and canaries can be implemented in observability.

There are two types of events:

- When actively initiated externally, such as a deployment, you use the Event API to send event to observability like hooks.

- You can capture or save specific sections of messages.

Most observability constraints can be addressed using events. While this can extend the scope of observability, it also introduces new architectural challenges. Observability can be duplicated on the CMDB and data side, or the observability can be larger than necessary, as discussed in Chapter 10.

1.3.5.1. Example 1

In this example, you organize an event store using event sourcing. Observability-based event sourcing improves on traditional event sourcing and has several advantages. You can reproduce failures and debug root causes.

You need a way to trace back and audit the root cause of an issue. Event sourcing is used to implement a root cause analysis data model, which is one of the important themes of this book. The design goals of event sourcing trace back to the root cause, recording events, and providing reproducibility, which is exactly what root cause analysis is all about.

Companies that provide payment services can also be audited.

- Can you determine your account balance at a specific point in time?
- How do you know that past and current account balances are accurate?
- How do you validate that your system logic is correct after the code changes?

A design that can systematically answer these questions is event sourcing, a technique developed from a domain-driven design.

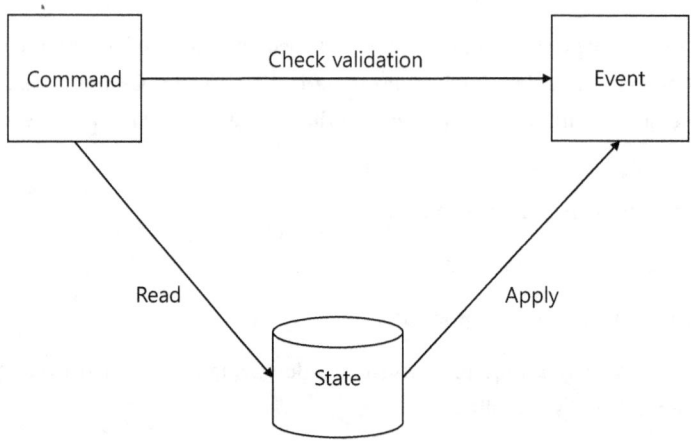

Figure 1-22.   Event sourcing flow

Event sourcing has important terminology, as shown in Figure 1-22.

- Command
- Event
- State

You might want to consider storing commands and events on local disk rather than in remote storage like Kafka. This prevents transfer times over the network. The event list is stored in a data structure that can only be appended to. Append is a sequential write operation, which is usually very fast. This works well with HDD because operating systems are usually heavily optimized for sequential read and write operations. Sequential disk accesses can sometimes be faster than random memory accesses.

By caching recent commands and events in memory, you can avoid reloading them from the local disk.

mmap technology is useful for implementing optimizations. With mmap, you can write to the local disk and automatically cache recent data in memory at the same time. mmap matches a disk file to a memory array. The operating system caches certain parts of the file in memory to speed up read and write operations. For operations on files that are append-only, all the necessary data is almost always in memory, which can speed up execution.

You've stored balance information in a relational database. However, as with the command and event store optimization plan, state information can also be stored on local disk.

You can use a file-based local relational database such as SQLite.

Instead of storing the current state, the event sourcing architecture keeps track of all events that change the state. Because it tracks all events that change the state of an order, you can recover the state of an order by replaying all events in order.

The mmap event store could have been written in Kafka if it weren't for the strict requirements on latency.

1.3.5.2. Example 2

This example shows how to create events using the BookInfo sample.

As shown in Figure 1-23, commercial observability is available for four services: productpage and details are not automated instrumentation, while reviews and ratings are automated instrument. productpage is manually instrumented with OpenTelemetry.

For example, a review captures the header and body of requests and responses processed within a rating. It converts them into events, stores them in an observability backend, and provides the ability to query them.

Events alone can provide more detailed analysis than other signals. While traces only output headers and logs output limited information, events capture headers and bodies, can query, and can be combined with other signals. These advantages, when combined with other signals, can solve many problems that were previously difficult to solve. Other signals and traces, such as RUM, can be used with events to fill in gaps and automate other signals. It's a good idea to connect traces and events across the board.

CHAPTER 1 RCA ESSENTIALS

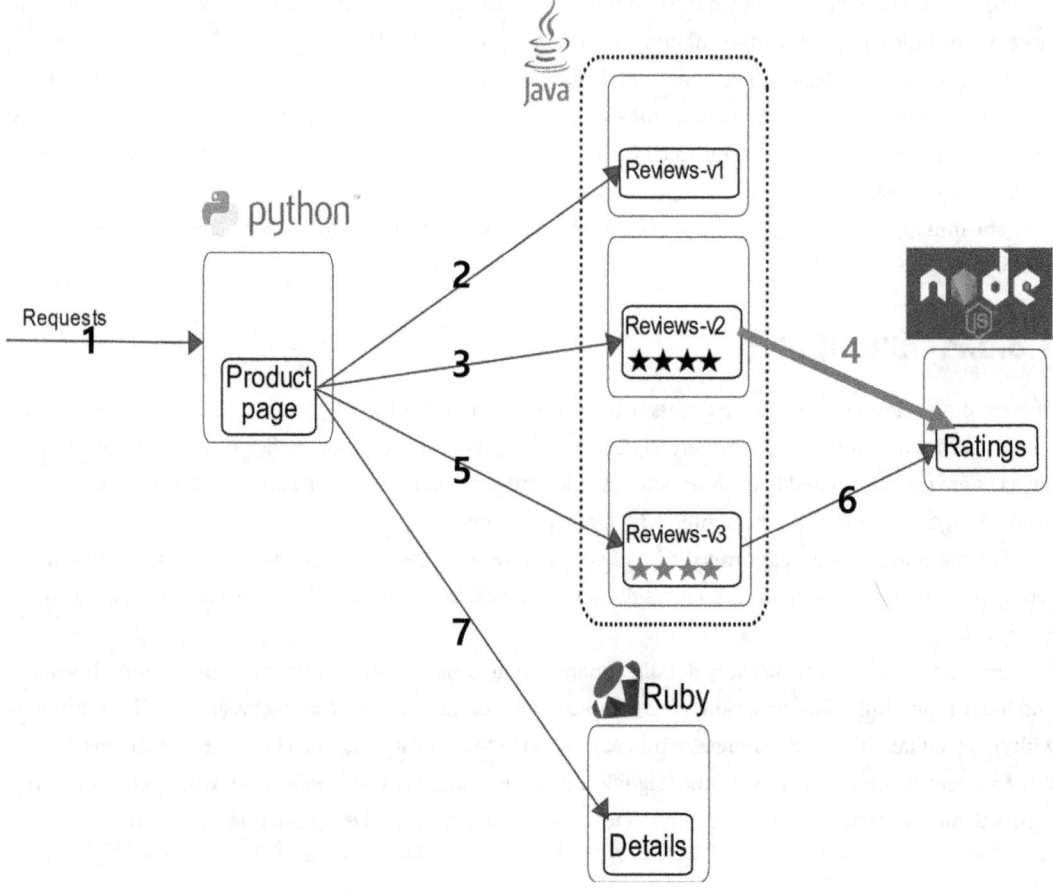

Figure 1-23. *Event process flow*

The following information can be obtained using the event:

- Requests and responses occur in seven segments.
- Events can be captured from 1-7.
- Events can separate requests from responses, collect them, and support a variety of protocols.
- You can collect the header and the body.

1.3.5.3. Example 3

The banking process is 2PC. Transferring funds, as shown in Figure 1-24, consists of two phases:

- In the first phase, the money is withdrawn from Bank A. This creates a payment ID 1 and a trace ID 01. Bank A uses a relational database, and data is committed after withdrawal. The fund transfer should be propagated to Bank B, but due to the nature of relational databases, the fund transfer cannot be traced.

- In the second phase, the deposit is made to Bank B. This creates a new trace ID 02 and uses the existing payment ID 1 as is.

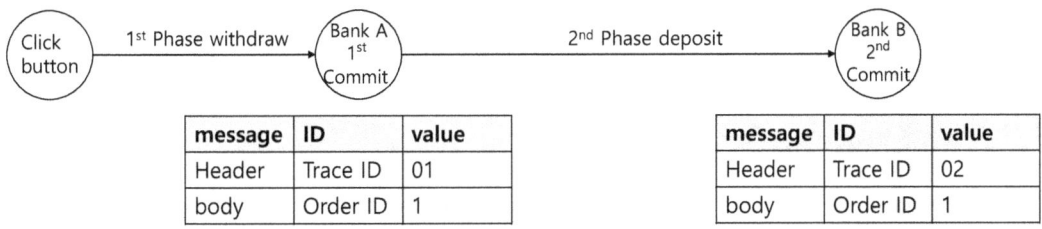

Figure 1-24. Combine multiple traces using a fund transfer event

The propagation failed, and although it was a single transaction, two traces were generated. There are technical limitations, and instrumentation is not always the right answer. Technical limitations should be considered whether they can be solved by business. Sometimes, using the event makes it easy to solve the problem. This captures events in the first phase and captures events in the second phase. It captures a total of two events. Then it outputs an fund transfer event containing two traces (withdraw, deposit) from the dashboard. The logic of the fund transfer query is simple:

- Group by the payment ID.
- Select the trace ID in chronological order.

Since the payment ID is not customer information, there is no security problem, and it can be captured as an event.

Events need to be thought of in a different light. Events are versatile, and they are the only signals that can be used in a business as well as a technical context.

1.3.5.4. Example 4

To understand orchestration, categories are more important than IDs. This is because product categories determine the granularity of orchestration. You can't understand the orchestration flow by looking at endpoints alone.

Multiple endpoints can exist within a single service, and even one endpoint can fulfill multiple types of orders.

In this case, you need to use events to capture the body and analyze the product category to identify the downstream microservice. The endpoints are the same, but the downstream microservices that are processed are different. Events can be used to identify product categories.

As you develop dashboards, you analyze your business by identifying services and endpoints. But endpoints alone don't tell the whole story. To understand the work, you need to utilize the message body. Only an event can capture the message body.

1.3.5.5. Example 5

Tracing is technical, not business. Even if the trace outputs an error, it's hard to understand which order or payment failed.

From a business perspective, it doesn't matter which trace ID prints an error. What matters is which order IDs are failing on which systems, how many orders are failing, and how much revenue is being lost due to this failure. Individual orders correspond to individual transactions, and individual transactions may consist of multiple E2E traces. The ability to convey business context using events is key to the observability success.

1.3.5.6. Example 6

Events can be used in various operational processes, including business requirements, and for deployment.

There are no limits to implementing events. You should be able to extend observability and demonstrate benefits at the business level. Events can also be utilized at a technical level. For example, to monitor releases at deployment time, you can compare them by release or version number of the application. This is not enough; it is important to understand when that release was deployed first.

Even in dashboards related to deployments like Canary, AB, and Bluegreen, it's more important to visualize the version list in chronological order than to simply compare version numbers.

Traces and logs don't have deployment times. Events include deployment times. Rather than developing a deployment dashboard using traces alone, you can develop a better dashboard by joining events and traces.

Sometimes, events are captured, but more often, they are fired externally like hooks and transferred to the observability agent using the API.

Suppose you want to compare two releases that were deployed 30 minutes ago. You need deployment and performance data. Observability has performance data, but not deployments. The deployments are on ArgoCD pipeline, and they don't send hooks to observability when they deploy. Observability doesn't understand if it's a regular deployment, an emergency patch, or a rollback. Observability has no deployment information, so there is no comparison. Events contain detailed deployment information.

1.3.5.7. Example 7

Because events only support HTTP and a few other protocols, they only measure some sections. It is more important to determine what the important sections are. Therefore, it is necessary to understand the business process. You don't need to collect all events in the E2E section, just the important few events.

Sometimes, it is technically impossible to propagate without headers, such as with relational databases. The relational database post-process creates a new trace. This is because tables do not have a default function to propagate headers. As database triggers are processed, events and traces can be captured. For example, by using events to collect the order ID in the body header, you can combine the two broken traces created before and after the relational database.

While processing hundreds or more spans, traces sometimes technically become broken, so it is useful to use events to combine multiple broken traces without changing your code.

Not only does this provide a way to bring business, but it also provides a way to overcome the technical constraints of trace.

There are cases where the event collection feature only supports HTTP, and the message protocol does not collect events. In this case, it is appropriate to develop an application to browse message detail in the message server queue and output it to the log.

1.3.5.8. Anomalies

The data sources for anomalies are events and logs, a la the RCA data model. Traces, which are located in the header, and metrics, which are aggregation data, are not suitable as data sources for an anomaly. If you assume that the number of resources in the public cloud for a service that spends $10 billion per month is 50,000 or more, it is difficult for SREs to manage this many resources manually, so they need to automate these using anomaly detection. Anomalies can be involve business and technical data, and there are no limits.

In general, business-level anomaly detection is more complex than technical anomaly detection. Rather than focusing on a single use case in detail, you need to understand the observability and anomaly detection scenarios that the SRE is looking for. Anomaly detection that can be deployed quickly and effectively to detect large-scale resources and services is best.

Users with previous experience with other anomaly detection systems can easily learn OpenSearch anomaly detection and develop and enhance their anomaly detection models. OpenSearch is designed to allow other models to be imported and deployed. Pipelines make it easy to process data and deploy and operate OpenSearch with minimal changes to existing models and Python APIs.

CHAPTER 1 RCA ESSENTIALS

1. In conjunction with live streaming, process real-time anomaly detection.

2. Support detectors for anomaly detection. Detector is an AI service that allows you to monitor and detect anomalies in time series data through batch and real-time detection without machine learning knowledge.

3. Utilize a variety of API and SQL, making it easy to develop and process further. You can use Python API and notebooks, as well as external machine learning frameworks like Keras.

4. OpenSearch provides anomaly detection management screens, visualization, and analysis. You can easily configure alerts and dashboards through the management screen.

5. Anomaly detection results are stored as an index within OpenSearch, and tools are provided to analyze them easily.

There are cases when OpenSearch anomaly detection is not the right fit.

- OpenSearch anomaly detection is focused on high productivity and easy anomaly detection development. If your anomaly detection involves complex rules and workflows or requires additional development based on complex requirements, OpenSearch anomaly detection is not for you.

- OpenSearch anomaly detection does not limit the applicable anomaly detection use cases, but it is better suited for implementing technical rather than business anomaly detection. OpenSearch anomaly detection is useful for metric correlation, k-NN semantic search, and RAG with generative AI.

- OpenSearch anomaly detection detects anomalies based on information collected in the index. Signals must be loaded into the index before anomaly detection can be applied. For example, anomaly detection is not recommended for data structures with parent-child relationships or complex overlaps, such as JSON. I recommend preprocessing and creating a flattened table structure first and then loading the signal data into the index.

Since OpenSearch is a forked project from Elasticsearch, it is implemented and works similarly to Elasticsearch's anomaly detection. There are some differences between Elasticsearch and OpenSearch anomaly detection, but most of the features are similar:

- For root cause analysis, OpenSearch provides metric correlation and k-NN algorithms.

- OpenSearch offers features like ratio analysis, category analysis, and population analysis, similar to the offerings by Elasticsearch.

- Similar to Elasticsearch unstructured analytics, observability in OpenSearch provides patterns and anomaly detection in logs.

- Elasticsearch inference provides a high degree of automation. OpenSearch will soon offer forecasting and inference capabilities as well.

- Similar to Elasticsearch record-level analytics, OpenSearch provides features and APIs that allow you to specify categories and search for anomalies. For specific fields, it provides aggregation functions such as sum, count, max, min, and average.

OpenSearch needs further development using the API to achieve Elasticsearch-level automation. Currently, OpenSearch's roadmap shows a number of AI and anomaly detection improvements.

1.3.6. Root Cause Analysis Data Model

So far, I have described the problems and limitations of various signals. Most readers will not be familiar with what I have described.

- For system resources, I identified eight signals from applications alone.

- Chapter 2 describes more than 14 correlations.

- Avoid developing multiple dashboards without standards for dashboards and SLOs. Multiple unorganized dashboards and SLOs are chaos. The dashboards and SLOs should have a clear baseline.

Observability is not easy. It's complicated. You spend a lot of time developing dashboards and SLOs, but they don't work as well as you'd hoped, and they add confusion. More is not better. A disorderly multitude only leads to chaos. Too many technologies and too much complexity are often the reason why observability projects fail.

In this book, you will develop one root cause analysis data model and one dashboard. I demonstrate that a single dashboard, without a data model, is sufficient to satisfy all production needs. Additional error and BPF dashboards may be required but are optional. You don't need a lot of SL and dashboards for observability. You need to manage complexity.

- Root cause analysis data models can store nanosecond-level events and latencies, are an excellent data source for AIOps, and can be utilized as an event store to provide reproducibility of anomaly detection and failures.

- We defined roughly 1,000 failures into 300 failure types. This can be used to reproduce failures in AIOps runbooks and root cause analysis data models.

- I'll join various signals and traces. I'll configure an event store to store signals and correlate them with other signals. I'll use them for root cause analysis.

CHAPTER 1   RCA ESSENTIALS

Root cause analysis data models can be extended in a variety of ways to compensate for the shortcomings of trace, as shown in Figure 1-25.

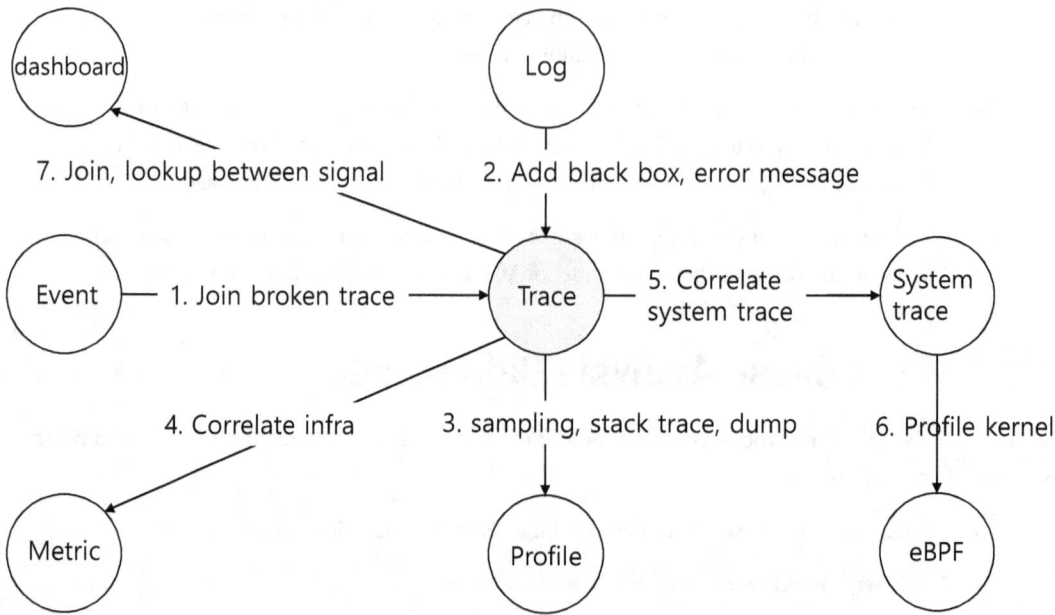

Figure 1-25. *Enhance RCA data model using correlation*

How do you overcome the drawbacks and maximize the advantages? There are seven challenges:

- **Connecting an broken trace:** Traces can be broken for technical reasons. The TCP protocol and relational databases have technical limitations in organizing traces. In a business process, a single transaction creates multiple traces. Think of an order—there's not just one click but many clicks, and each click creates a new trace. Events allow you to overcome the technology and business constraints. This is because events provide the ability to connect broken traces.

- **Augmenting non-instrumented traces:** Traces generate spans primarily for remote calls. Inter-threaded calls, black boxes, and most legacy agents don't generate spans. Instrumenting traces with a microservice focus is not enough to identify delays and failures. You can augment traces with trace context, which is printed in the logs. You create a trace using trace context and the ID recorded in the logs. You can join traces and logs in the dashboard.

- **Analyzing at the method level:** Traces have difficulty analyzing at the method level. Traces can only analyze the latency of methods. Profiles include call tree or stack trace, so you can analyze thread state, call count, and dependencies in detail. You can analyze threads and memory issues that traces can't. Root cause analysis is difficult without profiles.

- **Correlating to infrastructure context:** Span attributes require adding system context. As cloud availability zones, hosts, and Kubernetes are added, you can quickly jump to metrics in your infrastructure context if something goes wrong. While trace focuses on services, span attributes naturally extend beyond services by filling in the gaps. Out-of-the-box OpenTelemetry is lacking in span attributes. While problems can occur with services, problems can also overlap with infrastructure and system resources. It is useful to provide information about the resources used in the span attribute. For example, it is useful to print the memory utilization of the Java VM and the queue length of the CPU in the span properties.

- **Tying to system resources:** Joining traces, logs, events, and profiles allows for detailed analysis of your application, but it can't explain issues with system resources in your infrastructure. This is where system trace comes in. By joining distributed traces with system traces, you can understand nanosecond-level delays. Detailed issues with system resources output detailed system traces, including context switches, packet retransmissions, interrupts, disk access, and memory allocation.

- **Detailed analysis of the kernel:** While the system traces outputs events in chronological order without missing an event, it lacks a profile of the kernel's methods and system resources. When system traces are used in conjunction with BPF, 99th percentiles can be easily obtained, allowing you to make accurate judgments about nanosecond-level delays in method.

- **Using join and lookup between signals:** Additional agents may be required. The OpenTelemetry agent does not create spans when inter-thread passing occurs. Developing an agent that creates new spans in parallel, pool, scheduling, and elastic threads would fill the gap between OpenTelemetry and commercial observability. While it would be great if a single agent could do it all, there are limitations. Even if you have multiple trace IDs generated by multiple agents, the dashboard can display multiple trace IDs in chronological order using the payment IDs. The reason for the dashboard is that it provides queries, so you can work around the limitations of the signal. To work around the limitations of trace, you can use dashboards. Dashboards are a last solution. If you can't solve at the trace and event signal, you use dashboards to overcome observability constraints and limitations. Even if you don't have a data model configured, you can configure a root cause analysis dashboard with just a query.

Traces are similar to base tables for joins. The root cause analysis data model is also useful for connecting with other systems, as shown in Figure 1-26. I will design a root cause analysis data model and join the CMDB and SLO. Using the root cause analysis data model, you can troubleshoot issues with the CMDB, SLOs, alerts, and dashboards.

CHAPTER 1   RCA ESSENTIALS

Dashboards, SLOs, and CMDB require observability data. You can provide observability data to other systems in real time.

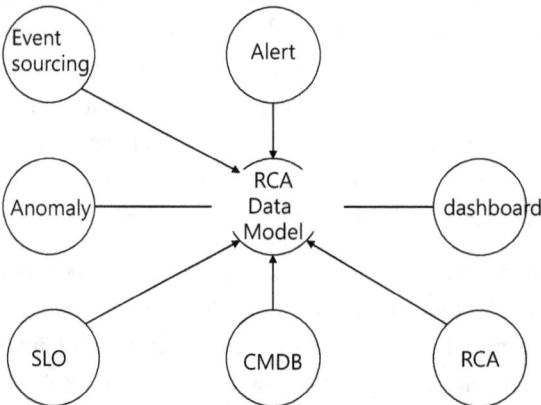

Figure 1-26. *RCA data model interface*

- Provide observability data to a variety of systems. Minimize preprocessing and provide accurate data in real time.

- The event store implemented with event sourcing is optimized for debugging, auditing, and root cause analysis and provides excellent reproducibility for failure.

- The event store can be deployed at a low cost and in a short period of time, assuming the individual signals are configured correctly.

Commercial observability is used to construct the root cause analysis data model, which is not easy to construct using only open source agents. Commercial observability agents provide data lakes and offer a variety of query capabilities, which you can leverage to further develop your event sourcing and organize your event store. Commercial observability agents are not enough, so you need to leverage open source agents at the right time and place.

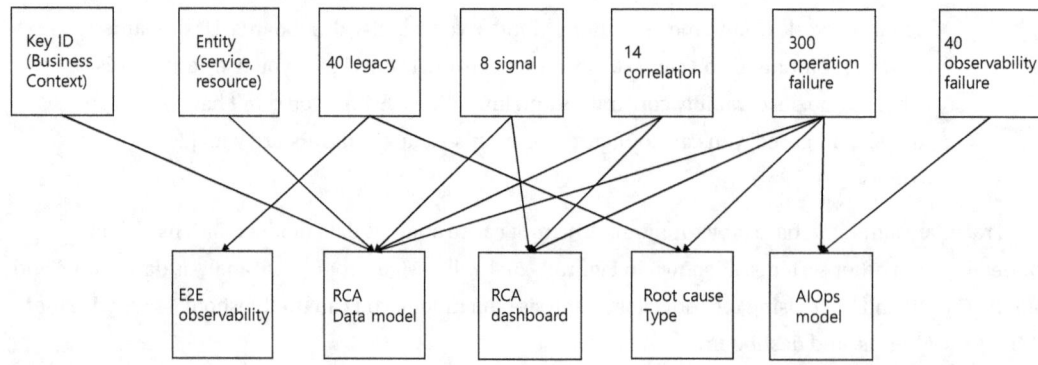

Figure 1-27. *RCA asset*

CHAPTER 1 RCA ESSENTIALS

The deliverables of this book are end-to-end observability—the RCA data model, the RCA dashboard, and the AIOps model. The materials used to generate the deliverables are based on 40 legacy applications, eight signals, 14 correlations, 300 failure runbooks, and 40 observability issues.

Once you understand the eight signals, you can analyze your applications and services. The benefits of observability don't end there.

- **Eight signals:** As shown in Figure 1-3, problems with the eight signals not being configured, correlation breaks, missing logs, and trace breaks are caused by the SRE configuring the signals incorrectly. When configured correctly, all signals are correlated and can be monitored in their entirety without missing or breaking. The SRE must understand the characteristics and constraints of the signals and configure observability.

- **System configuration and changes:** Entities contain service and resource information. Understanding entities eliminates the need to configure the CMDB as a separate system.

- **Business context:** By collecting events according to the key identity structure described in Figure 1-5, you can add most of the data processed in your business to your observability. If key IDs are missing, or if the structure and relationships are not organized, the architecture and developers are not developed properly. Security and privacy may limit your ability to collect data. Customer information is not needed for observability.

- **Kernel and system resources:** Observability currently does not provide detailed information about kernel and system resources. However, there are many ways to use open source to reduce costs and align with observability.

In telecom and banking, write paths are often unobservable. For example, simple processes such as product browsing and transaction history, which are read paths, have no problem enforcing observability. However, complex processes, such as order fulfillment in telecom and fund transfer in banking, are write paths, and observability often fails. This results in data not being collected and in difficulty configuring dashboards and alerts. Without accurate data collection, AI configuration is impossible and automation is limited. You will experience the limitations of off-the-shelf observability, which, despite the high cost, are simple. A large portion of this book is devoted to making instrumentation and solving data problems.

This book presents a range of technical challenges that have never been attempted before and shows successful results.

- Configuring E2E trace, including legacy and black box, and analyzing at the nanosecond level, from business to system resources.

- Configuring RAG and AI agents to automate anomaly detection and observability root cause analysis.

I think it's meaningful for many reasons to be the first to share a successful outcome.

CHAPTER 1   RCA ESSENTIALS

I will apply RAG, a modern AI technique, to the observability data model created by joining various signals to automate the root cause analysis process. I was surprised by the accuracy of the results and believe that AI will replace SRE. AI shows a much higher level of accuracy than SRE, and it is clear that this development will have a significant impact on observability in the future.

1.4. Summary

The book provides five deliverables, as follows:

- **Root cause types:** Distinguish between delays and failures, such as contention and queuing for system resources, replication and rebalancing in clusters, and the 99th percentile of kernel methods.

- **Root cause analysis data model:** Use correlations between events, distributed traces, and system traces to construct the data model needed for root cause analysis.

- **Root cause analysis and AIOps dashboards:** Create dashboards based on the root cause analysis data model and manage SLOs and failures.

- **AIOps model:** Create a runbook based on 300 production failures, root cause types, and runbooks and configure an automated AIOps model based on them.

- **E2E observability:** Configure E2E observability, including multiple legacies.

Being an SRE can be a challenging role. Here are some guidelines for becoming a successful SRE:

- SRE is a common interest, so you need to communicate with different organizations. It's not easy to make SRE work within an organization. Between infrastructure, network, security, and developers, it's not uncommon for SREs to get stuck and stagnate. You need C-level support, but it's important to be effective from the start and show the potential for success. You need to show that you can improve with other organizations.

- If the technology is new, there will be a lot of pressure, high resistance, and a high learning curve. You can't expect low-skill engineers to grow through individual learning alone. You need to find ways to support and motivate them to learn. Pressure alone won't solve the problem.

- Provide guidance to the existing workforce, but also challenge them to take the lead and show leadership. With the support of the CTO, create separate TFs or organize around common interests and allow engineering to flow more freely.

CHAPTER 1 RCA ESSENTIALS

- Bigger organizations tend to be more conservative. The best engineers' efforts and ideas may not be recognized by the organization. Even the best engineers can't do everything well, so collaboration is necessary. You need to bring your best engineers together and create an environment where they can work together. Even great engineers are likely to deliver mediocre results in a mediocre organization. You're likely to encounter a lot of pushback along the way, not only from developers, but also from within the SRE team.

- SREs spend a lot of time and effort troubleshooting at the system resource level. It's not uncommon for weeks of work to go by with no results or uncertain outcomes. There is a high probability of failure and even no outcome. Nevertheless, the effort and attitude should be respected. If everyone in the SRE team is only doing what works, it's impossible to analyze the root cause. Root cause analysis will be a difficult task if you don't have a constant spirit of challenge and passion.

- I'm an SRE, and there are many times when I don't perform well. It is difficult to improve by yourself, and it is only possible to jump to the next level and improve when the organization is at a certain level. You also need to have the foresight and discernment to choose a good organization and identify colleagues to work with. If the company is not ready to embrace positive change and improvement, the answer is to move to another good organization.

Observability requires an accurate understanding of the characteristics and constraints of individual signals, and compensating for constraints with correlations between signals. This is why developers and SREs who are used to logs and metrics have a hard time adapting to the new world of observability. Familiarity with metrics keeps them stuck at the level of simple monitoring, missing out on opportunities to modernize operations and improve the business. I believe that the reason organizations spend so much money on observability and don't see a return on their investment is not a problem with observability, but rather a problem with people not adapting to new concepts and methods.

This chapter has described new signals such as real user monitoring (RUM), profiles, events, debugging, and outliers. System traces and BPF are discussed later. It's complicated and difficult, but if you understand each of these signals one by one, you'll find that many of your unsolved problems will be solved.

CHAPTER 2

The RCA Approach

2.1. Introduction

This chapter describes 14 correlations between eight signals. Correlations simplify complex observability and allows for quick root-cause analysis.

The example in this chapter shows how to use the following:

- From distributed traces to system trace (eBPF)
- From events to traces
- From traces to logs
- From traces to profiles
- From logs to profiles
- From metrics to traces
- From RUMs to traces
- From events to anomaly detection
- From logs to traces
- From networks to traces
- From traces to metrics
- From traces to service maps
- From service maps to metrics
- From metrics to logs

The top two signals are important correlations. The core of this book is to develop a root cause analysis dashboard using two correlations. Once that's done, the rest is optional.

- From distributed traces to system traces
- From events to traces

CHAPTER 2   THE RCA APPROACH

In particular, two correlations are the most important. The top two correlations help align business and IT and improve root cause analysis, dashboards, and alerts. Distributed and system traces are the key to correlation.

Once you've successfully built the two correlations, root cause analysis is performed quickly and accurately, and reliability and MTTR can be significantly improved.

2.2. Using Correlations

Each signal is complex and hard to understand. If a signal is incorrect, it is difficult to correct it. With correlations, users can easily understand the signals. Correlations connect different signals and dashboards.

Incorrect correlation prevents joins and lookups in dashboards, and traces are detailed and choppy. It also leads to missing logs and noisy alarms. Signals become inaccurate, and accurate root cause analysis is difficult.

The goal is to reduce the complexity of observability and make it easy for developers to use observability. While it's important to provide a variety of dashboards and SLOs, core SLO and root cause analysis dashboards are more important.

Most signals are associated with a trace. For example, metrics, RUMs, profiles, and logs are associated with traces. Eight signals, including event, debug, and anomaly detection, are centered on traces. If the traces are not correctly organized, it is difficult to organize observability correlation. Traces are the first step to correlation. You shouldn't think of traces as the end of observability, but rather the start of observability.

For larger sites, it is more common to use commercial observability than to build observability from open source agents alone. While commercial observability is superior when considering productivity, it can be cost-prohibitive, so open source agents are often used appropriately. Grafana provides a great dashboard and correlation capability.

This chapter describes these correlations in order of importance.

If the trace is broken, you use events to connect it, and if a span is missing, you read it from the log and add it. You need to get the thread ID from every span and then correlate them with the thread ID in the system trace.

If the problem is not solved by the signal, you can use the dashboard to troubleshoot the correlation of the signal.

2.2.1. From Distributed to System Traces

There are many different correlations, but MTTR is an important metric for evaluating correlations. You need to consider which correlation should be prioritized to quickly and accurately analyze the root cause and solve the problem.

The system trace correlation is prioritized over the distributed trace. This is because it is the correlation that most closely matches the direction of this book.

This correlation is important because it connects applications and infrastructure. The industry doesn't have any concept of system traces.

You can use the same traces, profiles, stack traces, and logs that are used in application observability to correlate with infrastructure observability.

- **Traces:** A distributed trace can define a correlation with the infrastructure. The process ID, thread name, and thread ID file descriptors used by the application are defined with the span attribute. You can configure distributed traces and correlations by adding a trace context to the markers of system traces. By using PID between system traces in distributed traces and the same PID in the application's stack trace, you can understand the correlation between the application and the infrastructure. Kernel methods and system calls in system traces and application in stack traces are correlated by PID. You can monitor how the PIDs are passed over the network to the server via tcpdump.

- Non-blocking has many thread IDs. It is difficult to build correlations based on thread ID alone. Each agent has different support for trace specific threads. Therefore, it is difficult to correlate trace IDs with system traces. Trace ID is also often missing from logs. If you find it difficult to organize thread and trace IDs, you should output business-relevant IDs in span attributes and logs.

- You should configure the dashboard to include thread, trace, and transaction IDs so that all threads are not missing from the dashboard.

It would be useful to be able to generate spans of the processes in your infrastructure. Profiles, logs, and stack traces are useful, but they do not generate spans. This book uses KUtrace to generate a span of your infrastructure and correlate it to your application's distributed traces.

The duration of a method defines the number of calls to a method. They are not provided by traces but can be understood using stack traces and profiles. If you are unable to perform root cause analysis at the application level, you should review system traces. The KUtrace system trace of infrastructure observability provides nanosecond latency information by section, but it does not provide detailed information, such as the aggregation of methods and the number of calls. Therefore, it is necessary to use eBPF to fill in the gaps in KUtrace. Rather than solving all problems with a single KUtrace tool, it is more effective to look at various signals from different perspectives and perform root cause analysis.

This book proceeds with the root cause analysis from application to infrastructure in the following order.

For application observability, follow these steps:

1. Identify the scope of the problem outlined in the metric.

2. View the latency and error per segment in the distributed trace.

3. In the profile, check the number of calls per method and the duration per method.

CHAPTER 2   THE RCA APPROACH

4. The thread dump checks the thread state per thread.

5. Log for detailed error messages, supplementing existing signals for black boxes and legacy programs.

Infrastructure observability performs root cause analysis at the system resource level for problems that cannot be solved by application observability alone.

- Understand utilization, saturation, aggregation by resource, and CPU vs IO through metrics.

- Use the KUtrace system trace to identify problems with latency, scheduler, interrupts, and locks per segment.

- Check the kernel parameter and kernel log.

- Use the system utilities `ftrace` and `sftrace` to debug and identify events and methods.

- Check the eBPF profile for the number of calls per kernel method and the duration per method.

2.2.2. From Events to Traces

From an observability standpoint, events are more of a business signal than a technical signal.

This correlation is important because it connects business and technology.

The problem with traces is that they represent technical context, not business context. In many ways, trace is a very limited signal. These shortcomings can be improved with events.

A single event can contain multiple traces. For example, a single order can contain multiple trace IDs. Because you can't understand the business context from traces alone, it's useful to look at events.

The RCA critical path in this book can be organized into events, distributed traces, and system traces.

Events support HTTP, but have no problem supporting distributed traces initiated from the frontend. Events store only the ID in the body to find traces, but they can be built into structured queries. You don't want to capture every section like a trace, only the important sections.

Dashboards should describe your business processes, customers, and products, and correlate them to your technology. A long, meaningless list of SLOs is not a good dashboard. Your SLO dashboard should be business-based.

The signal called event is not yet described in OpenTelemetry and other standards. Commercial observability products such as Honeycomb and Dynatrace use events to enhance the value of observability. As shown in Figure 2-1, an event is the data in the header and body of an HTTP, but many other attributes can be added to an event.

CHAPTER 2   THE RCA APPROACH

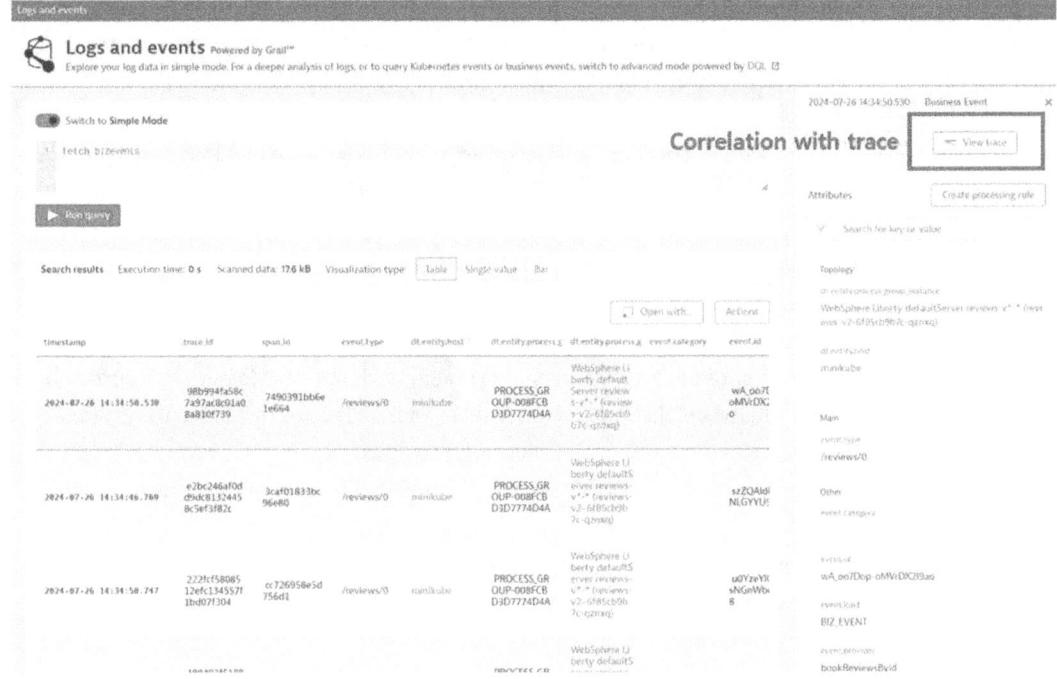

Figure 2-1. *The correlation between different signals in an event*

Events can also be understood as logs. From a data perspective, events and logs are similar: logs are free-format but managed by developers, while events are managed by SREs. Events can be captured in the body, or they can be captured in the body and appended to a header to be associated with a trace.

The benefit of commercial observability is that it is automated to add attributes from the body to the header or to capture, store, and manage the contents of the body and header.

2.2.3. From Traces to Logs

Traces are key signals for observability correlation and understanding problems with individual transactions.

A trace can correlate logs, and you can enrich the context with span attributes and baggage. With manual instrumentation, it is possible to construct a rich context. OpenTelemetry provides a way to add attributes even with automated instrumentation, and you can enrich context with baggage.

By including all events and adjusting the logging level to a lower level, logs can output more detailed debugging information.

While the correlation of logs in traces is important, it is also important to match and standardize trace IDs with other important IDs. This will help with further troubleshooting and analysis.

It is important to add the correct trace IDs to the log. In development, print dt.trace_id, dt.span_id, trace_id, and span_id to the log and enable all headers in the trace UI.

In the case of Dynatrace, `dt.trace_id` becomes the primary trace ID in log, and both `dt.span_id` and OpenTelemetry `span_id` must be added to logback. If you add only `dt.span_id`, you cannot see the instrumentation of OpenTelemetry `span_id` in the log.

Since logs are the most detailed signals, it's important to think about how to utilize them. Rather than trying to solve problems with traces alone, it is necessary to properly utilize logs that developers are familiar with.

The main attributes of the message header should be printed, and the trace ID in the log should be printed and compared in chronological order. In many cases, non-blocking, virtual threads, black box, legacy, inter-threaded calls, and trace alone are not enough for detailed analysis.

There are two types of spans: client and server spans. Client spans are divided into frontend and network spans. The latency output from a network span is enough to identify that latency is occurring on the network, but it does not tell you the detailed cause. You need to analyze latency by section using `traceroute` or analyze packets using `tcpdump` and Wireshark for root cause analysis.

After identifying latency in a trace, you should perform a detailed root cause analysis using profiles, logs, and system utilities.

The OpenTelemetry agent and commercial observability extend the language-specific log library, and the framework references the log library.

2.2.4. From Traces to Profiles

The latency, context, and trace outputs can help you troubleshoot performance problems in your application. However, they don't provide detailed information about whether your application is leaking memory or how well concurrency is being processed by the CPU, resource spikes, or virtual machine memory. You can only estimate from the trace charts and span messages. Flame graphs can help you understand how the span is processing resources like CPU and memory.

Profiles have many similarities to stack traces. While stack traces are very useful for analyzing problems and can be easily understood by developers, they are not easily understood by SREs who do not have access to the code. It is efficient to look at the stack trace whenever a problem occurs, and you should try to familiarize yourself with it.

OpenTelemetry traces do not correlate with stack traces. However, commercial observability provides a correlation between trace and stack trace. By using traces and stack traces together, you can apply traces at the code level.

- While traces can analyze individual transactions, it is difficult to analyze resources. Profiles provide information about resources, augmenting traces.
- Flame graphs are useful for comparing and analyzing changes in resources before and after code changes. They allow for detailed resource analysis, but it's difficult to specify individual transactions.

By configuring correlation, you can compensate for the weaknesses of each signal and reinforce its strengths.

You can see that the profile ID is defined in the span attribute. If you click the profile ID, you will be taken to the Pyroscope profile screen. Manually searching for traces and profiles is a cumbersome task. By simply implementing correlation, you can quickly and accurately perform root cause analysis.

The technical benefits include:

- Using trace to find the bottlenecked service and profile to dig deeper into its code.
- Visualizing the performance of the E2E of the request and individual code parts.
- Identifying service latency through traces. This supports profiles for causes such as database queries, API calls, or specific code inefficiencies.

In the Grafana dashboard, Jaeger and Tempo traces are correlated to Pyroscope profiles.

Flame graphs should provide not only visualization but also statistical information and the ability to make comparisons.

- **Profile:** Correlations from trace to profile provides a profile ID in the span attribute. When a profile ID is selected, the flame graph outputs the flame graph at that point in time. Grafana allows visualization of flame graphs, heatmaps, and histograms. PCP can write `bpftrace` one-liners for system calls and visualize the latency of kernel methods in BCC. Rather than building PCP separately, you can output BCC, `bpftrace`, and user-space applications together in the same dashboard in Grafana.
- **Stack trace:** A stack trace is similar to a profile. It is important for applications to understand the stack trace during the process and find the cause of performance degradation and latency. Stack traces output thread and process IDs. There is no information about the trace context. The stack trace outputs the details of what the application processes.

2.2.5. From Logs to Profiles

The profile outputs detailed information about the system internals processed by the application. It is also a good idea to go from trace to profile to understand and solve problems. You can go to the profile directly from the log using the profile ID. This is good when the log level is not detailed, or the debugging information in the log is not enough. Unlike profiles, logs are flexible, but they do not contain information about CPU or memory system resources because they are added by developers. Often, a profile is needed because logs lack information about CPU and memory.

Understand the problem with the code logic from the logs and check the profile to see if the code logic's resource management is appropriate and if there are resource constraints.

Since logs and profiles have different purposes, their shortcomings can be compensated for using correlation. Logs have no special format and can output whatever the developer wants. However, it is not easy to add information about system resources, and aggregation is difficult. However, it is easy to analyze individual transactions. The profile provides information about system resources and is good for high-level understanding because it provides aggregation.

2.2.6. From Metrics to Traces

Prometheus supports *exemplars*, which are samples of the traces provided by a metric. Metrics should include latency, throughput, and error rate by default. Automated instrumentation using the agent can automatically generate SLO.

Traces refer to individual transactions, so they don't show the big picture. Time series metrics show changes in traffic over time, which can help you understand the problem. The metric outputs an exemplar and provides a link to the trace.

2.2.7. From RUMs to Traces

A RUM is a system signal, but it can be used as a business signal. By correlating a frontend with a RUM and a distributed trace backend, you can trace each user's behavior, which enables business analysis.

In practice, the reason why RUMs are needed is that they often go from the frontend through CDN, load balancers, API servers, managed load balancers in the cloud, DNS servers in Kubernetes, and Kubernetes services, but they don't create traces. In reality, there are often failures along the way, but traces are often not configured. If each section is not measured and no span is displayed, it is difficult to identify the section, even if a failure occurs. Each segment is a single point of failure, so there is a high risk that all services will be disrupted.

RUM runs on real users, and RUM focuses on analyzing the user's experience.

From a technical perspective, it's similar to APM because it manages and improves the performance of the frontend. Think of it as frontend APM, and it's easy to understand.

- RUM occurs on the frontend and collects information such as network requests, page load times, and errors that occur on mobile or web. This is done to quantitatively evaluate the experience of users using the service and seek ways to improve it.

- RUM can also be correlated with logs and metrics and provides more value when it is correlated with traces to become an E2E trace.

- RUM provides clues to help you understand the problems users are experiencing so you can improve them. It can also be used as a site analysis and marketing tool for sites such as ABTest and Google Analytics. You can analyze session behavior and errors and recognize specific users. Based on the understanding of users, various business applications are possible. It supports not only the web but also mobile and various channels.

- RUM starts out with a technical purpose, but over time, it can be utilized as a marketing tool to achieve business goals.

RUM can be very helpful in understanding the user experience when problems occur. For example, users often experience service inconveniences due to high latency, mobile app crashes, and app interruptions, and RUM provides useful data and correlates to the backend for root cause analysis.

Rather than just thinking about RUM from a technical perspective, it is becoming more important as it is implemented in the business.

Correlating RUM and traces is important. This is because transactions that start on the frontend are propagated to the backend trace, allowing you to analyze the entire E2E. The trace analyzes the section after the API server, which cannot be said to be E2E without RUM. To correlate RUMs and distributed traces, you define the relationship between the user session in RUM and the distributed trace, create a trace in XHR, add the trace context to the header, and propagate it.

You can see detailed error messages in the generated log. The log contains the trace ID, session ID, and profile ID and provides the link URL for each signal. In this way, you can easily build correlations between RUMs and other signals.

For example, RUM outputs a direct correlation between the session ID of RUM and the trace ID of a distributed trace to the log. Session IDs include load and user actions. Each solution has a different configuration for correlating RUM and distributed traces.

In OpenTelemetry, RUM and trace are integrated, not separate.

Currently, RUM's OpenTelemetry specification is unclear, and the correlation of commercial observability with open-source RUM is a matter of implementation.

- OpenTelemetry RUM can generate multiple spans of resources, documents, and actions that generate events on the frontend. You can propagate traces to the backend and configure E2E traces that integrate the frontend and backend.

- Commercial observability sometimes provides a way to associate frontend resources, documents, and user actions with backend traces using cookies. This approach is difficult to correlate with traces instrumented on the API server.

- You can also define a correlation by outputting the session and trace IDs in the log.

2.2.8. From Events to Anomalies

This example uses OpenSearch for anomaly detection. OpenSearch's data sources can be logs and events in the RCA data model. Through anomaly detection, you can identify the specific event that caused the problem.

OpenSearch supports an anomaly detection engine that can identify anomalies when streaming data in real-time. Previously, I used a single stream detector, which had limitations. For example, a single stream detector can be used to sift through aggregated traffic from all IP addresses to alert users when an unusual spike occurs. However, in addition to aggregation, it is often necessary to identify anomalies in entities such as individual hosts and IP addresses. Each entity can work with different criteria. This means that they have different time series distributions (parameters such as size, trend, and seasonality).

Using a traditional monolithic model to detect anomalies will result in inaccurate results due to different baselines. OpenSearch can configure detectors for complex entities and customize the anomaly detection model.

OpenSearch anomaly detection identifies anomalies in events and stores the results in a result index. Through the result index, you can query or aggregate the results of anomaly detection. The anomaly uses the key used in the event so you can identify them.

2.2.9. From Logs to Traces

The main advantage of logs is their flexibility in containing a wide variety of information.

In order for observability to be more meaningful from a business perspective, it is important to utilize logs well. Traces are header-heavy, which limits their ability to convey business context. Compared to traces and logs, metrics are more difficult to define additional attributes. In observability, logs are the signals that can contain free context, and it is preferable to use logs to understand black boxes, whose context is difficult to understand with traces alone.

Logs are categorized into system logs and user logs. System logs refer to server infrastructure and application and web client logs, whereas user logs are logs of user requests.

User logs can contain session, trace, and profile IDs. The advantage of using a log is that it can be associated with traces, RUMs, and profiles.

The trace and profile IDs are outputted to the log so you can configure correlation with other signals in the log.

Error messages in the log are signs of failure that SREs pay attention to, so you configure metrics and logs to transfer alerts when errors are found. Since the log outputs so much information, it is difficult for users to understand it. By defining traces and correlation inside the log, you can easily identify traces.

Traces are only configured in the header, while logs are configured in the header and body. Logs have many limitations and are more difficult to customize. However, it is possible to add the necessary data to the body with a configuration file without modifying the code. Since it is easy and simple to analyze with log, if you need to improve observability in a short period of time, adding data to the body of log is more suitable.

When it comes to OpenTelemetry and commercial observability agents, the approach to supporting logs focuses on reusing existing language-specific libraries and extending their functionality.

Various trace contexts are output in the log, which have different notations depending on the trace standard. OpenTelemetry uses `trace_id` and `span_id`, commercial observability (`dt` is Dynatrace, `dd` is datadog) uses `dt.trace_id` and `dt.span_id`, and micrometer trace OpenTelemetry bridge uses `traceId` and `spanId`. The `x-` attribute is located in the message header and is used for trace, `x-dynatrace`.

In addition to correlation, you should try to match the results of the trace and log. Match not only the error messages, but also the error codes as much as possible.

The errors that the traces generate can be different from the errors that logs generate.

For example, the error generated by a span in the trace is more detailed because it is generated directly by microservices, while the error message and status code in the log is likely to be different because it reflects the end-user perspective.

The number of backend errors is high, and the number of frontend error codes is different. Error messages and counts are also different between signals.

If you ask which error message is more accurate between backend and frontend, it is a good idea to prioritize the error that is closer to the root cause, but it is also important to understand how the error negatively affects the user's perspective. A near-root cause error in a backend trace is different from a user-facing error in an API server. You need to manage both.

In the microservices structure, failures propagate, resulting in a variety of error codes. Errors should be considered from two perspectives:

- Which error is closest to the root cause? The closer you can get to the root cause, the easier it is to fix the problem.

- What is the impact of the error on your users? If the service has stopped or failed, you'll need to determine how many users are affected and retry to recover.

Technically, it is important to understand the root cause of the propagation of the failure, and business-wise, it is necessary to have accurate numbers and an understanding of the loss and impact of the failure. You can understand business errors and the impact of failures from logs, and you can understand root cause analysis and the exact section from traces when failure occurred. The correlation that supports these requirements is a log-to-trace correlation.

2.2.10. From Networks to Traces

Trace the HTTP traffic coming from L7. If you see an increase in errors such as latency, retries, and timeouts, you need to understand whether it's a problem with your infrastructure network or something internal to your application. L7 Protocol HTTP is not a stream like TCP, but HTTP is clearly separated into individual requests, connections, and sessions. You can include a trace ID in the HTTP header and map individual HTTP requests to metric exemplars.

You can't inject trace context into HTTP headers without an agent. To inject trace context into a frontend application like RUM, you can only generate trace context through automated instrumentation using an agent or manual instrumentation using an API.

The problem is that TCP and UDP are often freely customized by developers, making automated instrumentation difficult.

For example, a single HTTP request involves multiple packet transfers, including handshakes and DNS lookups. It is difficult to inject trace context directly into L3.

However, network-specific applications like Cilium can monitor a variety of protocols, including TCP, UDP, and TLS.

There is no meaning for a trace in a TCP header that consists of several packets.

If your application fails a transaction and retries it, and you don't have any data about the network, it will be difficult to troubleshoot the problem. Cilium provides detailed network data, making it easier to troubleshoot problems.

The scope of distributed traces is limited, and the service map is output due to the dependency on the application to propagate. Hubble UI complements the shortcomings of distributed traces and existing service maps and enables root cause analysis of the network.

CHAPTER 2   THE RCA APPROACH

The benefit of using Cilium and eBPF in conjunction with the trace is that you can quickly determine whether the network or the application is the problem. In production, when something goes wrong, you need to determine whether the problem is in the infrastructure or the application. Discussions and meetings with many different organizations can be tedious, difficult, and time-consuming, but if you can determine the problem upfront, it's a big help in troubleshooting.

2.2.11. From Traces to Metrics

Grafana provides the ability to move from traces to metrics.

The metric feature in trace allows you to see trends or aggregations of data related to each span. You can try it out by enabling the Metric Trace feature toggle in the Grafana configuration file.

1. Navigate to Explore and Query Trace. Each span now has a link to the query.

2. Clicking the link executes the query in the split panel. If the tag is configured, Grafana dynamically injects the value of the span attribute into the query. The query is executed over the selected time scope.

```
systemctl start grafana-server
/etc/grafana/grafana.ini

[feature_toggles]

tempoApmTable = true
traceToMetrics = true
```

By modifying the Grafana configuration file as shown in the previous configuration, you can enable the feature.

2.2.12. From Traces to Service Maps

Service maps are often used in infrastructure networks and traces. In the case of traces, they contain the execution paths of microservices. Grafana Tempo automatically generates service maps. You can specify various criteria to search for the nodes you want to analyze. While polystats give you an overall view of your infrastructure, service maps give you an overall flow of your application.

Grafana Tempo and OpenSearch observability provide SLO dashboards by default. It's useful to use SLO dashboards because they don't require any special development.

The Grafana APM dashboard displays basic SLOs such as error rate, throughput, and latency. You don't need to develop a separate SLO dashboard, and it displays the results along with the service map, which helps you understand which services are having problems or dependencies.

You should place multiple charts on your dashboard and use variables to match the values that the charts specify. If there is no connection between the charts, it's a good idea to use variables to connect them. SREs can further reduce MTTR by adding correlation.

You need to configure the correlation and dashboards to suit your requirements. It is also the role of the SRE to define these procedures.

2.2.13. From Service Maps to Metrics

A service map shows the relationships and dependencies between microservices. It is useful for understanding the overall flow, identifying the propagation of failures, and analyzing the root cause. However, there is also a disadvantage that when a large number of microservices are displayed on one screen, the complexity increases, making it difficult to understand the problem. Therefore, it is useful to output only the downstream and upstream services that are related to the service and perform critical path analysis.

Understanding the paths between services is meaningful, but paths alone are not enough to solve problems. You need information about how the individual microservice's output in the service map are being processed. Or you need to understand the state of other microservices that are involved. By clicking a node in the service map , you can understand the health of a specific microservice by outputting latency, throughput, and error rate.

2.2.14. From Metrics to Logs

The correlation between metrics and logs uses tags. It's common to use tags, but it's not recommended. You should use correlations rather than tags. After configuring the correlations described previously, you should configure tags as needed. While there are many advantages to using tags, the reality is that managing tens of thousands of tags can be challenging.

Metrics involve aggregation information, and logs involve debugging information, so they are different types of data. However, it would be helpful to understand the problem if the overall flow of metrics and the detailed data of logs were output together. However, metrics don't provide special sampling techniques for logs as the exemplar does. Metrics and logs cannot be correlated by specific ID, meaning there is no direct relationship between metrics and logs. You must explicitly specify the correlation using tags and labels. Grafana provides a correlation between metrics and logs by providing a synchronization button on the screen. If you drag and drop a metric at a certain point in time, the log and trace on the right will automatically look up the corresponding label and time period.

You should use as few tags as possible and organize your correlations. Well-organized correlations reduce the need to manually add tags.

I demonstrate using the most popular observability open sources—Grafana LTGM and OpenSearch.

2.3. Grafana Correlations

This section looks at Grafana's ability to define different correlations. It's not enough to understand them conceptually; you need to understand how they are implemented in your solution and configure them to suit your situation.

Depending on the dashboard version, you may encounter various issues such as not supporting correlation and conflicts with the Tempo version. The Grafana dashboard version released in Git works well without any problems, so I recommend using the Grafana version attached to the code whenever possible.

I will implement correlation in several ways using Grafana observability:

- Leverage correlation natively supported by Grafana. The correlation between logs and traces is implemented by leveraging Grafana's built-in functionality.

- Implementing the correlation standard. The correlation between metrics and traces is implemented by utilizing the standard exemplar, metric generator.

2.3.1. From Metrics to Traces

To manage exemplars, Prometheus allocates a separate space in memory to store them. Two settings are required when using an exemplar.

- Within the Grafana dashboard, there is a section for setting up the Prometheus data source, as shown in Figure 2-2.

- You need to set additional options at the Prometheus startup.

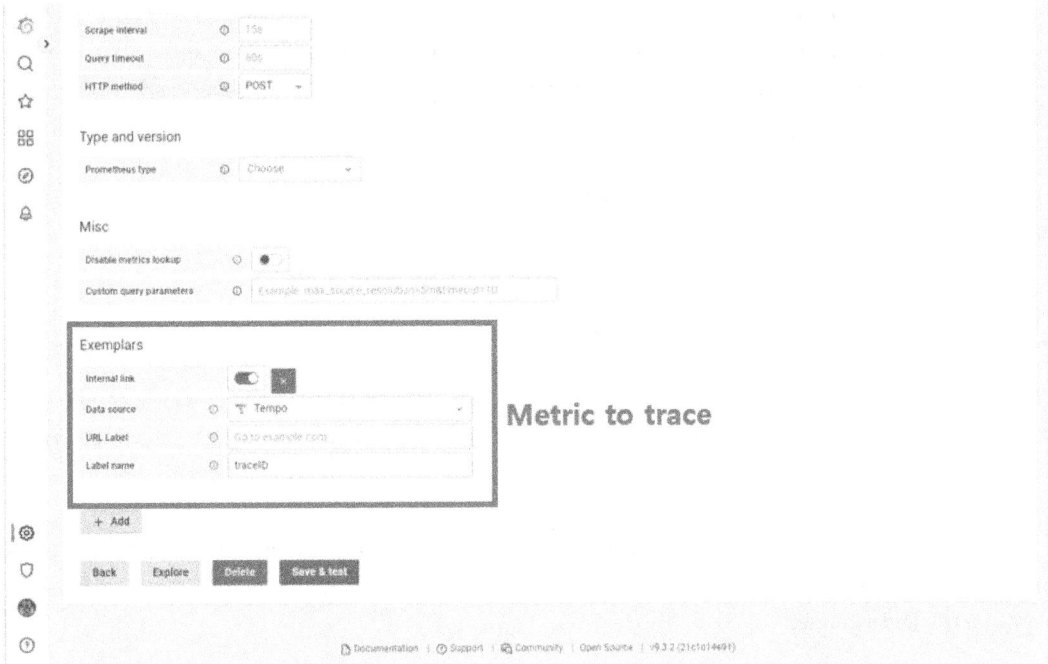

Figure 2-2. Setting up an exemplar in Grafana

An exemplar is a sampling of traces measured at a given time interval. Exemplars help identify high cardinality metadata from specific events within time series data. While metrics are great at providing an aggregation view of a system, traces provide a detailed view of a single request. Therefore, the two should be correlated to complement each other, and exemplars provide a way to correlate metrics and traces.

Let's say your website is experiencing a spike in traffic volume. More than 80 percent of your users are able to access your website in less than two seconds, but some users are experiencing slower than normal response times. To identify the factors contributing to the latency, you need to compare 99 quantiles. You should also identify slow transactions and analyze their traces in detail with exemplars.

- Exemplars are available in the Prometheus data source and must be enabled when using them.

- Prometheus allocates space to manage and store exemplars. The exemplar storage is implemented as a fixed-size circular buffer that stores exemplars in memory for all series. Enabling this feature allows you to store exemplars. You can control the size of the circular buffer using the exemplar in the configuration file block storage. An exemplar with only `traceID=< trace-id>` uses approximately 100 bytes of memory with in-memory exemplar storage. When the exemplar store is enabled, the exemplar is added to the WAL for local persistence.

- Grafana Mimir includes the ability to store exemplars in memory. Exemplar storage in Grafana Mimir is implemented similarly to that in Prometheus. Exemplars are stored as fixed-size circular buffers that store exemplars in memory for every series.
- OpenMetric officially supports exemplars.

It's important to learn about the metric generator, which provides the ability to automatically generate exemplars.

2.3.2. From Traces to Metrics

The metric generator is a Tempo component that generates metrics from traces and provides correlation capabilities with the generated metrics from ingested traces. The distributor writes the received spans to the ingester and metric generator. The metric generator processes the span, uses the Prometheus remote write protocol, and writes the metric to the Prometheus data source.

The metric generator runs multiple processors internally. Each processor collects spans and generates metrics. It generates various metrics such as bucket, sum, and count. Currently available processors are service graph and spanmetric:

- The service graph is a visual representation of the correlation between services in the Grafana dashboard.
- Spanmetric automatically generates metrics related to throughput and latency in Prometheus.

For correlation between metrics and traces, I recommend using exemplars. Developers can use the Prometheus API to develop exemplars. Spanmetric provides a simpler way to implement an exemplar.

- Spanmetric implements correlation by creating a metric from a span.
- Spanmetric generates metrics from collected trace data, including requests, errors, and duration (RED) metrics.

Spanmetric is an important and necessary feature because it generates metrics from traces. The generated metrics show application-level insights as long as the trace propagates through the application.

Spanmetric automatically adds exemplars to time series metrics, providing additional value in understanding your application.

Spanmetric works by examining all span received and counting the total number and duration of span for all dimensions. The dimensions can be service name, job, span type, status code, and attributes present in the span.

Spanmetric automatically generates the following metrics:

- **traces_spanmetrics_latency_bucket:** A histogram that calculates the latency of tasks. It automatically generates three metrics: Bucket, Count, and Sum.

CHAPTER 2   THE RCA APPROACH

- **traces_spanmetrics_calls_total:** A counter that counts requests and represents the number of calls.

The following are the metrics you need to add to your Prometheus options:

- web.enable-remote-write-receiver
- enable-feature=exemplar-storage

Most observability automatically generate latency, throughput, and error rate for a service and multiple endpoints within the service.

Quickly create SLO, enable exemplars, and service graphs.

In production, the question of whether to develop a metric or develop a trace to automatically generate a metric often arises. If you don't want to change your existing code, you can use spanmetric to generate important metrics quickly and without change.

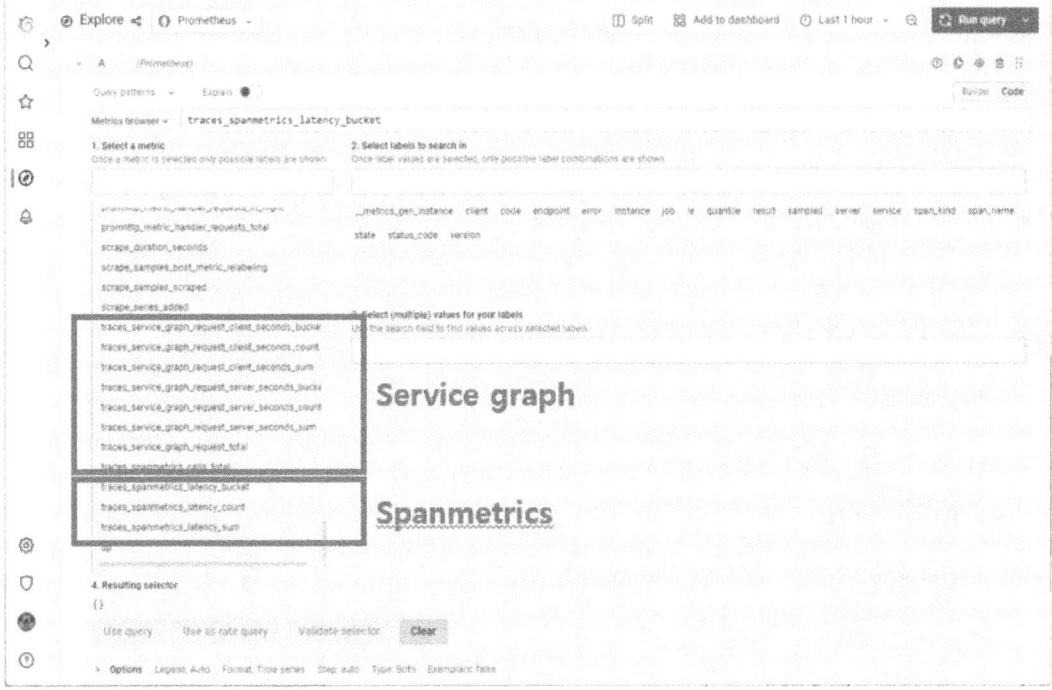

Figure 2-3. *Looking up a trace-metric in Grafana*

You can verify the trace_spanmetrics_latency_bucket, trace_spanmetrics_latency_count and trace_spanmetrics_latency_sum metrics, as shown in Figure 2-3.

111

CHAPTER 2   THE RCA APPROACH

2.3.2.1. Demo Configuration

The demo is done in a virtual machine and does not use Kubernetes. The applications required for this demo are Tempo, Loki, and Prometheus. This demo will automatically generate metrics from traces. Therefore, it uses spanmetric.

You need two hosts:

- Prometheus, Promtail, and Tempo will be installed on Server A.
- Loki will be installed on Server B.

Start Grafana on Server A:

```
systemctl start grafana-server
```

Start Tempo:

```
./binary/tempo -config.file ./binary/config.yaml
```

Launch Prometheus:

```
./binary/prometheus-2.39.1.linux-amd64/prometheus --config.file=./binary/prometheus-2.39.1.linux-amd64/prometheus.yml --enable-feature=exemplar-storage --storage.tsdb.max-block-duration=1m --storage.tsdb.min-block-duration=1m
```

Start Tempo:

```
./binary/tempo -config.file ./binary/tempo_config.yaml
```

Start Promtail:

```
./binary/promtail-local-config.yaml
```

Start the application:

```
./tracing-example 2>&1 | tee tracing-example.log
```

Start Loki at Server B:

```
./binary/loki-linux-amd64 --config.file=./binary/loki-local-config.yaml
```

Create a Tempo configuration file for a description of the configuration file.

- Set metrics_generator_enabled to true.
- metrics_generator_processors: [service-graphs, span-metrics]
- Set the remote write configuration to http://localhost:9090/api/v1/write. This is the address of Prometheus.

```yaml
multitenancy_enabled: false
search_enabled: true
metrics_generator_enabled: true

server:
  http_listen_port: 3200

distributor:
  receivers:
    jaeger:
      protocols:
        thrift_http:
        grpc:
        thrift_binary:
        thrift_compact:
    zipkin:
    otlp:
      protocols:
        http:
        grpc:

storage:
  trace:
    backend: local
    local:
      path: /tmp/tempo/blocks

metrics_generator:
  storage:
    path: /tmp/tempo/generator/wal
    remote_write:
      - url: http://localhost:9090/api/v1/write

overrides:
  metrics_generator_processors: [service-graphs, span-metrics]
```

Create a configuration file for Promtail. Configure it to read `tracing-example.log` as input and load it into Loki. Write a Prometheus configuration file.

This tracing-example is set up to scrape a custom metric:

```yaml
global:
  scrape_interval: 15s
  evaluation_interval: 15s
```

CHAPTER 2 THE RCA APPROACH

```
alerting:
  alertmanagers:
    - static_configs:
        - targets:
          # - alertmanager:9093

rule_files:
  # - "first_rules.yml"
  # - "second_rules.yml"

scrape_configs:
  - job_name: "prometheus"

    static_configs:
      - targets: ["localhost:9090"]

  - job_name: 'tracing-example'
    static_configs:
      - targets: ["localhost:8000"]
```

To summarize, the metric generator supports service graphs and spanmetrics, which allow you to automatically generate important metrics for microservices. Grafana makes these features available without additional development.

OpenTelemetry also now supports service graphs and spanmetrics. There is no dependency on specific solutions like Grafana.

Using the Node Graph in the Grafana dashboard, you can easily visualize the services graph, histogram, heatmap, exemplar, time series.

2.3.3. From Logs to Traces

In Grafana, you can set up a correlation from the logs to traces with a simple configuration, without any additional development. Figure 2-4 shows the screen for configuring the Loki data source in the Grafana dashboard. By using a derived field, you can implement log to trace correlation with the trace ID included in the output log.

CHAPTER 2   THE RCA APPROACH

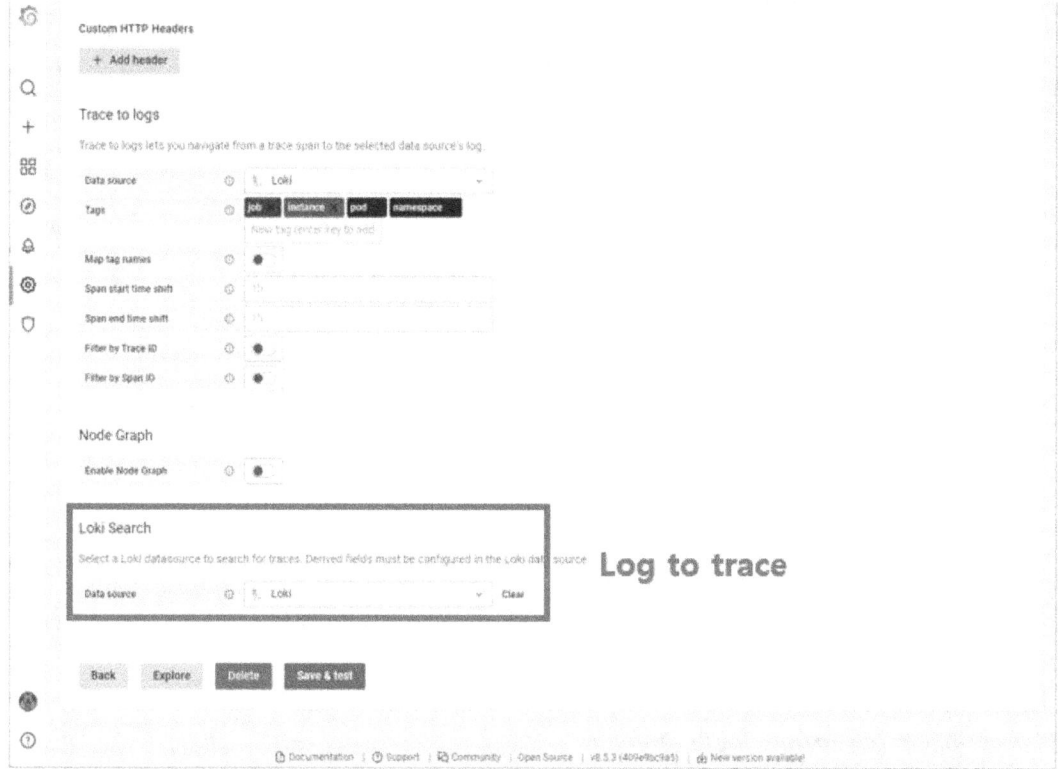

Figure 2-4. *Setting up log-trace in Grafana*

2.3.4. From Traces to Logs

You can implement trace-to-log by including a log in the trace context. A trace-to-log correlation can be implemented in Grafana with a simple configuration, as shown in Figure 2-5.

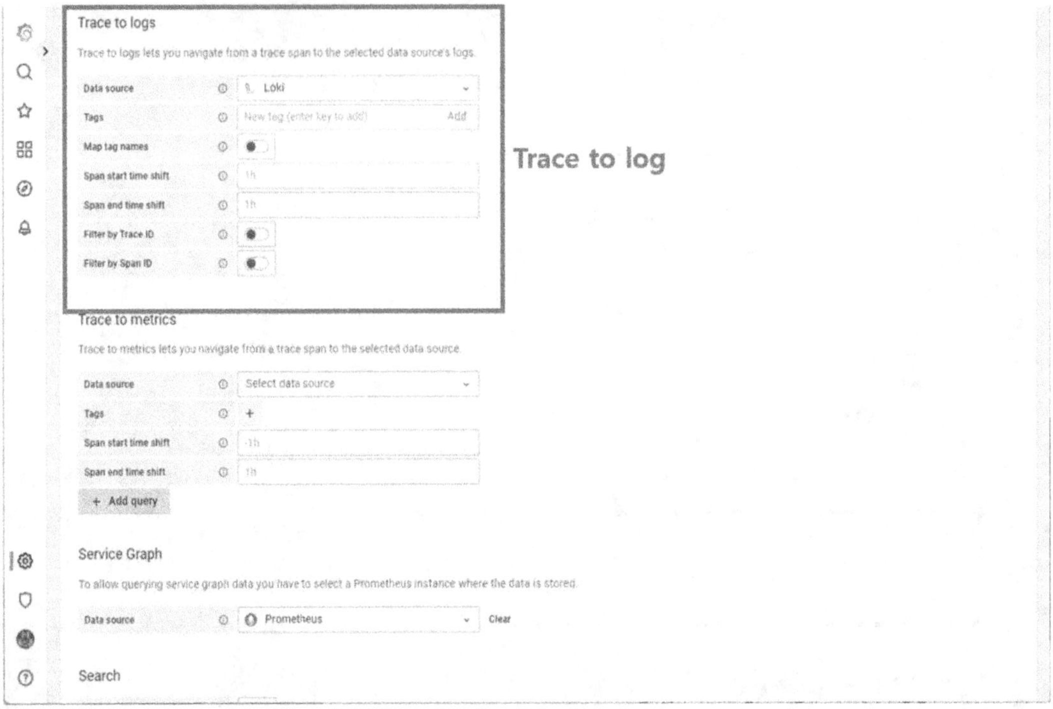

CHAPTER 2   THE RCA APPROACH

Figure 2-5. Setting up trace-log in Grafana

I recommend using the new version of the Grafana dashboard. Older versions often lack functionality or contain errors.

2.4. Using a New Stack

To demonstrate observability, you need an application with a frontend and a backend. This is because it is necessary to generate Telemetry. The demo requirements for observability are as follows:

- You need to provide a load generator. Observability requires a certain level of data. Without an automated load generator, manual traffic generation is difficult and time-consuming to validate observability data.

- It's not a good observability test if a lot of the traffic you to generate is only healthy. You need to mimic production, and you need to generate a certain amount of errors because observability is about finding the few that are a problem and fixing them out of tens of thousands of traffic.

From a developer's perspective, Docker is a useful runtime environment. Docker makes it easy to quickly and easily configure demos. If you use Docker to easily build and deploy without troubleshooting, it will be difficult to debug and analyze the cause and fix problems later on.

CHAPTER 2   THE RCA APPROACH

I prioritize Kubernetes for all demos wherever possible. Since Kubernetes is currently the standard for cloud-native runtime environments, it made sense to do everything related to observability in Kubernetes. Although it has the disadvantage of being significantly more complex than Docker, observability can achieve scalability, resiliency, and cost savings when running on Kubernetes. I believe that Kubernetes is the right environment for observability.

2.4.1. Introducing The New Stack (TNS)

The New Stack is a microservice that demonstrates observability of metrics, logs, and traces and consists of three layers: frontend, backend, and data management. It is a reference application that provides insights into how to develop and configure a modern observability technology stack and demonstrates the correlation between different signal of observability.

I configured the microservices with Grafana observability. Architecturally, the Grafana agent performs a role similar to that of the OpenTelemetry collector. I recommend using OpenTelemetry due to its vendor dependency:

- The frontend is an HTTP client, and the load is generated automatically by a load generator.

- The backend is responsible for receiving requests from the frontend and forwarding them to the data store.

- The data stored in the demo is not a database. It would be appropriate to implement a physical database such as MySQL, but for testing purposes, I developed an application that acts as a database.

The metrics, traces, and logs for TNS are as follows:

- metrics:
    - The TNS application provides metrics from the /metrkics endpoint and collects metrics through a scraping process. In addition to Prometheus metrics, it also provides OpenMetrics. OpenMetrics must be provided for the exemplar to be enabled. If you use the Grafana agent, the Grafana agent scrapes and writes the metrics to the Prometheus server using Prometheus remote write.
    - Prometheus can also scrape metrics directly from TNS, and the Grafana agent can be configured as a gateway to collect metrics, logs, and traces. In addition to the Prometheus server, any system that allows remote writing to Prometheus, such as Thanos or Cortex, can manage metrics.
    - To use exemplars, you need to use OpenMetric. To use it, run `go build` and `curl -H 'Accept: application/openmetrics-text' http://localhost:80/metrics | less` to collect and save the exemplar.

117

CHAPTER 2 THE RCA APPROACH

I implemented observability using the Weaveworks API. The client code looks like this: Create a client_request_duration_seconds metric of type histogram.

```
var requestDuration = promauto.NewHistogramVec(prometheus.HistogramOpts{
    Namespace:"tns",
    Name: "client_request_duration_seconds",
    Help: "Time (in seconds) spent doing client HTTP requests",
    Buckets: prometheus.DefBuckets,
}, []string{"method", "status_code"})
```

LB processes and extracts custom logic after TraceRequest. Each layer of TNS (LB, APP, DB) delivers traces to Tempo and stores the trace.

Each layer of the TNS (LB, APP, DB) writes standard output or standard errors to the log. Promtail collects the Kubernetes log files and passes the log to Loki. LB initializes trace. LB, APP, and DB initialize the log and trace it in a similar format.

APP is an API server, and it processes logic according to the three endpoints.

```
        s, err := server.New(serverConfig)
        if err != nil {
            level.Error(logger).Log("msg", "error starting server", "err", err)
            os.Exit(1)
        }
        defer s.Shutdown()
        databases, err := getDatabases(flag.Args())
        if err != nil {
            level.Error(logger).Log("msg", "error parsing databases", "err", err)
            os.Exit(1)
        }
        level.Info(logger).Log("database(s)", len(databases))

        app, err := new(logger, databases)
        if err != nil {
            level.Error(logger).Log("msg", "error initializing app", "err", err)
            os.Exit(1)
        }

        s.HTTP.HandleFunc("/", app.Index)
```

You have developed a custom metric and configured it to create an exemplar. DB adds an exemplar as follows. DB uses the ExemplarObserver interface and records the trace ID through the ObserveWithExemplar method.

```
func (db *db) Vote(w http.ResponseWriter, r *http.Request) {
        traceId, _ := tracing.Extract traceID(r.Context())
        start := time.Now()
```

```
        defer func() {
            elapsed := time.Since(start)
                if h, ok := db.votes.(prometheus.ExemplarObserver); ok {
                    h.ObserveWithExemplar(elapsed.Seconds(), prometheus.Labels{" traceID":
                    traceId})
                }
        }()
```

LB, APP, and DB provide the metric whose code looks like this:

```
func New(logger log.Logger, reg prometheus.Registerer) *db {
        return &db{
            logger: logger,
            fetches: promauto.With(reg).NewCounter(prometheus.CounterOpts{
                Name: "tns_db_fetches_total",
                Help: "Number of fetch requests handled by the database",
            }),
                posts: promauto.With(reg).NewHistogram(prometheus.HistogramOpts{
                    Name: "tns_db_post_time_seconds",
                    Help: "Time taken to submit new links to the database",
                }),
                votes: promauto.With(reg).NewHistogram(prometheus.HistogramOpts{
                    Name: "tns_db_vote_time_seconds",
                    Help: "Time taken to vote on links in the database",
                }),
                links: map[int]*Link{},
            }
}
```

It is configured to fail 40 percent of transactions for 30 seconds every five minutes. Because this logic is included, you get the sudden periodic spikes that you saw in the time series earlier. Because it is deployed in Kubernetes, it can generate a wide variety of errors.

Most of the applications in this book are configured to generate failures internally and to throttle errors to a certain rate. Because they run as microservices on Kubernetes, you can try different chaos engineering techniques and learn from analyzing the signals they collect.

1. Minimize the resources allocated to the pod and increase the traffic generated by the clients. Observe what failures occur.

2. If you delete certain Kubernetes deployments and pods, transactions will be lost, and you will see how they are recovered.

CHAPTER 2 THE RCA APPROACH

3. Create a service graph in your dashboard and measure throughput, latency, and error rate per service.

4. Logs should be enriched. The current output log is not sufficient for root cause analysis.

5. Change the latency to occur in individual microservices. It's also a good idea to generate more traffic from clients.

As you run the test multiple times, compare how it compares to past results and how it differs from the normal case.

2.4.2. Configure TNS

You need to deploy the instrumented three-layer (data layer, backend layer, and frontend layer) application to a Kubernetes cluster and monitor it. Then, a dashboard will be deployed to a Grafana instance for the visualization of performance metrics.

Next, you install and configure the demo application. The specific steps are as follows.

Launch Minikube:

```
minikube start --vm-driver=none --kubernetes-version v1.20.0 --memory=12000 --cpus=2
```

Add a chart:

```
helm repo add grafana https://grafana.github.io/helm-charts
```

Install Tempo:

```
helm upgrade --install tempo grafana/tempo
```

Install Prometheus:

```
kubectl apply -f prometheus-service.yaml
kubectl apply -f prometheus-deployment.yaml
kubectl apply -f prometheus-claim0-persistentvolumeclaim.yaml
cp prometheus.yml /tmp/hostpath-provisioner/default/prometheus-claim0
```

Install Loki:

```
kubectl apply -f loki-service.yaml
kubectl apply -f loki-deployment.yaml
```

CHAPTER 2   THE RCA APPROACH

Install Promtail. Save your `values.yaml`, as shown here:

```
config:
  clients:
    - url: http://loki:3100/loki/api/v1/push
```

Execute this `helm` command:

```
helm install promtail grafana/promtail -f values.yaml
```

Install Grafana. The version is 8.5.4. This is not a good way to install it. For example, it needs to be converted from YAML to `configmap`, or from YAML to Helm charts. Conversion is easy with open source tools, but it takes time.

```
kubectl apply -f grafana-service.yaml
kubectl apply -f grafana-deployment.yaml
kubectl apply -f grafana-claim2-persistentvolumeclaim.yaml
kubectl apply -f grafana-claim1-persistentvolumeclaim.yaml
kubectl apply -f grafana-claim0-persistentvolumeclaim.yaml
cp datasources.yaml /tmp/hostpath-provisioner/default/grafana-claim0
cp datasources.yaml /tmp/hostpath-provisioner/default/grafana-claim1
cp datasources.yaml /tmp/hostpath-provisioner/default/grafana-claim2
cp dashboards.yaml /tmp/hostpath-provisioner/default/grafana-claim0
cp dashboards.yaml /tmp/hostpath-provisioner/default/grafana-claim1
cp dashboards.yaml /tmp/hostpath-provisioner/default/grafana-claim2
cp -rf dashboards/ /tmp/hostpath-provisioner/default/grafana-claim0
cp -rf dashboards/ /tmp/hostpath-provisioner/default/grafana-claim1
cp -rf dashboards/ /tmp/hostpath-provisioner/default/grafana-claim2
```

Install the application:

```
kubectl apply -f .
```

In your web browser, go to `https://localhost:8080` to see the demo, the load generator. You can navigate to the Grafana dashboard to query the application logs, visualize metrics, and inspect trace.

Kubernetes writes the log file to the `/var/log/` folder.

You can navigate to Tempo by selecting the trace ID shown in Figure 2-6. This feature is generated by a field derived from the Loki data source.

121

CHAPTER 2　THE RCA APPROACH

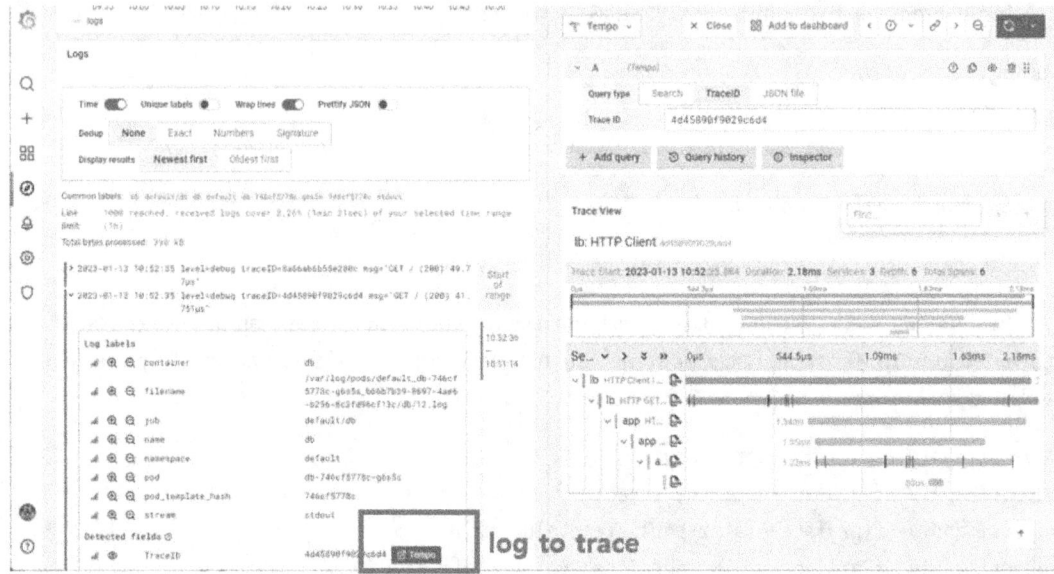

Figure 2-6.　*Moving from logs to traces*

Clicking Tempo will take you to the corresponding trace.

```
2022-08-16 23:28:52 level=debug traceID=6b34f1be8a986c7 msg="POST /post (302) 2.635115ms"
2022-08-16 23:28:52 level=info msg="HTTP client success" status=208 url=http://db/post durat
ion=2.362456mstraceID=6b34f1be8a986c7
2022-08-16 23:28:52 level=debug traceID=22c9f288f9ece1b0 msg="GET / (200) 2.857113ms"
2022-08-16 23:28:52 level=info msg="HTTP client success" status=200 url=http://db duration=
2.276518mstraceID=22c9f288f9ece1b0
2022-08-16 23:28:52 level=debug traceID=2a831e81ab2c380 msg="GET / (200) 3.169247ms"
```

2.4.3. TNS Correlation

The TNS correlation demo includes various correlations from metrics to traces, traces to logs, and logs to traces, and it shows how the application integrates with Grafana, Prometheus, Loki, and Tempo observability. It also includes prebuilt dashboards, load generators, and exemplars.

Figure 2-7 shows the dashboard of TNS. The dashboard, which typically consists of several charts, is organized as shown, and the screen is periodically refreshed to monitor the system.

CHAPTER 2   THE RCA APPROACH

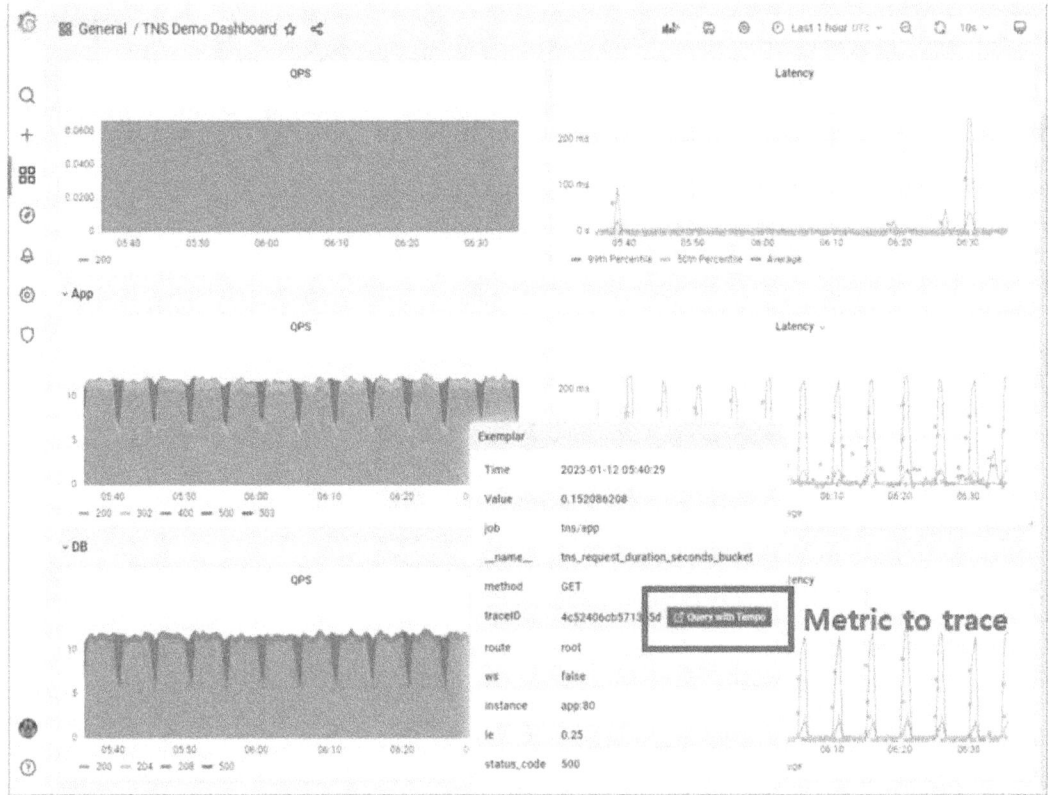

Figure 2-7. *The TNS dashboard screen*

2.4.3.1. Navigating from Metrics to Traces

Verify that Loki, Prometheus, and Tempo are running, the TNS demo is deployed to the Kubernetes cluster, and you need to configure the Prometheus data source in the Grafana dashboard.

Weaveworks middleware automatically outputs latency with exemplars. On the Prometheus screen, run a PromQL query and enable the exemplar as shown in Figure 2-8. This shows the latency for the TNS/APP.

CHAPTER 2   THE RCA APPROACH

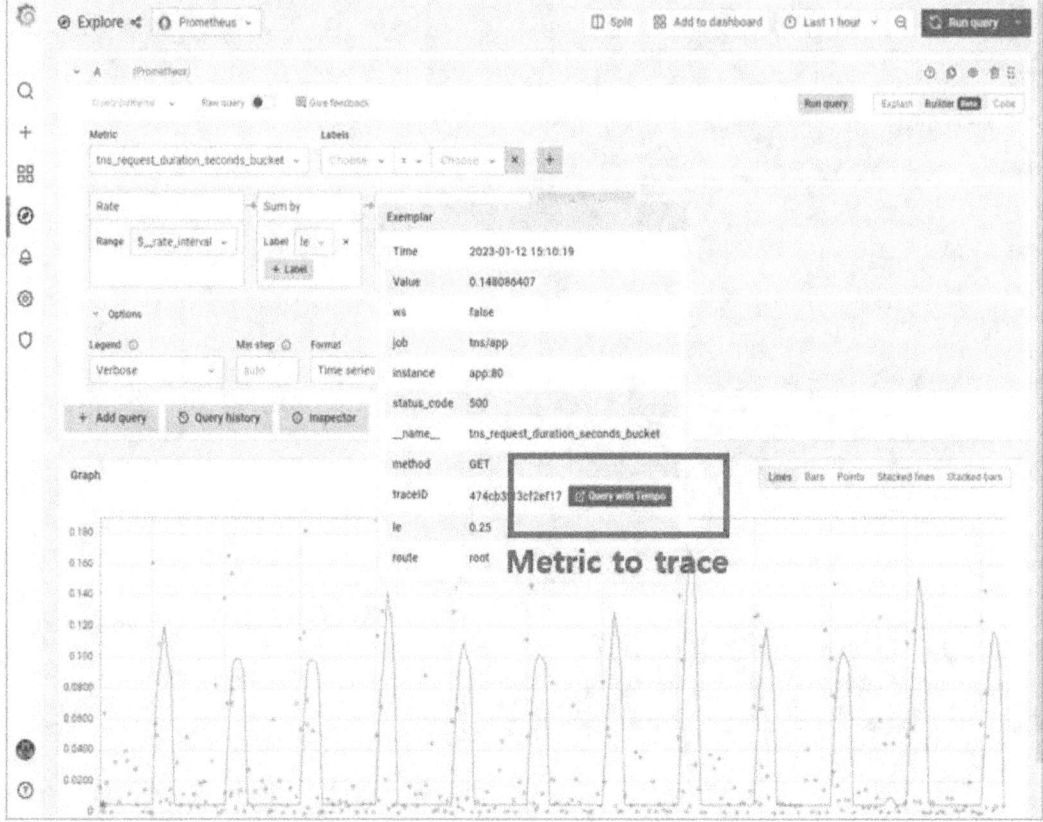

Figure 2-8. *The exemplar screen*

The load generator generates many transactions, some of which generate failed requests. The failed requests are output as exemplars. The exemplar is the point in the time series, which you can click to jump directly from metric to trace. The exemplar allows you to analyze the failed requests in detail.

```
histogram_quantile(.99, sum(rate(tns_request_duration_seconds_bucket{status_code="500"}
[1m])) by (le))
```

Enter a query and run it periodically, as shown in Figure 2-9.

CHAPTER 2   THE RCA APPROACH

Figure 2-9.   The Error Search screen

Transactions with 500 errors in the 99th percentile can be easily traced by enabling the printed exemplar. So you need to check the `tns_request_duration_seconds_bucket` for exemplars.

2.4.3.2. Navigating from Logs to Traces

The way to correlate traces from logs is to output the trace ID from the log. An important configuration is to set up a Loki-derived field to generate a URL link from the trace ID. Figure 2-10 shows the Loki data source configuration.

125

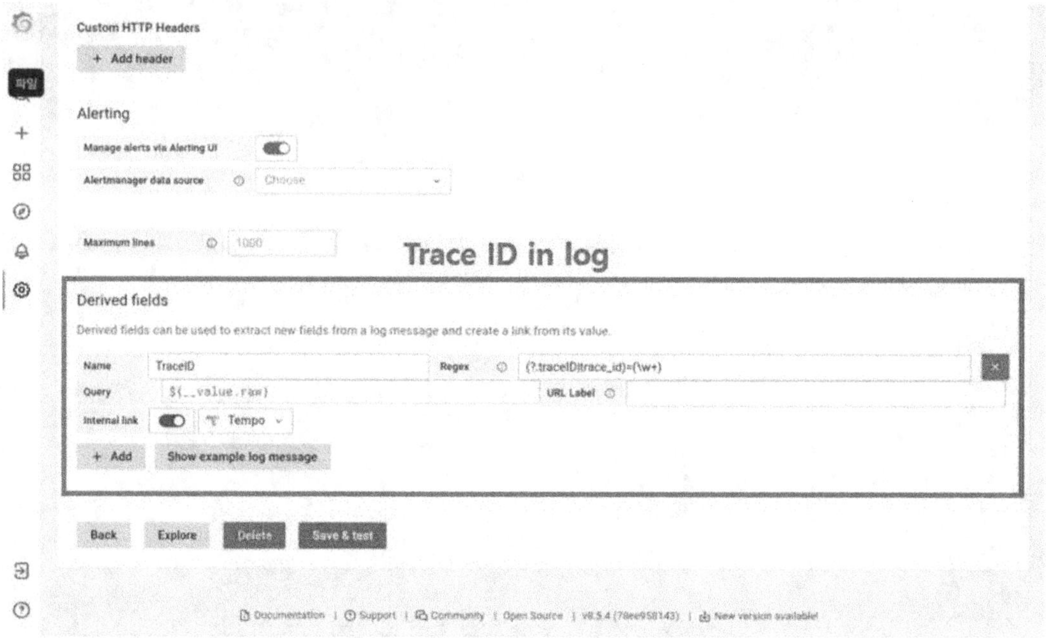

CHAPTER 2   THE RCA APPROACH

Figure 2-10. The Loki-derived field settings screen

The Grafana dashboard stores its internal configuration information in SQLite 3. It manages and associates the regular expressions and configuration information required by Loki, Tempo, and Mimir.

Extract the trace ID using a regular expression:

(?: traceID| trace_id)=(\w+)

In a query, enter the following values:

${__value.raw}

Next, I demonstrate how to correlate from logs to traces. If you want to display API requests that fail to go from APP to DB, query like this, as shown in Figure 2-11.

{ job = "default/db" } | logfmt

CHAPTER 2 THE RCA APPROACH

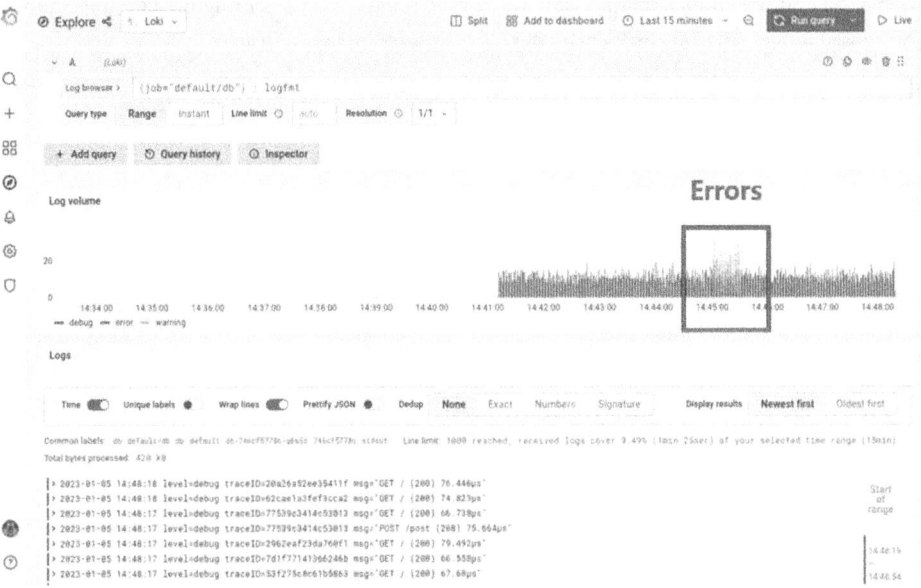

Figure 2-11. *The Log search screen*

To view the trace in the log line, click the Tempo button of the trace ID. You can see the corresponding trace output on the right in Figure 2-12. You can see the span where the problem occurred in the trace colored red. This is an error generated by the load generator for the demo.

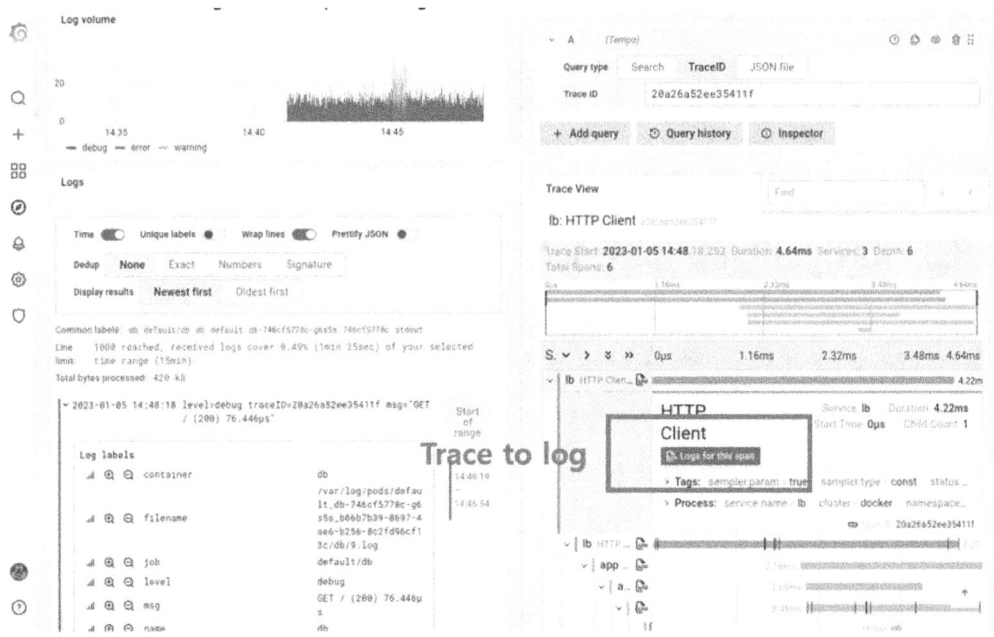

Figure 2-12. *Moving from log to trace*

CHAPTER 2   THE RCA APPROACH

Now, you look at the configuration to go from logs to traces. You can configure it on the Tempo data source, as shown in Figure 2-13. You can see the correlation from logs to traces.

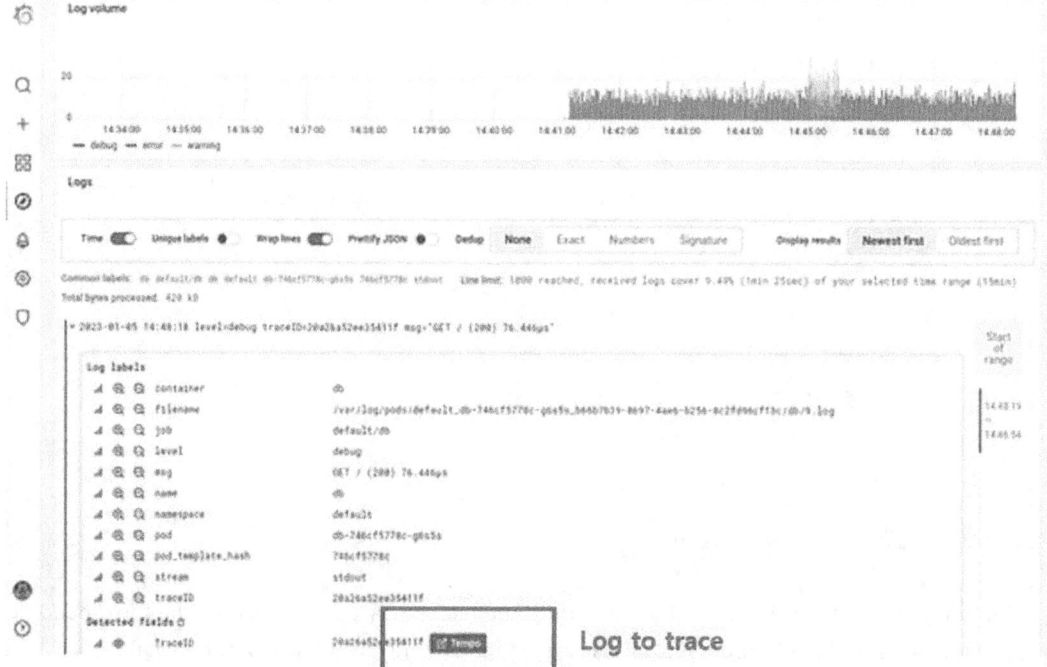

Figure 2-13. *The trace configuration*

When you select a specific span, you can see that the logs for this span are enabled. The TNS demo does not include spanmetric functionality to help you correlate from traces to metrics. I developed my own custom metrics instead of using spanmetric. You can easily implement correlation between traces and metrics by referring to the spanmetric configuration.

2.4.3.3. Navigating from Traces to Logs

The following guidelines describe how to move from metrics to traces to logs.

Select Prometheus in the data source and run the following query. The result is shown in Figure 2-14.

```
histogram_quantile(.99, sum(rate(tns_request_duration_seconds_bucket{}[1m])) by (le))
```

To analyze a particularly slow request, you can click exemplar:

CHAPTER 2 THE RCA APPROACH

Figure 2-14. *A custom metric*

If you analyze the graph in Figure 2-15, you can see that most transactions have no problems, but a small number of transactions have high latency. The exemplar is being output periodically with spikes.

Since exemplars are collected by sampling, they don't collect every metric, but they can be a good starting point for understanding the cause and fixing the problem.

CHAPTER 2 THE RCA APPROACH

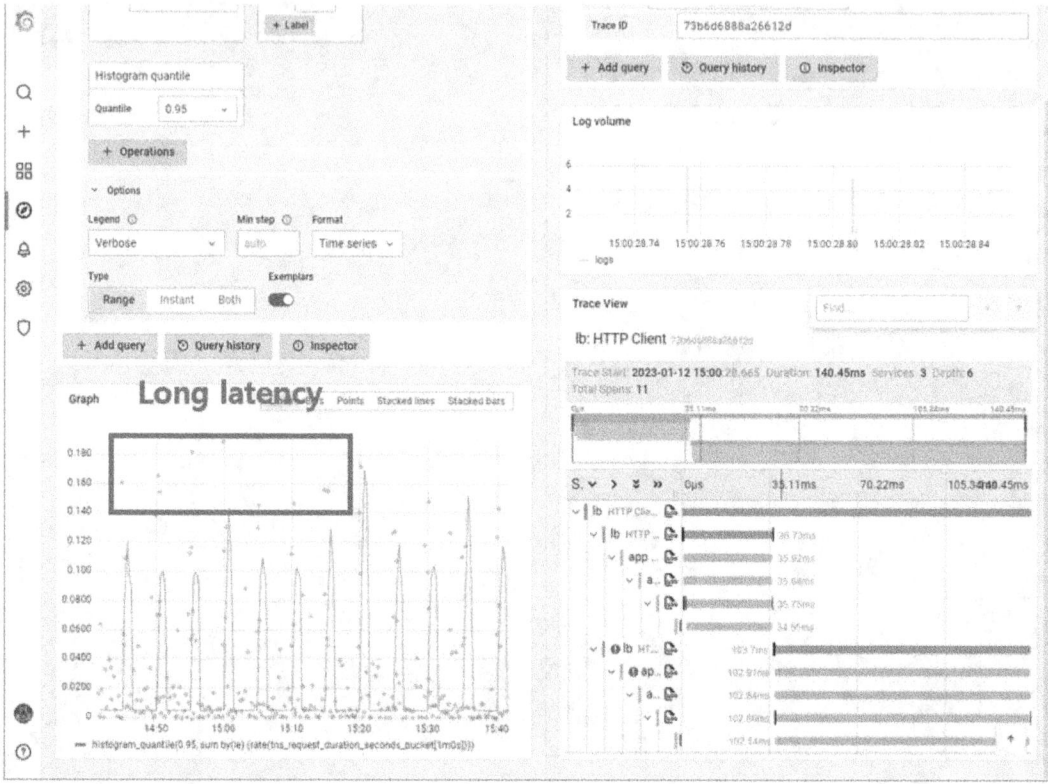

Figure 2-15. *Moving from metrics to traces*

Clicking on a specific exemplar will take you to the trace. The span can include log information, as shown in Figure 2-16. Compared to analyzing the log files, the trace provides richer contextual information, making it easier and faster for SREs to recognize problems.

CHAPTER 2   THE RCA APPROACH

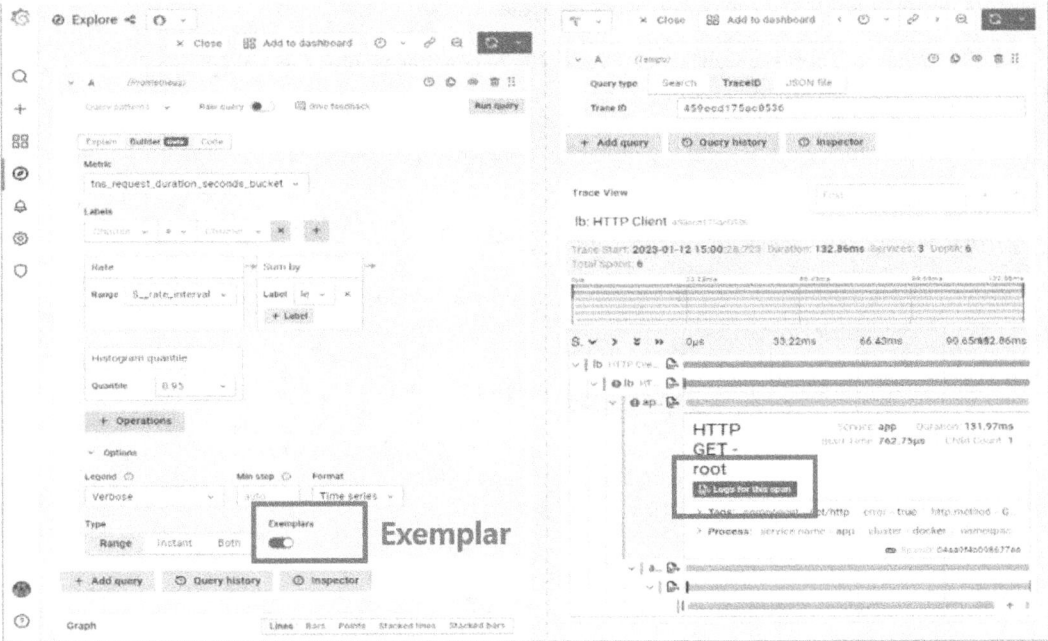

Figure 2-16. Moving from traces to logs

If you can't find the root cause based on the information in the span, you can go to the log file for debugging. Browsing the log files directly can be time-consuming and potentially inaccurate, but you can select a specific span to go directly to the logs.

Click the log icon on the span line to print the log details. It is recommended that problems be troubleshooted using traces whenever possible rather than logs. However, there are times when debugging is necessary, so the log is always useful, and it's a good idea to build a system to accurately collect and search for the data you need.

2.5. Grafana Observability

This example demonstrates the manual instrumentation of a Go application and analyzes the traces through logs and examples. The procedure for testing is as follows:

1. Deploy your application to a Kubernetes pod.

2. Your web server is running on port 8000.

3. Upon startup of a pod, Promtail collects the logs generated by the pod.

131

CHAPTER 2 THE RCA APPROACH

    4. Create an HTTP request and generate a trace.

    5. When you access a web server using CURL, it generates metric (request_latency_seconds).

    6. Each time you increment the Prometheus metric, you include the trace ID of the current request.

To enable an exemplar in your Go application, follow these steps:

    1. Create a metric on the web server and expose the Prometheus metric in OpenMetrics format.

    2. To visualize the traces associated with an exemplar, use a URL connection to Tempo.

Run the Go application and create a transaction using CURL:

```
curl http://localhost:8000/
```

Create an exemplar:

```
curl -H 'Accept: application/openmetrics-text' http://localhost:8000/metrics | less
```

If you want to see the output of the /metrics endpoint in OpenMetrics format, you must use the Accept HTTP header. Otherwise, you will get the default Prometheus format with no exemplar.

Log in to the Grafana dashboard http://localhost:3000/explore, select the Prometheus data source, and run the following query:

```
histogram_quantile(.99, sum(rate(demo_request_latency_seconds_bucket[1m])) by (le))
```

The results of the metric show that a small number of transactions are experiencing latency every five seconds. As you increase the traffic, you can see much more frequent spikes, as shown in Figure 2-17.

CHAPTER 2 THE RCA APPROACH

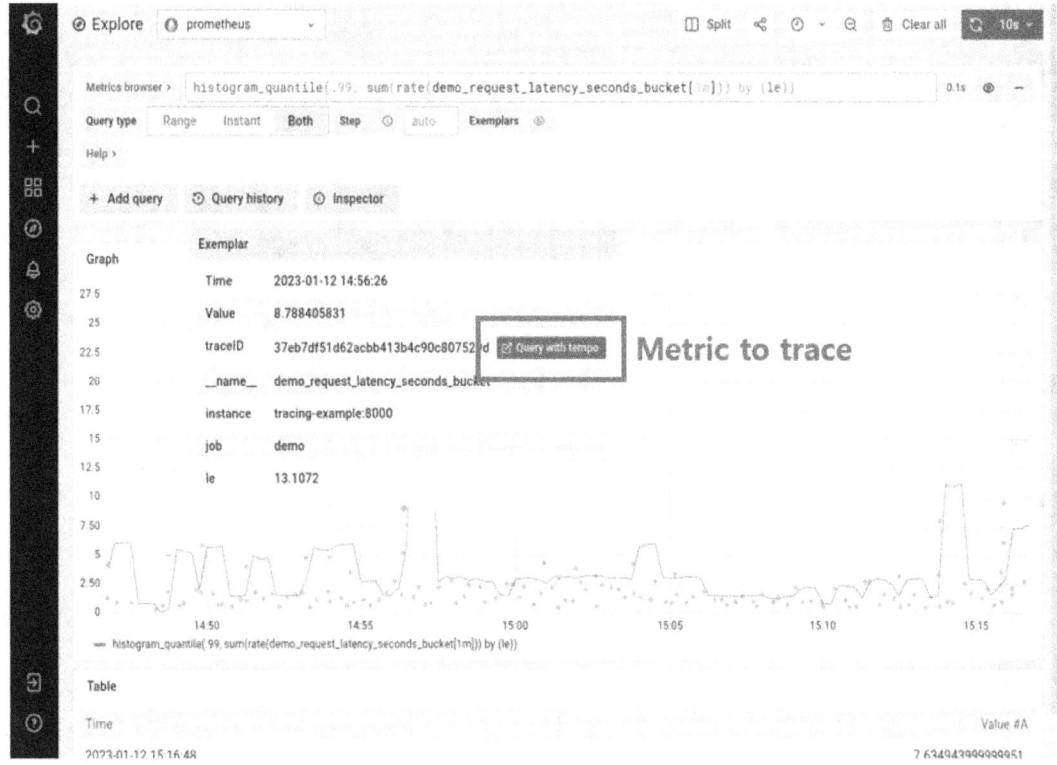

Figure 2-17. *Metric to trace correlation*

Moving on to Tempo, you can analyze the transaction in detail, as shown in Figure 2-18.

CHAPTER 2   THE RCA APPROACH

Figure 2-18.   *The log to trace correlation*

You can generate various errors, such as timeout due to latency and retries. Check to see if the errors are printed in the log.

2.5.1. Code Description

You can output the log by querying it like this:

{container_name="tracing-example"} | logfmt | latency > 1s

It's easy to search for the current trace ID in context.

To collect exemplars with Prometheus, you need to make sure that Prometheus can use the exemplar. The exemplar storage feature must be explicitly enabled using the --enable-feature=exemplar-storage flag. If you are using Prometheus helm charts, you can enable them by setting the following values.

```
server:
  image:
    repository: tomwilkie/prometheus
    tag: 0ea72b6a6
  extraArgs:
    enable-feature: exemplar-storage
```

134

CHAPTER 2 THE RCA APPROACH

The demo is a single Go application, and when you call the server with CURL, it generates server metrics:

```
var addr = "127.0.0.1:8000"
var tracer trace. tracer
var httpClient http.Client
var logger log.Logger

var metricRequestLatency = promauto.NewHistogram(prometheus.HistogramOpts{
    Namespace: "demo",
    Name: "request_latency_seconds",
    Help: "Request Latency",
    Buckets: prometheus.ExponentialBuckets(.0001, 2, 50),
})
```

Here's an implementation of trace:

```
func init tracer() func() {
        ctx := context.Background()
        driver := otlpgrpc.NewDriver(
                otlpgrpc.WithInsecure(),
                otlpgrpc.WithEndpoint("tempo:55680"),
                otlpgrpc.WithDialOption(grpc.WithBlock()),
        )
        exp, err := otlp.NewExporter(ctx, driver)

        bsp := sdk trace.NewBatchSpanProcessor(exp)
        tracerProvider := sdk trace.New tracerProvider(
 sdk trace.WithConfig(sdk trace.Config{DefaultSampler: sdk trace.AlwaysSample()}),
                sdk trace.WithResource(res),
                sdk trace.WithSpanProcessor(bsp),
        )

        otel.SetTextMapPropagator(propagation. traceContext{})
        otel.Set tracerProvider( tracerProvider)

    }
}
```

Use the `ExemplarObserver` interface and the `ObserveWithExemplar` method to record the trace ID. Specify a label to use to search for the trace ID in the Grafana dashboard.

If you use the default Prometheus HTTP handler, it exposes only metrics using the Prometheus format, which does not support exemplars. OpenMetrics is a specification that is based on the Prometheus format and supports exemplars. Prometheus knows how to collect metrics exposed in the OpenMetric format. Therefore, the Prometheus HTTP handler needs to be changed to support OpenMetric.

2.5.2. System Configuration

The demo application runs as a binary, but we also provide a docker image. Create a docker image as shown here.

The docker image uses alpine/curl:3.14.

In build.sh, modify it to docker build -t tracing-example:0.3.

```
# docker tag tracing-example:0.3 yohaim1511/tracing-example:0.3
# docker push yohaim1511/tracing-example:0.3
The push refers to repository [docker.io/yohaim1511/tracing-example]
b0ee9ccc0e44: Pushed
4ee472ad1e7e: Pushed
1ad27bdd166b: Pushed
0.1: digest: sha256:e475688d5d7d379b0f771ce06dca330348a103000f8acba78056367062eb7a64
size: 947
```

Check out the Docker image. If you are deploying to Kubernetes, you create a Deployment. A Kubernetes deployment looks like this:

```
apiVersion: apps/v1
kind: Deployment
    spec:
      containers:
        - image: yohaim1511/tracing-example:0.3
          name: tracing-example
          ports:
            - containerPort: 8000
          resources: {}
      restartPolicy: Always
status: {}
```

Use the following commands to build the application and test it locally. Build and run a Go application.

```
# go build
# ./tracing-example
listening tracer...
listening done...
listening...
ts=2022-07-04T04:46:18.184438519Z msg="http request" traceID=c0f0886f5dcbf929c25c94e6048ee
8d5 path=/ latency=102.612044ms
```

Build the application using the following command and test it locally:

```
CGO_ENABLED=0 GOOS=linux go build -a -installsuffix cgo -o app .
```

The configuration files for Prometheus and Tempo are almost identical to the previous demo.

This is the Tempo configuration file. Spanmetric has been excluded. We developed our exemplars and custom metrics and didn't use spanmetric:

```
multitenancy_enabled: false
search_enabled: true

server:
  http_listen_port: 3200

distributor:
  receivers:
    jaeger:
      protocols:
        thrift_http:
        grpc:
        thrift_binary:
        thrift_compact:
    zipkin:
    otlp:
      protocols:
        http:
        grpc:

storage:
  trace:
    backend: local
    local:
      path: /tmp/tempo/blocks
```

You need to add log settings.

Send a request to your backend application. If you're automating it, run it like this.

```
while true; do curl http://localhost:8000/; sleep 2; clear; done
```

The latency shown in the log is a good example to test anomaly detection. If you define sleep to be 0.1, you may notice a spike in latency. Anomaly detection can detect this latency and analyze the cause.

```
listening...
ts=2022-12-08T09:00:31.927275998Z msg="http request" traceID=a7d5fad55e0f1a68b21705b1b6988bb8 path=/ latency=102.121289ms
hello world
ts=2022-12-08T09:00:32.031244984Z msg="http request" traceID=a7d5fad55e0f1a68b21705b1b6988bb8 path=/ latency=414.046547ms
```

CHAPTER 2   THE RCA APPROACH

```
hello world
ts=2022-12-08T09:00:32.031742669Z msg="http request" traceID=a7d5fad55e0f1a68b21705b1b6988
bb8 path=/ latency=517.627752ms
```

Since it is an application, it is not difficult to generate errors and failures. For example:

1. If you kill a process abruptly, it will no longer be able to respond to requests from clients.
2. If you minimize your sleep time and send a large number of requests to the server, you will get a timeout, and the request will fail.

You can set things up so that the client can generate a lot of traffic with minimal latency, or you can set up your code so that the server processes with a certain probability. Changing values in your code and trying different tests are good ways to test.

```go
func shouldExecute(percent int) bool {
    return rand.Int()%100 < percent
}

func longRunningProcess(ctx context.Context) {
    ctx, sp := tracer.Start(ctx, "Long Running Process")
    defer sp.End()

    time.Sleep(time.Millisecond * 50)
    sp.AddEvent("halfway done!")
    time.Sleep(time.Millisecond * 50)
}
```

The log is formatted as follows:

```
ts=2023-01-12T05:43:30.689033161Z msg="http request" traceID=cb752735fbb4e8a7db8852e7611f92
9e path=/ latency=101.490632ms
```

Request an OpenMetric.

```
$ curl -H 'Accept: application/openmetrics-text' http://localhost:8000/metrics | less
```

Check the OpenMetric and see that the trace ID is printed, which is the same as the previous exemplar:

```
demo_request_latency_seconds_bucket{le="0.0001"} 0
demo_request_latency_seconds_bucket{le="0.1024"} 2 # { traceID="a7d5fad55e0f1a68b21705b1b698
8bb8"} 0.101191218 1.670490032030292e+09
demo_request_latency_seconds_bucket{le="0.2048"} 2
demo_request_latency_seconds_bucket{le="0.4096"} 3 # { traceID="a7d5fad55e0f1a68b21705b1b698
8bb8"} 0.309012213 1.6704900320308034e+09
```

CHAPTER 2   THE RCA APPROACH

```
demo_request_latency_seconds_bucket{le="0.8192"} 5 # { traceID="a7d5fad55e0f1a68b21705b1b698
8bb8"} 0.517619484 1.670490032031735e+09
demo_request_latency_seconds_bucket{le="1.6384"} 5
demo_request_latency_seconds_bucket{le="3.2768"} 5

demo_request_latency_seconds_bucket{le="2.74877906944e+07"} 5
demo_request_latency_seconds_bucket{le="5.49755813888e+07"} 5
```

The application I am demoing has a single microservice. To demonstrate observability, a single microservice is sufficient.

2.5.3. Setting Up Grafana

Loki's setup is shown in Figure 2-19. The derived field creates a link to the trace ID in the output log.

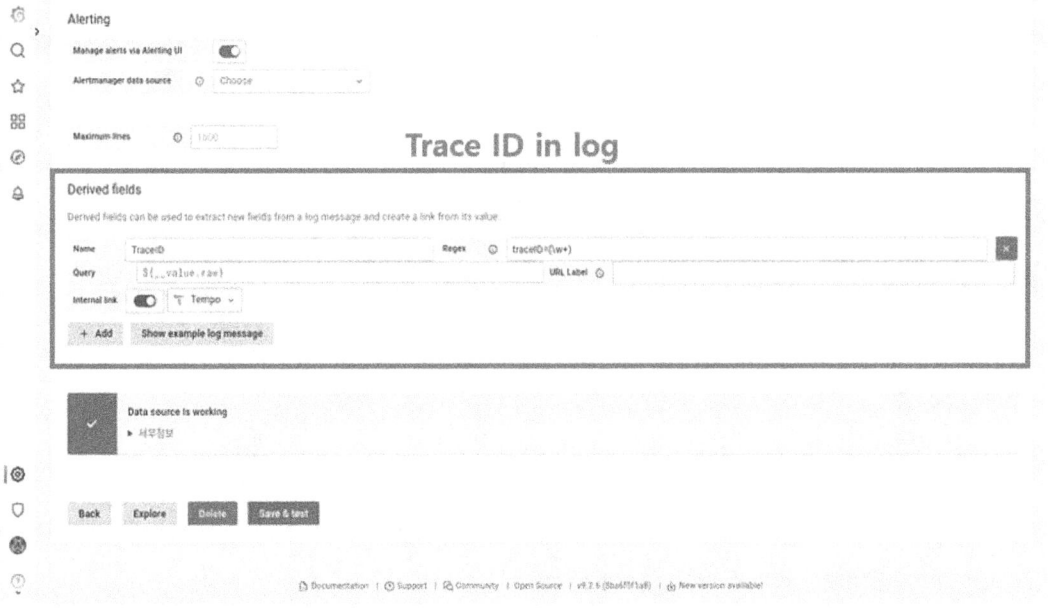

Figure 2-19. *Loki data sources*

The Prometheus settings are shown in Figure 2-20. Exemplar outputs a link to the trace ID in the time series chart.

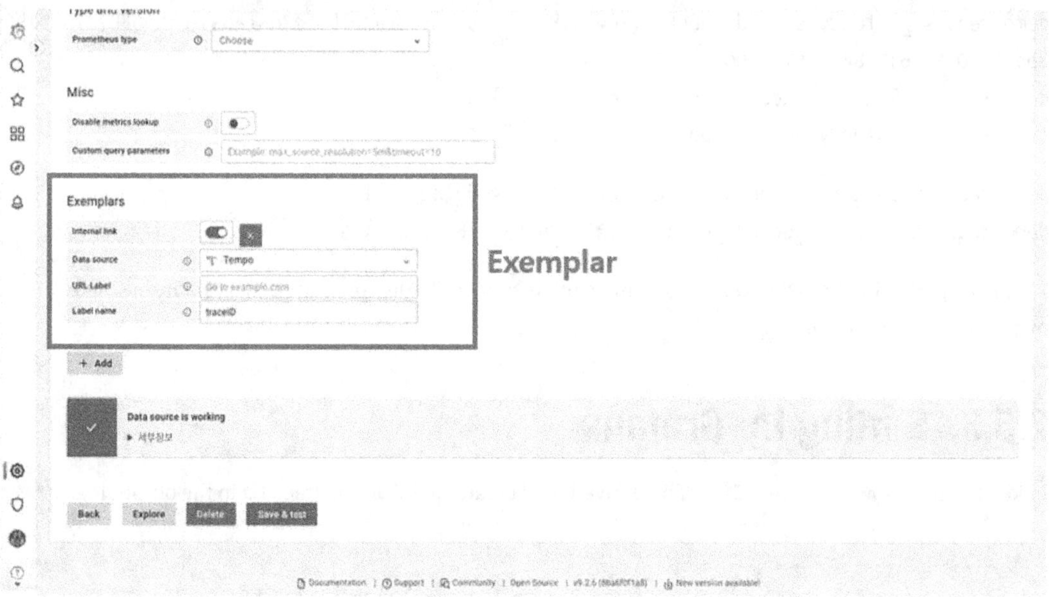

CHAPTER 2 THE RCA APPROACH

Figure 2-20. Prometheus data sources

The settings for Tempo are shown in Figure 2-21. Enable features such as service graph and Loki search.

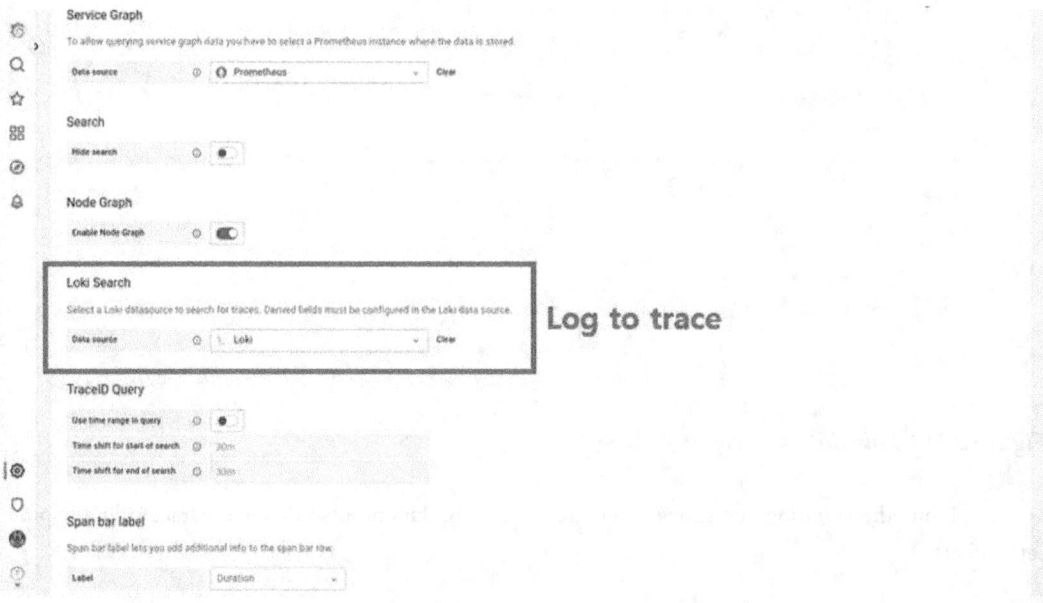

Figure 2-21. Tempo data sources

140

CHAPTER 2   THE RCA APPROACH

2.6. Running the o11y Shop Demo

This demo explains how to develop, build, and troubleshoot the problem.

- Build microservices using OpenTelemetry manual and automated instrumentation.
- Use OpenSearch to collect metrics, logs, and traces and implement observability. Also, understand the correlation with OpenSearch.

2.6.1. Demo Architecture

The architecture of the demo application is shown in Figure 2-22. It is developed in Python and consists of a number of microservices. All three demos are configured in Kubernetes.

- Developed using OpenTelemetry, it supports trace and log.
- It is based on Python Flask and works as a Kubernetes pod.

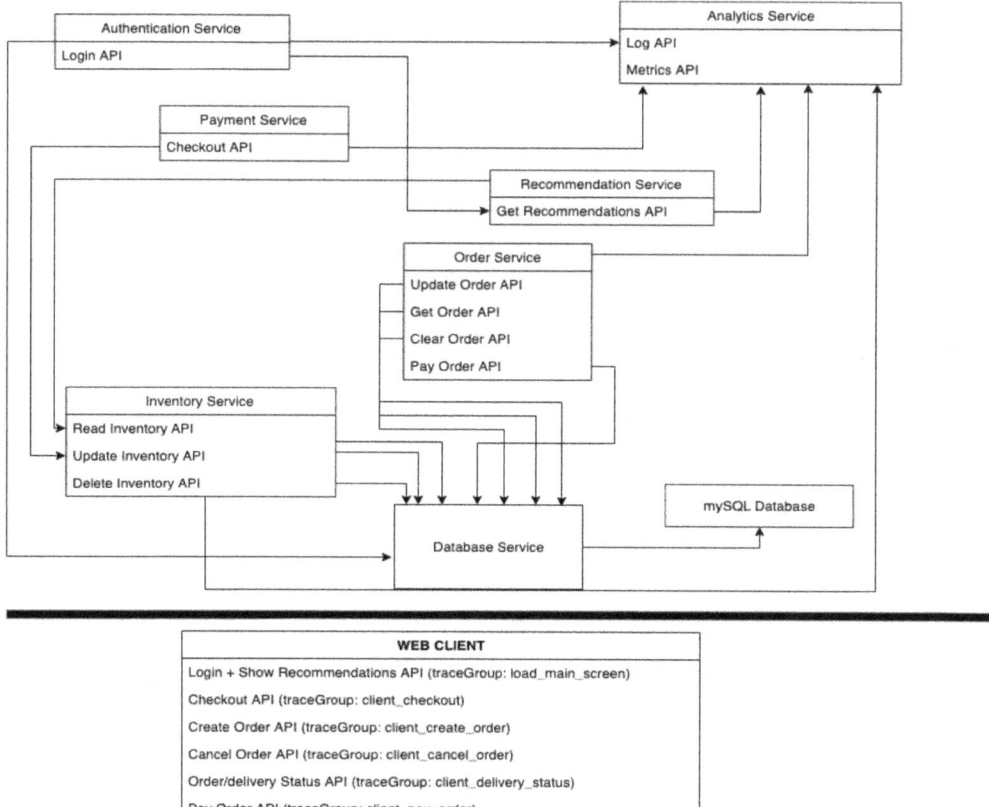

Figure 2-22. *The o11y demo configuration*

141

CHAPTER 2   THE RCA APPROACH

The services provided in the demo consist of eight microservices, including the client:

- inventoryService.py
- databaseService.py
- paymentService.py
- authenticationService.py
- recommendationService.py
- orderService.py
- analytics-service
- otel-collector

The client provides a number of APIs, as shown here:

- load_main_screen
- client_checkout
- client_create_order
- client_cancel_order
- client_delivery_status
- client_pay_order

All APIs call the /logs (analytics-service:8087) endpoint of the analytics service to log.

2.6.2. Demo Process

The demo has the following characteristics:

- Developed using OpenTelemetry, it supports trace and log.
- The web client application calls roughly seven REST APIs.
- MySQL defines various tables that are required for orders.
- analytics-service provides logs and metric APIs.
- It generates a lot of trace, including traces for load_main_screen, client_checkout, client_create_order, client_cancel_order, client_delivery_status, and client_pay_order.

The demo application implements a simple ordering scenario. Select the product and make payment. Finally, the order is finalized. As shown in Figure 2-23, three products are registered in the category and are available through the web screen.

CHAPTER 2   THE RCA APPROACH

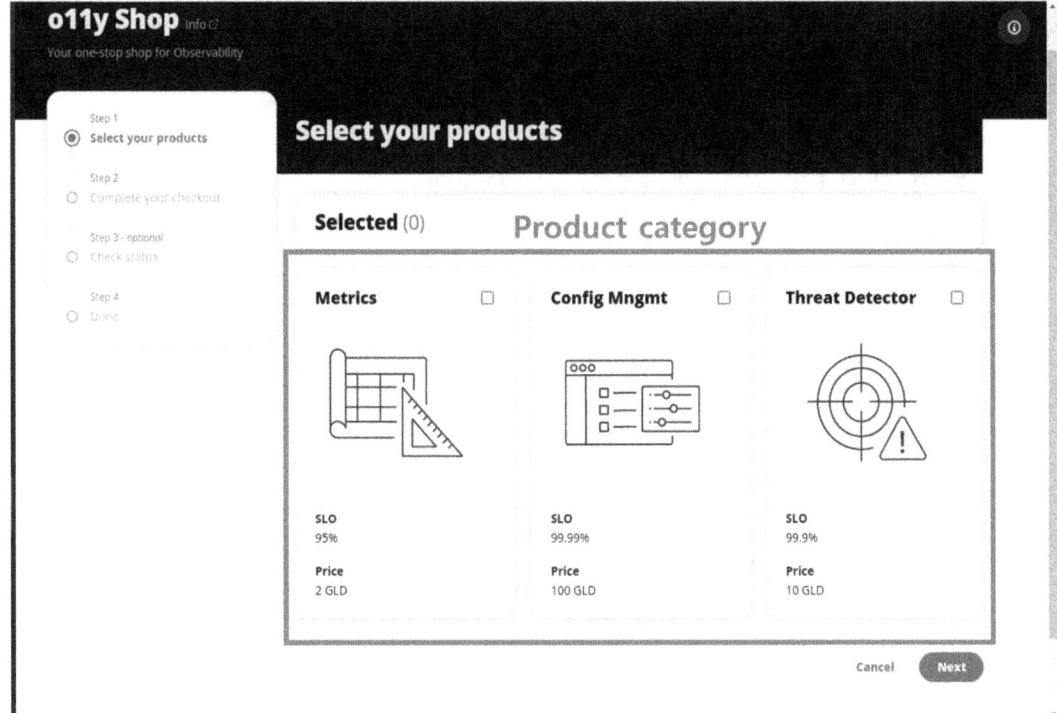

Figure 2-23. *The o11y Shop demo*

The order scenario consists of several steps, and each step generates trace and log information as it is processed. If you analyze the Kubernetes pod logs and the OpenTelemetry collector logs, you can see that they output detailed telemetry.

You can change the order status. Click the Get Order status button to display the order status. Click Cancel order to cancel the order.

2.6.3. Code Description

Import the following packages:

```
from opentelemetry import trace
from opentelemetry.instrumentation.logging import LoggingInstrumentor
from opentelemetry.instrumentation.flask import FlaskInstrumentor
from opentelemetry.exporter.otlp.proto.grpc. trace_exporter import OTLPSpanExporter
from opentelemetry.instrumentation.requests import RequestsInstrumentor
from opentelemetry.sdk.resources import Resource
from opentelemetry.sdk. trace import tracerProvider
from opentelemetry.sdk. trace.export import (
```

CHAPTER 2   THE RCA APPROACH

```
        ConsoleSpanExporter,
        SimpleSpanProcessor,
)
```

Configure the traceProvider and set it up for your application. This includes exporting logs to the OpenTelemetry collector over port 55680 and the OTLP protocol:

```
trace.set_tracer_provider(
    tracerProvider(
        resource=Resource.create(
            { {
                "service.name": "payment",
                "service.instance.id": str(id(app)),
                "telemetry.sdk.name": "opentelemetry",
                "telemetry.sdk.language": "python",
                "telemetry.sdk.version": pkg_resources.get_distribution("opentelemetry-sdk").version,
                "host.hostname": socket.gethostname(),
            }
        )
    )
)
```

Use LoggingInstrumentor to instrument your application. Insert the trace ID, span ID, and service name in the log for correlation:

```
LoggingInstrumentor().instrument(set_logging_format=True)
```

FlaskInstrumentor traces web requests in a Flask application:

- The FlaskURL rule pattern is used as the span name.
- The http.route span attribute is set to see only the URL rules that match the request.

```
        FlaskInstrumentor().instrument_app(app)
```

The trace HTTP request is generated by the Python request library:

```
RequestsInstrumentor().instrument( tracer_provider= tracerProvider)
```

To trace the transaction being processed, define it in your code as follows. The distributed trace starts a span with the following name:

```
with tracer.start_as_current_span("checkout"):
```

CHAPTER 2   THE RCA APPROACH

Other services implement instrumentation in a similar way.

The configuration file for the OpenTelemetry collector looks like this:

```
apiVersion: v1
kind: ConfigMap
metadata:
  name: otel-collector-config
  namespace: otel-collector
data:
  otel-collector-config.yml: |
    receivers:
      otlp:
        protocols:
          grpc:
            endpoint: 0.0.0.0:55680

    exporters:
      otlp/data-prepper:
        endpoint: data-prepper.data-prepper.svc.cluster.local:21890
        tls:
          insecure: true

    service:
      pipelines:
        traces:
          receivers: [otlp]
          exporters: [otlp/data-prepper]
```

Observability microservices must be able to generate errors. Eight microservices can be configured to generate errors internally. For example, the payment service can control the error rate by configuring ERROR_RATE_THRESHOLD.

```
logger = logging.getLogger(__name__)

error_rate_threshold = 100

app = Flask(__name__)
```

A good way to learn about observability is to make errors. This requires a kind of chaos engineering. Assume a failure and create a problem. Then use observability to discover the problem, analyze the cause, and repeat the process. I recommend doing this several times.

145

For example, you might have any of these problems:

- The span takes a long time or fails.
- You are experiencing latency due to excessive transactions.
- It throws timeouts.
- Multiple retries occur.
- You see an error in the log or an exception is processed.
- You notice anomalies in the log in your infrastructure.
- There is high utilization and saturation in infra.
- A particular microservice is overloaded with traffic, and it will fail and propagate the failure to other microservices.

These problems can be reproduced and tested directly in the demo application and in OpenSearch. When various failures occur, OpenSearch outputs meaningful data for root cause analysis.

Microservices run on Kubernetes, which provides various forms of reliability and availability.

- It's not set to autoscale, but you can manually increase the number of pods and distribute traffic.
- If you delete a pod, you will lose some transactions, but it will automatically re-create the pod and recover.
- By adding a proxy server, it's easy to add retries and circuit breaker functionality.

By default, Kubernetes provides the ability to reliably process large amounts of traffic.

2.6.4. Install the Demo

Configure your system and proceed as follows:

1. Install OpenSearch.
2. Install the OpenSearch dashboard.
3. Install a data prepper.
4. Install a Fluent Bit.
5. Install the OpenTelemetry collector.
6. Install nine microservices.

The installation script is available in YAML. I recommend installing with Helm charts. I provide the Helm charts and guidelines to make it easier.

CHAPTER 2   THE RCA APPROACH

Start Kubernetes 1.20 on Minikube:

```
minikube start --vm-driver=none --kubernetes-version v1.23.0 --memory=12000 --cpus=4
```

Currently, the installation script is available in plain YAML.
Install OpenSearch:

```
kubectl apply -f 01-config.yaml
kubectl apply -f 02-deployment.yaml
```

Install the OpenSearch dashboard:

```
kubectl apply -f 12-deployment.yaml
```

Install Data Prepper for a detailed configuration:

```
kubectl apply -f 21-config.yaml
kubectl apply -f 22-deployment.yaml
```

Install an OpenTelemetry collector for the metric:

```
kubectl apply -f 30-roles.yaml
kubectl apply -f 31-config.yaml
kubectl apply -f 32-deployment.yaml
```

Install the OpenTelemetry collector and application for trace:

```
chmod 755 apply-k8s-manifests.sh
./apply-k8s-manifests.sh
```

The application is already registered in the Docker hub.
See https://hub.docker.com/repositories/yohaim1511 for a list of registered Docker images. You can see the Docker registry in YAML.

Install the log pipeline. The installed Fluent Bit is not directly connected to OpenSearch, but through the Data Prepper. You can check the configuration set in Fluent Bit's output:

```
output-data-prepper.conf: |
    [OUTPUT]
        Name http
        Match * * Match
        Host data-prepper.data-prepper.svc.cluster.local
        Port 2021
        tls Off
        tls.verify Off
        Format json
        URI /log/ingest
```

147

CHAPTER 2   THE RCA APPROACH

In general, OpenSearch uses Fluent Bit to collect logs and metrics. The demo separates the pipeline that collects metrics from the pipeline that collects logs.

You can easily add functionality to collect logs, as shown here:

./apply-k8s-manifests.sh

You can also configure correlation in OpenSearch, as shown next. However, compared to Grafana, the correlation feature is lacking. You'll also find OpenSearch's screens lacking. You need to understand that the purpose is different.

2.6.5. Checking Results in OpenSearch

You need to check the results in OpenSearch. Grafana and OpenSearch also offer observability processes. Grafana observability focuses on correlating signals. OpenSearch observability focuses on various analytical functions centered on logs.

The demo consists of three pipelines:

- Trace pipelines with OpenTelemetry collectors
- Metric pipelines with OpenTelemetry collectors
- Log pipelines with Fluent Bit

The demo is configured in Kubernetes:

- The OpenTelemetry collector collects metrics and traces and passes them to the Data Prepper. The Data Prepper loads them into OpenSearch.
- Fluent Bit collects logs from microservices and delivers it to the Data Prepper. The Data Prepper loads it into OpenSearch.
- OpenSearch's pipeline architecture should be configured to pass data to the Data Prepper.

After creating several orders in the o11y application, you can check the traces and log in to OpenSearch. First, check the results of the traces.

OpenSearch observability provides detailed trace information and service maps. The service map is shown in Figure 2-24, and you can check the detailed performance of each service.

CHAPTER 2   THE RCA APPROACH

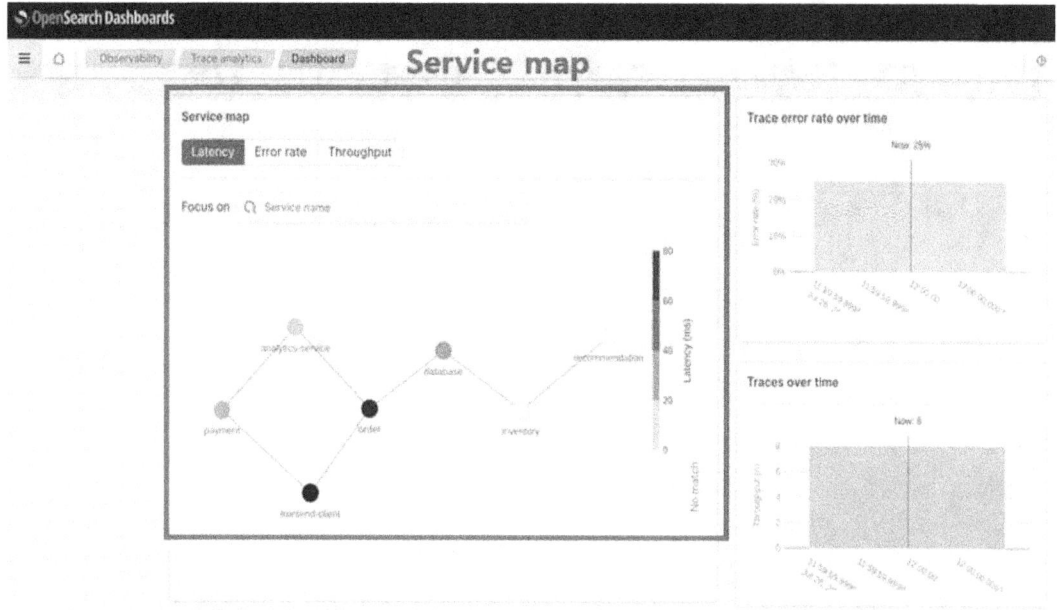

Figure 2-24. The OpenSearch service map

This provides the status of the processed trace and displays detailed information about the trace. It also displays detailed information about the number of spans, the duration, the trace messages, and the ratio, as shown in Figure 2-25.

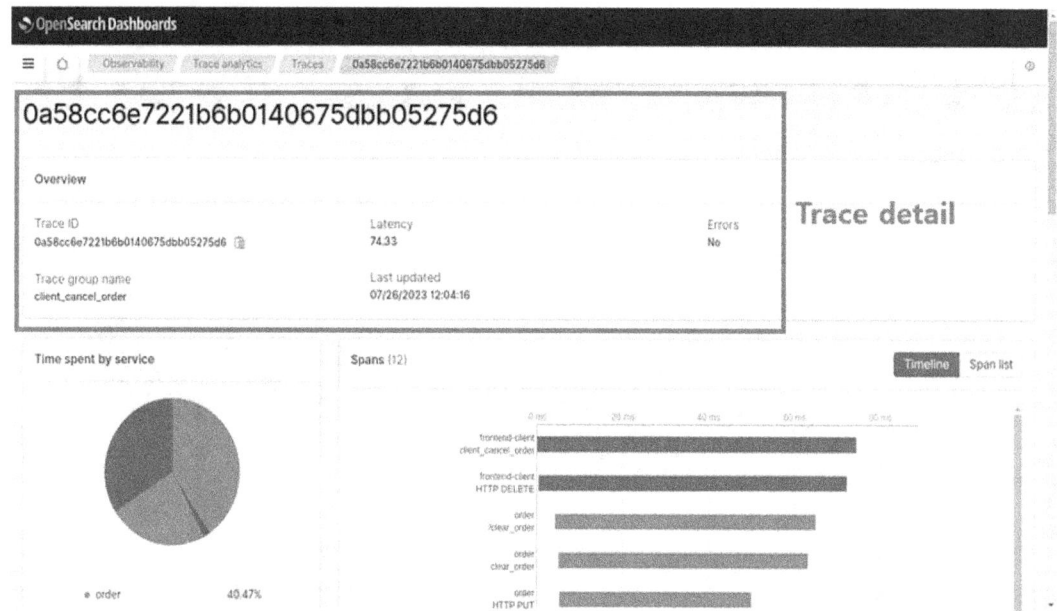

Figure 2-25. OpenSearch trace detail

CHAPTER 2   THE RCA APPROACH

Figure 2-26 provides information about individual traces as well as statistics per service.

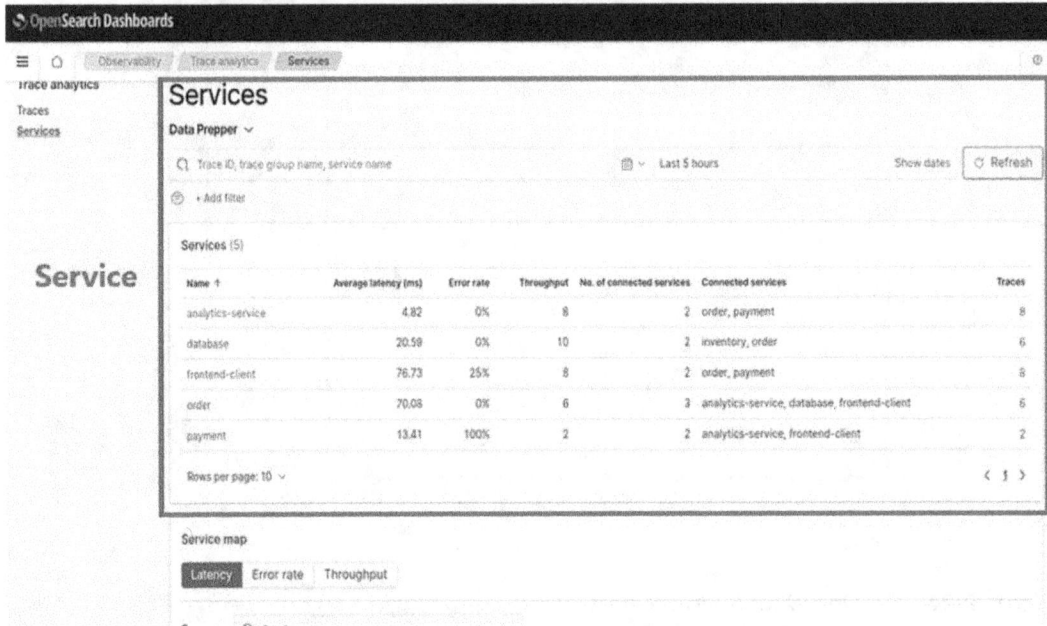

Figure 2-26. *The OpenSearch service screen*

This also provides detailed information on key SLO metrics: latency, error rate, and throughput. Check the result of log. It outputs not only log information, but also patterns and anomaly detection information; see Figure 2-28. OpenSearch provides the ability to create dashboards and alerts.

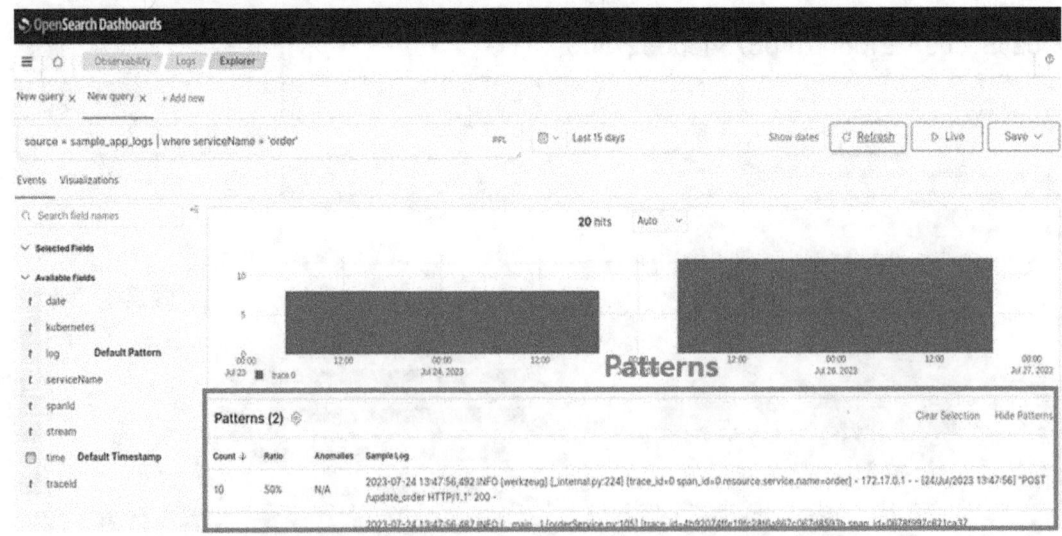

Figure 2-27. *The OpenSearch log search*

CHAPTER 2   THE RCA APPROACH

Loading metrics into Prometheus always leads to memory and disk problems. It's also a good idea to use OpenSearch to reliably manage your metrics, as shown in Figure 2-28. Don't use a separate exporter. You are collecting metrics through the OpenTelemetry collector and loading them into OpenSearch through the Data Prepper.

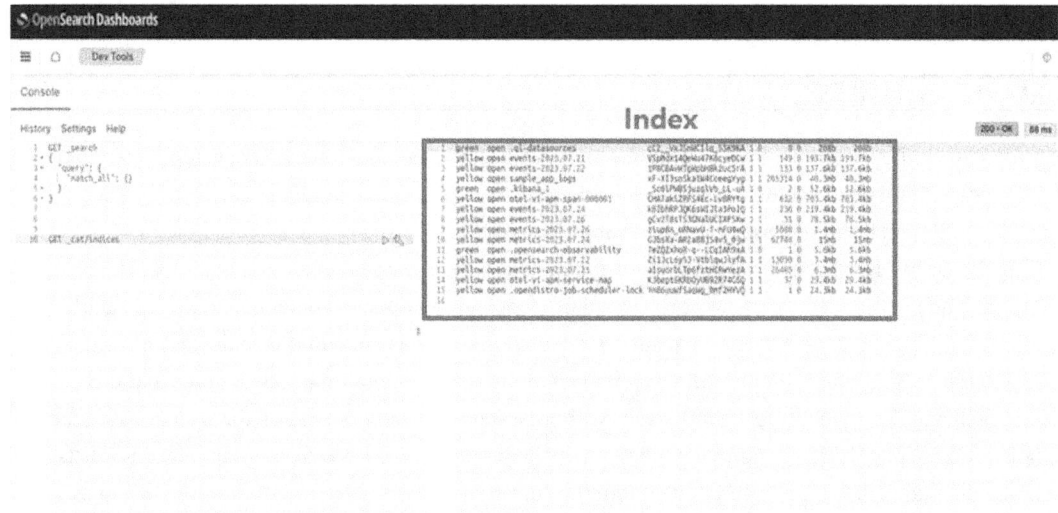

Figure 2-28. *The OpenSearch index lookup*

Figure 2-29 shows the screen for implementing correlation in OpenSearch. Compared to Grafana, it provides fewer correlation features.

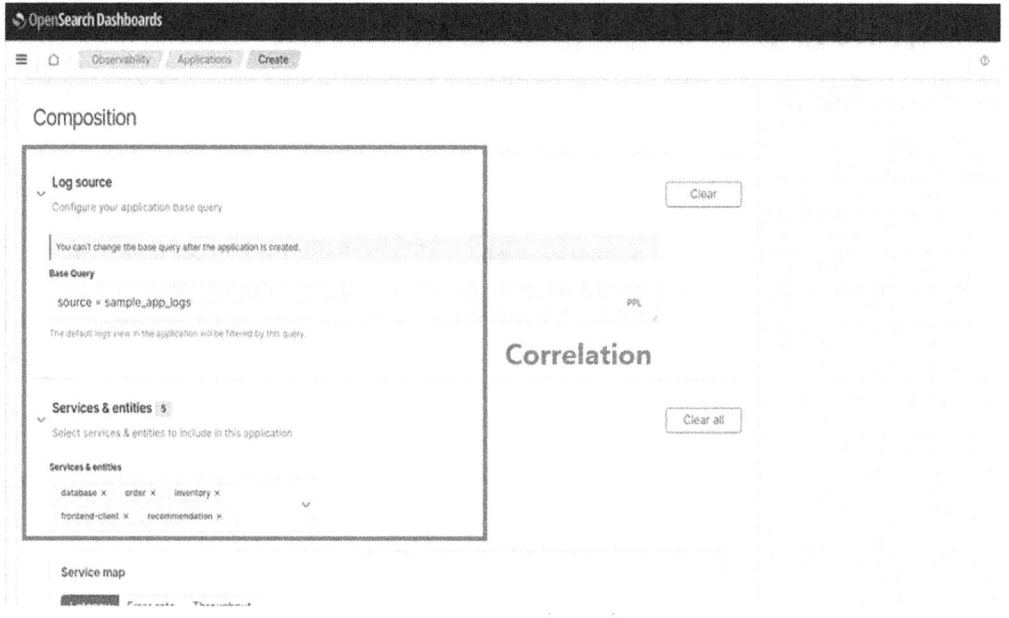

Figure 2-29. *The OpenSearch correlation*

151

To implement correlation, I recommend using Grafana. If your goal is AIOps or data analysis, I recommend using OpenSearch.

Using the Grafana dashboard, it is possible to correlate logs and traces using OpenSearch and Tempo. You can also correlate between Jaeger and Loki. There is no dependency on the solution, and correlation can be implemented in a variety of ways.

2.6.6. Summary

Correlation configuration requires collaboration with developers and architects. If developers output logs and traces without observability standards, it will be difficult for SREs to configure correlation. Therefore, developers should be guided to follow observability standards.

In the early days of observability, it was difficult to define correlation because signals were inconsistent, there were no tags and labels, IDs were not standardized, and there was no pipeline. As a result, alerts and anomaly detection were inaccurate, and root cause analysis was difficult due to the lack of context in logs and traces. The reason for inaccurate alerts and anomaly detection is the lack of process and effort to improve signals. You can't expect good results without a standard. Signals are also data. To improve data quality, you need to work on improving the signal itself over time. You need to adopt quality checklists and scorecards used in data quality and think about the current quality.

So far, I have described various correlations. When observability and AIOps are combined, many correlations can be configured. You don't need all of them, but it's important to understand what types of correlations are possible in order to implement them appropriately for SRE purposes. The goal of this chapter is to design a suitable root cause analysis process with a good combination of correlations.

2.7. Dashboard Visualizations

This section explains how to develop a successful dashboard that is different from the legacy dashboard configuration.

The easiest way to understand a problem is to visualize it on a screen. Developing a dashboard is a fundamental first step in organizing observability. The Grafana dashboard is open source and a favorite observability dashboard for SRE. Grafana supports a wide variety of charts. For root cause analysis, you need to understand how to use charts that are fit for purpose and allow for proper visualization of signals.

SLO require pre-aggregation. You can pre-aggregate using traces and logs as well as metrics. Pre-aggregation can be organized as a pipeline or a backend batch. Both approaches have their advantages and disadvantages.

Prometheus develops pre-aggregation as a recording rule, which is inefficient. You need a recording rule for each minute, hour, day, week, and month, making it difficult to develop more than 1,000 SLOs manually.

Now, let's look at the chart.

CHAPTER 2   THE RCA APPROACH

While the SRE dashboard relies heavily on time series charts, implementing correlation with a variety of charts can result in a user dashboard that is rich in context and makes sense of the signals. The following charts are useful for the visualization of observability signals:

- Service maps
- Polystats
- Heatmaps
- Histograms
- Time series
- Flame graphs
- State timelines
- Staters histories
- Stats
- Alert lists
- Annotations

Grafana is open source but can produce excellent charts and dashboards that rival commercial observability. I only discuss the most important charts available in Grafana.

2.7.1. Polystats

Polystats are great for expressing the number and state of your IT infrastructure in production, such as nodes and servers. See Figure 2-30.

CHAPTER 2   THE RCA APPROACH

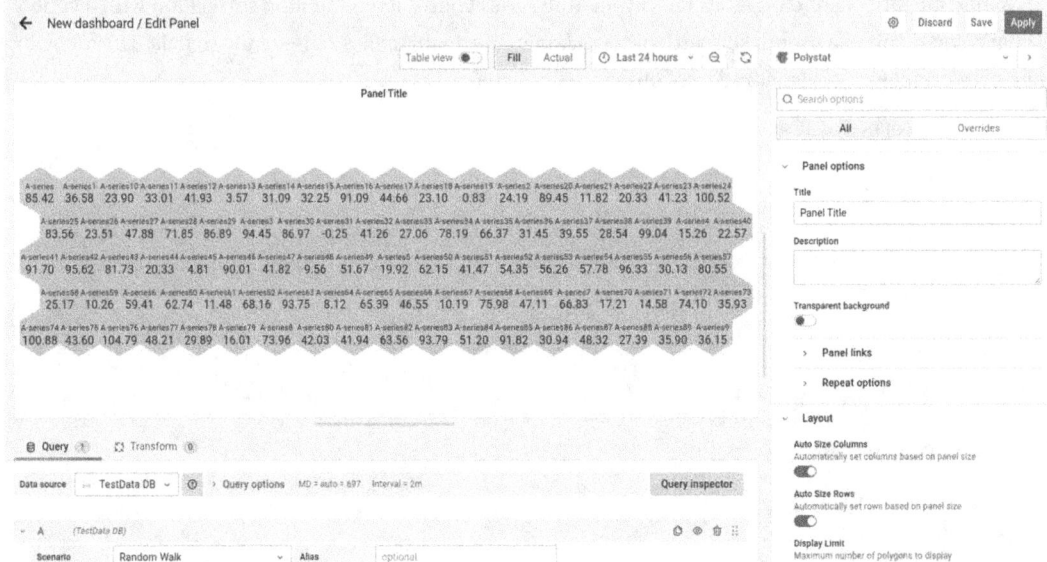

Figure 2-30. Polystats

The different colors make it easy to distinguish between normal and abnormal results and help you understand the problematic details in the overall picture. Details can include CPU, memory, disk, and more.

- Polystats are primarily used to monitor infrastructure. For example, they can be applied to nodes, VM, containers, and pods to monitor across your infrastructure. They can be used in conjunction with metrics from infrastructure-specific node exporters.

- I recommend applying polystats of infrastructure and service maps to networks and applications. Polystats and service maps are useful for providing a high-level view of your IT systems and can be used as a starting point for root cause analysis.

- I think it's inefficient to collect all infrastructure data. Hosts, containers, and pods have areas of overlap when it comes to resource usage. Containers and pods end up running on hosts, so they end up partitioning or sharing the same resources. The cost and efficiency of collecting infrastructure data should be weighed against the benefits.

    – Disk IO is a costly and systemic burden because of the amount of data it collects compared to other resources.

    – Compared to the metrics collected on the host, the metrics collected on containers and Kubernetes are limited. You need an appropriate way to overcome the limitations, and this is where eBPF and system trace come into play.

Polystats can be utilized for a variety of purposes, not only for infrastructure but also for services and applications. For example, you can create logical groups of services and express the SLO status of the group.

2.7.2. Service maps

A service map consists of nodes and edges. Service maps are referred to as network graphs and node graphs, as shown in Figure 2-31. They are suitable for representing dependencies between nodes in microservices and networks. Each node is associated with a metric, which can be further analyzed. Since failures tend to propagate, service maps allow you to understand the path and scope of the impact of a failure.

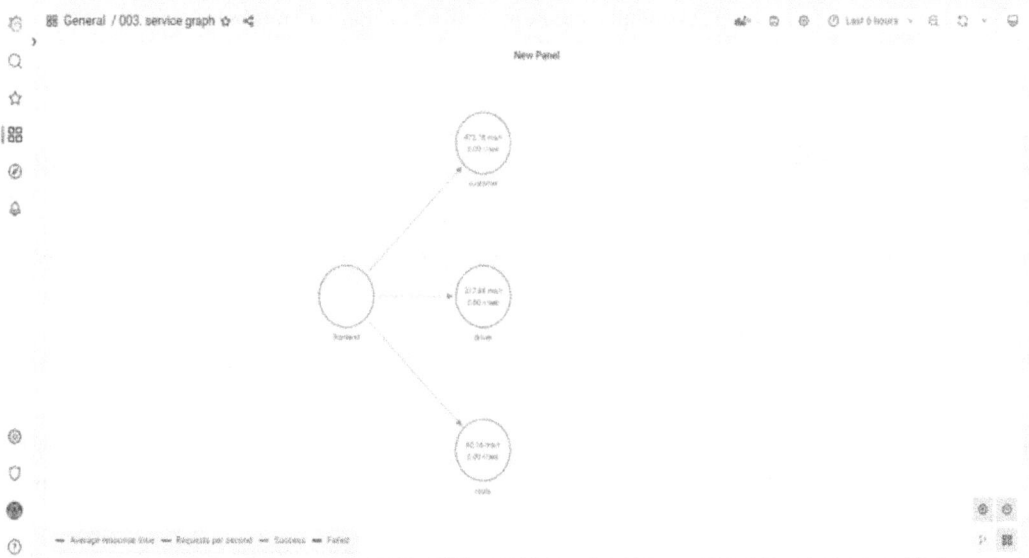

Figure 2-31. A service map

A service map is useful for representing the relationship between calls between microservices and the infrastructure network. Using service maps in both infrastructure and applications can help you understand flows and spot problems.

Service maps have the following limitations:

- There is no limit on upstream and downstream, so it will output all the paths you don't need, which makes it hard to make sense of too much data.

- If you don't output metrics for individual nodes, it's hard to analyze problems as they occur.

CHAPTER 2   THE RCA APPROACH

Misrepresenting a service map increases complexity and makes it harder to understand. I provide the following guidelines:

- Show the path the transaction was processed, focusing on upstream and downstream.
- Use metrics to enable further analysis of specific nodes.

Service maps are utilized by Tempo's microservices and Cilium's service maps. You can generate service maps from the OpenTelemetry collector and Tempo's metric generator. If you use a bucket in the service map as a data source, you can automatically output a service map chart.

In summary, service maps can abstract the network topology. Service maps are used to monitor infrastructure, especially networks and applications, to monitor the interactions between microservices. This helps you understand the overall context and is useful for root cause analysis.

2.7.3. Histograms

A histogram outputs a distribution within a specific time period. It uses buckets as the data source and outputs a distribution. It is used to sort transactions in a bucket (by duration). The distribution gives you an idea of the approximate load at any given time. For example, the 99th percentile is useful for determining how many transactions with unusually high latency are likely to cause problems.

Grafana's strength is that it doesn't require any additional preprocessing to create histograms, heatmaps, and service graphs. With the histograms created in Prometheus, you can easily create a variety of charts with just a few clicks.

Histograms are used to identify latencies and anomalies such as 95 percent or 99 percent, based on the performance distribution.

Histograms are important charts for visualizing the distribution of duration in percentiles. Because histograms use buckets, they only output data within a defined interval, making it difficult to see trends. To understand the overall trend, it's better to look at a heatmap first. When you output individual histograms by time period, the heatmap organizes the histograms for each time period. This makes it easier to understand if there is a problem with the histogram at a particular time. For example, you can easily find the 99th percentile where the problem occurred.

eBPF uses histograms and heatmaps to understand performance and latency. PCP uses histograms and heatmaps to represent performance.

2.7.4. Heatmaps

Heatmaps output multiple histograms as a time series, as shown in in Figure 2-32. They use buckets as the data source.

CHAPTER 2   THE RCA APPROACH

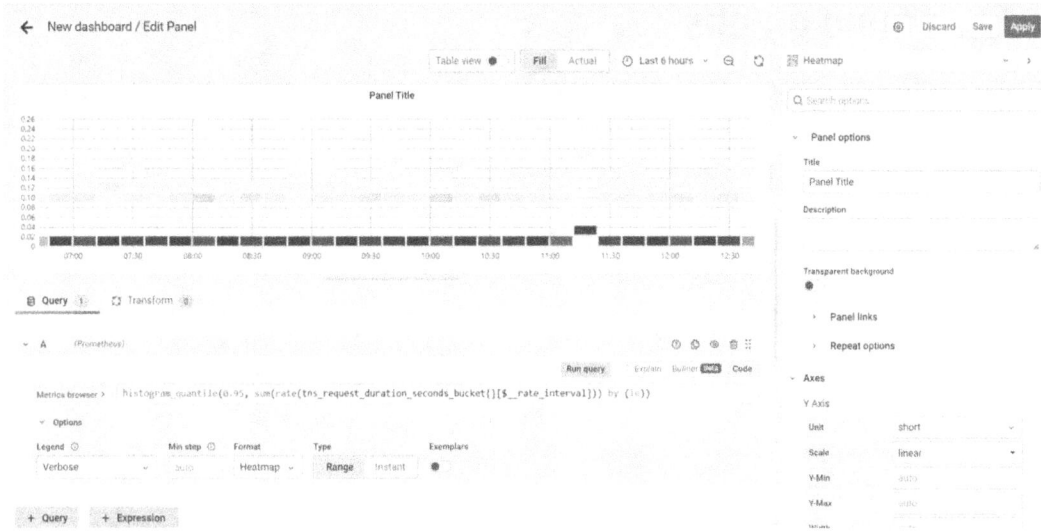

Figure 2-32. *A heatmap*

The y-axis is the latency category. The overall distribution over time is analyzed by a heatmap, while the detailed distribution at a specific time is analyzed by a histogram (i.e., a heatmap contains multiple histograms).

For example, the buckets generated by spanmetric can be used as a data source to generate histograms and heatmaps.

- This is similar to a time series but does not provide an exemplar.
- You can use the brightness of the colors to distinguish the differences.
- Include a histogram over time.

Heatmaps and histograms are important clues to understanding your infrastructure, application performance, and latency. Time series, histograms, and heatmaps with exemplars provide similar but different perspectives on latency.

PCP histograms automatically create the buckets needed for the histogram. Grafana allows you to visualize heatmaps without any preprocessing.

2.7.5. Time Series

Time series are the common charts. Time series can be output in a variety of ways. They can be used with rate, `histogram_quantile`, or you can enable exemplars. They can be used with buckets, sums, counts, and totals.

Time series represent exemplars, so they are useful for expressing the correlation between metrics and traces. You can also utilize tags and labels to express log and metric correlations.

157

CHAPTER 2   THE RCA APPROACH

2.7.6. Flame graphs

A common way to visualize a profile is to use a flame graph, as shown in Figure 2-33. Among the various signals, profiles can output the system resources most clearly. Defining the correlation between traces, logs, metrics, and profiles is an important task for root cause analysis.

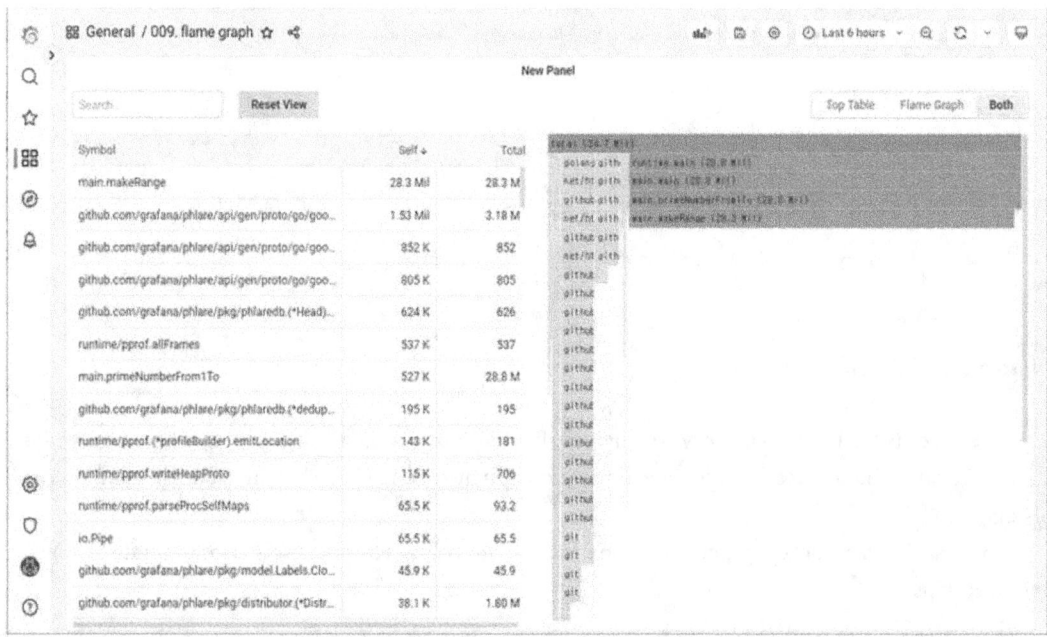

Figure 2-33. *A flame graph*

Flame graphs can be used for visualization of eBPF. To understand errors related to lower level resources such as threads and memory, it is not easy to analyze logs traces alone. This is where the profile flame graph comes in.

There are two ways to get to a profile from another signal:

- Log (from debugging point of view) to profile
- Trace (at the point of detailed transaction analysis) to profile

This book explains in detail the correlation between traces and profiles.

2.7.7. State Timelines

Time series charts have thresholds and no specific state. A state timeline has a state, and any data that contains a state can be visualized using a state timeline. Alerts have states. The state timeline chart outputs the state change of an alert as a time series, as shown in Figure 2-34.

CHAPTER 2   THE RCA APPROACH

Figure 2-34. A state timeline

I implemented the alert dashboard using the state timeline and status history. It is recommended to use it with alert list and stat. Nowadays, many dashboards include alerts, so you should familiarize yourself with the status history.

The SLO dashboard requires the following metrics:

- Different windows (minutes, hours, days, weeks, and months)
- Error budgets
- Burn rate

Alerts should be transferred if the error budget or burn rate exceeds a threshold, and visualization of the threshold exceedance is required. A state timeline is the most effective chart for this. It's also a great chart for complex and difficult SLOs like MTTR and MTTD. An active alert means that there is a problem with availability, or that it has not yet been resolved. You can get a rough idea of MTTR just by understanding the changing state of the alert on the state timeline.

Status history is similar to the state timeline mentioned previously but provides a different visualization. It has the following characteristics:

- You can define states by thresholds.
- You can output a different state if the threshold is exceeded or if the value changes.
- You can output the changes in state as a time series.

159

Even if you implement observability dashboards with commercial observability, you'll find that they are not as robust as Grafana and have limited functionality. In this case, Grafana can be a good alternative. Since Grafana provides a data source for commercial observability, you can utilize the benefits and charts of Grafana in conjunction with commercial observability. For example, it's useful to configure state timeline charts in conjunction with commercial observability.

2.7.8. Stats

Stats combine a time series and a counter. They output a numeric metric and a time series graph at the same time.

They are usually located at the top of the dashboard and are useful for metrics, graphs, and colors, in order to give an overview.

2.7.9. Traces

A trace chart consists of multiple spans, and each span is useful for understanding the process sequence of an application and measuring latency. Implementing a full E2E trace can be challenging in cloud-managed services and legacy environments. This book details how to understand the problems with traces and improve them.

2.7.10. Annotations

You use dashboards to visualize your infrastructure and application performance, but you can configure them for other purposes. For example, you can add information about security and networks, build deployments, errors, and more to your production. To understand the context, it's useful to utilize annotations.

The following tasks occur frequently in production, and you can use webhooks to transfer events externally:

- Resources are added from the cloud.
- The deployment runs on ArgoCD.
- An issue is registered in Jira.
- The job runs in the Terraform cloud.
- An event is raised in Git.
- Anomaly detection occurs.
- Errors and failure alerts are raised.

CHAPTER 2   THE RCA APPROACH

Annotating the webhook events you receive using a dashboard is a great way to understand context, as shown in Figure 2-35. For example, a deployment causes a failure, or a sudden resource spike occurs. It's not uncommon for the deployment to happen later, and the SRE will find the cause later. This is why information should be shared in annotations upfront. If you find it difficult to add annotations to the dashboard, it's useful to manage events and annotations in bulk with an annotation list.

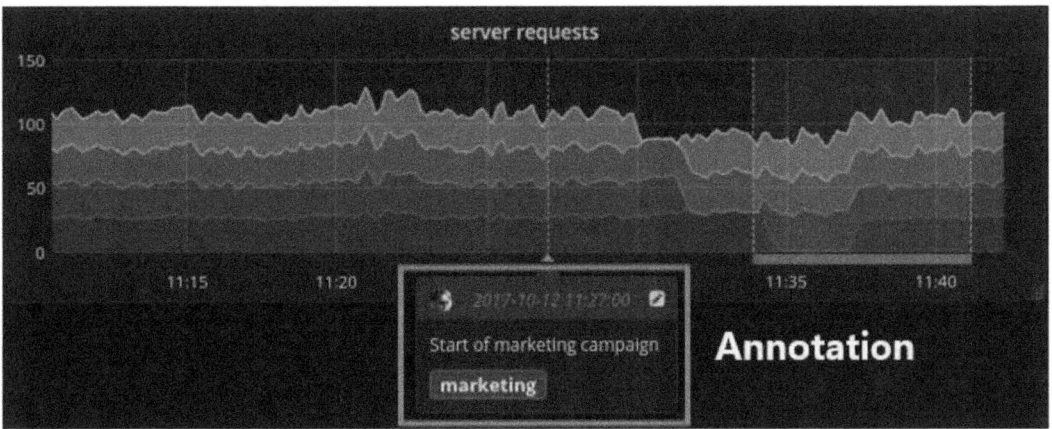

Figure 2-35. *Annotations*

2.7.11. Dashboard Development

The RCA dashboard is based on the RCA data model.

Alerts and dashboards are expressions of results. Accurate alerts and dashboards can only be configured if the signals are accurately defined, then ingested, transforms, and stored. Then you can query them and apply algorithms. If any step is configured incorrectly, it is difficult to configure an accurate dashboard.

Observability signals can be duplicated or lost due to pipeline failures. Signals are often misconfigured due to misunderstandings by the SRE.

RCA dashboards are not configured with a single log, as in the past.

I suggest the following guide for developing a dashboard. I have always succeeded in developing RCA dashboards this way.

Values included in the filter are not entered manually. They must be extracted from the signals through a query. Any complex process can extract data through a query and organize values within the filter. This is a very powerful and useful method. All processes on the dashboard should be automated by filter.

The root cause analysis data model and dashboard filters and join are at the heart of this book.

CHAPTER 2 THE RCA APPROACH

The table in the dashboard has the following characteristics (see Table 2-1):

- Request, order, and payment IDs are captured by events.
- 001 and 002 use the request ID and are simple actions, such as browsing a product.
- 003 uses the payment ID and is more complex, like a fund transfer.
- 004 uses the order ID and is more complex, like creating a new provision order.
- A trace ID contains a span ID, and the span ID has a one-to-one relationship with the thread ID. The thread ID contains the system trace ID.
- Each record contains latency issues, error messages, product categories, and system resources.

CHAPTER 2 THE RCA APPROACH

Table 2-1. The RCA Table Structure

Request ID	Order ID	Payment ID	TXN ID	Trace ID	Span ID	Thread ID	System Trace ID	System Span ID	Latency	Error Message	Product Category	Release	System Resource
001				001-A									
002				002-A									
		003		003-A									
		003		003-B									
	004			004-A									
	004			004-B									
	004			004-C									
			005	005-A									
			005	005-B									

163

CHAPTER 2   THE RCA APPROACH

As shown in Figure 2-36, the dashboard is simple to use.

- Users can select a critical process from the filters and select the request, order, and payment IDs. Important processes can include browse product, fund transfers, and provision new orders.
- Multiple trace and span IDs are output in chronological order.

You will need the following filters:

- Domains
- Critical processes
- Events

In addition to the filter, the following table is output:

- Trace ID
- Span ID
- Thread ID
- System trace ID
- System trace span ID

Thread ID forms the correlation between distributed traces and system traces. For example, a goroutine is a child thread, so you need to be able to identify the parent thread. For a goroutine, the context can include the parent thread or business ID and any metadata.

Monitoring goroutines is not a problem, but it can be difficult if the goroutine interacts with the kernel mode. If a goroutine calls a system call and something goes wrong, it's hard to identify, so you need to organize the correlation between the parent thread, the goroutine's thread, and the system call.

If you want to use multiple agents, they should have a clear purpose. It is very useful if other agents can fill in the gaps where commercial and OpenTelemetry agents do not support threads or are not instrumented. Correlations between multiple agents can be implemented using dashboard joins and filters.

Additional columns are joined with various dimensions:

- Latency
- Error messages
- Product category
- Deployment
- System resources

CHAPTER 2   THE RCA APPROACH

Having a large number of agents is not always a disadvantage. It's a negative because it can be unmanageable and confusing. If you have a lot of agents, you also have a lot of trace ID, so it's difficult to organize correlations between the agent trace ID, but the dashboard allows you to show most correlations.

Add these filters:

- Error or not
- Root cause type
- Alert
- Deployed or not

For a join to be configured successfully, a correlation must be configured. If the data is not configured correctly, the join will fail, and the dashboard will not be configured. For example, join logs to traces. If you do not understand what correlation exists, you cannot configure the join, and it is difficult to use dashboards and alert. The correlation is expressed in SQL as a join. Joining is very useful for increasing the value of data. Data exists only in specific signals. Like big data and NoSQL, it does not contain all the data in one table.

Determining the type of root cause based on nanosecond to microsecond delays is a challenging task. It is a challenge to distinguish and determine the type of problem between contention, waiting, and saturation in system resources, rebalancing and replication in clusters, and congestion in the network. In addition to the eight signals of observability, you need to understand and be able to identify the different root cause types—contention, waiting, congestion, rebalancing, and replication. However, I continue to discuss these methods in this book.

Joins, lookups, and filters are important techniques for constructing dashboards:

- You need joins to use correlations.

- You need to provide filters to make it easy to navigate to the data you want in a complex dashboard. Correlations are joins, but you shouldn't only configure joins. Filters need to be configured for searching.

- Rather than building dashboards with just one signal, as in the past, observability uses a variety of signals for dashboards.

Figure 2-36 shows a simple dashboard, but it uses different data than the traditional dashboard. Whereas the traditional dashboards were developed using only one metric signal, the observability dashboard uses eight or more signals to develop a single dashboard. Joining or looking up event, log, trace, and profile is very basic and involves different signals, not only in the output, but also between filters. The data in all dashboards is developed using all of the different signals.

165

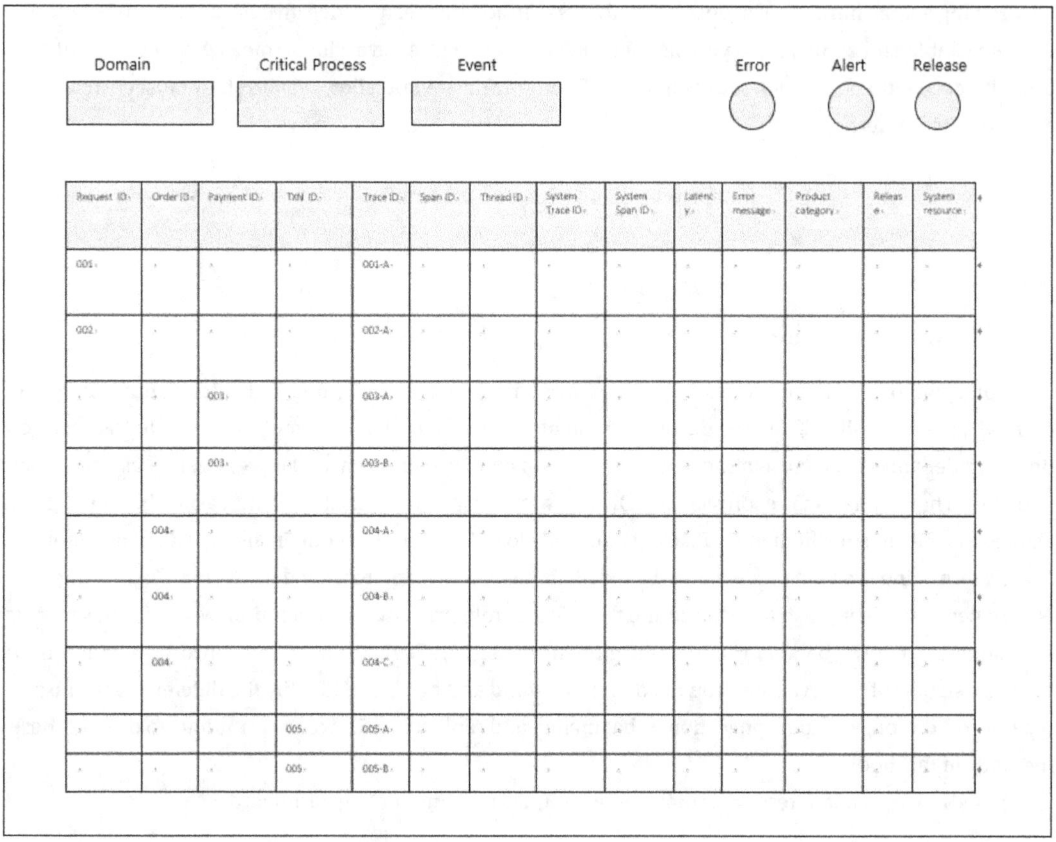

CHAPTER 2   THE RCA APPROACH

Figure 2-36. The RCA dashboard layout

The root cause analysis data model is joined with the CMDB and SLO. The root cause analysis data model is the core table of observability and can be joined with the CMDB to modernize IT operations.

Filters have the following characteristics:

- Add filters as search criteria for other filters.
- Add filters as search criteria for the value you want to output.
- All signals populate the filter with values, and the user can select these values.

In other words, you populate the filter with different signals, and the values selected in the filter become variables. Variables are added to the query as search criteria to organize the dashboard.

The RCA dashboard has a lot to offer, but its biggest advantage is that it can be the starting point for all dashboards.

You can join and filter different signals to understand the exact problem. Traditionally, only a single signal is used to output a simple SLO without user interaction. In comparison, the dashboard development introduced in this book is innovative and efficient.

CHAPTER 2   THE RCA APPROACH

- Dashboards can join various signals and output them. For example, events output business, and logs output internal information from the black box. By joining these signals, you can overcome the limitations of individual signals and display a variety of data, not just the technical aspects.

- Multiple filters can be used to restrict the output signals, allowing you to limit and narrow down the exact scope of the problem. You can quickly get to the problem you want.

- You can filter events to select businesses, applications, system resources, and all IT operations targets. You can define business IDs using service for microservices, resource IDs for system resources, and additional tags and then add them as data in the filter. For example, service IDs have a relationship with resource IDs, so it's a good idea to join services and resources.

I've covered various charts in this chapter. You can use the following charts to create a dashboard. Among the previous charts, I hope you will utilize the state timeline and annotations. They are important charts for SREs, but they are underutilized in practice.

In addition to the root cause analysis dashboard, in SRE, you need dashboards for visualization of SLOs, MTTR, and error budgets. You also need a USE and RED dashboard. These dashboards allow for clear visualization and understanding of signals.

- RED (Rate, Error, Duration)
- USE (Utilization, Saturation, Errors)
- Google SRE (Latency, Traffic, Errors, Saturation)

RED applies to services, USE applies to infrastructure, and Google SRE applies to both. To create a good dashboard, you must first define the correlation.

- It's a great way to organize a dashboard, showing the big picture first, and then showing a detailed chart at the bottom when you click a specific filter.

- You should have a filter at the top and configure it so that all charts within that dashboard dynamically change based on the scope and selection of the filter.

- Make sure that the charts output data consistently and appropriately to the topic. When organizing multiple charts in a dashboard, try to define the correlation between them.

Developing a variety of charts requires an understanding of the data sources that are mapped to the chart. For example, complex heatmaps and service maps don't require specific formulas to display. You just need to map the data source to the chart, and the chart will come out.

- Time series charts, heatmaps, and histograms use spanmetrics generated by the metric generator.

CHAPTER 2 THE RCA APPROACH

- Node exporters are used in polystats.

- You can select the metric (ALERTS, ALERTS_FOR_STATE) only when alerts are enabled. You need to scrape the Prometheus and Grafana servers when an alert is enabled.

- The service map utilizes the OpenTelemetry collector and metric generator. You can generate a spanmetric and a service map from the metric generator.

- While metrics and logs have been popular in the past, I recommend traces and events as data sources for observability dashboards.

A large number of meaningless SLOs and dashboards are developed, making them difficult and confusing to manage.

Once you have a good understanding of the internal data structure of the signals, you can quickly visualize the charts described previously without any preprocessing. An accurate understanding of the individual signals must precede visualization.

I'll explore Grafana's ability to define different correlations. When it comes to infrastructure, it's important to understand utilization and saturation rates for CPU, memory, disk, and network. SLO dashboards are essential for monitoring applications. The SLO dashboard includes basic error rate, availability, throughput, and latency. Depending on the domain and service type, it should also include error budgets and burn rates. For traditional industries, including legacy, error budgets, and burn rates, it can sometimes be overwhelming to apply, so they are not required. It is always useful to have a profile that allows you to monitor infrastructure and applications together, so I recommend correlating and profiles.

The dashboard should be more than just a visualization; it should consist of alerts to continuously improve as problems arise.

To build these types of dashboards, it's not enough to use Prometheus metrics alone. You need to connect to various data sources, such as Jira, the cloud, ArgoCD, Jenkins, and Git. And you'll need to use different types of charts, starting with time series charts.

The dashboards can be sophisticated, as shown here:

- They can add saturation rates from a basic infrastructure dashboard and improve with eBPF and Cilium.

- They can add error budgets and burn rates to application SLOs and elevate them at a service perspective.

- The Deployment, GitOps, and Issue Management dashboards are operational dashboards that use webhooks to collect and monitor operational data.

- Dashboards, alerts, SLOs, and error budgets should be automated, built, and deployed via Terraform or API.

2.8. Summary

In this chapter, you learned about two ways to define correlations: explicitly defining correlations between signals through their identities, or using machine learning to identify variables and define correlations between them. This chapter defined 14 correlations with key IDs between eight signals.

- Correlations can be used to quickly perform root cause analysis. Defining correlations makes it easier for developers to understand signals and configure dashboards and alerts. Signals differ in their purpose. Understanding them can be difficult.

- If the correlation is broken, it means that the signal is incorrectly configured or missing. Correlations can be used to validate the consistency of signals and improve their quality.

- It is possible to apply rules to automatically add tags. However, adding tags is mostly manual. It is inefficient to use tags and develop pipelines and interfaces. Correlation minimizes this manual work and allows you to leverage the power of observability signals alone.

In visualization, I described a variety of charts and root cause analysis dashboards. It is possible to apply charts in a common way without being limited to a specific dashboard solution. Before the visual output, it is necessary to organize a standardized data structure according to the root cause analysis data model. By organizing your data model according to the various correlations already described, you can use filters, joins, and lookups to develop a root cause analysis dashboard with a variety of signals.

Observability doesn't require many dashboards. In this book, you build two dashboards. This is because two dashboards are sufficient for root cause analysis. SREs should consider whether the existing dashboards they have spent a lot of time and money on are being underutilized, unimproved, and neglected.

A root cause analysis dashboard should provide context and a story to the user. It should give you an accurate understanding of the current context, help you understand what data you need to analyze further, and provide clues. A dashboard that simply lists metrics—ignoring cause and effect and correlation—is not meaningful. You need to develop dashboards that are clear about the meaning you want to convey to your users.

CHAPTER 3

Trace-Centric RCA

3.1. Introduction

Before I dive into the details of real-world industry problems, it's important to understand the correct way to organize observability by technology. This is because an understanding of the underlying technology will allow you to understand real-world problems and complex applications.

This chapter describes the workings of traces and the problems that arise when configuring them. The complexity and difficulty of configuring traces are common reasons why traces are often avoided. Developers who are used to logs often don't understand the effectiveness of traces and may even oppose them.

The following is a demonstration of the middleware.

- GCP PubSub: Passive instrumentation
- MQTT: Manual instrumentation
- Kafka: Automated instrumentation
- Azure SQS: Manual instrumentation
- Tibco EMS: Automated instrumentation
- Solaris JMS: Automated instrumentation
- Spring Cloud Stream: GCP PubSub binders fail, Solaris binders succeed only with OpenTelemetry
- Envoy: Automated instrumentation
- Gloo: automatic instrumentation
- Apigee: manual instrumentation
- Tibco EAI Server: Automatic instrumentation
- `webMethods` EAI Server: Automated instrumentation in commercial use
- WebSocket: Manual instrumentation

CHAPTER 3   TRACE-CENTRIC RCA

- RabbitMQ: Automated instrumentation
- AWS CloudFront: Manual instrumentation
- OpenTracing Shim: Automated instrumentation
- Batch: Automatically supported in commercial settings
- GraphQL: Automated instrumentation

Traces have many exceptions and complex requirements and require an understanding of many languages and protocols. If you need to trace to legacy systems, configuration becomes more difficult.

SRE monitors performance and identifies and improves latency. Traces shouldn't be the last step to observability, and observability should start with traces.

Before tracing, to understand the early symptoms of a problem such as latency, you had to use a variety of difficult utilities and metrics. Measuring latency on a per-section basis requires a lot of manual labor. If metrics didn't measure latency, logs were used. This is a technically difficult and time-consuming process.

The web servers, WAS, and Oracle databases of the past have changed to Kubernetes and cloud systems. This has brought a lot of changes in terms of development and operations. The performance tuning of the past needs to be changed and improved for observability. That doesn't mean that the old methods are wrong; it just means that they need to be improved to make them easier, faster, and more operational. The underlying theory is still important.

One of the reasons for adopting commercial observability is traces. Datadog and Dynatrace are commercially successful vendors with traces. This is because open source traces are not yet mature, have fewer features than commercial observability traces, and require vendor support. SRE is working to improve trace, but it's a difficult technology. To implement traces well, you need good internal engineers and vendor support. Using only commercial observability vendors leads to vendor dependency and higher costs, but if you implement observability using only open source, technical support is difficult, and the learning curve for internal engineers is high.

In addition to the distributed traces that occur between microservices, it is important to note the system traces that occur between system resources. There are no commercial observability implementations of system traces yet, and there is no specific technical standard. In this book, we will use KUtrace to organize system traces and correlate them with distributed traces.

This book contains many examples of traces. I have encountered various problems while implementing traces and observability in practice. I have tried to include the problems and solutions in this book. Most SREs currently implementing trace do not have best practices and probably lack reference material. Many companies don't have a lot of trace experts, and most of the time, they have to do a lot of technical verification and testing on their own.

I think this book minimizes this trial and error and explains cases with concrete results. Implementing a full E2E trace requires a lot of time and effort.

Most organizations have a variety of legacy applications that have played important roles in the past. There are CICS applications developed in Cobol on mainframes, and most organizations are using SAP ERP. Traditional on-premises solutions are being migrated to cloud SaaS and managed services. While there are many implementations of trace on a domain-by-domain and technology-by-technology basis, applying trace E2E, including microservices and legacy systems, is a huge challenge. Observability is not mature enough to support a complex legacy systems.

There is a wide variety of middleware in the enterprise. Basically, this includes API servers, JMS servers, EAI servers, mainframes, packaged applications, and SaaS, cloud-managed services. It is common to process important transactions on legacy systems. Startups may have fewer legacy systems, but medium-sized and larger companies that have been in business for a long time have a variety of legacy systems.

When it comes to technology these days, the focus is on startups and tech companies. However, most organizations have a lot of legacy systems. Adopting new technologies is more difficult for organizations with existing large legacies. It's not just a problem with the technology. It's a reluctance to adopt unproven or difficult technologies and an unwillingness to take on high risk. Due to the complexity and constraints of legacy systems, trace projects often fail. Rather than describing trace in an academic and theoretical way, it is more useful to share practical experiences of trying to improve the problems with trace in projects.

To an SRE, developers are collaborators and customers. You need to work with this mindset. If they are not willing to help and solve problems together, it is difficult to implement successful observability.

3.2. How Trace Works

The goal of this section is to explain the principles of agents' trace handling. Only by understanding the internal operation can you understand the causes of measurement failure and resolve bugs.

Observability starts with E2E traces. With a trace, you can quickly and accurately understand the latency and error of each section. You need to understand how traces work and be able to troubleshoot them in case the traces break or the instrumentation fails.

Automation and consulting services provided by commercial observability are great advantages, but focusing on the convenience of commercial observability can make it difficult to adopt open source in the future. In addition, many organizations experience difficulties in implementing observability for a variety of reasons, including organizational orientation, SRE technical preferences, and budget.

- Organizations typically use multiple observability solutions. Open source and commercial observability solutions often unintentionally go through multiple SREs and become unmanaged.

- The high cost of commercial observability limits the ability to take advantage of all that it has to offer. Commercial observability offers a lot of useful and convenient features, but you get what you pay for.

- To build observability using open source, you need to have the technical skills of your internal workforce. Technology needs to be internalized in development and operations. This internalization is difficult to achieve in the short term and takes time to build through culture and processes.

CHAPTER 3   TRACE-CENTRIC RCA

Even with commercial observability, E2E traces are difficult. Even the best trace solutions recognized by Gartner have been plagued by broken traces.

Problems arise for a variety of reasons, such as missing the benefits of traces because they are not configured correctly. When traces go wrong, it's hard to identify and validate the cause.

- When traces are configured with automated instrumentation, there is no way for an SRE with limited business knowledge to tell if a span is breaking and disconnecting in the middle, or if it is normal or abnormal. Developers lack understanding of observability and SRE lack business knowledge, so even if a span is abnormal, it's not easy to fix.

- Large organizations such as banking and telecom have a large number of transaction types. By configuring a trace, you can understand approximately how many spans are generated by a specific business process, and you can see if a specific service is interrupting or outputting the spans incorrectly.

When instrumentation malfunctions, it is difficult to analyze and fix the cause. Instrumentation problems are most often caused by the agent instrumenting the incorrect method or injecting the wrong bytecode because the method is unknown to the agent. Therefore, it is necessary to identify which methods the agent has attempted to instrument. Using profiles and debugging, you can troubleshoot bugs and unexpected instrumentation problems in the agent.

OpenTelemetry can debug the internals of the agent; it is open source, and you can analyze code and then quickly identify whether the instrumentation is incorrect. Commercial observability agents don't expose their internals to the outside world and are difficult to debug, so you need to look at the call tree and stack trace of the profile to make sure you are instrumenting the correct methods and debugging the spans being generated. You should also consider remote debugging. In the case of Java, the dependencies are complex, so the call tree helps you understand the dependencies, and the stack trace outputs thread information and timestamps.

Add a breakpoint and check to see if it creates a span.

You need observability naming conventions and processes along with development standards.

- Before you can technically fix anything, you need to understand what developers are trying to follow. If different development teams have different standards for observability, the SRE may end up with multiple different observabilities for different development teams. If there is a clear standard for observability and developers understand and adhere to it, it's possible to build enterprise-wide observability, but if not, you'll face a difficult situation. For observability to be successful, you need to think deeply about procedures and processes. Observability governance can be overwhelming, but it also requires procedures and processes to manage and improve complexity.

CHAPTER 3   TRACE-CENTRIC RCA

- Clearly define a structure, standardization, and naming convention for your signals. Before building observability, you need to have a clear understanding of your existing signals. Think about problems and work to improve them. It is best to configure standardization and naming conventions through pipelines and settings within observability without modifying code.

Traces are correlated with other signals. Even if the trace is wrong, the trace alone cannot validate the problem. You need to compare the trace with other signals and validate it.

You need to create procedures for validating and comparing signals. If a signal has a problem with consistency or a problematic signal that makes it difficult to construct a correlation, you need to figure out how to improve it. For example, if you have a transaction ID that is used throughout the E2E, you can query a specific transaction ID in the log in chronological order. By counting the number of lines of a specific transaction in the log, you can measure the approximate number of requests and responses.

- For example, you can see that a transaction is made with 20 requests and responses, and the transaction ID is added to the baggage in the trace.

- If you query the span count in the trace with that transaction ID, suppose it shows five spans.

- If there are 20 requests in the log, but only five spans in trace, you can guess that 15 spans are not instrumented or are incorrect. It's not hard to see that the spans included by the transaction ID are not accurately instrumented and need improvement.

It is not uncommon for spans to be interrupted for various reasons or for spans to be undetected and missing from the logs because they were not instrumented.

By comparing logs and traces, and counting and comparing, you can identify problems and pinpoint the cause of the problem and why. The log outputs a variety of IDs for upstream and downstream use. You can identify problems by comparing traces based on log counts and times, but if they are not standardized, the attribute naming is inconsistent, and the naming is different, you cannot compare logs and traces.

- Traces are similar to logs, but traces are easier to understand in context than logs. It is important to configure logs correctly, identify problems in traces based on logs, and understand the cause. It is difficult to verify using trace IDs, and when comparing logs and traces, you can use transaction IDs to compare the two signals. As explained, there are more trace contexts output in logs than in traces, so it is not easy to compare the exact count between logs and traces. You need to organize your logs carefully. Log attributes should be clearly defined and configured for accurate search. This is because you solve problems with traces based on logs. Logs are often wrong, and traces are often inaccurate. There's no good way to verify.

CHAPTER 3   TRACE-CENTRIC RCA

- RUM is directly correlated to traces, and RUM's session ID contains many trace IDs. If it outputs fewer span counts than expected, you can assume that there is a problem with the trace. If the transaction is generated on the frontend and passed to the backend, you can start with the RUM and analyze the distributed trace. However, many transactions are not generated by the client. Many transactions are created and completed on the backend. The number of trace contexts found in the log is higher than the number of span IDs found in the trace. The difference is even larger for non-blocking systems.

When configuring observability, there are many problems that can be encountered, and correlation can help solve them.

- The trace instrumentation failed, so you use the profile to identify the methods the agent tried to instrument.

- The trace breaks, and to fix it, you use logs to compare and verify against the trace.

You need observability for observability, and you need to be able to improve and solve internal problems with observability.

Observability, which joins a variety of signals, is more complex to configure than metrics and log-centric monitoring of the past. Misconfigurations are common.

Traces can be utilized in various fields, such as alerts, dashboards, data analysis, and anomaly detection, so analysis and design are important. Span attributes, span links, span annotations, and baggage should be carefully designed. Do not analyze observability using only dashboards. Observability requires more complex reports and MTTR calculations than the built-in metrics, so there is a need for data beyond the output on the screen.

Agents do not automatically configure span attributes and baggage, so these must be designed during the analysis and design process to improve observability. In fact, installing an agent is a short-term task, but span attributes need to be advanced by the SRE over a long period of time.

Figure 3-1 illustrates how trace works. There are three targets: microservices A and B and the observability backend. Microservices interact with each other, propagating and transferring the trace perspective.

CHAPTER 3 TRACE-CENTRIC RCA

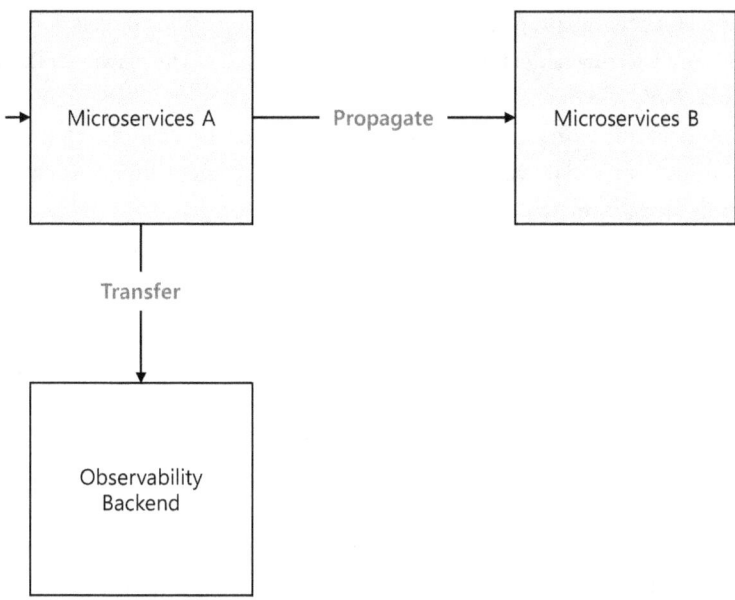

Figure 3-1. *The meaning of propagate and transfer in a trace*

Microservices perform three actions to implement trace:

1. **Validate the header:** When a message is propagated, it first checks if the trace ID exists in the header. If it doesn't exist, a new trace ID is created. If it does exist, the existing trace ID is reused and propagation occurs. If the header exists but is incorrectly formatted, an error is raised.

2. **Propagate to other microservices:** Microservices A makes a request to Microservices B. The header of the request message should define a trace context. The trace context contains the trace ID, the parent's span ID, and the span ID. The body of the message contains the business data. Due to the existence of various trace standards, there are cases where the header format is different between propagated traces. In this case, the headers are converted. For example, microservices may receive trace contexts in B3 format and propagate trace contexts in W3C format. The automatic conversion uses the SDK, and the manual conversion uses the composite propagator API. To summarize, Microservices A validates the headers of the requests. It then propagates a trace context to Microservices B. The trace context is located in the header of Microservices B's request.

3. **Transfer to observability backend:** Microservices transfer the trace context to the observability backend. The message includes the trace ID, parent span ID, span ID, start time, end time, service name, and various attributes. There is no header in the transferred message, only the body.

CHAPTER 3   TRACE-CENTRIC RCA

Note the distinction between propagating and transferring. Propagating targets downstream microservices, while transferring targets observability backend storage. The reason for this distinction is to avoid confusion and clarify semantics.

In general, I often use the terms upstream and downstream. Propagate is the interaction that occurs between the upstream and downstream, while transfer is the interaction that occurs between the observability backend and the microservices.

If you apply instrumentation to protocols and technologies that OpenTelemetry does not support, you will not get results. Suppose your application needs to propagate using a custom API or protocol. You would need to develop logic to measure the duration of the request and inject the trace context into the header of the protocol message. Then you would need to add logic to transfer it to the observability backend.

Propagation can be a problem in cases where publish and subscribe are separated, such as with message servers, special processing patterns such as batch instead of online, or where reads and writes are separated, such as NoSQL. Automated instrumentation would be great, but if it's not possible, you'll need to develop manual instrumentation using the API to inject and extract trace context into headers. Even if it is developed manually, applying manual instrumentation to many microservices requires code modifications and is inefficient. Eventually, manual instrumentation should be configured to become automated using the OpenTelemetry extension.

The trace contexts for publisher and subscriber work like this:

- The publisher injects the trace context into the header and publishes the message.

- The subscriber subscribes to the message and extracts the trace context located in the header.

Use cases that require converting between different trace standards often arise.

- Microservices A propagates a trace in B3 format. Microservices B receives the B3 format.

- Microservice A transfers to the collector in B3 format. The collector transfers to the backend storage in OTLP format.

By default, OpenTelemetry supports the following propagation formats:

- W3C trace context

- W3C baggage

In addition to the W3C, various propagators, such as B3, OpenTracing, and others are available. As shown in Figure 3-2, the message format for propagation and transferring is different. Propagating is more complicated than transferring. Propagation occurs using headers of various protocols, such as JMS and TCP, while transferring uses OTLP messages based on HTTP and gRPC protocols. The message format of propagate and transfer is as follows.

CHAPTER 3   TRACE-CENTRIC RCA

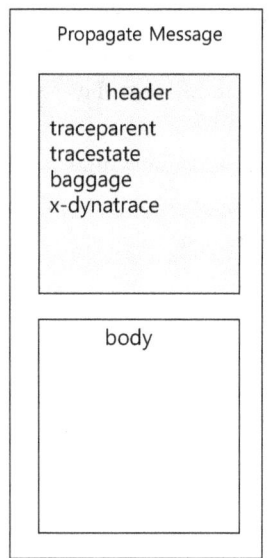 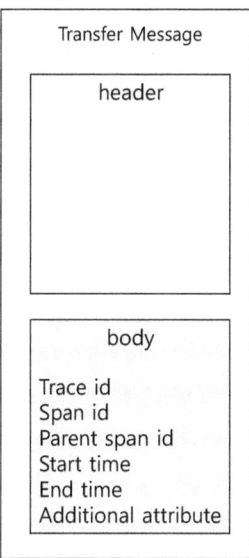

Figure 3-2. *Anatomy of a propagated and transferred message*

When implementing trace using only automated instrumentation, it is difficult to understand the internal operation. Initially, it is necessary to understand the internal behavior by using manual instrumentation and API as much as possible. Without understanding the internal operation, various trace problems arise, and it is difficult to propose solutions and detailed implementation plans. Understanding manual instrumentation is important. Automated instrumentation uses bytecode instrumentation and should be developed internally using manual instrumentation API.

Projects that use middleware, such as EAI and API servers, to integrate applications develop adapters. These adapters are often developed using client APIs. Trace is similar to this because it monitors the client. You'll need to instrument inbound, outbound, and server options. Generally you'll instrument clients (outbound) to create spans. Comparing difficulty levels, observability projects are more difficult than integration projects, which involve developing various adapters, interfaces applications, and legacy systems. This is because observability measures and monitors the various connectivity protocols.

Propagation is a common problem, so you need to keep improving for E2E traces. Legacy and middleware systems make propagation difficult. Implementing E2E traces and enforcing observability in organizations with diverse legacy and middleware systems is a challenge.

If you use commercial observability to automate your instrumentation, sometimes you may not be able to get it to work. In this case, I recommend that you try instrumenting with the OpenTelemetry agent. There are cases where instrumentation works with the commercial observability agent but not with OpenTelemetry. Conversely, it is often found that instrumentation that cannot be instrumented with commercial observability is instrumented with OpenTelemetry and propagated successfully.

CHAPTER 3   TRACE-CENTRIC RCA

There is a risk when using commercial observability. It is possible for OpenTelemetry to instrument and commercial observability to fail. In this case, the E2E trace will be broken in commercial observability. If you use commercial observability, you should prioritize commercial observability over OpenTelemetry when implementing traces.

When you install a commercial observability agent, it automates instrumentation, which increases productivity, but it also has side effects. All unnecessary traffic can be instrumented, or unknown traces can be instrumented and become noisy. Without a holistic understanding of the system, it is difficult to understand trace context when agents are configured on thousands of hosts.

When developing a trace, you may encounter many different exceptions. Since there are many cases where propagation does not work, it is important to understand the problem in order to provide an accurate solution. As the trace project progresses, additional development is often required due to the limitations of the agent technology.

3.2.1. Context

Before explaining the propagator, it is necessary to understand the context. In instrumentation, the context is the starting point. The term *context* is used in a variety of ways, which can be confusing.

OpenTelemetry logs and traces start with context.

- For logs, it is important to understand how they are processed by context, ThreadLocal (replaced by the OpenTelemetry agent), MDC, the Log4j log library, and the pipelines.
- For traces, it is important to understand context, propagation by propagators, transport by exporters, and inter-thread passing.

A context object is a mechanism for sharing data, including how it is processed by between thread or across service boundaries through propagation. You can get the current span using the context API anywhere in the code. Context objects are immutable data stores that provide a consistent API. Implementing context API varies by language, and many development languages have their own built-in context concept. The Context API provides developers with consistency when using OpenTelemetry.

- get_value: Extracts the value for a given key from the context. The only required parameter for a call is a key, and a context can be passed if necessary. If the context is not delivered, the value is extracted from the global context by default.
- set_value: Saves the value with the key given in the context. When storing a value in a specific context, the context parameter is also passed. Since the context is immutable, a new context object with the new value is returned when the method is called.

- **attach**: Enables API calls to be executed in a specific context environment. Specifies the current context with the passed context argument. The response value is a unique token and is used in the `detach` method.

- **detach**: Used to return to the previous state of the context and takes the unique token obtained by attaching as an argument. When the method is called, it returns to the original context specified just before the attach.

OpenTelemetry provides an object called context, which contains information about the trace:

- Stores trace information in context when implementing trace and logging. Propagates the context to the propagator.

- As in the case of worker threads, context propagation is processed by passing the context to another thread without the need for extraction and injection between internal threads. The worker thread can read the trace in the context. The implementation of trace worker threads varies by agent.

- When propagating the trace context downstream, extraction and injection occur using a propagator.

- When processing logs, the agent reads the trace from the context and passes the context to MDC.

This list summarizes the differences between, pass, propagating, and transfer:

- Crossing a service boundary is called propagation.

- The exchange of context between threads is called passing.

- Whenever possible, the distinction between propagation, transfer, and passing is used to clarify the meaning.

Context provides important information for debugging instrumentation. When instrumentation issues arise, start by analyzing the context. The context provides important information for debugging the instrumentation.

- The agent stores the instrumentation results in the context. When processing traces and logs, the context must be debugged.

- If trace information is not output from `boundedElastic`, a worker thread, or parallel threads, the context must be debugged.

When implementing traces and logs, store trace information in a context. Read the context and use it as a propagator to propagate it downstream across service boundaries.

CHAPTER 3   TRACE-CENTRIC RCA

Worker threads are implemented as pool, parallel, elastic, or scheduling threads. As in the case of worker threads, context propagation is handled by passing context to other threads without the need for extraction and injection between internal threads. The worker thread can read the trace of the context. The implementation of the trace worker thread is agent-specific.

- When propagating trace contexts downstream, extraction and injection occur using propagators.
- When processing logs, the agent reads the trace context from the context and passes the context to the MDC.

3.2.2. Propagators

The trace context is processed by propagators. It is important to understand propagators. If the upstream and downstream options use different trace header formats, they use the OpenTelemetry propagator.

- For automated instrumentation, you can configure different propagators in the SDK.
- For manual instrumentation, use the composite propagator API, which allows you to support a variety of trace formats.

A problem arises when if your observability does not support OpenTelemetry and supports a different trace format. In this case, you need to use a composite propagator and explicitly declare the trace standard you want to use. OpenTelemetry provides three type of propagators:

- **W3C propagator:** OpenTelemetry provides a text-based approach to injecting and propagating W3C trace context into HTTP headers.
- **Composite propagator:** Combines multiple propagators.
- **Baggage propagator:** Provides a text-based approach to inject OpenTelemetry baggage into HTTP headers and propagate it.

Propagation is a mechanism for exchanging context in header between services. It allows you to establish causal relationships across services that are distributed across network boundaries.

By default, OpenTelemetry uses the W3C context propagation standard. If an application instrumented with OpenTelemetry communicates with services that use different contexts, it is useful to configure additional propagators to correlate different trace between services. This is done by installing the propagator's package and using the OTEL_PROPAGATORS environment variable.

Traditionally, it uses B3 context propagation. It is used by Istio, Linkerd Service Mesh, and Spring Sleuth. Existing microservices use B3, and new microservices use OpenTelemetry W3C.

The core concerns are the main functions of the system. For example, fund transfers, deposits, and withdrawals. Cross concerns are features that can affect the entire system. For example, logging and security.

Propagators utilize context to inject and extract data into cross concerns such as traces and baggage.

Propagation is implemented through library-specific request interceptors and propagators. The interceptor detects requests to send and receive, and processes the extract and inject operations of each propagator. OpenTelemetry uses the term interceptor and commercial observability uses the term sensor.

I describe the propagators in detail in this order:

- Textmap propagators
- Composite propagators
- Deploying propagators
- Configuring propagators

3.2.2.1. Textmap Propagators

The propagator type is bound to a data type to propagate context data across service boundaries.

The propagator type currently provided is a textmap propagator. A textmap propagator is a string key and value pair that injects values into a carrier and extracts values from the carrier.

There are two types of carriers:

- Textmaps
- Byte arrays

OpenTelemetry uses textmaps.

A carrier is the medium used by a propagator to read and write values. Each propagator type defines a textmap or byte array as its carrier type.

To write values to a carrier and read values from a carrier, propagators must define inject and extract operations. Each propagator type must define a carrier type, and may define additional parameters.

For example, if you inject a value into the header of an HTTP send request, the required argument is

- The context: The propagator must first search the context for values (span context, baggage) or other cross-concerns.
- The carrier that holds the propagate field: For example, a message to send and an HTTP request.

When extracting a value from a received request, it extracts the value from the header of the HTTP request. The required arguments are

- The context
- The carrier holding the propagate field. The message to receive.

This returns a new context derived from the context passed as an argument. The extracted value can be a span context, baggage, or another cross-concern context.

In simple terms, a person (propagator) carries (propagates) a gift (context) in a bag (carrier). A gift (context) is placed (injected) into a bag (carrier). The type of the gift (text map) is read.

CHAPTER 3   TRACE-CENTRIC RCA

A textmap propagator injects and extracts cross-concern values as string keys and value pairs on a carrier. The carrier of the propagated data on both the client (injector) and server (extractor) is typically an HTTP request.

A trace can extend beyond a single process. This requires the trace's identifier to propagate context to remote processes.

To propagate a trace context, you need to register a propagator.

```
import (
  "go.opentelemetry.io/otel"
  "go.opentelemetry.io/otel/propagation"
)
...
otel.SetTextMapPropagator(propagation.TraceContext{})
```

Getters and setters are optional helper components used to extract and inject, respectively.

Injecting Textmaps

This injects a value into the carrier. When injecting, you can add an argument, which is a setter that sets the key/value pairs to propagate. The propagator can be called to set multiple pairs. These are the arguments you can define to inject data into the carrier.

Extracting Textmaps

This extracts a value from an incoming request. When extracting, you can add an argument, which is a getter that is called for the propagate key to be fetched. These are arguments that you can define to help extract data from the carrier.

3.2.2.2. Composite Propagators

You can choose to implement the propagator type as an object exposing inject and extract methods, or you can choose to split it into injectors and extractors. You should provide the ability to group multiple propagators of different cross concerns and utilize them as a single entity.

A composite propagator can be composed of a list of propagators or a list of injectors and extractors. The generated composite propagator calls the propagators, injectors, or extractors in the specified order.

If you want to propagate, define it like this:

```
set_global_textmap(CompositePropagator([tracecontext.TraceContextTextMapPropagator(),
B3MultiFormat()]))
```

Each composite propagator implements a specific propagator type, such as a textmap propagator, because different propagator types are likely to work on different data types.

OpenTelemetry provides a way to get propagators for supported propagation types. Depending on the language, the propagator can be set or used as a global accessor using dependency injection techniques.

The instrumentation library should call a propagator to extract and inject context. While this is not recommended, certain instrumentation libraries may use proprietary context propagation protocols or may be hard-coded to use a specific protocol. In these cases, you can avoid using the propagator provided by the instrumentation library and instead hardcode your own context extraction and injection logic.

Propagators should default to a composite propagator that includes the W3C trace context propagator and the baggage propagator. It should be possible to disable or override the preconfigured propagators.

3.2.2.3. Deploying Propagators

A list of official propagators that are maintained by the OpenTelemetry organization and should be distributed as OpenTelemetry extension packages.

- The W3C trace context can be deployed as part of the OpenTelemetry API.
- W3C baggage can be deployed as part of the OpenTelemetry API.
- B3
- Jaeger
- OT Trace
- Open Census Binary Format

Additional propagators that implement vendor protocols, such as the AWS X-Ray trace header protocol, should not be maintained or distributed with the OpenTelemetry repository.

If you only use W3C to propagate, you don't need a propagator. But reality requires a variety of propagators.

B3 is a popular trace standard used prior to OpenTelemetry. As you upgrade to String Boot 3, you may find yourself migrating Sleuth to OpenTelemetry. It is important to provide backward compatibility for existing B3.

B3 has both single and multiple header encodings. It also does not map directly to OpenTelemetry, including the debug trace flag, allowing spans of send and receive messages to share the same ID. To maximize compatibility between OpenTelemetry and the Zipkin implementation, the following guidelines for propagating B3 contexts have been established.

When extracting B3:

- You should try to extract the encoded B3 using single and multiple header formats.
- If the debug trace flag is received, it should be preserved and propagated with subsequent requests. When the debug flag is set, the OpenTelemetry implementation must set the sampled trace flag.
- You should not reuse X-B3-SpanId as a server-side span ID.

When injecting B3:

- You need to inject B3 using a single header format.
- You need to configure the default inject format to a B3 multi-header.
- OpenTelemetry does not support reusing the same ID on send and receive messages, so you should not propagate the X-B3-ParentSpanId.

3.2.2.4. Configuring Propagators

At the level of threads inside a process, we do not use the term propagate. Propagation occurs when an external call passes initiative outside the process and requires a propagator.

There are many different distributed trace standards, including Zipkin, Uber's OpenTracing Jaeger, Google's Open Census, CNCF-led OpenTelemetry W3C, AWS, and Datadog. OpenTelemetry supports various propagators such as W3C and B3. To do this, it provides a propagator API and supports interoperability with other trace standards.

To support different trace formats, propagators were introduced. OpenTelemetry provides a variety of propagators. Propagators are responsible for propagating traces between microservices. OpenTelemetry collectors, JavaAgents, SDK, and APIs include the ability to process and convert different propagators.

- SDK
- API
- Agent
- Collector

The implementation using Python is shown here:

```
pip install opentelemetry-propagator-B3==1.23.0
```

Use `OTEL_PROPAGATORS` in the SDK for automated instrumentation.

```
tracer = configure_tracer("CompositePropagator", "0.1")
set_global_textmap(CompositePropagator([tracecontext.TraceContextTextMapPropagator(),
B3MultiFormat()]))
```

You can set the `OTEL_PROPAGATORS` environment variable. Its allowed values are as follows:

- tracecontext: W3C trace Context
- baggage: W3C Baggage
- b3: B3 Single
- b3multi: B3 Multi

- Jaeger: Jaeger
- xray: AWS X-Ray
- ot trace: OT trace

The default configuration is the same as `OTEL_PROPAGATORS=" tracecontext, baggage"`. The SDK settings that are implemented with automated instrumentation are shown here:

```
export OTEL_PROPAGATORS=B3,B3multi,tracecontext,baggage
```

The collector settings are shown here:

```
receivers:
  otlp:
    protocols:
      grpc:
      http:
  jaeger: null
  prometheus: null
  zipkin: null
```

3.2.3. Propagating Trace

The trace context specifies two HTTP headers that are used to pass the context.

If the trace specification is not followed exactly, the trace will not work correctly. For example, the trace will be generated, but there will be problems with the span, or the trace will error and hang during propagation and transfer. If OpenTelemetry duplicates or omits any of the required conventions, the trace will not work properly. The trace ID, span ID, and parent span ID must be configured as required and propagated and transferred in accordance with the standards set by trace. The commercial observability agent automatically creates a trace context in the header and writes the trace ID into the log. Commercial observability uses its own telemetry semantic conventions and does not use the OpenTelemetry semantic conventions. This makes it difficult to understand the complexity of traces and spans if you are new to commercial observability.

- The OpenTelemetry carrier has a textmap format. And there are language-specific data structures (maps, dictionaries) that correspond to the format.
- Baggage is a common way to pass business context to traces. However, commercial observability don't use baggage, but instead adds data to the header in a key-value format in its own way.
- The concept of trace was designed around the HTTP protocol. The problem is that the propagation of the trace is interrupted by the existence of a message server. Manual instrumentation is required for this.

Span relationships or dependencies must be implemented. Define relationships between spans and dependencies between spans in a trace. If the parent span ID is empty, you can check that the trace is not propagated and has been not instrument.

The pass is primarily a manual instrument.

The agent has three functions: instrumentation, propagation, and transfer.

- Instrument the API and inject the trace context in the header.

- Propagate between upstream and downstream.

- Transfer traces to observability backend storage.

Automated instrumentation consists of agents. Different agents vary considerably in the scope of support and compatibility of development languages and protocols. Automated instrumentation automates the process of loading classes and injecting bytecode into entry points and the correct methods.

For popular frameworks like Spring Boot, instrumentation is not a problem because the agent already understands the classes and methods it instruments and injects. However, if it is custom-application by the developer or, for example, a newly launched managed service from a cloud vendor, the agent does not understand how it should instrument and inject, so it fails to create the span and misses it. If a span for a simple request and response fails to instrument, the span will be missed, but if it fails to propagate, the trace will be broken.

Manual instrumentation using the API is not recommended. Manual instrumentation requires code modifications and can be an operational burden. Frequent additional bytecode instrumentation can cause performance problems, requiring redeployment and ongoing management. Commercial observability provides features that make it easy to configure bytecode instrumentation. You select the classes and methods you want to instrument, and it adds bytecode instrumentation. It then creates a service that exposes the endpoint, similar to how it would be automatically discovered by an agent.

Assuming you have Microservices A, B, and C, Figure 3-3 shows how trace works.

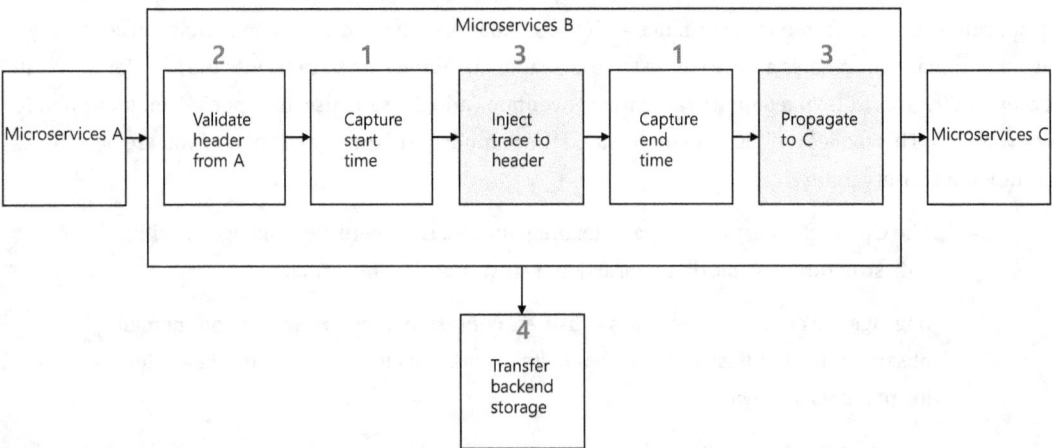

Figure 3-3. *Agent's process flow*

CHAPTER 3 TRACE-CENTRIC RCA

1. **Instrument:** Identify key methods within microservices and instrument the before and after of the methods.

2. **Extract:** Receive propagation from upstream and check if the context exists in the header. The propagate format should be checked. If the header is not propagated or is propagated incorrectly, the downstream will create a new trace. If the context doesn't exist, it creates a new context, and if it does, it extracts the existing context.

3. **Inject and propagate:** Inject the context in the header and propagate it downstream. If the propagation format is different, you need to specify a propagator downstream. If the upstream is sending to B3, it needs a B3 propagator.

4. **Transfer:** Transfer traces to backend storage. When transferring traces to an observability backend and propagating between microservices, always ensure that there are no compatibility problems with the propagation format and propagator.

To extract traces, the trace reads context from the protocol's message headers. Instrumentation logic is added before and after certain APIs, injecting context into the headers. Implementing trace introduces various exceptions, such as instrumentation in OpenTelemetry but not in commercial observability or different span results for different agents. Solving these problems requires debugging and explaining the results to developers and infrastructure engineers. Different agents may have different methods they understand, and different instrumentation on the methods may result in different results.

Message servers in Solace can support two types of message specifications. JCSMP uses `SolaceJCSMPTextMap`, and JMS uses `SolaceJmsW3CTextMap`. Developers can also develop manual instrumentation for JMS and JCSMP. Even with manual instrumentation, there are differences depending on the type of message.

Here is the manual instrumentation of the JMS publisher.

```
void howToCreateSpanOnMessagePublish(Message message, MessageProducer messageProducer,
Topic messageDestination, OpenTelemetry openTelemetry, Tracer tracer) {

final Span sendSpan = tracer
    .spanBuilder("mySolacePublisherApp" + " " + MessagingOperationValues.PROCESS)
    .setSpanKind(SpanKind.CLIENT)
    .setAttribute(SemanticAttributes.MESSAGING_DESTINATION_KIND,
    MessagingDestinationKindValues.TOPIC)
    .setAttribute(SemanticAttributes.MESSAGING_TEMP_DESTINATION, false)
    //.setAttribute(...)
    .setParent(Context.current())
    .startSpan();
```

189

CHAPTER 3 TRACE-CENTRIC RCA

```
try (Scope scope = sendSpan.makeCurrent()) {
    final SolaceJmsW3CTextMapSetter setter = new SolaceJmsW3CTextMapSetter();
    final TextMapPropagator propagator = openTelemetry.getPropagators().
    getTextMapPropagator();
    propagator.inject(Context.current(), message, setter);
    messageProducer.send(messageDestination, message);
} catch (Exception e) {
    sendSpan.recordException(e);
    sendSpan.setStatus(StatusCode.ERROR, e.getMessage());
} finally {
    sendSpan.end();
    }
  }
}
```

Here is the manual instrumentation of the receiver.

```
void howToCreateNewSpanOnMessageReceive(Message receivedMessage,
    Consumer<Message> messageProcessor,
    OpenTelemetry openTelemetry, Tracer tracer) {

final SolaceJmsW3CTextMapGetter getter = new SolaceJmsW3CTextMapGetter();
final Context extractedContext = openTelemetry.getPropagators().getTextMapPropagator()
    .extract(Context.current(), receivedMessage, getter);

try (Scope scope = extractedContext.makeCurrent()) {
    final Span receiveSpan = tracer
    .spanBuilder("mySolaceReceiverApp" + " " + MessagingOperationValues.RECEIVE)
    .setSpanKind(SpanKind.CLIENT)
    .setAttribute(SemanticAttributes.MESSAGING_DESTINATION_KIND,
    MessagingDestinationKindValues.QUEUE)
    .setAttribute(SemanticAttributes.MESSAGING_TEMP_DESTINATION, false)
    //.setAttribute(...)
    .setParent(extractedContext)
    .startSpan();

    try {
        messageProcessor.accept(receivedMessage);
    } catch (Exception e) {
        receiveSpan.recordException(e);
        receiveSpan
        .setStatus(StatusCode.ERROR, e.getMessage());
```

CHAPTER 3 TRACE-CENTRIC RCA

```
        } finally {
            receiveSpan.end();
            }
          }
       }
}
```

If trace and span are outputting incorrectly, the problem is most likely in your instrumentation. This could be due to incorrect instrumentation, missing instrumentation, asynchronous issues, or not supporting publish and subscribe.

If you expect three spans, the spans are generated as shown in Figure 3-4, but the spans are generated incorrectly. Instead of three spans, only one long span is output. Such spans are generated when the API server is not instrumented, or when communicating with external organizations that are not instrumented.

There can be multiple server spans in server. A single span is a simple representation, but it's better to have multiple spans. Two spans are inbound and outbound, and are connected to the outside world. Three spans consist of inbound, outbound, and threads connecting inbound and outbound.

Figure 3-4 shows a case where the API server appears as one long span. This is because the request and response failed downstream instrumentation, including the API server. The API server may have blocked the header from being processed, and in most cases, the trace context appended to the header was not understood and failed to propagate. If the header with the trace context is passed through, it will propagate downstream after the API server, and a span will be created.

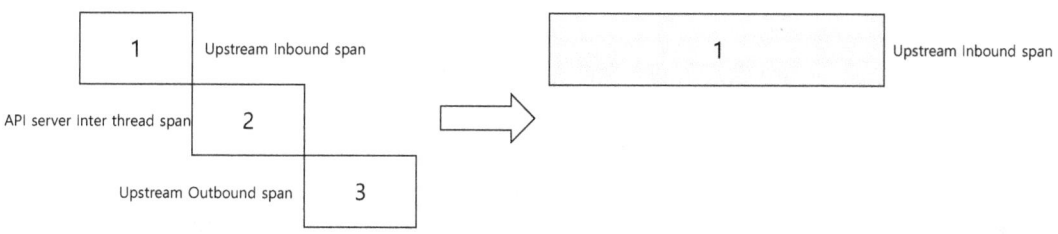

Figure 3-4. *API server trace case 1*

Figure 3-5 is a synchronous request and response call. Only two spans are output, one span is not output. The reason is that I did not instrument one span.

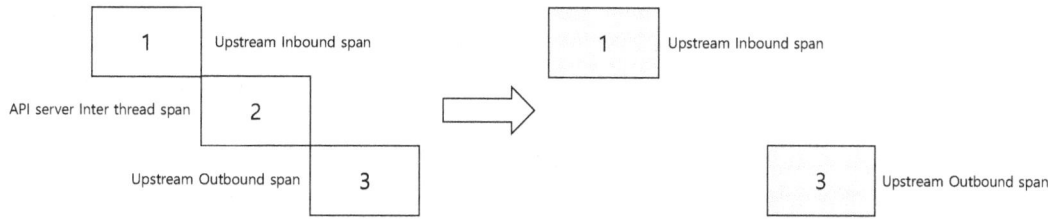

Figure 3-5. *API server trace case 2*

191

CHAPTER 3 TRACE-CENTRIC RCA

It only creates outbound spans. This is because it is not instrumented. The trace ID is not propagated downstream. The cause is often the API server, but it can also be the case that the downstream doesn't understand the context of the trace. And you received a response from the API server.

Internal threads are not instrumented. However, inbound and outbound spans are instrumented, so latency and propagation are not a problem.

Figure 3-6 shows that one trace should be generated, which is normal, but the trace does not propagate, creating two separate traces.

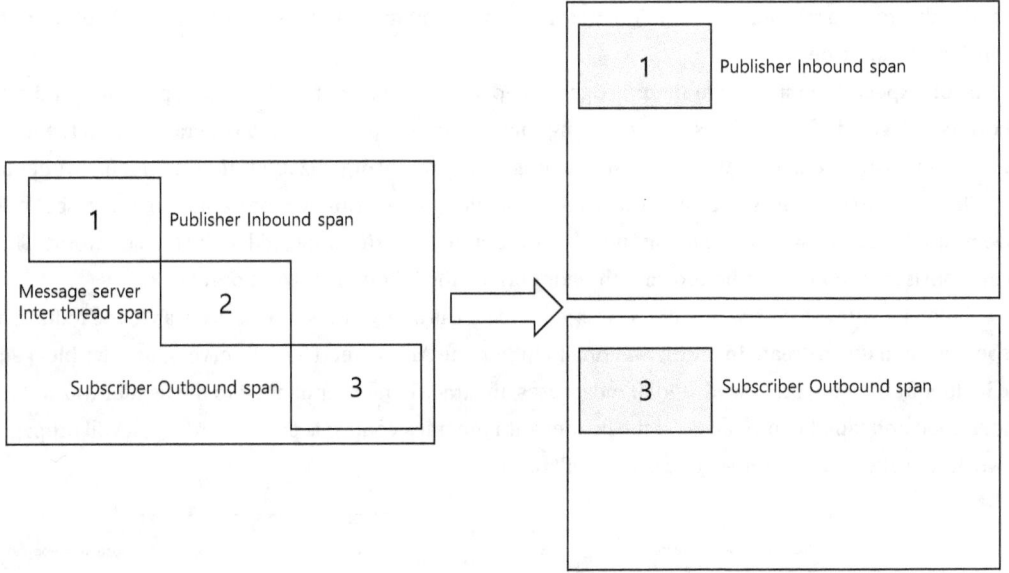

Figure 3-6. *Message server trace case 3*

If PubSub fails to propagate to a subscriber, it will output such a span.

With the correct instrumentation of the publishers and subscribers, propagation can generate spans correctly.

3.2.4. Propagating Baggage

There are many different components of trace. The basics are trace and span, but there are also events, baggage, attributes, decorators, link, states, exceptions, propagators, and more. Only the baggage is a header. The rest is not located in the header. It is only transferred. The `Request` attribute found in commercial agents is also only transferred.

In addition to the trace context, OpenTelemetry defines a baggage context. Just as the trace context is propagated across service boundaries to other microservices, the baggage context should also be propagated. While trace contains the technical context, baggage should contain the business context.

Transaction, request, and order IDs are located in the message body. The trace ID is not E2E from a user perspective. For example, a user must click at least two buttons to create and submit an order. Each click generates new trace ID, so an individual order action generates more than one trace ID. It is difficult to identify the user and the order based on the trace ID in the header alone. In the event of a failure, an incident is created, and the order ID is specified in the incident, but there is no corresponding ID in the header of the trace. You need to match the technical trace to the business order to ensure proper failure response. While baggage is useful, it is difficult to apply in practice—baggage is not automatically instrumented, requires custom development, and has a negative impact on runtime.

It is recommended that SREs manage the message header and developers focus on the message body. It's not good practice for SREs to see the entire message payload. Some developers print a lot of the log, but this is against security guidelines in banking and telecom.

If you output sensitive ID in traces and logs, emphasizing security alone can limit the scope of observability and make monitoring difficult. Unnecessary restrictions can negate the effectiveness of observability.

Baggage is not automated but can only be configured manually. Baggage context is not the only way to convey business context. OpenTelemetry has span attributes, and commercial observability provides its own approach.

Baggage is used primarily for search purposes in a trace, and it is recommended to search with the span attribute rather than baggage.

If your goal is a simple search, you'll want to lighten the header's load, so you'll want to use a different technique than baggage.

Baggage adds to the header, so it can make the header larger and negatively impact network traffic. The span attributes have no runtime impact as the header is not propagated; it's only used for transfer.

To summarize, baggage and `tracestate` can be applied to various purposes and propagated as headers. To search a trace, the span and request attributes are transferred to the backend storage.

The span attribute is difficult to apply to the entire E2E and can only be used for a specific span. Using automated and manual instrumentation, you can easily set the span attribute. Automated instrumentation using an agent can also easily add span attributes.

The development procedure for baggage is similar to the trace context and is processed as follows.

- A baggage is propagated through a textmap propagator. The propagator processes the extraction and injection of the context.

- A baggage is configured in the context, and you use get and set methods to process keys and values in the baggage.

Propagating a baggage on a message server is more complicated than propagating a baggage on HTTP. SQS servers can be configured with baggage, as shown here:

```
private void InjectContext(Message message, Activity? act)
{
    if (act != null)
    {
```

```
            PropagationContext context = new(act.Context, Baggage.Current);
             propagator.Inject(context, message,
                static (m, k, v) => m.Headers[k] = v);
    }
}
```

The Spring framework supports baggage, but it's common for it to support HTTP and not message servers.

3.2.5. OpenTracing Shim

The OpenTracing shim is a library that makes it easy to migrate from OpenTracing to OpenTelemetry.

This is useful if you have a large application with manually instrumented code. It can help perform the migration step by step because it allows the use of the legacy OpenTracing API on top of the new OpenTelemetry API.

Shim consists of a set of classes that implement the OpenTracing API and use OpenTelemetry configuration in the background. The purpose of these classes is to allow applications that are already instrumenting with OpenTracing to start using with minimal effort, without having to rewrite large portions of their code.

Shim processes the instrumentation, which is propagated in an OpenTracing format. Downstream, it uses the OpenTracing propagator.

```
@Path("/hello")
@ApplicationScoped
public class GreetingResource {

    @Inject
    io.opentracing.Tracer legacyTracer;

    @GET
    @Produces(MediaType.TEXT_PLAIN)
    @Traced(operationName = "Not needed, will change the current span name")
    public String hello() {
        // Add a tag to the active span
        legacyTracer.activeSpan().setTag(Tags.COMPONENT, "GreetingResource");

        // Create a manual inner span
        Span innerSpan = legacyTracer.buildSpan("Count response chars").start();

        try (Scope dbScope = legacyTracer.scopeManager().activate(innerSpan)) {
            String response = "Hello from REST";
            innerSpan.setTag("response-chars-count", response.length());
            return response;
```

```
        } catch (Exception e) {
            innerSpan.setTag("error", true);
            innerSpan.setTag("error.message", e.getMessage());
            throw e;
        } finally {
            innerSpan.finish();
        }
    }
}
```

It is an OpenTracing application with manual instrumentation.

- You need to remove the tracer annotation and insert OpenTelemetrySDK instead.

- The `@traced` annotation is replaced with the `@WithSpan` annotation, but note that this new annotation always creates a new span.

- You need to get an instance of the legacy tracer. Shim includes a utility class for this.

After making the changes, the code is compiled, and you can use the OpenTracing and OpenTelemetry APIs simultaneously.

```
@Path("/hello")
@ApplicationScoped
public class GreetingResource {

    @Inject
    io.opentelemetry.api.OpenTelemetry openTelemetry;

    @GET
    @Produces(MediaType.TEXT_PLAIN)
    @WithSpan(value = "Not needed, will create a new span, child of the automatic JAX-RS span")
    public String hello() {
        // Add a tag to the active span
        Tracer legacyTracer = OpenTracingShim.createTracerShim(openTelemetry);
        legacyTracer.activeSpan().setTag(Tags.COMPONENT, "GreetingResource");

        // Create a manual inner span
        Span innerSpan = legacyTracer.buildSpan("Count response chars").start();

        try (Scope dbScope = legacyTracer.scopeManager().activate(innerSpan)) {
            String response = "Hello from REST";
            innerSpan.setTag("response-chars-count", response.length());
            return response;
```

```
        } catch (Exception e) {
            innerSpan.setTag("error", true);
            innerSpan.setTag("error.message", e.getMessage());
            throw e;
        } finally {
            innerSpan.finish();
        }
    }
}
```

There are situations where it is difficult to use only OpenTelemetry. For example, when you are using a SaaS and it only supports OpenTracing and not OpenTelemetry. To propagate with the OpenTracing provided by the SaaS, you need to configure the global tracer of OpenTracing. In this case, I recommend using the OpenTracing Shim.

Commercial observability agents sometimes ds not accurately support OpenTracing Shim. Global tracers may not work, or unexpected instrumentation may occur. You might expect two spans should be created, but in some cases five spans are created. When using commercial observability only OpenTelemetry does not support OpenTracing Shim, which makes it difficult to configure traces.

You should configure it to prevent it from generating inaccurate spans, and analyze the profile to make sure it is instrumenting accurately.

If a span is invalid and it's instrumented incorrectly:

1. Use collectors to filter out specific spans.

2. Implement with manual instrumentation.

3. Exclude libraries that are instrumented by the OpenTelemetry agent.

4. If an unknown span is created by incorrect instrumentation, you need to apply a profile.

Analyze the methods instrumented with the profile. Identify the methods that are instrumented in your code and dependencies, and modify your code.

3.3. Propagating Managed Services

SaaS and managed services use externally provided services without building them. While this improves user convenience, managed services make it difficult to install agents, which makes it difficult to implement observability and trace.

There are many different types of middleware, and while many organizations use open source directly on-premises, they are increasingly migrating to managed services. Many managed services do not yet support OpenTelemetry.

CHAPTER 3 TRACE-CENTRIC RCA

Using observability within a managed service is appropriate, but managed service observability is isolated and difficult to connect with other external observability. You choose managed service observability because of price and reliability, but you end up paying more than you expected.

Trace prioritizes the instrumentation of clients over servers. Since you can't install an agent on a managed service, you need to instrument the client. In a microservices architecture, clients are upstream and developed as microservices, so you can configure observability. In this case, the managed service is upstream, propagating to downstream microservices. Transferring to an external observability backend is difficult. To propagate traces between distributed microservices, it is necessary to inject and extract them. If the API server and NoSQL are operated by a managed service, propagation and transfer are supported, but isolation can cause difficulties in configuring observability.

Managed services are limited in their ability to transfer. Using the AWS approach, you can use lambdas and CloudWatch logs for transfer.

1. Write the logs to CloudWatch.

2. Trigger the lambda and read the CloudWatch log.

3. The lambda can transfer.

Assuming you have a simple database, it makes a call to a downstream database and creates a span. The database is a server, but there is no instrumentation. It simply terminates with a request and response and creates only one span. As a result, it only measures the latency of the method.

- **API servers need two spans:** Inbound and outbound. Inbound is received from clients and outbound is sent to downstream microservices.

- **Message servers require two spans:** Publisher and subscriber. When a message server is instrumented, three spans are created: publisher, server, and subscriber.

Transferring to an external observability backend, such as an AWS API gateway, is not possible.

There are many restrictions on implementing propagation and transfer. Propagation and transfer are only within AWS.

Internal operations between threads must pass the trace context. If they don't, the trace is lost somewhere in the thread.

It is often not possible to generate a span, and this is not a big problem if you talk to the developer and agree on the span problem. Broken spans are an issue, not generating a span is not issue. It is not the goal of a distributed trace to generate a span for every segment. It is inefficient and expensive. Even if some spans are missing, you should strive to generate the correct span for critical sections and applications and configure E2E traces at a level that allows root cause analysis.

Managed services provide the ability to create and process events. For example, AWS lambdas can be used to capture events from a specific trigger. By capturing an event, you can transfer the trace context to an observability backend. The data to be transferred includes the trace ID, parent span ID, span ID, process start time, process end time, service name, and various other attributes to the observability backend. If your managed service does not provide the ability to propagate, you will need to modify microservices to add the trace context to the header. You should also propagate messages that are compatible with W3C formats.

CHAPTER 3   TRACE-CENTRIC RCA

The problems encountered when integrating trace into managed services are as follows:

- Propagating from RUM to a Managed Service API server
- Propagating from a Managed Service API server to microservices
- Transfer from a Managed Service API server to observability backend

Some commercial observability RUM solutions do not use distributed traces. It is similar to span, but does not follow the span format and is organized separately from distributed traces. In some cases, it is implemented by associating the internal ID of the RUM with the trace ID of the distributed trace. It may be difficult to connect RUM, managed service API servers, and microservices with traces. This is straightforward for traces between microservices, but there may be exceptions when connecting different technologies with traces.

As shown in Figure 3-7, it is normal for RUM, API servers, and microservices to generate spans at each interval. However, in commercial observability, you can see that RUM and API servers do not generate spans, and the trace starts in microservices.

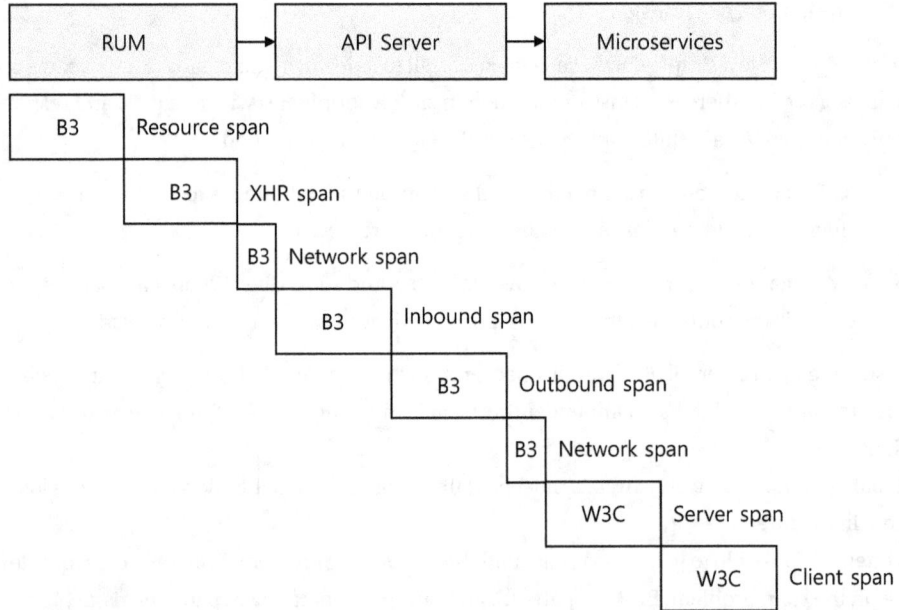

Figure 3-7. Propagating between different traces

If the trace format is different, you will experience difficulties in implementing propagation and transfer. If you use B3 for API servers and W3C headers for microservices, you will not be able to propagate. In such cases, you need to use a propagator.

Spans that are propagated must use headers from the same trace. If they use different headers, the appropriate propagator for the trace must be used.

If propagation fails, a new trace is created for each segment. If the trace fails to propagate in a particular span, the trace is aborted and disconnected. It is normal for a single trace ID to consist of multiple spans. However, if you create multiple separate trace ID, SRE analyzing the trace will experience confusion in understanding the context.

Managed services are less observable than you might think. If something goes wrong at the system resource level, it's hard to understand why. You need to design your application to supplement for the lack of observability.

Let's implement trace in managed services of AWS, GCP, and Azure.

3.3.1. AWS CloudFront Demo

CloudFront is a CDN. This demo is useful for connecting with API servers and various managed services. To conclude, the problem of converting between different trace signals is solved by configuring only a propagator.

This is a demonstration of propagating a trace context, for example, through a header between two services.

In Figure 3-8, the CloudFront uses B3 and the microservices use Spring Boot. Spring Boot is automatically instrumented using the OpenTelemetry agent. It identifies seven important behaviors in total.

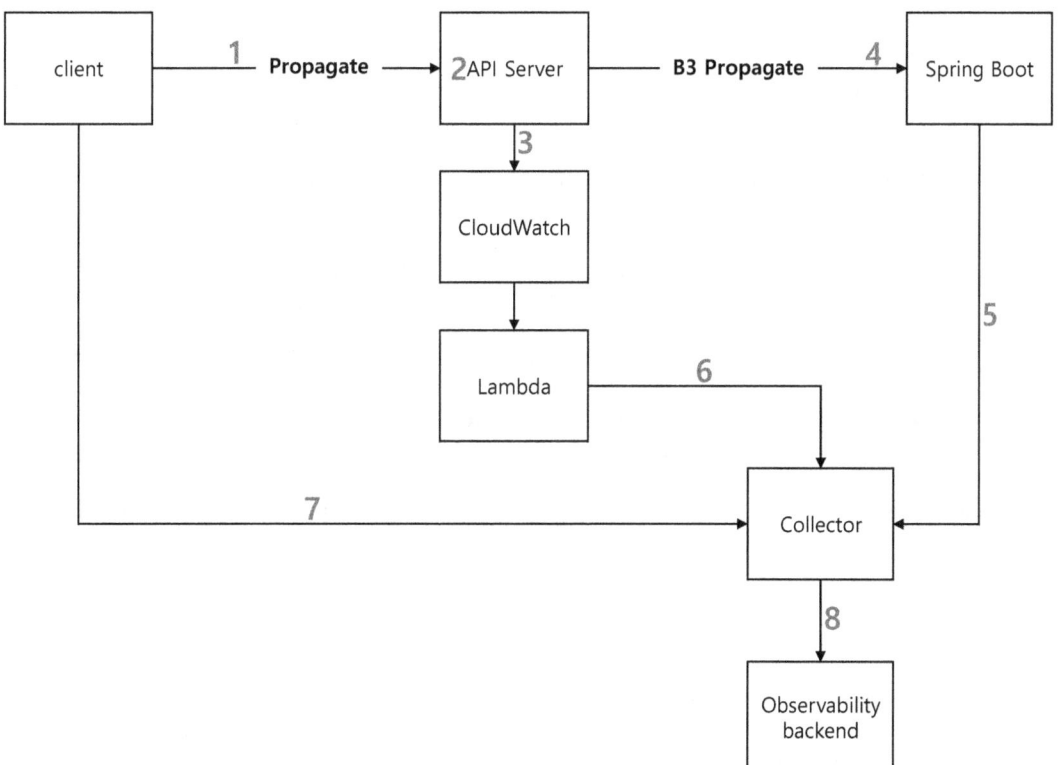

Figure 3-8. B3 Propagation flow

1. The client makes a request to CloudFront. CloudFront creates a new trace ID and span ID.

2. CloudFront propagates to B3 in the spring boot. It uses the already-created trace ID and creates new span ID.

3. CloudFront transfers to CloudWatch.

4. Spring Boot receives the B3 request. It uses the already created trace ID and creates a span ID. It uses the OpenTelemetry propagator to convert it internally to W3C.

5. Spring Boot transfers it to the OpenTelemetry collector.

6. Transfers from CloudWatch to the collector. It uses lambdas to collect events.

Two spans are created in CloudFront and Spring Boot within one trace ID. In the demo, the client does not create a trace. Sections 2 and 3 are the span to watch out for when implementing trace.

- Managed services like CloudFront natively support trace via AWS X-Ray, but not OpenTelemetry.
- Instead of tracing from CloudFront and the API server, you may want to trace from the client.

To meet these requirements, you can set up E2E trace with OpenTelemetry and additional development. Traces that start at the CloudFront are not E2E traces because latency and errors cannot be measured at the client. You need to develop transfer and propagation of your managed services.

- Using a propagator, you can solve the problem of propagation between different traces standard.
- It only supports AWS X-Ray, which makes it difficult to trace all the way through. Propagation can be accomplished by using the OpenTelemetry propagation API in CloudFront's script to configure the `traceparent` header. If transfer is an issue, you can use logs to solve this problem. Logs are easy to implement, so add the trace context to the logs. Using serverless methods, you can read the trace context from the log and send it to your backend observability.

Some load balancers, CDNs, and API servers that operate in the cloud can be scripted to augment their functionality. There is logic you can develop with scripts.

- **Propagate:** By creating a trace context, you can develop logic that propagates downstream.
- **Transfer:** After receiving a request from a client, it writes a log containing the request ID and the trace ID. Whenever a record with a new trace ID is written to the log, a FaaS-like lambda can trigger a change, transferring the trace context to external backend storage.

CHAPTER 3 TRACE-CENTRIC RCA

If the managed service supports distributed trace, OpenTelemetry B3-compliant messages can be transferred to the OpenTelemetry collector and downstream can use the OpenTelemetry B3 propagator to propagate trace context.

In addition to routing requests and responses, AWS CloudFront can implement additional propagation logic. Logic to propagate trace contexts downstream can be developed, as shown here:

- Create a trace context for the root span. The request ID generated by CloudFront, i.e., the `traceId` and `spanId` converted to hexadecimal strings, must be compatible with the B3 specification.

- The B3 `traceId` and `spanId` are attached to the header. The header is propagated to the OpenTelemetry JavaAgent.

- Set the sampling rate to 1. In production, set a ratio between 0 and 1 for performance.

When CloudFront returns a response to the end user, the response event is triggered. A log is generated with the CloudFront request ID, trace start time, trace end time, and a B3 propagate header.

- Write logs. Adding arbitrary attributes to the log can improve observability.

- Add the B3 header generated by the request to the response header.

Lambdas can be used to read the trace context of CloudWatch logs and transfer it to an external backend observability.

This demo is a simple Spring Boot controller. It uses a JavaAgent to process automated instrumentation. It receives a B3 propagate from CloudFront.

```
package com.example.demo;

import org.springframework.web.bind.annotation.GetMapping;
import org.springframework.web.bind.annotation.RestController;

@RestController
public class MainController {
    @GetMapping(path = "/")
    public String greet() {
        return "Hello World";
    }
}
```

To enable the OpenTelemetry JavaAgent, add the Java option when running the JAR file.

```
java -javaagent:/path/to/opentelemetry-agent.jar -jar app.jar
```

201

Inject the agent configuration as an environment variable:

- OTEL_EXPORTER_OTLP_ENDPOINT: The endpoint to which the OpenTelemetry JavaAgent transfers telemetry data. Configure the agent to transfer trace data to the OpenTelemetry collector via the gRPC protocol.
- OTEL_ TRACES_EXPORTER="otlp": The agent exports trace data in OpenTelemetry format.
- OTEL_PROPAGATORS="B3": The agent uses B3 to process the trace context in the request header.
- OTEL_ TRACES_SAMPLER="parentbased_always_off": The agent generates span data only if the preceding service turns on the sampling flag and transfers a trace context.

The collector is shown here:

```
receivers:
  otlp:
    protocols:
      grpc:
      http:
  jaeger: null
  prometheus: null
  zipkin: null
```

For managed services and black box type applications, it is useful to use the trace API and logs to generate spans. Use a log for areas where distributed trace instrumentation is difficult. It is recommended to apply traces only where the trace is possible and use a correlation of traces and logs for hard-to-trace areas.

It is useful to create a custom service after the profile to provide endpoints and create spans.

CloudFront and AWS API Gateway support a separate trace format called X-Ray. For transfer, the OpenTelemetry collector provides an X-Ray receiver, and for propagating, the OpenTelemetry agent supports an X-Ray propagator, so there is no problem processing traces. When using Micrometer traces, X-Ray, and OpenTelemetry W3C together, there may be conflicts between trace contexts. A single trace is recommended whenever possible.

3.3.2. GCP PubSub Demo

PubSub is used in event-driven applications, streaming analytics, and data integration pipelines that publish and receive messages. It is effective as a message-centric middleware for application integration.

Publishers communicate asynchronously with subscribers by broadcasting events rather than synchronous remote procedure calls.

The publisher publishes the event to the PubSub service, regardless of how or when the event is processed. PubSub then transfers the event to all services that subscribe to the event. PubSub's asynchronous integration increases the flexibility and robustness of the overall system.

PubSub is designed to scale horizontally; as the number of topics, subscriptions, or messages grows, it processes them by increasing the number of instances of the running server.

PubSub servers run in any Google cloud region in the world. This allows the service to provide fast, global data access and gives users control over where their messages are stored. PubSub provides global data access so that publishers and subscribers are unaware of the location of the servers they connect to or how data is routed through the service.

PubSub's load balancing mechanism directs traffic to the nearest Google cloud data center that is allowed to store data. Publishers from multiple regions can publish messages about a single topic with low latency. Individual messages are stored in a single region. However, a topic can have messages stored in multiple regions. When a subscriber requests a message topic, it contacts the nearest server for aggregation of data from topic and delivers it to the subscriber.

A PubSub message consists of fields with message data and metadata. You must specify one of the following in the message:

- **Message data:** This can be text or binary data. It represents the actual information you want to communicate between the publisher and subscriber. When using the REST API directly, the message data should be base64 encoded.

- **Order key:** This is an identifier that indicates which messages should be ordered. Messages with the same order key are transferred to subscribers in the order they were published. The order key is only needed if you want to transfer ordered messages.

- **Attribute:** This is an optional key and value pair that provides additional context and information about the message. The trace context is written to the attribute. They can be used to route, filter, and enrich message content. For example, you can add attributes such as a timestamp or transaction ID.

Figure 3-9 shows the trace for HTTP and Google PubSub.

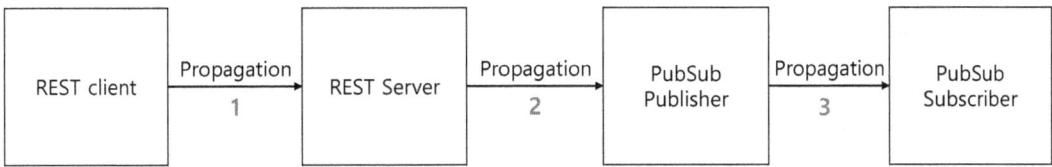

Figure 3-9. *GCP PubSub arc diagram*

CHAPTER 3   TRACE-CENTRIC RCA

One trace ID and multiple spans should be output:

- Make a REST request from the client to the server.
- Call the publisher.
- Call the subscriber.

Because the terminology can be confusing, I define the terms.

- Producers and publishers are referred to as publishers.
- Consumer and subscribers are referred to as subscribers.

REST calls are synchronous. The rest is processed as a PubSub event.

Asynchronous traces look like relay races. Within the same Golang service, traces are passed by ctx objects. Between services, traces are propagated by the traceparent HTTP header.

Per W3C standards, trace data is passed from the client to the server using HTTP headers.

traceparent: <version>-<trace-id>-<parent-id>-<trace-flags>

The header looks like this:

traceparent: 00-351772fff98e2108663b0d55f8eb5466-46158e065b2f87cb-01

- The trace version is 00.
- The trace ID is 351772fff98e2108663b0d55f8eb5466. This does not change during the lifecycle of the request.
- The parent's span ID is 46158e065b2f87cb. The span of the HTTP client that sent the request.
- The trace flag is 01. The only valid flag is 01, which means that the trace is sampled.

The E2E trace consists of the client, server, and PubSub:

- **Client-side:** HTTP clients can automatically serialize Go context objects with a trace header. When making a request, the HTTP client creates a new span using the URL as the span name.
- **Server-side:** Use Go Fiber. Fiber has middleware called otelfiber. This middleware automatically parses the trace header and creates a new span with the HTTP endpoint as the name. The new spans are stored in the fiber context (c *fiber.Ctx). You can convert the fiber context c to the Go context ctx by calling ctx = c.UserContext(). You can then create a child span from ctx. The span is created with the name /hello. In the helloWorld method, you create a child span named helloWorld.

CHAPTER 3 TRACE-CENTRIC RCA

- **PubSub trace:** Google PubSub does not provide a standard trace library, so you will need to develop your own manual instrumentation. For each message, you manually create a PubSub attribute called `traceparent`. Then, process the serialization and deserialization with your own library. Here is a demo for publishing a message:

```go
func BeforePublishMessage(ctx context.Context, tracer trace.Tracer, topicID string, msg *pubsub.Message) (context.Context, trace.Span) {
  opts := []trace.SpanStartOption{
    trace.WithSpanKind(trace.SpanKindProducer),
    trace.WithAttributes(
      semconv.MessagingSystemKey.String("pubsub"),
      semconv.MessagingDestinationKey.String(topicID),
      semconv.MessagingDestinationKindTopic,
    ),
  }
  ctx, span := tracer.Start(ctx, fmt.Sprintf("%s send", topicID), opts...)
  if msg.Attributes == nil {
    msg.Attributes = make(map[string]string)
  }

  otel.GetTextMapPropagator().Inject(ctx, propagation.MapCarrier(msg.Attributes))
  return ctx, span
}
func AfterPublishMessage(span trace.Span, messageID string, err error) {
  if err != nil {
    span.RecordError(err)
    span.SetStatus(codes.Error, err.Error())
  } else {
    span.SetAttributes(semconv.MessagingMessageIDKey.String(messageID))
  }
}
```

Trace in the header and publish the message.

```go
ctx, span := telemetry.BeforePublishMessage(ctx, tracer, topicName, &msg)
defer span.End()
messageID, err := topicObj.Publish(ctx, &msg).Get(ctx)
telemetry.AfterPublishMessage(span, messageID, err)
if err != nil {
  return err
}
```

205

CHAPTER 3   TRACE-CENTRIC RCA

This is a demo of subscribing to a message on a topic:

```go
type PubSubHandler = func(context.Context, *pubsub.Message)
func WrapPubSubHandlerWithTelemetry(tracer trace.Tracer, topicID string, handler PubSubHandler) PubSubHandler {
  return func(ctx context.Context, msg *pubsub.Message) {

    ctx, span := beforePubSubHandlerInvoke(ctx, tracer, topicID, msg)
    defer span.End()

    handler(ctx, msg)
  }
}
func beforePubSubHandlerInvoke(ctx context.Context, tracer trace.Tracer, topicID string, msg *pubsub.Message) (context.Context, trace.Span) {
  if msg.Attributes != nil {

    propagator := otel.GetTextMapPropagator()
    log.Info().Msg("Extracing traceparent from message attribute")
    ctx = propagator.Extract(ctx, propagation.MapCarrier(msg.Attributes))
  }
  opts := []trace.SpanStartOption{
    trace.WithSpanKind(trace.SpanKindConsumer),
    trace.WithAttributes(

      semconv.FaaSTriggerPubsub,
      semconv.MessagingSystemKey.String("pubsub"),
      semconv.MessagingDestinationKey.String(topicID),
      semconv.MessagingDestinationKindTopic,
      semconv.MessagingOperationProcess,
      semconv.MessagingMessageIDKey.String(msg.ID),
    ),
  }
  return tracer.Start(ctx, fmt.Sprintf("%s process", topicID), opts...)
}
```

The system configuration looks like this:

```
wget https://golang.org/dl/go1.18.1.linux-amd64.tar.gz
tar -xvf go1.18.1.linux-amd64.tar.gz

export GOROOT=/root/go
export GOPATH=/root/go/workspace
```

CHAPTER 3   TRACE-CENTRIC RCA

```
export PATH=$GOROOT/bin:/root/go/workspace/bin:$PATH
gcloud config set project infra-voyage-417702
export GOOGLE_APPLICATION_CREDENTIALS=
```

Build the application:

```
go build
```

Download the OpenTelemetry collector:

```
wget https://github.com/open-telemetry/opentelemetry-collector-releases/releases/download/v0.90.0/otelcol-contrib_0.90.0_linux_amd64.tar.gz
```

The configuration of the OpenTelemetry collector is shown here:

```
./otelcol-contrib --config developer.values.yaml
receivers:
  otlp:
    protocols:
      grpc:
      http:
exporters:
  logging:
    loglevel: debug
service:
  pipelines:
    traces:
      receivers: [otlp]
      exporters: [logging]
```

Configure the GCP SDK:

```
curl -O https://dl.google.com/dl/cloudsdk/channels/rapid/downloads/google-cloud-cli-468.0.0-linux-x86_64.tar.gz
tar -xf google-cloud-cli-468.0.0-linux-x86_64.tar.gz
./google-cloud-sdk/install.sh
./google-cloud-sdk/bin/gcloud init
```

Define the following environment variables:

```
gcloud config set project
export GOOGLE_APPLICATION_CREDENTIALS=
export GOOGLE_CLOUD_PROJECT=
gcloud components install pubsub-emulator
gcloud beta emulators pubsub start --project=
```

207

CHAPTER 3　TRACE-CENTRIC RCA

Now you can see the results of three spans. Here is the span for the REST request, which generates a trace ID:

```
InstrumentationScope github.com/gofiber/contrib/otelfiber semver:1.9.0
Span #0
    Trace ID           : 423c0359495a291950233be9dbcc8c2c
    Parent ID          :
    ID                 : 373c1356d9868163
    Name               : /publish
    Kind               : Server
    Start time         : 2024-03-25 22:55:37.853640892 +0000 UTC
    End time           : 2024-03-25 22:55:38.445027127 +0000 UTC
    Status code        : Unset
    Status message     :
Attributes:
     -> http.server_name: Str(api a)
     -> http.method: Str(POST)
     -> http.target: Str(/publish)
     -> http.url: Str(/publish)
     -> net.host.ip: Str(127.0.0.1)
     -> net.host.name: Str(localhost:3000)
     -> http.user_agent: Str(curl/7.68.0)
     -> http.request_content_length: Int(0)
     -> http.scheme: Str(http)
     -> net.transport: Str(ip_tcp)
     -> http.route: Str(/publish)
     -> http.status_code: Int(200)
    {"kind": "exporter", "data_type": "traces", "name": "logging"}
```

Here is the span for the publisher:

```
InstrumentationScope api-a
Span #0
    Trace ID           : 423c0359495a291950233be9dbcc8c2c
    Parent ID          : 373c1356d9868163
    ID                 : b65f1f3a552500a4
    Name               : source-topic send
    Kind               : Producer
    Start time         : 2024-03-25 22:55:38.285601061 +0000 UTC
    End time           : 2024-03-25 22:55:38.445015525 +0000 UTC
    Status code        : Unset
    Status message     :
```

CHAPTER 3   TRACE-CENTRIC RCA

Attributes:
     -> messaging.system: Str(pubsub)
     -> messaging.destination: Str(source-topic)
     -> messaging.destination_kind: Str(topic)
     -> messaging.message_id: Str(10789653045798033) InstrumentationScope api-b
Span #0
     Trace ID   : 423c0359495a291950233be9dbcc8c2c
     Parent ID   : b65f1f3a552500a4
     ID   : 388e79312451b0af
     Name   : source-topic process
     Kind   : Consumer
     Start time   : 2024-03-25 22:55:39.462594576 +0000 UTC
     End time   : 2024-03-25 22:55:39.462635945 +0000 UTC
     Status code   : Unset
     Status message :
Attributes:
     -> faas.trigger: Str(pubsub)
     -> messaging.system: Str(pubsub)
     -> messaging.destination: Str(source-topic)
     -> messaging.destination_kind: Str(topic)
     -> messaging.operation: Str(process)
     -> messaging.message_id: Str(10789653045798033)
     {"kind": "exporter", "data_type": "traces", "name": "logging"}

This is the span for the subscriber. One trace ID creates three spans.

InstrumentationScope api-b
Span #0
     Trace ID   : 423c0359495a291950233be9dbcc8c2c
     Parent ID   : b65f1f3a552500a4
     ID   : 388e79312451b0af
     Name   : source-topic process
     Kind   : Consumer
     Start time   : 2024-03-25 22:55:39.462594576 +0000 UTC
     End time   : 2024-03-25 22:55:39.462635945 +0000 UTC
     Status code   : Unset
     Status message :
Attributes:
     -> faas.trigger: Str(pubsub)
     -> messaging.system: Str(pubsub)
     -> messaging.destination: Str(source-topic)
     -> messaging.destination_kind: Str(topic)

```
    -> messaging.operation: Str(process)
    -> messaging.message_id: Str(10789653045798033)
   {"kind": "exporter", "data_type": "traces", "name": "logging"}
```

Manual instrumentation is a development process and needs guidelines. For this purpose, OpenTelemetry provides the OpenTelemetry Semantic Conventions. It is recommended that manual instrumentation and extension development adhere to the semantic conventions.

Within the same service, traces are carried by `ctx` objects. Between services, traces are passed by the `traceparent` header.

Create a source-topic topic for the publisher and a source-subscription for the subscriber. PubSub is the server, and the publishers and subscribers are the clients. So far, you have not instrumented the server but the client. The OpenTelemetry collector supports GCP PubSub, which allows you to create a server-side span, allowing the GCP PubSub server to operate as a white box. Check out the headers of a message published without a subscriber in Figure 3-10; you can see the trace context.

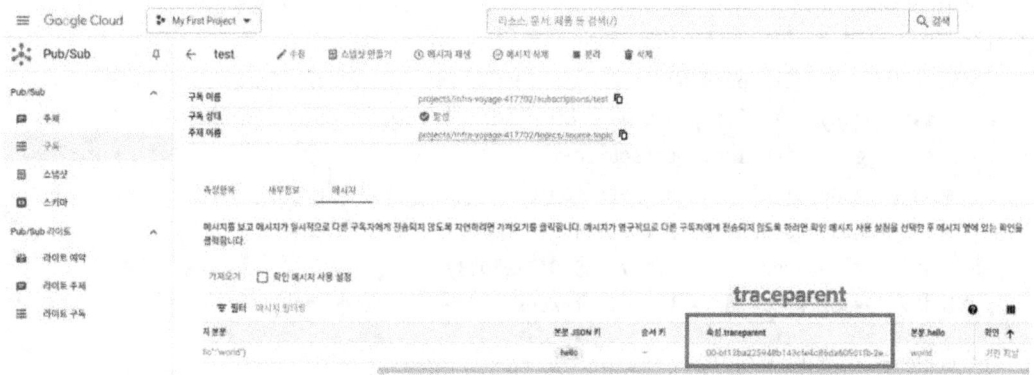

Figure 3-10. *Viewing trace results in the GCP*

The process after the backend microservices is called the *backoffice*. Message servers can be used backend microservices and the backoffice.

The traditional backoffice processes use batch schedulers and shell scripts, which makes it difficult to configure traceability and observability. However, by using a message server, E2E trace is possible, and it has the advantage of real-time processing.

You can use a variety of technologies to process the backoffice, but the recommended method is to use a message server. This allows you to organize E2E traces from frontend microservices, backend microservices, and backoffices.

There are two ways to process batches using the message server.

- How individual messages are published and subscribed
- How to bundle, publish, and subscribe multiple messages

When processing individual messages, add an attribute that records the identifier and batch size of all messages received. You need to create a trace per message and inject a unique trace context into each message.

You may want to aggregate data for analytics purposes, replicate subscribed data, or process it in batches. In these cases, it is not possible to process individual messages separately. The situation is further complicated in scenarios where a subscribed batch is split into multiple new batches, which are transferred to the next destination.

Using the span link, you can record the relationship so that you know if the message was received and what process it contributed to.

By default, it creates a batch processing trace that contains link to all the messages being processed. The link have attributes, and you can put important message metadata, such as delivery count, message ID, or inject time.

Message and batch processing is often performed by message client library frameworks. It is rarely possible to trace or measure the process calls through automated instrumentation. These scenarios vary widely from application to application, requiring manual instrumentation tailored to the specific use case and message system.

3.3.3. Azure SQS Demo

This section describes a demonstration of manual instrumentation of Azure SQS.

3.3.3.1. Instrumenting Your Publisher

The publisher is the component that is responsible for publishing messages to the broker. The sending a request to the broker and receiving a response from the broker indicating whether the message was successfully published is typically synchronous.

Depending on the messaging system and the publisher's needs, one publish request may contain one or more messages.

To trace this, you can trace the duration and status of the call when the message is published and debug individual requests.

3.3.3.2. Propagating the Trace Context

The context in the message should be propagated through the message header so that it can be propagated to subscribers.

You need to propagate the context of the message header so that it is passed on to the subscriber.

When you publish a message to a broker, you can uniquely identify the trace and the dispatch. A message is a payload with no prescribed structure or format that is delivered by the service. The `header` attribute is used to propagate the trace context, and the payload is kept in the `text` attribute.

CHAPTER 3 TRACE-CENTRIC RCA

3.3.3.3. Trace Publishers

To identify the broker, queue, and add other information, you need to create a new trace and put the message attributes in it.

It then injects context into the message and proceeds to publish it. If the message is successfully published, you can also record the information (message ID) returned by the broker. Use the Inject method to do so.

3.3.3.4. Trace Subscribers

Start by tracing individual messages to record when they arrive at your subscribers and how they are processed. This helps you debug problems by answering questions like, "Where is this message now?" or "Why did it take so long to process the data?"

- Request one or more messages from a queue. This processes the messages and deletes them from the queue when finished. If the process fails due to a temporary problem, the application does not delete the message.

- Instead of the application polling the queue, it can push messages to subscribers in response to client library callbacks. With callback-based transfers, the client library can provide the instrumentation, but with the polling-based model, you must write at least some manual instrumentation for the process by default.

- Instrument the message processing separately from the subscriber. Create traces to capture everything that happens in the process, including message deletions. Message deletions and changes are traced through SQS instrumentation.

- Extract context from the message and use it as the parent of the trace. Keep the link to maintain correlation. When a message is subscribed to and the processing is about to end, you can add a link to the message's trace context at that time.

- If too many messages are coming into the queue, and they're being produced faster than they're being consumed, the spacing of individual traces might suggest that the messages are spending time in the queue, but you can't know for sure. For individual message latencies, and for aggregations of latencies, also you can use metrics to see how quickly messages are published, processed, and deleted. You need to know how long messages stay in the queue and the size of the queue.

Now that you have an idea of how to instrument it, this application runs one publisher and three subscribers with observability.

When you send a request to a publisher at `http://localhost:5051/send`, it sends one message to the queue and returns the received information in response.

As you increase the number of subscribers, you can see how the metrics change. How do you know if your subscribers are working properly? You can start with subscriber latency and queueing metrics. Understand how many messages are waiting in queues on your message server and how long it takes for subscribers to read and process them. Topics are harder to monitor than queues. If you're using topics like Kafka, it's hard to understand the exact problem by looking at the number of messages waiting in a topic. You need to monitor the offsets per subscriber to make sure the distribution is even across multiple subscribers.

Now add an error by sending an invalid message to http://localhost:5051/send?malformed=true. Over time, you'll see the subscriber latency increase. You can see that the message is being subscribed to, processed, and failed repeatedly.

You can see that it tries to subscribe to messages about four times per second. Three of these attempts do not return a message, and the other one fails to process.

Open Jaeger (http://localhost:16686) and filter for traces with errors from subscribers.

You can see that four messages were subscribed and failed with errors. If you could add a link to this action, you would be able to navigate the trace for each individual message. In addition to the span link, you also use the message ID as a span attribute. Using this attribute, you can find the trace for one of these messages and analyze the problem in detail.

Based on this demonstration, the architecture in Figure 3-11 can be configured.

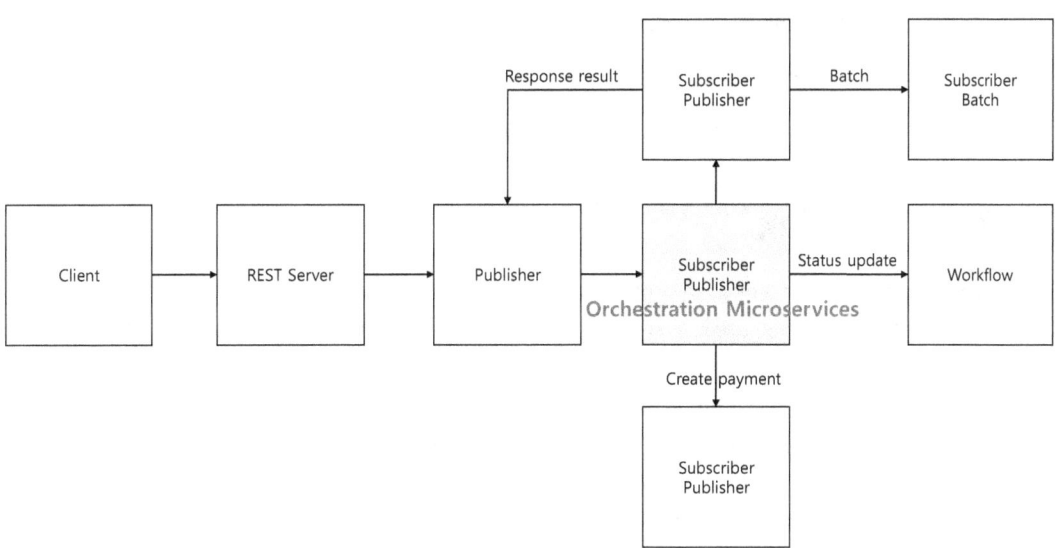

Figure 3-11. *Propagation of an Azure SQS span*

With the introduction of microservices, you'll often see architectural configurations like the one shown in Figure 3-11. The backend of the architecture is communicating via messages.

- Among the various microservices, the core are the microservices that perform orchestration. Orchestration microservices are loosely coupled with various microservices to update the state, execute batches, respond to results, and append key data. In Figure 3-11, the publisher plays the role of orchestration. The non-blocking and loosely coupled structure of the message server helps microservices isolate failures, prevents them from propagating, and ensures that the service can continue even if a microservice fails. Of course, if orchestration itself goes down, all services have the potential to go down.

- While REST server metrics include throughput, error rate, availability, and latency, message-based orchestration microservices require different metrics. With queues, you measure the number of pending messages, and with topics, you measure the LAG of subscribers with offsets. Certain queues and topics can be unusually large if they are not evenly distributed across publishers. For topics, it is difficult to measure the metric, but if there is no offset, it is a good idea to compare the throughput of publishers and subscribers.

This adds complexity to configuring a new layer of cross concerns in the header. Due to the nature of the implementation, all microservices and technology stacks propagate through the header, and cross concerns must be configured in the header. This involves adding an ID to the header and, if necessary, adding the ID in the message body to the header.

If you have a complex structure of queues and topics like the previous example, add the ID:

- Relationships between span require a parent span ID.
- The subscriber's span must have a link configured to the publisher's span.
- Add the message or service ID to the span's attribute.

3.3.3.5. Span Link

When routing messages to a queue, the upstream service may have an existing trace context injected into it. The default behavior in this case is to keep the context and propagate it. To correlate what happens to the message, you can add a link to the existing trace context of the message when publishing or subscribing to it.

Links allow a span to have multiple parents or provide another way to relate to multiple other spans at once. Without links, a span can only have one parent and multiple children and cannot be associated with spans from other traces.

Links are used in message server scenarios to represent receiving or processing multiple messages at once.

- When processing multiple messages, you need to extract the trace context and create a link from each message.
- You can then pass a collection of link.

Observability backends support links in different ways, so you may need to adjust your instrumentation based on your backend capabilities.

Span links do not connect broken traces; they explicitly define the relationship between spans.

When applied to a data pipeline, span links allow for the visualization of complex span structures. A span can have zero or more span links that are causally connected to other spans.

```
from opentelemetry import trace

tracer = trace.get_tracer(__name__)

with tracer.start_as_current_span("span-1"):

    ctx = trace.get_current_span().get_span_context()
    link_from_span_1 = trace.Link(ctx)

with tracer.start_as_current_span("span-2", links=[link_from_span_1]):
    pass
```

References output a span link, as shown in Figure 3-12.

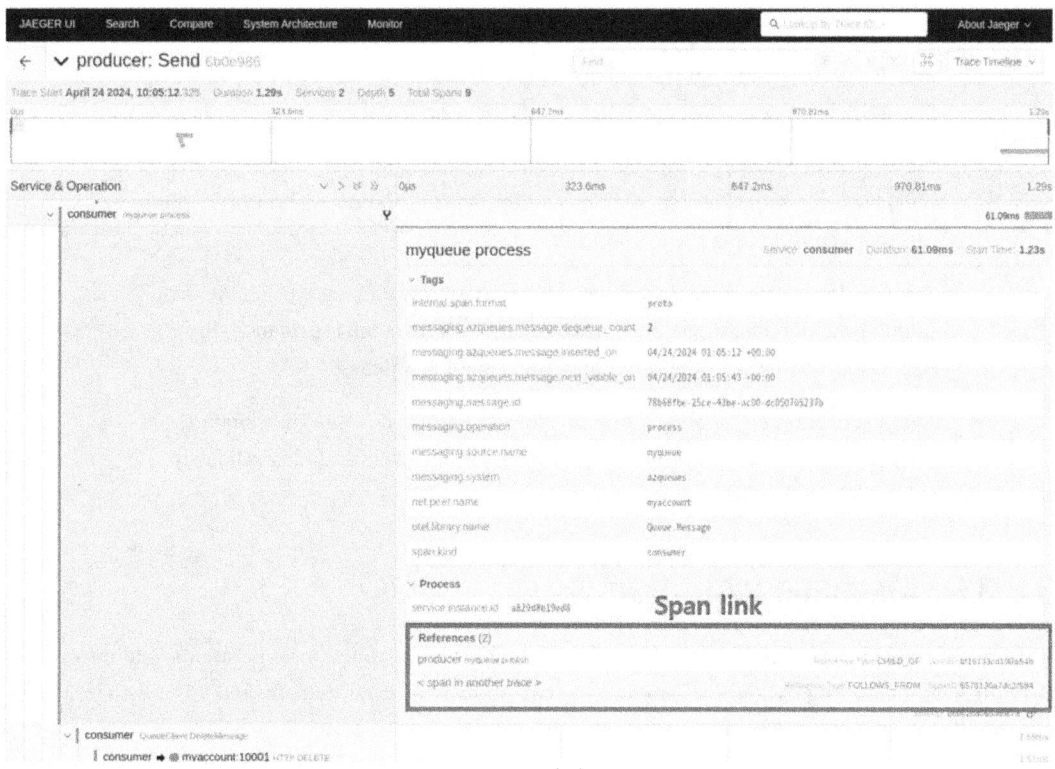

Figure 3-12. *A span link in a trace*

Chapter 3   Trace-Centric RCA

The message outputs the span link as shown here:

```
"traceID": "6b0e986eb1fa393aba0cf74ccede8884",
"spanID": "ee1f1372009db420",
"operationName": "HTTP POST",
"references": [
    {
        "refType": "CHILD_OF",
        "traceID": "6b0e986eb1fa393aba0cf74ccede8884",
        "spanID": "bf16133cd100a54b"
    }
],
```

Span links are great for scenarios where multiple jobs are combined into a single span. The single span is then split back into multiple spans. Links are useful for data pipelines that use asynchronous message servers and real-time streaming.

- **Map Reduce:** A span link correlates multiple parallel processes that are combined into a single process. The span link outputs the results of these parallel processes.

- **Message aggregation:** In systems like Kafka Stream, Span links correlate each message in a group of messages to an aggregated result, showing how individual messages contribute to the final output.

- **Transactional messages:** In scenarios where multiple messages using message queuing are part of a single transaction, span links correlate the relationship between each message and the overall transactional process.

- **Event sourcing:** The span link in event sourcing traces how multiple change messages contribute to the current state of an entity. Event sourcing is heavily utilized in this book.

3.3.3.6. Message Identifiers

Figure 3-13 should be improved by using links to trace subscription and process iterations, adding an attribute with the message ID received, so that you can find all the spans that affected this message. More observability backends are providing better support for links.

CHAPTER 3   TRACE-CENTRIC RCA

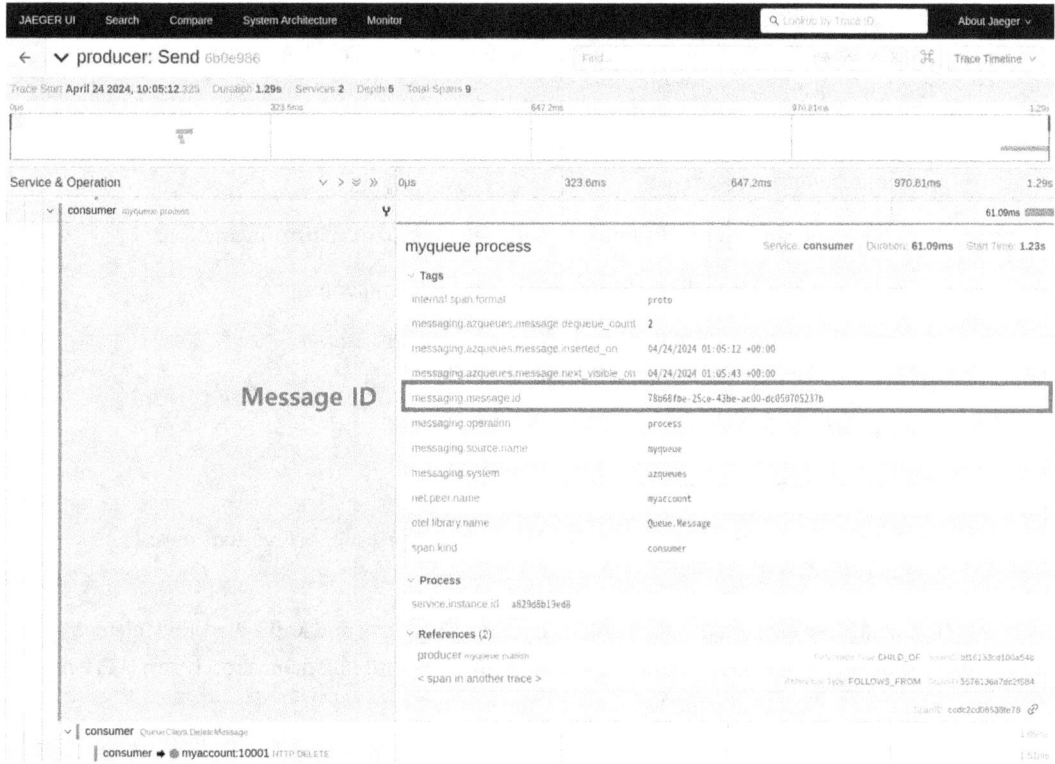

Figure 3-13. *Span attribute in a trace*

Message IDs correlate between publisher and subscriber and allow you to see how long the entire E2E process step. This lets you know if a subscriber is up and running, receiving and processing messages. To make it easy to find all the actions related to a particular message, you should be able to print the `messaging.message.id` attribute to span and identify it.

3.4. Propagating Message Services

Message servers are used to loosely couple systems and improve reliability. Because there are many types of message servers, instrumentation is often impossible. The SRE should understand and provide solutions for automated and manual instrumentation of message servers.

Message servers based on event-driven are flexible and scalable, but implementing traces is difficult.

Microservices are introduced, and message servers are widely used for event-driven and real-time processes. Message servers are also applied to CQRS, batches, and pipelines. For observability, it is difficult for the SRE to be in charge of traces. Since the event-driven pattern emphasizes flexibility, there are many different types of message servers for various purposes, which makes observability difficult. The list of message servers is as follows:

CHAPTER 3   TRACE-CENTRIC RCA

- IBM MQ provides instrumentation on the EAI server. MQ supports various platforms and development languages, including mainframe OS390 Cobol, AS400 RPG, and Tandem nonstop server TAL.

- WebSocket PubSub is a manual instrumentation in Java. It is used for two-way communication, such as chat.

- This book doesn't cover Redis PubSub, but it requires manual instrumentation.

- GCP PubSub was manually instrumented with a high temperature.

- OpenTelemetry supports Rabbit MQ.

- MQTT manual instrumentation is developed in Python. It is used in devices such as IoT.

- Azure SQS was instrumented manually.

- Spring cloud streams are supported by OpenTelemetry. It supports various message servers.

IBM MQ and JMS are explained in the banking demo in Chapter 4, and Kafka the OpenTelemetry are explained in the demo in Chapter 5. The GCP PubSub, Azure SQS, and JMS demos receive an HTTP request from a user and trace it through the publisher, topic, and subscriber to see the E2E trace.

In the past, we used MQ, but now there are too many open sources. SRE and architects should work together to set standards.

Kafka and JMS can create spans from publishers and subscribers.

- Kafka is mainly used for real-time data pipelines and event processing in microservices. Compared to other message servers, it is easily scalable and performs well.

- Kafka has four components. They are the broker, the topic, the publisher, and the subscriber.

- OpenTelemetry currently supports Kafka and generates traces.

OpenTelemetry supports JMS. JMS is used for application integration. While Kafka is widely used large cluster in cloud environments, legacy enterprise environments typically use JMS. It has the following components, which can be automatically instrumented using the OpenTelemetry JavaAgent.

- Message server

- Queues and topics

- Publisher

- Subscriber

JMS creates two spans—publisher and subscriber—but you can measure latency in queues and topics with metrics.

- Publisher's duration
- In a topic within the broker
- Subscriber's latency

JMS is a standard, and the API and specification are defined by Java, which means that developers use the same API to develop the client, so the code for developing JMS clients is the same. However, there are no restrictions on developing a JMS server. TIBCO EMS is developed in C, and vendor develops a JMS server that complies with the JMS standard specification in a different way. Due to this different internal structure, instrumentation of JMS servers is challenging. A prerequisite for automated instrumentation is that the client API is always the same, without any changes.

Therefore, except for the JMS server, including the queue, only the publisher and subscriber are instrumented, and spans are often created. Even if the server is not instrumented, the publisher and subscriber spans exist, so the latency waiting on the server can be approximated.

3.4.1. Solace JMS Demo

In addition to asynchronous communication, publishers and subscribers interact through a broker, which further complicates the situation.

Instead of waiting for the subscriber to process the message, once the message is sent to the broker, the work for the publisher is done. Depending on the scenario and application state, the subscriber can process it immediately, hours later, or days later.

Using OpenTelemetry spans and metrics for the broker are created. Previously, only the client created the span, but it can be configured so that the span and metrics of the server are created through server instrumentation.

- In addition to client instrumentation, server instrumentation is also required.
  Inbound is a server on the API server. Subscriptions are important for EAI servers because inbound is the server.
- The outbound is the client.

Basically, the publisher doesn't know if the subscriber exists, so any failure or latency in the pipeline is invisible to the publisher, which changes the way they look at latency, throughput, or error rate.

For example, if you only use HTTP calls, the latency of a request includes almost everything that happened with the request.

With the introduction of message servers, you need to measure E2E latency and identify failures between different components. For example, a real-time subscriber processes the latest messages, while a batch subscriber processes messages that were published a long time ago. In this case, the batch subscriber will have a long latency, and the real-time subscriber will have a small latency, but the long latency should raise suspicion of failure.

CHAPTER 3 TRACE-CENTRIC RCA

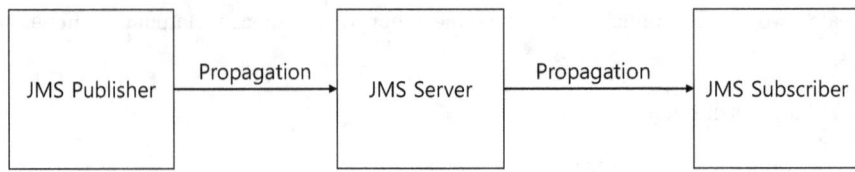

Figure 3-14. *Solace JMS service flowchart*

In Figure 3-14, the JMS message server is being processed as a white box. It generates only two spans: publisher and subscriber. But by tracing the JMS server as a white box, you can generate four spans. This principle applies to the GCP PubSub server, the Kafka broker, and the JMS server.

Even with OpenTelemetry's automated instrumentation, you can add span attributes and events. The latest automated instrumentation supports features that were previously only available with manual instrumentation. More features are being added to automated instrumentation.

You can configure Solace using the CLI, as shown here.

```
docker exec -it 2ee0ebc54b8f /usr/sw/loads/currentload/bin/cli -A
```

You need to check the trace context in the header of the JMS message. To demonstrate JMS, this example uses the Solace server.

```
receivers:
  otlp:
    protocols:
      grpc:

  solace:
    broker: [solbroker:5672]
    max_unacknowledged: 500
    auth:
      sasl_plain:
        username: trace
        password: trace
    queue: queue://#telemetry-trace
    tls:
      insecure: true
      insecure_skip_verify: true
```

Here's the result of the subscriber's execution:

```
# java -javaagent:opentelemetry-javaagent.jar -Dotel.javaagent.extensions=solace-opentelemetry-jms-integration-1.1.0.jar -Dotel.propagators=solace_jms_tracecontext -Dotel.traces.exporter=otlp -Dotel.metrics.exporter=none -Dotel.
```

CHAPTER 3   TRACE-CENTRIC RCA

instrumentation.jms.enabled=true -Dotel.resource.attributes="service.name= SolaceJMSQueueSubscriber" -Dsolace.host=localhost:55557 -Dsolace.vpn=default -Dsolace.user= default -Dsolace.password=default -Dsolace.queue=q -Dsolace.topic=solace/tracing -jar solace-queue-receiver.jar

```
Destination:                          Topic 'solace/tracing'
AppMessageID:                         ID:fe80:0:0:0:6641:d749:dba:9076%ens3380b318e
                                      eb6058e70:0
SendTimestamp:                        1713345943955 (수 4월 17 2024 18:25:43.955)
Priority:                             4
Class Of Service:                     USER_COS_1
DeliveryMode:                         PERSISTENT
Message Id:                           17
User Property Map:                    1 entries
  Key 'JMSXUserID' (String): default

Replication Group Message ID:         rmid1:30fc6-908abb10544-00000000-00000011
Tracing TransportContext:             {traceId=a3ca102ad6f675c8ff707910f0a220e2,
                                      spanId=e86b0c21aa07c345, sampled=true, traceState=}
Tracing CreationContext:              {traceId=a3ca102ad6f675c8ff707910f0a220e2,
                                      spanId=529b2367f3dd8fe8, sampled=true, traceState=}
XML:                                  len=12
  48 65 6c 6c 6f 20 77 6f   72 6c 64 21              Hello.world!
```

You can see that TransportContext and CreationContext have been added.

Here's the result of the publisher's execution:

java -javaagent:opentelemetry-javaagent.jar -Dotel.javaagent.extensions=solace-opentelemetry-jms-integration-1.1.0.jar -Dotel.propagators=solace_jms_tracecontext -Dotel.exporter.otlp.endpoint=http://localhost:4317 -Dotel.traces.exporter=otlp -Dotel.metrics.exporter=none -Dotel.instrumentation.jms.enabled=true -Dotel.resource.attributes="service.name=SolaceJMSPublisher" -Dsolace.host=localhost:55557 -Dsolace.vpn=default -Dsolace.user=default -Dsolace.password=default -Dsolace.topic=solace/tracing -jar solace-publisher.jar

You need to understand the meaning of the output in Figure 3-15.

- Create four spans. In conjunction with the OpenTelemetry collector, the Solace server can be monitored as a white box.

- Using automated instrumentation, the instrumentation and propagation are processed.

- The publisher and subscriber are displayed without any break, which means that the propagation was successfully processed.

CHAPTER 3   TRACE-CENTRIC RCA

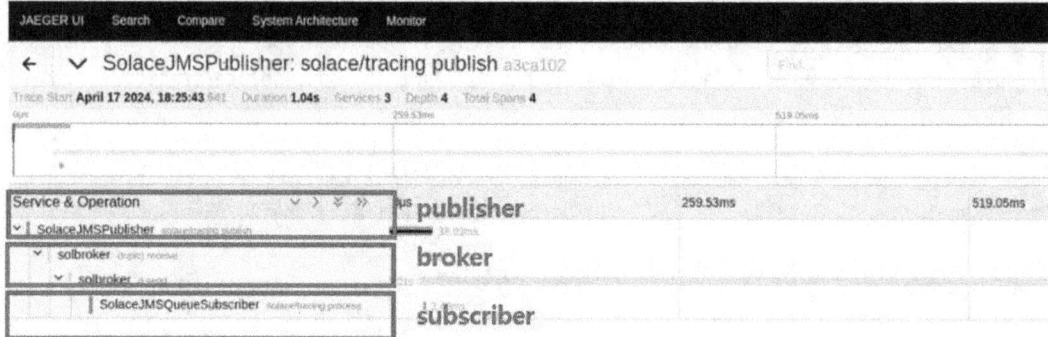

Figure 3-15. *Propagation of a Solace JMS span*

- The Solace demo uses the JavaAgent extension and the OpenTelemetry Collector.
- It consists of one publisher and one subscriber.
- To see the result, you need to check the trace ID and parent's span ID in the traceparent in the message header.

Figure 3-16 shows a span generated at several points, including the publisher, broker server, and the subscriber, and transferred to the OpenTelemetry collector.

Using OpenTelemetry, metrics are created for the broker.

Traditionally, only clients generate spans and configure server instrumentation to generate spans and metrics for the server.

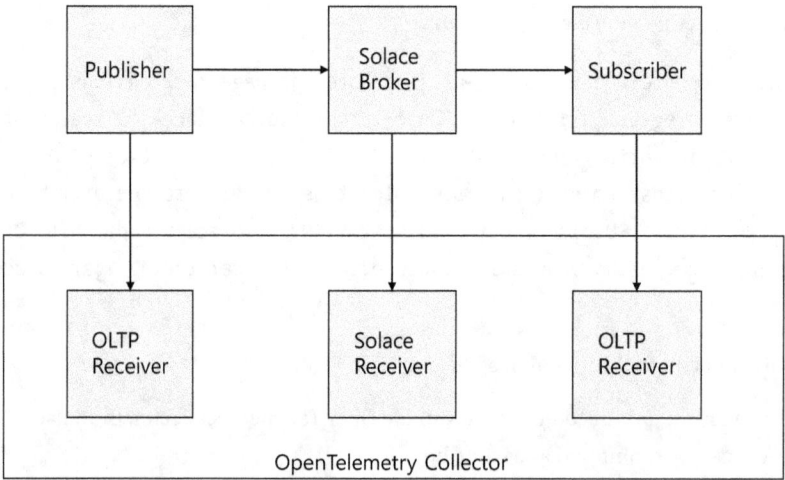

Figure 3-16. *Transferring between Solace and OpenTelemetry collectors*

3.4.2. TIBCO JMS Demo

You need server instrumentation and client instrumentation. The API server is inbound, it is the server; when outbound, it is the client. On an EAI server, subscriptions are inbound, and it is server.

The OpenTelemetry agent is an automated instrumentation and supports TIBCO EMS's JMS service. Configure the trace context in the JMS message header like the Kafka message header. Run the publisher.

```
java -javaagent:opentelemetry-javaagent.jar -Dotel.service.name=Producer -Dotel.traces.
exporter=otlp -Dotel.exporter.otlp.protocol=http/protobuf -Dotel.logs.exporter=none -Dotel.
metrics.exporter=none tibjmsMsgProducer -server localhost:7222 -queue "test.queue" test
```

Run the subscribers:

```
java -javaagent:opentelemetry-javaagent.jar -Dotel.service.name=Consumer -Dotel.traces.
exporter=otlp -Dotel.exporter.otlp.protocol=http/protobuf -Dotel.logs.exporter=none -Dotel.
metrics.exporter=none tibjmsMsgProducer -server localhost:7222 -queue "test.queue" test
```

The collector's configuration file is shown here:

```
receivers:
  otlp:
    protocols:
      grpc:
        endpoint: 0.0.0.0:4317
      http:
        endpoint: 0.0.0.0:4318
processors:
  batch:

exporters:
  logging:
    loglevel: debug

service:
  pipelines:
    traces:
      receivers: [otlp]
      processors: [batch]
      exporters: [logging]
    metrics:
      receivers: [otlp]
      processors: [batch]
      exporters: [logging]
```

CHAPTER 3   TRACE-CENTRIC RCA

```
logs:
  receivers: [otlp]
  processors: [batch]
  exporters: [logging]
```

Sometimes, automated instrumentation fails or does not perform as intended, so interpretation of the results is important. When validating span, considerations include:

- Check the contents of the header and make sure it propagates correctly. If propagation fails, check whether the trace is broken or interrupted. Propagation between distributed microservices is automated instrumented, and if automated instrumentation is not supported, it is developed by manual instrumentation. Automate the additional developed logic and manual instrumentation with extensions.

- Check for unexpected latency in span.

- Check the exceptions and errors raised in the trace.

- You need to check for uninstrumented and missing threads and spans.

- Identify the difference in the span between commercial observability and OpenTelemetry. Add propagators and `tracestates` to interface with other trace standards.

- Analyze whether attributes need to be added or whether context enrichment is needed.

Manual instrumentation requires a lot of labor to develop, so it should be analyzed carefully and designed to avoid manual instrumentation as much as possible.

Figure 3-17 shows that to determine whether a trace has propagated, you need to check the headers of the message for `traceparent` and `x-`. If there are other headers, you should check with the developer.

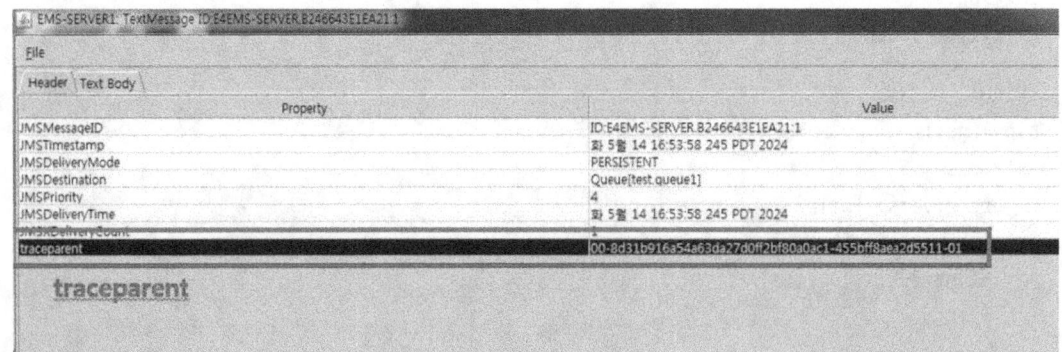

Figure 3-17. Checking the JMS header

TIBCO EMS and Solace demos support OpenTelemetry. Spring JMS is also supported. This is because it is not a vendor's independent protocol, but supports the standard.

As shown in Figure 3-17, you should check the `traceparent` header, troubleshoot the trace step by step, and check the trace ID output to the OpenTelemetry Collector.

3.4.3. MQTT Demo

MQTT is a publish and subscribe message protocol. MQTT is used in M2M and IoT. It is suitable for limited network environments, such as low bandwidth and low latency.

MQTT consists of a broker, a publisher, and a subscriber.

The part that publish to the broker to send and subscribe to messages is called the client. There are publisher clients and subscriber clients.

The publisher client and subscriber client do not send and receive messages directly but through a broker. This is done using topics. Topics have a similar layer structure to folders and files, using a forward slash (/) as a separator character.

Topics are arranged in a directory-like structure, with parent topics and child topics. If there are multiple clients within a parent topic, a subscriber client tells the broker that it subscribes to a topic of interest, and a connection is created to send and receive messages, much like creating a socket.

3.4.3.1. MQTT Operation

For MQTT to work, the publisher, subscriber client, and broker must be connected to a network where they can communicate with each other.

When a publisher client deploys a message in a topic, the broker publishes all messages in that deployed topic to all subscriber clients that have subscribed to that topic.

Subscriber clients subscribe to applicable messages from a topic in a periodically checked polling fashion, and subscriber clients can also unsubscribe to stop receiving messages from the broker for that topic. Subscriber clients can receive incoming messages from topics they have subscribed to and define conditions to control them based on the content published in those topics.

3.4.3.2. Propagating MQTT Trace Contexts

This example uses the `paho-mqtt` library as the MQTT client SDK. This is the most popular MQTT library in Python, but I can't find any automated instrumentation. So, you have to do manual instrumentation.

One of the difficulties with manual instrumentation of libraries that publish data is figuring out where to store the trace context. Define your own envelope as shown here:

```
{
  "trace_context": {
    "traceparent":"00-0af7651916cd43dd8448eb211c80319c-b7ad6b7169203331-01",
    "tracestate":"congo=BleGNlZWRzIHRohbCBwbGVhc3VyZS4"
```

CHAPTER 3 TRACE-CENTRIC RCA

```
  },
  "payload": ""
}
```

It is common practice not to enable the `tracestate` header on the message server when using the OpenTelemetry agent, but manual instrumentation can enable `tracestate`.

Inject the trace context when publishing and extract the trace context when subscribing. According to the draft W3C specification for MQTT trace contexts, there are two options (for JSON), depending on the version of the MQTT protocol you want to use.

- Use the payload of an MQTT v3 message and include the trace context at the root level along with other payload data.

- Using the MQTT v5 user attribute, embed a trace context. User attributes are a new feature in MQTT v5.

The approach uses MQTT v5 with user attributes. Now you can set up the trace, instrument the paho-mqtt library to propagate the trace context, and transfer the trace telemetry to the OTLP endpoint.

3.4.4. Kafka Demo

The gRPC and Kafka demos have implemented E2E traces. For example, in Figure 3-18, the REST client makes a request to the REST server, which creates a span. The REST server immediately propagates it to the Kafka publisher. The Kafka publisher propagates to Kafka subscribers. In this way, a single trace ID is used and propagated between the REST server, Kafka publisher, and Kafka subscriber.

There is a difference from the previous demos; there are multiple subscribers.

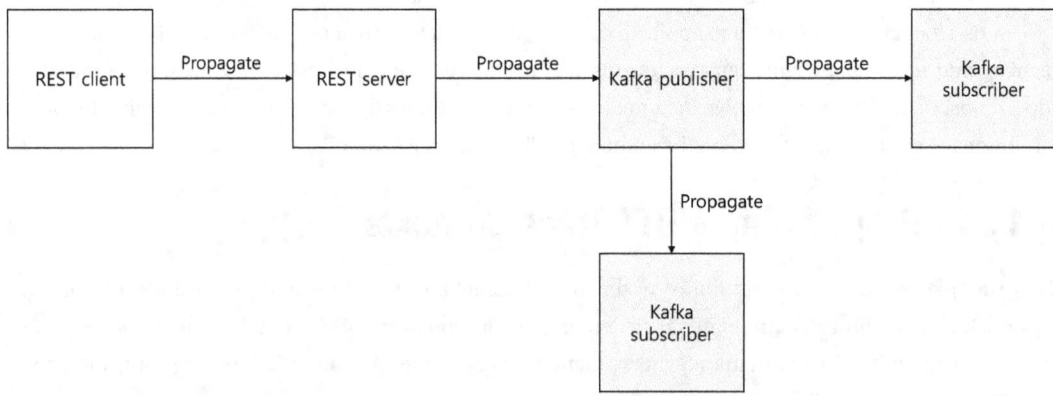

Figure 3-18. The Kafka flowchart

CHAPTER 3   TRACE-CENTRIC RCA

You should understand the meaning of the output in Figure 3-19.

- Notice that the publisher and subscriber are not separated from each other but are combined in a parent-and-child span relationship. Combined means that the propagation of the trace is successfully configured. If the publish and subscribe are separated, or the output is not displayed on the same screen, it means that propagation failed.

- One publisher and two subscribers are shown. If you compare the time when the other span are running, you can see that parallel processing is occurring. The publisher and subscribers are not affected by the process of the other span but are dependent on the parent span.

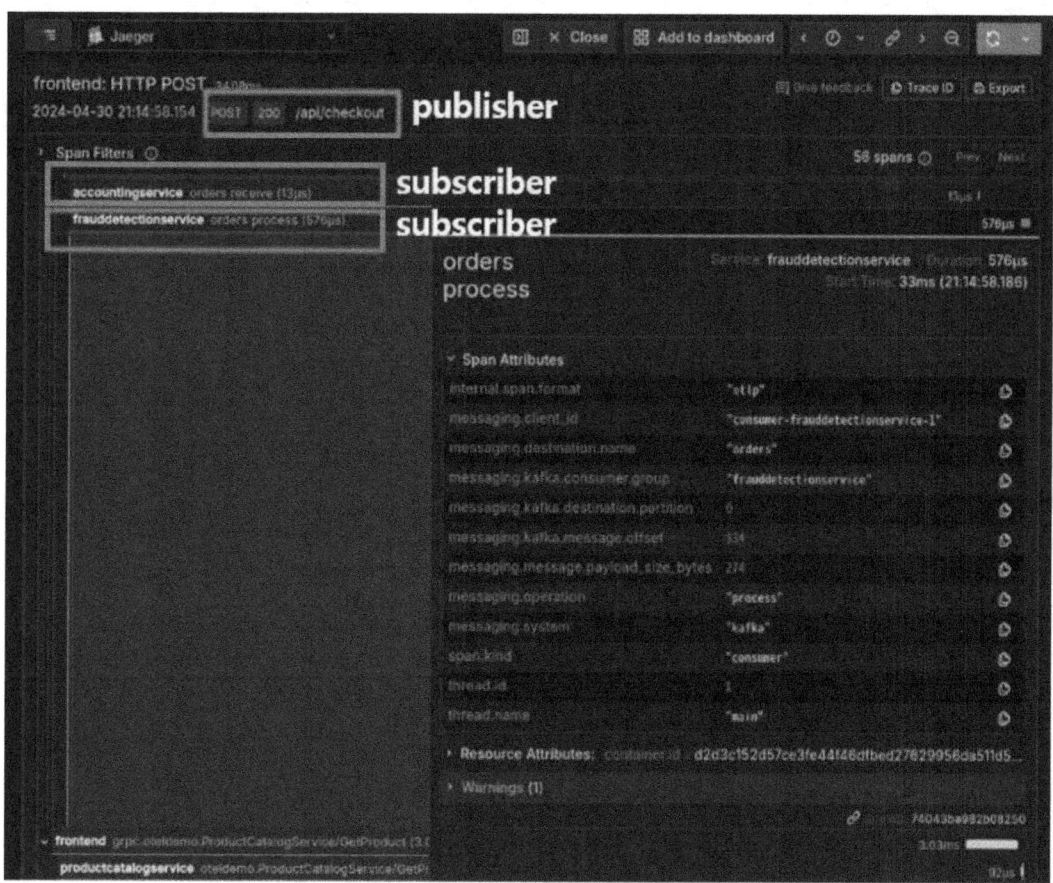

Figure 3-19. *Propagation of a Kafka span*

The Kafka broker server is a black box, and it does not create span. Only publishers and subscribers create spans, and by default, only two spans are created. With the OpenTelemetry collector Kafka receiver, it becomes a white box and can generate spans for the Kafka server.

227

CHAPTER 3 TRACE-CENTRIC RCA

As shown in Figure 3-20, the message server does not output `tracestate`, but only `traceparent`. The same can be seen in Kafka, Solace JMS, TIBCO JMS, and GCP PubSub. OpenTelemetry provides additional features over context propagation through `tracestate`, which means that it is not as easy to do this in message servers.

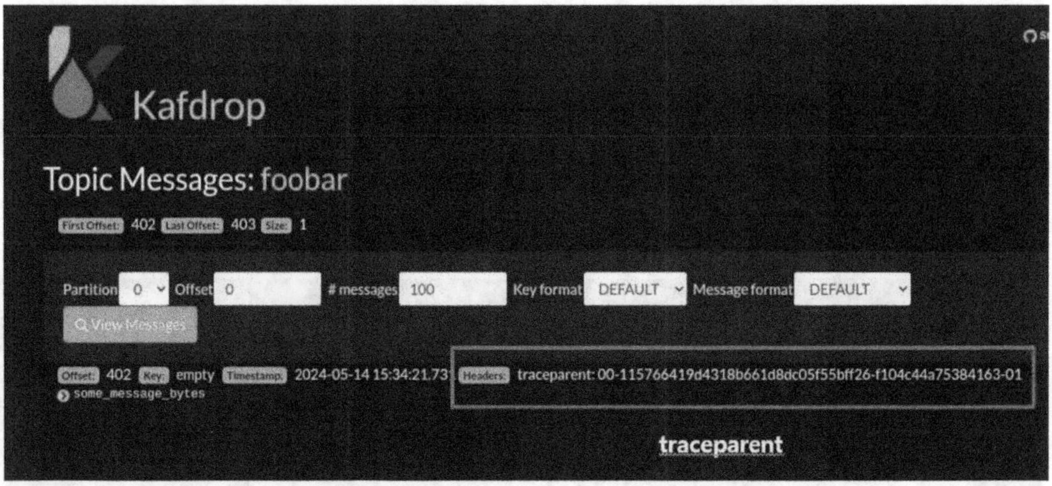

Figure 3-20. Verification of the Kafka header

You can see the `traceparent` for the publisher's message in the Kafka topic.

The OpenTelemetry JavaAgent does automatic Kafka instrumentation. Python does manual instrumentation.

When creating a Python Kafka message, you call the inject method on the header of the message.

```
propagate.inject(
    headers,
    context=trace.set_span_in_context(span),
    setter=_kafka_setter,
)
```

When reading a message, it extracts from the same headers.

```
extracted_context = propagate.extract(
    record.headers, getter=_kafka_getter
)
```

Event driven is difficult to implement trace. This is because propagating the context is difficult. Since publish and subscribe are separated, you have to add the trace context separately and propagate it.

The publisher injecting the Kafka header is shown here:

```
>>> producer.send('foobar', value=b'c29tZSB2YWx1ZQ==', headers=[('content-encoding', b'base64')])
```

The subscriber to extract the Kafka header is shown here:

```
>>> for msg in consumer:
...     print (msg.headers)
```

3.4.5. Spring Cloud Stream Demo

So far, you've looked at Solace, Kafka, and GCP PubSub. Message servers do not have a technical standard like HTTP and are proprietary implementations, so it is difficult to standardize them. Since most companies use multiple message servers, it is difficult to configure observability, so Spring Cloud stream abstracts individual message servers and provides the same API at a higher level. Regardless of the type of message server, you can configure an event-driven architecture with a common API.

Each message server provides a binder. Automated instrumentation results for various Spring Cloud streams using OpenTelemetry are shown here:

- Rabbit MQ: Success
- Kafka: Success
- Solace: The sink fails to find the parent's trace ID, but it partially succeeds. However, I used the OpenTelemetry extension and succeeded
- GCP PubSub: Failed

OpenTelemetry does not officially support Spring Cloud streams. However, you can see the instrumentation and propagation happening successfully.

The binders of cloud streams are implemented by the message server vendor, but if you analyze the internal logic, they use the existing message server's publish and subscribe. Kafka binders use Kafka protocols as they are. Therefore, OpenTelemetry supports Kafka's cloud streams.

If you compare the instrumentation results of the OpenTelemetry JavaAgent and a commercial observability agent, you may notice that the number of spans and the names of the instrumented methods are different. It is normal for different spans to be generated by different agents.

The processing order of cloud streams is source, process, and sink. In commercial observability, Solace SCS fails.

You can see the instrumentation of cloud streams in Solace using commercial observability, with two spans for Sink and one span for Process. The source is not being instrumented. The problem is that `Lambda$.run` is not instrumented, and it does not correctly recognize internal threads. This can prevent instrumentation at the specific thread level.

To debug the cause, it's a good idea to compare the results of a successful OpenTelemetry trace with the results of a failed commercial observability trace.

The results measured by the OpenTelemetry agent are shown in Figure 3-21.

CHAPTER 3   TRACE-CENTRIC RCA

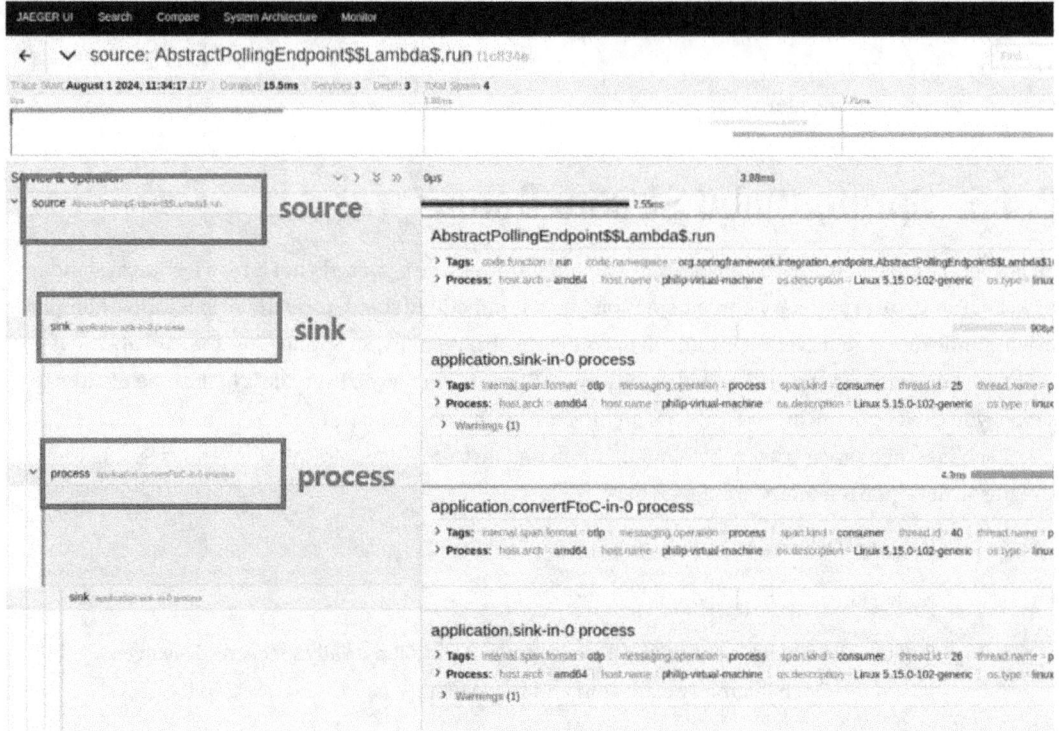

Figure 3-21. *Trace results for a Spring Cloud stream*

In the case of Solace, a trace is supported through the OpenTelemetry extension.

```
Destination:                           Topic 'sensor/temperature/fahrenheit'
Key 'solace_scst_messageVersion' (Integer): 1
  Key 'traceparent' (String): 00-4b14fe0ce9787f5606bc3f91150e7bcc-65f99fe121f9a271-01
  Key 'solace_scst_serializedHeaders' (String): ["id"]
  Key 'id' (String): rO0ABXNyAA5qYXZhLnV0aWwuVVVJRLyZA/
  eYbYUvAgACSgAMbGVhc3RTaWdCaXRzSgALbW9zdFNpZ0JpdHN4cLDshDyuTJwQbJRMzhmqAOO=
  Key 'solace_scst_serializedHeadersEncoding' (String): base64
  Key 'contentType' (String): application/json
  Key 'timestamp' (Long): 1723166795643

HTTP Content Type:                     application/json
Replication Group Message ID:          rmid1:30fc6-908abb10544-00000000-000005f8
Trace Context SMF Parameter:           {traceId=4048aece9afcbbea38f9909b81cff77d,
spanId=f461287be581e1ba, sampled=true, traceState=}
Binary Attachment:                     len=133
  7b 22 74 69 6d 65 73 74       61 6d 70 22 3a 31 37 32       {"timestamp":172
  33 31 36 36 37 39 35 36       34 31 2c 22 73 65 6e 73       3166795641,"sens
  6f 72 49 44 22 3a 22 36       30 31 31 65 33 31 30 2d       orID":"6011e310-
```

```
31 66 65 61 2d 34 39 65    63 2d 39 35 39 66 2d 30    1fea-49ec-959f-0
64 61 39 36 38 64 65 63    33 36 38 22 2c 22 74 65    da968dec368","te
6d 70 65 72 61 74 75 72    65 22 3a 37 32 2e 36 39    mperature":72.69
37 32 39 36 39 38 35 33    30 38 37 34 2c 22 62 61    729698530874,"ba
73 65 55 6e 69 74 22 3a    22 46 41 48 52 45 4e 48    seUnit":"FAHRENH
45 49 54 22 7d                                        EIT"}
```

If an OpenTelemetry agent supports instrumentation, you will see that instrumentation is also supported in the cloud stream. The agent is not instrumented by the higher-level cloud stream API but by the binder API. Since binders use the API of individual message servers internally, the OpenTelemetry agent discovers the instrumentation API through class loading and succeeds in instrumenting.

OpenTelemetry and commercial observability do not support GCP PubSub. When instrumentation fails, such as PubSub, debugging the problem is complicated because the higher-level API for cloud streams use AOP.

By default, OpenTelemetry does not support PubSub instrumentation. I tried the demo, but the instrumentation failed, and the trace was not propagated.

- OpenTelemetry instruments WebFlux and generates a trace ID.

- The propagation of the PubSub publisher fails, and a new trace is generated.

- You can find the traceparent in the topic, but the trace ID contains the trace ID of WebFlux. The WebFlux trace ID is found in the PubSub topic, not the trace ID of the PubSub publisher. The publisher instrumentation failed, and the injection failed.

- PubSub subscribers were not instrumented, and no extracts were made. Create a new trace ID.

Publishers often fail to inject into traceparent and fail. Even if the publisher successfully injects into the traceparent, it sometimes fails to extract the traceparent from the subscriber. See Table 3-1.

Table 3-1. SCS Trace in PubSub

	OpenTelemetry Trace ID	OpenTelemetry Span ID
WebFlux	1	1-1
publisher	1	1-2
PubSub Topics	1	1-1
subscriber	2	2-1

When instrumentation fails, it is important to analyze the cause.

Java often encounters problems in libraries related to dependencies. It is often the case that dependencies contain bugs or unexpected instrumentation occurs. Therefore, you should use profiles and debugging to understand dependencies.

CHAPTER 3   TRACE-CENTRIC RCA

If you look at the span ID in the PubSub topic, you can see that 1-1 is output. To analyze the cause, you need to profile and debug. This is because the agent is doing inaccurate instrumentation. By understanding the methods processed by the profile and using breakpoints to indicate which parts of your code are instrumented, you can identify the incorrect instrumentation points.

Commercial agent products have no code, and debugging the agent is difficult. OpenTelemetry agents support debugging and can be logged.

Configuring traces with commercial observability often results in spans that don't make sense. This is due to a failure in accurate instrumentation. It is important to identify the point in the code where the incorrect instrumentation occurred.

It is a cloud stream publisher for GCP PubSub.

```
@RestController
public class PublisherController {

  private final MessageChannel outgoing;

  public PublisherController(Channels channels) {
    outgoing = channels.outgoing();
  }

  @PostMapping("/publish/{name}")
  public void publish(@PathVariable String name) {
    outgoing.send(MessageBuilder.withPayload("Hello " + name + "!").build());
  }

}
```

You are a subscriber to GCP PubSub's cloud stream:

```
@Slf4j
@EnableBinding(Sink.class)
@SpringBootApplication
public class PubsubSubscriberApplication {

  public static void main(String[] args) {
    SpringApplication.run(PubsubSubscriberApplication.class, args);
  }

  @StreamListener(Sink.INPUT)
  public void handleMessage(Message<String> message) {
    log.info("Received: {}.", message.getPayload());
  }

}
```

The instrumentation is failing, and I'm getting unexpected errors. Further debugging is required.

- The header of the message is stored in the topic; using a profile, you should be able to identify exactly where the problem occurred.

- Cloud streams use AOP, which is hard to debug.

- The receiver will not be able to read the `traceparent` stored in the topic and will generate a new trace ID. Using the profile, you can find out which methods were instrumented and generated the span. Check the profiles and the call trees. For debugging, you can assign a breakpoint to a method and see if a span is generated. You can see the agent instrumenting and generating spans using the wrong method. You need to profile the internals of the binder. You should profile before debugging to understand the call tree and to debug.

- It is correct to instrument the binder, not the higher-level application code. You should start remote debugging, add breakpoints in several places, including the binder, and see when the span is generated. Since the instrumentation is incorrect, you need to debug which methods within the OpenTelemetry agent are being instrumented. If necessary, you should debug both the binder and the OpenTelemetry agent.

Because binders are dependencies, it is difficult to understand the logic that is handled in a dependency with simple debugging.

Cloud streams process publishing and subscribing in a lower level binder API, providing developers with a common, easy-to-use API.

Spring Cloud streams use the native protocols and API provided by message servers and do not use a separate message protocol. Binders use the existing message server-specific APIs. So I could see that Rabbit MQ, Solace, and Kafka, which OpenTelemetry supports, succeeded, and GCP PubSub, which OpenTelemetry does not support, failed.

Binders for all message servers are implemented independently per message server.

3.5. Propagating an EAI Server

EAI servers integrate a variety of legacy systems and black boxes. EAI can integrate with other legacy middleware such as BPM, MFT, MDM, and so on. If you are using an EAI server, you should instrument the EAI server to configure observability. This is a great way to improve observability in a short period of time.

Legacy systems do not support trace.

- Older legacy and packaged applications may not be able to be instrumented with traces at all.

- In some cases, you may be using Java, but using a version so old that OpenTelemetry is not currently applicable.

CHAPTER 3 TRACE-CENTRIC RCA

In this book, when trace is difficult, such as with legacy systems, I use the EAI server to interface the legacy system and create a span by instrumenting the inside of the EAI server. This is because it is difficult for OpenTelemetry to support various legacies.

Rather than instrumenting the legacy system directly, it is wise to instrument the EAI server that interfaces to the legacy system. This is because the EAI server processes complex legacy protocols and transformations.

- Traditional EAI servers are not observable, and many architectures are configured without traceability in mind, making trace impossible. Since EAI servers are developed in Java, you can use commercial observability agents for trace instrumentation.
- It is not easy to develop an extension to the EAI server to apply observability. It is not open source, so instrumentation is difficult.

Figure 3-22 shows the process section of the EAI server. SAP is connected through the webMethods EAI server. Assuming no webMethods instrumentation, SAP is represented by a single span. As shown in Figure 3-22, there are nine spans expected, but only five spans are output, making it difficult to measure and contextualize the response time of each section.

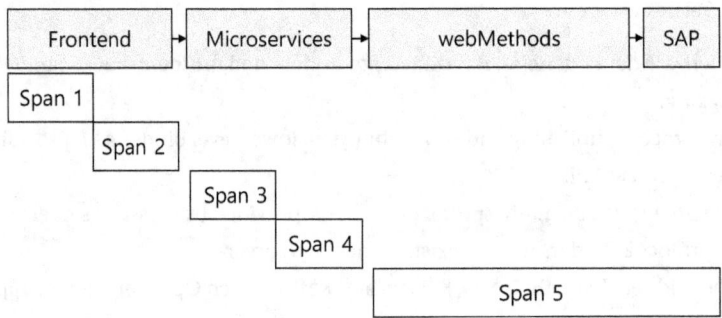

Figure 3-22. Problems with traces in the EAI server

Figure 3-23 shows the case where the trace is measured correctly. The trace ID is propagated, and it is an example of implementing an E2E trace. A trace ID is created in span 1, and the trace ID is being propagated. The EAI server should not create a new trace ID and should propagate the existing trace context.

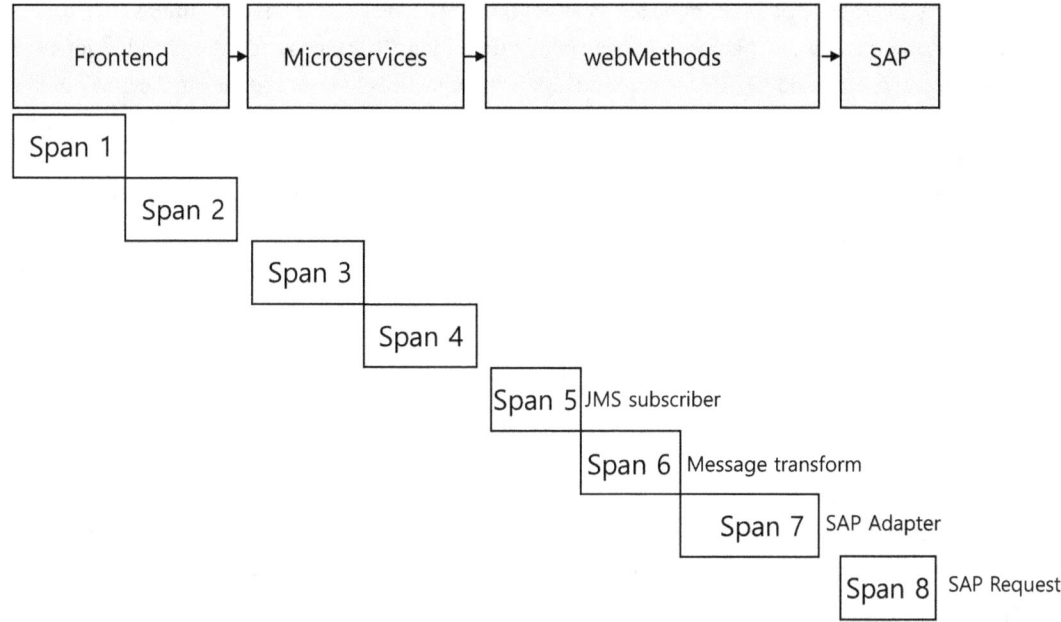

Figure 3-23. *Outputting the entire E2E to span*

The incorrectly configured trace generates four spans in spans 5-8, while the correctly configured trace generates a total of nine spans. By outputting the correct span for each segment, you can quickly understand the cause of the failure.

In general, the internal structure of the EAI server is processed as follows:

- The microservice publishes messages to the JMS server.

- The EAI server captures events from the source system and subscribes messages to from a queue.

- The EAI server subscribes for messages in the queue and transforms them. It sends the message to SAP, the target system of the EAI adapter.

Implementing a trace on EAI servers is complex and difficult. The first reason is that EAI servers are packaged in black boxes, so their internal structure is unknown. You need to use bytecode to inject logic to measure performance at the lower level. There are many classes that are difficult to understand, so finding the exact class and method to inject the bytecode into is a challenge.

Profiles allow you to see the dependencies and call trees whenever a method is called. You can view the class and method in the profile and instrument its bytecode.

It's common to measure the performance of methods through bytecode instrumentation. Since the EAI server is a commercial solution, its code is not publicly available, and instrumentation is difficult. You need to profile it to identify its internal methods and instrument them. There is no need to inject or extract headers between internal threads; OpenTelemetry intercepts and commercial observability sensors automatically recognize headers, allowing traces to be shared between threads.

CHAPTER 3   TRACE-CENTRIC RCA

Databases, packages, and mainframe legacy systems are black boxes, and it is often impossible to instrument legacy systems and packages. Instead of instrumenting the legacy system directly, developers often use microservices and EAI servers. The development language isn't Java, and the organization and development teams often disagree about enforcing traces. Instrumenting bytecode is an additional overhead and requires restarts.

Assuming it is possible to instrument the EAI server, it makes sense to use the EAI server rather than direct instrumentation of the legacy system.

Even if the instrumentation is automated with an extension, it complicates deployment. You'll need to restart after apply bytecode instrument.

You implement observability against the TIBCO `BusinessWorks` and `webMethods` integration servers. TIBCO officially supports OpenTelemetry, but `webMethods` does not yet support OpenTelemetry.

`WebMethods` are launched in JBoss WAS, and instrumentation is possible using agents.

The advantage of commercial observability is that it supports traces from TIBCO and `webMethods`. Many companies use EAI servers.

It is necessary to extract the trace context of requests coming to the EAI server via HTTP and JMS from external microservices. If the trace context already exists, it automatically extracts and propagates the trace context.

The BPM server provides workflow functionality. The BPM server manages cases by receiving requests to create new cases and sending status information to an external queue when a case is completed. The BPM server outputs the following information.

- New cases
- Completed cases
- Open cases
- Errors

The instrumentation of BPM servers is more difficult than EAI servers. Assuming that the processing of BPM internal workflows requires approval by an administrator, this manual processing can take a long time, so it is not suitable for trace.

To apply observability to BPM, BPM can return a case ID when a case is created and monitor it by updating the status of the case ID in a queue when the case is completed or an error occurs.

It is difficult to make BPM observable by using agents for trace alone. It requires a lot of customization.

- It outputs the status information of case start, case completion, and case error along with the case ID to a log.
- It reads the case ID from the log and creates a trace. It then adds the case ID to the baggage
- It uses events to combine multiple separate traces with the same case ID.

Rather than configuring E2E traces, it's more appropriate to combine broken traces. For example, the same case ID can contain multiple trace IDs to handle a single case. Where trace is difficult to apply, consider supplementing it with other signals, such as metrics and logs.

3.6. Propagation a Black Box System

Many legacy systems interface with use EAI servers. This book recommends legacy observability using logs in cases where trace is difficult, but if the black box plays an important role, it is also necessary to improve the black box to the level of observability.

Legacy systems refer to non-Linux platforms such as Tandem, AS400, OS390; package refers to SAP, Siebel, PeopleSoft. The black box refers to servers developed in Java or Python that do not support OpenTelemetry and whose internal structure is unknown.

- Check the status of threads created by the profile. It can identify that threads are created as the black box processes new requests and terminates when processing is complete.

- You can see the methods in the created thread. In an isolated environment, you can identify exactly what IO is being processed by the black box and how many calls are being made.

- If you have the source, check the variables in the method via remote debugging.

When you configure the agent on a black box, the automated instrumentation generates unknown span. It is difficult to understand which method or endpoint generated the span. In most cases, the cause of the problem is a lack of accurate instrumentation. This needs to be improved. Commercial observability can restrict spans from being created. Automated instruments in open source can disable spans by adjusting the dependency directly in the agent. However, side effects must be considered.

Commercial observability provides the ability to create custom services:

- Custom services use class loading, which allows you to specify an entry point and methods.

- Inject bytecode before and after the selected method and measure the latency of the method.

- The custom service creates a span from the selected method. If you use the HTTP protocol, expose an endpoint. The internal thread does not require propagation and recognizes the span from context. It then automatically recognizes the span.

Now that you have identified the method through profiling and debugging, you can create a service through custom services. The created service creates a span. If the protocol is HTTP or JMS, propagation is automatically configured. You can identify the `traceparent` and `x-` from the header.

237

CHAPTER 3   TRACE-CENTRIC RCA

Commercial observability uses custom services to provide observability to black boxes, and the OpenTelemetry extension can implement similar functionality.

There are two ways to apply observability to black boxes.

- **Log to configure observability.** If changing the log is difficult, use instrumentation with bytecode. You can use the legacy client API to read the header and body and write them to the log.

- **Analyze the internals with a profile, then configure debugging and trace.** You can also use the profile method to configure metrics such as number of calls, CPU and IO, latency, and utilization. By identifying the inbound and outbound methods, you can create two spans with bytecodes. Threads that process between inbound and outbound automatically pass context, which is joined by events when the spans are broken.

Many open source agents support OpenTelemetry as a top priority. Commercial observability requires vendors to develop custom instrumentation for various servers framework themselves. Another method is to extend the functions of the plug-ins, filters, policies, provided by the server framework and develop them further to support commercial observability.

If you need to instrument an API server that has no code and whose internal structure is unknown, profiling is the way to go. You can see the methods that process inbound and outbound calls in the call tree of the profile and create spans using bytecode. Since inbound and outbound methods pass context between threads, there is no need to inject or extract, and the trace will not be interrupted.

The instrumentation of the black box is summarized here:

1. Use an EAI server if possible.

2. Identify methods with profiles. Create a custom service.

3. Create multiple traces using logs and tie them together with events.

4. The black box uses the SDK to develop traces.

5. Identify methods with profiles. If the black box uses Java, the extension reads the `traceparent` and `tracestate` and generates the baggage.

6. Commercially bytecode instrumentation can add the parameters of the method to the header of the trace.

7. Write the key ID to the log using extension and create a trace from log.

If it consists of multiple steps, like ETL, use a combination of Steps 2 and 3 to instrument it.

3.7. Propagating Server Frameworks

There are various middleware servers in the enterprise, including API servers, channel servers, external servers, and EAI servers. Among the various middleware, API servers and EAI servers play an important role in implementing observability. EAI servers and API servers process message routing and protocol interface, and often do not support traces. When configuring observability, middleware often presents unexpected challenges. Implementing tracing in middleware requires considering a variety of exceptions.

To implement E2E tracing and observability, it is important to understand the domain and the product, but the domain cannot be understood in a short period of time. If you need to complete a trace project in a short period of time, it is better to take a middleware-centric approach. You can improve trace in a phased and incremental manner by addressing applications that don't support trace or have problems with span one by one.

It is different from the legacy middleware of EAI, BPM, ETL, MFT, and MDM.

A variety of middleware and server frameworks are used, as shown in Table 3-2.

Table 3-2. Various Middleware

Solution	Contents
Istio	Istio supports B3. Envoy proxy server supports OpenTelemetry.
nginx	Nginx supports OpenTelemetry.
Envoy proxy	The Envoy proxy server supports OpenTelemetry. Gloo is based on Envoy.
	If you experience latency when calling between microservices, you can measure the latency through envoys. After going through Envoy, create additional spans.
API server	Apigee only supports GCP Cloud Trace and B3 and may not support OpenTelemetry.
	AWS API Gateway only supports AWS X-Ray. There are a lot of limitations.
	If you are using a managed API server provided by AWS or GCP, trace support is limited. This is because they only support the internal observability backend and do not provide the ability to transfer traces externally. API servers play an important role in E2E trace, but since they can't be transferred externally, you can't create additional spans for them. Therefore, it is often difficult to measure latency for transactions coming from the frontend to the backend.
EAI server	TIBCO supports OpenTelemetry, but `webMethods` does not support telemetry internally. Only commercial observability agents support `webMethods`.

Microservices are not a problem when it comes to implementing trace.

Many middleware setups do not support traces, making observability difficult. To apply observability without code modifications, you need to understand and configure the middleware correctly. Unnecessary code modifications in microservices, or implementing microservices patterns and observability through custom and additional development, is not a good practice.

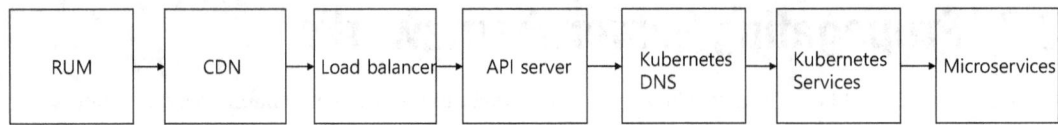

Figure 3-24. *Applications processed in a transaction*

As shown in Figure 3-24, a transaction may pass through various gateways, EAI servers, message servers, ingress servers, API servers, load balancers, proxies, and more as it is processed.

CDNs, load balancers, and API servers have a hard time instrumenting, propagating, and transferring traces to the external. Instead of direct instrumentation, they provide their own scripts, which must be configured to enable headers, propagate headers, write to logs, and transfer traces. In some cases, the server may not provide a script-based API, which means you may need to instrument bytecode, which will make the trace more complicated. Rather than always trying to instrument bytecode, if you can add functionality with scripts, you should use them.

It is necessary to check whether the middleware supports trace. API servers and EAI servers are often black boxes that don't release their source or are complicated to instrument. If the server doesn't support trace internally, it's difficult to apply an automatic instrument, and you'll need to implement manual trace. If it is developed in Java, you should use low-level bytecode instrumentation. Instrumenting API servers, EAI servers, and BPM servers with bytecode is not technically straightforward and can have unexpected side effects. If the middleware was developed in the past, it is unlikely to support distributed trace.

If you use API servers, how should you configure traces?

- The server framework should be developed to add the `traceparent` header, using a script. If you are using commercial observability, you will need to develop to add the `x-`header.

- Downstream microservices use the agent for automated instrumentation to process the `traceparent, x-`header.

- To start traces from the frontend, you need to inject traces from RUM. Commercial observability can add a trace context to a cookie in the header. The server framework extracts the frontend trace and propagates it downstream.

SRE should try to enable traces where possible, given the cost and effort involved. RUM, CDNs, north-south API servers, east-west API servers. Should support traces to help troubleshoot problems when they occur. I have experienced many failures in the previous sections during production.

If a trace starts with an OpenTelemetry `traceparent`, it is useful to use the OpenTelemetry `traceparent` until the end of the trace. For traces that start with `x-` in commercial observability, it is useful to use `x-` until the end. It is not a good practice to switch between `traceparent` and `x-` and configure interoperability with `tracestate`.

In recent years, many servers have supported OpenTelemetry out of the box. In this case, you can configure E2E traces without further development. Support for OpenTelemetry is a top priority for open source and commercial observability. You have to invest more money and time than with OpenTelemetry. This is because you can't use `traceparent`, and you have to configure `x-` in the header.

The middleware provides the ability to add filters or policies and scripts. The process for `traceparent`, `x-propagate` should use policies and filters. Consider the case in Figure 3-25:

- RUM uses the OpenTelemetry JavaScript, Swift, and Cotlin APIs to create spans and configure the starting point for traces. Commercial observability provides an SDK, which can be used to generate `x-`.

- The Apigee API server provides custom policies.

- AWS CloudFront provides a custom script.

- Istio offers custom filters.

You should understand the server framework and be able to configure headers as needed.

Often, you don't use `traceparent` but already use the `x-` header. They can be developed to support E2E traces by adding code to the server to filter out the `x-`.

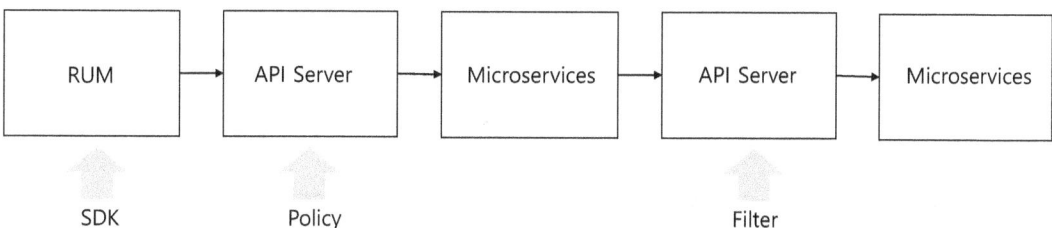

Figure 3-25. *Improving application-specific traces*

Manual instrumentation has many practical limitations. Assuming a large number of microservices are already in production and source changes are difficult, developers are not willing to accept additional development, such as modifying log files, adding trace API, or developing custom metrics. If you explain to a developer that observability is only possible by modifying the source, most developers will refuse to implement OpenTelemetry. Manual instrumentation is technically correct, but it has many limitations in practice. However, the more legacy-intensive the environment is, the more automated the instrumentation is.

3.7.1. Commercial Observability SDK Trace Demo

The commercial observability approach requires an agent and is difficult to operate without it. You should use the agent for automated instrumentation, but if commercial observability does not support instrumentation, you will need to develop manual instrumentation using the commercial observability SDK.

Figure 3-26 was developed with a commercial observability SDK and creates two spans: inbound and outbound.

CHAPTER 3   TRACE-CENTRIC RCA

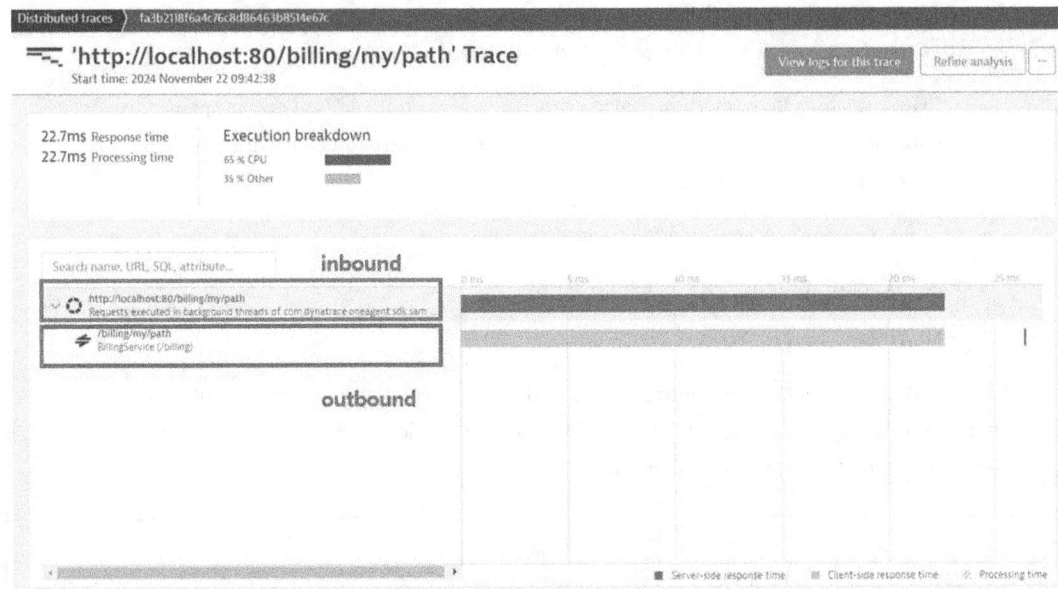

Figure 3-26. *Trace using the commercial observability SDK*

Compared to OpenTelemetry, commercial observability has a number of differences.

- Commercial observability has no concept of transfer, and no endpoint is provided for transfer. When the x-header is activated by manual instrumentation, the agent automatically recognizes it. It reads the trace context, and the agent transfers it. In commercial observability, the ability to automatically recognize traces is called a sensor. Commercial observability does not provide the ability to configure pipelines like OpenTelemetry collectors do. Pipeline functionality is embedded within the agent. Because commercial observability forces you to use an agent, implement transfer functionality through sensors rather than providing an endpoint. Commercial observability forces you to use the agent because the more agents you install, the more revenue you make.

- The commercial observability SDK only enables the x-header and does not enable the OpenTelemetry trace context. However, you can configure it and add it as a W3C header.

It is processed as shown in Figure 3-27, where the client is outbound, and the server is inbound.

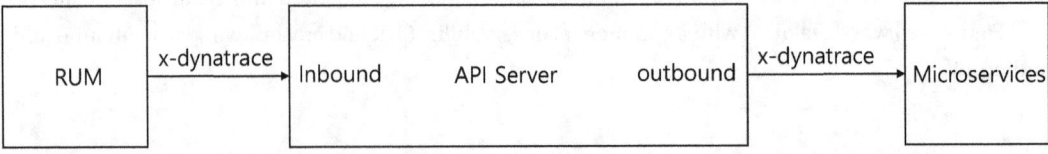

Figure 3-27. *Inbound and outbound with the commercial observability SDK*

242

CHAPTER 3   TRACE-CENTRIC RCA

From the API server's perspective, it's inbound if it's coming from the frontend, and it's outbound if it's going downstream. Notice that x- is enabled in the header, not in traceparent.

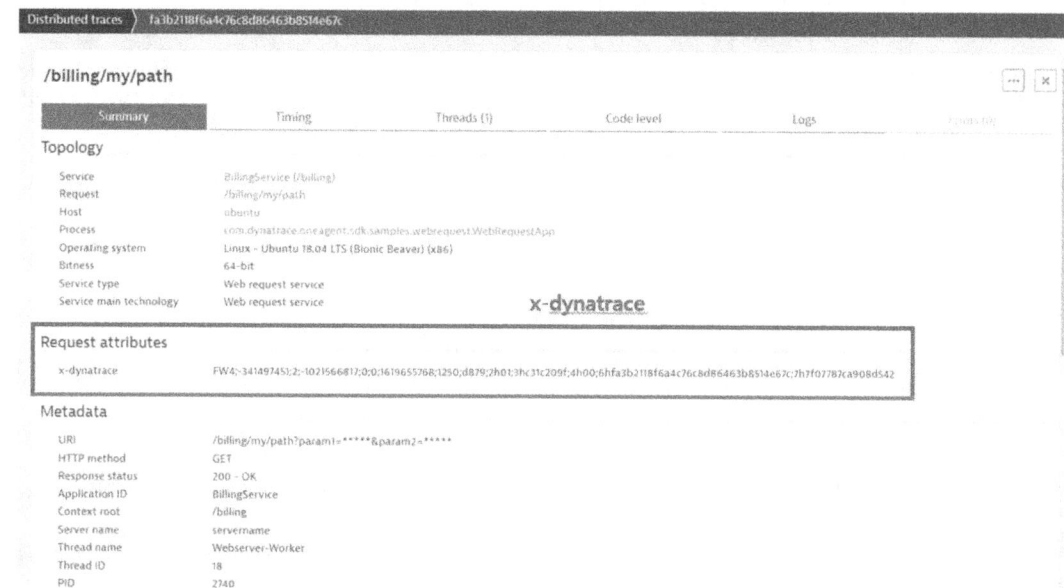

Figure 3-28. Trace results from a commercial observability SDK

In Figure 3-28, you can see that the x-header is enabled.

3.7.2. Micrometer Trace Demo

Spring Boot provides its own observability called *Micrometer*, which is used for metrics and traces. Micrometer traces support two methods: Zipkin Brave and OpenTelemetry.

If you need to upgrade to OpenTelemetry in Spring Boot, the configuration for micrometer-tracing-bridge-otel and opentelemetry-exporter-otlp is as follows.

```
<dependencies>
    <dependency>
        <groupId>org.springframework.boot</groupId>
        <artifactId>spring-boot-starter-actuator</artifactId>
    </dependency>
    <dependency>
        <groupId>org.springframework.boot</groupId>
        <artifactId>spring-boot-starter-web</artifactId>
    </dependency>
```

```xml
        <dependency>
            <groupId>org.springframework.boot</groupId>
            <artifactId>spring-boot-starter-test</artifactId>
            <scope>test</scope>
        </dependency>

        <dependency>
            <groupId>io.micrometer</groupId>
            <artifactId>micrometer-tracing-bridge-otel</artifactId>
        </dependency>
        <dependency>
            <groupId>io.opentelemetry</groupId>
            <artifactId>opentelemetry-exporter-otlp</artifactId>
        </dependency>
    </dependencies>
```

The correlation between log and trace is shown here. Add the trace context that you want to print to logging.

```yaml
tracing:
  url: http://localhost:4318/v1/traces

management:
  tracing:
    sampling:
      probability: 1.0

logging:
  pattern:
    level: "%5p [${spring.application.name:},%X{traceId:-},%X{spanId:-}]"
```

Commercial observability agents can automatically inject trace context into log files, or you can add trace context manually using MDC. There are often conflicts or compatibility problems between different trace standards. Enabling `micrometer-tracing-bridge-otel` OpenTelemetry in Micrometer and re-instrumentation in the OpenTelemetry agent is not recommended.

You should enable all the various trace IDs in your development environment and see the trace context written in the log. Be careful when generating OpenTelemetry format traces in Spring Boot and writing them to logs. Commercial observability agents generate x- trace IDs and write them to logs, so you need to understand and troubleshoot the different trace contexts.

In Spring Boot, it is more common to use Micrometer than Prometheus.

CHAPTER 3   TRACE-CENTRIC RCA

3.7.3. Commercial Observability Demo

This section describes how to configure an E2E trace between an upstream that only supports OpenTelemetry and a downstream configured with commercial observability. It describes how to interoperate OpenTelemetry with commercial observability. The upstream and downstream of the demo were developed with Spring Boot.

- The upstream uses the Micrometer OpenTelemetry bridge. It does not use a commercial observability agent.
- The downstream uses a Micrometer OpenTelemetry bridge. It uses a commercial observability agent.

In the following setup, propagation between upstream and downstream fails.

- The upstream and downstream transfer the trace context to the OpenTelemetry collector and do not transfer it externally.
- In commercial observability, only downstream traces are recognized; upstream traces are not.

Configure the system as shown in Figure 3-29.

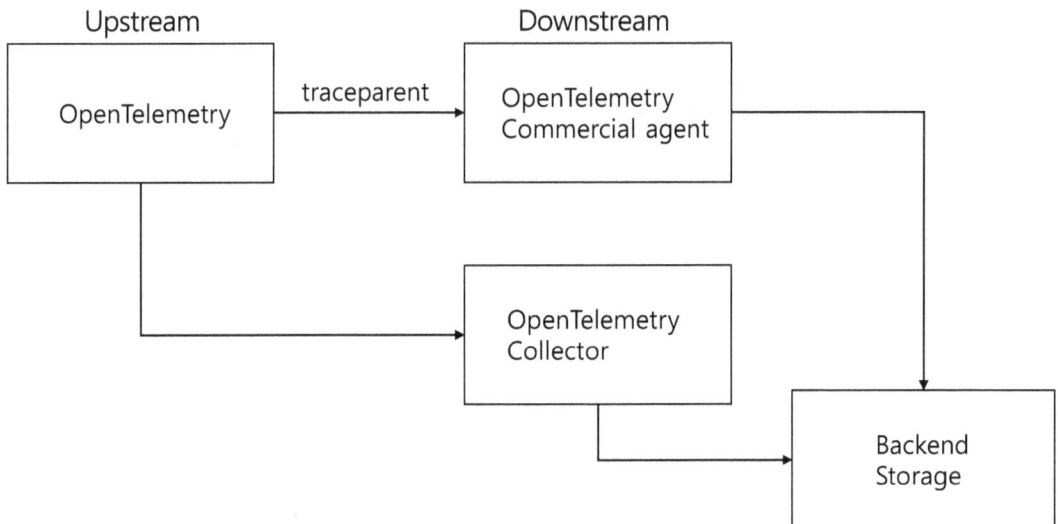

Figure 3-29. *Process flow for OpenTelemetry and commercial observability*

You can see that the upstream and downstream are connected using the OpenTelemetry collector, as shown in Figure 3-30.

CHAPTER 3   TRACE-CENTRIC RCA

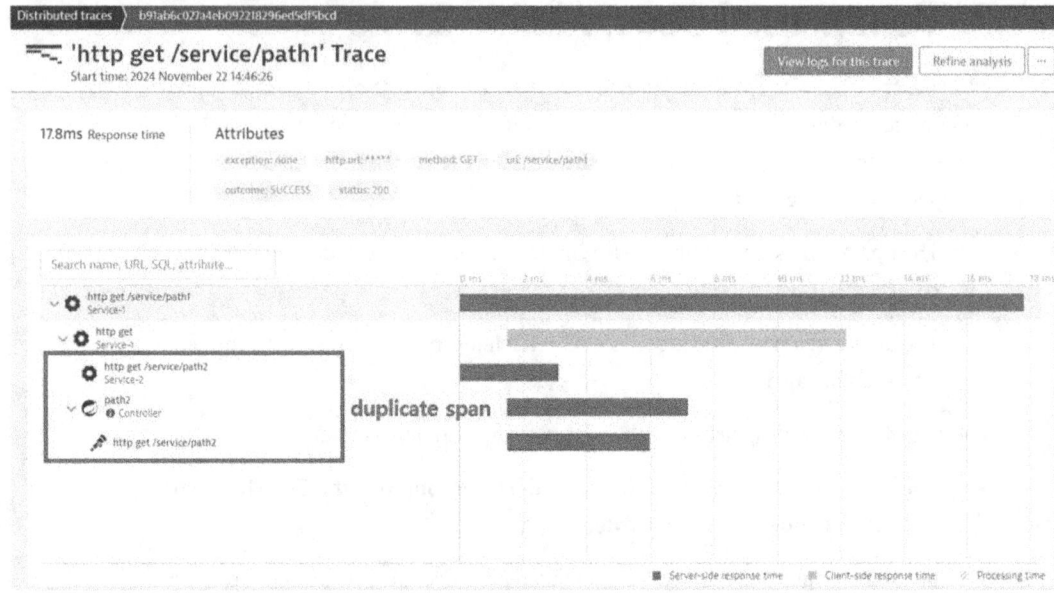

Figure 3-30. *Screen showing successful trace propagation*

The configuration to transfer the OpenTelemetry collector has changed to commercial observability.

In commercial observability, you can see the E2E traces upstream and downstream. However, you can see that there are duplicate traces downstream.

If there is no OpenTelemetry collector, it will fail to propagate between upstream and downstream and will only output the downstream span, as shown in Figure 3-31.

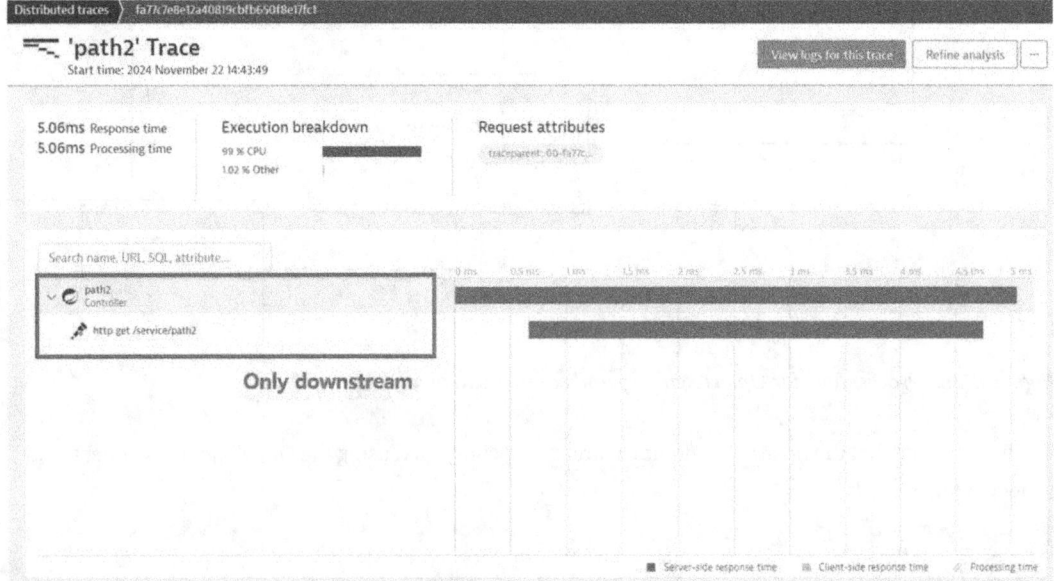

Figure 3-31. *Screen showing trace propagation failure*

The reason for the duplication in Figure 3-30 is that downstream, the Micrometer OpenTelemetry bridge is being used to transfer traces to the OpenTelemetry collector, and commercial observability is also sending OpenTelemetry back. I disabled the downstream OpenTelemetry bridge, and the problem was resolved.

Figure 3-32 shows that upstream and downstream should propagate to traceparent.

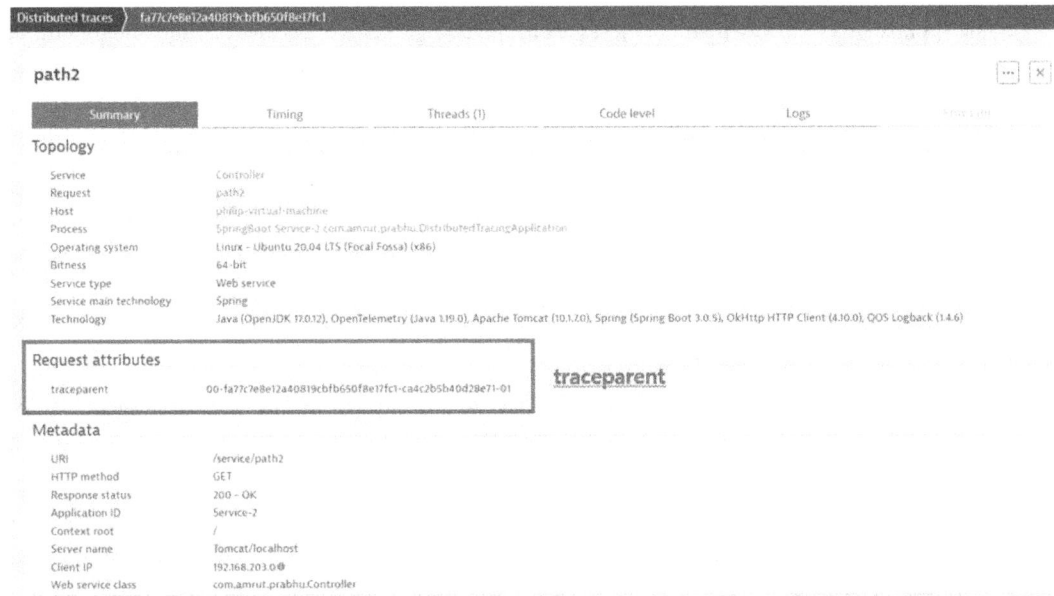

Figure 3-32. Detail screen showing successful trace propagation

Configuring OpenTelemetry and commercial observability to interoperate is more complex and difficult than configuring traces with OpenTelemetry alone. Configuring interoperation is different for each commercial observability.

3.7.4. WebSocket Demo

It is common for clients and servers to use gRPC or other protocols like WebSocket to communicate asynchronously when they establish a connection and then send messages to each other. Common use cases for this kind of communication include chat applications, collaboration tools, and data communicating in both directions in real time.

In chat, a call starts when a client initiates a connection and can last until the client disconnects, the connection goes idle, or network problems occur. In practice, this can last for days.

While the connection is alive, the client and server can write messages to each other on that network stream. This approach minimizes the overhead caused by DNS lookups, protocol negotiation, load balancing, authorization, and routing.

The downside is that you have to associate client messages with service responses and come up with your own semantics for metadata and status codes, which can make your application more complex.

Built-in instrumentation tools are not enough for observability. Manual instrumentation is required.

This demo is interesting because it manually instruments the publisher, subscriber, and server. This is applicable to API and message servers. So far, you've only instrumented the client, but in the case of WebSockets, you're developing the server and manually instrumenting it.

Some applications send independent messages within a single streaming call and want different traces to describe the individual messages. Other applications use streaming to publish multiple messages in batches and want one trace to describe everything that happens within a single streaming call.

With HTTP communication, a client must send a request to a server before the server can respond. If the server doesn't receive a request, it can't communicate with the client. To solve this problem, you need to use WebSocket communication, which allows you to communicate in both directions. Features such as chat, alerts, and trading cannot be implemented using HTTP communication. When building these features, you should use socket communication.

STOMP (Simple Text Oriented Messaging Protocol) is a protocol for efficiently publishing and subscribing to messages and is based on PubSub.

If you implement it using WebSockets alone, you have to implement it on your own because there is no standardized way to know what the request is, what format it is in, and how to process the message communication process.

Using STOMP as a protocol, the client and server define the format, type, and content of messages to communicate with each other. Therefore, you can clearly define the process of publishing and subscribing to messages, and you can use annotations such as `@MessageMapping` to manage endpoints separately when publishing messages without having to implement `WebSocketHandler` directly.

You can use the STOMP protocol through WebSockets in your Spring project to build a framework for publishing and subscribing messages, as shown in Figure 3-33.

The server exposes a WebSocket. Publishers connect to this WebSocket to send messages, and subscribers connect to the same WebSocket to receive messages. The Spring Controller helps convert message types and routes them to different targets.

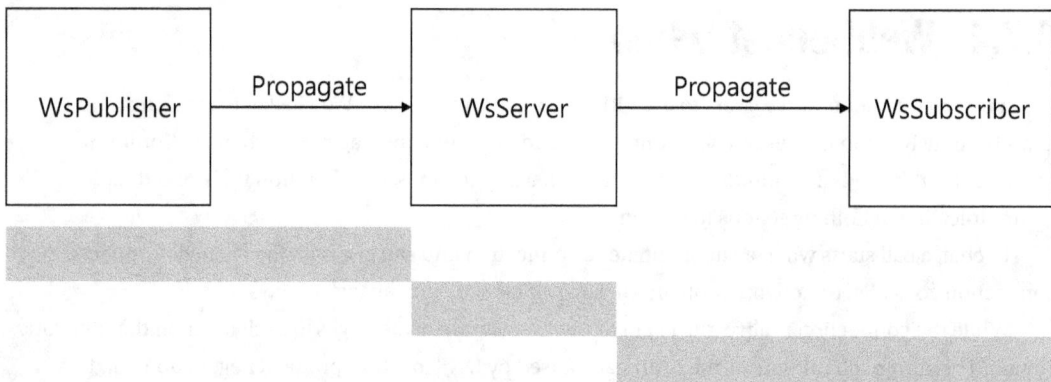

Figure 3-33. WebSocket trace flow

WsPublisher connects to WebSocket and publishes a JSON message in STOMP format to /app/tube.

The WsServerController contains a message mapping that converts messages into timestamped messages and sends them to /topic/messages. This is the "business" layer that contains the sophisticated message conversion.

WsSubscriber also connects to ws and creates a subscription to /topic/messages. When it receives a message, it logs its contents.

For simplicity of demonstration, I keep it as a monolithic Java process. In a real deployment, you can expect the three components to be deployed on separate hosts or containers.

Configure the OpenTelemetry agent and transfer it to the locally installed OpenTelemetry collector.

Then propagate the trace context and add some manual instrumentation to improve observability. First, add the following two OpenTelemetry dependencies to the build.gradle.kts file:

```
dependencies {
    implementation("io.opentelemetry:opentelemetry-sdk:1.21.0")
    implementation("io.opentelemetry.instrumentation:opentelemetry-instrumentation-annotations:1.22.1")
    ...
}
```

Starting with the publisher, the scheduled task calls WsPublisher.sendOne() every two seconds. You start by adding the @WithSpan annotation to this method.

```
@WithSpan(value="/app/tube publish", kind = SpanKind.PRODUCER)
private void sendOne() {
    ...
}
```

The annotation tells OpenTelemetry to create a new span each time the sendOne() method is called. The specification indicates that the span is a PRODUCER. Since this is the start of the publishing process, it has no parent and will be the root span in the trace.

The components downstream need to know the trace context, which contains the parent of the trace ID + span ID. But right now, the context is not propagated to STOMP, so you have to write a bit of code.

To do this, create a new instance of StompHeaders and set the message destination.

```
StompHeaders headers = new StompHeaders();
headers.setDestination("/app/tube");
```

Then, utilizing the OpenTelemetry API, you inject the current trace context into the context propagation mechanism, which is implemented as a textmap propagator.

```
GlobalOpenTelemetry.getPropagators()
    .getTextMapPropagator()
    .inject(Context.current(), headers, (carrier, key, value) -> {
```

CHAPTER 3 TRACE-CENTRIC RCA

```
        if(carrier != null){
            carrier.set(key, value);
        }
    });
```

The approach is that as a user, you don't need to know the internal operation of the propagation mechanism. For example, you don't need to see the name of the context header or the data type inside the propagated value. Lambdas simply act as small type adapters for specific implementations.

The routing method on the server side is `WsServerController.routeTube()`, which is annotated with Spring's `@MessageMapping`. You learned that you can add a `SimpMessageHeaderAccessor` parameter to the method to access the header in the subscribe message.

```
@MessageMapping("/tube")
public void routeTube(ExampleMessage exampleMessage, SimpMessageHeaderAccessor
headerAccessor) {
    ...
}
```

To get into the correct trace context, you need to implement an interface that allows you to get the header values from `SimpleMessageHeaderAccessor`.

```
static class HeadersAdapter implements TextMapGetter<SimpMessageHeaderAccessor> {
    @Override
    public String get(@Nullable SimpMessageHeaderAccessor carrier, String key) {
        return carrier.getFirstNativeHeader(key);
    }

    @Override
    public Iterable<String> keys(SimpMessageHeaderAccessor carrier) {
        return carrier.toMap().keySet();
    }
}
```

Now that you've created a textmap getter import, you can extract the incoming trace context from OpenTelemetry.

```
var traceContext = GlobalOpenTelemetry.getPropagators()
                    .getTextMapPropagator()
                    .extract(Context.current(), headerAccessor, new HeadersAdapter());
```

Make it current.

```
try (var scope = traceContext.makeCurrent()) {
    ...
}
```

CHAPTER 3 TRACE-CENTRIC RCA

Since the existing span has a parent, you want to create a new span to represent the routing task. When performing manual instrumentation like this, you'll often encounter this common pattern:

- Get the tracer.
- Create a span builder.
- Start the span.
- Make the new span the current span.
- Perform business logic.
- Exit the span.

This example selected SERVER, but you may need to select CONSUMER.

You can see that doRoute() injects the same default header method that was used for the publisher.

Server routing has been implemented. A new trace is created, and the context is added to the header of the routed message. The subscriber will receive the message.

The subscriber method is WsSubscriber.handleFrame(). This method subscribes to the STOMP message header and payload and a message object instance.

Just like I did with the router, I extract the subscribe trace context from OpenTelemetry. Instead of creating an internal class, I used an anonymous class and hid it in a method.

As before, I makeCurrent() the parent context, then create a new subscriber span within that context.

Let's check the results. Create one trace ID and a total of three spans. Create a span for the publisher. The trace ID is 91099e17c146196ba6f14bdfb2a42b57.

```
[otel.javaagent 2024-03-30 19:50:26:257 +0900] [pool-3-thread-1] INFO io.opentelemetry.
exporter.logging.LoggingSpanExporter - '/app/tube publish' : 91099e17c146196ba6f14bdfb2a
42b57 507f2448e48d351b PRODUCER [tracer: io.opentelemetry.opentelemetry-instrumentation-
annotations-1.16:1.22.1-alpha] AttributesMap{data={thread.name=pool-3-thread-1,
thread.id=22, code.namespace=com.splunk.example.WsPublisher, code.function=sendOne},
capacity=2147483647, totalAddedValues=4}
```

Create a span for the server:

```
[otel.javaagent 2024-03-30 19:50:26:259 +0900] [clientInboundChannel-10] INFO
io.opentelemetry.exporter.logging.LoggingSpanExporter - '/tube process' : 91099e17c
146196ba6f14bdfb2a42b57 e62e2a7afb9b920c SERVER [tracer: Custom_MessageMapping:]
AttributesMap{data={thread.name=clientInboundChannel-10, thread.id=62}, capacity=2147483647,
totalAddedValues=2}
2024-03-30 19:50:26.261  INFO 13589 --- [lient-AsyncIO-1] com.splunk.example.
WsSubscriber            : Subscriber received:
2024-03-30 19:50:26.261  INFO 13589 --- [lient-AsyncIO-1] com.splunk.example.
WsSubscriber            :    2024-03-30 19:50:26 | From: cash | Subject: rope
2024-03-30 19:50:26.261  INFO 13589 --- [lient-AsyncIO-1] com.splunk.example.
WsSubscriber            :    Body: Imagine the silhouette of a rope
```

CHAPTER 3   TRACE-CENTRIC RCA

Create a span for the subscriber:

```
[otel.javaagent 2024-03-30 19:50:26:261 +0900] [WebSocketClient-AsyncIO-1] INFO
io.opentelemetry.exporter.logging.LoggingSpanExporter - '/topic/messages receive' :
91099e17c146196ba6f14bdfb2a42b57 35478ae88fad434e CONSUMER [tracer: Custom_
MessageSubscriber:] AttributesMap{data={thread.name=WebSocketClient-AsyncIO-1, thread.id=41,
x-from=cash, x-subject=rope}, capacity=2147483647, totalAddedValues=4}
```

This is added to the subscriber span in the form of a custom attribute. You can add more observability details to your component.

You saw a demonstration of adding manual instrumentation to Spring to trace WebSocket-based STOMP protocol messages from the publisher, through the server, and finally to the subscriber. I demonstrated how to achieve trace context propagation by reading and writing message headers and specific usage of the OpenTelemetry Java API.

3.8. Using OpenTelemetry Extensions

Manual instrumentation is required for technologies not supported by OpenTelemetry. However, manual instrumentation is not the answer and should eventually be deployed as automated instrumentation via an extension.

Before you start this demo, I explain some basic concepts and terminology:

- **JavaAgent:** A tool that can be used to instrument the bytecode of class files in the JVM. JavaAgents are used for a variety of purposes, such as performance monitoring, logging, and security.

- **Bytecode:** This is the intermediate code generated by the Java compiler from Java code. This code is interpreted or compiled by the JVM to produce executable machine language code.

- **Byte**Buddy**:** This is a bytecode instrumentation library. It is used to create, modify, or adapt Java classes at runtime. In the context of JavaAgents, ByteBuddy provides a flexible way to modify bytecode. The OpenTelemetry agent uses `ByteBuddy` internally.

I previously distinguished between instrumentation and propagation. The API that implements instrumentation is `ByteBuddy`, and the API that performs propagation is OpenTelemetry. Now let's talk about how automated instrumentation works in `ByteBuddy`.

JavaAgents can be developed to instrument the performance of Java applications.

- In Java-based APM systems, most agents are developed using JavaAgents. The agent's role is primarily to collect performance data from the application.

- Bytecode instrumentation has long been a favorite technique for agent development. It helps you measure performance of legacy code and perform code coverage, without changing the existing source.

- OpenTelemetry uses JavaAgents. To provide additional instrumentation not provided by the OpenTelemetry agent, offer the OpenTelemetry extension. The extension provides bytecode instrumentation for various applications and works on top of the OpenTelemetry agent. When the extension provides additional instrumentation, the OpenTelemetry agent creates a span for it and processes the transfer.

- Instrumentation means extracting, injecting, and propagating, and is processed by the extension. To do this, the extension uses the JavaAgent API, the ByteBuddy instrumentation API, and the OpenTelemetry API. Propagation is processed by the OpenTelemetry agent.

Using OpenTelemetry and JavaAgents together, you can develop an OpenTelemetry agent to implement observability.

While you should try to reduce manual instrumentation as much as possible, there are times when it is necessary to use it. However, if you have legacy code, manual instrumentation may be difficult. In this case, you'll need to configure trace in two ways:

- If it's not Java, converting from log to trace is suitable.

- If it is Java, you need to configure the agent to configure a trace using bytecode instrumentation.

Various Java applications fail to extract spans. This is due to the agent's inability to instrument. If the instrumentation fails, analyze the cause with profiles. If you need additional instrumentation, you can develop it using extensions.

The rough structure of injecting bytecode and instrumentation using the agent is shown here:

- JavaAgent adds methods to measure performance before and after critical methods. It is possible to add the necessary logic using bytecode, without changing the existing source. It uses ByteBuddy at the higher level and ASM at the lower level.

- The extension handles the injection and extraction of trace context into the message header. It also handles propagation downstream.

- The OpenTelemetry agent generates the span for the extension's instrumentation content and handles the transport.

Commercial agents automate the entire process from service discovery to instrumentation. If the automated discovery instrumentation fails, you can manually configure a custom service.

After installation, the commercial observability agent automates the process of instrumenting your application and infrastructure and collecting signals. However, there are times when discovery fails, and some services don't work properly. For example, the agent may fail to configure the endpoint of a service because it doesn't support WebSockets, or the queue on a message server may not be recognized. With newer technologies, it is not uncommon for agent instrumentation to fail and for various message servers to fail to configure. With thousands of services and a wide variety of technologies, this can lead to undiscoverable and incorrect configuration.

OpenTelemetry discovery and instrumentation are done manually by SRE, so the SRE develops automation scripts and tools.

If manual instrumentation requires source changes for dozens of microservices, it's hard for the development team to accept the change. You need to guide the development team to implement automated instrumentation based on JavaAgents and extensions.

To measure durations without changing the existing source, the bytecode can be added and utilized for instrumentation. Most of the automation features offered by commercial observability use bytecode.

To solve trace problems, you need to understand the internal operation of manual instrumentation using API and automated instrumentation using agents. In fact, manual and automated instrumentation are not that different. Manual instrumentation is implemented using API, while automated instrumentation automates manual instrumentation.

OpenTelemetry uses JavaAgents and supports extensions for additional instrumentation. You need to understand the instrumentation of bytecode using ByteBuddy before OpenTelemetry and how to configure the JavaAgent. Finally, I show you how to configure the extension using OpenTelemetry.

3.8.1. Bytecode Instrumentation Demo

This section describes `ByteBuddy`, which is the basis of the extension.

There are many different libraries for bytecode instrumentation, but ByteBuddy is easy to use and has great features.

ByteBuddy is a code generation and manipulation library for creating and modifying Java classes during the runtime of Java applications. It describes what you can do with the `@Advice` annotation.

ByteBuddy's `Advice` method is described here:

- `@Advice.OnMethodEnter`: Annotated methods must be inlined before the ByteBuddy-matched method is called.

- `@Advice.This`: Indicates that the annotated parameter should be mapped to this reference of the instrumented method.

- `@Advice.Origin`: Indicates that the annotated parameter should be mapped to the string representation of the instrumented method.

- `@Advice.AllArguments`: Assigns an array containing all the arguments of the instrumented method to the annotated parameter. The annotated parameter must be of a type array.

- `@Advice.Argument(0 through n)`: This can be used to directly access the required method parameters. You can also change the arguments by setting the `readOnly` flag to `false` and setting new values.

CHAPTER 3 TRACE-CENTRIC RCA

- @Advice.FieldValue: Indicates that the annotated parameter should be mapped to a field in the scope of the instrumented method. You can also change the field by setting the readOnly flag to false and setting a new value.

- @Advice.OnMethodExit: Before exiting the instrumented method, the annotated method must be executed. The exception thrown is available via the @Advice.Thrown annotated parameter.

- @Advice.Enter: Annotated parameters should be mapped to the value returned by the advice method annotated with @OnMethodEnter.

- @Advice.Return: Annotated parameters should be mapped to the return value of the instrumented method.

First, run the application without @Advice.

```
public class Robot {
    private String name = "Casper";
    public String greetUser(String name ){
        System.out.println("Inside greetUser method . . . ");
        return "Hello " + name + "! I am " + this.name;
    }
}
```

The main method is shown here:

```
public class ByteBuddyExampleMain {
    public static void main(String[] args) throws Exception {
        String returnVal = (new Robot()).greetUser("John");
        System.out.println("return value: " + returnVal);
    }
}
```

When you run the code, you will see this output:

```
Inside greetUser method . . .
return value: Hello John! I am Casper
```

Let's instrument the Robot class with ByteBuddy and then run it again. A separate file has been added for instrumentation, and the main method has been changed to the following:

```
public class ByteBuddyExampleMain {

    public static void main(String[] args) throws Exception {
```

CHAPTER 3 TRACE-CENTRIC RCA

```java
        Class<?> type = new ByteBuddy()
                .redefine(Robot.class)
                .visit(Advice.to(MyAdvices.class).on(ElementMatchers.isMethod()))
                .make()
                .load(ClassLoadingStrategy.BOOTSTRAP_LOADER, ClassLoadingStrategy.Default.
                WRAPPER)
                .getLoaded();

        String returnVal = (String)type.getDeclaredMethod("greetUser", String.class).
        invoke(type.getDeclaredConstructor().newInstance(), "John");
        System.out.println("return value: " + returnVal);
    }
}
```

Implement the @Advice method as shown here:

```java
public class MyAdvices {
    @Advice.OnMethodEnter(suppress = Throwable.class)
    static long enter(@Advice.This Object thisObject,
                      @Advice.Origin String origin,
                      @Advice.Origin("#t #m") String detaildOrigin,
                      @Advice.AllArguments Object[] ary,
                      @Advice.FieldValue(value = "name", readOnly = false) String
                      nameField){

        System.out.println("Inside enter method . . . ");

        if(ary != null) {
            for(int i =0 ; i < ary.length ; i++){
                System.out.println("Argument: " + i + " is " + ary[i]);
            }
        }

        System.out.println("Origin :" + origin);
        System.out.println("Detailed Origin :" + detaildOrigin);

        nameField = "Jack";
        return System.nanoTime();
    }
```

```
    @Advice.OnMethodExit(suppress = Throwable.class, onThrowable = Throwable.class)
    static void exit(@Advice.Enter long time){
        System.out.println("Inside exit method . . .");
        System.out.println("Method Execution Time: " + (System.nanoTime() - time) + " nano
        seconds");
    }
}
```

You should see output like this:

```
Inside enter method . . .
Argument: 0 is John
Origin :public java.lang.String Robot.greetUser(java.lang.String)
Detailed Origin: Robot greetUser
Inside greetUser method . . .
Inside exit method . . .
Method Execution Time: 90445 nano seconds
return value: Hello John! I am Jack
```

Breakpoints don't work in the `Advice` method because the code is inlined directly into the target class by ByteBuddy. It's a good idea to keep these methods as small as possible.

I explained how to develop bytecode using ByteBuddy. ByteBuddy is used in conjunction with JavaAgents. The JavaAgent has `Premain`, `Agentmain`, and `Transformer` methods, which are used in conjunction with ByteBuddy `Advice`. The OpenTelemetry agent is developed using ByteBuddy, JavaAgent, and OpenTelemetry.

3.8.2. Extension Demo

Automated instrumentation is the process by which an agent modifies the bytecode of an application class to inject code. The agent does not modify the code directly but modifies the bytecode loaded into the JVM. This is done while the JVM is loading the class, so the modifications are applied at runtime.

Here's a brief description of the process:

- **Starting the JVM with an agent:** When starting a Java application, specify a JavaAgent with the `-javaagent` command-line option. This tells the JVM to load the agent before the application's main methods are called. At this point, the agent can set up a class file transformers.

- **Registering a class file converter with ByteBuddy:** The agent registers class file transformers with ByteBuddy. The converter is called whenever a class is loaded into the JVM. The converter receives the class's bytecode and can modify it before the class is actually used.

CHAPTER 3   TRACE-CENTRIC RCA

- **Bytecode conversion:** When a converter is called, it uses ByteBuddy's API to modify the bytecode. ByteBuddy allows you to specify transformations in a high-level representation instead of writing complex bytecode manually. For example, you can specify a specific class and method within the class you want to instrument and provide an interceptor that adds new behaviors to that method.

- **Transform byte code:** Suppose you want to measure the duration of a method. You can tell ByteBuddy to target a specific class and method and then provide an interceptor that wraps the method call. Whenever this method is called, the interceptor is called. First, the start time is measured, then the original method is called, and finally, the end time is measured, and the duration is output.

- **Using the transformed class:** After the agent sets up the transform, the JVM continues to load the class as usual. Each time a class is loaded, the converter is called to modify its bytecode. The application then uses these transformed classes but has the additional behavior injected through the interceptor.

Automated instrumentation with ByteBuddy modifies the behavior of Java classes at runtime, without requiring any direct changes to the code. This is useful for cross concerns such as logging, monitoring, or security, as the code can be managed and consolidated in a JavaAgent instead of being distributed throughout the application.

Here is an application for instrumentation. It simply asks you to enter text and then counts the number of words.

```java
package org.davidgeorgehope;
import java.util.Scanner;
import java.util.logging.Logger;

public class Main {
    private static Logger logger = Logger.getLogger(Main.class.getName());

    public static void main(String[] args) {
        Scanner scanner = new Scanner(System.in);
        while (true) {
            System.out.println("Please enter your sentence:");
            String input = scanner.nextLine();
            Main main = new Main();
            int wordCount = main.countWords(input);
            System.out.println("The input contains " + wordCount + " word(s).");
        }
    }
    public int countWords(String input) {
```

```
        try {
            Thread.sleep(10000);
        } catch (InterruptedException e) {
            throw new RuntimeException(e);
        }

        if (input == null || input.isEmpty()) {
            return 0;
        }

        String[] words = input.split("\s+");
        return words.length;
    }
}
```

Next, you need to run the applications and extensions. If you are starting with an application, use the OpenTelemetry agent to build and run it.

```
java -javaagent:opentelemetry-javaagent.jar -Dotel.metrics.exporter=otlp -Dotel.logs.exporter=otlp -Dotel.service.name=your-service-name -jar simple-java-1.0-SNAPSHOT.jar
```

Without instrumentation, nothing will happen. That's because the OpenTelemetry agent doesn't know what to instrument. The automated instrumentation works in that for well-known frameworks like Spring or HTTPClient, you can automatically inject trace code into those frameworks to get visibility.

The Java application has no prior knowledge of org.davidgeorgehope.Main. That class and its methods are custom applications by the developer. Fortunately, there is a way to add them, using the OpenTelemetry extension framework. The OpenTelemetry extension-related files are located in WordCountInstrumentation.java and WordCountInstrumentationModule.java.

You can see that the OpenTelemetry extension uses ByteBuddy, a library for instrumenting code. However, there are some key differences in how the code is bootstrapped.

The WordCountInstrumentation class is one of the instances of TypeInstrumentation.

TypeInstrumentation is grouped by applicable class loader and can only be enabled or disabled as a set.

The primary way to inject code using OpenTelemetry is inline. You can inject dependencies into the class loader using the InstrumentationModule configuration.

Inject the TypeInstrumentation and WordCountInstrumentation classes into the class loader.

```
@Override
    public List<String> getAdditionalHelperClassNames() {
        return List.of(WordCountInstrumentation.class.getName(),"io. opentelemetry.
        javaagent.extension.instrumentation.TypeInstrumentation");
    }
```

CHAPTER 3   TRACE-CENTRIC RCA

Another interesting part of the TypeInstrumentation class is its settings. An InstrumentationModule must have at least one name.

```
public WordCountInstrumentationModule() {
      super("wordcount-demo", "wordcount");
}
```

You can view the methods of this class to specify the order in which to load it relative to other instruments, if necessary; it extends TypeInstrumentation and specifies the class responsible for the instrumentation.

Now, take a look at the WordCountInstrumentation class, which extends TypeInstrumentation.

```
public class WordCountInstrumentation implements TypeInstrumentation {

    @Override
    public ElementMatcher<TypeDescription> typeMatcher() {
        logger.info("TEST typeMatcher");
        return ElementMatchers.named("org.davidgeorgehope.Main");
    }
}
```

The target class for instrumentation is defined in the typeMatch method, and the method you want to use for the instrument is defined in the transform method. I am targeting the Main class and the countWords method.

The onEnter and onExit classes tell you what to do when you enter the countWords method and what to do when you exit the countWords method.

```
@SuppressWarnings("unused")
    public static class WordCountAdvice {

        @Advice.OnMethodEnter(suppress = Throwable.class)
        public static Scope onEnter(@Advice.Argument(value = 0) String input, @Advice.
        Local("otelSpan") Span span) {

            Tracer tracer = GlobalOpenTelemetry.getTracer("instrumentation-
            library-name","semver:1.0.0");
            System.out.print("Entering method");

            span = tracer.spanBuilder("mySpan").startSpan();

            Scope scope = span.makeCurrent();

            return scope;
        }
```

The onEnter method sets up a new OpenTelemetry span, and the onExit method exits the span. When the method exits successfully, you get the word count and add it to the attribute.

```
@Advice.OnMethodExit(onThrowable = Throwable.class, suppress = Throwable.class)
    public static void onExit(@Advice.Return(readOnly = false) int wordCount,
                          @Advice.Thrown Throwable throwable,
                          @Advice.Local("otelSpan") Span span,
                          @Advice.Enter Scope scope) {

        scope.close();

        if (throwable != null) {
            span.setStatus(StatusCode.ERROR, "Exception thrown in method");
        } else {

            span.setAttribute("wordCount", wordCount);
        }

        span.end();
    }
```

Develop an extension using the OpenTelemetry API, like setAttribute.

There are two important things to note. The first is that you set the javaagent parameter to toopentelemetry-javaagent.jar. This will start the OpenTelemetry JavaAgent running before the code is executed.

Inside the JAR file, there should be a class with a premain method for the JVM to find. This will bootstrap the JavaAgent. As described, all compiled bytecode is filtered through the JavaAgent code by default, so you can modify the class before it is executed.

The second important point here is the configuration of javaagent.extensions, which loads the extensions. I built it to add instrumentation to this application.

Now you run the following command. Since I created this attribute in the span code as shown here with wordCount as the "Integer" type, I can automatically assign it as a numeric field.

```
span.setAttribute("wordCount", wordCount);
```

When you run the extension, you should see the following results:

```
InstrumentationScope instrumentation-library-name semver:1.0.0
Span #0
    Trace ID      : e898347a2a04a9691f8ba3b14e43c76f
    Parent ID     :
    ID            : 75af7fc7ecc6da59
    Name          : mySpan
    Kind          : Internal
```

CHAPTER 3   TRACE-CENTRIC RCA

```
    Start time       : 2024-03-31 02:10:03.77131869 +0000 UTC
    End time         : 2024-03-31 02:10:13.77182043 +0000 UTC
    Status code      : Unset
    Status message   :
Attributes:
    -> thread.id: Int(1)
    -> thread.name: Str(main)
    -> wordCount: Int(3)
    {"kind": "exporter", "data_type": "traces", "name": "logging"}
```

The implementation of the OpenTelemetry JavaAgent using the extension framework emphasized the agent's ability to inject trace code into the application to facilitate monitoring.

In general, the purpose of extensions is not only to instrument frameworks and protocols that are not instrumented by the agent, but also to minimize manual instrumentation and automate it. As an example of automation, an extension can be used to configure trace contexts and baggage contexts. If you need additional probes and health checks, you should include them in your extension as well. I don't recommend adding a lot of functionality to extensions, but extensions are a good way to go if you can't count on developer support.

You should first develop with manual instrumentation and understand the pattern of instrumentation in the logic. A good way to do this is to implement the manually instrumented logic as an extension and automate its instrumentation. Since the logic implemented as an extension is automatically instrumented, it does not require source changes and does not require developers to modify all microservices.

The instrumentation and extension approach is not the best way to go.

- Bytecode instrumentation using JavaAgents adds roughly 2 percent or more overhead with class loading and bootstrap.

- If you consider measuring the time before and after a critical method, to get current time requires a system call to the kernel's timer. There are two calls of 100 microseconds each.

- If you write the log to the file system, there is one system call. which takes roughly 200 microseconds.

- There is a 50-microsecond latency in the methods that calculate latency, inject, and extract.

If you add the latency of the system calls to write and get timestamp, you will have hundreds of additional microseconds of latency because many system calls are required over 10 microseconds. Before developing an extension, you should calculate the increased overhead and latency and minimize the impact on your service. Extensions aren't as cheap as you might think.

So far, I've described the ByteBuddy API and the OpenTelemetry extension API.

3.8.3. Debugging Extensions

When debugging, you need to choose between debugging the agent and the microservice.

You need to understand the roles of agents and extensions and approach the problem differently. If you encounter a problem with instrumentation, you should prioritize debugging the extension and agent.

Agent are more complex and difficult to debug than microservices.

However, the system-level debugging that SRE performs involves debugging the internals of the agent and the extensions.

There are cases where extensions developed for manual instrumentation fail to instrument or propagate incorrectly, and the need to analyze the agent internals in detail arises. However, the agent is also a system-level application that uses bytecode internally, so you need to understand and approach the system at a low level.

Commercial observability offers its own SDK and provides the ability to develop your own extensions that are not OpenTelemetry extensions. The problem is that the commercial observability SDK only supports manual instrumentation. The configuration of the commercial observability agent is not publicly available, so automated instrumentation is not possible. In this case, you need to use the commercial observability's SDK to develop a standard JavaAgent that enables automated instrumentation. JavaAgents developed with the commercial observability SDK should not create a `traceparent`. It should create an `x-`.

3.8.3.1. Advice Methods

The `Advice` annotation has an option to disable inlining, which allows breakpoints to work within the `Advice` method. This option should only be used for debugging.

Therefore, it is best to first debug the method that the `Advice` calls rather than the `Advice` method itself.

```
@Advice.OnMethodEnter(inline = false)
```

To debug the `Advice` method and agent initialization, use the following method.

```
System.out.println();
Thread.dumpStack();
```

You can output the modified class files to a directory where you can decompile them so you can see exactly what changes are happening. With an existing target directory defined, add the following to the JVM startup arguments.

```
-Dnet.bytebuddy.dump=/some/path
```

It is important to specify `-agentlib` to debug agent initialization code (e.g., `OpenTelemetryAgent`, `AgentInitializer`, `AgentInstaller`, and `OpenTelemetryInstaller`). You must specify `-javaagent:` JVM argument before the JVM argument and use `suspend=y`.

CHAPTER 3   TRACE-CENTRIC RCA

3.8.3.2. Enable Debugging

The following example shows the remote debugger configuration. The breakpoints should work for all code except the ByteBuddy advice method.

You need to add the jdwp option for remote debugging, as shown here:

```
java -agentlib:jdwp="transport=dt_socket,server=y,suspend=y,address=5000"
-javaagent:opentelemetry-javaagent-<version>.jar -jar app.jar
```

The trace data is generated in the build/native/agent-output folder.

Configure internal debug logging for the agent, as shown here:

```
-Dotel.javaagent.debug=true
```

You should be careful with debug logging because it negatively impacts the performance of your application.

3.9. Propagating Commercial Observability

Commercial observability also has its own set of pros and cons:

- Support for specific packages. In some cases, it supports EAI server and mainframe CICS, such as TIBCO and webMethods.

- The internal implementation logic of trace does not break and produces concatenated results with as little interruption as possible.

The most important technology in commercial observability and in observability implemented with OpenTelemetry is the agent. It is important to understand how they work and how to troubleshoot problems with them. Agents are used to instrument traces, but it is also important to know how to debug them to understand their problems and internal structure.

- I recommend enabling the log for E2E. For example, the IDs that should be written to the log are trace_id, span_id, dt.trace_id, dt_span_id, thread id, thread name, traceparent, tracestate, x-dynatrace, dtd, various cookies, and JSESSIONID in the header. If the trace ID is changed, empty, or abnormal, it is easy to find the abnormal section in the log.

- Commercial observability has provided its own headers and propagation methods since before OpenTelemetry and now provides a way to associate its own headers with OpenTelemetry headers. The commercial observability agent merges spans instrumented by various agents.

Sometimes, you'll use multiple trace standards together, such as Micrometer traces, x- trace IDs, and OpenTelemetry traceparent. In the process of implementing observability, you will experience agent chaos. This is the confusion caused by instrumenting multiple agents together. Resolving agent chaos varies from commercial observability to commercial observability, so it needs to be debugged and analyzed.

When using micrometer traces, OpenTelemetry agents, and commercial observability agents, there are three cases, as shown here:

- Micrometer trace provides a bridge. You can use `micrometer-tracing-bridge-brave` or `micrometer-tracing-bridge-otel`. In general, if `micrometer-tracing-bridge-otel` is used, it creates `traceparent` first. The commercial observability agent adds an `x-` and propagates the `traceparent`.

    - Using only the commercial observability agent generates `x-` and `traceparent`, and the two trace IDs are the same.

    - If Micrometer is used with the commercial observability agent, `x-` and `traceparent` are different.

    - When using Micrometer, the OpenTelemetry agent, and a commercial observability agent altogether, `x-` and `traceparent` are different.

Using the various agents together, the trace is analyzed as follows:

1. This is a case where propagation fails using OpenTelemetry alone but succeeds using commercial observability.

2. Sometimes propagation fails in commercial observability, and sometimes it succeeds in OpenTelemetry.

3. Commercial observability alone is not instrumentation, but OpenTelemetry can be instrumented to create more spans.

While I understand the benefits of commercial observability, it's common for developers and architects to have a strong preference for OpenTelemetry, which puts the SRE in a difficult position in Cases 2 and 3. SREs need to provide clear guidelines so that users of commercial observability don't spend too much time and effort. This can be done by explaining the internal behavior of the agent to users and working with them on solutions.

If you're spending a lot of money building observability with commercial observability and not getting the results you expect, this chapter will help you improve.

3.9.1. Automating Commercial Observability

Dynatrace provides a variety of automation features to support observability.

Commercial observability agents use sensors, so certain spans are generated. Server consumer have problems. Clients, internals, and producers are not accurately instrumented.

There are cases where the order, relationship, structure of spans is output incorrectly. For example, REST requests display the correct order of spans, but GraphQL displays the wrong order of spans, or the parent span ID is incorrect. You can define the order and role of spans, as shown in Figure 3-34.

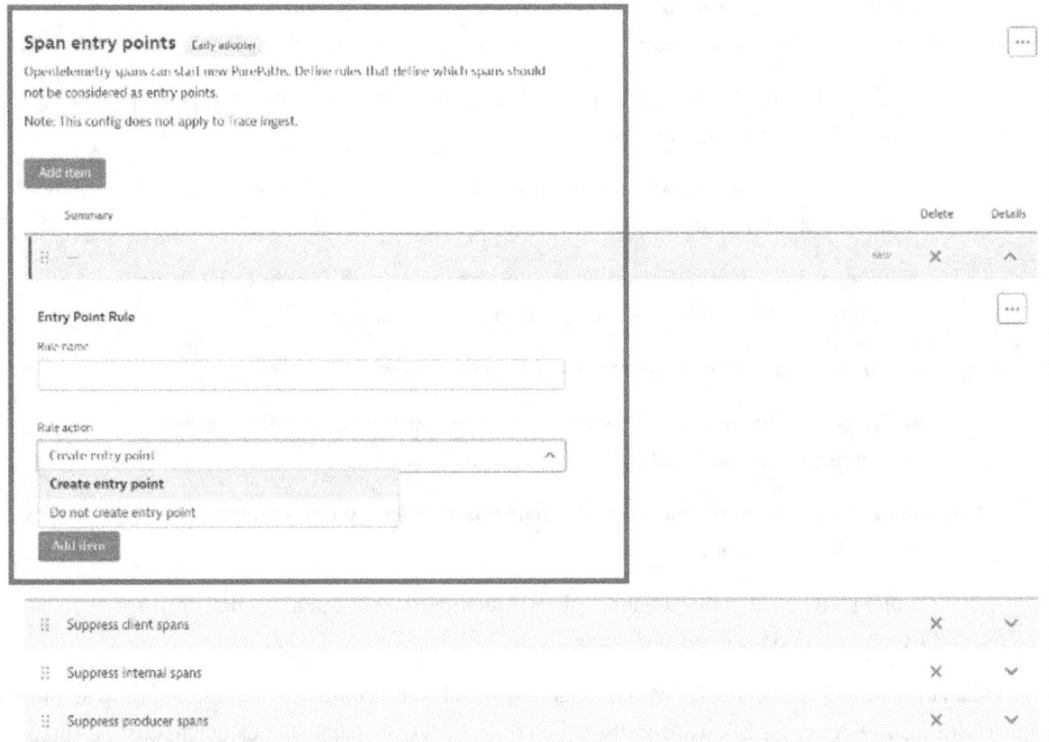

Figure 3-34. *Setting the span entry point*

Figure 3-35 provides the ability to define a `tracestate` for OpenTelemetry. Use OpenTelemetry traces to improve interoperability between different traces.

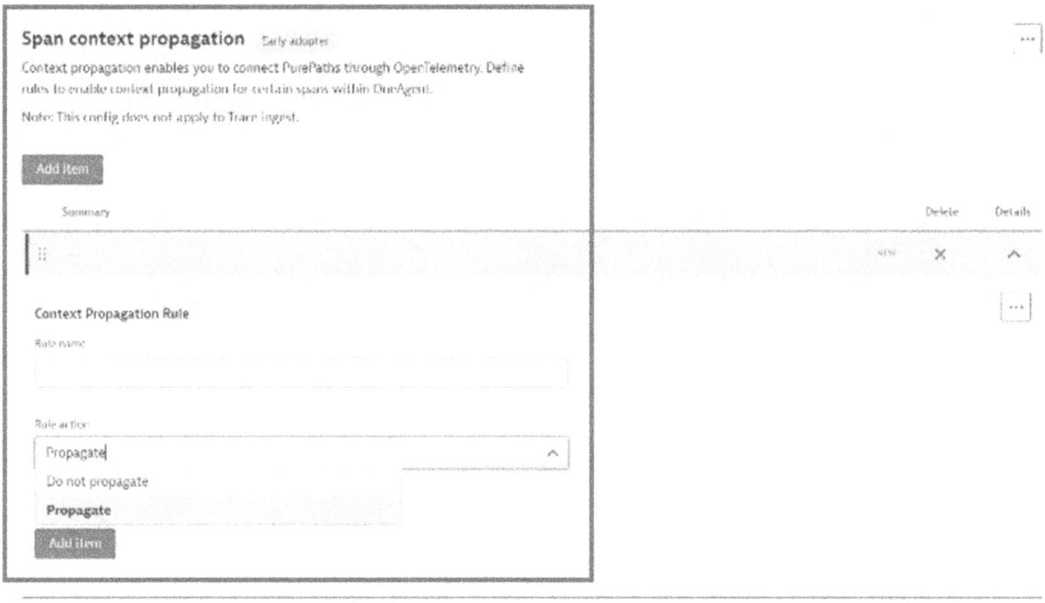

CHAPTER 3 TRACE-CENTRIC RCA

Figure 3-35. The tracestate automation feature

Figure 3-36 provides the ability to add Java methods and parameters to trace contexts and spans. They are only transferred to backend storage. This provides similar functionality to the OpenTelemetry span attribute, which makes it easy to identify and search for spans.

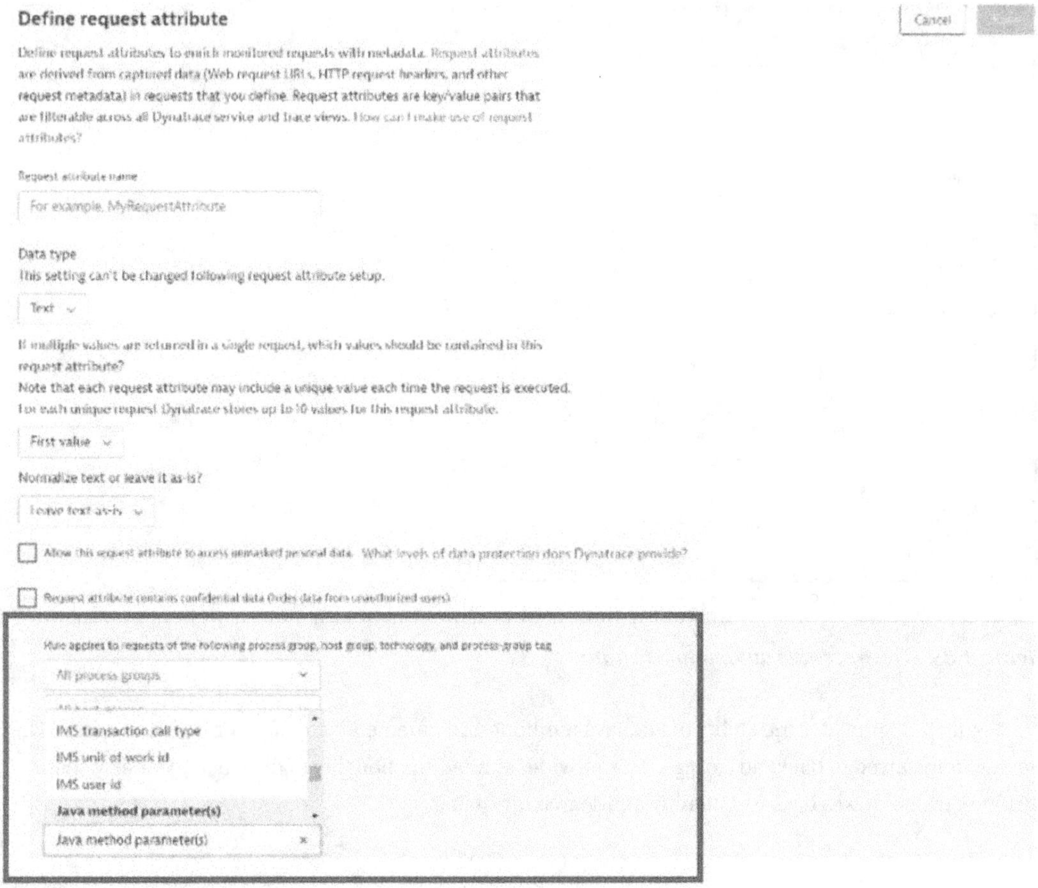

CHAPTER 3   TRACE-CENTRIC RCA

Figure 3-36. Adding request attributes

Figure 3-37 provides the ability to define events. An event captures the header and body of a message, which can be collected and analyzed.

CHAPTER 3 TRACE-CENTRIC RCA

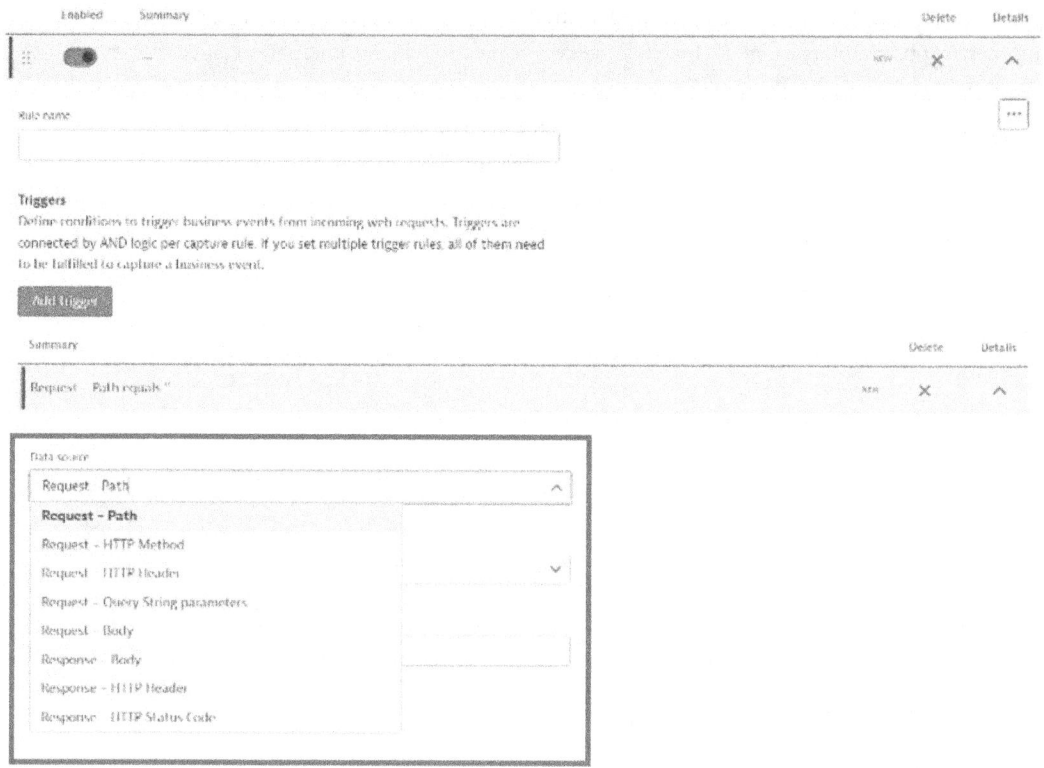

Figure 3-37. Adding an event

Figure 3-38 provides the ability to inject and extract trace contexts into the header of various applications. When the W3C trace context is enabled, it creates a `traceparent` and `tracestate` in the header.

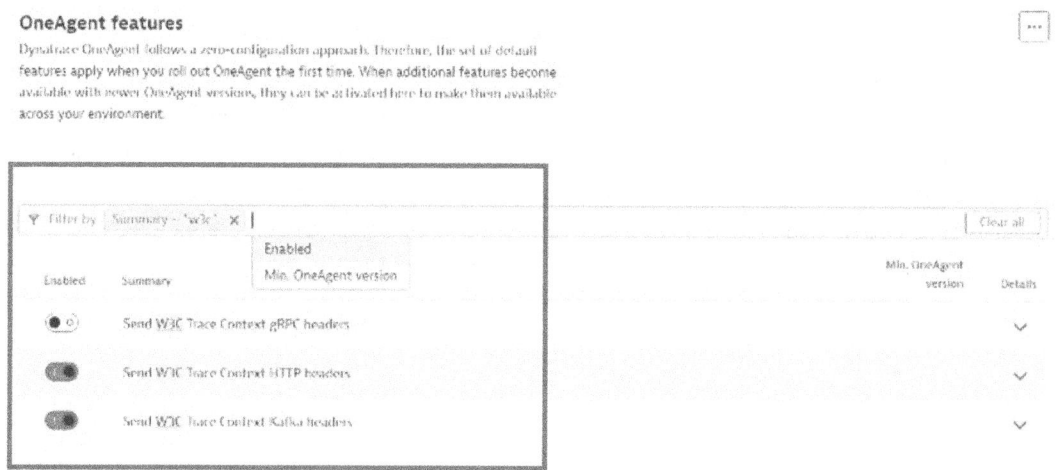

Figure 3-38. Enabling the agent feature

CHAPTER 3 TRACE-CENTRIC RCA

You can establish compatibility and propagation between the OpenTelemetry agent and the commercial observability agent. If OpenTelemetry is successful in instrumentation and commercial observability is successful, the OpenTelemetry span is copied to the span in commercial observability.

If you activate the function in Figure 3-39, side effects occur.

For example, inactivating the commercial observability agent means the instrument in Service B fails (see Table 3-3). In this case, the commercial observability trace ID does not output a value. OpenTelemetry will be able to successfully instrument and trace the entire E2E.

Table 3-3. Failed Propagation

	OpenTelemetry Trace ID	Commercial Observability Trace ID
Service A	1	2
Service B	1	
Service C	1	

If you activate Figure 3-39, an unexpected situation occurs. If commercial observability fails to instrument, copy the OpenTelemetry trace ID to the commercial observability trace ID. See Table 3-4.

Table 3-4. Inorrect Propagation

	OpenTelemetry Trace ID	Commercial Observability Trace ID
Service A	1	2
Service B	1	1
Service C	1	1

Eventually, the commercial observability trace ID is split into two, and the E2E trace fails.

Further development is required to instrument and propagate Services B and C in commercial observability, as shown in Table 3-5. This option is used to merge traces instrumented with OpenTelemetry and traces instrumented with commercial observability, but it can cause problems if only OpenTelemetry succeeds in instrumentation. To overcome this problem, you can consider `tracestate`. However, since the problem is caused by the failure of commercial observability instrumentation, manual or automated instrumentation should be developed using the commercial observability SDK.

Table 3-5. Correct Propagation

	OpenTelemetry Trace ID	Commercial Observability Trace ID
Service A	1	2
Service B	1	2
Service C	1	2

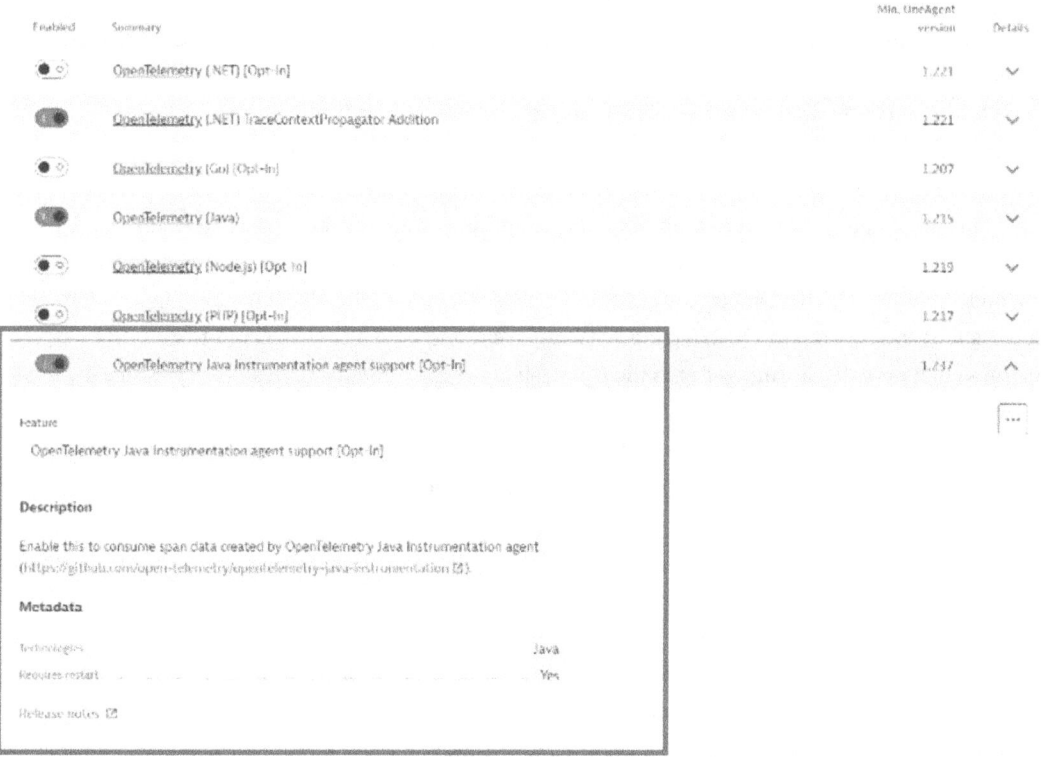

Figure 3-39. Setting up OpenTelemetry to propagate.

In addition to that, it offers a wide range of automation features. There is extensive implementation of bytecode instrumentation, as shown in Figure 3-39.

This provides automation to add a custom service if service discovery fails or to add a custom service. Even if it's a black box and you don't know what's inside, you can use profiles to see which methods are invoked by your request. If you specify the identified methods as custom methods, a span will be generated every time the request is processed. By analyzing with profile and applying bytecode, you can accurately generate spans and propagate traces even in the black box.

The agent provides a way to automatically or manually add trace context to a log. Whether the log is structured or unstructured, the agent provides a way to automatically add trace context and provides convenience. The manual method of adding trace contexts to logs is no different than the log MDC method.

3.9.2. Agent Chaos

By using multiple agents together, you will experience unexpected problems. You can use `tracestate` to troubleshoot problems.

It is not uncommon for commercial observability agents to fail to instrument or for traces to be broken. When using multiple agents, OpenTelemetry provides a solution using `tracestate`, but be aware that there are limitations.

`dt.trace_id` is written to the log, and `x-` is written to the message header.

In conclusion, if you are using commercial observability, you should prioritize the instrumentation of commercial observability over OpenTelemetry and instrument OpenTelemetry at a lower priority to maintain compatibility. Commercial observability supports `x-` trace context in the header, like `x-`. This allows propagation between microservices instrumented by commercial observability agents because they can understand `x-`. OpenTelemetry only uses `traceparent`, not the `x-`header. It is common for commercial observability to support both OpenTelemetry `traceparent` and `x-`, with `x-` being prioritized. The `x-` instrumentation results are merged with the OpenTelemetry instrumentation results to produce the final result of the trace.

The OpenTelemetry header is described first, followed by the commercial observability header.

OpenTelemetry has agreed on a new standard header called `traceparent`. This header is recognized as a standard header that should be passed by services.

`traceparent` contains all the fields needed to propagate trace contexts in a common format to support interoperability. This includes a unique 128-bit trace ID for distributed traces and a parent span ID. The `traceparent` can specify a given trace, and then propagate this data to downstream.

The trace context standard defines both the headers themselves and the values they can contain. The `traceparent` header contains the parent's span ID, which is the required information for enabling traces.

You need to define the sampling behavior that determines which traces are captured and which are not. This information is necessary because most trace systems only capture a fraction of all traces. This information is needed to ensure that the right traces are captured and that traces that will be discarded later are not captured. The `traceparent` is not the only header used in a trace. There is a second header called `tracestate`.

The `traceparent` header seems like it has everything you need to maintain transaction context within a distributed application. However, most implementations require more information than can be defined in the `traceparent` header.

`tracestate` is an optional header that can be used to propagate vendor-specific information. When a trace is propagated between two services instrumented through different vendors, the vendor-specific data for each service is added to the existing `tracestate`.

Pass a trace vendor-specific context in a list of key-value pairs. By using `tracestate`, you can interoperate with trace contexts used by other commercial observability. When setting a `tracestate`, you must use the `ot` key to include all in the entry, and the value must be a semicolon-separated list of key-value pairs.

```
ot=p:8;r:62
ot=foo:bar;k1:13
```

To keep the existing value, the set value must be updated or added to the `ot` entry of the `tracestate`. For example, if k wants to set an additional `k1:13`, `ot=p:8;r:62` becomes `ot=p:8;r:62;k1:13`. If the value of k1 already exists, `ot=p:8;k1:7;r:62` will be updated to `ot=p:8;r:62;k1:13`. The order does not need to be preserved.

A `tracestate` is similar to a label. The upstream injects the `tracestate` in the form of a key value. The downstream looks up the `tracestate` key values and extracts only the key values it needs.

To solve the problem of propagating trace contexts when using commercial observability, commercial observability supports the W3C trace context specification, which requires two standardized headers.

- `traceparent`: A header that identifies the trace ID and the parent's span ID.

- `tracestate`: Passes vendor-specific trace information and adds it like a label in the form of a key and value.

- `x-`: A unique header that is propagated to maintain backward compatibility with older commercial observability agents.

Dynatrace enables `tracestates` by default in HTTP. The upstream and downstream use `tracestate`, and the downstream's `tracestate` adds the upstream's reference to the `tracestate`.

The combination of these three headers allows the agent to propagate traces across the instrumented services. Figure 3-40 shows the flow of three scenarios.

- **Scenario 1:** In order to use `tracestate`, there is a condition. OpenTelemetry's instrumentation must succeed. Commercial observability uses `tracestate` to propagate the trace context of the instrumentation with OpenTelemetry.

- **Scenario 2:** This is when you use the OpenTelemetry agent and the commercial observability agent together. The OpenTelemetry agent creates a `traceparent`, and the commercial observability agent creates an `x-` context. The `x-` in commercial observability is of higher priority than OpenTelemetry `tracestate` to identify a trace.

- **Scenario 3:** The commercial observability agent supports both `x-` and `traceparent` and `tracestate`. Using `tracestate`, you can propagate to the commercial observability agent.

CHAPTER 3 TRACE-CENTRIC RCA

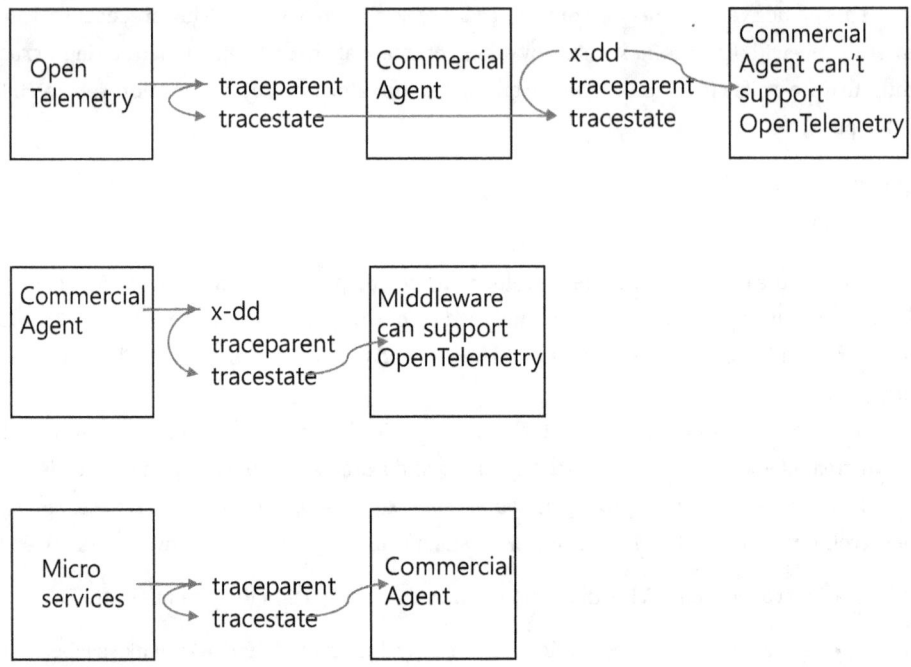

Figure 3-40. *Propagation between different traces*

You don't have to enable `tracestate` for all protocols, but only a few, mainly HTTP protocols. Automated instrumentation of message servers with OpenTelemetry does not create `tracestates` in most cases (Kafka, GCP PubSub, Solace JMS, TIBCO EMS, Spring Cloud Stream, and Azure SQS). Since there is no `tracestate` of the upstream, it is difficult to apply the `tracestate` of the downstream.

`tracestates` are most often manual instrumentation, not automated. Commercial observability is either automatically generated with `tracestate` rules applied or provides tools to automate it. Automation is still a work in progress. In open source, the methods that inject and extract `tracestates` need to be developed manually.

Commercial observability agents need to maintain compatibility with OpenTelemetry while allowing the vendor to take the lead. In terms of traces using the Spring Framework alone, OpenTelemetry offers more features than commercial observability. Commercial observability agents also support certain areas that OpenTelemetry does not, so it is best to use multiple agents together to maintain compatibility and scalability.

With so many benefits of OpenTelemetry, it's important to use multiple agents together.

3.9.2.1. The tracestate Demo

Vendor-specific trace formats can cause problems and break traces.

Different types of header formats can be used together in a trace context, In Figure 3-41, only span B is instrumented with commercial observability. Spans A and C are instrumented with OpenTelemetry—`traceparent` and `tracestate` exist. The trace is broken, and three trace IDs are created.

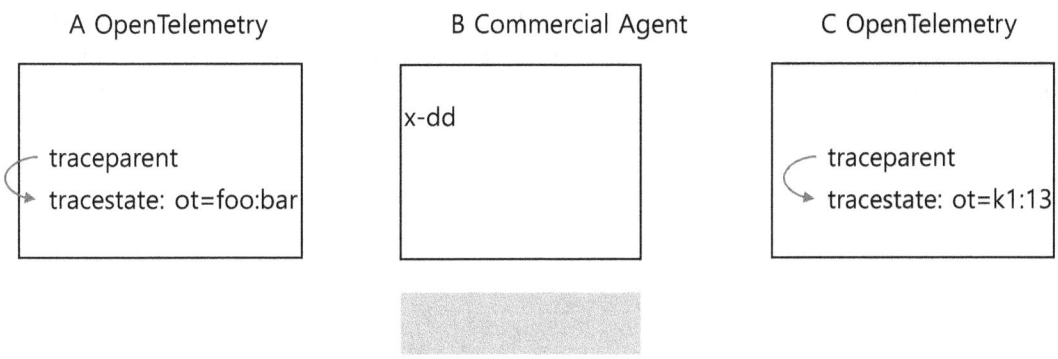

Figure 3-41. *Failure to propagate between traces of this type*

As the request travels from service A downstream to B and C, each agent must propagate its own trace context to the downstream services. However, if services are instrumented by agent that use incompatible headers, the trace context is not propagated properly between services. The result is individual traces with missing or broken spans.

Example 1

Using tracestate, you can see that the two different types of trace contexts are connected, as shown in Figure 3-42.

- Services A and B require OpenTelemetry agents configured, and Services A and B require tracestates.

- A vendor-specific tracestate is added to Service B's tracestate.

- The x- in commercial observability takes high-priority. Because differences can occur depending on commercial observability, you should understand the prioritization of internal trace contexts through the debugging process. The trace context used for traces in E2E is x-.

Figure 3-42 centers on Microservices B, instrumented with commercial observability and includes Spans A and C, instrumented with OpenTelemetry.

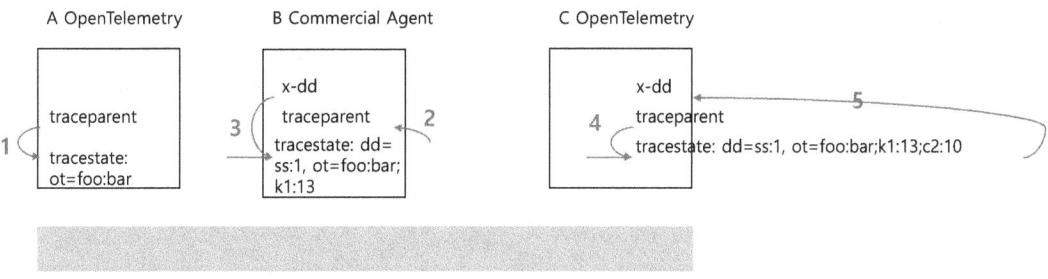

Figure 3-42. *Propagate types with tracestate*

CHAPTER 3 TRACE-CENTRIC RCA

Services A and C are associated with Service B using tracestate and propagate successfully. Even though the instrumentation of commercial observability fails, the commercial agent is not installed and there is no x- in A or C.

1. Service A adds traceparent to tracestate.

2. Service B copies from the propagated tracestate to the traceparent.

3. Service B adds x- to the tracestate.

4. Service C adds traceparent to tracestate.

5. Service C generates x- from tracestate.

In this way, Services A, B, and C can propagate the trace context.

With the introduction of the W3C trace context, Service B can now successfully receive the incoming trace header from Service A. It constructs a new tracestate header by adding its own vendor-specific ID.

Example 2

The upstream doesn't have x-, but it would require additional development to configure it to propagate using tracestate. Since x- is a feature only supported by commercial observability in Figure 3-43, commercial observability must be configured to recognize such propagation in traces. On the commercial observability, E2E traces must be configured around the commercial observability trace ID.

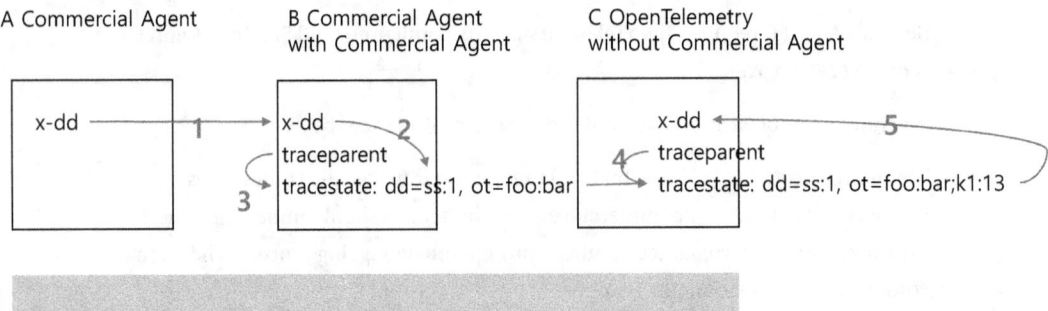

Figure 3-43. Propagate types with tracestate

You'll need to understand exactly where the trace breaks, and make sure your instrumentation propagates and debug it. It is best to instrument normally, without configuring a complex situation like tracestate, and given the additional development and maintenance of tracestate, this is not recommended.

1. Service A propagates x-.

2. Service B adds x- to the tracestate.

3. Service B adds traceparent to tracestate.

CHAPTER 3   TRACE-CENTRIC RCA

4. Service C adds `traceparent` to `tracestate`.

5. Service C generates `x-` from `tracestate`.

The downstream can be configured to be associated with the upstream by simply configuring `tracestate` without `x-`. Since the `tracestate` has the `x-` trace context of the upstream, you can create the `x-` manually.

1. If commercial observability is not installed, no `x-` header is generated.

2. If instrumentation succeeds, an `x-` and `traceparent` are created.

OpenTelemetry does not automatically generate `tracestates`, so development is required to propagate with downstream `tracestates`. Automation should be done using JavaAgents and extensions to avoid having to modify all microservices, and propagation and transfer should be considered.

- Agent chaos is caused by the use of multiple agents and the failure of instrumentation of commercial observability. to successfully instrument upstream. Commercial observability provides SDKs so you can develop instrumentation manually.

- If it is difficult to configure commercial observability upstream, manual instrumentation with OpenTelemetry should be done upstream to create a `tracestate`, which should be associated with the `tracestate` downstream.

In addition to `traceparent`, OpenTelemetry introduces a number of other concepts, including span attributes, span link, baggage, and `tracestate`. This book explains the differences between the various concepts and provides guidance for developing them for your purposes.

3.10. Summary

This chapter described how trace is applied in managed services, message servers, server frameworks, and EAI servers. SREs should understand the limitations of OpenTelemetry and commercial observability and provide appropriate guidance to developers.

The chapter explained how to develop manual instrument if automated instrument are not possible, and how to develop agents with OpenTelemetry extensions to automate manual instrument.

Developers are used to application-level programming, so system-level programming a system like an agent can be daunting. SREs may need to do some of the development themselves, or they may need to work closely with application developers.

While the techniques described in this chapter are certainly useful, it will take a lot of trial and error to put them into practice. In addition to the technology, you may face organizational opposition. Nothing an SRE can do in isolation, and without decision-making and full support from senior directors, it will be difficult to build momentum and create successful outcomes.

CHAPTER 3   TRACE-CENTRIC RCA

Technology is complex, but organizations are harder and more complex. I know because I've failed more often because of organization than technology. Both SREs and developers need to be passionate, open-minded, and collaborative.

If the SRE doesn't provide clear direction, root cause analysis will not succeed. I hope you learn from the various examples described in this book, convince your developers, and improve your operations with the right direction.

CHAPTER 4

Observability Practices by the Industry

4.1. Introduction

I have described how different technologies support observability. It's important to understand the limitations of the traces that OpenTelemetry currently provides, and it's necessary to develop and fill in the gaps. SREs should explain what developers don't understand and work with them to solve problems.

RCA is organized around two broad themes:

- How do you organize the relationships between business, applications, and infrastructure?
- How do you understand technology, data, and business processes to improve RCA?

While the previous chapters only discussed technology, this chapter discusses the challenges and real-world examples of applying observability to complex domains. In addition to the technology, this chapter also discusses domain-specific data and business processes.

Don't try to solve a problem with technology alone. While Chapters 3 and 4 primarily use distributed trace, it's very narrow-minded to try to identify and solve problems with trace alone. Whenever possible, you should try to understand the business and come up with solutions that take both technology and business issues into account.

The applications used in the bank demo are as follows:

- Tuxedo: A TP monitor used by UNIX.
- CICS: A TP monitor that runs on the IBM mainframe. In the demo, it manages cash and savings accounts.
- SAP ERP: An enterprise resource planning application, but in banking it is used as core banking. In the demo, it processes payment service.
- Customer MDM
- Oracle ERP

CHAPTER 4 OBSERVABILITY PRACTICES BY THE INDUSTRY

- Manage File Transfer

- SWIFT CASmf: SWIFT middleware that supports FTP, MQ protocol, and MT message formats for communicating with the SWIFT network. The CASmf SWIFT Server interfaces with the SWIFT network and processes business-to-business payment and foreign exchange transactions. The Global PAYplus Payment gateway uses Tuxedo internally and processes transactions with the CASmf via MQSeries.

- Lotus Notes

- IBM MQ: An industry-standard queue-based message server.

- DataStage ETL

- FileNet BPM

The applications used in the Telecom demo are as follows:

- TIBCO Order Management

- Portal infranet

- Siebel CRM

- PeopleSoft ERP

- MetaSolv M6

- Oracle ASAP

It is important to align the various legacies with modern technologies. This chapter organizes the following architecture:

- Configures a bank architecture that monitors EAI, BPM, MDM, MFT, and ETL middleware and legacy systems.

- Applies orchestration servers that handle distributed transactions to telecom processes.

- Configures and monitors ultra-low latency architectures for online gaming and trading.

The previous chapter discussed technical failures. In addition to technical failures, business and data failures are also common.

If the problem is not in the application code but in the deployment and testing procedures, you can improve the reliability of your service. The next step is to prepare for problems caused by data inconsistency. In domains with complex processes, it can be difficult to understand the problems caused by the data. This is why it's important to organize your dashboards for data inconsistency cases. Since observability provides charts for basic SLO, dashboards should be able to fill in the gaps.

Most failures are caused by defects in testing procedures and microservice functionality. Failures related to infrastructure are on the around 10 percent. Microservice failures are partial, meaning they are limited in scope and non-critical. If the failure is due to the deployment of a new microservice, identify and roll it back immediately. The root causes of microservice failures are difficult to resolve quickly, but the service is still available.

Service-level issues are easy, but when critical data conflicts and consistency issues arise, SREs and developers can't fix them alone; they need to be addressed by business experts who understand the data. Data inconsistencies require understanding and restoring the affected data, which is a difficult and time-consuming task to automate.

Infrastructure failures are pervasive and can affect any microservice contained within the infrastructure. Rolling back and restarting services won't fix the problem. The failure is likely to persist or recur somewhere unknown. Compared to individual microservice failures, data and infrastructure failures are harder to identify and take longer to resolve.

The basis of failure handling is not to quickly analyze the root cause but to quickly restore the service to normal. Restoration is prioritized over identifying the root cause.

Smaller services can be autoscaled, but be careful about applying autoscaling to legacy or black box systems.

Applications should always pay attention to concurrency and consistency. The problem with logic is that it often comes down to data concurrency and consistency. It's not a microservice problem, and just because it works doesn't mean the service is error-free. It could be that the batch that ran in the evening caused the data to be inconsistent.

If it's a data issue, it's more likely to be a bad development in the code. These are not issues that SREs can directly intervene and fix. However, they should be able to identify the type of issue, quickly assign the right person to resolve it, and guide them to a quick resolution. SREs should not only be concerned with availability, error rate, and latency but should also strive to improve the reliability of the service.

While technically addressing concurrency and consistency issues, the business case for reconciliation, ledger, and double-bookkeeping can be made to resolve data issues. Developers build retry and idempotent APIs. Concurrency and consistency are always needed, but consistency that implements distributed transactions is technically challenging. Instead of consistency, the problem is often solved by manual reconciliation and double-bookkeeping. If the data issues are small enough to be handled manually, they are handled manually. But if there are too many problems, it's time-consuming, and error-prone to be handled manually, then consistency should be implemented in an automated way. Rather than favoring technology alone, it's important to consider the business and find an efficient solution that combines possible solutions. Consider the different ways data can be processed accurately.

To maintain data consistency between services, it's important to ensure that requests are processed exactly once.

Maintaining data consistency between internal and external services typically utilizes idempotent and reconciliation processes. If the external service supports idempotent, then the same idempotent key should be used when retrying the transaction, such as a payment. However, even if the external service supports an idempotent API, you can't assume that the external system will always correct, so you can't skip the reconciliation process.

CHAPTER 4   OBSERVABILITY PRACTICES BY THE INDUSTRY

In addition to technical problems, root cause analysis requires an understanding of the business and product. To implement E2E trace, it is important to understand how traces are processed along with the business process. This requires collaboration with architects and business users, not just developers. In addition to technical expertise, SREs need to have the right attitude and business knowledge. They need to learn their terminology in order to talk to product owners and business analysts and solve problems together.

The work of an SRE is cross concern and requires collaboration with other organizations and constituents. Sometimes, it's not always best to solve problems technically, and sometimes, it's necessary to come up with business alternatives. You'll often run into situations where technology can't solve all the problems, so it's important to find ways to work together to solve them.

The basic architecture described in this book is outlined here:

- The frontend is not blocking, but non-blocking with Reactor.
- The backend uses a message server and is configured as event-driven.
- The database uses NoSQL.
- The backoffice and EAI are connected by message servers.
- Managed services, black boxes, and legacy systems need observability.
- The data pipeline uses a message server.

I believe that synchronous REST request and response and relational databases don't apply as much as they used to. Instead of synchronous, relational databases and blocking, the future trend is to use asynchronous, callback, event-driven messages, NoSQL, epoll, coroutines, schedulers, non-blocking, and graphQL, and these make up the to-be architecture that are introduced in this book.

1. The process of delivering requests to the server is not simply processed by a single thread.
2. This supports trace, but there are problems with logs, and this still needs to be improved.
3. Different agents behave differently. This confuses developers.
4. The more emerging the technology and the more flexible and dynamic the architecture, the harder it is to implement observability.
5. Agents often fail to instrument, are thread-unaware, or produce inaccurate spans.

This can happen if OpenTelemetry fails and commercial observability succeeds or if commercial observability fails and OpenTelemetry succeeds. It's great if both succeed, but it's a problem if only one succeeds. For example, with an OpenTracing Shim, only OpenTelemetry succeeds, but in a batch, only commercial observability succeeds. Some server frameworks that are deployed as extensions also only succeed with OpenTelemetry. The webMethod, TIBCO, only supported commercial observability. SREs should provide the right guidelines to developers; otherwise, it will start chaos.

CHAPTER 4   OBSERVABILITY PRACTICES BY THE INDUSTRY

Different industries have different requirements for observability. This chapter discusses the requirements of each industry with examples.

The demos are divided into banking, telecom, and online gaming.

- Industries with legacy systems: Banking and telecom
- Non-legacy industries: Online gaming

Historically, banking and telecom have required E2E tracing and distributed transactions. Even before the introduction of CQRS and Saga, they were processing E2E tracing and distributed transaction in different ways.

Let's implement the following demo on different domains:

- Banking implements E2E tracing.
- A Saga pattern will bring observability to telecom's distributed transactions and support rollback and revision processing.
- Online gaming will implement CQRS and cache to separate reads from write paths.

While open source has become mainstream, many banking organizations pay for and use commercial solutions. For example, EAI servers use TIBCO to implement application integration. EAI server requires adapter to work with a variety of legacy applications. Each adapter is implemented using the legacy application's client API.

It's common for organizations to have a variety of applications and protocols, and for E2E observability to work, they need to support a variety of technologies. If a problem occurs in the middle and the trace is stopped and broken, managing this diversity and complexity is the role of the SRE in implementing observability. Observability is a difficult technology.

Before SRE and observability, it is important to understand the domain. SLO and trace must be defined based on an understanding of the business. If you don't understand the business and domain, it's difficult to gather requirements, and you're more likely to end up with unclear and inaccurate observability.

SREs can't understand all the code and processes; they need to provide guidelines for business analysts and developers to build observability.

This chapter covers the following topics:

- Understanding observability practices and problems specific to each industry.
- Understanding E2E trace and distributed transaction processing, including legacy systems.
- Understanding the observability patterns that correspond to different microservices patterns.

CHAPTER 4   OBSERVABILITY PRACTICES BY THE INDUSTRY

4.2. Observability in Banking

In this section, you see how to configure an E2E trace in a fund-transfer process involving 30 legacies.

In the banking industry, a single transaction is processed by hundreds of requests. This complexity makes it difficult to quickly troubleshoot problems in the event of a failure. E2E traces are the starting point for troubleshooting problems.

Most of the demos in this book are optimized for microservices architectures. However, in the real world, legacy systems are already playing an important role. Legacy systems are a technical liability, but they contain experience and know-how and are an important asset for organizations. The microservice does not handle core functionality in complex domain such as banking or telecom, and you use the microservice as a gateway to support channels. The core functionality resides in the legacy system and is ultimately committed from the legacy system.

When introducing new microservices-based systems and perfecting observability, legacy systems and interfaces should always be considered. The preference is to take advantage of new technologies, represented by the cloud and Kubernetes, while effectively interfacing with existing legacy systems and incrementally improving the business and technology. Banking tends to be cautious and conservative from a cultural and organizational perspective. WAS and database monitoring have been mandatory, and microservices and observability are being adopted incrementally as they adopt newer technologies and improve their systems. Observability optimized only for microservices does not support existing legacy systems, making it difficult to use E2E trace.

The software used in the banking E2E trace demo and Telecom distributed transaction demo is not open source but uses commercial solutions, which makes it difficult for readers to test. The demo server has configured all the applications used in this book. For more information on how to use the app, add a comment in Git and I will provide you with a guide.

I will provide all the systems that can be demoed and tested in various ways, such as Git and YouTube.

4.2.1. The Bank Process

Data issues are not easily understood. This is because SREs have not been involved in data issues, and it is not easy for them to understand the high-level business processes. but the developer's understanding is narrow and often doesn't help solve the overall problem. This is why it's important to collaborate to solve the problem.

4.2.1.1. Concurrency

Banks use the term payment. A *payment* is an fund transfer and it involves two actions: a withdrawal and a deposit. Concurrency issues can arise with payments.

For example, how do you prevent double payments? Two issues need to be addressed:

- The same user can press the payment button multiple times.

- You have $100 in your account balance. A $100 withdraw in fund transfer is in progress, but a $100 utility bill payment has started at the same time.

There are two approaches to the first problem:

- **Client-side implementation**: Hide or disable the payment button after the client sends the request. This solves most double-click issues. However, it's not very reliable. For example, if a user disables JavaScript, then the client-side verification process can be bypassed.

- **Idempotent API**: Add an idempotent key to the payment API request. An API that produces the same result no matter how many times is called a duplicate API. Using the payment ID as an idempotent key solves the double payment problem.

Most queries in the system use the payment ID as a filtering condition.

Since the payment ID is the primary key of the payment table, no new records will be created that violate the uniqueness condition of the primary key. This avoids the double payment problem.

Based on the ACID attribute of the database, the data that the fund transfer transaction changed is not visible to the utility payment transaction until the fund transfer transaction is complete. Therefore, the utility bill payment transaction also completes the payment.

Both the fund transfer and the utility bill payment have been processed, and the balance is now -$100. To solve this problem, you need to utilize locks.

Using a lock on the database, you can solve the problem. However, this requires a lot of testing, as different databases may have different configurations for handling locks.

As soon as a user attempts to update a record, you immediately lock it to prevent simultaneous updates. Other users who want to update the record must wait for the user who first locked it to finish making changes and release the lock.

When you run a `SELECT FOR UPDATE` statement, the record returned by the `SELECT` is locked. If the fund transfer transaction ran first, the utility bill payment transaction must wait for fund transfer transaction to finish.

Because the fund transfer transaction locks the record first, the utility bill payment transaction's statement must wait for the fund transfer transaction to finish. After the fund transfer transaction finishes, the utility bill payment transaction can be processed.

Advantages:

- Prevents the application from updating data that is being changed.

- It is easy to implement and serialize all update operations to prevent conflicts. Locks are useful when data is in a highly volatile situation.

Disadvantages:

- Locks on multiple records can cause deadlocks. Writing deadlock-free application code can be complex.

- It's not very scalable. If a transaction leaves a lock unreleased for too long, other transactions cannot access the locked resource. This has a serious impact on database performance, especially if the transaction has a long lifetime or involves many entities.

4.2.1.2. Consistency

During the payment process, several services are called to maintain state information:

- The Payments service maintains payment data, including payment IDs such as non-redundant random numbers, payment amounts, and execution status.
- The Ledger holds all accounting data.
- The Accounts maintain users' account balance.
- Data can be replicated across multiple copies of the database for increased reliability.

In a distributed environment, communication between services can fail and result in data inconsistency. Let's take a look at the techniques used to solve data consistency issues in this payment process.

- A two-phase commit is a database protocol that guarantees atomic transaction execution across multiple databases and nodes. The idea is that all databases and nodes are guaranteed to finalize the transaction either successfully or unsuccessfully. If any databases fails, 2PC will rollback entire transactions. It's not a high-performance protocol.
- Saga is a collection of transactions that happen locally on each databases or node. When each transaction completes, it creates and sends a message that serves as a trigger to start the next transaction. If any transaction fails, Saga executes a sequence of transactions that undo all the results of the previous transaction.

While 2PC is a concept of satisfying the ACID property with a single transaction across multiple nodes, Saga should be viewed as relying on the resulting consistency because each step is a single transaction.

With 2PC, consistency can only be verified after the transaction is completed. A common method of verification is to compare internal records with bank statements. However, while this reconciliation may reveal that there is an inconsistency in the data, it doesn't tell you why the discrepancy occurred. Therefore, you need to build a system that is reproducible, called *event sourcing*.

4.2.1.3. Data Synchronization

Concurrency, consistency, and synchronization can be used interchangeably and raise the same issues. For the purposes of this book, I use my own definitions of these terms.

Concurrency occurs when multiple requests compete for a single resource, while consistency occurs when a long-running business processes committed multiple databases in a single transaction. Synchronization compares, validates, and matches data between the source and target database, such as it is caused by data discrepancy between operational and analytical database.

Data enters the operational system and is passed to the analytics system. The analytics system is comprised of four systems:

- **Change data capture**: Captures changes in real-time from the operational system database and sends them to the data warehouse.
- **Data warehouse**: ETL transforms and loads data from the data warehouse into a data mart.
- **Data mart**: Data marts are organized according to subject.
- **OLAP**: Aggregates and analyzes the data.

ETL handles the processing and loading of data between databases.

If records are missing along the way, or if a transformation goes wrong, users will see incorrect results. If the data is incorrect, you need to analyze the cause, reprocess it to match the data, and maintain data synchronization. It's not good practice for users to make arbitrary changes to the data, and you run the risk of creating other problems in the future.

Analytics systems, which consist of data pipelines, must ensure data synchronization. The operational system is the data source and must ensure accurate data through concurrency and consistency. If the analytics system is inaccurate, it is compared with the operational system to identify the discrepancy and achieve synchronization.

4.2.1.4. Reconciliation

When systems communicate asynchronously, there is no guarantee that messages will be delivered or that a response will be returned. This is a common problem in payment business processes, which often use asynchronous communication to increase system performance. External systems, such as credit rating agencies and central banks that interface with banks, also favor asynchronous communication. So, how do you ensure accuracy?

The answer is *reconciliation*, which is the process of periodically comparing the status of related services to make sure they match. It's typically the last line of defense for payment systems.

Every night, banks send reconciliation files to external banks and institutions. The reconciliation file lists the balance of a bank account and all the transactions that took place in that account during the day. The reconciliation system reads the details of the settlement file and compares them to the ledger system.

Reconciliations are also used to check the internal consistency of your payment system. For example, you can verify that the ledger and accounts have the same status.

Differences found during reconciliation are usually referred to the finance team for fixing manually. Possible discrepancy problems and solutions can be divided into three categories:

- **You know what type of problem it is, and you can automate the troubleshooting process**: You know the cause and how to fix it, and it's efficient to write an automation program. Engineers can automate reconciliation of inconsistencies.

CHAPTER 4   OBSERVABILITY PRACTICES BY THE INDUSTRY

- **You know what type of problem it is, but you can't automate the troubleshooting process**: You know the cause of the inconsistency and how to fix it, but the cost of automated reconciliation is too high. You have to queue the discrepancies and have your finance team fix them manually.

- **It's an unclassifiable type of issue**: You don't know how the discrepancy occurred. You have to queue these discrepancies and ask finance to investigate.

4.2.1.5. Bookkeeping

Ledger systems have an important design principle called *double-bookkeeping*. Double-bookkeeping is essential to any payment system and plays a key role in keeping accurate records. All payment transactions are recorded in two separate ledger accounts for the same amount. A debit is made from one account, and a credit is made to the other.

In a double-bookkeeping system, all transaction entries must total zero. If you add a dollar, someone else has to subtract a dollar. This system allows you to track the flow of funds all the way through and ensures consistency throughout the payment cycle.

A ledger is a financial record of payment transactions. For example, when a user pays a merchant $1, it creates a record of a $1 debit from the user and a $1 credit to the merchant. The ledger system plays a critical role in post-payment analytics, such as calculating total revenue or predicting future revenue.

4.2.1.6. Retries

Payment systems must be able to handle failed payments appropriately. Reliability and fault tolerance are key requirements for a payment system.

At every stage of the payment cycle, it's important to maintain accurate payment status. Whenever a failure occurs, you need to know the current status of the payment transaction and determine whether a retry or refund is required. You keep the payment status in a database table where you can only add data.

To handle failures, it's a good idea to have a retry queue and a failed message queue.

- **Retry queue**: Retryable errors, such as transient errors, are sent to the retry queue.

- **Failed message queue**: Messages that repeatedly fail to process are eventually sent to the failed message queue. This queue is useful for debugging and isolating problematic messages and inspecting them to determine why they were not processed successfully.

One of the most serious problems that can occur with a payment system is double-billing a customer. It's important to design your payment system so that a payment order is executed exactly once. A given operation is executed exactly once if the following requirements are met:

- It is executed at least once.

- It is executed at most once.

Let's take a look at how retries can be used to guarantee at least one execution, and idempotent checks can be used to guarantee at most one execution.

There are times when a payment transaction needs to be retried due to network errors or timeouts. Retry mechanisms can be utilized to ensure that any payment is executed at least once. Consider a scenario where a client tries to make a $10 payment, but the payment request keeps failing due to poor network connectivity. The network eventually recovers, and the request succeeds on the fourth try. If retry and idempotent keys are not configured, the same transaction could be processed multiple times.

It is possible that the batch was stopped the day before, preventing the payroll from going out. You can dismiss this as not being in the scope of SRE, but it's obviously devastating to service reliability.

It's also useful to understand exactly when something was processed, like a Kafka offset, and how to utilize it when reprocessing.

When introducing retries, it's important to decide on the interval and the retry number you want to retry.

- **Fixed interval**: Wait a certain amount of time before retrying.
- **Incremental interval**: Incrementally increase the time to wait before retrying by a specific amount.
- **Exponential backoff**: Increase the wait time before retrying by twice the amount of time from the previous retry. For example, if the request fails the first time, wait one second before retrying, two seconds for the second failure, and four seconds for the third failure.

Determining the appropriate retry strategy is difficult. There is no one-size-fits-all solution. However, a general guideline is that if a network issue is unlikely to be resolved in a short period of time, use exponential backoff.

4.2.1.7. Idempotence

Idempotence is a key concept for ensuring at most once execution. From an API perspective, idempotence means that a client can repeat the same API call multiple times and always get the same result.

To communicate between a client and a server, an idempotent key is typically a unique value that is generated by the client and expires after a certain amount of time. Many technology companies recommend UUID as an idempotent key, and they are widely used in practice. To ensure the idempotent of payment requests, you can add an idempotent key to the HTTP body.

Scenario 1

When a user clicks the pay button, a idempotent key is sent to the payment system as part of the HTTP request. The payment system treats the second request as a retry because it has previously received the idempotent key included in the request. In that case, the payment system returns the most recent status of the previous payment request.

If the payment service receives many requests with the same idempotent key at the same time, it processes only one of them and returns a 429 Too Many Requests status code for the rest.

One way to support idempotent is to utilize database-specific key constraints.

Scenario 2

A user clicks the pay button again after successfully processing a payment, but a network error prevents the response from reaching the payment system.

The payment service sends a non-redundant random number to the external organization, and the external organization returns a token that corresponds to that random number. This random number uniquely identifies the payment, and the token corresponds one-to-one to the random number. Therefore, the token is also uniquely identifiable to the payment.

If the user presses the pay button again, the payment is the same, and so is the token sent to the external organization. Since the external organization uses the token as the idempotent key, it recognizes the double payment and returns the previous execution result.

4.2.2. Bank Legacy Systems

Modern startups often implement microservices architectures and have no legacy systems, so they don't need complex EAI server. However, traditional banking and telecom have legacy systems. It is important to align the new microservices architecture with the legacy architecture in order to achieve seamless observability. Therefore, the previous chapters described the microservices architecture first, and this chapter will describe and interface the legacy architecture.

The banking business is divided into account and information systems. The account system is divided into domains such as deposit, loan, wealth management, foreign exchange, and cards.

Banking is legacy-heavy and processes monetary transactions, so data consistency is critical. If an error or inaccurate calculation is made in a banking transaction, the bank is liable for damages and loss of trust. Because many accounts are managed across multiple core banking systems, distributed transactions and rollbacks in case of failure are important to support consistency between accounts across transactions.

The banking industry has various business units. Therefore, there are different core banks for each business unit, and customers' accounts are managed in multiple core banks. Banking can sell various products, such as deposits, funds, and cards, to one customer, so it needs to be connected to various core banks to process them. The backend of banking is a complex mix of legacy and microservices. In the case of international banking, there is no standard technology architecture that is common to all business units. This is because each business unit started its business at a different time and adopted the appropriate technology architecture at that time.

A global banking organization runs its chart of accounts on a mainframe, and its database is an IMS-tiered database. With IMS running for more than 40 years, changing or migrating this legacy is a daunting task. Banking has been in business for a long time and is more legacy-intensive than other industries.

CHAPTER 4 OBSERVABILITY PRACTICES BY THE INDUSTRY

Popular middleware used in banking includes CICS, Tuxedo, MQ, and SWIFT, which are interfaced by adapter. Many legacy applications were developed using C and Cobol.

Korean banking has been using next-generation projects to consolidate core banking and legacy and replace it with new systems. While next-generation projects are risky, expensive, and inefficient, the benefits of technological innovation are clear.

When companies undergo mergers and acquisitions, start new businesses, or change leadership, it's hard to maintain technical consistency.

Korean banking is characterized by the fact that core banking is based on a commercial framework running on UNIX.

Korea often uses next-generation projects to downsize legacy systems and integrate work into next-generation systems. Foreign countries tend to use next-generation projects while improving decades-old systems. In the case of international banking, core banking is often operated on mainframes, and core banking on mainframes is operated with commercial frameworks.

International banking does not do the next generation, but maintains the existing legacy systems and uses service oriented architecture and microservices architecture to integrate new technologies with legacy systems. This improves the system incrementally. This often results in legacies that are more than 50 years old, and legacy systems often make it difficult to improve. The variety of legacy systems makes observability difficult.

In manufacturing, the number of parts in a finished product can be in the tens of thousands. To assemble a car, we need tens of thousands of parts and complex blueprints. Unlike manufacturing, banking doesn't have complex products but rather complex customer information. There are dozens of account types in banking, and customers' accounts are not managed in a single system but individually in a variety of systems, leading to duplication and consistency problems. Wealth, foreign exchange, card, fund, and deposit accounts are often managed in separate core banking systems. Querying a customer's account information often involves calling multiple core banking systems. Transactions are often processed in conjunction with various accounts, which requires distributed transaction processing. Where concurrency is the problem of multiple threads accessing a single resource, distributed transactions are about rollback and data consistency across multiple distributed systems.

The banking industry always faces challenges as they add observability to the various legacy applications and middleware.

Transactions in banking are divided into inbound and outbound transactions and consist of multiple stages of commitment. A funds transfer consists of an outbound request to an external banking system and an inbound request from the external banking system. A single transaction is composed and processed with a first commit to withdraw money and a second commit to deposit money.

In banking, you can't adopt a microservices architecture from the ground up. This is because the existing legacy architecture is still very much in place. Microservices architecture and open source have technical limitations in processing complex distributed transactions. The Saga pattern for distributed transaction processing is not yet mature. Banking already has used a variety of legacy middleware to process distributed transactions. Banking implements distributed transactions with CICS, Tuxedo, and Oracle databases. Banking uses the existing legacy 2PC distributed transaction processing without dependency on the Saga pattern.

CHAPTER 4   OBSERVABILITY PRACTICES BY THE INDUSTRY

By instrumenting the EAI server, you can save time and cost and achieve the technical objectives, rather than directly connecting to and instrumenting various legacy systems, as shown in Figure 4-1.

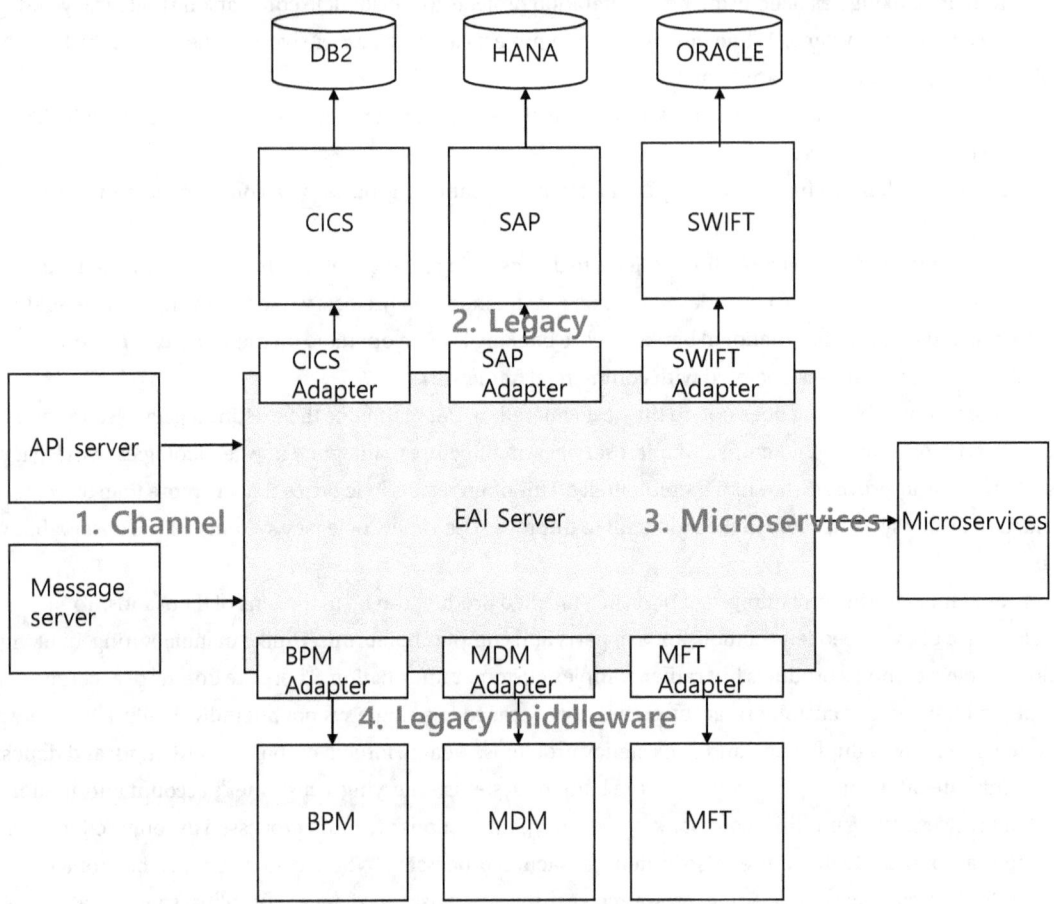

Figure 4-1. The EAI server integration process

Consolidating trace across E2E is an important feature provided by observability. However, it is difficult to organize E2E trace in real-world bank cases.

Various middleware is integrated into the EAI server. MDM, BPM, and MFT are closely interfaced to the EAI server. In other words, observability is configured, and a trace is generated through the EAI server.

If a single trace is broken and generates multiple separate trace IDs, root cause analysis becomes more difficult.

Existing monitoring tools are suitable for understanding the general pattern of failure using scatterplots, but it is difficult to understand the detailed latency and performance of each section.

This diversity makes it difficult to construct an E2E trace. In addition to black box and legacy systems that don't understand their internal operation, traditional message technologies like MQ and the CQRS microservices pattern are event-driven and loosely coupled. This dynamic and flexible architecture makes observability difficult.

Before adopting new technologies, architects and developers should share their pain points with SREs on the operational side.

From the introduction of traceability to its sophistication, it is necessary to share experiences with each other and make incremental improvements. If a system is opened only for flexibility and scalability to process large transactions, it is likely to cause difficulties from an operational perspective in the future.

It's better to talk to an SRE before you build a complex architecture and get feedback from each other than build a complex architecture and request that the SRE apply trace later. This often leads to awkward situations when development is complete, and the SRE wants to do instrumentation later.

Because microservices behave in a variety of ways, such as workflow, PubSub, event-driven, and batch, observability needs to account for a variety of exceptions. Trace is based on client instrumentation, but there are often ambiguous situations where there is no client in the architecture.

If it runs on the backend in a batch or is started by an async message event, like an EAI server, there is no client.

I demonstrate a full E2E trace implementation, incorporating legacy systems.

4.2.2.1. Tuxedo

Tuxedo is the industry standard for TP monitor, and you can develop applications using C, C++, COBOL, and Java to ensure 2PC and rollback. Tuxedo provides features such as transaction management, fault tolerance, and load balancing and acts as an application server. If CICS is the transaction processing monitor for mainframes, Tuxedo is the transaction processing monitor for UNIX. Using PowerBuilder and Delphi, you'll develop a Tuxedo client application.

Tuxedo uses the XA protocol to process complex distributed transactions and Tuxedo and Oracle databases to support 2PC. To this day, no other middleware supports XA and 2PC as well as Tuxedo, and it is widely used by most banking, telecom, and utility companies. The distributed transaction processing technology has a high barrier to entry and is not supported by open source.

Here are the components of Tuxedo:

- **Transaction Monitor Interface**: ATMI is an API to the Tuxedo system. It includes transaction, message processing, service interface, and buffer management.

- **Tuxedo service**: An application that can process requests from Tuxedo clients is called a Tuxedo service.

- **Tuxedo server**: A Tuxedo server is a process that manages a set of services. For clients requesting services, the Tuxedo server distributes each request from a Tuxedo client to the appropriate service. For service deployment, the Tuxedo server receives client requests, distributes them to service, and responds to the client.

- **Tuxedo client**: The Tuxedo client calls the Tuxedo method and library, collectively known as the Application Transaction Monitor Interface (ATMI). The client engages with the service only when necessary, disconnects from the service when the process is complete, and releases Tuxedo system resources for use by another client.

Tuxedo server and client communicate using a buffer. A buffer is similar to an IDL.

- **CArray**: A CArray is an undefined array of characters. For buffers of this type, the Tuxedo system does not interpret the meaning of the array. The length of a CArray must always be provided during publication.

- **FML32 buffers**: Tuxedo uses field buffers to define the format and layout of data transferred from the client to the server. The message returned by the ATMI creates a field buffer, and the Field Manipulation Language (FML) method is used to manipulate the message.

Tuxedo provides the following communication methods for messages between the client and server:

- **Synchronous**: The call to the method is blocked, and it is waiting for a response.

- **Asynchronous**: Does not wait for the requested service to complete. The client receives the result later.

- **Queue-based**: Through the Tuxedo messaging feature, the queue service provides the ability to store and search message.

- **Event-driven**: Register the event that needs to be called by an event broker and processes publication and subscription.

Tuxedo has the following gateway:

- Jolt is Tuxedo's Java client API.

- The WebLogic Tuxedo connector is a Tuxedo Java adapter provided by the WebLogic server.

- You can use the JMS C API to interface with the Tuxedo server.

- The TIBCO Tuxedo adapter provided by the EAI server uses the FML32 buffer to interface with the Tuxedo server.

There are many possible ways to do this, but the demo uses the FML32 and ATMI of the Tuxedo adapter to interface with the Tuxedo server.

The TIBCO Tuxedo Adapter interfaces with the Tuxedo server and acts as a client. The TIBCO EAI server can use OpenTelemetry for instrumentation. A span can be generated of all of the steps processed in conjunction with Tuxedo.

In order to start the Tuxedo server, you need to set various environment variables, as shown in the following code. When you run the Tuxedo server and application via `tmboot`, three processes start.

```
set TUXDIR=C:\bea\tuxedo8.1
set WSNADDR=//127.0.0.1:5000
set APPDIR=C:\tuxedo
set PATH=%TUXDIR%\bin;%APPDIR%;%PATH%
```

CHAPTER 4   OBSERVABILITY PRACTICES BY THE INDUSTRY

```
set TUXCONFIG=%APPDIR%\tuxconfig
set ULOGPFX=%APPDIR%\ulog
tmboot -y
Booting all admin and server processes in C:\tuxedo\tuxconfig
INFO: BEA Tuxedo, Version 8.1
INFO: Serial #: 650522264138-1214372389215, Expiration 2004-01-31, Maxusers 100
INFO: Licensed to: BEA Evaluation Customer

Booting admin processes ...

exec BBL -A :
        process id=364 ... Started.

Booting server processes ...

exec WSL -A -- -n //127.0.0.1:5000 -m 1 -M 10 -x 1 :
        process id=292 ... Started.
exec server -A :
        process id=1148 ... Started.
3 processes started.
```

Applying observability to a legacy system doesn't change the server application. Clients can be developed in a variety of languages and apply observability. Tuxedo's observability is implemented in the client, measuring latency between the client and server. If you can measure calls from inside the server to the database, you can create additional spans and perform detailed root cause analysis, but it requires a lot of testing because it can affect server processes. For observability, instrumentation on the client is a basic requirement.

The Tuxedo adapter becomes a Tuxedo client and calculates latency for requests to the Tuxedo server.

- The message server and client communicate using the FML message format. It is similar to COMMAREA in CICS and IDL in RPC.

- The Tuxedo adapter acts as a Tuxedo client, publishing input and output that conforms to the FML format with the Tuxedo server.

You can configure the request response schema required for the association based on FML, as shown in Figure 4-2.

CHAPTER 4   OBSERVABILITY PRACTICES BY THE INDUSTRY

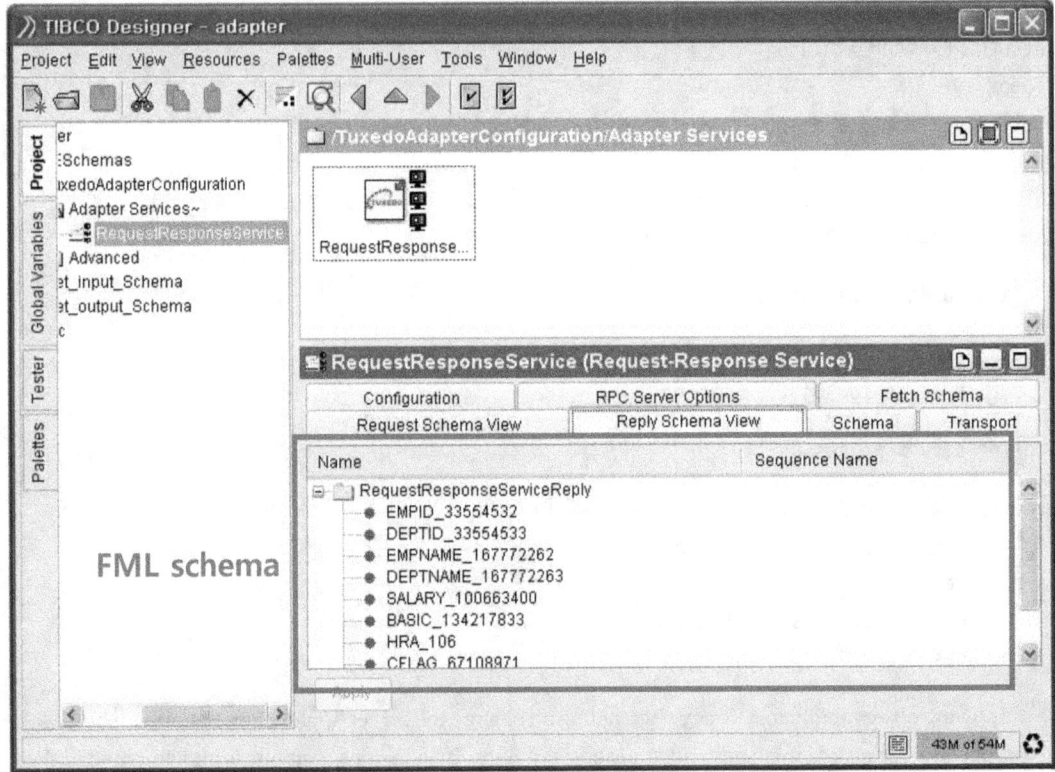

Figure 4-2. Tuxedo adapter configuration

Processes in the EAI server go through multiple steps to complete the process. Every individual step within a process should be measured in observability. A span should be created for each step. The latency, error rate, and throughput of each step must be measured in observability, so that you can respond to failure and perform root cause analysis.

Before OpenTelemetry and observability, it was difficult to output latency and throughput for each step. Traditional monitoring was limited to inside the EAI server. No technology existed that could trace the E2E as we attempt to do in this book.

Legacy professionals who have experienced the value of observability first-hand will agree that trace is an incredibly useful technology.

Tuxedo becomes the transaction manager and the EAI server becomes the resource manager, so you can configure two PCs with XA.

4.2.2.2. CICS

Banking is a classic domain that uses mainframes. Many banking organizations around the world are still using IMS middleware and tiered hierarchy IMS databases to deliver their services. More often than not, banking uses IMS TM (transaction manager) and DM (database manager), which are older than CICS and

CHAPTER 4 OBSERVABILITY PRACTICES BY THE INDUSTRY

DB2. Applications developed with PL1, which predates Cobol, run on proprietary protocols called SNA LU0 and LU6.2. CAPA is a core banking system developed by IBM in Japan, and before downsizing to UNIX, many Korean banks were implemented in this way.

The access channels of the core banking are internal terminal, internal system, and external organization, and the types of transactions supported differ depending on the access channel (see Table 4-1).

Table 4-1. Various Channels in Bank

Access Channel	Type	Description
Internal terminal	Terminal	The client program is written in C++ and connects to the gateway using TCP, which is connected to the core banking using SNA.
Internal terminal	ATM	The CAPA header is assembled at the branch and connected to the gateway using TCP.
Internal system	Server	This server is responsible for connecting the core banking and other systems. There are middleware, FEP, gateway servers.
External organization	Server	Connects to the account directly via X.25 or via the FEP server.

You need a server to process transactions requested from various channels, and CICS and IMS are middleware that run on the mainframe.

The network does not use TCP, but uses LU0 and LU6.2, and communicates SNA and TCP through the SNA server. SNA demo code is available for LU6.2 implementation with the IBM communication server.

The latest middleware is DB2 and CICS, and they use relational databases.

CICS stands for "Customer Information Control System". CICS is a mainframe-based TP monitor middleware to process distributed transaction and provide reliable banking services. CICS users submit transactions to be executed. A transaction consists of multiple applications that implement the required function.

The demo uses TXSeries, an open-systems version of CICS. It uses Cobol and C to develop applications and ensures compatibility with mainframe CICS. It also supports backend data storage, such as DB2 and VSAM (SFS). It creates and manages resources such as region listeners and filesystems. The developed demo Cobol application is registered as a program and transaction in TXSeries, and the Cobol application is deployed at runtime.

The CICS client can be implemented in a variety of ways. The traditional way is to use a 3270 terminal, as shown in Figure 4-3. In the past, business screens in banking were processed on 3270 terminals, although these days, they are more user-friendly and use the web.

Figure 4-3 shows the demo application running on a 3270 terminal.

CHAPTER 4   OBSERVABILITY PRACTICES BY THE INDUSTRY

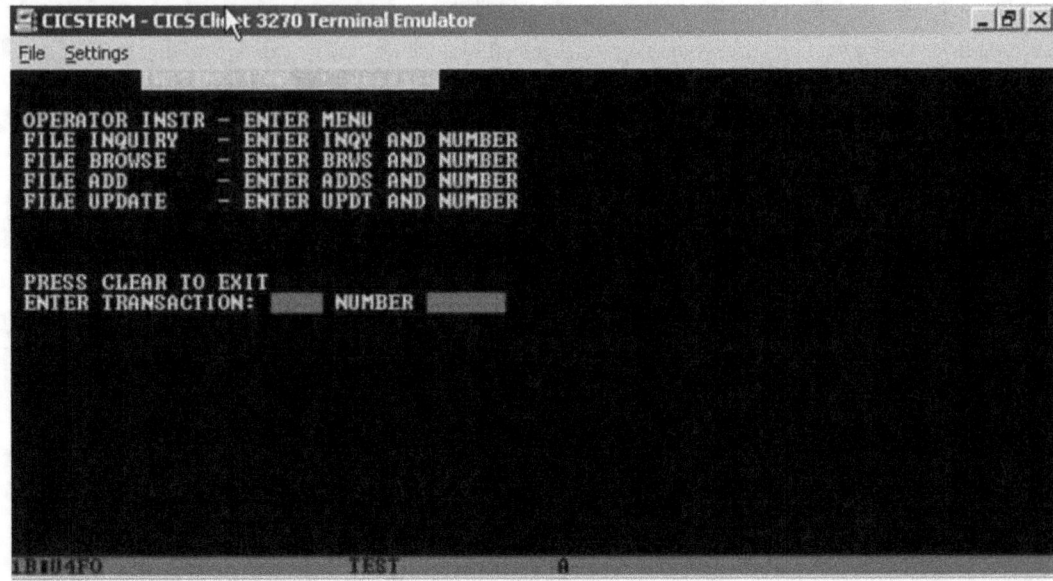

Figure 4-3. The 3270 terminal of the CICS demo application

OpenTelemetry does not provide a way to instrument applications developed in Cobol. CICS often has applications in Cobol, but there is no OpenTelemetry agent to support it. Given the conservative nature of banking, even if an agent were available, it is unlikely that any mainframe operator would agree to directly instrument a Cobol application.

Modifying CICS's Cobol source for manual instrumentation is not easy. Apart from the technical problems, it is not easy to get organizational buy-in. Therefore, the recommended approach is to instrument the application as a CICS client rather than instrumenting directly to CICS. Most CICS operators do not allow direct CICS connectivity for observability reasons, but validated clients will agree. In order to archive observability to CICS in a short period of time and at a low cost, you need to instrument in a validated way.

You can develop different types of client application using CICS Transaction Gateway (CTG), sockets, and more.

- Develop a Java application that calls the CICS Transaction Gateway. The CICS Transaction Gateway can be interface with CICS.

- Sockets can be used to interface with CICS.

- You can use the SNA C API to interface with CICS.

- You can interface with CICS through the TIBCO CICS adapter provided by the EAI server.

CICS supports socket communications. A program registered with CICS becomes a socket server, and the client is a socket client developed in various languages. The EAI server supports socket communication, so it can communicate with a socket server deployed as a CICS server. There are many ways to do this, but in the demo, a CICS Transaction Gateway and a CICS adapter are needed to implement observability.

CHAPTER 4 OBSERVABILITY PRACTICES BY THE INDUSTRY

A CICS Transaction Gateway requests and receives data from the CICS server via a Cobol copybook. CICS Transaction Gateways (CTGs) are often developed in Java. By using the OpenTelemetry agent to instrument a Java application deployed on a CICS Transaction Gateway, you can trace the transaction requested to the CICS server. Since the CICS server is assumed to be a black box, implementing trace through the CICS Transaction Gateway is a reliable method of observability.

With the OpenTelemetry agent, Cobol is not instrumentable, but Java is, so there is no problem implementing observability.

TIBCO EAI server provides a CICS adapter, which supports a direct interface to CICS or an interface via CTG. You can easily interface through the CTG. Therefore, observability is possible without a direct connection interface to Cobol and CICS. Many EAI servers do not support OpenTelemetry yet. However, webMethods and TIBCO EAI servers support OpenTelemetry instrumentation.

- TIBCO supports OpenTelemetry. Individual steps within a TIBCO process generate spans.

- webMethods do not support OpenTelemetry. Commercial observability provides the ability to instrument webMethods, which can be used to generate spans.

You need to find a way to instrument your EAI server, either through OpenTelemetry or commercial observability.

In the future, more EAI servers will support OpenTelemetry, and it will be easier to implement E2E trace and observability.

Here's how it works under the hood:

- CTG interfaces with programs and transactions in CICS through the CICS ECI interface.

- The CICS adapter uses the CTG API internally to interface to the CTG.

When the UCC and CICS server communicate, port 1435 is used by default, and if the program is developed in C, it will call directly from the UCC to the CICS server without a Java gateway. If you use the 3270 client to test program registered on the CICS server, use port 1435.

For Java program, the Java gateway is called using the 2006 port, followed by an internal call from the Java gateway to the UCC, followed by a call to the CICS server. The Java gateway and UCC are collectively referred to as CTG.

This demo requires the configuration of the CTG, the CICS server, and the TIBCO CICS adapter. First, configure the CICS adapter.

- Enter the CTG host and port.

- To run a CICS program, you must enter the user information registered with CICS.

- The transaction type is SXEX.

- For the CTG Server Name, enter the information for the CICS resource.

CHAPTER 4   OBSERVABILITY PRACTICES BY THE INDUSTRY

The EAI server can be connected directly to CICS, or it can be intermediated by CTG. In the demo, the EAI server is connected using CTG, as shown in Figure 4-4.

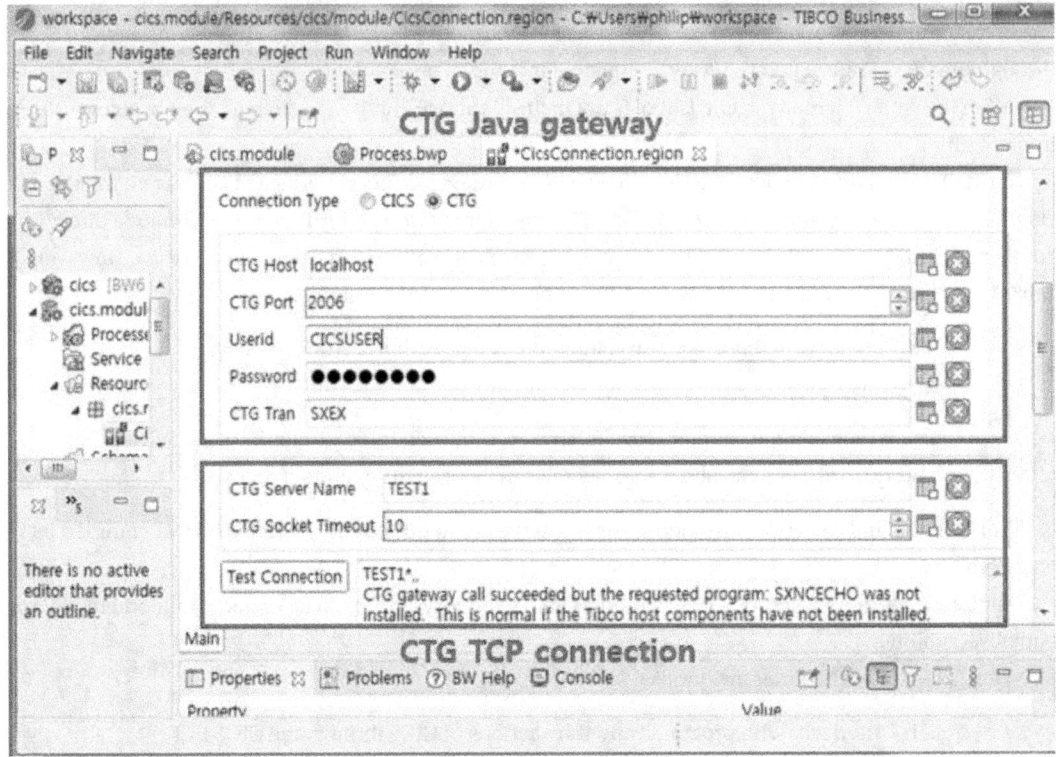

Figure 4-4. *Connection for the CICS CTG adapter*

Set up a CICS server:

- The protocol uses TCP.

- The initial transaction is optional and specifies a CEMT managed transaction.

- For the host name, enter the IP address of CICS.

Set up a CTG:

- Connect to CTG on port 2006.

- The protocol uses TCP.

- For the host name, enter the name of the CICS server. For the port, enter 1435, and then click the Done button.

While the legacy system is highly reliable, there is a chance that failures will occur as it tries to interface with new systems. Legacy systems also need observability to respond to failures and understand the cause. Legacy systems provide a variety of ways to interface. Direct instrumentation is best, but changing a legacy system can be challenging due to organizational and technical constraints, so I recommend using a gateway or an EAI server to configure observability.

There are four types of interfaces between legacy systems and EAI servers: request and response, subscription, publication, and request and response from the legacy system. This book focuses on the simplest—request and response and publication.

4.2.2.3. SAP ERP

SAP is the most commercially successful ERP and is used by most companies both domestically and internationally. It provides the business processes that companies need, such as logistics, accounting, and more. Aside from the frontend, where you serve customers, most of the backoffice is organized in SAP.

It has migrated from CICS Cobol applications to open Tuxedo C, and many legacy applications are being consolidated and migrated to SAP. More recently, SAP has been configured and operated in the cloud. SAP is used in a variety of industries, including banking, where the SAP Core Banking Solution is also used.

Tuxedo and CICS are middleware and do not include processes. SAP does include processes, and you can customize them to fit your requirements.

SAP has a complex architecture internally. The demo does not describe the internal complexity of SAP but rather the SAP client library for implementing observability. SAP consists of a NetWeaver application server and a HANA database. The NetWeaver application server receives requests from external clients and calls methods on the SAP server. SAP provides APIs in different ways. The SAP client can use the SAP API to interface with the SAP server.

The TIBCO SAP Adapter has an internal implementation of the SAP API and can communicate with the SAP server as a SAP client. The TIBCO EAI Adapter supports the following SAP integration interfaces:

- **Business Application Programming Interface (BAPI)**: BAPI is an externally provided method in a SAP business object. This interface is suitable for processing real-time queries and updates to the SAP server.

- **RFC (Remote Method Call)**: Allows you to call RFC-enabled SAP ABAP functions from the external system. Functionally similar to BAPI, but does not interface to a SAP business object.

- **ALE/IDoc**: ALE facilitates event-driven, asynchronous data interfaces.

BAPI, RFC. ALE/IDoc are available, but the demo uses the RFC method, as shown in Figure 4-5. To interface to the SAP server, you will develop a SAP client using the RFC and OData protocol.

CHAPTER 4   OBSERVABILITY PRACTICES BY THE INDUSTRY

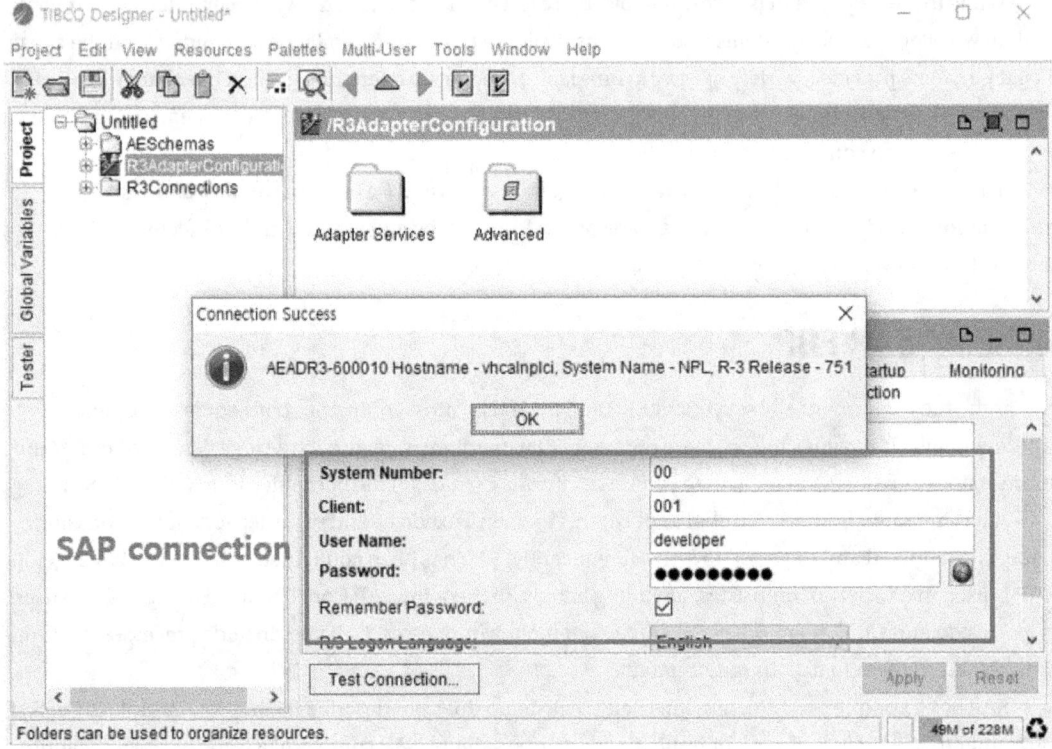

Figure 4-5. *Connection information for the SAP adapter*

You can use the OData client to call the NetWeaver application server, or you can use the RFC client library to call the RFC method on the SAP server directly. Since the RFC client is developed in JCO Java and OData provides a Java API, you can use the OpenTelemetry agent to generate traces.

- The OData client forwards requests to the NetWeaver server. It uses the HTTP protocol, similar to REST.

- Using the JCO Java library, you call the RFC program on the SAP server directly. This is the most common interface method in the past.

As with CICS and Tuxedo, it is useful to instrument the client that interfaces to the legacy rather than directly instrumenting the SAP server. The clients used in the demo are JCO and TIBCO SAP adapter. The TIBCO EAI server interfaces with the SAP adapter. By directly instrumenting the EAI server and SAP adapter, you can create a span.

Since JCO is a Java library, it needs to be configured in classpath. Enter the SAP connection information and check that the connection works.

Figure 4-5 shows the process of configuring a connection to the demo SAP server using the SAP adapter.

CHAPTER 4 OBSERVABILITY PRACTICES BY THE INDUSTRY

SAP RFC are components provided by SAP. SAP's internal function is developed as RFC. EAI server calls RFCs to interface with SAP. The EAI server and the SAP adapter are clients of the SAP server. By instrumenting the SAP adapter, observability can measure the requests that are passed to the SAP server.

Interfacing is about understanding the server and engaging with it using client technology. Observability is about measuring the client's request and response in the middle. Therefore, an SRE familiar with observability needs to understand the structure of the server and client and the various protocols.

When you select an RFC in the SAP adapter, it automatically generates the schema required for input and output, as shown in Figure 4-6.

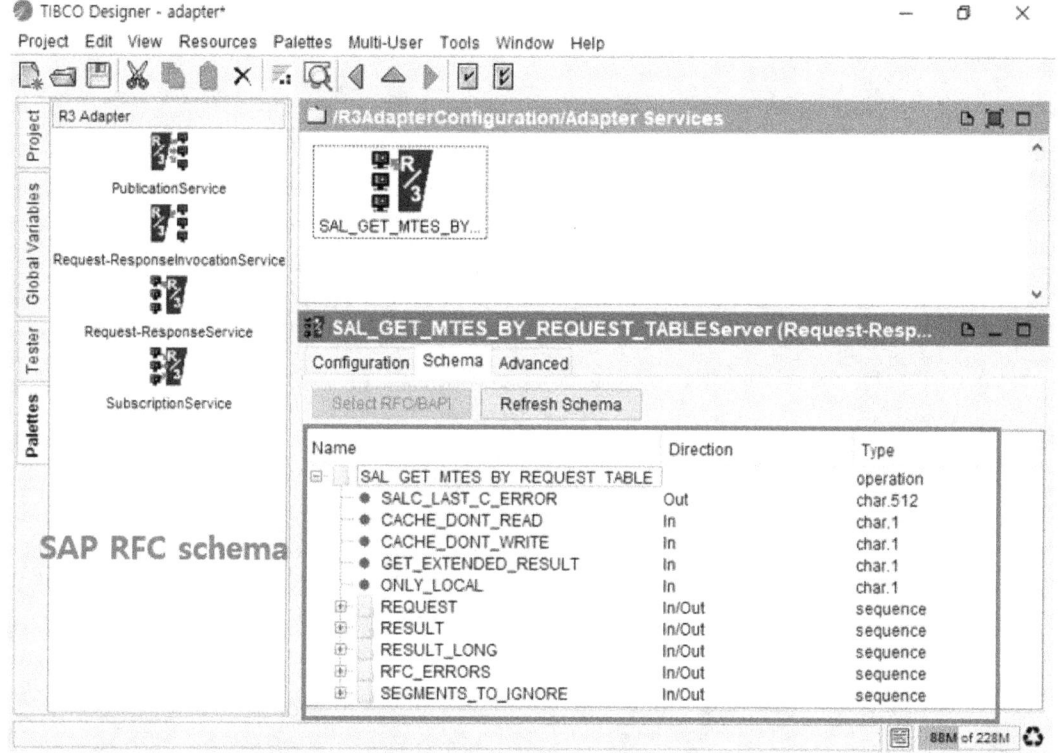

Figure 4-6. *The schema for a SAP adapter*

When you select a specific RFC, it automatically generates the necessary schemas for the input and output. You can see that the behavior is similar to Tuxedo's FML32. The client automatically generates the required schema for request and response, and the client requests the SAP server with request and response according to the schema format. Trace measures the duration of the request and response.

SAP, Siebel, and PeopleSoft business applications use components internally to organize business processes. They provide components externally. EAI servers can interface with components. CICS and Tuxedo, on the other hand, provide SDKs to develop schemas without including components under the hood.

4.2.2.4. Customer MDM

Banking systems manage the customer master. In the master data, there are product masters and customer masters, where the product master includes raw materials, semi-finished products, finished products, services, and so on. Product masters can contain other product masters (raw materials and semi-finished products) and form a bill of material (BOM). Product masters have attributes and define relationships between product masters. Product information is required by many different systems, so when a product is released or changes occur, the product master data is distributed and synchronized.

As shown in Figure 4-7, the customer MDM server provides a REST API to interface with the external system, and you can use the EAI server development tool to develop the interface process.

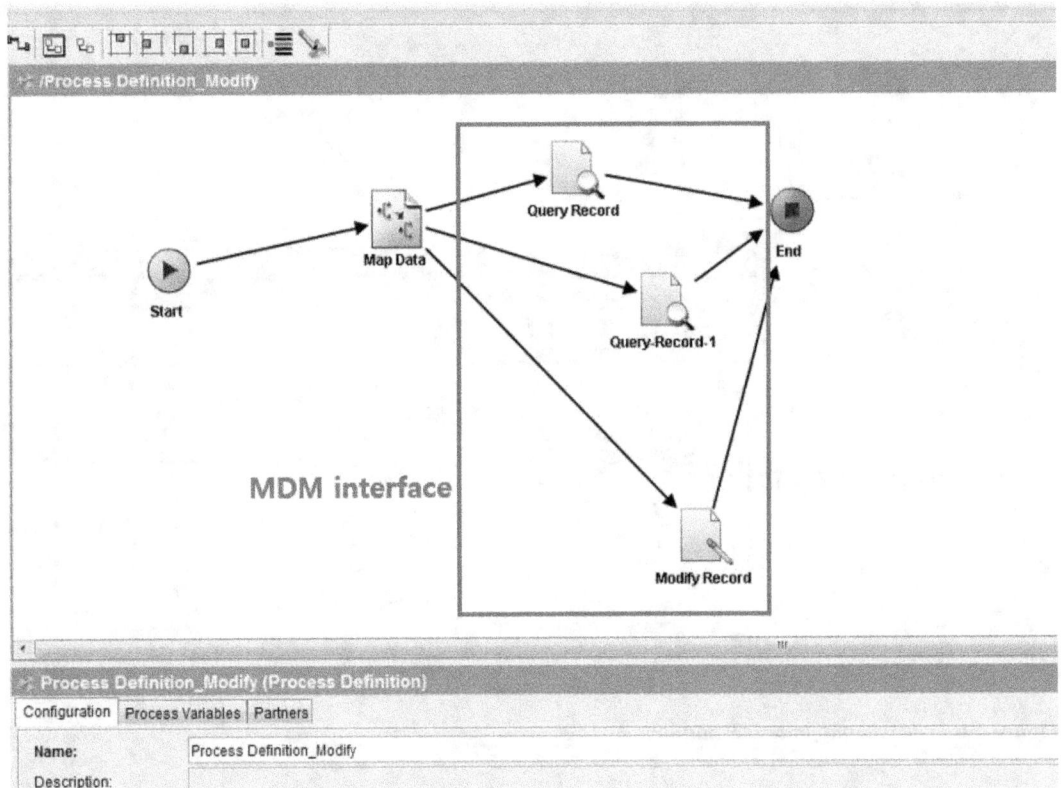

Figure 4-7. *Processes in customer master management data*

Customer data has different characteristics than product data. You need to improve alignment and eliminate duplicates. Customers, partners, and vendors are defined in the customer master. Customer masters are used by businesses with long-standing legacy operations, such as the banking industry. This minimizes request and interfaces from various external systems and reduces the load on the legacy system. With similar data being managed in multiple systems, there are likely to be problems with data consistency.

CHAPTER 4   OBSERVABILITY PRACTICES BY THE INDUSTRY

By organizing it in a master data system, you can improve the consistency of customer data. In banking, customers often have multiple accounts, making the process of querying them complex and resource-intensive. A customer master can improve both performance and data consistency. Customer masters require real-time processing, so observability and traceability are critical.

There are many applications that require master data or need to be synchronized. Examples include customer management and core banking. If a customer's information changes in other systems, the master data needs to reflect the change. These interfaces need to be managed and organized efficiently, and it is useful to interface to the master data through an EAI server.

The TIBCO MDM server is a master data management application that can ensure the consistency, completeness, and accuracy of master data across organizations, enterprise systems, and partners. It provides a way to manage and synchronize master data within an organization. TIBCO MDM is based on a flexible business process automation framework that uses workflows and business rules:

- Data is managed in repository. The repository defines the syntax and semantics of the data and provides secure access to the data.

- You can define business processes and rules to manage information, such as publishing it to other systems or trading partner.

TIBCO MDM provides a REST API and supports external connectivity. The TIBCO EAI server can easily interface with the MDM server using the external API provided by the MDM server. By instrumenting the EAI server, you can measure the MDM server's request.

Along with the EAI server, data pipeline (ETL), master data management (MDM), managed file transfer (MFT), and business process management (BPM) contain critical data and processes. If they support traceability and observability, they help the organization understand and operate their data and processes. These applications often do not support modern OpenTelemetry and observability. This book shows you how to interface an instrumented EAI server with MDM, MFT, and BPM and instrument various servers.

Legacy middleware includes customer MDM, product MDM, BPM, EAI, API management, batches, MFT, and ETL, with EAI being the centerpiece and interfacing all legacy middleware. Each legacy middleware product typically has hundreds to thousands of processes running.

4.2.2.5. Oracle ERP

SAP's strength is in manufacturing, while Oracle ERP has many examples in accounting and finance. Oracle first launched its application suite in the late 1980s with financial software. By 2009, it had expanded into supply chain management, human resource management, warehouse management, customer relationship management, call center service, product lifecycle management, and many other areas.

Oracle offers the most successful database, but it also offers a wide range of application and middleware options.

Figure 4-8 shows the Oracle ERP, which also provides a separate client-server based form.

305

CHAPTER 4 OBSERVABILITY PRACTICES BY THE INDUSTRY

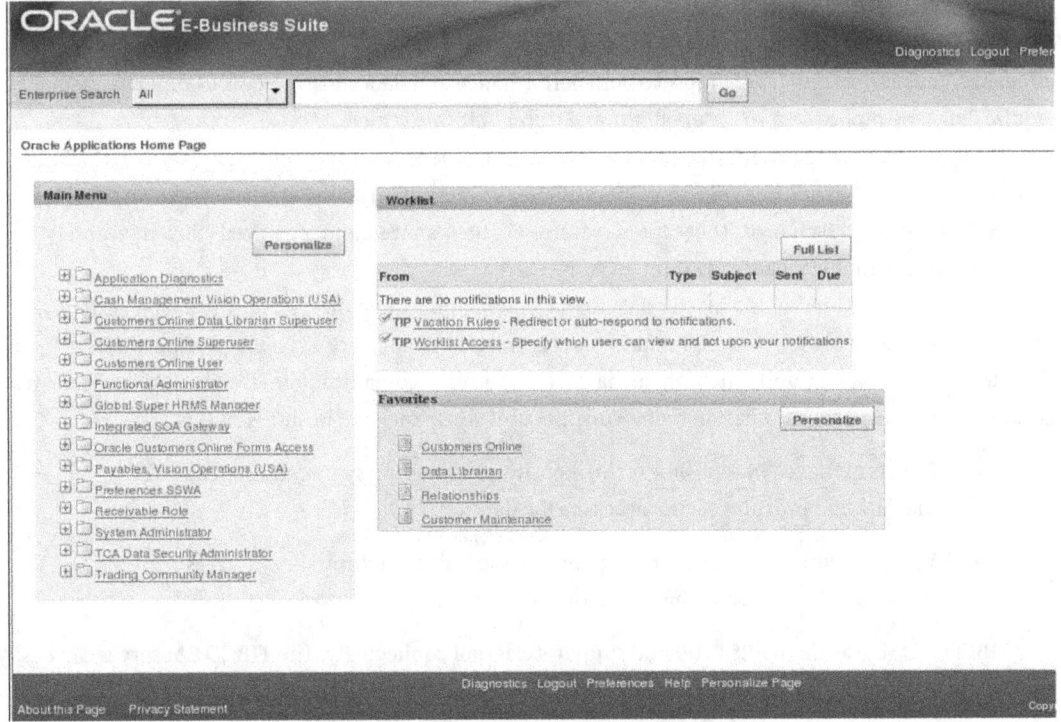

Figure 4-8. *User screen in Oracle ERP*

ERP manages critical process and data, so it needs to be interfaced to other applications in the enterprise. Oracle ERP stores data in the Oracle database, and the EAI server uses the TIBCO database adapter to interface with Oracle ERP.

Oracle ERP provides an interface table for the external interface. Triggers in the Oracle database are used to process events. The database adapter uses ODBC to interface with the table.

Figure 4-9 shows setting up the ODBC driver to interface with Oracle ERP.

CHAPTER 4   OBSERVABILITY PRACTICES BY THE INDUSTRY

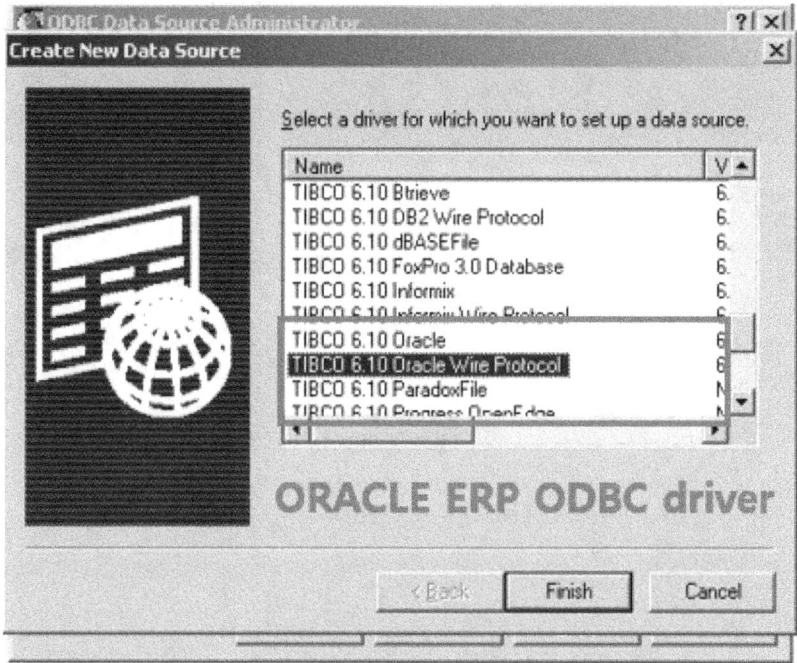

Figure 4-9. Oracle ERP adapter configuration

Legacy provides technologies for many different types of interfaces. It can be standard or non-standard. To interface with legacy, you need to provide different types of adapters.

4.2.2.6. Managed File Transfers

Banking requires thousands of batches and file transfers. Traditionally, batch schedulers like Control-M were used to transfer files over FTP. Due to the nature of FTP, file transfer is not guaranteed, and redelivery, monitoring, and security are weak.

The number of file transfers is so large that it is difficult to recognize or manage problems when they occur. Therefore, there is a separate server to manage file transfers, called MFT. The MFT server provides reliable file transfer, security, and scheduling.

You can develop a process for transferring files within the EAI server, as shown in Figure 4-10.

CHAPTER 4　OBSERVABILITY PRACTICES BY THE INDUSTRY

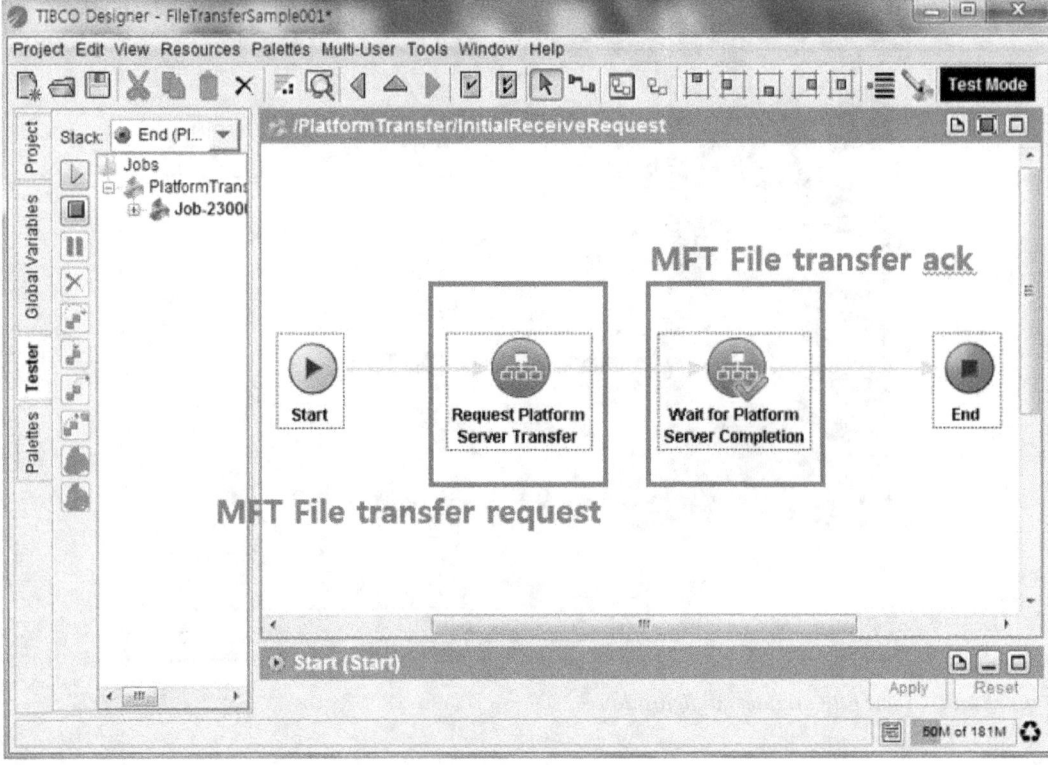

Figure 4-10. *The MFT process*

The MFT server provides logs and history information about file transfers and can set policies for redelivery in case of transfer failures. To process file transfers, an MFT agent is installed on each host, and file transfers are performed between the agents. An MFT agent is used for basic file transfer, but if the MFT server needs complex file transfers with other application, they can be processed through an EAI server. The EAI server, in conjunction with the MFT server, can develop processes for file transfer. The MFT server provides APIs to manage file transfer, and external parties can use the MFT server's REST API to initiate the file transfer process and manage its status.

4.2.2.7. SWIFT

SWIFT is an organization that provides an automated payment processing system to send and receive banking messages quickly and securely between banks around the world. You use Swift to do transactions between domestic and international banks. Banks connect to the Swift network and follow the MT message format to send and receive data.

SWIFT users include banking institutions, such as brokers, dealers, or investment managers, securities, foreign exchanges, money markets, treasuries, and trade operations. Every SWIFT user is identified on the SWIFT network by a unique address, called a banking identification code (BIC). To exchange messages over the SWIFT network, every user must have at least one unique BIC.

CHAPTER 4 OBSERVABILITY PRACTICES BY THE INDUSTRY

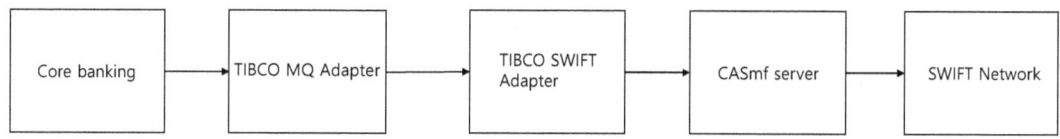

Figure 4-11. SWIFT flow

In Figure 4-11, the CASmf server is configured in the SAA and is legacy middleware for connecting to the SWIFT network. SWIFT's Common Application Server (CASmf) is the middleware that the SWIFT Alliance server connects to in order to transfer SWIFT messages.

There have been some recent changes to SWIFT. SWIFTNet is a network that replaces the existing X.25 protocol-based network used by the SWIFT community. The SWIFT Alliance Gateway (SAG) is the interface for accessing SWIFTNet and provides various connectivity features for the SWIFTNet users.

In this demonstration, you use the CASmf interface to communicate with a SWIFT Alliance Server (SAA). CASmf uses a MAPID, a name given to each instance of the message application, to establish communication between the user application and the SAA. The MAPID is defined on the user host and in the SWIFT interface.

CASmf provides an API to the user application developer. Using the API, the user's host environment can communicate with the SWIFT interface to establish a real-time session. Once a real-time session is established, messages can be exchanged. The API can open, close, or abort a session and send or receive data. The CASmf software uses TCP/IP as the communication protocol.

The CASmf server provides a C API to send and receive MT messages. A SWIFT adapter is a CASmf client that uses the CASmf C API. The SWIFT adapter interfaces with SWIFT through the CASmf server.

Since the transactions processed by SWIFT are large, all transactions should be observable and rollback in case of failure.

Usually, there is a core banking system inside the banking system that manages payments and foreign exchange, and the EAI server transfers messages in MT format to the SWIFT network via CASmf.

It is also used for foreign exchange transactions between individuals, but it is more commonly used for corporate banking, including large-amount foreign exchange transactions. If there is a problem in corporate banking, it will cause great losses, so it is necessary to establish a highly reliable SWIFT interface system.

The configuration of CASmf is shown in Figure 4-12, and after startup, the MAPIDs in the figure are configured.

309

CHAPTER 4 OBSERVABILITY PRACTICES BY THE INDUSTRY

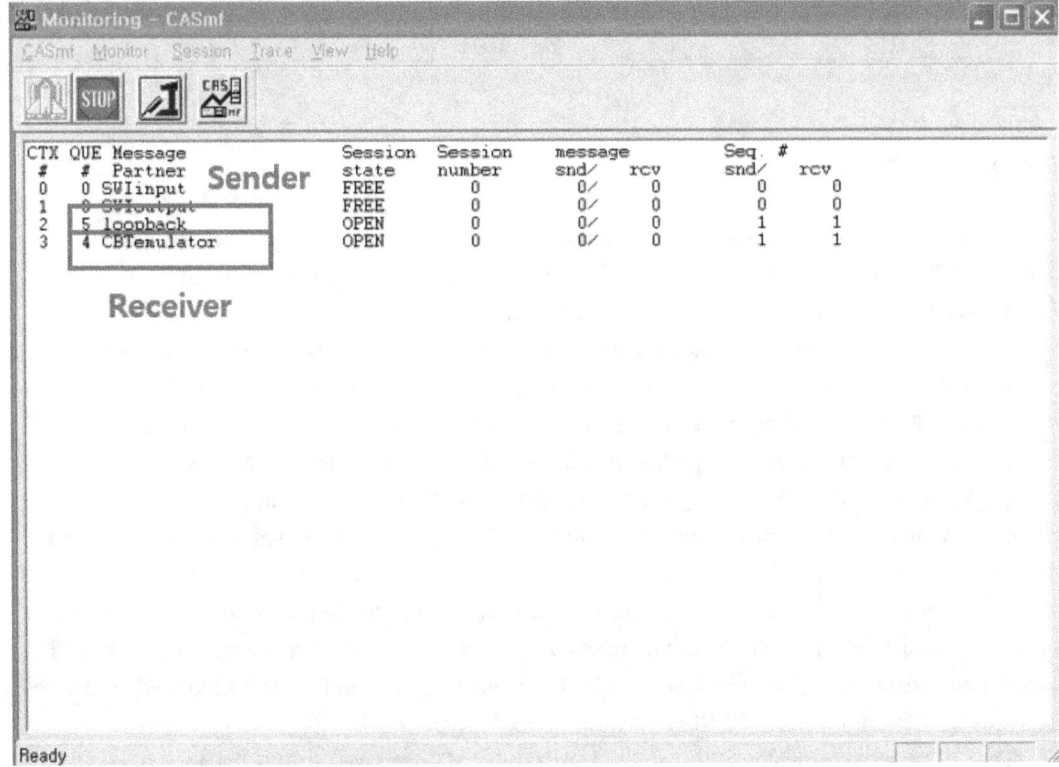

Figure 4-12. The CASmf administration

In this demo, loopback and CBTemulator are used.

- Loopback is the MAPID used to send.

- CBTemulator is the MAPID used to receive.

You can see that the SWIFT CASmf adapter has started. The SWIFT adapter configures the connection with CASmf. The integration process within the TIBCO EAI server consists of many steps, including request, response, and transformation of various input and output. The individual step is represented by span and instrumented with OpenTelemetry. You can see the results of the span in the demo.

The EAI server provides the ability to easily develop integration processes by drag and drop. Since many organizations have more than 4,000 integration processes, it is more productive and easier to use a development tool than to develop code directly. EAI, BPM, and ETL provide drag-and-drop development tools.

Figure 4-13 shows that by using a SWIFT adapter, you can develop an integration process for sending to and receiving from CASmf.

CHAPTER 4 OBSERVABILITY PRACTICES BY THE INDUSTRY

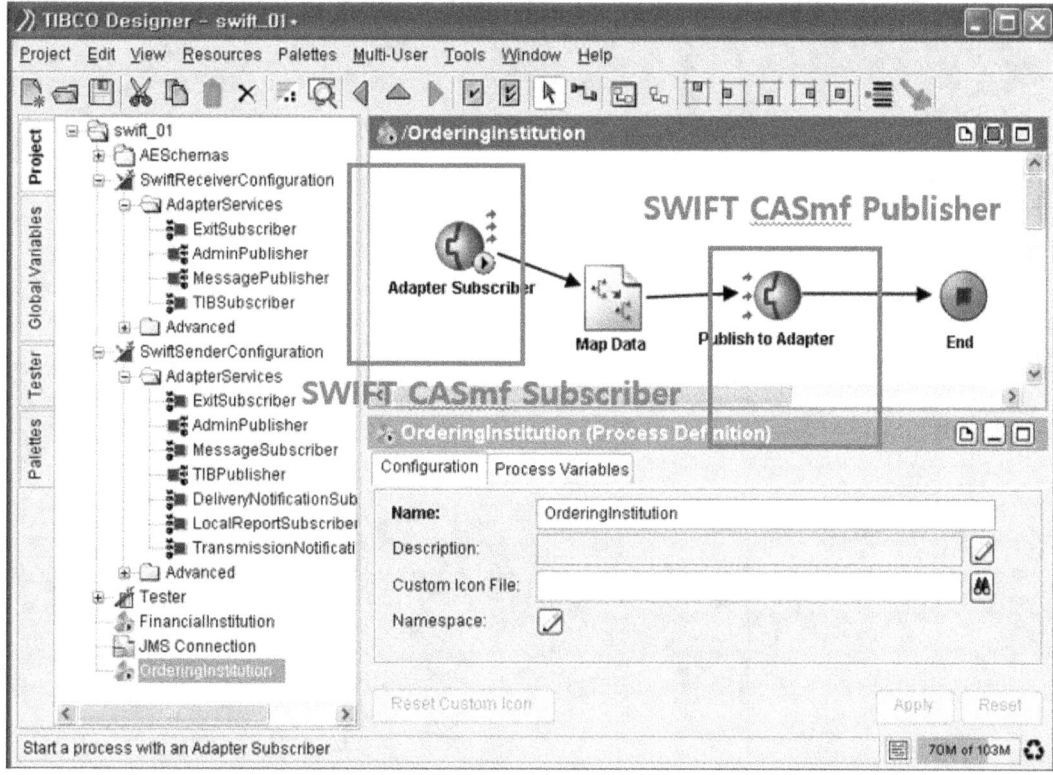

Figure 4-13. SWIFT integration process

4.2.2.8. Lotus Notes

Lotus Notes is IBM's groupware, which was popular before Microsoft Outlook. Lotus Notes provides software for enterprise collaboration, including email, calendaring, documents, and more. Lotus Notes requires integration with other enterprise applications such as ERP, CRM, and SCM. Lotus Notes manages its own database, which consists of documents, forms, and views.

- **Document**: A Lotus Notes database was created using forms. A document contains fields that hold the data for an object instance. In Figure 4-14, you can see the schema being created in the document.

- **Form**: Defines how the document is edited, displayed, and printed.

- **View**: Displays summary information from multiple documents. Using View, you can search, sort, and relate information in the database.

CHAPTER 4　OBSERVABILITY PRACTICES BY THE INDUSTRY

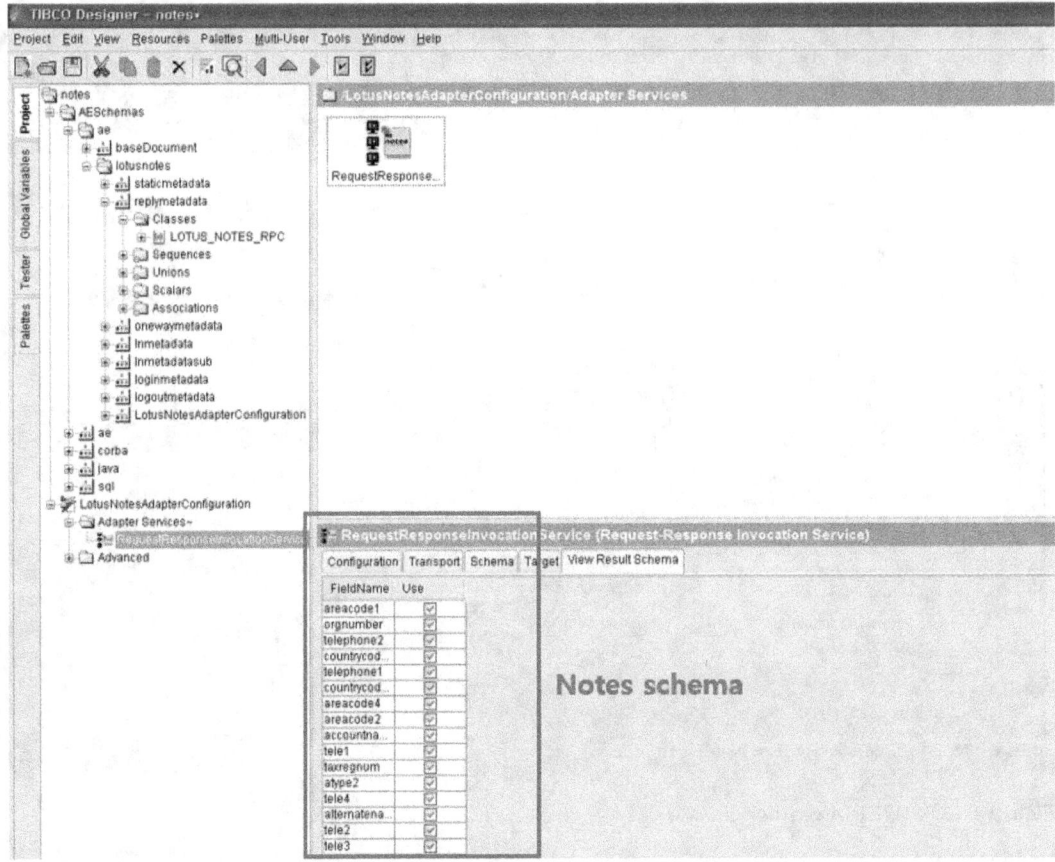

Figure 4-14. Notes adapter configuration

The Notes database must have templates (view, form) for the TIBCO Lotus Notes adapter in order to be able to interface with the TIBCO EAI server. The template is made up of .nsf files that come with the installation of the Notes adapter.

Lotus Notes agent is used only by the publication service and the request and response call service. The agent process document is published to the Lotus Notes database. Every agent runs a Java class that is imported when you define the agent. The agent class file is maintained in the ADLN_HOME/lib/agents directory. To use an agent, you must import it into the database using the Lotus Notes Designer.

HTTP agent:

- The HTTP Publisher Agent notifies the publisher that the event will be published, using the host name and port number specified in the Lotus Notes event.

- The port number must match the HTTP port to receive Lotus Notes events on the field on the Adapter Services tab of the Lotus Notes adapter instance configuration.

CHAPTER 4 OBSERVABILITY PRACTICES BY THE INDUSTRY

Polling agent:

- The polling publisher agent sends documents to the inbox without notifying the adapter. The publisher continuously polls the outbox for unpublished events.

4.2.2.9. IBM MQSeries

IBM MQ is a message server that can be used for inter-application communication. With IBM MQ, applications in different environments can exchange data asynchronously using queue.

In the past, developers used MQSeries as a message-based middleware. After Java was introduced to enterprise systems, JMS was used, and recently, various message servers such as Kafka have been used in the cloud and with Kubernetes.

In banking, it's common to see MQ, JMS, and Kafka all being used. MQ is heavily used in legacy systems, so its instrumentation is important. The EAI server processes publishing and subscribing to messages through an MQ adapter.

MQ supports its own MQ API and the JMS API. This demo uses the MQ API and interface to an MQ server using an MQ adapter. The MQ adapter implements observability.

A queue manager manages multiple queues. Publishers publish messages to the queue, and subscribers subscribe to messages in the queue. You need to specify a queue manager and a queue name.

MQ is organized as follows The MQ adapter is responsible for subscribing to messages in the queue or publishing messages to the queue. The MQSeries Manager screen is shown in Figure 4-15.

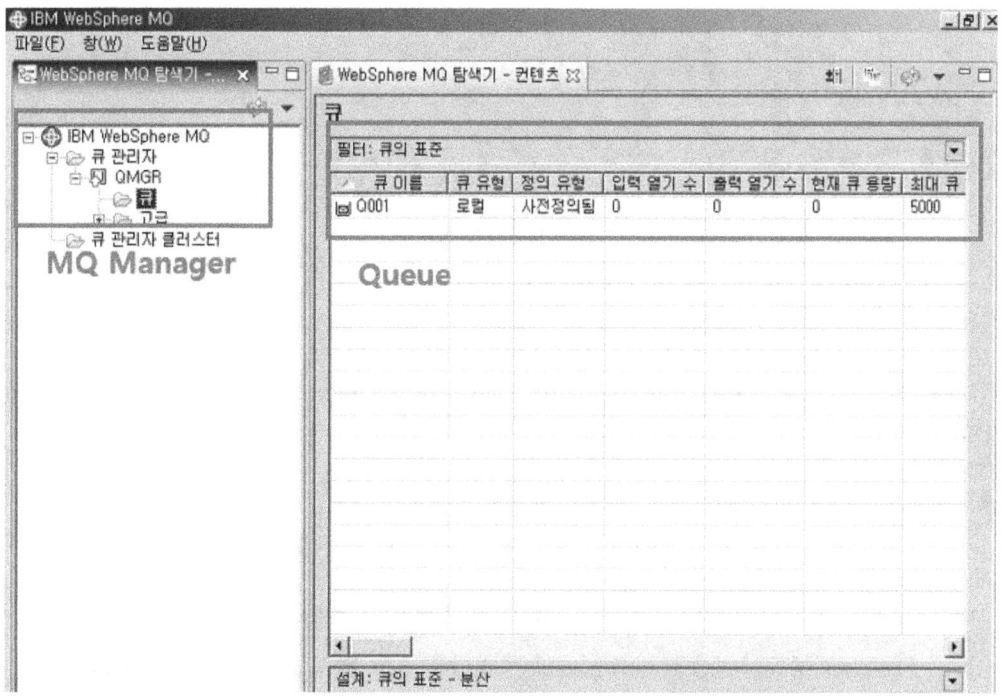

Figure 4-15. MQ management

CHAPTER 4   OBSERVABILITY PRACTICES BY THE INDUSTRY

4.2.2.10. DataStage ETL

ETL is necessary to develop data pipelines. In large organizations, there are thousands of processes configured on the EAI server. In a medium-sized organization, you might see more than 3,000 pipelines configured on the ETL server.

In addition to microservices observability, you also need observability in your data pipeline.

Figure 4-16 shows the palette provided by the DataStage Designer that you can drag and drop to develop your data pipeline.

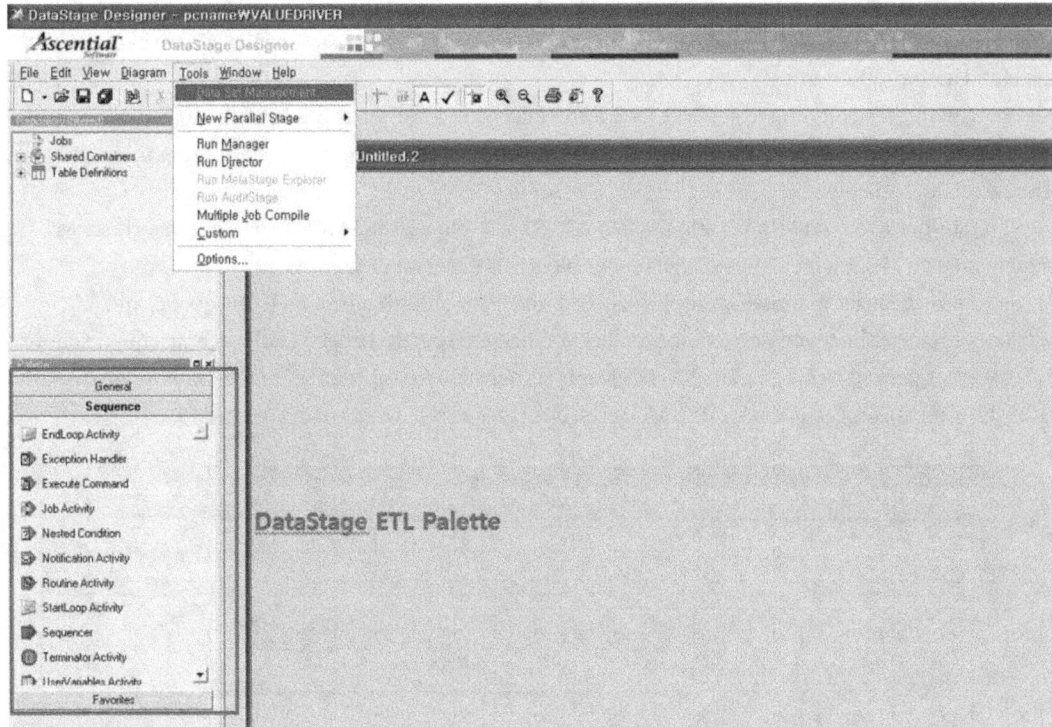

Figure 4-16. *DataStage development*

Legacy ETLs like DataStage do not provide the same observability as OpenTelemetry. You can register and monitor pipelines internally, but it's not a standardized monitoring system, so it's hard to connect externally. Legacy ETLs are limited by the difficulty of manual instrumentation. With otel-cli, it is possible to create spans from shell scripts.

The data pipeline is processed using message servers such as Kafka, but most of the time, it is tied to a database.

Data pipelines need to approach observability in a different way than microservices.

- Each time a data pipeline runs, it creates a thread, which behaves like a Job. A job contains multiple steps. Each step interfaces with the database using JDBC and ODBC. To apply observability to your data pipeline, you need to create spans at the thread level.

314

CHAPTER 4 OBSERVABILITY PRACTICES BY THE INDUSTRY

- If your data pipeline is developed in Java or can be further developed like Apache Airflow and GCP dataflow, you can create a span with a declaration like a span annotation.

- For ETL developed in Java, JDBC is used to connect to the source and target databases. OpenTelemetry can be used to create spans.

- The simplest and easiest way is to create traces from logs rather than use complex internal instrumentation.

For now, I briefly describe legacy middleware, and in the final chapter, I discuss failure cases in detail.

4.2.2.11. FileNet BPM

Businesses have a lot of data and processes, and organizations use them to process a variety of activities. Many of these processes are not automated or are only partially automated. Business process management involves technologies and tools to manage and automate business processes performed by people, applications, and external sources.

Figure 4-17 shows a palette provided by FileNet that you can drag and drop to develop your workflow.

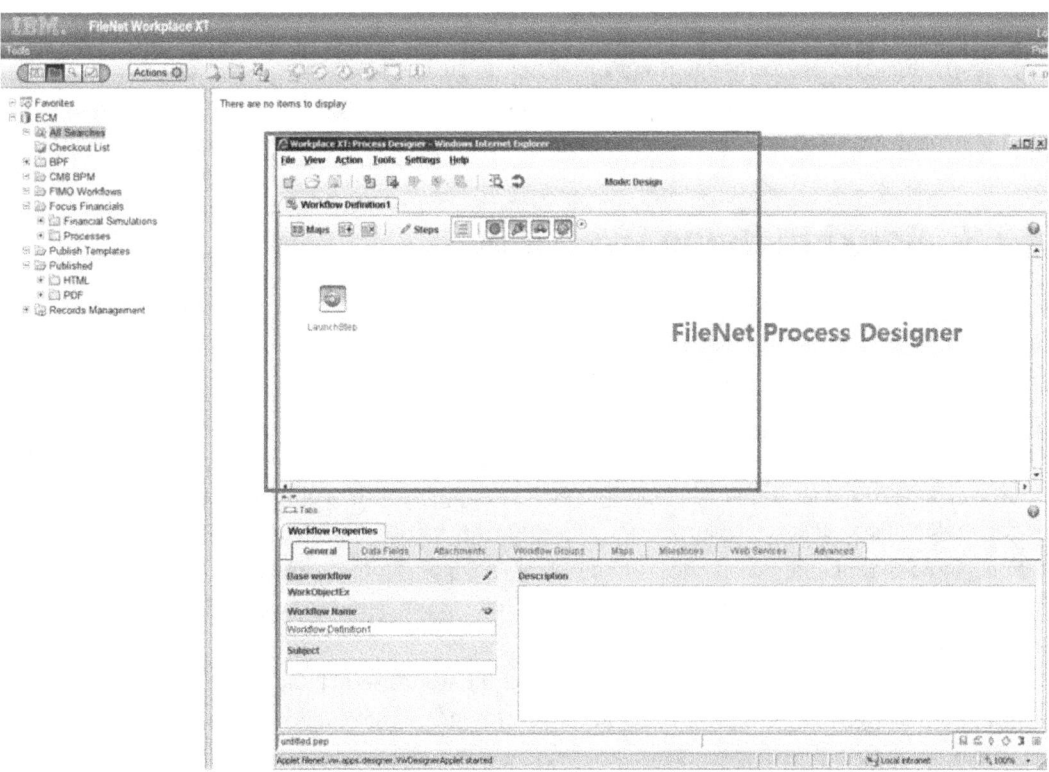

Figure 4-17. FileNet process development tool

The BPM server provides a REST API that can be called externally. The EAI server can interface to the BPM server and output the duration of the BPM server as a span.

If possible, observability and trace should be applied to the BPM server, but in practice, this is not easy. The BPM server is middleware, but they are not systems that process transactions in real-time. They are processed in multiple steps over a long period of time by users within the process. It is important to use trace to understand latency and error, but the long process of a BPM server is not suitable for applying trace. When a black box like the BPM server is involved, it becomes difficult to organize an E2E trace.

Most business applications include Salesforce, ServiceNow, and Workday. They contain internal workflows, and it is difficult to apply trace given the process of workflow, the difficulty of instrumentation, and the specificity of the UI.

The workflow in the BPM server creates a Case ID and updates the status information to the message server. The status update should contain various information, including the Case ID.

Assuming the Case ID is generated by the BPM server, you can analyze the request to understand how many cases were created. Once the workflow is completed and the status updates are analyzed, you can measure the number of completed cases. By comparing the number of inputs and outputs, you can understand how many cases are currently being processed by the BPM server. It's also a good idea to measure the number of cases created, the number of cases in process, and the number of completed cases as metrics and output them to a dashboard.

For black boxes that are not traceable, you should be able to analyze the input and output of the black box using metrics and logs. Rather than applying a trace to the black box, you can improve observability through other signals. It is also possible to configure trace to microservices before and after the BPM server in a limited way. You need to understand the limitations of trace and find ways to improve your work.

4.2.3. Banking Demo Overview

Banking has a lot of legacy, black box, and external integration systems, making it difficult to configure E2E trace. This demo uses the EAI server to apply distributed trace to multiple legacies.

There is a wide variety of middleware in banking. MCI for channel integration, FEP for external integration, EAI server for application integration, API server for API integration, and MFT for file transfer are functionally similar but used for different purposes in different areas. The middleware I focus on is the API server and EAI server. Traditional EAI servers do not support modern observability.

It is difficult to develop an OpenTelemetry extension for every application to apply observability. It would be costly and time-consuming. If your EAI server supports observability, you can configure E2E observability. For banking observability, it is important to configure the correct observability in the middleware.

A single order that a customer creates in your application consists of hundreds of requests and responses. Creating a new account or family accounts owned by a customers in telecom is a complex internal process. I use OpenTelemetry to instrument the E2E and demonstrate detailed traces and profiles.

CHAPTER 4 OBSERVABILITY PRACTICES BY THE INDUSTRY

The application process is no longer composed of a handful of servers and clients but rather a backend that interfaces between various applications and finally delivers responses to the client. In this process, the backend is often composed of decades of legacy systems, so it's a flexible mix of new technology and legacy. Organizing this into observability is not easy.

This demo works with microservices and API servers, including the legacy and EAI servers described so far. The banking architecture in the demo is divided into five main areas: microservices (frontend, backend), EAI server, core banking, and backoffice.

- The microservices architecture is divided into two areas. Frontend microservices use non-blocking Reactor, and backend microservices use events in the message server, which is interfaced to the API server.

- Core banking legacy architecture is interfaced to the EAI server.

- There is a backoffice that processes batches and external interfaces.

In Korea, this is categorized into channels, core banking, external, and backoffice, but international banking is different. The main purpose of integrating the four areas is to propagate them together under a single trace ID. The advantages of E2E trace are as follows:

- It's easy to understand which specific section within the E2E is having problem.

- You can understand latency and throughput in each section.

It is difficult to root cause a trace alone, and it is essential to correlate individual sections with a more detailed profile.

Problems that can occur with E2E trace include these:

- The backoffice consists of a legacy black box, an EAI server, a TCP server, a BPM server, an MFT server, and a batch scheduler, with no instrumentation configured by default. If the batch and data pipeline use a message server, observability can be configured.

- Since the batch scheduler running in the backoffice is a disconnected process from a business perspective, it is difficult to propagate trace from the backend to the batch. In this case, I recommend using a message server. The message server can be used to periodically process messages stored in the batch scheduler and understand the trace context through the message server. When implementing E2E trace, if propagation is not possible due to relational databases and batches, use the message server to propagate.

While banking can trace E2E from the channel to core banking, extending traceability to the backoffice can be challenging. This is because the backoffice contains many black boxes and legacy and is often not instrumented. It is possible to trace E2E with payment and order IDs rather than trace IDs, but sometimes it is not practical because it requires legacy modifications. If a trace is not supported, other signals can be used to configure observability, such as events and logs.

CHAPTER 4   OBSERVABILITY PRACTICES BY THE INDUSTRY

EAI servers must support a variety of protocols and technologies. Different legacies use unique protocols, making it difficult to interface using standard technology alone. The EAI server provides adapters to support legacy systems. Even if you don't instrument the individual legacy, you can instrument the legacy if you instrument the EAI server that is interfacing with the legacy. Instrumenting legacy systems is not the purpose of observability; legacy systems should be viewed as black boxes. If the EAI server supports OpenTelemetry, you can create a span of all the detailed process steps.

Enterprise applications have many different, complex structures:

- **Client**: There are different client types, such as web and app. They are measured in RUM.

- **API server**: Receives requests from clients and routes them to microservices.

- **Microservices**: Developed in a variety of development languages and implemented in Python in the demo.

- **EAI server**: Interfaces with the API server. I use the TIBCO EAI server and integrate various legacy systems.

- **Legacy system**: The legacy of banking was comprised of SAP, CICS, and SWIFT. They process deposits, loans, and foreign exchanges.

Banking is all about payments, cards, loans, cash advances, and wealth management. In Korea, we use the term account system, but international banking uses the term payment system. Korean banking terms are categorized into deposit, loan, and foreign exchange, which are different from international banking terms.

There are more than 10,000 microservices in banking, and from an overall application perspective, microservices make up about 20 percent of the total. The other 80 percent is dominated by black box, legacy, batch, and data pipeline systems.

In addition to outbound processing, the banking domain should also consider inbound processing. For example, in the case of a fund transfer, an amount withdrawn from Bank A should be deposited to Bank B. Conversely, a withdrawal from Bank B should be deposited to Bank A. It needs to be able to process transactions in both directions. Withdrawals and deposits are processed consecutively, ensuring data consistency, and are processed as 2PC distributed transactions.

All interfaces with legacy systems are processed through the EAI server.

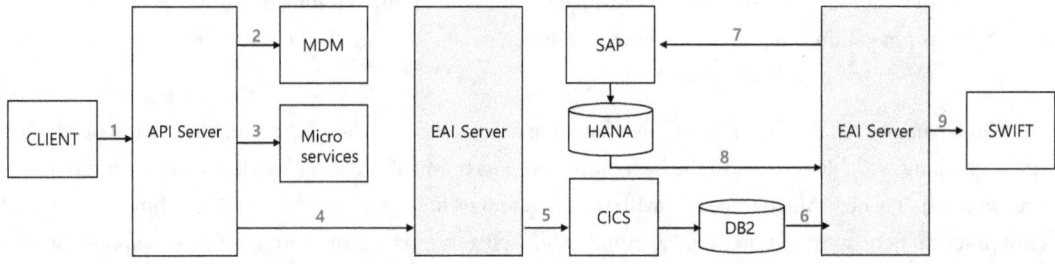

Figure 4-18. *Banking demo flow*

CHAPTER 4   OBSERVABILITY PRACTICES BY THE INDUSTRY

The banking architecture is a complex orchestration of message servers, with the EAI server in the middle. This is shown in Figure 4-18.

If the EAI server and message server do not support trace or context is lost, it becomes difficult to understand the root cause of a failure. In addition to being technically non-blocking, asynchronous, and event-driven, the process is complex, making it difficult to understand the context of interactions between microservices. A single transaction creates hundreds of spans, so in the event of a failure, it is difficult to understand which span is causing the problem and why.

Many requests and responses are called repeatedly between microservices and legacy systems and when problems occur, it can be difficult to identify them and understand the cause. Often, it's not even possible to come up with a solution. Microservices is not a simple distributed system with three layers but a complex process where transactions are terminated after interacting with roughly more than 20 applications, and microservices is only a small part of the overall process. Observability in banking is challenging because there are dozens of legacy systems and black boxes that are impossible to instrument. Even if you configure observability, the problem is not easy to solve, but the more complex it is, the more essential it is to adopt observability.

What happens if number 2 in Figure 4-18 is not instrumented? What changes would be required to the overall trace if it were changed to GCP PubSub, which is not instrumented, instead of Kafka?

As long as it is a request and a response, there is no problem if the instrumentation fails. The trace will show the request and response as "unknown host," and only one long span will be generated.

The purpose of the banking demo is to

- Propagate legacy and microservices with trace.

- Understand the black boxes that are not instrumented in legacy and know how to apply trace to them.

- Instrument the EAI server to measure the legacy's latency.

In banking, there is a distinction between the frontoffice and the backoffice. Figure 4-18 shows only the frontoffice and does not detail the backoffice, which includes connecting SWIFT to an external organization. In banking, the frontoffice alone is not the entire E2E. It is more accurate to say that the frontoffice and backoffice are combined to form the E2E.

Banking requires a two PC commit. This is because when you withdraw from Bank A, you make a deposit to Bank B. For example, a transfer consists of a withdrawal and a deposit. If only the withdrawal succeeds but the deposit fails, you'll have a critical problem. To avoid such problems, all banking transactions, including payments and settlements, require verification. Backoffice legacy typically processes payments, settlements, and reconciliations.

The backoffice consists of black box applications developed in Delphi and PowerBuilder. Unlike Java, it is technically difficult to apply trace. If there are too many black boxes, trace is often broken, making it difficult to organize E2E trace. If it is difficult to trace, other signals such as logs and events should be used to configure observability.

In the past, it was difficult to monitor at the distributed trace level, but now that E2E trace is open source, I think it's a game changer for engineers.

CHAPTER 4   OBSERVABILITY PRACTICES BY THE INDUSTRY

It is possible to implement a trace of a complex application, as shown in Figure 4-18. The roles of the API server and EAI server are important in organizing the trace, and the banking demo breaks it down into nine phases, each of which is described in detail. Technically, the entire E2E is traceable, and observability is demonstrated through manual and automated instrumentation.

1. From RUM to API server
2. From Kafka to API server
3. From microservices to API server
4. From API server to EAI server
5. From EAI server to CICS
6. From DB2 to EAI server
7. From EAI server to SAP
8. From HANA to EAI server
9. From EAI server to SWIFT

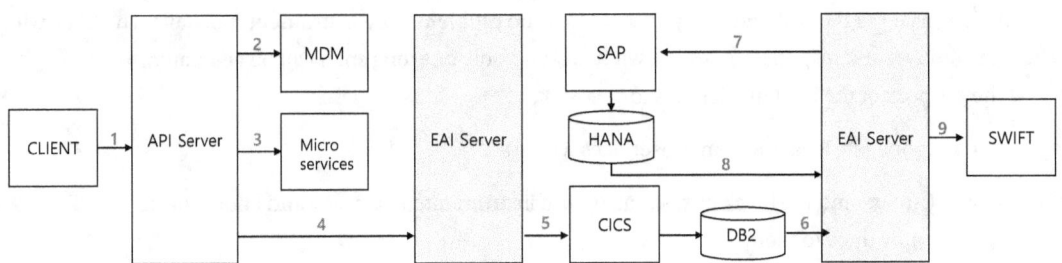

The sequence is as follows:

- Number 1 is implemented with gRPC. The client is a gRPC client, and the API server acts as a gRPC server. The API server is responsible for receiving client requests and routing them to the backend.

- Number 2 uses Kafka to organize publishers and subscribers. It uses manual instrumentation. OpenTelemetry can be used to instrument Kafka as well as other applications such as Redis, Mongo, and others.

- Number 3 consists of a Flask and uses automated instrumentation.

- In Number 5, the EAI server processes the association with the legacy. While the legacy is the core application, new services are best implemented in microservices. It is important to minimize the load on the legacy as much as possible.

While banking has problems with customer data, telecom has problems with product data. Product attributes change orchestration flow logic and process orders differently. Suppose the trace from the API server has two spans, as shown in Figure 4-19.

CHAPTER 4 OBSERVABILITY PRACTICES BY THE INDUSTRY

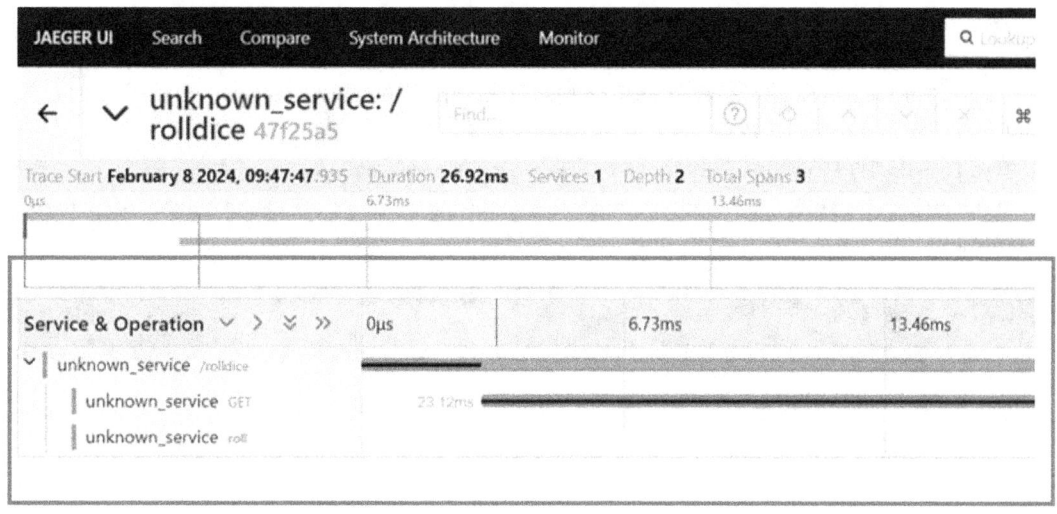

Figure 4-19. *The span on the API server*

In Figure 4-20, the number of steps in the EAI server is ten. Every step in the EAI process creates a span. The process on the EAI server creates ten spans.

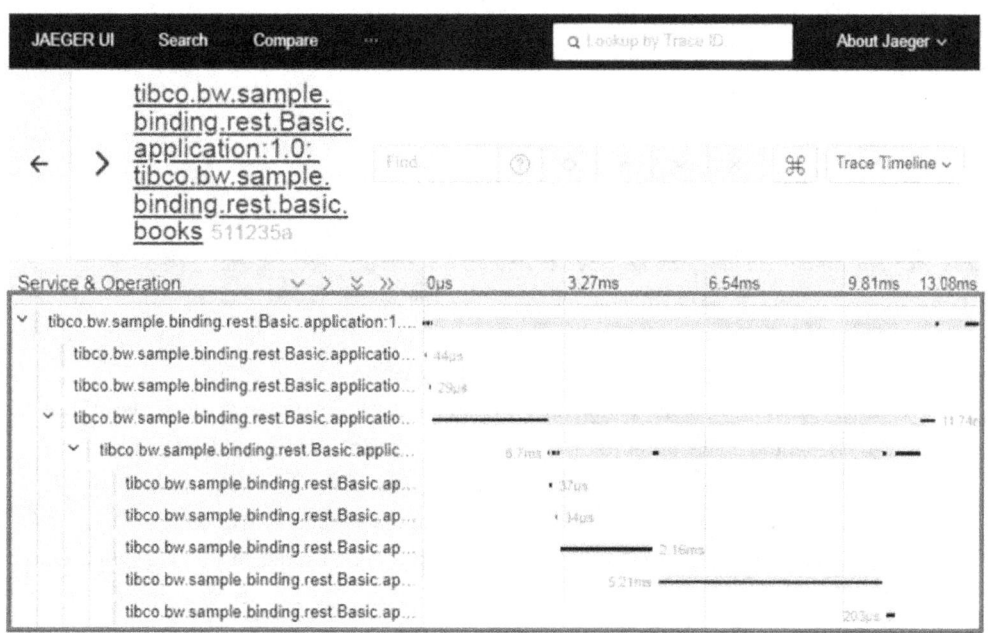

Figure 4-20. *The span on the EAI server*

321

When the two separate processes are merged, the result is shown in Figure 4-21. This is because all requests and responses, including the API server and EAI server, are represented by multiple spans in a single trace. The span of two API servers and ten EAI servers are combined to create a single trace. The number of span in the trace is 12.

If you use the HTTP protocol within the EAI server, it will propagate,

If you include backoffice transaction (transfers from the backend to SWIFT), the number of spans is even higher.

Figure 4-21. The span of an integrated API server and an EAI server

Commercial observability offers different capabilities for instrumenting some black boxes, so it is important to check if each commercial observability supports legacy instrumentation.

OpenTelemetry Java and Python provide APIs for manual instrumentation at a lower level. The demo uses Python. So, you should check the support before selecting an instrumentation language.

I would like to share my experience and knowledge of E2E trace.

Step by step, I describe Figure 4-21 and finally implement the banking E2E trace.

TIBCO EAI server did not support OpenTelemetry in past versions. It recently added support for OpenTelemetry. It is still in its early stages and has some limitations. The EAI server supports a variety of processes. Simple requests and responses are fine, but complex event processing between applications can cause problems with OpenTelemetry.

4.2.4. From RUM to API Server

If the gRPC client also performs instrumentation, a span is created. The API server source implemented with gRPC is shown here:

```python
import logging
from concurrent import futures

import grpc
import requests

from opentelemetry.instrumentation.requests import RequestsInstrumentor

from opentelemetry import trace
from opentelemetry.instrumentation.grpc import GrpcInstrumentorServer
from opentelemetry.sdk.trace import TracerProvider
from opentelemetry.sdk.trace.export import (
    ConsoleSpanExporter,
    SimpleSpanProcessor,
)

import helloworld_pb2
import helloworld_pb2_grpc

trace.set_tracer_provider(TracerProvider())
trace.get_tracer_provider().add_span_processor(
    SimpleSpanProcessor(ConsoleSpanExporter())
)

grpc_server_instrumentor = GrpcInstrumentorServer()
grpc_server_instrumentor.instrument()

class Greeter(helloworld_pb2_grpc.GreeterServicer):
    def SayHello(self, request, context):
        url = "http://jsonplaceholder.typicode.com/posts/1"
        response = requests.get(url)
        response_json = response.json()
        print(response_json)
        return helloworld_pb2.HelloReply(message="Hello, %s!" % request.name)

def serve():
    server = grpc.server(futures.ThreadPoolExecutor())
    helloworld_pb2_grpc.add_GreeterServicer_to_server(Greeter(), server)
    server.add_insecure_port("[::]:50051")
```

```
    server.start()
    server.wait_for_termination()
if __name__ == "__main__":
    logging.basicConfig()
    serve()
```

The client's request looks like this:

```
import requests
from opentelemetry.instrumentation.requests import RequestsInstrumentor
url = "http://jsonplaceholder.typicode.com/posts/1"
response = requests.get(url)
response_json = response.json()
print(response_json)
```

You shouldn't run it with python3; you should run the collector and run it with opentelemetry-instrument python3 to output the trace.

```
opentelemetry-instrument python3
```

Start the collector:

```
# docker run -p 4317:4317    -v /tmp/otel-collector-config.yaml:/etc/otel-collector-config.yaml    otel/opentelemetry-collector:latest    --config=/etc/otel-collector-config.yaml
```

The demo developed a Python client and used it like RUM.

4.2.5. From API Server to Kafka

The API server is associated with many different applications. It is necessary to trace the calls to Kafka.

I am not instrumenting the Kafka server but rather the publisher and subscriber that correspond to the client.

Here's the instrumentation for Kafka. Kafka uses version 2.2.0:

```
pip install opentelemetry-api
pip install opentelemetry-sdk
pip install opentelemetry-instrumentation-kafka-python
pip install kafka-python
```

Export to the console:

```
from opentelemetry import trace
from opentelemetry.sdk.trace import TracerProvider
```

```
from opentelemetry.sdk.trace.export import (
    SimpleSpanProcessor,
    ConsoleSpanExporter,
)
from opentelemetry.instrumentation.kafka import KafkaInstrumentor
def instrument(*args, **kwargs):
    provider = TracerProvider()
    simple_processor = SimpleSpanProcessor(ConsoleSpanExporter())
    provider.add_span_processor(simple_processor)
    trace.set_tracer_provider(provider)
    KafkaInstrumentor().instrument()
```

Here's the Kafka publisher:

```
from tracing import instrument
instrument()
from kafka import KafkaProducer
producer = KafkaProducer(bootstrap_servers='localhost:9092')
for _ in range(1):
    producer.send('foobar', b'some_message_bytes')
    producer.flush()
```

This is the subscriber to Kafka:

```
from tracing import instrument
instrument()
from kafka import KafkaConsumer
consumer = KafkaConsumer('foobar', bootstrap_servers='localhost:9092')
for msg in consumer:
    print(msg)
```

4.2.6. From API Server to Microservices

Configure your Flask server as shown here:

```
pip install 'flask<3' 'werkzeug<3'
```

The source for automated instrumentation of Flask and exporting to the collector is shown here. Because it is automated instrumentation, it does not include the OpenTelemetry API in the code.

```
from random import randint
from flask import Flask, request
import logging
```

CHAPTER 4   OBSERVABILITY PRACTICES BY THE INDUSTRY

```python
app = Flask(__name__)
logging.basicConfig(level=logging.INFO)
logger = logging.getLogger(__name__)

@app.route("/rolldice")
def roll_dice():
    player = request.args.get('player', default = None, type = str)
    result = str(roll())
    if player:
        logger.warn("%s is rolling the dice: %s", player, result)
    else:
        logger.warn("Anonymous player is rolling the dice: %s", result)
    return result

def roll():
    return randint(1, 6)
```

Install the Python OpenTelemetry library:

```
pip install opentelemetry-distro
```

The OpenTelemetry collector uses 0.93.0:

```yaml
# /tmp/otel-collector-config.yaml
receivers:
  otlp:
    protocols:
      grpc:
exporters:
  # NOTE: Prior to v0.86.0 use `logging` instead of `debug`.
  debug:
    verbosity: detailed
processors:
  batch:
service:
  pipelines:
    traces:
      receivers: [otlp]
      exporters: [debug]
      processors: [batch]
    metrics:
      receivers: [otlp]
      exporters: [debug]
      processors: [batch]
```

CHAPTER 4   OBSERVABILITY PRACTICES BY THE INDUSTRY

```
logs:
  receivers: [otlp]
  exporters: [debug]
  processors: [batch]
```

The following commands cause SSL handshake errors. If you start the collector and Jaeger at the same time, the ports will conflict. Therefore, the collector uses Docker.

```
opentelemetry-instrument \
    --traces_exporter console,otlp \
    --metrics_exporter console \
    --service_name your-service-name \
    --exporter_otlp_endpoint 0.0.0.0:4317 \
    python myapp.py
```

Start the collector as shown here:

```
docker run -p 4317:4317 \
    -v /tmp/otel-collector-config.yaml:/etc/otel-collector-config.yaml \
    otel/opentelemetry-collector:latest \
    --config=/etc/otel-collector-config.yaml
```

You should check `opentelemetry-collector-contrib`.
The port uses 4317 6831 14250.

```
pip install opentelemetry-exporter-otlp
```

To perform automated instrumentation in Flask, you need to run the following command. It is possible to export to the collector without using a separate exporter API by running the following command.

```
export OTEL_PYTHON_LOGGING_AUTO_INSTRUMENTATION_ENABLED=true
opentelemetry-instrument --logs_exporter otlp flask run -p 8080
```

By default, `opentelemetry-instrument` exports traces and metrics via OTLP/gRPC and transfers them to `localhost:4317`, which is being received by the collector.

Use the instrumentation library to process automated instrumentation:

```
export OTEL_PYTHON_LOGGING_AUTO_INSTRUMENTATION_ENABLED=true
opentelemetry-instrument --logs_exporter otlp  python3 greeter_server.py
```

Using the OpenTelemetry API, you can perform manual instrumentation of the Flask server. An additional span is created for the Flask server.

```
from flask import Flask
from opentelemetry.instrumentation.flask import FlaskInstrumentor

app = Flask(__name__)
```

```
FlaskInstrumentor().instrument_app(app)

@app.route("/")
def hello():
    return "Hello!"

if __name__ == "__main__":
    app.run(debug=True)
```

4.2.7. From API Server to EAI Server

REST calls from the instrumented Flask server are propagated to EAI server.

This is important because it is the span that propagates the API server and EAI server together. The two servers are interfaced using the REST standard. For protocols supported by OpenTelemetry, this can be propagated without problems. The API server is instrumented and includes a trace context in its header.

The EAI server is configured to support OpenTelemetry. If a request coming into the EAI server injects a trace context, the EAI server extracts the trace context and processes the propagation inside the EAI server. So, the API server and EAI server are integrated into one trace ID. No additional development is required for this, and with a simple configuration of the EAI server, it is possible to trace E2E between the API server and the EAI server.

```
import requests

from opentelemetry.instrumentation.requests import RequestsInstrumentor

class Greeter(helloworld_pb2_grpc.GreeterServicer):
    def SayHello(self, request, context):
        url = "http://jsonplaceholder.typicode.com/posts/1"
        response = requests.get(url)
        response_json = response.json()
        print(response_json)
        return helloworld_pb2.HelloReply(message="Hello, %s!" % request.name)
```

This demo uses HTTP, but in practice, I use JMS to propagate the API server and EAI server.

4.2.8. From EAI Server to Legacy System

Bringing observability to a legacy system is a big challenge for many reasons.

CHAPTER 4   OBSERVABILITY PRACTICES BY THE INDUSTRY

- There are cultural differences between legacy organizations and SRE organizations in terms of building observability. Legacy organizations are closed, and it's hard to change them.

- There is a long history of technical debt, and OpenTelemetry is difficult to instrument for legacy and black box systems.

From a legacy perspective, microservices is a new territory. Just as a young developer may be familiar with microservices and have no knowledge of Cobol and ABAP, a senior developer may be in the opposite situation. To implement observability, the SRE's will alone is not enough to trace the E2E. At the end of the day, there needs to be a commitment and support at the enterprise level to build observability into the legacy.

Direct instrumentation of the legacy provides a more accurate latency measurement than instrumenting the EAI server. Technically, direct instrumentation of the legacy is difficult. Considering productivity and development labor, instrumenting the EAI server is a good idea. Use traces to automatically instrument the EAI server and create spans for steps in the EAI process.

The adapter configuration can be configured within the EAI server, or it can be configured on the legacy server. If it's configured on the legacy server, the adapter is via JMS, and propagation occurs.

Remote calls require injecting and extracting, but there is no need to propagate context between threads in the same process. The `Context` object passes context to other threads.

There are multiple threads within a process, and a thread is created each time the process runs. There is no complex propagation. The call between the JMS server and the EAI server is a remote call, in which case propagation occurs.

The instrumentation of inter-thread calls and IPC is agent-specific.

You should output the trace context to the log and think about improvement. If the EAI server does not generate OpenTelemetry, you can use profiles to identify the methods called by the step and instrument them to generate traces and logs. The code you instrument should include logic to handle context.

The EAI server provides adapter to interface legacy system. EAI server supports connectivity with various legacy systems such as SAP and CICS.

The EAI server minimizes coding and provides tools to drag and drop the integration process, as shown in Figure 4-22.

1. Configure the adapter for interfacing the source and target applications.

2. Add functionality for transform, look up, and validate the messages.

CHAPTER 4   OBSERVABILITY PRACTICES BY THE INDUSTRY

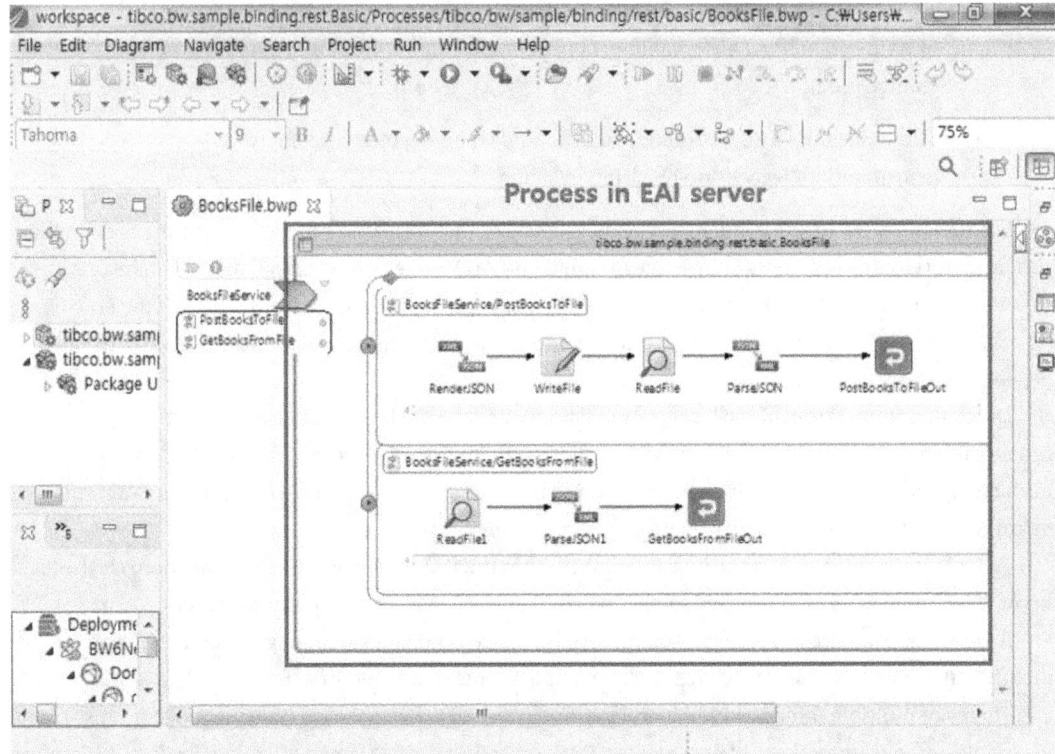

Figure 4-22.   *TIBCO EAI server development tool*

4.2.9. Transfer to Jaeger

Spans generated by automated instrumentation from the EAI server and API server are transferred to the OpenTelemetry collector. However, in the demo, they are transferred to Jaeger and the collector manually.

I discussed propagating and transferring earlier, and the application needs to transfer to the observability backend. Transfers can be implemented through API development. For automated instrumentation, you can use an agent to specify it as an environment variable and then transfer it to a collector. Since the entire E2E is instrumented with OpenTelemetry, you can instrument the entire E2E with a single trace ID.

Managing library dependencies is complicated in Python. OpenTelemetry is also a changing specification, so you may find that things don't always work.

This is explained in detail at https://opentelemetry.io/docs/languages/python/exporters/.

The JaegerExporter uses port 6831, and the collector Jaeger exporter uses port 14250.

The EAI server creates a thread when it receives a request. The EAI server calls multiple methods in one thread and creates a span for each step of the method in the integration process. Since it passes context from Method A to Method B through an internal thread, there is no propagation, but it is difficult for automatic instrumentation and requires development by manual instrumentation.

CHAPTER 4 OBSERVABILITY PRACTICES BY THE INDUSTRY

```
from opentelemetry import trace
from opentelemetry.exporter.jaeger.thrift import JaegerExporter
from opentelemetry.sdk.resources import SERVICE_NAME, Resource

from opentelemetry.sdk.trace import TracerProvider
from opentelemetry.sdk.trace.export import BatchSpanProcessor

#trace.set_tracer_provider(TracerProvider())

trace.set_tracer_provider(
TracerProvider(
        resource=Resource.create({SERVICE_NAME: "my-helloworld-service"})
    )
)

jaeger_exporter = JaegerExporter(
    agent_host_name="localhost",
    agent_port=6831,
)

trace.get_tracer_provider().add_span_processor(
    BatchSpanProcessor(jaeger_exporter)
)

tracer = trace.get_tracer(__name__)

with tracer.start_as_current_span("foo"):
    with tracer.start_as_current_span("bar"):
        with tracer.start_as_current_span("baz"):
            print("Hello world from OpenTelemetry Python!")
```

When using Grafana Tempo, the collector settings are as follows:

```
exporters:
  otlp:
    endpoint: tempo:4317
    tls:
      insecure: true
```

Jaeger supports OTLP, and it supports the 4317 port:

```
exporters:
  prometheus:
    endpoint: "0.0.0.0:8889"
    const_labels:
      label1: value1
```

331

CHAPTER 4 OBSERVABILITY PRACTICES BY THE INDUSTRY

```
  debug:

  zipkin:
    endpoint: "http://zipkin-all-in-one:9411/api/v2/spans"
    format: proto

  otlp:
    endpoint: jaeger-all-in-one:4317
    tls:
      insecure: true
```

You can export to Jaeger. Jaeger uses 1.53.0:

```
from opentelemetry import trace
from opentelemetry.exporter.jaeger.thrift import JaegerExporter
from opentelemetry.sdk.resources import SERVICE_NAME, Resource
from opentelemetry.sdk.trace import TracerProvider
from opentelemetry.sdk.trace.export import BatchSpanProcessor
trace.set_tracer_provider(
    TracerProvider(
        resource=Resource.create({SERVICE_NAME: "my-hello-service"})
    )
)
jaeger_exporter = JaegerExporter(
    agent_host_name="localhost",
    agent_port=6831,
)
trace.get_tracer_provider().add_span_processor(
    BatchSpanProcessor(jaeger_exporter)
)
tracer = trace.get_tracer(__name__)
with tracer.start_as_current_span("rootSpan"):
    with tracer.start_as_current_span("childSpan"):
            print("Hello world!")
```

Export to an OTLP supported by the collector:

```
from opentelemetry import trace
from opentelemetry.exporter.otlp.proto.grpc.trace_exporter import OTLPSpanExporter
from opentelemetry.sdk.resources import Resource
from opentelemetry.sdk.trace import TracerProvider
from opentelemetry.sdk.trace.export import BatchSpanProcessor
```

```
resource = Resource(attributes={
    "service.name": "service"
})

trace.set_tracer_provider(TracerProvider(resource=resource))
tracer = trace.get_tracer(__name__)

otlp_exporter = OTLPSpanExporter(endpoint="http://localhost:4317", insecure=True)

span_processor = BatchSpanProcessor(otlp_exporter)

trace.get_tracer_provider().add_span_processor(span_processor)

with tracer.start_as_current_span("foo"):
    print("Hello world!")
```

The instrumentation to implement the transfer can be done in two ways.

- Develop an application to transfer manual instrumentation to Jaeger and OTLP. Configure an OTLP receiver in the OpenTelemetry collector to send traces to an endpoint and an exporter in the collector to transfer to Jaeger and OTLP. Since Jaeger supports OTLP, it is also possible to transfer directly to Jaeger, bypassing the collector.

- The automated instrumentation uses the OpenTelemetry agent, and the endpoint information for the transfer is defined in the environment variables. The agent can transfer traces to the endpoints in the provided environment variables without development.

Transferring is relatively easy compared to propagating.

The bank has frontend microservices, backend microservices, core banking, backoffice, SWIFT, ledger, reconciliation, and bookkeeping as backoffice.

I configured observability with EAI servers for frontend, backend, and core banking.

Interface externally with gateways including the backoffice and SWIFT. The backoffice and SWIFT are configured for observability with the EAI server.

The E2E trace is a challenge. The EAI server also has a 2PC requirement. Sometimes they require N-PC.

At the bank, batching is critical. Except for pipelines that run on a scheduler at a set time, they often run like batches. This is difficult with commercial batch schedulers like Control-M, but batch schedulers are often developed in parallel threads with spring batches and elastic threads, or they are handled in crontab. Developers also use a lot of message servers these days. The commercial batch scheduler is too expensive to license, so you can develop an open source batch scheduler and introduce observability.

4.3. Observability in Telecom

Telecom processes distributed transactions and involves complex orchestration. There are many limitations when organizing E2E observability.

Even pure tech companies have products. Despite the importance of technology, no company is without a product and customer. Products contain a company's strategy. There are systems in place to design the product and sell it to the customer, and the company needs business processes to do so. SREs need to understand the basic business processes and the strategy of a company. If you only understand the technical part, it's not easy to communicate with people in the organization. You need to understand the customers, the products, and the business in order to convince and lead them. To process and improve real-world failures, technology alone is not enough. In complex, customer-driven domains like banking and telecom, you need to understand more than just the technology.

A wireline or wireless telecom has over 10,000 products and releases new products every month. The system that sells these products is called an order system.

These systems launch complex and diverse products, such as wireline and wireless combined products and family discounts. They also manage complex hierarchy customer and product data. They develop an orchestration server to handle multiple wireline and wireless order in a single way. Telecom order processing is more complex than bank fund transfers, but it also shows a more flexible and innovative way to develop.

It is the role of the Telecom orchestration server to activate orders received from customers.

The concept of event-driven orchestration is used a lot in the work of telecom. It consists of a message server and many microservices.

Telecom orchestration is characterized by the following features:

- Distributed transaction processing with compensation
- Create orchestration plans based on product masters
- Handle complex revision and cancellation orders while preserving the customer's existing assets
- Support for complex product and customer structures like combined products
- Loosely coupled, difficult to migrate

These features are difficult to handle in orchestrations developed simply as microservices. Telecom orchestration is at a different level than other industries. These requirements are unique to telecom that don't even exist in banking and trading.

The banking demo was all about applying observability to different legacy with E2E trace and EAI server. The telecom demo was about distributed transaction processing and complex order orchestration, explaining how observability would be implemented. Having worked in various domains, I have a personal opinion that telecom's order processing is the most complex and challenging. Telecom has a lot of legacy systems and a loose coupling of microservices architecture.

CHAPTER 4   OBSERVABILITY PRACTICES BY THE INDUSTRY

The process of rollback and event sourcing for distributed transactions is a complex topic. It is not a problem of concurrency, such as mutexes in a single database, but managing data consistency of transactions from many applications and databases in business processes. Distributed transactions can be processed in two ways.

- Use TP-monitor to manage multiple databases with the XA protocol and process 2PC.
- The message server can orchestrate multiple applications, and compensation can be processed in the event of a rollback.

The telecom demo uses orchestration and a message server. It explains how compensation is processed when a rollback occurs. Roughly, it is processed in steps, as shown here:

- Compensation cancels the transaction being processed.
- It compares the differences between the old and new transactions.
- Performs reprocessing on the differences.

It's important to understand that rollbacks happen when something goes wrong more often than normal.

Implementing a reliable Saga pattern is difficult, and you have to use a commercial orchestration server. I describe examples that are directly applicable in practice.

Figure 4-23 illustrates how the orchestration server supports trace:

1. The system that captures the order generates an order ID and a trace ID when the order is submitted and sends it to the JMS queue.
2. The orchestration server creates components according to the orchestration plan.
3. The task executes the compensation for the created components and sends them to the JMS queue.
4. The EAI server subscribes to the components in the JMS queue.
5. The EAI server uses an adapter to connect to the legacy system.
6. It sends to the JMS queue in the fallout when a failure occurs.
7. If the administrator determines that it is a technical failure, fallout management attempts to reprocess.

By default, the order system, JMS server, EAI server, and fallout management support trace. If no intervening orchestration servers, components, or tasks restrict message headers, the propagation of traces is handled successfully. Propagation occurs on Steps 1, 3, 4, 5, 6, and 7 (not 2).

CHAPTER 4   OBSERVABILITY PRACTICES BY THE INDUSTRY

Analyzing Figure 4-23, traces propagate on Steps 2, 4, 6, 7, 8, 9, 11, 12, 13, and 14. Steps 3, 5, and 10 do not propagate, but they are not critical because they are internal operations that occur between threads. Since the process is long and complex, it is important that there are no breaks, and some can be omitted.

The downside is that most orchestration servers and EAI servers are currently difficult to monitor together. Trace enables full observability of the integration of orchestration and EAI server. You need to support trace throughout the order's processing and organize distributed transactions based on it.

The telecom orchestration demo is not open source but uses commercial software, which makes it difficult to test. I make the demo and system available in other ways.

For example, suppose that the number of request in the system that a new order for a combined wireless and wireless product generates is over 500. The wireline order consists of 500 requests and responses, and you are processing the 300th request.

- The customer has already submitted an order. Due to personal reasons, that customer creates a revision order to cancel or change the existing order.

- In the case of a cancelled order, the orchestration server executes only the requests that require an Undo of the 300 requests. The other requests that have already been processed need to be rolled back.

- While you were processing 300 requests, a revision order was submitted by the user. In this case, you need to cancel the 300 requests you've processed so far and restore the previous state. First, undo the 300 requests. In the restored state, reprocess the 300 requests that contain the changes. This is the same as redoing 300 requests. The redo is done—it will do the remaining 200 and complete the 500 requests.

- When all requests have been fulfilled, mark the order status as complete.

- Calculating the process is Do 300 (process) + Undo 300 (cancel) + Redo 300 (reprocess) + Do 200 (process), with a total throughput of 1,100 requests processed. The order is fulfilled. The total number of spans, including system traces, is 1,100 x 100, which is 11,000.

E-commerce does not process cancellations in this way, and other domains have simple cancellation and revision processes compared to telecom. Why is telecom's order fulfillment so complicated?

- The customer has existing assets. The new order should be processed without conflicting with the existing assets, and there should be no problems with data consistency.

- If the number of error is small, it is possible to correct them manually by an operator without automating distributed transactions. However, manual work is error-prone, and if the number of errors to be processed is high, it is necessary to automate them with a system.

- The work of telecom requires a variety of network equipment, engineer visits, and construction. As telecom processes are complex, so are orders to cancel and change them.

CHAPTER 4   OBSERVABILITY PRACTICES BY THE INDUSTRY

The orchestration server wants to implement distributed transactions with event sourcing and the Saga pattern. However, there is no open source support for distributed transactions. Vendors have been selling orchestration servers that process distributed transactions for a long time, while not exactly implementing event sourcing and the Saga pattern.

Banking companies configured the Tuxedo domain, processed distributed transactions on the EAI server, and implemented 2PC. Many telecom companies use TP-monitor to process distributed transactions with 2PC rather than compensation. In Korea, they prefer not to process distributed transactions with compensation and use 2PC.

2PC configures the Tuxedo domain for processing and requires an Oracle database.

Compared to banking, telecom orders require complex orchestration. In the banking demo, the API server and EAI server played an important role in implementing observability. The orchestration server used in the telecom demo is an engine that processes compensation and interfaces with various systems. The telecom demo uses an orchestration server to illustrate how trace observability can be improved. The telecom task is as follows:

- The foundation of telecom is the network. Wireline and wireless network require equipment that is managed by an inventory system. Telecom facilities require physical space and a design to install and configure them. Construction is required to build the telecom facility on site as designed.

- Customers subscribe to wireline and wireless services and pay for what they use. Billing is calculated based on assets and usage.

- The telecom product is a combination of wireline, wireless, and broadcasting and can be billed and discounted with various accounts, such as family and other.

- Telecom has complex product attributes and structures. Various discounts and combinations are offered, and operations teams need to support new product launches. Bundles and promotions are processed all the time, so product changes are frequent, and product information must be accurately distributed to other systems.

- Telecom requires a variety of equipment and device. For example, a modem must be shipped to the customer's address, and the equipment must be installed. Depending on the equipment, telecom services are available only after a complex activation process.

- There are many canceled or revision change orders when processing orders. Manual work is time-consuming, can't process many things at once, and is prone to errors. You need to automate your work to improve productivity and accuracy.

- You need fallout management for when order processing fails. You need support for handling customer complaints, activation process delays, and failures.

- In addition to product and customer master data, you need to manage master data for services and resources on your network.

CHAPTER 4 OBSERVABILITY PRACTICES BY THE INDUSTRY

Depending on the type of customer you're dealing with, whether it's an individual or a business, the processes and products are very different. For telecom, selling to individuals is a completely different process than selling to businesses, and selling to businesses is more complex. Dealing with enterprises involves fewer transactions, larger amounts of money, and more complex processes.

Observability is a technology used in production, but in practice, it requires both a business understanding and a technical understanding of the application. To communicate effectively with other development organization, you need to understand the business and the application, and the better you understand them, the better you can configure observability. Within the SRE team, there are systems engineers who focus on root cause analysis, and there is also a role for SREs to facilitate communication with other departments. You'll need to collaborate with developers and business people and work to explain and convince other departments of the benefits of observability. Unless you're a startup with a small number of people, you'll need to collaborate with various organizations and people to make decisions, which can be a complex process.

The work of telecom can be broadly categorized into business support systems (BSS) and operational support systems (OSS). Telecom provides a variety of services, including wireline, wireless, and broadcast, and in order to provide these services, they use facilities that need to be installed and configured, which is the OSS area. Since you pay for the services you use, it is important to measure how much you use and bill for it.

Banking is organized into two main areas: microservices and legacy systems. In telecom, the division is business and network, and it's common to orchestrate both areas separately.

In banking, API and EAI servers are important, and in telecom, orchestration servers and EAI servers that process orders are important.

The orchestration server includes the following two features:

- Order fulfillment orchestrates processes in business support systems.

- Network provisioning orchestrates the processes of the operational support system.

Once the orchestration of order fulfillment is complete, the orchestration of network provisioning is then processed. The generated result after orchestration is called a component. In other words, the orchestration server orchestrates the component. The orchestration server dispatches components to the legacy system and manages the order and state of the component.

In the past, telecom used commercial observability to customize its order system rather than developing its own. Telecom purchased commercial observability for billing and customer management and customized it. As described, this is because of the complexity of the business and the technical limitations and difficulties that are not supported by open source. The applications that show the characteristics of telecom are as follows:

- Oracle BRM is a billing software that processes rating and billing.

- Oracle M6 is a network inventory. It designs and configures services and resources.

- Siebel is a customer management application. It manages customer information and creates orders.

- PeopleSoft is an enterprise resource planning application. It manages the workforce.

CHAPTER 4　OBSERVABILITY PRACTICES BY THE INDUSTRY

Telecom uses a variety of legacy and packaged applications. Legacy systems often play an important role in the overall business process. Although SREs don't have to deal with legacy systems directly, it is a process of E2E trace and often the cause of failure, so it is necessary to familiarize yourself with important legacy applications.

The EAI server processes the interface between the legacy application and the orchestration server.

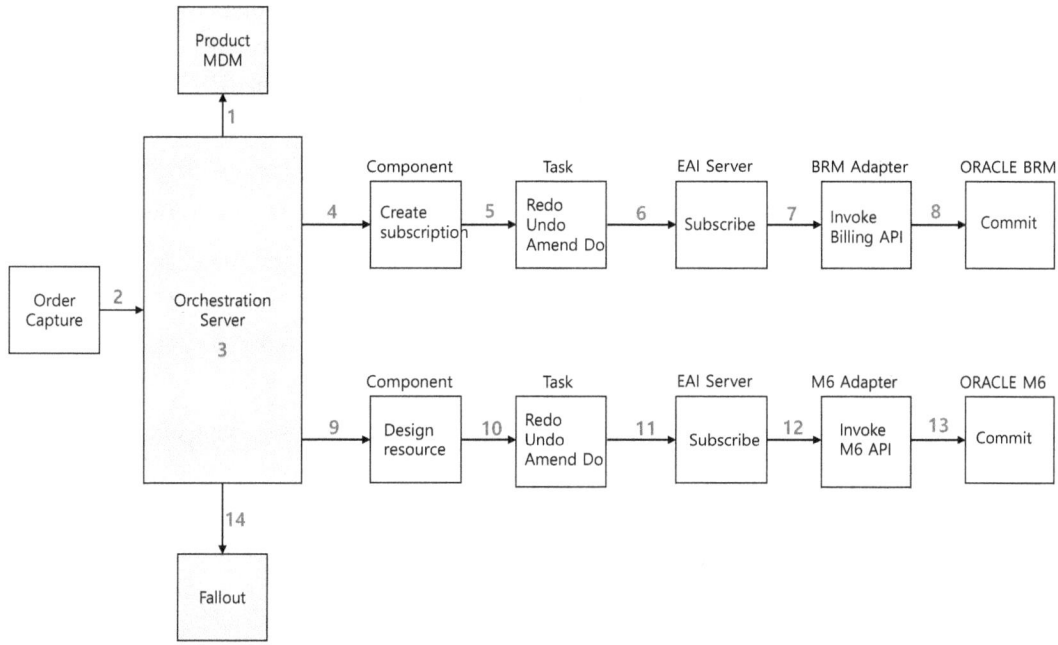

Figure 4-23. *Orchestration server's compenstation flow*

The telecom's processing is more complex than routing on an API server; it creates components and orchestrates them. See Figure 4-23. It implements compensation and organizes distributed transactions through the orchestration server.

1. The order system can create an order or change an existing order. It submits the created order to the orchestration server. After submission, orchestration starts.

2. The orchestration server processes order fulfillment and network provisioning. The orchestration server creates components based on product attributes and publishes them through the JMS message server. The task reads the component and handles the compensation logic. The EAI server subscribes to the component from the JMS server.

3. The EAI server processes logic and interfaces with various legacy systems, such as billing and inventory.

339

CHAPTER 4   OBSERVABILITY PRACTICES BY THE INDUSTRY

4. When the legacy is done processing, it passes the response to the EAI server, which passes the status to the orchestration server.

5. As well as request and responses being processed through the EAI server, this creates multiple spans. Internal logic is processed by the orchestration server, components are published to the JMS message server, and EAI processing interfaces to the legacy system are created as spans. Traces can be monitored. The orchestration server only manages the sequential processing of components and the status of publish, subscribe, and order, while the EAI server handles the legacy interface, and the processing logic is custom-developed in the legacy interface.

Operationally, the orchestration server processes order fulfillment and network provisioning processes:

- Based on the attribute of the product included in the submitted order, a number of components are created that are required by the orchestration. Examples of components include creating a customer, starting a billing cycle, and activating equipment.

- Add the goods and services included in the order to the customer's account. Create the customer's goods (assets) in the billing system.

- While order fulfillment and network provisioning have business differences, they are technically processed by the same orchestration server.

- Assign and manage tasks to engineers to deliver or install telecom equipment.

- Inventory the configuration information (services and resources) of the installed wireline and wireless networks.

- Activate the goods and services included in your order on various network devices.

Create and process orders exist in a variety of industries. Orders are created by combining customer and product master data; the order is the transactional data that combines various master data, and orders have a complex layer structure. Different industries and process have different types of orders. Orders in telecom are more complexly organized than in other industries.

- It's more complicated and difficult to process existing orders than create new ones. The product that a customer is already using is called an asset or a subscription. A change order changes an existing asset, so it's complicated to process a cancellation. Asset data should not be inconsistent. Assets are distributed across multiple legacy systems. Therefore, distributed transactions are required.

- The data structure of customers and products has a layered and complex relationship. Telecom combines various products and sells them in promotions and bundles. Products contain various attributes. Different pricing and discount policies are applied to products.

CHAPTER 4   OBSERVABILITY PRACTICES BY THE INDUSTRY

- Customer data can be organized into groups, like a family. Members of a group can be added or removed dynamically. When changes are made, such as additions and removals, additional discounts are applied. Product and customer data is organized into groups and dynamically added or excluded. This requires complex rules when capturing the order.

- When processing a wire order, there are times when the order fails due to a technical failure or the customer changes their mind and cancels the order. In this case, a revision order is submitted, and the orchestration server must process the rollback and compensation.

It is more common to create a change order with assets already created than to process a new order with no new assets. While processing the change order, multiple cancellation and revision are often requested. This is why telecom orders are more complex than orders in other industries, and it is technically difficult and complex to implement these requirements.

The orchestration server uses the TIBCO telecom order solution, and a demo is conducted. E2E trace and observability are also available for telecom. Basically, the core Microservices, JMS server, and EAI server support OpenTelemetry and create span, so detailed analysis of latency, throughput is possible for each section.

E2E observability in telecom is more difficult than it sounds, but the introduction of OpenTelemetry has made it possible.

Order processing for combined wireline and wireless products in telecom is very complex. The number of requests in a single order can be in the hundreds, including order status updates. The number of spans in a revision order, which is more complex than new activation and number porting, is even higher. The number of systems involved in an order often exceeds 50, including network equipment. A lot of network equipment is activated because it requires a variety of additional services. As you can see, telecom orders are complex and require observability to monitor them. It is important to analyze the logic and interfaces that are processed in order fulfillment and network provisioning, and to troubleshoot problems. For example, a telecom order involves approximately 500 spans and 50 applications, so a high level of observability is required to troubleshoot errors.

The value of the E2E trace can be realized by applying it to complex processes rather than simple ones. Events must be used to resolve the constraints of observability.

4.3.1. Telecom Architecture

It is important to understand that the telecom demo is architected differently than the banking demo.

The architecture of the telecom E2E observability demo processes orders.

While a new order in telecom is a single transaction, the internally generated span is a complex process with hundreds of spans. It must implement the Saga pattern, support rollback, and process the revision order.

CHAPTER 4 OBSERVABILITY PRACTICES BY THE INDUSTRY

Depending on the vendor's orchestration server, trace may not be supported, so there are a number of approaches you can use, as explained here.

The first method uses a script on the orchestration server. The orchestration server does not support trace. You can implement the E2E trace by adding the order ID of the message body in JMS to the header. The component created by the orchestration server contains the order ID. Whenever a message is published to the JMS queue, an order ID and a trace ID are generated together, and the order ID contains multiple trace IDs.

The second method creates multiple traces within an order ID. Use events to combine multiple traces with the same order ID. By capturing multiple components with events, you can capture multiple trace and order IDs. Propagating trace context between components, tasks, JMSs, and EAI servers is no problem.

While trace IDs help troubleshoot technical problems, order IDs allow you to monitor the status and progress of orders across the E2E. See Figure 4-24.

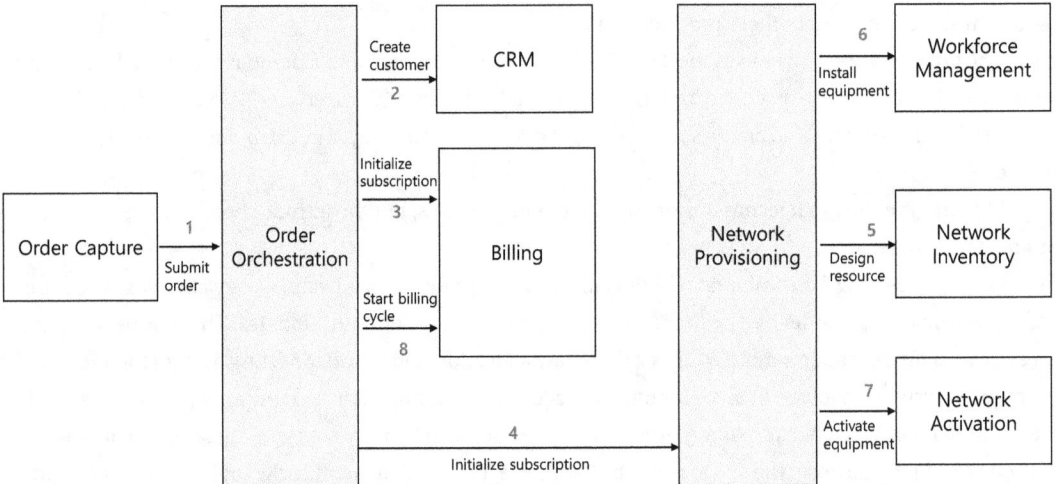

Figure 4-24. *Telecom demo flow*

However, the telecom demo implements rollbacks and revisions in a similar way to the Saga pattern. Historically, telecom has used a Saga-like pattern to process cancel and revision orders in complex order operations, such as new wireline-wireless combination. Many people think that the Saga pattern is new, introduced with microservices, but it was used 20 years ago to process orders and distributed transactions in a similar way.

Compared to e-commerce orders, telecom orders are complex.

- In addition to business-level order fulfillment, telecom adds network provisioning. Like telecom order orchestration, e-commerce is processed by an order system that creates, publishes, and subscribes components, communicating asynchronously with various applications. Network provisioning is a telecom-specific task.

- Telecom needs to process distributed transactions. Korea Telecom uses 2PC to process distributed transactions. However, international telecom uses distributed transactions as an orchestrated process that implements compensation. It is necessary to determine whether an order can be canceled through PoNR (Point of No Return) and process complex revisions, cancelations, and rollbacks.

4.3.1.1. Distributed Transactions

In a distributed system, a transaction can involve processes on multiple nodes. Distributed transactions are a way to atomically bundle these processes into a single transaction. There are two implementations of distributed transactions: 2PC and the Saga pattern.

2PC

This relies on the TP monitor and database itself. The most commonly used algorithm is a two-phase commit. For example, to run 2PC between heterogeneous databases, all databases must meet the X/Open XA standard. The main problem with 2PC is that locks can remain locked for a long time while waiting for messages from other nodes, resulting in poor performance.

Saga

Saga is one of the most popular distributed transaction solutions and is a de facto standard in microservice architectures. All operations are ordered. Each operation is executed as an independent transaction in its own database.

Operations are executed in order from first to last. When one operation is completed, the next operation is initiated.

If an operation fails, the entire process is rolled back through compensation transactions in reverse order from the failed operation to the first operation. Thus, Saga distributed transactions must prepare a total of 2n number of transactions.

- Run *n* number of transactions.
- Run n number of compensations.

There are two types of Saga patterns:

- **Decentralized**: In a microservice architecture, all services involved in a Saga distributed transaction subscribe to events from other services to perform components, which is a fully decentralized coordination method.
- **Centralized**: A single coordinator ensures that all services execute their operations in the correct order.

The bank example used an EAI server, but most sites are not fully decentralized and often implement a mix of partially decentralized and centralized orchestration, even with decentralized orchestration, designed for a core microservice that orchestrates downstream microservices.

How you choose to orchestrate depends on your business needs and goals. Because services communicate asynchronously with each other in a decentralized orchestration approach, every service must maintain a state machine internally to determine what to do as a result of events raised by other services. This can be difficult to manage if you have a lot of services.

Normally wireline and wireless telecom use the centralized approach.

Note that the two phases in 2PC are one transaction, whereas in Saga, each phase is a separate transaction.

In 2PC, when the second phase starts, all local transactions are incomplete, while in Saga, when the second phase starts, the first phase local transactions have been completed. In other words, the second phase of 2PC ends by aborting or committing the unfinished transaction, while the second phase of Saga executes a new transaction that rolls back the result of the previous transaction when an error occurs.

This is called compensation-based distributed transactions. Implement the undo procedure as business logic. The advantage is that it is database-agnostic. The disadvantage is that the business logic at the application layer must manage and handle the complexity of distributed transactions.

The application can see the intermediate results of these independent local transactions. In contrast, for distributed transactions such as database transactions or 2PC, the executor is the Tuxedo TPmonitor, and the application does not know the intermediate results of the execution.

Data inconsistencies always occur during distributed transaction executions. The operations in Saga must be executed in order. If there are no latency requirements or the number of services is small, Saga is a good choice for microservice architectures.

Telecom uses Saga and 2PC together. The customer management system and billing are connected with 2PC, and the entire order process is organized in Saga.

4.3.1.2. Telecom Reference

A simple description of 2PC is that TP is controlled by TM (transaction monitor) and RM (resource manager) by XA (extended architecture). These technical specifications are not open source, and 2PC has dependencies on specific commercial software. For example, only Tuxedo is used for the transaction process monitor, and Oracle is used for the database support 2PC. Most databases do not provide XA functionality.

When it comes to orders that process monetary transactions, consistency is key. Billing and customer management systems process monetary transactions and need to ensure data consistency and integrity while processing canceled orders. There is a requirement for distributed transactions between billing and CRM, which can be implemented as 2PC or compensation.

In a telecom order system, a customer creates an order and submits it to an orchestration server, which retries if an error occurs in processing the order and reliably processes rollbacks and changes if a canceled order is submitted. If an order is not completed and is in the middle of being processed, the customer can request changes to the order. These orders are called revision orders or in-flight orders. The orchestration server must support order types for flight, revisions, cancellations, changes, and so on.

CHAPTER 4 OBSERVABILITY PRACTICES BY THE INDUSTRY

The terms EAI server and orchestration server are often confused, so I define what they mean.

- An EAI server process consists of a number of steps.
- The orchestration server analyzes product attributes and orders and creates a number of components. Component have different granularities.
- A task processes the logic of the component.
- Compensation on the orchestration server is handled by the task.

If you mix up the component, task, and step, it's hard to understand what's going on. They should be clearly distinguished. Communication with the bank uses the EAI server. The communication uses an orchestration server.

Process Revision Order

Compensation occurs when you process a revision order, and you process the revision order and any changes to an existing order.

- Revision orders are recognized via order keys and validated via lifetime policies and PoNRs.
- Significant element: Recognize revision order and changes from existing orders and compensate for any changes.
- Create and compare orchestration plans for revision orders and change existing orders with that information.
- With a revision order, amend the existing order.
- Process components since the time of the revision and new components that came into the revision.

Compensation Types

Here's how to calculate compensation types. Compensation isn't as difficult as you might think. You determine the type of compensation by comparing the components of the original order and the revision order. See Table 4-2.

Table 4-2. Deciding on Compensation Types

Existing Order	Revision Order	Compensation Types
Exists	Does not exist	Undo
Does not exist	Exists	Amend Do
Exists	Exist, no change found	No compensation required
Exists	Exist, change found	Redo

345

CHAPTER 4   OBSERVABILITY PRACTICES BY THE INDUSTRY

Different types of compensation must be defined: Undo, Redo, Amend Do, None. The basic Undo provided by the Saga pattern is not enough to fulfill complex compensation requirements.

The compensation type determines what type of compensation the component will make. The actual compensation is performed by the task related to the component.

- **Undo**: Occurs when a component exists in the existing order but does not exist in the revision order (already performed and completed in the existing order).

- **Amend Do**: This occurs when a component does not exist in the existing order but does exist in the revision order.

- **Do**: Occurs when a component does not exist in the existing order but does exist in the revision order. This is similar to Amend Do but performed after compensation is complete.

- **Redo**: Existing and revision orders are the same component, but this occurs when there is a significant element change. Similar to Update. It is also possible to Do after Undo, but various exceptions must be considered.

- **No compensation required**: Components that exist identically in existing and revision orders, with no significant element changes.

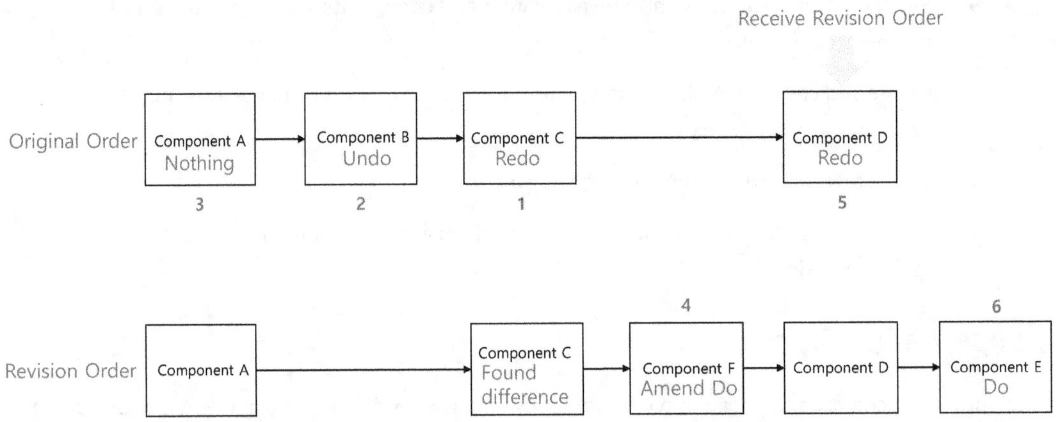

Figure 4-25. Revision processing using compensation

Steps 3 2 1 4 5 6 are processed in order. Roll back the original order and process the revision order. Redo D, and then do the rest of E. Then compare the existing order to the revision order.

- The compensation type is determined at the orchestration level through a comparison of components.

- Once the compensation type is determined, the compensation is determined by the compensation that maps to the component.

- The determination of the compensation type is based on a comparison of the orchestration plans of the existing order and the revision order.

CHAPTER 4   OBSERVABILITY PRACTICES BY THE INDUSTRY

Orchestration plans read the attributes of the products in an order, and then determine how many components to create and the dependencies between components.

If you analyze the order process in Figure 4-25, you can configure the compensation types, as shown in Table 4-3.

Table 4-3. *Compensation Result*

	Existing Order	Revision Order	Compensation Types	Process
Component A	Exists	Exist, no change found	No compensation required	Create customer
Component B	Exists	Does not exist	Undo	Create wireline subscription
Component C	Exists	Exist, changes found	Redo	Create wireless subscription
Component D	Exists	Exists	Redo	Activate network
Component E	Exists	Exists	Do Run after compensation completes	Start billing cycle
Component F	Does not exist	Exists	Amend Do	Create inventory

Design the compensation as shown in Table 4-3 and process the revision orders.

Once the compensation type is determined by comparing the components of the original and revision orders, as shown in Figure 4-25, the task implements the determined compensation type.

Designing and developing compensation is not complicated. The Saga pattern fills in the gaps in the solution where the pattern alone is lacking. Compensation includes some of the logic required for orchestration and a lot of configuration.

The task reads the component and executes the required compensation. Tasks handle the following compensation. The actual entity that performs the compensation is the task.

- **Do**: This is how general tasks are processed and is also used to process revisions for Undo, then redo and Amend Do.

- **Redo**: This occurs for a task that you want to redo when there is a change in the executed task compared to the revision order.

- **Undo**: Sets the Undo compensation for the task to be canceled compared to a change order, such as a cancel or revision order, on a task that has already been performed.

- **Amend Do**: When there is a new task in a change order, an Amend Do is fired.

The detailed logic for the compensation is implemented in a task. New components generate new trace IDs.

In orchestration, you organize components that have different granularities. The granularity is the order as an entire order and includes header and body, line item, order header, order body, and message header and body.

The message is divided into a header and a body, and the body is in turn divided into the order header and the body of the order. The header of an order contains the customer's name, contact information, address, and account. This information is then used to create a customer's account.

- When you add a subscription to a customer's account at billing time, you need line items, not headers. Define granularity at the line-item level rather than granularity for the entire order. Because billing deals with sensitive monetary information, the process changes line items if there are any changes and cancels the corresponding line item if a deletion is found.

- The customer management system creates an account. When you create a customer account, you need a large granularity: the entire order. When the billing cycle starts, you need line items, which means different components require different granularity, and you need to understand the component and choose the granularity.

- The installation of network equipment should not be handled on an line item basis but should be completed in a single visit (i.e., the granularity is the entire order, not the line item). Engineer visits are PoNR and prevent revision processing.

Select Undo, Redo, No Compensation Required for the compensation type, and determine the granularity of the component based on your understanding of the work.

It is necessary to configure the granularity of the component correctly to avoid additional parsing of messages in the task.

Compensation occurs when a change to an existing order is required. Compensation is also required when an order fails. For example, when processing an order, it fails due to technical reasons. This process is called fallout management, and it is reprocessed with compensation.

So far, I have described the process of revision and rollback used in orchestration servers. If the microservices Saga pattern is to be utilized in practice, it should be implemented with a similar concept. Since the Saga pattern is an immature technology, processing complex distributed transactions is not feasible at this point. The distributed transactions required in the telecom business are complex with many exceptions, so it is difficult to implement the Saga pattern alone.

4.3.1.3. Order Systems

Telecom orders are different from orders in other industries because the process is dynamic. For example, orders for new activations, number porting, and add-on services are more complex than e-commerce orders. The number of products is small, around 10,000. Enterprise orders in telecom are more complex than consumer orders because they require design and construction for network equipment.

I use the Saga pattern to demonstrate distributed transaction processing. In practice, it is best to avoid implementing distributed transactions in microservices as much as possible. While 2PC has the advantage of minimizing manual interactions and automation, it is highly complex and has many vendor dependencies and limitations.

I implement a wireline and wireless telecom activation process using TIBCO Order Fulfillment.

The orchestration server defines fulfillment rules and processes and automates everything from order submission to service activation within the network.

- **TIBCO Order Fulfillment**: Allows you to orchestrate orders based on metadata specified in your product catalog.

- **TIBCO Network Provisioning**: Implements provisioning processes and capabilities for services and resources that automate the allocation of basic network services. Not used in the demo.

- **TIBCO Product Catalog**: Provides catalog functionality to define and manage the lifecycle of products and services. Used in the demo in conjunction with TIBCO Order Fulfillment.

Provide a demo where you can create and submit an order, as shown in Figure 4-26:

- Apply for the telecom plan and add-on services. You want to purchase and complete your order.

- Provide the ability to create, change, or cancel order.

- Submit the order to the orchestration server.

If you order a wireless product, your order is processed immediately. However, if you order a wireline product, the modem needs to be configured after the engineer visits. Therefore, you can see in Figure 4-26 that the order is not completed immediately but is waiting for the engineer's visit.

CHAPTER 4 OBSERVABILITY PRACTICES BY THE INDUSTRY

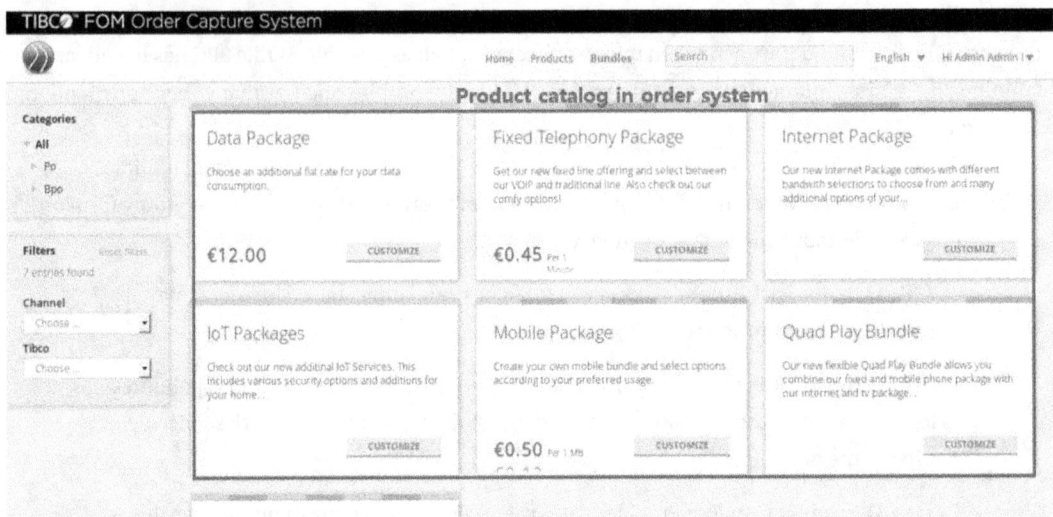

Figure 4-26. The order capture demo system

You can submit cancel and revision orders:

- On the Create Order screen, select a wireline product.

- Select an Internet package from the wireline offerings, and change the Install attribute to Yes.

- Since wireless communication requires no manual labor, the order is completed one minute after you submit it.

It must be tied to an EAI server. Develop logic to interface with billing and inventory using the EAI server.

4.3.1.4. Master Data

In the banking demo, I discussed the customer master. The telecom demo focuses on the product master.

The core of telecom BSS is the billing and customer management system. The important data of both systems are customers and products, and customers and products are managed as master data.

In previous telecom architecture setups, billing used to be the main system, and CRM was provided as a module for billing. While this architecture reduces complex interfaces, it doesn't lend itself to a modern distributed architecture. By including all operations in a single system, it lacks flexibility and scalability. Nowadays, billing and customer management are organized separately. This means that product and customer master data are managed separately in billing and customer care. Since the same data is managed by different applications, there is a need to synchronize the data. Master data is used to eliminate duplicates and manage data quality. Customer master data is used to reduce the legacy load and eliminate duplication.

In telecom, the structure and attributes of products are complex, and products are regularly deployed to various systems. Order fulfillment and network provisioning are generated orchestration based on the product master data.

Orchestration plans are created based on the attributes of a product. Changes to attributes can change the flow of orchestration, so changes to product MDM are also managed by master data.

No separate product master system is built, and product master management is included within the orchestration server.

4.3.1.5. Managing Fallout

Various exceptions and errors occur while processing orders. While orders for wireless products can be fulfilled within minutes, orders for wireline products can take days to process. Orders can be changed for a variety of reasons, such as a customer changing their mind and switching to a different product or canceling the order altogether. There are a number of exceptions, such as the billing system becoming unavailable during the order or the customer care system going down.

In general, there are three cases where compensation is required

- You want to make changes to an in-progress order,

- You want to cancel an order that hasn't been completed and is in-progress.

- An in-progress order fails, and you want to reprocess it.

If the order failed during processing, you can also use a revision order to cancel the order. If the order is complete, you should create a change order, not a revision order. Unexpected errors can occur during processing, and fallouts can occur.

If the order fails in the third case, you need to analyze the cause and reprocess the order, and the system that supports this is called *fallout management*. The fallout is processed internally and organized into workflows and message server.

If an order fails midstream, don't immediately roll it back or cancel it. Use fallout management to determine if it's a technical error and retry or if it's a business error, and discuss the problem with the product owner. Log the fallout in a trouble ticket in your CRM and communicate the failure and order activation status to the user.

You need to provide the ability to resolve fallouts and reprocess failed orders, which is usually done by the workflow in conjunction with the orchestration server. In the event of a fallout, the user logs into the workflow to analyze the cause of the fallout and retry.

The fallout management screen outputs a list of orders that are in a fallout state, and users can manually cancel or request to reprocess them. Different types of fallouts are processed differently. For example, technical fallouts are resolved by retrying. Business fallouts are compensated by creating a revision order or rolling back to a canceled order.

No separate fallout management system is built; the fallout management system is embedded within the orchestration server. The way fallouts are handled is internally organized into workflows and message servers.

CHAPTER 4   OBSERVABILITY PRACTICES BY THE INDUSTRY

Fallout is sometimes included in the orchestration server, but it can also be implemented separately as a BPM. In TIBCO's case, I implement fallout in a separate BPM.

4.3.2. Order Orchestration

The order orchestration server is responsible for creating and managing components and interfacing to the EAI server and workflow server.

By default, orchestration servers do not create spans. Only message servers and EAI servers create spans. The trace ID does not support E2E trace, but if you add the order ID to the span annotation, span attribute, and baggage, you can implement trace, including the orchestration server and EAI server.

A typical order application uses multiple IDs:

- **Session ID**: Generated when accessing the web and apps.
- **Trace ID**: Generated when a user clicks a specific button on the web and in the app.
- **Order ID**: Used only during the order process.
- **Request ID**: Used to process general transactions other than orders, such as product and order history inquiries.

The wireline and wireless telecom demo identifies orders by the order ID. Individual orders contain multiple trace IDs. When an order is submitted, an order ID is generated, and a component generated by the order orchestration server propagates the order ID and trace ID on the Java Message Service server and the EAI server.

The order ID is managed in the body, not the header.

You can configure E2E trace in several ways. Use the request ID to retrieve a product from the catalog. If it is placed in the body of the message, like the request ID, it will not be interrupted or broken if the microservices' protocol changes. If it is placed in the header, you need to manage the request ID so that it propagates throughout the E2E.

Order IDs are used to manage multiple trace IDs in an order.

In addition to traces, you can use events and logs to configure spans that are interrupted or missing:

- The first approach, I have yet to experience an orchestration server that supports OpenTelemetry. Further custom development is needed. Although the orchestration server does not support trace instrumentation, you can use scripts to add the trace context of the W3C trace context to component. The JMS server and EAI server support instrumentation, so you can propagate traces generated by components without interruption.

- The second approach uses events to collect order and trace IDs. You can output the trace ID in chronological order based on the order ID. This is the simplest way to implement trace on orchestration server.

- The third approach uses the log to collect order and trace IDs.

CHAPTER 4   OBSERVABILITY PRACTICES BY THE INDUSTRY

If your orchestration server does not support OpenTelemetry instrumentation, a single order can generate approximately 50 or more trace IDs using the first approach. Ideally, you want to create one trace per order using the second approach through the scripts and development provided by the orchestration serve. You can configure E2E trace with an orchestration server, a JMS server, and an EAI server by adding a trace context.

Figure 4-27 shows the orchestration server. The administration screen prints detailed information about individual components. The order orchestration management screen is similar to the distributed trace screen. You can monitor the status, duration, and fallout of individual component. The following information is available on the management screen:

- Component flow and status information
- Relationships and impacts between components
- E2E orchestration progress

Figure 4-27 is similar to a Gantt chart or sequence diagram. To monitor the order of processing and latency, you monitor each order or component.

Order IDs can be used to spot orders with high latency or to identify orders with errors. You should identify the section of the order where the problem occurred and analyze the section using the trace ID for RCA on the EAI server and legacy.

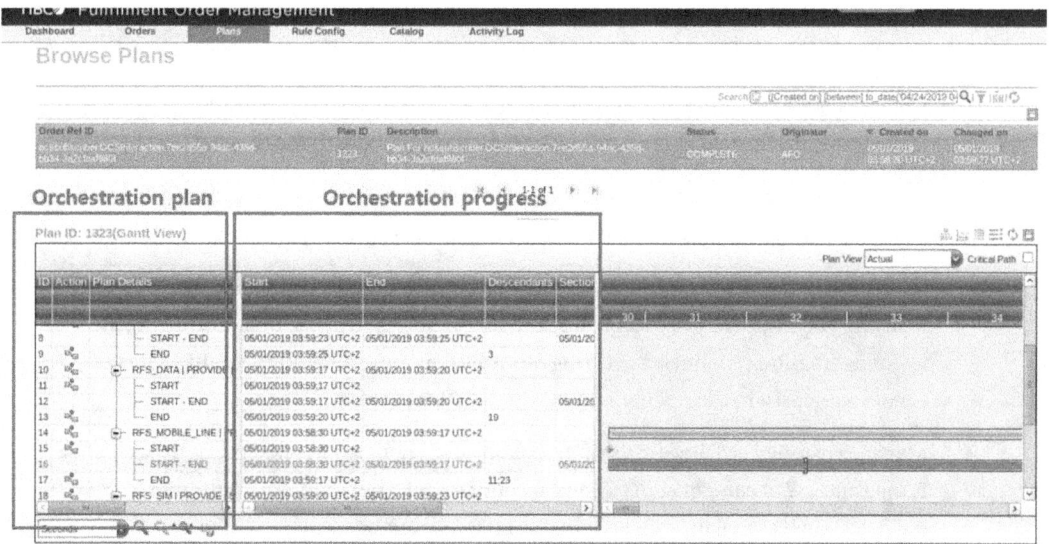

Figure 4-27. Orchestration server administration

This displays the flow between component processed by the orchestration server and displays detailed component information in order. For example, the billing system's component can help you understand latency and errors.

353

4.3.2.1. Billing

The subscription, rating, and billing components processed by telecom billing are as follows:

- **Subscription**: Billing customers have a variety of assets, such as plans, add-ons, and devices they are using. You need to add and change assets to the customer's account. During the order orchestration process, you need to start the billing cycle before the order is closed.

- **Rating**: Billing is not processed directly by the CDR. It is processed by a preprocessing system associated with the telecom CDR equipment. Before CDR is post-processed to billing, invoices are preprocessed to create a file format that billing can recognize. Pre-paid options use a processing module called AAA, while post-paid options are processed through CDR preprocessing.

- **Billing**: Billing calculates a rating for customers based on their usage and generates invoices at various intervals throughout the week and month. Based on the generated invoice, billing the customer is necessary. Calculating a rating is usually done in conjunction with various backends, such as refunds and settlements.

If billing goes wrong, the following use cases can occur:

- Customers receive inaccurate billing or are unable to use the service due to a lack of activation.

- In case of incorrect order processing, the customer will use the service after activation, but since there is no rating, the customer can use the service for free.

Oracle Billing Revenue Management (aka BRM, previous portal infranet) is a subscription, rating, and billing system for telecom service providers. BRM provides the following key features:

- Rating calculates how much to bill for service usage and subscriptions. If you measure and discount events in batch and real-time, you can use Pipeline Manager to configure BRM pipelines. Recurring monthly fees are evaluated by the BRM server. Create a price list in the pricing center, which defines the rates.

- Manage customer balances. Customer balances are updated in real time as usage is measured. You can perform various accounts receivable actions on customer balances, such as making adjustments and offering refunds.

- In customer management, you create subscriber accounts and manage customer accounts. Accounts are stored in the BRM database. You can create and deactivate accounts and manage the product offerings that customers have purchased.

- Generate reports. You can use BRM reports to analyze customer usage and plan your product offerings.

CHAPTER 4 OBSERVABILITY PRACTICES BY THE INDUSTRY

- BRM can bill customers for using and subscribing to the service. You can configure online billing (charging upfront fees in real-time) and offline billing (charging based on usage recorded in CDR files).

- Billing generates invoices each month that include the amount of the plan and collects payment. The BRM includes all billing for the customer in the invoice. You can request payments using various payment methods, such as credit card or email. Users can automate the process using the client UI or API.

EAI servers can be associated with BRM in a variety of ways, as shown in Figure 4-28.

- TIBCO BRM Adapter
- BRM JCA Adapter
- SOAP Web Services

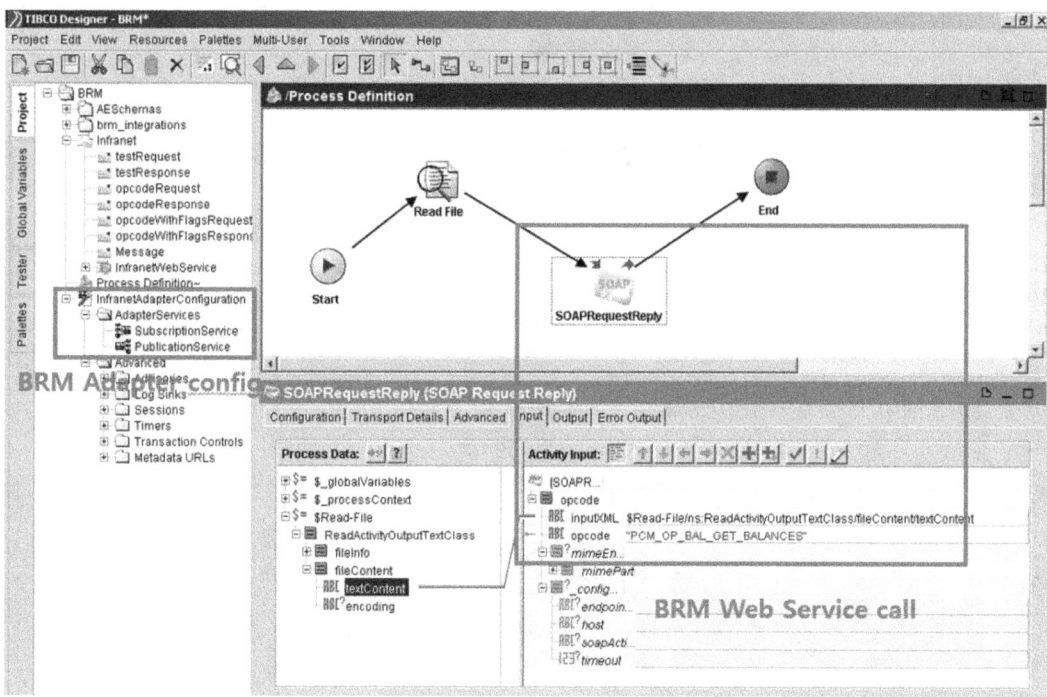

Figure 4-28. *The BRM interface*

The TIBCO BRM adapter used in the demo has the following components:

- The EAI Plugin for an infranet EAI framework is an application built with the EAI manager framework to provide access to infranet event data.

- The infranet data manager is a custom data manager for infranet that allows infranet client applications to call RPC operations.

355

CHAPTER 4   OBSERVABILITY PRACTICES BY THE INDUSTRY

The Infranet EAI plugin service is used by clients to call request and response operations. External applications can execute Opcode by sending requests to the infranet.

- The adapter receives the request.
- Iv converts external data to an infranet FLIST.
- It calls the corresponding Opcode to execute the required business function.
- A response is returned from BRM to the adapter.
- The result is sent back to the client.

Using the TIBCO development tool, you can configure request and response actions to call the infranet Opcode. The BRM client looks like in Figure 4-29.

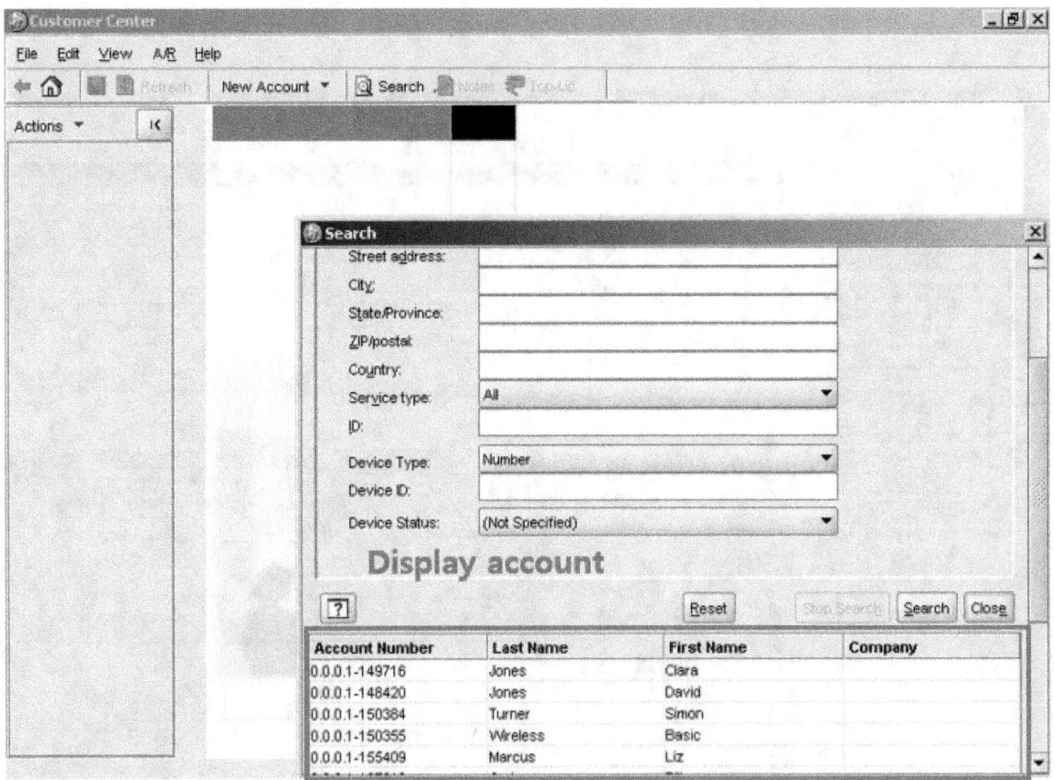

Figure 4-29. The BRM billing client

4.3.2.2. CRM

While developers now favor SaaS-based CRMs like Salesforce, telecom used to be a large user of Siebel CRM. Siebel supports the lifecycle of customer management. Basically, it manages different types of processes and data, such as products, customers, and orders. Here's how telecom's CRM process look:

- You can manage leads and opportunities for your customer audience.

- In the initial pre-sales phase, you process quotes.

- You can create orders through sales orders.

- After the order is fulfilled, you proceed with after-service.

- You can manage business service requests and technical trouble tickets.

Siebel is configurable by industry, and telecom includes order management, trouble ticket management, account management, service request management, call center management, product management, and customer master management by default.

Siebel CRM provides an application development tool called Siebel Tools, which allows you to create object definitions and develop Siebel applications.

The following are the main object types in the Business layer:

- **Business component**: Represents a business entity in an enterprise and consists of several fields that characterize it. For example, contact, company address, or activity.

- **Business object**: Represents a functional area of an enterprise that consists of one or more business components. For example, an Opportunity business object consists of opportunities and their associated contacts, activities, products, and issues.

- **Integration object**: This allows you to express integration metadata in Siebel business objects in a common structure that the EAI infrastructure can understand. They are logical objects that represent multiple business objects in a single entity.

The demo does not cover events as complex as publish and subscribe. From a trace perspective, asynchronous publishing and subscription can be complex to propagate. Requests and responses are simple to instrument and propagate in trace.

Figure 4-30 shows the Siebel user screen, which has been changed to an open UI in the latest version.

CHAPTER 4   OBSERVABILITY PRACTICES BY THE INDUSTRY

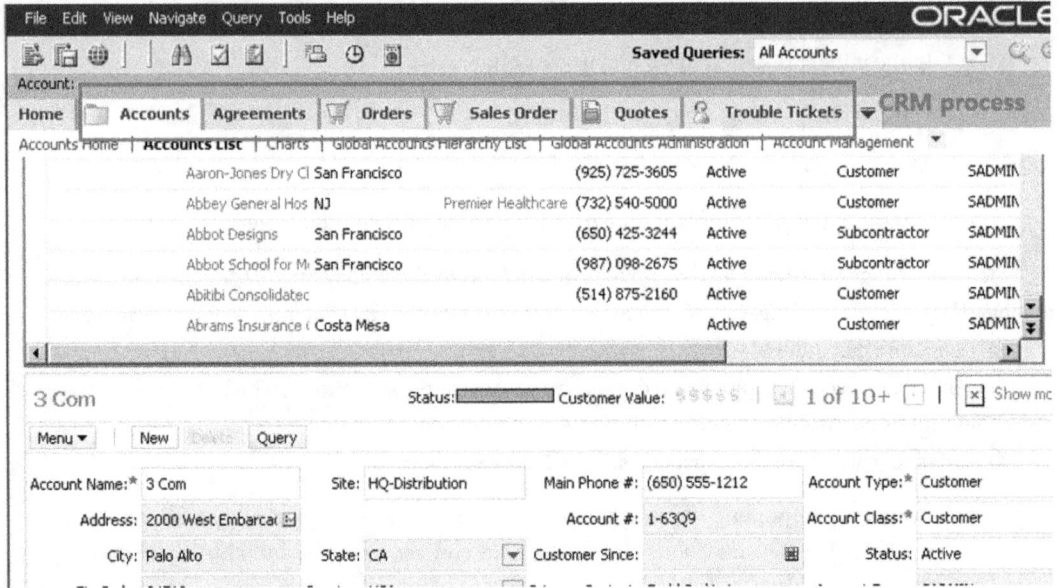

Figure 4-30. *Siebel CRM UI*

The connection information for the Siebel adapter is shown in Figure 4-31. The Siebel adapter uses a Siebel Java library internally.

Just as SAP is organized into BAPI and RFC, Siebel is organized into business components and business objects. When you select the business component and business object you want to call, it automatically generates the IO schema.

CHAPTER 4   OBSERVABILITY PRACTICES BY THE INDUSTRY

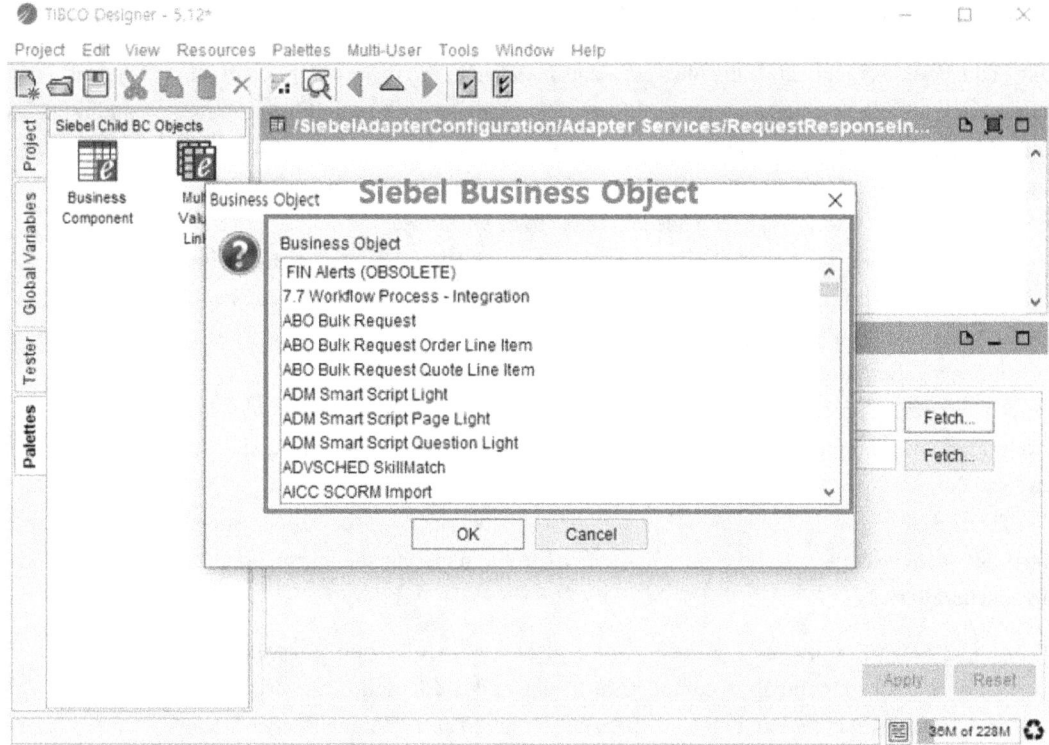

Figure 4-31. Siebel adapter configuration

You can see that the Siebel adapter is nicely configured.

4.3.3. Network Provisioning

Network provisioning is the process of organizing the inventory required for telecom network configuration and activating network equipment corresponding to services. TIBCO FOS was used to process order fulfillment, and the network provisioning module in TIBCO FOS was used to configure the processes required for network provisioning. The Operational Support System (OSS) interfaces with the following legacy systems"

- M6 is network inventory.
- PeopleSoft is an enterprise resource planning application, and it's especially famous for its role in HR management.

CHAPTER 4   OBSERVABILITY PRACTICES BY THE INDUSTRY

4.3.3.1. Network Inventory

One of the key telecom assets is the physical assets installed in the region. Examples include wireless repeaters on building rooftops, telecom cables on the ocean floor, and wireline telecommunications cables underground and over roads. These physical resources are associated with logical services, such as phone numbers and IP addresses, which means that a system is needed to organize and manage the physical resources and logical services, which telecom refers to as *inventory*.

Telecom requires the installation and construction of facilities in various physical spaces, and to maintain them, an inventory system is built. The network provisioning process creates and activates resources and services in the inventory. The physical network equipment and services are then activated for the order activation process.

The activation process requires various interactions with the resources and services defined in these inventories. For example, within the scope of the circuit's available bandwidth, it allocates the customer's assets to the resources and services in the inventory.

Figure 4-32 shows the Metasolv M6 inventory solution that allows telecom to automate and manage the order, service activation, and service assurance (problem management) processes. Metasolv consists of several modules:

- **Network provisioning**: Facilitates the delivery of a full scope of services, from simple circuit assignments to complex line design and configuration. Service providers know exactly what their customers have ordered and what their network can support.

- **Network design**: Integrates the geographic, physical, and logical dimensions of the network and manage equipment. You can design a variety of network topologies and equipment in your inventory.

- **Trouble management**: Supports the reporting, track, and resolution of problems related to the delivery of telecom products and services. Traces reported problems from initial identification to resolution

- **Interface management**: Supports the exchange of information between the Metasolv solution and the service provider's legacy systems.

- **Task management**: Enables you to process task and workflow across your organization. It provides the ability to manage the provisioning plans required to manage the flow of tasks and information in the network provisioning process.

CHAPTER 4 OBSERVABILITY PRACTICES BY THE INDUSTRY

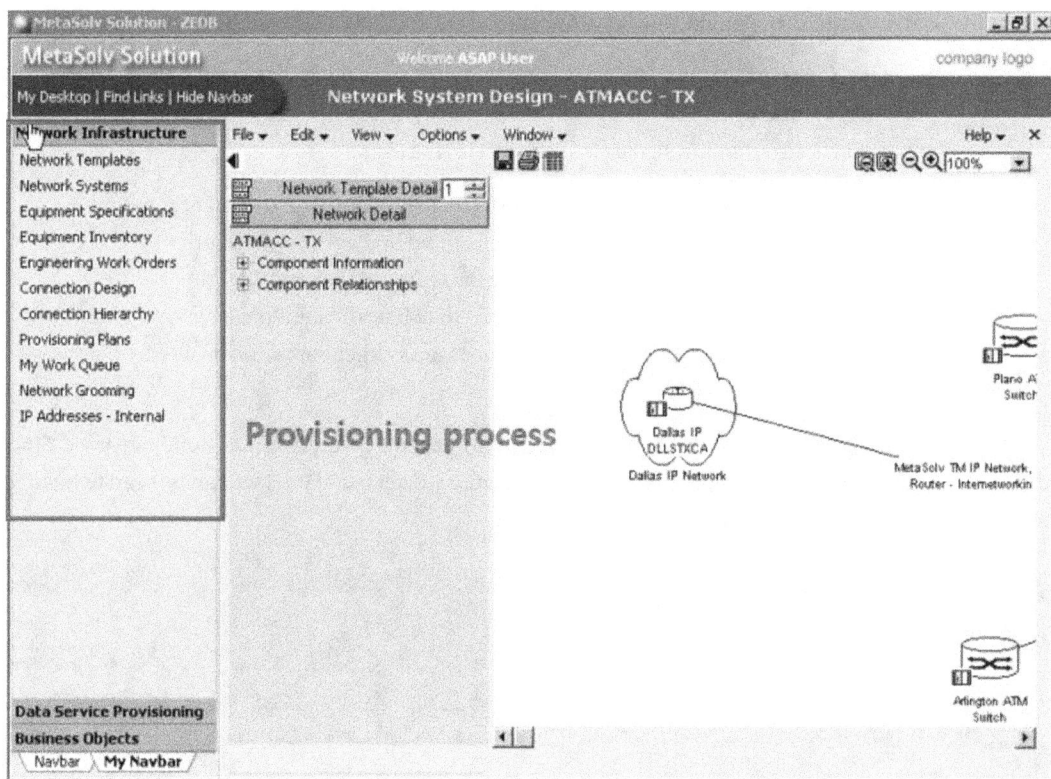

Figure 4-32. Designing a Metasolv resource

Another process within network provisioning is the activation of network equipment. The interface between the network provisioning server and the telecom wireline and wireless equipment is mainly done using telnet. The demo does not show equipment activation.

Using the Metasolv API

The Metasolv interface architecture provides APIs to access specific information in the Metasolv Solution database. The Metasolv API is an IDL file that provides a way to communicate with Metasolv solutions and is available on all platforms that support CORBA.

Metasolv has defined predefined signals called application events.

Understanding Events

An *event* is something important that happens within the workflow of a task management or application.

361

CHAPTER 4 OBSERVABILITY PRACTICES BY THE INDUSTRY

The task management implements two types of events:

- **Application events** are predefined within a Metasolv solution and occur at a fixed point in the workflow. Application events are from the Metasolv solution to external applications via outbound signals associated with the event.

- **Gateway events** provide a mechanism for inserting hooks into the task management. Gateway events are defined by the application and set in the Metasolv solution database using the user interface provided by the task management. Unlike application events, which can only occur within the Metasolv solution, gateway events be defined in the Metasolv solution database as either outbound or inbound events.

It is recommended to use application events and gateway events to interface and configure trace. Since Metasolv is processed on top of WebLogic, as shown in Figure 4-33, it uses JMS. JMS can be used to interface between Metasolv and external applications.

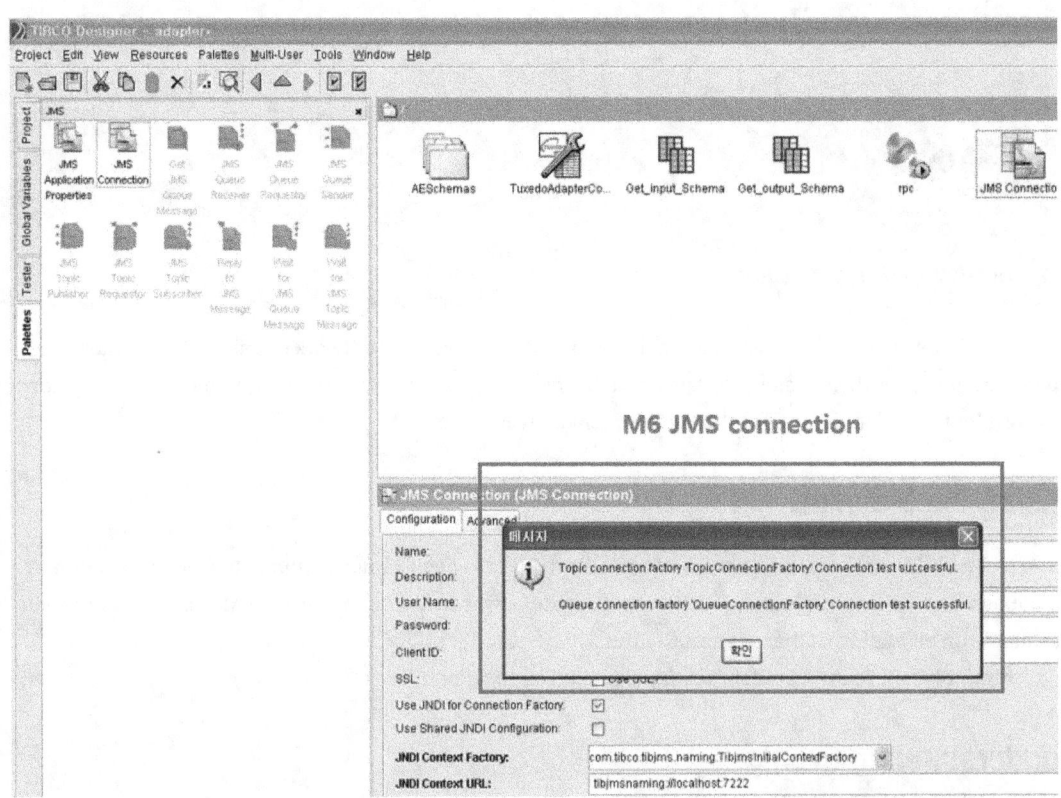

Figure 4-33. Interface using WebLogic JMS

CHAPTER 4 OBSERVABILITY PRACTICES BY THE INDUSTRY

4.3.3.2. Workforce Management

WFM assigns tasks to network engineers. For example, the engineer might go to a location and install a modem. They might use a solution that specializes in workforce management, or leverage the workforce management capabilities within your ERP. Wireless doesn't require a site visit for equipment installation or service. However, wireline and enterprise offerings require an engineer to go to your site and assist with installation and configuration. WFM selects the right engineer and assigns tasks, or you can request an engineer visit if you have problems with the equipment or need additional service.

PeopleSoft supports the integration of legacy with PeopleSoft within the enterprise, as shown in Figure 4-34.

- **Component interface**: The component interface allows external applications to use PeopleSoft business logic. Component interfaces are ideal for use in PeopleSoft environments that require tightly coupled integrations to send data in real-time.

- **Integration broker**: An integration broker that uses application message technology to integrate with third-party applications.

PeopleSoft is internally composed of Tuxedo, Jolt, and the Weblogic Web Application Server. The TIBCO PeopleSoft Adapter does not interface directly to Tuxedo but to PeopleSoft through Jolt.

The PeopleSoft tool is a development tool, and you can see the preregistered services.

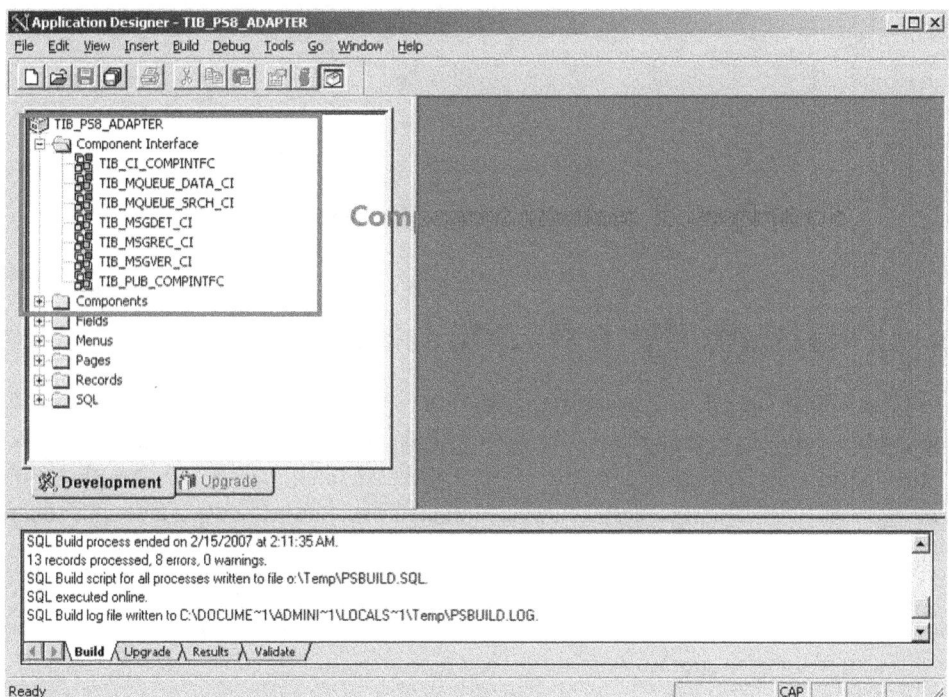

Figure 4-34. *The component in the PeopleSoft development tool*

363

PeopleSoft provides a way to call components from the legacy.

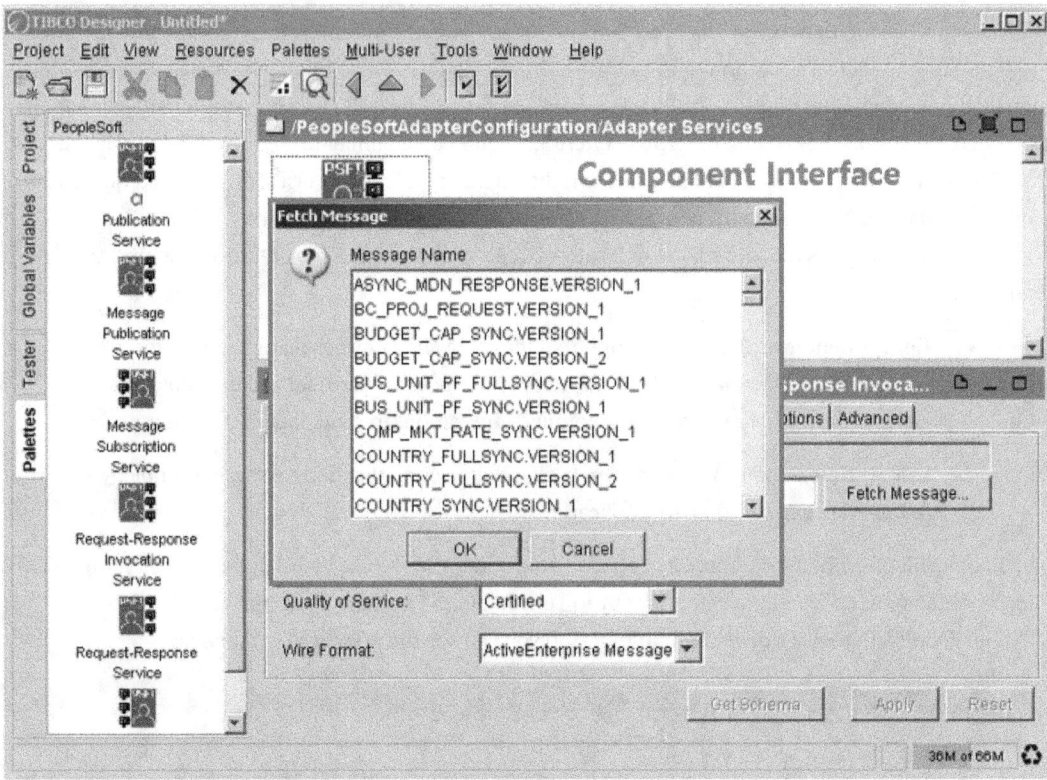

Figure 4-35. PeopleSoft Adapter Configuration

It automatically generates an IO schema for a developer, as shown in Figure 4-35.

4.4. Observability in Online Games

This section explains a demonstration of applying observability to an online game architecture. Unlike banking and telecom, online games have no legacy and need to provide high-volume, global services. Online gaming has a different approach to observability than traditional industries. Online gaming also has different requirements than other industries, such as multitenancy, Kubernetes operators, and Kubernetes cluster autoscale.

There are many differences between the development and operation of games and other industries. While there is an advantage in not having a legacy, gaming requires the development of ultra-low latency servers and a lot of tuning to improve performance and reduce costs.

4.4.1. Game Operation

Observability is a cross-concern, so it is favorable to build multi-tenants. Microservices make it difficult to distinguish between service boundaries, so multitenancy is often not practical in other industries. Since games are released by different game studios, it can be cost-effective for the SRE to build centralized observability rather than building separate observability for each studio. In many cases, each studio has its own SRE, and developers often build observability according to their own preferences without standards. This often results in duplication of effort and uncontrolled costs. Since studios work on different games, it's a good environment to configure multi-tenants that can be centrally managed to reduce costs. Kubernetes lends itself to multi-tenant configurations and provides the infrastructure. Grafana basically supports multi-tenancy, and OpenSearch can also be configured. Online games use the cloud, but they are typically deployed and run on virtual machines. Increasingly, games are being run on Kubernetes.

4.4.1.1. Kubernetes Operators

For online games that are not console games but are played by many users, you need to manage user sessions. This can be automated using Kubernetes operators.

Kubernetes operators are well suited to the lifecycle of online games. Develop operators that support the game lifecycle and manage Kubernetes resources. Users use the UDP protocol to connect to the game. You need to allocate resources for one game room in one pod to a large number of players.

A game server creates a Pod for an hour of a game room; multiple players (clients) join the pod to play the game, and the pod is deleted after the game ends. This pod lifecycle is different from other industries.

To support this unique architecture, you can automate with operators. Online games don't have legacy and black box, but they do require a lot of customization to configure their online game lifecycle.

4.4.1.2. Multi-Kubernetes Clusters

Cloud vendors offer managed game servers. Google's game server, Agones, is open source. Network latency is important for FPS games. Network latency is one of the most important metrics for global services. Since it is important to reduce network latency, it is difficult to operate a centralized Kubernetes cluster for global service and create multiple Kubernetes clusters distributed across multiple regions. You need to manage multiple Kubernetes clusters. You need to measure the network latency of users and route them to specific global clusters accordingly.

Large online games run game servers across tens of thousands of pods in multiple Kubernetes clusters. Agones Game Server supports multiple Kubernetes clusters and provides the ability to autoscale Kubernetes clusters. While autoscaling is typically processed at the node and pod level, online games need to autoscale Kubernetes clusters to manage user traffic dynamically.

4.4.1.3. Resource Provisioning

The gaming industry is well-positioned to adopt new technologies. There is less technical debt and less risk in adopting new technologies. If the game is successful, it will experience global services, high traffic, and aggressive tuning of systems. DevOps could set up systems with Terraform and Ansible. Assuming the game doesn't do well, they can scale back and delete resources a few days later. Online games provide a global service, and the configuration of the system is dynamic and elastic, depending on the success of the game. Kubernetes and the cloud are well-suited to organize this dynamic provisioning of resources. In other industries, once a service is launched, it is maintained and managed for a period of time, even if the sizing of resources varies depending on the number of users. Online games require dynamic resource provisioning. Terraform and Ansible automate resource provisioning.

4.4.1.4. Monolithic Architecture

Games have a monolithic architecture, except games that use a lot of microservices.

Online games operate differently than other industries. The lifecycle of game development is different from the typical software development lifecycle. Game architecture does not use microservices. The servers and clients of a game are implemented monolithically, not as microservices. Online games typically consist of a client app and various types of servers, such as NPC servers, proxy servers, log servers, and so on, but they are not developed using the microservices pattern. Games are developed in C++. However, the architecture for operating the game heavily utilizes Kubernetes and the cloud. Other applications besides games use microservices, and they favor Kubernetes over Java. Spring Boot is not often used, as the complex Java-based framework is not suitable.

The game server runs the game and manages the game sessions.

4.4.1.5. CQRS

The CQRS pattern is a common model for supporting this process, separating reads and writes in the system. Writes affect a single normalized entry, whereas queries can look up unnormalized data. For example, you might use PostgreSQL for persistent transactional storage but use Elasticsearch for index lookup queries.

Many open source architectures built on microservices have also implemented CQRS internally, as shown in Figure 4-36.

Clusters are configured, and since Grafana LGTM and Apache Druid are architected to separate reads and writes by default, most customers already apply CQRS.

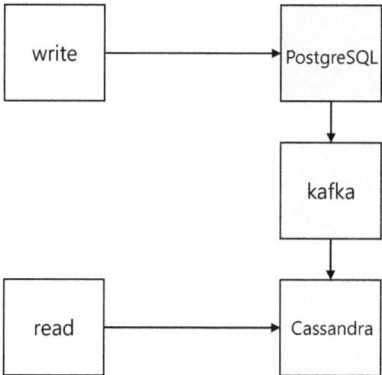

Figure 4-36. *The CQRS process*

Let's say data is entered into a database on the write path, and a commit is made. Due to the nature of relational databases, it is difficult to inject trace context into tables.

In CQRS, data is added to the write path. You need to update the read path and synchronize the reads and writes. The relational database in the write path does not have a separate header, so the read path does not receive the trace context of the write path.

You need to think about how to pass trace context. It goes through a message server, is committed in a relational database, and then the event is forwarded to another application. Banks have a similar problem.

Even if CQRS is technically difficult to observe and trace, it may not be a problem in practice. For example, suppose the write path is a direct deposit, and the read path is an account inquiry. The direct deposit and the account inquiry are separate transactions and should be configured as separate traces. For account inquiry, CQRS must be configured because the current balance must be synchronized between RDB and NoSQL, but it does not need to be implemented as a trace. If this is technically difficult to implement, it is a good idea to solve the problem in a business-like way.

A transaction is committed to the core banking database, and the same transaction continues to be processed in the backoffice. In the middle, the trace is interrupted by the core banking RDB. It is also useful to use a message server to propagate messages to the backoffice.

4.4.1.6. Online Game Demos

The demo architecture in Figure 4-37 is utilized to collect game event data and interact with external partners. The demo is an application that supports the streaming of game broadcasts. Game broadcasts are special events and occur regularly. When a game broadcast ends, the service goes into a stop state and requires no infrastructure. Kubernetes and the cloud are ideal for processing these events.

This is because you don't have to maintain the system all the time, which reduces costs, and you can elastically and flexibly scale resources to meet spikes in traffic. It can autoscale, and it provides the benefits of global services from different regions that the cloud provides. There are four core services, as shown in Figure 4-37:

CHAPTER 4   OBSERVABILITY PRACTICES BY THE INDUSTRY

- API server
- Ingester
- redis
- Kafka

Banking, telecom, and online games have slightly different process patterns and architectures, but the goal is the same: reliability. Kafka was chosen to process large volumes of traffic. Kafka and Redis are often used when building observability. Redis cache is utilized for reads, and Kafka is useful for processing large logs and reprocessing failures.

Compared to other message servers, Kafka is stable and performs well. The relational database is not suitable for processing large amounts of traffic, so it is implemented as a Redis cache. By using a Redis cache, you can improve performance and reduce costs. If you process using relational databases, you will have to pay a lot more in operating costs than Redis.

To explain the process in the demo, the game server fires various events during the game's playing. For example

- Fires a gun.
- Takes damage.
- Acquires an item.
- Restores health.

The log server collects a large number of events from the game server. The log server publishes large real-time events to Kafka. The API server performs two-way communication with multiple partners. It provides event details and aggregation to external partners. The event process of the online game demo is as follows:

1. The log server publishes the event to Kafka.
2. The ingester subscribes to the event.
3. The ingester stores the event after aggregation.
4. The ingester send message to API server.
5. The API server transfers events to external partners.
6. The external partner requests aggregation to API server.
7. The API server processes the aggregation and serves it to external partners.

The online game demo transfers events generated by the log server to Kafka. This architecture is a common pattern used in many industries, not just online games. For example, a trading firm generates orders with an architecture similar to Figure 4-37.

CHAPTER 4 OBSERVABILITY PRACTICES BY THE INDUSTRY

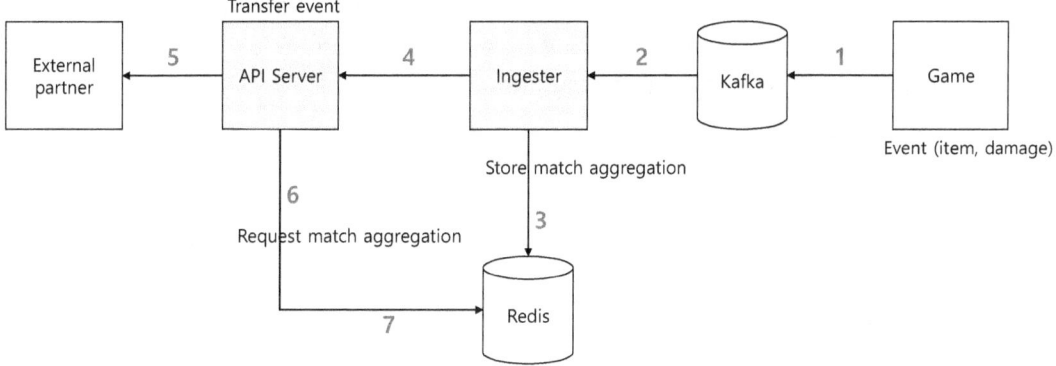

Figure 4-37. Online game demo

It creates two types of traces for every section:

- The first trace is processed in the order 1, 2, 3, 4, 5.
- The second trace is processed in the order 6, 7.

The features and architecture of the demo are described here:

- It implements a CQRS architecture with separate writes and reads. Observability supports the Golang, Kafka, and Redis used in the demo and E2E traces.

- Kafka's advantage is that it can be configured for parallel processing based on large clusters to process a large number of events. Kafka is not suitable for sequential processing. If you run only one topic and the consumer is single-threaded, sequential processing is possible but not efficient.

- It supports a variety of key-value format databases, not just Redis. Dynamo Database, a cloud-managed service, is also available.

- An API server acts as both a server and a client. When sending messages to external partners, it acts like a client and requests POST. You can use Kafka to connect with external partners, but a standards-compliant REST-based client is more effective.

- The API server receives various aggregation requests from external partners, processes the aggregation in Redis, and returns the results to the external system.

The online game demo supports E2E traces, as explained here:

- The microservices in the demo were developed with Golang, so you need to support Golang's instrumentation, as well as their Kafka and Redis instrumentation, to create spans. For manual instrumentation, provide Otelsarama for Kafka and redisotel for Redis.

CHAPTER 4   OBSERVABILITY PRACTICES BY THE INDUSTRY

- The nature of online games favors manual rather than automated instrumentation. This is because tuning is important, and the number of microservices is small, so it is important to optimize through manual instrumentation.

- The ingester creates a span when it reads an event from Kafka.

- The ingester stores the event data in Redis, which creates a span.

- It is responsible for delivering events to API clients. The ingester and API server create a span. The API client forwards the event to the external partner. The API server acts as a client, and requests transferred to external partners generate spans.

- The API server receives aggregation requests from external partners. It creates spans for the request and response and creates spans when making queries to Redis.

4.4.2. Game Observability

The observability architecture for online games is different from that of other industries. This section breaks it down.

4.4.2.1. Logs

In online games, logs are more special than other signals and are utilized in different ways. Online games collect different types of logs.

- The game is a backend process that receives and processes requests from client apps. A log server is separately located, and the log server collects logs from the game. By separating the game and the log server, more stable game operation is possible, and problems can be solved by analyzing the log when they occur.

- Observability in online games is mainly based on logs. In addition to the game backend, there are various servers in the game operation, such as servers for provisioning game processes, session servers to collect and manage clients, proxy servers to route UDP traffic, and databases to sell items. Some of these servers can be traced, but most of them only utilize logs.

- Your game manages three types of logs. There are infrastructure logs, event logs from the game, and logs from the client app. Infrastructure logs can be used to analyze the performance of the game server and the network latency, and decide whether to increase infrastructure. Client logs can be used to check network quality for failures such as app crashes, service failures, or disconnections during the game. It could also be a problem with the mobile device, so use it to improve service for quality and user experience. The event log collects events that occur during the game and manages logs of players buying and selling items. This can be utilized for marketing and planning recommendation machine learning.

- It's important to manage sessions. For example, in an online FPS game, after users join the game, they wait for a while. When the game server reaches a certain number of users, it assigns them to a game session, and the game runs for a certain amount of time. The trace only manages the process of assigning users to game sessions, while the log is used to collect and capture the status of the game play. Because this is an FPS game, you don't apply trace to collect events such as health being restored by items or bullets being fired between users. In-game event processing and failures that cause the mobile app to crash are processed using logs. The purpose use of traces and logs are separate.

4.4.2.2. Metrics

Basically, it is important to measure latency, utilization, and proper distribution and allocation of resources. The lifecycle that games operate in is different from that of other industries, requiring different observability and metrics.

- Important metrics for the demo are the latency and duration of the ingester and API server.

- The log server is the Kafka publisher, and the ingest is the Kafka subscriber. You also need to manage Kafka lag and Redis TPS latency. Theoretically, Redis processes 100,000 TPS per second.

- If the game server transfers a lot of events, Kafka will have performance problems. You monitor metrics for the partitions of Kafka's brokers and topics. Measure the number, offset, and latency of the messages being loaded into the topic. You should also measure the performance of individual partitions, not just the high-level broker, because the number of replicas can cause performance degradation on a particular partition. Improve performance on slow or problematic partition.

- Ingester is a Kafka subscriber. It monitors lag, rebalancing, and more.

- You may want to configure a cache for each pod where your game is served. If you're only playing for an hour, this isn't a problem because you won't lose much data in a game failure. However, if your game is running for several days, you don't want your game to go down and lose data. Even if your game goes down, you should be able to recover data from the cache. Repeatedly creating and deleting hundreds of pods a day will have a negative impact on your Redis cluster, including rebalancing. You should be able to quickly provision independent a Redis server, which supports only one pod without configuring a Redis cluster.

- It is important to minimize latency in your network. You should measure latency when deploying game servers in cloud regions.

CHAPTER 4   OBSERVABILITY PRACTICES BY THE INDUSTRY

- The database used by the game is configured for sharding. It improves performance and provides high availability against failure. You should monitor sharding and backup processes through metrics.

4.4.2.3. Traces

Use a demo similar to the online game demo to configure observability.

- Configure CQRS and connect microservices and process events through Kafka.
- Since online games are legacy-free, it is rare for instrumentation to fail or traces to break. In most cases, you can configure an E2E trace.

The demo configured with the architecture in Figure 4-38 outputs the same trace results from OpenTelemetry and commercial observability.

The trace clearly shows the processing order, so you can understand the internal processing process.

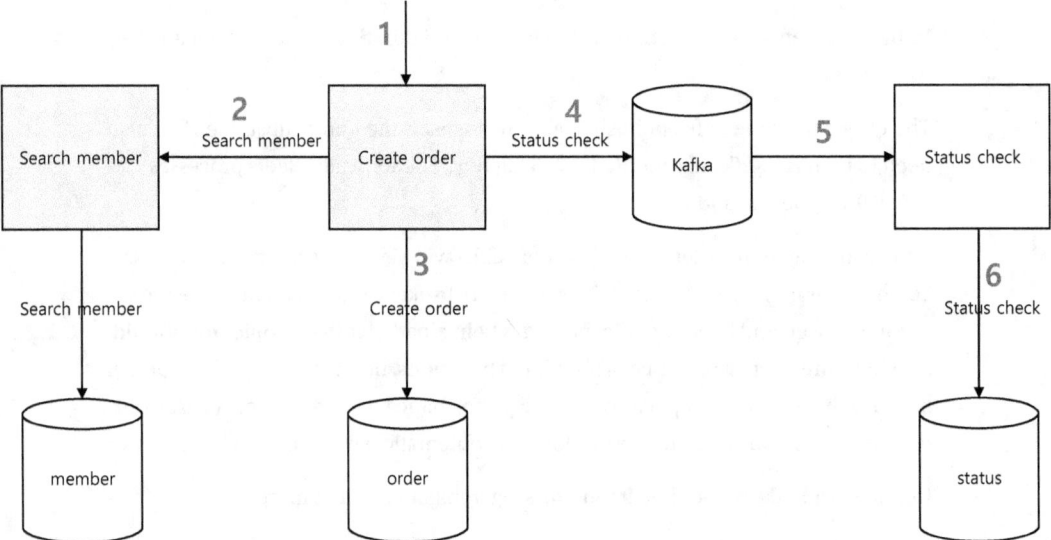

Figure 4-38. The process of the microservices demo

The details of the spans in Figure 4-39 are shown here:

- SQL is processed with two inserts and one select.
- Kafka's one publisher and one subscriber are processed.
- The web request is executed as 1 POST and 1 GET.

The demo runs on Kafka, a relational database, and Spring Boot. OpenTelemetry supports trace of the applications used.

CHAPTER 4 OBSERVABILITY PRACTICES BY THE INDUSTRY

No legacy systems and a simple architecture using a modern tech stack.

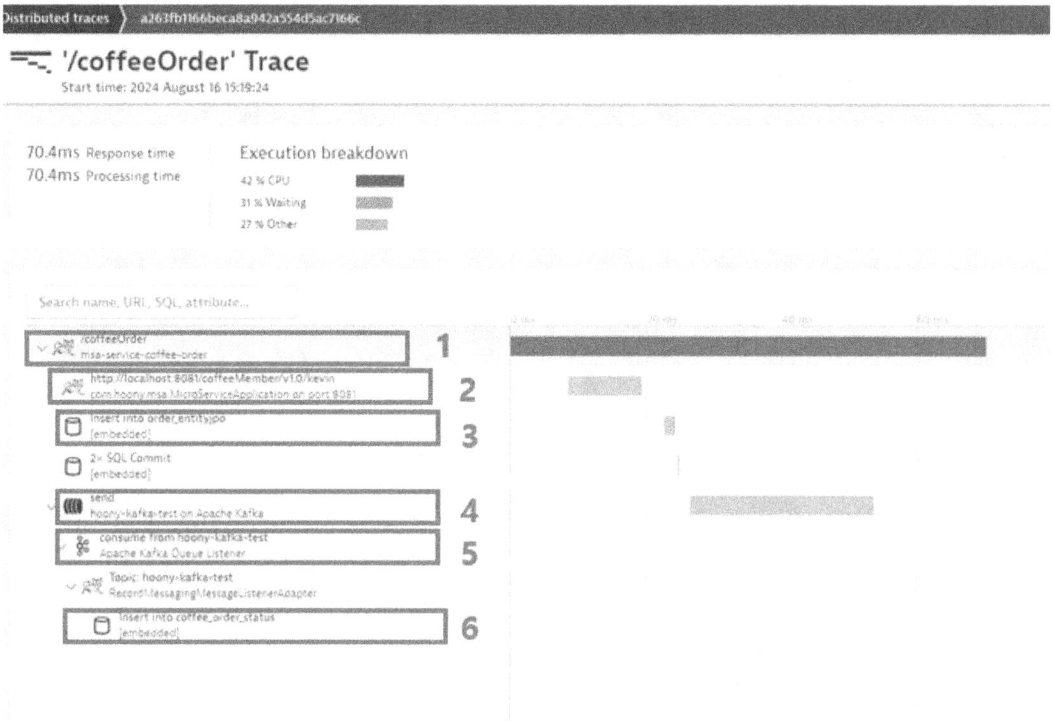

Figure 4-39. Propagating a successful span

4.4.2.4. Debugging

Remote debugging with development tools is useful. Analyzing the source internals of open source is not easy. Sometimes bugs cause operational difficulties, insufficient documentation makes it difficult to understand, and sometimes errors in open source are not easily resolved. Remote debugging is a great way to understand the internal structure of a system. Since you can specify breakpoints directly in the runtime environment (not production), it's easy to analyze the cause. Whether your application is running on Kubernetes or in a pod, you should have no problem processing remote debugging.

Applications running in Kubernetes pods also have no problem with remote debugging.

It's important to make good use of remote debugging during the development phase. Run as a normal user.

```
export DISPLAY=:0.0
```

CHAPTER 4   OBSERVABILITY PRACTICES BY THE INDUSTRY

Install DLV:

```
go get github.com/go-delve/delve/cmd/dlv
```

Compile the application as shown here:

```
GOFLAGS=-mod=vendor CGO_ENABLED=0 GOOS=linux go build -o ./build/api-server/api-server -gcflags="all=-N -l" ./cmd/api-server/

GOFLAGS=-mod=vendor CGO_ENABLED=0 GOOS=linux go build -o ./build/debugtool/debugtool -gcflags="all=-N -l" ./cmd/debugtool/

GOFLAGS=-mod=vendor CGO_ENABLED=0 GOOS=linux go build -o ./build/event-sim/event-sim -gcflags="all=-N -l" ./cmd/event-sim/

GOFLAGS=-mod=vendor CGO_ENABLED=0 GOOS=linux go build -o ./build/streaming-stats-ingest/streaming-stats-ingest -gcflags="all=-N -l" ./cmd/streaming-stats-ingest/
```

Start the binary with DLV:

```
# dlv --listen=:2345 --headless=true --api-version=2 --accept-multiclient exec ./build/streaming-stats-ingest/streaming-stats-ingest
API server listening at: [::]:2345
2022-08-03T15:03:17+09:00 warning layer=rpc Listening for remote connections (connections are not authenticated nor encrypted)

3:03PM INF New Event Handler. Allowed Events: map[LogGameStatePeriodic:true LogHeal:true LogMatchEnd:true LogMatchStart:true LogPlayerKillV2:true LogPlayerMakeGroggy:true LogPlayerPosition:true LogPlayerRevive:true LogPlayerTakeDamage:true] subsystem=EventHandler system=eSportsStatsIngest
```

The GoLand settings are shown here. Experienced SREs are used to analyzing code while debugging. Of all the signals, debugging is the strongest. Debugging can be used when analyzing kernel code, not just application code.

4.5. Trading Observability

Trading is organized into brokerages and exchanges, as shown in Figure 4-40.

- The brokerage creates the order and sends it to the exchange.
- The exchange receives the order and executes the trade.

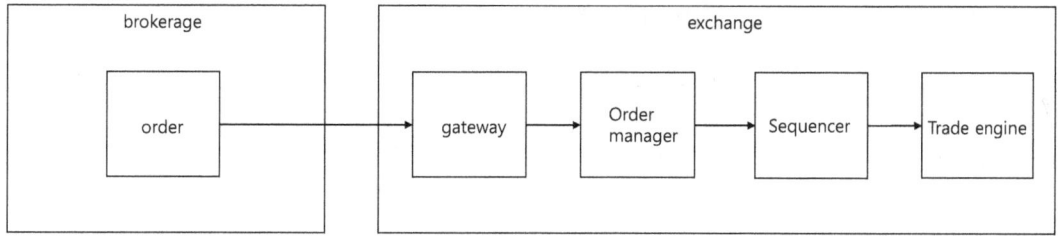

Figure 4-40. Trading flow

Brokerage and exchange applications are ultra-low latency applications and are implemented differently than traditional development. Session-based gaming, credit card authorization, brokerage orders, exchange trading, autonomous and driving are implemented with ultra-low latency. While the Spring Boot framework and Nginx are typical servers, ultra-low latency has a number of characteristics that make it different from typical servers.

4.5.1. Designing Ultra-Low Latency

Measuring latency at the nanosecond level is one of the main topics of this book. Developing ultra-low latency applications fits the topic and deserves to be explained in detail.

Ultra-low latency doesn't generate IO, such as disk access, and uses IPC most of the time.

In the bank demo, you configured E2E trace with legacy, and in the telecom demo, you configured distributed transactions using the Saga pattern. The trade demo goes into more detail about event sourcing. E2E trace, Saga patterns, and event sourcing are challenging but important topics.

4.5.1.1. Memory Allocation

Dynamic memory allocation is very common in complex, large-scale applications. It is important to understand that there are many steps involved each time a dynamic memory allocation operation is called, and this can cause performance degradation in the application.

Dynamic memory management allows applications to manage dynamically sized blocks of memory that are determined at runtime. For example, it allocates, moves, and frees release memory. However, it is not suitable for ultra-low latency applications that require very strict performance, considering the actual internal implementation and its impact on performance. During dynamic memory allocation, the allocated memory exists in the heap and is returned to the heap when the memory is released. However, in reality, dynamic memory management is not simple, and small mistakes in application implementation can cause subtle memory leak problems and performance problems in critical paths.

Dynamic Memory Allocation Phase

The OS maintains available heap memory blocks using two linked lists: the free list of currently unallocated heap memory blocks and the allocated list of allocated heap memory blocks. When a request for a new memory block comes in, the freed list is searched until a memory block of sufficient size is found to process the request. Then, some or all of the memory blocks are moved from the freed list to the allocated list, and the currently allocated memory address is returned to the caller.

During the lifecycle of the program, there may be countless operations to allocate and deallocate arbitrary amounts in arbitrary order. These operations may cause holes in the deallocation list when previously allocated memory is returned to the deallocation list between blocks of still allocated memory.

The concept of creating holes in the list of released heap blocks is called *memory fragmentation*. In rare cases, a lot of fragmentation can occur, and there may be so many holes that the memory is wasted, and each hole is too small to satisfy the request, so the holes cannot be used to satisfy the dynamic memory allocation request. There are several techniques and strategies for collecting and consolidating these chunks, which the allocator calls periodically to prevent heap fragmentation.

Memory leaks are another problem with dynamic memory allocation, where memory blocks are allocated but not used and are not released by the application, so they are not returned to the free pool. This is called a memory leak, and it can cause a surge in memory usage, performance degradation due to a large memory footprint, and even cause the OS to terminate the process leaking memory or drain all processes that need to allocate dynamic memory.

In summary, dynamic memory management comes with application complexity, the potential for bugs, overhead, and latency, and can cause performance problems due to memory fragmentation.

Pre-Allocation-Based Memory Management

Let's take a look at some alternatives to dynamic memory management. This section looks at a way to achieve this without suffering from the performance problems of dynamic memory management provided by the OS while maintaining the flexibility of allocating and deallocating an arbitrary number of elements at runtime.

Stack Memory Limit

This is to limit dynamic memory allocation on the heap. In other words, if there is something that can be allocated on the stack, it should be used first, such as setting an upper limit on the number of elements and having local variables that can process up to that number of elements on the stack. This eliminates the disadvantages of using dynamic memory allocation whenever an unknown number of elements is needed.

Memory Pool

When the type of an object is known, it is often much more efficient to create a memory pool, allocate large memory blocks, and manage memory directly from software. Because the type and size of the object are known, using a template makes the actual memory pool implementation common but very efficient.

Also, since the size of each element is fixed, there is no need to worry about hole/memory fragmentation. In addition, since it is possible to use LIFO stack-style deallocation/allocation instead of linked lists, cache performance is likely to be much improved.

4.5.1.2. Cache

This mainly explains the perspective of improving memory access and allocation latency.

First, let's take a look at the memory layer structure of modern architectures. Starting with the storage closest to the processor, which has the lowest access latency but also the lowest cost and storage capacity, I move through the various levels of cache in the processor registers.

When an application requests data for the first time, it may not be available in registers or caches, loaded from main memory to L0 to L4 cache. Data is loaded in one page or several kilobytes at a time, rather than a few bytes at a time, so subsequent references to the same data result in cache hits and significantly lower access latency.

The best case scenario is when the data is already in the L0/L1 cache and the access time drops below one nanosecond.

The important point here is that applications with a much higher cache hit ratios perform much better in terms of memory access than applications with a much lower cache hit ratios.

How can you monitor CPU L1 and L2 cache misses and GPU memory bandwidth? To analyze cache misses, the CPU profiles provided by the CPU manufacturer are ideal. Kernel-based system traces and eBPF are not enough to understand memory bandwidth and L1 cache misses, which are configured differently by each manufacturers. System trace and eBPF can only distinguish between main memory and CPU cache. SREs need to understand the limitations and constraints and suggest alternatives. System trace and eBPF have limitations, and behavior inside specific hardware requires the use of vendor profiles and system utilities. To control the L1 cache, you must use the C and C++ SDK provided by the manufacturer. Java SDKs are not typically available.

Pre-Fetch-Based Alternatives for Performance Improvement

I explained the impact of cache hits on memory access performance. Therefore, to make the most of cache performance, ultra-low latency application developers should focus on writing cache-friendly code, the most important aspect of which is the locality principle, which basically explains why caching is more efficient when related datasets are placed close to each other in memory. You should be aware of the size of each cache, the amount of data that goes into the cache line, and the cache access time for a specific architecture.

Temporal Locality

Temporal locality is the principle that if a specific memory location has been accessed, it is likely that the same location will be accessed again soon. Therefore, according to this principle, it is reasonable to cache recently accessed data because it is likely to be accessed again and is likely to still be cached at that point.

Spatial Locality

Spatial location refers to the principle of placing related data close to each other. Generally, the memory loaded into RAM is fetched in chunks larger than the application requests, and the hard disk drive and CPU cache are fetched in a similar manner. The reason for this is that the application code is often executed continuously instead of moving randomly through memory addresses, so the program is likely to need large chunks of data taken from the previous instance. Therefore, it is likely to create cache hits or memory hits instead of fetching data from the disk.

Cache-Friendly Data Structures and Algorithms

It is important to be aware of caches and cache performance when designing data structures and algorithms, and to adjust the design in a way that maximizes cache usage and performance, especially for ultra-low latency applications.

Utilizing the Implicit Structure of Data

Data that is fetched from the main memory and cached in the cache bank is fetched in blocks. Therefore, when a specific element of a matrix is accessed, elements close to that element in memory locations are also fetched and cached. By utilizing this order, calculations that require subsequent elements to be accessed can be performed with fewer memory accesses because the elements are already found in the cache line.

In the context of C++, virtual functions are generally avoided when writing ultra-low latency applications because the compiler cannot determine which method implementation will be called at compile time, making it impossible to inline the method and preventing the processor from fetching data in advance, which makes many compiler optimizations impossible, especially important ones. Therefore, if a particular method is not called frequently, there will be far more cache misses during lookup.

4.5.1.3. Context Switching

Context switching is a useful feature for most applications that have a good mix of user input, disk IO, and CPU-intensive processing. Without context switching, it would be impossible for modern operating systems to support multitasking. The most important aspects are multitasking, OS interrupt handling, and switching between user mode and kernel mode.

Multitasking

All modern operating systems have a task scheduler that switches one process for another to be processed by the CPU. There can be many reasons why a running process is switched, for example, when a process has finished, when an IO or synchronization operation has been suspended, or when waiting for input from a thread or disk. The reason that a thread or process can be switched is to prevent a single CPU-intensive thread or process from monopolizing all CPU resources and preventing other pending tasks from being completed.

Processing Interrupts

Interrupt-based data flow is common in most modern architectures. When a process needs to access a resource, such as reading or writing something from a disk I/O or a NIC, the process does not wait for the operation to complete, consuming CPU resources until the operation is complete. This is mainly because disk and network I/O operations are much slower than CPU operations, resulting in a huge waste of CPU resources.

In an interrupt-based architecture, these processes initiate IO operations and are blocked by those operations. The scheduler switches to those processes and resumes other processes that are waiting. The OS installs interrupt handlers in the hardware to handle request completion by interrupting the running process when the operation is complete and waking up the process that initiated the request.

Switching Between User and Kernel Mode

When part of the work in the kernel space is performed, the interrupt handler is called with the necessary signal, and a new process is allocated some CPU resources to start processing the data. The actual data processing is usually done in user space and depends on the application itself. Some instructions called by a process running in user space may force a switch to kernel mode. In most systems, this switch does not invoke a context switch, but in some systems, a context switch may occur when switching between user mode and kernel mode.

Let's look at some of the tasks involved in context switching, specifically saving the state of the currently executing thread or process and restoring the state of the next thread or process to be executed as determined by the task scheduler.

- To save the state of the current process, the state must be saved in what is often referred to as the PCB (process control block). This includes registers, stack pointers (SP) registers, program counters (PC), and memory maps.

- There may be several steps to flush the cache and flush the TLB, which converts virtual memory addresses to physical memory addresses.

- Restoring the state to execute the next thread is the opposite of saving the state, which is restoring the registers and data contained in the PCB for the thread to be restored.

Now that you have some background on context switching, let's look at why context switching is not suitable for ultra-low latency applications.

Basic CPU Task Scheduler Behavior

The default CPU task scheduling algorithm of a multicore server is often not the most suitable scheduling mechanism for ultra-low latency. Various task scheduling mechanisms consider various factors, such as maintaining the fairness of CPU resources allocated to all executable threads, improving energy consumption efficiency, and maximizing CPU throughput/efficiency by executing the shortest tasks first or the longest tasks first.

This often conflicts with the tasks that are important for ultra-low latency applications.

High-Cost Operations when Switching Contexts

This is performed to save the PCB of a thread that is being removed from the CPU when a context switch occurs and to restore the PCB of the thread that will be scheduled on that CPU. Some steps are very computationally intensive in the case of context switches. I explained task scheduling, which is one of the overheads of context switching. Flushing the TLB and cache during context switching is also a costly operation. Cache and TLB invalidation is another operation when performing context switching. The new code replaces the space used by the old code, and it takes longer to fetch the new code from memory and bring it into the cache. These are called cache misses. This cache invalidation step causes the next thread or process to incur a significant number of early cache misses, slowing down the resumption of the process that was allocated CPU resources after the context switch.

The next section discusses how to design and configure ultra-low latency applications with the goal of avoiding or minimizing context switches as much as possible.

Fixing Threads to CPU Cores

By explicitly implementing CPU isolation and fixing important or CPU-intensive threads to specific cores, you can ensure that hot threads experience little to no context switching.

Prevent Preemption by System Calls

The problem is that system calls that block disk or network IO block the calling thread and cause a context switch followed by a kernel interrupt. One solution to minimize these context switches is to reduce the use of blocking system calls as much as possible. Another solution describes kernel bypassing. By avoiding context switches by trading off system call overhead for CPU utilization, system calls can be avoided altogether as far as network IO operations are concerned.

4.5.1.4. Locks

When/why is locking necessary?

From a software development perspective, programming with locks is not simple. Even a simple task of deleting something from one data structure and inserting it into another data structure is difficult to reproduce in a multi-threaded application.

In other words, bugs related to or caused by locking depend on the timing of the operation and the code path. Overall, they can be very subtle and difficult to reproduce, such as deadlocks. Therefore, debugging applications that use synchronization mechanisms is a very difficult task.

It is important to strike an optimal balance between lock overhead (additional memory/CPU resources to use the lock) and lock contention (when a thread tries to acquire a lock that has already been acquired by another thread/process), which depends on the problem domain, design, solution implementation, and low-level architecture design.

Overhead and Performance Locking

Using lock requires additional resources, such as memory space for locking and CPU resources for initializing, acquiring, and releasing locks. Although the possibility of contention is rare, every place where locks are used to protect access to shared resources introduces additional overhead.

Lock Contention

Lock contention occurs when a process or thread tries to acquire a lock that is already held by another thread. The more granular the locks, the less contention but the higher the lock overhead.

Any threads waiting to acquire the lock must wait until the lock is released, causing queue delays. More importantly, if one of the threads in the list dies, hangs, blocks, or enters an infinite loop, the thread waiting for the lock will now wait forever, causing the entire system to fall into a deadlock.

Deadlocks

If the thread holding the lock is not completed, there is a possibility of a deadlock scenario in which all other threads waiting to acquire the lock will wait forever. However, a deadlock is described as tasks wait to acquire a lock held by another process. A simple example is when Process-1 holds Lock-A and attempts to acquire Lock-B, while Process-2 holds Lock-B and attempts to acquire Lock-A. Without external action, the two tasks will remain stuck forever.

Priority Inversion

Priority inversion is a scenario in which a thread or process with a lower priority holds a shared lock with a thread with a higher priority. When a thread with a lower priority holds the lock, the progress of the thread with a higher priority may be slowed or interrupted. This is because a low-priority process that holds a lock may not be selected by the scheduler to run because of its low priority, but it may block from acquiring the lock whenever a high-priority process is selected to run, preventing it from progressing.

Priority inheritance is one solution, where a process with a higher priority is waiting for a process with a lower priority due to the shared lock. The scheduler assigns the same priority or the highest priority to the process with the lower priority. The goal is to minimize the worst-case time and prevent a deadlock when a priority inversion scenario occurs.

Building applications that use the synchronization mechanism is complex, adding overhead for each lock instance and lock operation, and there are special scenarios where there is a risk of deadlock and system slowdown, requiring special solutions. Therefore, locking is often inefficient and costly, and given its characteristics of blocking, unblocking, and context switching, it is often not the preferred mechanism for ultra-low latency applications.

Prototype for a Lock-Free Data Structure

This prototype designs a lock-free data structure to avoid all the problems and inefficiencies that arise when using synchronization primitives in ultra-low latency applications. Since it is generally difficult to design generalized lock-free algorithms, the common approach is to design lock-free data structures (such as lock-free lists, stacks, queues, maps, and queues). These lock-free data structures can then be used in ultra-low latency applications where interaction or data sharing between different threads is required. Let's design and understand the details of a producer-consumer data structure without locks. A producer-consumer data structure is basically a queue in which producers can write data and consumers can read data; a common operation when passing data between ultra-low latency components.

4.5.1.5. Kernel Bypass

This section describes how to improve the performance of User Datagram Protocol (UDP) sockets that process data updates using kernel bypass technology and Transmission Control Protocol (TCP) sockets that send outbound requests. Basically, kernel bypassing significantly reduces latency by eliminating the expensive context switch and mode switch between kernel mode and user mode, as well as the redundant copying of data from the network interface card (NIC) to user space.

Network processing is driven by a thread that wants to read data coming in on a UDP or TCP socket block when the system calls/interrupts or reads calls of the non-kernel bypass design. The blocked thread is then switched to context and woken up by the interrupt handler when data is available on the socket. Switching the context of the thread and switching from kernel mode to user space adds latency every time a packet is read, making this inefficient.

In the case of applications, these packet reads occur millions of times throughout the day, so the delay can accumulate and significantly reduce performance. In addition, since the data is copied from the NIC buffer in kernel space to the application buffer in user space, the additional copy is another source of delay. A similar copy mechanism exists for outgoing UDP or TCP packets.

The alternative to eliminating the latency that occurs in socket programming, making it unsuitable for ultra-low latency, has two aspects: rotating on the CPU core of the user's space and zero-copy of received and sent data. To support these two functions, a special NIC and an application programming interface (API) that supports these functions are required.

User Space Rotation

An alternative to blocking and context-switching designs is to have the calling thread rotate in user space, continually polling for UDP or TCP sockets that are enabled for kernel bypass. Polling is a good compromise because it is strictly user space—i.e., there are no system calls or kernel time. In this design, NIC buffers mirrored in user space are constantly polled for new packets.

Zero Copy

After user space rotation, copying from the NIC kernel space buffer to the process user space buffer is not necessary. This is also part of the NIC, and as soon as a packet arrives, the NIC buffer is forwarded directly to the user space, eliminating the need for a separate copy step. In kernel bypass terminology, this absence of copying is referred to as zero copy.

Kernel Bypass Latency

The UDP read/write time without kernel bypass latency is between 1.5 and 10 microseconds, and with kernel bypass, the latency is between 0.5 and 2 microseconds. The TCP read/write time also shows a similar performance improvement, except that it is slightly slower.

4.5.1.6. Memory-Mapped Files

A memory-mapped file is a mirror of a file in virtual memory. The mapping between the physical file and the associated memory space allows an application composed of multiple threads to read the file by directly reading and modifying the memory to which the file is mapped, the OS processes the commit of changes to the memory to the file on the disk. Among other tasks, it updates the memory mapping when the file on the disk is changed. The application itself does not need to manage these tasks.

In C, memory-mapped files are created using the mmap() system call, which allows reading and writing files on the disk by reading and writing memory addresses.

There are two types of memory mapping files:

- Persistent memory mapping files
- Non-persistent memory mapping files

Persistent Memory-Mapped Files

Persistent memory-mapped files should be thought of as memory maps for which the file exists on disk or will exist. When an application finishes working with a memory map of a file, the changes are committed to the actual file on disk. This is a convenient and efficient method for applications that work with large files or need to store partial processing results in a file.

Non-Persistent Memory-Mapped Files

Non-persistent memory-mapped files are similar to temporary files, which exist only in memory and are not associated with actual files on disk. Therefore, they are not files but rather memory blocks that look like memory-mapped files. They are mainly used for storing temporary data and sharing data using shared memory between processes (i.e., inter-process communication—IPC).

CHAPTER 4   OBSERVABILITY PRACTICES BY THE INDUSTRY

Let's take a look at some of the advantages of memory-mapped files. They are related to performance and access latency, which are very important for applications.

- **Improved I/O performance**: This is a given, but the biggest advantage is improved I/O performance. Accessing a memory-mapped file is much faster than a system call to read and modify something on disk. In addition, the OS handles the task of reloading/writing files to disk, which can be done efficiently at the optimal time.

- **Random access and lazy loading are faster**: Accessing a specific location of a large file on a disk is slow because it requires finding the correct location to read/write. However, using a memory-mapped file is much faster because the application has direct read/write access to the data in the file in memory. Updates have also been made, so no additional temporary copies are needed. When you cross a page boundary, the entire next page is brought into memory, so locating it in memory is slow, but in-memory operations on the next page are very efficient.

- **They can support large files with a small amount of RAM**: This is achieved by loading small pages into memory when data is accessed. This prevents loading large files into memory, which can cause other performance problems such as cache misses and page faults.

- **Optimized OS management page file management**: The latest OSs are systems that process the virtual memory manager an important virtual memory management tasks, so the memory mapping and paging processes are very efficient. For this reason, the OS can manage the memory mapping process very efficiently and select the optimal page size.

- **Parallel access**: Using the memory-mapped area allows simultaneous read/write access to the file from multiple threads. Therefore, parallel access is possible in this case.

Disadvantages of memory-mapped files include these:

- A cache miss basically occurs when the code/data required by a running process cannot be used from the cache bank and must be fetched from the main memory. A page fault is a similar concept, but the difference is that the OS must fetch data from the disk when data is not available in the main memory. Page faults are the biggest problem with memory-mapped files. They usually occur when a memory-mapped file is not accessed sequentially. If a page fault occurs, the thread will wait until the I/O operation is complete, which slows down the process.

- If address space availability is a problem, too many or large memory-mapped files can cause the OS to run out of address space, which can exacerbate the page fault situation.

4.5.1.7. System Calls

Some privileged commands/system calls can only be performed in kernel space, and they are intentionally designed to prevent malicious user applications from executing the desired commands and damaging the entire system. From the application's point of view, the inefficiency is that when a system call must be made, the kernel mode must be switched, and a context switch must be performed, which slows down the system, especially when system calls occur frequently in important code paths.

The OS kernel still manages user-space applications and policies the resources that the applications can access. The virtual memory space is also divided into kernel space and user space. Physical memory does not distinguish between the two spaces, but the OS controls access. User space cannot access kernel space, but the opposite is also true: kernel space can access user space.

If a process running in user space needs to execute a system call such as disk I/O, network I/O, and so on, it does so through a system call. A system call is a part of the kernel interface that the kernel exposes to user space processes. When a system call is invoked in a user-space process, an interrupt for the system call is first transferred to the kernel. The kernel finds the correct interrupt handler for the system call and executes the handler to process the request. When the interrupt handler is complete, processing continues with the next set of tasks.

In general, code running in kernel space runs at the same speed as code running in user space. The difference in performance is due to the fact that code running in kernel space runs faster when there is a system call, while code running in user space must switch to kernel mode when a system call occurs, which can trigger a context switch that is slower and more expensive. Therefore, for user applications, it is recommended to minimize the use of system calls and eliminate them altogether where possible.

Another example is `clock_gettime()`, which internally calls system calls. Ultra-low latency applications can cause a lot of system calls because they update the time very frequently.

Overall, there are many opportunities to eliminate or minimize system calls from user space applications in the process of developing ultra-low latency applications. All you need to do is think about which methods are being called, whether they are calling system calls, and whether there is a better way to perform the same function without calling system calls, at least as far as the code in critical hot paths is concerned.

This is designed to minimize system calls by loading files into memory and allowing processes to delay/control the frequency at which they directly modify memory and commit changes to disk. Another example of completely eliminating system calls from network read/write operations is kernel bypass.

It is important to note that some of the improvements are achieved by eliminating copies of unnecessary data buffers.

4.5.1.8. Logging

The fundamental problem with logging and statistical calculations related to ultra-low latency applications is that they are very slow operations. Logging involves some level of disk I/O, which is the slowest operation.

CHAPTER 4   OBSERVABILITY PRACTICES BY THE INDUSTRY

Calculating statistics can be complex and expensive due to the nature of the calculation itself. Another reason for the slow calculation of statistics is that they often include a rolling window of past observations. These characteristics make both operations too inefficient to perform on hot/critical threads.

Let's discuss the architecture of an efficient logging and statistics infrastructure suitable for the processes that make up low-latency applications.

Signals used for ultra-low latency observability are considered as logs first. Various benchmark tools and profiles are used. First, it is best to move the logging and statistics calculation threads out of the critical threads. Then, you can control the activation frequency of the logging and statistics calculation threads according to the specific characteristics and expected usage of the ultra-low latency application, checking system usage, and determining how real-time the logging and statistics calculation will be.

This uses a lock-free data structure and non-persistent memory-mapped files to transfer data from the critical thread to the logging thread to prevent locking, and it is ideal to pin the logging and statistics calculation threads to self-contained CPU cores to prevent context switches on the hot path and to use persistent memory mapping files to reduce the time spent on disk I/O and control when writes occur on disk.

Ultra-low latency applications are highly dependent on very low average latency performance and low-latency variations of their components, so it is especially important to regularly measure the performance of each component. As various components of ultra-low latency applications change and improve, there is always the potential for unexpected latency, and without a robust and detailed performance management system, these harmful changes can go unnoticed.

Ultra-low latency applications are composed of components that operate in nanoseconds and microseconds. This means that the performance measurement system itself must have extremely low additional latency. This is very important to ensure that calling the performance measurement system does not change the performance itself.

For this reason, performance measurement tools and infrastructure for ultra-low latency applications have the following characteristics:

- The measured values are very accurate.
- The overhead itself is very low.
- They often call special CPU instructions to make the target architecture very efficient.
- They use non-trivial methods to measure performance, such as mirroring and capturing network traffic, inserting fields into outbound traffic to link it with inbound traffic, and using hardware timestamping on NIC and switch.

Certain code blocks/paths should not be targeted for optimization because they are executed very rarely and certain code blocks/paths should be targeted for optimization because they are executed very frequently. The key to finding these hot paths/critical codes is to measure performance regularly in an accurate and efficient manner.

4.5.1.9. Network

This involves bandwidth, throughput, and packet speed/size.

Bandwidth is the theoretical number of packets exchanged between two hosts. The speed at which communication reaches its intended target is called *throughput*. The main difference between the two is that throughput measures actual packet transfer, not theoretical packet transfer. The average data throughput shows how many packets arrive at the target. To provide high-performance services, packets must reach their target effectively. It is very important not to lose packets.

When evaluating and measuring network performance, *packet size* and *packet speed* are two important criteria to consider. Network performance depends on the settings of these parameters. Throughput values increase in proportion to packet size and decrease until they reach a saturation value. Increasing the packet size increases the amount of data transferred, thereby increasing throughput.

Increasing the packet rate improves network throughput because increasing the packet rate increases the amount of data, which increases throughput. When the maximum throughput of an interface is reached, buffering may occur when multiple receive interfaces try to transfer outbound packets to the same send interface.

The main function of a switch is to route packets. If there is too much incoming data, it may take longer to process the data than the time it takes for the data to arrive at the switch. To avoid losing data, it is essential to have a buffer. This buffer stores data that is waiting to be processed. The switch's main role is to receive packets from the input port. It then looks up the destination to get the output port and puts the packet in the output port queue. A large stream of data going to an output port can saturate the output port queue. If there is too much data in the queue, the latency increases significantly. If the buffer is full, data may be lost.

One of the important problems is head-of-line (HOL) blocking. This problem occurs when a packet that wants to leave the queue causes many packets to wait in the queue, which can increase latency or reorder packets. In practice, when many packets are blocked in a queue, the switch continues to process other packets going to other outputs, which prevents the packets from being received in order.

It's important to understanding packets in the transmit/receive (TX/RX) path. The steps that a packet goes through are as follows:

1. The NIC receives the packet and checks to see if the MAC address matches its own MAC address. If it does, the NIC processes the packet.

2. The NIC then checks that the FCS is correct.

3. Once these two checks are complete, the NIC uses direct memory access (DMA) operations to copy the packet to the buffer responsible for receiving data.

4. The RX buffer is a ring buffer, which is a data structure that uses a fixed-size buffer. DMUs speed up memory operations by allowing I/O devices to bypass the CPU and exchange data directly with the main memory.

5. Then, the NIC triggers an interrupt so that the CPU can process this packet. The interrupt handler recognizes the interrupt and moves data from the network to a buffer for subsequent processing in the lower half. The processor switches from user space to kernel space, looks up the interrupt descriptor table (IDT), and then calls the corresponding interrupt service routine (ISR). It then switches back to user space. These operations are performed at the NIC driver level.

6. Then, when the CPU has some spare capacity, it starts the soft-IRQ. It switches from user space to kernel space. The driver allocates a socket buffer, or SK buffer (also known as an SKB). An SKB is an in-memory data structure that contains the packet header. This includes a pointer to the packet header and the payload. For every packet in the buffer, the NIC driver dynamically allocates an SKB, updates the SKB with the packet header, removes the Ethernet header, and then passes the SKB to the network stack. A socket is an endpoint for sending and receiving data at the software level.

7. The network layer checks the IP address and checksum and removes the network header. When checking the IP address, the address is compared with the route lookup. If some packets are fragmented, this layer is responsible for recombining all the fragmented packets. Once this is done, the next layer is processed.

8. The transfer layer is specific to the TCP (or UDP) protocol. This layer queues the packet data in the socket read queue. It then signals that the message can be read from the read socket at the end.

4.5.1.10. Compiler

In an ultra-low latency system, the compiler can help optimize the loops, which are the parts of the code that consume the most time. This is an important part of reducing execution time while increasing memory usage and cache utilization.

Executable File Formats

Compilers and linkers convert high-level programs into executable file formats that are suitable for the target OS. The OS parses the executable file to figure out how to load and run the program. In Windows, it is an executable file (PE), but in Linux, it is an executable and linkable format (ELF) file. Each OS has a loader. The loader determines which chunks of the program on the disk to load into memory. The loader allocates the scope of virtual addresses that the executable file will use. It then starts execution at an entry point and calls the main function defined by the programmer. In terms of memory, it is important to remember that the OS uses virtual memory to protect processes from each other. All executable files run in isolation in their own virtual address space.

Static and Dynamic Links

Many executable programs have dependencies on external code libraries. There are two ways to integrate this code into the program to process these external dependencies. The first is to build a standalone binary by statically linking all the code. The second is to dynamically link the external code so that the OS inspects the executable file to determine which libraries are required to run the program and load them separately.

Linkers align application code and dependencies into a single binary object through static linking. This binary object contains all dependencies. For example, many programs use the glibc library on Linux. If these programs are statically linked, a lot of memory is wasted on repeatedly storing the same dependent libraries. Static linking has the important advantage that the compiler and linker can work together to optimize all function calls, including those to objects imported from external libraries.

Dynamic linking allows the linker to create a smaller binary file in which the location of dependent libraries is replaced with stubs. The dynamic linker loads the appropriate shared object from disk at application startup to load the corresponding library. The library is loaded into memory only if it is needed for dependencies. When multiple running processes use the same library, the memory of the library code can be shared by multiple processes. The library functions are indirectly referenced when called through the procedure linkage table (PLT). This indirect reference can increase overhead, especially if short functions in the library are called frequently. Typical ultra-low latency systems use static linking where possible to avoid this overhead.

4.5.1.11. Programming Languages

So far, I have explained how to develop ultra-low latency at the system resource level. There are various guidelines for developing ultra-low latency depending on the development language.

C++ is mainly used to develop ultra-low latency applications. Tuning is required for the JVM using Java. For ultra-low latency development by language, refer to the development documentation.

4.5.2. Ultra-Low Latency Reference

Latency is a critical issue for exchanges. The average latency should be low, and the overall latency distribution should be stable.

There are two ways to reduce latency:

- Reduce the number of tasks that run on the critical path.
- Reduce the duration of each job. For example, reduce network and disk usage and the execution time of each job.

Keep only the most necessary components on the critical path. Even logs are kept off the critical path to reduce latency.

4.5.2.1. Application Tunning

The trade path includes the following components:

- Gateway
- Order manager
- Sequencer
- Trade engine

This section describes the gateway, order manager, and sequencer, excluding the trade engine.

Gateways

Gateways are latency-sensitive. They need to be lightweight. They need to deliver orders to the right destination as quickly as possible.

Client gateway vary with different types of clients. The main considerations are latency, trading volume, and security. For example, institutions provide a significant portion of liquidity to exchanges and require very low latency. One extreme example is a co-location engine. This is trade engine software that a broker runs on a portion of servers rented from the exchange's data center.

Order Managers

The event loop is an interesting concept. Its main task is to continuously poll for actions to execute through a `while` loop. To meet strict latency requirements, only the tasks that are most critical to achieving the goal should be processed inside this loop. The goal is to reduce the execution time of each component to ensure that the overall execution time is predictable.

Sequencers

Before sending an order to the trade engine, it is labeled with an order ID and with the order ID that the trade engine has finished processing. In other words, there are two sequencers—an input sequencer and an output sequencer—each of which maintains its own order. The order ID that the sequencer creates should be a sequential number that makes it easy to spot missing items.

Here's why we stamp order ID on incoming orders and outgoing run commands.

- Faster recovery and replay
- Guaranteed correct first-time execution

The sequencer doesn't just generate an order ID; it also acts as a message queue. It creates two message queues: one to send messages to the execution engine and another to send messages back to the order manager. It can also be viewed as an event store for order and execution history.

This is similar to having two Kafka event streams connected to the trade engine—one for incoming orders and the other for outgoing execution records. In fact, if Kafka's latency was low and predictable, you could have used it in the Sequencer implementation.

When following an event-sourcing architecture, all messages use the same event store. The items held in the event store have a sequence field. The sequencer puts the value of this field in the event store.

Each event store has only one sequencer. Having multiple sequencers is bad because they compete for permission to write to the event store. There is no time to waste on lock contention, so the sequencer is the only write operation that orders events before sending them to the event store. The sequencer also acts as a message store, but it only does one simple thing, and it's very fast.

In exchange for trade engine, you can configure orders to be processed in chronological order, or you can run only one process to prevent locks from occurring. If a brokerage has 1,000 stocks, you can configure 1,000 processes per stock to process each stock sequentially.

KRX uses a message server. Sequential processing is important.

4.5.2.2. CPU Tunning

To maximize CPU efficiency, the event loop is implemented as a single thread and is locked to a specific CPU core. Pinning the application loop to the CPU has significant benefits.

There is no context switching. The CPU is fully allocated to process the order manager's event loop.

There's only one thread updating state, so there's no need to use locks and no lock contention.

The downside of locking the CPU is that it makes coding more complex. Engineers need to carefully analyze the time each task takes to ensure that it doesn't occupy the application loop thread for too long. Otherwise, subsequent tasks may not be executed on time.

4.5.2.3. Network Tunning

You assume that the components of the critical path run on separate servers connected over the network. The round-trip network latency is about 500 μs. If the critical path has many components communicating over the network, the total network latency increases to single-digit ms. Sequencer is also an event store that stores events on disk. Even if you design efficiently to take advantage of the performance benefits of sequential writes, disk access latency is still in the tens of ms.

When you consider both network and disk access latency, the total latency is in the tens of ms.

Exchanges have reduced the total latency of critical paths to tens of μs, primarily by reducing or eliminating network and disk access latency. By placing everything on the same server, they eliminate the network. Communication between components on the same server is via mmap, an event store.

4.5.2.4. Memory Tunning

mmap refers to a POSIX-compliant UNIX system that maps files into a process's memory.

mmap provides a high-performance memory-sharing mechanism between processes. The performance benefits are even greater when the files to be mapped to memory are located in /dev/shm. When you perform an mmap on a file located in /dev/shm, no disk IO occurs when accessing shared memory.

CHAPTER 4   OBSERVABILITY PRACTICES BY THE INDUSTRY

Take advantage of this to avoid disk access as much as possible on critical paths. The idea is to use mmap on the server to implement a message bus for components on the critical path to communicate with each other. This communication path never touches the network or disk, and messages take less than a μs to send. This, combined with event sourcing in an event store created using mmap, allows exchanges to build low-latency microservices on their servers.

The critical path does not store order records in a database. To increase performance, it executes trades in memory and utilizes hard disk or shared memory to store and share order records. In particular, orders are stored in sequencers for fast recovery, and data archiving is performed after the market close.

4.6. Summary

Operations are more complex than development, and observability is a highly specialized area even in operations. It's not just about collecting metrics and log signals and presenting the results in a dashboard. Continuous improvement and tuning can reduce costs, improve performance, increase customer satisfaction, and ultimately contribute to the success of the organization.

- The bank demo showed how E2E trace can be applied to a variety of legacy middleware. The bank demo of connecting and monitoring legacy applications such as SAP, Tuxedo, and Siebel and legacy middleware such as EAI, BPM, MDM, and MFT has not been covered in any other book. Based on my own experience and success, I prove that observability and trace can be successfully applied to complex legacy systems.

- The telecom demo is more complex than banking. I know, because I've had my share of failures in large telecom ordering projects. The most challenging issue in telecom ordering projects is distributed transaction processing. While banks' distributed transactions are limited to a few systems, such as various core banking systems, telecom distributed transactions involve dozens of legacy systems within an order, combined with 2PC and complex compensation. Not only are they complex to implement, they are also prone to problems and even more difficult to monitor. Since there are no books describing distributed transactions with compensation, the telecom example uses the Saga pattern to provide a concrete example of how distributed transactions are handled. I also presented various limitations and solutions.

- Developing games and ultra-low latency applications is new and exciting in many ways. The development and operation methods are completely different from microservice development. Game companies run their games by customizing most of the basic functions provided by Kubernetes, while their architecture, develop, and operate in the opposite way to microservices. While ultra-low latency may not be universal, the need for ultra-low latency will only increase as industries and our way of life become more automated, like with autonomous driving. As engineers and SREs, this is something we need to pay attention to.

CHAPTER 5

OpenTelemetry Demo

5.1. Introduction

While the benefits of observability are clear, it requires expertise in many areas, has a high learning curve, and is technically complex and challenging. Even with observability, it is difficult to get meaningful results as expected because there is a lot of noise. You need to understand your signals and use anomaly detection and AIOps to reduce noise and improve accuracy.

Traditional application monitoring is application-centric, lacking insight into the many problems and dependencies between cloud providers, networks, storage, databases, and applications. This chapter introduces a new observability technology called *live debugging*, which is a powerful profile based on E2E distributed traces and stack traces.

The data that needs to be managed grows exponentially. Systems become more complex and user expectations continue to rise. This means it becomes increasingly difficult for operators to understand what's happening. They need a solution to regain control and contain the complexity they are exposed to. The solution must meet the following requirements:

- It must be standards-based and open source to reduce costs. OpenTelemetry provides a standardized technology for telemetry.
- It must have lower complexity and require a smaller learning curve.
- It must be user-friendly and provide easy-to-use management tools.
- It must use code to automate and increase reusability. It should use open source to automate the deployment and configuration of observability.
- It should reduce operational and development costs and minimize financial losses due to failure.

Observability solutions allow developers and operators to seamlessly move between metrics, logs, traces, and profiles to comprehensively measure the various operations an organization is performing, reducing the mean time to recovery and increasing Apdex (a frontend metric that measures user satisfaction).

In recent years, a variety of solutions have been introduced for SRE. Data lakes and AIOps have been introduced to automate observability, and deployments and pipelines have been equipped with anomaly detection and self-healing capabilities.

CHAPTER 5   OPENTELEMETRY DEMO

Throughput and latency are the most basic metrics.

- Metrics output the quantiles, while profiles output the mean.
- The profile roughly distinguishes between total duration, CPU duration, IO time, latency, and self time. Latency can be interpreted in a variety of ways, and it is not straightforward to distinguish exactly how much time is spent waiting at the nanosecond level due to context switches and interrupts. If you look closely, traces, metrics, and profiles have different ways of calculating time and different meanings. It is important to understand these differences and their consequences.
- Total duration has a similar meaning as latency, but it is technically different. It is important to distinguish between total duration and CPU duration. Once you understand total duration and CPU duration, you can estimate IO time and other latencies.

5.2. Overview

The previous chapter explained how to use SQL to understand and find problems. SQL is a powerful data analysis tool. The demo in this chapter is the official OpenTelemetry demo. It runs on Kubernetes and is presented as a reference application. I introduce useful features that are not mentioned in the official documentation and enhance various observability features. This demo:

- Describes the agent and instrumentation libraries for OpenTelemetry automated instrumentation. Microservices, Kafka, Redis, and Envoy developed in various languages are used as demonstrations.
- The OpenTelemetry Collector is an observability pipeline. This demo describes the various correlation features provided by the OpenTelemetry Collector, including exemplar, spanmetric, and service graphs.
- Applies the profile to microservices written in Java, Golang, and Python.
- Generates errors using feature flags. Analyzes metrics for differences before and after an error. Describes how to design and configure SLOs.
- Configures Promscale and automates root cause analysis using SQL. The goal of this chapter is to perform root cause analysis using dashboards and SQL.
- Grafana organizes observability with OpenSearch.
- Provides technical direction for OpenTelemetry, including logs, span attributes, anomaly detection, and legacy integration.

CHAPTER 5 OPENTELEMETRY DEMO

As shown in Figure 5-1, there is a complex interconnection between various microservices. There are load generators, feature flags, automated instrumentation, and more. OpenTelemetry is constantly adding new features, which are reflected in the demo.

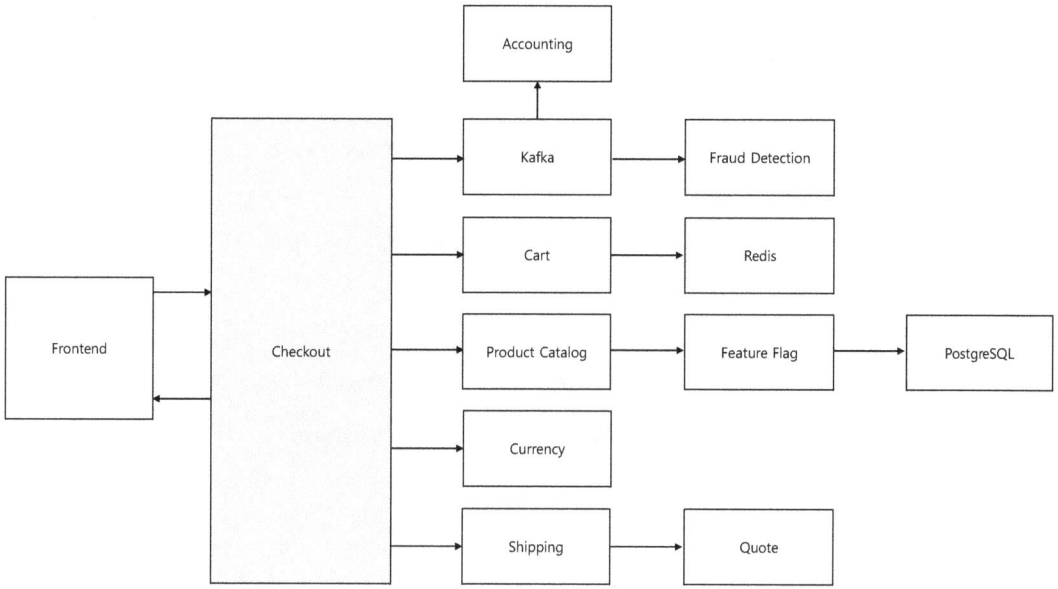

Figure 5-1. *Microservices flow*

The OpenTelemetry demo is similar to the architecture of the banking demo described in Chapter 4, but this one is simpler because it is legacy-free. The demo allows you to try new features and learn as you go, customizing as appropriate to meet your needs.

The official demo of OpenTelemetry has the following features:

- Describes the architecture and configuration of OpenTelemetry. Describes how observability can be applied in various ways in a large microservices environment. The number of microservices in OpenTelemetry is 15. Microservices are written in 12 different development languages and generate traces and metrics.

- The generated signals are transferred to the OpenTelemetry Collector. The observability backends are Prometheus and Jaeger. The OpenTelemetry Collector transfers signals to Prometheus and Jaeger.

- You can use Locust for automated load testing to create loads.

- You can generate traces for Kafka and Envoy. This is a recent addition to OpenTelemetry. Kafka uses the OpenTelemetry JavaAgent to support automated instrumentation. The checkout service is the publisher. Accounting and fraud detection are subscribers. The cart service uses Redis.

- Feature flags can be used to validate SLO, load testing is supported, and more.

395

CHAPTER 5 OPENTELEMETRY DEMO

- Microservices alone, with the exception of OpenTelemetry, are worth the price. You can configure commercial observability agents to connect with various observability backends.

- Includes SDKs, collectors, and other complex configurations.

- RUM and trace have been propagated. Many microservices are being instrumented automatically using agents or manually using API.

The OpenTelemetry demo application was created to demonstrate the OpenTelemetry API SDK. The goal of this application is to provide a demonstration of OpenTelemetry components as well as serve as a framework for end users, vendors, and others.

- Provide developers with sample applications that can be used to learn OpenTelemetry instrumentation.

- Provide observability vendors with a demo platform that can be customized.

- Demonstrate the functionality and use of the OpenTelemetry API and SDK.

Here is a general description of the components in the demo application:

- Applications
- Pipelines
- Deployment
- Feature flags
- Load testing

Each component is described in detail next.

Applications:

- Most of the demo applications are microservices-based applications, such as e-commerce sites. The application consists of multiple services that communicate with each other over gRPC and HTTP and run on Kubernetes.

- Each service is instrumented with OpenTelemetry to collect traces and metrics.

- Each service implements the same gRPC endpoint, but can communicate with services written in different languages.

- Each service communicates with the feature flag service to enable/disable errors. This illustrates how telemetry can help solve problems in distributed applications.

Observability pipelines:

- To avoid dependency on a specific observability backend, it provides a lot of functionality in the collector. For example, it provides exemplars. Previously, exemplars were only available in Grafana Tempo, but with collectors, you can implement exemplars independently of a specific observability backend.

CHAPTER 5 OPENTELEMETRY DEMO

- By extending the functionality of the default pipeline with observability, you can add an AIOps pipeline with Promscale.

- Simple integration with Grafana LGTM as well as Jaeger and OpenSearch. Configure pipelines for metrics and traces. The pipeline consists of three parts: receiver, processor, and exporter.

- The receiver receives data from the Microservices as gRPC.

- Processors make up the spanmetric and batch processors. Processors provide various features to improve the performance of pipelines and process large amounts of data. In production, it is essential to apply critical parameters.

- The exporter transfers to Prometheus and Jaeger.

Feature flags:

- They consist of a number of services that provide a feature-flag configuration utility for your application. They consist of a browser-based client interface and backend services. The role of the client is to allow operators to visualize the available feature flags and switch their states. The server provides a feature flag catalog where key application services can register their current state and targeting rules.

- You can set four feature flags: recommendation cache, product catalog failure, cart service failure, and ad service failure.

- The `featureflags` component is implemented as an Erlang+Elixir/Phoenix service. The feature flag catalog is stored in a database. Kubernetes accesses feature flags by configuring port forwarding.

Feature flags (also known as *feature toggles*) allow you to enable certain features at runtime without deploying new code. This technique allows you to change features at runtime without changing the source and allows for more sophisticated experiments.

Deployment:

- All services run on Kubernetes. OpenTelemetry collectors are deployed via the OpenTelemetry operator and run in sidecar and gateway mode. Signals from each pod are routed from the agent to the gateway, which transfers them to the open source trace and metric visualization tools by default.

- Non-Kubernetes deployments are deployed via Dockerfiles, and you monitor not only the application's trace/metrics, but also the Docker containers via the Docker stat receiver.

Locust load testing: Locust uses its own greenlets, which allow you to write tests like Python code instead of using callbacks or other mechanisms.

Locust makes it easy to run distributed load tests across multiple machines. It is event-driven, so a single process can process thousands of concurrent users. There may be other tools that can make more requests per second on certain hardware, but Locust's low overhead makes it a good tool for testing concurrent workloads.

5.3. Observability Demo

As I refine the OpenTelemetry demo, I'll cover a variety of application observability topics that I haven't covered before.

The telemetry that OpenTelemetry can provide is very useful for diagnosing problems in distributed systems. Here, you look at a scenario that shows how to move from higher level metrics and traces to determine the source of a memory leak.

To run this scenario, you need to deploy the demo application and enable the Recommended Cache feature flag. After enabling the feature flag, run the application for about ten minutes so that the data can be populated.

The first step in diagnosing a problem is to determine if you have one. Check the metrics dashboard provided by a tool like Grafana.

The demo provides two dashboards. One is to monitor the OpenTelemetry Collector, and the other includes several queries and charts to analyze the latency and request rate of each service.

The dashboard contains a number of charts:

- Recommended services (CPU and memory)
- Service latency (powered by spanmetric)
- Error rate

The recommended services are generated from OpenTelemetry metrics exported to Prometheus, while the service latency and error rate charts are generated by the spanmetric processor in the OpenTelemetry Collector.

The recommendation service seems to have some abnormal behavior (spikes in CPU utilization and long tail latency in the 95th and 99th percentile histograms). You can see a spike in memory utilization for this service.

The problem of memory leaks is a simple scenario of increasing memory, but it also causes CPU spikes. If the memory leak continues, the memory will eventually reach its limit. This will cause a full garbage collection to be processed continuously, and you will see CPU spikes.

It is useful to use profiles to further analyze CPU and memory problems. If the root cause is related to garbage collection, comparing the normal and abnormal cases in the profile can help you find the leaky method.

Later, I'll demonstrate applying profiles to a recommendation service. The recommendation service has metrics, traces, and profiles all applied.

Jaeger allows you to search the trace and display the latency. You may have noticed an increase in latency in your frontend requests. Jaeger allows you to search and filter to include only traces that contain requests for referral services.

You can sort by latency to quickly find a specific trace that took a long time. Click a trace in the right pane to see a waterfall view. You can see that the recommendation service is taking a long time to complete its work, and by looking at the details, you can understand what's going on.

In the waterfall view, you can see that the app.cache_hit attribute is set to false and the app.products.count value is very high.

Back in the Jaeger search UI, filter to the dropdown called Featured in the Services and search for app.cache_hit=true in the Tags box. Requests tend to be faster when they are used in a cache. Now search for app.cache_hit=false to compare the latency.

Since this is an artificial scenario, you know where to look for the underlying bug in the code. I propose three methods of root cause analysis.

- Use dashboards similar to how many commercial observability offerings do. Service graphs and polystats give you an understanding of your overall IT operations, and you can analyze histograms and heatmaps and correlate signals to quickly find the cause.

- The data stored in Promscale is structured and uses SQL to analyze it. Rather than looking at a bunch of charts, the advantage of using SQL is that you can uncover hidden insights not found onscreen and automate your know-how. Describe a number of SQL that can be utilized for metrics, traces, and log signals.

- There are ways to automate using machine learning. The data collected in Promscale is of good quality and lends itself well to automation with machine learning. The more data you collect and the larger your scale, the more you can improve accuracy by automating with machine learning.

For small-scale observability, root cause analysis using screens is suitable, and if you plan complex and large-scale observability in the future, I recommend an architecture that can analyze data using SQL.

Next, I demonstrate screen-centric and SQL-centric root cause analyses.

5.3.1. Profile Support

The profile is implemented using Pyroscope. Let's apply the profile to two services:

- Python supports the recommend service
- Golang is a product catalog service

Pyroscope is configured as an openTelemetry extension to implement trace and correlation, obtaining profile IDs through automated instrumentation and adding profile IDs to the span attribute in the trace.

CHAPTER 5　OPENTELEMETRY DEMO

You can collect profiles in two ways, as shown in Figure 5-2. The product catalog and recommendations are implemented.

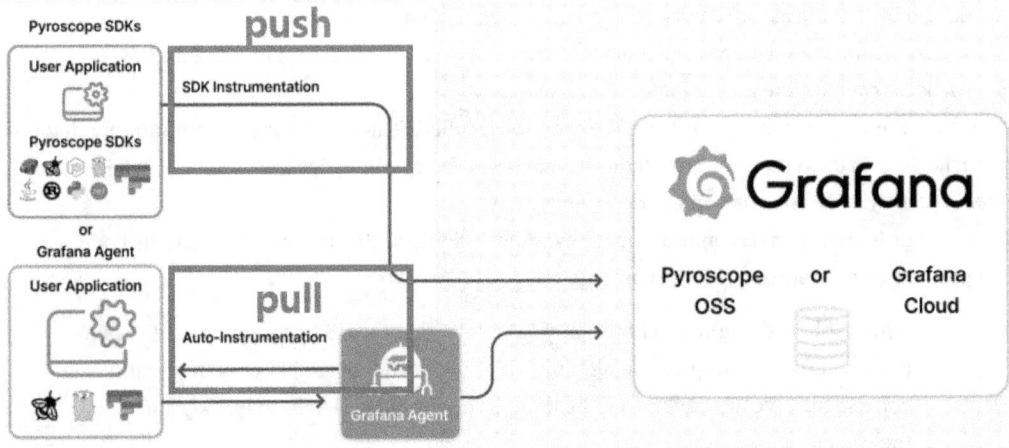

Figure 5-2. Two methods of profile instrumentation

The pull method is simple to implement. The push method can be implemented by adding the following source. No special logic is implemented; just add Pyroscope's endpoint to the existing source to collect and transfer profiles.

```
pyroscope.Start(pyroscope.Config{
    ApplicationName:   "example.golang.app",
    ServerAddress:     "<URL>",

    BasicAuthUser:     "<User>",
    BasicAuthPassword: "<Password>",

    ProfileTypes: []pyroscope.ProfileType{
      pyroscope.ProfileCPU,
      pyroscope.ProfileInuseObjects,
      pyroscope.ProfileAllocObjects,
      pyroscope.ProfileInuseSpace,
      pyroscope.ProfileAllocSpace,
    },
})
```

CHAPTER 5   OPENTELEMETRY DEMO

For example, the `pull` method used by Go periodically collects profiles from the `/debug/pprof/*` endpoint. The Grafana agent uses the `pull` method to collect profiles from Pyroscope's endpoints. The `pull` method corresponds to automated instrumentation, while the `push` method corresponds to manual instrumentation using the API.

You can define various correlation processes in this demo:

- You can go from trace to profile.

- You can navigate from log to profile.

You can implement correlation by choosing a method that suits your architecture. Since logs provide debugging information, it is also possible to move from logs to profiles.

From a root cause analysis process perspective, it makes more sense to navigate from traces to profiles.

Grafana dashboards provide flame graph charts as a plugin. In the Grafana dashboard, you can integrate it into the Grafana dashboard or output a flame graph independently.

Grafana supports a variety of languages, including Java, Python, and Golang, and can collect and analyze profiles without modifying the source.

5.3.1.1. Recommended Services

This demo runs a Python application and profiles the CPU. By using feature flags and profiling, you can easily understand the changes in resources.

This service is responsible for getting a list of recommended products to the user, based on the existing product ID that the user is browsing. It is developed in Python. After modifying the recommendation service, you can build and deploy it.

```
docker compose up -build
```

Add `pyroscope-io==0.7.1`:

```
import pyroscope

pyroscope.configure(
        application_name = "simple.python.app",
        server_address = "http://pyroscope:4040",
)
from metrics import (
    init_metrics
)

cached_ids = []
first_run = True

class RecommendationService(demo_pb2_grpc.RecommendationServiceServicer):
    def ListRecommendations(self, request, context):
```

401

```
        prod_list = get_product_list(request.product_ids)
        span = trace.get_current_span()
        span.set_attribute("app.products_recommended.count", len(prod_list))
        logger.info(f"Receive ListRecommendations for product ids:{prod_list}")
```

Add pyroscope-io==0.7.1 to the docker-compose file:

```
pyroscope:
    image: 'pyroscope/pyroscope:latest'
    ports:
      - '4040:4040'
    command:
      - 'server'
    depends_on:
      - recommendationservice
    logging: *logging
```

Profiles like Pyroscope still have limitations. For example, Python does not provide a memory profile, only a CPU profile. There are still language-specific limitations to profile functionality.

5.3.1.2. Catalog Services

This service returns information about products. You can use this service to get all products, search for a specific product, or return details about a single product.

You need to install the Pyroscope library:

```
go get github.com/pyroscope-io/pyroscope/pkg/agent/profiler
```

You also need to add a profile to your source, as shown here:

```
func main() {

        pyroscope.Start(pyroscope.Config{
          ApplicationName: "ProductCatalogService",
          ServerAddress:   "http://pyroscope:4040",
        })
```

Modify ProductCatalogService as shown here:

```
import (
        "context"
        "fmt"
        "io/ioutil"
        "net"
```

```
"os"
"strings"
"sync"
"time"

pyroscope "github.com/pyroscope-io/pyroscope/pkg/agent/profiler"

pb "github.com/opentelemetry/ opentelemetry -demo/src/productcatalogservice/
genproto/oteldemo"
"github.com/sirupsen/logrus"
"go. opentelemetry.io/contrib/instrumentation/google.golang.org/grpc/otelgrpc"
"go. opentelemetry.io/contrib/instrumentation/runtime"
sdkmetric "go. opentelemetry.io/otel/sdk/metric"
healthpb "google.golang.org/grpc/health/grpc_health_v1"
```

Configuring a profile for the OpenTelemetry demo is not complicated. By automating the build and deployment, it's easy to use profile.

Prior to the Pyroscope acquisition, Pyroscope did not support Tempo and was tied to Jaeger. Since Pyroscope was acquired by Grafana, many improvements have been made:

- It supports correlation with Tempo traces.
- It is integrated into the Grafana dashboard.

5.3.1.3. Pyroscope and Tempo

Pyroscope profiles are slightly different from commercial observability profiles. In Figure 5-3, Pyroscope provides a link URL to the Pyroscope profile ID in the span, while commercial observability provides detailed profile information for the methods in the span.

CHAPTER 5 OPENTELEMETRY DEMO

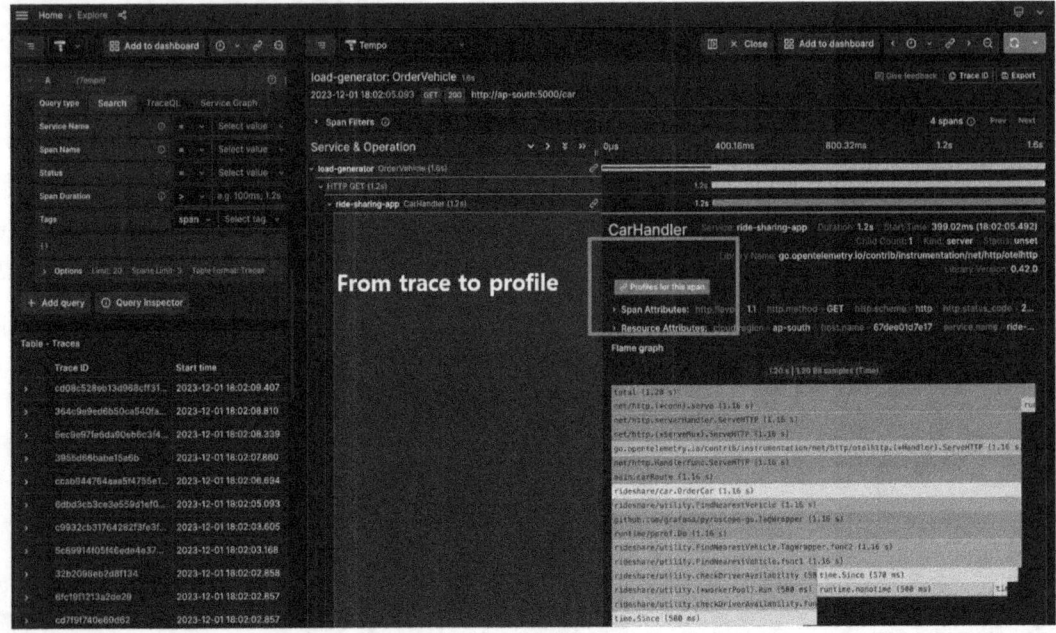

Figure 5-3. *The correlation between pyroscope and tempo*

Pyroscope supports integration with Tempo. Since Pyroscope was added to the Grafana labs, it has been integrated into Tempo and the Grafana dashboard. In the Grafana dashboard, it is possible to define Pyroscope as a data source (see Figure 5-3). This enables correlating between traces and profiles within Grafana dashboards.

In the Grafana dashboard, the left side displays a list of traces, and the right side shows the details of a specific trace. If you click a span, you can see that a flame graph is displayed as an attribute of the span.

It is possible to go to Pyroscope and analyze the detailed profile, but by printing and comparing the profile in span, it is also possible to perform a quick root cause analysis. It can compensate for the shortcomings of trace such as lack of debugging and difficulty in analyzing the system. See Figure 5-4.

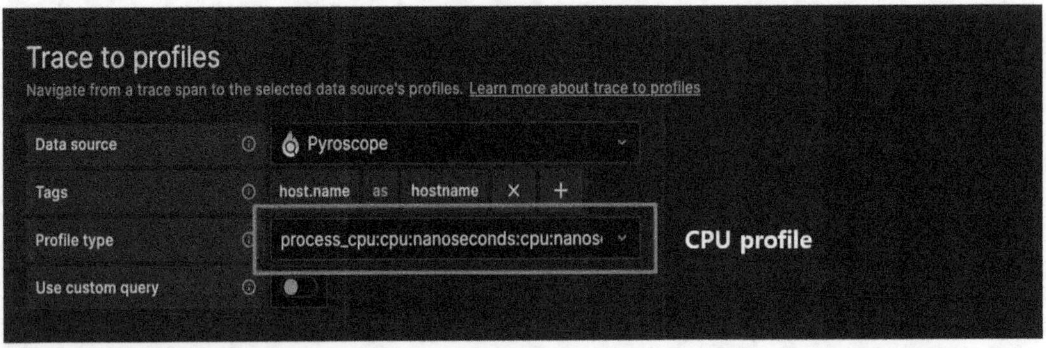

Figure 5-4. *The correlation configuration*

CHAPTER 5 OPENTELEMETRY DEMO

In Grafana, you can configure the data source for Pyroscope and the settings for the trace data source provide settings to configure profile and correlation.

5.3.2. OpenTelemetry Agent

In the OpenTelemetry demo, the agent was used in the following cases:

- The Pyroscope used in the profile demo is implemented as an OpenTelemetry extension. Pyroscope uses bytecode instrumentation and implements trace-to-profile correlation by extending the span attribute in the trace to add the profile ID.

- OpenTelemetry JavaAgent officially supports Kafka and Kafka Streams. OpenTelemetry officially supports envoys. Envoys receive requests from load generators and route them to the frontend.

The OpenTelemetry agent will be an alternative to the existing Java Micrometer and Prometheus exporters. The agent can be used to automatically generate traces, metrics, profiles, and logs. Automated instrumentation makes it easy and fast to implement observability without development.

You can configure the JavaAgent as shown here:

```
-javaagent:/root/Downloads/opentelemetry-javaagent.jar
-Dotel.traces.exporter=jaeger
-Dotel.resource.attributes=service.name=router
```

5.3.3. SLOs

SLOs are not simple. Rather than defining SLOs based on availability and latency, I suggest the following approach:

1. Understand the product. The product includes the company's strategy and direction.

2. Understand the process. Identify critical paths and prioritize processes.

3. Understand the data. Ensure that the data is collected and loaded correctly. Ensure that the joins and lookups are possible and measure data quality.

4. Design the IT architecture, dashboards, and SLO.

The dashboard and SLOs should be based on an understanding of the domain and detailed processes, and the root cause analysis data model contains most of the key data. The details are technical, but you should plan the overall dashboard flow and story to reflect your business.

CHAPTER 5 OPENTELEMETRY DEMO

There are two types of dashboards:

- Root cause analysis dashboards and core SLOs focus on E2E observability and are developed by SRE. They are great for identifying and calculating MTTD and MTTR. Developing a lot of dashboards is not a good direction. You should strive to reduce the number of dashboards and enhance your root cause analysis dashboards.

- Business-specific dashboards focus on specific areas that developers are responsible for. The root cause analysis dashboard and the developer's business dashboard should be linked. URL links should be provided so that you can navigate between the dashboards.

You should first use the root cause dashboard to understand the overall context, and then move to the business-specific dashboards to understand the problem from a different perspective.

The SRE should provide clear guidelines for root cause analysis. Just like the root cause analysis data model and dashboards already described, it's important to provide a baseline. Only when the baseline is clear can developers join the data model and develop the detailed dashboards needed for their specific business. If the baseline is unclear, developers will be confused, standardization will be difficult, and confusion will increase.

- The root cause analysis dashboard does not output SLO. It gives you the ability to select errors and deployments, and search by filters. It helps users to understand if it is divided into frontend, microservices, orchestration, backend, database, and backoffice. Multiple layers should represent the business flow within a single dashboard screen.

- Business-specific dashboards should output SLO. Assuming that multiple layers make up a process, each layer will have a different SLO. For example, the frontend outputs user sessions, actions, and user satisfaction as real user monitoring, while the microservice outputs the availability, error rate, and latency of the API server and microservice. Message servers care more about the number of messages queued and any subscriber lag. The backend includes the error rate of the database, slow queries, data consistency, and so on. Batches in the backoffice need to manage the processing status and error rates of batches managed by different batch schedulers, which means that different tiers need different SLOs and should be clearly organized in a dashboard so that you can pinpoint the problem areas.

Assuming that different tiers make up a process, each tier has different SLO needs. Dashboards need to reflect that different processes require different SLO. Viewing a browse order history and creating an order require different handling from a system perspective. It is difficult to organize multiple business process into one and the same template and SLO pattern, requiring multiple patterns and dashboard templates.

Backend SLOs include error rate, throughput, latency, and availability. Because availability can mean many different things, you'll see many different availability calculations. A simple availability can consist of a probe to a complex MTTR. Depending on the level of availability, it can consist of several steps.

- Kubernetes probes are the simplest example of availability. They measure simple health checks, liveness, and readiness. You can use CloudProbe, which is open source, to measure the availability of many different infrastructures and protocols, not just Kubernetes.

- In conjunction with proxy and API servers, you can measure application status codes and SLO.

Measure the error rate from the user's perspective:

- The Google SRE book describes various Prometheus availability formulas. I recommend that you refer to them to improve your availability.

- You can use the percentage or rate of successful requests to get the error budget.

- The most complex and best availability is tied to MTTR and MTTD.

It makes sense to measure availability in the API server because all requests are forwarded to the API server.

Failures occur in the CDN, the API server, and the load balancer, so you can get availability from RUM. It's not easy to measure the KPI of Apdex. In frontend RUM, you measure Apdex.

Apdex is a frontend metric that measures user satisfaction with the response time of web applications and services. It is a simplified service level agreement that allows you to see how satisfied users are with your application through metrics such as the Apdex score and dissatisfaction rate instead of traditional metrics such as average response time.

Sometimes the number of errors from the logs, metrics, and traces do not match. For example, if an error is printed in the log but not in the trace, the SRE might miss it. If the error message is different between signals, it can be difficult to understand the error. If the number of errors in the log is 5, but the number of errors in the trace is 1, it will take a long time for the SRE to determine the error.

It is necessary to separate user perspective errors from root cause analysis errors.

- The API server's status code is tied to the backend. This is best viewed as an SLO for customer service. For example, it could mean availability of customer service. If your API server does not support traces, but supports metrics and logs, use them to create an SLO.

- The error code in trace can help you understand the exact reason why an error occurred. This can be used for root cause analysis and to calculate SLOs for each service.

There is no problem with different error messages and different error counts between logs and traces. They have different meanings and perspectives, and these differences help you improve customer service and root cause analysis.

You need to think about which signals you want to understand errors. It is important to have a clear baseline for errors, noise, and exceptions across signals. Exceptions, errors, and alerts should be configured so that they are consistent with each other.

On the backend, it might be a 500 error, but on the user-facing API server, it might be 400. You want to match the error codes as much as possible, but you don't have to fix them if they're different.

You must also distinguish between technical errors and business errors. You need to accurately measure the failure. While SREs can't modify your code, it's important to make sure that you're processing exceptions correctly, outputting error messages correctly, and avoiding performance degradation due to unnecessary logging. While it is possible to disable and ignore certain errors and exceptions, developers need to develop their code accurately.

Error codes can have different results when measured on the backend than when measured on the frontend. Backend error codes should be prioritized for root cause analysis.

- From a customer service perspective, it is useful to manage the error rate and availability of RUM and API servers.

- From an SRE perspective, it's useful to use traces to measure the error rate of the backend.

In the demo, if you use kubectl port-forward svc/my-otel-demo-frontendproxy 8080:8080, you can see that the feature flags are output as normal by Kubernetes. You can use feature flags to enable errors. After configuring with feature flags, Grafana will see that the number of errors in the recommendation service increase over time.

Guidelines for defining SLOs, error budgets, and burn rates are shown in Figure 5-5.

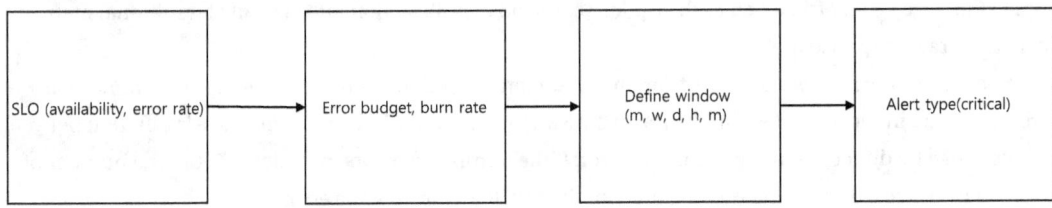

Figure 5-5. *The SLO configuration process*

Here is a use case to illustrate the error budget:

```
SLI error: Request status code >= 300
Period: 30 days
SLO: 99.9
Error budget: (100-99.9) = 0.1
Total number of requests in 30 days: 10000
Number of error requests allowed: 10
```

The SLO is 99.9, so if you receive 1,000 requests, you will be satisfied 99.9 percent of the time with only one error. If the total number of requests in a 30-day period is 10,000, you want to allow no more than ten errors. The error budget will be ten or less, or 9.99 to be exact. The Google SLO book explains how to set up multiple windows and calculate multiple alerts based on the burn rate.

CHAPTER 5   OPENTELEMETRY DEMO

- If you are using Prometheus to get error budgets and burn rates, you will need to define multiple burn rules. Due to the need to implement alerts for multiple windows, it is recommended to use an open source SLO generator rather than implementing recording rules directly.

- Using Grafana's alert list and state history charts is a great way to visualize SLOs, burn rate, and MTTx.

- Error budgets and burn rates are important, but it is also important to implement MTTx, with advanced availability. It's hard to generalize because error budgets don't work for every company. However, availability is important for both technical and business teams.

- Histograms output distributions and do not output details about individual requests. For example, they does not output the number of transactions that took more than one second for last five minutes. In this case, you need to use a counter. Quantiles only return percentages, which are difficult to use to calculate SLO. Histograms do not output durations.

Promscale returns the value corresponding to the percentile. You can see the exact delay time. To get an error budget, you need to measure the number of errors. There are two ways to get the number of errors and requests:

Error budgets can be expressed as two types: duration and count. Count is relatively simple, while duration is more complex.

- You can get the number of errors from the counter metric, which returns the error code. You calculate the error budget by dividing the number of errors by the total number.

- It is also possible to get the number of errors from a duration. However, finding the number of errors based on duration is tricky. If you want to find the number of errors in a specific quantile, you can't just use the quantiles because histograms are cumulative. For example, say you want to find the number of errors using the 100th percentile - 99th percentile method. You can use a formula to get the number of counts in a specific quantile. This could be implemented as follows, but it's not a good idea.

    ```
    sum(increase(demo_request_latency_seconds_bucket{le="0.4096"}[20m])) - sum(increase(demo_request_latency_seconds_bucket{le="0.1024"}[20m]))
    ```

- Rather than calculating this with a histogram, it is useful to use a counter metric such as duration or throughput to get the number of transactions that exceed a few seconds (i.e., you can get the number of transactions that exceed a latency of one second from the counter).

CHAPTER 5   OPENTELEMETRY DEMO

I use availability a lot for error budgeting. It's not always easy to agree on an error budget with other teams.

The purpose of an error budget is to help you make deployment decisions and prioritize with the business. If the current state is below the error budget, it can provide guidance to the development team that they should stabilize the current system rather than develop new features. If production continues to experience failures and is unstable, the error budget can explain that stabilization is a priority.

Burn rate should be used in conjunction with error budget. You can configure alerts through burn rate.

While it is possible to quantitatively measure the monetary cost of a failure by collecting events, it is preferable to measure the cost of the error budget.

You need to implement various windows and alerts.

- In the Google SRE chapter, I described multi-windows and multi-alerts. The burn rate implemented is hard-coded into the recording rules. You can modify the burn rate to suit your requirements. I recommend looking at `https://sloth.dev/` for open source examples.

- The reason that different types of windows are defined is to keep costs down and the system running efficiently. Querying the aggregation of week, month, and year windows would be expensive and slow. Using pre-aggregations for each window, you can quickly respond to user queries. With limited retention, data tiering becomes easier to manage. The process of these windows is implemented through Prometheus recording rules.

You may be using SumoLogic and then migrating to Datadog. When migrating observability to other products, the main migration targets are SLOs, alerts, and dashboards.

- Use OpenSLO.

- Use the SLO generator.

You can join and filter different signals to determine the exact problem and failure. Traditionally, only a single signal is used to output a simple SLO without user interaction. In comparison, the dashboard development introduced in this book is innovative and efficient.

- Dashboards can join various signals and output them. For example, events output business, and logs output internal information from the black box. By joining these signals, you can overcome the limitations of individual signals and display a variety of data, not just the technical data.

- Multiple filters can be used to restrict the output signals, allowing you to limit and narrow down the exact scope of the problem. You can quickly get to the problem you want.

CHAPTER 5 OPENTELEMETRY DEMO

- You can filter events to select business, application, system resources, and IT operations targets. You can define critical business IDs using service for microservices, resource IDs for system resources, and additional tags, and add them as data to the filter. For example, service IDs have a relationship with resource IDs, so it's a good idea to join services and resources.

I've discussed various charts. I hope you will utilize the state timeline and annotations. They are important charts for SREs, but they are underutilized in practice.

In SRE, you need dashboards for visualization of SLOs, MTTR, availability, and error budgets. You also need USE and RED dashboards. These dashboards allow for clear visualization and understanding of signals.

- RED (Rate, Error, Duration)
- USE (Utilization, Saturation, Errors)
- Google SRE (Latency, Traffic, Errors, Saturation)

RED is applicable to services, USE is applicable to infrastructure, and Google SRE is applicable to both services and infrastructure. To create a good dashboard, you must first define the correlation between the charts.

- It's a great way to organize a dashboard, showing the big picture first, and then showing a detailed chart at the bottom when you click a specific value.

- You should have a filter at the top, and configure it so that all charts within that dashboard dynamically change based on the scope and selection of the filter.

- Make sure that the charts output data in a consistent manner that is germane to the topic. When organizing multiple charts in a dashboard, you should try to define the correlations between them.

Developing a variety of charts requires an understanding of the data sources that are mapped to the chart. For example, complex heatmaps and service maps don't require specific formulas to display. You just need to map the data source to the chart, and the chart will come out.

- Time series charts, heatmaps, and histograms use spanmetrics generated by the metric generator.

- Node exporters are used in polystats.

- You can select metrics (ALERTS, ALERTS_FOR_STATE) only when alerts are enabled. To scrape this, you need to scrape the Prometheus and Grafana servers when an alert is enabled.

- The service map utilizes the OpenTelemetry Collector and metric generator. You can generate a spanmetric and a service map from the metric generator. If you use a bucket in the service map as a data source, you can automatically output a trace chart.

- While metrics and logs have been popular in the past, I recommend traces and events as the data sources for observability dashboards.

CHAPTER 5   OPENTELEMETRY DEMO

Once you have a good understanding of the internal data structure of the signals, you can quickly visualize the charts described previously without any preprocessing. An accurate understanding of the individual signals must precede visualization.

I'll explore Grafana's ability to define different correlations. You need to understand how they are implemented in this solution and configure them to suit your context.

When it comes to infrastructure, it's important to understand utilization and saturation rates for CPU, memory, disk, and network. To monitor applications, SLO dashboards are essential. The SLO dashboard includes basic error rates, availability, throughput, and latency. Depending on the domain and service type, it should also include error budgets and burn rates. For traditional industries, including legacy, error budgets, and burn rates can sometimes be overwhelming, so they are not required. It is always useful to have a profile that allows you to monitor infrastructure and applications together, so I recommend correlating and using profiles.

The dashboard should be more than just a visualization; it should consist of alerts to continuously improve as problems arise.

To build the dashboards mentioned previously, it's not enough to use Prometheus metrics alone. You need to connect with various data sources such as Jira, the cloud, ArgoCD, Jenkins, and Git. And you'll need to use different types of charts, starting with time series charts.

Along with building your system, you will build dashboards using Grafana's default dashboards. The dashboards can be sophisticated, as shown here:

- Add saturation rates from a basic infrastructure dashboard and improve with eBPF and Cilium.
- Add error budgets and burn rates to application SLO and elevate them to a service perspective.
- The Deployment, GitOps, and Issue Management dashboards are operational dashboards that use webhooks to collect and monitor operational data.
- Dashboards, alerts, SLOs, and error budgets should be automated, built, and deployed via Terraform or API.

So far, I've been talking about traces, and the signals used in the dashboard are basically metrics. Rather than configuring the trace dashboard from scratch, I recommend starting with metrics first. The components of an SLO, availability, duration, throughput, and error rate, are important.

- It is important to understand that different types of applications require different metrics to be measured. For web frameworks, availability, duration, throughput, and error rate SLOs are appropriate, while for publish and subscribe, the number of pended messages is useful, and for batch, error rates and throughput are useful. If reads and writes are separated, cache hits and slow queries should be managed for reads, while speed and pipeline throughput are useful for writes.

CHAPTER 5 OPENTELEMETRY DEMO

- It is good to apply error budgets and burn rates in addition to basic SLO, but review whether it is necessary depending on the characteristics of the service and organizational structure. Error budgets and burn rates should not be used to hold people accountable, but are recommended for decision-making on whether to deploy new services, improve the quality of existing services, and schedule management. It is not a good practice to develop SLO error estimates and burn rates manually. They should be generated in batches using a generator. This is a time-consuming task because it requires many windows.

- I recommend configuring separate dashboards for tickets, incidents, errors, and alerts.

- In addition to the application dashboard, you need an infrastructure dashboard. You need to see utilization and saturation. From a network perspective, I also recommend Cilium.

- You should avoid developing custom metrics. Once the Application, Infrastructure, Alert, and Ticket dashboards are complete, the next task is to configure the Anomaly Detection, Deployment, and Configuration Management dashboards.

- Select critical tasks and develop a dashboard that outputs business and technology together.

- Minimize detailed technology and business dashboards and develop them as needed. Select the most important tasks and develop dashboards that show business and technical outputs together. Create dashboards that provide an overview of the user journey.

If you fail to optimize your log dashboard, you could be paying a lot of money. Consider different ways to reduce costs, and be careful not to spend too much money.

- If an error is found in the log, sending an alert is the most basic alert.

- You can create metrics from logs. Use metric over login dashboards.

- Use recording rules that take into account time windows. For example, when applying error budgets, pre-aggregation can save money.

It is recommended that observability dashboards be configured using traces rather than metrics or logs. I explain how to configure dashboards with traces using Promscale.

There are two main types of errors: business and technical. Understanding business process tasks is limited, but you should at least be able to quickly recognize errors and determine whether they are technical or business task errors.

CHAPTER 5   OPENTELEMETRY DEMO

5.3.4. OpenTelemetry Collector

Observability operations require high availability of pipelines and design patterns. OpenTelemetry Collector supports various design patterns for reliability. For example, it supports throttling, buffers, retries, batch processing, and rate limiting.

In addition to the OpenTelemetry Collector, there are many other pipelines, including FluentD, Fluent Bit, Promtail, Datadog vectors, Kafka connectors, and more. However, the Collector is superior in terms of functionality and compatibility. In the following demo, Collector supports exemplars, multitenants, and service graphs.

Figure 5-6 provides an overview of the OpenTelemetry Collector component utilized by the OpenTelemetry demo application. It also highlights the flow of observability data (trace and metric) within the system.

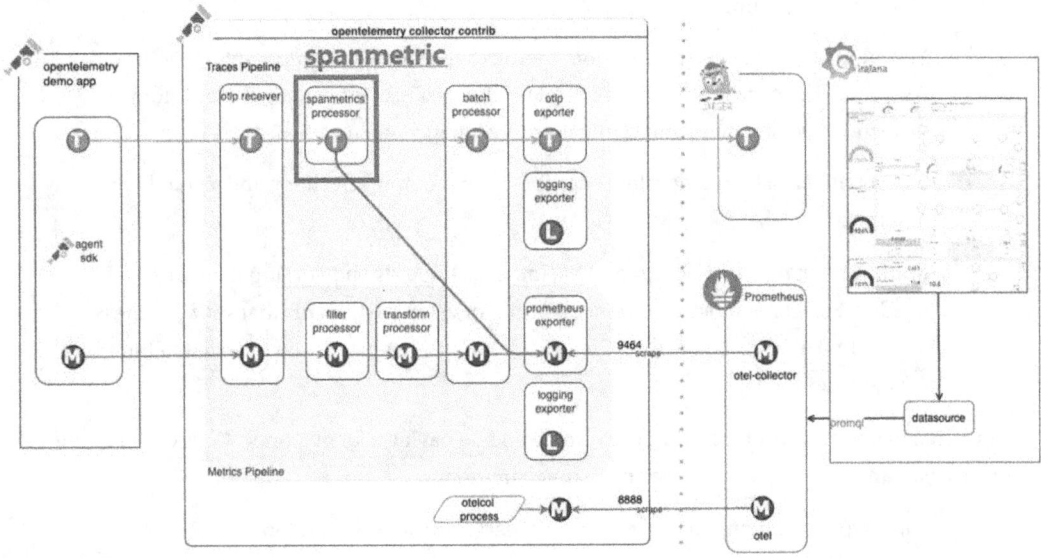

Figure 5-6. Flowchart of the OpenTelemetry demo

Monitoring data flow through OpenTelemetry Collector is important for several reasons. Understanding the data received, such as sample counts and cardinality, is essential to understanding the internal behavior of the Collector.

Application-specific performance dashboards with spanmetric are useful.

Initially, only Grafana Tempo supported spanmetrics, but now OpenTelemetry Collector supports spanmetrics as well. You can create spanmetrics and measure SLOs for microservices without dependency on backend storage.

Here is the configuration file for the OpenTelemetry Collector associated with Promscale. You can see that spanmetric is defined:

```
exporters:
  otlp:
    endpoint: '{{ include "otel-demo.name" . }}-jaeger-collector:4317'
    tls:
      insecure: true
  prometheus:
    endpoint: '0.0.0.0:9464'
    resource_to_telemetry_conversion:
      enabled: true
    enable_open_metrics: true
  otlp/promscale:
    endpoint: "tobs-promscale:9202"
    compression: none
    tls:
      insecure: true

processors:
  spanmetrics:
    metrics_exporter: prometheus
```

Metrics are used to monitor both send and receive data flows. These metrics are created by the OpenTelemetry Collector process, exported to port 8888, and scraped by Prometheus. The namespace associated with these metrics is `otelcol` and the job name is labeled `otel`.

Labels can serve as a useful tool to identify specific metrics, allowing you to differentiate metrics within the overall namespace.

5.3.5. RUM

The standard specification for RUM is not yet finalized. It measures different types of clients. RUM has a complex architecture because it needs to provide APIs and backend storage for each type of client.

The scope of RUM is ambiguous. Some solutions create distributed traces directly from the client. The demo provides a React web-based UI and API path based on Next.JS.

The web-based UI is provided by the frontend instrumented for web browsers. OpenTelemetry instrumentation is included as part of the Next.js component in `Pages/_app.tsx`. See Figure 5-7.

CHAPTER 5 OPENTELEMETRY DEMO

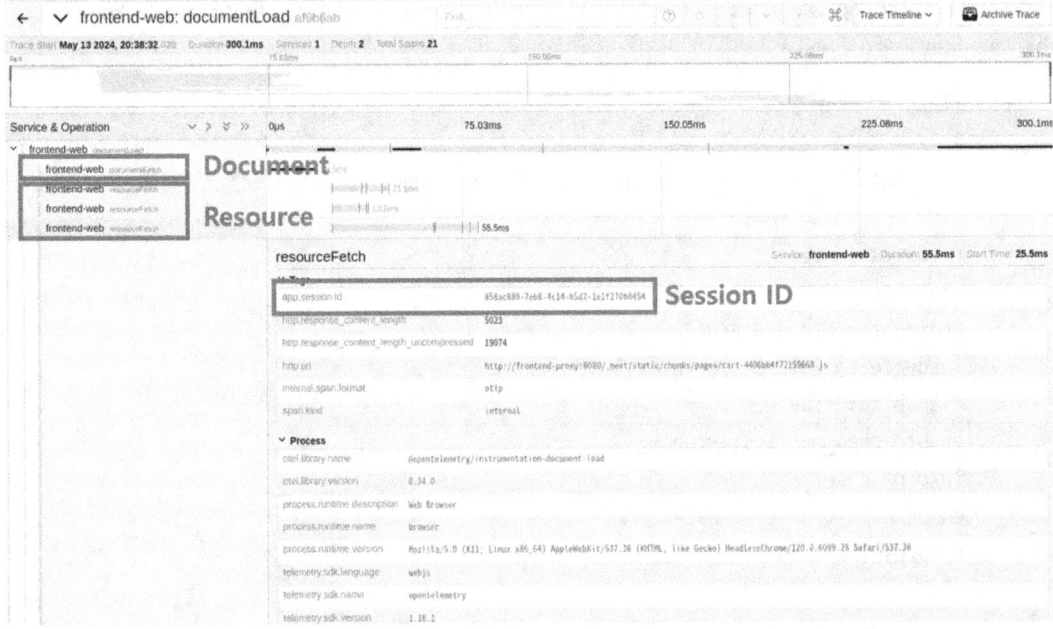

Figure 5-7. A trace generated by RUM

In OpenTelemetry, a RUM is equivalent to a distributed trace. The user's XHR, document, and resource fetches are generated with spans. You can also use Session IDs from logs. RUM is generated with spans from resource and document fetches.

- The demo creates a session ID. It performs an action (e.g., clicking the Complete Order button) and calls the backend.

- The load generator starts the transaction, but does not implement an E2E trace. It calls the frontend only.

- frontend-web is the microservice for the frontend, and it implements fetching resources and documents. It calls the frontend microservice.

- A frontend is a microservice in the backend, and the frontend interfaces with other backend microservices. It plays the same role as an API server.

Import and initialize the instrumentation from the sources shown here:

```
import Frontend tracer from '../utils/telemetry/Frontend tracer';

if (typeof window !== 'undefined') Frontend tracer();
```

CHAPTER 5   OPENTELEMETRY DEMO

The utils/telemetry/Frontend tracer.ts file does the following:

- Initializes the provider.
- Sets up OTLP export.
- Registers a trace context propagator.
- Registers the frontend automated instrumentation library.

The browser transfers the data to the OpenTelemetry Collector, which is likely on a separate domain, so the CORS header is also set.

Figure 5-8 shows how to use RUM to create a trace context on the frontend and propagate it to the distributed traces.

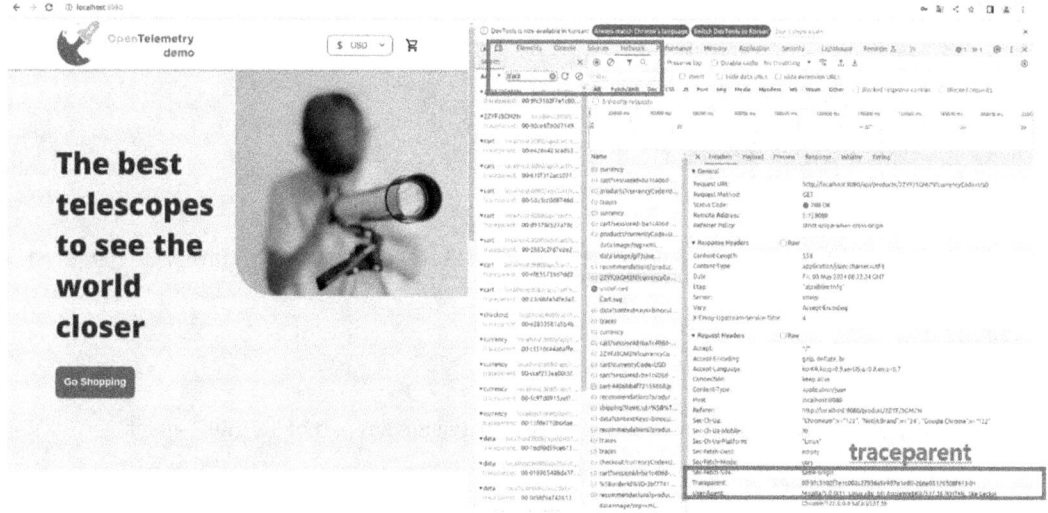

Figure 5-8. *Verifying the trace ID*

To pass the Synthetic_request attribute flag for the backend service, the applyCustomAttributesOnSpan method is added to the instrumentation-fetch library span attribute in such a way that it is included in the browser span.

For browser spans to be collected, you must also specify the endpoint location of the OpenTelemetry Collector. The frontend proxy defines the path to the OpenTelemetry Collector with the prefix /otlp-http path. You can configure the endpoint of the OpenTelemetry Collector by setting the following environment variables in the frontend component:

```
components:
  frontend:
    envOverrides:
      - name: PUBLIC_OTEL_EXPORTER_OTLP_TRACES_ENDPOINT
        value: http://otel-demo.my-domain.com/otlp-http/v1/traces
```

5.3.6. Automated Instrumentation

The OpenTelemetry demo supports both automated and manual instrumentation. Java, Golang, and Python support automated instrumentation well, but each language has its own limitations.

The SDK is initialized using the `init tracerProvider` method. This is the source that propagates the baggage:

```go
func initTracerProvider() *sdktrace.TracerProvider {
    ctx := context.Background()

    exporter, err := otlptracegrpc.New(ctx)
    if err != nil {
        log.Fatal(err)
    }
    tp := sdktrace.NewTracerProvider(
        sdktrace.WithBatcher(exporter),
        sdktrace.WithResource(initResource()),
    )
    otel.SetTracerProvider(tp)
    otel.SetTextMapPropagator(propagation.NewCompositeTextMapPropagator(propagation.TraceContext{}, propagation.Baggage{}))
    return tp
}
```

The gRPC service receives gRPC requests that are instrumented as part of the gRPC server.

```go
var srv = grpc.NewServer(
    grpc.StatsHandler(otelgrpc.NewServerHandler()),
)
```

The service makes multiple send gRPC calls, all of which are instrumented by wrapping the gRPC client with instrumentation.

```go
func createClient(ctx context.Context, svcAddr string) (*grpc.ClientConn, error) {
    return grpc.DialContext(ctx, svcAddr,
        grpc.WithTransportCredentials(insecure.NewCredentials()),
        grpc.WithStatsHandler(otelgrpc.NewClientHandler()),
    )
}
```

Kafka (Sarama) writes the processed results to a Kafka topic, which is then processed by other microservices in turn.

```
saramaConfig := sarama.NewConfig()
producer, err := sarama.NewAsyncProducer(brokers, saramaConfig)
if err != nil {
    return nil, err
}
producer = otelsarama.WrapAsyncProducer(saramaConfig, producer)
```

5.3.7. Commercial Observability Demo

There are situations where commercial observability agents and OpenTelemetry agents operate together.

- Commercial observability agents have a different semantic convention, which makes them harder to understand.

- They provide their own profile rather than a flame graph. The span of a trace is associated with its own profile and provides the ability to debug at the code level.

- Since the naming may conflict with existing trace IDs in the log, a naming standard should be established and guidelines provided to developers.

- The commercial observability RUM is implemented in a different way than OpenTelemetry's RUM.

- OpenTelemetry collectors are not required, and commercial observability agents can recognize traces generated by OpenTelemetry agents.

You can configure the demo using Dynatrace, as shown in Figure 5-9.

CHAPTER 5   OPENTELEMETRY DEMO

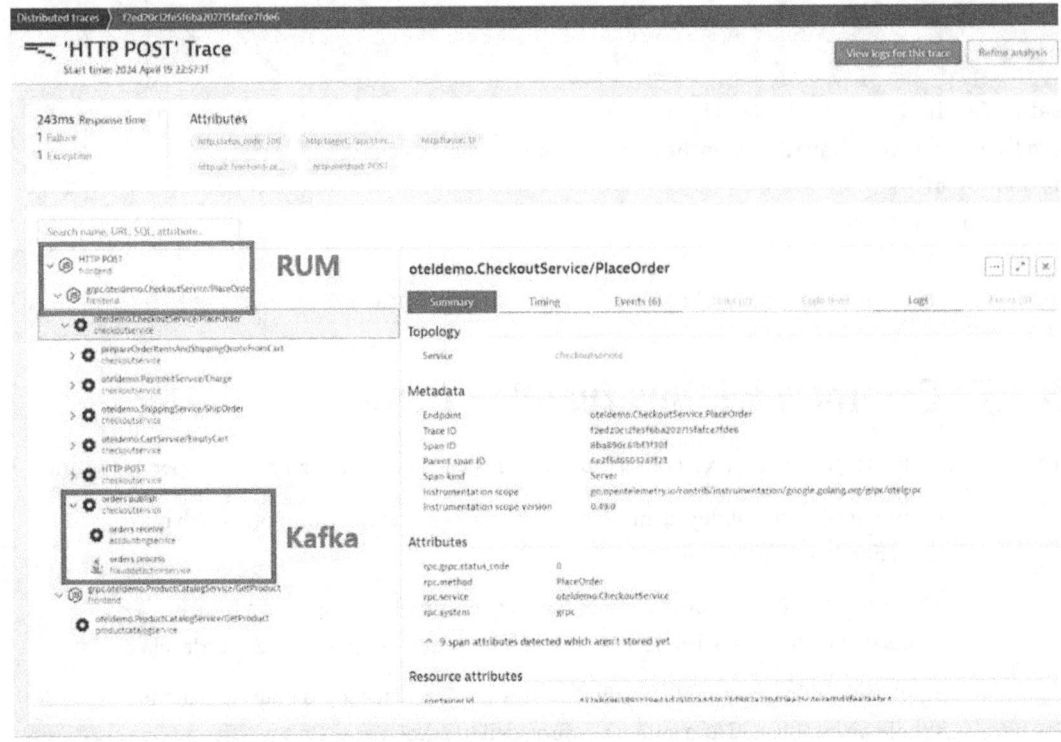

Figure 5-9. *E2E trace of commercial observability*

Next, navigate to src/otelcollector/otelcol-config-extras.yml. This file contains the configuration that will be merged with the collector's configuration. Copy the following contents to the file:

```
exporters:
  # otlp/http exporter to Dynatrace.
  otlphttp/dynatrace:
    endpoint: "${DT_OTLP_ENDPOINT}"
    headers:
      Authorization: "Api-Token ${DT_API_TOKEN}"

processors:
  cumulativetodelta:
  filter/histograms:
    error_mode: ignore
    metrics:
      metric:
        - 'type == METRIC_DATA_TYPE_HISTOGRAM'
```

```
service:
  pipelines:
    traces/dynatrace:
      receivers: [otlp]
      processors: [batch]
      exporters: [otlphttp/dynatrace]
    metrics/dynatrace:
      receivers: [otlp, spanmetrics]
      processors: [filter/histograms, batch, cumulativetodelta]
      exporters: [otlphttp/dynatrace]
    logs/dynatrace:
      receivers: [otlp]
      processors: [batch]
      exporters: [otlphttp/dynatrace]
```

This configuration exports traces, metrics, and logs to Dynatrace using OTLP. It also includes a spanmetric processor that generates request, error, and duration (RED) metrics from span data. All the necessary components are available directly from the OpenTelemetry Collector included in the demo application.

To view the metrics, open the Metric view in the left navigation. You should see a variety of metrics. Filter using `calls.count` to see the metrics generated by the spanmetric connector.

One of the most recent additions to the demo application is the log. To access the logs from Dynatrace, go to the Log Viewer page. Select one of the log lines and a sidebar with available attributes will appear. Select View Trace to associate a log line with a trace and see in detail which requests (distributed trace) led to this log line. The trace and log correlation are the `trace_id` and `span_id` attributes, which the OpenTelemetry library attaches to each log message when available.

5.3.8. Live Debugging

Debugging is technically the most powerful observability method. While not defined as a standard by OpenTelemetry, commercial observability agents offer live debugging.

Debugging in DevTools is the most basic debugging method. You debug your Go source in DevTools. See Figure 5-10.

CHAPTER 5 OPENTELEMETRY DEMO

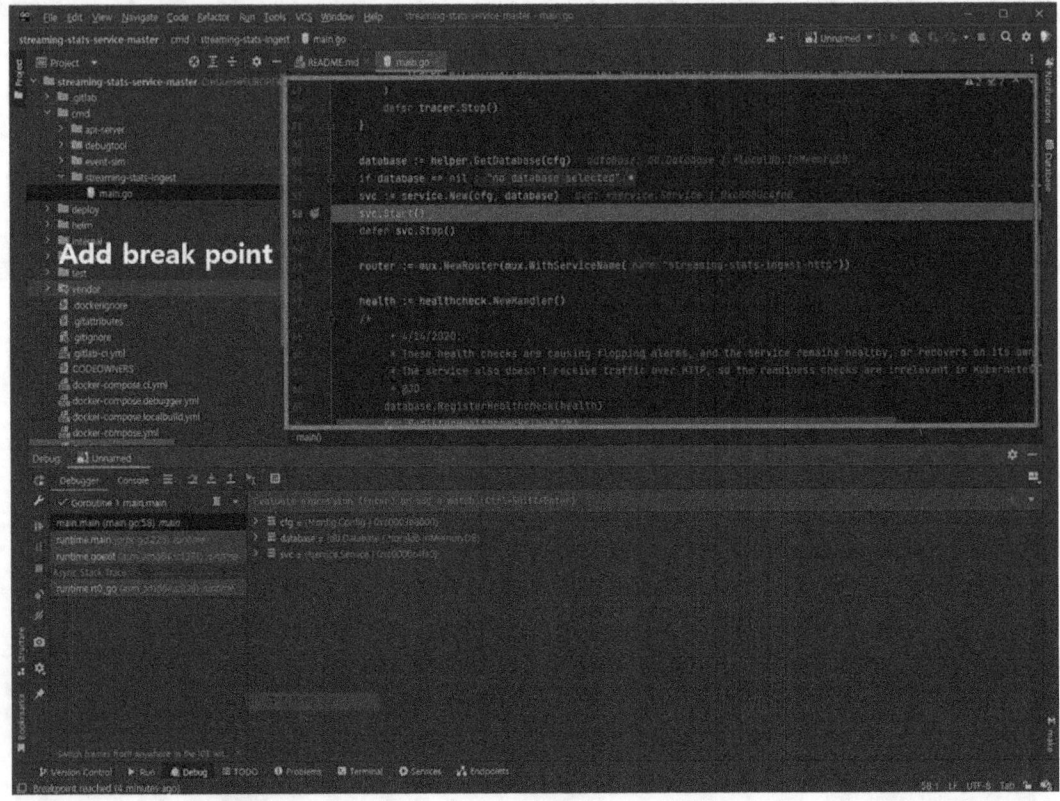

Figure 5-10. *Setting breakpoints when debugging GoLand remotely*

Remote debugging of JetBrains GoLand uses GO dlv, which allows you to access and debug your Go application from your IDE.

```
FROM golang:1.13.8 AS build-env

RUN go get github.com/go-delve/delve/cmd/dlv

ADD . /dockerdev
WORKDIR /dockerdev

RUN go build -gcflags="all=-N -l" -o /server

# Final stage
FROM debian:buster

EXPOSE 8000 40000

WORKDIR /
COPY --from=build-env /go/bin/dlv /
COPY --from=build-env /server /
```

CHAPTER 5 OPENTELEMETRY DEMO

```
CMD ["/dlv", "--listen=:40000", "--headless=true", "--api-version=2", "--accept-
multiclient", "exec", "/server"]
```

Run a Kubernetes pod and debug the application in the pod with `dlv`:

```
kubectl --kubeconfig=/root/.cache/JetBrains/GoLand2021.3/kubernetes/dockerdev-
kubernetes-debug/api-provider/config logs web-585b464d65-znxwp --container=dockerdev-web
--namespace=default --follow=true
API server listening at: [::]:40000
2022-04-13T10:39:33Z warning layer=rpc Listening for remote connections (connections are not
authenticated nor encrypted)
2022/04/13 10:40:49 main.go:57: trying to connect to the db server (attempt 1)...
2022/04/13 10:40:49 main.go:21: starting server...
```

You need to set the port of the Kubernetes service. The screen in Figure 5-11 shows you how to run a specific module of the API server remotely and debug `dlv` in the development tool.

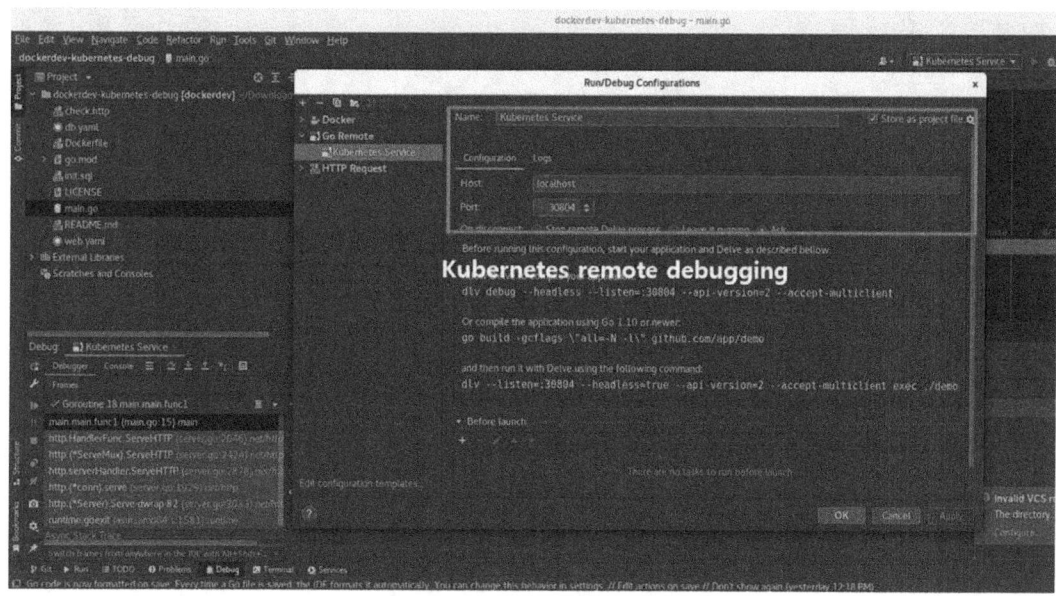

Figure 5-11. GoLand remote debugging setup

5.3.9. Baggage Context

On the frontend microservices, you can utilize OpenTelemetry baggage to determine if the request is a synthetic request from the load generator. A synthetic request creates a new trace, as shown in Figure 5-12.

CHAPTER 5   OPENTELEMETRY DEMO

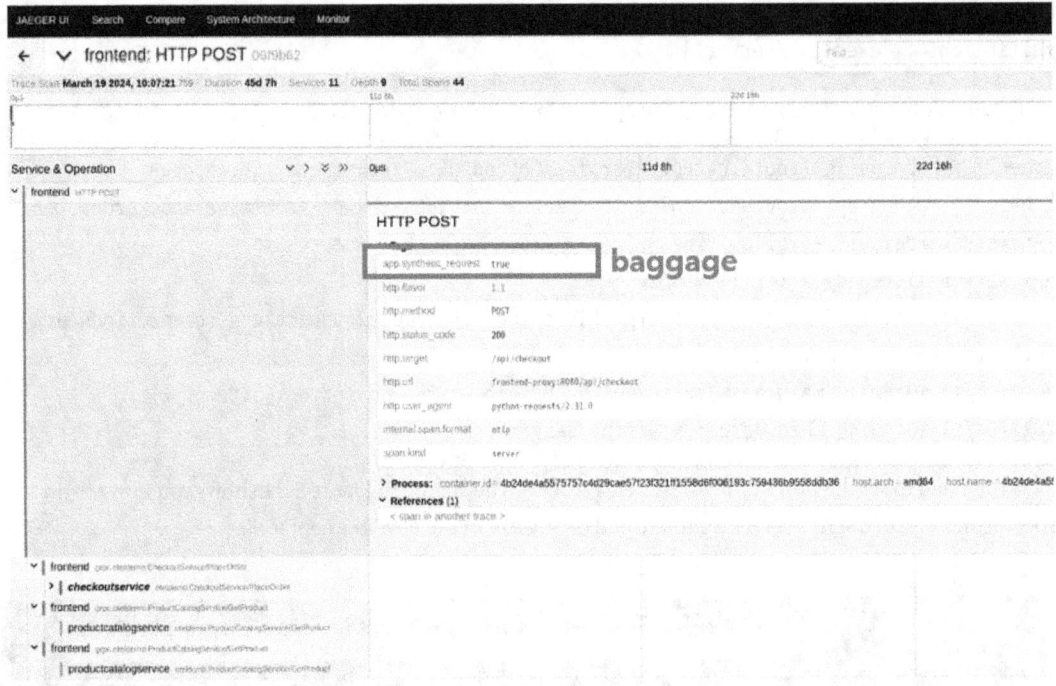

Figure 5-12. Checking baggage

In Figure 5-12, you can see that app.synthetic_request is set to true.

To determine if a baggage item is set, you can leverage the propagate API to parse the baggage header and utilize the baggage API to get or set the entity.

```
ctx = baggage.set_baggage("synthetic_request", "true")
context.attach(ctx)
```

It is important to understand the difference between span attributes and baggage: span attributes allow you to include additional information in each span, while baggage allows you to pass additional information across multiple spans and use baggage when you need to share data in the trace. The span attribute is used for transfers only, whereas baggage is used when propagated as a header.

5.3.10. Span Attributes

You need to design a data structure for IDs and attributes. The demo explains how to do this. Automated instrumentation signals alone are not enough and should be used to add IDs and attributes to advance observability and AIOps. Correlations, IDs, and attribute schemes are a great way to improve observability data analysis.

CHAPTER 5 OPENTELEMETRY DEMO

Individual microservices have the following characteristics.

The demo is a simple:

- Ad, Cart, Fraud Detection, Quote, and Recommendation support logs.
- Frontend Payment supports baggage.
- Frontend Fraud Detection supports a span link.
- Checkout is the most important microservice, and it interfaces with many microservices.
- Ads support exemplars.

You can configure the following feature flags. You can validate various scenarios in conjunction with anomaly detection and chaos engineering:

- The Checkout service generates app.payment.transaction.id, app.order.id, and app.shipping.tracking.id.
- The Frontend and Checkout services create various transactions. Define various IDs such as order and payment IDs.
- The Checkout service is an orchestrating microservice and it creates multiple spans. It creates one span per method.
- The Frontend service generates app.request.id and app.session.id.

The span attributes and feature flags are listed in Table 5-1.

Table 5-1. The Span Attribute for the Feature Flag

Microservices	Feature Flag	Span Attribute	Whether to Log
Ad	Generate errors for GetAds	app.ads.category app.ads.contextKeys app.ads.contextKeys.count app.ads.count app.ads.ad_request_type app.ads.ad_response_type	Log
Ad	Trigger full garbage collection in the Ad service		
Ad	Generate high CPU load To demonstrate CPU throttling, set a CPU resource limit		

(*continued*)

Table 5-1. (*continued*)

Microservices	Feature Flag	Span Attribute	Whether to Log
Cart	Generate an error for an empty cart	app.cart.items.count app.product.id app.product.quantity app.user.id	Log
Product Catalog	Generate an error for a GetProduct request with a product ID (OLJCESPC7Z)	app.product.id app.product.name app.products.count app.products_search.count	
Recommendation	Exponentially growing cache causes memory leaks	app.filtered_products.count app.products.count app.products_recommended.count app.cache_hit	Log
Payment	Generate an error when calling the charge method	app.payment.amount app.payment.card_type app.payment.card_valid app.payment.charged	
Checkout	Use the wrong address when calling the PaymentService service; it looks like the PaymentService service is unavailable	app.cart.items.count app.order.amount app.order.id app.order.items.count app.payment.transaction.id app.shipping.amount app.shipping.tracking.id app.user.currency app.user.id	
Load Generator	The home page starts to flood with a huge amount of requests that can be configured by changing the status flagged JSON		

(*continued*)

CHAPTER 5 OPENTELEMETRY DEMO

Table 5-1. (*continued*)

Microservices	Feature Flag	Span Attribute	Whether to Log
Kafka	Kafka queues are overloaded, causing subscriber-side latency to spike at the same time		
imageSlowLoad	Product image loading on the frontend is slow, using envoy error injections		

Various span attributes are defined, and anomaly detection rules are defined based on these attributes.

The attributes added to span can be used for aggregation of anomaly detection and for metrics, alerts, and complex calculations—see Table 5-2.

Table 5-2. Span Attribute for Anomalies

Service Name	Span Attribute
Frontend	app.cart.size
	app.cart.items.count
	app.cart.shipping.cost
	app.cart.total.price
	app.currency
	app.currency.new
	app.order.total
	app.product.id
	app.product.quantity
	app.products.count
	app.request.id
	app.session.id
	app.user.id
Quote	app.quote.items.count
	app.quote.cost.total
Shipping	app.shipping.cost.total
	app.shipping.items.count
	app.shipping.tracking.id
	app.shipping.zip_code

CHAPTER 5   OPENTELEMETRY DEMO

Anomaly detection, chaos engineering, and feature flags provide similar functionalities from different perspectives. Feature flags are application-specific, chaos engineering is infrastructure-specific, services are complex and require additional attributes, and the span attribute is a good fit.

You can add attributes to an automatically instrumented span. You can get the current span from the context during code execution.

```
Span span = Span.current();
```

Add an attribute using `setAttribute` to the span. In the `getAds` method, multiple attributes are added to the span.

```
span.setAttribute("app.ads.contextKeys", req.getContextKeysList().toString());
span.setAttribute("app.ads.contextKeys.count", req.getContextKeysCount());
```

Using trace to improve value from a technical perspective, such as root cause analysis, is not the only way to improve value, but you should also think about business effects. Baggage and span attributes can be applied in various ways, such as via IDs, amounts, transactions, revenue, and cost of loss for failures.

You could use Google Spanner, but it doesn't recognize attributes. For example, without the query information in the span, it cannot understand what the span is processing. In this case, you need to add attributes to the span. By adding attributes, you can understand the process of the span, and you can query it and utilize it for various purposes

Commercial observability agents provide similar technologies such as request attributes rather than baggage and span attributes.

Figure 5-13 is a demonstration of configuring a separate header called Request Attributes.

CHAPTER 5 OPENTELEMETRY DEMO

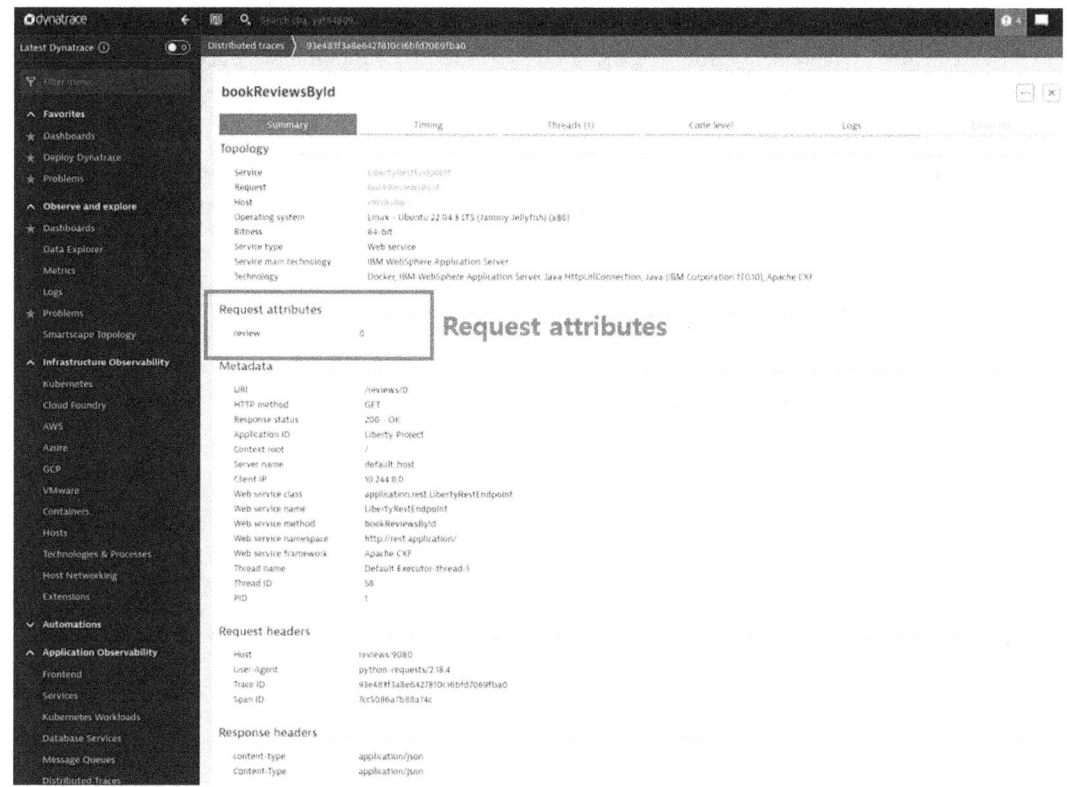

Figure 5-13. *Request Attributes feature in commercial observability*

5.3.11. Span Annotations

Along with the previously discussed span link, the span attribute, baggage, is an important technical concept in traces. Let's consider the baggage span annotation from a business perspective.

Even if you implement E2E traces, you can't often determine which order ID failed. For example, it's hard to explain how many orders fail, how many users are affected by a failure, and how much damage and impact it has on them based on traces alone. Technical context alone is not enough; business context needs to be added. Single customer E2E journeys are composed of many E2E traces, meaning that a journey can only be meaningful if it contains many E2E traces and is expressed within the business.

Span annotations make it easy to create a span. It is better to resolve using the span link to clarify the relationship between spans, and the span attribute to define the business meaning. It is OpenTelemetry's direction to use baggage instead of the span attribute, but given the development labor, network traffic and maintenance of baggage added to the header, span attribute is more appropriate than baggage in most cases.

When a user takes an action, such as clicking a button, they call the backend API. Multiple web pages make up a single order. For example, a user creates an order, pays for it, and processes shipping. If this is processed in the order of order, payment, and shipping and consists of three parts, it will generate at least three trace IDs. If there is a problem with processing the payment, you won't be able to understand which order it is. The order, payment, and shipping must have an order ID in addition to a trace ID to determining the E2E order process.

Suppose the number of spans in the order trace is 100, the number of spans in the payment trace is 50, and the number of spans in the shipping trace is 50. The order process contains three trace IDs and consists of 200 spans in total. You need an ID that can semantically combine the three different trace IDs and the order IDs should be defined in the baggage or span attribute.

The span annotation helps you go beyond the E2E trace.

There are times when users want to create their own span for their code without making significant changes to the code.

You can create a method span using WithSpan. To create a span for one of your methods, you can annotate the method with @WithSpan.

```
import io.opentelemetry.instrumentation.annotations.WithSpan;

public class MyClass {
  @WithSpan
  public void myMethod() {
      <...>
  }
}
```

Whenever an application calls a method with an annotation, it creates a span representing that span and provides any exceptions. By default, the span name will be <class name>.<method name> unless a name is provided as an argument to the annotation.

Once a span is created for a method, you can annotate the method parameters with the @SpanAttribute annotation to automatically add them as attributes to the span.

```
import io.opentelemetry.instrumentation.annotations.SpanAttribute;
import io.opentelemetry.instrumentation.annotations.WithSpan;

public class MyClass {

    @WithSpan
    public void myMethod(@SpanAttribute("parameter1") String parameter1,
        @SpanAttribute("parameter2") long parameter2) {
        <...>
    }
}
```

CHAPTER 5 OPENTELEMETRY DEMO

Unless specified as an argument to an annotation, attribute names are derived from parameter names when compiled into .class files. This is done by passing the -parameters option to the javac compiler.

```
@WithSpan("getAdsByCategory")
  private Collection<Ad> getAdsByCategory(@SpanAttribute("app.ads.category") String category) {
    Collection<Ad> ads = adsMap.get(category);
    Span.current().setAttribute("app.ads.count", ads.size());
    return ads;
  }
```

Using @WithSpan and @SpanAttribute minimizes source changes (see Figure 5-14). Baggage requires manual instrumentation, but span annotations using @WithSpan and @SpanAttribute can be applied with automated instrumentation. You can create a span with @WithSpan and @SpanAttribute.

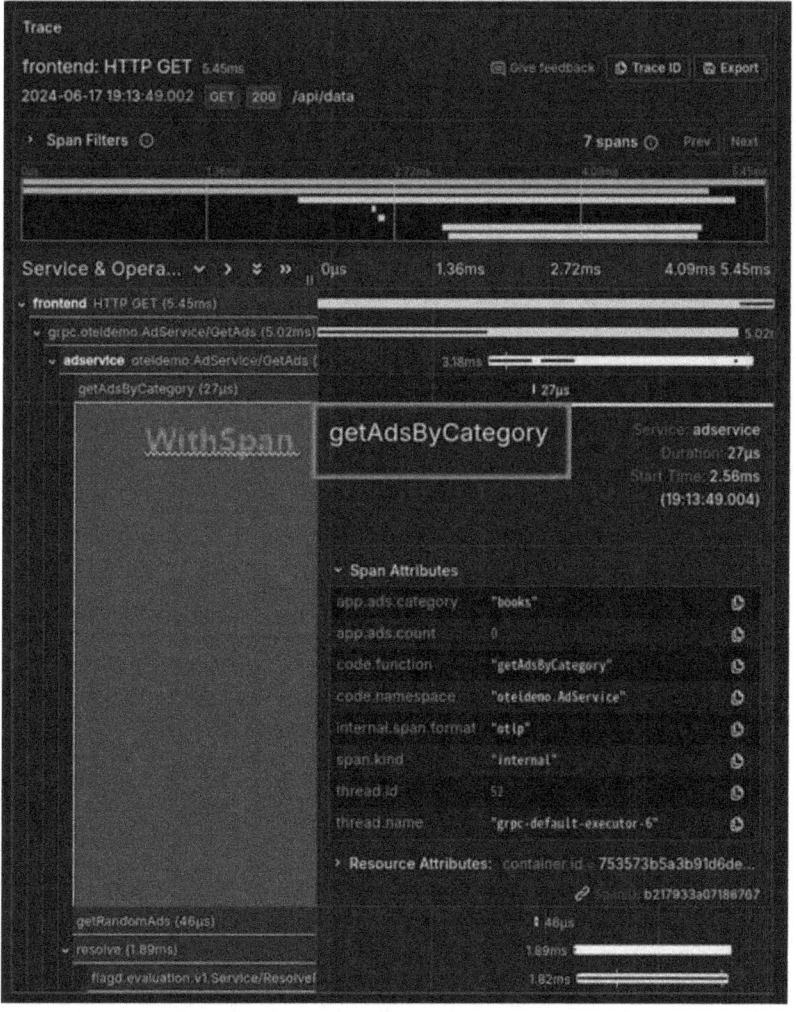

Figure 5-14. *Span annotation created using WithSpan*

CHAPTER 5   OPENTELEMETRY DEMO

Automated instrumentation can also use the span attribute, and you can use `attributesprocessor` on the collector.

The `attributesprocessor` option can read the body of a log and generate a span. Generating spans from logs is a good practice if you are using a managed service that does not support traces.

Micrometer traces and OpenTelemetry agents can use annotation to create spans. This is not automatic instrumentation, but manual instrumentation. Some threads cannot be spanned using automatic instrumentation alone. You can use annotations to manually create spans for threads.

5.3.12. Promscale Kubernetes

The OpenTelemetry Collector consists of two pipelines. The first pipeline is configured for connectivity with Grafana observability. The second pipeline is the AIOps pipeline, which consists of Promscale and Jaeger for data analysis and automation (see Figure 5-15). It is configured to receive signals from microservices and transfer them to the two pipelines in parallel. Grafana LGTM supports correlation for observability, but it stores data in its own uninterpretable format (a Prometheus-compatible file format) in object storage, so there is no need to configure a separate data pipeline for subsequent processing. Grafana does not allow data pipelines to process blocks stored in object storage.

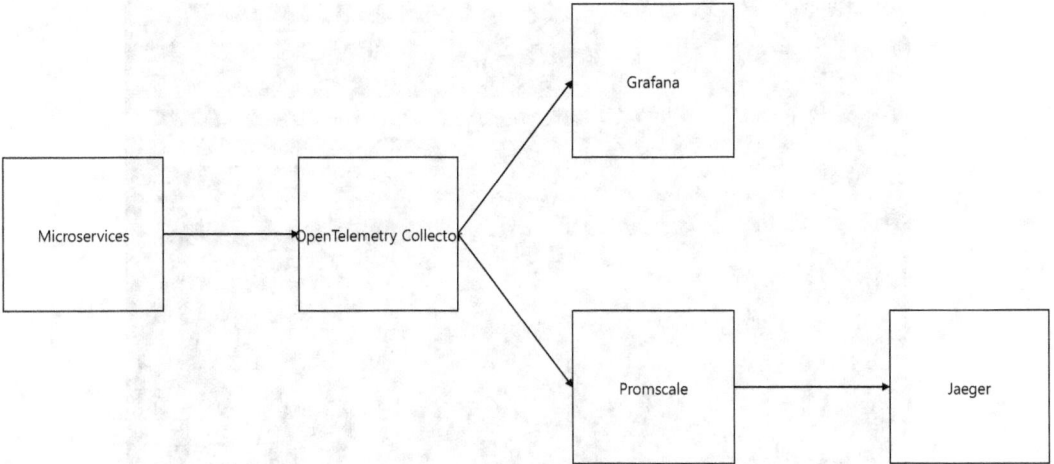

Figure 5-15. *The AIOps pipeline architecture*

So you need to configure Promscale and Jaeger. This book provides Promscale versions of Kubernetes deployments. You can deploy and configure your environment in different ways. For production, I recommend configuring Promscale with TOBS.

TOBS is a tool that makes it easier to install observability stacks into Kubernetes clusters. The current stack includes Prometheus, Jaeger, OpenTelemetry Collector, Promscale, Timescale database, and more.

- TOBS is complex to configure and configures Fullstack, including demo microservices, `kubernetes-prometheus-stack`, and the OpenTelemetry Collector.

CHAPTER 5 OPENTELEMETRY DEMO

- Aside from the kubernetes-prometheus-stack, I also provide a simple TOBS for testing.

The installation process is as follows.

Start Kubernetes:

```
minikube start --vm-driver=none --kubernetes-version v1.23.0 --memory=19000 --cpus=4
```

Install cert-manager:

```
kubectl apply -f https://github.com/cert-manager/cert-manager/releases/download/v1.9.0/cert-manager.yaml
```

Add the Helm repository:

```
helm repo add timescale https://charts.timescale.com/
```

Set a Grafana password:

```
adminUser: admin
# To configure password externally refer to https://github.com/grafana/helm-charts/
blob/6578497320d3c4672baB3a3c7fd38dffba1c9aba/charts/grafana/values.yaml#L340-L345
adminPassword: asdf1234test5678
```

Configure TOBS:

```
helm install tobs --wait --timeout 30m timescale/tobs -f values.yaml
```

Add the OpenTelemetry repository:

```
helm repo add open-telemetry https://open-telemetry.github.io/opentelemetry-helm-charts
```

Modify the OpenTelemetry Collector:

```
otlp/promscale:
      endpoint: "tobs-promscale:9202"
      compression: none
      tls:
        insecure: true

  service:
    pipelines:
      traces:
        processors: [memory_limiter, spanmetrics, batch]
        exporters: [otlp, logging, spanmetrics, otlp/promscale]
```

CHAPTER 5 OPENTELEMETRY DEMO

Install the OpenTelemetry demo:

```
helm install my-otel-demo open-telemetry/opentelemetry-demo -f values.yaml
```

TOBS is complex, so I provide a simpler Promscale Helm chart that is easier for readers to test. TOBS charts contain many pods, so you should organize them so that you can easily deploy only the pods you need.

```
# kubectl get pod
```

NAME	READY	STATUS	RESTARTS	AGE
alertmanager-tobs-kube-prometheus-stack-alertmanager-0	2/2	Running	1 (3h11m ago)	3h21m
alertmanager-tobs-kube-prometheus-stack-alertmanager-1	2/2	Running	1 (3h11m ago)	3h21m
alertmanager-tobs-kube-prometheus-stack-alertmanager-2	2/2	Running	0	3h21m
jaeger-d464f6f5c-m7s5h	1/1	Running	0	142m
my-otel-demo-accountingservice-6cbbdf77df-9sk7h	1/1	Running	0	3h
my-otel-demo-adservice-76cc5ddc9c-25hfv	1/1	Running	0	3h
my-otel-demo-cartservice-7ccc74fd46-88cqw	1/1	Running	0	3h
my-otel-demo-checkoutservice-d7c8f74d9-8dzn5	1/1	Running	0	3h
tobs-connection-secret-1-qdlh6	0/1	Completed	0	3h22m
tobs-kube-prometheus-stack-operator-5474f557d6-9ggg8	1/1	Running	0	3h22m
tobs-kube-state-metrics-fb47c77b4-l5bvn	1/1	Running	0	3h22m
tobs-opentelemetry-collector-8d7898dd5-vtnqc	1/1	Running	0	3h7m
tobs-prometheus-node-exporter-vzj86	1/1	Running	0	3h22m
tobs-promscale-b698bf467-lhcft	1/1	Running	7 (3h13m ago)	3h22m

Install Java if necessary:

```
apt install default-jre
curl -fsSL https://dbeaver.io/debs/dbeaver.gpg.key | sudo gpg --dearmor -o /etc/apt/trusted.gpg.d/dbeaver.gpg
echo "deb https://dbeaver.io/debs/dbeaver-ce /" | sudo tee /etc/apt/sources.list.d/dbeaver.list
sudo apt update && sudo apt install dbeaver-ce
```

Install dbeaver if necessary:

```
wget https://dbeaver.io/files/dbeaver-ce-latest-stable.x86_64.rpm
sudo rpm -Uvh ./dbeaver-ce-latest-stable.x86_64.rpm
```

When configuring Promscale, consider the following.
Note 1:

- The OpenTelemetry demo works with version 0.26.

CHAPTER 5 OPENTELEMETRY DEMO

- The OpenTelemetry Collector requires the `cert-manager` to be installed first.
- Promscale has problems with restarts, so PV configuration is required.

Note 2:

Failure in the OpenTelemetry Collector due to unnecessary replicas being set up. Change this to `false`:

```
- "--metrics.high-availability=true"
```

Change `replicas` to 2:

```
replicas: 2
```

Install TOBS:

```
helm install tobs --wait --timeout 30m timescale/tobs -f values.yaml
```

Configure OpenTelemetry:

```
helm repo add open-telemetry https://open-telemetry.github.io/opentelemetry-helm-charts
```

Modify the OpenTelemetry Collector as shown here:

```
  otlp/promscale:
    endpoint: "tobs-promscale:9202"
    compression: none
    tls:
      insecure: true

  prometheusremotewrite:
    endpoint: "http://tobs-promscale:9201/write"

service:
  pipelines:
    traces:
      processors: [memory_limiter, spanmetrics, batch]
      exporters: [otlp, logging, spanmetrics, otlp/promscale]
    metrics:
      exporters: [prometheus, prometheusremotewrite, logging]
```

The Prometheus metric is not output to Promscale. The span is loaded. You need to add Prometheus to the collector.

Note 3:

TOBS's PostgreSQL is not initially connected, so the following settings are required.

CHAPTER 5 OPENTELEMETRY DEMO

Connect to Promscale:

```
$ kubectl get secret --namespace default tobs-tsdb-credentials -o jsonpath="{.data.PATRONI_SUPERUSER_PASSWORD}" | base64 --decode
gwAeYR9hsIGCYhCc
```

Here are the access accounts:

postgres/gwAeYR9hsIGCYhCc

psql log in:

```
RELEASE=tobs
kubectl exec -ti $(kubectl get pod -o name -l role=master,release=$RELEASE) psql
```

Run the query to see the Promscale table:

```
postgres=# show search_path
postgres=# select schema_name from information_schema.schemata;
      schema_name
------DOUBLEHY
PHEN------DOUBLE
HYPHEN------DOUB
LEHYPHEN--
 pg_toast
 pg_catalog
 public
 information_schema
 _timescaledb_cache
 _timescaledb_catalog
 _timescaledb_internal
 _ps_trace
 ps_tag
 ps_trace
 pg_temp_29
 pg_toast_temp_29
(36 rows)

postgres=# set search_path to ps_trace

postgres-# \d
        List of relations
```

```
 Schema | Name  | Type | Owner
ps_trace | event | view | postgres
ps_trace | link  | view | postgres
ps_trace | span  | view | postgres
(3 rows)
postgres-# select * from span
```

Note 4:

The current collector configuration has no remote writes. The OpenTelemetry demo's Prometheus outputs `calls_total` and `latency`, but the TOBS Prometheus does not.

```
metrics:
        exporters: [prometheus, prometheusremotewrite, logging]
```

The collector does not export to TOBS; it only transfers to Prometheus in the OpenTelemetry demo. You need to add the following:

```
prometheusremotewrite:
        endpoint: "http://tobs-promscale:9201/write"

    service:
      pipelines:
        traces:
          processors: [memory_limiter, spanmetrics, batch]
          exporters: [otlp, logging, spanmetrics, otlp/promscale]
        metrics:
          exporters: [prometheus, prometheusremotewrite, logging]
```

In Promscale, you can see that the `calls_total` and `latency` metrics are output.

```
prometheus:
        endpoint: '0.0.0.0:9464'
        resource_to_telemetry_conversion:
          enabled: true
        enable_open_metrics: true
```

You need to configure Jaeger queries:

```
---
# Jaeger Promscale deployment
apiVersion: apps/v1
kind: Deployment
metadata:
  name: jaeger
```

```
    namespace: default
    labels:
      app: jaeger
    spec:
      containers:
        - image: jaegertracing/jaeger-query:1.30
          imagePullPolicy: IfNotPresent
          name: jaeger
          args:
          - --grpc-storage.server=tobs-promscale:9202
          - --grpc-storage.tls.enabled=false
          - --grpc-storage.connection-timeout=1h
          ports:
            - containerPort: 16686
              name: jaeger-query
          env:
            - name: SPAN_STORAGE_TYPE
              value: grpc-plugin
---
# Jaeger Promscale service
apiVersion: v1
kind: Service
spec:
  selector:
    app: jaeger
  type: ClusterIP
  ports:
  - name: jaeger
    port: 16686
    targetPort: 16686
    protocol: TCP
```

Prometheus and Promscale are physically separated. The Prometheus remote write is used to load trace data into Promscale. Prometheus remote writes are implemented in the OpenTelemetry Collector and do not require configuration of a separate Prometheus server. Promscale belongs to PostgreSQL. The Grafana data source defines the PostgreSQL, and the data is available via a query.

5.3.13. Promscale SQL

For SQL-centric data analytics, Promscale is best.

Commercial observability does not use SQL, but provides a separate query language. SQL provides methods such as lookup and join. The data pipeline of observability processes columns in the order of lookups, adding columns, and joining. It is similar to a typical ETL pipeline.

Promscale can configure data searches, analytics, aggregations, machine learning, and AIOps in conjunction with Promscale. These are discussed in the next chapter.

The trace SQL being demonstrated is shown here:

- SQL for aggregation of request ratios.
- SQL for aggregation of the error rate.
- SQL for aggregation of latency.
- SQL for aggregation of service dependencies.
- SQL for aggregation of the upstream spans.
- SQL for aggregation of upstream and downstream dependencies.

SQL for aggregation of request ratios provides a general overview of the performance of the service and reveals common problems that may require attention. The queries are provided as Git.

SQL for aggregation of the error rate provides detailed data about the performance of a service so that you can quickly identify specific problems with that service related to throughput, latency, and error rate. The query is provided as a Git.

With SQL for aggregation of latency, the query is provided as a Git.

With SQL for aggregation of service dependencies, spanmetrics that calculate latency and service graphs that output impact are important data for troubleshooting performance problems.

The service graph helps you understand the problems that arise from calls between services and how they are processed.

As described previously, the demo created two types of service graphs.

- Cilium created a service graph centered on infrastructure and network.
- The OpenTelemetry Collector created a service graph of the application

With two types of service graphs, you can understand and analyze the impact and dependencies across microservices. Queries are provided as Git.

With SQL for aggregation of the upstream spans, an upstream dependency is a real-time service graph that includes upstream services. This allows you to quickly identify the impact of a failure in a particular service and see if an upstream service is causing problems in a downstream service.

CHAPTER 5 OPENTELEMETRY DEMO

```sql
-- nodes
WITH RECURSIVE x AS
(
    SELECT
        trace_id,
        span_id,
        parent_span_id,
        service_name,
        span_name
    FROM ps_trace.span
    WHERE $__timeFilter(start_time)
    AND service_name = '${service}'
    AND span_name = '${operation}'
    UNION ALL
    SELECT
        s.trace_id,
        s.span_id,
        s.parent_span_id,
        s.service_name,
        s.span_name
    FROM x
    INNER JOIN ps_trace.span s
    ON (x.trace_id = s.trace_id
    AND x.parent_span_id = s.span_id)
)
SELECT
    md5(service_name || '-' || span_name) as id,
    span_name as title,
    service_name as "subTitle",
    count(distinct span_id) as "mainStat"
FROM x
GROUP BY service_name, span_name
```

This is SQL for aggregation of downstream dependencies.

Downstream dependencies are service graphs that include downstream services in the overall service. They allow you to solve problems such as how downstream services and tasks affect the performance of upstream services. Queries are provided by Git.

Here are some things to consider when analyzing observability data using SQL:

- Metrics contain data from your infrastructure and applications.

- Create one table per metric. 100 metrics require 100 tables. Identify only important metrics and store them in Promscale. It is not easy to determine correlations and propagate failure between various metrics. Use a metric correlation algorithm.

- Trace SQL contains various performance, latency, and error data such as latency, error rate, and duration of the application. Trace is limited in scope since it only includes applications. Most alerts, dashboards, and SLOs use trace SQL.

- Use trace SQL for complex data analysis. You can get better results and accuracy than when using metric SQL.

- Promscale does not support logs.

I used trace SQL to output the state and aggregations of a simple application. You can use it to solve many of the problems you encounter when implementing observability.

- You need to identify the transaction and the specific section of the trace where the problem is occurring where span is not propagating correctly. Querying span directly is a great way to troubleshoot these problems. You can check for abnormal span counts.

- By querying the trace directly, you can determine the overall transaction and the state of the trace. SQL is useful for generating aggregations and statistics, which can be used to measure observability maturity and MTTR. By easily querying individual transactions, a variety of applications are possible.

5.4. Summary

This chapter described the new technologies that OpenTelemetry provides. There are many architects and developers who favor OpenTelemetry. It's important to understand that, while there are many advantages to OpenTelemetry, there are also many limitations. If you're looking to modernize complex IT operations with more than just logs and traces, improve your CMDB, leverage complex data, and automate with AI, there's only so much you can do with OpenTelemetry. It's better to modernize IT operations and improve root cause analysis as quickly as possible with all available solutions, without bias and without hesitation.

CHAPTER 6

Infrastructure RCA

6.1. Introduction

OpenTelemetry and commercial observability focus on application observability and only partially support infrastructure observability. Some APMs only support WASs (Web Application Servers) and specific databases. Even APMs that support E2E monitoring only support part of the application. I've personally thought about the need for alternatives many times, and this chapter describes many of the things I've thought about. I have implemented infrastructure observability using only open source.

So far, the book has focused more on application observability than on infrastructure. This is not to discount the importance of infrastructure, but rather because I believe that the right approach to observability is to start with the application in a top-down fashion.

- First, you need to configure application observability with E2E traces. Infrastructure observability takes longer to analyze and is more technically complex to resolve than application observability. It may provide fewer performance improvements than application observability, and it is more likely to fail because it doesn't identify the root cause. Nevertheless, if you don't fix the problem in your infrastructure, you run the risk of it recurring in the future. It puts you in a precarious position where you must always be careful and cautious in development and production.

- Developers and infrastructure teams are separated, and SREs are responsible for improving reliability across applications and infrastructure. When a failure occurs, it must be identified as an application-level problem. It cannot be assumed to be an infrastructure problem without higher level diagnostics. Considering a cost-effective approach, it makes sense to start with application observability to determine the root cause and, if possible, resolve the problem with application observability alone. If necessary, infrastructure observability should be used to perform root cause analysis. Saving money and time is important. By using profiles and system utilities around system traces, you should try to quickly identify root cause analysis that occurs in the infrastructure.

CHAPTER 6 INFRASTRUCTURE RCA

- Application observability calculates losses at a smaller scale than infrastructure, on a per-service or microservice basis. Applications are at the scope of a few pods, whereas infrastructure is at the scope of a million hosts, and infrastructure is at the scope of a large data center. If you can minimize latency and improve performance with infrastructure observability, that equates to a significant cost savings. Improving CPU utilization by 10 percent, or identifying and patching a bottleneck causing latency and saving half a second, doesn't just apply to individual microservices. It applies to every host in the entire data center, not just a specific cluster. For a data center that spends tens of billions of dollars over a few years, that means savings in the billions.

There's a lot of new terminology in infrastructure observability and it's important to understand it. Table 6-1 outlines this terminology.

Table 6-1. *Concepts in Infrastructure RCA*

Terminology	Description
System call	An action that enters the kernel space from the user space. System calls are located halfway between user space and kernel space and act as an interface.
User space	Linux categorizes resource access and execution permissions into user and kernel spaces. With user spaces: • The behavior and state of your applications are influenced by the code you write. • User applications run in user space and have limited access to memory space and no direct access to hardware.
Kernel space	With kernel spaces: • When kernel code is executed, it is possible to call methods inside the kernel. • Control your hardware with unrestricted access to memory space.
File descriptor	When you open a file, the kernel returns a file descriptor, and you must pass that file descriptor to the kernel when you run a file operation. Once the kernel has this number, it can find all the information about the file corresponding to that number and complete the file operation.
ftrace	Prints detailed kernel behavior, including interrupts, scheduling, and kernel timers. Displays the called method, call stack, and the process executing the method. Used for kernel debugging.
strace	Analyzes system calls. You can check the order and relationship of various system calls, such as `write()` and `read()`. Use `strace` if you suspect that your application is behaving abnormally.
tracepoint	Represents a hook for the event of interest. Representation of an event that can occur in many places in your code.

(continued)

Table 6-1. (*continued*)

Terminology	Description
eBPF	It can be used in production because it has less overhead compared to `strace` and `ftrace`, and it provides detailed profile information compared to system utilities.
BCC	It is a high-level profile framework developed for using eBPF. The BCC repository contains more than 70 eBPF tools for performance analysis and troubleshooting problems. You can install BCC on your system without having to write any BCC code, and then run the tools that come with BCC.
bpftrace	It is a new tool that provides an advanced language for developing eBPF tools. The relationship between BCC and `bpftrace` is complementary: `bpftrace` is ideal for simple but powerful one-liners and short, customized scripts, while BCC is ideal for writing complex scripts or daemon programs and can be used in conjunction with the library.

It is impossible to describe the system utilities, eBPF, and the Linux kernel in a single chapter. The purpose of this chapter is to describe an effective approach for successful infrastructure observability.

As shown in Figure 6-1, a service is composed of multiple layers, and the functionality of each layer directly or indirectly affects and propagates to other layers. Each layer has different errors. However, it's not always clear that each layer is an isolated error. This chapter does not discuss cluster-level rebalancing and sharding. I only discuss the kernel and infrastructure resources shown in Figure 6-1.

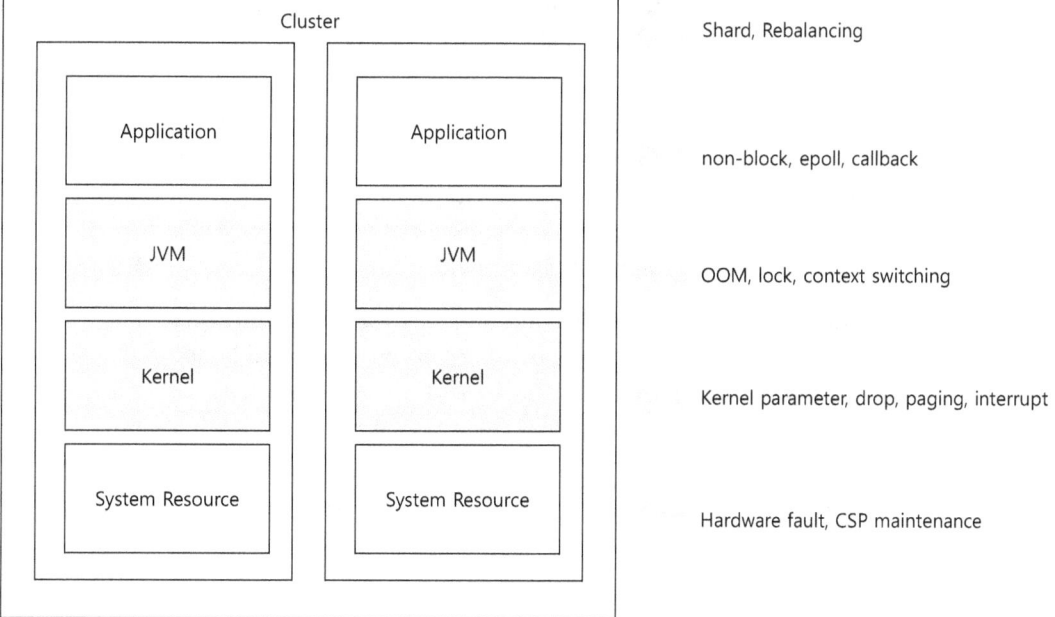

Figure 6-1. Types of failures by layer

CHAPTER 6   INFRASTRUCTURE RCA

Failures overlap and propagate. Bottom-up root cause analysis, starting with the infrastructure and working back to applications, is time-consuming. The infrastructure is better suited for long-term monitoring, but it can be expensive and inefficient due to unnecessary over-collection. Collecting all the signals without understanding them is not useful. In this chapter, you see how to configure infrastructure observability to reduce costs and aid in root cause analysis.

The signals of observability are buildable, like Lego blocks, and they can be connected to fill in the gaps. If you don't understand whether the problem is in the application or infrastructure, you need to be cautious in your troubleshooting approach. You should first try to identify the root cause analysis using application observability. Before I shift the perspective from application to infrastructure observability, consider system traces.

Unlike distributed traces, traces used by infrastructure observability are called system traces. Use KUtrace, `strace`, and `ftrace` to configure system traces. Infrastructure observability prioritizes system traces over other signals. It is possible to understand exactly where the problem occurred, collect various events from the kernel and system resources, and represent them as spans in the system trace. While conceptually similar to distributed traces, the implementation is different. To bridge the gap between distributed traces and system traces, services in applications and resources in infrastructure are conceptually distinct but correlated. By understanding the services in distributed traces and the resources in system traces, you can quickly perform root cause analysis.

Aside from system resources such as CPU, memory, disk, and network, it is important to understand Linux and Java. The Linux kernel is a popular OS. Many enterprise applications are developed in Java, and understanding the Java virtual machine is essential to identifying and solving problems. The Linux kernel is described in detail in this chapter, and the Java virtual machine is described in detail in another chapter. The Linux kernel and the Java virtual machine have similar internal process behavior and a similar approach to observability.

Failures that occur in higher-level services contain meaningful identifiers. The trace and request IDs included in the service help to reduce the scope of the problem. You can determine the propagation of the failure through the service map. Lower-level identifiers such as the thread ID and the file descriptor can be used to correlate the distributed traces of the service with the resources in the system traces.

There are four main aspects to infrastructure observability:

- **Align with application observability:** Understand the constraints and limitations of distributed traces. Traditional distributed traces output application-level information and lack information about lower level resources. You need to switch to infrastructure observability and use system traces. Use eBPF profiles for details that system traces do not provide. If you need to collect difficult bugs or failures at the system level, you should use system traces to analyze them, checking CPU, memory, storage, network, kernel, VM, framework, database, and applications, in that order.

- **The Linux kernel:** An understanding of the Linux kernel is important and you should be able to analyze various kernel parameters and system calls. If you are experiencing problems with system resources, use system traces such as KUtrace, `ftrace`, and `strace` to identify the areas and methods within the kernel that are causing latency. eBPF collects signals from the Linux kernel, providing more detailed lower-level observability than traditional signals. Develop `bpftrace` to easily write customizable BCC and one-liners using various languages. Use eBPF to measure the latency of methods and troubleshoot problems. Consider system traces and eBPF as a complement to existing performance utilities and as an alternative for easily understanding performance and latency. Compared to traditional utilities, system traces and eBPF make it easier to visually understand the results, and they can also output detailed information that traditional utilities may not be able to instrument. There is no problem with using existing utilities to configure infrastructure observability, but the problem with existing system utilities is that they have a high overhead. KUtrace enables system trace with low overhead. You can write multiple eBPF programs using shell scripts and Python and configure them to trigger only when certain conditions are met. This reduces the scope of the instrumentation or the number of calls. If an agent behaves like a daemon and has higher overhead than necessary, running the program in batches at specific points in time minimizes the load and impact on the system and allows you to analyze the cause using eBPF.

- **eBPF:** Supporting new infrastructures like containers and hypervisors, more complex networks, and multiple development languages is a challenge. It is necessary to identify latency and failures in complex infrastructures such as the cloud, hypervisors, and Kubernetes. System utilities provide detailed infrastructure information that observability can't provide, which can be very helpful in troubleshooting problems. System utilities often lack support for development languages, hypervisors, and containers so consider using eBPF as an alternative. While traditional system utilities are powerful and have many advantages, they are not well suited for root cause analysis of new technologies like Kubernetes. Even with commercial observability, observability of Kubernetes is difficult compared to traditional VM and containers.

- **Network:** In cloud and Kubernetes native environments characterized by microservices, the network is a single point of failure, and its failure is catastrophic. eBPF has particular strengths with network security. When a failure occurs in the network, troubleshooting it is complex and difficult. Using eBPF helps you quickly understand and resolve network failures. If latency occurs on a specific network segment, KUtrace can create system traces in the segment, and Cilium can generate a service map based on the network and help you understand the latency and problems between various services. L3 and L7 networks can be analyzed in detail in conjunction with the trace. `tcpdump` and `wireshark` can analyze packets and help you understand retransmissions and latency problems in your network.

CHAPTER 6   INFRASTRUCTURE RCA

6.2. System Traces

There are many system utilities available. Among them, I recommend the KUtrace, `strace`, and `ftrace` system traces.

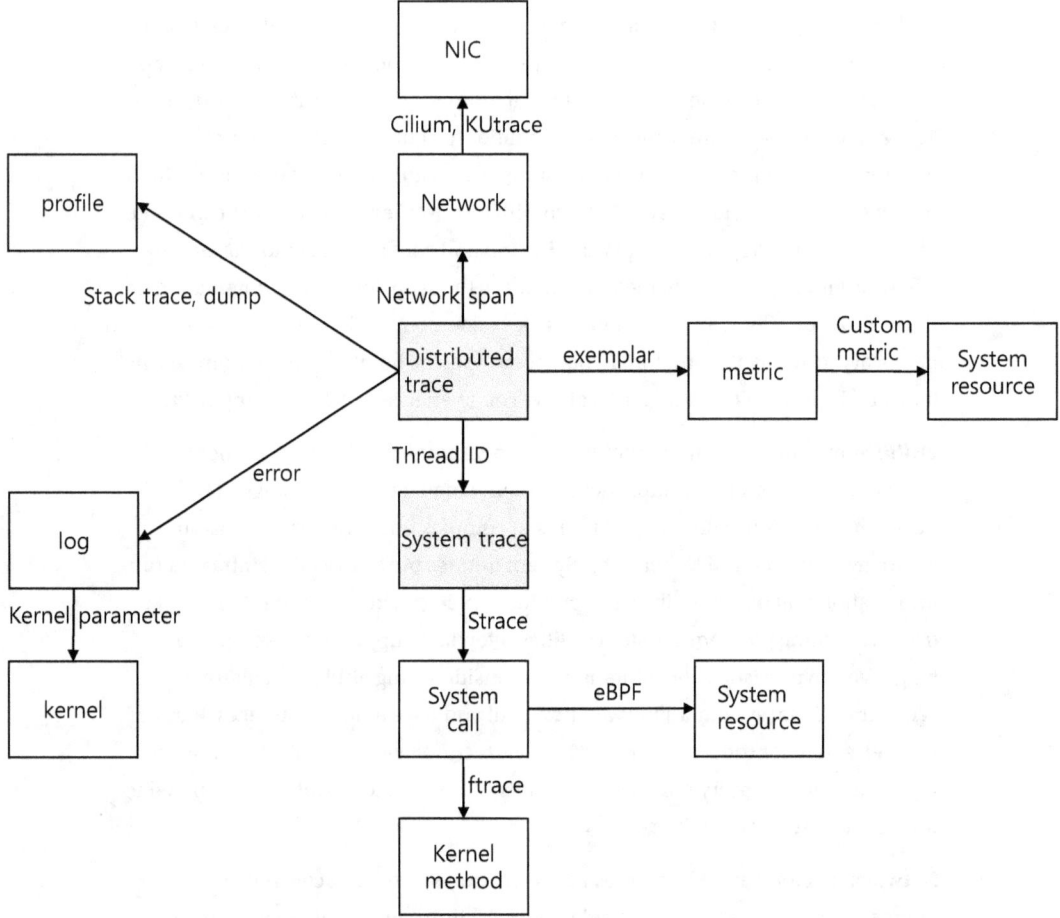

Figure 6-2. Relationship between two observables

To understand the various failures that occur at a low level, consider the competencies required of an SRE. Observability is not the domain of a few performance experts, and it's important to look beyond the single topic of performance to achieve the common goal of improving reliability. The SRE team alone can't achieve this goal, and it requires a collaborative effort from a variety of organizations, including developers, architects, testers, and operators. Observability is a framework that can include and unify this diversity. Observability is not only about technology, but also about being collaborative, automated, easy to use, and quick to perform root cause analysis.

CHAPTER 6 INFRASTRUCTURE RCA

Infrastructure observability can extend application observability, as shown in Figure 6-2, and it can identify root causes and suggest solutions.

The E2E trace described in this book means that the correlation between the distributed trace of the application and the system trace of the infrastructure is configured.

This chapter uses system utilities and system traces to augment the existing root cause analysis process and walks through the process shown in Figure 6-2.

Gray shows application observability and white shows infrastructure observability. I added the scope of infrastructure observability to the scope of application observability for which E2E traces are configured.

1. Use traces and metrics rather than logs to configure alerts.

2. If you experience latency and errors, trace them to identify the exact point where the problem occurred.

3. The metric should narrow down the scope of the problem. Overlap different metrics and analyze them as a time series.

    A. Infrastructure metrics analyze utilization and saturation according to the USE methodology.

    B. Analyze critical SLOs such as availability, throughput, latency, and error rate.

4. Microservices call each other, and failures propagate, so you need to understand the process between microservices.

5. Start application observability.

    A. Analyze the profile.

        i. Check the sampling of CPU, memory, IO, locks, and queries.

        ii. Analyze the stack trace for thread state, call frequency, and duration. Analyze thread dumps if necessary.

    B. Analyze the log.

        i. Analyze debugging messages and errors that are not printed to trace.

        ii. Most threads are not printed in trace. Check the log to see which threads are present.

6. Infrastructure observability analyzes metrics. Since it is difficult to perform root cause analysis using metrics alone, once a suspected problem is identified, you need to analyze system traces using KUtrace. Use system utilities to understand CPU load first.

    A. Before using `ftrace` and eBPF, use KUtrace to understand the process, latency, and events per section.

B. Determine the types of jobs that are causing the load. Analyze the ratio of CPU and IO processes. If the CPU ratio is high, analyze it in terms of CPU usage. If the IO ratio is high, you should look at the behavior and investigate the resources and IO involved. If the User and System resources are high, analyze the CPU.

   i. If the user space ratio is large, analyze the application and database.

   ii. If the kernel space ratio is large, analyze the system call and the kernel.

   iii. Identify the problem by looking at the CPU profile and the flame graph.

C. Next, analyze your network. Check the latency of each network segment.

   i. Analyze kernel parameters, such as retransmission, keepalive, and time wait, that correspond to the kernel network.

   ii. Analyze retries, timeouts, and more for microservices.

   iii. Use KUtrace to analyze latency by segment, `tcpdump` to analyze packets, and Cilium to analyze network metrics.

D. Analyze memory.

   i. Analyze full garbage collection and paging occurrences. Analyze memory dumps if necessary.

   ii. Analyze virtual memory, cache, memory settings, and more.

   iii. Analyze swaps, NUMA, and more.

E. Analyze the disk.

   i. Analyze operations that involve disk IO on files, such as merging, sorting, compressing, buffering, and flushing.

   ii. Analyze filesystem and disk IO.

F. If various resources fail to identify the problem, analyze the kernel.

   i. Use `strace` and `ftrace` to identify the methods in the kernel that are causing the latency.

   ii. Use eBPF BCC `funclatency` and `funccount` to determine which methods are causing latency. Use `bpftrace tracepoint` to measure the performance of methods and events and determine latency.

7. Complement infrastructure observability. Containers and hypervisors are difficult to analyze with existing system utilities.

    A. Check out the Kubernetes tools provided by eBPF and apply them.

8. Errors that occur in clusters are different from kernel and application errors. You need specialized monitoring tools from your vendor.

CHAPTER 6 INFRASTRUCTURE RCA

So far, I've built application observability based on E2E traces. This is the first step to successful observability and is technically critical. If distributed traces are broken, root cause analysis of infrastructure observability becomes difficult. Without infrastructure observability, application observability is limited. Even if distributed traces are successful, it is difficult to perform accurate root cause analysis without infrastructure observability.

If the application and infrastructure are disconnected and the correlation is not clear, root cause analysis is difficult.

By using distributed traces for application observability and system traces for infrastructure observability in combination with eBPF profiles and network observability, you can build observability that covers all systems in your applications and infrastructure. Using distributed traces with system traces such as ftrace and KUtrace is a good combination for root cause analysis and E2E observability.

The areas shown in Figure 6-3 are currently supported by observability. Other than the grayed-out areas, observability is difficult for distributed traces and logs.

Figure 6-3 is a single microservice, and it is normal to create about two spans. However, it creates one span and writes one trace context to the log. There are three kinds of threads in the log, but only one thread is being identified. At the lower level of the kernel, scheduling, interrupts, and IO are happening through system calls, but most of the information is not visible. Current observability only collects and monitors about 10 percent of the data. The goal is not to collect all the data and make it 100 percent. You need to understand the full scope and possibilities and be able to collect signals as needed for root cause analysis.

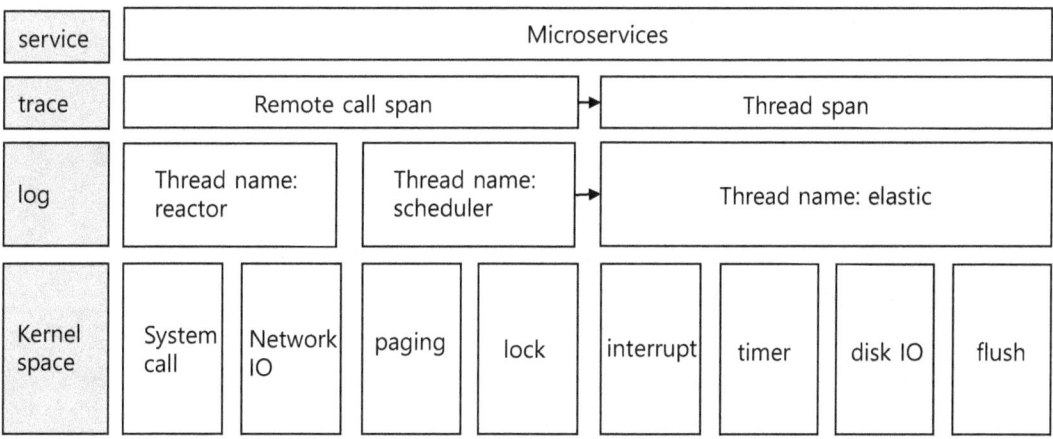

Figure 6-3. *Detailed process sequence for applications and infrastructure*

As shown in Figure 6-3, the limitations of OpenTelemetry and application observability are clear and need to be addressed. As shown in the banking trace example, the number of spans within a single trace ID can often be 300 or more. One span calls dozens of kernel methods. The number of kernel methods processed within a single span that processes external calls over the network can be in the dozens, which means that even if it appears as a single span in a distributed trace, it can be printed as dozens of spans in a system trace. As an SRE who needs to understand the internals of the system, you should be able to identify latency when a problem occurs in a specific method within the system.

CHAPTER 6   INFRASTRUCTURE RCA

You don't always need to enable system traces and collect spans because you need to save money. You can enable them briefly, only when a problem occurs, and you can apply system traces in a limited scope, not E2E.

6.2.1. KUtrace

KUtrace is open source and supports system traces. It also generates infrastructure-level spans. It captures all switches between the user space and kernel space, including all system calls, interrupts, and context switches, and it shows them with a timestamp. At 200,000 events per second per CPU core, the CPU overhead is less than 0.5 percent, which is about ten times faster than tools like `ftrace`. The recorded information is also written to the megabyte kernel trace buffer. You can check the latency of various system resources, including CPU, memory, disk, and network.

For each event, KUtrace records only four bytes. This includes a 20-bit timestamp and 12 bits of the event number, for a total of four bytes. To switch the trace into meaningful information, you need to do some post-processing, which shows what the core is doing every nsec. You can also use markers to manually add annotations to code in kernel space or user space.

- The user space library controls traces through a custom program.
- When you stop trace, the measured binary trace data is written to a file on disk.
- When this file is post-processed, the timestamped events are converted to their respective CPU core durations.
- The end result of the post-processing is a JSON file.
- In the final post-processing step, you load the JSON into a timeline for each CPU so that it can be converted into HTML, which provides the user interface.

KUtrace captures all events that occur separately by core ID and process ID and creates a span, which is helpful for root cause analysis. Markers can be used to add context, such as file descriptors.

Distributed traces and system traces have similarities, as explained here:

- Similar to the distributed trace, the KUtrace system trace breaks down the process and visually displays the spans where latency occurs.
- If distributed traces require you to understand what you're doing, system traces require you to understand the kernel.
- A system trace can identify in which section, latency is occurring. However, it lacks information about the kernel methods. It doesn't provide histograms of throughput and duration per method. The `bpftrace` program can be developed to fill in the gaps in the system trace.

6.2.1.1. Configuration

Installing and configuring KUtrace can be difficult for engineers who are not familiar with kernel compiles, patches, and the Linux module development. Use the following steps to install and configure KUtrace. Errors will occur in virtualized environments, so I recommend installing it on a host environment.

1. Upgrade the kernel to kernel 6.1.12 on CentOS 9.
2. Apply the KUtrace kernel patch from 6.1.12.
3. Install the module after applying the kernel patch.
4. Build KUtrace_control and postproc, for example.

Configure the required libraries:

```
yum install ncurses-devel redhat-rpm-config rpm-build openssl openssl-devel bison flex make gcc bc elfutils-libelf-devel bison flex dwarves
```

Copy the configuration file:

```
$ cp -v /boot/config-$(uname -r) .config
```

Save the kernel configuration:

```
$ sudo make menuconfig
```

Make additional settings:

```
$ scripts/config --disable SYSTEM_TRUSTED_KEYS
$ scripts/config --disable SYSTEM_REVOCATION_KEYS
$ scripts/config --set-str CONFIG_SYSTEM_TRUSTED_KEYS ""
$ scripts/config --set-str CONFIG_SYSTEM_REVOCATION_KEYS ""
```

Build the kernel code:

```
make -j4
```

Install the module:

```
sudo make modules_install
```

Install the kernel:

```
sudo make install
```

Restart 6.1.12 and verify the kernel:

```
$ uname -a
```

CHAPTER 6 INFRASTRUCTURE RCA

You need to make sure KUtrace is checked in your make menuconfig. Copy linux-6.1.12-patches.txt and apply the kernel patches:

```
patch -p1 < linux-6.1.12-patches.txt
```

Verify the results:

```
patching file arch/x86/Kconfig
patching file arch/x86/entry/common.c
patching file net/ipv4/tcp_output.c
Hunk #2 succeeded at 1400 (offset 3 lines).
patching file net/ipv4/udp.c
Hunk #2 succeeded at 970 (offset -7 lines).
Hunk #3 succeeded at 2455 (offset -7 lines).
root@ubuntu:/usr/src/linux-6.1.12# make menuconfig
```

Select KUtrace:

```
make menuconfig
```

Compile the code:

```
make -j4
```

Install the module:

```
make modules_install
```

Install the patched kernel:

```
make install
```

Restart and build the KUtrace module:

```
sudo make -C /lib/modules/6.1.12/build M=/root/software-dynamics/KUtrace-master/linux/module modules
```

Install the module:

```
sudo insmod kutrace_mod.ko tracemb=20 check=0
```

Check the module:

```
# lsmod | grep kutrace_mod
kutrace_mod            20480  0
```

Build the control and postprocessing:

```
cc -O2 kutrace_control.cc kutrace_lib.cc -o kutrace_control
```

CHAPTER 6 INFRASTRUCTURE RCA

Verify the results:

```
# ll
-rw-r--r-- 1 root root   1211 Nov 13 01:02 basetypes.h
-rw-r--r-- 1 root root    111 Nov 13 01:02 build_control.sh
-rwxr-xr-x 1 root root  53840 Nov 13 01:47 kutrace_control*
-rw-r--r-- 1 root root    908 Nov 13 01:02 scrape_syscall_linux.sh
```

Set permissions with chmod -R 777:

```
# ./build_postproc.sh
```

View the file you built:

```
# ll
-rw-r--r-- 1 root root   3714 Nov 11 05:25 base40.cc
-rw-r--r-- 1 root root   1211 Nov 11 05:25 basetypes.h
-rwxr-xr-x 1 root root    613 Nov 11 05:25 build_postproc.sh*
-rw-r--r-- 1 root root    693 Nov 11 05:25 build.sh
-rwxr-xr-x 1 root root  35560 Nov 13 02:01 checktrace*
-rw-r--r-- 1 root root  39801 Nov 11 05:25 checktrace.cc
-rw-r--r-- 1 root root 216467 Nov 11 05:25 d3.v4.min.js
```

To start a trace, use KUtrace_control:

```
./kutrace_control
```

At the prompt, type goipc<cr>, and at the next prompt, type stop<cr>.

- Go: Starts trace.
- GOIPC: Starts a trace that also includes the cycle-by-cycle instructions for each time span.
- GOLLC: Starts a trace that also includes the last level cache misses for each time span.
- GOIPCLLC: Uses IPC and LLC in alphabetical order here.
- Stop: Stops the trace and writes the raw trace binary to a disk file.

It should be visualized so that operators can understand the process and latency of system resources. It is difficult to build infrastructure observability with system utilities alone.

Once the trace is processed, you can generate the resulting file. For example, create the ku_20240709_152922_dclab-2_11686 trace file.

Use postproc3 to generate ku_20240709_152922_dclab-2_11686.json and ku_20240709_152922_dclab-2_11686.html.

```
$ ./postproc3.sh ku_20240709_152922_dclab-2_11686.trace "description"
```

CHAPTER 6　INFRASTRUCTURE RCA

You'll need to install additional libraries before compiling:

sudo apt-get install libpcap-dev

Build a user demo application:

./compile_all_user.sh

Verify that the demo application was created correctly:

```
# ll
-rw-r--r-- 1 root root     3728 Oct 28  2021 base40.cc
-rw-r--r-- 1 root root     1221 Oct 28  2021 basetypes.h
-rw-r--r-- 1 root root     3729 Oct 28  2021 disk_readhog.cc
-rwxr-xr-x 1 root root    28088 Nov 17 04:49 dumplogfile4*
-rw-r--r-- 1 root root     6689 Oct 28  2021 dumplogfile4.cc
-rwxr-xr-x 1 root root   102912 Nov 17 04:49 eventtospan3*
```

There are so many different types of problems that can occur with system resources and the kernel. KUtrace supports them, but it is not possible to describe them all in this book. To understand KUtrace in detail, I recommend Richard Sites' *Understanding Software Performance*. Richard Sites' papers and various lectures are also useful. In this book, you'll learn how KUtrace visualizes and prints out issues with CPU, memory, network, and disk.

A correlation must be established between system trace and distributed trace. There are three ways to correlate with distributed trace:

- Marker: Using the KUtrace library, you can add additional context.

- Thread ID

- RPC ID: The microservice uses HTTP. By using the parent protocol, you can monitor the child protocols as well. For example, if you test an HTTP endpoint, you can also monitor DNS, TCP, and RPC.

Markers and RPC IDs are implemented as Java agents, so they are configured to be injected automatically. It is also useful to configure them with the span attribute.

KUtrace outputs the following information:

- Start and end events of transactions (added by the RPC library)

- Normal execution: user processes, system calls, interrupts, memory faults, and idle loops on the CPU

- Slow execution: CPU clock frequency counts, IPCs, exits in a slow lazy state

- Freezes: Context switching, lock IDs (added by the lock library), and RPCs acting as a queue (added by the queue library)

- Various interrupts: Timer, disk, Ethernet
- Packets handled when sending and receiving on the network
- Wakeups and context switching handled by the scheduler

Contention, waiting, and interference can occur due to incorrect development, bugs, or incorrect system configuration. In development, only exceptions and errors can be identified, and contention, waiting, and interference are difficult to identify by debugging during development. This is because they occur in the process of processing transactions, consuming system resources. Bugs and defects are a serious type of root cause. Waiting and contention are always not problems; they can be a normal part of the process. If contention, waiting, or interference is frequent or prolonged, you should consider it abnormal and identify it, determine the cause, and resolve it.

In addition to the eight signals of observability, there are nine types of unusual root causes that can occur with system resources:

- **Exceptions:** Throw an exception or print a status code unambiguously.
- **Errors:** Either they are not exceptioned and become errors, or the program is unable to process normally and is forced to terminate. Errors can range from thread failures to kernel crashes.
- **Contentions:** Multiple threads trying to access a single resource, causing a delay.
- **Waiting:** A thread can resume from idle, or it can be unallocated and wait during scheduler and context switching.
- **Interruptions:** An unintentional interruption in the middle of processing, such as an interference.
- **Saturations:** The amount of queuing that cannot yet be processed.
- **Congestions:** A situation where the network bandwidth is exceeded or errors occur while processing a large amount of traffic.
- **Bugs:** Unknown software errors. Internal logic is implemented incorrectly, causing data inconsistencies. These might also contain functional errors.
- **Faults:** A failure can occur on outdated hardware or contain defective equipment.

The nine signals have nanosecond processing times, and some of them look similar, making it difficult and confusing to distinguish them accurately. But you should try to distinguish them.

If you don't handle exceptions, they can become errors. Exceptions and errors are the types of root causes that developers encounter.

System resources are used to saturation. Excessive loads that exceed NIC bandwidth is congestion, cache misses are waits, disk and Ethernet interrupts are interference, but in some cases they can be contention, or overlapping with queuing, delay. The types of problems are not always clear-cut and can sometimes be mixed. It is not important to clearly categorize the root cause, but rather to propose a comprehensive solution that takes into account the number of different cases.

CHAPTER 6   INFRASTRUCTURE RCA

While contention, waiting, and interference are most often delays, not failures, these root causes can cause retries and timeouts in an service.

How do you call root causes other than errors and delays when they occur? It's a good practice to call root causes precise counts and names of problems rather than unambiguous errors. It's true that root causes overlap and occur in parallel with sequences, making it difficult to distinguish between them, but if you don't have a clear distinction, you can't offer solutions. So you should try to define the types of root causes and distinguish them when they occur.

6.2.1.2. Waiting

Waiting is a type of delay, and it occurs not only on the CPU, but also on disk, network, and memory. Waits can occur for a variety of reasons, including scheduler, IO, and locking issues. The goal is to minimize the number and duration of unnecessary waits.

- On a hyperthreaded CPU, the only bottlenecks are the instruction patch, instruction execution unit, and cache and memory shared with the core. With a single thread, the bottleneck is only in the cache and memory shared with the core.

- If the child threads don't get a fair share of CPU time, or if the threads don't actually start at program startup, the program will delay.

- This is likely to include small delays due to all cores in the CPU being in use, delays in cores waking up from idle, or the nature of schedulers that are not perfectly fair.

Thread scheduling is an important topic. With KUtrace, you can measure the behavior of each CPU core every nsec that the kernel or user code executes. Measurements include user program and kernel code, all interrupts, and waiting loops. Not only does this capture all the duration it takes to process a transaction, but it can also explain why it is waiting instead of executing. The trace also includes page faults, kernel threads, and unrelated interrupts that cause long latencies that developers may not have considered. KUtrace is an effective tool for capturing the reasons why transactions are slow.

As you run the example, note the dynamic interaction between threads. Run a group with many child threads. The scheduler running on four cores will not do anything until there are at least five threads, so you can identify groups with five threads.

After the parent thread bash.3562 runs the child threads shedtest.3573, 3574, 3575, 3576, and 3577, it waits for all threads to complete before running the six threads on the far right in Figure 6-4. The CFS scheduler selects threads based on the number of active threads and CPU cores, as indicated by the small squares in Figure 6-4. However, contrary to what you might expect, it does not allocate time in a round robin fashion.

CHAPTER 6   INFRASTRUCTURE RCA

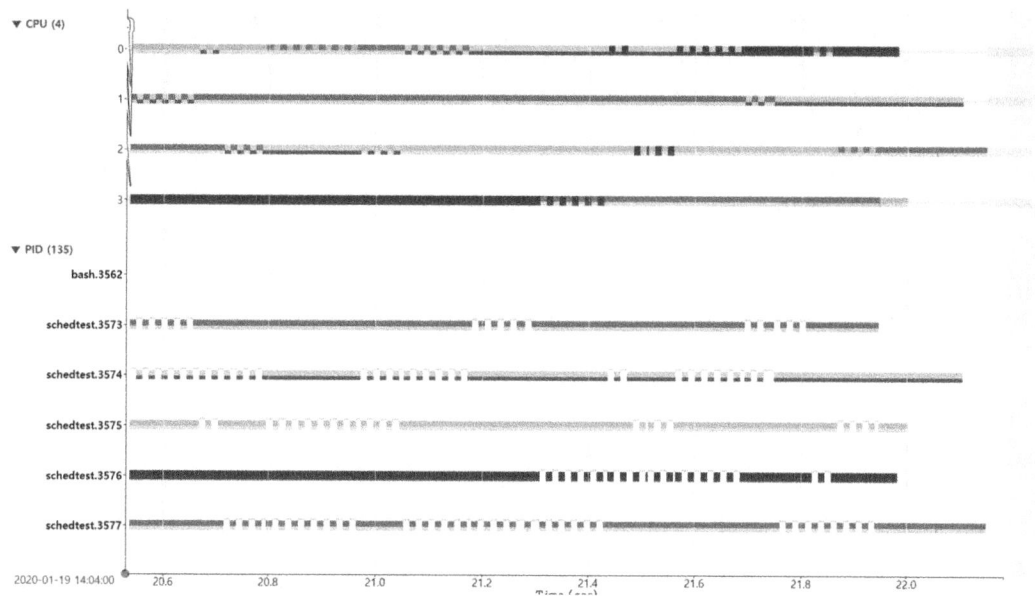

Figure 6-4. *Thread scheduling*

Some threads may be allocated time and then wait until the next time, while other threads may be allocated time repeatedly in succession before waiting. This pattern is not constant and varies each time the program runs.

At first, it looked like the five child threads would finish at about the same time. However, thread 3573 finished first, and thread 3577 finished last. The scheduling of five processes on four CPUs is not completely fair, and you can see the subtle differences in Figure 6-5.

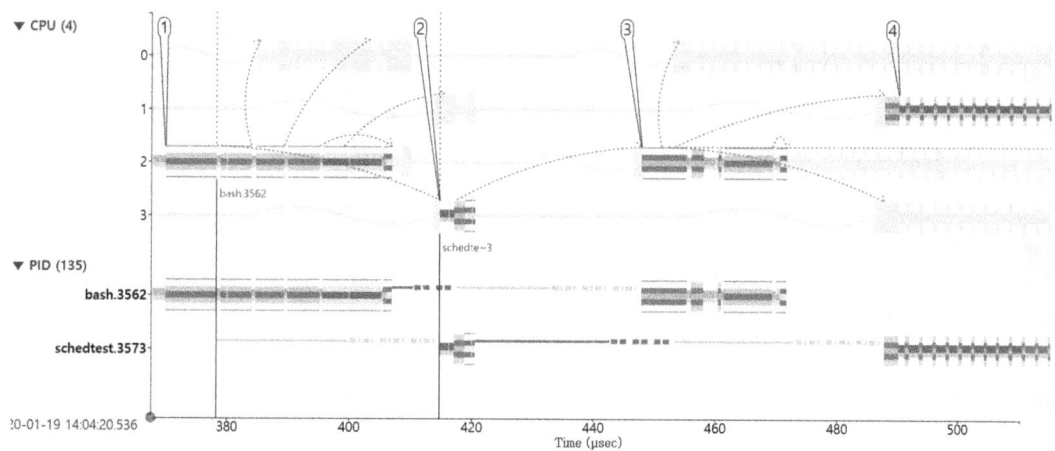

Figure 6-5. *Visualization of a clone call*

To create five child processes, the bash.3562 program calls clone five times, but the calls are staggered in time. In Figure 6-5, we are scheduling five processes on four CPUs, and we see process 3573 running three times in a row for 130 usec, with a latency of 30 usec.

All five child threads are not started at once, and the CPU idle time constraint is exceeded. The excess time is caused by the CPU cores taking longer to exit idle, which is also a problem with not running or running slowly. This shows the steps to run the first child thread, schedtest.3573.

The first four are executed in order on CPU 2, but the parent process is preempted by the fourth executed process. The parent process calls the fifth clone call on CPU 1.

Processing by the scheduler affects the cache as well as the CPU. It is necessary to understand how the CPU interacts with the cache:

- Thread A waits until it can be restarted on the same CPU core it was running on before. Thread A is briefly blocked and restarts from its cache. However, if Thread B runs on that CPU core while Thread A is blocked, Thread A must be restarted with a cold cache. If another CPU is idle while Thread A is waiting, the work-preserving scheduler might move it to that core to run.

- Moving Thread A from its old CPU core X to another idle core Y usually causes Thread A to experience a cache miss. If X and Y share the L1 cache, such as with hyperthreads, then moving Thread A to run on core Y is free and will always execute immediately. If X and Y do not share an L2 cache and instead share an L3 cache, the scheduler will have to wait roughly tens of usecs before moving thread A to CPU core Y. Due to context switching, the thread moves to a different core. The scheduler starts the thread. It reads the previously processed data from the cache. If the cache is shared, there is no problem, but if it is not, there is a cache miss (delay) and the thread is ready only after the data is initialized (delay).

- Idleness can also be ignored by the scheduler. The scheduler makes an autonomous decision, hence the CPU wait.

- CPU 0 and CPU 2 are on the same physical core, so there is no cold cache cost when threads move between them.

Context switching involves many tasks, including thread state management, blocking, idle state management, and cache management on resumption.

6.2.1.3. Congestion

Congestion is commonly used in networks. This involves waiting due to congested network hardware. Congestion occurs because traffic exceeds the bandwidth of a single Ethernet link on a client device.

- Delays can be caused by kernel or network hardware. You need to understand the delay between calling the kernel in user mode and receiving bits, or between bits arriving on the wire and being brought into user mode.

CHAPTER 6   INFRASTRUCTURE RCA

- Optimizations can be made to pass interrupts to the CPU core to forward packets to multiple ring buffers connected to different CPU caches. To handle high volumes of flow, interrupts signaling packet arrival are merged so that they occur less frequently.

Delays can occur in both transmitting and receiving. It is not uncommon to see slowdowns caused by network congestion due to outbound traffic outstripping line bandwidth. Why are transmissions, including both sending and receiving, delayed?

- There is a delay of about 200usec before an Ethernet interrupt occurs. This is because the BH:tx soft interrupt handler is trying to put more packets into the ring buffer.

- If there is no network traffic contention on the client, there shouldn't be a long delay before sending the request packet. However, there may be a delay before the packet arrives at the server and the NIC can issue an interrupt to the CPU.

- After that, you can observe the packets via tcpdump. The reason interrupts are delayed is to avoid overloading the CPU with a series of interrupts that occur faster than it can process. Instead of delaying interrupts, they are merged and packets are stacked so that the CPU can process them efficiently.

In production environments, programs are often allocated bandwidth and prioritized for transmission to reduce delays due to congestion. Congestion can cause packets to be reordered, retransmissions to occur, or packets to be dropped.

Interrupt delays can be improved by changing ethtool's rx-usecs argument and preventing nanosleep from misbehaving to reduce the time interval between RPCs.

Network sends and receives use a lot of resources and are processed internally in a complex way. Networks are a good place to illustrate the use of KUtrace. For example, a network that sends and receives with KUtrace applied looks like this, as shown in Figure 6-6.

1. The resource is processed by the user space client program.
2. The resource is processed by the client's kernel space code.
3. Over a network line.
4. The resource is processed by the server's kernel space code.
5. The resource is processed by the user space server program.

It should be possible to monitor applications in user space as well as in kernel space.

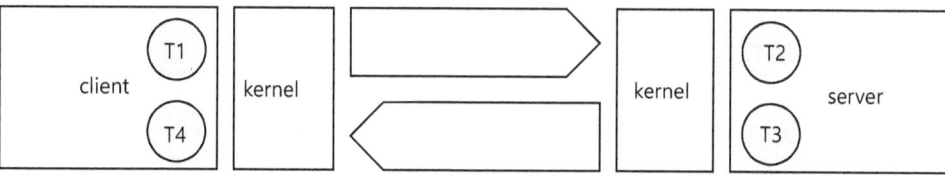

Figure 6-6. *The network process*

461

CHAPTER 6 INFRASTRUCTURE RCA

Latency is measured from T1, the time a user space client program sends a request, to T4, the time it receives a response. Latency can be caused by user code, kernel code, network equipment sending, or network equipment receiving.

With KUtrace, I explain to what level you can analyze network latency and processes.

- To describe the send process, a request travels through many layers of software and hardware to get from the client to the server. It starts in the user code, which calls the write() system call and runs the kernel's TCP/IP transport code to create a list of packets, which are inserted into a transfer queue. The packets in the queue are placed in a main memory buffer and transferred to the line where the transport network interface is the physical link.

- To describe the receive process, the receiving NIC on the other side puts the incoming packet into the main memory ring buffer and sends an interrupt to the CPU. When the hard interrupt routine is executed, it immediately processes the interrupt routine BH:rx and exits. Soft interrupt routines execute TCP/IP receiving code, such as system calls or calls to the recvform poll. The read system call passes the data to the user's code; without the read system call, the packet data is buffered in the kernel.

To investigate network performance impact, I use a timeline with times T1, T2, T3, and T4 to represent timing in Figure 6-6. Four timestamps are applied:

- Client user space
- Client kernel space
- Server user space
- Server kernel space

The timestamping process is detailed next. Outbound occurs on the client and inbound occurs on the server.

The client looks like this:

- Clients in the user space record timestamps.
- Outbound tcpdump timestamps capture a portion of an outbound packet and stamps it just before it is transferred. It is logged when the packet enters the transfer queue or ring buffer.

The server looks like this:

- Inbound tcpdump captures a portion of an inbound packet, receives it, and records a timestamp. When the code in the TCP/IP protocol processes a packet, it gives it a timestamp.
- The server in user space records timestamps.

CHAPTER 6 INFRASTRUCTURE RCA

There are two possible causes of latency in the network, as explained here:

- On client equipment, outbound packets may have to wait in a software transfer queue or wait in the NIC's hardware ring buffer for a while if the NIC buffer is full.

- On server equipment, a packet may be delayed by an interrupt for tens of usecs before the CPU is notified that it has arrived. Once the arrival of a packet is detected, the packet is held in the kernel's software queue for the purpose of merging interceptors, ensuring ordering, and other reasons. If network traffic is not congested on the client, the packet is not latched before being sent. The packet arrives at the server and can be delayed before the NIC issues an interrupt to the CPU. The reason interrupts are latched is to prevent the CPU from being overwhelmed by a series of interrupts that occur faster than it can process. Instead of latency, interrupts are merged and packets are stacked so that the CPU can process them efficiently.

KUtrace outputs the detailed process as described, and it can help you identify network latency at the low-level. It is useful for understanding system calls and system traces. It outputs the results of system calls in the D3 format.

For every event of a remote call that occurs between systems over the network, KUtrace creates dozens of spans. In the case of distributed traces, only one span for remote call is created, making root cause analysis difficult, but system traces create dozens of internal spans that belong to the one span of distributed traces. RPC IDs are generated for external calls, and root cause analysis is possible by associating them with the process IDs.

Using the example program, let's match the `tcpdump` time to the KUtrace time on each machine, then run the program and generate the results. Figure 6-7 shows the results for a typical 4KB sink RPC operation. The server's results are shifted by 7.17 msec to closely align with the client time. Network traffic is shown from CPU 0, with outbound messages (tx) coming from CPU 0 slightly upward, with the dashed lines showing the approximate spacing of the packets.

Inbound messages (rx) are slightly offset from CPU 0. The message can be multiple packets (3 for a 4KB request and 690 for a 1MB request), and only the first packet containing the message header contains the timestamp.

CHAPTER 6   INFRASTRUCTURE RCA

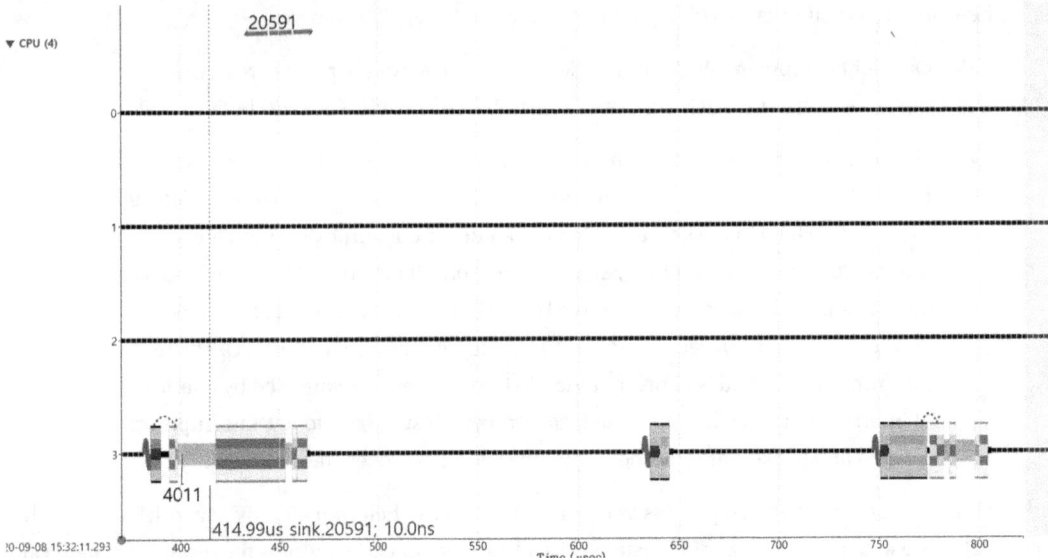

Figure 6-7. Monitoring sent client packets

The client records the timestamp of the KUtrace request in RPC 20591 in the first vertical line. And tcpdump records the timestamp of the first sent packet.

tcpdump is an application that collects events and visualizes them. On the right, tcpdump records the timestamps of the packets it receives on the second vertical line. KUtrace plots the response timestamps on the second sink vertical line. In the middle, you can see an Ethernet interrupt from CPU3, which processes a TCP ACK packet sent by a client not shown in Figure 6-7. The time scale in Figure 6-7 does not make it easy to distinguish the interval between packets from the client.

CHAPTER 6 INFRASTRUCTURE RCA

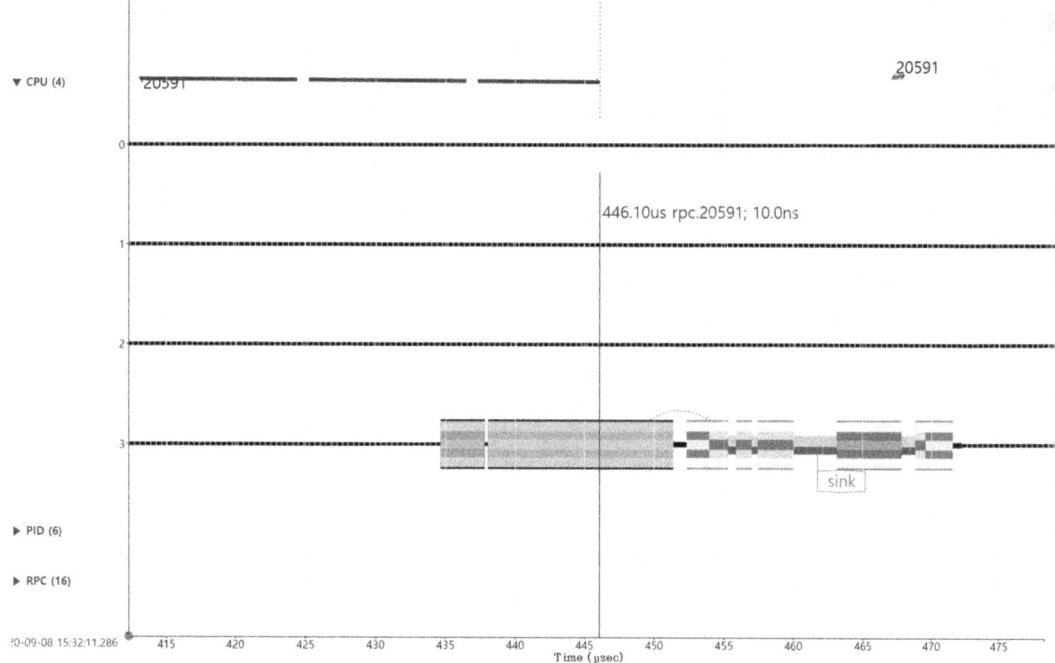

***Figure 6-8.** Monitoring received server packets*

Three request packets arrive from the server, the interrupt handler wakes up the server program, and then four vertical lines appear again. The vertical lines represent the timestamps of the received packets from tcpdump, the timestamps of the requests and responses from KUtrace, and the timestamps of the sent packets from tcpdump, respectively. There is also a TCP ACK packet on the far right of the server that is not shown in Figure 6-8. This packet is a response packet, and it is processed as an interrupt by CPU 3 at 600usec.

KUtrace collects and visualizes various events such as network packets, disk blocks, threads, and interrupts. These features of system trace compensate for the shortcomings of distributed trace and help you trace both applications and the infrastructure.

6.2.1.4. Saturation

When starting out with infrastructure observability, it makes more sense to use Prometheus rather than any system utilities. For example, the Prometheus node exporter is useful for Linux hosts, cAdvisor is useful for containers, and kube-state-metrics (KSM) is useful for monitoring Kubernetes.

Since you already understand utilization, this section discusses utilities that measure saturation. Saturation indicates waiting, which can lead to latency.

CHAPTER 6   INFRASTRUCTURE RCA

vmstat

The `vmstat` tool shows other system metrics in addition to CPU and memory. When run with an argument value of 1, the tool outputs a one-second summary.

The columns to check are the following:

- R: The number of processes running on the CPU and the number of processes waiting for their turn. This value is more useful than load average in determining whether a CPU is saturated because it does not include IO information. If the value of R is greater than the number of CPUs, it indicates saturation.

- Free: The available memory in kilobytes. If the number has a very large number of digits, it means you have plenty of free memory.

- SI and SO: Swap in and swap out. If these values are non-zero, you are out of memory.

- us, sy, id, wa, and st: A breakdown of the average CPU time for all CPUs. In order from front to back, these are user time, system time, idle, and IO wait.

iostat

This `iostat` tool shows the IO metrics of disk devices. Note that the output result column for each disk device is processed with line breaks, making it difficult to read. It includes the following metrics:

- r/s, w/s, rkB/s, wkB/s: The number of reads and writes delivered to the device and the KB read and written per second. These metrics can be used to characterize workloads.

- The average await IO time in milliseconds. This includes both the time the application waited and the time it took to process. If the average time is higher than expected, it may suggest that the device is saturated, or it may indicate a problem with the device.

- argqu-su: The average number of requests forwarded to the device. A number greater than 1 may be evidence of saturation.

- %util: Device usage. This is a percentage of business, showing how much time the device was working each second. It does not show usage from a capacity planning perspective because devices can work in parallel as requested. While it can vary by device, a reading above 60 percent typically indicates poor performance. A reading close to 100 percent indicates saturation.

In the kernel, latency is the time spent in the block layer scheduler queue and the device dispatch queue. Duration is the time from a request being made to the device until it is completed. This can include time spent waiting in queues on disk devices.

Latency is the total time from when the IO is inserted into the OS queue to when it completes. Latency is most important because if the IO were synchronous, the application would have to wait all of this time.

Disk utilization may be the most relevant metric for planning usage; for example, if a disk's utilization is close to 100 percent, you can assume you have a performance problem. However, disk utilization is the OS's calculation of the time the disk is doing something, and it doesn't account for virtual disks made up of multiple devices and queues on the disk. This can make disk utilization numbers misleading in some situations.

This includes when a disk with 90 percent utilization becomes capable of accepting workloads that far exceed the extra 10 percent. Utilization is still useful as a clue, and it's a metric you can always use. However, time spent waiting and saturation metrics are better measures of disk performance problems.

niostat

niostat is a network utility. This tool outputs network interface statistics and is designed like iostat.

It contains saturation-related statistics that combine error information. The -u option prints out read and write utilization, so you can see if either is reaching its limits.

6.2.1.5. Delay

Page faults are considered to be waiting to use memory.

- A runnable process waits to use memory. This is because the data the process wants to use may be paged out, and it may need to access a page table that is being accessed by another process.

- Before a memory allocation fails, the operating system starts paging out dirty pages, causing significant slowdowns and memory waits.

If the time is too long to be described as a simple wait, it is better characterized as a delay. It's not an IO, an instantaneous wait by the scheduler, but a long wait that is considered a delay.

A page fault is a type of interrupt, and context switching, timer interrupts, and disk interrupts occur before and after the page fault. When a fault occurs, the CPU is blocked or interrupted and waits. This is a delay.

The paging of the example program is paging_hog for 20 msec before the 177 chunks are fully disk-swapped to 178 chunks.

It occurs before 200 chunks (8000MB/40MB = 200) or 40MB memory allocations on an 8GB memory system. The trace shows that it starts right after allocating 177 chunks (7.08GB). The paging_~1 (paging_hog), shown on the left in Figure 6-9, runs on CPU 2 and causes 12,240 page faults, leading to a zero-page state. Then, in the middle, a swapping daemon called kswapd0 (kswapd0~0) starts on CPU 0. This daemon remains CPU-allocated for most of the rest of Figure 6-9.

CHAPTER 6   INFRASTRUCTURE RCA

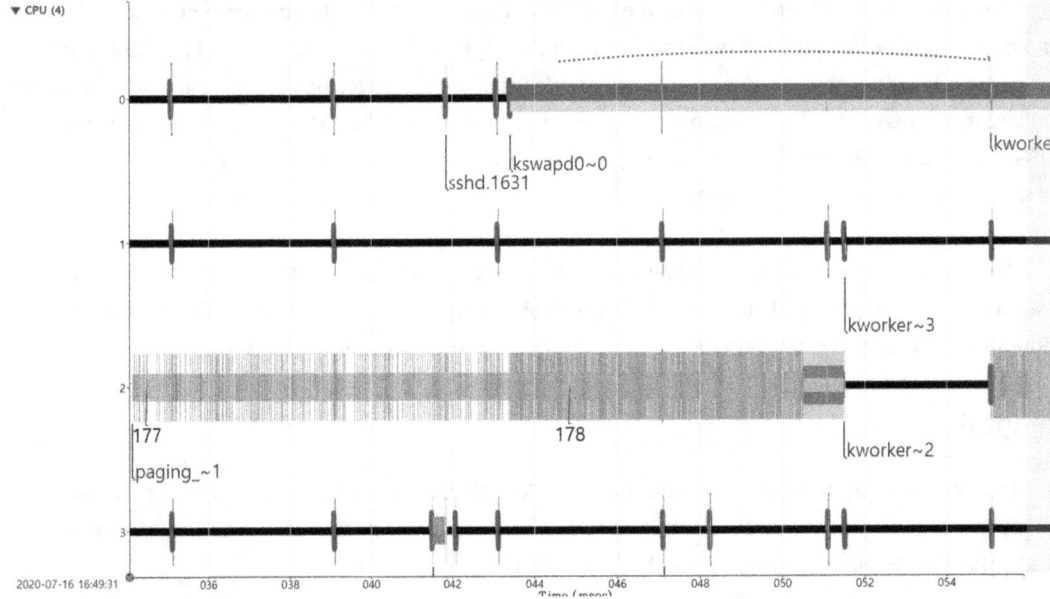

Figure 6-9. *The page fault process*

The main memory is not completely exhausted when kswapd0 starts, but there is not enough free space, so the swapper starts and tries to allocate ahead of when the memory is used. This is because the allocation of 178 chunks succeeds, causing 1240 page faults. Then a page fault occurs from 51 msec to 1 msec, and paging_~1 (paging_hog) stalls from 55 msec to 3.5 msec. There is no memory wait before the long page fault.

6.2.1.6. Interference

There are disk, Ethernet, and timer interrupts. Interrupts are classified as interference. IPC can help you understand when something is running slowly and provide detailed reasons for the interference between programs.

Different programs use different resources and therefore interfere differently. A program that is noticeably slow is probably using more than half of a shared resource. If two programs are using the same resources and bottlenecking, they can interfere with each other. If running multiple copies of the same program is not a problem, interference is unlikely.

Cycles per instruction (CPI) is an important measure that shows CPU utilization and how the CPU is utilizing its clock cycles. You can also use the inverse, which is IPC (instructions per cycle).

A high CPI means that the CPU is often delayed due to memory accesses. A low CPI means that the CPU does not delay and has high instruction throughput. These metrics show you where to best focus your performance tuning efforts.

Synchronizing disks: A process in a runnable state waits for disk access when it wants to write data that has not yet been delivered to disk or that can no longer be buffered in memory by the filesystem.

CHAPTER 6   INFRASTRUCTURE RCA

You can see how your code interacts with the OS, and you can also understand the disk itself. Figure 6-10 shows a complete sync operation. The example program calls the sync system call. This system call does not return until 900 msec has passed. During this latency, the disk interrupt, BH:block, occurs 60 times. These occurrences are very evenly spaced. It appears that one interrupt occurs per disk rotation, so there will be one occurrence per track on which a write was performed. The sync code in the example program executes only 12 times.

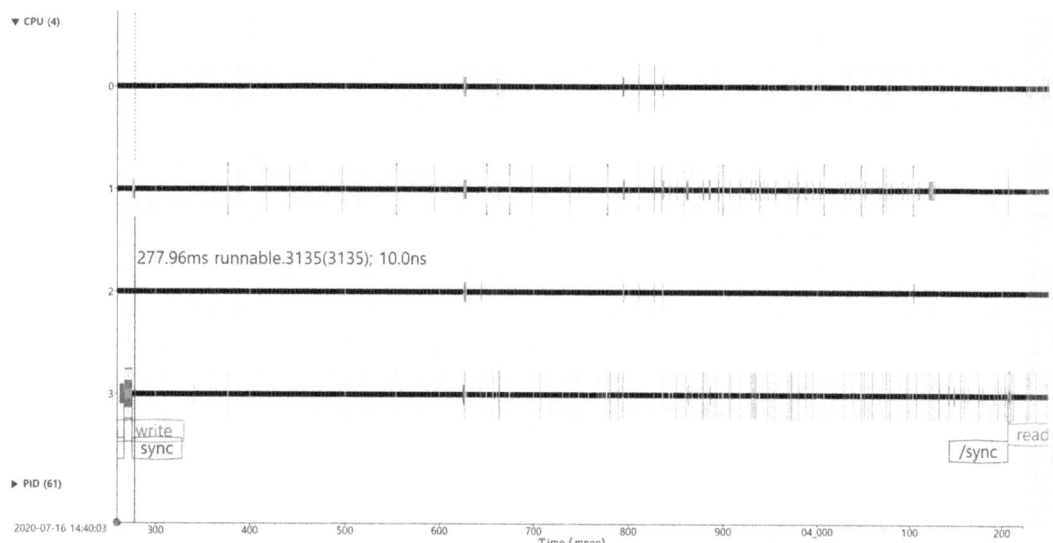

Figure 6-10. *The sync system call for synchronization*

These 12 times are not evenly spaced, as shown by the 12 vertical lines in Figure 6-10. The first vertical line marks the start of the SYNC system call, and the last vertical line marks the completion of the SYNC system call. The other ten times continue the SYNC but have unpredictable dynamic interactions, with more than 70 wakeup bursts.

Because the kernel filesystem buffers all data in main memory, the write system call must return a small number of msecs after it is called to modify the user's buffer. Next, the system call sync operation transfers the actual data to disk: one sync system call contains multiple disk interrupts. The rest of the time is spent sending IO requests to the disk hardware, to find the right location in the track buffer, make the transfer, and send the interrupt.

Disk blocks don't appear in the user buffer all at once at the end, but rather through the read system call. This is because of the time required to locate each block on disk. Block reads take seek time because the disk must be seeked before reading.

6.2.1.7. Contention

If you have a lot of interference, like with disks, you can make improvements as follows:

- By distributing interrupts across multiple CPU cores, you can achieve a higher transfer rate than if one CPU is the bottleneck, handling all the interrupts.

- In terms of CPU time spent on transfers, one core consumes about 1 percent of the total CPU time. Very little CPU is needed for IO processing.

- Running two programs in parallel takes more time than running them sequentially. This is because running two programs in parallel not only requires splitting a saturated resource in half, but also requires additional work to be done. In some cases, this means more seek, and in other cases, it creates additional work to refill cache lines or TLBs.

- Smaller transfers are devastating to performance.

- Sharing resources causes a steep slowdown. Small transfers and resource sharing should be avoided.

Lock contentions

Figure 6-11 shows the interaction of the contested lock, where thread 6736 holds the lock on the shared data indicated by the pink arrow, until it releases the lock at 525.15 usec and wakes up the waiting thread. The dashed line shows the wakeup behavior.

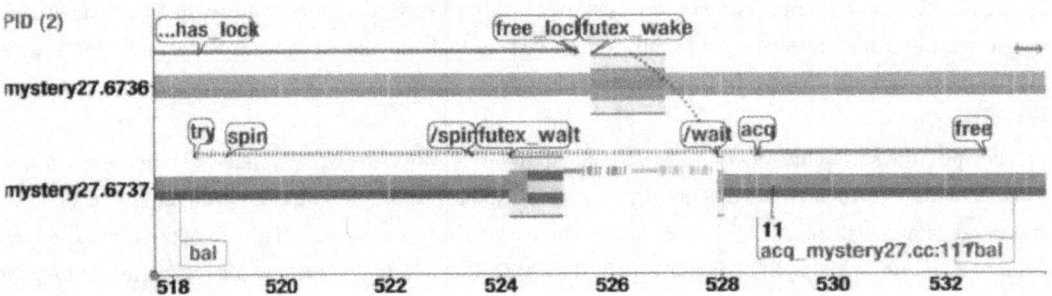

Figure 6-11. Lock contention

Thread 6737, in the bottom left of the figure, starts the Balance transaction. It tries to acquire a lock but fails because thread 6736 has acquired the lock, so it retries 5 usec later and is blocked by futux(wait). The yellow line shows the CPU waiting to be reallocated.

Lock contention refers to locks that are almost all contested, effectively preventing parallel execution. Rather than focusing on how many locks are held, I focus on how quickly a thread that was not holding a lock can acquire a lock. From a transaction latency perspective, the time it takes to acquire a lock is an important issue.

- The term *lock contention* means that there is almost always contention, and performance does not improve with multithreading.

- The term *lock capture* means repeatedly acquiring and releasing a lock before another thread can acquire it.

- The term *starvation* refers to a thread that is unable to acquire a lock for a long time, even if no other thread is holding it for a long time.

These three problems will almost always occur in a highly contentious locking system if you don't design for them. You'll end up with complex situations where interrupts and blocks occur together, or where contention, delays, and waits occur together. Over time, even lock systems that don't have many contentions tend to have more and more contentions.

System traces are useful for understanding where delays are occurring in a transaction, but they have limitations when analyzing methods within code or 99th percentile analysis. System traces can help you identify where delays are occurring, but you need to profile them in detail with BPF. BPF provides excellent profile capabilities that complement system trace.

If your environment is difficult to configure using KUtrace, consider ftrace. If ftrace is not available, use strace. If all else fails, eBPF should be considered, but if your organization has never traced system resources before, eBPF alone is not enough for root cause analysis. Clearly, there is a multi-year accumulation of unidentified and unresolved potential problems.

If observability is not organized correctly, root cause analysis is difficult. It relies on mere guesswork. Many organizations still use only metrics. There's a reason that metrics are not discussed in this book. Moving away from metrics is the beginning of improved observability.

6.2.2. ftrace

KUtrace is recommended if possible, but if the conditions are not met, ftrace should be used instead. ftrace also provides powerful trace capabilities.

KUtrace does not support all OSs, and there may be compatibility problems with the Linux version. If you are using a GPU in addition to a CPU, it is useful to use ftrace.

I use ftrace to identify the event and method that is causing the latency.

You should understand the output of strace to trace system calls and ftrace to trace kernel methods and be able to identify them in your code.

- Check the system call number and identify the methods that are processed in kernel space and user space.

- You can identify the kernel code being processed by the ftrace event and method name.

Utilizing `ftrace` and `strace` can provide useful debugging information in these cases:

- When you want to verify that a system call has been properly raised in user space
- When a system call occurs in user space and you want to check if the system call handler has been executed in kernel space
- When you want to check the arguments passed to a system call handler and the error message when the system call handler is executed

The `ftrace` event name tells you what code inside the kernel is outputting the event. sched event can see the behavior of the process being scheduled:

- `sched_switch`: Context switch behavior
- `sched_wakeup`: Behavior to wake up a process

The name of the method that outputs the `ftrace` for each event has the following format:

`"trace_" + "ftrace event name"`

For example, the `sched_switch` event outputs information about the scheduling of a process when the `trace_sched_switch` method is executed.

To search for code that outputs a `sched_switch` event, search the kernel code with the keyword `trace_sched_switch`. You can find the `trace_sched_switch` method in `core.c`.

```
static void __sched notrace __schedule(bool preempt)
{
    struct task_struct *prev, *next;
    unsigned long *switch_count;
    unsigned long prev_state;
    prev_state = prev->state;

    next = pick_next_task(rq, prev, &rf);
    clear_tsk_need_resched(prev);
    clear_preempt_need_resched();
    trace_android_rvh_schedule(prev, next, rq);
    if (likely(prev != next)) {

        ++*switch_count;
        psi_sched_switch(prev, next, !task_on_rq_queued(prev));
        trace_sched_switch(preempt, prev, next);
        /* Also unlocks the rq: */
        rq = context_switch(rq, prev, next, &rf);
    } else {
        rq->clock_update_flags &= ~(RQCF_ACT_SKIP|RQCF_REQ_SKIP);
        rq_unlock_irq(rq, &rf);
```

```
        }
        balance_callback(rq);
}
```

The __schedule() method outputs the scheduling behavior of the process. From this, you can see that the context switch is processed when the __schedule() method executes the context_switch(rq, prev, next, &rf) method.

To use ftrace, you need to modify the value of Kernel hacking > tracers through menuconfig and rebuild it. If, during the KUtrace installation, you compiled the kernel and installed a new kernel, you can use ftrace without any additional configuration.

Events and methods in the kernel code are structured according to naming conventions. Understanding these conventions makes it easier to understand the code and solve problems quickly.

ftrace provides the following events to trace the behavior of a system call.

- sys_enter
- sys_exit

Using ftrace, you can collect these events. You need to enable the sys_enter and sys_exit events using the following commands.

```
echo > /sys/kernel/debug/tracing/set_event
sleep 1
echo "set_event"

echo 0 > /sys/kernel/debug/tracing/tracing_on
sleep 1
echo "tracing_off"

echo nop > /sys/kernel/debug/tracing/current_tracer
sleep 1
echo "current_tracer nop"

echo 1 > /sys/kernel/debug/tracing/events/raw_syscalls/sys_enter/enable
echo 1 > /sys/kernel/debug/tracing/events/raw_syscalls/sys_exit/enable
echo "syscalls event enabled"

echo 1 > /sys/kernel/debug/tracing/tracing_on
echo "tracing_on"
```

Run this command to collect the event of the system call.

Run the following command to create an ftrace log.

```
#!/bin/bash

echo 0 > /sys/kernel/debug/tracing/tracing_on
echo "ftrace off"
```

CHAPTER 6 INFRASTRUCTURE RCA

```
sleep 3

cp /sys/kernel/debug/tracing/trace .
mv trace ftrace_log.c
```

You can see the system calls in the ftrace log.

The system call starts with the message sys_enter. When a system call occurs in user space, the execution flow changes to kernel space, and the system call handler calls a kernel method. Depending on the type of system call, internal kernel methods are called. After completing this process, ret_fast_syscall is executed to return to user space. The sys_exit message prints the ftrace log at this point.

This section explains how to check the system call number. NR 120 message means the system call number. NR 3 message means that system call number 3 has been executed.

```
#define __NR_read  (__NR_SYSCALL_BASE + 3)
#define __NR_clone (__NR_SYSCALL_BASE + 120)
```

The system call handler methods corresponding to 120 and 3 are named unistd-common.h.

You can find it in the header file.

```
SYSCALL_DEFINE5(clone, unsigned long, clone_flags, unsigned long, newsp,
        int __user *, parent_tidptr,
        unsigned long, tls,
        int __user *, child_tidptr)
```

Note that the system call handler is the sys_clone() method. Check the following ftrace message and the arguments seen in the method declaration.

```
sys_enter: NR 120 (1200011, 0, 0, 0, 76F81046, 0)
```

The system call handler for system call number 3 is the sys_read() method.

```
SYSCALL_DEFINE3(read, unsigned int, fd, char __user *, buf, size_t, count)
{
    return ksys_read(fd, buf, count);
}
```

Check the following ftrace message and the arguments seen in the method declaration.

```
sys_enter: NR 3 (1200011, 0, 0, 0, 76F85214, 0)
```

Most system call handler methods are created with the convention sys_. You can see that the system call handler for the read() method called from user space is the sys_read() method.

There is a lot of information generated by ftrace, which can be difficult to understand and analyze. Therefore, you can use open source tools for monitoring and visualization ftrace to improve your understanding of complex ftrace system calls. One such recommended tool is traceshark. Figure 6-12

CHAPTER 6 INFRASTRUCTURE RCA

shows its user interface. It includes a graphical viewer for ftrace and Perf events that can be captured by the kernel. It visualizes the following events:

- cpu_frequency
- cpu_idle
- sched_migrate_task
- sched_process_exit
- sched_process_fork
- sched_switch
- sched_wakeup
- sched_rface of traceshark

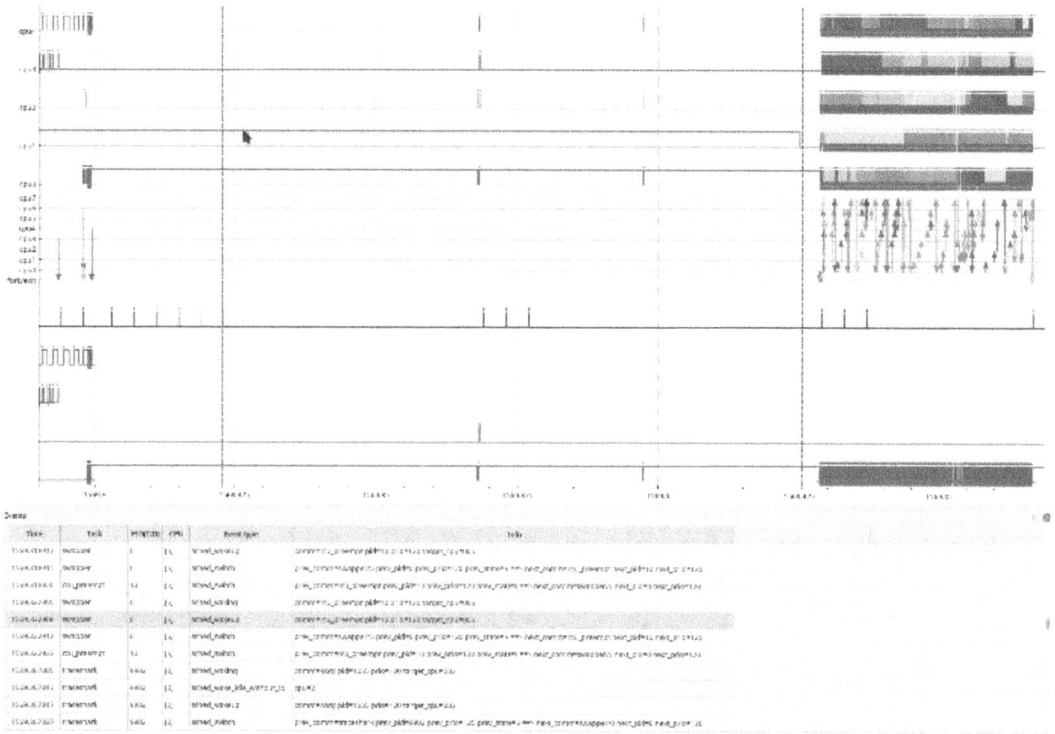

Figure 6-12. The traceshark UI

- wakeup_new
- sched_waking

CHAPTER 6 INFRASTRUCTURE RCA

Important events are cpu_frequency, sched_process_fork, sched_switch, and sched_wakeup. Perfetto is also a useful trace visualization tool.

6.2.3. Kubeshark

Kubeshark is a service map. For detailed latency measurements on different network segments in Kubernetes, kubeshark is useful. See Figure 6-13.

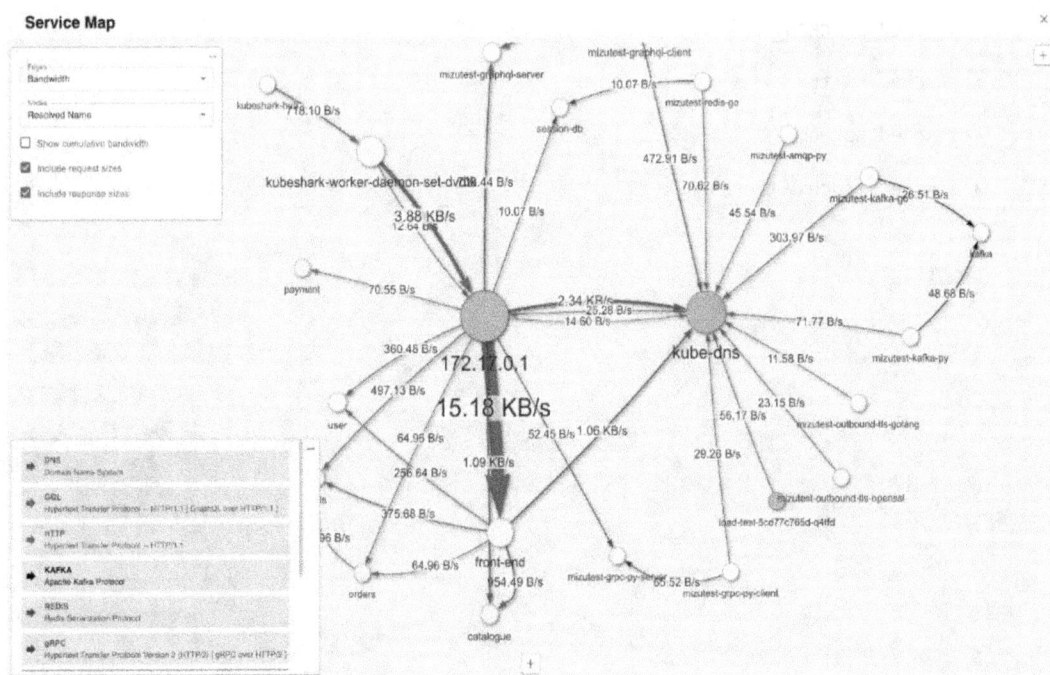

Figure 6-13. The kubeshark UI

Rather than using Kubeshark and traceshark, you should understand how to use them in the process of root cause analysis and utilize them as an important part of the big picture of observability.

6.2.4. System Utilities

The requirements of observability as defined in this book are that developers and business analysts can collaborate together. System utilities are useful for root cause analysis, but when used frequently, they are difficult to collaborate with and automate, and are not well suited for AIOps and anomaly detection. However, observability suffers from a lack of infrastructure and detailed system information, so system utilities compensate.

CHAPTER 6 INFRASTRUCTURE RCA

This section describes the process for root cause analysis using system utilities. Important system utilities include stack traces, CPU, network, Java, and system traces, each of which is discussed next.

Collecting stack traces:

- `jstack(pstack)`: Collects stack traces. This allows you to identify the threads that are causing the problem and determine the cause.

CPU:

- `vmstat`: Allows you to understand the overall health and load of your system. It also provides information about the CPU and other IO, such as memory and disk.

- `lsof`: Provides information about the files that generate disk IO.

- `perf`: Included in the Linux kernel, it is a CPU profile tool. It provides a variety of performance measurement techniques. It shows the number of events, high-impact methods, and event values on a per-method basis.

- `mpstat`: A command that provides detailed information about each CPU core, useful on multi-core systems.

- `top`: This is a command that prints information about the currently running process.

    - `us`: This shows the CPU utilization in user space, which is the part where applications on the kernel that use system calls run. This value may increase when the application is running and the actual implementation uses a lot of CPU.

    - `Sy`: CPU utilization in kernel space. The `sy` value increases in environments where context switches occur frequently or there are many forks. The `sy` value may increase if the web application and middleware use a lot of CPU processing. For example, web servers such as Apache HTTP Server and nginx can quickly process encryption and decryption of AES, which is widely used as a TLS encryption algorithm in HTTPS connections, on the CPU. Using this can increase the `sy` value because the kernel processes more on servers that create and delete many HTTPS connections.

    - `Ni`: Each Linux process has a priority. Use the `ps` command to check the nice value, which indicates which process should be switched to the priority. In a heavily loaded daemon process, performance can be reduced to allocate CPU resources to other high-priority processes. The nice value is the priority value referenced by the scheduler.

    - `Id`: This is the percentage of CPUs that are not being used. When you want to know the approximate utilization of the CPU, refer to the value obtained by subtracting the idle value from 100, which is the sum of the other values.

Chapter 6 Infrastructure RCA

- If the thread is not processed in a multi-threaded manner, the process cannot perform other processing until the IO processing is completed. WA indicates the CPU utilization of a process that is waiting for IO processing on a disk within the process.

- Wa: A high wa value indicates that there are many processes waiting for disk read and write operations to complete. When operating a web application, you should change the design so that the disk is not read and written or make changes to reduce reading and writing as much as possible.

- ST: is a value that indicates the CPU utilization rate used in a virtualized environment. The CPU recognized by the VM is a virtual CPU created by virtualization technology, and it processes the operation using the CPU resources on the host side only when physical CPU resources are required. However, since the host OS also uses the context switch to run the process, CPU resources may not be allocated when the VM is needed. If multiple VM are assigned to the same CPU core, the presence of a process with a high CPU load in a VM will affect the performance of other VM. The value that represents this is "available but unallocated CPU time."

Network:

- `netstat`: Monitors the currently open sockets and their status. You can determine the status of connections between local and external addresses.

- `nslookup`: Sends a query to a DNS server and outputs the IP address and other information for that domain.

- `tcpdump`: Allows you to analyze packets. Use with `wireshark`.

Java:

- JSTAT: Analyzes your garbage collection.

- JMAP: Collects Java heap memory.

System traces:

- `strace`: Analyzes a system call.

- `ftrace`: Analyzes kernel methods.

- KUtrace: Supports system traces and generates spans for infrastructure observability.

Supporting and collaborating with alerts and dashboards is important. `strace` is difficult to visualize, while `ftrace` can visualize health information similar to a time series. System utilities have unclear thresholds, and alerts are difficult to define. For infrastructure observability, it is difficult to understand thresholds, and it is useful to utilize alerts within anomaly detection.

The term *system trace* is not a standard term in the IT industry, but the traces used in infrastructure observability are called system traces.

- strace traces a system call and writes it as text to stderr, a file. Depending on how many system calls are called, the overhead can be high. strace may be better suited for inspecting programs offline rather than in real time.

- ftrace provides the ability to trace kernel methods, which means it is used for debugging the kernel. It is not designed to look at interactions with user programs, but it is useful for analyzing kernel activity.

- ftrace is powerful, but when very large amounts of data are logged, it significantly reduces the overall system speed. There is a lot of CPU and memory overhead, so be careful. It is useful for finding kernel bugs in an offline environment.

Trace technologies such as strace, ftrace, and stack trace have a high overhead if used incorrectly, so they should be used with caution in production and limited to troubleshooting. For this reason, eBPF is an alternative. It is useful to identify methods with strace and ftrace in a development environment, and use eBPF in production to trace the latency of methods and measure their performance. To distinguish the functions of the tools, strace and ftrace are traces, and eBPF is a profile. It's not a good idea to start with profiles when doing root cause analysis. You need to narrow down the scope of the problem, which is difficult and time-consuming with profiles. You need to use all traces to understand the problem in segments. You need distributed traces of application observability, which I've already discussed, but there are no similar traces for infrastructure. That's why this book describes system traces.

Various perf, sar, and vmstat system utilities are provided for a high-level understanding of performance.

First, be sure you understand CPU usage, then analyze other resources in turn. vmstat measures the system, user, IO wait, and idle metrics. Typically, User is high, but if System is higher than 30 percent, it is best to analyze the system.

6.2.5. How the Kernel Works

The Linux kernel provides most of the system utilities, and you can use them to debug your system. You should know the method call flow and data structure of the application as it works.

- Information about which processes and threads are running the method
- The latency, distribution, throughput, and execution time of a method

In a distributed trace, it is output as a single span, but in a lower level kernel, there may be multiple calls. To understand the results of system traces, and to understand the root cause of your infrastructure, you need to understand the Linux kernel. When an error or failure occurs, you need to be able to identify the root cause.

CHAPTER 6   INFRASTRUCTURE RCA

You should be able to identify what is output to the system trace and profile. KUtrace outputs the following concepts as spans:

- Unusual calls to methods inside the kernel
- Kernel synchronization
- Schedulers that process context switches
- Interrupts
- System calls
- Thread state
- Timers
- NUMA

If you're having problems with any of these targets, you're likely experiencing latency.

Without a basic understanding of these targets, it is difficult to understand the results of system trace and profile and identify latency. Various system utilities such as KUtrace and eBPF are just tools to identify latency, but without understanding the concept, successful infrastructure observability is difficult.

Thread state, context, and scheduling are important concepts that are used in the kernel, VM, and Reactor frameworks. The kernel is complex, but it is the foundation of the VM and server frameworks. Understanding the kernel will make it easier to understand the Java VM described later. I want to emphasize that while it's important to understand the application technology, like Java Reactor, it's equally important to understand the underlying technology, like the kernel and virtual machine.

6.2.5.1. CPU and IO

When disk processes IO, no CPU intervention is required. While the disk is processing IO requests, the kernel is scheduling the CPU to perform other tasks.

For example, CPU and disk IO runs as explained here:

- The CPU starts Thread A, and requests disk-related IO, such as reading a file.
- Since disk IO is very slow compared to CPU speed, Thread A cannot proceed until the IO request is finished processing. At that point, Thread A stops running.
- The CPU is allocated to Thread B, which is in the ready state. Thread B starts running.
- The disk starts to process the IO requested by Thread A.
- The CPU and disk both process their work independently. When the disk finishes processing the IO request, the CPU continues to execute Thread A.

The tasks executed by IO and CPU are two independent tasks with no dependency on each other, so they can be processed in parallel. Understanding the load is a prerequisite for root cause analysis. You can use various system utilities to understand the load. For example, you can use `vmstat`.

When monitoring CPU usage, it is measured separately for System, User, IO Wait, and Idle. The approach depends on the utilization of each segmented area.

- **System:** CPU usage for system calls in kernel space. System calls are methods related to process control, device management, file and network management, input and output processing, system information and time management. Generally, system utilization is less than 30 percent of the total usage, so if you see high system utilization, use system call monitoring tools and stack trace tools. You can check what types of system calls are occurring in which code.

- If system utilization is high, you need to analyze the system call. The system call outputs the process and thread IDs and a file descriptor.

    - Using the thread ID, you can understand the relationship between lower-level system calls and the application's stack trace. To do this, use the `strace` system call monitoring tool and stack trace tools such as `jstack` and `pstack`. OpenTelemetry trace does not provide stack traces, but commercial observability provides stack traces within traces.

    - The network and file processes generate file descriptors. In blocking calls, thread and file descriptor information is simple, but non-blocking calls create multiple threads, which complicates understanding the relationship of file descriptors.

- **IO Wait:** A process or thread has been allocated a CPU and is ready to use it, but is currently waiting for IO to complete and is therefore unable to use the CPU. Once a thread is blocked and off-CPU waiting for an event, the thread typically returns to the CPU only when a wakeup event occurs. In the example of disk IO, a thread may be blocked from a filesystem read operation that generates IO, and that thread is later woken up by a worker thread that processes a completion interrupt. This is not actual CPU usage, but rather the amount of CPU that is unavailable due to waiting for IO, which is roughly less than 20 percent of CPU usage. Therefore, if you see a high IO Wait percentage, you may have an excessive amount of IO or disk utilization as a problem.

- If IO Wait is high, analyze other resources other than CPU, such as disk. If you suspect that the problem is not at the application level, but at a lower level of the infrastructure, you need to take a cautious approach. This is because infrastructure problems are hard to narrow down, broad in scope and subject matter, difficult to assign a cause, and time-consuming to resolve. You should start by looking at IO Waits and performing a detailed analysis of the load, excluding CPU.

CHAPTER 6   INFRASTRUCTURE RCA

- **User:** This is the CPU usage used to run general methods other than system calls. For Microservices or database servers, it is normal for User CPU utilization to be higher than other parts of the stack. To examine the potential for improvement, you can use the CPU profile tool to identify the threads in a process with high CPU utilization and collect the stack for analysis.

- If User is high, the problem is likely in the application. After identifying the busy processes and threads, you can use profile to analyze them. If the profile is not enough, you should use system utilities.

6.2.5.2. Processes

Linux is divided into user space and kernel space, and the two spaces are connected through system calls in the middle. Processes running on Linux can be broadly categorized into user-level processes and kernel-level processes

- **User processes:** With the help of a library (glibc) that creates processes in user space, you make a request to the kernel to create a process.

- **Kernel processes:** Create a kernel process by calling the kthread_create() method inside the kernel.

When you create a process, you call the _do_fork() method. When you call the fork() method in user space, you request the kernel to create a process with the help of a library provided by Linux. When the Linux-provided library code is executed, it raises a system call, and the Linux kernel layer calls the sys_clone() method, which is the system call handler for the fork() method.

- The user-level process calls the fork() and pthread_create() methods in user space. With the help of the glibc Linux library file, it requests and creates services from the kernel.

- In order for a user-level process to request any service from the kernel, it must execute a system call.

- Kernel-level processes run in kernel space. You can create a process by calling the kernel's kthread_create() method.

6.2.5.3. Kernel Data Structure

The kernel contains many structures. Understanding the structure helps you understand the process of the kernel.

Structures that store process attribute information and execution flow are important. For the data structure that manages processes, the object is called a task descrubber and is represented by the task_struct structure. This structure stores attribute information such as memory resources used by the process, process name, duration, the process ID, and the address of stack.

Execution flow of a process is the stack space, which contains the thread_info structure at the top address of the stack. Each process has its own stack, with one thread_info structure per process. It stores detailed execution information about the process, such as:

- Contextual information
- The set of registers that were executed immediately prior to scheduling
- Process detail runtime information

The difference between the task_struct and thread_info structures are as follows:

- The task_struct structure stores attributes for CPU architecture-independent process management.
- The thread_info structure stores detailed attributes of the process that are dependent on the CPU architecture.

Different CPU architectures have different implementations. Each CPU architecture requires a thread_info structure. For example, if a call fails on a manufacturer, you need to be able to understand it down to the thread_info structure level to solve the specific CPU problem.

For example, a thread takes less time to perform a context switch than a process. This is because threads share address space for file descriptors, files, and signaling information with other threads in the process to which they belong. Unlike a process, which has its own address space, a thread shares an address space with other threads in its thread group. However, from the kernel's perspective, threads are managed equally with other processes.

6.2.5.4. Stack Traces

The stack traces provide details about the running processes. In the stack trace, you can see the resource usage and duration of methods by process and thread. You should analyze the most resource-intensive processes and methods first. Processes and methods that consume fewer resources and make fewer calls are likely not a serious problem. The processes that use the most resources are more likely to be causing the problem, and fixing them will have the greatest impact.

The output of the stack trace is complex, but understanding it is important for root cause analysis.

The stack trace has thread ID (LWP_ID) information, and the system call also has thread ID information, so you can analyze the application and system call together. For example, if you find a thread that is using too much CPU, you can see what the thread is doing in the system call monitoring, and in the stack, you can see what the thread is doing and what method code it is executing.

A run-queue is a scheduling data structure that manages processes running on a CPU in order to become executable.

Before a process can run on the CPU, it must be inserted into a run-queue. The scheduler calculates the priority among the run-queued processes and selects the next process.

Using stack trace and system utilities, you can determine which processes are taking up CPU and how many processes are currently waiting in the run-queue.

CHAPTER 6 INFRASTRUCTURE RCA

The scheduler frequently accesses the run-queue data structure to check the list of processes waiting to be executed and to check process information related to scheduling. Thus, the run-queue manages and stores the overall information about the execution flow of processes on a Linux system.

This is because the run-queue data structure provides a list of processes that are waiting to run, as well as a list of processes that are running and taking up CPU.

The useful information in a stack trace is the state of the thread. This can help you understand what the thread is processing at that point in time. For example, in Java, threads have different states, as shown in Figure 6-14.

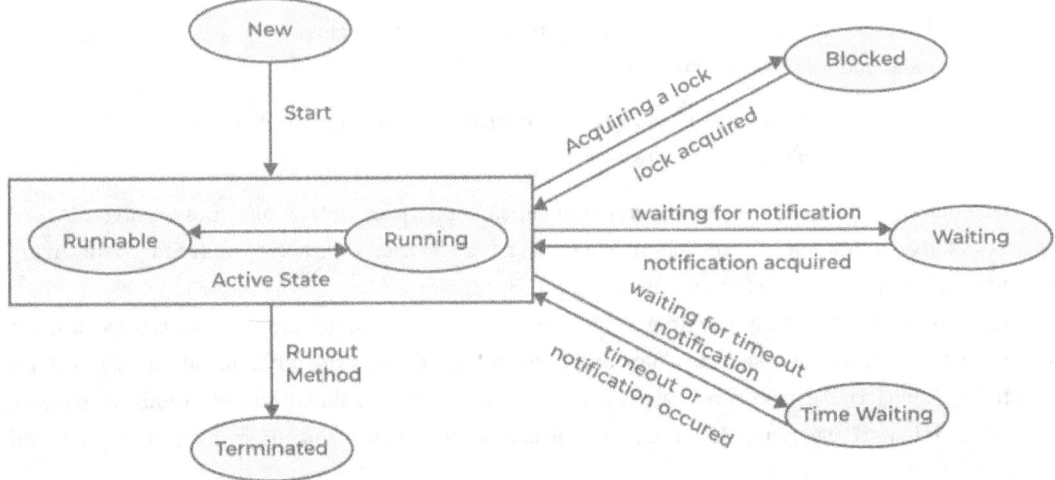

Figure 6-14. *The flow of switches in Java thread state*

In the case of Java, after being inserted into a run-queue, there are two types of processes in the TASK_RUNNING state: those that are waiting to run, and those that are running and occupying CPU.

Waiting to execute and running are different states, but Java only prints TASK_RUNNING and does not print thread state in detail. Different languages have different thread state models, and there are more than ten thread states observed in lower level kernels than Java. Implementations vary, and there are differences between virtual machines and kernels. There are many different kernel and many different VM, so you have to understand the differences.

The process is created and then changes to the TASK_RUNNING state, inserting itself into the run-queue. The scheduler selects the highest priority process from the queued processes and runs it on the CPU.

In order to occupy CPU, it must first change to the TASK_RUNNING state, which means it becomes a candidate process for execution. It is inserted into the run-queue to be selected by the scheduler.

Failure Case 1

The most problematic thread states are RUNNABLE and BLOCKED. WAITING can also be a problem, but since WAS is mostly configured as a thread pool, it is mostly in WAITING when there is no request on WAS.

Infinite loops and unresponsive external storage, such as SQLs, have one thing in common: they continuously occupy one thread. The difference is whether the CPU is occupied or not. An infinite loop occupies the CPU at full, while waiting does not occupy the CPU, but the RUNNABLE state is maintained, causing the problem of running out of threads or running out of available connections to the database connection pool.

If a thread's state is RUNNABLE for an extended period of time, it is suspected to be abnormal. If a large number of threads are RUNNABLE for a long period of time without taking up CPU, the service might crash due to lack of available threads and connections. You need to find the cause of the prolonged RUNNABLE state. It could be internal, but it is more likely to be external, such as downstream microservices becoming unresponsive or SQL responses being delayed.

While it's possible that some of the stack in the socket read state is actually reading the data it received, it's more likely that socket programs are using wait I/O, waiting for another server or process to finish processing. After an application requests the other party to process data, it immediately calls the socket read method to receive the results of the process and waits within the socket read method for the response. Therefore, if you see a lot of processes or threads in the socket read state, you can assume that the other process or server is making long or frequent calls.

The wait caused by waiting for another process to process will eventually have to be reduced, either by improving the duration within that process, or by calling it less frequently.

Failure Case 2

The API server uses a thread pool. If a downstream goes down due to failure and there is no appropriate timeout, the API server's thread is RUNNABLE and waits for a response from the downstream. If a new request comes in, the API server can't spawn a thread and process the request. Resources remain and utilization is low, but threads are exhausted and service becomes impossible. This can happen if the IO Wait is high, the number of RUNNABLE threads is high, or there are many unnecessary waits.

If you see a lot of BLOCKED states and high latency, suspect a lock. You should analyze the stack trace and system calls.

Thread ID and time information should be included in the output so that you can measure performance on a per-thread basis. During low traffic times, WAS threads are often in the WAITING state. It is abnormal if resource usage is low and there are many WAITING states during high traffic times.

6.2.5.5. System Calls

The foundation of Linux debugging is understanding how system calls flow from user space to kernel space. System calls describe in detail who makes them, when they happen, and how they work.

A system call is executed when an application running in user space requests some service to the kernel. A user application requests a service the kernel in the following situations.

- When you want to access the filesystem to read or write to a file
- When you want to get process information, such as the PID
- When you want to get system information

To do this, you raise a system call, moving the execution flow from user space to kernel space.

You can debug the detailed behavior of a system call with `strace` and `ftrace` to see the detailed arguments and return values when it is executed.

To properly understand system calls, you need to look at the entire flow from user space, where the system call is issued to kernel space and where the system call handler is executed.

- User applications need to call the `open()`, `write()`, and `read()` methods to access the filesystem to open, write and read files, or the `fork()` or `exit()` methods to create or terminate processes. When you call a low-level method on a Linux system, the assembly code inside the GNU C library is executed. This results in a system call.

- When a system call is executed, it moves into kernel space and accesses the system call table. From the system call table, it branches to the system call handler method corresponding to the system call number. The system call handler methods that are called depending on the system call behavior are as follows.

  - Virtual filesystems: `sys_open()`, `sys_write()`, and `sys_read()`

  - Create and terminate processes: `sys_clone()` and `sys_exit_group()`

The kernel's system call handlers work like this:

1. While executing a system call in user space, check for errors in the arguments passed to it. This is because an application developer in user space may incorrectly pass arguments to a system call.

2. Depending on the type of service requested from user space, kernel internal methods are called.

3. Return the information requested by the user application in a format such as a string, or return the requested type.

6.2.5.6. File Descriptors

UNIX and Linux use something called a *file descriptor* when using sockets or files, and looking up a process's file descriptor usage can give you a better understanding of the process by showing you what servers the system is networked with and what files it's working with.

For example, if the handshake is successful on the webserver, you can call the `accept` method to get the connection, which you can further obtain as a file descriptor. Once you have the file descriptor, you can use it to communicate with the user.

If there is no file descriptor available, the thread is blocked and suspended.

It is not known in advance whether the I/O device corresponding to a file descriptor is in a readable state. It is inefficient for developers to implement this logic themselves to manage file descriptors. This functionality is provided by the kernel, which uses I/O multiplexing to tell you when a file descriptor can be read and written.

CHAPTER 6   INFRASTRUCTURE RCA

To obtain a file descriptor provided by the kernel, follow these steps. The type of file descriptor can be network-related or file-related.

- Call a specific method and request an available file descriptor from the kernel.
- The method returns the available file descriptor.

There are three techniques for doing this: select, poll, and epoll.

- While poll has an unlimited limit of 1024 file descriptors, it has the problem of degrading performance as the number of file descriptors increases.
- epoll has a list of file descriptors ready to go, and it passes the list of file descriptors to the thread.

When network-based API servers and microservices interact with database servers or other systems, there are many file reads and writes. In the case of WAS or web servers, there are failures due to the lack of file descriptors, such as not being able to connect to the network or not being able to open files. In those cases, you can get the following useful information by looking up the file descriptor.

- Current usage relative to file descriptor value
- Determine if the file descriptor setting needs to be increased
- File descriptor usage type statistics

If you find that you are using file descriptors unnecessarily, or are using them a lot, you should modify your settings or program.

On Linux, file descriptor information can be found in the /proc/pid/fd and /proc/pid/fdinfo directories, where the status information of each process is managed. The file descriptor status of a process can be queried with the lsof command.

Because stack trace information and file state information are point-in-time information, if a file is opened and closed instantaneously rather than continuously, the state information may not be accurate, and the number of reads and writes may not be known. To get this information, you need to monitor the system calls that occur in network and files. Thread ID information can categorize system calls by thread, so you can understand which server or file operation took a long time.

- If it is a threaded program, analyze it by thread ID.
- When monitoring network and files, focus on file descriptors.
- When analyzing failures, it is important to know the return value of the method and whether an error occurred, so analyze the thread ID and file descriptor together.

The system call doesn't indicate which server the network connection it's processing is connected to. For file operations, if you have already opened a file before monitoring, you won't know which file it is. This is because when performing a system call, the network and file processing methods work with file descriptors. When you open a file, you are given a file descriptor, and then you perform file operations such as reading or writing with the file descriptor value.

CHAPTER 6   INFRASTRUCTURE RCA

If a file was opened before the system call was monitored, you can't tell which file it is because you only see the file descriptor value in the monitoring results. If you use a command like `pfiles` to view the network and file status of a process, you can get additional information, including the filename, hostname, and port number of the file descriptor value.

6.2.5.7. Scheduling

CFS is a scheduler that tries to execute processes that are waiting to run as fairly as possible based on their priority. To understand the details of how CFS works and its algorithms, it is important to understand the following concepts

- Time slices
- Prioritization

CFS gives each process a unit of time to run, called a time slice. A time slice is an OS term for a duration granted to a process by the scheduler. A process is context switched when it has exhausted its given time slice.

The main reason for managing processes with time slices is to give all processes that are waiting to run a chance to run on the CPU as much as possible. Without time slices, it would be difficult to manage the execution units of processes.

From a scheduler's perspective, a time slice is a unit for managing the duration of a process. When a process exhausts its time slice, the scheduler marks it as a candidate for preemptive scheduling. A process that is marked for preemptive scheduling is context switched.

Priority is one of the criteria by which the CFS scheduler selects the next process at context switch. The CFS scheduler processes high priority processes as follows:

- The first thing it does is run it on the CPU.
- Allocates many time slices.

Preemption scheduling is a method of interrupting processes running on a CPU to allow higher priority processes to run on the CPU. By managing process execution with preemption scheduling, higher priority processes wait less often, which can increase the overall responsiveness of your system.

The scheduler compares the priority of Process A with the priorities of Process B. If it determines that Process B has a higher priority than Process A, it frees Process A from the CPU and runs Process B on the CPU.

When the kernel initiates preemptive scheduling:

- After interrupt handling: After running an interrupt handler, before returning to the process that stopped running.
- After system call handling: After processing a system call method before returning to user space.

6.2.5.8. Context Switches

Scheduling and multitasking techniques in Linux kernel arose because a CPU can only run the code of one process at a time. The software module that manages multiple processes and gives them rules so that they can run on the CPU in an efficient alternating order is called a scheduler.

When a process starts running on a CPU, it doesn't run on the CPU continuously; it runs, stops, and starts again. The process occupies the CPU, constantly switching between running and waiting to run.

The process of selecting a process to run on the actual CPU from among the many processes that exist in memory is called scheduling. The scheduler decides which process to select and in what way. For example, it selects one of the processes that is in the waiting-to-run (TASK_RUNNING) state and puts it in the CPU-running (TASK_RUNNING) state.

Scheduling refers to the criteria or algorithm that replaces a currently running process with a new one, and it works independently of CPU architecture.

On the other hand, context switches behave differently on different CPU architectures. This is because a context switch removes the process currently running on the CPU and populates it with a new process to run.

Context refers to the state information in which a process is running. The term context switch means to change the context.

The context first refers to the process itself, which the process is running. When a process runs on a CPU, a set of CPU registers are populated with details about the method it is currently executing. The register set that contains the details of the process execution is itself the context.

A context switch is an action that frees a process running on the CPU and allows a new process to run on the CPU. It is the scheduler's job to choose which process to run next based on priority.

Suppose you have a Threads A and B, and Thread A is currently running

- When a timer inside the system generates an interrupt signal, the CPU receives the interrupt signal and pauses the execution of the current thread.

- Next, you switch from user space to kernel space and start running the program that processes timer interrupts in the kernel.

- The program that processes the timer interrupt determines if the CPU time slice allocated to Thread A has been used up, and if there is time left, it returns to user space and continues execution.

- When Thread A's time slice is used up, the CPU should be allocated to Thread B.

Thread A and Thread B can belong to different processes, and the address spaces of the different processes are different.

The CPU is switched from Thread A to Thread B, and the main part of this operation involves saving the CPU context information of Thread A and restoring the CPU context information of Thread B.

Every Linux thread has a corresponding process descriptor, the task_struct structure, and the thread_struct structure within it is responsible for storing CPU context information.

CHAPTER 6 INFRASTRUCTURE RCA

When the CPU switches from Thread A to Thread B, it first stores the CPU context information of the running Thread A in Thread A's descriptor, and then restores the context information stored in Thread B's descriptor to the CPU.

6.2.5.9. Kernel Synchronization

A critical section is a block of code that, if executed by more than one process, can cause a concurrent access problem. The beginning and end of a specific block of code should be executed by only one process.

Suppose Process A is in the middle of executing code, and Process B is executing the same block of code. This can be considered a situation where A and B are approaching the critical section at the same time. This situation where two or more processes are executing code in a critical section at the same time is called a race condition.

To ensure that only one process executes the critical section, you should lock the critical section to prevent race conditions.

To explain why a race condition occurs, an SMP system with four CPUs on a Linux system can have different processes running in parallel on the four CPUs. This can lead to a situation where processes running on different CPUs access the same code or method.

This phenomenon is called concurrency. SMP systems are a natural condition for concurrency to occur.

Concurrency and race conditions have similar meanings. Concurrency refers to running the same code on two cores in an SMP system. A race condition is when a process on two cores executes a critical section in a concurrency environment.

When you encounter a race condition, the process to resolve it is as follows

- Determine why the race condition occurred
- Analyze which code sections are critical using kernel logs or memory dumps
- Decide which kernel synchronization method to use, such as spinlock or mutex

You need to lock critical sections that can be contaminated by race conditions so that only one process can execute them. The kernel supports a variety of features to accomplish this, but the most popular methods in the Linux kernel are spinlocks and mutexes.

6.2.5.10. Interrupt

To understand the behavior of the Linux kernel, it is necessary to know the details of interrupts.

Interrupts are one of the ways peripherals communicate with the kernel, and are a mechanism for a CPU to notify the Linux kernel of event that have occurred to it. Interrupts can occur for a variety of reasons, such as when the keyboard is pressed. Interrupts can occur for the following reasons:

- The signal handler registered in user space executes the interrupt handler and then starts processing.
- A race condition interrupt occurs asynchronously, polluting the code in the critical section.

- Performance problems that cause kernel panics or system slowdowns are often associated with interrupt behavior.

Post-interrupt techniques are often applied when processing network packet communication or multimedia.

The Linux kernel immediately instructs the CPU to process the packet at the stage when the packet is received by the NIC. This is called an interrupt. Polling, which checks whether packets arrive at regular intervals, can also be considered, but this is not efficient, and instead, interrupts are used.

Efficient packet processing is possible by processing interrupts only when they arrive, without periodically checking hardware devices such as NICs. There are two types of interrupts: hardware interrupts, which require immediate processing such as packet processing or keyboard input, and soft interrupts, which are executed with a delay.

A hardware interrupt is used for packet processing that occurs when a packet is received, and a soft interrupt is used for the process of interpreting protocols such as TCP/UDP.

The Linux kernel provides IRQ threads, soft IRQ, and tasklets.

The reason for the post interrupt technique is that interrupt handlers must execute code in a short and concise manner. If an interrupt handler takes a long time, most systems will misbehave. It is possible to accidentally write code in an interrupt handler that takes a long time.

Interrupt Use Case 1

If there is no interrupt signal, everything works as normal, and the CPU starts executing the next machine instruction. When an event appears from some device that requires CPU processing, it must decide whether to process it or not. This is where prioritization comes into play. If the priority of the interrupt signal is not higher than the program currently running, the interrupt may not be processed.

1. When Thread 1, which is running on the CPU, initiates a system call to request input or output, the OS pauses the execution of Thread 1 and assigns the CPU to Thread 2. Thread 2 starts running.

2. At this point, the disk is operational and ready for data, and DMA directly transfers data between the device and memory. When this data transfer is complete, it notifies the CPU using the interrupt mechanism, and the CPU pauses the execution of Thread 2 and processes the interrupt.

3. The kernel has seen that the input/output operations requested by Thread 1 have been processed, so it decides to reallocate the CPU back to Thread 1, which will eventually continue running from where it left off.

The key is that when the disk processes an IO request, the CPU doesn't wait on the spot and runs Thread 2 according to the kernel scheduling. In the process, it maximizes the resources of the OS, devices, DMA, and interrupts.

CHAPTER 6　INFRASTRUCTURE RCA

Interrupt Use Case 2

Process 2 continues to run, and Process 1 continues to wait. When the system's timer sends a timer interrupt signal after Process B has been running for a certain period of time, the CPU jumps to the interrupt handling method. At this time, the OS thinks that the duration of Process B is long enough and puts it in the ready queue, and at the same time, it takes Process A out of the ready queue and allocates CPU. Process 1 continues to run.

Note that the OS paused Process B by putting it in the ready queue because it used up its allotted time, not because it requested blocking input or output.

6.2.5.11. Timers

Using the timer methods provided by the kernel, you can perform the following actions as background tasks:

- The scheduling methods use the timer methods provided by the kernel to control the process.
- The system time is periodically updated by receiving timer interrupts.
- Run the Soft IRQ Timer service periodically to manage dynamic timers.

To understand the overall execution flow of the kernel timer, you need to know the structure of Soft IRQ. The execution steps of the TIMER_SOFTIRQ service in Soft IRQ are as follows

- When a timer interrupt occurs, it requests a Soft IRQ called TIMER_SOFTIRQ.
- The Soft IRQ calls the run_timer_softirq() method, which is the TIMER_SOFTIRQ handler.
- The run_timer_softirq() method processes a dynamic timer registered in a global variable called time_base.

It is necessary to check whether unnecessary interrupts and timers are running. This is because it will be delayed.

Timer are often processed together with interrupts, making it difficult to analyze the interrupt and timer. For detailed analysis, use ftrace. Various ftrace events are provided. ftrace traces the behavior of the kernel, which is defined as an event.

Dynamic timers are an important feature of the kernel and provide the following events:

- timer_start: Registers a dynamic timer
- timer_cancel: Unregisters a dynamic timer
- timer_expire_entry: Information just before executing the dynamic timer handler
- timer_expire_exit: Information immediately after executing the dynamic timer handler

/kernel/time/timer.c for the code. Print ftrace's timer_expire_entry and timer_expire_exit event logs before and after the fn(timer) method. With this ftrace log, you can measure the time that the dynamic timer handler has been running.

```
trace_timer_expire_entry(timer, baseclk);
fn(timer);
trace_timer_expire_exit(timer);
```

It also provides a tracepoint, which is specified as timer_expire_entry. You can see the code in /trace/events/timer.h:

```
TRACE_EVENT(timer_expire_entry,

    TP_PROTO(struct timer_list *timer, unsigned long baseclk),

    TP_ARGS(timer, baseclk),

    TP_STRUCT__entry(
        __field( void *,        timer    )
        __field( unsigned long, now      )
        __field( void *,        function )
        __field( unsigned long, baseclk  )
    ),

    TP_fast_assign(
        __entry->timer    = timer;
        __entry->now      = jiffies;
        __entry->function = timer->function;
        __entry->baseclk  = baseclk;
    ),

    TP_printk("timer=%p function=%ps now=%lu baseclk=%lu",
        __entry->timer, __entry->function, __entry->now,
        __entry->baseclk)
);
```

The system periodically generates timer interrupts, and each time an interrupt is processed, the kernel has the opportunity to decide whether to suspend the current thread. This is why developers don't need to explicitly specify when to pause a thread and release resources from the CPU.

The CPU detects the interrupt signal and executes the interrupt handling program inside the kernel. The interrupt handling method determines if the process is ready to run, and if it is, it continues to run the process. If not, it suspends the process, and the scheduler schedules another process that is ready.

The program that processes the timer interrupt determines if the CPU time slice allocated to Thread A has been used up, and if there is time left, it returns to user space and continues execution. If Thread A's time slice is used up, the CPU should be allocated to a thread such as Thread B.

Taking an idle process as an example, when an idle process is suspended by a timer interrupt, the interrupt handling method checks if there is a ready process in the system, and if not, it continues to execute the idle process.

Even if a program has an infinite loop, the kernel can still control the scheduling of the process by timer interrupts, and the presence of an infinite loop does not cause a problem with the kernel.

6.2.5.12. Memory

When Java has OOM problems, it's usually due to poor development, configuration, and bugs in the application. Eventually, full garbage collection occurs, and CPU utilization spikes. This is a common failure. You can analyze memory dumps to find the methods that are leaking.

If you create too many threads, context switches occur frequently, which increases latency. Resources are used to create new threads. Eventually, you'll run out of memory and your Kubernetes pod will crash, but it will restart automatically. This process repeats itself. You need to fix the root cause, and increasing the number of thread pools or increasing the memory of the pod is not the solution. Using flame graphs to compare duration and memory usage before and after code changes can help you troubleshoot the problem.

6.2.5.13. Disk

Rather than theoretical explanations, let's break down the disk problem by describing a failure that occurred in production.

The failures are as follows:

- Cassandra compression failed.
- Cassandra CPU utilization on a particular node suddenly increased.
- The API server associated with Cassandra was no longer able to process user requests.

The cause analysis failed because observability was not configured on the API server and Cassandra cluster. Analyze the cause of why the compression failed. Although metrics will output that the compression failed.

We speculated that the Cassandra shard was down, causing rebalancing to occur, which caused the latency, but there was no problem with the balancing ratio of the Cassandra shard.

It's important to understand what kind of load compression is causing CPU utilization to increase, although I suspect it has more to do with IO than CPU. You need to analyze the sudden increase in CPU utilization. If you analyze the processes and threads in the stack trace, can see the thread name. You can use the profile to identify methods that are called frequently and have long durations. Analyze how often the method is called and why the latency is increasing. It could be a Cassandra bug, a bug in the virtual machine or the kernel, or it could be a patch.

The order of requests for compaction is as follows

- The application calls the user method.
- The system call is called.
- The virtual filesystem within the filesystem is processed.
- The system within disk IO is processed.

You need to know at what point the compression goes down. The processing a block is off-CPU, and the wakeup event changes the state to on-CPU and uses CPU. If you see a sudden spike in CPU utilization with low IO, it's likely on-CPU. If the problem is not caused by the CPU, you need to analyze the IO. Compaction goes through filesystem and disk IO to the physical disks. Filesystems and disk IOs consist of many processes. If you need a detailed analysis of disk IO and filesystems, eBPF measures the latency of each process.

Cassandra's latency propagated to the API server, and the API server was no longer able to process new requests. You need to analyze the API server's stack trace. Analyze how individual threads on the API server are interact with Cassandra, the thread status, and the duration of the threads.

Root cause analysis fails because observability is not in place. If you enforce infrastructure observability across all resources, you will spend a lot of money. Without infrastructure observability, root cause analysis becomes difficult. Considerations for enforcing infrastructure observability include the following:

- Prioritize critical systems.
- Unvalidated agents can increase overhead and decrease reliability. Pre-validation of agents is required.
- Register the system utility as a batch and collect profiles periodically.
- Flexible use of sampling and retention to lower overhead and reduce costs.

All tasks processed within a cluster have a priority. If more resources are needed for a higher priority task, the lower priority task that was being performed on the same equipment can be terminated to secure the resources. If a task is performed for about an hour, there is a high risk that the task will end to make room for high-priority processes. It should be configured to withstand unexpected frequent task termination.

6.2.5.14. Network Applications

A network application starts with code in user space and then passes through the code in the kernel space and network equipment. On the server, it is received as code in the kernel space and finally passed to code in the user space. Latency is generated by the code in user space, but latency can also be generated by the client kernel code, the server kernel code, and interfaces between the user code and the kernel code and the network equipment.

CHAPTER 6   INFRASTRUCTURE RCA

Sending and receiving is processed in the Linux kernel code:

- **Sending data:** Once a socket is created, the user can send data to it by requesting SYS_WRITE(). SYS_WRITE() calls SOCK_WRITEV() and SOCK_AIO_WRITE() registered in the file operation structure. It calls the method registered in the SOCKET data structure for the OPS variable SENDMSG. Assuming you are using TCP/IP, the registered method is inet_sendmsg(). You have entered the INET layer. The INET layer calls the methods registered in the variable named sendmsg in the sock data structure. Here, a method called tcp_transmit_skb() is registered. This method creates the sk_buff, performs any necessary initialization, and calls the methods registered in the queue_xmit of the tcp_sock data structure. Here, the ip_queue_xmit() method is registered. The ip_queue_xmit() method creates an IP header in the sk_buff structure, finds the corresponding net_device structure with the network equipment name, and calls the method registered in the field named hard_start_xmit. To do this, the Linux kernel manages the net_device structure through a list starting from the dev_base variable.

- **Receiving data:** To receive data, the user can request a SYS_READ() on the socket. SYS_READ() calls SOCK_READV() or SODK_AIO_READ() registered in the file operation structure. This method calls the method registered in the INET_RECVMSG of the OPS variable in the SOCKET data structure, which in turn calls the SOCK_COMMON_RECVMSG() method. You have entered the INET layer. This method calls a method called tcp_recvmsg(), which enters the TCP layer. if network equipment data is received, an interrupt is raised and el3_interrupt() is called. This method makes the received data into an sk_buff, adds it to the net_device structure, calls netif_wake_queue(), and causes ip_rcv() to be performed. When ip_rev() is called, it looks at the IP header and decides if this packet is from itself or if it needs to be retransmitted. If it is, it calls ip_local_deliver(); if it needs to be retransmitted, it calls ip_forward().

It refers to the kernel parameters of the network, and the parameters have a lot of influence on the performance and failure of the network. Incorrect and unmanaged parameters can cause failures, so be careful.

There are active and passive closers, and the one that disconnects first is called the active closer. The reason it matters who disconnects first is that the active closer creates a TIME_WAIT socket.

What kind of problems can be caused by a large number of TIME_WAIT sockets? First, application timeouts due to local port exhaustion can occur. Linux has a kernel parameter called net.ipv4.ip_local_port_range, which serves to specify the scope of local ports needed to communicate.

When a process requests the creation of a socket to communicate with the external, the kernel assigns one of the values defined in net.ipv4.ip_local_port_range to the local port that the socket will use. If all local ports are in the TIME_WAIT state at this time, the application will not be able to communicate with the external because there are no local ports available for allocation, and the application may experience a timeout.

Frequent TCP connections and disconnections can also slow down the responsiveness of the service. This is how sockets work in the kernel:

- The kernel assigns the application one port number from the list of local ports it manages that it can use.

- The application requests the kernel to create a socket with the assigned number.

- The kernel creates a socket with that information. The socket is created with a source IP and port, a target IP and port, and a set of four values, and that socket is unique inside the kernel, meaning there is no other socket with the same four values.

- If the socket creation completes successfully, the kernel will pass a file descriptor for your application to use to access the socket.

When you actively close a socket that has been used in this way, it remains in the TIME_WAIT state, which means that under normal circumstances it cannot be used again until it is released from the TIME_WAIT state and returned to the kernel. If a large number of local ports are in the TIME_WAIT state in this way, and there are no more ports available, the local ports will be exhausted and unable to communicate with the server.

The way to deal with local port exhaustion is through kernel parameters.

- net.ipv4.tw_reuse is a parameter that allows you to reuse the TIME_WAIT socket on the local port you use on the way out.

- net.ipv4.tw_recycle is a parameter that allows the server to quickly reclaim and recycle the TIME_WAIT socket.

The connection pool method can also prevent reckless use of local ports and improve the responsiveness of your service.

You can't eliminate TIME_WAIT sockets, but you can reduce them by using keepalives. A *keepalive* is a feature that allows you to keep a session open even after the request ends. For example, if you have a series of GET requests coming in every two seconds, it's more economical to establish a single session, keep it open, and process the requests continuously rather than establishing a new session every two seconds.

The kernel parameters required to keep TCP keepalive are listed here:

- net.ipv4.tcp_keepalive_time

- net.ipv4.tcp_keepalive_probes

- net.ipv4.tcp_keepalive_invl

The ability to maintain a connection between two ends at the kernel level, which can reduce unnecessary TCP handshakes and prevent invalid connections.

TCP keepalive is intended to maintain the connection between the two ends, while HTTP keepalive is intended to keep the connection open as long as possible. If both values are 60 seconds, TCP keepalive will check every 60 seconds to see if the connection has been maintained, and if it has received a response, it will continue to maintain the connection. However, the application will keep the connection for 60 seconds, and if no request is received after 60 seconds, it will disconnect.

CHAPTER 6　INFRASTRUCTURE RCA

There are many kernel parameters related to retransmissions and network-related kernel parameters. If they are improperly set, failure can occur. The following application timeouts should be set to account for retransmissions.

- **Connection timeout:** Occurs when retransmission occurs during the TCP handshake process
- **Read timeout:** Occurs when requesting data over a tied session

It is recommended to set the connection timeout to 3 seconds and the read timeout to at least 300 ms so that the timeouts in your application can withstand at least one retransmission.

If you think it's network latency, use system utilities such as netstat and traceroute to analyze the cause. If that doesn't work, you should use tcpdump and wireshark to analyze packets and measure the latency of the server-client network. tcpdump collects packets by specifying an IP address and port. wireshark can analyze packets from various protocols.

ulimit sets limits on the resources that a process can use. Most middleware, as well as database applications such as MySQL, can read and write files to process them efficiently. In an environment where many packets are processed, many connections are created, and the number of files opened at the same time increases. In such a situation, the limit should be increased in advance because the demon may suddenly terminate and cause a failure.

The value that is often encountered when operating a web service is Max Open Files. This is the maximum number of files that can be opened by the process with the open(2) flag. When the process opens the file with open(2), the Linux kernel assigns a number called a file descriptor to the file as an interface for the process to handle it. The process can read and write files to the OS by specifying this number.

The Linux kernel has a table that manages the status of files along with the file descriptor. An entry is added to the file table when open(2) is executed, and the entry is deleted when close(2) is executed.

This interface can be used to read and write physical files, as well as to use sockets using the system call socket(2).

In Linux, when receiving a packet, the listen(2) system call is used to wait for a socket connection, and if the connection is successful, communication is started with accept(2). At this time, accept(2) takes one from the queue of pending connection requests and establishes a connection. In the case of TCP sockets, the sockets handled by listen(2) are responsible for waiting to receive SYN packets and create connections.

The queue of connection requests waiting to be processed is called the *backlog*, and net.core.somaxconn is a kernel parameter that sets the size of this queue. If the size of the backlog is exceeded, the Linux kernel considers that a new connection cannot be made and discards the packet. Therefore, in an environment that processes many HTTP requests simultaneously, even if there are sufficient resources, it may not be possible to process simultaneous connections.

Net.ipv4.ip_local_port_range: The client side requires a port for packet communication, and the port area that dynamically allocates this is called *ephemeral ports*. In Linux 5.4, 32768-60999 are used by default. The client dynamically allocates and uses the available ports among ephemeral ports.

When a server connects to a database such as MySQL or another system, the client side can also reuse the previously used port. Ephemeral ports can be exhausted when the client tries to create as many connections as possible to perform as many processes as possible.

MTU is the maximum size that can be transferred on the corresponding network interface. When transferring packets larger than the MTU value, the packets are divided into the MTU size and transferred.

The maximum MTU size was 1,500 bytes. However, as communication speeds have increased and the size of files sent and received has also increased, the cost of splitting files up to 1,500 bytes has increased. In general, the MTU can be extended to 9,000 bytes.

When operating microservices, MTU settings have little effect. The MTU must be set on all devices, including the client and server that exchange packets, and even the network equipment in the path. Even if the MTU of the server is set to 900 bytes, if the network equipment is 1,500 bytes, the packets will be split up to 1,500 bytes by the network equipment in the path.

6.2.6. Kernel Development

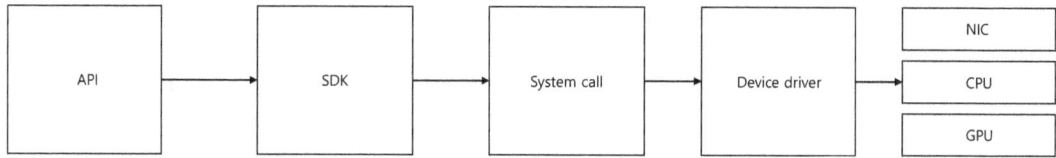

Figure 6-15. *The kernel flow*

If a problem occurs and you try to solve it with development, it will take a lot of time and cost. Nevertheless, the advantages of lower-level development are strong. The Linux kernel explains the system resources and the process of processing.

In Figure 6-15, it is processed in four steps.

1. **Hardware:** Hardware can process instructions in machine language. Assemblies are mainly used, and hardware vendors provide instructions and assemblies in documents. Developers do not develop assemblies themselves, but use higher-level APIs.

2. **Device drivers:** The kernel recognizes the CPU, GPU, and NIC hardware and processes IO and instructions in conjunction with each piece of hardware. The kernel requires device drivers for the hardware, and in Linux, device drivers can be developed using modules.

3. **System calls:** It may be necessary to develop system calls in response to new device drivers. The SDK and API provided to the developer are processed in the user space. The system call links the provided API and the device driver.

4. The hardware vendor provides the device driver, system calls, SDKs, and APIs and provides detailed guidelines. The user can easily install the driver, and the developer can develop additional applications using the provided APIs.

CHAPTER 6   INFRASTRUCTURE RCA

It is easy to develop device drivers without having to understand complex assemblies. Linux provides modules, and hardware vendors provide SDKs and APIs.

A closer look at the code for KUtrace shows that it is structured similarly to these four steps. It consists of examples developed with device drivers, system calls, SDKs, and KUtrace APIs, and it collects events at each step to create a span.

KUtrace has limitations. KUtrace supports various CPU architectures, including x86, Raspberry Pi ARM, FreeBSD, RISC-V, and Android. However, it does not support NVIDIA GPU.

Drivers are specific to a certain hardware. The kernel is hardware-independent and has some areas that are used commonly, but there are also parts that are hardware-dependent. When using KUtrace, there are still cases where hardware-dependent parts are not supported.

With KUtrace, you can monitor all processes except for the hardware. If you think there is a problem with the hardware, you can use the benchmarks and profiles provided by the vendor or use specialized debugging tools to check for equipment defects and malfunctions. If there is a problem with the hardware, it will eventually propagate to the application in the user's space, but it is not a good way to identify hardware problems at the end user. If you suspect that there is a software fault, KUtrace is a great help in resolving problems by clarifying device drivers, system calls, and system traces of the SDK. If it is not a software fault, it is useful to profile the hardware. In this book, monitoring the hardware inside is not included in infrastructure observability.

6.2.6.1. Module Development

Linux provides a mechanism called dynamic kernel modules. Most of the kernel's functions can be implemented as modules. For example, filesystems, device drivers, communication protocols, and new system calls can be implemented as modules. Modules are dynamically loaded into memory when needed. Therefore, memory can be used efficiently by loading specific kernel functions into kernel space only when they are needed.

Modules can make the kernel light by implementing only the functions that are essential to the kernel space. Generally, functions closely related to hardware, such as context switches, address translations, system call processing, and device drivers, are implemented in the kernel space. Using modules makes it possible to create a smaller kernel and load and use many functions when needed. Using modules eliminates the need to compile the kernel source directly when adding new features to the kernel.

Modules operate in kernel space and use variables or functions defined inside the kernel. Therefore, when writing a module program, you need to insert some header files used by the kernel. Insert the `Kernel.h` and `module.h` header files. The module must write a function that will be called automatically when it is loaded into the kernel. The `Module_init()` and `module_exit()` macros allow you to specify the names of these functions arbitrarily. In the end, `hello_module_init()` is executed when the module starts, and the `hello_module_exit()` function is executed when it ends. Both functions print characters using a kernel internal function called `printk()`.

If you created a device driver when the concept of modules did not exist, you had to recompile the kernel because the kernel had changed. The kernel compilation process is a time-consuming task. Since the concept of modules was introduced, modules can be installed and uninstalled without this process. This is the module where you can register or unregister devices. For example, use the following function when registering a character-type device.

```
int register_chrdev(unsigned int major, const char *name, struct file_operations *fops);
```

For now, you don't need to know what this function does. First, let's see how modules are registered. Let's create a very simple module. Write the following code as you would write it in C programming.

```
#include <linux/module.h>
#include <linux/kernel.h>
#include <linux/init.h>

static int __init my_init(void){
    printk("hello, kernel!\n");
    return 0;
}

static void __exit my_exit(void){
    printk("goodbye, kernel!\n");
}

module_init(my_init);
module_exit(my_exit);
```

The three header files at the top (linux/module.h, linux/kernel.h, and linux/init.h) must be included.

module_init, which is initialized when you install the module for the first time, and module_exit, which is called when you uninstall the module, are defined in module.h. You can pass the parameters of these macro functions to the functions you have defined. You can see what they do here:

```
#define module_init(x)  __initcall(x);
//...//
#define module_exit(exitfn)                                      \
    static inline exitcall_t __maybe_unused __exittest(void)     \
    { return exitfn; }                                           \
    void cleanup_module(void) __copy(exitfn) __attribute__((alias(#exitfn))));
```

Did you learn about constructors and destructors in object-oriented programming? Isn't the initialization of an object done in the constructor, and the finishing touches, such as releasing resources, done in the destructor? You can think of it as having a similar role.

printk is used to print the contents of a message from a kernel module. You can view kernel messages with the dmesg command. Note that it is printk, not printf!

Anyway, if you have written the code, you need to compile it using a makefile. Here's how to do this:

```
KERNDIR=/lib/modules/$(shell uname -r)/build
obj-m+=mymodule.o
objs+=mymodule.o
PWD=$(shell pwd)

default:
    make -C $(KERNDIR) M=$(PWD) modules

clean:
    make -C $(KERNDIR) M=$(PWD) clean
    rm -rf *.ko
    rm -rf *.o
```

Programming in the kernel area is a difficult task, and it allows you to perform detailed operations. For example, you can also hook system calls through kernel modules. As I mentioned earlier, modules are part of the kernel and do not necessarily have to act as device drivers.

6.2.6.2. Device Driver Development

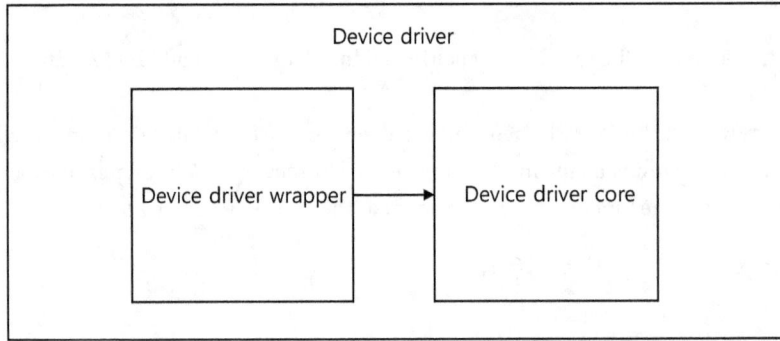

Figure 6-16. *Device driver flow*

You can add a new device driver or change the existing device driver content. In particular, using module programming, new drivers can be added without modifying or compiling the existing kernel code.

The term *device driver* refers to software that is used to run devices that exist as hardware. The hardware, called a device, can be used with any OS or even in an environment without an OS. However, since the way OSs manage device drivers is different, it is difficult to create a device driver that works on all OSs. Therefore, when writing a device driver, it is desirable to separate the hardware-specific code and the OS-specific code required to run the device, as shown in Figure 6-16.

- Linux's device driver consists of a device driver core for a specific piece of hardware and a kind of reference to make the core available in Linux. Device driver cores are written to match the characteristics of the hardware by referring to the hardware manual.

- The wrapper must register the created core in the kernel so that the Linux kernel can recognize it, and connect the functions of the core with the functions that the user task will call in order to make the user task accessible through the device file. The Linux kernel has predefined the functions that the driver wrapper should provide. In other words, device driver developers do not need to worry about which functions to provide for user tasks, but only provide the functions that are already defined in the file operation data structure.

6.2.6.3. NVIDIA GPU Development

The processing process of the CPU and that of the NVIDIA GPU are similar. See Figure 6-17.

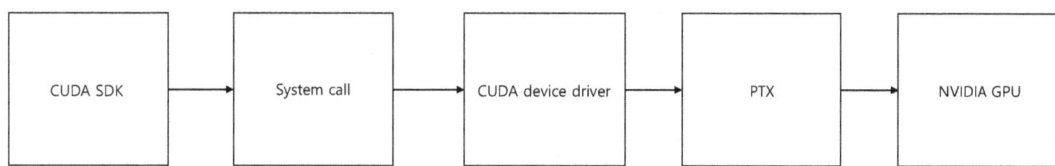

Figure 6-17. *NVIDIA flow*

NVIDIA CUDA provides drivers for NVIDIA GPUs and APIs for developers. CUDA helps general developers use GPU parallel computing easily. CUDA includes device drivers, low-level APIs, system calls, and the CUDA SDK. Developers use the CUDA API to develop parallel processing applications.

It has long been possible to overclock CPUs, and CPU manufacturers recommend using only about 70 percent of the CPU to operate stably. DeepSeek improves the performance of lower-level GPUs. However, DeepSeek makes full use of the GPU and is designed to operate similarly to overclocking.

In addition to CUDA, NVIDIA GPUs also provide lower-level API such as Parallel Thread Execution (PTX). DeepSeek uses PTX to enable fine-grained control of NVIDIA GPUs at a much lower level than typical CUDA code. CUDA also uses PTX internally, but it is not known how much optimization has been done. NVIDIA exclusively provided it, and developers habitually used CUDA. DeepSeek uses PTX instead of CUDA to optimize kernel and user space and process them much faster. It is similar to developing drivers and SDKs based on PTX.

It is quite possible to use assembly to optimize PTXs like DeepSeek, and to develop DeepSeek's own device drivers, system calls, APIs, and SDKs. Moreover, it is a good idea to find out that CUDA's optimization is insufficient and to make the most of the GPU.

Similar to CPUs, profiles and benchmark programs are used to compare performance between GPUs or to analyze problems. GPU can also measure floating-point operations, memory bandwidth, and energy efficiency, just like CPUs. However, due to the nature of GPUs, they operate in a different way from CPUs. GPUs are strong in parallel processing and process thousands of threads simultaneously on hundreds of cores.

The way the GPU processes IO, interrupts, locks, context switches, memory allocation, and internal GPU caches is different from that of the CPU. I recommend that you learn about and understand the GPU in detail.

6.3. eBPF

eBPF is useful for Linux observability. You can use eBPF to instrument the kernel and identify problems in the kernel. You configure eBPF-based observability with PCP.

With system trace, you can trace events that occur on various system resources and visualize them as a span. You can measure the latency of each span and identify problems.

Among the system utilities, `strace` and `ftrace` support system trace. Although the features provided by system utilities are powerful, they have high overhead to be used in production, so they are suitable for debugging in a development environment.

System traces are useful for understanding the overall flow of processes and identifying problems, but it is difficult to understand the reason for latency in specific methods and events in the kernel code.

With system traces, you can narrow down the scope of the problem and get closer to the root cause. The next step is to quickly and simply understand the root cause by looking at the 99th percentile latency of the method, number of calls, call tree, and stack trace. The tool for this is profile, and you will use eBPF profile to measure the performance of events and methods in low-level Linux kernel code.

Sitting inside the kernel, eBPF executes code instructions in an isolated environment. In this way, eBPFs are similar to JavaAgents, which execute machine code compiled from high-level programming languages. This is because the bytecode instrumentation and profiling methods described for JavaAgents are similar to eBPFs.

- **Instrumentation:** Bytecode instrumentation in Java is similar to static and dynamic instrumentation using `tracepoint` and `kprobe`.

- **Profile:** eBPF uses a histogram to output latency. The Java profile measures latency as a histogram and can be debugged in a variety of ways.

The entry point, JIT compiler, and class loading provided by JVM are similar to eBPF.

The compiled code (eBPF program) is run through the eBPF verifier. The verifier checks if the code is safe to run in the kernel. If the code is safe, the eBPF program is loaded into the kernel. The Linux kernel also has a JIT compiler for eBPF instructions. The JIT compiler converts the program to eBPF bytecode immediately after it is verified, reducing the burden of performing this conversion at runtime. This means that eBPF programs can be put into the kernel without restarting the system.

BPF trace supports multiple event sources to provide visibility. Dynamic instrumentation allows you to insert instrumentation points into your application. Because dynamic instrumentation works without code modification, it imposes no overhead when the instrumentation is not in use. It is commonly used to instrument the start and end of a method. Dynamic instrumentation is also similar to the technique used by debuggers to insert breakpoints.

The final component of eBPF is the eBPF map, which is used by the kernel and user space to share resources. The eBPF map is a bidirectional data structure for sharing data, meaning that both the kernel and user space can read and write to it. Several data structures are used in eBPF.

Do you need eBPF, even though you have existing system utilities?

While there is some overlap with System Utility, eBPF offers many features that System Utility does not. There are more tools in eBPF than in System Utility, and it provides more detailed profile capabilities. If you are familiar with System Utility, you should use it first. Use eBPF if System Utility does not provide the functionality you need, or if you need low-level debugging.

6.3.1. BCC and bpftrace

BCC can write eBPF programs in C, while `bpftrace` provides its own high-level language. Both tools use LLVM IR and LLVM libraries under the hood to compile to eBPF.

Programming directly with eBPF commands, or using LLVM IRs, is the domain of developers working inside BCC and `bpftrace`.

Because it is difficult to code eBPF commands directly, tools have been developed that allow you to code eBPF commands using high-level languages. Examples include BCC and `bpftrace`.

BCC is the first framework developed for using eBPF. It provides a C language programming environment for writing kernel eBPF code and Python and C++ programming environments for writing user-level interfaces. BCC is the origin of `libbcc` and the current `libbpf` library, which provide the ability to instrument multiple events with eBPF programs.

`bpftrace` is a new development method that provides an advanced language for developing eBPF tools. `bpftrace` code is very concise and allows you to quickly measure kernel performance.

To understand the Linux kernel, it is recommended that you practice it yourself, as shown here:

- Kernel compilation and patching
- Kernel module development
- Developing system calls

Kernel compilation and patching are not comparable to eBPF because they are code modifications and upgrades. However, kernel modules are similar to eBPF in that they operate in kernel space instead of user space. See https://blog.ippon.tech/ebpf-and-kernel-modules-whats-the-difference for more information.

KUtrace is developed using a kernel module. While KUtrace has about ten times less overhead than `ftrace`, it has inherent limitations because it was developed as a module.

CHAPTER 6   INFRASTRUCTURE RCA

Even small overheads have a cost that cannot be ignored when installed in a data center or cluster. In a data center that pays 100 billion, 1 percent overhead is equivalent to 1 billion. Even system traces developed as modules can have side effects under heavy load.

Overhead requires additional performance and drives up production costs in a pay-as-you-go cloud environment. Aside from eBPF, there aren't many alternatives to reliably and inexpensively measuring latency and performing root cause analysis.

By incorporating eBPF into a performance analysis tool, you can leverage the programmability of eBPF to analyze performance in the way you want. Using an eBPF program, you can calculate any latency you want and perform statistical summaries in any way you want.

The advantage is that histogram generation can be done in the kernel context, which greatly reduces the amount of data copied to user space. The resulting efficiency gains make it possible to use eBPF in production.

If you are not using eBPF, this is the process of generating histogram statistics.

1. Start instrumentation for disk IO events in kernel space.
2. Each event in kernel space writes an event to the `perf` buffer. If `tracepoint` was used, the recorded information includes metadata fields about disk IO.
3. Periodically copy a buffer of all events from kernel space to user space.
4. For each event in user space, analyze the byte fields of the event metadata. Other fields are ignored.
5. Generate a histogram for that byte field in user space.

For IO-heavy systems, Steps 2-4 have a high performance overhead. It is easy to understand if you think of transferring 10,000 disk IO trace records per second to the user space program and summarizing them.

If you are using eBPF, this is a very small program.

1. Start instrumentation for disk IO events in kernel space and plug in a very small eBPF program you wrote.
2. Run the eBPF program on each event in kernel space. This program takes only the byte fields and stores them in a user-specified eBPF map histogram.
3. Read and print the eBPF map histogram once in user space.

This method avoids copying the event to user space and having to process this information again. It also doesn't copy unused metadata fields.

I have briefly described the internal structure of eBPF. Many tools are available that are built on top of eBPF, and SREs should familiarize themselves with them. These tools are often necessary and useful in the process of root cause analysis and troubleshooting problems.

While eBPF provides the ability to visualize with flame graphs, histograms, and heatmaps, it is difficult to visualize with spans.

CHAPTER 6　INFRASTRUCTURE RCA

The eBPF `bpftrace` and BCC tools measure performance and latency, and they can quickly and accurately identify where latency is occurring. This requires knowledge of the kernel and lower level systems, which is why I explained how Linux processes this internally.

In this section, I explain infrastructure observability by excluding system traces and using only existing system utilities and eBPF.

- Understand the approximate order in which the Linux kernel executes. Look at the latency over a large scope. Use `ftrace` and `strace` together. When tracing from user space through an application, `strace` is used to identify system calls, and when tracing from kernel space, such as receiving network packets, ftrace is used to identify kernel methods. First, use `ftrace` and `strace` to get a general understanding and identify problems, and then use BCC and `tracepoint` for detailed analysis. System utilities and eBPF should both be considered.

- You can trace the detailed behavior of interrupts, scheduling, and kernel timers.

- BCC is recommended as a first step. Some useful BCCs are `funclatency`, `funccount`, and `stackcount`. Use `funccount` and `funclatency` to identify the methods in your kernel code that are causing problems.

- Finally, instrument with `tracepoints`. Use static or dynamic instrumentation and measurement of the event. Using thread IDs and symbols, develop additional logic and check the `tracepoint` log. Check the kernel method enhanced with `stackcount`. `kprobe` and `tracepoint` are provided, so once the method is identified, instrumentation is not difficult.

The following prior knowledge will help you identify latency in the kernel:

- Accurately identifying events and methods is difficult. Instrument the identified event with a `tracepoint`.

- Visualize latency using a histogram and measure the 95th percentile latency.

- In order to instrument a specific method within a detailed process, an understanding of the kernel code is required.

You need to know how to use eBPF's BCC and `tracepoint`, and how to measure the latency of the methods.

6.3.1.1. Analyzing Tracepoints

kprobe is a debugging system that exists within the Linux kernel. With kprobe, you can dynamically add programs of your choice to the entry and exit points of kernel methods. This gives you access to most of the kernel's code.

Tracepoint can instrument more than 1,000 events and kprobe can instrument more than 5,000 methods.

CHAPTER 6   INFRASTRUCTURE RCA

Since there are more than 1,000 `tracepoints`, kprobe can perform a lot of instrumentation.

Whereas a kprobe is a dynamic point that exists on a per-method basis, a `tracepoint` is a more statically defined event. A kprobe can be attached to any area of the kernel.

The literal meaning of kprobe and `tracepoint` is points for probe and trace, and the kernel already provides developers with the ability to instrument specific points and methods. By instrumenting these points, developers can understand the latency for specific events and methods.

eBPF is a profile, not a trace. The output format is a metric. Despite the previous explanation of the difference between trace and profile, the term trace is often used with eBPF, which can be confusing.

BPF uses `tracepoint` for instrumentation, so it uses some of the techniques of trace. Not to be confused, eBPF's profiles can capture events and methods in the kernel.

The Linux kernel has many such conventions, and they help you understand how the kernel processes things. To search for `ftrace` events in the code, you identify system call handler methods in `unistd-common.h`. This section describes how the `tracepoint` instrumentation is implemented in the kernel code.

A `tracepoint` is an instrumentation method for the kernel, and a `tracepoint` has a number of events that can be traced. `tracepoints` make instrumentation of kernel methods easy.

If you understand the method you want to instrument and want more detailed instrumentation, it is useful to instrument methods rather than events. The correct approach to instrument is to search for the event, instrument the event if it exists, and search for the method if the event does not exist.

You can trace the kernel methods with kprobes, but the problem is that methods change as the kernel evolves, so this is not a stable way to trace methods. Also, kernel methods can sometimes be inlined.

If the method is inlined, you can't easily kprobe it. It's not impossible, but in this case you have to figure it out from the body of the method where the inline code starts.

The /sys/kernel/debug/tracing/events directory indicates the available trace subsystems.

Individual subsystems can define multiple events. For example, this is seen in the .net subsystem.

```
$ sudo ls /sys/kernel/debug/tracing/events/net
enable                    netif_receive_skb
filter                    netif_receive_skb_entry
napi_gro_frags_entry      netif_receive_skb_exit
napi_gro_frags_exit       netif_receive_skb_list_entry
napi_gro_receive_entry    netif_receive_skb_list_exit
napi_gro_receive_exit     netif_rx
net_dev_queue             netif_rx_entry
net_dev_start_xmit        netif_rx_exit
net_dev_xmit              netif_rx_ni_entry
net_dev_xmit_timeout      netif_rx_ni_exit
```

A directory is a recognizable event in network processing.

If you look at enable and filter, notice that they are labeled rw. The enable file is used to enable a probe or set of probes. You can enable an event with the appropriate enable file.

CHAPTER 6   INFRASTRUCTURE RCA

You can also filter events using filter expressions.

```
$ sudo ls -al /sys/kernel/debug/tracing/events/net/netif_rx
total 0
drwxr-xr-x.  2 root root 0 Oct 18 10:20 .
drwxr-xr-x. 20 root root 0 Oct 18 10:20 ..
-rw-r--r--.  1 root root 0 Oct 18 10:20 enable
-rw-r--r--.  1 root root 0 Oct 18 10:20 filter
-r--r--r--.  1 root root 0 Oct 18 10:20 format
-r--r--r--.  1 root root 0 Oct 18 10:20 id
-rw-r--r--.  1 root root 0 Oct 18 10:20 trigger
```

There are a few additional files. ID is a unique identifier that can be used to attach to a specific tracepoint.

```
$ sudo cat /sys/kernel/debug/tracing/events/net/netif_rx/id
1320
```

This format describes the fields used by the tracepoint. Each tracepoint outputs a message that can be displayed by the trace tool. It defines a set of fields that are populated by the trace argument.

```
$ sudo cat /sys/kernel/debug/tracing/events/net/netif_rx/format
name: netif_rx
ID: 1320
format:
    field:unsigned short common_type; offset:0; size:2; signed:0;
    field:unsigned char common_flags; offset:2; size:1; signed:0;
    field:unsigned char common_preempt_count; offset:3; size:1;signed:0;
    field:int common_pid; offset:4; size:4; signed:1;

    field:void * skbaddr; offset:8; size:8; signed:0;
    field:unsigned int len; offset:16; size:4; signed:0;
    field:__data_loc char[] name; offset:20; size:4; signed:1;

print fmt: "dev=%s skbaddr=%p len=%u", __get_str(name), REC->skbaddr, REC->len
```

Note how the device name, SKB address, will appear in the formatted message.

The tracepoint probe type instruments a static instrumentation point in the kernel. The format is as follows:

tracepoint:tracepoint_name

The tracepoint _name field contains the name of the tracepoint, which consists of the class and event name. For example, net:netif_rx corresponds to tracepoint_name, and it is used as tracepoint:netif_rx when instrumenting with bpftrace.

CHAPTER 6   INFRASTRUCTURE RCA

You need to know how to find tracepoints in the kernel code. For example, let's look at where the netif_rx tracepoint is located. It is common for tracepoints to be called via trace_<tracepoint_name>, so you need to find trace_netif_rx().

In net/core/dev.c, you can see the following:

```
static int netif_rx_internal(struct sk_buff *skb)
{
    int ret;

    net_timestamp_check(netdev_tstamp_prequeue, skb);

    trace_netif_rx(skb);
...
```

You can see that tracepoint is called with struct sk_buff * as an argument. From this sk_buff *, the fields described in format are populated, and the field values are available in the formatted trace event output.

The tracepoint is defined in a header file under include/ trace/events. The netif_rx tracepoint is defined in include/trace/events/net.h.

Each tracepoint definition is organized as follows:

- TP_PROTO: The method prototype used to call the tracepoint is TP_PROTO. In the case of netif_rx(), the structure is sk_buff *skb.

- TP_ARGS: Argument names.

- TP_STRUCT__entry field definition: Corresponds to the field that is assigned when the tracepoint is triggered.

- TP_fast_assign: Takes an argument to tracepoint (skb), setting the field values (skb len, and skb pointer).

- TP_printk: Displays the trace message using the corresponding field value.

A tracepoint defined via TRACE_EVENT specifies all of the above, but it can also define an event class that shares fields, assignments, and messages. In fact, netif_rx belongs to the event class net_dev_template, so its field assignments and messages come from that event class.

You should avoid incurring performance overhead for tracepoints that are no longer in use. The overhead of disabled tracepoints should be as small as possible. If the required compiler feature (asm goto) is supported, it works like this

- At kernel compile time, instructions are added to the tracepoint points. The actual commands used depend on the architecture.

- A tracepoint handler is added at the end of the method that traverses an array of registered tracepoint probe callbacks.

CHAPTER 6 INFRASTRUCTURE RCA

When a trace tool enables `tracepoint` at runtime, the `tracepoint` callback array is modified to add new callbacks for the trace tool and synchronized via RCU.

If the trace tool disables `tracepoint` at runtime, the `tracepoint` callback array is modified to remove the callbacks and synchronized via RCU.

6.3.1.2. Using bpftrace

There are many tools available and many combinations possible. This book uses `bpftrace` and `tracepoint` for instrumentation, but procedures and tools may change depending on the reader's environment.

For example, measure the duration of a READ system call.

- SYS_ENTER_READ: Defined at the beginning of the READ system call, it is used to capture the arguments of the READ system call and store them in a hash map.

- sys_exit_read: Defined at the end of a read system call and is used to process the results of the read system call, such as checking if the read data is HTTP traffic and transferring an event.

While developing the OpenTelemetry extension, I already described injecting code before and after a method and measuring its duration. Through class loading in Java, you instrumented the bytecode by selecting the entry point and method you wanted to instrument. eBPF using `tracepoint` is also instrumented in a similar way to the OpenTelemetry extension.

```
tracepoint:syscalls:sys_enter_read
{
    @start[tid] = nsecs;
}

tracepoint:syscalls:sys_exit_read / @start[tid] /
{
    @times = hist(nsecs - @start[tid]);
    delete(@start[tid]);
}
```

You can see the results in a histogram format, as shown here:

```
Attaching 2 probes...
 ^C

@times:
[256, 512)         326 |@                                                    |
[512, 1k)         7715 |@@@@@@@@@@@@@@@@                                     |
[1k, 2k)         15306 |@@@@@@@@@@@@@@@@@@@@@@@@@@@@@@@                      |
[2k, 4k)           609 |@@                                                   |
```

[4k, 8k)	611	@@
[8k, 16k)	438	@
[16k, 32k)	59	
[32k, 64k)	36	
[64k, 128k)	5	

6.3.1.3. Analyzing Kernel Code

If you are familiar with Java bytecode instrumentation, `tracepoint` will give you a different approach to instrumentation. I believe that Linux kernel instrumentation methods like `tracepoint` are a skill worth learning.

`tracepoint` is used for kernel static instrumentation. It traces calls that developers insert into logical locations in the kernel code, which are subsequently compiled into the kernel binary.

Maintaining `tracepoints` is a burden for kernel developers, so their scope of use is limited compared to kprobe. The advantage of `tracepoints` is that they provide a stable API. You should use `tracepoint` first whenever possible, and only use kprobe when it is not sufficient.

Let's look at sched:sched_process_exec through a use case. When running a Linux utility program, the process calls the `fork()` and `exevc()` system call methods.

- sched_process_fork: Creates a process
- sched_process_exec: Runs a process
- sched_process_exit: Exits a process
- sched_process_free: Frees process resources

BPF is a profile, which is used to understand performance and latency, and debugging is the process of understanding the code. SRE also needs to understand the code to be able to perform root cause analysis.

The method is named sys_execve(). Because the sys_execve() method is a handler method for the execve system call, you can deduce that the execve() system call occurred in user space. Based on this information, you know that the execve() system call was executed in user space after the `fork()` system call.

You can find the code at /kernel/syscalls/sys_execve.c.

```
int sys_execve(const char *path, char *const argv[], char *const envp[]) {
  int fd = sys_open(path);
  if(fd < 0) return fd;
  process p;
  int ret = load_binary(fd, &p);
  if(ret < 0) return ret;
  sys_close(fd);
  if(create_elf_info(&p, argv, envp)) return -EFAULT;
```

```
  asm volatile(
    "mov [rip + kernel_stack], rsp;"

    "xor rbp, rbp;"
    ".byte 0x48;"
    "sysretq"
    :: [entry]"r"(p.entry + p.load_addr), [rsp]"r"(p.rsp)
    : "r11", "rcx"
  );

  return -EPERM;
```

include/trace/events contains the header files for tracepoints. The following are included in sched.h:

```
#define TRACE_SYSTEM sched
[...]
TRACE_EVENT(sched_process_exec,
TP_PROTO(struct task_struct *p, pid_t old_pid,
struct linux_binprm *bprm),
TP_ARGS(p, old_pid, bprm),
TP_STRUCT__entry(
__string( filename, bprm->filename)
__field( pid_t, pid )
__field( pid_t, old_pid )
),
TP_fast_assign(
__assign_str(filename, bprm->filename);
__entry->pid = p->pid;
__entry->old_pid = old_pid;
),
TP_printk("filename=%s pid=%d old_pid=%d", __get_str(filename),
__entry->pid, __entry->old_pid)
);
```

The code specifies the trace_SYSTEM as sched, and the tracepoint name as sched_process_exec. The next line specifies metadata, including the format string from TP_printk().

It is also available at runtime through the format files for each tracepoint in the located in /sys. For example:

```
# cat /sys/kernel/debug/tracing/events/sched/sched_process_exec/format
name: sched_process_exec
```

CHAPTER 6 INFRASTRUCTURE RCA

```
ID: 298
format:
field:unsigned short common_type; offset:0; size:2; signed:0;
field:unsigned char common_flags; offset:2; size:1; signed:0;
field:unsigned char common_preempt_count; offset:3; size:1; signed:0;
field:int common_pid; offset:4; size:4; signed:1;
field:__data_loc char[] filename; offset:8; size:4; signed:1;
field:pid_t pid; offset:12; size:4; signed:1;
field:pid_t old_pid; offset:16; size:4; signed:1;
print fmt: "filename=%s pid=%d old_pid=%d", __get_str(filename), REC->pid,
REC->old_pid
```

The trace tool uses this format file to understand the metadata associated with a tracepoint. The tracepoint is called via trace_sched_process_exec() in the kernel code in fs/exec.c. The system call handler, sys_execve(), is called, and then the exec_binprm() method is executed.

- do_execveat_common()
- exec_binprm()

The trace_sched_process_exec() method displays the location of the tracepoint. You can see the code in /fs/exec.c.

```
static int exec_binprm(struct linux_binprm *bprm)
{
pid_t old_pid, old_vpid;
int ret;

old_pid = current->pid;
rcu_read_lock();
old_vpid = task_pid_nr_ns(current, task_active_pid_ns(current->parent));
rcu_read_unlock();
ret = search_binary_handler(bprm);
if (ret >= 0) {
audit_bprm(bprm);
trace_sched_process_exec(current, old_pid, bprm);
ptrace_event(PTRACE_EVENT_EXEC, old_vpid);
proc_exec_connector(current);
}
[...]
```

Print the behavior of the process starting execution as a sched_process_exec event in ftrace.

6.3.1.4. BCC Tools

https://github.com/iovisor/bcc/blob/master/t describes a variety of BCC tools. While it is difficult to understand all of the tools in detail, you should have a general idea of their capabilities so that you can quickly utilize them in the future.

- runqlat
- runqlen
- funclatency
- softirqs

The runqlat Tool

runqlat is a BCC and bpftrace tool that measures CPU scheduler latency, often referred to as execution queue latency. This tool is useful for finding and quantifying CPU saturation issues, when something is demanding more CPU resources than it can service. The metric that runqlat measures is the amount of time each thread spends waiting for its turn on the CPU.

runqlat works by instrumenting scheduler wakeup and context switch events to determine how long it takes for a process to wake up and enter the running state. These events can be very frequent, exceeding 1 million events per second in production.

The runqlen Tool

The BCC and bpftrace tools sample the length of the CPU execution queue, aggregate how many tasks are waiting for an order, and display this as a histogram. This tool can be used to identify the characteristics of an execution queue latency problem, or just to do a quick calculation.

I refer to the execution queue length as a secondary performance metric and the execution queue latency as the primary performance metric. Latency directly affects performance. Consider a situation where you're standing in line to check out at a store. Why does the length of the queue matter, or the actual time you spend waiting? runqlat is more important. So why use runqlen?

runqlen can further characterize the issues found by runqlat and explain how the latency is increasing. runqlen uses periodic sampling at 99Hz intervals, while runqlat traces scheduler events. This sampling incurs negligible overhead compared to runqlat's scheduler trace. In general production, I recommend using runqlen first to identify issues and then runqlat ad hoc analysis to quantify latency.

BCC Tools

funclatency can measure latency and is an important metric in performance analysis of both kernel and user space applications. It provides insight into how long a particular method takes to execute.

CHAPTER 6 INFRASTRUCTURE RCA

- **Identify performance bottlenecks:** High latency can indicate inefficiencies or problems within your code that need to be optimized.

- **Ensure system responsiveness:** In real-time systems or latency-sensitive applications, it is essential to understand and minimize method latency to maintain responsiveness.

- **Profiles and benchmarking:** By measuring the latency of various method, developers can benchmark their systems and compare the performance of different implementations or configurations.

- **Debugging and diagnostics:** If you experience unexpected behavior or performance degradation in your system, measuring method latency can help you pinpoint the source of the problem.

Both kernel space (e.g., system calls, file operations) and user space (e.g., library methods) functions can profile latency, providing a comprehensive view of system performance.

funclatency is an eBPF program designed to measure the latency of a method by connecting to the entry and exit points of the method. The program uses kprobes and kretprobes for kernel methods and uprobes and uretprobes for user space methods to measure the start and end times of method execution.

- **Entry method:** Measures the current timestamp when the method is entered and stores it in a start map keyed by the process ID.

- **Exit method:** Calculates latency by subtracting the stored start time from the current time. The result is then categorized into a histogram, which is incremented to record the occurrence of the corresponding scope of latency.

funclatency can be measured in user space and kernel space.

To profile the latency of a user space method, such as the read method of the libc library, you can run the following command:

```
# ./funclatency /usr/lib/x86_64-linux-gnu/libc.so.6:read
tracing /usr/lib/x86_64-linux-gnu/libc.so.6:read...
tracing func read in /usr/lib/x86_64-linux-gnu/libc.so.6...
Tracing /usr/lib/x86_64-linux-gnu/libc.so.6:read.  Hit Ctrl-C to exit
^C
    nsec              : count     distribution
       0 -> 1         : 0         |                                        |
       2 -> 3         : 0         |                                        |
       4 -> 7         : 0         |                                        |
       8 -> 15        : 0         |                                        |
      16 -> 31        : 0         |                                        |
      32 -> 63        : 0         |                                        |
     128 -> 255       : 0         |                                        |
```

```
    512 -> 1023       : 0        |                                          |
  65536 -> 131071     : 651      |*****************************************+|
 131072 -> 262143     : 107      |******                                    |
 262144 -> 524287     : 36       |**                                        |
 524288 -> 1048575    : 8        |                                          |
8388608 -> 16777215   : 2        |                                          |
Exiting trace of /usr/lib/x86_64-linux-gnu/libc.so.6:read
```

To profile the latency of a kernel space method, such as vfs_read, run the following command:

```
# sudo ./funclatency -u vfs_read
Tracing vfs_read. Hit Ctrl-C to exit
^C
     usec              : count     distribution
        0 -> 1         : 0         |                                          |
        8 -> 15        : 0         |                                          |
       16 -> 31        : 3397      |*****************************************|
       32 -> 63        : 2175      |************************                  |
       64 -> 127       : 184       |**                                        |
     1024 -> 2047      : 0         |                                          |
     4096 -> 8191      : 5         |                                          |
  2097152 -> 4194303   : 2         |                                          |
Exiting trace of vfs_read
```

This command profiles the execution of the specified method in user space or kernel space, and outputs a histogram of the observed latencies to show the distribution of the method's duration.

The ftrace Tool

Let's compare vfs_read to ftrace and strace.

You can check the available events and functions in /sys/kernel/debug/tracing/available_filter_ functions and /sys/kernel/debug/tracing/available_events. Similar to kprobe and tracepoint, ftrace also performs root cause analysis centered on events and functions.

Many system calls support virtual filesystem-related functions, and the vfs_read() method is called from the kernel. First, I describe ftrace.

```
Echo 0 > /sys/kernel/debug/tracing/tracing_on
sleep 1
echo "tracing_off"

echo 0 > /sys/kernel/debug/tracing/events/enable
sleep 1
echo "events disabled"
```

CHAPTER 6   INFRASTRUCTURE RCA

```
echo function > /sys/kernel/debug/tracing/current_tracer
sleep 1
echo "function tracer enabled"

echo 1 > /sys/kernel/debug/tracing/events/raw_syscalls/sys_enter/enable
echo 1 > /sys/kernel/debug/tracing/events/raw_syscalls/sys_exit/enable
echo "syscalls event enabled"

echo vfs_read > /sys/kernel/debug/tracing/set_ftrace_filter
sleep 1
echo "set_ftrace_filter enabled"

echo 1 > /sys/kernel/debug/tracing/options/func_stack_trace
echo 1 > /sys/kernel/debug/tracing/options/sym-offset
echo "function stack trace enabled"

echo 1 > /sys/kernel/debug/tracing/tracing_on
echo "tracing_on"
```

Most system call handlers execute virtual filesystem interface methods that start with `vfs_read`.

If you run the command and create an `ftrace` log, you would see the `sys_read()` and `vfs_read()` methods in the `ftrace` log. Since most system call handlers are created with the `sys_` convention, you can see that the system call handler for the `read()` method called from user space is the `sys_read()` method.

The strace Tool

This section describes how to use `strace` to debug system calls. `strace` provides the following features:

- Prints the name of the method that calls the system call in the `glibc` library
- Returns the value after running a system call

The log of the `strace` looks like this

```
openat(AT_FDCWD, "/root/simple.txt", O_RDWR)           = 3
read(3, "", 256)                                       = 0
write(3, "CentOS 9!\n", 16)                            = 16
lseek(3, 0, SEEK_SET)                                  = 0
read(3, "CentOS 9!\n", 256)                            = 16
write(1, "\320\256\3228read again \n", 16Ю 8read again
) = 16
write(1, "[+]read buffer: CentOS 9!\n", 32[+]read buffer: CentOS 9!
) = 32
write(1, " \n", 2
)                                                      = 2
```

CHAPTER 6　INFRASTRUCTURE RCA

```
close(3)                                                              = 0
clone(child_stack=NULL, flags=CLONE_CHILD_CLEARTID|CLONE_CHILD_SETTID|SIGCHLD, child_
tidptr=0x7f72050327d0) = 61366
write(1, "start execution of parent process"..., 34start execution of parent process
) = 34
getpid()                                                              = 61365
getppid()                                                             = 61363
write(1, "strace testing ppid:61363 pid:"..., 39strace testing ppid:61363 pid:61365
) = 39
nanosleep({tv_sec=2, tv_nsec=0}, strace: Process 61366 attached
 <unfinished ...>
[pid 61366] write(1, "start execution of child process"..., 33start execution of
child process
) = 33
[pid 61366] getpid()                                                  = 61366
[pid 61366] getppid()                                                 = 61365
[pid 61366] write(1, "strace testing ppid:61365 pid:"..., 39strace testing ppid:61365
pid:61366
) = 39

[pid 61366] nanosleep({tv_sec=2, tv_nsec=0},  <unfinished ...>
[pid 61365] <... nanosleep resumed> 0x7fffd40bfe80) = 0
[pid 61365] exit_group(0)                                             = ?
[pid 61365] +++ exited with 0 +++
<... nanosleep resumed> 0x7fffd40bfe80)                               = 0
exit_group(0)                                                         = ?
+++ exited with 0 +++
```

The result can be understood as shown here:

- It called the `fork()` method, which called the `clone()` method in `glibc`.
- In the `read()` method, note from the internal code of the `printf()` method that it calls the POSIX write system call.
- When you call the Linux low-level method `sleep()`, it calls a system call method within the `glibc` library called `nanosleep()`.

Measuring method latency with eBPF BCC provides a detailed understanding of the performance of user space and kernel space code.

This example measures the latency of various `softirqs`.

```
# ./softirqs -d
Tracing soft irq event time... Hit Ctrl-C to end.
```

519

CHAPTER 6 INFRASTRUCTURE RCA

```
^C
softirq = net_rx_action
     usecs               : count     distribution
         0 -> 1          : 0        |                                        |
         2 -> 3          : 0        |                                        |
         4 -> 7          : 0        |                                        |
         8 -> 15         : 0        |                                        |
      8192 -> 16383      : 8770     |****************************************|
     16384 -> 32767      : 1780     |********                                |
     32768 -> 65535      : 216      |                                        |
     65536 -> 131071     : 4        |                                        |

softirq = run_timer_softirq
     usecs               : count     distribution
         0 -> 1          : 0        |                                        |
         2 -> 3          : 0        |                                        |
       128 -> 255        : 0        |                                        |
       256 -> 511        : 2        |                                        |
       512 -> 1023       : 366      |*********                               |
      1024 -> 2047       : 1525     |****************************************|
      2048 -> 4095       : 629      |****************                        |
      4096 -> 8191       : 87       |**                                      |
      8192 -> 16383      : 1        |                                        |
```

Sometimes you only need the number of events and not the distribution. You can use the --C or --events option.

```
# ./softirqs.py -C
Tracing soft irq events... Hit Ctrl-C to end.
^C
SOFTIRQ         TOTAL_count
block                    5
tasklet                  6
net_rx                 402
sched                 5251
rcu                   5748
timer                 9530
```

I briefly described system utilities and eBPF. The overall direction and approach was explained, but the details are lacking. I recommend further learning through related books.

System utilities and eBPF can be confusing, as there are many different tools available. I would like to explain this approach. The ftrace, eBPF, and KUtrace system utilities all have different purposes. There are different choices to suit different purposes and priorities: debugging, production overhead, visualization.

- It is important to understand that eBPF is a profile and KUtrace is a system trace, so the usage and results are different. KUtrace offers many advantages and should be considered first over eBPF.

- The next step is to use bpftrace to write a simple tracepoint one-liner. You can add more features than the BCC tool, so this allows you to measure more granular performance than just methods. If tracepoint does not support events, check if kprobe supports the method. For more complex requirements, you can use the Python, high-level libraries provided by BCC to develop your application.

I recommend using a visualization tool like traceshark, KUtrace, or PCP.

PCP supports BCC and bpftrace, and it manages real-time and historical data.

6.3.2. PCP

There are not many solutions that allow you to write and visualize one-liners with bpftrace and visualize the results of BCC tools and system calls as histograms, heatmaps, and flame graphs. I recommend that SREs use the CLI. However, in large-scale production where automation is required, using only the CLI is inefficient. To make data easy to understand, you need to provide visualizations. It is integrated with Grafana, and you can configure the eBPF dashboard with various charts. For example, you can configure various BPF correlations in the Grafana dashboard, such as applying variables along with the application profile.

- A wide range of users should be able to use these tools together and collaborate.

- It's easy to integrate with Prometheus and easy to develop alert rules.

- Be able to manage data over long periods of time and analyze trends and details.

- To process large volumes of traffic, it can be tied to Redis and is easy to scale.

- BCC and bpftrace are supported out of the box, and you can write your own one-liners.

PCP provides metrics by default that can be extended with your own plugins or agents.

PCP's stateless model is lightweight and powerful. Because the client processes all state management, sampling rates, and computation, the overhead on the host is negligible.

6.3.2.1. Introduction

Using PCP as a data source, you can visualize most of the BCC and bpftrace metrics provided by PCP through Grafana. You can show historical data, or you can show real-time metric data.

Figure 6-18 shows that a PCP contains three components. They are data sources, server processes, and dashboards. The data source provides real-time and historical data. The server process collects data from the data source and transfers it to the dashboard. The dashboard outputs charts such as flame graphs and histograms.

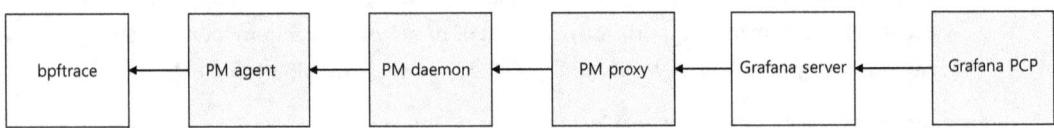

Figure 6-18. *PCP flow*

PCP data sources:

- The PCP Redis data source provides fast, scalable time series capabilities. It is intended for querying historical data across multiple hosts and supports filtering based on labels. Queries are sent to a proxy, which queries metrics from the Redis database.

- The PCP vector data source shows real-time host metrics. This includes support for individual hosts and containers. The PCP Vector data source connects to a proxy, requesting live metrics directly from the daemon. In this case, the metrics are stored temporarily in the browser, and the metric values are lost when the browser tab is refreshed.

- The PCP bpftrace data source supports using the bpftrace script. You can connect to the bpftrace agent and run a bpftrace script on the host.

The server process is made up of various daemons, including agents, daemons, proxies, loggers, and more.

- The monitored host runs a daemon that communicates with the agent.

- Daemons are the core component of PCP. They typically run on the target host and manage the collection of metrics from a large number of agents.

- The logger daemon records the metrics of the daemon and stores them in storage.

- The proxy searches for new data generated by the logger and stores it in Redis.

- Proxy is a Prometheus exporter. PCP provides metrics based on Prometheus. You can scrape metrics from /metrics. This is the same as normal Prometheus scraping.

In the case of node exporters, the built-in features are complicated and it is difficult to add the features you need. With PCP, you can easily add the features you want and visualize them with Grafana. PCP is recommend over node exporters if you want to save money on observability and want detailed kernel data. For example, the node exporter provides a large number of metrics, and sometimes you may not need a specific metric. The node exporter also allows you to exclude metrics you don't need. PCP makes it simple to add new features and make changes at the kernel level.

The proxy is a Prometheus exporter. You can scrape metrics from /metrics, as shown in Figure 6-19. PCP provides metrics externally in a variety of ways, such as through Openmetric.

```
# TYPE kvm_efer_reload counter
kvm_efer_reload{hostname="localhost.localdomain",machineid="e95c31c264ab40ea9d659932ca428e78",domainname="localdomain"} 0
# PCP5 kvm.exits 95.0.1 u64 PM INDOM NULL counter count
# HELP kvm_exits Number of guest exits from I/O port accesses.
# TYPE kvm_exits counter
kvm_exits{hostname="localhost.localdomain",machineid="e95c31c264ab40ea9d659932ca428e78",domainname="localdomain"} 0
# PCP5 kvm.fpu_reload 95.0.2 u64 PM INDOM NULL counter count
# HELP kvm_fpu_reload Number of reload fpu(Float Point Unit).
# TYPE kvm_fpu_reload counter
kvm_fpu_reload{hostname="localhost.localdomain",machineid="e95c31c264ab40ea9d659932ca428e78",domainname="localdomain"} 0
# PCP5 kvm.halt_attempted_poll 95.0.3 u64 PM INDOM NULL counter count
# HELP kvm_halt_attempted_poll Number of times the vcpu attempts to polls.
# TYPE kvm_halt_attempted_poll counter
kvm_halt_attempted_poll{hostname="localhost.localdomain",machineid="e95c31c264ab40ea9d659932ca428e78",domainname="localdomain"} 0
# PCP5 kvm.halt_exits 95.0.4 u64 PM INDOM NULL counter count
# HELP kvm_halt_exits Number of guest exits due to halt calls.
# TYPE kvm_halt_exits counter
kvm_halt_exits{hostname="localhost.localdomain",machineid="e95c31c264ab40ea9d659932ca428e78",domainname="localdomain"} 0
# PCP5 kvm.halt_successful_poll 95.0.5 u64 PM INDOM NULL counter count
# HELP kvm_halt_successful_poll The number of times the vcpu attempts to polls successfully.
# TYPE kvm_halt_successful_poll counter
kvm_halt_successful_poll{hostname="localhost.localdomain",machineid="e95c31c264ab40ea9d659932ca428e78",domainname="localdomain"} 0
# PCP5 kvm.halt_wakeup 95.0.6 u64 PM INDOM NULL counter count
# HELP kvm_halt_wakeup Number of wakeups from a halt.
# TYPE kvm_halt_wakeup counter
kvm_halt_wakeup{hostname="localhost.localdomain",machineid="e95c31c264ab40ea9d659932ca428e78",domainname="localdomain"} 0
# PCP5 kvm.host_state_reload 95.0.7 u64 PM INDOM NULL counter count
# HELP kvm_host_state_reload Number of full reloads of the host state
# TYPE kvm_host_state_reload counter
kvm_host_state_reload{hostname="localhost.localdomain",machineid="e95c31c264ab40ea9d659932ca428e78",domainname="localdomain"} 0
# PCP5 kvm.hypercalls 95.0.8 u64 PM INDOM NULL counter count
# HELP kvm_hypercalls Number of guest hypervisor service calls.
# TYPE kvm_hypercalls counter
kvm_hypercalls{hostname="localhost.localdomain",machineid="e95c31c264ab40ea9d659932ca428e78",domainname="localdomain"} 0
# PCP5 kvm.insn_emulation 95.0.9 u64 PM INDOM NULL counter count
# HELP kvm_insn_emulation Number of insn_emulation attempts.
# TYPE kvm_insn_emulation counter
kvm_insn_emulation{hostname="localhost.localdomain",machineid="e95c31c264ab40ea9d659932ca428e78",domainname="localdomain"} 0
# PCP5 kvm.insn_emulation_fail 95.0.10 u64 PM INDOM NULL counter count
# HELP kvm_insn_emulation_fail Number of failed insn_emulation attempts.
# TYPE kvm_insn_emulation_fail counter
kvm_insn_emulation_fail{hostname="localhost.localdomain",machineid="e95c31c264ab40ea9d659932ca428e78",domainname="localdomain"} 0
# PCP5 kvm.invlpg 95.0.11 u64 PM INDOM NULL counter count
# HELP kvm_invlpg Number of invlpg attepts.
# TYPE kvm_invlpg counter
kvm_invlpg{hostname="localhost.localdomain",machineid="e95c31c264ab40ea9d659932ca428e78",domainname="localdomain"} 0
```

Figure 6-19. *Metric in PCP*

The PCP dashboard uses the Grafana PCP plugin, which allows you to analyze BCC and `bpftrace` with Grafana dashboards. Historical and real-time metrics are available.

You can output real-time host metrics using the PCP vector data source, as well as output historical metrics for multiple hosts, using the PCP Redis data source. The advantage of PCP is that you can write `bpftrace` one-liners and output the results to a dashboard. This allows you to measure performance optimized for your specific application.

6.3.2.2. Configure PCP

The demo is on Red Hat Linux. Proceed in the following order:

```
$ setenforce 0
```

CHAPTER 6 INFRASTRUCTURE RCA

Proceed with the BCC installation:

```
$ ./Install
[Sun Sep 10 08:18:15] pmdabcc(79912) Info: Initializing, currently in 'notready' state.
[Sun Sep 10 08:18:15] pmdabcc(79912) Info: Enabled modules:
[Sun Sep 10 08:18:15] pmdabcc(79912) Info: ['netproc', 'runqlat', 'biolatency', 'tcptop', 'tcplife']
[Sun Sep 10 08:18:15] pmdabcc(79912) Info: Configuring modules:
[Sun Sep 10 08:18:15] pmdabcc(79912) Info: netproc
[Sun Sep 10 08:18:15] pmdabcc(79912) Info: runqlat
[Sun Sep 10 08:18:15] pmdabcc(79916) Info: biolatency
[Sun Sep 10 08:18:15] pmdabcc(79916) Info: tcptop
[Sun Sep 10 08:18:15] pmdabcc(79916) Info: tcplife
[Sun Sep 10 08:18:15] pmdabcc(79916) Info: Helpers registered.
Updating the Performance Metrics Name Space (PMNS) ...
Terminate PMDA if already installed ...
Updating the PMCD control file, and notifying PMCD ...
Check bcc metrics have appeared ... 1 warnings, 1 metrics and 0 values
```

Check the installed BCC modules:

```
$ pminfo bcc
bcc.disk.all.latency
bcc.runq.latency
bcc.proc.io.net.tcp.duration
bcc.proc.io.net.tcp.rx
bcc.proc.io.net.tcp.tx
bcc.proc.io.net.tcp.dport
bcc.proc.io.net.tcp.daddr
bcc.proc.io.net.tcp.lport
bcc.proc.net.udp.recv.calls
bcc.proc.net.udp.send.bytes
bcc.proc.net.udp.send.calls
bcc.proc.net.tcp.recv.bytes
bcc.proc.net.tcp.recv.calls
bcc.proc.net.tcp.send.bytes
bcc.proc.net.tcp.send.calls
[root@localhost bcc]#
```

Install bpftrace:

```
$ cd /var/lib/pcp/pmdas/bpftrace && sudo ./Install
Updating the Performance Metrics Name Space (PMNS) ...
```

```
Terminate PMDA if already installed ...
Updating the PMCD control file, and notifying PMCD ...
Check bpftrace metrics have appeared ... 23 metrics and 22 values
[root@localhost bpftrace]# pminfo bpftrace
bpftrace.scripts.runqlat.data.usecs
bpftrace.scripts.runqlat.data_bytes
bpftrace.info.scripts
bpftrace.control.stop
bpftrace.control.start
bpftrace.control.deregister
bpftrace.control.register
```

bpftrace and the PCP profiles can be used to measure performance and understand the problem. The reason you need PCP is that it makes bpftrace easy to develop and visualize. It provides tools for storing data and visualizing it.

Automating the various tools mentioned in BCC and bpftrace is not straightforward. Therefore, it is best to set alerts on PCP to monitor them.

6.3.2.3. PCP Demo

This demo describes how to use PCP and bpftrace together to graph low-level kernel metrics. If you can get values from the kernel into an eBPF map (key/value data used to store data in an eBPF program) in a bpftrace script, you can use PCP to graph them.

To test if the bpftrace agent is installed properly, try the following:

```
pmrep bpftrace.scripts.runqlat.data_bytes -s 5
```

Five samples of run queue latency measured in microseconds are displayed.

```
b.s.r.data_bytes
        byte/s
           N/A
       586.165
       590.276
       588.141
       589.113
```

Using the bpftrace agent, which works with the PCP, you can start working on integrating with Grafana.

- To enable PCP bpftrace in Grafana, you need to create a user that can run valid bpftrace scripts.

- Click Configuration, then click Data Sources. Click Add Data Source, scroll to the bottom of the page where PCP bpftrace is located, and then click Select.

CHAPTER 6   INFRASTRUCTURE RCA

- In the URL field, enter http://localhost:44322, and under Auth, click Basic Auth.
- Basic Auth Details appears. Enter the username for metrics and the password.
- Click the Dashboards icon and select Manage. The list displays a dashboard named PCP bpftrace System Analysis.
- You will see various metrics. Click the dropdown next to CPU usage and click Edit.
- When executed, you can see that the query is the actual bpftrace script, and @ cpu adds data to the eBPF map, which is populated with a histogram of CPU data representing CPU usage. Grafana takes this eBPF map and graphs it.

Let's see how to use the bpftrace script to graph kernel data, such as the number of PIDs per second.

```
BEGIN
{
    printf("Tracing new processes... Hit Ctrl-C to end.\n");
}

tracepoint:sched:sched_process_fork
{
    @ = count();
}

interval:s:1
{
    time("%H:%M:%S PIDs/sec: ");
    print(@);
    clear(@);
}

END
{
    clear(@);
}
```

The core parts of the script you need are explained here.

- Basically, it counts the number of times sched_process_fork is called and stores it in an eBPF map that can be graphed.
- Let's get started with creating a panel to graph. Back on the PCP bpftrace System Analysis dashboard page, there is an Add Panel button. A new panel with two buttons appears. Click the Add Query button.

CHAPTER 6   INFRASTRUCTURE RCA

- Select PCP bpftrace. In the text box for Query A, enter the bpftrace script.

- Returning to the PCP bpftrace System Analysis board, you can see that the metric is graphed in the dashboard.

You need a way to provide bpftrace scripts to users without having to run the bpftrace scripts. The bpftrace agent package provides this functionality. The bpftrace script stored in /var/lib/pcp/pmdas/bpftrace/autostart is loaded with the PCP metric when the bpftrace agent is loaded.

Edit /var/lib/pcp/pmdas/bpftrace/autostart/pidpersec.bt.

```
tracepoint:sched:sched_process_fork
{
    @ = count();
}
```

Because you did not name the eBPF map, name the map root.

```
pmrep bpftrace.scripts.pidpersec.data.root -s 5
```

Output the following result:

```
b.s.p.d.root
       /s
      N/A
    3.984
   31.049
    0.000
    0.000
```

This shows the number of processes per second. Since it's a standard PCP metric, you can import it into Grafana and graph it without having to grant special permissions to Grafana users.

- Click the dashboard icon, and then click Manage.

- Click PCP Vector Host Overview.

- Click the Add Panel button, then in the new panel, click Add Query.

- There is a dropdown menu next to the word Query. Select PCP Vector from this menu and type bpftrace.scripts.pidpersec.data.root into the query.

- Click the General icon and set the Processes per Second heading.

- Returning to the PCP Vector Host Overview dashboard, you can see the eBPF map from the bpftrace script graphed by a normal user without special permissions.

bpftrace provides a way to expose kernel metrics to Grafana's graphs. Using bpftrace scripts in this way means that they will run continuously

6.4. Chaos Engineering

Unlike with applications, infrastructure problems can be major failures. Chaos engineering can proactively identify infrastructure failures and improve infrastructure reliability. Chaos engineering and anomaly detection are better suited for infrastructure observability than for applications.

During production, microservices may experience latency or go down. If users experience inconvenience, you should try to resolve it quickly. SREs don't get rattled by this level of failure, because there are times when the infrastructure fails and all services go down.

- A large utility company had a problem while patching network equipment. There was no rollback and all services were down for over two days.

- A large banking organization experienced a failure of its API server, load balancer, and security services, which caused customers to experience service inconvenience for three days.

- An e-commerce store was experiencing a database and cache server outage, resulting in a prolonged service interruption.

There is a problem with the infrastructure—network, load balancers, API servers, databases, cache servers. The chaos engineering I am talking about involves network failures.

Typical microservices communicate on L7. I create a failure on L3 through the chaos mesh. Although the failure occurs at L3, it will affect L7, and eventually you will see latency increase in the microservices.

Chaos engineering involves intentionally introducing errors and faulty scenarios into a distributed system to test its resilience. This provides insight into the reliability of the system. Utilizing this approach, ensure that your product accurately identifies various failure scenarios.

- Create a latency. In a distributed system, latency is the sum of network latency and frontend and backend application latency. In some cases, you need to measure network and application latencies separately. You need a tool that can analyze the latency of each section in detail.

- The TCP retransmission mechanism can occur when packets are out of order, or when there is insufficient bandwidth available to send and receive packets. To easily reproduce this behavior, use chaos meshes.

- Generate packet drops in the network. As packet loss occurs, you can understand how it affects your transactions.

6.4.1. Overview

To improve reliability in production, and to make it easier to generate failures and errors in the test environment, chaos engineering is a great way to go.

- Chaos mesh makes it easy to create network latency, retransmission, and loss of packets.

- Chaos mesh and Cilium network policies can be used to create losses precisely where microservices communicate with each other.

- It provides a great opportunity to make sure your SLO and metrics are configured correctly, and to make improvements.

Chaos engineering is the field of experimenting with systems to build systems that can withstand sudden failures, even in production.

How much confidence can you have in a complex system that you've deployed to production? Even if all the individual services within a distributed system are working properly, the interactions between them can produce unexpected results. These results make the distributed system itself inherently chaos.

The definition of chaos engineering is as follows:

- Chaos engineering is the principle of experimenting with a system to build confidence in its ability to handle the chaos that occurs in production.

- Many factors can affect reliability, and as a chaos engineer, you can focus on establishing evidence of how resilient the system is under unexpected and unavoidable circumstances.

- The sole purpose of chaos engineering is to provide evidence of vulnerabilities in a system.

The real world is unpredictable, so it may seem unnecessary to intentionally cause problems. Accidental configuration changes and power outages affecting data centers are just a few events that have caused large-scale problems around the world. Especially in distributed systems, dependencies can lead to errors that can be difficult to explain during normal development.

You need to identify weaknesses in advance that may manifest themselves as abnormal behavior throughout the system. System weaknesses can take the following forms:

- Inappropriate response when a service is unavailable

- Excessive retries due to incorrectly set timeout values

- Failure of backend systems to process large volumes of traffic

- Failures that propagate

Before these things impact the customer experience in production, you need to proactively address their most critical weaknesses. You need a way to manage the chaos inherent in these systems, increase their flexibility and speed, and make them reliable for deployment in production.

By observing the behavior of the system in controlled experiments, you need to understand the failures that are likely to occur.

With the aim of specifically addressing uncertainty in large-scale distributed systems, chaos engineering facilitates the discovery of system weaknesses through experiments. These experiments follow four steps:

CHAPTER 6 INFRASTRUCTURE RCA

1. Extract measurable system outputs and define normal behavior as steady state.
2. Assume that this steady state will continue in both the control and experiments.
3. Introduce variables that reflect real-world events, such as server failures, storage malfunctions, and network outages.
4. Find the steady-state difference between the control and experiments and disprove the hypothesis.

The harder it is to deviate from the steady state, the more confidence you can have in the behavior of the system. If weaknesses are found, they can be improved before they appear in the actual system.

The following principles describe the ideal application of chaos engineering, based on the experimental process described previously.

- **Make hypotheses about steady state and behavior.** Emphasis should be placed on measurable system outputs rather than internal attributes of the system. Outputs measured over a short period of time represent the steady state of the system. Overall system throughput, error rate, and latency percentiles can be key metrics that indicate health. When conducting experiments, focus on the behavioral patterns of the system, and chaos engineering will validate that the system is working properly.

- **Apply a variety of real event variables.** Chaos variables reflect real-world events. Prioritize events based on their potential impact or expected frequency. Consider hardware failures such as server outages, software failures such as incorrect responses, and non-
failure events such as traffic spikes or system scaling. Any event that can disrupt the steady state is a potential variable in chaos experiments.

- **Run experiments in production.** Your system will behave differently depending on your environment and traffic patterns. Since utilization patterns can change at any time, it is necessary to sample real traffic. To ensure reliability in how the system runs and relevance to the system as currently deployed, Chaos engineering prefers to run experiments directly on production traffic.

- **Automate to run experiments continuously.** Running experiments manually is not only labor-intensive, it's also unsustainable. You need to automate your experiments and run them continuously. Chaos engineering is about building automation into your system to support orchestration and analysis.

- **Evaluate the scope of propagation and risk.** Experiments in production can cause unnecessary inconvenience to customers. While there should be some tolerance for short-lived negative impacts, it is the responsibility and obligation of the chaos engineer to minimize and contain the significant damage that experiments can cause to multiple systems.

Chaos engineering is a powerful tool that has already changed the way people design and engineer software, and it's happening in some of the largest operations in the world. Chaos deals primarily with the uncertainty of these distributed systems. The principles of chaos can be applied at scale and quickly, and they deliver high-quality experiences that customers value.

Chaos engineering offers many benefits. It can be improved on the topics mentioned here:

- **Separate signals:** For those of us who collect a lot of data and need to apply it to automation and AI, it's useful to be able to quickly and easily generate errors and warning data.

- **Validate alerts:** If you generate a large number of alerts indiscriminately, they can become unnecessary noise. You need a process to validate and verify the data generated before it becomes noise.

- **External maintenance:** Due to the nature of the cloud, CSPs do a lot of maintenance and patching internally. If the application is not tested beforehand, or if there is no exception processing, it will experience unintended failures.

- **Change management:** New applications can cause problems, but if you don't have a clear understanding of the risks and dependencies of your existing environment or other applications with complex dependencies, it's hard to avoid errors and failures. The more complex the dependencies, the more likely it is that changes will cause failures due to a lack of understanding of other dependencies. It is important to have a clear understanding of the scope of failure propagation through multiple tests.

Before deploying an application to production, putting it through a variety of stress, functional, and integration tests can help you forecast the behavior of your application in a broad scope. However, in some situations, this can be difficult to reproduce outside of production. Through chaos engineering, engineers can learn and explore system behavior. The goal of these experiments is to ensure that the system is robust enough to withstand errors.

Chaos engineers run experiments in production, but it is important to understand that one of the principles of chaos engineering is to not cause unnecessary inconvenience to users, to control experiments, and to limit their scope.

The experiment creation cycle is as follows:

- It starts with a known good or healthy system.

- A hypothesis is then proposed to explain the impact of the experiments on the system state.

- The proposed experiments are executed on the system.

- Validate the impact on the system by verifying that the forecast matches the hypothesis. The validation phase provides an opportunity to identify any unexpected side effects of the experiments. If it behaved worse than expected, what was the reason? If it worked better than expected, what happened? It is important to understand what happened, especially if the results were better than expected.

- Once validated, the system is improved, and a new cycle begins. Ideally, these experiments can be automated.

6.4.2. Demo

This demo requires a complex configuration, but you need to understand how to demo, accurately reproduce, and measure problems in a runtime environment close to production.

In the demo, latency on L3 failure propagates to L7 and the application. It is important to be able to recognize and differentiate between problems on L3. The root cause is L3. It is difficult to identify L3 latency from distributed traces alone. This is where Cilium and Hubble come in.

The latency caused by the infrastructure can propagate, causing the application to become latent. The latency will increase and a timeout error will occur. It will retry the specified number of times. Chaos mesh-generated losses interfere with traffic destined for a particular pod. Traffic forwarded to the target pod adds latency, but it is not considered a drop. To create drops, I recommend using network policies.

- Support Kubernetes and host environments.
- Accurately inject faults into Kubernetes pods.
- Compare previous configurations and manage settings.
- Compare and manage the results of your experiments.
- By combining multiple experiments, create more complex, realistic experiments.
- While Cilium only allows for network-specific chaos engineering, chaos meshes allow for many different types of experiments.

Injecting faults using chaos meshes is more powerful and useful than Cilium. Download utilities like TC when configuring your Docker image. For more complex configurations, I recommend using the official Docker image with TC.

6.4.2.1. Setting Up Chaos Meshes

Configure the tools needed for chaos engineering on Linux.

Run the test on CentOS:

```
$ modinfo sch_netem
filename:       /lib/modules/3.10.0-1127.el7.x86_64/kernel/net/sched/sch_netem.ko.xz
license:        GPL
retpoline:      Y
rhelversion:    7.8
srcversion:     577020F076652D84055CCE4
depends:
```

```
intree:          Y
vermagic:        3.10.0-1127.el7.x86_64 SMP mod_unload modversions
sig_key:         69:0E:8A:48:2F:E7:6B:FB:F2:31:D8:60:F0:C6:62:D8:F1:17:3D:57
sig_hashalgo:    sha256
```

You need to create specific failures, make sure that errors are logged appropriately, and ensure that metrics and traces are output.

Configuring an environment for specific conditions and calculating SLO is a difficult and complex task, but with chaos engineering, it can be done easily. This code checks the available network interfaces:

```
$ sudo lshw -C network | grep 'logical name'
    logical name: ens33
    logical name: br-a52f0434f2a3
    logical name: docker0
    logical name: br-97c2fa53daa2
```

Feature flags are useful, but if you want to create a variety of failures, chaos engineering is a good way to go.

In order to perform observability effectively, you need to be able to introduce a variety of errors. It is repeatedly checked to see if it outputs the correct signal under various failures.

Install a chaos mesh into Kubernetes. I've focused on network chaos, but kernel chaos, JVMchaos, and IOchaos are also useful.

- **PodChaos:** Simulates pod failures, including node restarts, persistent unavailability of a pod, and failure of a specific container in a specific pod.

- **StressChaos:** Simulates CPU race conditions or memory race conditions.

- **IOChaos:** Simulates IO failures in application files, such as IO latency, read, and write failures.

- **TimeChaos:** Simulates a time jump exception.

- **KernelChaos:** Simulates kernel errors, such as application memory allocation exceptions.

Network faults:

- **NetworkChaos:** Simulates network failures such as network latency, packet loss, packet failure, and network partitions.

- **DNSChaos:** Simulates DNS failures, such as DNS domain name parsing failures and returning incorrect IP addresses.

- **HTTPChaos:** Simulates HTTP communication failures, such as HTTP communication latency.

CHAPTER 6 INFRASTRUCTURE RCA

Platform faults:

- **AWSChaos:** Simulates AWS platform failures, such as AWS node restarts.
- **GCPChaos:** Simulates GCP platform failures, such as GCP node restarts.

Application errors:

- **JVMChaos:** Simulates JVM application errors such as method call latency.

As shown in Figure 6-20, chaos meshes make it easy for hosts and Kubernetes to create network packet drops and more.

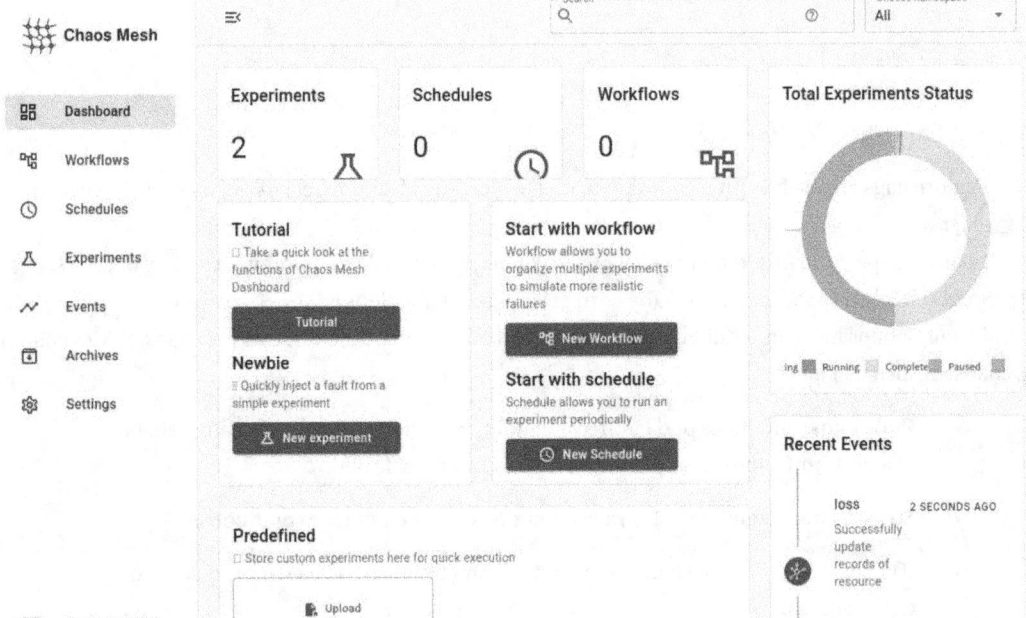

Figure 6-20. *Chaos types in a chaos mesh*

You can create a variety of experiments, as shown in Figure 6-21. You can monitor the status of your experiments.

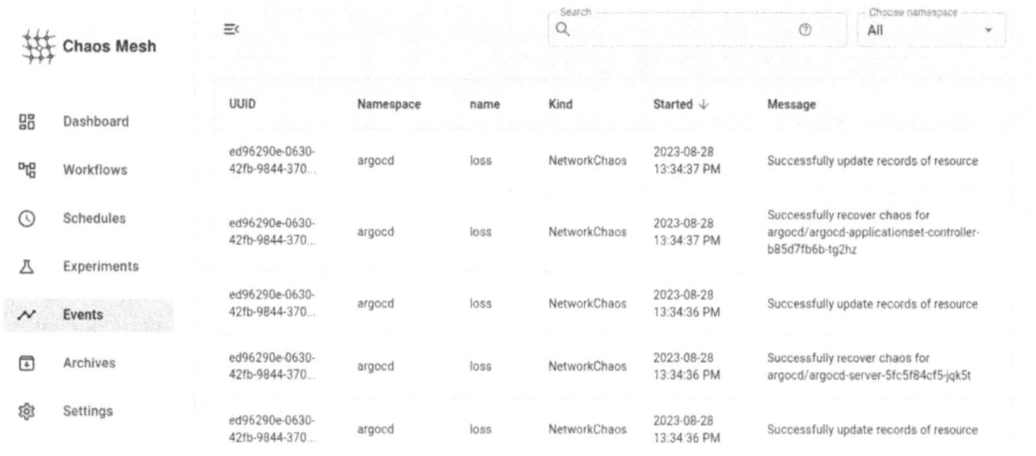

Figure 6-21. Experiments with chaos mesh

Chaos messages are also processed well by the host and Kubernetes with no problems.

Chaos mesh can easily reproduce Kubernetes packet loss, and it's possible to limit the failure to precisely a specific pod.

The reason for the latency in Kubernetes is that the tc is configured inside the Docker image. Since you are not testing the host network, you do not need to configure the host TC.

Create a 1 percent network loss using TC as shown here:

```
sudo tc qdisc add dev ens33 root netem loss 90%
```

This command can also be used to set up a configuration directly on the host network.

You can check the retransmission status like this:

```
netstat -s |grep -i retransmitted
netstat -napo | grep -i time_wait
sysctl -a | grep -i retries
```

6.4.2.2. Configure Kubernetes

The L3 demo uses chaos meshes to create losses within the Kubernetes pod. You will notice that fewer bytes are transferred than usual. You may notice that the latency of your application increases. Currently, there is no timeout setting in the application.

There is latency in the Hubble UI and Cilium metrics. For example, if you disconnect Linux from the network, you will see a drop in the Hubble UI.

You should also use your existing Linux network utilities. While eBPF and the Grafana dashboard provide user-friendliness, network utilities can fill in the gaps.

CHAPTER 6   INFRASTRUCTURE RCA

If you increase the latency for the network interface, you'll see these results.

- Reduced total number of requests processed
- Increased latency

To test latency, use the following command. This uses the `tc` utility inside the container to add a 0ne-second latency to all traffic sent and received over interface eth0.

```
$ kubectl exec grocery-store tc qdisc add dev eth0 root netem delay 1s
```

In Grafana's Application Metrics dashboard, you can see that the time series of the number of requests has decreased, and the latency quantiles have increased. The histogram of the latency distribution has changed over time, showing an increase in the number of requests falling into buckets with longer durations, as shown in Figure 6-22.

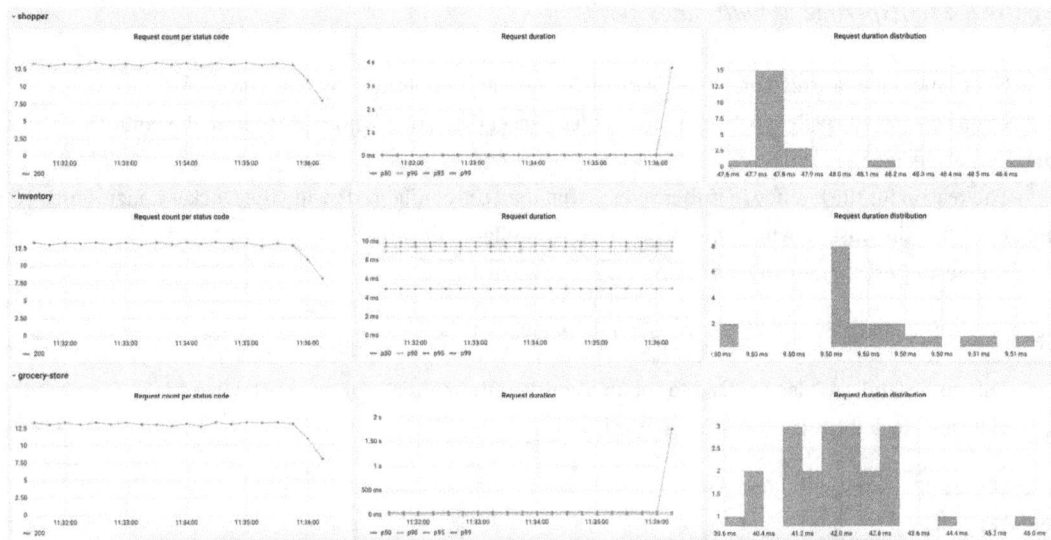

Figure 6-22. *Dashboard outputting latency*

Depending on how you run your tests, there are a variety of chaos engineering possibilities.

- As you increase the load and latency on the frontend microservices, the total latency increases and the throughput increases incrementally. The latency does not propagate to the backend microservices.
- As you increase the load and latency on the backend microservices, you can see that the total latency increases, the throughput increases, and when a certain throughput is reached, the latency that started on the backend propagates to the frontend. As the resources allocated to individual microservices process the load and reach the limit, you can see that the services that exceed the allocated resource limit are taken down and restarted.

Propagation can occur from upstream to downstream and from downstream to upstream. Measuring the 99th percentile from the frontend and user perspectives is not sufficient for root cause analysis. Frontend error rates are useful, but latency is more likely to be systemic.

You need to identify exactly where the change in latency occurred. The metrics can help you understand the scope of the problem, and searching for traces for that service can reveal what happened. The correlation between the metrics and the traces provided by the exemplar can help you quickly identify the problem by giving you specific traces to investigate in the metric.

The network emulator feature can simulate many other symptoms, such as packet loss, rate limiting, and reordering, and it can create latency. However, the network is not the only thing that can cause problems for your system.

Chaos mesh was used to increase the error rate, and latency was simply increased. The network should monitor RTD roundtrip latency, saturation, and packet loss. Chaos mesh provides several network-specific features. You can control the kernel to regulate bandwidth, packet loss, and ordering.

6.4.2.3. Retransmission Analysis

It is useful to monitor network sections when latency occurs. Start analyzing the server, client, and network segments separately. In the distributed trace, span separates the sections by type, which helps you identify the latency.

If you suspect the problem is in the server side, start by understanding the scope of the latency (application or infrastructure) and the type of load (CPU or IO).

If the problem is on a packet of the network, you should use `tcpdump` and `wireshark` to measure it on a section-by- section basis.

If you have a problem at L3, you need metrics or system utilities for L3 to understand what is causing the latency. Once you understand that the retransmission occurred through metrics, you need to do a root cause analysis of why it happened.

Retransmissions can occur for a variety of reasons. It could be a problem with the network itself, but misconfiguration of firewalls, switches, and load balancers can also cause retransmissions. When new equipment is added or configuration changes are made, packets should be analyzed and checked for retransmissions.

Understanding packets is complicated, so filtering and searching is necessary. This is where `wireshark` comes in handy.

- You can filter packets by session. If you select Follow TCP Stream, only that stream is filtered, with all other packets that are not related to that stream being discarded. You can see the E2E process, including the handshake, until you get a 200 response. TCP Stream is especially helpful when trying to figure out what caused a particular packet to happen. When an RST packet appears out of nowhere, if you can see the process leading up to it with TCP Stream, you can understand what caused it to happen.

- Provides options to determine if any of the packets contain a specific string of characters. The Frame Contains option is used when you want to find packets that contain a specific word among the packets.

CHAPTER 6 INFRASTRUCTURE RCA

If you know where the retransmitted packet should have been in the original packet flow, you can calculate the process latency caused by the retransmission. In TCP theory, the retransmission algorithm is controlled by TCP's SEQ and ACK numbers. The original and retransmitted packets match the SEQ number in TCP and the data size.

The IP header contains the SEQ and ACK numbers to confirm the order of data received and provide retransmission algorithms for missing and latency packets. SEQ and ACK tell the other party the order of the data you are sending (SEQ) and the data information you received correctly (ACK).

- **SEQ:** The SEQ number is the same as the position number in the data, so it is used to order the data.

- **ACK:** The ACK number indicates the SEQ number that should be retransmitted in the event of a miss. Retransmission is done by transferring data with the SEQ number that matches the ACK number that the other party keeps sending.

If a three-way handshake is processed normally, the SEQ and ACK are as shown in Table 6-2.

Table 6-2. A Three-Way Handshake

Number	SEQ	ACK	Flags
1	0		SYN
2	0	1	SYN-ACK
3	1	1	ACK

As shown in Figure 6-23, TCP transfers data, and the receiving end sends an ACK to say that it received the data.

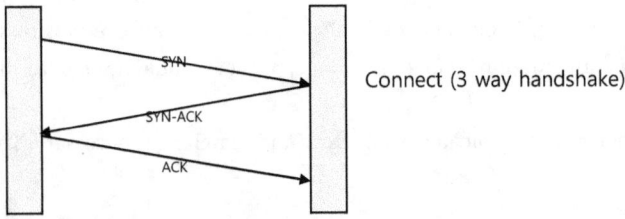

Figure 6-23. Three-way handshake

Use a three-way handshake in the connection creation step, as shown in Figure 6-24.

- When Host A connects to Host B, it transfers a SYNC flag segment to Host B, and the connection status becomes SYN_SENT.

- After receiving the SYN flag segment, Host B sends an ACK flag segment to Host A for the SYN and the received SYN, and the connection status becomes SYN_RECV.

CHAPTER 6 INFRASTRUCTURE RCA

- When Host A receives a SYN+ACK flag segment from Host B authorizing the connection, it changes the state to ESTABLISH, indicating that the connection is complete. When Host B also receives an ACK and becomes ESTABLISH, it is ready to send and receive data.

- The application sends and receives data with the send() and recv() commands.

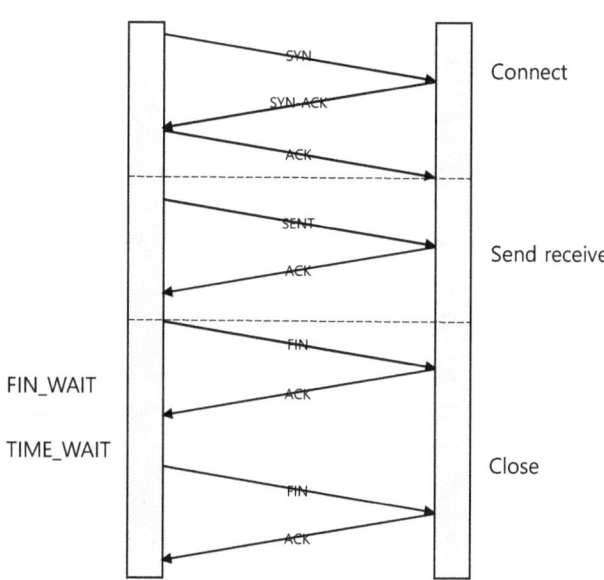

Figure 6-24. The network state changes

Retransmission Case 1

The retransmission process is illustrated in a three-way handshake shown in Table 6-3.

Table 6-3. Retransmission Case 1

Number	SEQ	ACK	Data Size	Flag	Retransmission or Not?
1				ACK	
2	900	1500	200		
3					
4	900	1500	200		retransmission
5	1500			ACK	

CHAPTER 6 INFRASTRUCTURE RCA

Analyzing the table, it looks like this:

- Numbers 2 and 4 have the same data size as the SEQ. It is the same packet, and Number 4 is a retransmission of Number 2.

- I sent packet 2, but there was no ACK that it was received, so I retransmitted the same packet again in Number 4. An ACK packet acknowledging receipt of all packets came back in response in Number 5.

- The time difference in Steps 2 through 4 is the latency.

Use a four-way handshake to terminate the connection.

- Host A sends a `FIN` flag segment to Host B when the operation is complete, and the state becomes `FIN_WAIT1`. When Host B receives the `FIN` flag segment, it enters the `CLOSE_WAIT` state, waiting for the `close()` command to be called, and emits a response ACK for the `FIN`.

- When Host A receives an ACK for `FIN`, the state changes to `FIN_WAIT2`. If it does not receive a `FIN` flag segment from Host B for a certain amount of time, the state changes to `TIME_WAIT`. When `close()` is called on Host B, the `FIN` flag segment is passed to Host A, and the state becomes `LAST_ACK`.

- Host A receives the final `FIN` flag segment, so it closes the network connection and sends a final ACK flag segment to Host B in response to the `FIN`. Host B receives the ACK and closes the network connection.

Retransmission Case 2

The process of a four-way handshake is shown in Table 6-4.

Table 6-4. Retransmission Case 2

Number	SEQ	ACK	Data size	Flag	IP ID	Retransmission or Not?
1	1	1	499		1	
2						
3	4000	500		FIN	4	
4	1	500	1499		5	Retransmission
5	500	1500		ACK	2	

CHAPTER 6   INFRASTRUCTURE RCA

Analyzing the table, it looks like this:

- Number 4 is a retransmission. There are no packets with the same SEQ or data size (assuming they were collected from SYN). The first packet was lost in the transfer.

- Number 3 has a larger SEQ number than Number 4. This means that it is later in the sending order.

- The IP ID used by wireshark is the only IP packet identifier, and it has an incremental value based on the order in which it is transferred, so a larger value indicates a packet that was sent later in time.

- Number 3 should be sent after the retransmission packet according to the SEQ, but by the IP ID, it is the first packet sent.

- The cause is that it didn't get an ACK, so it transferred the packet three times and then retransmitted the packet.

Detailed root cause analysis is possible, but it requires a long learning curve and requires an experienced SRE and infrastructure engineer. Without an SRE, developers have to understand basic infrastructure problems, such as whether retransmissions are causing latency.

6.5. Network Observability

eBPF is installed as a sandbox in the kernel, which allows you to filter packets.

A classic example of eBPF being used is the filtering used by tcpdump. An extension of this is eBPF, which is built into the Linux kernel and processes requests simply through system calls without any changes to the system.

Figure 6-25 shows that traditional packet processing incurs unnecessary overhead by going through the IP table in the kernel and user space, as shown on the left, while eBPF is embedded in the kernel and can process filtering for packets at the kernel level.

CHAPTER 6 INFRASTRUCTURE RCA

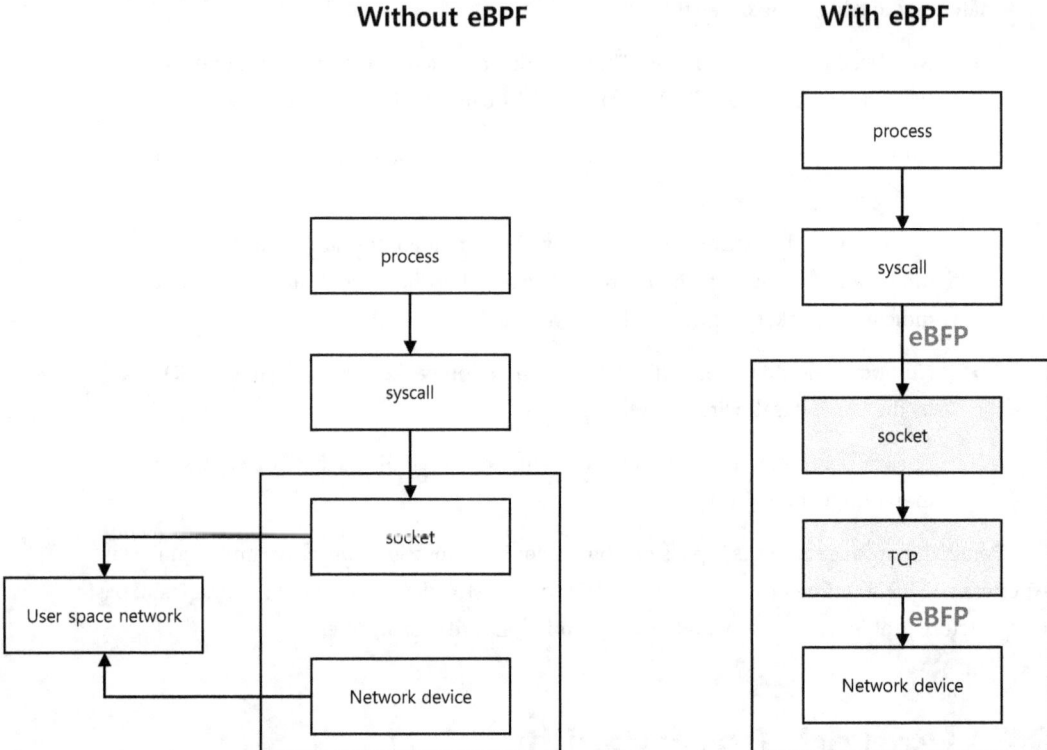

Figure 6-25. Comparison of traditional and Cilium methods

In addition to reducing dependency on IP tables, here are some reasons to use eBPF in Kubernetes:

- With traditional IP table rules, the number of rules grows as the number of services and pods grows, so every rule must be checked until it matches. This takes a lot of time and introduces latency. When an update to the rules in an IP table occurs, it takes a lot of time to replace the rules in the entire IP table. Nowadays, we do continuous deployment, which means that new microservices are deployed, which means that the IP table is updated. Although you haven't measured the latency, you assume that if you have 10,000 microservices, the latency of the IP table for them is significant. This latency will affect the latency of the user service. On the other hand, eBPF does not use IP tables, and packets can be processed through eBPF to eliminate the aforementioned problems.

- With eBPF, packet traces and network statistics at the pod and container level are possible.

6.5.1. Introduction

eBPF shows strengths in networking and security. At this point, it supports a subset of application languages and is primarily used for observability in standardized infrastructures like Linux.

As distributed systems have evolved, so has the abstraction of the network layer. Two of the most promising technologies in this area are eBPF and Cilium, which provide kernel-level insight into everything Linux touches.

Hubble and service discovery provide network visibility and generate granular signal data for observing events at the kernel level. Today, eBPF and Cilium simplify the operation of complex Kubernetes networks, and when problems arise, detailed signals enable quick troubleshooting.

Understanding failures and configurations in a Kubernetes network can be challenging. With Cilium, you can reduce the complexity and make it easy to debug. Cilium provides the following network policy and monitoring capabilities:

- With Cilium network policies, network testing is simple and easy. Previously, with chaos engineering and network emulators, you could randomly generate latency and loss. Network testing is complex and time-consuming. Cilium can test and configure accurately and reliably.

- To measure latency, it is inefficient to configure distributed traces using agents on every network hop. With Cilium, you can see latency and errors in your network and applications. It supports monitoring across the E2E of the network, and Cilium can be coupled with distributed traces.

Troubleshooting the root cause of a network outage is difficult. However, with Cilium, you can generate signals that are clearly segmented by technology area, get clear meaning of each segment, understand how they propagated, and quickly perform root cause analysis.

If you experience resource exhaustion, low application throughput, or high latency, there are many possible causes. Due to the large number of IO processed by microservices, it is difficult to accurately determine whether a problem is caused by the microservices application or the network.

I chose Cilium because of its root cause analysis of the infrastructure and network. With Cilium, you can manage L3, L7, and applications in a unified way, and you can determine exactly where problems occur and perform root cause analysis.

Reducing scope of problem is important. If you can confirm that there are no problems on your L3 or L7 network, you can focus more on your application and minimize MTTR.

6.5.2. Metrics

Cilium is a container network interface (CNI) for securing and load-balancing network traffic in Kubernetes environments. As a CNI provider, Cilium gives you more control over how you build applications and monitor traffic and extends your existing network capabilities. For example, a Kubernetes installation uses a traditional firewall and Linux-based network utilities like IP tables to filter traffic between pods based on

IP addresses or ports. However, in such environments, the high rate of change between pods and their IP addresses makes it more difficult to manage network communications using standard firewall rules.

Cilium alleviates these problems by allowing you to build application-aware network policies. For example, policies can leverage container, pod, or service metadata. These measures replace traditional firewalls and support cross-cluster communication, enabling advanced design patterns such as multi-region database architectures.

By leveraging eBPF, you can provide security and networking features to the Linux firewall without changing any code. With eBPF, Cilium provides enhanced management capabilities and can be flexibly managed based on the workload of the cluster. Cilium reduces network complexity and provides a variety of metrics to help administrators easily understand problems. Cilium provides a variety of metrics.

Cilium and Hubble generate metrics that provide better insight into how Kubernetes processes requests. The Hubble platform consists of a standalone relay service and server instance that generates network-level metrics per pod. This data can be viewed through Hubble's available UI or CLI.

The advantage of Cilium is that you can manage L3 TCP and L7 HTTP in a unified way.

6.5.2.1. Total Number of Requests

Key metrics: http_requests_total, dns_queries_total

You can observe the HTTP and DNS traffic on your network at a high level. These values can fluctuate based on application usage, such as throughput spikes during business hours, but a sudden drop in either metric indicates a connectivity problem. To pinpoint the source of the problem, you can utilize Hubble to troubleshoot each layer of the request, such as TCP connections and DNS queries.

DNS and TCP monitoring for HTTP requests can be profiled. Cilium is provided as metrics, so it is less detailed than profiles.

6.5.2.2. Total Number of Drops

Key metrics: drop_count_total, http_responses_total, dns_responses_total

With alerts for drop_count_total and http_responses_total, you can detect early signs of connectivity problems at various network layers. For example, a sudden spike in the total number of packets dropped (drop_count_total) could indicate a problem with Layer 3 (L3) policies. Layer 3 sets the basic networking rules for communication between endpoints. On the other hand, an increase in the number of 5xx (http_responses_total) or SERVFAIL (dns_responses_total) response codes can signal that Layer 7 (L7) policies are not configured to allow traffic.

6.5.2.3. Durations per Second

Key metric: http_request_duration_seconds

http_request_duration_seconds can alert an endpoint to a sudden influx of API calls. This activity causes a steady increase in latency until the Cilium agent limits the request and returns a response code to the initial requestor. By comparing this value to the Cilium_api_limiter_processing_duration_seconds metric, you can determine if Cilium is attempting to control the rate of API calls to a particular endpoint.

CHAPTER 6   INFRASTRUCTURE RCA

In most cases, a rate-limiter will mitigate traffic to protect against resource shortages or service interruptions. However, if requests for a particular resource are frequently throttled, you may need to take additional measures. For example, optimizing certain services to make API calls less frequently can help prevent them from hitting the rate limits that Cilium configures.

6.5.3. Hubble

To efficiently troubleshoot performance degradation problems like service latency, you need a good understanding of pod-to-pod and client-to-client communication. Hubble collects and aggregates network data from all pods in your environment, providing data on request throughput, status, errors, and more. Hubble also integrates with OpenTelemetry to export log and trace data from the Cilium-managed network to third-
party monitoring platforms.

Because Cilium can control traffic at Layers 3, 4, and 7 of the OSI model, Hubble allows you to monitor multiple levels of network traffic, such as TCP connections, DNS queries, and HTTP requests, across a cluster or mesh of clusters. To accomplish this, Hubble utilizes two main components: servers and Hubble relays.

Figure 6-26 shows the Hubble component. A Hubble server runs with a Cilium agent on each cluster node. Each server provides an observation service to monitor pod traffic and a peer service to trace Hubble instances on other nodes.

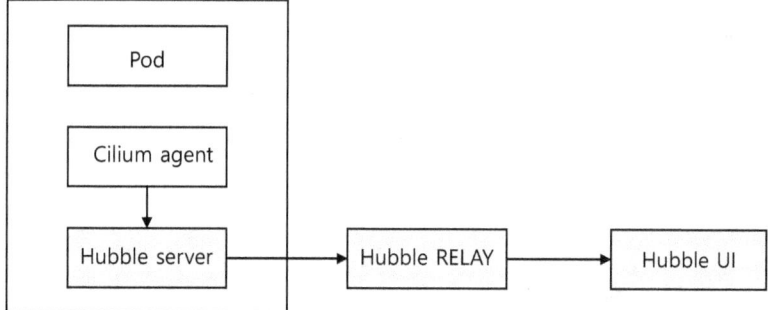

Figure 6-26. *The Hubble component*

Hubble Relay is a component that collects network flow data from each server instance and makes it available to the Hubble UI and CLI via a set of APIs.

The Hubble platform is automatically deployed with Cilium, but it is not enabled by default. You can enable it by running the following command on your host:

```
Cilium hubble enable
```

The output uses the Hubble CLI. You can also check the status of Hubble and Cilium by running the Cilium status command. You should see output similar to the following:

545

```
$ Cilium status
    /¯¯\
 /¯¯\__/¯¯\    Cilium:         OK
 \__/¯¯\__/    Operator:       OK
 /¯¯\__/¯¯\    Envoy DaemonSet: disabled (using embedded mode)
 \__/¯¯\__/    Hubble Relay:   disabled
    \__/       ClusterMesh:    disabled

DaemonSet Cilium     Desired: 1, Ready: 1/1, Available: 1/1
Deployment Cilium-operator Desired: 1, Ready: 1/1, Available: 1/1
Containers: Cilium-operator    Running: 1
            Cilium             Running: 1
Cluster Pods: 16/16 managed by Cilium
Helm chart version: 1.13.0-rc2
Image versions Cilium quay.io/Cilium/Cilium:v1.13.0-rc2: 1
               Cilium-operator quay.io/Cilium/operator-generic:v1.13.0-rc2: 1
```

If one of the services fails to start, the command output shows an error status. This problem can occur if the primary node is running out of memory. Allocating more memory and restarting Cilium may help resolve the problem.

6.5.3.1. Hubble CLI

Hubble's CLI extends the visibility provided by standard kubectl commands, such as kubectl get pods, to provide more network-level details about requests. You can view this information with the hubble observe command, which allows you to monitor traffic coming in and out of your pods to verify that your policies are working as expected. For example, you can see all requests dropped between services using the following command:

hubble observe --verdict DROPPED

May 12 13:35:35.923: default/service-a:58578 (I D:1469) -> default/service-c:80 (ID:851) http-request DROPPED (HTTP/1.1 PUT http://service-c.default.svc.cluster.local/v1/endpoint-1)

For example, you can see that the request was dropped because of the L3/L4 policy.
This indicates that Cilium is managing the traffic appropriately.

6.5.3.2. Hubble UI

The Hubble UI abstracts the L3 network as a service and outputs it to the service map. Cilium provides its own service map screen. Hubble UI captures all network traffic, regardless of protocol, and provides a visualization of the network topology.

CHAPTER 6 INFRASTRUCTURE RCA

While the CLI provides insight into networking issues in individual pods, you still need visibility into how a problem is affecting the entire cluster. The Hubble UI provides high-level service maps for monitoring network activity and policy behavior, so you can better understand how your pods interact with each other. Service maps are especially useful for monitoring large environments because they can automatically capture the interdependencies between Kubernetes services. With this level of visibility, you can verify that your network is routing traffic to the appropriate endpoints.

Hubble UI is a web interface that can automatically search for service dependency graphs at L3/L4 and L7 layers, with user-friendly visualizations and data flows filtered into service maps. It outputs a protocol-agnostic network topology and service map.

Figure 6-27 shows the Hubble UI. It resembles a network topology and displays the interactions between each service in terms of network traffic. The service map has the advantage of displaying not only the HTTP protocol, but also many other protocols, including OpenSearch and Kafka, DNS, and TCP. In case of a drop, it displays the request, service, and section where the drop occurred in real time.

The Hubble UI automatically discovers Elasticsearch, Kafka, Zookeeper, and other services that support L3 and whose latency is difficult to measure without application instrumentation. Logic is processed at the kernel level without complex instrumentation, allowing for lightweight and detailed analysis.

Figure 6-27. *Service map in the Hubble UI*

Grafana also provides a service map, but it is generated by traces. The Grafana service map has its drawbacks. Kafka, Elasticsearch, Zookeeper, and DNS servers are not listed in the service map. It is not easy to output load balancers, CDNs, or API servers. Microservices are the main focus of the service map. Tracing requires instrumentation, but instrumentation is difficult for many black boxes and applications. Since trace-centric service maps have limitations, it is useful to use a network-based service map like Cilium to compensate.

If there is a network failure or latency in the network, Hubble's service map will show the problem. The problems displayed in the Hubble UI also affect the distributed traces, which output errors. The Hubble UI makes it easy to understand network and trace errors.

CHAPTER 6 INFRASTRUCTURE RCA

The trace only outputs to services that propagate successfully and does not include any other scope. The scope of traces is limited because of the black box and the many legacy and external connections. Hubble UI overcomes these limitations and provides monitoring capabilities at a wider scope than distributed traces.

Hubble's service map is based on network process paths, and external services are also included in the service map. You can see latency and errors by network segment. Since there is no trace ID, it is difficult to identify individual transactions. It is useful to recognize the problem area in the Hubble UI and then drill down into specific traces in the distributed trace.

The Hubble UI also provides simple filtering capabilities. Hubble has difficulty analyzing packets of tcpdump and wireshark, but it can identify problems when they occur. The service map is intended to quickly identify problems, and if you need more detailed analysis, you should use tcpdump and wireshark, and use kernel parameters and system utilities to analyze problems in your network.

6.5.4. The Grafana Plugin

The Grafana plugin is provided with a basic service map. The Grafana dashboard, shown in Figure 6-28, enhances Cilium's monitoring capabilities and allows you to correlate metrics with other signals. Metrics can reveal anomalies in both your network and Cilium, and Cilium provides a variety of Prometheus metrics for agents, policies, and more.

The Grafana dashboard can be used for Hubble data sources. While the Hubble UI operates independently, the Grafana dashboard can be analyzed in conjunction with other signals, which is useful when constructing correlations.

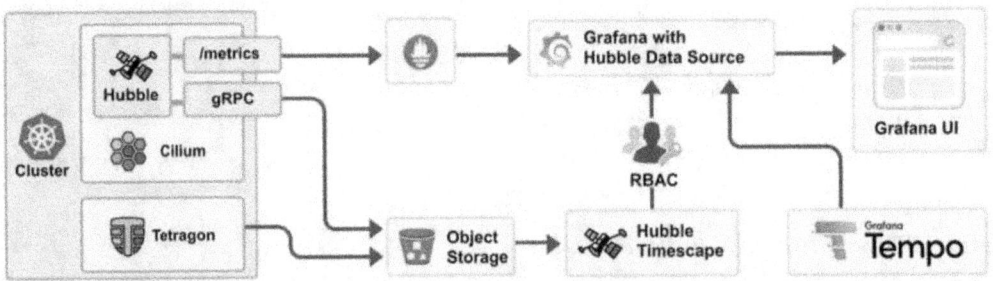

Figure 6-28. The flowchart of the Hubble Grafana data source

Hubble's Grafana plugin provides a service map.

- **Service map:** Displays communication paths and HTTP protocol metrics between services. The dashboard has a service map that shows the communication paths between workloads and Cilium ingress. This dashboard makes it easy to see the status of each workload and the ratio of requests between workloads. By clicking each workload, you can see detailed metrics for the percentage of requests, 95th percentile latency, average latency, and percentage of failed requests.

- **Dashboard:** This tracks Hubble HTTP connections by namespace. In addition to providing a visual communication path service map, it charts HTTP metrics such as duration, error rate, and latency.

The Cilium Grafana dashboard provides dashboards for L3, L7, and various components of Cilium.

6.6. The Cilium L7 Network

Cilium complements distributed traces and provides visibility into black boxes and legacy systems. It focuses on observing the connectivity and performance between cloud-native applications.

- It's difficult to gain connectivity observability for modern cloud-native workloads.
- The new and exciting eBPF in the Linux kernel has enabled a better approach.
- The eBPF-based Cilium project has become the de facto new standard for secure, observable connectivity within Kubernetes environments.

This section takes a closer look at some specific examples of how to combine Cilium's rich connectivity observability data with Grafana Lab's LGTM.

6.6.1. Introduction

There are many benefits to switching to building a microservices architecture, but in a world where a single click from a user can trigger dozens or hundreds of API calls internally, any fault, overcapacity, or latency in the connection can negatively impact your application.

Modern infrastructure platforms like Kubernetes dynamically schedule different replicas of a service in large multi-tenant clusters. This architecture makes it very difficult to pinpoint where a workload with connectivity problems can run.

Even if the nodes are identified, the multi-tenant nature of containers means that application developers no longer have direct access to system resource-level network tools (`netstat`, `tcpdump`).

6.6.1.1. Layered Connectivity

The development team receives a report of application errors or slowdowns and believes the network is to blame. The platform team sees no signs of a problem in the infrastructure components they manage and believes the problem may be at the application layer. Or maybe the problem is in the underlying physical or cloud provider network.

Comprehensive connectivity observability requires visibility into multiple networking layers.

The idea is that network connectivity is designed in a series of "layers" called the OSI networking model. While the details of the model are not important, you may hear people talk about Layer 2 (Ethernet), Layer

CHAPTER 6   INFRASTRUCTURE RCA

3 (IP), Layer 4 (TCP), and Layer 7 (applications). The goal of each layer is to abstract away the details of the layers below it. This is useful if it processes well and without problems, but it also means that layering hides faults in lower layers.

The end result is that comprehensive connectivity observability cannot be achieved by observing only a single layer, nor can it be done simply in an application. Comprehensive connectivity observability requires the ability to see all layers and correlate between them.

6.6.1.2. Isolating Noise

Even a multi-tenant Kubernetes cluster can easily run thousands of different services, each of which has multiple service replicas scheduled across hundreds of worker nodes. As a result, the underlying connectivity is "noisy" for operators trying to observe the connectivity of a single application.

Historically, the IP address or subnet of an application running as a physical node or VM on a dedicated VLAN and subnet was often a meaningful way to identify a specific applications. This meant that IP-based network logs or counters could be analyzed to build a meaningful description of application behavior. However, with modern infrastructure platforms like Kubernetes, containerized workloads are constantly being created and destroyed, and as a result, these platforms treat IP addresses as ephemeral identifiers that are not tied to applications.

The important point here is that for connection observability in applications, IP is not a meaningful identifier for connections. All observability must be done in the context of a meaningful service ID. For workloads running on Kubernetes, this service ID can be derived from the metadata labels associated with each application (`namespace=tenant-jobs, service=core-api`). For services external to Kubernetes, there is no label metadata, but the resolved DNS name to access the external service (`api.twilio.com` or `mybucket.s3.aws.amazon.com`) is often the appropriate format, and the service ID can be used.

Along with other forms of higher level ID, such as API metadata, service IDs are useful "context" for understanding a particular error or behavior.

With pointing out problems and signal vs. noise issues in mind, it's easier to understand where existing mechanisms for observing connectivity fall short.

- Traditional network monitoring devices are limited in many ways. Because they are centralized devices, they quickly become bottlenecks, and their observability typically lacks a meaningful concept of service IDs for connections.

- The cloud provider network flow logs (VPC flow logs) are not a centralized bottleneck, but they are limited to network-level visibility, so they lack both service ID and API layer visibility. Because they are tied to the underlying infrastructure, they are inconsistent across cloud providers.

- Linux host statistics contain some data about network errors, but in a Kubernetes cluster, they can't distinguish between multiple service IDs running as containers on a given node. The OS also lacks understanding of the service IDs of remote targets and has no visibility into the API layer.

CHAPTER 6   INFRASTRUCTURE RCA

- Modifying the application code to export metrics, logs, or traces for each connection can provide meaningful application and API layer visibility, but there is no visibility into faults or bottlenecks at the network layer (TCP, IP, or Ethernet layers). There is also no service ID for incoming connections.

- Sidecar-based service messages, such as Istio, provide rich API layer observability without modifying application code, but they are costly in terms of resource consumption, performance impact, and operational complexity. Service messages have limited visibility into connections "outside" the mesh, and because proxies only work at the API layer, they lack visibility into faults or bottlenecks at the network layer.

As far as service identity-aware network and API layer observability, eBPF is supported by Linux distributions and provides a secure and efficient way to inject kernel-level intelligence into applications. It does this by means of "eBPF programs" that run without interruption whenever an application calls standard Linux OS functions for network access, file access, or program execution.

Instead of leveraging legacy kernel network features like IP table, Cilium is built using the eBPF native approach.

Cilium creates in-kernel eBPF programs based on the ID of the workload. These eBPF programs export observability data to the Grafana LGTM stack.

Cilium utilizes eBPF to ensure that connection observability data is associated with the application's higher level service ID on both sides of the network connection, not just the IP address. And because eBPF works at the Linux kernel layer, this added observability doesn't require any changes to the application itself or the use of heavy, complex sidecar proxies. Instead, Cilium is transparently injected under existing workloads, scaling horizontally within a Kubernetes cluster.

Cilium leverages eBPF to ensure that connection observability is tied to the application's high-level service ID, not just its IP address.

6.6.2. Cilium Architecture

Cilium recognizes service IDs and generates connectivity metrics and events. It pairs backend observability, such as the Grafana LGTM stack, with Cilium's powerful connectivity observability. This section looks at specific examples of how this powerful combination can help Kubernetes platform teams monitor connectivity or troubleshoot common problems.

6.6.2.1. Golden Signals

There are three key metrics for understanding the health of your HTTP connections, sometimes referred to as the HTTP golden signals.

- HTTP request rate
- HTTP request latency
- HTTP response codes/errors

CHAPTER 6 INFRASTRUCTURE RCA

Cilium can extract this data without making any changes to the application, and it aggregates these metrics based on long-term, meaningful service IDs rather than based on IP.

If the application team is experiencing faults with application connectivity, these HTTP golden signals can clearly highlight whether the root cause is at the API layer (a problem that the application team needs to process) or at a lower layer of the network stack (the layer that manages the infrastructure team).

And going back to the "signal vs. noise" problem, the fact that they're tagged with meaningful service IDs means that platform or application teams can quickly focus on just the service tagged with the team name or a specific service, without having to know where the container for the service is located or running.

6.6.2.2. Detecting Problems

Errors can exist at any layer of the network stack. When connectivity problems occur at non-API layer components of the networking stack (DNS errors, firewall drops, and network latency/congestion), application teams typically have limited ability to clearly identify if an underlying network problem has occurred.

Consider an application where users reported performance degradation and application layer timeouts for a short period of time a few hours ago. The application logs show no problems, and the application's CPU load was not unusually high. Could a network problem be the cause?

Using Cilium's kernel-level observability, you can extract what can be considered the TCP golden signals and aggregate these metrics based on meaningful service IDs.

- Bytes sent and received at the TCP layer
- Retransmission of TCP layer to measure loss and congestion at the network layer
- TCP RTT "round-trip-time" to represent network layer latency

6.6.2.3. Propagating Traces

Network and API layer observability data can also be used to enable multi-hop network traces with applications propagating standard trace identifiers via HTTP headers.

The following run a demo of a Kubernetes cluster running Cilium, Grafana, Prometheus, and Grafana Tempo.

6.6.3. Demo

Using Cilium network policies to cause errors, it is possible to trigger drops through policies. Network policies use L3 and L7 HTTP protocols and can be configured to apply only to specific pods. You can see the error in the application trace. You won't get timeout errors, but you will get latency. This approach is similar to chaos engineering. You only need to change the policy without modifying the application. The current policy does not cause drops, but simply increases the error rate of network traffic coming into a particular application.

Cilium makes it easier to test SLOs. Traffic to any pod can be throttled, and Cilium makes it easier to cause failures. Policy-driven network operations have many advantages.

Cilium provides a service map by default. It outputs connections such as Kafka and Zookeeper that the existing service map does not provide, although it has the disadvantage of limited output to the Kubernetes network.

Here's how to install the Hubble Grafana plugin.

```
plugins:
  - isovalent-hubble-datasource
```

Cilium provides correlation with traces. It measures the latency of HTTP calls to the source or target.

By configuring policies, you can introduce latency into HTTP communications or randomly throw errors. Cilium can correlate application traces with the transaction that caused the problem in L7 and see how network issues are affecting the application and causing errors.

When running applications in an environment like Kubernetes, you need good observability. However, for many organizations, it can be difficult to update existing applications to provide the desired observability. Using the Hubble L7 observability feature within Cilium, you can get observability metric for your applications without modifying your code.

This demo demonstrates how Cilium provides observability metrics for your application and how you can use the Grafana dashboards provided by Cilium to gain insights into how your application is behaving. It deploys Cilium along with Grafana and Prometheus on Kubernetes.

This demo demonstrates the correlation between application traces while generating L7 failures. To do this, it uses Cilium L7 network policies. Updating Helm, including the policy, increases the error rate and introduces latency. The application retries frequently because the error rate of the network policy has changed.

Cilium L7 manages HTTP connections from source to target. It shows the E2E trace from the application perspective, including the latency of the L7 network.

6.6.3.1. Configure

Utilities such as `git`, `helm`, `kind`, `yq`, `Jq`, `kubectl`, and `Cilium-cli` should be installed.

```
git clone https://github.com/aiops/Cilium-grafana-observability-demo
cd Cilium-grafana-observability-demo
```

Using KIND, I set up a Kubernetes cluster. This will create a KIND cluster without a default CNI, so you can use Cilium.

```
kind create cluster --config kind-config.yaml
```

Next, you need to add a few Helm repositories:

```
helm repo add Cilium https://helm.Cilium.io
helm repo add ingress-nginx https://kubernetes.github.io/ingress-nginx
```

CHAPTER 6 INFRASTRUCTURE RCA

```
helm repo add prometheus-community https:// prometheus -commu nity.github.io/helm-charts
helm repo add open-telemetry https://open-telemetry.github.io/opentelemetry-helm-charts
helm repo add minio https://operator.min.io
helm repo add grafana https://grafana.github.io/helm-charts
helm repo add strimzi https://strimzi.io/charts
helm repo add elastic https://helm.elastic.co
```

To avoid problems installing the Cilium service monitor, install the Prometheus operator CRD before Cilium:

```
helm template kube-prometheus prometheus-community/kube-prometheus -stack --include-crds \
  | yq 'select(.kind == "CustomResourceDefinition") * {"metadata": {"a-NNotations":
{"meta.helm.sh/release-name": "kube-prometheus ", "meta.helm.sh/release-namespace":
"monitoring"}}}' \
  | kubectl create -f -
```

This also creates a monitoring namespace where Cilium will install the Hubble Grafana dashboard.

```
kubectl create ns monitoring
```

6.6.3.2. Deployment

This demo uses KIND to install Cilium. It deploys Cilium, ingress-nginx, Prometheus, Tempo, and Grafana. Next, install jobs-app to demonstrate the Hubble HTTP metric.

```
MASTER_IP="$(docker inspect Cilium-grafana-observability-demo-control-plane | jq '.[0].
NetworkSettings.Networks.kind.IPAddress' -r)"
helm upgrade Cilium Cilium/Cilium \
   --version 1.13.0-rc2 \
   --install \
   --wait \
   --namespace kube-system \
   --values helm/Cilium-values.yaml \
   --set ku beProxyReplacement=strict \
   --set k8sServiceHost="${MASTER_IP}" \B
   --set k8sServicePort=6443
```

Check your pods and run the Cilium status if everything is up and running.

```
kubectl get pods -n kube-system
Cilium status --wait
```

Use ingress-nginx to access Grafana. Next, verify the pods, and if everything is up and running, run the Cilium status.

CHAPTER 6   INFRASTRUCTURE RCA

```
helm upgrade ingress-nginx ingress-nginx/ingress-nginx \
  --install \
  --wait \
  --namespace ingress-nginx --create-namespace \
  --version 4.1.3 \
  --values helm/ingress-nginx-values.yaml
```

Change the OpenTelemetry operator and collector.

```
helm upgrade opentelemetry-operator open-telemetry/ opentelemetry-operator \
  --install \
  --wait \
  --namespace opentelemetry-operator --create-namespace \
  --version 0.15.0 \
  -f helm/ opentelemetry-operator-values.yaml
kubectl apply -n opentelemetry-operator -f manifests/otel-collector.yaml
```

Transfer the trace to Tempo via the collector.

```
helm upgrade tempo Grafana/tempo \
  --install \
  --wait \
  --namespace tempo --create-namespace \
  --create-namespace \
  --version 0.16.2 \
  -f helm/tempo-values.yaml
```

Prometheus collects and stores the metrics generated by Hubble, and Grafana visualizes the metrics.

```
helm upgrade kube-prometheus prometheus-community/kube-prometheus -stack \
  --install \
  --wait \
  --namespace monitoring --create-namespace \
  --version 40.3.1 \
  --values helm/prometheus-values.yaml
```

You can access Grafana from a browser (http://grafana.127-0-0-1.sslip.io) using admin as the username and password as the password.

Install jobs-app. Then, deploy jobs-app with the L7 Cilium network policy. Hubble will generate metrics based on HTTP flows and generate traces.

```
helm upgrade kube-prometheus prometheus-community/kube-prometheus -stack \
   --install \
   --wait \
   --namespace monitoring --create-namespace \
   --version 40.3.1 \
   --values helm/prometheus-values.yaml
```

Configure a Helm chart.

```
helm dep build ./helm/jobs-app
helm upgrade jobs-app ./helm/jobs-app \
  --install \
  --wait \
  --create-namespace \
  --namespace tenant-jobs \
  -f helm/jobs-app-values.yaml
```

To view Cilium network policies, do the following:

```
kubectl get Ciliumnetworkpolicy -n tenant-jobs -o yaml
```

6.6.3.3. Demo

Verify that Hubble is up and running. Automatically generate traffic internally to the demo application. The demo consists of two applications (Elasticsearch and Kafka) and four microservices:

- Coreapi
- Crawler
- Loader
- Resume

1. Coreapi is a RESTful HTTP API used by resumes, recruiters, and job postings. It manages the creation, search, and listing of resumes and jobs in Elasticsearch. The coreapi is stored in Elasticsearch. Elasticsearch stores resumes and job postings.

2. Crawler periodically generates a random resume and sends it to the loader via gRPC.

3. Loader is a gRPC service that submits resumes to Kafka's resume topic to be processed by the resume service.

CHAPTER 6 INFRASTRUCTURE RCA

4. Resume subscribes to the resume Kafka topic, and submits a resume to coreapi. Job postings use the coreapi to list job openings in the web UI and allow candidates to submit resumes. Recruiter can use the coreapi to list candidates and view their resume.

Deploying coreapi

All of the items in the dashboard require no instrumentation from your application and are using Hubble HTTP metric. To deploy coreapi, in the dashboard, locate the target workload variable at the top of the page and select Loader.

Configure the crawler to create more resumes and try running more than one crawler replica to increase request traffic.

```
helm upgrade jobs-app ./helm/jobs-app --namespace tenant-jobs --reuse-values -f helm/jobs-app-increased-request-rate.yaml
```

In the Grafana dashboard, you can see that as the crawler's resume creation rate increases, the request rate also increases. Go back to the Target workload variable at the top of the page and select coreapi. You'll see that the request rate for coreapi also increases.

Identifying errors in external services

With the service ID metadata associated with the metric, the application or platform team can quickly investigate network layer signals related to the application in problem. Demos require periodic communication with external networks. If you arbitrarily block the network, you can immediately see drops occur. Drop errors are visible in the Hubble UI. You can create drops by simply configuring network policies. Latency is not a drop, but I use the term drop when a transfer fails.

You notice that the alert service in `tenant-jobs` has increased TCP retransmissions (network layer packet loss), but only while communicating externally with `api.twilio.com`. If the duration of the error matches the time of the reported application issue, the development team can check the Twilio service status page to see if there was a known service outage during that time and determine that the problem was external.

Increased coreapi Error Rate

Next, you'll deploy the new configuration and use the metrics to see the change in error rate. You can see that the error rate increases due to the coreapi configuration change.

```
helm upgrade jobs-app ./helm/jobs-app --namespace tenant-jobs --reuse-values -f helm/jobs-app-increased-error-rate.yaml
```

Next, deploy the new configuration and use the metric to see the change in latency.

```
helm upgrade jobs-app ./helm/jobs-app --namespace tenant-jobs --reuse-
values -f helm/jobs-app-increased-request-duration.yaml
```

Due to the coreapi configuration change, there is an increase in latency.

Injecting multiple failures and comparing them is not enough to analyze the cause. By correlating traces, it is easier to perform root cause analysis.

The Grafana dashboard shows error codes for all inbound connections to the core-api application service in the tenant-jobs namespace. It's only being accessed by another service, resumes, and it's easy to see that the connection was good at first, but then a API layer problem started to occur, as evidenced by the increase in HTTP 500 on the service connection. This is a clear metric that indicates an API layer problem that needs to be addressed by the application team running the core-api and resumes services.

6.6.3.4. Propagating Traces

If your application exports a trace header, Hubble extracts the trace ID from the HTTP header. You can export this as an exemplar along with the Hubble HTTP metric and configure it so that you can correlate from the metric to the trace in Grafana.

The jobs-app uses OpenTelemetry, which supports trace generation. Next, let's deploy jobs-app with traces enabled. Add the trace as shown here:

```
helm upgrade jobs-app ./helm/jobs-app --namespace tenant-jobs --reuse-
values -f helm/jobs-app-enable-tracing.yaml
```

In the HTTP latency by source and target panel, look for exemplars represented by dots, along with a line graph visualization. Each exemplar represents the duration of a single request and is linked to a trace ID.

The service map is interesting because it not only displays microservices using L7, but also Kafka, Elasticsearch, and Zookeeper on a single screen. If you want to call external SaaS services or use gRPC, it is not easy to output to service map, but Hubble UI supports it.

A client span can include a network span, and outputs separate client, server, and network spans so that SRE can respond to failures. By displaying the different types of spans, you can accurately understand the latency in your network.

It is difficult to understand the problem by looking at the change in error rate based on the response code, such as 2xx normal, 4xx client error, and 5xx server error. Traces can accurately distinguish the time spent by network latency in the client span if the client and server spans are separated and the instrumentation is configured correctly.

For example, suppose your core-api service shows a spike in request latency.

Notice the small green boxes that are Grafana exemplars for individual HTTP requests between resumes and core-api. Clicking an individual exemplar with a high latency value will bring up a window that gives you an option called Query with Tempo, which is an LGTM stack component for querying and visualizing traces.

CHAPTER 6　INFRASTRUCTURE RCA

By clicking this button, the user is taken to the trace details of Tempo. In this case, it indicates that failures and retries are likely the cause of the high latency.

When you hover over an exemplar in Grafana, you will see metadata about the metric. One of these fields is the trace ID, and clicking it brings up a link to view the trace in Tempo, as shown in Figure 6-29.

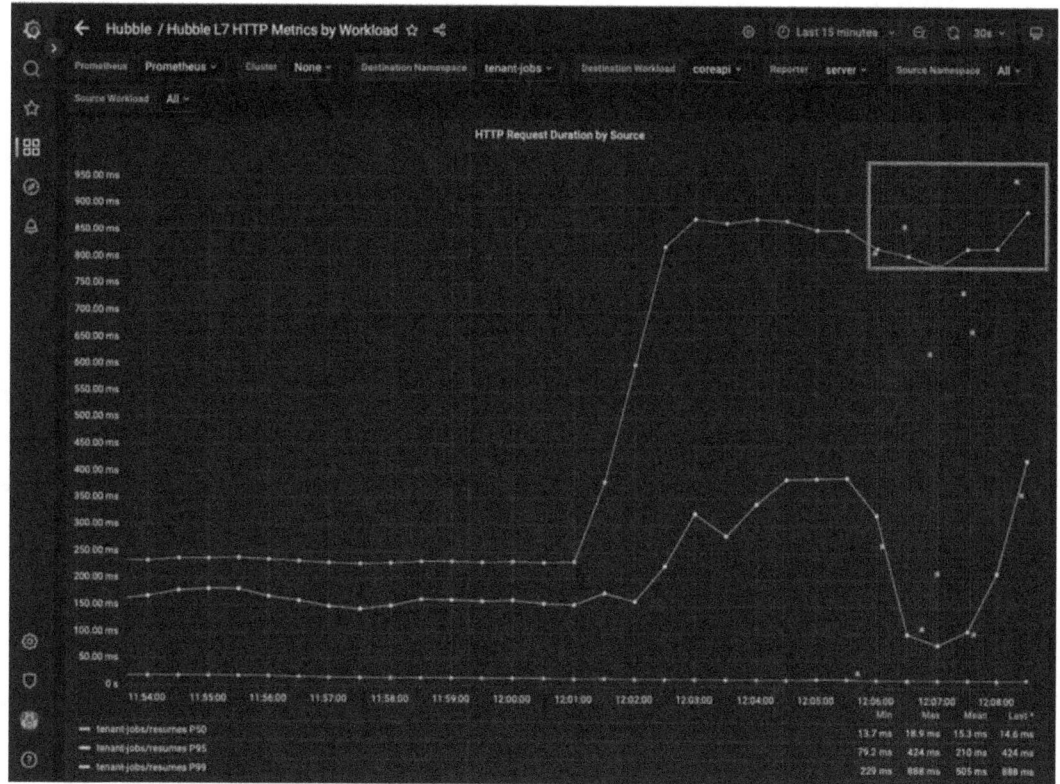

Figure 6-29. *Associating distributed traces with Cilium*

Find some exemplars and open them in Tempo. You should see that some requests are slower than others, and some requests fail and are retried on the client.

The request fails, and after a few retries, you can see that a trace that succeeds.

The demo supports E2E traces at the microservices level. If you have a small number of microservices, you can configure distributed traces without any special restrictions. However, if the Kubernetes DNS server goes down and the service stops, is it possible to perform root cause analysis using only distributed traces?

Distributed traces are difficult to analyze for cause, but in the Hubble UI, you can see that the DNS server is down. While it is important to implement E2E traces, it is even more important to understand the limitations of E2E traces and how they can be augmented.

- With Cilium's L7 network policies, you can gain insight into how your applications are behaving without changing them and without sidecars.

- Cilium improves on this process by integrating trace with Hubble.

559

CHAPTER 6   INFRASTRUCTURE RCA

With the introduction of Kubernetes and the cloud, the networks for customer service has become more complex.

It goes through load balancers, CDN servers, API servers (north-south), the cloud load balancer, the Kubernetes DNS server, the Kubernetes Kubeproxy, the Kubernetes Service, the API server (east-west), and microservices. Only microservices support traces. Due to the structure of the network, it is SPOF, and if a failure occurs in a certain section, it is not easy to determine which section caused the failure. Distributed traces provide insufficient information for root cause analysis of the network.

You should be able to understand where the problem is happening. Even if it's not in the scope of traces or instrumentation, you should apply observability, including the entire black box, security, and network.

The agents used by trace are typically instrumented at the API level of the development language rather than the kernel, and this imposes a number of limitations.

While OpenTelemetry's capabilities are incrementally improving, black boxes and security protocols like LDAP are still difficult to trace. In fact, failures are more likely to occur in black boxes and legacy systems, which are unobservable networks, where they can propagate into large-scale failures.

Hubble service maps are network-based, analyzing and visualizing external and internal communications. This is a great way to extend the scope of distributed traces and compensate for their shortcomings. Cilium has built-in support for distributed traces. A typical process is to recognize the general flow and problems from the Hubble service map and understand the latency of each section through Grafana traces.

6.7. Cilium Add-ons

DevOps and observability are constantly evolving, and it's a process of figuring out where the gaps are and how to fill them.

Cilium has a lot to offer. It basically provides observability for L3 and L7 networks, but it also has a lot more features, like service mesh, multi-Kubernetes networks, ingress, and more. This demo focuses on the most important features rather than trying to understand all of them.

- Cilium policies
- Multi-Kubernetes clusters
- Service meshes
- Ingress

Cilium is often compared to Istio. Istio also supports network policies, multi-Kubernetes clusters, service mesh, and ingress. It is interesting to compare Istio, which is configured as a sidecar, to Cilium, which is implemented as CNI and eBPF. Let's compare the pros and cons from the Cilium perspective.

6.7.1. Network Policies

In the previous demo, I explained how to create failures on L3 and L7 and test them. This time, I use Cilium network policies to create drops, identify the problems they cause, and understand how to perform root cause analysis. This time, I won't use chaos engineering to create failures, just policies.

Install Cilium:

```
minikube start --vm-driver=none --kubernetes-version v1.20.0 --memory=16000 --cpus=2
--network-plugin=cni --cni=false
Cilium install --version 1.13.0-rc2
```

Check the status of Cilium:

```
$ Cilium status
    /¯¯\
 /¯¯\__/¯¯\ Cilium:        OK
 \__/¯¯\__/ Operator:      OK
 /¯¯\__/¯¯\ Envoy DaemonSet: disabled (using embedded mode)
 \__/¯¯\__/ Hubble Relay:  disabled
    \__/   ClusterMesh:    disabled

DaemonSet Cilium Desired: 1, Ready: 1/1, Available: 1/1
Deployment Cilium-operator Desired: 1, Ready: 1/1, Available: 1/1
Containers: Cilium-operator Running: 1
            Cilium Running: 1
Cluster Pods: 16/16 managed by Cilium
Helm chart version: 1.13.0-rc2
Image versions Cilium quay.io/Cilium/Cilium:v1.13.0- rc2: 1
               Cilium-operator quay.io/Cilium/operator-
               generic:v1.13.0-rc2: 1
```

Install Hubble:

```
Cilium install --version 1.13.0-rc2
Cilium hubble enable --ui
Cilium hubble ui
```

Go to http://localhost:12000.

```
export HUBBLE_VERSION=$(curl -s https://raw.githubusercontent.com/Cilium/hubble/master/stable.txt)
HUBBLE_ARCH=amd64
if [ "$(uname -m)" = "aarch64" ]; then HUBBLE_ARCH=arm64; fi
```

CHAPTER 6 INFRASTRUCTURE RCA

```
curl -L --fail --remote-name-all https://github.com/Cilium/hubble/releases/download/$HUBBLE_
VERSION/hubble-linux-${HUBBLE_ARCH}.tar.gz{,.sha256sum}
sha256sum --check hubble-linux-${HUBBLE_ARCH}.tar.gz.sha256sum
sudo tar xzvfC hubble-linux-${HUBBLE_ARCH}.tar.gz /usr/local/bin
rm hubble-linux-${HUBBLE_ARCH}.tar.gz{,.sha256sum}
```

The Star Wars demo is an L3 and L7 demo. Using policies, you can create drops. This is a great demo to check out Cilium's L3 and L7 metrics.

It also provides ingress functionality, including routing and security, and can be interfaced to an envoy proxy server.

```
helm upgrade jobs-app ./helm/job s -app --namespace tenant-jobs --reuse-
values -f helm/jobs-app-enable-tracing.yaml
```

Results are available in the Hubble UI and can be visualized in conjunction with Grafana.

The Star Wars-inspired demo has three microservices applications: a Death Star, a TIE Fighter, and an X-Wing.

- The Death Star application runs an HTTP web service on port 80. To balance the load of requests to the Death Star across two pod replicas, it is exposed as a Kubernetes service. The Death Star service provides a landing service so that Imperial ships can request to land.

- The TIE Fighter pod represents the client service for landing requests from Imperial ships.

- X-Wing represents services on Alliance ships. It provides various security policies, such as access control, for the Death Star landing service.

The demo includes Kubernetes deployments for three services. Each deployment is identified using the Kubernetes labels (org=empire, class=deathstar), (org=empire, class=tiefighter), and (org=alliance, class=xwing). It also includes a deathstar-service that performs traffic load balancing for all pods with the label (org=empire, class=deathstar).

Kubernetes deploys pods and services in the background. When you run kubectl get pods and svc, it tells you the progress of the job. Each pod goes through several states until it reaches a point where it is ready to run.

Each pod is represented in Cilium as an endpoint of the local Cilium agent.

Because I haven't yet imported the network policy that selects the pods, send and receive policy enforcement is still disabled on all pods.

From the perspective of the Death Star service, only ships with the org=empire label are allowed to request a landing. There is no rule enforced, so both X-Wing and TIE Fighters can request to land.

6.7.1.1. Enforcing L3/L4 Policies

For using Cilium, the endpoint IP address is irrelevant when defining security policies. Instead, you can define security policies using the labels assigned to the pods. The policy is applied to the pod based on the label, regardless of when or where it runs in the cluster.

I start with a default policy that restricts requests to land on the Death Star to ships with the label (org=empire). This way, ships without the org=empire label are not even allowed to connect to the Death Star service. This is a simple policy that only filters IP protocols (network layer 3) and TCP protocols (network layer 4), so it is sometimes referred to as an L3/L4 network security policy.

```
apiVersion: "Cilium.io/v2"
kind: CiliumNetworkPolicy
metadata:
  name: "rule1"
spec:
  description: "L3-L4 policy to restrict deathstar access to empire ships only"
  endpointSelector:
    matchLabels:
      org: empire
      class: deathstar
  ingress:
  - fromEndpoints:
    - matchLabels:
        org: empire
    toPorts:
    - ports:
      - port: "80"
        protocol: TCP
```

Cilium network policies use an endpointSelector to match pod labels to identify the source and target to which the policy applies. This policy whitelists traffic transferred from any pod with the label (org=empire) on TCP port 80 to the Death Star pod with the label (org=empire, class=deathstar). This is illustrated in Figure 6-30.

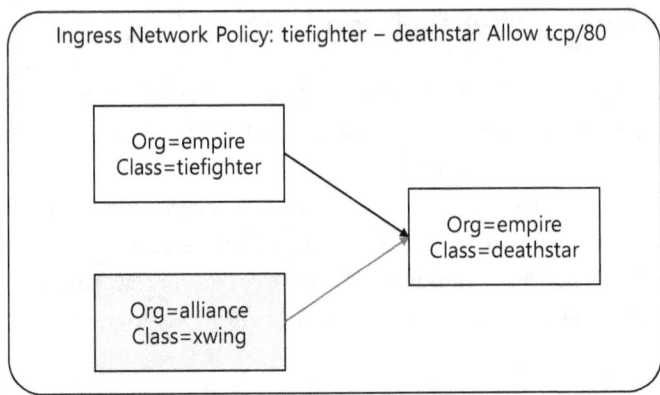

Figure 6-30. Creating an L3 failure

To apply an L3/L4 policy, do the following

```
$ kubectl create -f https://raw.githubusercontent.com/Cilium/Cilium/1.14.5/examples/
minikube/sw_l3_l4_policy.yaml
Ciliumnetworkpolicy.Cilium.io/rule1 created
```

It works as expected. The same request running on the xwing pod fails.

```
kubectl exec xwing -- curl -s -XPOST deathstar.default.svc.cluster.local/v1/request-landing
```

6.7.1.2. L7 Policies

In the previous simple scenario, it was sufficient to give the TIE Fighter/X-Wing full access to the Death Star's API, or no access at all. However, to provide security between microservices, you need to restrict each service that calls the Death Star's API to generate only the necessary HTTP requests.

For example, consider that the Death Star service exposes a maintenance API that should not be called from any Imperial ship.

Cilium can enforce HTTP layer (L7) policies to limit the URLs that TIE Fighters can reach. The following is a policy file that extends the original policy by restricting the type to only making POST /v1/request-landing API calls, and disallowing all other calls (including PUT /v1/exhaust-port).

```
apiVersion: "Cilium.io/v2"
kind: CiliumNetworkPolicy
metadata:
  name: "rule1"
spec:
  description: "L7 policy to restrict access to specific HTTP call"
  endpointSelector:
    matchLabels:
```

```
      org: empire
      class: deathstar
ingress:
- fromEndpoints:
  - matchLabels:
      org: empire
  toPorts:
  - ports:
    - port: "80"
      protocol: TCP
    rules:
      http:
      - method: "POST"
        path: "/v1/request-landing"
```

Update an existing rule to enforce an L7-aware policy to protect the Death Star using the following code:

```
$ kubectl apply -f https://raw.githubusercontent.com/Cilium/Cilium/1.14.5/examples/minikube/sw_l3_l4_l7_policy.yaml
Ciliumnetworkpolicy.Cilium.io/rule1 configured
```

Because this rule is built on an ID-aware rule, traffic from pods without the `org=empire` label will continue to be dropped, causing the connection to timeout.

```
kubectl exec xwing -- curl -s - XPOST deathstar.default.svc.cluster.local/v1/request-landing
```

- The Hubble metric outputs the drops that occur on TCP.

- In the event of a drop, L7 will throw a timeout, which can be seen in the error code. You can check the SLO and trace where the latency occurs.

- L3 monitors RTT, which indicates network speed and latency, and retransmission metrics, which indicate the number of times a packet is lost.

- To monitor L7, check the error codes in HTTP and the latency between the source and target. Check the amount of data being transferred.

- When a failure occurs, you can determine where the failure is occurring. L7 and microservices are sampled with traces, and you can quickly identify where latency is occurring.

CHAPTER 6   INFRASTRUCTURE RCA

6.7.2. Multi-Cluster

Running multiple Kubernetes clusters provides routing and load balancer functionality. For example, I used to use Istio for multi-Kubernetes and service mesh, but Cilium is a good alternative because it is lightweight and can run at the kernel level.

In this section, you see how to configure two Kubernetes clusters using KIND and deploy microservices on each cluster.

Cluster mesh extends the networking data path across multiple clusters. This allows endpoints on all connected clusters to communicate while supporting policies. Kubernetes annotations enable load balancing.

```
$ ./kind-Cilium-mesh-up.sh
=> Creating the clusters...
Creating cluster "kind-Cilium-mesh-1" ...
 ✓ Ensuring node image (kindest/node:v1.21.2) 🖼
 ✓ Preparing nodes 📦📦📦
 ✓ Writing configuration 📜
 ✓ Starting control-plane 🕹
 ✓ Installing StorageClass 💾
 ✓ Join ing worker nodes 🚜

DaemonSet Cilium Desired: 3, Ready: 3/3, Available: 3/3
Deployment clustermesh-apiserver Desired: 1, Ready: 1/1, Available: 1/1
Deployment Cilium-operator Desired: 1, Ready: 1/1, Available: 1/1
Containers: Cilium Running: 3
             Cilium-operator Running: 1
             clustermesh-apiserver Running: 1
Cluster Pods: 8/8 managed by Cilium
Image versions Cilium-operator quay.io/Cilium/operator-generic:v1.11.0-rc3@sha256:bdaa42d80f
8a11c5af398bc1f0c6e7656a05a6be0895a3c931a3bd3c41db7ebe: 1
             clustermesh-apiserver quay.io/coreos/etcd:v3.4.13: 1
             clustermesh-apiserver quay.io/Cilium/clustermesh-
             apiserver:v1.11.0-rc3: 1
             Cilium quay.io/Cilium/Cilium:v1.11.0-rc3@sha256:176e0B3f8354d8705ae6d7527
             da606fa14f7ed4aa553848670d5aee7b1063ed3: 3
$ kubectl run --restart Never --rm -it --image giantswarm/tiny-tools tiny-tools -- /bin/
sh -c 'for i in $(seq 1 10); do curl http://rebel-
base/; done'
{"Galaxy": "Alderaan", "Cluster": "Cluster-2"}
{"Galaxy": "Alderaan", "Cluster": "Cluster-1"}
{"Galaxy": "Alderaan", "Cluster": "Cluster-2"}
```

```
{"Galaxy": "Alderaan", "Cluster": "Cluster-1"}
{"Galaxy": "Alderaan", "Cluster": "Cluster-2"}
pod "tiny-tools" deleted
```

In the past, I used Istio to configure multi-Kubernetes clusters. The problem was that the sidecar caused the cost to increase dramatically as the cluster grew, the network structure to become complex, and performance to degrade. I was unable to deploy to production and rolled back Istio. Cilium makes it easy to configure and operate multi-cloud clusters.

6.7.3. Service Meshes

Cilium provides a wide range of features for running Kubernetes networks and infrastructure. With the introduction of distributed applications, additional visibility, connectivity, and security requirements have emerged. Applications communicate over untrusted networks across the cloud and on-premises boundaries. Understanding application protocols requires load balancing, resiliency becomes critical, and security must evolve to a model where the sender and receiver can authenticate each other's identities. In the early days of distributed applications, these requirements were addressed by injecting the necessary logic directly into the application. Service meshes extract this functionality from the application and make it available as part of the infrastructure for all applications to use, no longer requiring changes to each application.

Cilium provides a service mesh. It comes with an Envoy proxy server as a sidecar, which simplifies the complex network operations required to run microservices. The problem is with sidecars. Every pod needs to have a sidecar, which is expensive. Istio has many limitations, such as only supporting L7 and complicating existing container networks.

If you need a lightweight way to implement a service mesh, Cilium is a good alternative. Cilium integrates L3 and L7, provides well organized metrics, and has a variety of different but well modularized features. L7 is tied to traces. When problems occur in the network, it's easy to find the root cause and respond quickly. Cilium runs at the Kubernetes CNI level, not as a sidecar, so you don't have to pay extra for it.

```
$ kubectl get pods -n Cil i um-test --show-labels -o wide
name ready status restarts age ip node nominated node readiness gates la bels
client-7b78db77d5-wkwcp 1/1 Running 1 (6d5h ago) 6d5h 10.0.0.227 minikube <none> <none>
kind=client,name=client,pod-template-hash=7b78db77d5
client2-78f748dd67-49tsv 1/1 Running 1 (6d5h ago) 6d5h 10.0.0.192 minikube <none> <none

$Cilium connectivity test
  iSingle-node environment detected, enabling single-node connectivity test
  iiMonitor aggregation detected, will skip some flow validation steps
ℤ [minikube] Waiting for deployments [client client2 echo-same-node] to become ready...
```

CHAPTER 6   INFRASTRUCTURE RCA

⌛ [minikube] Waiting for CiliumEndpoint for pod Cilium-test/client-7b78db77d5-wkwcp to appear...
[=] Test [client-egress-l7-method]
......
 [=] Test [to-fqdns]
....

✅ All 31 tests (151 actions) successful, 0 tests skipped, 1 scenarios skipped.

Cilium's mesh features are lightweight and uncomplicated. They don't require a sidecar like Istio, and routing and operations are done at the kernel level.

6.7.4. Ingress

Cilium provides Kubernetes ingress capabilities. Nginx is useful but lacking in features, and you have to pay for commercial observability to use it. Istio ingress has rich routing capabilities and monitoring, but you must have Istio to use Istio ingress. Providing ingress at the CNI level allows for simpler network configuration than Istio.

Compared to Kubernetes and Istio ingress, Cilium ingress has many advantages.

- It uses eBPF profiles, making it easy to monitor and debug.
- Because it uses CNI, it's simple to configure and performs well.

```
$ kubectl get svc
name type cluster-ip external-ip port(s) age
deathstar ClusterIP 10.101.249.78 <none> 80/TCP 6d4h
details ClusterIP 10.99.26.149 <none> 9080/TCP 3m16s
kubernetes ClusterIP 10.96.0.1 <none> 443/TCP 6d5h
productpage ClusterIP 10.104.200.132 <none> 9080/TCP 3m16s
ratings ClusterIP 10.103.18.170 <none> 9080/TCP 3m16s
reviews ClusterIP 10.99.156.8 <none>     9080/TCP 3m16s
$ kubectl get ingress
name class hosts address ports age
basic-ingress Cilium * 80 24s
$ kubectl get pod
name ready status restarts age
deathstar-54bb8475cc-2c6kc 1/1 Running 0 126d
deathstar-54bb8475cc-5dngp 1/1 Running 0 126d
details-v1-7586964646-mz4r6 1/1 Running 0 120d
productpage-v1-8fcbd56fd-h8dnv 1/1 Running 0 120d
ratings-v1-5f6df8bf7d-l84xl 1/1 Running 0 120d
```

```
reviews-v1-7667d45f6b-ztqg7 1/1 Running 0 120d
reviews-v2-9db565b6b-nch5d 1/1 Running 0 120d
reviews-v3-6b56856b7d-4dcfc 1/1 Running 0 120d
tiefighter 1/1 Running 0 126d
xwing 1/1 Running 0 126d
```

So far, I've discussed application, infrastructure, and network observability. Since a lot of time is spent on validating new hypotheses and features, it would be helpful for SREs to have resources

6.8. Summary

Along with Chapters 4 and 10, this is a key chapter in the book. Infrastructure observability is an extension of application observability and provides critical data for AIOps automation. Most commercial observability offerings do not fully support infrastructure observability.

BPF alone does not provide the context needed for root cause analysis. For example, it is possible to identify outliers in custom metrics in Prometheus time series data and find kernel methods that consume system resources and cause delays in the kernel, but it will take a long time and a lot of trial and error. This chapter described methods and procedures for using correlation, system trace, and BPF to reduce this trial and error.

No book explains exactly what causes delays, so system trace with KUtrace is the first step. System trace is more important than distributed trace and serves as a correlation between distributed trace and BPF profiles. It is important to distinguish contention, congestion, delay, waiting, and interference through system.

In recent years, many legacy systems have migrated to the cloud, to managed systems, and to SaaS. System administrators no longer need to understand system resources to operate large systems. This is because system resources are managed by cloud CSPs like Google and Microsoft. Because you no longer need to have a deep understanding of the system (the vendor takes care of it for you), you lose the opportunity to learn about system resources. I wonder how this will change in the future.

CHAPTER 7

Anomaly Detection

When an error occurs in an application during production, a common response is to roll it back. The average time to resolution for applications is shorter than the average time to resolution for infrastructures. Infrastructure errors are difficult and complex in many ways. They're not errors in code. The error code is also unclear. It is difficult to understand the log.

Application observability is relatively easy to understand and clear because failures caused by applications are monitored through SLO. Commercial observability, which originated in APM, supports application observability. In infrastructure, the signals themselves are ambiguous and it is difficult to determine the error of a system resource. It is necessary to proactively detect and understand small latencies that occur in infrastructure system resources. Small nano-second latencies are often not identified by operator. Commercial observability and OpenTelemetry still lack capabilities to support infrastructure observability.

Technically, there are a lot of differences between application and infrastructure, and from an organizational perspective, there is a distance. You suspect that it is a root cause and a problem because it is a different organization, but it needs to be approached with caution and care.

Anomaly detection is not limited to infrastructure, but can be applied to a wide variety of fields. I believe that anomaly detection can enhance infrastructure observability and is an extension of infrastructure observability. Infrastructures have tens of thousands of resources; this is not uncommon and is beyond the scope of an SRE's direct management. Compared to application failures, infrastructure failures are larger in scope and more difficult to troubleshoot, so anomaly detection would benefit from being able to proactively recognize risks at the infrastructure level. Anomaly detection focuses on infrastructure and its various resources rather than on applications.

Working on a large-scale anomaly detection and AIOps project can be costly and the results aren't as good as you think they would be. Let's think about the causes of this:

- Trace is limited in scope because it is application-oriented and does not support infrastructure. Errors that occur outside the scope of trace cannot be collected and measured. Although system trace is provided, anomaly detection has not yet been implemented in system trace.

- Observability does not collect most of the parameters and hardware resources related to the kernel. There are technical limitations.

- Commercial observability focuses on application observability and does not sufficiently support infrastructure observability.

CHAPTER 7   ANOMALY DETECTION

- Anomaly detection in commercial observability and AIOps' focus on accuracy has led to defensiveness in the anomaly detection engine. It's important to provide a variety of feedback from time to time, even if it's noisy or has low confidence and accuracy. The product is still immature.

- AIOps has a classification model for 100 limited root causes. For example, when an error occurs, the AIOps classification model analyzes the cause of the error and makes a decision based on the limited classification model. It is not generative AI, but simply matches the classification.

- SREs lack the technology to supplement for the shortcomings of commercial observability. Commercial observability is closed and organized like a black box.

- Exceptions and errors must be accurately logged. Accuracy decreases as noise increases, so anomaly detection must be configured to learn and make accurate inferences by improving the signal and accurately describing errors. It is useful to introduce a scorecard to continuously measure and improve data quality.

The retransmission example in the previous chapter demonstrated that microservices work in Kubernetes. Identifying retransmissions in Kubernetes is more complex than identifying retransmissions on a host. It is difficult to measure Kubernetes retransmissions based on legacy network utilities. A good anomaly detection scenario would identify retransmissions on a specific segment of the Kubernetes network before the application experiences latency. The problem with current anomaly detection and AIOps is that they don't identify retransmissions at the Kubernetes network level, and focus only on latency in the application level. Commercial observability only identifies retransmissions that occur on the host.

Despite retransmissions not being a hard problem, commercial observability does not yet technically identify Kubernetes retransmissions. It's not just retransmissions that are not identified; most Kubernetes and kernel problems are not identified by anomaly detection and AIOps, and anomaly detection projects fail to deliver using commercial observability.

Performance latency occurs because a small number of resources are accessed by many processes and are designed to maximize process utilization within limited resources. Resources and processes have a minority:majority relationship, and performance latency is caused by the scheduling of multiple processes against limited resources. Anomaly detection and AIOps should monitor the relationship between resources and processes, preferably at the lower level, as part of root cause analysis. Identifying only the latency in a higher level application is not a valid anomaly detection method. Latency is not a root cause analysis because the latency that occurs at the lower level propagates to the higher level. If the anomaly detection assumes that the problem is only in the application, it is misleading the SRE.

The approach of this chapter is as follows.

- Through anomaly detection, infrastructure-level latency and failures are identified in real-time.

- Application-level latency and failures are identified in real-time with SLO and thresholds.

CHAPTER 7   ANOMALY DETECTION

- SREs perform root cause analysis through application and infrastructure observability.

- Root cause analysis is automated with AIOps.

Application observability and system trace have their limitations. Let's say application observability fails to analyze the root cause. The next step is to apply infrastructure observability. If you don't have knowledge of infrastructure observability, you can only perform application observability and not root cause analysis, and the problem will recur in the future. Without root cause analysis, you don't know when and under what circumstances the problem will reoccur, so you'll be operating in the hope that it doesn't escalate into a major failure.

For the purposes of this chapter, anomaly detection is defined as follows:

- You don't need business-critical, sophisticated anomaly detection; you need anomaly detection that can be quickly applied to your infrastructure.

- Anomaly detection does not require a threshold. Defining application-level SLO is difficult for infrastructure. The number of infrastructure resources is large, and defining a threshold is labor intensive. Infrastructure anomaly detection allows you to automatically identify anomalies without threshold and configure the alert and dashboard.

Infrastructure observability and anomaly detection are complementary technologies.

Rather than implementing anomaly detection using machine learning alone, validation using SQL can deliver more accurate results.

OpenSearch offers a wide range of features. In addition to basic text analysis, observability, anomaly detection, and vector databases are useful features. This chapter explains OpenSearch anomaly detection and the Vector database. I chose OpenSearch for anomaly detection for the following reasons:

- It provides a variety of APIs and makes it easy to configure anomaly detection.

- It is easy to configure anomaly detection dashboards and alerts.

- With the provided notebook, it's easy to develop with other machine learning frameworks.

- It has strengths in log analysis and can combine traces and metrics managed by observability.

This chapter discusses the following topics of OpenSearch:

- OpenSearch anomaly detection development

- Using the OpenSearch anomaly detection API

I do not recommend using OpenSearch anomaly detection alone to configure inference-based anomaly detection. SQL provides good capabilities for anomaly detection. I recommend using a combination of SQL and the inference provided by OpenSearch anomaly detection to implement the anomaly detection required for observability. Anomaly detection should be configured in a way that allows for incremental validation and incremental accuracy.

CHAPTER 7   ANOMALY DETECTION

7.1. SQL Anomaly Detection

Anomaly refers to a feature that is different from other members of the same group. In data terms, it refers to records that are different from the rest of the data and raise suspicion; similar words are outliers, novelties, noise, and deviations. Anomaly detection can be done literally to detect anomalies and as an intermediate step in a larger analytics project.

The process of finding anomalies is the same regardless of what caused them, but in order to resolve them, you need to understand exactly what the root cause of the anomaly is so you can respond correctly.

Anomalies can signal anomalous transactions, network intrusions, structural faults in the product, weaknesses in policies, or use of the system in ways that developers never intended. Anomalies can be caused by malicious users abusing the system, but they can also be caused by customers using the product in unintended ways.

SQL is a versatile and powerful language that is useful for a wide range of data analysis.

Writing anomaly detection in SQL has the advantage that it's easier to understand why a particular record was processed as an outlier than rules or machine learning, and even if the database changes, SQL is unaffected and always performs the same behavior.

There are times when SQL is not useful. SQL doesn't provide sophisticated statistical analysis like Python. It does provide some standard statistical methods, but in some databases, even moderately complex statistical calculations can be time-consuming. It also takes time to load data when performing data analysis in the database, so SQL may not be a good choice if you need to know immediately whether an anomaly is present, such as for anomalous transaction detection or intrusion detection. In this case, a typical anomaly detection procedure is to perform an initial analysis in SQL to determine the minimum, maximum, and average values in the normal scope, and then perform real-
time monitoring using real-time data. If an outlier pattern is detected during monitoring, the streaming service can be set up to process it.

There is another case where SQL is inappropriate for anomaly detection. SQL code operates on a static rule base. While it's great for dealing with data from well-known fields, it can't automatically adapt its analysis conditions to rapidly changing types of anomalous patterns. This is where rules and machine learning come in.

There are several ways to detect outliers in the dataset itself:

- Using an ORDER BY clause to sort the data to find outliers.

- You can also use a GROUP BY clause to find outliers by determining the frequency of each value stored in a field.

This is how to use SQL's statistical methods to find outliers that fall outside the usual scope.

7.1.1. Anomaly Detection Method

I described the sort, percentile, and standard deviation methods in metric SQL and trace SQL. Even if you are familiar with SQL, many readers are not familiar with time series analysis, anomaly detection, and cohort analysis using SQL. Therefore, I explain anomaly detection with SQL.

The first thing you do when working with a dataset is profile it. *Profiling* is the process of understanding your data before you start analyzing it.

7.1.1.1. Frequency

The best way to understand the specific fields in your dataset is to check the frequency of occurrence of each value per field. Frequency checks are useful for finding out if a particular value is likely to occur or if there are unexpected values and, if so, how they might have gotten in. This can be used for any data type, including string, number, and date, and is also useful for finding sparse data.

Specify the field you want to profile in a GROUP BY clause and use count(*) to get the number of each value in the field.

Frequency plots are a way to visualize the frequency of values in a dataset. They typically represent the values of the profile target field on the x-axis and the frequency of each value on the y-axis.

7.1.1.2. Sort

The basic way to find outliers using SQL is to sort the data with an ORDER BY clause. By default, the ORDER BY clause sorts data in ascending order. The ORDER BY clause allows you to sort data by one or more columns at a time, and you can specify a separate sort order for each column, either ascending or descending.

7.1.1.3. Percentile

Visualizing the results of sorting data, both overall and by group, is a great way to find anomalies, especially when there are extreme values mixed in with the data. Quantifying the distribution of your data gives you a new way of looking at it.

There are many methods for calculating percentiles:

- median
- percent_rank
- percentile_cont
- percentile_disc
- ntile

Percentile means the percentage of the data that is smaller than a certain value. The median, which is the 50th percentile, is when half of the data is greater than the value and half of the data is less than that value.

CHAPTER 7   ANOMALY DETECTION

When checking the distribution of data, we often want to check the median. To do this, many databases support the `median` method. It takes as an argument the field whose median you want to check and returns the value that corresponds to the median of the values in that field.

The `median` method is supported by most databases, but if it is not, you can use the `ntile` method. Both the `median` and `ntile` methods are window methods, meaning that they perform operations across multiple rows and return a single value as a result. The `ntile` method takes the number of sections you want to divide as an argument and divides the data, using the `PARTITION BY` clause and `ORDER BY` clause if necessary.

Interval is a useful way to profile continuous values. Instead of counting the number of records for each value, you group them based on the scope of the value. These groupings are called *buckets*, and you can count the number of records that fall within their scope. The size of the bucket can be flexible depending on the purpose of your analysis, such as making them all close together or varying the number of records in each scope so that they are similar.

While the `ntile` method is better suited for intervals, the `percent_rank` method can be used to see the continuous distribution of your data, create a report on its own, or used for other analysis later. The `ntile` and `percent_rank` methods are computationally expensive to use on large datasets because they require every row to be sorted for calculation, so it's better to filter only the data you need from the table.

The `percent_rank` window method provided by SQL returns the percentile of each row value in a given partition. It is used without arguments and performs the operation on all rows specified in the query. Because it is a window method, it uses the `ORDER BY` clause to set the sorting direction. The `percent_rank` method also uses the `PARTITION BY` and `ORDER BY` clauses.

When using the window method, the `PARTITION BY` and `ORDER BY` clauses are not required in some cases, but it's better to use the `ORDER BY` clause to specify the sort order unless you have a specific reason not to do so. On the other hand, you must use the `OVER` clause. First, you use the `percent_rank` method in the subquery to calculate the percentiles. Then you count them in the outer query. You should calculate the percentile with the `percent_rank` method before doing any other aggregation to get accurate results.

In addition to percentiles, SQL's `ntile` method divides the data into *N* buckets and determines which bucket each row belongs to.

If you want to calculate the value corresponding to a specific percentile in the entire dataset, rather than finding the percentile or Nth percentile of each row, use the `percentile_cont` or `percentile_disc` method. Both are window methods, but the syntax is slightly different, such as using a `WITHIN GROUP` clause.

The `percentile_cont` method returns an interpolation of the value when there is no exact value in the dataset that corresponds to the specified percentile, while the `percentile_disc` method finds and returns the closest value to that value. For large datasets or datasets consisting primarily of continuous values, there is often no practical difference between the two methods, but it is best to judge which one will yield the desired analytical results and choose the more appropriate one.

Finding percentiles or N-quantiles in a dataset provides a quantitative basis for finding anomalies. You can learn how to use percentile values to process anomalies in your dataset. However, looking at percentiles only gives you a value that falls between 0 and 100 percent; it doesn't tell you how much a particular value deviates from the norm.

CHAPTER 7 ANOMALY DETECTION

7.1.1.4. Standard Deviation

Standard deviation is used to identify extreme values in a dataset. The standard deviation is the degree to which values are spread out in the data. A small standard deviation means that the values in your data are close together, while a large standard deviation means that the values in your data are spread out widely.

The typical standard deviation methods provided by most databases are the stddev_pop and stddev_samp methods.

- The stddev_pop method calculates the standard deviation of populations. Use it when the dataset is representative of the entire population, such as when analyzing all customer data.

- The stddev_samp method calculates the standard deviation of a sample. Unlike when calculating the standard deviation of populations, it is divided by N-1 instead of N in the formula. This has the effect of making the standard deviation value larger and therefore less accurate.

For example, if you are analyzing sample data from a survey, you can use the stddev_samp method. In practice, when analyzing large datasets, there is little difference between the results of the stddev_pop method and the stddev_samp method.

Use these methods to express the difference between each value in the dataset and the mean in standard deviation units. This value is called the *jet score* and is used to standardize the data. Values above the mean have a positive jet score, and values below the mean have a negative jet score.

7.1.2. Anomaly Types

In this section, you learn how to recognize anomalies by dividing them into three categories: value, count or frequency, and presence. When you find a value that appears to be an anomaly in your profile results, or when you suspect an anomaly exists for any number of reasons, you can check for the presence of an anomaly from these three aspects. Depending on the data domain, certain values may be outliers, or they may be typical.

7.1.2.1. Exceptional Values

When you think of anomalies, you probably think of extremely high or low outliers. However, sometimes outliers are actually values that are located in the center of the overall data distribution.

Finding anomalous values is important, but to analyze them well, you need to understand why they occurred and what other attributes are relevant to the anomaly.

CHAPTER 7   ANOMALY DETECTION

7.1.2.2. Number and Frequency of Exceptions

It is useful to measure counts and frequencies to identify anomalies.

- Sometimes anomalies are not just individual values, but patterns or clusters of anomalies.
- There are several conditions that determine if a particular cluster is an anomaly. The conditions are context-dependent. They are utilized to find anomalous clusters based on time, location, and other attributes.
- Events that occur with uncommon frequency over a short period of time are considered exceptional events.

To find these anomalies, you need to look for differences that are out of the ordinary.

Once you've identified common patterns in your data, you can build on them to look for unusual patterns. Analytics basically involves iterating through the steps of profiling the data, understanding the data based on domain knowledge, and drawing insights from the results of queries.

To find out how often a particular value is an anomaly in your data, you need to iterate through the queries and data by varying the granularity of the values. You start with a coarse granularity, then narrow it down to a finer granularity, then back to a specific scope of data, or look at the data with a different attribute. This is a common process in data analysis, and SQL is a great tool for doing this iterative work.

7.1.2.3. Missing Data

An unusually high number of events can be an anomaly. Conversely, don't forget that no event occurrences can also be an anomaly. Calculate the time from the last event to the current time to check for missingness.

When investigating anomalies, use queries to look for patterns and repeat the process of verifying the results. Obvious outlier values are easy to spot. Query the entire dataset, including the outliers, to get a sense of the different attributes (time, source) and build a basis for judging them as outliers. Then check the records to see if there are any unusual values in a particular attribute.

7.2. Machine Learning Anomaly Detection

Anomaly detection requires procedures and a management system. This is because there are differences from the existing SLO method, and it is a process for implementing AIOps.

You configure anomaly detection in five steps, as shown here:

1. Analyze patterns and measure frequency.
2. Define the anomaly levels. You can define anomalies at different levels: individual records, populations, buckets (sets) at specific times of day, or categories.

CHAPTER 7 ANOMALY DETECTION

3. Define the anomaly feature. Understand the business and technology and define any composite features.

4. Define anomaly determination. Judge anomalies with grades and confidence, not thresholds.

5. Analyze the anomalous results.

Infrastructure observability is broad in scope, high in number of resources, and expensive to monitor. Anomaly detection can reduce costs and improve overall infrastructure observability.

This list describes what machine learning anomaly detection can do for you. It also describes real-time and batch anomaly detection and explains how to analyze anomaly results and configure alerts and dashboards:

- Anomaly detection based on machine learning is used a lot, and it constitutes a variety of anomaly detection applications, such as application cost, network security, system scaling, latency and failure forecasting. There is no problem with anomaly detection even if it is not a time series, but observability-based anomaly detection is based on time series data. Anomaly detection works without baselines and thresholds.

- Anomaly detection comes in two types: real-time and batch. Real-time anomaly detection detects anomalies in a set window (typically every 5-10 minutes). OpenSearch provides RCF algorithm for real-time anomaly detection, which can identify anomalies with high accuracy. This allows for immediate response to the highly volatile and unexpected anomalies characteristic of real-time data without the need to train new models.

- RCF anomaly detection is unsupervised learning, and the results of anomaly detection are stored in the OpenSearch internal index. The operator can analyze the internal index through SQL queries and develop further processes. RCF is used to collect anomalies, and once the results are accumulated, the collected anomalies can be trained to create a supervised learning model.

- Algorithm-based anomaly detection can sometimes fail to specify the exact anomaly. For example, if you are implementing anomaly detection in an ordering processing, it may not provide the exact Order ID of the anomaly, only the time period in which it occurred. If 1,000 orders are generated per second, finding anomalies among them is not straightforward. OpenSearch anomaly detection stores anomaly detection results in the user results index. You can use categories (order, gender, region, age) to target anomalies and perform SQL follow-up processes to identify anomalies. This compensates for the weaknesses of algorithm-based anomaly detection and identifies anomalies quickly and accurately.

CHAPTER 7 ANOMALY DETECTION

The data source for anomaly detection are logs and events. Trace only supports applications, so it is not suitable for infrastructure observability. Profiles are text-like, unstructured, and not suitable for anomaly detection. The best signal for anomaly detection is a structured log.

Promscale stores metrics and traces in a structured way. Within Promscale, metrics are organized into multiple tables, and traces are organized into a single span table.

You can create a new table per metric. For example, if the scraping target increases, the metric table grows by the number of metrics. The trace table uses only one spanmetric table, so the number of tables does not change.

The reason that metric and trace are not suitable for anomaly detection is that it is difficult to add the attributes needed for anomaly detection. A log is better suited for anomaly detection because it has more degrees of freedom.

Anomaly detection should be implemented with a large number of unsupervised learning instances. In terms of number, a large number means over hundreds.

Unsupervised learning has many advantages over supervised learning. The reasons for using unsupervised learning in anomaly detection are as follows.

- Dozens or more detectors can be configured for infrastructure anomaly detection. Developing multiple supervised learning models requires a lot of time and development.

- Observability data has high data consistency and low errors such as duplicates. Under the assumption that the data quality is good, high accuracy anomaly detection results can be obtained by unsupervised learning alone.

- Adding a large number of labels by hand is time-consuming. Unsupervised learning does not require labels. Detectors can be quickly constructed using only time series data.

Given realistic resource constraints and desired outcomes, unsupervised learning is a good way to get started with anomaly detection. Once the results of unsupervised learning stabilize and you want to take it to a higher level of sophistication, I recommend combining it with supervised learning.

There are three types of patterns that the detector identifies as anomalies, as shown here:

- **Time base:** Understands the historical behavior patterns of a system and identifies anomalies when it starts to behave differently from the past. Time series data is trained to recognize anomalies when a pattern that is different from the past occurs.

- **Profile:** If a component starts to behave differently from other components, it is identified as an anomaly. In other words, it detects outlier patterns that are relatively different compared to others.

- **Rare events:** Identifies anomalies when previously unseen patterns begin to appear. Detects when a statistically rare pattern occurs.

7.2.1. Example 1: Internet of Things

The temperature of a refrigerator can be continuously traced to alert the user to dangerous temperatures for food or medicine, so that the user can take action to avoid them. Each entity has a category field that describes it, and the category field is an attribute of that entity. The serial number of a refrigerator is a category field that uniquely identifies the refrigerator.

- **Geography:** 5°C is normal for Seattle, but winter temperatures in the tropics are likely to be unusual.
- **User behavior:** A user might open the refrigerator door multiple times, causing the temperature to spike. The duration and frequency of spikes can vary based on user behavior.

By grouping temperature data into regions and users, you can detect different regional temperatures and user behavior.

7.2.2. Example 2: Security

Consider an intrusion detection system that identifies an increase in failed login attempts in the authentication logs. Username and host IP are category fields used to determine who is accessing the host.

- Hackers can guess user passwords through brute-force attacks, and not all users on the same host IP can be targeted.
- The number of failed logins varies by host at any given time, for any given user.

Create a baseline (number of failed logins) for each user on each host and monitor changes to the baseline.

7.2.3. Example 3: IT Operations

This examples monitors access traffic per shard of a distributed service. Shard ID is a category field and entity is a shard. A distributed system usually consists of shards that are connected.

Operators only care about the number of shards and that they are evenly distributed across the shards. When a shard outage occurs, retries increase and traffic on dependencies increases significantly. However, the increase in traffic is difficult to detect because only the dependency shards are affected. Changes in many IO metrics, including network bandwidth, are detected.

The traffic of the dependency shard can reach 64 times the normal level, while the average traffic of all shards can only grow by a small constant (less than 2).

You can monitor if shards are failing or evenly distributed.

CHAPTER 7   ANOMALY DETECTION

The simple case described here is an example of infrastructure observability using anomaly detection. OpenSearch anomaly detection provides three demo datasets for training and testing:

- Web log
- E-commerce order data
- Airline operational data

This allows you to test and understand OpenSearch anomaly detection in a short period of time. Each data contains anomalies, so by creating an anomaly detection detector, you can automatically identify and test anomalies. You can also create anomalies by randomly updating the documents in the sample data, and you can verify the functionality of anomaly detection in various ways.

The anomaly detection flow is shown here. The demo uses web log sample data.

- Create a detector that analyzes an index of time series data.
- After configuring a detector, you can run a detector job that reports an anomalies.
- You can use the resulting index to trigger alerts or create dashboards.

Create a detector:

- Create a job that detects anomalies in the number of requests split by status code. This can tell you if your system is experiencing high traffic or server errors.
- Name the index sample_data_logs and select the Timestamp field as Timestamp.
- The detector interval defines how often the detector collects data. The shorter the interval, the closer to real-time it is and the more resources it consumes. Keep it at ten minutes.

Create a feature:

- Create a feature that counts the number of response.keyword values.
- By setting response.keyword as a category, you can split the results by response code.

Run the detector:

- You can run the job in real time or through history. Select Historical to see results for the current dataset because it is a static sample.
- You can see the expected and actual number of documents in the feature breakdown chart.
- The anomaly grade is the severity of the anomaly (0 to 1). This is useful for setting alerts based on the impact of the anomaly.

CHAPTER 7   ANOMALY DETECTION

You can use the same data to configure different anomaly detections. For example, if you see an unusual increase in network traffic from a particular IP or OS, you can identify it as an anomaly. Select Bytes for the feature and OS for the category. After configuring the categories, the anomalies for each category are displayed in different colors at the top (see Figure 7-1).

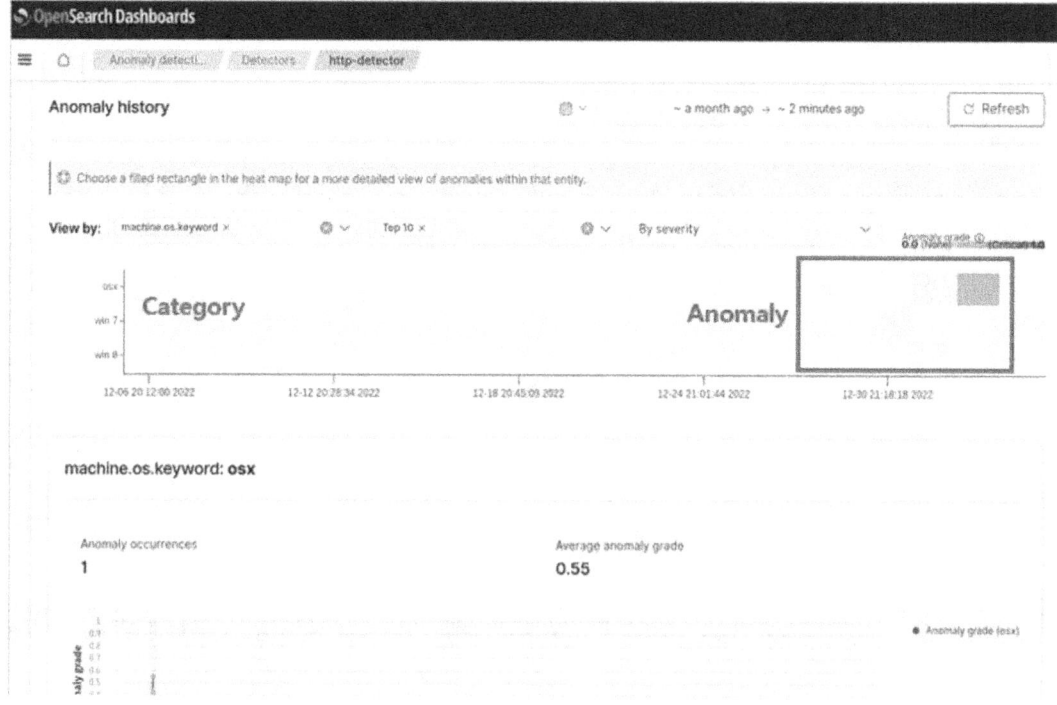

Figure 7-1. Viewing real-time anomaly detection results

When you click a specific category, the average, total, and maximum values will be output, as shown in Figure 7-2.

583

CHAPTER 7　ANOMALY DETECTION

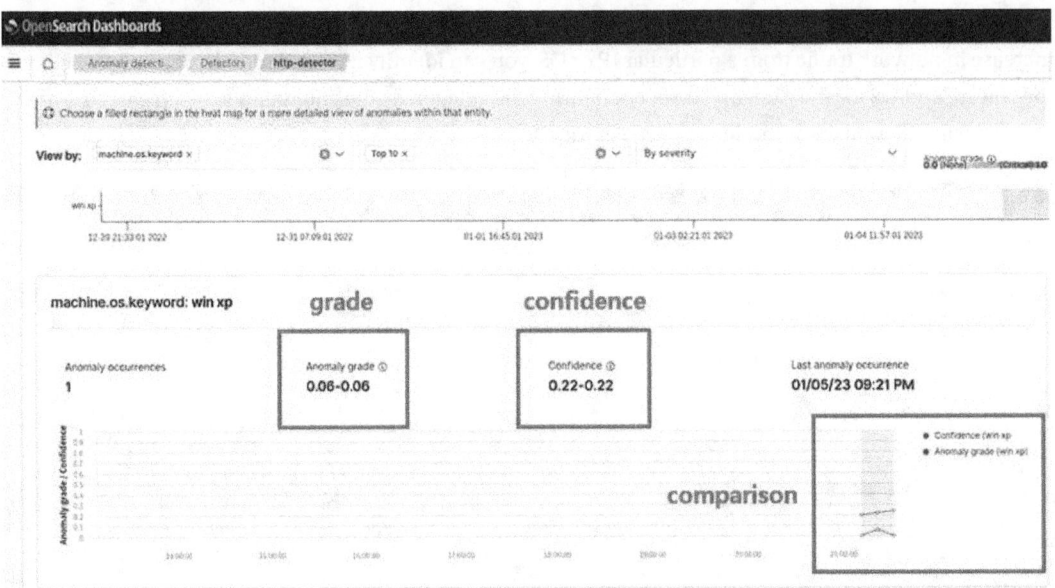

Figure 7-2. Aggregation analysis by category

You can evaluate the confidence (0.22) and anomaly grade (0.06) values and determine whether there is an anomaly. See Figure 7-3.

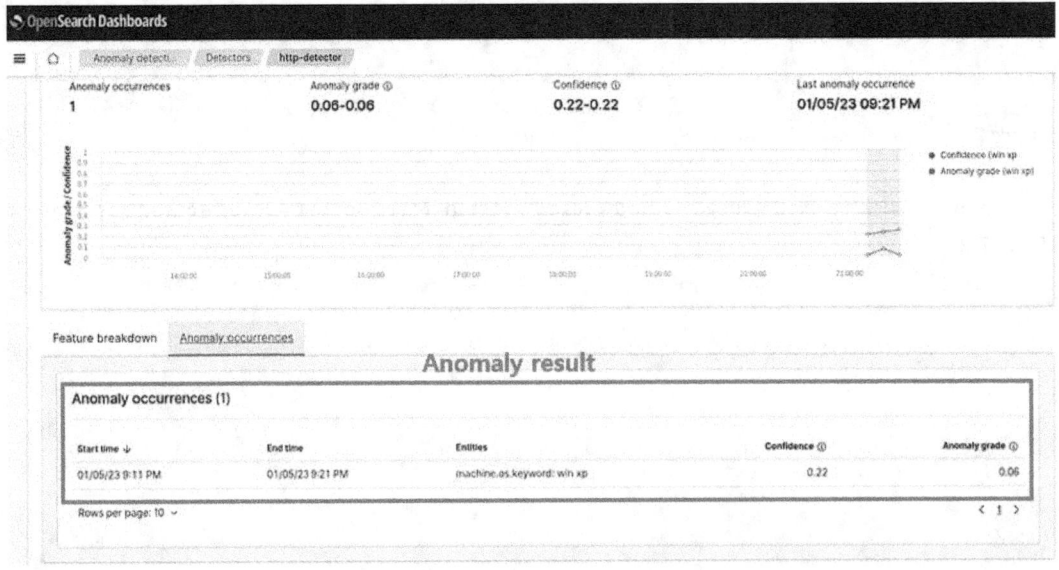

Figure 7-3. Anomaly grade and anomaly confidence analysis

There are roughly five types of anomaly detector configurations provided by anomaly detection:

- Ratio analysis
- Category analysis
- Populations analysis
- Pattern analytics
- Bucket analytics

7.2.4. Ratio Analysis

This section looks at counting methods that can detect changes in event rates over time. Detecting changes in event rates has many important use cases, including the following

- Suddenly finding tons of error messages in your log files
- Detecting a sharp drop in the number of orders processed by your online system
- Identifying excessive access attempts, such as a sudden increase in the number of login attempts for a specific user ID

In the detector, you define the requirements for the anomaly you want to detect. Inside detector, there are methods to select the features of the target.

For the count method, the feature is the occurrence rate of the event over time. This method counts the number of documents obtained from the index query results. We usually think of anomaly detection in terms of spikes, but not only high numbers like spikes, but also lower numbers than usual can also be a problem.

Count metrics alone can be used to forecast frequency. If the data point includes state and attributes, you can combine the count and state to get accurate anomaly detection results.

7.2.4.1. Use Case 1

Rate and change analysis primarily uses the count method.

Anomaly detection captures abnormal patterns in time series data. This can be done using regular queries and filters, but the problem is that the values you use to define "too much" and "too little" can change based on context, event date and time, amount of data, and more. An anomaly might be a high number in one case, and a low number in another. Capturing context with static thresholds can complicate queries.

On top of that, things can change: the amount of data grows or shrinks or user behavior changes. Maintaining thresholds, patterns, and rules becomes very complex.

CHAPTER 7　ANOMALY DETECTION

Instead of setting these thresholds yourself, anomaly detection allows you to use "anomaly detection models" to trace unusual events based on current data, instead of static thresholds. So you just configure the "what" you want to trace, and the model processes the "how."

OpenSearch uses Random Cut Forest (RCF), a machine learning algorithm, to analyze data in real-time, establishing anomaly grades and confidence levels to define how common an event is based on the current dataset.

Using the count method, you saw how easy it was to detect a set of obvious anomalies related to the overall percentage of occurrences of an event in an index over time.

7.2.4.2. Use Case 2

This is a demo using max. It processes anomaly detection on CPU usage data and creates a detector.

- Select the index containing the CPU usage log files you want to identify anomalies from as the data source.
- Set the detector interval to two minutes. This interval defines how long the detector collects data, in minutes.
- In the Window delay, add a one-minute latency. This latency adds a duration to ensure that all data within the time period is present.

The Live anomaly section shows anomalies that occur when data is ingested.

Now that you've created a detector, you'll create a monitor that will call an alert to transfer a message to Slack when it detects CPU usage that meets the conditions specified in the detector settings:

- Anomaly grade threshold
- Anomaly confidence threshold

Alerts differ from the traditional approach of setting a threshold and measuring anomalies.

The goal of anomaly detection is not to specify individual thresholds. Rather, anomaly detection should be able to identify an optimized threshold.

Instead, it does not have a specific threshold, but evaluates how abnormal the data points are and how confident it is in the calculated grade.

Anomaly detection can be text or categories, but for accuracy, numbers are the way to go. Let's take a look at methods that can help you detect changes in numeric fields in your data.

The metric method is the easiest detection to understand because it works on numeric fields and returns a numeric value:

- MIN, MAX, MEAN, and MEDIAN: These methods return, as you would expect, the minimum, maximum, mean, and median values for all numbers observed in the field of interest in the bucket span.

CHAPTER 7 ANOMALY DETECTION

- To ensure that these methods are meaningful, it is recommended to have as many numeric samples per bucket span as possible.

- It is also important to note that metric methods process data sparsity as null, meaning that even if the data is sparse and there are unobserved bucket spans, the lack of data does not degrade the statistics of the field of interest. Therefore, these metric-based methods do not have a thesis or a nonce.

- The Sum method returns the sum of all the numbers within the bucket span for the field of interest. Use the non-null version to avoid processing the lack of data as zero, which will inevitably drag down the sum value when there is sparse data.

7.2.4.3. Use Case 3

If you had selected sum(bytes) on the sample_data_logs index, you would have seen that the requests generated a larger amount of bytes in transfer on the web server. This is reasonable if you think that an increase in the number of requests to the web server would be associated with an increase in the number of bytes being transferred.

Developers can develop custom expressions based on additional requirements. For example, you can use distinct count to analyze populations and cohorts.

7.2.5. Category Analysis

While it is common for anomalies to be individual entities, groups or categories can be identified as anomalies. In many categories, it is possible to identify a specific category in which a problem is an anomaly.

For example, you can categorize by age or gender to get accurate results. For system resources, organize categories by resources such as CPU and memory usage, and then apply operations (sum, max) to identify anomalies. Split categories are based on fields that can be categorized.

7.2.5.1. Use Case 1

If you analyze the sample e-commerce index, you can see that the sum method on the taxful_total_price field is split by the category.keyword field.

The analysis is performed for the category of every item in your e-commerce store—for example, by categories of men's clothing or women's accessories.

Over time, the anomaly detection shows only the top ten most anomalous categories and color-codes the categories where anomalies occur. The men's clothing category was the most anomalous category on November 9, with $2,250 in revenue.

7.2.5.2. Use Case 2

This use case specifies an index that contains access count and response time data for airline websites:

- For the event_rate field, use the count metric to analyze the anomaly for the number of connections, and select the response-time field. Use the max method to analyze the anomaly for latency based on the maximum value of response time.
- Choose the airline to learn about each airline's website separately, so you can aggregate the data for each airline.
- When you find an anomaly, specify the field that is most relevant to the anomaly.

By categorizing the data into airline websites and access hosts with, you can identify which airline and which access host are involved when an anomaly occurs.

To organize categories, OpenSearch provides category fields. The fields you select can be organized as features.

7.2.6. Analyzing Populations

There are two ways to determine an anomaly:

- Determine how significantly behavior changes over time. Identify outliers in long-term trends that deviate from established trends.
- Determine whether something is significantly different when compared to other entities in the population. Identify an anomalous application among a large number of normal applications.

When analyzing populations, you may want to look for systems that are logging more than other similarly configured systems:

- There is a misconfiguration that causes many errors to occur in the system or application log files.
- Systems that can be compromised by malicious code can be instructed to suppress logging, which can significantly reduce log volumes.
- The log volume is decreasing because the system is disconnected or failing.
- A change to the logging level setting causes logs to take up more disk space.

When it comes to analyzing user behavior, populations are often used to compare behaviors among users:

- **Automated users:** Instead of typical human behavior or usage patterns, automated scripts can exhibit significantly different behavior patterns in terms of the rate, duration, and variety of events generated. Whether you're looking for crawlers trying to harvest products and prices for your online catalog or detecting bots spreading misinformation on social media, automated identification of automated users can help.

- **Snoopers:** Whether it's a real human trying to take over or a piece of malicious code doing reconnaissance, snoopers can do a wide range of things in the hopes of matching something or finding an entry point.

- **Malicious users:** After the reconnaissance phase, malicious users or malicious code will actively wreak havoc and engage in active measures, such as denial of service, brute force, and theft of valuable information.

7.2.6.1. Use Case 1

This example could find customers who spend significantly more than your average customer. Whether you're interested in proactively investigating potential fraud or increasing your marketing to your wealthiest customers, you should look for these outliers. By selecting the `customer_full_name.keyword` field in the e-commerce index, you can create a populations job. Since the field selected is a name, you can't split it into categories. The detector selects the sum of the `taxful_total_price` field, which is the total revenue for the individual orders placed by the individual.

In the list of the most anomalous users (in this case, users with large spending per unit of time), the user named Wagdi Shaw, who ordered $2,250 worth of goods, is the largest. Unlike category analysis, which identified categories, populations analysis identifies individual anomalies. Population analysis can be powerful and is often used in use cases that target individual entities.

7.2.6.2. Use Case 2

You can evaluate the system load of 1,000 servers or processes to identify if there are any anomalies in real time:

- Out of 10,000 users accessing your webserver, can you identify those who behave differently?

- Out of 2,000 FTP processes, can you identify those that behave differently?

- Out of 10,000 webservers, can you identify those that have different patterns of system load?

CHAPTER 7 ANOMALY DETECTION

Solving this problem is important, but it is a difficult problem to solve even for experienced professionals.

Security experts may consider a logged-in user who downloads a lot of data compared to other users as a potential threat, but determining whether it's an anomaly for them to download 20MB or 100MB in five minutes is a problem beyond the reach of humans, as it requires learning and profiling the past behavior patterns of all users and comparing them to other users.

Even with traditional rule-based or statistical modeling approaches, user behavior is constantly changing and requires constant attention. In theory, the modeling will always miss something because it needs to be updated every time the behavior changes.

7.2.6.3. Use Case 3

If you calculate the amount of traffic by IP using `CLIENT IP` and `TOTAL BYTE` from the server logs provided in the example, you can identify users who are downloading more than usual.

HTTP data exfiltration is a hacking threat that uses the standard protocol HTTP to steal data from websites. This threat is one of the most difficult to detect:

- On an online site with 100,000 visitors per day, an attacker enters the same channel as other users over HTTP and exfiltrates data. It's not easy to distinguish the attacker from other legitimate users requesting data.

- If a user requests more than 10MB ten times in one minute, set an anomaly detection rule. It is difficult to apply anomaly detection if it is an online promotion period and normal users also make such requests.

- If you see a high concentration of access to certain URLs, you can assume that this is not normal. The hacker could have been trying to steal data by randomizing the connection paths. There are many ways to hide behind 300,000 visitors, making it difficult for security experts to identify anomalies on high-traffic sites.

7.2.7. Pattern Analytics

OpenSearch supports anomaly detection in text log files through machine learning-based pattern analysis.

After indexing, it provides a pattern analysis feature that automatically measures counts from the saved logs.

Patterning and data profiling are best done before anomaly detection. The core of anomaly detection is the detector, which requires various analyses and configurations to define the exact detector. Even if you don't have basic knowledge of the data in the log, the patterns are automatically analyzed when the data is saved, so it is best to configure the detector by referring to them.

7.2.7.1. Use Case 1

When infrastructure has a problem, it will eventually go through the process of searching the logs around the time of the problem to identify exactly what the problem is. (For example, searching for error status codes.)

By searching for error messages or status codes after a problem has already occurred, it is not possible to proactively detect the occurrence of potentially problematic logs in advance.

Perhaps the solution is to learn the pattern of all the logs that are generated and identify in real time if there are any that are not generated under normal circumstances.

By taking log data (system load, access time, and data export volume) and determining that it behaves differently compared to the past or compared to other components with the same role, the example can automatically identify the event with a probability value.

7.2.8. Bucket Analysis

This section summarizes the results of all anomaly detection jobs per time bucket. It indicates how anomalous that time bucket is:

- Analyzing bucket results is useful if you measure many metrics and have dynamic thresholds.
- At the bucket level, how normal was this time interval for this job compared to other time intervals?
- It is used to better understand unusual entities within a time scope. What is the most unusual entity and when was it unusual?

To summarize, it is important to properly use the record level for the short term and the bucket level for the long term. They compensate for each other's shortcomings.

7.2.8.1. Use Case 1

Notice the `clientip` and `response.keyword` fields in the server log example. The `response.keyword` value is 404. This is relevant because it gives the user an immediate clue as to what the 30.156.16.164 address was doing during the anomaly detection. If you examine this unusual IP address, you can see that 100 percent of the requests resulted in a 404 response code.

Therefore, the 404 value is highly significant. This is because 100 percent of requests are 404s. You can then analyze how abnormal the 404 values are over time. In this demo dataset, there are hundreds more 404s over time, but most of them are not associated with an anomaly.

7.2.8.2. Use Case 2

Insert fake documents into the indexes monitored by the anomaly detection job, then wait for the alert to fire. These documents show a spike in requests from an unusual 0.0.0.0 IP address that generates a 404 response.

- You need to determine the current time in UTC. Documents stored in OpenSearch indexes are stored in UTC, so you need to know the UTC time. To determine this, use the OpenSearch development tool console.

- Insert a new document into the sample_data_logs index with the current time, change the value of the timestamp field accordingly, and insert it at least 20 times in the developer tool console.

- To make the URLs all unique, use a script to randomize the field values in the _update_by_query API call, so that you can dynamically modify the document you just entered.

- By checking the appropriate times in the dashboard, you can verify that you have correctly generated a large number of unique and random requests from fake IP addresses.

If you are waiting for the anomalous behavior you entered to be discovered by anomaly detection tasks and alerts, you can think about when you should expect those alerts to occur.

If a given job has a one-hour bucket, a ten-minute frequency, and a query latency of one to ten minutes, you should expect the alert to occur between 1:12 PM and 1:20 PM local time.

It is for an anomaly detection job that counts the number of events for an individual response.keyword (404 document spikes are exceeding expectations) and correctly identifies clientip=0.0.0.0 as an anomaly.

7.3. Analyzing the Results

Alerts and dashboards can be developed using the identified anomalies and measured anomaly detection results. Using the collected anomalies, you can advance to supervised learning anomaly detection.

Anomaly detection machine learning outputs a confidence and grade score. Setting thresholds in machine learning anomaly detection is not a good idea. If the system is being opened for the first time, the thresholds are unknown to the developers and SREs and are difficult to set. It is a good idea to use unsupervised anomaly detection to find the appropriate threshold.

- Understanding the pattern first helps you understand the data.

- Before configuring the detector, SQL is used to profile and process SQL anomaly detection.

- Various anomaly detections can be configured, including frequency, populations, categories, and time-based buckets.

- The collected data can be used to improve the accuracy of anomaly detection through supervised learning.

7.3.1. How to Analyze Your Results

Anomalies can be considered from a variety of perspectives:

- Analyze individual data points and records. For example, determine if the number of anomalies increases during certain times of day.

- Analyze how individual anomalies differ from other anomalies within the same populations.

- Analyze what categories you need to pay attention to in order to identify anomalies.

- Analyze buckets. For example, analyze whether anomalies at a particular time of day are different from anomalies at other times of day. Store data points from a specific time period in a bucket and analyze the bucket for anomalies.

Rather than simply judging an anomaly based on count, frequency, or value, it is necessary to compare and analyze the difference between the before and after time periods and other anomalies before judging it as an anomaly.

OpenSearch uses anomaly grade and anomaly confidence to determine the severity of an anomaly.

- **Anomaly grade:** A number between 0 and 1 that indicates how abnormal a data point is. An anomaly grade of 0 indicates "no anomaly," while a non-zero value indicates the relative severity of the anomaly.

- **Anomaly confidence:** This is an estimate of the probability that a reported anomaly grade matches the expected anomaly grade. Confidence increases as the model observes more data and learns about data behavior and trends. It is important to understand that confidence is separate from model accuracy.

Anomaly grade and confidence are used to define triggers. They are values between 0 and 1.

The anomaly grade indicates the severity of the anomaly: A rating of 0 means that the forecast is not an anomaly.

Confidence measures whether an entity's model has observed enough data to include enough unique real-world data points. If the confidence value of one model is greater than the confidence of another model, the anomaly in the first model has observed more data.

There is a record level and a bucket level. You can measure the score for each level and determine the presence or absence of anomaly based on the score. The confidence level calculated by the machine learning algorithm gives you an idea of how accurate it is.

CHAPTER 7   ANOMALY DETECTION

From a time series data perspective, individual anomalies are referred to as data points; from an anomaly detection perspective, individual anomalies are referred to as entities.

7.3.2. Results Analytics API

The anomalies identified by the detector are stored in the results index:

- Once you create the user result index, it creates the index according to the naming convention and stores the anomaly detection results.
- Without categories, more anomalies are searched, but it is difficult to identify the exact anomaly and generate a lot of noise.
- Defining a category field creates a category on the y-axis within the anomaly detection screen.
- When using the API, the GET method also has a body and behaves like a POST.
- The anomaly detection sample index does not have a user result index, so it is difficult to analyze the results. You need to use the sample demo provided by OpenSearch. You can test the result index using OpenSearch samples.

The number and duration of data collected will determine the anomaly results and affect the accuracy. Make sure you have enough data and process anomaly detection over a long window. This is because what may appear to be an anomaly in a five-minute window may not be a problem in a 24-hour window.

You can analyze anomaly detection results in two ways:

- Since you cannot directly query the result index in OpenSearch, you need to create an index pattern to query an anomaly. After an index is created with an index pattern, you can use the _search API to query the index for anomalies, or add anomaly results to a dashboard.
- The results index stores anomaly detection results in JSON format. You can use Python to handle the JSON and develop reports that meet requirements.

Analyzing results onscreen is the most effective way to do this, but if you need to customize or associate results, use an API. Here are three important APIs:

- Find the detector task.
- Search the detector results.
- Search for high anomalies.

Without a category, it's not easy to find anomalies. The reason for having categories is to make it easier to quickly find the anomaly that is the real problem.

CHAPTER 7   ANOMALY DETECTION

For example, let's say you run a retail store. The field could be the amount, the category could be the region of the retail store, and the age range of the customer is another category. Having categories makes it easy to identify which orders have anomalies. The best way to identify them is to use the API.

detector contains tasks. real-time detection does not keep task ID in anomaly results, so task ID will be null.

The sample data provided by OpenSearch is continuously fed with data, and after configuring the detector, you can see that outliers are automatically identified.

You can update the data arbitrarily to generate more frequent anomaly detections.

```
POST /opensearch_dashboards_sample_data_logs/_doc/4zeUgYUB-CylDo66mtj2?pretty
```

Bytes to 1111114529. This is clearly an abnormal byte size.

```
{
        "agent" : "Mozilla/5.0 (X11; Linux x86_64; rv:6.0a1) Gecko/20110421
        Firefox/6.0a1",
        "bytes" : 1111114529,
        "clientip" : "54.190.60.72",
        "extension" : "deb",
        "geo" : {
          "srcdest" : "IN:PK",
          "src" : "IN",
          "dest" : "PK",
          "coordinates" : {
            "lat" : 40.84365472,
            "lon" : -72.63178917
          }
        },
        "host" : "artifacts.opensearch.org",
        "index" : "opensearch_dashboards_sample_data_logs",
        "ip" : "54.190.60.72",
        "machine" : {
          "ram" : 16106127360,
          "os" : "osx"
        },
        "memory" : null,
        "message" : "54.190.60.72 - - [2018-07-22T06:15:34.660Z] \"GET /beats/metricbeat/
        metricbeat-6.3.2-amd64.deb_1 HTTP/1.1\" 200 4529 \"-\" \"Mozilla/5.0 (X11; Linux
        x86_64; rv:6.0a1) Gecko/20110421 Firefox/6.0a1\"",
        "phpmemory" : null,
        "referer" : "http://twitter.com/success/james-m-kelly",
        "request" : "/beats/metricbeat/metricbeat-6.3.2-amd64.deb",
```

```
          "response" : 200,
          "tags" : [
            "success",
            "info"
          ],
          "timestamp" : "2022-12-25T06:15:34.660Z",
          "url" : "https://artifacts.opensearch.org/downloads/beats/metricbeat/
          metricbeat-6.3.2-amd64.deb_1",
          "utc_time" : "2022-12-25T06:15:34.660Z",
          "event" : {
            "dataset" : "sample_web_logs"
          }
}
```

Response 200, but an abnormal increase in bytes is identified as an anomaly.

You can view the results onscreen, but you can also use the API to get the results.

Find the detector task. It provides two APIs:

- GET _plugins/_anomaly_detection/detectors/tasks/_search

- POST _plugins/_anomaly_detection/detectors/tasks/_search

Instead of HISTORICAL_HC_ENTITY, you can also select HISTORICAL_SINGLE_ENTITY. Enter search criteria such as task_type, is_latest. The request looks like this:

```
{ {
  "query": { "query".
    "bool": { "true
      "filter": [].
        { {
          "term": { "term".
            "detector_id": "-JQNMIUBXTb6s6wMdsxa"
          }
        },
        { {
          "term": { "term".
            "task_type": "HISTORICAL_HC_ENTITY"
          }
        }
      ]
    }
  }
}
```

CHAPTER 7 ANOMALY DETECTION

This returns all results for the search query:

- POST _plugins/_anomaly_detection/detectors/results/_search/ to search only the default results index, you can use the search API

- POST _plugins/_anomaly_detection/detectors/results/_search/<custom_result_index> to search both the custom result index and the default result index, you can add a custom result index to the search API

For example, a request for POST _plugins/_anomaly_detection/detectors/results/_search/opensearch-ad-plugin-result-flight-detector would look like this:

```
{ {
  "query": { "query".
    "bool": { "true
      "filter": [].
        { {
          "term": { "term".
            "detector_id": "-JQNMIUBXTb6s6wMdsxa"
          }
        },
        { {
          "range": { { "1".
            "anomaly_grade": { }
              "gt": 0
            }
          }
        }
      ]
    }
  }
}
```

Omit the response. It returns results only when called with a localhost, as shown here:

```
import requests
import json

url = "http://localhost:9200/_plugins/_anomaly_detection/detectors/tasks/_search"

payload = json.dumps({
  "query": { "query".
    "bool": { "true
      "filter": [].
```

CHAPTER 7 ANOMALY DETECTION

```
    { {
      "term": { "term".
        "detector_id": "g6soKoUB6uQCBPJHMrsW"
      }
    }
   ]
  }
 }
})
headers = {
  'Content-Type': 'application/json'
}
response = requests.request("POST", url, headers=headers, data=payload)

print(response.text)
```

Look for high anomalies:

- GET _plugins/_anomaly_detection/detectors/<detectorId>/results/_topAnomalies?historical=false

- GET _plugins/_anomaly_detection/detectors/-JQNMIUBXTb6s6wMdsxa/results/_topAnomalies?historical=true

A call that requests *N* jobs with high anomaly detection scores, starting at a specific timestamp, looks like this:

```
{ {
  "size": 3,
  "category_field": [].
    "FlightDelayType"
  ],
  "order": "severity",
  "task_id": "_pQNMIUBXTb6s6wMdszS",
  "start_time_ms": 1668956466818,
  "end_time_ms": 1671548466818
}
```

The response is shown here:

```
{ {
  "buckets" : [ ].
}
```

Basic anomaly detection results do not provide information about specific entities. Therefore, preprocessing is required to narrow the scope using categories:

- POST _plugins/_anomaly_detection/detectors/results/_search/opensearch-ad-plugin-result-log-detector

The request looks like this:

```
{ {
  "query": { "query".
    "bool": { "true
      "filter": [].
        { {
          "term": { "term".
            "detector_id": "g6soKoUB6uQCBPJHMrsW"
          }
        }
      ]
    }
  }
}
```

You can then search for the exact anomaly.

7.4. Configuring Anomaly Detection

RCF is an unsupervised algorithm that models the data streams it receives. The algorithm calculates anomaly grades and confidence score values for data points. These values are used to distinguish anomalous changes from normal variations.

Anomalies are abnormal changes in the behavior of time series data. For example, in IT infrastructure, anomalies in memory usage metrics can help detect early signs of system failure.

7.4.1. Configuring OpenSearch Anomaly Detection

In the OpenSearch dashboard, select Anomaly Detection. To test with sample streaming data, you can try one of the preconfigured detectors on the sample dataset.

Configure OpenSearch anomaly detection as shown in Figure 7-4. Here's a brief summary of the process:

1. Develop a pipeline to collect the log and event and store them in an index.
2. Create a detector and run it.

CHAPTER 7   ANOMALY DETECTION

3. Analyze the resulting index.

4. Develop alerts and dashboards.

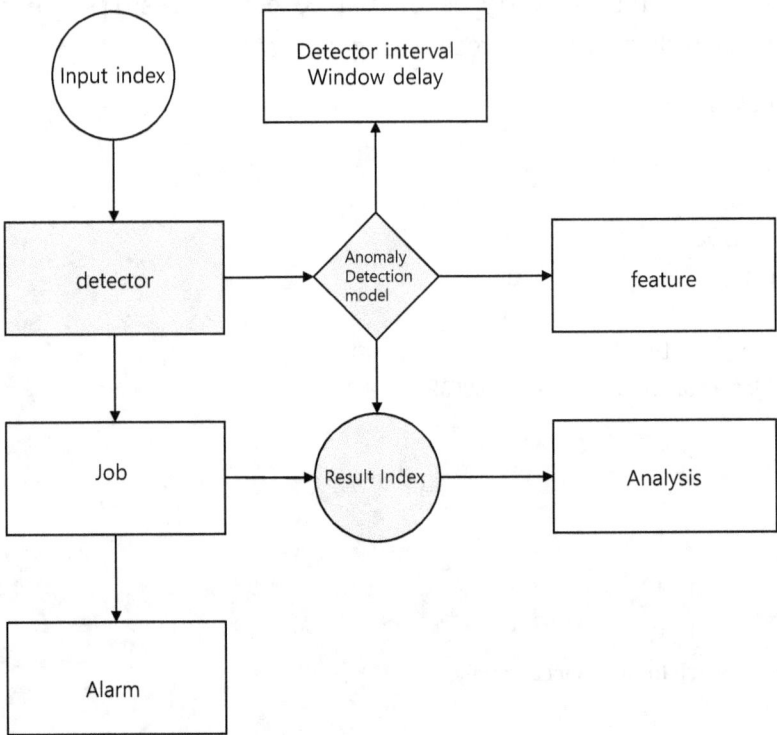

Figure 7-4. *OpenSearch anomaly detection process*

7.4.1.1. Step 1: Create a Detector

A detector is an individual anomaly detection task. You can define multiple detectors, all of which can run concurrently, each analyzing data from different sources.

1. Select Create Detector.

2. Add detector details. Enter a name and a short description.

3. Specify the data source. Under Data Source, select the index you want to use as the data source.

4. Specify a timestamp. Select the timestamp field in the index

5. Define the job settings. In the task settings, define the detector interval, which is the time interval during which the detector collects data.

The detector aggregates data at this interval and then sends the aggregated results to the anomaly detection model. When you set this interval, the detector aggregates. fewer points. The anomaly detection model uses singling, a technique that uses consecutive data points to generate samples for the model. This process requires a certain number of aggregated data points at consecutive intervals.

6. To add duration to the data collection, specify a window latency value.

    This value tells the detector that the data is not being ingested into OpenSearch in real time, but that there is a certain latency involved. To move the detector interval to account for this latency, set the window latency.

    For example, suppose the detector interval is ten minutes and data is ingested into the cluster at a typical latency of one minute. Suppose the detector is triggered at 2:00. The detector tries to get the last ten minutes of data from 1:50 to 2:00, but because of the one-minute latency, it only gets nine minutes of data and misses the data from 1:59 to 2:00. If you set the window LATENCY to one minute, the interval window moves to 1:49-1:59, and the detector gets all ten minutes of the detector interval time.

7. Specify a custom result index.

    To store anomaly detection results in your own index, specify the user index where you want to store the results. Add the opensearch-ad-plugin-result- prefix to the index name you enter. For example, if you enter abc as the result index name, the final index name will be opensearch-ad-plugin-result-abc.

7.4.1.2. Step 2: Configure Your Model

Add a feature to the detector. A *feature* is a field in an index that you want to check for anomalies. A detector can find anomalies in one or more features. For each feature, you must select an aggregation method: average(), count(), sum(), min(), or max().

For example, if min() is selected, the detector will focus on finding anomalies based on the minimum value of the feature. If average() is selected, the detector will find anomalies based on the average value of the feature.

Multi-feature models relate anomalies. It is important to note that the performance of the model deteriorates as the dimensionality increases. Adding more features can negatively impact the precision and recall of the model. Choosing the optimal feature set is usually an iterative process. By default, the maximum number of features in a detector is five.

Set up category fields for high cardinality.

- Category fields use dimensions such as IP address, product ID, and country code to categorize or segment a time series. This allows you to drill down to see anomalies within each entity in the category field, helping you isolate and debug problems.

- To set up a category field, select Enable Category Fields and select a field. A field supports a specific number of unique entities. Use the following equation to calculate the recommended total number of entities supported in your cluster:

```
(data nodes * heap size * anomaly detection maximum memory percentage)
/ (detector's entity model size)
```

For example, for a cluster with three data nodes, each with a JVM heap size of 8GB, a maximum memory ratio of 10 percent, and an entity model size of 1MB in the detector, the total number of unique entities supported is as follows:

$$(8.096 * 10^9 * 0.1/1mb) * 3 = 2429$$

If the actual total number of unique entities is greater than the calculated number (in this case, 2429), the anomaly detector tries to model additional entities. The detector prioritizes entities that occur more frequently and are more recent.

Setting the size of the shuffling tile sets the number of aggregation intervals for the data stream to be considered in the detector window. It is best to choose this value based on your actual data to see which value produces the best results for your use case.

The anomaly detector expects the singleton size to be in the scope of 1 to 60. The default singling size is 8. I do not recommend choosing 1 unless you have more than two features. Smaller values can result in better recall, but they can also result in false positives. Larger values can be useful for ignoring noise in the signal.

Preview sample anomalies and adjust feature settings if necessary. For sample preview, the anomaly detection plugin selects a small number of data samples (one data point every 30 minutes) and uses interpolation to estimate the remaining data points.

- Load the sample dataset into the detector.
- The detector uses this sample dataset to generate a sample preview of anomaly results.
- You can review the sample preview and use it to fine-tune your feature configuration to get more accurate results.
- Select Preview Over Sample.

If you don't see any out-of-sample results, check your detector interval and make sure you have more than 400 data points for some entities during the preview period.

7.4.1.3. Step 3: Set Up the Detector Job

To start a real-time detector to look for anomalies in your data in near real time, select Start Real-Time Detector Automatically.

To perform historical analysis and find patterns in a long window of historical data (weeks or months), select Run Historical Analysis Search and then select a date scope (at least 128 search intervals).

CHAPTER 7 ANOMALY DETECTION

Using historical data, you can also evaluate the performance of the detector to further fine-tune it. Before moving to a real-time detector, I recommend experimenting with historical analysis using different feature sets and checking the accuracy.

7.4.1.4. Step 4: Analyze the Results

The shorter the interval, the faster the model goes through the singling process and the faster it starts generating anomalous results. If a detector has been pending in the "initialization" state for more than a day, perform an aggregation of the existing data to see if any data points are missing. If the aggregation reveals many missing data points, consider increasing the detector interval.

Use the following visualization to analyze the anomaly:

- The anomaly overview (real-time) and anomaly history displays the anomaly grade, using the corresponding confidence measure.

- Feature analysis displays features based on an aggregation method. You can change the date and time scope of the detector. When you select a point in the feature line chart, the feature output, the number of times the field appears in the index, and the expected value, which is a forecast for the feature output, are displayed. If all is well, the output and expected value are the same.

- Anomaly occurrence shows the start time, end time, confidence, and anomaly grade for each detected anomaly item.

Selecting a point on the anomaly line chart displays the feature contribution, which is the percentage of the feature that contributes to the anomaly.

After setting the category field, a heatmap chart is displayed. The heatmap correlates results for anomalies. The chart is empty until you select an anomaly entity. You can also see a line chart of anomalies and features for the time period of the anomaly (anomaly_grade > 0).

If you have set up multiple category fields, you can filter and sort the fields by selecting a subset of the fields. When you select a subset of fields, you can view the parent values of one field that share a common value with another field.

For example, if you have a detector whose category fields are IP and Endpoint, you can select Endpoint from the View by drop-down menu. Then select a specific cell to overlay the top 20 IP values in the chart.

7.4.2. Detector Considerations

Before creating a detector, consider the following configurations:

- **Filters:** Filters select the data you want to analyze based on some condition. The demo filter selects requests in the HTTP request log that have a status code of 400 or later. The 4xx and 5xx classes of HTTP status codes indicate that the request was returned with an error. You can then create an anomaly detector for the number of error requests. .

- **Category field:** Every entity has a feature that describes it. The category field provides the category of that feature. For example, you would specify the Process and Host fields to monitor a specific process on a specific host.

- **Detector interval:** Aggregate data within a certain interval and run the model on the aggregated data. As mentioned earlier, OpenSearch anomaly detection is best suited for dense time series that can be sampled uniformly. You should make sure that you have data in at least most of the intervals. Longer intervals smooth out long-term and short-term workload fluctuations, which can lead to longer detection latencies because they are less likely to introduce noise. Shorter intervals are faster to detect, but you may find expected workload fluctuations instead of anomalies. You can configure your time series with different intervals and observe which interval reduces noise while maintaining anomalies. Use the default ten-minute interval.

- **Feature:** This is an aggregation of values extracted from monitored data. They are transferred to the model to measure the degree of anomaly. For example, you might be interested in the garbage collection time field aggregated through the average method.

- **Window latency:** If the value is not configured correctly, the detector can analyze the data before the late data arrives in the cluster. In this case, the window latency is 0 because all the data was collected in advance.

7.5. Summary

Infrastructure observability collects metrics by default.

Infrastructure anomaly detection includes network, kernel, and system resources. In the case of the kernel, it is not straightforward to collect events such as interrupts and context switches from the kernel. You need to narrow the scope of the events you collect. This is because collecting unnecessarily many events is costly and makes it difficult to accurately determine anomalies.

Applying anomaly detection to infrastructure observability requires scoping and cost reduction. You need to clearly define your goals and targets, and it's not a good idea to collect all signals without a plan. Rather than collecting signals from your infrastructure all the time, you should be flexible enough to collect them on demand or only during certain periods of time. It is more effective to collect signals in a sampling fashion. Anomaly detection can also be differentiated from observability in the signals and events collected.

Rather than applying anomaly detection to all hosts, VM, and containers, configure anomaly detection based on the importance and priority of the service. For examples, include resources with a high probability of recurrence, failed root cause analysis, or newly configured resources.

Depending on the data being collected, a lot of preprocessing is required:

- **Traces:** It is difficult to use input data collected from KUtrace and ftrace as anomaly detection input. This requires a lot of preprocessing.

- **Metrics:** Metrics collected through the Prometheus exporter are in the form of gauges and counters. When stored in Promscale, they are structured. They need to be preprocessed to be used as anomaly detection input.

- **Profiles:** Data collected through PCP is stored in Redis. PCP supports gauges and counters for metrics, as well as histograms. You can use system traces to narrow the scope, and only profiles of specific methods are stored.

Automation is not complete with anomaly detection. Anomaly detection and LLM will combine to automate root cause analysis.

Anomaly detection alone is not enough for root cause analysis, and automation isn't done yet. Anomaly detection is organized based on ML, but it does not explain why the problem occurred. Measuring confidence in the identified anomalies is the key to anomaly detection. It is the role of developers and SRE to analyze the root cause of anomalies. To automate the analysis of anomalies, LLM is the technology you need. ML anomaly detection alone does not complete the root cause analysis, which means that ML anomaly detection and LLM can be used together to automate root cause analysis. LLM is described in detail in the final chapter.

CHAPTER 8

Analyze RCA Data

In recent years, the term *observability* has become popular and widespread. Instead of observability at the application and infrastructure level, there is a movement toward observability in data.

- While observability has traditionally been focused on data and MLOps pipelines, we are now seeing observability applied to LLM.

- Database reliability engineering is moving into the realm of traditional database administrators.

- In Chapter 4, service and application data was collected using distributed trace, and in Chapter 6, infrastructure data was collected using system trace. In addition, various other data, such as events, anomaly detection, and profiles, were collected. This chapter explains how to analyze and utilize the data collected in this way.

Even with open source, E2E trace is possible. The commercial observability advantage is that it offers many features that utilize the data. This is because open source does not yet have a clear solution for how to utilize observability data.

Since observability is the subject of this book, it may be more appropriate to discuss the topic of database observability rather than the utilization of observability data. As an engineer who builds and improves observability in the field, I decided it would be more meaningful to focus on how to utilize observability data rather than database observability, which already has a clear direction.

While this chapter focus on applications and infrastructure, data is an important area that cannot be overlooked. To identify latency and improve performance, observability must be applied to data as well. In this chapter, I explain how to utilize data for observability in three ways:

- **Search:** Supports keyword-oriented search and semantic search using the OpenSearch Vector database.

- **Analytics:** Promscale allows you to structure traces and metrics and analyze them with SQL.

- **Aggregation:** Organize data lakes based on observability data and aggregate complex data.

CHAPTER 8   ANALYZE RCA DATA

The goal of IT operations is to automate the operation of IT systems, reduce costs, and effectively support and accelerate the business to achieve its objectives. IT supports the business by minimizing manual effort and failure and maximizing availability and reliability. It should also minimize unnecessary costs and expenditures and provide measures to improve performance and use resources efficiently.

Once observability is in place and your applications and infrastructure are stabilized, it's time to start thinking about how you're going to use your observability data. Basic uses include dashboards, SLOs, error budgets and burn rates, alerts, automated and advanced anomaly detection, AIOps, and more.

For observability, you need to generate a variety of reports and deliverables. For example:

- Complex SLO availability reports that include service dependencies
- Costs for error budgets, burn rates, and losses for failures

In this case, a simple search is not enough to generate a report. Observability is time series data, and the nature of time series data limits the ability to write complex queries. You can only search for simple time series data through dashboards and screens.

The inability to construct complex queries limits the ability to analyze, aggregate, and join data. If you're not just monitoring, but you're using observability to build AIOps or automate and modernize your operations using a CMDB, the existing observability backend alone is not enough to utilize the data; it requires additional configuration.

Analytics, aggregations, and joins require separate long-term storage like a data lake. Time series databases with retention of only a few months cannot store observability data for long periods of time. The goal of this chapter is to learn how to go beyond simple searching of data with observability to complex analysis, aggregation, and joining.

The direction of observability data analysis is as follows:

- Analyze observability data using trace. Enrich with metrics.
- Logs, which require a lot of preprocessing, have a low priority compared to other signals. Metrics and traces should be prioritized for dashboards whenever possible, and logs should be used when there are constraints that are difficult to process with existing signals. Logs are utilized by AIOps RAG.

Since the purpose of observability is root cause analysis, search functionality should be prioritized. If there are other purposes besides search, it is appropriate to organize separate storage and provide data analysis and aggregation.

Developers talk about the need for indexes because they are used to using them in log analysis, but in observability, they focus more on label-centric search without indexes, like Grafana's Loki.

- I prefer Elasticsearch, but it's expensive and cluster management is complex if you're only looking for observability. It is not suitable for running on Kubernetes, requires a lot of internal validation when making changes to the cluster, is time-consuming to autoscale, and lacks scalability of write paths.

- If you're using logs for various data analytics aggregations and SIEM considerations, an index is a great way to go, but if you're just looking for observability, a log solution is great.

- Indexes are more expensive to store and take longer to retrieve. Considering the purpose of observability, there is no need to spend a lot of money on indexes. The nature of logs requires a lot of development labor, including preprocessing.

- Logs are limited in developing rules with thresholds and configuring alerts.

- Developing complex SLOs and MTTRs requires a lot of preprocessing and development.

I believe that observability should not be log-centric. Traces should be the starting point, and correlations should be built around them. Logs are expensive and should be a low priority. I'm not denying the importance of logs, but developers are already familiar with them, so continuing to perform root cause analysis with logs will delay the adoption of new observabilities and cause problems with change management. Traces are not the end of observability. They are just a starting point. By configuring various correlations, you can reduce MTTR and improve root cause analysis.

Service failure, even for a short period of time, can have a huge impact on your business. You need to be able to forecast problems in advance or recover as quickly as possible to minimize inconvenience to your users. You should always be looking for ways to reduce recovery time and increase reliability, and observability is a great way to do that. But don't stop at observability; analyze the observability data you collect to uncover hidden insights and make improvements.

This chapter explains anomaly detection and AIOps. Before you get into the complex technology, it's important to understand and utilize the data.

The set of tasks described previously all come down to data utilization. You need to understand how to collect unstructured observability data, how to transform it into structured data, and how to use SQL to search, analyze, and aggregate observability data.

You need to implement a data pipeline and think about how you will store and query your data. Pipelines ingest data. Promscale and OpenSearch structure unstructured logs, metrics, and traces and store them in a format that can be SQL-queried. SQL can be used to process search, analysis, and aggregation of the data and visualization of the results.

With commercial observability, it is difficult to take data out and repurpose it. Commercial observability provides a limited, isolated, and siloed environment. The AIOps model of commercial observability also makes it difficult to leverage external data. Even if it is partially possible to export via API, commercial observability is a sandbox. SRE should consider whether commercial observability is right for them in terms of utilizing observability data.

Because observability is a nascent and immature technology, it often requires additional customization. Even with commercial observability, there are often gaps in the out-of-the-box dashboards and charts, or the need for additional data analysis and algorithms.

CHAPTER 8   ANALYZE RCA DATA

This chapter analyzes observability data for root cause analysis. Understanding root cause analysis through screens is still a good way to go. However, it's important to understand how to automate using SQL, machine learning, and more to make root cause analysis faster and easier.

You should strive to construct structured, SQL-enabled datasets. Data analytics, anomaly detection, machine learning, and AIOps all start with structured data.

The overall flow of data utilization, as described in this chapter, is as follows

- Analyze your data
- Aggregate the data
- Search for the data
- AIOps

The data flow is search, analysis, and aggregation, but AI has changed the direction of search to semantic and neural network search, so I discuss search later.

The difficulties of analyzing data for root cause analysis are as follows:

- Data comes in many different types. Schemas change frequently, specific tags are not defined, and specifications for data schemas are not defined, making it difficult for SREs to understand them.
- The internal structure of the data overlaps, is irregularly formatted, or is too complex. This complexity makes it difficult to generate structured queries.

Applying SQL and AIOps to a variety of signal data and getting accurate results is a challenge.

Chapter 2 analyzed root cause analysis through user screens. This time, as a first step toward automating root cause analysis, you will see data-driven root cause analysis using SQL and machine learning. First, I explain SQL data analysis.

You should be able to store the collected observability data in various databases and utilize it for your purposes.

This is why SREs who solve problems and data engineers who need to utilize observability data need to collaborate.

To describe the most common dashboard configurations, you need two types of dashboards on the operational side. On the technical side, you need a dashboard that shows whether the application's processes and pods are being processed correctly. On the business side, you need a dashboard that shows whether the customer's orders or transactions are being processed correctly.

Traditionally, we use metrics for technical dashboards and logs for business dashboards. They are not technically detailed and require a lot of preprocessing and development labor. I recommend using traces and events for observability dashboards. You can use traces for technical dashboards and event for business dashboards. This is consistent with the direction of this book on data analysis.

8.1. Analyzing SQL Data

Recently, commercial observability has been adding capabilities for data analytics within observability. In addition to data analytics capabilities, data lakes and pipelines for observability are being improved internally. For example, Dynatrace Grail collects and stores various signals and provides query capabilities to users.

In order to implement AIOps in the future and achieve a high level of automation, you need a system that can collect, store, and analyze a variety of data. A data lake that can collect and query data is critical to the success of AIOps, anomaly detection, and data analytics. This is because preprocessing is necessary to collect and structure data accounts for more than 80 percent of data projects. Algorithms and visualization are important, but the data must be structured and easily queried by users. This is where OpenSearch and Promscale come in.

- **OpenSearch:** Forked Elasticsearch and developed OpenSearch on AWS. It manages logs, provides anomaly detection, and uses a Vector database.

- **Promscale:** Promscale is open source, developed by Timescale, and uses PostgreSQL to store and retrieve traces and metrics.

From a process perspective, traces are central, but from a data perspective, metrics are central. By configuring all signals to be converted to metrics, it is easy to implement visualizations, SLO calculations, and alerts.

All signals are converted to metrics: RUM, log, trace, profile.

- For traces, Promscale creates a single trace table. All trace data is stored in that table. Traces are useful for application-level observability. Services and applications use traces, while infrastructure uses metrics to analyze the data.

- Metrics are stored differently. A metric table is created for each metric. For example, if there are 100 metrics, 100 metric tables are created. You need as many tables as you have metrics.

- RUM contains the same data as traces. Additional data is written to the log file.

- Profile data is converted to a metric.

- Log data is stored in a table in OpenSearch.

The converted metric has many uses. It can be used as a source for SLOs, alerts, anomaly detection, visualization, and machine learning.

The data collected through observability is essentially time series data. Therefore, it is necessary to understand time series data analysis techniques:

- Time windows
- Cumulative values
- Seasonality analysis

CHAPTER 8   ANALYZE RCA DATA

8.1.1. Time Windows

Time series data is often noisy, which hinders the ability to find meaningful patterns. As a denoising method, you need to learn about rolling time windows to analyze trends by setting multiple bins.

Rolling a time window is also known as a moving calculation. Moving averages are the most common of the moving calculations, but SQL allows you to apply any aggregation method, not just averages. Time window rolling is used in a wide variety of analytics, including stock price analysis, macroeconomic trends, ratings surveys, and more.

There are a few important considerations for time rolling calculations:

- **The window size.** The window size refers to the number of time bins to include in the calculation, and a larger window will smooth out noise because it includes more time. However, this reduces sensitivity, making it less desirable for data where it's important to identify short-term fluctuations. Conversely, a smaller window size can be more sensitive to changes in short periods of time, but at the cost of being more susceptible to noise.

- **The aggregation method.** With SQL, you can calculate move totals, move counts, move mins, and move maxs. The number of moves is useful for things like active user metrics, while the minimum and maximum moves can be used to preview the extremes of your data and plan your analysis.

- **The segmentation or grouping of the data contained within the window.** In some cases, you may need to set up windows on a yearly basis, or use a moving calculation based on user groups or data values. Partitioning is done through the window method and the PARTITION BY clause or by grouping.

There are two main ways to calculate time window rolling:

- Using self-JOIN with any database.
- Using the window method, which is not supported by all databases.

I use a window method option called the FRAME clause to fine-tune which records to include in each window. By default, all records that fall within the window are included, which is fine for most purposes, but for movement calculations, you need more fine-
grained scoping.

The window method has several options for performing calculations, including the PARTITION BY clause and the window FRAME clause. These allow you to perform complex calculations with relatively simple syntax.

8.1.2. Cumulative Values

It's common to set the pixel size to a fixed value for window rolling calculations such as moving averages. In addition to moving calculations, there are ways to analyze time series using cumulative values over years, quarters, months, and so on. Cumulative values use a fixed-size window, but the calculation is performed by gradually increasing the window size from a starting point.

Calculating cumulative values is simple using window methods. You can use the SUM aggregation method to calculate total sales YTD.

The PARTITION BY clause sets up windows based on the month or week.

In time series analysis, we often use the ORDER BY clause to sort by date fields. If the table you are analyzing does not store data in date order, omitting the ORDER BY clause can lead to incorrect results. Therefore, it's a good idea to sort using the ORDER BY clause even if you think the data is already sorted.

8.1.3. Seasonality Analysis

Seasonality represents a regularly recurring pattern at regular intervals. Unlike other noise, seasonality in data can be forecast. Just as seasonality is reminiscent of the recurring seasons, so too are these recurring patterns in datasets. New application deployments, regularly configured security patches, network equipment upgrades, and internal maintenance by cloud vendors are examples of recurring patterns. These repetitive tasks introduce latency or cause system changes internally, such as backup and recovery processes. Temporary spikes due to deployments, rebalancing of clusters, and sequential restarts of nodes can be monitored with time series data. Restarts are failures from a system perspective, even if they are maintenance that the administrator is aware of. In that case, it's a failure that's already recognized and managed. Seasonality doesn't have to be seasonal—it can be annual or even minute-by-minute.

Graphical visualization of time series data is useful for understanding patterns such as seasonality and cycles.

Comparing current values to E2E values is a useful way to denoise and compare seasonality analysis. However, there are times when a single E2E value is not sufficient for comparison. This is the case when the previous E2E value was affected by a specific event and stored an atypical value. For example, if you want to compare Monday's data to last Monday, but last Monday was a public holiday, you can't just compare the two and use that data for analysis.

Similarly, when comparing the current month's data to the same month in the previous year, consider whether there were problems in the previous month, such as economic problems, bad weather, or power outages. To reduce the impact of noise from these specific events, it's a good idea to compare the current value to at least two previous E2E values.

In time series analysis, when seasonality is involved, denoising is often necessary to accurately analyze trends. By utilizing multi-bin analysis, you can see the denoised trend, which can help you understand what is characteristic of a particular time period.

8.2. Using Promscale

Most commercial observabilities provide their own query language to allow you to query the signals collected by the observability. For example, you may want to aggregate the number of spans within a trace ID that are experiencing an error. The term *span count* is commonly used, and it provides query functions for various analyses and aggregations by span. However:

- There are many cases that do not support querying the span count.
- There are many cases where queries cannot be used to identify problems or analyze the results of the trace.
- It also does not support direct querying of data stored in object storage.

Querying span counts isn't as simple as it sounds. You need span counts to build dashboards, alerts, and other things that you need in the real world, not just simple SLO.

There are two main types of signals that Promscale processes: metrics and traces. Since profiles and RUM are converted to metrics, they can be categorized as metrics from a data analysis perspective. Only when they are stored as structured data can they be searched, analyzed, and aggregated using SQL queries.

The preprocess of structuring observability data is harder than it sounds:

- There are four types of metrics: counters, gauges, histograms, and summaries. Because the metric data type is not structured like JSON, it is difficult to apply SQL to it. For example, a counter can have many different labels attached to it. Histograms are structurally similar to schemaless data and it's hard to define a fixed schema for them.

- Logs are text. Sometimes they are structured as JSON, but often they contain unstructured text. This requires complex text preprocessing. You can use regular expressions for this, but they are difficult to understand and manage. If you have a full-search index like OpenSearch, text analysis is easy.

- The trace is structured using JSON, but it is a complex structure that overlaps. Preprocessing such as flattening is required to process QL. Internally, arrays and maps are used to represent the structure of traces, so querying them with SQL is not straightforward.

Processing everything as text is not a good idea. A lot of development effort is required. To summarize, observability data is characterized by the following features:

- Structured data, like JSON, or unstructured data, like text.
- The schema is dynamic, variable, and schemaless.
- This data is a complex structure with overlapping structures. It includes parent-child relationships, key and values, and arrays.

PostgreSQL provides features for anomaly detection, time series analysis, and more, but OOB can't process the complex data structures of observability. Even if you store Prometheus metrics and Jaeger trace signals in PostgreSQL, they are difficult to structure and cannot be queried.

The question is how to transform unstructured observability data into a structured form. You need to provide users with queries that allow them to retrieve the data they want in SQL. There's been a lot of thought about how to structure observability data with technology. Promscale is one useful way to do this.

To apply SQL to observability data, you can use Promscale.

- Promscale provides maps (keys and values) and arrays. It's complex because objects and arrays overlap, it's compatible with Prometheus metrics and Jaeger formats, and it provides a variety of user-defined methods.

- Commercial observability offers a wide variety of query languages and good user-friendliness. However, it offers non-standard query languages. It requires a separate learning curve and creates problems with external integration. Promscale supports ANSI SQL, a standardized technology.

- Promscale is aimed at analyzing data. It's more complicated than searching for data, but it's not about implementing aggregations like pre-aggregation and multi-dimensional drill-down.

Promscale uses SQL to analyze data and supports the development of various dashboards Here are some of Promscale's advantages:

- SQL provides a variety of methods to analyze data in detail.

- Easy backup and recovery using snapshots and more.

- You still get the all benefits of a PostgreSQL relational database.

Here are some of Promscale's drawbacks:

- It has problems with sharding config and retention, and it is difficult to store large amounts of data. No support for object storage.

- It has poor performance on aggregation queries. It is inefficient to process aggregation queries on metrics and trace data over long periods of time. Since PostgreSQL is not aggregation-specific, it is useful to pair it with a solution that specializes in aggregation, such as Druid.

- The roadmap for Promscale managed services offered by Timescale is unclear.

- Database experts develop custom methods. Promscale augments the functionality of PostgreSQL and allows developers to add custom methods.

CHAPTER 8   ANALYZE RCA DATA

8.2.1. Promscale Features

There are many open source backend storage solutions that are 100 percent compatible with Prometheus. However, Promscale is superior to other open sources in many ways, including its proven performance based on PostgreSQL.

- Using the Prometheus remote write provided by the OpenTelemetry collector, you can save metrics within Promscale.
- Promscale requires Timescale internally. Timescale is a time series database and uses PostgreSQL internally.
- Promscale can be configured as the backend storage for storing traces. Using the Jaeger exporter in the OpenTelemetry collector, distributed traces can be implemented using only the Jaeger UI.
- Promscale acts as CDC change data capture between observability and the data lake. For long-term storage, it connects with Druid.

Here is the process for storing a metric in Promscale:

1. The node exporter collects resource information in a node.
2. The OpenTelemetry collector scrapes metrics from the node exporter.
3. Write remotely to Promscale using the OpenTelemetry collector.
4. Transfer the Prometheus metric to a timescale.
5. The timescale is stored in PostgreSQL.
6. Users retrieve the stored metric using the same connection information and as PostgreSQL.

Here is the process for saving a trace to Promscale:

1. The OpenTelemetry agent transfers traces to the OpenTelemetry collector using the OTLP protocol.
2. The OpenTelemetry collector transfers traces to Jaeger.
3. Jaeger uses Promscale as backend storage for traces. Jaeger stores traces in Promscale.
4. Transfer Jaeger traces to the timescale.
5. The timescale is stored in PostgreSQL.
6. Users can view traces using the Jaeger UI or query traces in Grafana PostgreSQL.

8.2.2. The Promscale Method

Given the specificity of Prometheus metrics and trace data, Promscale provides custom methods called *hypermethods*. The most commonly used Promscale methods are listed in this section:

- percentile_cont
- approx_percentile
- percentile_agg

The default methods provided in Prometheus do not allow you to get values (e.g. response time, throughput) for specific quantiles. Promscale provides methods by default.

8.2.2.1. percentile_cont

To calculate the percentile, use the percentile_cont method. You can also find the 50th percentile or median. For example, to find the median temperature, do the following:

```
SELECT percentile_cont(0.5)
  WITHIN GROUP (ORDER BY temperature)
  FROM conditions;
```

8.2.2.2. approx_percentile

Calculate an approximate percentile using the uddsketch algorithm. Estimate an approximate percentile value from a uddsketch aggregation.

For example, given a sample containing numbers from 0 to 100, estimate the first percentile value:

```
SELECT
  approx_percentile(0.01, uddsketch(data))
FROM generate_series(0, 100) data;
```

Percentile analysis is useful, but it has one major drawback. It requires the entire dataset to be stored in memory. This means that such analysis is only possible for relatively small datasets, and even then it can take longer to compute.

The approximate percentile hypermethod improves on these problems. Combined with materialized views, which take up storage space and refresh automatically, it can produce results almost instantly.

8.2.2.3. percentile_agg

To create an intermediate aggregation from the raw data, use percentile_agg. This intermediate aggregation can be used to compute results.

Multiple intermediate aggregates can be combined using rollup().

Percentile aggregation creates a continuous aggregate that stores percentile aggregate objects.

```
CREATE MATERIALIZED VIEW foo_hourly
WITH (timescaledb.continuous)
AS SELECT
    time_bucket('1 h'::interval, ts) as bucket,
    percentile_agg(value) as pct_agg
FROM foo
GROUP BY 1;
```

The following is an example of using percentile approximation. It warns about response times that exceed the 95th percentile.

```
WITH "95th percentile" as (
    SELECT approx_percentile(0.95, percentile_agg(response_time)) as threshold
    FROM response_times
)
SELECT count(*)
FROM response_times
AND respon se_time > "95th percentile".threshold;
```

You can see the use of these mentioned methods in the metric and trace SQL demos.

8.3. Promscale Demo

In Promscale, a metric is not fixed schema. If a tag changes, the schema changes as well. A table is created in PostgreSQL for each metric. If there are 10,000 metrics, 10,000 tables must be created. Managing a large number of metric tables is therefore a burden on the database.

There are two approaches to save a metric:

- Create one table per metric. If there are 1,000 metrics, 1,000 tables are created. When collecting metrics from an exporter, you need to filter the metrics.

- Create a common metric table, such as latency and throughput tables, and all microservices store SLOs in the common table. You don't need to create tables for each metric, and you can reduce the number of tables, but it is difficult to look up SLOs based on tags and labels.

Commercial observability uses the second approach, but due to the low product maturity, there are many problems when querying.

Commercial observability sometimes uses a configuration that creates tables by request count, error count, and latency, and it stores multiple services in a common metric table. This structure can reduce the number of metric tables, but it will be difficult to support complex metric requirements. Often, metrics require custom metrics that add multiple dimensions or use complex formulas. There are limitations to storing metrics from multiple services in a common metric table.

Organizing storage for metrics is not straightforward because scope across applications and infrastructure. Creating a table per metric or managing multiple services in a metric table has its advantages and disadvantages.

Metrics should be stored with aggregation by windows, such as day, week, month, and year. In Prometheus, you can use recording rules for pre-aggregation to store aggregation information on a per-window basis.

The metric schema is not fixed, so metric queries need to change depending on the metric type. The trace schema, on the other hand, is fixed. In Promscale, traces store the span information of all microservices in a single table. The way metrics and traces are stored is different. Metrics such as utilization, saturation, custom metrics, and latency can be measured using queries. You need to make sure that the dimension is constructed and searched using the span attribute and additional data such as baggage. The trace data stored in Promscale is raw data corresponding to individual transactions. To output it as a time series, it is useful to use the spanmetric to convert it to a metric and output the time series.

Since the subject of the trace is limited to application performance, it can be reused without requiring many changes to the query.

You need to understand how to use Promscale SQL to query and analyze data. More specifically, let's look at metric and trace SQL.

Metrics are centered on utilization and saturation and store time series. Traces are centered on SLO and store latency, duration, and availability.

8.3.1. Metric SQL

Whereas traces focus on the performance of an application, metrics include data across IT operations, including infrastructure and applications.

PromQL is the default way to query Prometheus metrics. However, it has the following problems:

- Not as flexible as SQL. Data is hard to process.
- There is a learning curve to learn `promql`.
- It is difficult to join with other signals like trace and log.
- It is difficult to extract large amounts of data in conjunction with pipelines.

The advantages of using Promscale include the following:

- Data is stored in a defined schema. Data can be quickly extracted from tables organized by metric.
- It allows you to back up and snapshot your data. It also supports downsampling.
- SQL is useful for searching and analyzing time series, anomaly detection, cohorts, and experiments.

- It is processed in SQL, so you can see the results intuitively. Complex aggregations such as multi-dimensional drill-downs, slices, and TopN are possible.
- It's also easy to create data marts in PromQL and connect them with pipelines. PromQL can also process machine learning directly in PostgreSQL.

8.3.2. Metric SQL Demo

8.3.2.1. Configure

Testing with Kubernetes can be quite overwhelming. For the Promscale demo, I test in Docker.

```
version: '3.0'

services:
  db:
    image: timescale/timescaledb-ha:pg14-latest
    environment:
      POSTGRES_PASSWORD: password
      POSTGRES_USER: postgres

  promscale:
    image: timescale/promscale:latest
    restart: on-failure
    depends_on:
      - db
    environment:
      PROMSCALE_DB_URI: postgres://postgres:password@db:5432/postgres?sslmode=allow
      promscale_tracing_otlp_server_address: ":9202"

  hotrod:
    depends_on:
      - jaeger-collector
    image: jaegertracing/example-hotrod:1.37.0
    environment:
      jaeger_endpoint: http://jaeger-collector:14268/api/traces
    ports:
      - "8080-8083:8080-8083"

  jaeger-collector:
    depends_on:
      - promscale
    restart: on-failure
```

```
image: jaegertracing/jaeger-collector:1.37.0
environment:
  SPAN_STORAGE_TYPE: grpc-plugin
  GRPC_STORAGE_SERVER: promscale:9202
```

You can generate traffic on HotROD and check the Promscale running status, as shown here:

```
$ kubectl get deployment
name ready up-to-date available age
db 1/1 1 1 9d
hotrod 1/1 1 1 9d
jaeger 1/1 1 1 9d
my-release-grafana 1/1 1 1 6d17h
otel-collector 1/1 1 1 9d
prometheus 1/1 1 1 9d
promscale 1/1 1 1 7d1h
$ kubectl get pod
name ready status restarts age
db-64599c9555-jkl7k 1/1 Running 9 (7d1h ago) 9d
jaeger-767895 d884-hztwf 1/1 Running 16 (7d1h ago) 9d
otel-collector-685f4745c5-gwtp6 1/1 Running 0 7d1h
prometheus-66fffd9d69-ktk7v 1/1 Running 13 (7d1h ago) 9d
promscale-d9956d94c-g254z 1/1 Running 4 (7d1h ago) 7d1h
```

Configure the HotROD demo. Transfer HotROD directly to Jaeger without a collector and transfer the Promscale with a collector.

```
docker-compose up
```

Create a load on HotROD using microshim. Demos for metric SQL and trace SQL are available in Docker.

8.3.2.2. SQL

This provides a variety of query demos. I recommend that you study the demos and try to apply complex queries.

Provides SQL for metric analysis:

- Query the `cpu_hours_total` value for the tenant team.
- Compare the 95th percentile latency of HTTP requests by tenant.
- Query the `cpu_usage` metric.
- Query to show the number of data points in each series.

CHAPTER 8 ANALYZE RCA DATA

- Aggregate the CPU usage over the past year by namespace.
- Query only metrics in the product namespace or metrics with pods that start with the letters ab.
- Query the 99th percentile of memory usage per container in the default namespace.
- Look up containers with low memory utilization through the 99th percentile.
- Visualize the go_gc_duration_seconds metric.
- Compute the time for go_gc_duration_seconds and the 99th percentile of the time series.

Suppose you want to use SQL to get the value of cpu_hours_total{__tenant__="team"}.

```
SELECT
   * The
FROM
   prom_metric.cpu_hours_total
WHERE
   labels ? ('__tenant__' == 'team');
```

In PromQL, all queries must aggregate the data within each time series before performing any other aggregations.

Say you want to compare the 95th percentile latency of HTTP requests by tenant. Compare all requests from one tenant to other tenants.

```
SELECT
   val(__tenant__id) as tenant_name,
   percentile_cont(0.95) WITHIN GROUP (ORDER BY value) as p95,
FROM
   prom_metric.http_re quests_total
GROUP BY __tenant__id
```

The cpu_usage metric is queried like this:

```
SELECT
 time,
 value,
 jsonb(labels) as labels
FROM "cpu_usage";
```

CHAPTER 8   ANALYZE RCA DATA

A query that shows the number of data points in each series would look like this:

```sql
SELECT
 jsonb(labels(series_id_)) as labels,
 count(*)
FROM "cpu_usage"
GROUP BY series_id;
```

For example, here's a query that aggregates median CPU usage over the past year by namespace:

```sql
SELECT
 val(namespace_id) as namespace,
 percentile_cont(0.5) within group (order by value)
AS median
FROM "cpu_usage"
WHERE time > '2019-01-01'
GROUP BY namespace_id;
```

For example, if you only want metrics from the production namespace or metrics with pods that start with the letters ab, you can use OR.

```sql
SELECT avg(value)
FROM "cpu_usage"
WHERE labels ? ('namespace' == 'production')
      OR labels ? ('pod' ==~ 'ab*')
```

You can easily get the 99th percentile of memory usage per container in the default namespace:

```sql
SELECT
  val(used.container_id) container,
  percentile_cont(0.99) within group(order by used.value) percent_used_p99
FROM container_memory_working_set_bytes used
WHERE labels ? ('namespace' == 'default')
GROUP BY container
ORDER BY percent_used_p99 ASC
LIMIT 100;
```

Now find containers with low 99th percentile memory utilization or over-provisioned Kubernetes containers:

```sql
WITH memory_allowed as (
  SELECT
    labels(series_id) as labels,
    value,
```

623

```
    min(time) start_time,
    max(time) as end_time
  FROM container_spec_memory_limit_bytes total
  WHERE value != 0 and value != 'NaN'
  GROUP BY series_id, value
)
SELECT
  val(me mory_used.container_id) container,
  percentile_cont(0.99)
    within group(order by memory_used.value/memory_allowed.value)
    AS percent_used_p99,
  max(memory_allowed.value) max_memory_allowed
FROM container_memory_working_set_bytes AS memory_used
INNER JOIN memory_allowed
    ON (memory_used.time >= memory_allowed.start_time AND
        memory_used.time <= memory_allowed.end_time AND
        eq(memory_used.labels,memory_allowed.labels))
WHERE memory_used.value != 'NaN'
GROUP BY container
ORDER BY percent_used_p99 ASC
LIMIT 100;
```

Visualize go_gc_duration_seconds.

```
SELECT
  jsonb(v.labels)::text as "metric",
  time AS "time",
  value as "value"
FROM "go_gc_duration_seconds" v
WHERE
  $__timeFilter("time")
ORDER BY 2, 1
```

Calculate the 99th percentile of the time and time series for go_gc_duration_seconds:

```
SELECT
   val(pod_id) as pod,
   percentile_con t(0.99) within group(order by value) p99
FROM
   go_gc_duration_seconds
WHERE
   value != 'NaN' AND val(quantile_id) = '1' AND pod_id > 0
```

```
GROUP BY
  pod_id
ORDER BY
  p99 desc;
```

For infrastructure, alerts, and general applications, use metric SQL, and for performance of the application, use trace SQL.

8.3.3. Trace SQL

Grafana Tempo supports spanmetrics through its metric generator. Using the spanmetric process in the OpenTelemetry collector, you can generate spanmetrics. Jaeger also provides spanmetric functionality. The table described here is similar to the spanmetric tables in trace. A trace table is an individual transaction and a collection of spans. A spanmetric is an aggregation of spans into an SLO-appropriate metric. The various attributes and dimensions defined in the trace context should be preserved during the conversion to metric, and should be organized so that they are searchable.

Create PostgreSQL tables corresponding to the Prometheus metric names. For Jaeger, create the latency_bucket, calls_total, and span tables.

- calls_total
  - A counter that counts the total number of spans per unique set of dimensions. The number of errors can be identified by the status_code label. This can be used to calculate the percentage of invalid calls by dividing the metrics with status_code labels equal to STATUS_CODE_ERROR by the total number of metrics.

- latency
  - Composed of several basic Prometheus metrics that represent histograms. Due to the labels associated with these metrics, you can generate histograms for latency

- latency_count
  - Contains the total amount of data points in the bucket.

- latency_sum
  - Contains the sum of all data points in the bucket.

- latency_bucket
  - Contains the number of data points whose latency is less than or equal to a predefined time. You can configure the amount of buckets by changing the latency_histogram_buckets array in the OpenTelemetry collector configuration.

8.3.4. Trace SQL Demo

This chapter uses the Promscale OpenTelemetry demo, which consists of seven microservices.

Microservices are developed in Python and offer two types of demos: automated and manual instrumentation.

8.3.4.1. Configure

The system configuration uses Prometheus remote write to store traces in Promscale. It is 100 percent compatible with Jaeger queries, so you can output trace graphs from the Jaeger UI. Here is how the data is processed:

- The microservices demo application transfers signals to an OpenTelemetry collector with a spanmetric processor.
- The OpenTelemetry collector transfers the span to Jaeger, which stores it in Promscale.
- Send the metrics generated by the spanmetric processor to Promscale.
- Configure Jaeger to query and visualize traces and metrics from Promscale, and deploy other components.

The Jaeger installed here is configured as an all-in-one:

```
$ kubectl get deployment
name ready up-to-date available age
db 1/1 1 1 9d
jaeger 1/1 1 1 9d
otel-collector 1/1 1 1 9d
prometheus 1/1 1 1 9d
promscale 1/1 1 1 7d1h
$ kubectl get pod
name ready status restarts age
db-64599c9555-jkl7k 1/1 Running 9 (7d1h ago) 9d
jaeger-76 7895d884-hztwf 1/1 Running 16 (7d1h ago) 9d
otel-collector-685f4745c5-gwtp6 1/1 Running 0 7d1h
prometheus-66fffd9d69-ktk7v 1/1 Running 13 (7d1h ago) 9d
promscale-d9956d94c-g254z 1/1 Running 4 (7d1h ago) 7d1h
```

Rather than using Kubernetes, this example uses Docker. No complicated configuration, just a simple way to get started:

```
docker-compose up
```

CHAPTER 8 ANALYZE RCA DATA

8.3.4.2. SQL

Trace only requires the span table. It provides useful SQL as shown here:

- Retrieves traces for the filtered time period.
- Retrieves traces from each ten-second bucket in the time period.
- Retrieves the top ten slowest traces in the time period.
- Generates a histogram for the trace period.
- Outputs the 95th percentile over time.
- Calculates the total duration of each ten-second bucket of work in the time period.
- Searches for all spans upstream from all traces in the specified time period.
- Searches for all spans downstream from a specific scope of spans.
- Analyzes the structure of the upstream call tree.
- Creates a downstream graph.

The query to get upstream and downstream is useful, and I recommend making it more applied.

Filter by time of day

You can also get the number of traces in the filtered time period. Since a single trace can have multiple spans, you only count the root span.

```
SELECT count(*) as nbr_ traces
FROM ps_ trace.span s
WHERE $__timeFilter(s.start_time)
AND s.parent_span_id IS NULL -- only root spans
```

It is important to understand how many traces are collected in each ten-second bucket in that window. As long as all traces are collected, the number of traces is the same as throughput.

While time_bucket is a timescale method, you can use date_trunc to achieve essentially the same result. time_bucket is more powerful and flexible.

```
SELECT
    time_bucket('10 seconds', s.start_time) as time,
    count(*) as nbr_ traces
FROM ps_ trace.span s
WHERE $__timeFilter(s.start_time)
AND s.parent_span_id IS NULL
GROUP BY time
ORDER BY time
```

CHAPTER 8   ANALYZE RCA DATA

Slow queries

The top ten slowest traces in that duration should be understood. The duration of each root span is the duration of the trace, since the duration of the root span includes all its children.

```
SELECT
    s.trace_id,
    s.duration_ms
FROM ps_ trace.span s
WHERE $__timeFilter(s.start_time)
AND s.parent_span_id IS NULL
ORDER BY s.duration_ms DESC
LIMIT 10
```

Latency histogram

In Figure 8-1, the duration of the root span is the same as the request latency. This code creates a histogram for duration.

```
SELECT
    s.trace_id,
    s.duration_ms
FROM ps_trace.span s
WHERE $__timeFilter(s.start_time)
AND s.parent_span_id IS NULL
```

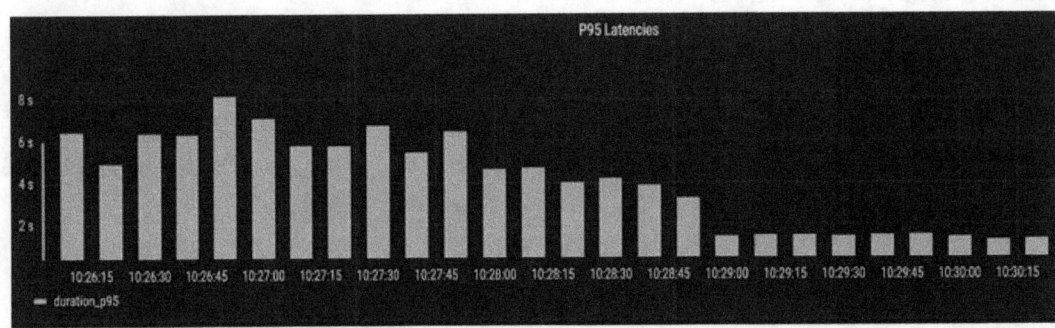

Figure 8-1. 95th percentile

Latency changes over time. Figure 8-2 shows the latency heatmap.

```
SELECT
    time_bucket('10 seconds', s.start_time) as time,
    approx_percentile(0.95, percentile_agg(s.duration_ms)) as duration_p95
```

```
FROM ps_trace.span s
WHERE $__timeFilter(s.start_time)
AND s.parent_span_id IS NULL
GROUP BY time
ORDER BY time
```

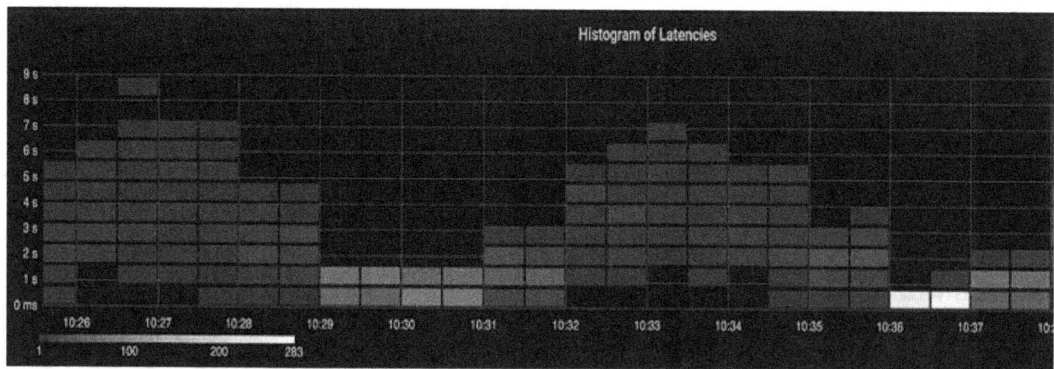

Figure 8-2. Latency heatmap

You can see how the latency heatmap changes over time. Now look at the heatmap of latency for every ten-second bucket. This will give you the variability over time.

```
SELECT
    time_bucket('10 seconds', s.start_time) as time,
    s.duration_ms
FROM ps_trace.span s
WHERE $__timeFilter(s.start_time)
AND s.parent_span_id IS NULL
```

Duration pie chart

The duration of each span includes the time spent in the span itself and the time spent in child spans. You can calculate the duration of a span by excluding its child spans. You do this by subtracting the sum of the durations of the child spans.

I use a pie chart where each slice of the pie corresponds to a task operation. The value is the total duration spent on that operation over the filtered time period. It tells you which code in the whole system takes the longest.

```
SELECT
    s.service_name || ' ' || s.span_name as operation,
    sum(
        s.duration_ms
```

CHAPTER 8 ANALYZE RCA DATA

```
        coalesce(
        (
            SELECT sum(k.duration_ms)
            FROM ps_ trace.span k -- kids
            WHERE k. trace_id = s. trace_id
            AND k.parent_span_id = s.span_id
            AND $__timeFilter(k.start_time)
        ), 0)
    ) as total_exec_ms
FROM ps_ trace.span s
WHERE $__timeFilter(s.start_time)
GROUP BY s.service_name, s.span_name
```

Duration table

For each job, you can calculate the average duration and 95th percentile duration. The query is provided as a Git. Figure 8-3 shows the duration ratio.

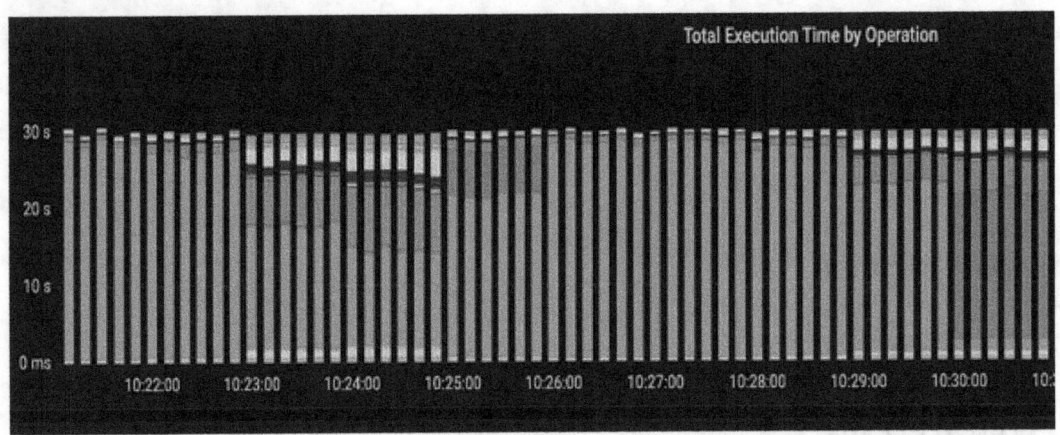

Figure 8-3. Duration ratio

What if you wanted to know which tasks have the biggest impact on latency? You can calculate the total duration spent on each task in each ten-second bucket within the time period. Stacking these values will show you which jobs are contributing the most to latency over time.

```
SELECT
    time_bucket('10 seconds', s.start_time) as time,
    s.service_name || ' ' || s.span_name as operation,
    sum(
        s.duration_ms
        coalesce(
```

CHAPTER 8 ANALYZE RCA DATA

```
        (
            SELECT sum(k.duration_ms)
            FROM ps_ trace.span k
            WHERE k. trace_id = s. trace_id
            AND k.parent_span_id = s.span_id
            AND $__timeFilter(k.start_time)
        ), 0)
    ) as total_exec_ms
FROM ps_ trace.span s
WHERE $__timeFilter(s.start_time)
GROUP BY time, s.service_name, s.span_name
ORDER BY time, total_exec_ms
```

Given a service name and a span name, you can use recursion to find all span upstream in the trace for a given time period.

Downstream span tables

By reversing the direction of recursion, you can search for downstream executions from a given span. You can identify all spans that are called directly or indirectly by a given span. The query is provided as a Git.

Upstream span graphs

As applications become more complex and accumulate microservices, the overall application service map becomes too complex to understand individual nodes and loses the main benefit of an intuitive overview of system state.

To deal with the constraints of a service map built only with edges between adjacent nodes, you aggregate the trace data and visualize it as a service map (see Figure 8-4). The query is provided as a Git.

CHAPTER 8   ANALYZE RCA DATA

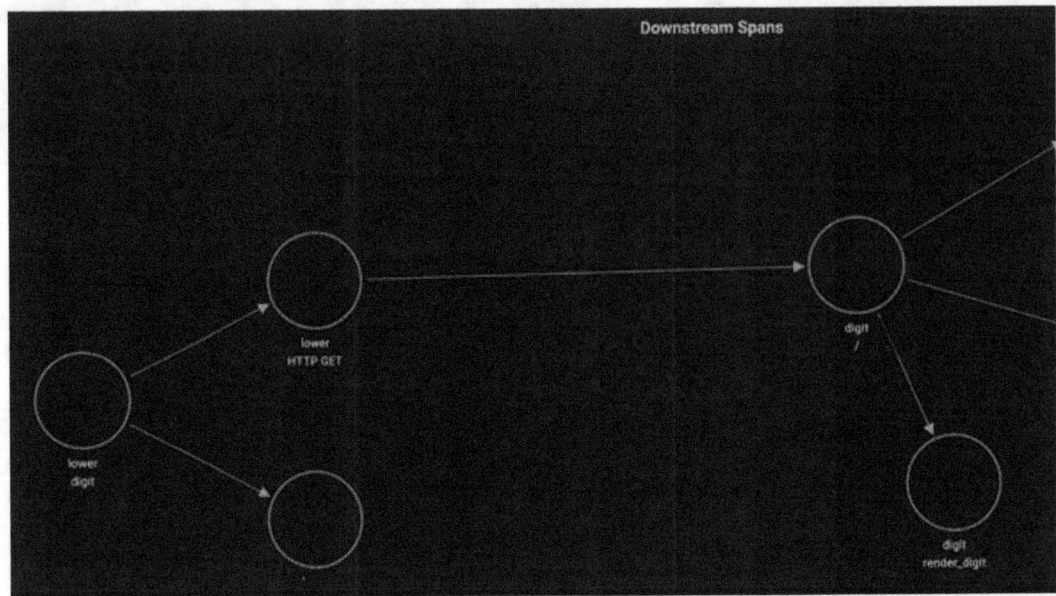

Figure 8-4.   Service graph

Developers who want to understand the upstream and downstream dependencies of a service, will get a clearer picture of the actual dependencies between the upstream and downstream of the service, as well as any neighboring nodes.

The upstream and downstream tables are great, but it's hard to visualize the structure of the calls. You can use Grafana's service map panel to draw the path of the upstream and downstream call tree. The service map panel requires two queries. The first query identifies unique nodes. The second query identifies unique edges. To accomplish this query, you only need to make minor changes to the queries you already have:

```
WITH RECURSIVE x AS
(
    SELECT
        s.trace_id,
        s.span_id,
        s.parent_span_id,
        s.service_name,
        s.span_name
    FROM ps_trace.span s
    WHERE $__timeFilter(s.start_time)
    AND s.service_name = '$service'
    AND s.span_name = '$span_name'
    UNION ALL
```

```
    SELECT
        p.trace_id,
        p.span_id,
        p.parent_span_id,
        p.service_name,
        p.span_name
    FROM ps_trace.span p
    INNER JOIN x
    ON (p.trace_id = x.trace_id
    AND p.span_id = x.parent_span_id)
    WHERE $__timeFilter(p.start_time)
)
SELECT DISTINCT
    concat(x.service_name, '|', x.span_name) as id,
    x.service_name as title,
    x.span_name as "subTitle"
FROM x
```

Downstream span graphs

Creating a downstream graph is basically a one-line change to the two queries used in the upstream graph. Once you have both the upstream and downstream graphs, you can visualize the position of a given span in the execution path from the perspective of that span.

8.4. Summary

The weakness of open source observability is in data analysis and aggregation. On the other hand, commercial observability's strength is in data analysis, aggregation, and automation.

Open source observability has limitations in aggregating, analyzing, and automate data. To develop complex data applications and visualizations, time series data does not provide a wide range of functions, but it can analyze real-time observability data. Representing time series charts with metrics is basic, but it cannot satisfy the diverse and complex requirements of observability.

Observability requires monetizing failure losses, complex dependencies between failures, and event analysis of builds and deployments. Traditionally, CMDBs have been used to support these requirements. Today, CMDBs are still utilized as an advanced operational practice in many leading tech companies. However, because CMDBs are built in isolation, they require a lot of manual development, such as interface, pipeline, and tag. While CMDBs have their pros and cons, observability offers a great alternative.

CHAPTER 8 ANALYZE RCA DATA

Observability provides a data lake where you can join and look up not only time series, but also various signals. By storing signals together in a single repository, you avoid the shortcomings of individual signals. Rather than relying on a single signal, you can optimize dashboards for root cause analysis by combining multiple signals within a single dashboard.

Observability data lakes make it easy to develop dashboards that can support complex operational requirements, not just performance. In addition to utilizing data, you can automate using AI. The E2E data lifecycle, from search analytics aggregation to predictive inference, can be addressed with the observability data lake, eliminating the need for complex pipelines and interfaces. I go into more detail about this in the final chapter.

CHAPTER 9

Aggregate RCA Data

Observability signals are big data. To analyze them, you used Grafana and OpenSearch. I explained SQL for analysis, and the next step after analysis is aggregation. In this chapter, I explain how to aggregate the signal data collected from observability.

Observability data can be stored long-term and used for a variety of purposes. It is worth thinking about the need for an observability data lake. An observability data lake manages the following data:

- Holds metric types such as counters and histograms.
- Logs, RUM, traces, and profiles are converted to metrics and stored.
- Keeps preliminary aggregation based on time windows.

Promscale is a PostgreSQL database, so it has retention limitations. It has the advantage of transaction support, replication, backup, and recovery, but large aggregations require a separate engine. Promscale is more about analytics than aggregation, and it falls into the CDC role. In the end, you need a separate engine for data storage and aggregation.

There will be more technical discussions about analyzing observability data. If the initial focus of observability was on building and stabilizing the system, you will want to make good use of it and advance it. In this chapter, I share the case of applying Presto and Druid to aggregate observability data. Understanding the examples will help you avoid trial and error. First, I introduce the Presto case.

Is it necessary to explain data aggregation? This chapter is necessary for the following reasons:

- Promscale has problems with scalability, so you need an alternative.
- Sharing my trials and errors is definitely worth it.
- I introduce observability into a complex open source system and configure Java observability by profiling the internal structure.

9.1. The Presto Case Study

Most companies store data in multiple databases. ETL is a useful technique for replicating data, but company policies may not allow you to use ETL to replicate data, and it can be difficult to load new data and reflect changes each time.

CHAPTER 9   AGGREGATE RCA DATA

Initially, Presto was a query engine used by over 1,000 Facebook data analysts to analyze a 300PB (petabyte) data warehouse. Presto doesn't store any specific data, but rather connects to external databases. It can query files on HDFS and S3, and it supports many different types of storage.

Presto has the ability to join and query different databases using the same query. Data can be stored in a variety of ways, such as documents, key values, and streams.

Presto's strength is joins. If you need joins, Presto is great. Join are also necessary for processing observability data, as it is often necessary to join different signals.

For data projects, it's important to choose the right engine for the right purpose.

- I considered using BigQuery instead of Presto, but I decided to use Presto for cost savings, as I like to use open source without vendor dependency.
- While joins and aggregations are relevant for the read path, it's important to consider the write path as well. For example, the most important aspect of the write path is indexing, which is handled differently by different engines. Presto is an ELT, not an ETL, so it doesn't require a separate write path configuration. It can build simply.
- The goal is to build a flexible system that takes full advantage of object storage, uses open source to keep costs down, and uses a variety of ad hoc queries such as joins.

Presto features include:

- Excessive memory usage is a drawback of Presto, but since there is no indexing involved, it is relatively lightweight. It doesn't have complex read and write configurations like Druid, and it is useful for ad hoc queries based on data catalogs.
- The advantage is that you can use AWS S3 and your data catalog as is. It supports overlapping queries and flattening methods, but it lacks the performance of complex aggregations and is expensive to scan when using object storage.
- Not suitable for batches that require long duration. AWS Glue, which is based on Presto, will timeout and fail if the job is not processed within 15 minutes.
- It does not have caching capabilities and relies on third parties to provide caching.
- It provides machine learning capabilities for simple data analysis.
- Certain connectors are feature-rich. Connectors are provided to join different data sources.

This demo collects OpenTelemetry data, loads it, and uses Presto for aggregation. Technically, you need data storage to collect and manage the signals. This demo will store the signal data first. Next, you need to query with SQL and visualize the results.

- Signal storage
- Signal metadata

CHAPTER 9   AGGREGATE RCA DATA

- Signal query engine
- Signal dashboard

Each topic is described in detail:

- **Backend storage of signals:** Use AWS S3. In addition to S3, you can configure an architecture that is independent of vendor dependencies.

- **Manage signal metadata:** Signal data is loaded into object storage. AWS Glue's data catalog is a good fit. OpenTelemetry provides a standardized schema. Based on the format of the stored telemetry signals, a schema is created. It is structured and managed as a table.

- **Signal query engine:** It includes a query engine that can run standard SQL. You can call the query engine through an API available in many languages.

The Presto-based data architecture you'll build in this chapter is shown in Figure 9-1.

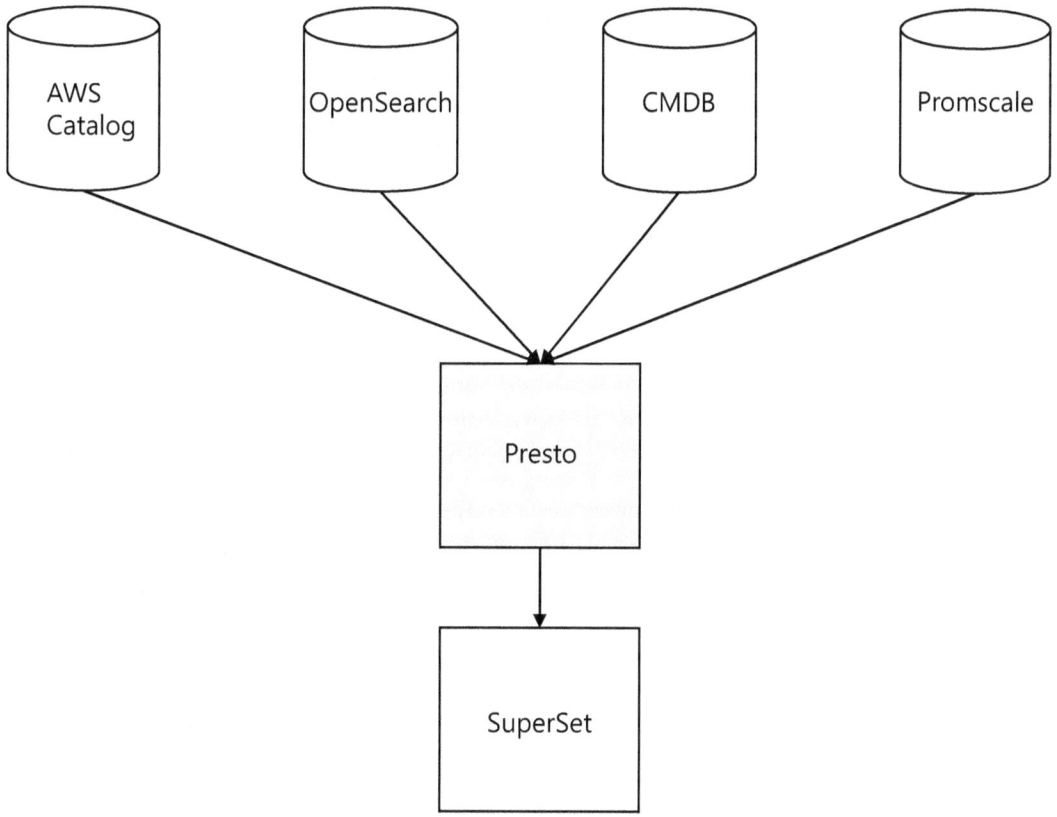

Figure 9-1. *The Presto federated query*

CHAPTER 9 AGGREGATE RCA DATA

When the number and volume of data sources in an enterprise is small, it's useful to build a centralized data lake to ingest data from a variety of sources and consolidate it into one place. However, as the company grows and builds various systems, the number of data sources may become too large, the data sources may exist on different networks, the number of data pipelines may grow exponentially, and the scheduling of jobs may become complex. In addition, data platforms often have rapidly increasing operational costs. This centralized approach becomes inefficient.

There are a lot of Prometheus and Elasticsearch instances running, and unified search was not easy. Presto offers a good alternative.

- Prometheus provides most of the metrics you need for infrastructure and application monitoring. You can query the data through the REST API and Presto.

- Manages logs, traces, metrics, and more in object storage. Using hives, you can create external tables for object storage and aggregation of observability data.

- Supersets dynamically develop dashboards with multiple charts. Supersets provide an excellent API, which can be leveraged to create charts and dashboards. Supersets use Presto to query and visualize results.

Using the Presto Prometheus plugin, you can aggregate the matrix.

In a typical organization, there are many duplicates of Prometheus, Elastic, and Grafana. You need to integrate and aggregate them. Federated queries connect to various data sources and support join queries.

9.1.1. Analytics Frameworks

- Hive:
    - Distributed applications on Hadoop are designed from the ground up to be highly scalable and fault tolerant. Since the premise is to utilize thousands of pieces of hardware, failure of any part of it is routine, and the system stem is built to continue the process as a whole.
    - Hive is a query engine that was developed as an extension of that, running large batch processes on a consistent basis. In particular, heavy processes such as processing data or creating column-oriented storage tend to have a long duration, making them ideal for running on Hive.

- Presto
    - Because Presto specializes in executing queries, it is not well suited for structuring data that is centered on processing text. Column-oriented storage is also not suitable. You're better off using Hive and Spark to structure your data.
    - Presto's queries consume a lot of resources in a short amount of time, so if you push it too hard, it won't be able to run other queries. It's best to leave time-consuming batches to hives and split clusters so that Presto has plenty of time for queries.

CHAPTER 9   AGGREGATE RCA DATA

In this chapter, you perform the following tasks:

- Structure the object storage as a hive and create tables. (Collected logs are stored in object storage.) Using Hive SQL, query the contents of the object storage.

- Use Presto to join collected data based on observability, network, resource, and other associations. Use the superset dashboard to explore your data and perform the initial tasks required for analysis.

Store unstructured data in object storage, for example. In the process of processing the data, a schema is defined and it can be analyzed by converting it into structured data.

Unstructured data, or schema-less data, collected from each application is stored in distributed storage. Data collected in distributed storage cannot be aggregated with SQL, so you need to convert the schema into structured data in a clearly tabular format.

First, I discuss structured data creation with Hive and interactive querying with Presto. Let's see how the data pipeline is organized and processed.

First, you structure the data stored in distributed storage and store it in a column-oriented storage format. I use hives because this is a heavy process that involves reading in and processing a large number of text files.

Presto can be used to execute queries using column-oriented storage to reduce duration .

The information for each table created in the hive is stored in a special database called the *hive metastore*. Let's take a closer look.

Start the hive and define an external table with CREATE EXTERNAL TABLE.

Most query engines, including Hive, are capable of aggregating text files without bringing the data in-house, as MPP databases do. For example, all CSV files contained in the path you specify as an external table will be loaded and aggregated.

However, aggregation of CSV files as they is inefficient. It's not exactly fast, either, since the text is read in every time you run a query. Convert the table to ORC format, which is a column-oriented storage format. In Hive, you can specify a storage format for each table. Create a new table and store all the data read from the external table.

The conversion to ORC format will take some time, but the aggregation of the tables after the conversion will be reduced. The file size will also be reduced by a tenth or less compared to the original CSV file.

By converting text data to column-oriented storage in this way, the aggregation of data is greatly improved.

9.1.2. OpenTelemetry Data Model

The *data model* describes the detailed layout and data structure for metrics, traces, and logs. For developers with experience with Elastic, it is similar to the Elastic Common Schema (ECS). The OpenTelemetry Data Model is a standardized message and data format designed to make it easy to correlate metrics, traces, and logs, and it is designed to be vendor-neutral. It is also compatible with the gRPC protocol buffer.

CHAPTER 9   AGGREGATE RCA DATA

Without a data model, even if the transport protocol is the same, the schema would change every time, adding complexity, maintenance, and development challenges to the applications and observability that communicates telemetry.

Developers and architects can save time and money by not having to design standardized message formats for telemetry, and they avoid the confusion caused by schema changes when analyzing continuously loaded OpenTelemetry data.

Designing a robust message and data model is important from an application and data architecture perspective, and the benefits of the OpenTelemetry Data Model are clear.

The OpenTelemetry Data Model for metrics consists of protocol specifications and semantic conventions for the delivery of pre-aggregated metric time series data.

- The data model is required when importing data from and exporting data to existing systems.
- It also supports technical specifications designed to generate metric indicators from other signals, such as spans or log streams.
- The data model is designed with a variety of charts and visualizations in mind, and it is designed to be suitable for data transformations.

Compatibility with existing data models is also taken into account. For example, popular existing metric data formats, such as the Prometheus format, can be unambiguously converted to the OpenTelemetry data model. I include specifications for how to support the popular Prometheus metric types used today and how to maintain compatibility with OpenTelemetry types.

Trace is consolidated into the new OpenTelemetry trace rather than maintaining the various existing trace standards, and logging is enhanced to augment the logging of telemetry while maintaining the availability of various language-specific logging libraries.

The OpenTelemetry Collector is designed to accept metric data in a variety of formats, to transfer data using the OpenTelemetry data model, and then to export it to existing systems. The data model can be converted to the Prometheus remote write protocol without loss of functionality or semantics through well-defined transformations of the data, including the ability to automatically remove attributes and reduce histogram resolution.

The data model has the following characteristics:

- Defines the OTLP OpenTelemetryProtocol and vendor-agnostic semantic conventions that telemetry can support.
- Defines the representation of the components that form a particular signal. It provides details about the fields that must be present in each component and describes how all components interact with each other. The data model also describes how the data should behave to developers implementing the standard.

CHAPTER 9 AGGREGATE RCA DATA

Here is an example of an OpenTelemetry trace message. It contains a variety of objects, including events, attributes, resources, and links, along with context. I explain what each of these objects means.

```
{
    "name": "opentelemetry trace",
    "context": {
        "trace_id": "0x4b6c50bc5c49e82fddc196b8a905768f",
        "span_id": "0xec8f0a64e3206a8c",
        "trace_state": "[]"
    },
    "kind": "SpanKind.CLIENT",
    "parent_id": "0x8f395001df358d3f",
    "start_time": "2022-12-26T13:40:07.727380Z",
    "end_time": "2022-12-26T13:40:07.740846Z",
    "status": {
        "status_code": "OK"
    },
    "attributes": {
        "http.method": "GET",
        "http.flavor": "1.1",
        "http.url": "http://localhost:5000/products",
        "net.peer.ip": "127.0.0.1",
        "http.status_code": 200
    },
    "events": [
        {
            "name": "events sent",
            "timestamp": "1970-01-01T00:00:00.000000Z",
            "attributes": {
                "url": "http://localhost:5000/products"
            }
        }
    ],
    "links": [],
    "resource": {
        "telemetry.sdk.language": "python",
        "telemetry.sdk.name": "opentelemetry",
        "telemetry.sdk.version": "1.10.0",
        "net.host.name": "philip-virtual-machine",
        "net.host.ip": "127.0.1.1",
```

CHAPTER 9   AGGREGATE RCA DATA

```
        "service.name": "client",
        "service.version": "0.1.2"
    }
}
```

Here is an example of an OpenTelemetry log message. It is common to define log messages in the format shown here. The general direction of OpenTelemetry logs is to add correlation and telemetry information, such as traces, to existing log message formats.

```
{
    "body": "opentelemetry log",
    "name": null,
    "severity_number": "<SeverityNumber.INFO: 9>",
    "severity_text": "INFO",
    "attributes": {},
    "timestamp": "2022-12-26T13:23:06.035780Z",
    "trace_id": "0x4ca66f7dfefc05fd9b8823dafd48bf1c",
    "span_id": "0x5df7437bac087fab",
    "trace_flags": 1,
    "resource": "BoundedAttributes({'telemetry.sdk.language': 'python', 'telemetry.sdk.name': 'opentelemetry', 'telemetry.sdk.version': '1.9.0', 'net.host.name': 'philip-virtual-machine', 'net.host.ip': '127.0.1.1', 'service.name': 'shopper', 'service.version': '0.1.2'}, maxlen=None)"
}
```

Here is an example of an OpenTelemetry metric message. OpenTelemetry metrics are more complex than Prometheus metrics, and there are more types of metrics available.

```
{
  "attributes": "",
  "description": "",
  "instrumentation_info": "InstrumentationInfo(client, 0.1.2, https://opentelemetry.io/schemas/1.9.0)",
  "name": "opentelemetry metric",
  "resource": "BoundedAttributes({'telemetry.sdk.language': 'python', 'telemetry.sdk.name': 'opentelemetry', 'telemetry.sdk.version': '1.10.0', 'net.host.name': 'philip-virtual-machine', 'net.host.ip': '127.0.1.1', 'service.name': 'shopper', 'service.version': '0.1.2'}, maxlen=None)",
  "unit": "ms",
  "point": {
    "start_time_unix_nano": 1672061810649043615,
    "time_unix_nano": 1672061810650148037,
```

```
    "bucket_counts": [
      0,
      0,
      0,
      0,
      1,
      0,
      0,
      0,
      0,
      0,
      0
    ],
    "explicit_bounds": [
      0.0,
      5.0,
      10.0,
      25.0,
      50.0,
      75.0,
      100.0,
      250.0,
      500.0,
      1000.0
    ],
    "sum": 30.760162,
    "aggregation_temporality": 2
  }
}
```

9.1.3. Presto's Features

Batch query engines like Hive are great for large-scale data processing involving large amounts of output, but they are not well suited for interactive data processing that involves executing small queries multiple times. Presto is an interactive query engine that aims to reduce the latency of query execution.

- Pluggable storage

    – Presto is characterized by its pluggable storage design. In a typical MPP database, storage and compute nodes are tightly coupled, meaning that aggregation cannot begin without first loading data. Presto, on the other hand, does not have dedicated storage, so it reads data directly from various data sources, just like a hive.

- Presto can import tables registered in the Hive metastore. This makes it ideal for purposes such as aggregation of structured data created by Hive. In order for Presto to perform at its best, the original storage must be a column-oriented data structure.
- Presto is specifically optimized for ORC-formatted loads and places them on highly scalable distributed storage for maximum performance.
- In addition to the Hive metastore, Presto can reference many other data sources as tables. For example, you can join a fact table on distributed storage with a master table in MySQL in a single query.

- Optimize CPU processes
  - It is a system specialized in executing SQL, which analyzes queries, generates an optimal execution plan, and converts them into Java bytecode. The bytecode is distributed to Presto's worker nodes, and it is compiled into machine code by the runtime system.
  - Execution of the code is multi-threaded, running hundreds of tasks in parallel on a single machine. Reading from column-oriented storage is also parallelized, with data being processed as it arrives. Therefore, the speed at which data is read determines the duration of the query, as long as there is enough memory and CPU resources.
  - A Presto cluster is always waiting for Presto and only Presto, and it uses all the resources of the machine to run queries. If it runs out of resources, later queries must wait for earlier queries to finish. This introduces latency, so the Presto cluster must always be in a free state.
  - Because Presto queries can't be interrupted once they start running, you shouldn't run queries that are too large; they can consume most of your resources, making it impossible to run other queries. However, most queries exit in a short amount of time, freeing up resources, so you shouldn't notice a problem.

- Speedup by in-memory processes
  - Unlike Hive, Presto does not write to disk during the execution of a query. It processes all data in memory, and if it runs out of memory, it will either wait until more is available or fail with an error. In this case, you need to increase the memory allocation by changing settings, or rewrite the query to reduce memory consumption.
  - Even if the amount of data handled is large, the memory consumption does not increase proportionally. For example, aggregation of data by GROUP BY is a simple iterative process, so the memory consumption is almost fixed.
  - It works well to run what you can in memory, and leave only some data processes that really need to be on disk to hives and the like. Large batch processes that take hours and combinations between huge tables should be on disk.

Figure 9-2 shows Presto's join and aggregation processes.

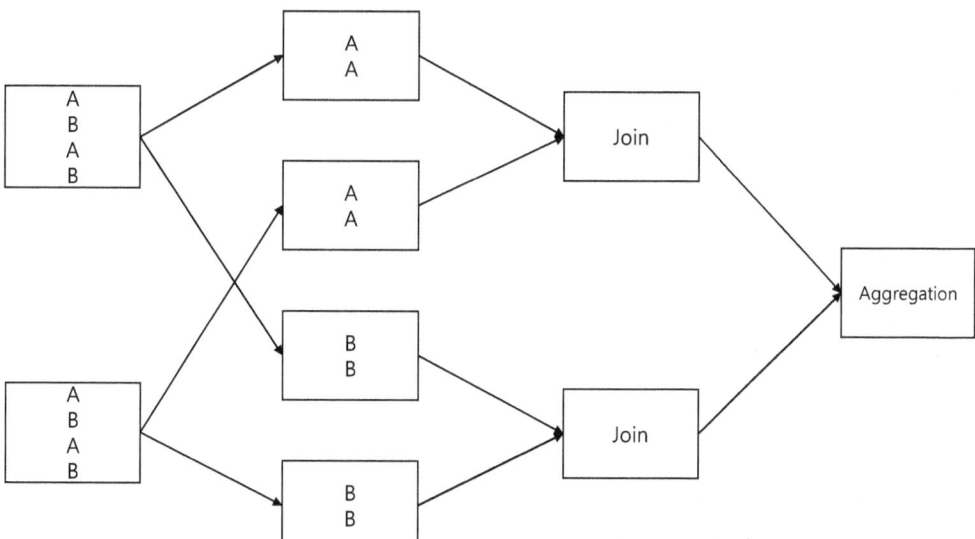

Figure 9-2. Join and aggregation processes in Presto

- Combining tables often consumes a large amount of memory, especially when combining two fact tables, which requires keeping a very large number of join keys in memory. Presto performs distributed joining by default, where data with the same key is gathered on the same node.

- Distributed concatenation involves network communication to transfer data between nodes, which often results in latency for queries. If one table is small enough, you can also use broadcast concatenation to significantly improve throughput. In this case, all the data in the table being joined is copied to each node.

- When combining multiple dimension tables in a single fact table, such as in a star schema, the dimension tables are often small enough to fit in memory. This makes combining the tables much faster because you only need to copy them once initially, and you don't have to rearrange the fact tables.

- Column-oriented storage aggregation
  - This structure also allows Presto to perform very fast aggregation of column-oriented storage. In fact, if you load a table in ORC format, you can see that aggregation can take less than a second for data volumes with millions of records.

9.1.4. Presto's Configuration

Install Presto:

```
wget https://repo1.maven.org/maven2/com/facebook/presto/presto-server/0.264/presto-server-0.264.tar.gz
wget https://repo1.maven.org/maven2/com/facebook/presto/pr e sto-cli/0.264/presto-cli-0.264.jar
```

Write config.properties:

```
node-scheduler.include-coordinator=true
http-server.http.port=8580
query.max-memory=5GB
query.max-memory-per-node=1GB
query.max-total-memory-per-node=2GB
discovery-server.enabled=true
discovery.uri=http://localhost:8580
```

Write jvm.config:

```
-server
-Xmx16G
-XX:+UseG1GC
-XX:G1HeapRegionSize=32M
-XX:+UseGCOverheadLimit
-XX:+ExplicitGCInvokesConcurrent
-XX:+HeapDumpOnOutOfMemoryError
-XX:+ExitOnOutOfMemoryError
-Djdk.attach.allowAttachSelf=true
```

Create a node.properties:

```
node.environment=production
node.id=presto
node.data-dir=/root/binary/presto-server-0.264/
```

Authorize:

```
chmod +x presto-cli-0.264-executable.jar
```

Run the query:

```
/presto-server-0.264/etc/catalog
```

Set up Presto:

```
# ./presto-cli-0.264-executable.jar --server localhost:8580 --catalog glue
```

In the following configuration, you can see that the metastore for the Hive is AWS Glue. I am not using the Hive query engine internally; I am only using Hive for metadata.

At the time of design, it was intended to be a service similar to AWS Glue service. BigQuery is relatively expensive, so I ruled it out and decided to use Presto, an open source version of Glue based on AWS S3. If you configure it like it's shown here, you can use S3, utilize the Glue data catalog as metadata, and configure only the query engine to run on local Kubernetes.

```
connector.name=hive-hadoop2
hive.metastore=glue
hive.non-managed-table-writes-enabled=true
hive.metastore.glue.region=ap-northeast-2
hive.metastore.glue.aws-access-key=
hive.metastore.glue.aws-secret-key=
```

If you get this Presto error—deserializer does not exist: org.openx.data.jsonserde.JsonSerDe—download this file:

```
wget http://www.congiu.net/hive-json-serde/1.3.6-SNAPSHOT/cdh5/json-serde-1.3.6-SNAPSHOT-jar-with-dependencies.jar
```

Copy the json-serde-1.3.6-SNAPSHOT-jar-with-dependencies.jar file. It's located in the plugin, lib folder.

Set up an AWS data catalog:

```
CREATE EXTERNAL TABLE schema (
  description string,
  foo struct<bar:string, level1:struct<l2string:string, l2struct:struct<level3:string>>,
  quux:string>,
  wibble string,
  wobble array<struct<entry:int, entrydetails:struct<details1:string, details2:int>>>)
ROW FORMAT SERDE 'org.openx.data.jsonserde.JsonSerDe'
LOCATION 's3://bucketname/foldername/';
```

Complex JSON must be supported. Simple JSON is no problem, but JSON with complex structures will not be recognized by the crawler and will fail. Tables should be created to fit the schema structure, as shown here.

You must add the org.openx.data.jsonserde.JsonSerDe option to successfully create the catalog. blog.json is stored in s3://bucketname/foldername/. Create the database in default folder and the tables in s3:/ /bucketname/foldername/.

CHAPTER 9   AGGREGATE RCA DATA

```
CREATE EXTERNAL TABLE sesblog (
  eventType string,
  mail struct<`timestamp`:string,
              source:string,
              sourceArn:string,
              sendingAccountId:string,
              messageId:string,
              destination:string,
              headersTruncated:boolean,
              headers:array<struct<name:string,value:string>>,
              commonHeaders:struct<`from`:array<string>,to:array<string>,messageId:string,
              subject:string>
              >
  )
ROW FORMAT SERDE 'org.openx.data.jsonserde.JsonSerDe'
LOCATION 's3://bucketname/foldername/'
```

The original plan was to use an AWS crawler to automatically recognize the schema from the file and create structured tables.

JSON contains iterated arrays and overlapping structures.

Complex arrays need to be flattened. UNNEST (unpacking an array) is a method that returns an array in rows, and when you unpack the resulting array, you can get the row corresponding to each item in the array.

Sometimes you want to output STRUCT and ARRAY types as individual rows like a normal record. To do this, use UNNEST.

```
# ./presto-cli-0.264-executable.jar --server localhost:8580 --catalog glue
presto> show schemas;
       Schema
--------------------
 default
 demo
 information_schema
(3 rows)

Query 20230827_235710_00000_4xc8r, FINISHED, 1 node
Splits: 19 total, 19 done (100.00%)
0:05 [3 rows, 44B] [0 rows/s, 8B/s]

presto> select * from default.schema;

Query 20230827_235729_00001_4xc8r, FAILED, 1 node
Splits: 17 total, 0 done (0.00%)
0:10 [0 rows, 0B] [0 rows/s, 0B/s]
```

CHAPTER 9 AGGREGATE RCA DATA

Query 20230827_235729_00001_4xc8r failed: deserializer does not exist: org.openx.data.jsonserde.JsonSerDe

```
presto> select * from default.schema;
 description | foo | wibble | >
-------------+-----------------------------------------------------------------------+---
-----+--------------------->
 my doc | {bar=baz, level1={l2string=l2val, l2struct={level3=l3val}}, quux=revlos} | 123 |
[{entry=1, entrydeta>
 my doc | {bar=baz, level1={l2string=l2val, l2struct={level3=l3val}}, quux=revlos} | 123 |
[{entry=1, entrydeta>
```

You can see that AWS Athena successfully outputs the same results. Without using Presto, the process in AWS Athena looks like this The purpose of Presto is to process data like Glue, while reducing costs by using an open source query engine, and taking advantage of the cloud by using S3 and the AWS Glue data catalog.

Figure 9-3 shows a pipeline that combines Presto and Glue data catalogs.

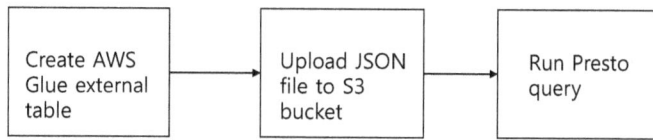

Figure 9-3. *The Glue data catalog processing using Presto*

The AWS data catalog ensures compatibility with the Hive metastore and contains information about Glue's metadata. Athena reads tables and columns from the data catalog and processes queries in S3, where the actual data is stored.

It is common to encounter schemas that change frequently or dynamically during production. The OpenTelemetry schema is JSON and can change frequently. For OpenTelemetry metrics, it is more schema-less.

Using observability, developing queries and organizing the schema change process are complex and challenging tasks.

External tables can be created in the Glue data catalog, uploaded to S3, and queried using Presto. This can significantly reduce query costs and S3 storage costs. See Figure 9-4.

CHAPTER 9   AGGREGATE RCA DATA

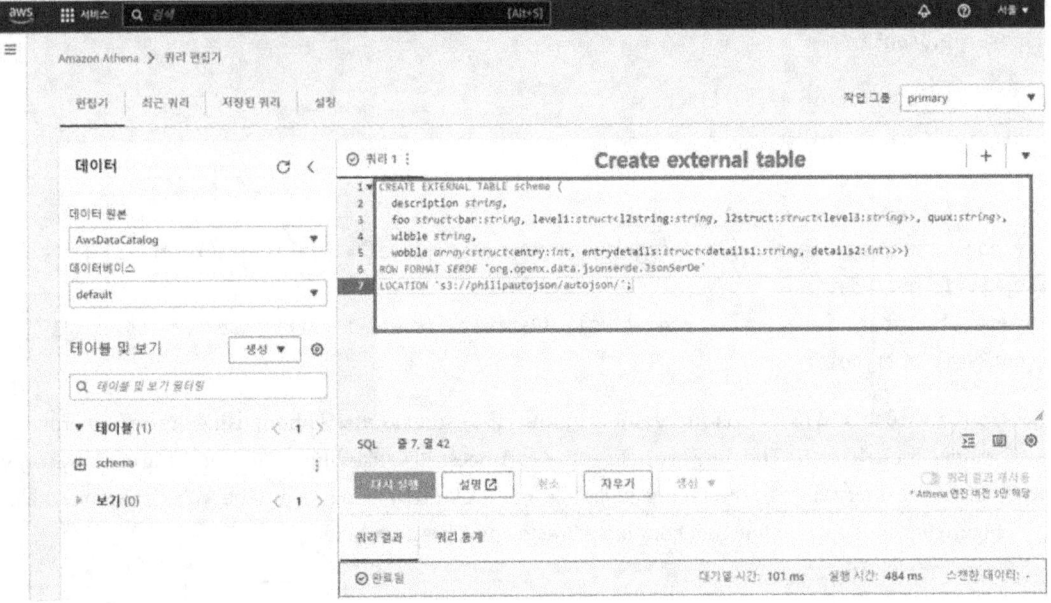

Figure 9-4. Data catalog in AWS

It is more accurate to say that Presto was unfit for purpose than that it was badly lacking in aggregation of data. It's memory intensive, which is great for ad hoc and ELT. I tested Presto because of the performance and scalability I experienced with AWS Glue, but I don't think it's a good fit for an observability data lake.

Time-consuming batch processes should, in principle, use hives. When a denormalized table reaches hundreds of millions of records, exporting it to an analytics system alone takes a significant amount of time. In this case, the performance of the query engine itself doesn't have much of an impact on the final duration. In this case, using a batch system can be a more efficient use of resources.

NoSQL is optimized for processing JSON, but there are pros and cons to using Presto for JSON processing. When organizing a data lake, it is important to structure complex JSON correctly. While it would be nice to be able to process unstructured, schema-less, or dynamic formats that are always changing, it's a challenge.

9.2. The Apache Druid Case Study

If you're running open source in a cluster, you're probably facing a lot of challenges. If you are running an open source cluster with little documentation, you should think twice about putting it into production. If you encounter a problem or suspect a bug during production, you need to analyze the cause and fix it, and observability will help you do that.

In this section, you apply observability to understand why Druid is a good fit for observability data aggregation and to understand the internal structure of Druid.

Because the problems I focus on in this book are at the lower levels of the system, I have not discussed in detail the problems of large clusters. Failures in large clusters in production are common. I explain the problems of large clusters through Druid.

With an understanding of Druid, I discuss root cause analysis of large clusters. It is important to understand the complex internal structure of Druid and how to troubleshoot problems as they arise.

While Presto is useful for ad hoc queries, Druid processes pre-aggregation and is more useful for static queries based on predefined dimensions. They have different requirements and are used for different purposes.

Aggregation has a different purpose than analytics.

Analytical SQL queries are different from aggregation SQL queries. If you only consider simple GROUP BY and TopN (rearrange GROUP BY results) methods, aggregation queries must support necessary and complex OLAP features such as rollup, slice, dice, and drilldown.

Because of the different computational structure required by aggregations, separate solutions are needed to process and optimize them.

When choosing a data engine, it's all about purpose. You should choose an engine that is optimized for your needs, whether it is search, analytics, or aggregation. It is a characteristic of databases that the same query takes 0.1 seconds on Engine A, but takes 10 seconds or more on Engine B. It's not a matter of supporting a specific SQL method, but understanding the characteristics of the engine to process large transactions.

- Search has an algorithm, and even inaccurate results should be processed with a short response time compared to analytics.

- Average, Max, Min, Group, and Frequency are simple analytics, while GROUP BY and Distribution are also used for analysis.

- Rollups, pre-aggregation, sliced dices (analyzing only some dimensions), drilldowns (expanding the aggregated data again), and TopN are examples of complex aggregations.

Druid is aimed at aggregation of categories and numerical data. Since they are different systems with different purposes, it is not appropriate to compare them. Instead, it is important to understand the purpose and benefits of each solution.

The choice of open source should be based on an understanding of the nature of the data, the purpose, its application, and the SQL query plan. Here is a brief understanding of the following features:

- Schema-less searches
- Index methods
- Rollups

CHAPTER 9   AGGREGATE RCA DATA

9.2.1. Schema-Less Searches

These searches provide full-text search for documents without schema, and are often needed for access to raw event-level data. While OpenSearch is strong in search, it is building out its capabilities for analytics and aggregation. OpenSearch's resource requirements for data ingestion and search are much higher than Druid's. JSON has overlapping, layered relationships. It is not suitable for relational databases.

9.2.2. Index Methods

The biggest difference between Grafana Loki and OpenSearch is how they index data. Loki is designed to keep indexing low, while OpenSearch indexes all data in all fields, and each indexed field has a dedicated, optimized data structure. The simplicity of indexing in Loki makes it cost-effective and performs well. However, you lose the rich text search capabilities that OpenSearch offers.

9.2.3. Rollups

OpenSearch does not support summarizing/rollup of data at ingestion. The data that needs to be stored can be compressed up to 100 times the actual dataset. Druid focuses on OLAP workflows. Druid is optimized for fast aggregation and ingestion at low cost and supports a wide range of analytical tasks. Druid provides some basic search support for structured event data, but does not support text search. Druid does not support unstructured data. Measures must be defined in a Druid schema so that summarization/rollups can be performed.

Understanding Druid is a good example of observability. You can understand the internal structure of a large cluster and get experience with performance tuning.

9.2.4. Druid Components

Apache Druid stages data from the storage to the compute layer. Before you run a query, the data is already there. It automatically performs node balancing, and workloads are automatically redistributed to the changed nodes.

As new data comes in, it can be analyzed at the compute layer before sending it to storage. This makes Druid useful for analyzing real-time data. This is why Druid is so popular for analyzing streaming data.

Druid's tables are partitioned into segments and stored on data nodes in a compressed form as columns. When a query comes in, the query node distributes the workload, extending parts of the query to each relevant server and returning a single result. This makes it possible to process large amounts of data, billions of new columns, and interactive queries from thousands of concurrent users.

Druid is composed of various nodes:

- Real-time nodes
- Historical nodes

CHAPTER 9　AGGREGATE RCA DATA

- Broker nodes

- Coordinator nodes

Druid, like any other large cluster, has reads and writes separated, and is processed by multiple microservices interacting with each other. See Figure 9-5.

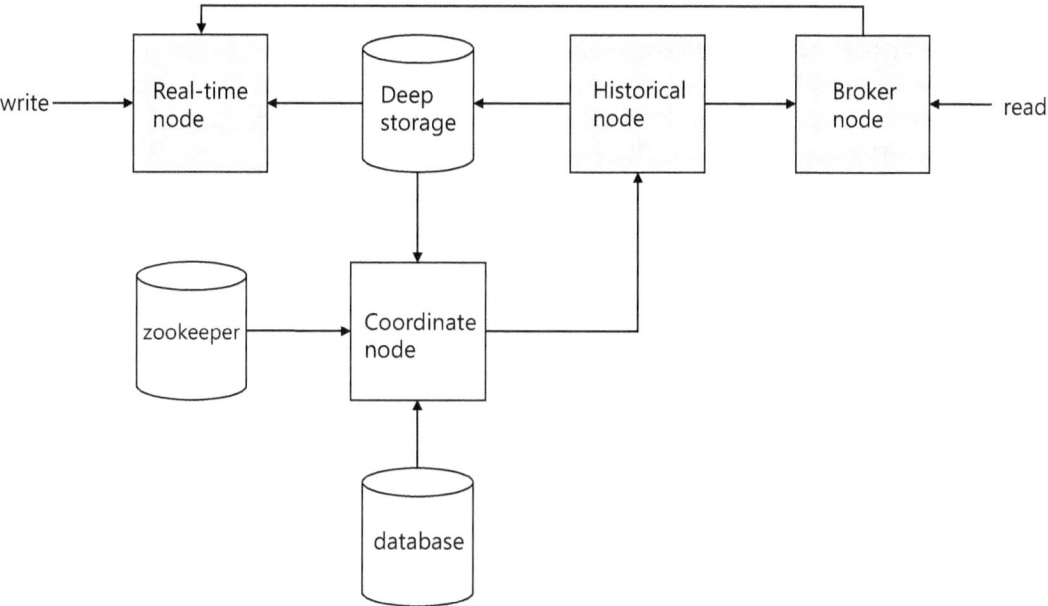

Figure 9-5. *Component relationships in Druid*

Broker nodes are responsible for user queries. Data indexed in batches is fetched from Historical nodes. Communication between components inside Druid is handled by the zookeeper.

Druid is pre-aggregation and dimensionally configurable. You can pre-aggregate and post-aggregate based on timestamps. Dimensions are fields that can be filtered and grouped. It's not a good idea to create a new aggregation every time for large amounts of data, such as monthly aggregations. You should archive the aggregations that have already been made and give users the ability to drill down.

If you are serving your service externally, you should configure SQL optimized for your dimension configuration so that Druid is preconfigured to process it quickly. If Druid has to process queries that it doesn't expect, it will have a negative impact on performance. Examples include frequent requests for full scans, or needing to load a specific segment from deep storage into Historical because the data does not exist in Historical. Druid's performance varies a lot depending on the type of query. Users should be guided to configure queries that process predefined dimensions rather than ad hoc like Presto. Frequent use of ad hoc queries in Druid will have a negative impact on the entire cluster.

CHAPTER 9 AGGREGATE RCA DATA

A *segment* is a unit of indexing file that is stored in Druid's time-based indexing, and the storage unit can be optimized according to user queries. When collecting data to be stored, the segment granularity defined in the indexing specification determines the storage unit. For example, if the segment granularity is an hour, indexing creates segment files (shards) by hour. The recommended segment size for Druid is between 300MB and 700MB. If the segment file grows larger than this scope, sharding is required.

9.2.4.1. Real-Time Nodes

The real-time node family is responsible for ingesting and querying event streams, as shown in Figure 9-6. These nodes process only recent events within a short time scope and periodically forward them to deep storage. The procedure is as follows

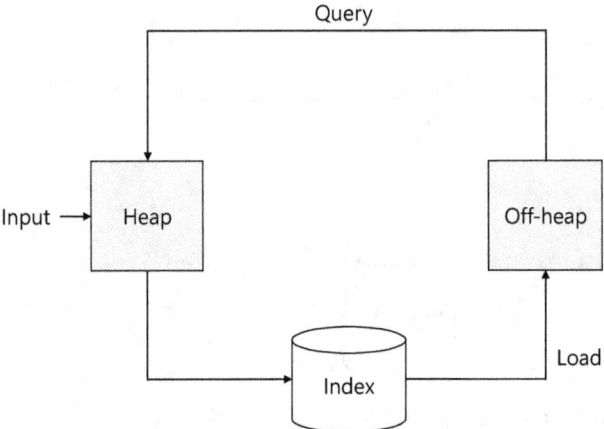

Figure 9-6. *The Druid read path*

- Incoming events are indexed in memory and can be used for queries immediately.
- Data in memory is regularly written to disk and converted to an immutable (read-only) columnar format.
- The stored data is loaded into off-heap memory, so it remains queryable.
- Indexes stored on disk are periodically merged to form data segments, which are then moved to deep storage.

In this way, all events obtained with real-time nodes remain queryable as they exist in on-heap or off-heap memory before and after disk storage (queries are passed to both indexes in memory and indexes stored on disk). This real-time node capability allows Druid to perform real-time data ingestion. As events occur, they are immediately queried.

Real-time nodes report their online status and the data they are processing to the main keeper for organic behavior with other nodes in the Druid cluster.

654

CHAPTER 9 AGGREGATE RCA DATA

9.2.4.2. Historical Nodes

The Historical node family is responsible for loading and processing read-only data segments (blocks) generated by real-time nodes. These nodes download read-only segments from deep storage and process queries against them (data aggregation/filtering). There are no race conditions between them—they simply load, drop, and process segments as directed by the main keeper.

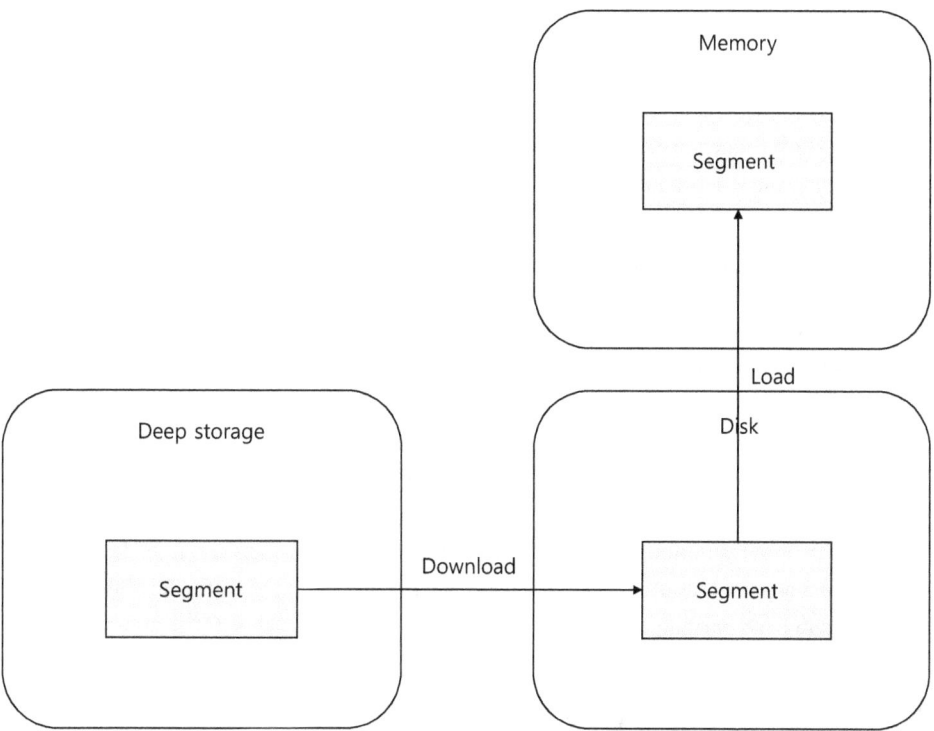

Figure 9-7. The process for Historical nodes

When a Historical node receives a query, it first checks its local cache, which holds information about which segments already exist for it. If the information about a segment is not in the cache, the node downloads the segment from deep storage. The segment is then declared in the main keeper and becomes a queryable object, and the node performs the requested query on this segment. See Figure 9-7.

Historical nodes can guarantee read consistency because they only deal with read-only data. Read-only data blocks also enable a simple parallel model. Historical nodes can scan and aggregate read-only data blocks simultaneously without interfering with each other.

Like real-time nodes, historical nodes report their online status and the data they are processing to the main keeper.

9.2.4.3. Broker Nodes

Through the metadata reported to the zookeeper, the broker nodes know which segments are queryable and where each of them is stored. The broker nodes specify the path of the input queries, ensuring that each query reaches the correct historical or real-time node. They then aggregate the results from each of the historical and real-time nodes and return the final query result to the caller.

Broker nodes use caches to increase resource efficiency. If a query requires multiple segments, the broker node first checks for segments that already exist in its cache and forwards the query to the historical and real-time nodes where they are stored. When historical nodes return results, the broker node stores them in its cache on a per-segment basis for later use. Data from real-time nodes is not stored in the cache, so requests for real-time data are always forwarded to real-time nodes. This is because the data from real-time nodes is variable, and storing their results in a cache is not reliable.

9.2.4.4. Coordinator Nodes

The coordinator node family is primarily responsible for managing and distributing historical node data. The coordinator node determines which historical nodes will perform queries against which segments, and it instructs them to load new data, drop stale data, replicate data, and move data to balance the load. This enables a distributed group of historical nodes to process data quickly, efficiently, and reliably.

Like all other Druid nodes, the coordinator node maintains a zookeeper connection to the cluster to stay aware of its status. Coordinator nodes also maintain a connection to a MySQL database, which manages additional computational parameters and configuration information, such as creation, destruction, and replication rules for segments in the cluster. To ensure the reliability of a Druid cluster, the coordinator nodes are redundant, and typically only one coordinator node is active.

9.2.5. Performance Improvements

The basics of performance tuning are monitoring input and output, observing traffic to change parameters, and allocating enough resources to avoid unnecessary bottlenecks.

So far, I haven't discussed how to tune a cluster of shards and diagnose problems. Most of the focus has been on understanding the problems and causes of single resources and applications. Failures at the cluster level are a different type of failure than the ones discussed so far. For example, it is difficult to identify and discover failures using traces and profiles. It is not an application error like microservices, and it is difficult to judge only by the input and output of resources such as CPU memory. It is a resource problem between multiple applications and systems, including lower levels such as Java virtual machine and kernel, but beyond their scope, and it is a cluster-level failure that occurs in the process of organizing a large-scale distributed system.

The challenge with using open source is tuning. Large data analytics platforms have similar internal behavior. In this chapter, I explain how to improve the performance of Druid.

CHAPTER 9 AGGREGATE RCA DATA

Most of the performance tuning needed was related to I/O:

1. Cache in broker and historical
2. Tiering in historical
3. Tasks of the middle manager
4. Indexing, compression, and merging of segments in deep storage
5. Improving slow queries
6. Pipeline improvements for Kafka and more
7. Application profiles

It doesn't make sense to describe the exact parameter values for performance tuning. Each site has different requirements and system architecture. This chapter describes how reads and writes are processed to handle large amounts of data.

The read path looks like this:

1. Users request queries from the router. When a large number of requests is sent to the router, latency starts at the router. The router is a web server and forwards the user's query to the broker.
2. The broker analyzes the request query and searches the cache. The broker is responsible for sending requests to the middle manager and the historical node and aggregating the results.
3. The broker requests current data from the middle manager.
4. The broker requests historical data from the historical node.
5. The historical node searches the cache, and if no data is found, it searches deep storage.
6. The broker receives responses from the middle manager and the historical node, merges the results, and forwards them to the router.

The write path is as follows:

1. The middle manager gets data from Kafka or other data sources.
2. The middle manager does pre-aggregation.
3. The task creates an index.
4. Tasks create segments in deep storage.

CHAPTER 9 AGGREGATE RCA DATA

This is because understanding the approach, rather than understanding the specific parameters, allows you to understand how to tune any system in the future.

- The clusters of OpenSearch, Grafana Loki, Thanos, and Jaeger are not different from Druid. They are roughly 70 percent the same.

- Reads and writes are decoupled. Writes manage state, so when the number of nodes changes, rebalancing occurs, so frequent autoscales can affect write reliability. Writes are careful about setting parameters, such as the number of shardings, Reads, however, are more flexible to autoscale. In Kubernetes operations, writes are deployed to stateful sets and reads are deployed to deployments.

- For reads, you should configure the cache to use as much of it as possible, and look for slow queries to analyze and tune for causes. This is because there are different ways to write optimized queries for your system depending on your needs, whether it's search, analytics, or aggregation.

- On writes, most indexes are created internally. You may encounter performance slowdowns while building indexes, so you should break them down as granularly as possible to understand where they are slowing down and configure them to change parameters or increase resources.

- It's also fast because it's already aggregated by dimension through pre-aggregation.

- It should be configured to prevent unnecessary full scans from occurring. Separate storage by tenants. Storage is tiered, which means you want to segment your data as much as possible. Managing storage in isolation by tenant and by storage tier can save you money.

- You need to consider pre-aggregation, cache processing, and time window processing. It is useful for the query engine to modify the query in the desired format. No matter how strong your distributed parallelism is, unnecessary IO will slow down performance.

- When running on Kubernetes, each pod must have the correct resource allocation. In particular, incorrect memory configuration will cause pods to crash frequently.

A lot can be learned by understanding the system and tuning it appropriately. Through tuning, SREs optimize systems and fix things that are broken. An SRE should be able to look at code, debug, and have a lot of experience tuning.

The difficulties with tuning Druid are as follows:

- Druid is organized in the form of microservices. Each microservice communicates and interacts with the others in a complex way, so problems with some microservices can cause overall performance degradation. The complexity of the configuration means that it takes a long time to troubleshoot problems.

- Druid interacts with various data stores such as cache, object storage, relational databases, zookeeper distributed configuration management, and messages. In addition to Druid microservices, you need to monitor metrics and logs from various data stores. You can configure compression, merging, downsampling, multitenant, and data tiering. Druid supports extensions to extend its functionality.

- Druid does not provide metrics by default. After installing the extension, you must configure an emitter and exporter to provide Druid metrics externally.

With so many metrics, it's important to pick the ones that matter.

9.2.5.1. Write Paths

To run a large cluster like Druid, memory is important, but in some cases, CPU computation is necessary. Each component—such as the historical, middle manager, and broker nodes—requires different types of resources depending on how it processes data. Broker is CPU-centric, historical is memory-centric because it loads large amounts of data into memory, and middle manager is relatively IO-intensive and CPU-intensive because it compresses incoming data and performs frequent merges and flushes. Since each component has different resource requirements, you should understand the characteristics of each component before allocating resources.

For example, if you are running Druid on Kubernetes, you need to be careful with memory sizing. If you allocated 15GB (gigabytes) of memory for the historical node, your pod should have at least 17GB to avoid memory problems. Druid stores its cache off-heap, so it is not subject to memory reclamation by garbage collection. If the off-heap memory setting is incorrect, an OOM occurs, causing the pod to restart.

Data fed through Kafka resides in memory for a while before being written to disk. In the event of a failure, there is a chance that the data buffered in memory will be lost. To prevent data loss and avoid redundant reprocessing from Kafka, you use partitions and offset configurations.

The most important thing about the write path is

- Ingesting
- Indexing (pre-aggregation)
- Creating a segment
- Tiering

Druid can roll up data as it is ingested, reducing the amount of incoming data to store on disk. Rollups are a form of summarization or pre-aggregation. Rolling up data can significantly reduce the size of the data to be stored and reduce the number of rows by many orders of magnitude. In exchange for the efficiency of rollups, you lose the ability to query individual events.

At ingest time, rollups are controlled by the rollup setting in granularitySpec. Rollups are enabled by default. They combine all rows with the same dimension value and timestamp value into a single row.

CHAPTER 9   AGGREGATE RCA DATA

When rollups are disabled, Druid does not perform any form of pre-aggregation and loads each row as is. This mode is similar to databases that do not support rollups. To store each record as is without a rollup summary, set rollup to `false`.

Use rollups in the following cases:

- When you want optimal performance or have strict storage constraints
- When you don't need raw values for high-cardinality dimensions

Conversely, disable rollups if either of these are true:

- When you need results for individual rows
- When you need to run a `GROUP BY` or `WHERE` query on all columns

If you have conflicting requirements for your use case, you can create multiple tables with different rollup configurations for each table.

While it is possible to process windows in the pipeline, it is also possible inside Druid, so you should consider it.

When Druid middle manager's ingest rate slows down, it's not easy to understand whether it's a problem with Kafka resources or an internal Druid issue. Furthermore, Druid middle manager does not create consumer groups, so it is not easy to analyze performance when there is a Kafka problem.

Creating Indexes

Creating indexes in Druid involves segments and determining the proper size of segments, compression, and merging is important.

The Druid Indexing Service is a high-availability distributed service that runs indexing-related tasks. Indexing jobs are responsible for creating and terminating Druid segments. The Indexing service is composed of the following components: Peons that can run single jobs, the middle manager that manage the peons, and overloads that manage the distribution of jobs to the middle manager.

- When writing to object storage, it's important to organize your blocks and consider things like the size of your compressed blocks.

- Druid organizes dimensions through pre-aggregation at index process time. Latency in the write path is caused by the inbound traffic pipeline, index creation, and storage in object storage. By segmenting the write path, it is necessary to verify and identify whether the latency is caused by the index creation process, the way the disk is stored, and each section where latency occurs.

- Batching and buffering should be applied from the time it enters Druid from the pipeline, and if traffic enters without this configuration, you can experience severe write latency.

- Create the segments that store the disk, and the merging and compression of the segments occurs.

Creating a Segment

Since Druid uses object storage, you need to analyze the metrics of object storage while tuning. There is a lack of metrics provided by S3, and it is difficult to analyze the cause based on the number of calls to the AWS S3 PUT and GET API. If you use AWS S3 in production, you may experience frequent tearing, frequently block creation and compression at the point of storage, or unnecessary full scans queries. You're likely to experience performance problems with object storage. Using metric-rich minio in a test environment, you need a way to analyze metrics and logs.

Rather than using S3 in a development environment, you should use minio to see how Druid interacts with object storage, what inputs and outputs it generates, and what events it generates. Then you tune it. I recommend tuning Druid's storage processes through debugging before deploying to AWS S3 in production.

Object storage is directly related to the tiering and slow queries discussed later. Although reads and writes are logically separated, it's important to understand that they interact a lot with each other.

9.2.5.2. Read Path

The main topics covered in the read path are

- Tiering
- Caching
- Querying
- Multitenancy

Tiering

Tiering is a difficult setting. Data retention rules allow you to configure Druid to honor data retention policies. A data retention policy specifies what data to keep and what to delete from the cluster.

Set the capacity and duration for loading data from object storage to memory. Druid supports load, drop, and broadcast rules. Each rule is a JSON object.

You can configure a default set of rules to apply to all data sources, or you can set specific rules for specific data sources.

You can specify which data to keep or delete in the following ways:

- **Duration:** Segment data specified as an offset from the current time.
- **Interval:** Use a fixed time scope.

Archiving rules are persistent, meaning they remain in effect until you change them. Druid stores archiving rules in the metadata store. The key is to configure it to avoid unnecessary loading. Loading from object storage, due to unexpected user queries, will degrade performance and cost money.

Failures and poor pipeline organization often lead to problems where the incoming data increases or decreases.

CHAPTER 9   AGGREGATE RCA DATA

Caching

Caching is many orders of magnitude faster than object storage. I recommend using caching to dramatically improve performance and lower costs. However, caches are difficult to operate and require experience operating with many exceptions. Druid provides caching in the read path. Druid uses a broker on the read path and historical uses a cache .

Caching is used to improve read performance. This can be measured by the cache hit rate. Due to the nature of time series data, the cache hit rate is relatively low compared to other domains.

Druid manages its cache using Java off-heap or using something like Redis. The basic behavior is that when it receives the same query, it doesn't execute a new query, but returns the results it already has in its cache.

The problem is Java offheap. Java offheap only provides cache information as a metric, and since it only outputs a hit rate, you can't determine if a particular query hit the cache. With Redis's hit rate, you can easily analyze how a particular query interacts with the cache and why the cache hit rate is low. While I recommend using Java off-heap in production, you should at least use Redis in your development environment to tune your cache and queries for problems.

While a Druid cache is useful, it makes sense to configure the cache internally on the backend microservices that generate the queries. Reducing the number of Druid requests is useful.

Querying

Internally, all Druid SQL queries are converted to queries in the JSON-based Druid native query format before they are executed on the data node. While you can use Druid SQL for most purposes, familiarity with native queries is useful for writing complex queries and troubleshooting performance problems.

Druid uses SQL optimized for aggregation. When you run a query, the plan outputs the query type. In general, query engines are specialized for their purpose and have preferred queries.

1. In Druid, the type of query has a significant impact on performance.

2. Druid does pre-aggregation and provides additional dimensionality, so your queries should reflect this when writing them.

3. Unnecessary full scans slow down performance and cost extra money.

4. Fixed-dimensional queries have an advantage over ad hoc.

5. They are processed by pre-aggregation depending on the window.

Multitenancy

You can implement multitenancy. In this case, each tenant is separated and stored in object storage. Multitenancy is an efficient way to run your system.

- If you need different retention intervals for different departments, you can configure retention to set different intervals for different tenants.

- If you look up data from entire organizations, you're scanning unnecessary data, which increases your scan costs. You can save money by using multitenancy to look up only specific tenants. Avoid full scans.

- Suppose your total data is 10TB and your tangent is 1TB. Once the tenant is set up, you don't need to query 10TB, you only need to query 1TB to get the results you want, and you can improve speed by querying less data.

- You can set different tiering and security policies for different tenants. If you don't differentiate between tenants, it's difficult to apply different policies to different tenants.

Multitenancy in observability is difficult because applications make complex calls over service boundary, making it difficult to define and separate boundaries, and because there is no standardization. It has unclear boundaries and many common services. Since there is a lot of IO in the cluster and many tuning parameters, it is naturally difficult to operate the system.

9.2.6. Druid Observability

The architecture of Druid you've seen so far implements the microservices pattern. The Druid components are as follows:

- The Coordinator service manages the availability of data in the cluster.

- The Overload service manage the allocation of data collection workloads.

- The broker processes user requests in the read path.

- The Router service is optional. It routes requests to brokers, coordinators, and overloads.

- Data loaded from the Historical node services object storage.

- The Middle Manager ingests the data.

CQRS, gateways, and caches are used internally. The way to understand Druid is to apply observability. By analyzing Druid's metrics, logs, traces, and profiles, you can understand its internal structure and tune its performance.

To get an accurate understanding of Druid, you should configure it to output as many signals as possible. To do this, you need to enable the Prometheus exporter, and then request logging, traces, emitters, logs, JMXs, and profiles.

Remote debugging is a great way to understand how the API works. You can specify your own breakpoints and see the values of variables on a line-by-line basis. Combined with the Chrome developer tools, it's a convenient way to find problems in your frontend.

1. Prometheus exporter

2. Emitters

CHAPTER 9   AGGREGATE RCA DATA

   3. Caches

   4. Logs

   5. JavaAgent

   6. Object storage

9.2.6.1. Metrics

You should collect metrics for

- Druid
- redis
- Kafka
- Minio object storage

To integrate with S3 Minio and Redis, you need to install a Druid extension. An extension is similar to a plugin.

Add -D to the java command. Here's how to install Druid's extension and configure the Redis cache.

```
java -cp "lib/*" -Ddruid.extensions.directory="extensions" -Ddruid.extensions.hadoopDependenciesDir="hadoop-dependencies" org.apache.druid.cli.Main tools pull-deps --no-default-hadoop -c org.apache.druid.extensions.contrib:prometheus-emitter:25.0.0

java -classpath "lib/*" org.apache.druid.cli. Main tools pull-deps -c org.apache.druid.extensions.contrib:druid-redis-cache:25.0.0
```

```
druid.cache.type=redis
druid.cache.host=localhost
druid.cache.port=6379
druid.broker.cache.useCache=true
druid.broker.cache.populateCache=true
```

```
yum install redis
systemctl start redis
```

```
npm install -g redis-commander
```

Druid metrics use emitters and the Prometheus exporter by default. You can limit the metrics output from your application via the emitter before exporting.

CHAPTER 9 AGGREGATE RCA DATA

Here's how to configure metrics in Druid:

```
druid.monitoring.monitors=["org.apache.druid.java.util.metrics.JvmMonitor", "org.apache.druid.client.cache.CacheMonitor", "org.apache.druid.java.util.metrics.JvmThreadsMonitor","org.apache.druid.java.util.metrics.SysMonitor","org.apache.druid.java.util.metrics.JvmCpuMonitor","org.apache.druid.server.metrics.EventReceiverFirehoseMonitor"]

druid.extensions.loadList= ["druid-hdfs-storage", "druid-kafka-indexing-service", "druid-datasketches", "prometheus-emitter", "druid-multi-stage-query"]
```

You need to start the Druid exporter:

```
# ./druid-exporter
time="2023-05-03T04:42:03-04:00" level=info msg="Druid exporter started listening on: 1234"
time="2023-05-03T04:42:03-04:00" level=info msg="Metrics endpoint - http://0.0.0.0:1234/metrics"
time="2023-05-03T04:42:03-04:00" level=info msg="Druid emitter endpoint - http://0.0.0.0:1234/druid"
time="2023-05-03T04:42:03-04:00" level=info msg="Successfully collected data from druid emitter, druid/historical"
time="2023-05-03T04:42:03-04:00" level=info msg="Successfully collected data from druid emitter, druid/historical"
```

Here's how to configure an exporter in Druid:

```
druid.emitter.http.recipientBaseUrl=http://localhost:1234/druid
druid.emitter=http

export DRUID_URL="http://localhost"
export PORT="1234"
```

Due to the large number of Druid components, the number of metrics available via exports is also large. You need to increase the collection interval or allocate enough memory to Prometheus.

The minio metric is organized as follows:

```
wget https://dl.min.io/client/mc/release/linux-amd64/mc
chmod +x mc

# ./minio server /mnt/data --console-address ":9001"
S3-API: http://192.168.244.146:9000 http://192.168.122.1:9000 http://127.0.0.1:9000
RootUser: minioadmin
RootPass: minioadmin

# ./mc alias set myminio http://192.168.244.146:9000 minioadmin minioadmin
# ./mc admin prometheus generate myminio
```

665

CHAPTER 9 AGGREGATE RCA DATA

```
- job_name: minio-job
  bearer_token: eyJhbGciOiJIUzUxMiIsInR5cCI6IkpXVCJ9.eyJpc3MiOiJwcm9tZXRoZXVzIiwic3ViIjoi
bWluaW9hZG1pbiIsImV4cCI6NDgzNjA5MTYzM30.e4suNpUqXZJXFgo991EP_hdjdSKKR99B-87h11WsQMcQUCU
z9LU-5vrK1vXJYVCEU3muXmXIXlY-87uYotRBOQ
  metrics_path: /minio/v2/metrics/cluster
  scheme: http
  static_configs:
    - targets: ['192.168.244.146:9000']
```

curl https://localhost:9000/minio/v2/metrics/cluster

Druid Middle Manager periodically ingests Kafka. It creates tasks internally

The task performs indexing, creates segments in a distributed node system, and writes to disk on each node.

export MINIO_PROMETHEUS_AUTH_TYPE="public"

./minio server /mnt/data --console-address ":9001"

./mc alias set myminio http://192.168.244.146:9000 minioadmin minioadmin

./mc admin prometheus generate myminio

Here's how to configure S3 in Druid:

```
druid.storage.type=s3
druid.storage.bucket=druidbucket
druid.storage.baseKey=druid/segments
druid.s3.accessKey=
druid.s3.secretKey=
druid.s3.protocol=http
druid.s3.enabePathStyleAccess=true
druid.s3.endpoint.signingRegion=us-east-1
druid.s3.endpoint.url=http://127.0.0.1:9000
```

Druid can collect metrics using the Prometheus exporter.

9.2.6.2. Logs

Druid logs should also be collected. Druid is divided into system logs and user logs. System logs generated by Druid components configured like various microservices should be collected and log levels should be adjusted for detailed debugging and troubleshooting. In addition to that, the read path generates additional user logs, which should be collected by enabling plans and request logging.

CHAPTER 9 AGGREGATE RCA DATA

- Plans

- Request logging

```
2023-04-28T12:36:04.888Z 127.0.0.1 {"queryType":"segmentMetadata","dataSource":{"type":"table","name":"wikipedia"},"intervals":{"type":"segments","segments":[{"itvl":"2016-06-27T00:00:00.000Z/2016-06-28T00:00:00.000Z","ver":"2023-04-18T07:19:37.853Z ","part":0}]},"toInclude":{"type":"all"},"merge":false,"context":{"defaultTimeout":300000,"finalize":false,"maxQueuedBytes":5242880,"maxScatterGatherBytes":9223372036854775807,"queryFailTime":1682685664681,"queryId":"6e0ee9e7-421d-449e-bd63-18a57f1eb1f1","timeout":299818},"analysisTypes":[],"usingDefaultInterval":false,"lenientAggregatorMerge":false,"granularity":{"type":"all"}}    {"query/time":244,"query/bytes":1237,"success":true,"identity":"allowAll"}
2023-04-28T12:36:04.631Z {"queryType":"segmentMetadata","dataSource":{"type":"table","name":"wikipedia"},"intervals":{"type":"segments","segments":[{"itvl":"2016-06-27T00:00:00.000Z/2016-06-28T00:00:00.000Z","ver":"2023-04-18T07:19:37.853Z","part":0}]},"toInclude":{"type":"all"},"merge":false,"context":{"queryId":"6e0ee9e7-421d-449e-bd63-18a57f1eb1f1"},"analysisTypes":[],"usingDefaultInterval":false,"lenientAggregatorMerge":false,"granularity":{"type":"all"}}    {"query/time":558,"query/bytes":-1,"success":true,"identity":"allowAll"}
2023-04-28T12:36:13.403Z
```

Druid metadata contains information about the schema, not the execution of the query.

The metric has no information about what queries were executed, so you can't find specific queries that are performing poorly.

Most databases provide plans to extract information from slow queries. In some cases, this is not appropriate to provide as a metric, and plans are more useful.

Druid can export plans. Since plans are created as files, it is necessary to preprocess the contents of the file. TSV and CSV files can be obtained with OpenSearch and analyzed quickly and easily. You need to analyze the query duration, query parameter, query type, and cache hits. Measure the time it took to process the query and print out the query that took the longest time.

To analyze logs, I recommend OpenSearch over Loki. OpenSearch automatically creates indexes for you, so you can quickly analyze text like logs. Loki is relatively lacking in aggregation features.

Slow queries and per-query latency should be logged.

The Druid service can also log the query requests it processes. The request log contains information. You can use the error information in the request log to monitor performance and identify bottlenecks. Logging is disabled by default.

Logging can be done in a variety of ways, such as transferring it to another web server or writing it to a local file.

9.2.6.3. Trace

The trace provides data to help you understand the internal processes and latency.

CHAPTER 9   AGGREGATE RCA DATA

A Druid application works like many microservices, consisting of multiple components. Druid components are clearly separated into processes. Druid uses Jetty internally. You can use trace to analyze latency between microservices at the Jetty WebServer level. OpenTelemetry allows for instrumentation, but is not very helpful for troubleshooting failures.

Druid provides a variety of metrics and logs, and profiles can fill in the gaps. It is useful to use profiles rather than traces to improve Druid's performance.

When building a system with unfamiliar and poorly documented open source, the main task is to improve performance. Since Druid is a package and a predeveloped open source, you don't need to modify much of the source itself. For example, it's not very common to encounter bad memory leaks or slow performance due to unoptimized operations. It is possible to improve performance by modifying parameters, and finding the optimal parameters is difficult.

Without knowing the internal structure, it is difficult to understand the meaning of many parameters in the configuration file, which often leads to misbehavior in complex cluster configurations. Profiles are the most powerful way to analyze your application. They are already stable and open source, so they don't have many bugs. However, traces and profiles are useful for understanding and troubleshooting problems that arise when changing configuration files.

Use -D to enable JMX. Incorrect instrumentation can lead to incorrect profiles.

- Understand the order and internals of the method process when instrumentation goes wrong and problems with signals occur.
- Errors occurred in an unknown method or dependency.
- Compare performance and differences at the method level before and after parameter changes.
- Flame graphs alone are not enough to solve the problem; use profiles such as VisualVM.

```
# vi jvm.config
total 12
-rw-r--r--. 1 501 games 231 Dec 22 2022 jvm.config
-rw-r--r--. 1 501 games 40 Dec 22 2022 main.config
-rw-r--r--. 1 501 games 1286 Dec 22 2022 runtime.properties

-server
-Xms4g
-Xmx4g
-XX:MaxDirectMemorySize=8g
-XX:+ExitOnOutOfMemoryError
-XX:+UseG1GC
-Duser.timezone=UTC
-Dfile.encodin g=UTF-8
-Djava.io.tmpdir=var/tmp
```

```
-Djava.util.logging.manager=org.apache.logging.log4j.jul.LogManager
-javaagent:/root/Downloads/opentelemetry-javaagent.jar
-Dotel.traces.exporter=jaeger
-Dotel.resource.attributes=service.name=historical
```

Since Druid is open source and provides code, configuring remote debugging in conjunction with your development tools is a great way to understand its internals.

9.2.6.4. Profiles

This section briefly describes Flame graph profiles.

Continuous profiles minimize overhead, but you can collect and analyze profiles for a while without running them all the time like a daemon agent.

For Java, the result of profile is a stack trace. They can affect running services. You need to obtain stack traces without overhead.

Operators don't agree on what configures an agent. Commercial observability agents do not open overhead data, so there is nothing to explain the internal overhead to operators.

It is possible to configure the application itself like Pyroscope to output flame graphs, but if your infrastructure team and application staff do not allow a profile, or if your situation does not allow it, I recommend using a short-term utility like the one shown here:

```
sudo -u aws jcmd

sudo -u aws java -jar sjk.jar stcap -p 11745 -o druid-${pid}.std -t 30s -i 50ms

# java -jar sjk.jar stcap -p 7534 -o druid-${pid}.std -t 30s -i 50ms
Restarting java with unlocked package access
Writing to /root/druid-NNN.std
Collected 600
Collected 1080
Collected 1560
Collected 69000
Collected 69600
trace dumped: 69600

sudo -u aws java -jar sjk.jar flame -f druid-NNN.std -o druid-flame-${pid}.html

# java -jar sjk.jar flame -f druid-NNN.std -o druid-flame-${pid}.html
Restarting java with unlocked package access
Input files
  ./druid-NNN.std

69600 samples processed
```

CHAPTER 9   AGGREGATE RCA DATA

Since Druid is developed in Java, you can utilize Java Mission Control and VisualVM to get a more detailed understanding of the system's internal structure.

In Kubernetes, you must use the Druid operator to operate. Clusters consisting of microservices running on Kubernetes are difficult to operate. Non-disruptive rolling updates, version upgrades, and system patches require restarting the cluster and delivering services as non-disruptively as possible. Without operators, managing these complex operations is difficult and prone to failure.

9.3. Java Observability

The kernel interacts directly with all system resources, including CPU, memory, disk, and network. It's important to understand the load, and I split the load into CPU and IO. These principles apply equally well in Java.

Class loading, bytecode, and JIT compilers are important in the Java virtual machine, but I'll talk more about profiles, threads, coroutines that fit the observability theme.

There are two situations where profiles are useful:

- You don't understand the internal structure, so analysis is required.

    1. Understanding the order and methods that are processed, such as the call tree and stack trace, duration, thread status.

    2. Instrumenting the wrong method,

    3. Understanding the method that causes latency, waiting time, and self time.

- You understand the internal structure, but you want to dig deeper. You can perform root cause analysis with detailed profiles such as memory, locks, SQL slow queries, number of calls per method, 95th percentile latency per method, and stack counts.

In the process of root cause analysis, the kernel and its various system utilities and overheads were explained. Java is described in a similar approach, but with a more limited focus on CPU using profiles. Once you understand the CPU profile approach, you can apply the same to various system resources, such as memory, locks, JDBC, and IO.

Presto only exists to read, but Druid requires both reading and writing. Compared to Presto, Druid is more complex and difficult. Java observability is better suited to the complexity of Druid. To troubleshoot the internal problems of a complex Java application like Druid, you need to understand how to debug and profile Druid within Java. The goal is to understand the approach to how to profile a Java application. When you adopt open source and encounter a lower level problem or bug, you need to profile and debug to solve it. If you can't solve it, you need to introduce managed services or work around the failure.

Druid metrics contain information about internal processes per component and provide detailed information. You need to understand the internal structure. Log and trace don't help you understand the internal structure. This situation is most often encountered when customizing and using open source.

Even if you adjust the log level, it will output limited information. Since Druid doesn't require any development, the logs you add only include system logs, not user logs. When running an open source like Druid, it is useful to focus on metrics and profiles.

It is difficult to debug at the system resource level with metrics alone, but metrics can help you determine whether a problem is internal or external to Druid. Debugging the code directly from scratch is time-consuming, so you can profile it before debugging to get a rough understanding. System resource problems require a profile.

Different types of systems require different signals. For example:

- Microservices start with metrics and traces.

- Black box and legacy systems use logs.

- Open source options start with metrics and profiles.

- The database starts with metrics and traces and analyzes the plan.

To analyze the internals of an open source, you need to understand the lower level resources. Since trace is application level, it is not suitable for analyzing lower levels system resource.

To summarize, you should know the difference between sampling, profiles, and dumps, and use them appropriately.

If you use profiles without defining dependencies, the overhead is high. That's why I prioritize sampling. The call tree from sampling is useful, but depending on the profile, the number of calls and latency may not be output. Profiles can be used for detailed analysis when sampling is insufficient. If your application hangs or is in an unserviceable state, you should create and analyze multiple dumps. The stack traces in the dumps output the state of the threads, which can help you understand the problem. The open source profiles provide useful plugin features, such as adding real-time bytecode instrumentation to your code, but they are limited in functionality. For advanced network and NoSQL analysis, you'll need to purchase a commercial profile.

9.3.1. Java CPU Profile

Due to the overhead of analyzing the Linux kernel runtime, I used KUtrace and eBPF.

The same situation occurs in Java. Gathering detailed internal data or profiling frequently called methods has a large overhead.

- No matter how low overhead a method is, if it is called a lot, it will incur overhead. You should measure how many times the method you want to monitor is called—for example using funccount in eBPF—and then decide whether to sample it.

- The stack trace is detailed, but using thread dumps to extract the stack trace adds latency to the application due to overhead.

Existing profiles provide more detail than new observabilities because they are language-specific and have been refined over time.

CHAPTER 9   AGGREGATE RCA DATA

Druid is difficult to tune and has a complex architecture. Druid has a number of internal components, but the clusters it is configured with are diverse and complex. You need to understand and work with other clusters and their IO, including Redis, Kafka, and object storage. You'll also need to manage distributed configuration information using metadata and zookeepers.

Print the Java process in the Druid. You can check the settings for Java parameters, as shown in Figure 9-8.

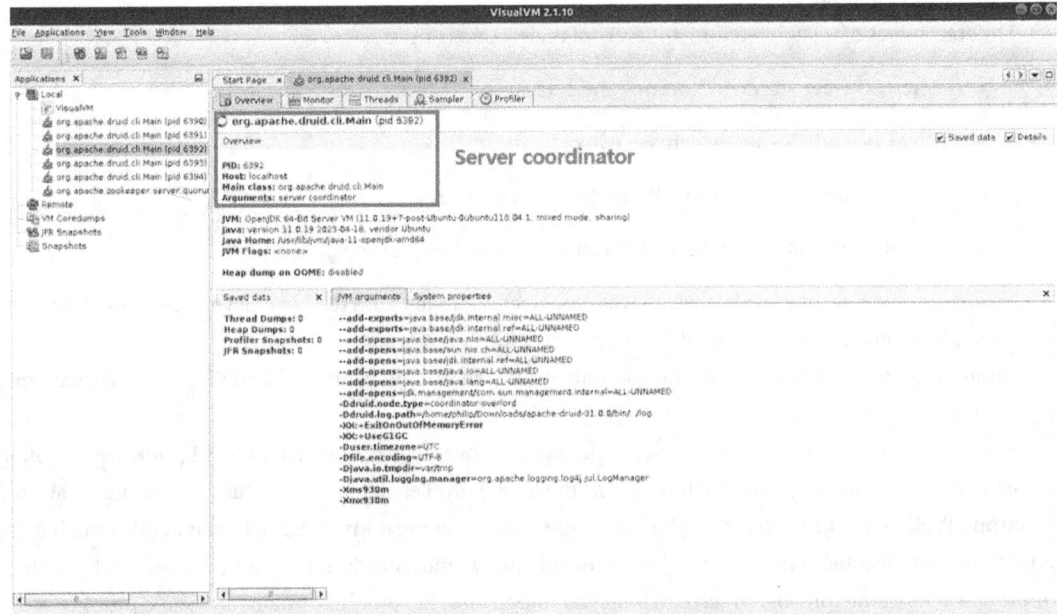

Figure 9-8. *Parameters of a Java process*

Sampling is a way to understand the code that your application runs. With a rough understanding of what's going on inside the application, you should use a profile to see if further analysis is needed. For this reason, sampling is always utilized prior to profiling an application and is often sufficient on its own.

Sampling happens in two steps:

- By sampling, you can understand what code is running and which parts need to be analyzed in more detail. Profiling is a resource-intensive process. If the overhead of profiling the entire code is too high, before you do a profile, you should filter the packages and classes you want to focus your investigation on. The execution first will give you a good idea about which parts of your application to focus on.

- Once sampling is complete, you can determine if a profile is needed, and if so, use it to get more information about the execution of a particular piece of code.

You can profile to get more information about the execution. But before you can do that, you need to know which parts of the code to profile,

672

CHAPTER 9   AGGREGATE RCA DATA

The advantage of sampling is that it provides more detailed information with lower overhead than profiling, so it is useful to use sampling to understand the problem before profiling, and finally profile if the problem cannot be solved by sampling.

This outputs information about the CPU, heap, threads, and garbage collection of the Java processes in the Druid. See Figure 9-9.

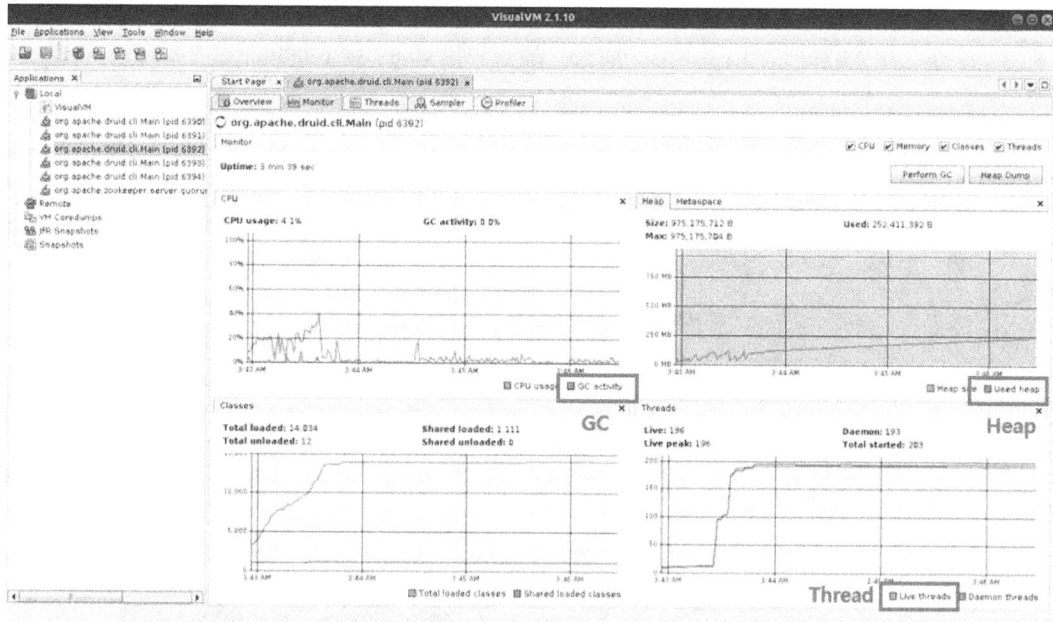

Figure 9-9.   Monitoring CPU and memory

Sampling is observing an application as it uses system resources. You can find problems by VisualVM, such as memory leaks and zombie threads.

Zombie threads that remain running after the application finishes executing, consuming system resources, but the threads they created are still running. These threads are called *zombie threads* because they don't do anything and remain running. They are just using CPU resources.

There are many inferences that can be made from just looking at resource usage. VisualVM also shows the amount of CPU resources used by the garbage collector.

- The CPU usage of garbage collection can help you understand your application's memory allocation problems. If garbage collection is taking up an unusually large amount of CPU resources, you should suspect a memory leak. This is because full garbage collection consumes most of the CPU resources.

- If you notice that your garbage collection is not using any CPU resources, and your application is consuming a lot of processing power but not processing anything, this is usually a sign of zombie threads, which is the result of a concurrency problem.

673

CHAPTER 9 AGGREGATE RCA DATA

- It is using very little memory. This also means that the application is not doing anything. Concurrency is likely the root of the problem. There's no garbage collection happening

It is important to use VisualVM to visually understand how threads are running. A chart of threads, as shown in Figure 9-10, is similar to the Grafana state timeline chart already described. The state timeline chart does not just show the degree of change in a time series, but represents a change in state. In most cases, this will give you clues as to which threads you should be concerned about.

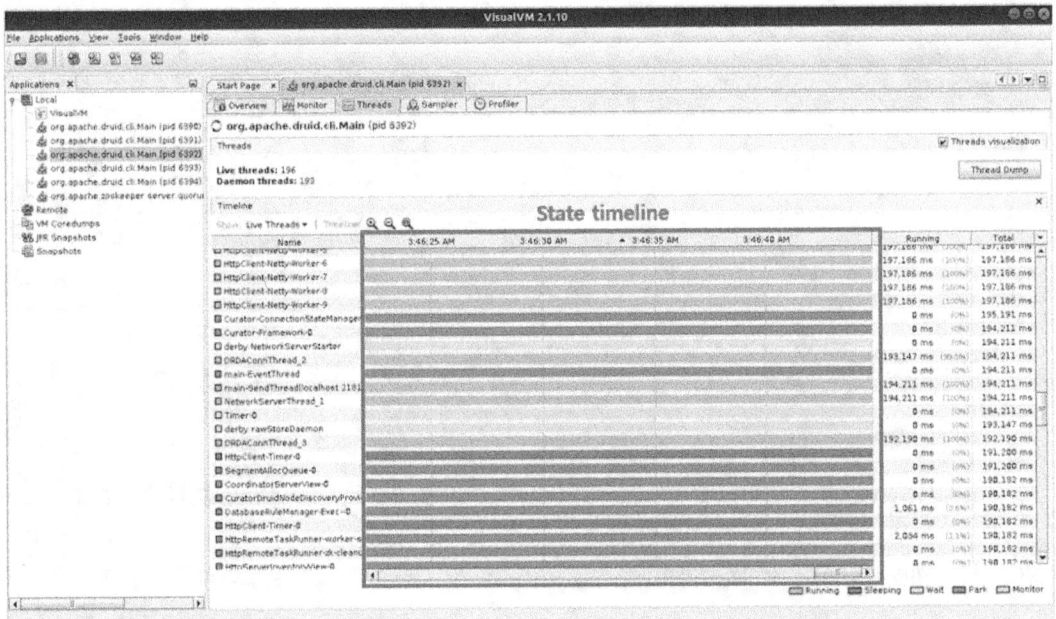

Figure 9-10. Monitoring thread status

Understanding the problem of resource consumption is important. You need to be able to quickly distinguish and understand correct application behavior from anomalous behavior.

I gave each thread a name. The names `Thread-0` and `Thread-1` given to each thread by the JVM are not very helpful in identifying them. It is better to name the threads so that you can identify them as soon as possible.

If you have a synchronization block, you'll notice that it interrupts execution from time to time to ensure that only one thread is running at a time.

- Threads are marked as not running continuously, blocked, waiting, or asleep.
- Threads can also run concurrently; if they're shaded at the same time, they're running concurrently.

Garbage collection tries to delete unused data from memory, but if there's not enough space to store new data, it throws an OOM error.

CHAPTER 9   AGGREGATE RCA DATA

The OOM error stack trace doesn't necessarily point to the code causing the problem. Since there is only one heap memory space allocated to the application, any thread can cause problems. There may be some unlucky threads that were the last to try to claim the memory space and got an error.

If you look at a healthy application with no memory leaks, you can see that the graph goes up and down. The application is allocated the memory it needs, the garbage collector deletes unnecessary data, and so on. You can understand that the increase and decrease in memory is not being affected by memory leaks.

However, if the memory is filling up and the garbage collector doesn't seem to be cleaning it up, you may have a memory leak. If you suspect a memory leak, you should continue to investigate further by watching the dump.

The sampling provides four essential details:

- **Executed methods:** When investigating a problem, sometimes you don't know which parts of your code are executed, and sampling can help you determine that. By sampling, you can see what code is running in the background. This helps you determine which parts of your application to investigate.

- **The total duration of the method:** This information can give you an idea of which parts of your code are causing potential latency problems. You can understand the latency for each method.

- **CPU time:** This tells you if the code is waiting for something.

- **Understand memory consumption:** Analyze the problems related to memory.

In VisualVM, click the CPU button to start sampling, and you will see a list of all the threads and their stack traces. VisualVM intercepts the execution of the process, showing all called methods and their approximate duration (see Figure 9-11).

Sampling can give you clues when you don't know where to start debugging.

675

CHAPTER 9 AGGREGATE RCA DATA

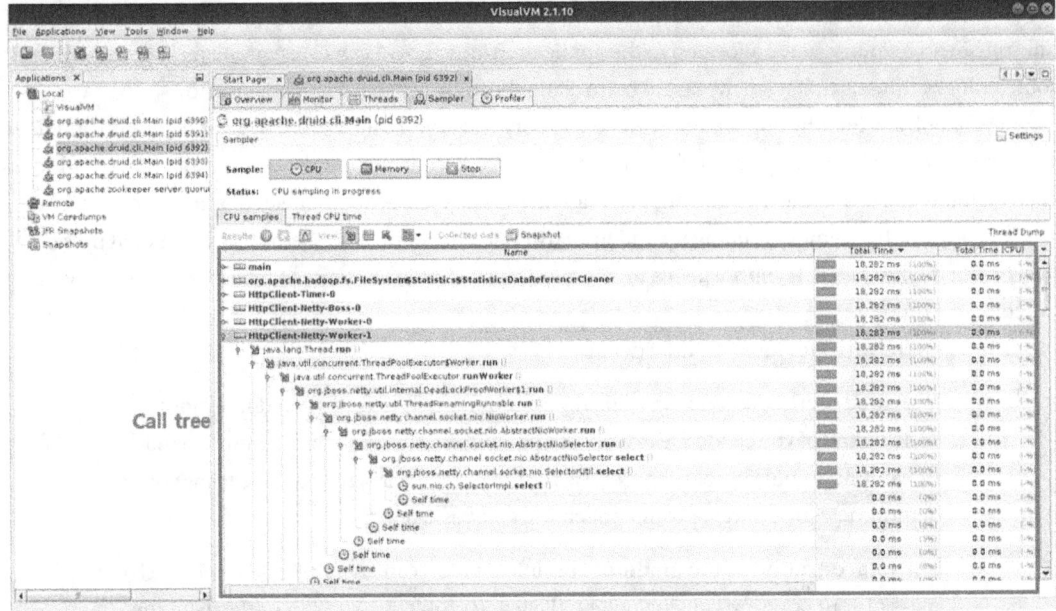

Figure 9-11. Duration by method

To start debugging, you need to decide where to take your breakpoints. By sampling before debugging, you can identify the points in your code that need to be debugged.

This displays all the stack traces that your application has executed. You can use the stack trace to find out what code your application has executed and if it has a long duration.

The stack trace displays all methods and the sub-methods they call in layers, so you can quickly find the code you're looking for when investigating a particular feature.

Let's take a look at the stack trace to see what information it provides. You can easily see what code is being executed by expanding the stack trace until you get to the method you want to investigate. When investigating the cause of latency, you can expand the stack trace to see the maximum duration.

CPU time and duration should be clearly distinguished. If a method consumes CPU time, it means that it is working. If a method consumes very little CPU time but has a long duration, it's likely that the method is waiting for something. Without doing anything, you need to figure out what your application is waiting for.

If the duration is CPU, IO time, and other latency, you can subtract the CPU time from the duration that VisualVM outputs to get an idea of the other latency, including the IO (see Figure 9-12).

If you expand the stack trace, you can see which methods have been running, and for how long. It shows the time spent per method call. Based on this, you can determine what caused your application to slow down.

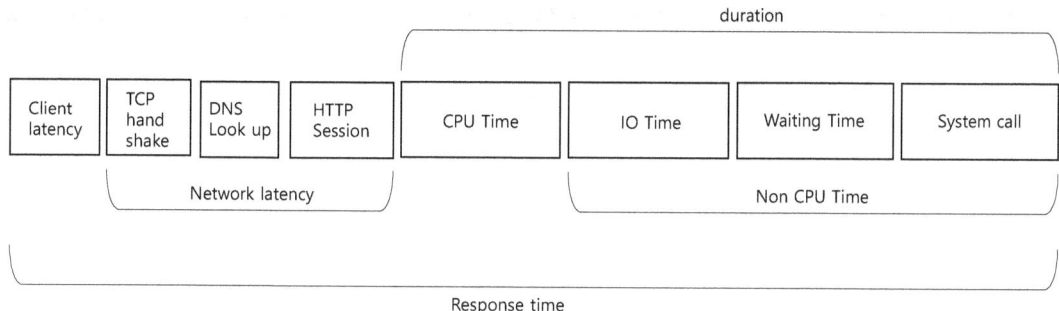

Figure 9-12. Measuring various latency types

It is important to understand and distinguish various times in detail, such as response time, duration, CPU time, and IO time. In this book, duration terms have been used as much as possible to reduce confusion.

If the CPU time is 0, it means that the application spent time waiting for something without doing anything.

Sometimes it's not enough to know what code is being executed. To really understand the logic, you need more information. Sampling doesn't tell you how many times a method is called.

When profiling an application, you should analyze only the parts that you need to investigate, instead of examining the entire code. Profiling is a resource-intensive task, and it will take an enormous amount of time.

Referencing the entire code of an application is a huge waste of time and resources. When profiling a large application, you should limit the scope of the code you intercept as much as possible (see Figure 9-13).

You should always profile against a small number of packages and define a filter for which classes to profile before you profile.

The thread state of the stack trace, variables during debugging, and methods in the profile all provide important data for understanding internal operations.

When the application is executed, all methods are called in the dependency. The application implements abstractions, so the problem that occurs in the package with dependencies cannot be understood just by looking at the code. The profile must be used at runtime.

Profiles are not commonly used in production. For this reason, I use JMC, which has better profile capabilities and is less demanding on the application.

JFR is a monitoring and event-based information gathering framework built into hotspot virtual machines. VisualVM also supports JFR. Oracle emphasizes its always-on capabilities. In production, the impact of JRF on throughput is less than 1 percent, sometimes described as *zero performance overhead*. In addition, the JFR monitoring process can be turned on and off at any time without restarting the application. The monitoring operation itself is also transparent to the application. No application code needs to be modified, and no specific agent needs to be running alongside it.

When an event occurs, all context data is stored in memory or in a specified file in the form of a log, so only data from recent events is available. JMC reads event data from memory or files to analyze performance.

CHAPTER 9 AGGREGATE RCA DATA

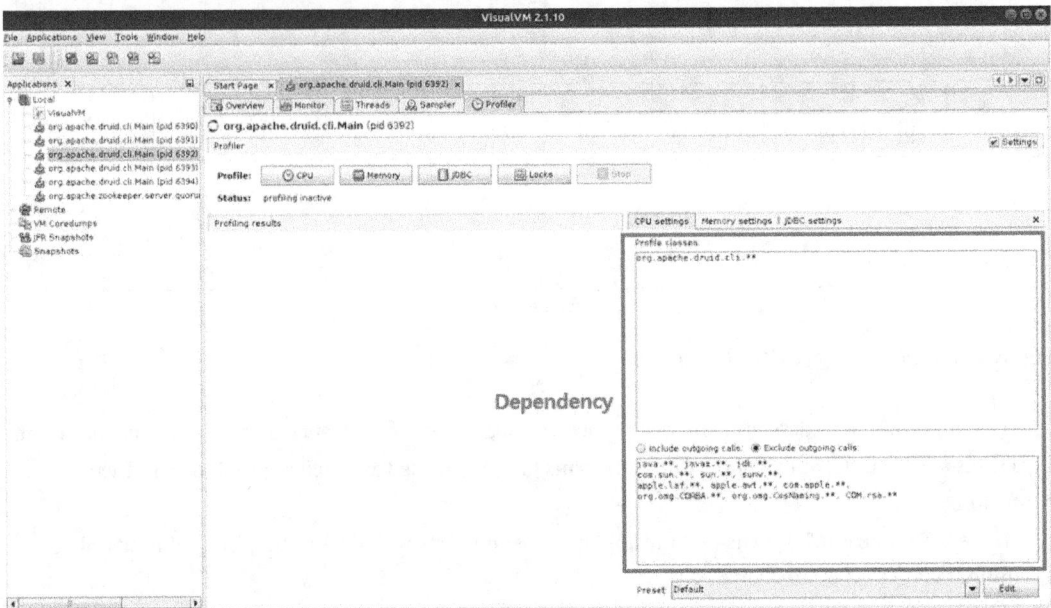

Figure 9-13. *The profile of CPU, memory, queries, and locks*

An unnecessarily large number of calls in a profile can be a problem. It is necessary to improve by looking at the number of calls and the latency per call together. This is because even if the latency is large, if it is only called once, it may be given a low priority.

You can intercept queries before your application sends them to the database, so you can understand what queries are executed on the database.

To compute slow queries, you preprocess the plan logs, which are automatically output by profile (see Figure 9-14).

CHAPTER 9 AGGREGATE RCA DATA

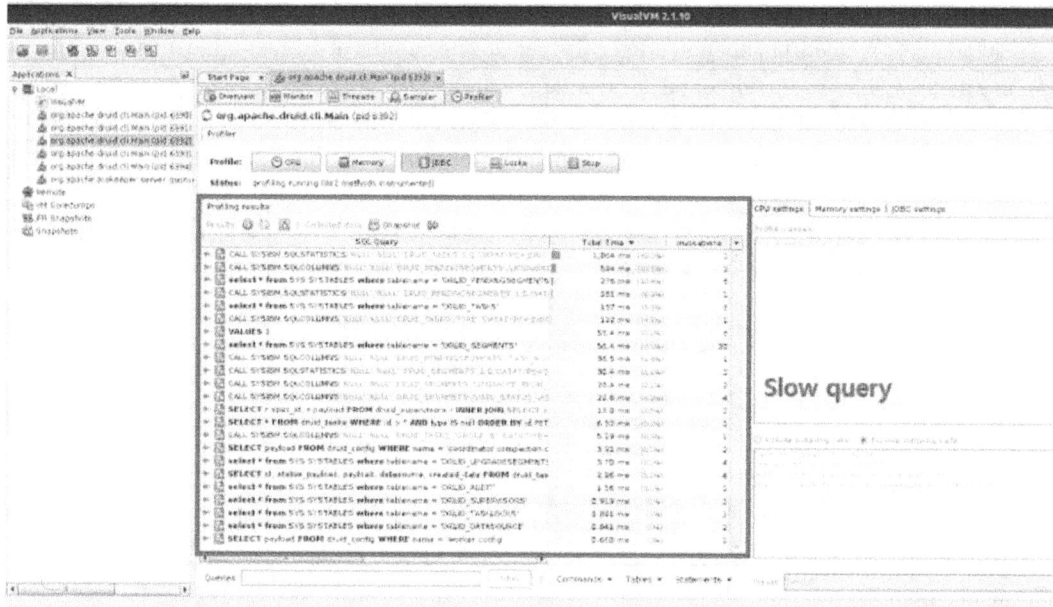

Figure 9-14. Query-specific duration

Profiles provide useful functionality for your network. When you call the HTTP endpoint:

- You can see that a three-way handshake occurs on the socket, and after the connection is established, and various events occur, such as receiving.

- DNS lookup occurs.

- HTTPS adds interactivity depending on how you authenticate.

It would be nice to have this information in a trace context, but it is not supported by automated instrumentation. Using profiles will help you monitor events occurring in Layers 3, 4, and 7 and help you understand the problem.

You should be able to identify whether the problem is in the application or, if it's a network issue, at what layer. Importantly, you should be able to analyze alongside the application to identify the scope and location of the problem. When infrastructure, applications and networks are separated, monitoring is difficult, and troubleshooting takes time.

Plans, thread dumps, and memory dumps are helpful for root cause analysis, although they are complex and only experienced SREs can understand them. Profiles provide visualization of the results and make it easier to understand the meaning.

Most developers try to use logs or a debugger to investigate these problems. The downside of using logs to investigate this kind of problem is that it's hard to identify which query is the problem in the first place. In a real-world scenario, an application requests all kinds of queries, some of which are made to the database multiple times, and most of them are long and have many parameters. With profiles, you can see all the queries and quickly find the problem by looking at the duration and number of times.

CHAPTER 9 AGGREGATE RCA DATA

The detail you can get from a profile is the number of times a method is called. Sampling gives you the total duration of a method, but not how often it was called. The number of calls is important information for spotting methods that are too slow or being misused.

SREs who understand the code will agree that profiles are more important than SREs who don't know the code. The more you know, the better you can identify problems. Stack traces and call trees are great for finding inefficient code.

While the stack trace is good because it is presented in intuitive text, it is not sufficient for quickly understanding the relationship between objects and method calls. The call tree focuses on the relationship between objects and method calls.

Profiles analyze the lock and view the thread information:

- Which threads lock other threads
- Number of times a thread is locked
- The amount of time a thread was interrupted without running

It is also possible that the method is not waiting for something else. Self time refers to the duration of the method itself.

If the self time is greater than the total CPU time, the thread is likely locked by another thread. You should analyze the number of locks, their latency, and the relationship between the locked thread and the thread that caused the lock.

If the method appears to be waiting on itself, rather than waiting for something external, the thread is likely locked. To find out why the thread is locked, you need to further profile and analyze the execution of your application.

Thread A waits for Thread B to do something, and Thread B waits for Thread A to do something, and so on, and never executes. When this happens, the application freezes.

Since a deadlock can cause the process to completely freeze, you can't use sampling or profiling techniques. You can investigate by collecting a thread dump, which records all threads for a particular JVM process and statistics about their state.

CHAPTER 9 AGGREGATE RCA DATA

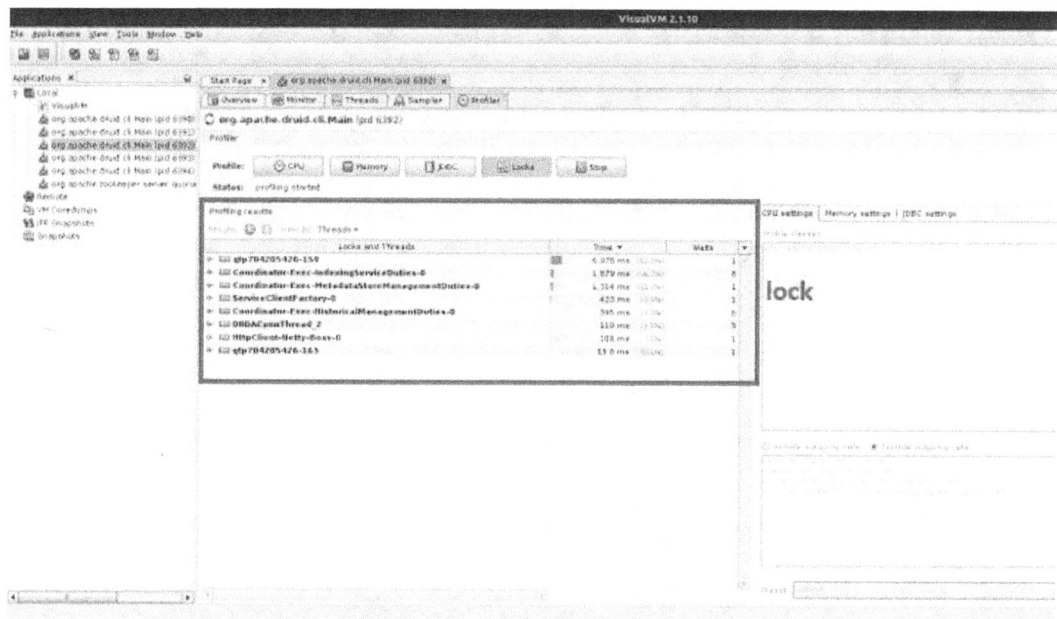

Figure 9-15. *Contents of a per-thread lock*

Instead of analyzing locks during execution, if you want to analyze the thread state of your application, you can get a thread dump and read it, which will tell you which threads affected each other and caused the application to freeze (see Figure 9-15).

Thread dumps can be obtained by using a profile like VisualVM or by calling the JDK built-in tools directly from the command line (see Figure 9-16).

CHAPTER 9　AGGREGATE RCA DATA

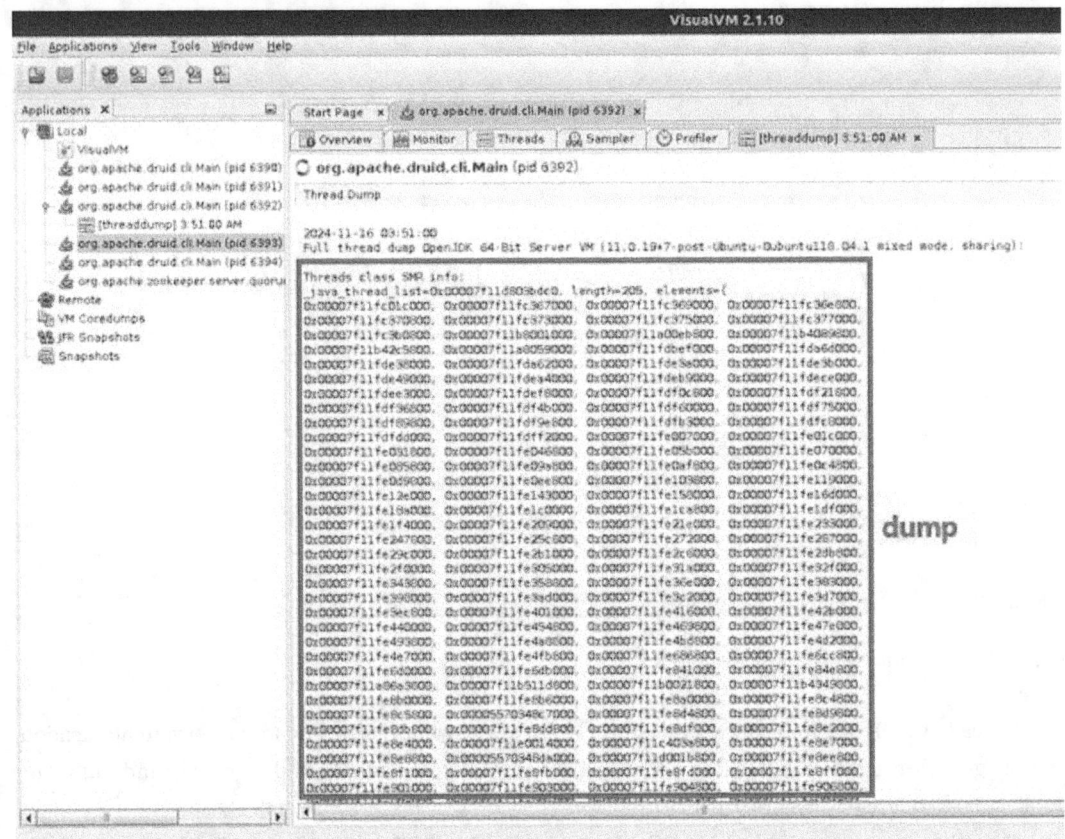

Figure 9-16. Thread dump

Since Java threads are wrappers of kernel threads, you can find out which kernel threads are running in the background. Once you've identified the thread, you need to analyze the details you're interested in, and a thread dump can give you three pieces of information: thread priority, CPU time, and total time. The OS assigns a priority to each thread it is running. If the thread dump shows that the thread priority assigned by the OS is low, meaning that the thread hasn't done as much work as it should have, then the total will be much higher than the CPU time. The total indicates how long the thread was alive, while the CPU time indicates how well the thread was working.

Status descriptions are valuable information about what's happening to a thread. Status are named like Running, Waiting, and Blocked. Describe what state the thread is in at that point in time.

It is important to understand that a thread dump provides just as much detail as a lock profile. A lock profile shows the dynamic mechanics of execution. A thread dump is at a point in time, while a profile shows how parameters change during execution.

VisualVM provides a memory profile feature, which is the similar as a CPU profile. Druid and the Java framework have IO with the network and filesystem. When interacting frequently with files and networks in Java, Java NIO is heavily used. VisualVM provides plugins for IO and network profiles.

The advantage of VisualVM is that it offers a wide variety of plugins. For example, B trace uses the instrumentation of hotspot VM to dynamically insert debugging code that wasn't in the original code. This debugging code does not interfere with the behavior of the target program, which is very useful for running programs. The ability to dynamically insert debugging code is useful. Since it is processed at the nanosecond level, it is difficult to identify the exact method at runtime using only the stack trace and call tree. After modifying the source, view just the plugin without having to build and deploy it. You can identify exactly which method is running at the nanosecond level.

The call stack, parameters, and return value output are the most basic uses. Many plugins are available and easy to add.

9.3.2. The Java Virtual Machine

For computationally intensive workloads, the goal is to keep the CPU utilization of user space close to 100 percent. There should be plenty of resources available.

For example, vmstat shows the number of context switches that occurred, so running the vmstat command can show the real-time impact of context switches. If a process has a high rate of context switches despite low CPU utilization in the user space, it's likely that it's experiencing blocking, locks, or race conditions.

It is not possible to identify the cause based on vmstat output alone. It outputs the status of IO operations as is, so you can identify IO problems. However, to detect race conditions in real time, you need something like VisualVM, which shows the thread status of the executing process. The profile tool, which samples the stack and shows the blocking code, is also useful.

The hotspot JVM allocates memory to user space at startup. This eliminates the need for system calls to allocate memory. To process garbage collection, kernel space is rarely used. Garbage collection uses CPU resources in user space and does not affect the utilization of kernel space.

If a JVM process is using 100 percent of the CPU in user space, and vmstat shows a constant CPU utilization of 100 percent, but the utilization is being consumed in user space, you should analyze whether it is the JVM GC or user code that is consuming the CPU.

File IO is often a problem for overall system performance. For example, memory can be processed through virtual memory, but there is no equivalent for IO that developers can abstract away. You need to be able to identify how IO occurs in your application. If you have an application that is IO intensive on the host, you can analyze it with basic counters provided by tools like iostat.

The JVM provides an OS-independent execution environment. However, even the most basic services, such as thread scheduling (getting time information from the system clock), require access to the OS.

These features are implemented as native methods with the native keyword. Native methods are written in C, but can be accessed like any other Java method. The common interface to process this is called the Java native interface.

Figure 9-17 shows an easy example of getting the system time.

CHAPTER 9   AGGREGATE RCA DATA

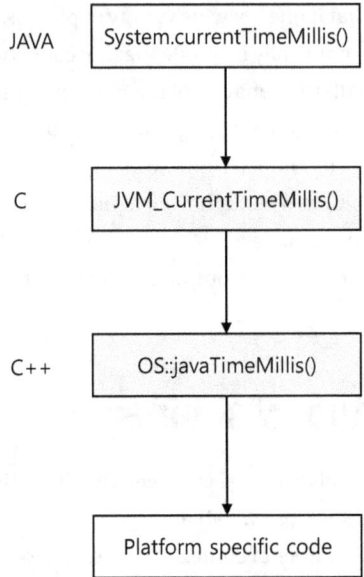

Figure 9-17. *The internal processes of a Java virtual machine*

The os:javaTimeMillis() method processes the logic implemented in the Java static System. currentTimeMillis() method. The actual code is written in C++, but it is accessible from Java via a C code bridge. In the hotspot, the native method System.currentTimeMillis() is mapped to a JVM entry point method called JVM_CurrentTimeMillis(). This mapping relationship is set up in the JNI java.lang. System.registerNatives() included in the java/lang/System.c file.

JVM_CurrentTimeMillis() calls the method corresponding to the VM entry point. Although it is a C method, it is an exported C++ method that follows C calling conventions. This method is defined in the OS namespace and has OS dependencies. Although platform-independent, Java calls services provided by the underlying OS and hardware.

9.3.3. Coroutines

Synchronous calls are simple to understand and monitor. The problem is asynchronous, non-blocking callbacks.

9.3.3.1. Callbacks

In synchronous calling, the entire operation is processed in the thread that called the method, whereas in asynchronous calling, the processing of the operation is split into two parts.

- The first part is processed by the thread that calls the method.
- The second part is not processed in the thread that calls the method, but in another thread.

The second call is out of your scope of control, and only the caller knows what to do. In situations like this, callback methods are a necessary behavior.

In a callback method, the other module knows when to do something, so it needs to pass the information it knows to the other module via a callback method.

Complex asynchronous callback code requires careful attention to callback pitfalls. A way to combine the efficiency of asynchronous callbacks with the readability of synchronous callbacks is with coroutines.

9.3.3.2. Blocking

Blocking and non-blocking are used in programming to call methods. A blocking call is when a thread is suspended. In general, blocking is mostly IO related.

- The time it takes for the disk to complete one track seek input/output request is measured in ms.
- CPU clock frequencies have already reached the GHz level

When a thread performs these IO operations, it must relinquish control of the CPU to another thread while the IO process is running so that it can perform other tasks. When the IO operation is complete, the CPU control is returned to the thread so that it can continue to execute the next task. During the time between losing and regaining CPU control, the thread is blocked and paused.

Thread A is blocked with IO and paused, and the CPU is allocated to Thread B.

While Thread B is running, the OS allocates CPU back to Thread A when it sees that its IO work is complete. The OS must efficiently allocate CPU usage time between each thread to maximize the CPU's resources.

The problem is that motivated is blocked, and unmotivated is complicated.

- Compared to blocking synchronous calls, you can see that writing code for asynchronous IO is not intuitive.
- IO operations are so slow that synchronous calls threads to block.

A way to start an IO operation without pausing the calling thread is to use non-blocking.

9.3.3.3. epoll

In Linux, everything is treated as a file. Programs all use file descriptors to perform IO operations. How do you process multiple file descriptors at the same time?

It's not a good idea to process each file descriptor sequentially. The OS manages the directives and passes them to the application. Instead, the OS watches a number of socket file descriptors on behalf of the application, and when data comes in, the OS passes the available file descriptors to the application. This is called IO multiplexing, and Linux uses epoll.

9.3.3.4. Coroutines

When a coroutine suspends itself, it saves its running state and resumes from the saved state to continue running.

In fact, the kernel space can pause a program at any part of the code. However, there is no behavior for timer interrupts in user space, so developers must explicitly specify in their coroutines where they want to pause and relinquish resources from the CPU using a reserved word like `yield`.

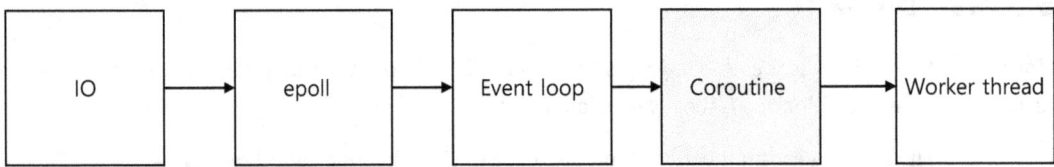

Figure 9-18. Coroutine-based non-blocking process

The worker thread processes without blocking (see Figure 9-18). If a coroutine is blocked due to RPC processing, the worker thread processes a new coroutine. Regardless of whether a coroutine is blocked or not, it should not be blocked in order to continue processing in the middle of an event loop or worker thread.

Isn't this similar to how the OS schedules threads? Threads can also be paused, and the OS will first save the thread's execution state before proceeding with the scheduling of other threads. The paused thread is then reallocated CPU resources, and the thread continues to run as if it had never been paused.

Because coroutines are implemented in user space, they can be interpreted as threads in user space. Developers can directly control when a coroutine runs and pauses.

The worker thread can be implemented in many ways; it can be a scheduler microservice message server.

The CPU detects the interrupt signal and executes the interrupt handling program inside the OS. The interrupt handling method determines if the process is ready to run, and if it is, the interrupted process continues to run. If not, the process is suspended, and the scheduler schedules another process that is ready.

Go provides goroutin, Kotlin provides coroutines, and Java provides virtual threads. In Java, virtual threads are not yet technically mature, so there are other alternatives to applying coroutines now.

Coroutines and worker threads may use different components, such as message servers, depending on the architect. Instead of using coroutines to be non-blocking, you can use message servers to be loosely coupled with the backend. An epoll receives the request from the frontend, and an event loop passes the request to the backend.

One of the important roles of coroutines is to enable asynchronous programming in a synchronous way. For example, WebFlux is a non-blocking development approach and has a high learning curve. This is because it requires a different development approach than traditional blocking. This is compared to non-blocking, virtual threads, which are similar to coroutines and are easier to learn and simpler to develop.

Once you enable virtual threads inside the Spring framework, no code changes are required. WebFlux, on the other hand, requires new learning and development.

The difference is that when a coroutine is paused, the worker thread is not blocked. This is the main difference between blocking with threads and coroutines.

When a coroutine is paused, the worker thread switches to run another coroutine that is ready, and when the service assigned to the paused coroutine responds and returns the results of its process, it is again ready and waiting for its turn at scheduling.

When another coroutine returns CPU control with an RPC request, the worker thread executes the other ready coroutine. Even if a coroutine makes an RPC call in a blocking manner, the worker thread is not blocked, thus achieving the goal of efficient use of system resources.

Similar to coroutines, non-blocking WebFlux is processed similarly. If your worker thread is a Reactor scheduler, and you use parallel threads, your worker thread will not be blocked by WebFlux. WebFlux is stable but has a high learning curve. Coroutines and virtual threads have a low learning curve, but Java's virtual threads are not yet stable. Whatever technology you use, it's important to configure your backend so that it doesn't block. From an observability perspective, WebFlux, virtual threads, and coroutines are still difficult to manage.

Kernel threads are created and scheduled by the kernel. The kernel allocates CPU computational resources based on thread prioritization. Coroutines are an unknown component to the kernel, and the kernel allocates CPU time according to threads regardless of how many coroutines are created. It can decide which coroutines to run within the time allocated to a thread, which is equivalent to allocating CPU time from user space. Because this allocation occurs in user space, coroutines are sometimes referred to as user threads.

9.3.4. Implementing Threads

There are two main ways to implement threads. You can use the kernel thread implementation, or you can use a user thread implementation.

9.3.4.1. Kernel Threads

Kernel threads are threads that are directly supported by the OS kernel, which is responsible for mapping the tasks of threads to their respective processes. This allows the OS to process multiple things at the same time.

Programs typically do not use kernel threads directly, but instead use lightweight processes, which are a high-level interface to kernel threads. Lightweight processes are what we usually call threads. Because each lightweight process relies on kernel threads, kernel threads must be supported before lightweight process can exist. The one-to-one relationship between lightweight processes and kernel threads is called the one-to-one threading model.

With the help of kernel threads, each lightweight process is scheduled as an independent unit. If one lightweight process is blocked by a system call, the entire process is not affected and continues to work.

CHAPTER 9   AGGREGATE RCA DATA

Lightweight processes have two limitations:

- First, because it is implemented based on kernel threads, various thread operations such as creation, destruction, and synchronization are performed by system calls. Since system calls involve switching between user space and kernel space, the execution cost is relatively high.

- Second, because one lightweight process maps to one kernel thread, lightweight processes consume a certain amount of kernel resources. Therefore, there is a limit to the number of lightweight processes a system can support.

9.3.4.2. User Threads

Since all threads can be viewed as a type of user thread unless they are kernel threads, lightweight processes are also user threads. However, lightweight processes are always kernel-based and rely on system calls for many of their operations, which means they are less efficient and don't have the benefits of user threads.

User threads point to thread libraries entirely in user space. Therefore, the kernel is unaware of the existence of user threads and how they are implemented. The creation, destruction, synchronization, and scheduling of user threads are all processed entirely in user space, without any help from the kernel. If implemented properly, there is no need to switch to kernel space at all.

Switching load on kernel threads is the cost of context saving and restoring. There are a number of cost-saving techniques that developers can try if they bring the context saving and restoring work to the developer.

Coroutines have the disadvantage that a lot of things have to be implemented at the developer level.

The advantage of user threads is that they don't require any support from the kernel, but the disadvantage is that they don't get any support from the kernel either. All thread creation, destruction, synchronization, scheduling must be processed by the user program.

User threads are difficult to implement well, but if done well, they can be effectively processed at low cost and high performance.

Recently, many new programming languages that claim to be highly concurrent are using user threads. This includes the Go language.

9.3.4.3. Java Threads

Java threads are mapped directly to kernel threads in the kernel, Therefore, the hotspot is not involved in the scheduling of the threads. The kernel takes care of that process—when to suspend or wake a thread, how much process time to allocate to a thread, and which process core to assign the thread to are all decisions made and performed by the kernel.

In preemptive scheduling, the duration of each thread is assigned by the system. Threads don't get to decide when to switch. The system can control thread duration, preventing a single thread from bringing a process or the entire system. Java uses preemptive scheduling.

The scheduling of Java threads is done automatically by the system, but you can advise the kernel to allocate more or less duration to a particular thread.

However, thread prioritization is not a very reliable method of coordination. Since Java threads in a JVM are mapped to kernel threads, it is the kernel that determines thread scheduling. kernel provide a concept of thread prioritization, but it doesn't necessarily match the prioritization of Java threads.

The Java virtual machine has traditionally adopted a one-to-one kernel thread model. The mapping of Java threads to kernel threads naturally leads to high switching and scheduling costs, and severely limits the number of threads the system can accommodate.

9.3.5. The Virtual Thread Demo

Virtual threads are cheap to context switch. Threads have a stack memory size of up to 2MB by default, so there is a lot of memory movement during context switches, and their creation requires communication with the kernel for scheduling, so they are not cheap to create because they use system calls. See Figure 9-19.

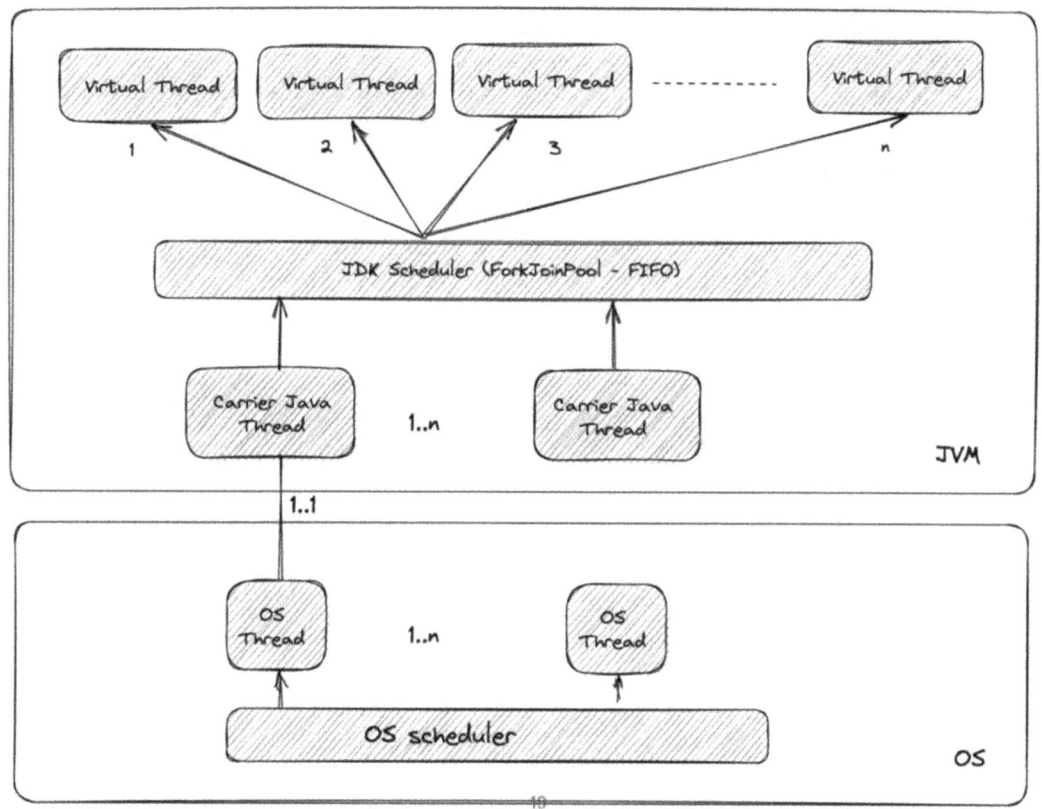

Figure 9-19. *The process of a virtual thread*

Java's traditional concurrency doesn't work well with microservices. Virtual machines use a one-to-one kernel thread model. As Java threads are mapped to kernel threads, context switches and scheduling costs increase and severely limit the number of threads the system can accommodate. In monolithic applications, the duration of a single request was relatively long and the cost of context switches was not significant. But now, the duration per request is very short and there are many of them. Eventually, the user context switch load approaches the load of the computation itself and becomes wasteful.

Traditional threadpools typically have a capacity of a few dozen to 200. When millions of requests are sent to these threadpools, the switch loss is significant, even if the system can process them.

The cost of scheduling a kernel thread is the cost of switching between user space and kernel space, which is primarily the cost of responding to interrupts and then storing and restoring execution information.

Virtual threads coexist with the traditional thread model and provide a new concurrency model. With the addition of virtual threads, Java's thread model has changed, as shown in Figure 9-19.

Virtual threads have an N:1 relationship with Java threads. If one virtual thread blocks, the Java thread continues the work of the other virtual threads it is attached to. In this way, kernel threads execute application code without context switches.

However, because virtual threads are created by the JVM, they make fewer calls to kernel regions such as system calls, and their memory size is only 1 percent of that of a regular thread, so they have a lower context switch cost than threads.

The virtual thread is referencing a Java thread, and when it runs, it is mounted on the Java thread and enqueued into the `ForkJoinPool` for scheduling. You can see this process through the profile.

The advantage of virtual threads is that the JVM can handle the scheduling of virtual threads on its own, reducing the cost of context switches and making them more efficient. However, there are cases when virtual threads are pinned to a Java thread and cannot take advantage of the benefits. There are two ways to do this: using synchronized within the virtual thread or using native methods via JNI.

The lifecycle and state changes of a virtual thread are shown in Figure 9-20.

CHAPTER 9 AGGREGATE RCA DATA

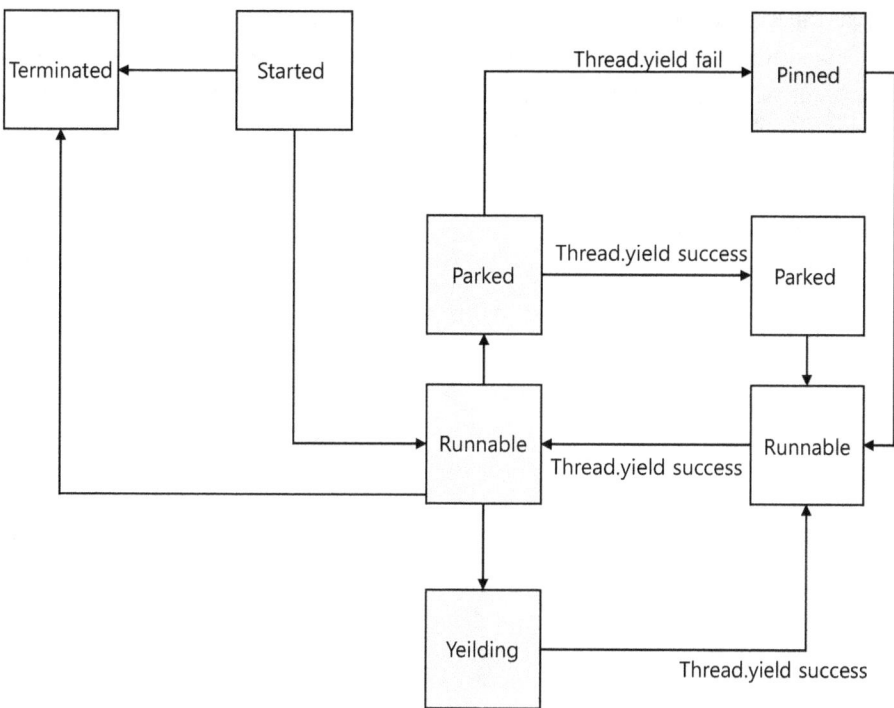

Figure 9-20. *The status of virtual threads*

In the profile, you can see that the thread's state changes, and it changes to PARKED.

Presto, Druid, Kafka, OpenSearch, and Hadoop are developed in Java and use NIO.

In the profile, you can isolate a virtual thread from other threads, determine the number of virtual thread calls it requests, and identify the stack trace.

Virtual threads are a challenging topic because the technology has gotten so far ahead in development that operations has been an afterthought, and it's not easy to monitor even basic threads with observability. Most commercial observability vendors are either developing or planning to develop virtual thread capabilities. If you are currently using virtual threads, you should use system utilities to monitor them, not observability. While Java is a mature technology, it is still improving, and commercial observability does not fully implement non-blocking, reactors, or virtual threads. It's a new technology, and we still need to wait.

9.3.5.1. Spring Boot Virtual Threads

For virtual threads to work, you need JDK 23, Spring Boot 3.2.

To use virtual threads in your application, add the following attributes to the application. properties file:

```
spring.threads.virtual.enabled=true
spring.threads.virtual.enabled.manually=false
```

CHAPTER 9 AGGREGATE RCA DATA

Note that virtual threads do not replace all standard threads. These settings are relevant for asynchronous work with Spring MVC and Spring WebFlux because the frameworks have been adapted for virtual threads. For example, they are used to process the @Async method when @EnableAsync is enabled.

The controller that received the request waits 300 milliseconds, then starts a simple application for Spring Boot 3.2 and Java 23 that provides the current thread ID.

```java
public class VirtualThreadController {
    private static final Logger LOGGER = LoggerFactory.getLogger(VirtualThreadController.class);
    public static final int SLEEP_TIME = 300;

    @GetMapping("/")
    public String getResponse(){
        try {
            TimeUnit.MILLISECONDS.sleep(SLEEP_TIME);
        } catch (InterruptedException e) {
            LOGGER.error(e.getMessage());
        }

        long threadId = Thread.currentThread().threadId() ;
        return String.valueOf(threadId);
    }
}
```

Create a request as shown here:

```
$ curl http://localhost:8080
```

If there is no request, no virtual thread is created, as shown in Figure 9-21.

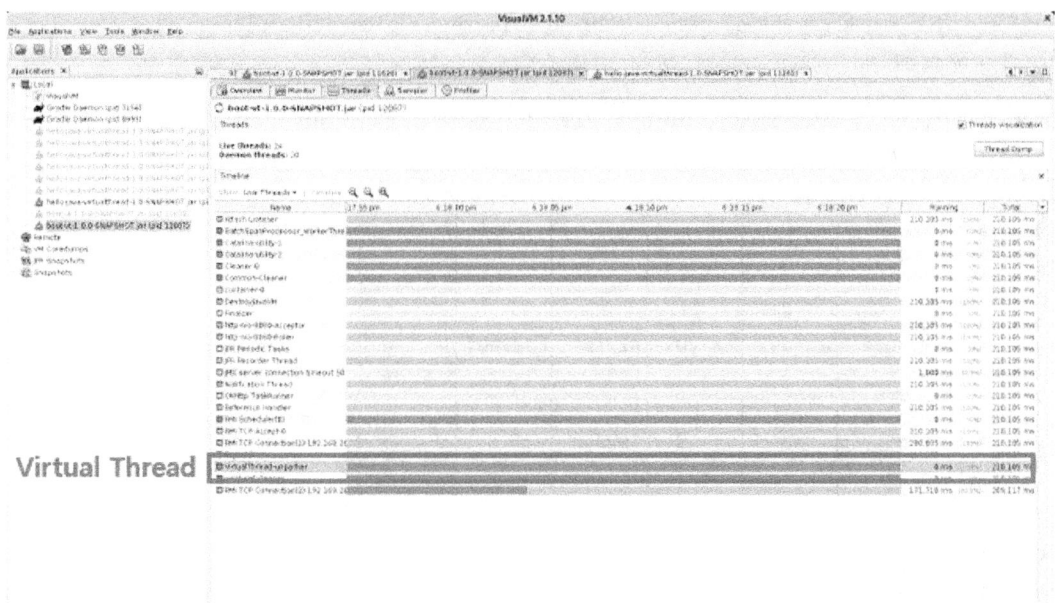

Figure 9-21. *The VirtualThread-unparker thread's profile*

As the request is processed, you can see the virtual thread being created. When you set up virtual threads in Spring Boot, you can see that the VirtualThread-unparker thread is configured, as shown in Figure 9-22.

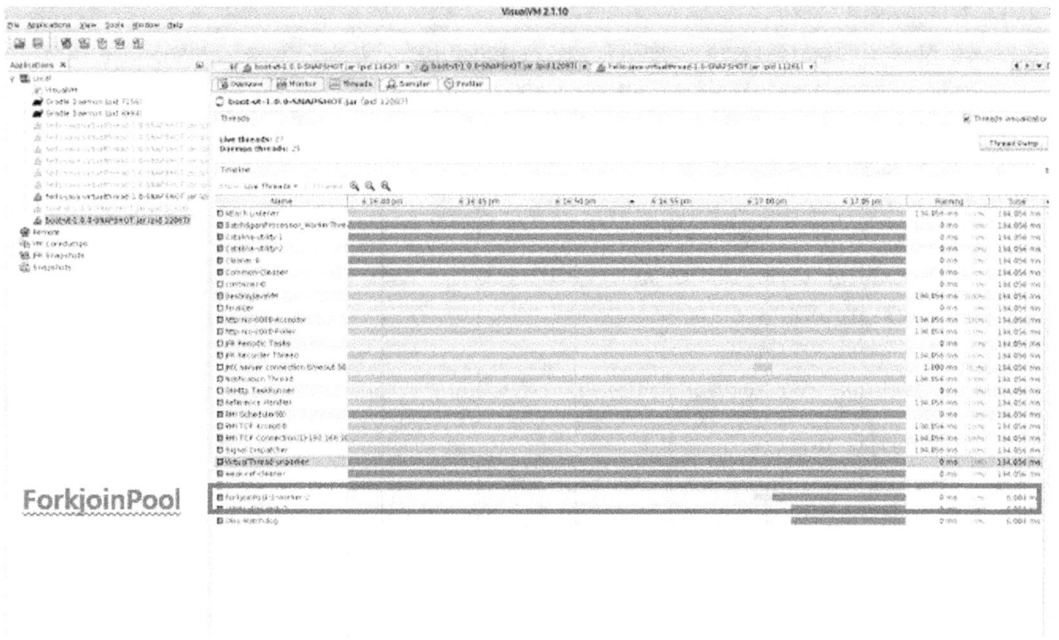

Figure 9-22. *Processing the ForkjoinPool-1-worker virtual thread*

CHAPTER 9 AGGREGATE RCA DATA

The virtual thread generates a trace. The thread on the server is `tomcat-handler-0`.

The results from OpenTelemetry are shown here:

```
2024-12-13T09:29:00.948+1100    info    traces {"kind": "exporter", "data_type": " traces",
"name": "debug", "resource spans": 1, "spans": 1}
2024-12-13T09:29:00.949+1100    info    ResourceSpans #0
Resource SchemaURL: https://opentelemetry.io/schemas/1.24.0
Resource attributes:
     -> host.arch: Str(amd64)
     -> host.name: Str(192-168-203-142.tpgi.com.au)

     -> telemetry.distro.version: Str(2.10.0)
     -> telemetry.sdk.language: Str(java)
     -> telemetry.sd k.name: Str(opentelemetry)
     -> telemetry.sdk.version: Str(1.44.1)
ScopeSpans #0
ScopeSpans SchemaURL:
InstrumentationScope io.opentelemetry.tomcat-10.0 2.10.0-alpha
Span #0
     trace ID : ca0f2be20b77d9dc8fba62aee5bdb05b
     Parent ID :
     ID: ef568b2aea3af748
     Name : GET /
     Kind : Server
     Start time : 2024-12-12 22:28:56.660791321 +0000 UTC
     End time : 2024-12-12 22:28:57.10500201 +0000 UTC
     Status code : Unset
     Status message :
Attributes:
     -> user_agent.original: Str(curl/7.76.1)
     -> network.peer.port: Int(37480)
     -> network.protocol.version: Str(1.1)
     -> url.scheme: Str(http)
     -> thread.name: Str(tomcat-handler-0)

     -> thread.id: Int(37)
     -> http.response.status_code: Int(200)
     -> http.route: Str(/)
     { "kind": "exporter", "data_type": " traces", "name": "debug"}
```

In Demo 1, you saw that Spring Boot virtual threads support profiles and traces.

9.3.5.2. Java Socket Virtual Threads

This section demonstrates a Java socket server and client.

The example consists of two classes. EchoServer is a server program that listens on a port and starts a new virtual thread for each connection. EchoClient is a client program that connects to the server and sends the typed message.

EchoServer responds to EchoClient with input over the socket. EchoClient reads and displays the data passed back from the server. EchoServer can serve multiple clients simultaneously, with one virtual thread for each client connection.

```java
int portNumber = Integer.parseInt(args[0]);
    try (ServerSocket serverSocket = new ServerSocket(portNumber)) {
        while (true) {
            Socket clientSocket = serverSocket.accept();

            Thread .ofVirtual().start(() -> {
                try (
                        PrintWriter out = new PrintWriter(clientSocket.
                        getOutputStream(), true);
                        BufferedReader in = new BufferedReader(new
                        InputStreamReader(clientSocket.getInputStream()));
                ) {
                    String inputLine;
                    while ((inputLine = in.readLine()) != null) {
                        out.println(inputLine);
                    }
                } catch (IOException e) {
                    e.printStack trace();
                }

            });

        }
    } catch (IOException e) {
        System.out.println("Exception caught when trying to listen on port "
        + portNumber + " or listening for a connection");
        e.printStack trace();
    }
}
```

The EchoClient creates a socket and connects to the EchoServer. It reads the user's input from the standard input stream, writes the text to the socket, and passes the text to the EchoServer.

CHAPTER 9   AGGREGATE RCA DATA

```
String hostName = args[0];
        int portNumber = Integer.parseInt(args[1]);
        try (
                Socket echoSocket = new Socket(hostName, portNumber);
                PrintWriter out =
                        new PrintWriter(echoSocket.getOutputStream(), true);
                BufferedReader in = =BufferedReader
                        new BufferedReader(
                                new InputStreamReader(echoSocket.getInputStream()));
        ) {
            BufferedReader stdIn = new BufferedReader(new InputStreamReader(System.in));
            String userInput;

            while ((userInput = stdIn.r eadLine()) != null) {
                out.println(userInput);
                System.out.println("echo: " + in.readLine());
                if (userInput.equals("bye")) break;
            }
        }
```

OpenTelemetry fails to instrument the socket. You can see that there are no spans being created. The server runs like this:

```
# /root/jfr-thread-pinning-spring-boot/jdk-23/bin/java -javaagent:/root/jfr-thread-pinning-spring-boot/target/opentelemetry-javaagent.jar -Dotel.service.name=virtualthread -Dotel.logs.exporter=none -Dotel.metrics.exporter=none -jar hello-java-virtualthread-1.0-SNAPSHOT.jar 1111
```

The client runs like this:

```
# /root/jfr-thread-pinning-spring-boot/jdk-23/bin/java -javaagent:/root/jfr-thread-pinning-spring-boot/target/opentelemetry-javaagent.jar -Dotel.service.name=client -Dotel.logs.exporter=none -Dotel.metrics.exporter=none -jar hello-java-virtualthread-2.0-SNAPSHOT.jar localhost 1111
```

The client and output the results as shown here:

```
1
echo: 1
2
echo: 2
```

The server's profile screen is shown in Figure 9-23.

CHAPTER 9   AGGREGATE RCA DATA

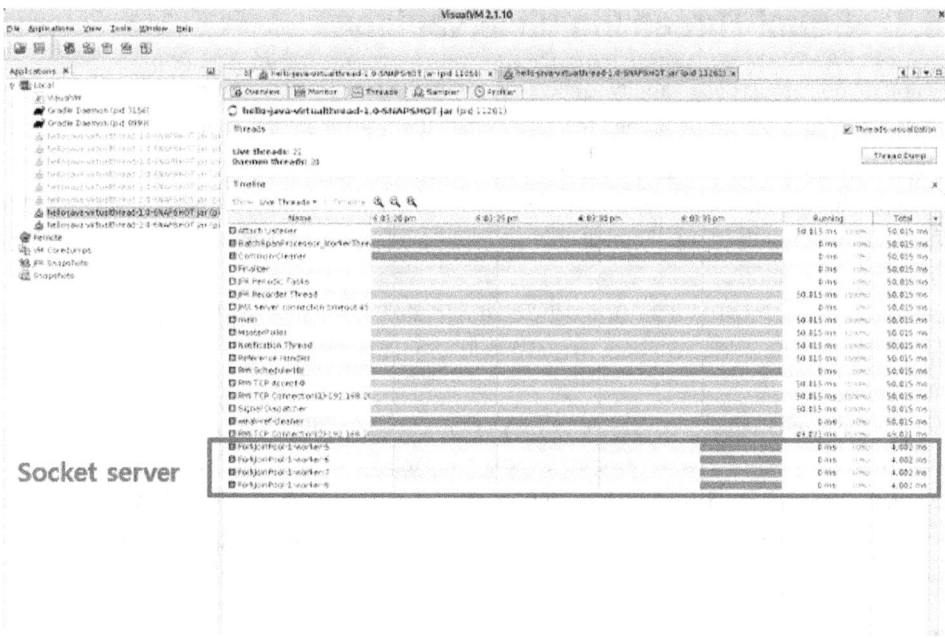

Figure 9-23. *The EchoServer profile*

The client profile screen is shown in Figure 9-24.

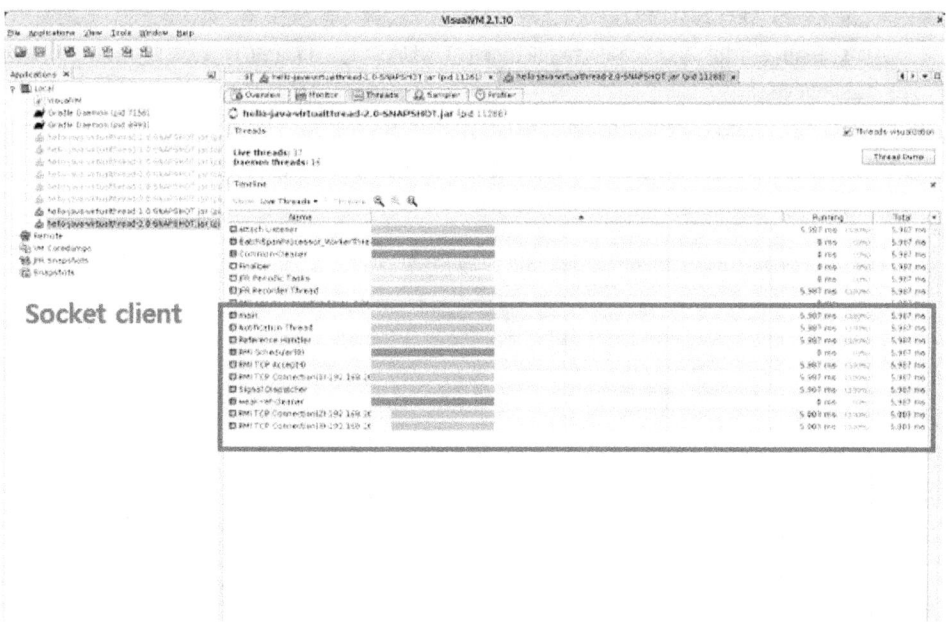

Figure 9-24. *The EchoClient profile*

If trace is not supported, such as for sockets, use profiles and logs to configure observability.

9.3.5.3. Virtual Thread Pin Observability

This section demonstrates observability to solve the problem of pins in virtual threads.

A virtual thread can become pinned to a Java thread, limiting the main benefit of virtual threads, which is the ability to mount and unmount Java threads. This is known as the virtual thread pin problem.

When a virtual thread enters a synchronized method, monitor ownership is assigned to the virtual thread's Java thread, not the virtual thread. If the virtual thread performs blocking operations, the Java thread is not freed but pinned.

Monitoring pins is important for virtual thread observability. You need to detect pins in real-time, understand the exact duration of pin events and details about their causes, and display pin problems in a dashboard.

Along with virtual threads, Java 21 comes with a new JFR event called `VirtualThreadPinned`. This event is generated when a pin occurs and can contain additional metadata such as stack traces and event duration.

Java 14 introduces Java Flight Recorder (JFR) event streaming, which allows applications to use JFR events. This gives you a lot of flexibility when processing these events. Use a logger to log the events and provide them as observability metrics.

```java
@Override
    public void start() {
        if (!isRunning()) {
            running.set(true);

            rs = new RecordingStream(); // (1)
            rs.enable("jdk.VirtualThreadPinned").withStack trace(); // (2)
            rs.onEvent(
                    "jdk.VirtualThreadPinned",
                    ev -> log.warn("Thread pinning detected! {}", ev) // (3)
            );

            rs.setMaxAge(Duration.ofSeconds(10)); // (4)

            rs.startAsync();
        }
    }

    @Override
    public void stop() {
        if (isRunning()) {
            rs.close();
            running.set(false);
        }
    }
```

CHAPTER 9   AGGREGATE RCA DATA

- The Start() method is an interesting one. First, it creates a RecordingStream to initialize the JFR recording session.

- Explicitly enable the jdk.VirtualThreadPinned event you are interested in. If you use withStack trace(), the stack trace is also logged.

- It provides a simple handler method. This method simply logs the received RecordedEvent object containing details about the recorded JFR event.

- It prevents the application from accumulating events, which can lead to memory leaks.

It then sends a request.

```
$ curl -X POST localhost:8080/pinning
```

The information printed to the log is as follows:

```
2024-12-12T22:21:37.260+11:00 WARN 6438 --- [jfr-thread-pin ning-spring-boot] [ Event Stream 1] m.j.p.JfrVirtualThreadPinnedEventHandler : Thread 'web-vt-0a4765c9-6765-4141-9792-f36728d74e9b' pinned for: 245ms at 2024-12-12T22:21:36.327028205, stack trace:
    java.lang.VirtualThread#parkOnCarrierThread: 689
    java.lang.VirtualThread#parkNanos: 648
    java.lang.VirtualThread#sleepNanos: 807
    java.lang.Thread#sleep: 507
    com.mikemybytes.jfr.pinning.ThreadPinningController#sleep: 36
    com.mikemybytes.jfr.pinning.ThreadPinningController#lambda$pinCarrierThread$0: 27
    com.mikemybytes.jfr.pinning.ThreadPinningController$$Lambda+0x00007fd8e07729d0.1333344259#run: -1
    java.lang.Thread#runWith: 1596
    java.lang.VirtualThread#run: 329
    java.lang.VirtualThread$VThreadContinuation$1#run: 209
    jdk.internal.vm.Continuation#enter0: 320
    jdk.internal.vm.Continuation#enter: 312
    jdk.internal.vm.Continuation#enterSpecial: -1
```

You can see how long it took. You can also find the eventThread that caused the event. The stack trace is limited to the top five items by default. In most cases, this is not enough.

You can extract the event processing part into a dedicated JfrVirtualThreadPinnedEventHandler. This separates the event-specific logic from the JFR recording session.

Figure 9-25 shows the virtual thread creation and the result of the process. The difference with the previous virtual thread demo is that the JFR Event Stream is enabled during the thread.

CHAPTER 9 AGGREGATE RCA DATA

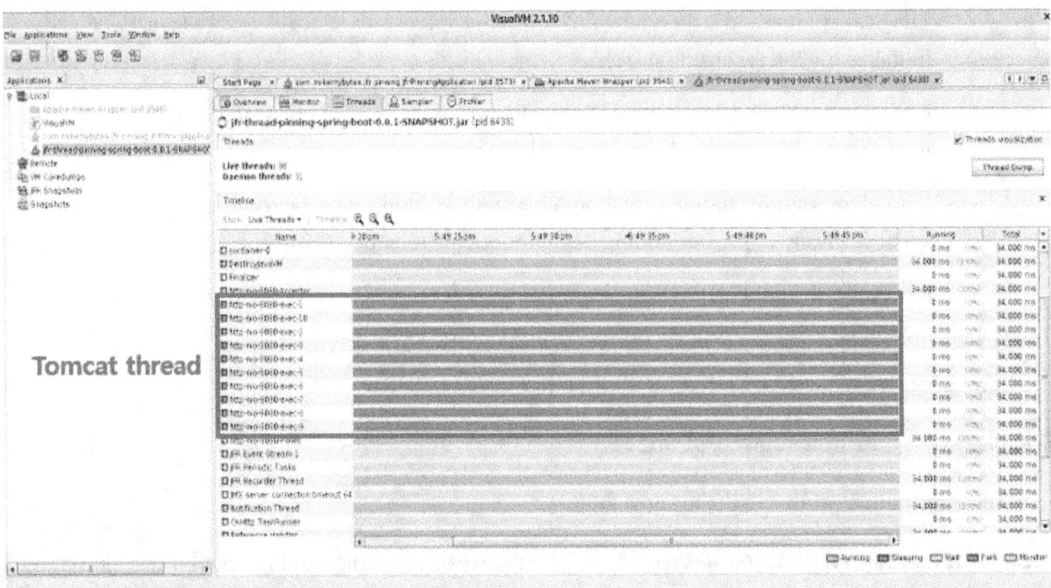

Figure 9-25. *The JFR event stream thread results*

Before sending a request, you can only see the tomcat thread (http-nio-8080-exec), no virtual threads.

In Figure 9-26, you can see that ForkjoinPool-1-worker starts in the PACK state when it receives the request.

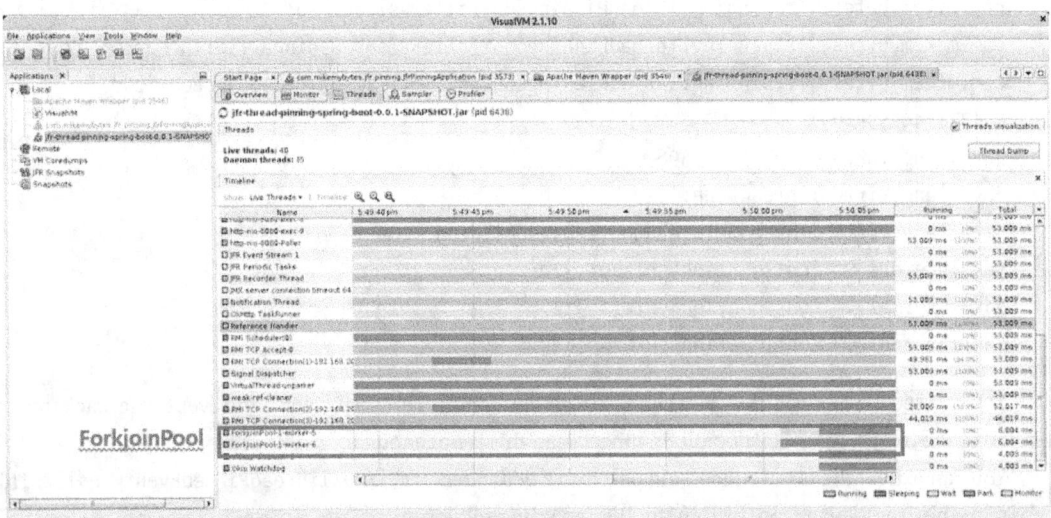

Figure 9-26. *ForkjoinPool-1-worker virtual thread results*

CHAPTER 9   AGGREGATE RCA DATA

You already know that displaying only the top five stack trace entries isn't enough, so you need to adjust the output. The RecordedObject class, which RecordedEvent extends, organizes the stack depth. The PrettyWriter class used internally is not available because it is not exposed in the jdk.jfr module. In this way, you can customize the stack trace.

The handler class provides the duration as a micrometer timer. The timer also acts as a counter, so you can also get the number of registered events.

```
void handle(RecordedEvent event) {

    var thread = event.getThread() != null ? event.getThread().getJavaName() : "<unknown>";
    var duration = event.getDuration();
    var startTime = LocalDateTime.ofInstant(event.getStartTime(), ZoneId.systemDefault());
    var stack trace = formatStack trace(event.getStack trace(), STACK_TRACE_MAX_DEPTH);

    log.warn(
        "Thread '{}' pinned for: {}ms at {}, stack trace: \n{}",
        thread,
        duration.toMillis(),
        startTime,
        stack trace
    );

    var timer = meterRegistry.timer("jfr.thread.pinning");
    timer.record(duration);
}

private String formatStack trace(RecordedStack trace stack trace, int maxDepth) {
    if (stack trace = = null) {
        return "\t<not available>";
    }
    String formatted = "\t" + stack t r ace.getFrames().stream()
        .limit(maxDepth)
        .map(JfrVirtualThreadPinnedEventHandler::formatStack traceFrame)
        .collect(Collectors.joining("\n\t"));
    if (maxDepth < stack trace.getFrames().size()) {
        return formatted + "\n\t(...)";
    }
    return formatted;
}

private static String formatStack traceFrame(RecordedFrame frame) {
    return frame.getMethod().getType().getName() + "#" + frame.getMethod().getName() + ": "
        + frame.getLineNumber();
}
```

701

CHAPTER 9 AGGREGATE RCA DATA

The output JFR metric is shown in Figure 9-27.

Figure 9-27. *The metric for virtual threads*

JMC provides better virtual thread profile capabilities than VisualVM.

- You can use jcmd for debugging, and the JMC JFR outputs virtual threads as the thread type. VisualVM cannot distinguish between virtual threads and Java threads, whereas JMC can do so clearly. JMC also outputs the stack trace of the virtual thread.

- Enable the jdk.VirtualThreadStart and jdk.VirtualThreadEnd events through JDK mission control or through a custom JFR configuration.

Using virtual threads works just as well in Tomcat and in Spring MVC.

The advent of virtual threads suggests that you don't need to use a non-blocking thread model like WebFlux. In fact, in non-CPU-centric environments, they perform just as well as non-blocking models.

I don't think virtual threads are stable enough for production yet. It's something to watch with interest.

If you have more IO than CPU, or need to process large volumes, virtual threads are a good alternative with small changes, either with the new WebFlux non-blocking with new development.

Virtual threads support metrics, traces, and the need to supplement logs with JFR and MDC. Profiles can categorize virtual threads and output stack traces, but need to be enhanced.

It's risky to operate with a new technology like virtual threads when observability isn't ready for it. You should introduce new technologies cautiously, with careful scrutiny and validation that observability supports the technology.

9.3.6. Spring WebFlux Demo

In blocking IO communication, tasks that remain until the thread processes them are blocked and they wait until the task is finished. In non-blocking IO communication, threads are not blocked.

Spring WebFlux implements non-blocking and uses an asynchronous, non-blocking IO-based server engine like Netty to process many requests with a small number of threads, which makes efficient use of CPU and memory, allowing you to process a lot of traffic with fewer resources. See Figure 9-28.

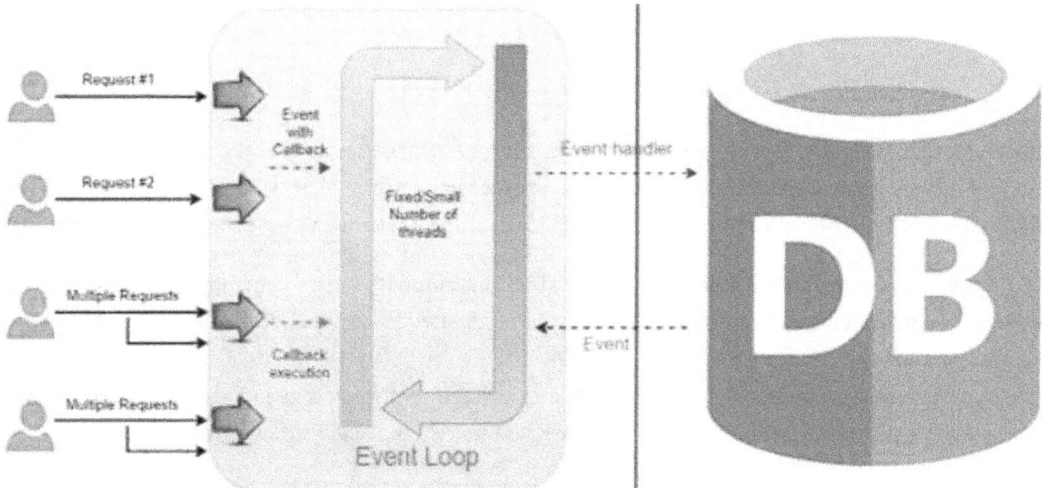

Figure 9-28. *Spring WebFlux process flow*

WebFlux is simpler than traditional development methods for non-blocking, callbacks, and asynchronous development, but you should learn the Reactive development method.

The event loop continues to run on a single thread, and since all operations are processed as events, whether it's a client request, database IO, or network IO, when an event occurs, it registers a callback for that event and moves on to processing the next event.

- The request handler receives incoming requests from the client.
- It pushes the received request to the event loop.
- Event loops register callbacks for costly operations, such as network and database operations.

CHAPTER 9   AGGREGATE RCA DATA

- When the task completes, it pushes the completion event to the event loop.
- It calls the registered callback to pass the result of the process.

The demo uses Brave during the micrometer trace, which generates the trace in B3 format. Since the client and server both use B3, you need to configure the OpenTelemetry collector to transfer.

Enable the OpenTelemetry zipkin receiver. You don't need a separate zipkin server; just start the OpenTelemetry collector.

```
docker run -p 4317:4317 -p 4318:4318 -v /root/otel-collector-config.yaml:/etc/otel-collector-config.yaml otel/opentelemetry-collector:latest --config=/etc/otel-collector-config.yaml
```

Start the frontend microservices:

```
java -javaagent:/root/sleuth-webmvc-example/target/opentelemetry-javaagent.jar -Dotel.service.name=frontend -Dotel.exporter.otlp.protocol=http/protobuf -Dotel.logs.exporter=none -Dotel.metrics.exporter=none -jar brave-example-webflux6-micrometer-1.0-SNAPSHOT-exec.jar
```

Start the backend microservices:

```
java -javaagent:/root/sleuth-webmvc-example/target/opentelemetry-javaagent.jar -Dotel.service.name=backend -Dote l.exporter.otlp.protocol=http/protobuf -Dotel.logs.exporter=none -Dotel.metrics.exporter=none -jar brave-example-webflux6-micrometer-1.0-SNAPSHOT-exec.jar
```

The OpenTelemetry agent recognizes the Zipkin B3 instrumentation and attempts to transfer the Zipkin server. The OpenTelemetry collector receiver must be configured for zipkin. Use the exporter to transfer to backend storage.

In development, it is important to pay attention to what trace format is included in the header where propagation is processed as long as is present. If x-B3 is found in the header, downstream microservices should use the OpenTelemetry agent to configure a B3 propagator.

Commercial observability ignores traditional B3, instrumentation of upstream and downstream microservices, and generates and propagates x-.

Even if you use the OpenTelemetry agent, it will not be applied. You can see that micrometer traces are prioritized.

9.3.7. Non-Blocking Reactor Demo

Future architectures may consist of WebFlux configuring non-blocking IO for frontend microservices, message servers for backend microservices for an event-driven architecture, or coroutines (virtual threads) and R2DBC. See Figure 9-29.

But the problem lies in observability. There are limitations to configuring observability.

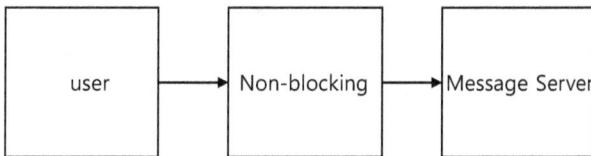

Figure 9-29. *The flow of non-blocking with message servers*

For example, some `reactor-http-epoll` generate spans and, in case of agent, some `scheduling-1` do not generate new spans but keep the existing ones. `boundedElastic` does not generate spans and does not write the trace context to the log. Each agent behaves differently. In conclusion, trace supports asynchronous non-blocking threads, but with limitations in logging.

There are also problems processing the trace context. For example, OpenTelemetry logs and MDC recognize threads in scheduling-1, but commercial observability doesn't even recognize scheduling-1 threads. There is a big difference between a thread being searched by logs and not being searched at all. There are many areas where traces and profiles alone do not identify problems, that different agents instrument different results, and that different trace contexts are written to logs. This confuses SREs in their root cause analysis.

Java has a number of concepts that provide context. ThreadLocal and MDC are two examples. Non-blocking makes it difficult to use ThreadLocal because threads change with frequent context switches, so Reactor provides a separate way to manage context.

Context is information that is needed in a specific situation. A Reactor's context is a store in the form of keys and values that is propagated between Reactor components, such as operators. Propagation means that the context is propagated from upstream to downstream, so that each operator in the operator chain has the same access to the information in that context. Contexts in Reactors are somewhat similar to ThreadLocals, but unlike ThreadLocals, which are mapped to individual threads of execution, Reactors are mapped to Subscribers, meaning that whenever a subscription occurs, a single context is created that is associated with that subscription.

The recent trend is moving from Spring MVC and JPA to Spring WebFlux and Reactor. OpenTelemetry officially supports Reactor, Reactor Netty, Spring WebFlux, and R2DBC.

Here are some common threads you'll see in production:

- Apache Tomcat (`http-nio-8080-1`): Synchronous Spring Boot applications running on Tomcat create the `http-nio-8080` thread. If it processes `@Async` asynchronously, it creates a `task-1` thread.

- WebClient (`HttpClient@7a860e9a-146`): The WebClient uses an event loop model to implement concurrency. If you run the WebClient on Reactor Netty, it shares the event loop used by Netty. In this case, you may not notice much difference in the `reactor-http-epoll` threads that are created. WebClient is also supported by Servlet 3.1+ containers like Jetty, but it works differently. Depending on whether you are using WebClient or not, you will notice that there are additional threads created by the WebFlux application running Jetty.

CHAPTER 9   AGGREGATE RCA DATA

- boundElastic-evictor-1: The scheduler in Reactor is similar in meaning to the scheduler used in the OS. Reactor's scheduler is responsible for managing the threads used for asynchronous programming. It is not a scheduler that manages batches. You use the scheduler to control which threads are processed. Schedulers can be used to minimize problems such as race conditions between threads. Schedulers.boundedElastic creates a thread pool based on ExecutorService and uses a fixed number of threads in it to process tasks, returning the threads when they finish and reusing them. In Reactor, the Schedulers class defines the execution model and where execution takes place. The Schedulers class provides different execution contexts, such as elastic and parallel. It provides different types of thread pools, which are useful for different tasks. Using the existing ExecutorService, you can create your own scheduler at any time. The boundedElastic scheduler is a thread pool that dynamically adjusts the number of worker threads based on the workload. It is optimized for IO-bound tasks such as database queries and network requests and is designed to process large volumes of short-lived tasks without spawning too many threads or wasting resources. By default, the maximum size of a boundedElastic thread pool is the number of available processors multiplied by ten, but you can configure it to use a different maximum size if needed. By using an asynchronous thread pool like boundedElastic, you can avoid thread exhaustion and excessive resource usage due to the limited nature of the thread pool, and the elasticity of the pool allows you to dynamically adjust the number of worker threads based on the workload.

- Parallel: While boundedElastic is optimized for blocking IO, parallel is a scheduler that is optimized for non-blocking IO and creates as many threads as there are cores. reactor-http-epoll is received by parallel and the rest of the processing is done by the parallel thread pool. Using a parallel scheduler allows multiple tasks to run simultaneously in different threads, which can better utilize CPU resources and process a large number of concurrent requests, improving performance and scalability. However, memory usage can increase, and if you exceed the maximum number of worker threads, the thread pool can become exhausted. Therefore, the decision to use a parallel thread pool should be based on the specific needs of your application and the tradeoffs.

- scheduling-1: The thread of the spring scheduler.Scheduling is to tell a job to perform at a specified period of time. Spring Boot makes scheduling and batching simple by using the @Scheduled annotation.

- pool-4-thread-1: The thread created by ExecutorService. ExecutorService is a Java library provided to efficiently process multiple tasks in parallel. You only need to specify a task to the ExecutorService, and it uses thread pool to execute and

CHAPTER 9 AGGREGATE RCA DATA

manage the task. Tasks are managed in a queue. If there are more tasks than threads in the thread pool, the unexecuted tasks are stored in the queue and assigned to the threads that have completed execution and are executed sequentially.

- `reactor-http-epoll`: The `reactor-http-epoll` thread is the thread that processes Netty requests. In Linux, epoll is a Linux API used to efficiently detect a large number of socket IOs and process the events. This operation is referred to as multiplexing. epoll supports both blocking and non-blocking modes. Netty uses epoll internally. Netty uses selectors internally to implement high-performance IO because selectors are the wrapper implementation of epoll. So when a new connection comes in, Netty behaves similarly to epoll—it adds the connection socket to the socket list, watches for changes, and performs IO on it. The event loop supports several methods depending on the OS: NIO, epoll, and KQueue. In the past, `reactor-http-nio` was output as a thread name, which has been changed to `reactor-http-epoll`. In Spring, epolls, event loops, and coroutines do not create separate threads. Instead, epoll, event loop, and coroutine are combined and processed in a single `reactor-http-epoll` thread.

When you run the demo, the output from VisualVM is shown in Figure 9-30. The boundElastic, Parallel scheduler is visible in the thread list, but it has not been created. You can see a single `reactor-http-epoll-2` thread running.

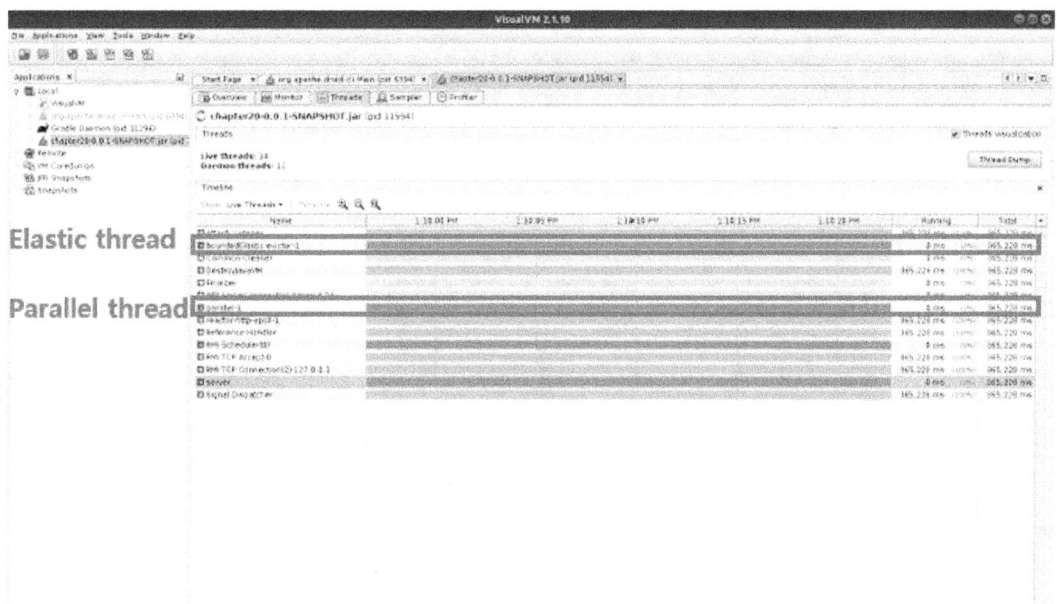

Figure 9-30. *The WebFlux thread profile*

707

CHAPTER 9 AGGREGATE RCA DATA

Use curl http://localhost:8080/v10/books/1 to generate the request. Figure 9-31 shows reactor-http-epoll being created and the request being processed.

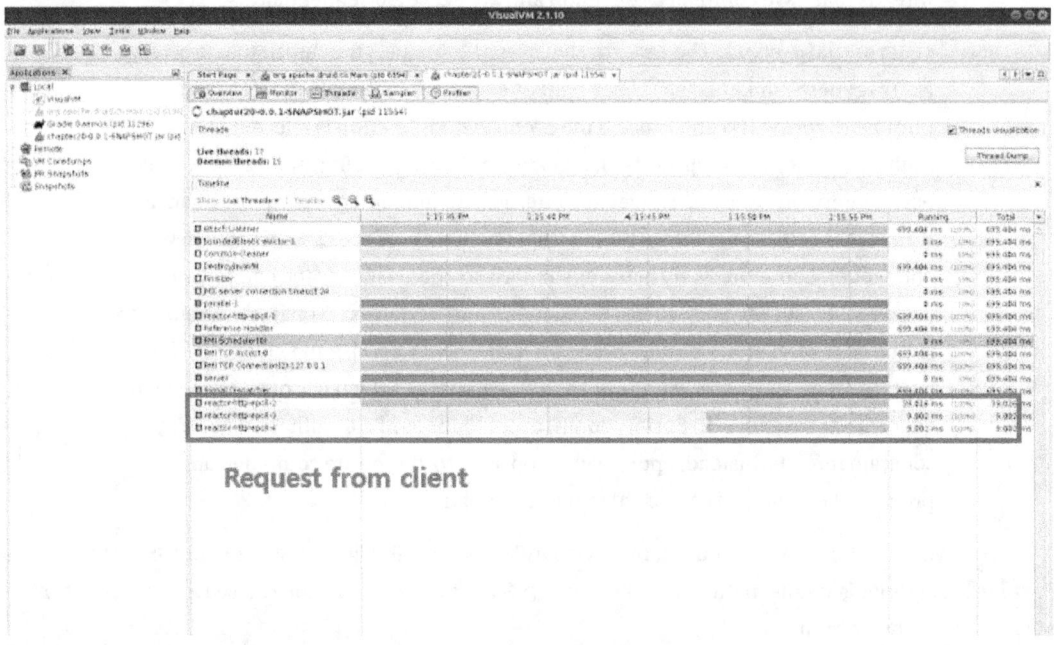

Figure 9-31. *Results of the reactor-http-epoll process*

When you print the results of trace in Grafana, you see Figure 9-32. Two spans are generated for the reactor-http-epoll thread, and one span is generated by the CURL request. In total, the Grafana trace shows that three spans were generated.

CHAPTER 9   AGGREGATE RCA DATA

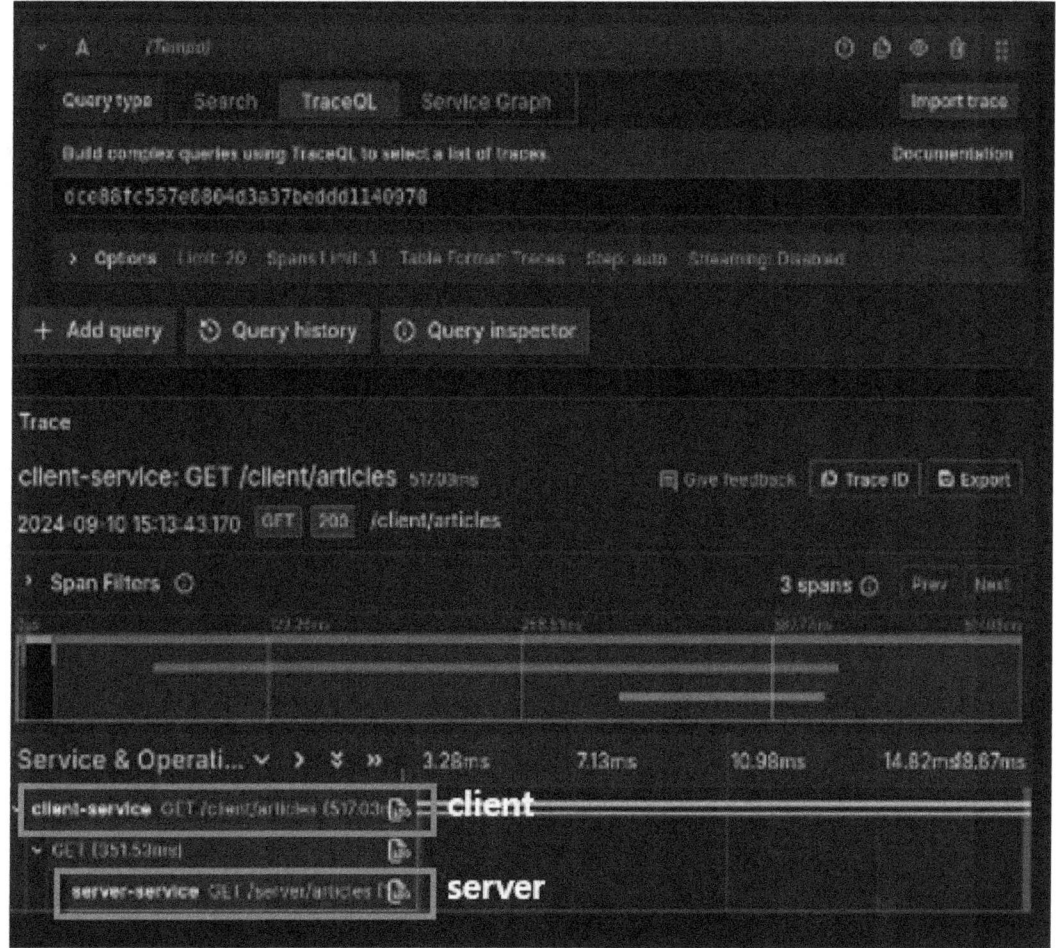

Figure 9-32. *Results of the Grafana trace*

If you suspect that spans are not being generated correctly on a particular thread, you can monitor VisualVM, the trace screen. The following is the result of instrumentation of an application that implements WebClient and R2DBC.

Commercial observability may only generate Netty spans and not R2DBC spans. This is because they are not instrumented. However, OpenTelemetry does generate R2DBC spans. The spans that are only measured in OpenTelemetry are merged into the commercial observability trace, so that all spans are output without any problems across the E2E.

WebFlux creates a span when it receives a request from the client, and R2DBC creates a span when it connects to the database. In total, you create spans for two `reactor-http-epoll` threads.

```
ScopeSpans #0
ScopeSpans SchemaURL:
InstrumentationScope io.opentelemetry.r2dbc-1.0 2.7.0-alpha
```

709

CHAPTER 9 AGGREGATE RCA DATA

```
Span #0
    trace ID : 43f4f8cce11731be8ff04c5292acbef3
    Parent ID : ce0c21e10bc45fc4
    ID: c6ad7b867b511842
    Name : SELECT testdb.book
    Kind : Client
    Start time : 2024-09-10 05:31:51.165442288 +0000 UTC
    End time : 2024-09-10 05:31:51.234798197 +0000 UTC
    Status code : Unset
    Status message :
Attributes:
     -> db.user: Str(sa)

     -> db.name: Str(testdb)
     -> thread.name: Str(reactor-http-epoll-2)
ScopeSpans #1
ScopeSpans SchemaURL:
InstrumentationScope io.opentelemetry.netty-4.1 2.7.0-alpha
Span #0
    trace ID : 43f4f8cce11731be8ff04c5292acbef3
    Parent ID :
    ID : ce0c21e10bc45fc4
    Name : GET /v10/books/{book-id}
    Kind : Server
    Start time : 2024-09-10 05:31:50.790832 +0000 UTC
    End time : 2024-09-10 05:31:51.382949804 +0000 UTC
    Status code : Unset
    Status message :
Attributes:
     -> user_agent.original: Str(curl/7.68.0)
     -> network.protocol.version: Str(1.1)

     -> thread.name: Str(reactor-http-epoll-2)
     -> url.path: Str(/v10/books/1)
     -> server.address: Str(localhost)

     -> network.peer.port: Int(56572)
     { "kind": "exporter", "data_type": " traces", "name": "logging"}
```

To monitor this asynchronous non-blocking, various signals must be used appropriately. Metrics uses micrometer traces to monitor Netty threads. Logs should use the Reactor context for MDC. Developers should ensure that Reactor contexts are propagated to the MDC.

9.4. Summary

Since there was no detailed root cause analysis of the cluster, I used Druid to explain the internal behavior of the cluster and possible delays.

Recently, Prometheus, Grafana, and so on are developed in Golang, but most clusters (HDFS, Kafka, Elastic, Druid, Presto, etc.) are developed in Java. In the enterprise, open source clusters that process data as well as microservices are often configured in Java, and commercial solutions are often developed in Java. Java is still important, and applying observability to Java is important.

Understanding Java profiles is more important than analyzing metrics and logs. While it's important to understand latency and performance issues with Java profiles, you can understand the internal operations of the system. The profile will help you understand the root cause of the microservice, not the root cause of the observability configuration.

It's important to understand the failures as well as the successes. Presto is a failure because it is not well suited for aggregating data, does not provide advanced aggregation functions, and is better suited for joining distributed databases.

Druid is better suited for multidimensional analysis with pre-aggregation. However, it is not suitable for processing text data.

With the recent popularity of LLM, the need to collect and manage textual unstructured data is increasing. Each data engine is often specialized for a specific purpose, such as joins, aggregations, or unstructured text. There is no one data engine for all data types.

CHAPTER 10

AIOps RCA

AI is a key technology for root cause analysis and operational automation. This final chapter explains how to automate root cause analysis using machine learning algorithms. It also explains how Generative AI and RAG can be applied to AIOps. To apply machine learning, you will utilize OpenSearch.

Generative AI has made it easy to automate sophisticated tasks. For anomaly detection, you used the RCF algorithm. This chapter discusses k-NN, metric correlation, text embedding, and LLM (Large Language Model) algorithms.

You used Grafana to implement observability, but anomaly detection and AIOps are based on OpenSearch.

- Grafana is used for observability because you can configure multi-tenant and object storage. You can easily and quickly perform root cause analysis through various correlations.

- OpenSearch is used for anomaly detection and AIOps because it has built-in anomaly detection, provides the algorithms and Vector database needed for AIOps, and is easy to integrate with LangChain. OpenSearch is great for searching and analyzing large volumes of text.

This chapter utilizes OpenSearch for many purposes:

- Collect traces, logs, and metrics and implement observability
- Anomaly detection with the RCF algorithm
- Vector database
- Metric correlation
- k-NN semantic searches
- RAG

Grafana is easy to configure for correlation and multi-tenant uses. The features that OpenSearch offers are optimized for implementing AIOps. It struggles with technologies like Generative AI.

- OpenSearch supports not only local storage, but also object storage and various tiering features.

- OpenSearch provides text analytics, semantic search, and Vector database capabilities. It offers a variety of agents and tools for RAG.

While we achieved meaningful results by configuring E2E traces, we also discussed the limitations of traces and how to compensate for them. For small systems, root cause analysis can be done with just a few SREs. But the larger you get, the more legacy and black boxes you need to automate. Hiring more and more SREs and increasing headcount is not the answer.

Observability signals were collected and stored in Promscale and Druid. You collected various black box and legacy logs and stored them in OpenSearch. Using the collected data, you need to automate infrastructure and application observability.

- Anomaly detection supports infrastructure observability.
- Distributed trace only supports application observability.
- Events support business.
- Observability data analysis and aggregation support infrastructure and applications, but there are many limitations.
- AIOps must fill the previously mentioned limitations and provide detailed support for both applications and infrastructure.

Before you learn to automate, let's talk about the limitations of observability and AIOps built with commercial observability and OpenTelemetry.

10.1. AIOps Limitations

Using AIOps, you learn why root cause analysis fails. Current observability partially supports infrastructure observability and focuses on application observability.

You need to understand exactly what the root cause is. Don't confuse cause and result. Nano-second latency, errors, and failures are results. They are not the cause. Consider the following example. Sometimes AIOps reports that the result is the cause.

10.1.1. Example 1

There are no threads in the thread pool with a `WAITING` state. All threads are `RUNNABLE`, and there are no more threads available to support new requests.

Cause: No threads are available in the thread pool. You need to change the settings of the thread pool.
Result: Increased more latency and a timeout error occurs.
Solution: Check the available resources and increase the number of thread pools.

AIOps should describe the cause and provide a solution. For example, the root cause analysis of AIOps is as follows.

The thread state of the microservices associated with the downstream is RUNNABLE for a long time. Even if you change the thread pool to increase the number of threads, you will still run out of threads. The solution is to make sure that the RUNNABLE state is not processed for a long time. The RUNNABLE state should be completed and changed to WAITING. The scheduler can use the threads in the WAITING state. To do this:

- Reduce the timeout on the upstream to 4 seconds.
- Certain methods in downstream need to be improved. Improve to respond within 1 second to minimize failures.

I've described a simple example. AIOps needs to understand the cause and be able to answer the SRE accurately.

1. If AIOps says that the latency is coming from upstream, they are wrong.
2. If AIOps says, "We don't have enough threads and need to increase the thread pool," they are wrong.
3. If it's a bug or logic issue in your application, allocating more resources to the pod and increasing the number of thread pools is not the right answer to the failure.

Most AIOps answer as above. A good approach is to profile and identify the methods that are causing the latency or manage the connections. For the failure problem, most AIOps answer as above.

I can't find a cause for the problem. The cause is a delay downstream. This is an incorrect answer and should be answered at the next level down.

- Timeouts need to be improved.
- You need to change the kernel network parameters.
- You need a profile of downstream methods.

10.1.2. Example 2

Memory kept growing in the older generation of the JVM heap, causing multiple full garbage collections in the morning. Users experienced significant latency.

Solution: The API server is down due to an OOM.

GA (Google Analytics) 360 was patched on the API server two days ago. A new deployment has occurred. Due to this internal GA360 instrumentation bug, memory was increased in the older generation.

AIOps doesn't know if there is a bug in the GA360 patch. However, the deployment occurred two days ago, and it identifies a small increase in memory, a problem with older generations in JVM, and transfers an alert. However, AIOps says that garbage collection is happening frequently and transfers an alert. It doesn't describe it as full garbage collection. It doesn't explain how the problem is happening in either the new or old generation.

CHAPTER 10   AIOPS RCA

The alert that AIOps should transfer should specify that memory management and garbage collection started happening after a certain deployment, and that the root cause was a deployment two days ago,

Garbage collection is an result, not a cause. AIOps did the incorrect root cause analysis.

The root cause is that the new deployment increased memory utilization and garbage collection was not working properly. Garbage collection not working properly is an effect, and the new deployment caused the problem, so it's the cause. AIOps should answer that the deployment is the cause. If they answer that full garbage collection is the problem, they are confusing cause and effect.

Why do AIOps projects fail? Let's look at some examples.

10.1.3. Example 3

Nginx is a popular application server. It has the following important parameters:

- **Worker process:** The worker process, which follows the number of CPU cores.
- **Worker connections:** worker_connections is 1024, which follows the number of file descriptors.
- **epoll**: epoll is recommended over select and poll.
- **Multithreading:** worker_aio_threads, which are asynchronous IO threads. For example, to manage disk IO.
- **TCP Fast Open**: Processes TCP handshakes overhead.
- **TCP_nodelay, TCP_NOPUSH:** Optimize TCP packets.

Other key parameters include the keepalive timeout, keepalive requests, file caches, and SSL/TLS improvements.

It operates as a multi-process-single thread, but uses an event-based architecture, allowing each process to process requests and responses from multiple clients in parallel.

It runs as a master process and its sub-processes, the worker processes. It is the worker processes that receive requests, while the master process is responsible for controlling and managing the work processes. Each worker process processes requests and responses from clients in parallel on an event basis.

- **Non-blocking IO:** Non-blocking IO and multiple IOs are used to process IO based on requests and responses in parallel and with high throughput. File I/O is in a blocking state, waiting for data to arrive. Non-blocking IO can be used to avoid blocking.
- **Multiplexed IO:** Multiplexed IO is a technology that processes multiple file descriptors simultaneously, and it can be used with select, epoll, and kqueue. When one of the file descriptors becomes available for IO, it receives a notification and can process it efficiently. In Linux, epoll performs better than select, so nginx uses epoll by default.

- **Single thread:** Although there are differences depending on the language, IO is generally called using a blocking system call. Since the processing is blocked due to the system call, the process is handled by a coroutine. While the process inside the coroutine is blocked, the process of another coroutine can be executed to utilize resources. This technology is called asynchronous IO. Since threads are not used, only one CPU can be used by a single worker process, and multiple worker processes are generally run to increase processing performance. The number of worker processes can be specified by changing the worker_processes setting, and if it is set to auto, it is automatically stores them according to the number of CPU cores.

- **Compression:** A compressed response can be returned using gzip for HTTP client requests. If Accept-Encoding, gzip is present in the request HTTP header. The response body can be compressed using gzip to reduce the response size because the client can use gzip.

It is difficult to generalize because it depends on the web service or response size, but when the HTTP response is compressed with gzip, the size is about one-fifth of the original. When the response size is smaller, the response can be returned faster. This has a very significant performance impact even in mobile environments with unstable networks. In addition, since the network accounts for a large portion of infrastructure costs, reducing the transfer volume can reduce costs.

AIOps can also handle slow clients by buffering requests and responses. The downstream only needs to focus on communication with nginx, so the problem of client speed is solved.

To process requests and responses for large files, the request body and response body are written to disk as temporary files. However, since the recording of temporary files can be a burden on the server, servers that receive large files should monitor the server to determine when and which file IO occur. Buffering of requests can be adjusted by changing the client_body_buffer_size or client_body_temp_path settings. If the file IO is high, you can write to memory by specifying client_body_temp_path as a directory mounted with tmpfs.

nginx has a setting to disconnect from the upstream every time. If you want to maintain the connection and reuse it, you should use HTTP/1.1 and set the Connection header to an empty string.

Keepalives can reduce the processing of upstream and connection. The keepalive settings include keepalive_connections, which specifies the number of connections maintained, and keepalive_request, which specifies the maximum number of requests that can be processed until the connection is closed. If a server processes a large number of requests, frequent connection regeneration can reduce the server's performance or cause it to malfunction due to high load.

Recently, it has become common to communicate using TLS encryption such as HTTPS. In TLS, you can use the ssl_session_cache setting to cache session information by sharing Session ID. In nginx, you can use ssl http2 by changing the listen setting, and you can use the AES-NI feature to quickly process encryption and decryption of AES, which is widely used in TLS. Using kTLS, a TLS technology within the kernel, encryption and decryption can be processed within the kernel, resulting in more efficient performance without the need for memory copying.

CHAPTER 10   AIOPS RCA

In this book, the terms file descriptor, epoll, non-CPU IO, TCP handshake, keepalive, IO scheduler are familiar. To understand what these values mean, you need to understand kernel parameters and system calls. Setting the defaults may not be a problem, but if you modify your application and kernel parameters, `nginx` should reflect the changes appropriately. These parameters are critical to performance and can be the starting point for major failures if set incorrectly. If `nginx` fails before traffic is routed to microservices, it becomes a SPOF.

For example, suppose there is a failure downstream. Too many requests. The failure propagates to `nginx`, and `nginx` experiences severe latency. You restart downstream, but the cause is unknown, and while checking various parameters, you realize that you are running out of worker connections or have a large keepalive timeout.

AIOps needs to understand the causes and provide solutions.

- It should guide you as to which methods and queries downstream are wrong.
- `nginx` should be able to tell you that some parameter is incorrectly set and is causing the problem.

If AIOps only provides guidance at the level of latency and service failure, it doesn't help with root cause analysis. However, current AIOps does not answer the question of root cause analysis.

The `nginx` metric OSS is free, but it's not enough to address the complex failures and propagation of `nginx`. You need to pay for Plus to operate `nginx`, but the metrics provided are application-level metrics. However, some of the parameters described previously are kernel parameters, while others are highly related to system calls. If the application observability agent only monitors the application and lacks support for the infrastructure, it is difficult to analyze the cause of latency and failure caused by kernel parameters, network settings, and system calls. Since the agent does not collect data, it is recognized as out of scope from an AIOps perspective. The agent supports Java applications, virtual machines, and some host metrics. If the problem is external to Java, it is outside the scope of AIOps and it becomes difficult to perform root cause analysis.

Commercial observability offers an extension for monitoring `nginx`, but it's limited and lacks the metrics offered by `nginx` Plus.

It is difficult for AIOps to analyze the internal latency and failures that occur in nginx. Parameters are system resources or kernels. Limited root cause analysis is performed on microservices. The scope of data collection is limited to the application. It is not a root cause analysis, but it is implemented to identify the latency occurring in microservices and transfer alerts.

Commercial observability and OpenTelemetry lack lower-level system monitoring and correlation with applications.

Evaluating the failures you've experienced, it looks like this:

- When assessing failure severity, infrastructure observability is more severe than application observability.
- In terms of frequency of failures, kernel internal bugs are less frequent. Microservices are relatively more buggy, and the frequency of failures in application observability is higher.

CHAPTER 10 AIOPS RCA

- If you analyze the list of failures, you'll find that they're more often related to build deployment, poor testing, and unreasonable feature development schedules than performance issues. The latency issues mentioned in this book may not be a big problem in production.

- Observability does not support load balancers, CDN, clusters consisting of sharding, or complex data pipelines. There are still many applications that observability does not support.

Since application observability is a small part of root cause analysis, it is questionable whether it is appropriate to implement AIOps based on it.

For AIOps to be successful:

- Application-centric observability alone is not enough; you need to include infrastructure observability.

- In addition to performance and failure-focused observability, you also need deployment and configuration information from across your operations.

The role of AI to provide the desired data and help SREs analyze and make decisions accurately. At this point, it is difficult for AIOps to perform root cause analysis and draw conclusions. It is recommended that SREs take the lead in root cause analysis and AIOps be used as an assistant to provide important data in a timely manner. The problem is that AIOps lacks the technical capabilities to collect and analyze data.

AIOps is useful for organizations with simple business processes, fewer black boxes and fewer legacy systems, but industries like banking and telecom, with complex business processes and more legacy systems, will find AIOps less effective. The varying complexity of SRE will limit the effectiveness of AIOps.

Especially in banking and telecom, where there is a lot of legacy, data is disrupted and not easy to join and utilize. There is a lot of data, but not enough useful data. In the previous chapter, you organized the data to be joined and utilized through traces and events. In this chapter, you automate it using AI.

The overall scope is Promscale metric correlation, and the detailed root cause is RAG OpenSearch.

In this chapter, you'll implement an AIOps demo with two aspects.

The root cause analysis method described in the previous section uses service maps and polystats to get a rough idea of what is wrong with a service. It is not an automated method, but the SRE manually performs the root cause analysis using the screen or SQL.

You want to identify problematic metrics that differ across multiple application and infrastructure metrics. The goal is to automate the process of identifying discrepant metrics, rather than manually, so that the root cause can be identified quickly and accurately.

Use observability to perform root cause analysis of failures in your applications and infrastructure. Use metric correlation to help reduce the scope of the failure.

- **Traces:** Provide insight into individual transactions and can identify error and error messages more accurately than other signals.

- **Metrics:** Traces and metrics are structured and stored in Promscale and Druid. Use them to develop metric correlation.

719

To apply the algorithm, the following conditions are required

- Data must be structured and organized to be queried.
- Data should be organized in the form of numbers or categories, not text.
- A time series is not required, but a column that includes time is useful.
- Signals collected from various data sources should be converted into something as metric-like as possible.

Rather than asking AI about a broad scope of topics, you'll get better results if you ask it about specific, targeted topics. The goal is to identify the area, such as application, or infrastructure where the problem is occurring. Complex and specific questions create a knowledge base rather than metric correlation, so you should ask difficult and complex questions to your root cause analysis QA.

Correlation analysis uses structured data and is suitable for machine learning and anomaly detection. Root cause analysis questions and answers use unstructured data and are implemented as RAG.

Rather than directly querying the problem, it is necessary to accurately identify and narrow down the problem. For large scopes, you can narrow down the scope with correlation analysis, and for small scopes, you need to understand the problem in detail with LLM.

The platform in this book uses OpenSearch to automate root cause analysis in two ways.

To understand the root cause, prepare questions. The next step is to identify the root cause from the question and answer system implementing LLM and Generative AI.

Failure data across configuration, deployment, and IT operations, including observability, should be managed in the LLM. For example, failure solutions and SRE know-how should be accumulated in the LLM.

The burden is on the preprocessing, but you have the freedom to customize the contents of the log. Logs can contain infrastructure, application, and business data. For legacy systems and black boxes that don't support metrics and traces, logs are the only way to go. If you want to implement observability with just traces and metrics, you'll have a hard time. In this case, you need to collect logs. Use log data stored in OpenSearch to develop Generative AI.

The architecture of the root cause analysis will lead to two approaches.

- Using LangChain and LLM
- Using OpenSearch and the LLM

Now that I've covered observability in detail, let's talk about CMDB.

10.2. AIOps Correlation

Successful AI services are all about accuracy. How you organize your technical architecture is secondary; you need to ensure a certain level of accuracy. For example, 85-92 percent accuracy is the minimum required to serve users and ensure satisfaction and trust.

Using a metric correlation algorithm, you can identify the data that stands out as different among the various data collected. Understanding the differences is the starting point for AIOps.

The correlation described in AIOps is a different kind of correlation.

- **Correlation between signals:** There is a relationship between different signals, and the relationship is correlated by an ID. For example, in the correlation between traces and profiles, the span attribute contains the profile ID. The scope of correlation between signals is limited to observability.

- **Metric correlation:** Select metrics from a set of metrics that contain different contexts. You can select metrics that are significantly different, rather than common. In addition to observability, you should utilize a variety of data generated during IT operations, such as deployments and changes.

When SRE find discrepant metrics, they analyze why the discrepancies occur. They can analyze the technical process in chronological order and determine if it is the root cause.

In production, the resources involved in the problem are too numerous and complex, and there are dependencies between service and resources. It's beyond what SREs can understand and manage. It's hard to understand what's involved using only service maps and polystats. By automating metric correlation, you can understand dependencies, impact.

Commercial observability such as Elastic, Honeycomb, and Dynatrace provide user screens for root cause analysis. There is a limitation because there is not enough data for root cause analysis and only a few dependencies can be checked on the screen.

While there are differences between solutions, observability offers a variety of RCA capabilities.

- **Honeycomb and Elasticsearch:** This is the case of forecasting the correlation between metrics. The event correlation algorithm finds events in a set of metric data. The algorithm defines an event as a time window in which multiple metrics display abnormal behavior at the same time. Given a set of metrics, the algorithm counts the number of events that occurred at the time each event occurred and determines which metric is associated with each event. Traditional root cause analysis methods include organizing multiple metrics in a dashboard and comparing multiple charts in chronological order.

- **Dynatrace:** Exceptions, errors, problems, and alerts, in that order. When an error is found, it is transferred to the AIOps engine (Davis) and the root cause is forecasted through Davis' root cause analysis. While experience has shown high accuracy, there are obvious limitations and constraints. It is unable to respond to complex failures and the answers are limited and not diverse.

- **Prometheus:** Prometheus provides methods to forecast metrics. You can also use `predict_linear` to forecast metrics. By using this method, it is possible to output the trend of multiple metrics in a single chart. `predict_linear(v range-vector, t scalar)` uses simple linear regression to estimate the value of a time series t seconds from now based on a scope vector. The metric type must be a gauge.

CHAPTER 10   AIOPS RCA

The OpenTelemetry Collector pipeline feeds data to ML and LLM, as shown in Figure 10-1.

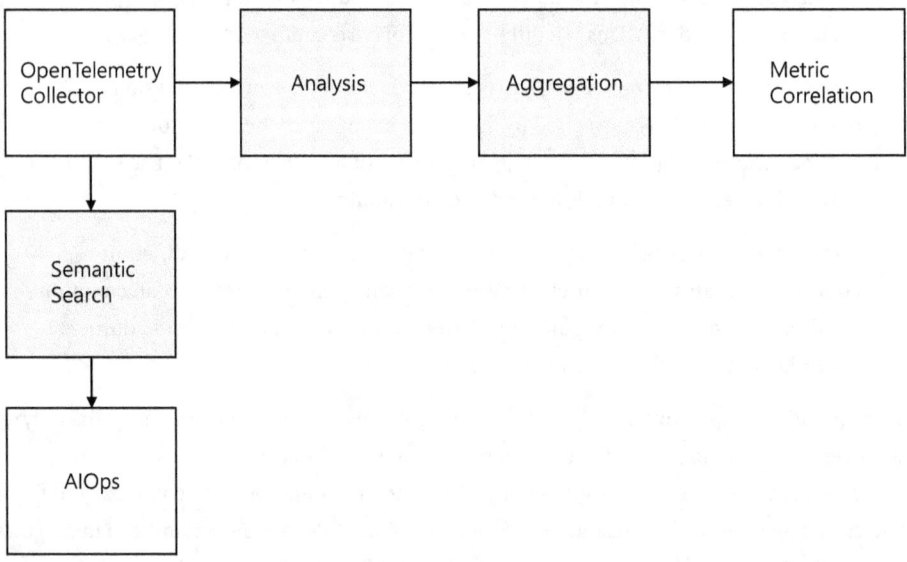

Figure 10-1. The process of searching, analyzing, and aggregating data

A variety of signals can be used to develop AIOps correlations. Traces, logs, and metrics should be considered for root cause analysis.

You should minimize preprocessing as much as possible and select suitable signals

Through comparisons between various metrics, metric correlation identifies which applications and systems are experiencing problems. METRIC CORRELATION can identify anomalies at a level larger than traditional buckets and individual record levels.

To enable the metric correlation algorithm, update the following cluster settings:

```
PUT /_cluster/settings
{ {
  "persistent" : {
    "plugins.ml_commons.enable_inhouse_python_model": True
  }
}
```

The metric correlation input is an M x T array of metric data, where M is the number of metrics and T is the length of each individual sequence of metric values.

When you enter a metric into the algorithm, it assumes the following

- For each metric, the length of the input sequence is the same, T.
- All input metrics must have the same set of corresponding timestamps.
- The total number of data points is M * T <= 10,000.

CHAPTER 10 AIOPS RCA

In the following example, enter the number of metrics (M) as 3 and the number of time steps (T) as 128.

```
POST /_plugins/_ml/_execute/METRICS_CORRELATION
{"metrics": [[-1.1635416, -1.5003631, 0.46138194, 0.5308311, -0.83149344, -3.7009873,
-3.5463789, 0.80134094]]}
```

The API returns the following information:

- event_window: Event interval
- event_pattern: Intensity score across time periods and overall severity of the event
- suspected_metrics: Set of metrics involved

Each entry corresponds to an event found in the metric data. The algorithm finds one event in the input data of the request, as shown in the output of event_pattern, which has a length of 1. event_window shows that the event occurred between time 52 and 72. Finally, suspected_metrics shows that the event is related to all three metrics.

```
{ {
  "function_name": "metrics_correlation",
  "output": { "output".
    "inference_results": [].
      { {
        "event_window": [
          52,
          72
        ],
        "event_pattern": [0, 0, 0, 0, 0, 0, 0, 0, 0, 0, 0, 0, 0, 0, 0, 0, 0, 0, 0,
          0, 0, 0, 0, 0, 0, 0, 0, 0, 0, 0, 0, 0, 0, 0, 0, 0, 0 , 0, 0, 0, 0, 0, 0, 0,
          3.99625e-05, 0.0001052875, 0.0002605894, 0.00064648513, 0.0014303402, 0.002980127,
          0.005871893, 0.010885878, 0.01904726, 0.031481907, 0.04920215, 0.07283493,
          0.10219432, 0.1361888, 0.17257516, 0.20853643, 0.24082609, 0.26901975, 0.28376183,
          0.29364157, 0.29541212, 0.2832976, 0.29041746, 0.2574534, 0.2610143, 0.22938538,
          0.19999361, 0.18074994, 0.15539801, 0.13064545, 0.10544432, 0.081248805, 0.05965102,
          0.041305058, 0.027082501, 0.01676033, 0.009760197, 0.005362286, 0.0027713624,
          0.0013381141, 0.0006126331, 0.0002634901, 0.000106459476, 4.0407333e-05, 0, 0, 0, 0,
          0, 0, 0, 0, 0, 0, 0, 0, 0, 0, 0, 0, 0, 0, 0, 0, 0, 0, 0, 0, 0, 0, 0, 0, 0,
          0, 0, 0, 0, 0, 0, 0, 0, 0, 0, 0, 0, 0, 0, 0, 0, 0, 0, 0, 0, 0],
        "suspected_metrics": [0,1,2]
      }
    ]
  }
}
```

CHAPTER 10   AIOPS RCA

10.2.1. AIOps Correlation Demo

This section contains an introduction to the metric correlation algorithm. It includes a demonstration using data from the Server Machine dataset, and a description of the algorithm configuration and output.

10.2.1.1. Step 1: Install the Packages

In the terminal, install the following packages:

```
%load_ext autoreload
%autoreload 2
# !pip install pandas matplotlib numpy opensearch-py
```

Then define the client settings and features:

```
cluster_url = 'https://localhost:9200'

def get_os_client(cluster_url = CLUSTER_URL,
                  username='admin',
                  p assword='admin'):
    """
    Get OpenSearch client
    :param cluster_url: cluster URL like https://ml-te-netwo-1s12ba42br23v-ff1736fa7db98ff2.elb.us-west-2.amazonaws.com:443
    :return: OpenSearch client
    """
    client = OpenSearch(
        hosts=[cluster_url],
        http_auth=(username, password),
        verify_certs=False,
        timeout = 30
    )
    return client
```

Connect with the ml_common client:

```
from opensearch_py_ml.ml_commons import import MLCommonClient
ml_client = MLCommonClient(client)
```

10.2.1.2. Step 2: Prepare Your Data

```
df_pd = pd.read_csv("data/smd_data.csv", header=None)
df_pd
```

CHAPTER 10 AIOPS RCA

This case considers an example of a server machine dataset. As the name suggests, the data are performance metrics collected from industrial servers. The servers sometimes suffer performance degradations that show up in the metric data. In this case, you will assume the role of an operations engineer investigating the recent metric data to understand if and how these problems occurred.

While individual metrics can show very different behavior, it is essential to correlate problems across metrics in order to detect and diagnose server issues. First, let's visualize the data you'll be working with in this case study. It consists of nine metrics observed at 1,000 timestamps. Each metric time series has been normalized so that the values are between 0 and 1.

```
M, T = df_pd.shape

plt.figure(figsize=(12,4))
cm = plt.get_cmap('Dark2')
vals = np.array(M)[::-1]

for i in range(M):
    plt.plot(df_pd.iloc[i], color = cm(vals[i]))

plt.title('Example metrics from the Server Machine Dataset')
plt.ylabel('Normalized metrics value')
plt.xlabel('Timestamp')
```

Figure 10-2 shows the result.

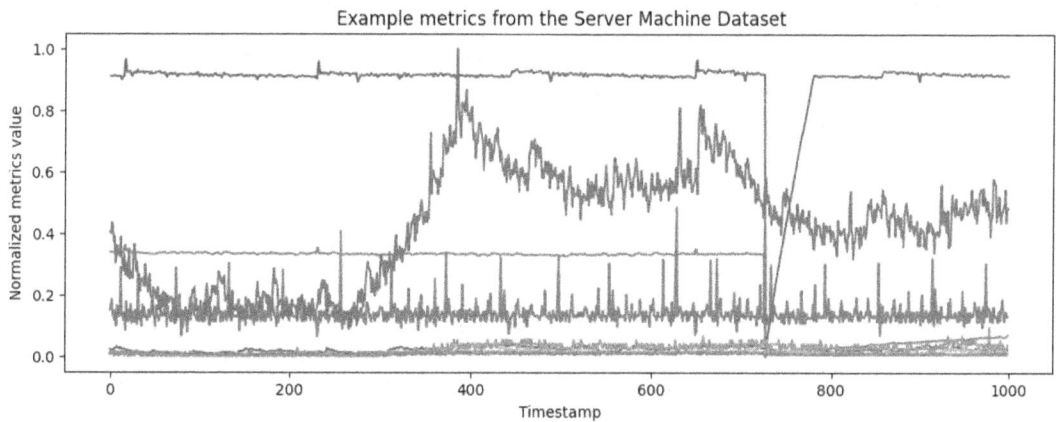

Figure 10-2. *Normalized metric*

10.2.1.3. Step 3: Metric Correlation

The metric correlation algorithm looks for events in a metric dataset. Here, an event is defined as a time window during which multiple metrics simultaneously display abnormal behavior. Given a time scope and a total set of metrics, the metric correlation algorithm automatically determines how many events occurred, when they occurred, and which metrics are associated with each event. The algorithm requires no prior training and minimal configuration.

CHAPTER 10   AIOPS RCA

Let's see how this works on the server machine dataset example.

```
df_pd = pd.read_csv("data/smd_data.csv", header=None)
df_pd
```

Now, through the execute API, you can run the metric correlation algorithm on this data.

```
results = ml_client.execute(
    algorithm_name = "METRICS_CORRELATION",
    input_json = input_json
)
```

The result is provided as a list, where each component of the list is an event that the algorithm found in the data. If the list is zero in length, the algorithm did not find any events in the given input data.

In this case, the algorithm searches for two events.

```
len(results['output']['inference_results'])
```

Every event is represented by a dictionary, with three fields

- **Event window:** A list consisting of the start and end index values of the event. Describes when the event occurred.

- **Suspected metrics:** A list containing an index of all metrics that were part of the event. This describes which metrics were correlated during the event.

- **Event pattern:** An array of length T where each value represents the relative strength of the event at that timestamp. This roughly represents the time the algorithm focused on to define the event.

```
results['output']['inference_results'][0].keys()
dict_keys(['event_window', 'event_pattern', 'suspected_metrics'])
```

10.2.1.4. Step 4: Visualize Your Results

In this step, you implement a plotting function that uses each of these fields to visually display the event. This method displays all of the input data, but highlights the metric associated with the event and shades the interval in which the event occurred. It also displays the pattern of the event.

Now you can easily visualize the two events found in your data.

```
plot_event(results['ou tput']['inference_results'][0], df_pd)
```

Figure 10-3 shows the result.

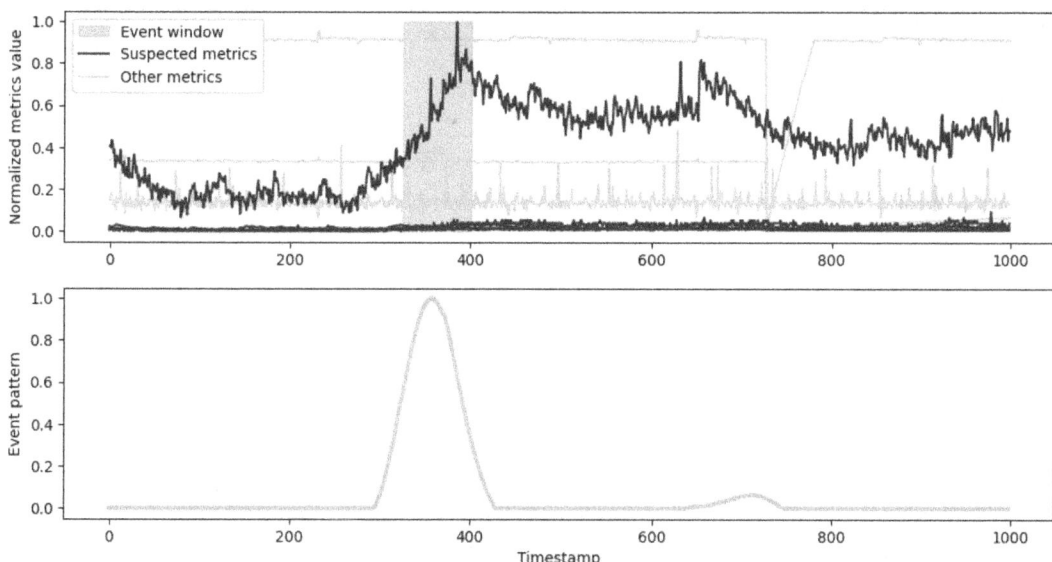

Figure 10-3. *Outputting the event pattern*

```
print("Event window for second event", results['output']['inference_results'][1]['event_
window'])
```

```
print("Suspected metrics", results['output']['inference_results'][1]['suspected_metrics'])
```

The first event occurs between timestamps 325 and 401 and is characterized by a large spike that can be clearly seen in the first plot of the data. However, the algorithm found and correlated several other metrics that show more subtle changes during this period.

In this plot, you can see that only one metric contributes significantly to the event, but if you look closely without the main metric, note the changes in other metrics over the same period. To show this visually, I've plotted the other metrics:

```
ixs = [x for x in results['output']['inference_results'][0]['suspected_metrics'] if x!=6]
event_start, event_end = results['output']['inference_results'][0]['event_window']
plt.figure(figsize=(12, 4))

for i in ixs:
    plt.plot(df_pd.iloc[i], alpha=0.8, color = cm(vals[i]))

plt.fill_between(results['output']['inference_results'][0]['event_window'], 0, 0.1,
color='skyblue', alpha=0.6)
plt.show()
```

727

CHAPTER 10 AIOPS RCA

Figure 10-4 shows the result.

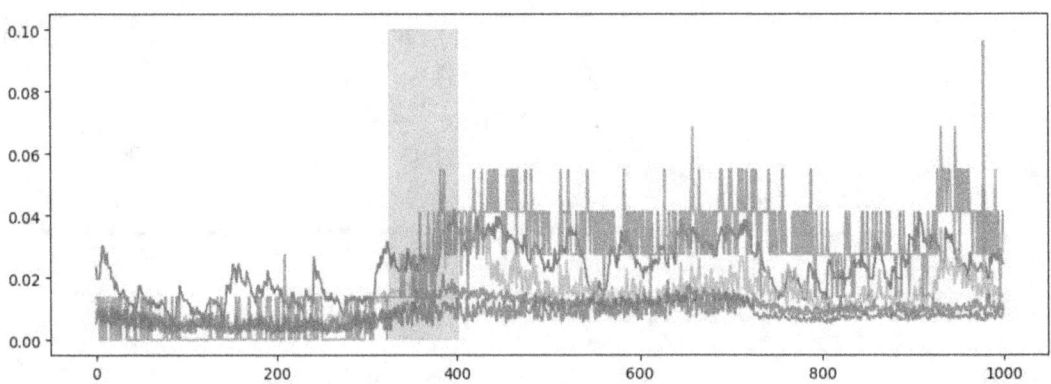

Figure 10-4. *Outputting multiple metrics*

Next, we'll plan a second event.

```
plot_event(results['output']['inference_results'][1], df_pd)
```

Figure 10-5 shows the result.

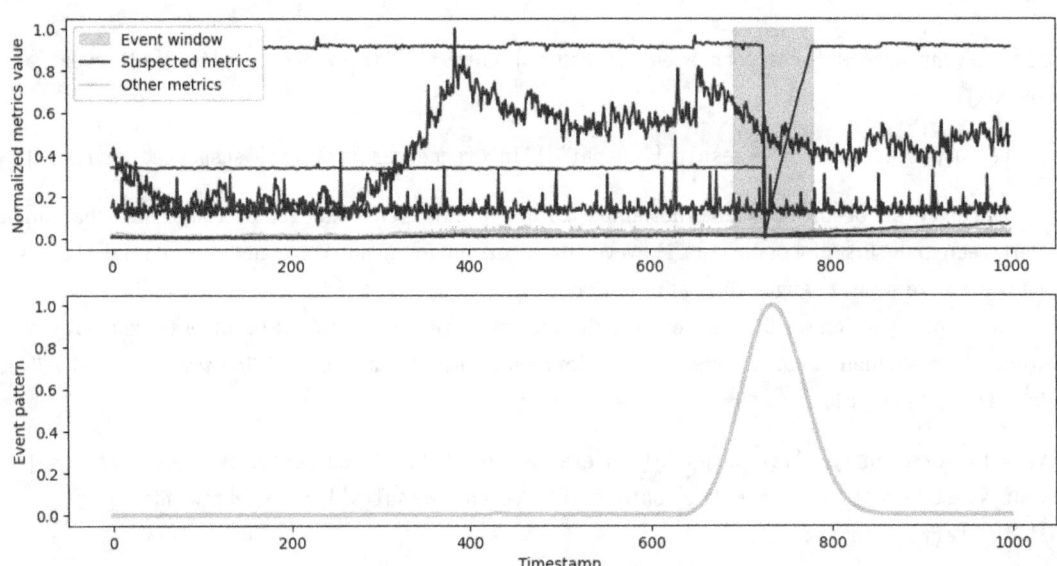

Figure 10-5. *Outputting the second event*

```
print("Event window for second event", results['output']['inference_results'][1]['event_window'])

print("Suspected metrics", results['output']['inference_results'][1]['suspected_metrics'])
```

The second event occurs between timestamps 692 and 780, and it captures the sharp dip that was again clearly visible in the initial plot. Here, the drop is automatically correlated with a second, smaller drop, with several metrics changing behavior from rising to slow rising during this interval.

10.3. IT Operation Data

AIOps requires a variety of operational data, including CMDB. The failure to collect the data required for AIOps leads to poor results.

As described earlier, observability data is being ingested through a data pipeline, structured for search, analysis, and aggregation. It's stored in a data lake.

- In previous experience with many data projects, how structured the data is and how it is preprocessed makes a big difference in the results. Structured data like metrics and traces use structured algorithms and supervised learning. Promscale and Druid, described in the previous chapter, are already structured.

- Anomaly detection uses unsupervised learning. Anomaly detection is similar to pattern analysis and lends itself to simple classification and inference. Many logs are indexed, processed, and structured in OpenSearch.

- AIOps can be applied to a variety of use cases, including root cause analysis. It can be extended using structured logs and external knowledge bases. Use logs and configure them as Generative AI.

Let's think about the data you need for AIOps.

1. Define the categories of IT operations.
2. Derive subject and data by category.
3. Determine if data is being collected and output correctly.

The bottom line is that commercial observability AIOps fails because of a lack of data, and the downside of commercial observability is its closed nature. It's a closed environment where you want to combine the accumulated experience and existing know-how within the organization to produce the best results, but it's hard to connect with external learning data. It does not provide the ability to add external learning data to commercial observability AIOps, and there are many technical constraints to exporting data from commercial observability. In many ways, commercial observability AIOps is hard to succeed.

Because AIOps requires a lot of data, it requires a variety of systems and pipelines to be organized, as shown in Figure 10-6.

The scope of AIOps is as follows. For root cause analysis to be successful, the following data is required.

- Infrastructure and application observability
- Deploying builds

CHAPTER 10   AIOPS RCA

- Configuring CMDB
- Jira issue management
- Organization and contact information

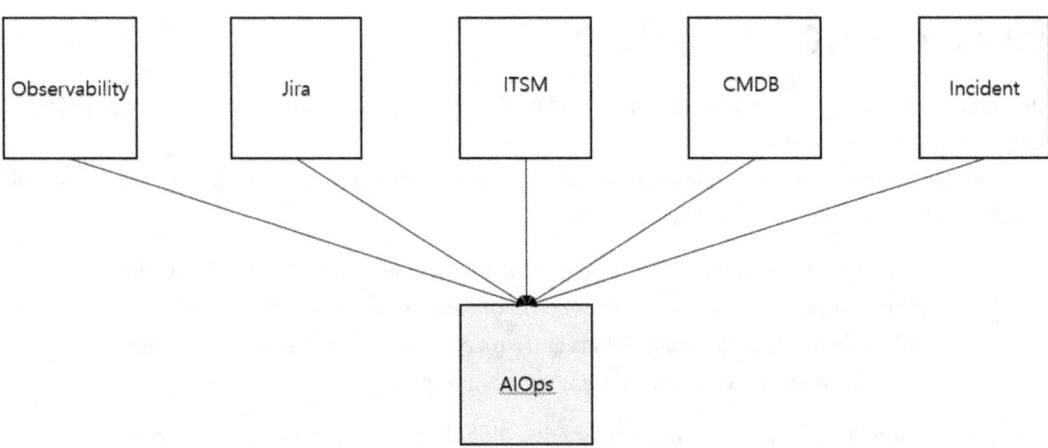

Figure 10-6. Data sources in AIOps

You need to have a lot of SREs with technical expertise in-house. Most business-oriented companies, unless they are tech companies, don't have that internal know-how. The focus on personal work does not provide time to analyze kernel and system resources for a long period of time. It is difficult to grow in banking and telecommunications, even they are good companies, because there is no environment where you can focus in detail and build your skills, and colleagues are not cooperative.

There is currently no commercial observability that provides the data required for AIOps. Know-how is hard to build in a short period of time.

There are many applications of AIOps for analyzing failures. For example, suppose a user's mobile app is experiencing high latency and low Apdex, and the question is: Which area of the network, application, or database is causing the problem? Commercial observability AIOps analyzes the internal call path of the system in chronological order to determine where the problem initially occurred and how it affects other areas. It distinguishes between where the problem first occurred and where it propagated, and it forecasts the root cause analysis. The root cause analysis process involves a variety of data. If AIOps uses only observability data, only a limited set of topics will be understood by AIOps. IT operations require more topics and data. In addition to application and infrastructure observability data, you need CMDB, deployment, and more.

Observability is a small part of the larger scope of IT operations. Currently, observability is focused on applications and partly on infrastructure. AIOps requires data on a variety of topics beyond observability.

- **Deploy your builds:** Integrate with Git, Jenkins, and ArgoCD to annotate or list deployment and rollback information. Visualize sudden spikes with annotations.

- **Maintenance:** Manage rolling updates and outages due to maintenance.

- **Jira tickets:** Manage high-priority issues and incidents.

- **Availability:** By using probes to monitor various endpoints, you can proactively respond to failures.

- **MTTR:** Manage the lifecycle of errors and failures, support root cause analysis and recurrence prevention and knowledge sharing.

- **Alerts:** By displaying alerts in a state timeline, you can understand their status and lifecycle.

- **Anomaly detection:** Anomaly detection is associated with dashboards and alerts by default.

- **Resource and service management:** Manage changes to resource configurations in Terraform and Cloud. In conjunction with newly created resources and services, you can configure automated discovery.

- **Costs:** Manage costs by key resources and services. You can discover where costs are suddenly increasing.

It is necessary to consider whether CMDB or observability is suitable for AIOps configuration. In the past, IT operations were centered on CMDB, but observability, including performance management in APM, is evolving into a platform. Data that should have been managed in the CMDB is being managed in observability in a duplicate manner. Deployments, changes, and probes required for operation are supported by observability, so it is functionally redundant with CMDB, and data is also redundant.

Depending on the type of data you have at hand, there are a variety of automation possibilities.

- The data sources for metric correlation are structured data, such as metrics and traces. Metrics can be applied to both infrastructure and application, but traces are limited to applications.

- The data sources for anomaly detection are unstructured data, such as logs and events. It is difficult to make a clear distinction because logs can also be structured data. Events are closer to the business and applications than infrastructure.

- Metric correlation and anomaly detection can be automated using AI. The root cause analysis data model described previously already contains data throughout in a structured form. In terms of accuracy, the root cause analysis data model is more accurate than AI. It can be used as the most accurate data source.

The root cause analysis data model is constructed by joining multiple tables and embedding it in a Vector database that only measures similarity can be inaccurate.

The dashboard is organized as shown in Figure 10-7. It consists of two parts: the top part, which uses machine learning-based anomaly detection, and the bottom part, which implements LLM prompts. This dashboard:

- Provides various anomaly detection based on the subject, and the user can select the subject. You can also use metric correlations.
- Identifies anomalies through time series graphs.
- Enters questions about the identified anomalies at the prompt.
- LLM answers the root cause analysis.

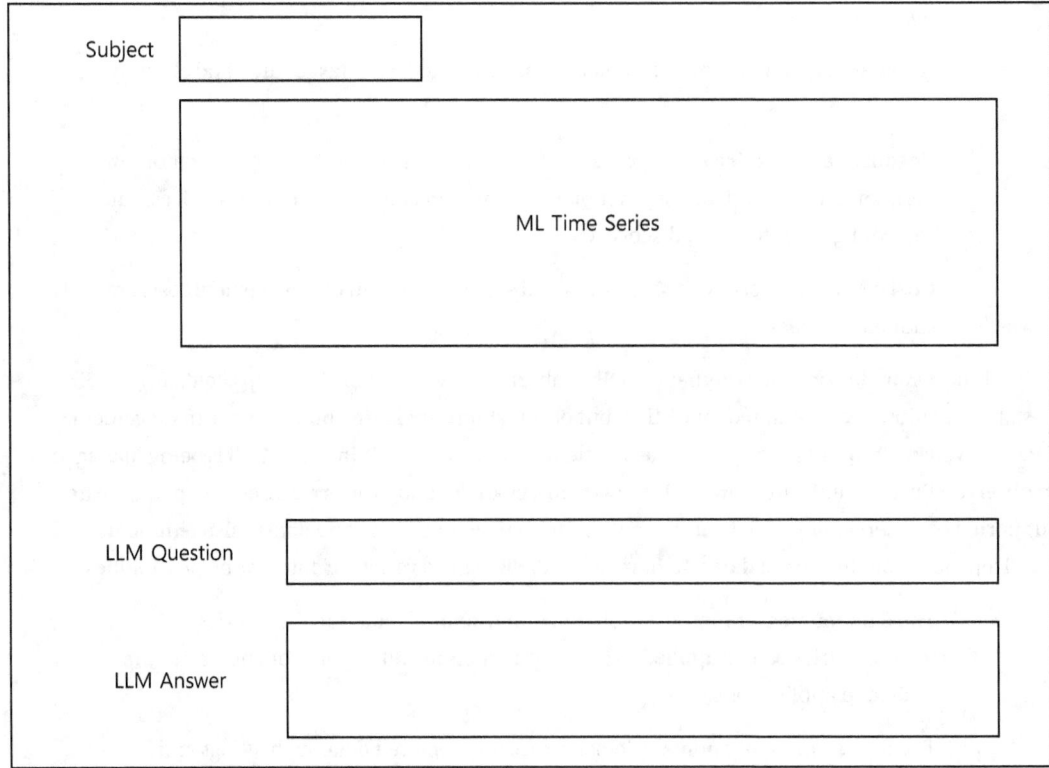

Figure 10-7. The AIOps dashboard

The user needs to have the experience and knowledge to view the results and judge the results of the root cause analysis.

It is not useful to have a large number of dashboards. An AIOps dashboard can be embedded in a root cause analysis dashboard. It uses the root cause analysis and failure list tables and attempts to join them. A small number of necessary and useful dashboards are enough to improve and automate operations.

The data required for the AIOps dashboard is managed in the knowledge base and LLM in the Vector database.

I recommend using commercial observability solutions whenever possible, but it has limitations for configuring AIOps dashboards.

- Commercial observability solutions are not scalable. It is difficult to add data. It needs to be flexible and extendable through continuous improvement.

- Open source and commercial observability solutions collect limited data from within the organization. They fail to trace all the way through, or don't understand the observability data model.

It's impossible to accurately identify the cause of a failure at first glance. You need to understand the big picture and narrow it down. While there are dozens of commercially observability failure and error categories, they are limited in describing the wide variety of failures. In this book, there are hundreds of categories of failures. It is difficult to accurately infer hundreds of failure categories with a classification model alone.

Anomaly detection and metric correlation using machine learning were not used to infer disorder categories. Machine learning was used to understand context and reduce scope before inferring failure categories. LLM was used to predict the failure category and to answer detailed questions. No single algorithm handles all the different inferences, but each algorithm does what it does best.

Traditional monitoring tries to reduce noise by setting thresholds and sending alarms when a failure occurs. If the signal is accurate, it accomplishes its purpose at some level. But observability needs to include more. It involves entities, so that you can clearly identify the failed service or resource and easily look up the services and resources it depends on. It should clearly distinguish between errors and exceptions, clearly identify where the error is occurring in the backend through trace, and easily understand the user impact of the error. All of this data needs to be accurately collected, stored in observability, and queried so that you can join different signals to get the exact data you need. Anomaly detection and root cause analysis should be automated with AI. The amount of data managed by observability is larger than you might think. Observability is evolving to the center of IT operations.

Before AIOps, it's important to collect data and structure it so that it can be queried. AIOps requires high quality data.

- A runbook that describes the causes and solutions for various failures.

- Data that allows for root cause analysis

- Includes historical failure data and should be configured for reproducibility. Event sourcing is a good solution. The events, commands, and states in event sourcing match the requirements of AIOps.

Observability requires joining with various data, including CMDB. Within observability, you can build a root cause analysis data model and join with data from other systems.

Data analytics can be done Promscale and via Druid, but I provide two ways to do it using event stores.

Rather than starting with complex and time-consuming services like AIOps and anomaly detection, it's important to use dashboards early on to understand the overall flow and data. Ideally, you should use dashboards to understand your data and processes and switch to AIOps as you gradually automate them. If you jump straight into AIOps and anomaly detection without analyzing your processes, data, and existing

CHAPTER 10   AIOPS RCA

problems, the SRE will not be able to determine if anomalies and problems are identified whether correct or not. The SRE's internal capabilities need to be enhanced to the point where they are able to judge the accuracy of the conclusions generated by AIOps. This is because AIOps is often wrong.

Grafana connects various data sources and enables visualization. You can recognize problems, set thresholds and alerts, and improve your understanding of your data by looking at it directly.

- Configuration information for services and resources
- Access control and permissions
- Upgrades and updates
- Security
- Organizations
- Application endpoints
- Business processes
- Knowledge bases
- Communication
- Infrastructures

Observability data manages data such as latency, performance, and errors. AIOps should include a variety of data, including observability. AIOps use cases are not unique, and many are easily encountered and automated in normal IT operations.

It's important to learn the use cases for AIOps. Alerts are a simple concept, but reducing the noise in them is a difficult task. Alerts are used extensively for SLO, anomaly detection, and more, so AIOps is the way to go.

- How often and how many alerts are reactivated
- Categorize the cause of the alert
- Determine the frequency of occurrence per hour per alert
- Time to resolve per alert
- Time to initial response per alert
- Whether duplicate alerts are occurring
- Accuracy and reliability of alerts
- Lifecycle management per alert
- Are the alerts noisy or not
- Automatic assignment of alert channels

- Alert's severity rating
- Dynamic threshold measurement

Alerts are used with formulas for MTTR, availability, error budget, and burn rate.

Alerts are more of an final result, the process is defining and collecting signals. If an alert is inaccurate, it is most often because there is a problem with the signal. Don't confuse the result with the cause. Improving the cause is more important, and as the cause of signal is refined and improved in quality, the result of the alert will naturally improve.

Errors have a similar lifecycle to alarms. However, the same root cause analysis can contain many different errors. A root cause can have a small number of errors, but many errors can occur because of the propagation and nesting of errors. Application errors and infrastructure errors overlap, and errors at the network layer can also overlap. It is useful to separate errors into user-facing errors that affect the availability of the service and root cause errors that occur earlier in the chronological order.

- Frequency and number of errors
- Error codes and status codes
- Percentage of errors per service
- Root cause of errors
- Determine the type of error: user or root cause
- Determine if the error is business or technical
- Dependency of the error
- Whether the error is propagating

Anomalies, alerts, and errors are typically managed in observability, while incidents and issues are heavily used in Jira.

Alerts, errors, incidents, and so on have statuses. In addition to measuring thresholds, you need to manage and visualize the state.

Recently, I've seen AIOps implementations using Slack to implement ChatOps.

Incidents:

- Incident assignment ratio by operator
- Assign incidents to the right operator
- Determine if the error code is correct
- Determine if a rollback is required
- Estimate the time required to resolve the issue

The information that should be recorded in deployments, changes, oncalls, and issues in the organization. The organization is always changing, so it needs to be synchronized when changes occur.

CHAPTER 10 AIOPS RCA

There are two types of AI services: ML and LLM. The most important part of ML is data preprocessing. ML preprocessing is the process of structuring data. Most ML projects focus on preprocessing.

LLM also requires preprocessing. It is the process of structuring and cleaning the data before storing it in vectors. Writing a runbook, providing the underlying data, and organizing the knowledge base well are important tasks for LLM preprocessing and improve the accuracy of LLM.

It is common for various deployments, such as rolling updates, rollbacks, canary, AB, BlueGreen, and so on, to send hooks to observability, which become events in observability.

Organizations include:

- System operators
- Developers
- Teams and individuals
- Roles

It's still common for organizations to manage in Excel and update it whenever changes occur.

Costs:

- Forecasting costs for reserved resources
- Increase in the number of resources in a particular category
- Resource utilization increases or decreases dramatically

In the case of the cloud, I recommend downloading it as a CSV and adding it to your expense management database rather than calling the API.

Resources:

- Forecast resource growth
- Determine whether a resource is needed
- Determine whether traffic is evenly distributed across resources
- Automated and manual tags
- Whether a resource is utilized
- Categorize unallocated resources

Entities such as services, resources, and tags are managed in the CMDB, but can now be ingested by observability agents.

Performance:

- Select the service that is closer to the root cause among multiple services
- Identify outliers
- Determine the severity of the failure

- Impact analysis
- Dependency analysis
- Analyze whether the failure is propagating
- Calibrate and automatically improve the accuracy of traces and spans

In addition, you need configuration information, change information, service and resource information, catalogs, and more. IT operations are broad, and there are many different operating systems. The CMDB collects, centrally stores, and manages most of the data used in operations.

The companies with the best failure response and operational capabilities are those that have a well-organized CMDB. Observability alone does not improve fault response and operational capabilities. Observability helps you focus on problem identification and resolution, but it doesn't improve organization, business processes, and communication.

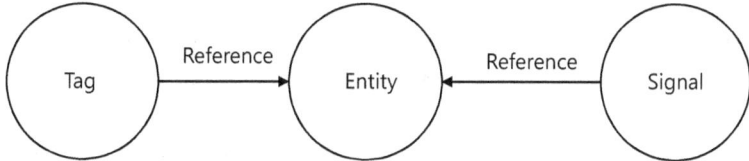

Figure 10-8. The relationship between entities

Services and resources that are configured by agents are not signals. They are the metadata of the signal, as shown in Figure 10-8. Tags are added to entities, not signals. The use of tags should be minimized wherever possible and configured to extend correlation. Observability can be a source for services, resources, and so on. Such an architecture minimizes linkages and is simpler to operate and maintain.

OpenTelemetry does not automatically discover resources, services, or other entities. Automatic discovery is one of the advantages of commercial agents.

10.3.1. Using CMDB

A CMDB is a configuration management database, a file that clarifies the relationships between the hardware, software, and networks used by an IT organization.

It is master data and must manage attributes, relationships, and versions. This is not a simple change, but an incremental one, so additional changes must be managed.

It is master data and must manage attributes, relationships, versions, and so on. This is not a simple change, but an incremental one, so additional changes must be managed.

A CMDB stores information about the configuration of items such as hardware, software, systems, facilities, and even employees. This configuration data can include interdependencies between items, each item's change history, and its class and attributes (e.g., type, owner, criticality). It is the job of the IT organization to define what needs to be traced and how to trace it.

Within the CMDB, these trace items are called configuration items (CIs). As defined by ITIL 4, a CI is "any component that needs to be managed to deliver an IT service." Examples of CIs include routers, servers, applications, and virtual machines.

The goal of a CMDB is to provide the information needed to make better business decisions and run efficient ITSM processes. By keeping all configuration information centralized, operators have a better understanding of critical CIs and their relationships. A CMDB is important for impact analysis, root cause analysis, legal compliance, incident management, and change management.

10.3.1.1. CMDB Benefits

Siloed data and outdated information are key problems that CMDB solves. Before implementing a CMDB, most organizations had a variety of data spread across multiple systems, making it impossible for owners to see all CIs and their dependencies at a glance, and even harder to know what information is current and what is outdated.

For this reason, teams don't understand critical context when making decisions. This can impact risk assessment and reporting, decision-making, slow down issue resolution, and ultimately cost the business in financial and reputational terms.

For example, suppose CI A's data is in one department and CI B is in another. CI B is dependent on CI A to function properly, but when CI A's department decides to switch offline for maintenance, there's no way to know the impact on CI B. CI B is dependent on CI A to function properly.

It can cause nothing but confusion among teams. In the worst case, it can turn into a major incident. All you need to avoid these scenarios is an effective CMDB.

10.3.1.2. Operations

CMDB improves a number of core ITSM practices, including changes, incidents, and problem management.

1. In change management, a CMDB can forecast users, systems, and other CI that may be affected, improving risk assessment. In regulated industries, it can also support compliance, helping teams manage controls and providing a clear audit trail.

2. In incident management, a CMDB can help you identify the changes that caused an incident and resolve it faster. Incident records can be linked to related CIs, so teams can trace incidents over time along with the affected assets.

3. In problem management, CMDB supports root cause analysis, allowing teams to get to the heart of a problem faster. It can also support proactive problem management by helping teams identify assets that need to be upgraded to reduce service costs and unplanned downtime.

CMDB reduces complexity, prevents errors, improves security, and helps ITSM practices like change and incident management run smoothly.

CHAPTER 10 AIOPS RCA

In addition to signals through discovery, comprise entities such as services and resources. Entities contain many relationships and attributes between them. Entities serve as metadata for the signals that are collected. The problem is that there may be differences or conflicts with the entities, such as services and resources defined in the CMDB. Through the discovery of observability, various operational activities can be improved.

- Creating and changing services and resources: It does not collect entities directly from Kubernetes, but rather collects changed entities through the agent's discovery.
- Used for deployments and releases such as BlueGreen and Canary.
- Used for failure responses, such as runbooks and alerts.

AIOps requires a variety of data to be successful. Observability alone is not enough to enable AIOps.

- Observability does not support kernels, system calls, black boxes, or clusters. Limited data is collected.
- AIOps requires other important data besides application observability data. CMDB data helps with root cause analysis.

Failures happen for a variety of reasons. Failures due to changes in applications and infrastructure are more common than failures due to overload.

- After deploying a new feature and release, failures can occur due to bugs in the feature. Most failures are deployment-related.
- Kubernetes supports rolling updates. During rolling updates, latency can occur, or errors can cause retries. Even in simple deployments, most observability can't distinguish between rolling update errors and critical deployment errors.
- Internal maintenance can be caused by infrastructure as well as applications, and failures can be caused by external cloud and SaaS maintenance.
- You can also change the network configuration in an external telecom.
- The infrastructure team may make changes to aging hardware, authorized developers may create new resources, or there may be failures in applying feature upgrade patches.

It is more important to understand whether changes have occurred at the IT operational level and how they affect observability before focusing on the specific problem of observability.

AIOps fails because of the lack of poor data quality.

- AIOps is better organized around the CMDB than observability.
- AIOps should be implemented in a way that integrates CMDB and observability.
- A knowledge base should be organized that includes root causes and solutions.

CHAPTER 10 AIOPS RCA

Organize your CMDB to enable a high level of automation. Connect with observability and configure AIOps, as shown in Figure 10-9.

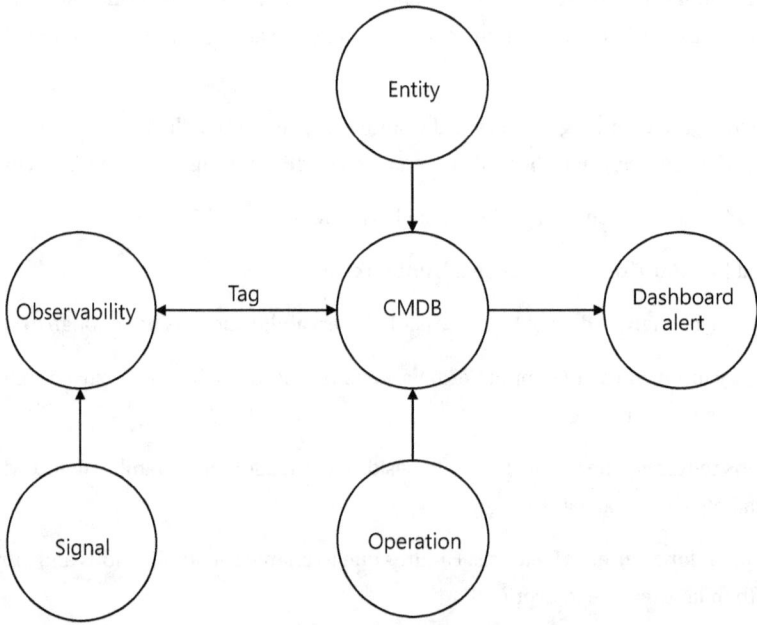

Figure 10-9. *The relationship between observability and CMDB*

- You can tag entities automatically or manually.
- Entities include virtual machines, Kubernetes, host servers, databases, and more, and unlike signals, entities are configured precisely.

CMDB collects entities through APIs. You spend a lot of money to develop a CMDB, and it's inefficient. Observability provides a better solution for organizing a CMDB. Observability uses agents, so it is more specific and automatable than CMDB. APIs are great for collecting information about resources, services, and so on, but they are sometimes parsed directly from GitHub, and are difficult to collect without the help of infrastructure. With an observability data lake, SRE can look up entities in the infrastructure and utilize them for various purposes without the help of other teams. This is a great way to save time and money.

CHAPTER 10   AIOPS RCA

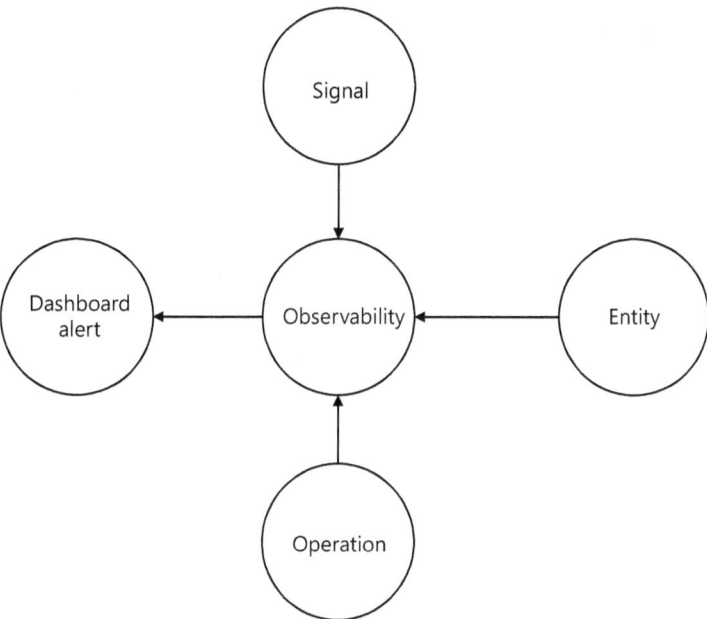

Figure 10-10. *AIOps centric observability*

As observability manages services and resources instead of CMDB, future changes in operational architecture are anticipated. This is illustrated in Figure 10-10,

While runbooks are based on customer-specific standardized failures, and specific failures need to be refined, everything in this book is intended to be used as a source for runbooks and AIOps.

More detailed runbooks should be written for the failures described so far, tied to business processes, and provided to AIOps. Only then can AIOps succeed.

The foundation of AIOps is good data collection. If it's not collected, it's hard to measure, hard to analyze, and hard to automate. Even if it is collected, it needs to be preprocessed into a format that AI can understand. In LLM, you need to write a runbook. Microservices alone don't collect enough data and need to include legacy.

AIOps will only be successful if the scope of data collection and utilization extends to legacy.

In Kubernetes and cloud environments, systems are always changing. Dynamic system changes are prone to failure and difficult to manage. An example is autoscaling.

In practice, you often don't have the data you need for AIOps.

- Data is not being collected.
- You're not sure if the data exists, and you don't know where it is.
- The data exists, but it takes months to actually utilize it.

As a solution, observability can be a great single source of truth.

10.3.2. Autoscaling

When you apply non-blocking options to accommodate more traffic, you can't forecast what happens on the backend.

If you're not serving an unspecified number of people, you have a set number of users, and you can predict your traffic, there's not much reason to use autoscale. The more dynamically the system is configured, the more unstable it becomes.

Kubernetes can scale the number of pods by checking CPU utilization or other metrics. This is called the *Horizontal Pod Autoscaler* (HPA), and it is a controller that checks the metrics you specify and automatically increases or decreases ports to get the number of replicas of pods needed based on load.

This book does not provide detailed explanations and labs for autoscaling clusters by adding and subtracting nodes, but only explains and provides labs for autoscaling pods by adding and subtracting pods.

HPA autoscales pods and can be used to scale pods for the following resources, including replica sets.

- Deployment
- ReplicaSet
- Replication controller
- StatefulSet

Autoscale can be applied to various components within a Grafana observability. For example, distributor, querier, query-frontend, and gateway are set to autoscale, and each component constitutes a separate hash ring.

There are many ways to autoscale. AWS has provided autoscaling based on EC2 virtual machines. However, since virtual machines combine network and storage centered on the OS, there is a high dependency, and the large capacity required for autoscale takes a long time to replicate. When scaling applications horizontally, it is difficult to achieve horizontal scaling, which is ineffective in terms of cost and resource optimization because it extends to unnecessary parts. Containers overcame these shortcomings and provided a solution.

Containers are small, simple to replicate, and only run applications. They are loosely coupled with other complex infrastructure, making them ideal for horizontal autoscaling. In fact, many commercial applications from IBM and Oracle have been redeveloped to support containers, drastically changing their existing architecture to support containers. Autoscale is better for performance and resource utilization when scaling horizontally on a container-by-container basis.

It is important that autoscale scales pods horizontally and evenly distributes user traffic to the scaled pods.

- Flow to increment pods based on measured metrics
    - To measure metrics, you use a metrics server, but it has the limitation that it only supports CPU and memory metrics. Therefore, we usually use Prometheus adapter, KEDA Kubernetes event-driven autoscaling to collect/manage application metrics.
    - HPA increases the number of pods based on the measured metric information.

- A flow that distributes a user's traffic to each pod

    - The process of autoscaling, which involves engaging with autoscaled pods based on measured metrics and delivering real services to users, is a complex task.

    - User traffic flows through the frontend and into the Kubernetes service.

    - Pods that have been autoscaled should be easily spotted, and the load should be evenly distributed across the pods.

    - You need to configure a production environment with a load balancer in front of your Kubernetes service.

Scale your application from multiple perspectives. There is horizontal scaling by adjusting the number of pod replicas, vertical scaling by adjusting the resource requirements for pods, and scaling the cluster itself by changing the number of cluster nodes. While all of these operations can be performed manually, Kubernetes provides a way to automatically perform scaling based on load.

Kubernetes automates the orchestration and management of applications composed of many containers by maintaining declaratively expressed requests. However, due to the continuously and frequently changing nature of most workloads, it is not easy to know how the state of a request should be reflected. Figuring out exactly how many resources a container will demand—as well as how many replicas a service needs to adequately meet service levels at any given time—requires a lot of time and effort. Fortunately, Kubernetes makes it easy to change the resources of a container, the number of service replicas requested, and the number of nodes in a cluster. These changes can be done manually or, given certain rules, in a fully automated way.

In addition to maintaining fixed pod and cluster configurations, Kubernetes can monitor external load and capacity-related events, analyze its current state, and scale itself to the desired performance. Let's take a look at the different ways this behavior is possible and how to combine scaling approaches.

Kubernetes provides a variety of features and techniques for finding the best settings for your application.

The dynamic nature of most workloads, which change over time, makes it difficult to set fixed scaling, but cloud-native technologies like Kubernetes allow you to create applications that adapt to changing loads. With Kubernetes' autoscaling, you can define the capacity of different applications in terms of how much they can process different loads, rather than a fixed capacity. The simplest way to enable this behavior is to use HPA to scale the number of pods horizontally.

Consider creating an HPA for a deployment. For the HPA to be effective, it is important to declare the `spec.resources.requests` limit on the deployment. Another requirement is to enable a metrics server that aggregates resource usage data across the cluster.

CHAPTER 10 AIOPS RCA

Now let's look at how HPA can replace human operators to ensure autoscaling. At a high level, the HPA controller continuously performs the following steps:

- Get metrics for pods that are scaled according to the HPA definition. It does not read metrics directly from the pod, but from the Kubernetes Metrics API, which provides aggregated metrics. The resource metric at the pod level is taken from the Kubernetes metrics API, and all other metrics are taken from the Kubernetes custom metrics API.

- Calculates the number of replicas needed based on the current metric value and the requested metric value to target.

Metric calculation and implementation are further complicated by the need to account for multiple running instances of pods, deal with multiple metric types, and even account for a variety of exception cases and fluctuating values. For example, if multiple metrics are specified, HPA evaluates each metric individually and suggests the largest value, meaning that when the calculation is complete, the final output is an integer that is less than or equal to the "requested threshold" but greater than or equal to the "requested number of replicas" that will be autoscaled.

The types of metrics that HPA evaluates include standard metrics and custom metrics.

- **Standard metrics:** Declared as .spec.metrics.resource[:].type, the same as resources, and represent resource usage metrics such as CPU and memory. Standard metrics are the easiest type of metric to use, typically provided by metric servers and the like.

- **User-defined (custom) metrics:** Custom metrics are declared as .spec.metrics.resource[:].type, the same as objects or pods, and require different advanced cluster monitoring settings for each cluster. A custom metric of type Pod describes, as the name implies, a specific pod metric, while an object of type Object can describe any other object. Custom metrics are done with the Aggregated API server at the custom.metrics.k8s.io API path and are available in various metrics adapters such as Prometheus.

Autoscaling is a rapidly evolving area of Kubernetes, and each detail can have a big impact on the overall behavior of autoscaling.

- Use a combination of pod-level autoscale and node-level autoscale. The pod-level autoscaler creates the number of additional pods specified in the deployment and reaches a threshold of nodes. The node-level scaler creates a new node and continues to create new pods on the new node. To summarize, the pod autoscaler grows pods first, and then the node (cluster) autoscaler grows nodes as appropriate for the situation.

CHAPTER 10   AIOPS RCA

- Failures occur during decreasing pods and nodes rather than increasing pods and nodes, so it is important to set detailed parameters for scale-in. It is common for different sites to have different types of traffic and therefore different parameters for scale-in. Through various tests, you should select autoscale parameters based on the increase and decrease of traffic and resources.

- While I recommend developing custom metrics and using Prometheus for advanced autoscale, if you have a microservice-based application with complex interconnections, I recommend starting with a primary resource (CPU, memory) based autoscale. Due to the complex interactions and dependencies between microservices, applying autoscale using custom metrics is a challenging task.

- The node autoscaler provides most of the automation, so there is often no need for manual intervention on the part of the operator. However, dain, cordon, taint, PDBpod disruption budget, and affinity are useful commands . Grafana Observability Helm charts basically use the metrics server to autoscale CPU, memory, and PDB. You can use KEDA to sophisticate it to suit your needs.

10.3.2.1. Prometheus Adapter

This section continues with a detailed description and hands-on lab of the Prometheus adapter, this time in theory.

- Let's say you have a frontend webserver that can autoscale based on the number of HTTP requests per second it receives by writing a configuration for the Prometheus adapter.

- Before we begin, I instrumented the frontend server using the `http_requests_total` metric. This metric is exposed as a single label method that categorizes requests by HTTP verb.

- You have configured Prometheus to collect metrics and add the `kubernetes_namespace` and `kubernetes_pod_name` labels to represent your respective namespace and pod.

Query Prometheus and you'll see a series that looks like this:

```
http_requests_total{method="GET",kubernetes_namespace="production",kubernetes_pod_name="frontend-server-abcd-0123"}
```

The adapter processes metrics in the following ways:

- Discovery first searches for available metrics.
- Association identifies the Kubernetes resource that each metric is associated with.

745

CHAPTER 10 AIOPS RCA

- Naming figures out how to expose to the custom metrics API.
- Querying finally figures out how to query Prometheus to get the actual number.

```
rules:
  custom:
    - seriesQuery: '{__name__=~"^some_metric_count$"}'
      resources:
        template: <<.Resource>>
      name:
        matches: ""
        as: "my_custom_metric"
      metricsQuery: sum(<<.Series>>{<<.LabelMatchers>>}) by (<<.GroupBy>>)
```

So far, you've set up a Prometheus adapter. Now let's set up a Kubernetes HPA.

```
apiVersion: autoscaling/v2beta1
kind: HorizontalPodAutoscaler
metadata:
  name: autoscaling-app-hpa
  namespace: custom-metrics
spec:
  scaleTargetRef:
    apiVersion: apps/v1beta1
    kind: Deployment
    name: autoscaling-deploy
  minReplicas: 1
  maxReplicas: 5
  metrics:
  - type: Object
    object:
      target:
        kind: Service
        name: autoscaling-service
      metricName: http_requests
      targetValue: 5
```

10.3.2.2. Prometheus Adapter Demo

Figure 10-11 shows how the Prometheus adapter works.

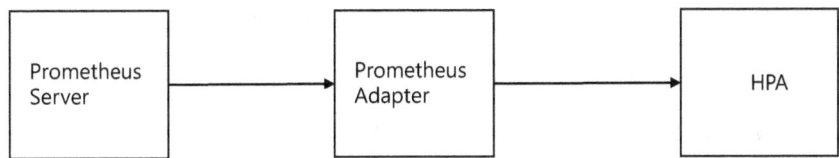

Figure 10-11. Autoscale flow in Prometheus

This example uses the Prometheus adapter:

```
minikube start --vm-driver=none --kubernetes-version v1.15.0 --memory=12000 --cpus=4
```

Use the monitoring namespace:

```
kubectl create namespace monitoring
```

Install the operator:

```
# helm install prom --namespace monitoring stable/prometheus-operator
WARNING: This chart is deprecated
manifest_sorter.go:192: info: skipping unknown hook: "crd-install"
NAME: prom
LAST DEPLOYED: Tue Aug 30 14:54:36 2022
NAMESPACE: monitoring
STATUS: deployed
REVISION: 1
```

Check the installed pods:

```
# kubectl get pod -n monitoring
name ready status restarts age
alertmanager-prom-prometheus-operator-alertmanager-0 2/2 Running 0 51s
prom-grafana-55846bb94f-lbs46 2/2 Running 0 85s
prom-kube-state-metrics-db84fc9d-5wmdv 1/1 Running 0 85s
prom-prometheus-node-exporter-5w22g 1/1 Running 0 85s
prom-prometheus-operator-operator-8678d58858-jl9lj 2/2 Running 0 85s
prometheus-prom-prom-prometheus-operator-prometheus-0 3/3 Running 1 42s
```

Configure port forwarding:

```
kubectl port-forward svc/prom-prometheus-operator-prometheus 9090:9090 --namespace monitoring
```

Use the custom-metrics namespace:

```
kubectl create namespace custom-metrics
```

CHAPTER 10   AIOPS RCA

You can retrieve registered custom metrics using the following commands:

kubectl get --raw "/apis/custom.metrics.k8s.io/v1beta1/" | jq | grep pods/

The adapter determines which metrics to expose and how to expose them through the discovery rules. Each rule runs independently (so the rules must be mutually exclusive) and specifies each step the adapter must take to expose metrics from the API.

Each rule can be divided into four parts.

- Discovery specifies how the adapter should find all Prometheus metrics for this rule.

- Association specifies how the adapter determines which Kubernetes resource a particular metric is associated with.

- Naming specifies how the adapter exposes metrics from the custom metrics API.

- Querying specifies how to translate requests for specific metrics from one or more Kubernetes instances into queries to Prometheus.

Let's take a closer look at discovery, naming, and querying.

Discovery

Manage the process of discovering the metrics you want to expose in your custom metrics API. Discovery has two settings. They are seriesQuery and seriesFilters.

seriesQuery specifies a Prometheus seriesQuery (passed to Prometheus's /api/v1/series endpoint) that will be used to find a subset of Prometheus series (series, metric-name) in the first place. The adapter removes the label values from this series and then uses the resulting metric-name-label-name combination later.

In most cases, seriesQuery is sufficient to limit the list of Prometheus series. It is useful to perform additional filtering on metric names (especially when two rules may overlap). In this case, you can use seriesFilters. A list of series is returned from seriesQuery and then returned as metric names filtered through filters.

```
# match all cAdvisor metrics that aren't measured in seconds
seriesQuery: '{__name__=~"^container_.*_total",container!="POD",namespace!="",pod!=""}'
seriesFilters:
  - isNot: "^container_.*_seconds_total"
```

Naming

This manages the process of converting Prometheus metric names to metrics from a custom metrics API and vice versa by the name field.

CHAPTER 10   AIOPS RCA

This is controlled by specifying a pattern to extract the API name from the Prometheus name field and a transformation for the extracted value. The pattern is a regular expression specified in the matches field, which defaults to .*.

Let's look at an example:

```
# match turn any name <name>_total to <name>_per_second
# e.g. http_requests_total becomes http_requests_per_second
name:
  matches: "^(.*)_total$"
  as: "${1}_per_second"
```

Querying

This manages the process of actually getting the values for a particular metric. It's controlled by the metricsQuery field.

The metricsQuery field is a Go template that is transformed into a Prometheus query with a call to the Custom Metrics API, the result of which is returned as a metric name, a group resource, and one or more objects from that group resource.

- **Series:** Metric name.
- **LabelMatchers:** A comma-separated list of label matchers that match the given object.
- **GroupBy:** Contains the group resource labels used by LabelMatchers.

In general, I recommend using Series, LabelMatchers, and GroupBy fields.

The query should return one value for each requested object. The adapter uses the label of the returned series to associate the given series with the corresponding object.

```
# convert cumulative cAdvisor metrics into rates calculated over 2 minutes
metricsQuery: "sum(rate(<<.Series>>{<<.LabelMatchers>>,container!="POD"}[2m])) by (<<.GroupBy>>)"
```

For testing purposes, name it metricName: http_requests and create a Deployment, Service, ServiceMonitor, and HPA.

```
cat <<EOF | kubectl apply -f -
apiVersion: apps/v1beta1
kind: Deployment
metadata:
  name: autoscaling-deploy
  namespace: custom-metrics
spec:
  replicas: 1
```

749

CHAPTER 10   AIOPS RCA

```
    template:
      metadata:
        labels:
          app: autoscaling
          release: prom
      spec:
        containers:
        - name: autoscaling
          image: quay.io/brancz/prometheus-example-app:v0.1.0
          ports:
          - containerPort: 8080
---
```

Check the application's metrics provided in /metrics, as shown in Figure 10-12.

Figure 10-12. *The Metrics screen in Prometheus*

In the Prometheus Metrics screen, look up the http_requests_total metric to see the results, as shown in Figure 10-13.

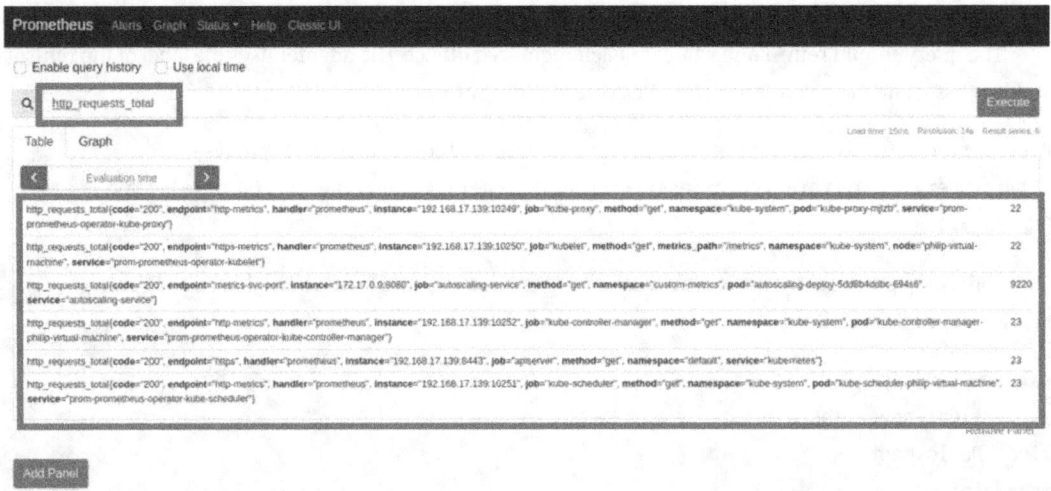

Figure 10-13. *The Metrics screen in Prometheus*

Configure port forwarding:

```
kubectl port-forward svc/autoscaling-service 3000:80 --namespace custom-metrics
```

Create a load:

```
while true; do wget -q -O- http://127.0.0.1:3000; done
```

Verify that the HPA is functioning normally:

```
# kubectl get hpa -n custom-metrics
name reference targets minpods maxpods replicas age
autoscaling-app-hpa Deployment/autoscaling-deploy 95196m/5 1 5 5 43m
```

View detailed logs and results from HPA:

```
# kubectl describe hpa -n custom-metrics
Metrics: ( current / target )
  "http_requests" on Service/autoscaling-service (target value):  18734m / 5
Min replicas: 1
Max replicas: 5
Deployment pods: 5 current / 5 desired
Conditions:
  Type Status Reason Message
  ---- ------ ------ ------ -------
  AbleToScale True ReadyForNewScale recommended size matches current size
  ScalingActive True ValidMetricFound the HPA was able to successfully calculate a replica count from Service metric http_requests
  ScalingLimited True TooManyReplicas the desired replica count is more than the maximum replica count
  Normal SuccessfulRescale 45s horizontal-pod-autoscaler New size: 2; reason: Service metric http_requests above target
  Normal SuccessfulRescale 30s horizontal-pod-autoscaler New size: 4; reason: Service metric http_requests above target
  Normal SuccessfulRescale 15s horizontal-pod-autoscaler New size: 5; reason: Service metric http_requests above target
```

10.3.2.3. KEDA

KEDA monitors the event source and feeds that data to HPA to rapidly scale the resource. Each replica of the resource actively pulls events from the event source. Deployments and StatefulSets are the most common ways to scale workloads with KEDA. KEDA and its extensions Deployments/StatefulSet allow you to scale based on events while maintaining a rich connection and processing semantics with the event source.

CHAPTER 10 AIOPS RCA

This allows you to define Kubernetes deployments or StatefulSets that KEDA will scale based on scale triggers, as shown in Figure 10-14. KEDA monitors those services and automatically scales resources based on events that occur.

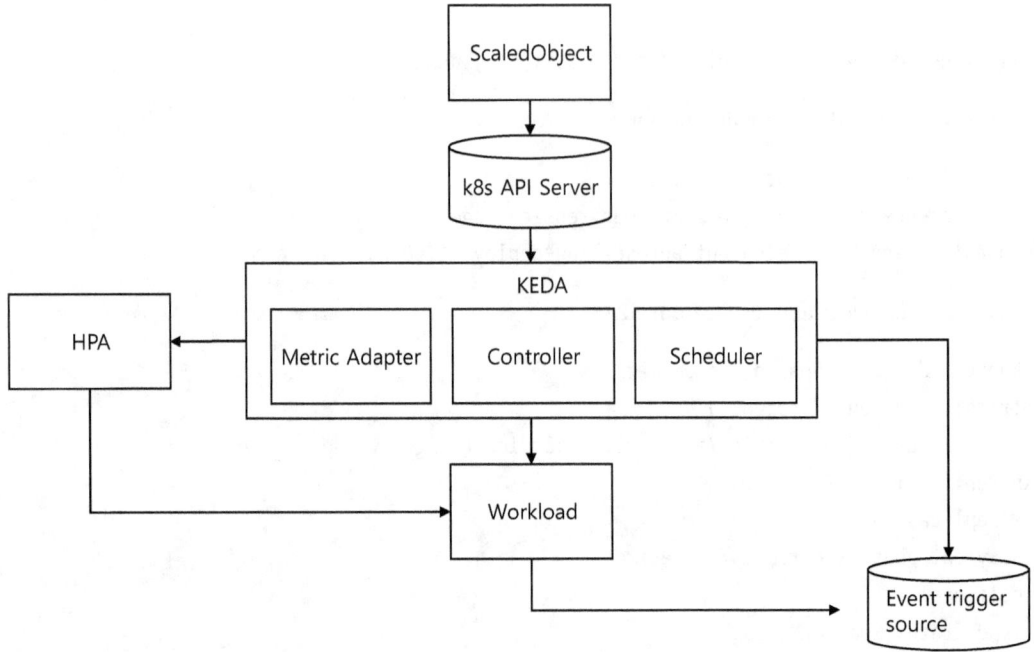

Figure 10-14. *KEDA's lifecycle*

For example, if you want to use KEDA as an event source with Apache Kafka, the workflow might look like this:

- If there are no pending messages, KEDA extends the deployment to zero.
- A message arrives, and KEDA detects it as an event and activates the deployment.
- When the deployment starts running, one of the containers connects to Kafka and starts fetching messages.
- As more messages arrive in a Kafka Topic, KEDA can feed this data to HPA for horizontal scaling.

```
apiVersion: keda.sh/v1alpha1
kind: ScaledObject
metadata:
  name: sample-app
spec:
  scaleTargetRef:
```

```yaml
    kind: Deployment # Optional. Default: Deployment
    name: sample-app # Mandatory. Must be in the same namespace as the ScaledObject
  pollingInterval: 15 # Optional. Default: 30 seconds
  cooldownPeriod: 30 # Optional. Default: 300 seconds
  minReplicaCount: 1 # Optional. Default: 0
  maxReplicaCount: 5 # Optional. Default: 100
  triggers:
  - type: prometheus
    metadata:
      serverAddress: http://prometheus-server.default.svc.cluster.local
      metricName: nginx_ingress_controller_requests
      threshold: '15'
      query: http_requests_total
```

The advantage of KEDA over other autoscales is that it provides a variety of data sources. While Metric Server only supports computing resources such as CPU and Prometheus Adapter supports Prometheus, KEDA can directly measure and autoscale metrics from various resources such as Redis, Kafka, and Prometheus. In addition, KEDA is simple to configure and has fewer compatibility problems. The Prometheus Adapter requires compatibility with the Prometheus ecosystem and Kubernetes, so I recommend using KEDA whenever possible.

10.3.2.4. KEDA Demo

The Prometheus adapter can only measure Prometheus metrics. It is not directly tied to other system metrics, is complicated to set up, and has compatibility problems. For these reasons, I recommend KEDA.

In the real world, we use KEDA rather than the Prometheus adapter. I recommend using KEDA rather than the Prometheus adapter whenever possible. I provide KEDA labs, as shown here.

Here are the contents of a scale object. You use a custom resource called a scale object to automatically create and control HPAs.

The autoscale will be based on the value measured in the http_requests_total metric. Currently, the thread is set to 10.

```yaml
apiVersion: keda.sh/v1alpha1
kind: ScaledObject
metadata:
  name: sample-app
spec:
  scaleTargetRef:
    kind: Deployment # Optional. Default: Deployment
    name: sample-app # Mandatory. Must be in the same namespace as the ScaledObject
```

CHAPTER 10   AIOPS RCA

```
    pollingInterval: 15 # Optional. Default: 30 seconds
    cooldownPeriod: 30 # Optional. Default: 300 seconds
    minReplicaCount: 1 # Optional. Default: 0
    maxReplicaCount: 5 # Optional. Default: 100
    triggers:
    - type: prometheus
      metadata:
        serverAddress: http://prometheus-server.default.svc.cluster.local
        metricName: http_requests_total
        threshold: '10'
        query: http_requests_total
```

When you try to access the sample-app, you'll see the http_requests_total metric count increase. Check the ScaleObject and PodToscaler:

```
# kubectl apply -f scale.yaml
scaledobject.keda.sh/sample-app configured
# kubectl get scaledobject
name scaletargetkind scaletargetname min max triggers authentication ready active fallback age
sample-app apps/v1.Deployment sample-app 1 5 prometheus True True False 211d
```

Identify autoscaled applications. After a certain number of pods, the number of pods starts to increase.

```
# kubectl get hpa
name reference targets minpods maxpods replicas age
keda-hpa-sample-app Deployment/sample-app 44667m/5k (avg) 1 5 3 21m
# kubectl get pod
name ready status restarts age
prometheus-alertmanager-58d64b84db-jv4dk 2/2 Running 0 128m
prometheus-kube-state-metrics-5547d95bd-htz9r 1/1 Running 0 128m
prometheus-node-exporter-7s2lb 1/1 Running 0 128m
prometheus-operator-6bf9dd7f76-sq565 1/1 Running 2 211d
prometheus-pushgateway-85679964b8-s6q46 1/1 Running 0 128m
prometheus-server-6bfb6b68-kzfv5 2/2 Running 0 128m
sample-app-7cfb596f98-h4ww4 1/1 Running 1 211d
sample-app-7cfb596f98-lfpqr 1/1 Running 0 97m
sample-app-7cfb596f98-nwj44 1/1 Running 0 111m
```

Here's the result after autoscale:

```
# kubectl get hpa
name reference targets minpods maxpods replicas age
```

```
keda-hpa-sample-app Deployment/sample-app 25/50 (avg) 1 5 5 12m
# kubectl get pod
name ready status restarts age
prometheus-alertmanager-58d64b84db-jv4dk 2/2 Running 0 122m
prometheus-kube-state-metrics-5547d95bd-htz9r 1/1 Running 0 122m
prometheus-node-exporter-7s2lb 1/1 Running 0 122m
prometheus-operator-6bf9dd7f76-sq565 1/1 Running 2 211d
prometheus-pushgateway-85679964b8-s6q46 1/1 Running 0 122m
prometheus-server-6bfb6b68-kzfv5 2/2 Running 0 122m
sample-app-7cfb596f98-h4ww4 1/1 Running 1 211d
sample-app-7cfb596f98-h5w8n 1/1 Running 0 58m
sample-app-7cfb596f98-lfpqr 1/1 Running 0 91m
sample-app-7cfb596f98-nwj44 1/1 Running 0 105m
sample-app-7cfb596f98-v6c2l 1/1 Running 0 74m
```

You can continue to test KEDA by arbitrarily changing the set threshold. Autoscale is closely tied to deployment and performance.

Performance:

- Anomaly or not?
- Determine the severity of the failure
- Impact failure analysis
- Analyze service and code dependencies
- Analyze whether a failure propagates
- Calibrate and automatically improve the accuracy of the traces and spans

In addition, you need configuration data about changes, services and resources, catalogs, and more. The scope of IT operations is wide, and there are many different operating data. The CMDB collects, centrally stores, and manages most of the data used in production.

Companies with the failure handling and operational capabilities are those with well-organized CMDB. Observability alone does not improve failure handling and operational capabilities. Observability helps you focus on identifying and resolving problems, but it doesn't improve your operation processes, or reliability, MTTR, MTTD, or collaboration.

10.4. The Failure List Data Model

Technology isn't the key to AIOps. Data is more important. LLM, RAG, and other technologies are not enough to make AIOps successful. While it is important to summarize and organize the various errors described so far, failure cases and error records can be used as an important source of data for AIOps implementation.

CHAPTER 10 AIOPS RCA

I've described the key applications and system resources used in IT operations, and how telemetry can be used to collect and ingest signals from them. In order for Generative AI to answer correctly, you need to build a knowledge base, enrich the prompts to help Generative AI analyze the cause, and provide rich hints to LLM. The knowledge base and hints will be the failure list data model described in this book.

The reasons why AIOps and anomaly detection fail are not as complicated as you might think. It's because the knowledge base and hints are either not available or are inaccurate. For AIOps to be successful, it needs accurate data and must be loaded into the Vector database.

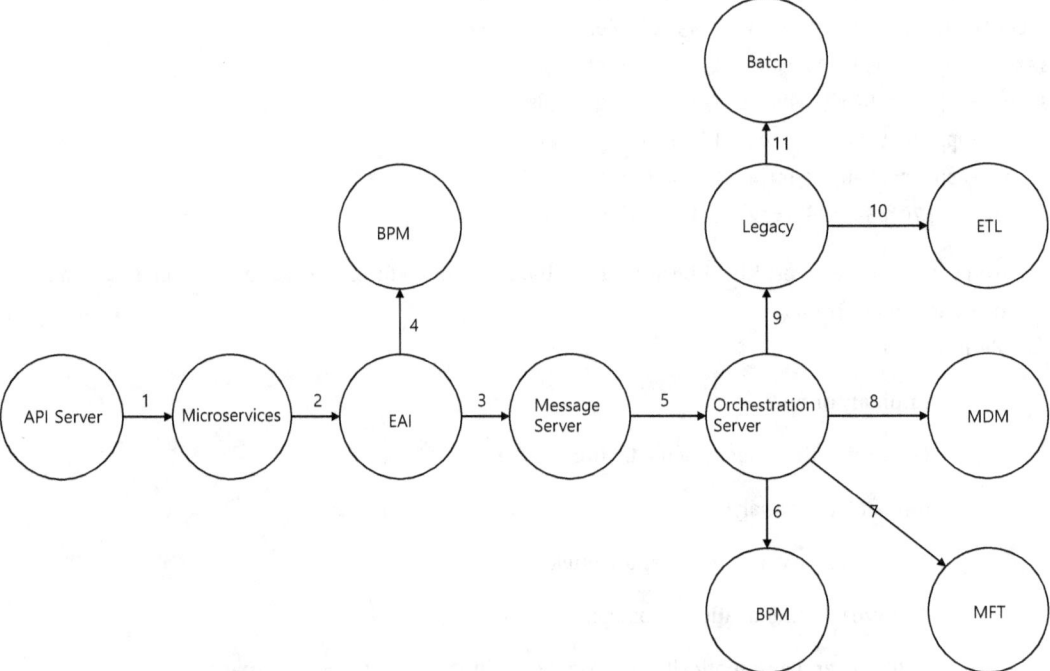

Figure 10-15. *Legacy middleware in transaction processing*

Corporate businesses with large transaction amounts for individual transactions are often processed by BPM, EAI, MFT, and legacy middleware.

The processing flow is as follows (see Figure 10-15):

1. Apply policies to requests received from the client and route them to the microservice.

2. The microservice generates an event and sends it to the EAI server.

3. The EAI server subscribes to the event, transforms the message, and sends it to the message server.

4. The EAI server creates a case for the BPM server, and the user starts workflow and approves the case on the BPM server.

5. The message server is loosely coupled with the orchestration server. The way things are handled on the backend uses message-based events. The orchestration server decomposes messages and sends them to various legacy servers.

6. Messages that fail to process are sent to the BPM server, which generates a fallout. In case of technical errors, they can be reprocessed if necessary.

7. Send files via MFT.

8. Customer MDM checks for customer data duplication.

9. The orchestration server requests messages from the legacy.

10. The ETL server processes the data pipeline that's loaded into the legacy.

11. The batch server handles the batching of the legacy.

In the case of financial and telecom companies, transactions are processed through a variety of legacy middleware. Rather than simple lookups, complex tasks like payments and orders are typically handled as events using message servers.

In this book, I've described the following failures. Automated AIOps should be able to identify similar failures. Here's how they are categorized. Here are the 11 large categories, each of which contains many subcategories:

1. **Microservices**: If you're using multi-cloud, you need to communicate between different clouds, which can complicate security.

2. **Legacy middleware**: EAI, ETL, MDM, MFT, BPM, and batch are examples of legacy middleware.

3. **Legacy applications**: I provide demos for SAP, Siebel, and Tuxedo, but do not recommend direct legacy observability. I instrument legacy indirectly through EAI servers, kernels, and virtual machines.

4. **Server frameworks**: Server frameworks include API servers, message servers, CDNs, load balancers, and so on.

5. **Clusters**: ElasticSearch, Kafka, Redis, and Kubernetes form clusters of multiple nodes.

6. **System resources**: Failures occurring in the kernel, CPU, memory, disk, or network.

7. Data pipelines

8. Data consistency

9. Observability

CHAPTER 10 AIOPS RCA

10. Databases
11. Clients

There are 11 large categories, 50 medium categories, and about 400 small categories.

- Large categories can be microservices, server frameworks, data pipelines, and so on.
- Medium categories can be EAI, ETL, MDM, MFT, BPM, and batch, using legacy middleware as an example.
- Small categories can be individual failure cases, as described next.

Large and medium categories are handled by anomaly detection and metric correlation. Small categories are handled by LLM.

In many cases, it is not possible to instrument using commercial agents, so manual instrumentation is required for development. I have described various manual instrumentation development solutions. The various agents are complementary and often not instrumented, so additional bytecode instrumentation is required to collect signals.

E2E tracing is important, but so are failures along the way. This is because failures can occur at any point along the way. Figure 10-16 illustrates how various legacy middleware can be tied together around an EAI server and configured for observability. Understanding the processing flow can help you identify critical sections and troubleshoot failures.

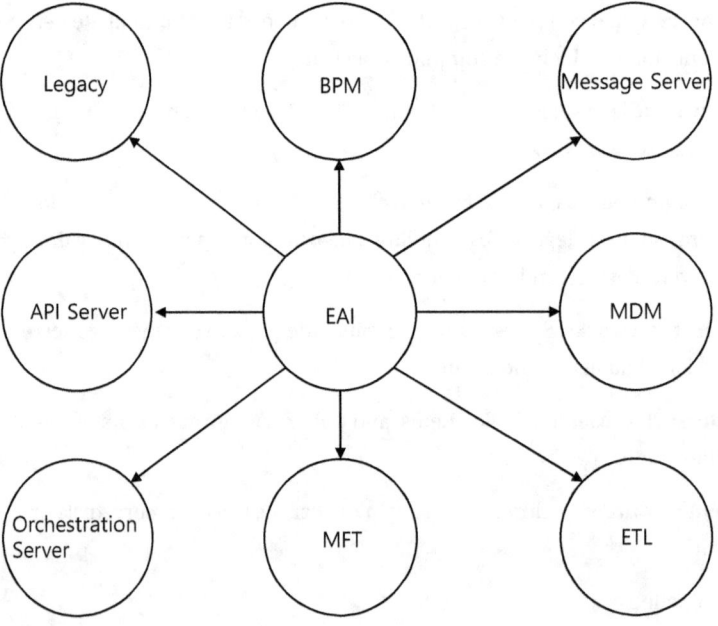

Figure 10-16. *The EAI server-centric AIOps*

Microservice failures are not unique. It is not the purpose of this book to describe only these failures. The range of failures is wide and the problems are diverse.

10.4.1. System Resource Failures

Delays in clusters are due to replication, rebalancing, and so on, whereas delays in system resources are due to contention, interference, and so on.

10.4.1.1. Networks

In a microservice architecture, network failures can be a SPOF. Commercial observability lacks network monitoring capabilities, and the introduction of Kubernetes has complicated network configuration. Table 10-1 lists the network failures.

Table 10-1. Network Failures

Number	Description
1	Network packet order is reversed
2	TIME_WAIT disconnects a large number of sockets and runs out of local ports
3	CLOSE_WAIT fails to CLOSE on client, misconfiguration results in zombie connections
4	Keepalive reuses connections
5	epoll, misconfigured number of file descriptors
6	Difficult-to-analyze, low-level networks such as L3 and packets
7	New network equipment is misconfigured and slows down
8	Limit the number of connections to a host on request
9	Reuse connections to the same host
10	IP tables, DNS servers cause delays
11	L4 load balancer, browser cache
12	Retransmit network packets
13	RST flag errors
14	CDN's static content handling

10.4.1.2. System Resources

System resources include CPU, memory, disk, and kernel, which are subject to various delays and errors. The scope of failure is large, and many services are affected by delays and failures. See Table 10-2.

Table 10-2. System Resource Failures

Number	Description
1	Memory swap
2	Memory reallocation
3	Increased CPU L1/L2/L3 cache misses
4	Low cache hit rate
5	Misconfigured kernel parameters
6	NUMA configuration
7	Frequent system call delays
8	Memory page faults

10.4.1.3. System Traces

Commercial observability focuses on delays and failures that occur in applications and services, and it does not provide the ability to identify delays and traces that occur in system resources. With system trace, you can identify the following delays and failures (see Table 10-3):

- Contentions
- Waiting
- Interferences
- Saturation
- Congestion
- Bugs
- Faults

Table 10-3. Kernel Failures

Number	Description
1	Does not support BPF
2	Merges, sorts, compresses, compacts, buffers, flushes, paging, locks, and so on behave incorrectly
3	No support for system utilities and system trace
4	Supports exceptions and errors only; does not support contention, greed, interference, saturation, congestion, bugs, or faults
5	Difficult-to-analyze waits such as scheduler waits, L1/L2 cache misses, context switches, idle states with frequent IO, thread states (Runnable), and so on
6	Difficult-to-analyze outgoing and incoming packets, wait on NICs, congestion when bandwidth is exceeded, incoming interrupts, and so on
7	Disk/Ethernet/timer interrupts, disk synchronization, block creation, and so on can measure interference with IPC, but observability does not support IPC
8	Difficult-to-analyze lock contention, lock capture, lock starvation, and so on
9	Setting kernel parameters such as file descriptor, ulimit, MTU, `local_port_range`, `tw_resuse`, `tw_recycle`, and so on
10	High IO Wait, System ratio
11	High in-CPU saturation, difficult to measure `runqlen` and `runqlat`
12	High overhead due to frequent method calls
13	Use profiles for slow queries, locks, heap usage, IO, and CPU waits

10.4.1.4. Ultra-Low Latency

Ultra-low-latency applications are architected differently than traditional development approaches like Spring. Ultra-latency can be achieved in a variety of ways, including CPU, memory, compiler, and network (see Table 10-4).

Table 10-4. Ultra-Low Latency Failures

Number	Description
1	Difficult-to-analyze static memory allocations such as memory pools, stack memory designations, and so on
2	Minimize cache misses and virtual functions and minimize latency
3	Minimize delays caused by context switching, such as pin threads to a core or preventing preemption from system calls
4	Minimize locks with locks, races, lock-free data structures, priority inversion, and more
5	Minimize latency with kernel bypasses like zero copy, user-space rotation, and more
6	Improve performance with memory mapping files
7	Ultra-low-latency applications configure observability with logs
8	Improve network performance with switch queuing and HOL configuration
9	Improve performance with static links, executable formats, and more
10	Minimize unnecessary network calls and operate within a single server
11	Minimize context switching, lock contention, and IO, freeze CPU and mmap memory for better performance

10.4.1.5. JVMs

Java fails because of threads, memory issues, poor development practices, and more. See Table 10-5.

Table 10-5. JVM Failures

Number	Description
1	Incorrect GC selection
2	Pin virtual threads
3	Designing long critical sections
4	Delays due to incorrect sequential processing
5	Poor performance due to resource constraints
6	Bad retry logic
7	Frequency and number of full-garbage collections
8	CPU spikes and latency due to full-garbage collection
9	OOM memory leaks
10	Low memory, constantly referenced and not garbage collected
11	Errors in the dependency library
12	Increased overhead due to large dependency scope when profiling
13	Difficult-to-analyze thread state with stack traces
14	Runnable is long-running, causing delays in queuing
15	Blocked for a long time and a lock occurs
16	Understanding dependency with call trees
17	Number of thread pools that are too large or too small
18	If you set memory to small, GCs will occur more frequently
19	Running out of resources due to a high thread count
20	Delays due to context switching with an incorrect thread pool

10.4.2. Cluster Failures

We categorize cluster failures as shown in Table 10-6. Clusters provide multiple ways to overcome failures. If some nodes go down or become unavailable, the service should not be affected, with only a small delay.

- WAL, the number of replicas
- Buffering and batches
- Rebalancing

CHAPTER 10 AIOPS RCA

- Shards, partitions
- Compression, merging
- Tiering
- Skew and distribution
- Quorum consensus
- Gossip, Heartbeat
- Cache of reads: Misconfiguration of the cache and propagation of cache failures
- Flush and block size
- Scale-out of write and read paths
- Data conformance: Provides offset, 2PC processing, and sequential processing
- Cluster operations: upgrades, backups, and cluster configurations

Table 10-6. *Cluster Failures*

Number	Description
1	Frequency and number of flushes when handling IO
2	Configuring WAL and the number of replicas
3	Skew, data throughput imbalance
4	Unfair shard distribution
5	Rebalancing delays
6	Improve performance and reduce costs with partitioning
7	Clusters do not autoscale
8	Frequency and count of merge, compress, and sort processing
9	High IO activity causes congestion and interference, resulting in delays, timeouts, and errors
10	Scale-out delay for write paths
11	Bootstrap delay at startup
12	Only read paths can be scaled out
13	Using k8s operators when upgrading
14	Using cache to improve read path performance

(continued)

Table 10-6. (continued)

Number	Description
15	Use tiering to manage storage and save money
16	Failures when adding and changing nodes such as HDFS
17	Delays in Redis backups and restores
18	Consistency issues such as lost or duplicate messages in the pipeline
19	Message lost due to incorrect Kafka offset
20	Only certain shards are saturated due to distribution issues
21	Frequent pull-scans due to lack of caching or pre-aggregation
22	Tiering (hot, warm, cold) setup errors
23	Kubernetes etcd, API server down due to excessive pod creation
24	StatefulSet provisioning delays
25	Docker's disk IO and object storage scans are expensive, and many metrics take a long time to process
26	Failure due to mismatched upgrade order and status between components in a cluster
27	Upgrading API servers, etcd servers, DNS servers, and so on in a k8s cluster causes operational disruption
28	Observability does not support cluster monitoring
29	Poor performance only on certain topics within a Kafka cluster
30	Communication between shards in a cluster exceeds or congested network bandwidth
31	No multi-tenant support for clusters

10.4.3. Server Framework Failures

10.4.3.1. API Servers

The API server applies policies to requests and routes traffic to the backend, as shown in Figure 10-17.

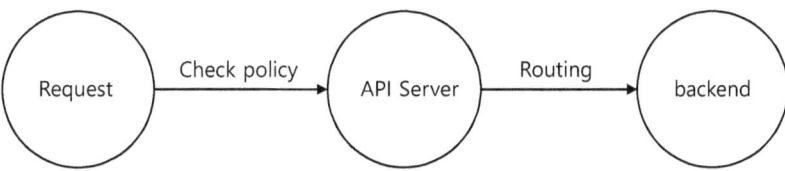

Figure 10-17. API server processing

API server failures can be as follows (see Table 10-7):

- The API server must be configured to prevent upstream and downstream failures from propagating.
- The API server uses a database for configuration information and logs. If the database fails, the failure propagates to the API server.
- Incorrect use of rate limits, circuit breakers, and caching can cause this to happen.

Table 10-7. API Server Failures

Number	Description
1	Circuit breakers; rate limit malfunction takes down entire cluster
2	Frequent failure propagation
3	Zombie threads occur
4	Certificate expiration

Unlike web servers, which are generally stateless, API servers manage state and fail because of it.

Kernel parameters, switches, CDNs, and network configurations can also affect the failure of an API server.

10.4.3.2. Message Servers

Message server failures are outlined in Table 10-8.

Table 10-8. Message Server Failures

Number	Description
1	GCP PubSub misbehavior in Spring SCS
2	No Kafka support for rate limits, and so on, only HTTP-oriented
3	Message server tracestate requires manual instrumentation
4	Spring SCS only supports OpenTelemetry via extensions, not commercial observability
5	Increase in the number of pending messages
6	Many message servers only support manual instrumentation
7	Topics without offsets are difficult to monitor

Message servers are a constraint when configuring observability because their protocols are not standard, which can often require manual instrumentation.

- The number of unprocessed and pending messages in the JMS queue increases.
- The retransmission flag is misconfigured in the JMS header, and message delivery is not guaranteed due to conflicts and checkpoints.
- Kafka offsets are misconfigured, causing messages to be lost or duplicated in the event of a failure. Duplicates increase the number of messages.
- Messages are lost in the event of an abnormal termination.
- Messages are lost because they expire.
- If an error occurs, the exception and the exception handling for the error must be configured correctly.

10.4.4. Legacy Middleware Failures

This can break legacy and packaged applications. However, commercial observability can be added to the header of a trace using bytecode. Legacy middleware can be a big hindrance because it is often associated with many different applications and is a common service.

A list of legacy middleware is shown here:

- EAI
- BPM
- Customer and product MDM
- MFT
- ETL
- API gateways
- Orchestration servers
- Batches processed by EAI, ETL, and MDM

Failures in legacy packages are difficult to explain and are beyond the scope of this book. I focus more on legacy middleware.

10.4.4.1. The EAI Server

The EAI server subscribes to events from the source application and sends them to the target application, as shown in Figure 10-18. It supports various adapters for this purpose. They are mainly used to connect applications.

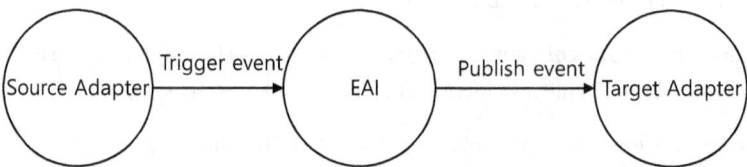

Figure 10-18. *The EAI server processing*

The EAI server failures are listed in Table 10-9.

Table 10-9. *EAI Server Failures*

Number	Description
1	Confirmation and checkpoints matter when resending messages, and configuring resend flags in messages
2	EAI and ETL are all about memory mins and maxes
3	Message conversion and validation failures
4	Invalid retries, timeout settings
5	Lost abnormal shutdown messages
6	Messages are lost due to incorrect exception handling
7	Incorrect false retransmissions when EAI exception handling fails

- Retransmissions, checkpoints, and confirmations must be implemented correctly, and data consistency must not be compromised.

- Failures in the source and target applications, propagating through the EAI process and causing errors. No data loss should occur.

- Failure to create new threads for requests can occur. Increase the number of threads or increase the throughput of the target application.

- Configure exception handling correctly. You should be able to identify exceptions and errors and reprocess them.

- Set the number of retries and timeouts.

- Set sufficient minimum and maximum memory for instances.

- If the order of stopping and restarting the cluster is incorrect, messages can be lost.

- This can result in incorrect transformations or incorrect message validation.

To instrument on the EAI server, use a profile to identify the method. You can implement instrumentation that adds bytecodes as a way to pass data stored in the context to the next step.

The EAI servers—Tipco and WebMethods—are not much different. The behavior and architecture are similar. For ETL, Talend, Informatica, and Data Stage are not different from each other. BPM and MDM are also similar in terms of errors that occur by product.

10.4.4.2. The BPM Server

The BPM server is called from the outside to create a case, and the user approves the steps in the workflow to complete the case, as shown in Figure 10-19. This integrates with various external systems, such as forms on the BPM server that link to external portals, or status updates that are sent to a queue.

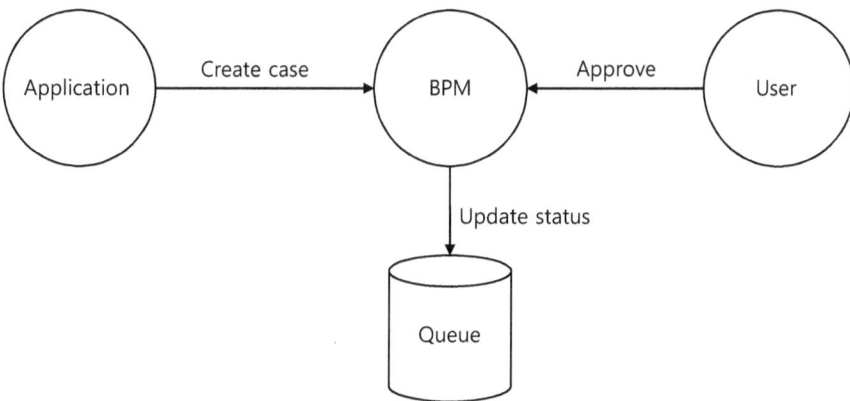

Figure 10-19. BPM Server processing

The BPM server can fail in the following ways

- Message servers and external applications fail when responding to requests.

- When processing fails, the error queue is configured to analyze the error and retry.

A case is created by an external request, and status updates are sent to the queue on the message server. There are cases where the case fails because there is a problem with data conjugation such as RPA rather than simple linkage. Errors such as inclusion in the portal and security occur.

Use an external screen instead of using the BPM screen as it is. Most of the time, it is connected with BPM API.

There is a lot of development, such as managing the status of steps, and the possibility of errors is high. Cases may fail due to data consistency issues rather than case creation.

Only the header manages the trace ID, but in the case of BPM, it is manual measurement to manage the body, and it is limited to configure the BPM frontend RUM and backend for trace.

CHAPTER 10 AIOPS RCA

Temporal BPM supports OpenTelemetry, just as TIBCO recently added support for OpenTelemetry.

10.4.4.3. The ETL Server

ETL pipelines can extract from source data and enrich the data with joins and lookups during processing (see Figure 10-20). It completes the pipeline after loading into the target database. It is utilized for a variety of purposes, including data warehouses, data marts, data lakes, and real-time streaming.

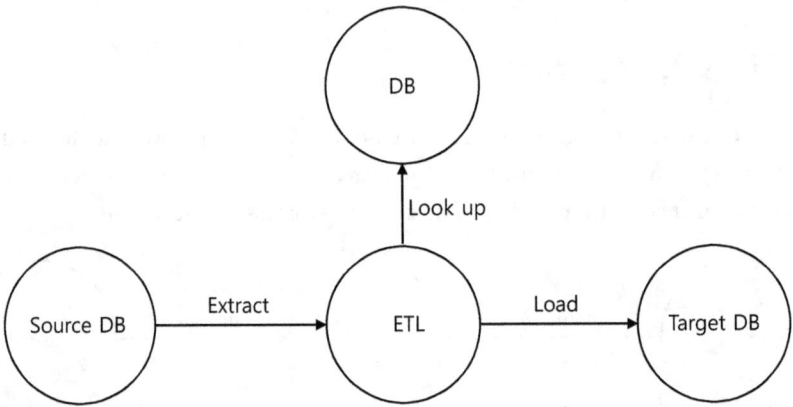

Figure 10-20. ETL Server processing

ETL server failures are listed in Table 10-10.

Table 10-10. ETL Server Failures

Number	Description
1	Incorrect configuration of thread count for EAI, ETL, and API gateways
2	In ETL, the number of fetches from the source and commits to the target is important, and slowing down in the middle causes memory shortages

- Accurately handling increments and decrements is difficult.
- Bugs in the pipeline can lead to missing and lost data.
- Data inconsistencies can require reprocessing.
- Schema changes can cause errors in pipeline processing.
- The number of patches in the source, the number of commits in the target, and the amount of data in memory since the pipeline stores data in memory after fetching data should be considered.
- The batch server is having problems and ETL jobs are not running.

- Performance degradation because things not being processed in time and affecting subsequent processing.

- Loading to the target fails. Some data is loaded successfully. In this case, you need to reprocess the data that failed to load, or reprocess it from the beginning. A variety of reprocessing options are required.

10.4.4.4. The MFT Server

The MFT server installs agents on all servers that need to transfer files and manages trusted file transfers between agents. The MFT server manages file transfers. For example, it directs file transfers to agents or manages the configuration required for file transfers.

Use MFT when you need to transfer a large number of files and need to ensure retransmission and security. See Figure 10-21.

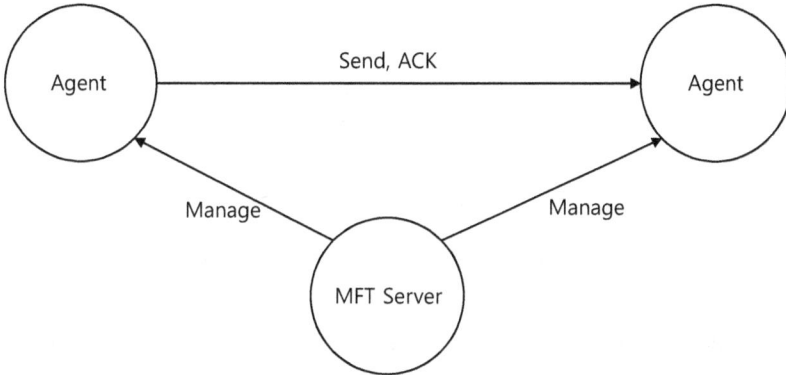

Figure 10-21. *MFT server processing*

MFT server failures can be as follows:

- Network switch changes, reducing the amount of data transferred per second

- The agent does not send ACKs, causing unnecessary file retransmissions.

- When the agent restarts and many file transfers are processed simultaneously, the internal network bandwidth may run out. The agent is unstable and fails frequently.

MFT processing doesn't load the entire file into memory, but instead sends it in chunks. It provides security and guarantees retransmission to external networks.

MFT agents must support a wide variety of platforms, which leads to frequent bugs.

MFT is agent-to-agent communication and does not use FTP. It uses its own protocol optimized for large file transfers, retransfers, and security. See Table 10-11.

Table 10-11. MFT Server Failures

Number	Description
1	MFT uses ACKs and retransmission errors
2	MFT manages MTU, bandwidth per section
3	MFT uses a lot of bandwidth, causing network interference and congestion
4	MFT manages backup files separately, so that you can use them in case of failure

Batch server failures are listed in Table 10-12.

Table 10-12. Batch Server Failures

Number	Description
1	Support for retries on batch errors
2	Observability does not support batch servers and requires modifications to batch scripts

- A predecessor batch fails, and subsequent batches fail to run.

- Observability is decoupled from the batch server, or the batch job is difficult to monitor.

- Batch fails to terminate on time, fails during processing, a batch job fails to start, negatively affects other batch jobs, hangs instead of terminating, or completes processing but terminates abnormally.

There are several types of batches:

- Registered with Cron to periodically process a shell script. Add an open source that supports OpenTelemetry in the shell script.

- Registered with Airflow to manage all processing. OpenTelemetry supports Airflow.

- Use a spring scheduler to create batch jobs as threads. OpenTelemetry can have issues with thread handling, but it is well supported in most cases.

- Legacy batches are registered with Control-M and often have tens of thousands of batch jobs.

Is it possible to use observability on legacy middleware to identify and resolve the failures mentioned? The answer is—it is difficult.

- It's often not open source, and its internal structure is not publicly available and therefore incomprehensible. Legacy has internal monitoring, but it's hard to integrate, and most legacy middleware doesn't support observability.

- Observability supports logs and metrics for some middleware, but middleware typically has complex internal processing and many external interactions. When something goes wrong, it's hard to understand the cause and requires an understanding of the business.

Failures can be caused by data inconsistencies, operator error, or bugs in the solution.

10.4.5. Data Pipeline Failures

Databases are categorized into relational databases and NoSQL. Table 10-13 lists the data pipeline failures.

Table 10-13. Data Pipeline Failures

Number	Description
1	Number of database connections
2	Low TPS due to unoptimized queries
3	Duplicates, sets, and unnecessary queries
4	Improved small patch count, commit record count, and query call count
5	Sessions, connections, and resources not returned after processing
6	Reprocessing because records are missing or there are issues with data consistency

Data observability applies trace to data pipelines. Like ETL, batches can be handled similarly. Data pipelines vary from

- ETL
- Dataflow, Apache Beam
- Glue
- Airflow
- Spark
- Flink
- Kafka Connect
- Confluent

To bring observability to your pipeline, it's not a good idea to approach it as an individual technology. If you can't instrument with agents, use logs. And then there's the conversion from logs to traces.

By default, the pipeline outputs the jobs and step IDs to the log. For each step, the time is output. If you automatically recognize an index like OpenSearch, you can search for a job ID by time and convert steps to spans.

Create a trace with a job ID and create steps as spans. Log-based preprocessing is required. It was developed in many languages, not just Java, making automated instrumentation difficult. You need to understand the limitations of Python, managed services, and relational databases.

10.4.6. Data Consistency Failures

Handling complex order and payment processes involves a variety of servers working together, and the potential for data inconsistencies is high.

- If a process fails in the middle of processing, you need to retry, cancel, and more.
- Bugs and errors in the application can also cause problems with data consistency.
- Administrators can manually correct data inconsistencies more than automated methods.
- You should implement a variety of ways to validate data consistency.

10.4.6.1. Orchestration Server Failures

Orchestration server failures are handled through fallout management.

- Failures that occur after the point of no return (PoNR) must be handled manually. If handled manually, this can cause problems with data consistency.
- Orchestration engages with multiple applications. It provides fallout management. When data consistency issues arise in the orchestration overhead, rather than in individual systems, resolution is complex and time-consuming.
- Data migration is complex and requires procedures to validate data consistency.

The orchestration server is too complex compared to the product maturity of the orchestration server, resulting in excessive additional development of the orchestration. While there are bugs and various limitations, most failures in orchestration servers are related to data consistency. It's not just about distributed transaction processing between two databases; it's about orchestrating dozens of applications and databases. In the process of doing so, data can become corrupted.

Combined products require a lot of rules. For example, if multiple products and tasks are shared by a family, the discounts offered need to change when a family member is added or removed.

10.4.6.2. MDM Servers

MDM servers are used to synchronize data or to validate consistency. There are two types of MDM servers

Customer MDMs can validate customer data for duplicates and improve data quality, as shown in Figure 10-22. Financial firms use customer MDMs to reduce legacy load and manage data quality.

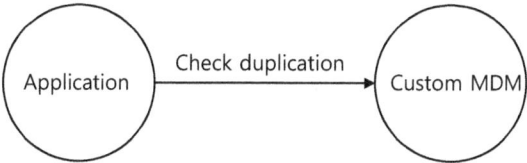

Figure 10-22. Customer MDM server processing

Product MDMs distribute product data to different systems and make the same product and pricing data available to applications in the enterprise (see Figure 10-23). Products contain many attributes, and the product structure is hierarchical. Telcos develop more than 10,000 products, with many attributes and complex structures. Product MDMs are used to reduce complexity and improve the consistency and ease of distribution of product data.

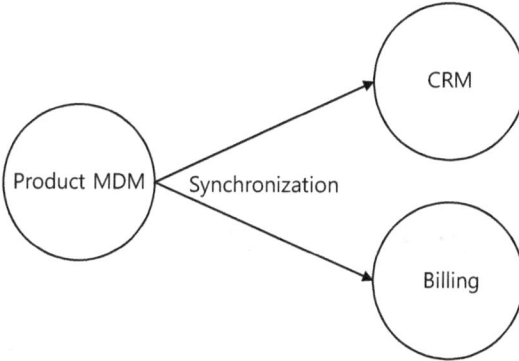

Figure 10-23. Product MDM server processing

MDM server failures include:

- To release a new product, the product needs to be deployed to various servers. Deployments can fail or have errors.

- It is more stable than cache and can manage the change history of customer master. You can manage MDM server failures and delays by connecting with various systems in real time.

In addition to the assets a customer owns, they are allocated discounts and usage that are shared with other customers. Additional discounts are offered when families are combined. For example, a family that was previously able to download 50G will be able to share the increased usage to 100G. Table 10-14 shows the data consistency failures.

CHAPTER 10   AIOPS RCA

Table 10-14. Data Consistency Failures

Number	Description
1	Revisions are not processed when existing, and non-new assets exist
2	Issues when adding discounts to a combined family deal or sharing resources between families
3	Propagation in the event of an external organization failure
4	Fallout processing sometimes fails
5	Multiple identical orders are submitted, resulting in duplicates and unsupported equality
6	Orders are not fulfilled in chronological order, and the ranking is reversed
7	Noisy with the wrong threshold
8	Incorrect distributed transaction processing causes problems with data consistency
9	No sequential processing, parallelization

In telecom and banking, data inconsistency is a common problem. Data inconsistencies like the previous one are very serious errors.

- Incorrect interest is paid to customer accounts, or incorrect direct deposits are made.
- Billing errors result in incorrect invoices being sent to customers.

10.4.7. Microservices Failures

Failures can propagate between distributed microservices due to poor development practices. Failures should be proactively minimized during microservice development through deployment and testing. MTTR and rollback in case of failure are important, but they should be preceded by activities to prevent them. See Table 10-15.

Table 10-15. Microservice Failures

Number	Description
1	Configuring database locks when handling concurrency
2	Deadlocks and contention
3	Healthcheck and probe errors
4	Disk and filesystem errors
5	Miss Redis cache
6	Setting timeouts and retries
7	API calls change the order of processing, reprocessing due to failures and the delays they cause
8	Delays due to frequent and long locks
9	Failure to create threads upstream due to downstream failure and insufficient thread count
10	Frontend call order control errors
11	Deployment errors
12	Lack of testing
13	Using the wrong data structure for large data overwhelms system resources
14	Incorrect network configuration causes poor performance for certain methods
15	Analyze performance with stack traces, analyze time-consuming methods, and analyze counts and weights
16	Check for invalid or unnecessary system calls
17	Bad logging patterns and excessive log output
18	Increased latency due to string processing and number conversion
19	Minimize exclusive locked sections
20	Apps crashes and freezes frequently

10.5. The Observability Failure Case

I have described various errors in the process of operating applications and system resources. In order to accurately identify delays and failures that occur during operation, observability must be configured correctly. This section describes the various errors that occur when building observability. See Table 10-16.

Table 10-16. Observability Failures

Number	Description
1	Most server frameworks preferentially support OpenTelemetry, commercial observability lack compatibility
2	AWS X-Ray, GCP Cloud Trace do not support OpenTelemetry
3	Commercial observability always requires an agent, and the tracestate configuration is complex
4	Commercial observability supports CICS, IMS, and various EAI servers
5	Commercial observability provides bytecode instrumentation and can be automated
6	The agent does not instrument legacy middleware
7	Commercial observability has multiple ways of storing signals, it's not yet unified
8	Observability AIOps only supports basic root cause analysis, not complex analytics
9	Commercial observability collects limited signals, making root cause analysis and AIOps configuration difficult
10	Logs are not indexed, just simple search capabilities
11	Incorrect correlation of RUM, logs, and so on
12	Restrictions on the API server due to cookies from RUM
13	Managed services, legacy protocols, and so on don't support instrumentation, and agents are difficult to install
14	Join and lookup fail because signals are not integrated
15	Events don't support multiple protocols
16	Traces only instrument the client, not the server
17	Out of memory in the agent
18	Lack of validation of invalid or broken traces
19	Bytecode instrumentation only supports Java, not other languages
20	Multiple agents' trace contexts exist in the logs
21	RUM, distributed trace, and system trace are separated, making it difficult to trace the E2E observability
22	Orchestration servers and legacy middleware don't support trace
23	Tabs, filters, joins, and lookups in dashboards are not supported
24	Metrics output from JMX, Prometheus, and so on are different and missing important metrics
25	Node exports are heavy, Docker disk info is too slow, and collecting too many metrics causes delays
26	No support for virtual threads, netty, or coroutines

(continued)

CHAPTER 10 AIOPS RCA

Table 10-16. (*continued*)

Number	Description
27	OOM in the agent
28	Delays and OOM in the pipeline
29	Inaccurate metering can increase unexpected resource usage and cause anomalous behavior
30	No or incorrect instrumentation in the agent
31	Crashing because of reserved words in logs
32	Collecting too many metrics and logs is costly
33	GraphQL, and so on; span order reversed
34	Cannot omit certain spans
35	Limited dashboard filter functionality
36	Difficult to pre-aggregate by SLO window
37	Difficulty joining observability with external CMDB
38	No support for joining, looking up, and filtering different signals in dashboards
39	TCP, relational databases do not support trace
40	Commercial observability's trace conventions differ from OpenTelemetry, leading to confusion and inaccurate labeling of queue names
41	Agent does not support MDC on a specific thread
42	Commercial agents use sensors instead of propagators, and uses unsupported trace endpoints
43	No support for modern technologies like OpenTracing Shim, Spring Boot, and so on
44	Commercial observability does not support the ability to convert heterogeneous traces like propagators do
45	Commercial agents do not support exhaust being added to headers
46	Only one long span is output, or spans are missing in the middle
47	Difficult to understand results when using OpenTelemetry with commercial agents
48	Incorrect metering creates additional spans
49	No support for custom metrics
50	Inter-agent trace interference and propagation
51	Understanding the thread/alert lifecycle with the state timeline

(*continued*)

CHAPTER 10   AIOPS RCA

Table 10-16. (*continued*)

Number	Description
52	Instrumentation failures prevent results from being output to the OpenTelemetry context
53	Inconsistent trace context due to lack of a standard log policy
54	Doesn't support system trace, lacks system utilities, kernel parameters, or infrastructure monitoring capabilities
55	Errors in automatic discovery of services and resources
56	No integration between RUM and distributed trace

- Only the log write path can be configured in a pipeline to handle large amounts of data using a message server such as Kafka. Other signaling can cause messages to be lost in the event of a failure.

- Excessive traffic can cause delays in indexing or cause OOM in the pipeline and backend servers.

- Frequent OOM errors in the agent.

- Frequent pull-scans on read paths, resulting in frequent memory outages and performance degradation.

Frequent failures during operations and errors are caused by misconfiguration.

- It can be categorized into agents, pipelines, read paths, and write paths.

- Agent's measurement and signal data matching errors occur frequently.

The overall data model for observability is as follows:

- Key business ID, such as order ID and payment ID

- Entities such as services and resources

- Eight signals collected from applications and services

- System resources collected from the kernel and hardware

Figure 10-24 shows the data managed by observability. As you can see, observability already contains a lot of data. By utilizing and automating it, you can automate your IT operations.

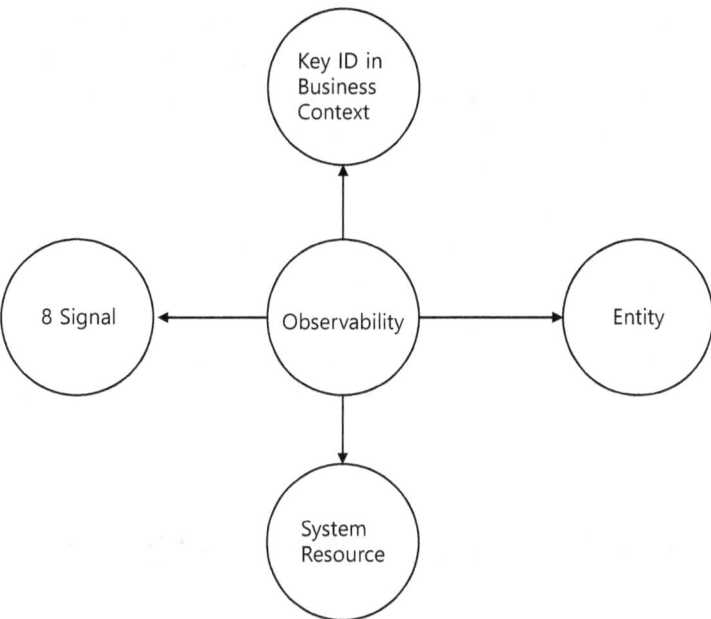

Figure 10-24. Observability data structure

Many developers and SREs think that data is missing or that they don't have the data they need, but observability already includes all the data from the business and applications. You can output more detail than any business report. There's no need to build a CMDB, and no need for tags, data pipelines, or API interfaces. Observability is the single source of truth, and you should take advantage of it to reduce costs and improve productivity.

Create a failure list data model based on what you've learned so far.

Large Category (Failure Scope)	Medium (System)	Failure Type	Small (Failure Content)
Legacy middleware	EAI	Data consistency	Confirmation, checkpoints matter when resending messages, and configuring resend flags in messages
Legacy middleware	EAI	Resource allocation	EAI, ETL is all about memory min and max
Legacy middleware	EAI	Data consistency	Message conversion and validation failures
Legacy middleware	EAI	Invalid configuration	Invalid retries, timeout settings
Legacy middleware	EAI	Data consistency	Lost abnormal shutdown messages
Legacy middleware	EAI	Data consistency	Messages are lost due to incorrect exception handling
Legacy middleware	EAI	Data consistency	Incorrect false retransmissions when EAI exception handling fails

CHAPTER 10   AIOPS RCA

You must use RAG to join the root cause analysis data model and the failure list data model. There are no keys to join between the root cause analysis data model and the failure list data model. In the root cause analysis data model, you can see which applications and databases are failing. However, because there are no specific tags and ID, the relationship between the two tables is invisible. You can check for errors directly in the root cause analysis data model by the SRE, and check the root cause analysis at the prompt.

If you can identify the application name in the error message, it will help the SRE generate prompts based on that. The legacy name is defined in the span generated by the step on the EAI server, or the database name can be found in the span generated by the step on the ETL server.

Since there are relationships between entities, this allows you to see the dependencies between entities. You can also retrieve the data you need from the relationships between entities and signals.

The root cause analysis data model also includes system traces, so you can understand failures that occur in system resources.

10.6. Retrieval-Augmented Generation (RAG)

The goals of this section are to understand and develop various RAGs used in AIOps implementations.

Retrieval-Augmented Generation (RAG) has emerged as an AI technology that combines efficient data search with LLMs (large language models) to generate accurate and relevant responses. RAG has gained traction with users because it reflects the high accurate information, reducing inaccuracies and illusions in responses.

The goal of this section is to organize AIOps using RAG and develop two types of RAG.

- LangChain is an open source way to configure RAG. You'll learn about the components of LangChain and develop RAG using simple agents and tools.

- Using OpenSearch, quickly implement a production-ready RAG.

The RAG process takes these steps when a question is asked by a user:

- Semantically close words or sentences will have vectors with close values. In this step, you vectorize the user's question.

- Get sentences by searching a vector of user input in a database. This allows you to get multiple similar sentences. They are not accurate and cannot combine various pieces of knowledge. The language model can generate more accurate answers from information it

- Combine sentences and questions from the search results, build a prompt, and call the language model to ask the question and get an answer.

It targets data analysis of observability and does not explain LangChain in detail.

10.6.1. LangChain

LangChain is an open source library that supports application development utilizing LLM.

In LangChain, you can combine different modules to create applications that perform complex tasks. The core of LangChain is the agent.

LangChain's agent module inferred what is required as an answer from the user's input, selected and executed the necessary tools, and create the optimal answer.

LangChain has tools that serve to endow LLM with knowledge.

If you're building an application like ChatGPT, and you're just having a conversation, the Open API is enough. You don't need LangChain. Where LangChain is helpful is when you want your LLM to utilize external knowledge or computational power. By connecting a web search function to the LLM with LangChain, the LLM can search the web to get the latest information and answer questions that cannot be answered using only their own knowledge.

LangChain provides a variety of modules to help you develop applications using LLM. Modules can be used individually, or you can combine them to build complex applications.

The main modules are as follows:

- **LLM:** Common interface for calling LLM
- **Prompt templates:** Create prompts based on user input
- **Chaining:** Connecting the input and output of multiple LLMs and prompts
- **Agent:** Decide which features to execute and in what order based on user requests
- **Tools:** Specific functions performed by the agent.
- **Memory:** Memory holdings of chains and agents

Prompt templates, chains, and memory are not discussed in detail. Agents and tools are described in detail.

10.6.1.1. Models

LangChain provides a common interface to utilize different LLMs in the same way.

LangChain's LLM class is a common interface for calling LLMs. This makes it easy to switch between the LLM used by your application. However, few LLMs have enough language understanding to take full advantage of LangChain's capabilities, usually limited to GPT-4 and GPT-3.5.

Begin by initializing the LLM:

```
from langchain.chat_models import ChatOpenAI

# LLM Preparation
chat_llm = ChatOpenAI(
    model _name="gpt-3.5-turbo", # model ID
    temperature=0 # randomness
)
```

Call the LLM:

```
from langchain.schema import (
    SystemMessage,
    HumanMessage,
    AIMessage
)

messages = [
    HumanMessage(content="how to get cache hit rate?")
]
result = chat_llm(messages)
print(result)

messages_list = [
    [HumanMessage(content=" Why are only certain transactions experiencing high latency?")],
    [HumanMessage(content=" To find slow queries in OpenSearch?")]
]
result = chat_llm.generate(messages_list)

# output text
print("response0:", result.generations[0][0].text)
print("response1:", result.generations[1][0].text)

# of tokens used
print("llm_output:", result.llm_output)
```

10.6.1.2. Prompt Templates

Prompting is a very important module in LLMs to get the best answers.

An prompt template in LangChain is a template for generating an answer from user input. The prompt template contains information such as instructions to the LLM, questions for the LLM, and example answers to help the LLM create better answers.

When developing applications with the LLM, developers don't typically pass user input directly to the LLM. Instead, you can inject user input into prompt phrases that have been shown to return good answers, and then pass them to the LLM.

10.6.1.3. Chains

Chains are modules that allow you to connect the input and output of multiple LLM or prompts. Chains are composed of prompt templates, models, arbitrary methods, other chains.

Chains are modules for chaining the input and output of multiple LLM or prompts. used LLM and prompt templates on their own, but in real-world applications, they are chained together.

10.6.1.4. Agents

An agent is a module that decides which functions to execute and in what order based on the user's request. Chains perform predetermined functions, but agents vary the functions they perform based on the user's request.

Agents alternate between inferring reasons for behavior and acting on those reasons. Actions affect the external environment, gathering new information as observations. Inferences do not affect the external environment, but instead affect internal states by inferring context and updating information useful for future inferences and actions.

The agent's process flow is as follows:

- **Input:** How users assign tasks to agents.
- **Inference:** The agent thinks about what to do.
- **Action:** The agent determines which tools to use and the inputs to the tools.
- **Observation:** Observe the output of the tool.

Repeat this process until the agent determines that the task is complete.
Initialize:

```
from langchain.agents import load_tools
from langchain.chat_models import ChatOpenAI

# Prepare the tool
tools = load_tools(
    tool_names=["serpapi", "llm-math"], # tool names
    llm=ChatOpenAI(temperature=0) # LLM to use for initialization of the tool
)
```

Create memory:

```
from langchain.chains.conversation.memory import ConversationBufferMemory

memory = ConversationBufferMemory(
    memory_key="chat_history",
    return_messages=True
)
```

Create an agent:

```
from langchain.agents import initialize_agent

agent = initialize_agent(
    agent="conversational-react-description", # set agent type
    llm=ChatOpenAI(temperature=0), # LLM to use for agent initialization
```

```
    tools=tools, # tools
    memory=memory, # memory
    verbose=True # Print verbose information
)
```

Run the agent:

```
agent.run("What caused the spike?")
```

10.6.1.5. Tools

To perform complex tasks in the agent, you need the right tool.

A tool is a specific function that an agent performs in its behavior during its process. It acquires new information by observation by influencing the external environment. Tools serve to endow LLMs with knowledge and computational capabilities.

- **Knowledge:** Web search, knowledge base
- **Compute:** Calculate numbers, run programs

To prepare tools, specify an array of tool names in load_tools(). Some tools require an LLM to initialize the tool, in which case you pass it in the LLM parameter.

```
from langchain.agents import load_tools
from langchain.chat_models import ChatOpenAI

# Prepare the tool
tools = load_tools(
    tool_names=["google-search"],
    llm=ChatOpenAI(temperature=0)
)
```

Create memory:

```
from langchain.chains.conversation.memory import ConversationBufferMemory

memory = ConversationBufferMemory(
    memory_key="chat_history",
    return_messages=True
)
```

Create an agent:

```
from langchain.agents import initialize_agent
```

```
agent = initialize_agent(
    agent="zero-shot-react-description",
    llm=ChatOpenAI(temperature=0),
    tools=tools,
    memory=memory,
    verbose=True
)
```

Run the agent:

```
agent.run("What is the MTTR formula?")
```

10.6.1.6. Memory

Memory is a module used by inference during the agent's process flow. It stores information inside the agent that is useful for future inferences and actions. Specifically, it can remember conversations between the agent and the user and use that information to decide what to say next.

Examples include chat AI remembering past conversations and using them to make inferences about what to say next.

Memory allows you to remember the past conversations of a chain or agent and incorporate that information into the current conversation.

The main memory provided by LangChain is as follows.

- ConversationBufferMemory: Memory that uses all conversation history

Create memory:

```
from langchain.memory import ConversationBufferMemory

memory = ConversationBufferMemory()
memory.chat_memory.add_user_message("Collect metrics.")
```

Gets a memory variable:

```
memory.load_memory_variables({})
```

So far, you've learned about the main components of a LangChain.

AIOps requires a variety of components to make it work. Vector databases, agents, tools, models, and many other components are used together in LangChain, so knowledge of them is required. In order to provide services in operations, you need to combine components well, which requires a lot of experience. Compared to LangChain, OpenSearch is more automated and helps you easily deploy components into production.

10.6.2. Searching Observability Data

The Vector database is used for searching observability data. The basic activities in utilizing data are search, analysis, and aggregation. I have already discussed data analysis and aggregation. This section explains how to search semantic data using the Vector database. The search technology required in AIOps is different from previous search technologies:

- **Analyze observability data:** Use Promscale. Collect observability data and structure metrics and traces for analysis.

- **Aggregate observability data:** Use Druid to process long-term storage and complex aggregations.

- **Search for observability data:** Use the Vector database. Configure semantic search to search by meaning, rather than traditional keyword search.

To implement RAG, you need agents, tools, and a Vector database. Reusable agents and tools are provided and can be developed as needed. The Vector database is required to organize the knowledge base.

Machine learning allows you to create embedding models. Embedding encodes any type of data into a vector that captures its context. This allows you to search for neighboring data points to find similar data.

A vector embedding is a mathematical representation of a set of data points in a low-dimensional space that shows their underlying relationships and patterns. Embeddings are often used to represent complex data types like images, text, and audio in a way that makes them easier for machine learning algorithms to process. Rather than being defined by experts, they are self-discovered by the model as it trains on large datasets, learning complex patterns and relationships that would be difficult for humans to identify. This allows models to utilize embeddings to make forecasts or decisions based on the underlying patterns and relationships between data.

It adds the additional capability to efficiently and quickly look up nearest neighbors in an N-dimensional space. It is powered by a k-NN index and is built with algorithms like HNSW and IVF.

Vector databases can be combined with generative text models to develop intelligent agents that provide interactive search experiences. Vector databases can complement Generative AI models and support external knowledge bases for AIOps.

The more accurate the results, the slower the query response time is likely to be. Real-world vectors can have hundreds of dimensions instead of two, and comparing thousands of them using a distance metric is time-consuming. Therefore, the Vector database consists of three processes: indexing, querying, and post-processing.

- **Indexing:** Vector databases use algorithms such as PQ, LSH, or HNSW to index vectors. This process maps vectors to data structures, allowing for faster searches.

- **Querying:** Vector databases compare the index query vector with the index vectors in the dataset and find the nearest neighbors.

- **Post-processing:** If necessary, the Vector database searches for the final nearest neighbors in the dataset and post-processes them to return the final results. This process may involve reranking the nearest neighbors, using different similarity measures.

The Vector database provides a way to operationalize embedding models. Within the model, the k-Nearest Neighbor (k-NN) index efficiently searches vectors, applies a distance method such as cosine, and ranks the results based on similarity.

OpenSearch uses the Okapi BM25 algorithm to calculate document scores. BM25 is a keyword-based algorithm that performs well on queries containing keywords, but does not capture the semantic meaning of query terms. A semantic search, unlike a keyword-based search, considers the meaning of a query in the context of the search, which is why semantic search performs better for queries that require natural language understanding.

Semantic searches utilize vector similarity when searching, which has the advantage of finding semantically similar documents, but the disadvantage is that they may return fewer relevant documents than a keyword search, which compares strings. To compensate for this drawback, you can use a hybrid search, which is a combination of a keyword search and a semantic search.

Semantic searches allow you to use embeddings in your search documents to improve the relevance of your search results.

Given a set of points (vectors) and a query, the problem of k-NN is to find the k points in the set that are closest to the query, which is relatively simple compared to other ML techniques. The approach is to compute the distance from the query for each vector in the set.

The problem with this approach is that it is difficult to scale. The runtime search complexity is $O(Nlogk)$, where N is the number of vectors and k is the number of nearest neighbors. This may not be noticeable when the contains thousands of vectors, but it becomes noticeable when the size grows to millions. Using the exact k-NN algorithm can speed up the search, but at higher dimensions.

10.6.2.1. OpenSearch Vector Database

OpenSearch is a Vector database with a k-NN plugin, which can be implemented in various use cases such as semantic searches, RAG to use LLM, and recommendation searches. The OpenSearch k-NN plugin provides the ability to use the k-NN algorithm within the OpenSearch cluster.

In this section, you see how to run a k-NN workload on OpenSearch. First, you need to create an index. An index is an easily searchable way to hold a set of documents . For k-NN, the "mappings" in the index tell OpenSearch which algorithm and parameters to use.

Each of the three engines used in approximate k-NN search has unique attributes that make it more reasonable to use than the others in a given situation.

- **Non-Metric Space Library:** NMSLIB implements the HNSW algorithm.

- **Facebook AI Similarity Search:** FAISS implements both the HNSW and IVF algorithms.

- **Lucene:** Implements the HNSW algorithm.

In general, NMSLIB and FAISS should be the optional choice for large-scale use cases. Lucene is a good option for smaller deployments, but it offers benefits such as smart filtering, where the optimal filtering strategy (pre-filter, post-filter, or exact k-NN) is automatically applied depending on the situation.

OpenSearch uses the Approximate k-NN algorithm from the NMSLIB, FAISS, and Lucene libraries to power k-NN searches.

With the k-NN OpenSearch plugin, OpenSearch collects documents with vectors as k-NN field types.

```
sudo bin/opensearch-plugin list
```

It's easy to install OpenSearch k-NN.

```
sudo bin/opensearch-plugin install opensearch-k-NN
```

The OpenSearch k-NN Plugin

The k-NN plugin supports three ways to get neighbors.

- Use Approximate k-NN for large indexes with no pre-filtered queries.
- Use scoring scripts for small bodies and pre-filtered queries.
- To calculate the score, use a painless script if you need to use the distance function.

The Vector Search Algorithm

A simple way to find similar vectors is to use the k-NN algorithm, which calculates the distance between the query vector and other vectors in the Vector database. The scoring script and painless script search methods use the Exact k-NN algorithm internally. However, for very high-dimensional datasets, this creates a scaling problem that reduces the efficiency of the search. Approximate k-NN search methods can overcome this problem that reorganize the index more efficiently and reduce the dimensionality of the searchable vectors.

There are a variety of Approximate k-NN search algorithms, including locality-sensitive hashing, tree-based, cluster-based, and graph-based. OpenSearch implements two Approximate k-NN algorithms: Hierarchical Navigable Small World (HNSW) and Inverted filesystem (IVF).

- The HNSW algorithm is one of the most popular algorithms for searching artificial neural networks. The core idea of the algorithm is to build a graph with edges connecting index vectors that are close to each other. When searching, this graph is partially traversed to find the closest neighbors to the query vector. In order to progress the search towards the query's closest neighbors, the algorithm always visits the candidate closest to the query vector first.

- The IVF algorithm separates the index vector into a set of buckets and then searches only a subset of these buckets to reduce search time. if the algorithm randomly splits the vector into multiple buckets and searches only a subset of them, the approximation is poor. Therefore, the IVF algorithm uses an improved approach. First, it assigns a representative vector to each bucket before starting indexing. When a vector is indexed, it is added to the bucket with the closest representative vector. Vectors that are closer to each other are placed in roughly the same bucket or a nearby bucket.

Using the Approximate k-NN method, let's collect some documents to search. You will use the word embedding demo. The vector array values will be generated using the word embedding library.

The most relevant attributes are

- **Dimension:** The amount of dimensionality the vector will have.

- **space_type:** The spatial method used to calculate the distance between vectors.

- **ef_construction:** The size of the dynamic list used in k-NN. Higher values provide better precision, but also slow the indexing process down.

- **m:** The number of bidirectional links the plugin will create. This will affect memory usage, so keep it between 2 and 100.

```
PUT test-k-NN
{ {
  "set tings": { {
    "index": { "index".
      "k-NN": True,
      "k-NN.algo_param.ef_search": 100
    }
  },
  "mappings": { "mappings".
    "properties": { "properties".
      "product_vector": { "product_vector".
        "type": "k-NN_vector",
        "dimension": 4,
        "method": { "method".
          "name": "hnsw",
          "space_type": "l2",
          "engine": "nmslib",
          "parameters": { "parameters".
            "ef_construction": 128,
            "m": 24
          }
        }
      }
    }
  }
}
```

CHAPTER 10 AIOPS RCA

Now collect some example documents:

```
POST _bulk
{ "index": { "_index": "test-k-NN", "_id": "1" }
{ "product_vector": [1, 5, 5, 4], "price": 10.00, "name": "Hygienic sand" }
{ "index": { "_index": "test-k-NN", "_id": "2" }
{ "product_vector": [5, 4, 4, 4, 4], "price": 25.00, "name": "Pet supplies pack" }
{ "index": { "_index": "test-k-NN", "_id": "3" }
{ "product_vector": [7, 9, 9, 9, 9], "price": 500,"name": "Catapult" }
{ "index": { "_index": "test-k-NN", "_id": "4" }
{ "product_vector": [1, 1, 2, 1], "price": 5,"name": "Hot Wheels Car" }
```

Each component of the vector array is a dimension that represents a feature of the document. Thousands of different dimensions can be computed.

```
GET test-k-NN/_search
{ {
  "size": 2,
  "query": { "query".
    "k-NN": { "k-NN".
      "product_vector": { "product_vector".
        "vector": [2, 3, 5, 6],
        "k": 2
      }
    }
  }
}
```

The dimensionality attribute of the mapping supports up to 10,000 dimensions. Suppose that after training the model, the vector representation for "cat" is [2,3,5,6].

- **Size:** The amount of results to return.
- **K:** The amount of neighbors to return for each graph.
- **Vector:** A vector representation of the document being searched.

Searching for Approximate and Exact K-NNs

The OpenSearch k-NN plugin provides three methods to obtain k-NN from a vector index. They are Approximate k-NN, scoring script (exact k-NN) and painless script (exact k-NN).

Approximate k-NN

The first method uses Approximate k-NN, which uses one of several algorithms to return an Approximate k-NN for the query vector. Typically, these algorithms provide performance benefits such as lower latency, smaller memory usage, and more scalable search, but at the expense of index speed and search accuracy. Approximate k-NN is the best choice for searches on large indexes (hundreds of thousands of vectors or more) that require low latency.

If you want to significantly reduce the number of vectors to search for in a k-NN search, you can apply a filter to the index. This feature is only available for Lucene and Faiss engines using HNSW.

Approximate k-NN cannot be pre-filtered. For example, after running k-NN, if you want to filter products by price, you can use a post-filter clause.

```
GET test-k-NN/_search
{ {
  "size": 2,
  "query": { "query".
    "k-NN": { "k-NN".
      "product_vector": { "product_vector".
        "vector": [2, 3, 5, 6],
        "k": 2
      }
    }
  },
  "post_filter": { }
    "range": { { "1".
      "price": { "price".
        "lte": 20
      }
    }
  }
}
```

With this query, no pet supply packs are returned due to price.

Scoring script k-NN (Exact k-NN)

The scoring script is to run an Exact k-NN search on the knn_vector field or fields that can represent binary objects. With this approach, the k-NN search can be run on a subset of the vectors in the index (also known as a pre-filtered search). This approach is preferred when searching or pre-filtering on small document bodies is required. Using this approach for large indexes can result in high latency.

With this approach, you can apply filters before executing the nearest neighbor search. For this reason, it does not scale well, but it is useful for dynamic search cases where the index body may vary based on different conditions.

```
PUT my-k-NN-index-1
{ {
  "mappings": { "mappings".
    "properties": { "properties".
      "product_vecto r": { "product_vector".
        "type": "k-NN_vector",
        "dimension": 4
      }
    }
  }
}
```

To use this index for both scoring scripts and approximations, you need to set k-NN.index: true and set k-NN.space_type. The query looks like this:

```
GET my-k-NN-index-1/_search
{ {
 "size": 4,
 "query": { "query".
   "script_score": { 1
     "query": { "query".
       "match_all": {}
     },
     "script": { "script".
       "source": "k-NN_score",
       "lang": "k-NN",
       "params": { "params".
         "field": "product_vector",
         "query_value": [2.0, 3.0, 5.0, 6.0],
         "space_type": "cosinesimil"
       }
     }
   }
  }
 }
}
```

Painless scripts (Exact k-NN)

The third method adds the distance method as a simple extension that can be used for more complex combinations. Like the scoring script, this method can be used to perform an Exact k-NN search, where each vector in the index is compared against the others, and it also supports pre-filtering. This approach has slightly slower query performance compared to the scoring script.

This method allows you to change the distance method value and score. You can choose from a list of available methods and, for example, multiply the score values or include other fields from the document in the equation. All methods take a field name and a vector value as parameters.

See the following example:

```
GET my-k-NN-index-1/_search
{ {
  "query": { "query".
    "script_score": { 1
      "query": { "query".
        "match_all": {}
      },
      "script": { "script".
        "source": "1.0 + cosineSimilarity(params.query_value, doc[params.field])",
        "params": { "params".
          "field": "product_vector",
          "query_value": [
            7.9,
            2.9,
            4.9,
            4.9
          ]
        }
      }
    }
  }
}
```

This script runs the cosine similarity method, calculates the scores, and then sums the totals to 1.0.

I have covered various algorithms and techniques used to perform approximate k-NN searches. There is no perfect algorithm or approach that optimizes all metrics at once. HNSW, IVF, and PQ each allow you to optimize different metrics in a k-NN workload. When choosing which k-NN algorithm to use, you should first understand the requirements of your use case and then tune the algorithm configuration to meet them.

10.6.2.2. LangChain Vector Database

Configure the vector database in OpenSearch and query the Vector database from the LangChain application.

Install the Python library:

```
pip ins tall opensearch-py
```

To use Open AI embeddings, you need the OpenAI API:

```
import os
import getpass

os.environ["OPENAI_API_KEY"] = getpass.getpass("OpenAI API Key:")
```

Create an embedding:

```
from langchain.document_loaders import TextLoader

loader = TextLoader("../../../../state_of_the_union.txt")
documents = loader.load()
text_splitter = CharacterTextSplitter(chunk_size=1000, chunk_overlap=0)
docs = text_splitter.split_documents(documents)

embeddings = OpenAIEmbeddings()
```

Process scoring scripts with user-defined parameters:

```
print(docs[0].page_content)

docsearch = OpenSearchVectorSearch.from_documents(
    docs, embeddings, opensearch_url="http://localhost:9200", is_appx_search=False
)

query = "What did the president say about Ketanji Brown Jackson"
docs = docsearch.similarity_search(
    "What did the president say about Ketanji Brown Jackson",
    k=1,
    search_type="script_scoring",
)

print(docs[0].page_content)
```

Process painless scripts:

```
docsearch = OpenSearchVectorSearch.from_documents(
    docs, embeddings, opensearch_url="http://localhost:9200", is_appx_search=False
```

```
)
filter = {"bool": {"filter": {"term": {"text": "smuggling"}}}}
query = "What did the president say about Ketanji Brown Jackson"
docs = docsearch.similarity_search(
    "What did the president say about Ketanji Brown Jackson",
    search_type="painless_scripting",
    space_type="cosineSimilarity",
    pre_filter=filter,
)
print(docs[0].page_content)
```

By combining internal data stored in OpenSearch with external LLM such as OpenAI, it is possible to deliver highly accurate results. By embedding the data and documents and storing them in the Vector database, the LLM can understand and answer the stored documents, which can be utilized for root cause analysis.

10.6.3. OpenSearch AIOps

Like LangChain, RAG can be configured quickly and without development using OpenSearch. OpenSearch manages the embedding model and provides the Vector database. It provides the agents and tools that are the main components of RAG.

After supporting and resolving failures in your practice, write a report of your findings or a failure report. Once the failure report is well organized, you can categorize the failure. It can become a well-organized playbook at the infrastructure and application level. You need to organize the reports, turn them into a knowledge base, and use them to respond to failures and reduce MTTR. Generative AI and RAG are useful tools to facilitate this process.

The basic principle of operation is processed by creating a knowledge base with playbooks and asking questions to Generative AI. Therefore, it is of utmost importance to create a knowledge base so that Generative AI can give accurate answers.

- Chaos engineering generates good data in the test environment. The errors and signals generated are utilized as a knowledge base for the Vector database.

- Use snapshots in production. Promscale, OpenSearch, and others support snapshots. They are useful for archiving and recreating past failures.

By providing Generative AI with error messages and tuning data, it can perform root cause analysis. While the amount of documentation is important, Generative AI can give good answers with a small number of high-quality documents. This book provides many demonstrations, and through chaos engineering, you can obtain many error messages and tuning data. By storing them in a Vector database and asking questions based on accurate data, Generative AI can answer accurately.

By using OpenSearch, RAG development time can be reduced. This is because OpenSearch provides tools and agents that were developed directly by LangChain as modules that do not require development.

Given the complexity of the Vector database and agent configuration, OpenSearch provides excellent features for AIOps implementations.

OpenSearch minimizes development and provides a wide range of tools and agents. AIOps configuration is as simple as setting it up.

1. You can register and manage models. You can automate model management through connectors.

2. It provides a basic Vector database and modeling tools, as well as more complex tools and agents such as RAG and PPL.

In this chapter, you'll develop different types of RAG.

- **Root cause analysis RAG:** Simplified configuration of agents without using a Vector database. Looks up indexes and ties them to external LLM. Uses OpenAI and AWS Bedrock.

- **Observability RAG:** Configures complex agents and use OpenAI.

- In addition, you'll configure reranking and guardrail RAG.

This was tested in May 25, 2025, but there is a version risk that it will not work in the future. This should be considered in your lab.

You can improve accuracy a bit by using certain techniques. But I think the real problem lies in the data, and I focused more on the data itself than on specific techniques.

I believe that the hybrid search, various RAG, and Vector databases provided by OpenSearch are sufficient to achieve satisfactory results.

Build a RAG application that serves OpenSearch k-NN indexes as a knowledge base for a large language model (LLM). I use semantic search for data retrieval.

RAG is exactly what it sounds like: searching for the information you need and generating it by augmenting the prompts. OpenSearch RAG are functionally similar to LangChain RAG, but are more automated. OpenSearch RAG is processed in the following order:

1. Get the data you want to search from the data source, make it into embedding vectors through the embedding model, and store it in the Vector database.

2. Search for data related to the request in the Vector database where you stored the data to be retrieved and reflect the results in a prompt.

3. Search the Vector database for information relevant to the user's request that came in through the user interface and combine it with the user's request to complete the prompt.

Since anomaly detection and metric correlation are already configured, you can add RAG to organize AIOps with OpenSearch.

This section explains how to configure, develop, and use different types of RAG, agent.

- **Data search:** An algorithm to search the Vector data stored in a knowledge base.
- **Data ingest:** Data that is ingested in real-time or in batches needs to be stored in vector form. This is called vector embedding and requires a model for embedding. Clearly, adding data in real time is a big challenge. Managing a large Vector database requires a lot of system resources. As data is ingested, the vectors are constantly changing slightly.
- **LLM models:** Connectors are needed to interface to external LLM model. OpenSearch is a non-standard connector, and MCP is the standard that is often mentioned these days.
- **Agents:** Two tools are needed for vector search and LLM prompt.

In this section, I demonstrate various configurations with OpenSearch.

- **Observability:** Traces, logs, and metrics can be configured with Grafana. It is difficult to query the repository directly, but with OpenSearch, traces are stored in an index, so it is possible to join them with logs.
- **Anomaly detection:** Supports real-time anomaly detection, and the results of anomaly detection are stored in the index, so various visualizations are possible using query.
- **RAG:** It can link embedding models and LLM model, and it provides agent and tool.
- **Vector database:** Provides a semantic searchable Vector database.
- **Machine learning algorithms:** Metric correlation uses algorithms provided by OpenSearch.
- **SIEM:** Using OpenSearch for security and network management. SIEM uses internal rules to identify threats. RAG can be used to explain the identified threat.
- **Chatbot:** The chatbot provided by OpenSearch is implemented with RAG and LLM.

Additional applications include multi-tenant support. Indexes are stored in S3 object storage for long-term storage. There is a built-in cache to improve performance.

OpenSearch is more useful than other open sources for managing structured and unstructured data simultaneously, or for a variety of purposes.

The downside is that it doesn't provide a lot of correlation and has a high learning curve.

Traditionally, the index pipeline uses an embedding model to process data for embedding and then indexes the data. Then, the backend API system performs a semantic search after embedding the search keywords.

With the semantic search provided by OpenSearch, the search query is vectorized and k-NN is used to return the closest vector in the corpus.

CHAPTER 10 AIOPS RCA

Configure the OpenSearch RAG in the following order.

- Registering and deploying text embedding models
- Creating a pipeline
- Creating a k-NN index
- Creating a connector for an external LLM model
- Registering and deploying external LLM models
- Registering and running the agent

When registering and deploying text embedding models, you need to register two models: a text embedding model and an LLM model (see Figure 10-25). To facilitate the search for vectors, you need a text embedding model. Use one of the pretrained models provided by OpenSearch.

- Input from users or systems can be delays and errors identified in the root cause analysis data model, anomaly identified through anomaly detection, and problems identified through metric correlation.
- The data stored in the Vector database can be a list of 400 failures.
- The agent enriches the prompts by comparing the delays and errors in the input, the root cause analysis data model, with the failure list in the Vector database.
- The enriched prompts are passed to the LLM, which responds by generating a final answer.

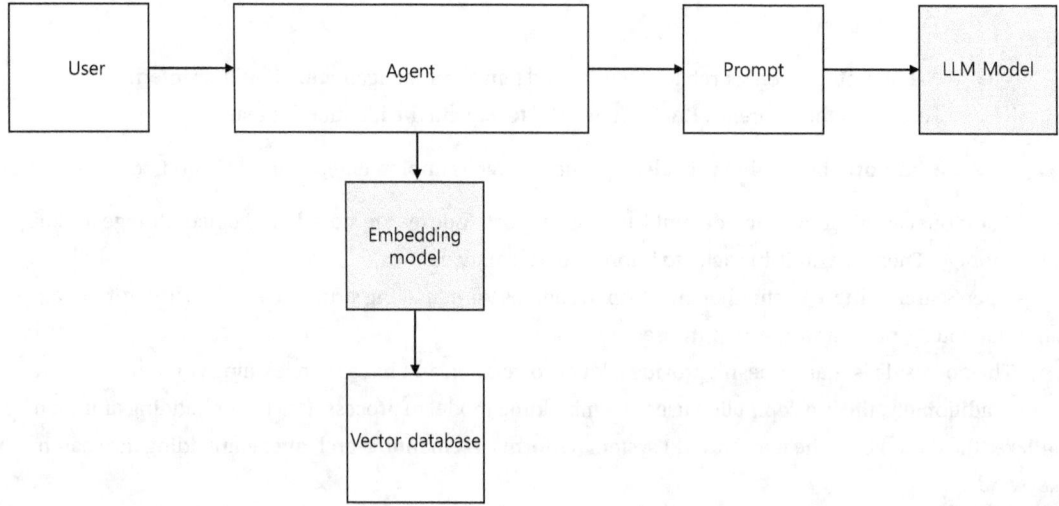

Figure 10-25. RAG components

Each of the components described in Figure 10-25 has many choices depending on your requirements. Depending on which components you choose, the architecture will be different. This complexity makes RAG difficult to learn.

- **Data:** RAG uses Vector databases, but many types of databases are possible. The advantage is that it can be a relational database, structured, unstructured, natural language processing, anomaly detection, SIEM, observability, machine learning, IT operations, knowledge base, root cause analysis, semantic search, or chatbots. The ability to read data from various tasks and apply RAG immediately simplifies system configuration and enables various RAG with little cost and labor. Combining OpenSearch RAG with various data sources is useful when the results of a data source are difficult to understand or when internal knowledge can be combined to produce higher-level results. Your knowledge base should be organized in business domains, not just technology. Without a business context, it is difficult to identify and solve technical problems. The reason I chose OpenSearch is that it provides a variety of data sources, which makes it easy to configure RAG for different purposes and organize AIOps.

- **Agents:** A basic agent sequentially processes multiple tools. As a more complex agent, ReAct is able to understand the context in which LLM are working, and to omit or selectively handle the necessary tools. A more sophisticated agent is the plan-execute agent, which is a separate planner agent that plans and an executor agent that executes, making it ideal for automating complex tasks. Root cause analysis RAG is similar to the ReAct agent, and observability RAG is similar to the plan-execute agent.

- **Post-processing:** You can configure multiple agents to collaborate between them. You can also utilize tools like n8n that make it easy to link AI agents and RAG. Reranking and guardrails are some of the post-processing actions that should be considered.

You need to register two models: a text embedding model and an LLM model. First, register the text embedding model.

To store and search contextual information, you need to convert text into embedding vectors, which is where the embedding model comes in.

It is the process of searching the Vector database for information relevant to the user's request that came in through the user interface, and then combining it with the user's request to complete the prompt.

Clone from https://github.com/opensearch-project/opentelemetry-demo.

Testing was done on CentOS, not Ubuntu. CentOS is recommended if possible. Before running Docker Compose, run the following command:

```
export OPENSEARCH_USER=admin
export OPENSEARCH_PASSWORD=Corr#ecthorsebatterystaple1
export OPENSEARCH_INITIAL_ADMIN_PASSWORD=Corr#ecthorsebatterystaple1
```

CHAPTER 10 AIOPS RCA

As a first step, register the text embedding model and create a pipeline that references the text embedding model. Create an index that references the pipeline.

```
PUT _cluster/settings
{
    "persistent": {
        "plugins.ml_commons.only_run_on_ml_node": false,
        "plugins.ml_commons.native_memory_threshold": 100,
        "plugins.ml_commons.agent_framework_enabled": true
    }
}
```

Set up a cluster to configure the OpenSearch RAG, as shown in Figure 10-26.

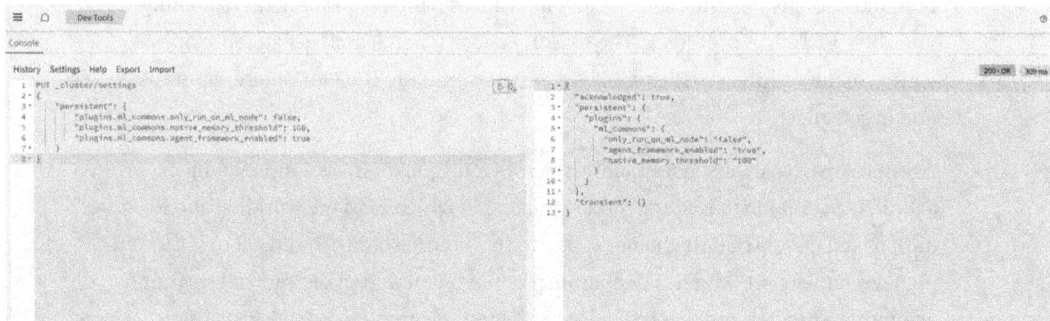

Figure 10-26. Cluster configuration

Register the embedded model in OpenSearch.

This example uses the model huggingface/sentence-transformers/all-MiniLM-L12-v2, which generates a dense vector embedding of 384 dimensions. To register and deploy the model, you need to send the following request:

```
POST /_plugins/_ml/models/_register?deploy=true
{ {
  "name": "huggingface/sentence-transformers/all-MiniLM-L12-v2",
  "version": "1.0.1",
  "model_format": "TORCH_SCRIPT"
}
```

Register the embedding model, as shown in Figure 10-27.

CHAPTER 10 AIOPS RCA

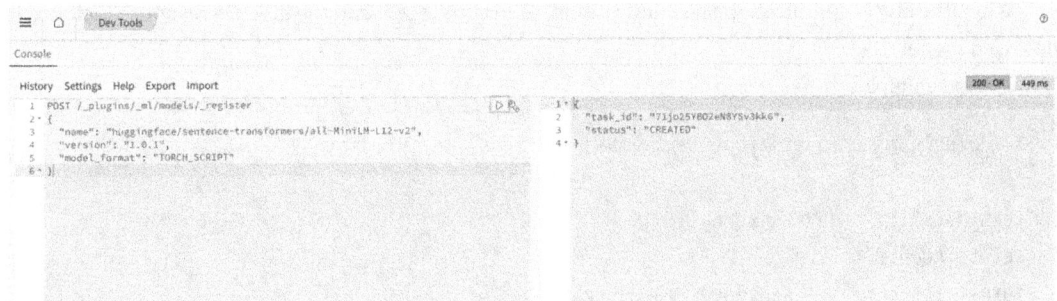

Figure 10-27. *Registering the embedding model*

GET /_plugins/_ml/tasks/your_task_id

Confirm the embedding model, as shown in Figure 10-28.

Figure 10-28. *Confirming the embedding model*

Deploy the model:

POST /_plugins/_ml/models/your_text_embedding_model_id/_deploy

Deploy the embedding model, as shown in Figure 10-29.

Figure 10-29. *Deploying the embedding model*

803

CHAPTER 10 AIOPS RCA

When the task is complete, the task status changes to Completed, and the task API response includes the deployed model ID.

Test the model:

```
POST /_plugins/_ml/models/your_text_embedding_model_id/_predict
{
  "text_docs":[ "today is sunny"],
  "return_number": true,
  "target_response": ["sentence_embedding"]
}
```

Test the embedding model, as shown in Figure 10-30.

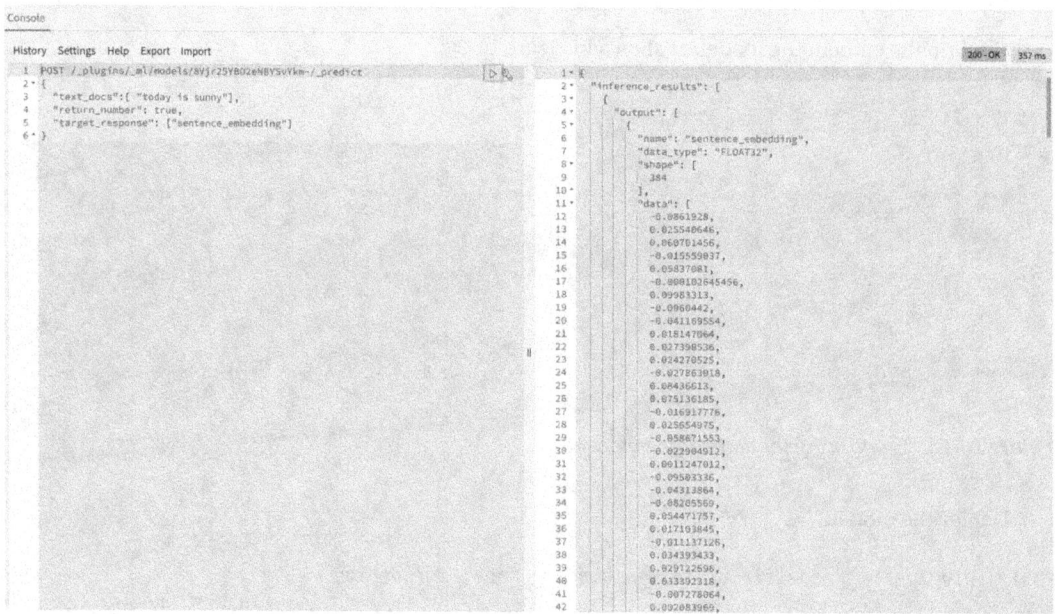

Figure 10-30. *Testing the embedding model*

Register and demo various LLM models such as OpenAI.

To vector embed text, set up a pipeline. The pipeline identifies the text field and writes the result to the embedding field. Create a pipeline by specifying model_id in the following request.

```
PUT /_ingest/pipeline/test_population_data_pipeline
{
    "description": "text embedding pipeline",
    "processors": [
        {
            "text_embedding": {
                "model_id": "your_text_embedding_model_id",
```

```
            "field_map": {
                "population_description": "population_description_embedding"
            }
        }
    }
  ]
}
```

If the model status shows DEPLOYED in the development tool or RESPONDING in the OpenSearch dashboard, you can use the model ID to build a pipeline. Make sure to replace the model ID with the unique ID generated for the model deployed in your domain.

Create a pipeline, as shown in Figure 10-31.

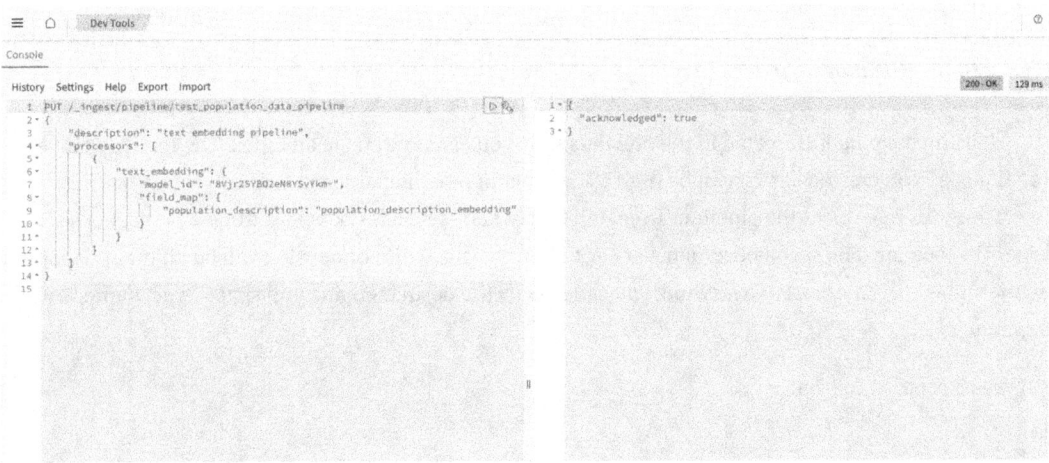

Figure 10-31. *Creating a pipeline*

A pipeline is a series of processors that are applied to a document when it is indexed (see Figure 10-31). Each processor in the pipeline can perform tasks such as filtering, transforming, and enriching data. Let's utilize the text_embedding processor.

Now ingest the data into an OpenSearch index. In OpenSearch, vectors are stored in a k-NN index. You can create a k-NN index by sending a request.

You can define index mappings with the configured default pipeline, as shown in Figure 10-32. Ensure that the vector field is declared as knn_vector and that the dimensions are appropriate for the deployed model.

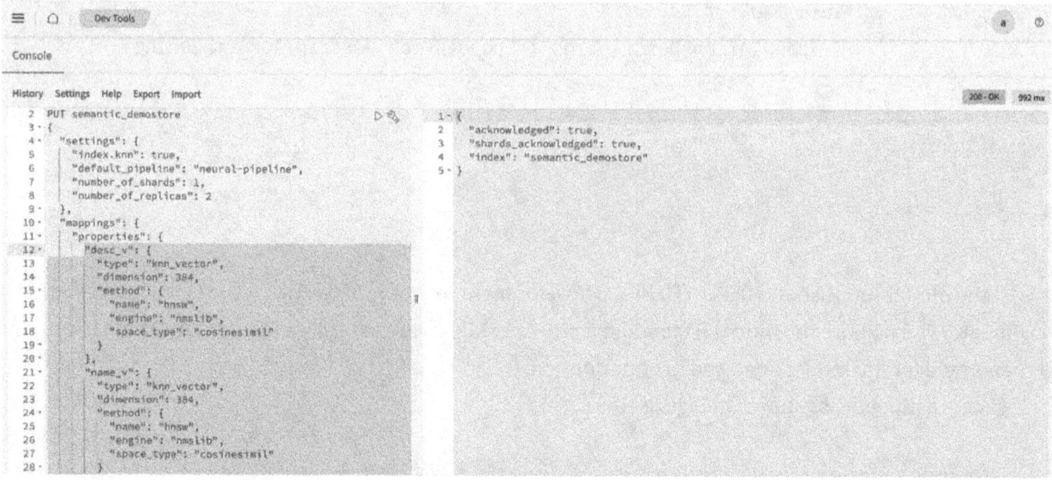

CHAPTER 10 AIOPS RCA

Figure 10-32. Creating an index

Utilizing the pipeline created in the previous step, you can now create an index. The test-pipeline-local-model you created earlier can be used as the default pipeline for the index.

The index references the pipeline. To search for backers, set index.knn in settings to "index.knn": true. The type must be specified as knn_vector to index vectors, and dimension will be different depending on the embedding model. For a method, you can specify the desired engine and space_type, name, and parameters.

```
PUT test_population_data
{
  "mappings": {
    "properties": {
      "population_description": {
        "type": "text"
      },
      "population_description_embedding": {
        "type": "knn_vector",
        "dimension": 384,
        "space_type": "cosinesimil"
      }
    }
  },
  "settings": {
    "index": {
      "default_pipeline": "test_population_data_pipeline",
      "knn": "true"
```

```
      }
    }
}
```

Create an index, as shown in Figure 10-33.

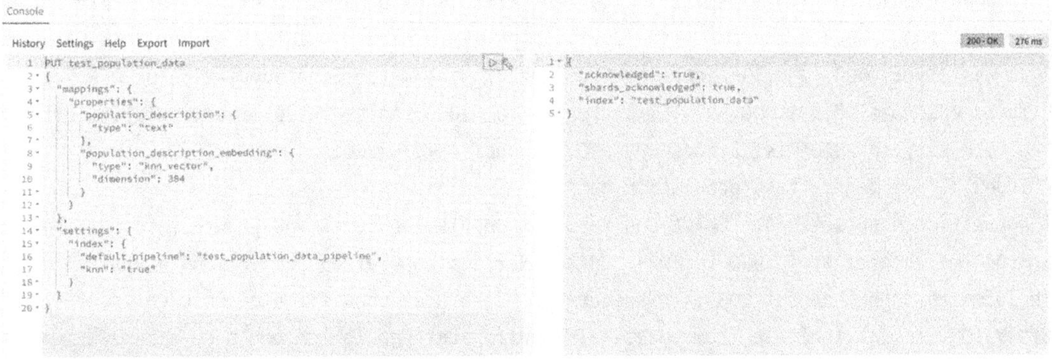

Figure 10-33. Create an index

Utilizing the pipeline created in the previous step, let's create an index. The test_population_data you created earlier can be used as the base pipeline for the index.

The index will reference the pipeline. To search for the vector, set the settings to "index.knn": true, the type must be specified as knn_vector to index vectors, and the dimension will vary depending on the model you are embedding. For the method, you can specify the desired engine and space_type, name, and parameters.

The data added in this step is the list of failures described previously.

When building a RAG pipeline, it is important to correctly split vector store documents into chunks by optimizing the chunk size of specific content and selecting LLMs with the appropriate context length. In some cases, a complex chain of multiple LLMs may be required.

Setting the right chunk size is critical to RAG performance because the success of the RAG pipeline depends in large part on finding the right context for generation during the search phase. The search phase typically examines a small chunk of the original text, rather than the entire document.

The entire prompt must fit into the LLM's context pane. Don't make the chunk size too large, and balance it with the expected query size. Experiment with different chunk sizes, but a typical value should be between 100 and 600 tokens, depending on the LLM.

```
POST _bulk
{"index": {"_index": "test_population_data"}}
{"population_description": "Chart and table of population level and growth rate for the
Ogden-Layton metro area from 1950 to 2023. United Nations population projections are also
included through the year 2035.\nThe current metro area population of Ogden-Layton in 2023
is 750,000, a 1.63% increase from 2022.\nThe metro area population of Ogden-Layton in 2022
was 738,000, a 1.79% increase from 2021.\nThe metro area population of Ogden-Layton in 2021
```

CHAPTER 10 AIOPS RCA

was 725,000, a 1.97% increase from 2020.\nThe metro area population of Ogden-Layton in 2020 was 711,000, a 2.16% increase from 2019."}
{"index": {"_index": "test_population_data"}}
{"population_description": "Chart and table of population level and growth rate for the New York City metro area from 1950 to 2023. United Nations population projections are also included through the year 2035.\\nThe current metro area population of New York City in 2023 is 18,937,000, a 0.37% increase from 2022.\\nThe metro area population of New York City in 2022 was 18,867,000, a 0.23% increase from 2021.\\nThe metro area population of New York City in 2021 was 18,823,000, a 0.1% increase from 2020.\\nThe metro area population of New York City in 2020 was 18,804,000, a 0.01% decline from 2019."}
{"index": {"_index": "test_population_data"}}
{"population_description": "Chart and table of population level and growth rate for the Chicago metro area from 1950 to 2023. United Nations population projections are also included through the year 2035.\\nThe current metro area population of Chicago in 2023 is 8,937,000, a 0.4% increase from 2022.\\nThe metro area population of Chicago in 2022 was 8,901,000, a 0.27% increase from 2021.\\nThe metro area population of Chicago in 2021 was 8,877,000, a 0.14% increase from 2020.\\nThe metro area population of Chicago in 2020 was 8,865,000, a 0.03% increase from 2019."}

Add a list of failures, as shown in Figure 10-34.

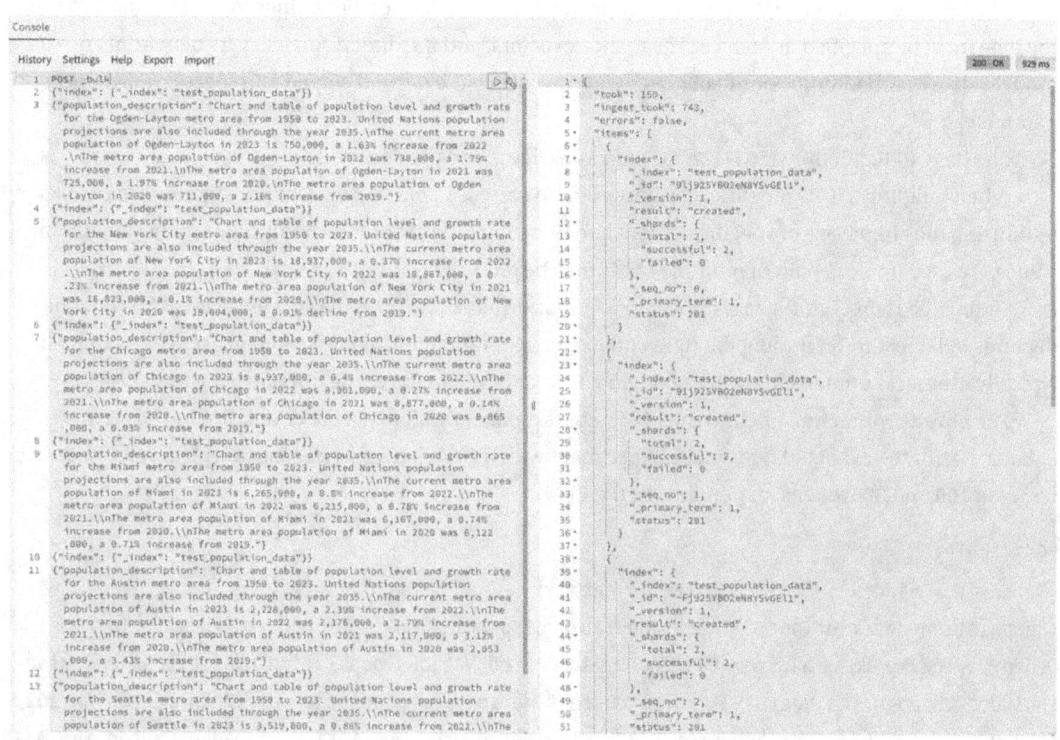

Figure 10-34. Adding a list of failures

The first model is already complete.

To use semantic search, you need to set up an LLM model (see Figure 10-35). I recommend that you configure an LLM connector to the LLM service or a third-party alternative. Starting with OpenSearch version 2.9, the LLM connector integrates with semantic search to simplify and automate the task of converting search queries into vector embeddings, removing much of the complexity of vectorization and search.

Now you will configure the second model. Create a connector for the external LLM model, and then register and deploy the external LLM model.

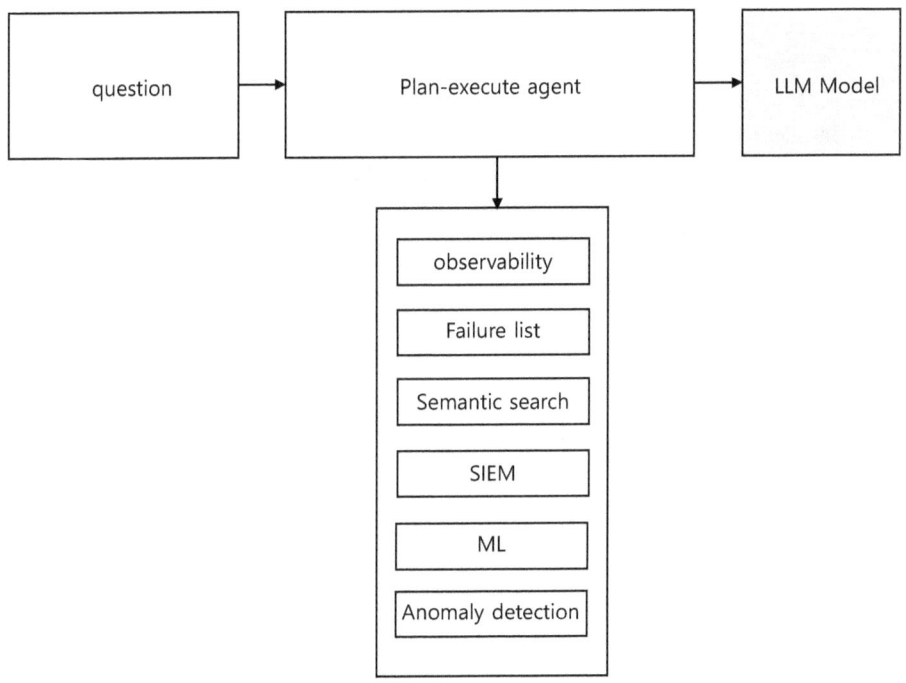

Figure 10-35. The flow between the connectors and the LLMs

Let's learn how to configure connectors to simplify complex indexing and search procedures. If you use the internal model, you don't need a connector, but if you use the external model, you do.

Configure the OpenAI connector as shown here.

```
POST /_plugins/_ml/connectors/_create
{
    "name": "OpenAI Chat Connector",
    "description": "The connector to public OpenAI model service for GPT 3.5",
    "version": 1,
    "protocol": "http",
```

CHAPTER 10 AIOPS RCA

```
    "parameters": {
        "endpoint": "api.openai.com",
        "model": "gpt-3.5-turbo"
    },
    "credential": {
        "openAI_key": "..."
    },
    "actions": [
        {
            "action_type": "predict",
            "method": "POST",
            "url": "https://${parameters.endpoint}/v1/chat/completions",
            "headers": {
                "Authorization": "Bearer ${credential.openAI_key}"
            },
            "request_body": "{ \"model\": \"${parameters.model}\", \"messages\":
            ${parameters.messages} }"
        }
    ]
}
```

Create an LLM connector, as shown in Figure 10-36.

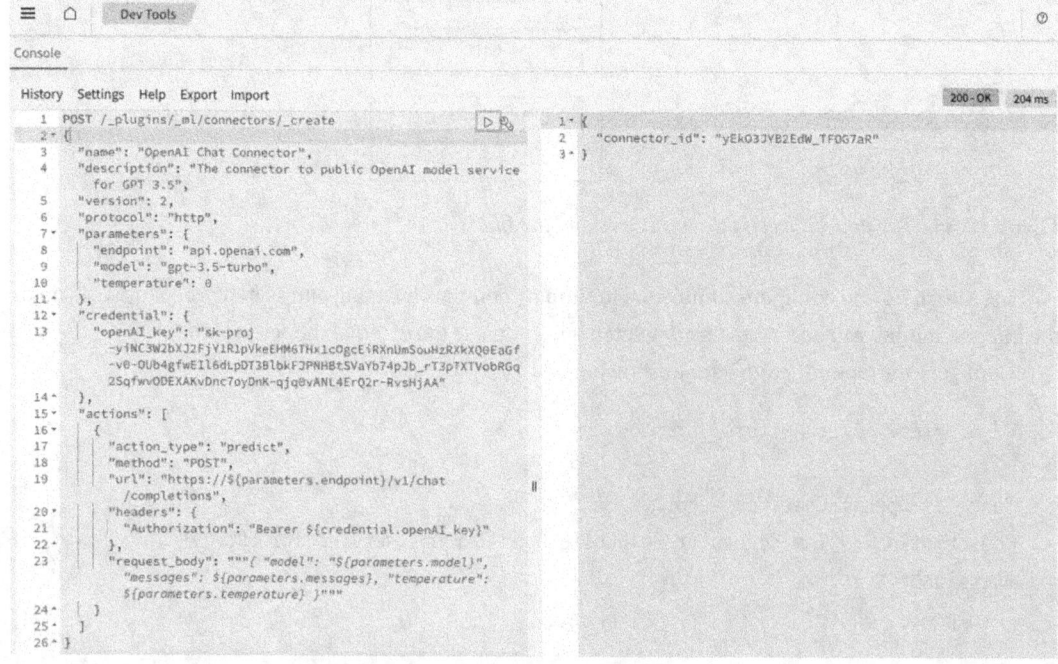

***Figure 10-36.** Creating an LLM connector*

810

CHAPTER 10 AIOPS RCA

The OpenSearch connector eliminates the need to implement separate embedding logic in the backend application for indexing and searching data. It uses a model with a pipeline to automatically embed data and perform semantic searches based on it. As a result, this approach significantly reduces the complexity of the system while improving the quality of the search.

```
{
  "connector_id": "a1eMb4kBJ1eYAeTMAljY"
}
```

By default, OpenSearch allows you to create your own connectors to connect with third-party LLM platforms.

You need to deploy a model and create a model ID through the LLM connector. You only need to provide OpenSearch with a model name that uniquely identifies the model connection.

It manages the deployment and hosting of embedding models, which can then be used to enrich semantic search queries in OpenSearch. Once the connector is created, it hosts the model, and OpenSearch is used to perform search queries based on the inference results.

You need an LLM to generate responses to user questions.

Like the text embedding model, an LLM needs to be registered and deployed to OpenSearch.

```
POST /_plugins/_ml/model_groups/_register
{
  "name": "openai_model_group",
  "description": "A model group for open ai models"
}
```

As with the text embedding model, you need to register the LLM and deploy it to OpenSearch.

```
POST /_plugins/_ml/models/_register?deploy=true
{
    "name": "openAI-gpt-3.5-turbo",
    "function_name": "remote",
    "model_group_id": "JUaOTZIBH2qLnqOGgrfx",
    "description": "test model",
    "connector_id": "LEa1TZIBH2qLnqOG-rfb"
}
```

Now register and run the agent This means the models, tools, and agents described in LangChain. Tools refer to registered models. An agent contains and runs multiple tools.

Build a RAG application using an interactive flow agent. Using the text embedding model and model you already created, create a flow agent. This flow agent runs the VectorDBTool and then runs `MLModelTool`.

The flow agent runs the configured tools sequentially in the order you specify. In this example, two tools are used to create the agent.

- **VectorDBTool:** The agent uses this tool to search for OpenSearch documents related to the user's question. It collects the information into the OpenSearch index. It deploys a text embedding model that converts text into vector embeddings to facilitate vector searches. OpenSearch converts the collected documents into embeddings and stores them in the index.

- **MLModelTool:** You provide the agent with a user question, and the agent constructs a query from the question, runs a vector search in the OpenSearch index, and passes the retrieved relevant documents to the MLModelTool. The agent runs the MLModelTool tool to connect to a large language model (LLM), sends the user query enriched with OpenSearch documents to the model, and the LLM answers the question based on its knowledge and the documents provided.

VectorDBTool is configured with the model ID of the text embedding model created for searching vectors. `MLModelTool` consists of the created LLM model.

When configuring agents and tools, refer to the model ID of the embedding models and LLM models you have already configured.

```
POST /_plugins/_ml/agents/_register
{
  "name": "Test_Agent_For_RAG",
  "type": "flow",
  "description": "this is a test agent",
  "tools": [
    {
      "type": "VectorDBTool",
      "parameters": {
        "model_id": "JoOnTZIBOZlO6yHYy_Oy",
        "index": "my_test_data",
        "embedding_field": "embedding",
        "source_field": [
          "text"
        ],
        "input": "${parameters.question}"
      }
    },
    {
      "type": "MLModelTool",
      "description": "A general tool to answer any question",
      "parameters": {
        "model_id": "Oka5TZIBH2qLnqOGOrdr",
        "messages": [
```

CHAPTER 10 AIOPS RCA

```
        {
          "role": "system",
          "content": "You are a professional data analyst. You will always answer a
            question based on the given context first. If the answer is not directly shown
            in the context, you will analyze the data and find the answer. If you don't know
            the answer, just say you don't know."
        },
        {
          "role": "user",
          "content": "Context:\n${parameters.VectorDBTool.output}\n\
            nQuestion:${parameters.question}\n\n"
        }
      ]
    }
  }
]
}
```

OpenSearch returns the newly created agent ID:

```
{
  "agent_id": "fQ75lIOBHcHmo_czdqcJ"
}
```

To run the agent, send the following request. Since you configured the agent to accept parameters, when you register it, you need to provide this parameter in the request. This parameter represents a user question that you created.

```
POST /_plugins/_ml/agents/879v9YwBjWKCe6Kg12Tx/_execute
{
  "parameters": {
    "question": "what's the population increase of Seattle from 2021 to 2023"
  }
}
```

It inferences the answer to the question based on the data collected and shows the result.

```
{
  "inference_results": [
    {
      "output": [
        {
          "name": "MLModelTool",
```

813

```
                "result": """{"id":"chatcmpl-ADvINGOAgRu8zo8TQKiQjeDu1XAhH","object":"chat.
                completion","created":1.727881871E9,"model":"gpt-3.5-turbo-0125","choices":
                [{"index":0.0,"message":{"role":"assistant","content":"To calculate the population
                increase of Seattle from 2021 to 2023, you can subtract the population of Seattle
                in 2021 from the population of Seattle in 2023.\n\nPopulation of Seattle in 2023
                \u003d 3,519,000\nPopulation of Seattle in 2021 \u003d 3,461,000\n\nPopulation
                increase \u003d Population of Seattle in 2023 - Population of Seattle in 2021\
                nPopulation increase \u003d 3,519,000 - 3,461,000\nPopulation increase \u003d
                58,000\n\nTherefore, the population of Seattle increased by 58,000 from 2021 to
                2023."},"finish_reason":"stop"}],"usage":{"prompt_tokens":482.0,"completion_
                tokens":132.0,"total_tokens":614.0,"prompt_tokens_details":{"cached_
                tokens":0.0},"completion_tokens_details":{"reasoning_tokens":0.0}}}"""
            }
        ]
    }
  ]
}
```

Endpoints are provided by agents, not tools. The agent is the orchestrator of many tools.

If your data is structured, not text, you shouldn't organize it as a vector. It should be organized in a structured form, like SQL. LLMs can also handle structured and unstructured data. Structured text should be integrated within the agent, using SQL tools. Using vectors to retrieve data such as UUID reduces accuracy.

So far, I've covered the basics of RAGs. You'll now proceed with the demo.

10.6.3.1. Observability RAG

Root cause analysis RAG makes the agent process two tools sequentially, but observability RAG does not process tools sequentially, but dynamically.

OpenSearch provides many features for observability.

- Multi-tenant support is built in.

- OpenSearch requires a collector to work with OpenSearch, whereas before it required a Data Prepper.

- With FluentBit, you can capture HTTP messages and store them in OpenSearch. You can utilize them like events and join them with trace.

- OpenSearch is a basic trace and log, but you can store various signals in the form of log. You can collect and join various signals in OpenSearch, a feature not available in Grafana LGTM.

- OpenSearch does not provide service discovery.

If you are experiencing issues with trace, you have three solutions to choose from

- Combine broken traces using events.
- Convert from logs to traces.
- Implement bytecode instrumentation.

These methods can also be used in OpenSearch to solve trace problems.

In this demo, traces and logs are used as data sources instead of the root cause analysis data model. By using the root cause analysis data model, data consistency issues can be resolved, and system resources and entities such as CPU and kernel can be identified. This demonstration is more limited than the root cause analysis RAG, but focused on illustrating complex agent functionality.

You can configure RAG using observability data source, including log and trace. The tool doesn't specify a particular index, so you can configure the agent flexibly by organizing your knowledge base on an index or adding tools.

OpenSearch 3.0 introduces the *plan-execute-reflect agent*, which is a powerful new capability that breaks down complex problems, selects and executes tools autonomously, and adapts through reflection.

The plan-execute-reflect agent provided by OpenSearch is the same concept as the plan-and-execute agent.

Plan-execute-reflect agents are designed to solve complex tasks that require iterative reasoning and step-by-step execution. These agents use one large language model (LLM)—the planner—to create and update a plan to execute each individual step using a built-in conversational agent.

A plan-execute-reflect agent works in three phases:

- **Planning:** The planner LLM generates an initial step-by-step plan using the available tools.
- **Execution:** Each step is executed sequentially using the agent and the available tools.
- **Reevaluation:** After executing each step, the planner LLM reevaluates the plan using intermediate results. The LLM can adjust the plan dynamically to skip, add, or change steps based on new context.

The plan-execute-reflect agent stores the interaction between the LLM and the agent in a memory index. In the following example, the agent uses a `conversation_index` to persist the execution history, including the user's question, intermediate results, and final outputs.

The agent automatically selects the most appropriate tool for each step based on the tool descriptions and current context.

The agent currently supports reevaluation only after each step. This allows the agent to dynamically adapt the plan based on intermediate results before proceeding to the next step.

The new agent framework includes several notable improvements:

- A plan-execute-reflect agent that systematically breaks down and executes complex multi-step tasks
- Native Model Context Protocol (MCP) support for integration with external AI tools
- Enhanced tool selection and execution capabilities
- Asynchronous execution support for managing long-running tasks efficiently

I dive into a practical observability use case that showcases the true power of this new agent framework. You'll see firsthand how it can automatically investigate service failures in a microservices application a typically time-consuming and complex process. You'll see how the agent can:

- Break down a complex investigation into logical steps.
- Automatically select and use appropriate tools.
- Analyze multiple data sources (logs, traces, metrics).
- Provide clear, actionable insights.

Now let's explore the capabilities and workflow of the plan-execute-reflect agent.

The plan-execute-reflect agent is a long-running agent designed for complex, multi-step tasks. This agent is capable of breaking down a complex task into a series of simple steps (plan), executing each step (execute), and optimizing its plan based on intermediate step results (reflect). It uses a separate executor agent for the execution of substeps.

Key features of this agent include the following:

- Adaptive planning that evolves based on intermediate results
- Flexibility to use different models for planning and execution phases by specifying your own executor agent during registration
- Asynchronous execution capability for handling long-running workflows in the background (when `async=true`)
- Built-in MCP client functionality allowing connections to multiple MCP servers
- Standardized tool communication through function calling
- Support for custom prompts, enabling specialization for specific use cases such as building an observability agent or research agent (using the WebSearchTool)

Figure 10-37 illustrates the execution flow of the plan-execute-reflect agent.

CHAPTER 10　AIOPS RCA

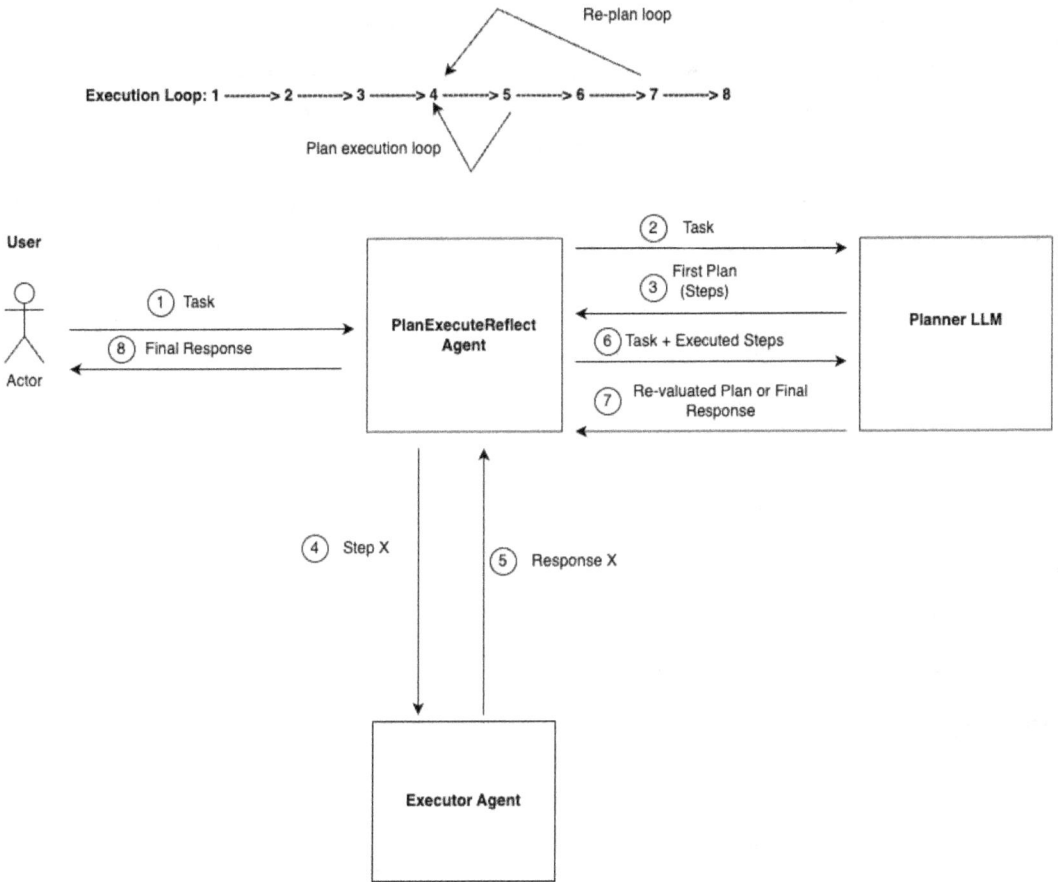

Figure 10-37. The plan-execute-reflect flow

The workflow consists of the following steps:

1. A user provides a task to the plan-execute-reflect agent.

2. The plan-execute-reflect agent forwards the task to the planner LLM.

3. The LLM returns a plan.

4. The plan-execute-reflect agent forwards the first step of the plan to the executor agent.

5. The executor agent executes the steps and returns the response.

6. The plan-execute-reflect agent forwards the result of the executed step and the original plan to the planner LLM.

817

7. The planner LLM either returns the final result or a refined plan.

8. If the planner LLM returns the final result, the result is returned to the user. Otherwise, the planner LLM returns a new plan and executes Steps 4–7 until it has enough information to complete the task and return the result.

The strength of the plan-execute-reflect agent is its flexibility. The demo uses built-in tools to investigate cart failures, but the agent can support a variety of tools. For example, you can use WebSearchTool to perform a detailed investigation.

The current plan-execute agent is similar to a LangChain, but in the future, it will be advanced to the level of a LangGraph. OpenSearch plans to enhance the functionality of the plan-execute agent as follows:

- Parallel tool execution
- Multi-reflection strategies
- Human in the loop
- Ability to cancel running tasks
- Agent execution checkpoints

The `plan-execute-reflect` agent uses OpenAI.

```
POST /_plugins/_ml/connectors/_create
{
    "name": "My openai connector: gpt-4",
    "description": "The connector to openai chat model",
    "version": 1,
    "protocol": "http",
    "parameters": {
        "model": "gpt-4o"
    },
    "credential": {
        "openAI_key": ""
    },
    "actions": [
        {
        "action_type": "predict",
        "method": "POST",
        "url": "https://api.openai.com/v1/chat/completions",
        "headers": {
            "Authorization": "Bearer ${credential.openAI_key}"
        },
```

```
            "request_body": "{ \"model\": \"${parameters.model}\", \"messages\": [{\"role\":\
            "developer\",\"content\":\"${parameters.system_prompt}\"},${parameters._chat_history:-}
            {\"role\":\"user\",\"content\":\"${parameters.prompt}\"}${parameters._interactions:-
            }]${parameters.tool_configs:-} }"
        }
    ]
}
```

Note the connector ID; you'll use it to register the model:

```
POST /_plugins/_ml/models/_register
{
    "name": "Bedrock Claude Sonnet model",
    "function_name": "remote",
    "description": "Bedrock Claude 3.7 sonnet model for Plan, Execute and Reflect Agent",
    "connector_id": "etRC_ZYBgSi1HZubvLl_"
}
```

Note the model ID; you'll use to register the agent:

```
POST _plugins/_ml/agents/_register
{
  "name": "My Plan Execute and Reflect agent with Claude 3.7",
  "type": "plan_execute_and_reflect",
  "description": "this is a test agent",
  "llm": {
    "model_id": "fNRC_ZYBgSi1HZub8bmd",
    "parameters": {
      "prompt": "${parameters.question}"
  }},
  "memory": {
    "type": "conversation_index"
  },
  "parameters": {
    "_llm_interface": "openai/v1/chat/completions"
  },
  "tools": [
    {
      "type": "ListIndexTool"
    },
    {
      "type": "SearchIndexTool"
    },
```

CHAPTER 10 AIOPS RCA

```
    {
      "type": "IndexMappingTool"
    }
  ]
}
```

OpenSearch 3.0 introduces the ability to execute agents asynchronously. Because this agent is long running, you can execute it asynchronously by providing the `async=true` query parameter.

Note the task ID and memory ID. You'll use task ID to query for the result and the memory ID to track interactions between the agent and the LLM.

```
POST /_plugins/_ml/agents/ftRD_ZYBgSi1HZubL7lq/_execute?async=true
{
  "parameters": {
    "question": "How many flights from Beijing to Seattle?"
  }
}
```

OpenSearch responds with the task information. Let's check the status of the task by querying the tasks endpoint:

```
GET _plugins/_ml/tasks/cMpD_ZYBrHbyBa1aX8Jf
```

Once the agent has completed execution, you should receive a response.

Figure 10-38 shows the Observability RAG OpenAI result.

Figure 10-38. Observability RAG OpenAI result

The agent identifies that the root cause of the problem is a Redis connection issue. It highlights repeated failures to connect to the Redis backend, visible in the service logs and traces, and links to specific log entries showing ECONNREFUSED errors. The response also includes a step-by-step explanation of how the agent analyzed the traces and logs to identify the failure. By automating root cause analysis, the agent effectively reduces the time spent on manual troubleshooting, showcasing how it can resolve complex issues and empower teams to quickly find solutions.

Conclusion

I showed you how to use the plan-execute-reflect agent to troubleshoot and identify the root cause of a cart failure in the OpenTelemetry demo application. By breaking down a high-level task into smaller steps and executing them iteratively, the agent provides a powerful and flexible way to automate complex reasoning workflows. This approach is particularly useful for observability and operational intelligence use cases where multi-step diagnosis is needed.

The plan-execute-reflect agent demonstrates how intelligent automation can simplify root cause analysis. By combining OpenTelemetry observability data with LLM-based reasoning, OpenSearch can now assist you in debugging complex, multi-service systems with just a single prompt.

While you have experience with root cause analysis and AIOps using a variety of commercial observability, the capabilities provided by OpenSearch Observability RAG is flexible and highly accurate. Where commercial observability are often closed and non-customizable, opensource observability RAG are a good alternative.

CHAPTER 10　AIOPS RCA

Traces and log signals tend to focus on applications and services. Detailed names of business processes and system resources should be added to the OpenSearch index. Noise in the knowledge base should be minimized and data quality should be improved. Accurate data should be provided so that the plan-execute-reflect agent can produce combined results from various aspects of applications, business processes, and system resources.

10.6.3.2. RCA RAG

While the OOTB OpenSearch RAG is close to RAG's standard procedure, RCA RAG is an adaptation of RAG for OpenSearch.

- Instead of using vector embeddings, it uses OpenSearch's indexes. The contents of the failure list need not be stored as vectors.
- The agents and tools responsible for input and output have been changed to generative_qa_parameters.
- It changed the Vector database ingest pipeline to a RAG pipeline.
- It improved memory functionality within RAG. Specific failure lists can now be loaded directly into memory.

This demo uses OpenAI to configure the LLM.

Conversational searching allows you to ask questions in natural language and refine the answers by asking follow-up questions. Thus, the conversation becomes a dialogue between you and the LLM. For this to happen, instead of answering each question individually, the model needs to remember the context of the entire conversation.

RAG retrieves data from the index and history and sends all the information as context to the LLM. The LLM then supplements its static knowledge base with the dynamically retrieved data. In OpenSearch, RAG is implemented through a search pipeline containing a `retrieval_augmented_generation` processor. The processor intercepts OpenSearch query results, retrieves previous messages in the conversation from the conversation memory, and sends a prompt to the LLM. After the processor receives a response from the LLM, it saves the response in conversation memory and returns both the original OpenSearch query results and the LLM response.

```
PUT /_cluster/settings
{
  "persistent": {
    "plugins.ml_commons.memory_feature_enabled": true,
    "plugins.ml_commons.rag_pipeline_feature_enabled": true
  }
}
```

CHAPTER 10 AIOPS RCA

RAG requires an LLM in order to function. To connect to an LLM, you need to create a connector. The following request creates a connector for the OpenAI GPT 3.5 model:

```
POST /_plugins/_ml/connectors/_create
{
  "name": "OpenAI Chat Connector",
  "description": "The connector to public OpenAI model service for GPT 3.5",
  "version": 2,
  "protocol": "http",
  "parameters": {
    "endpoint": "api.openai.com",
    "model": "gpt-3.5-turbo",
    "temperature": 0
  },
  "credential": {
    "openAI_key": "<YOUR_OPENAI_KEY>"
  },
  "actions": [
    {
      "action_type": "predict",
      "method": "POST",
      "url": "https://${parameters.endpoint}/v1/chat/completions",
      "headers": {
        "Authorization": "Bearer ${credential.openAI_key}"
      },
      "request_body": """{ "model": "${parameters.model}", "messages": ${parameters.messages}, "temperature": ${parameters.temperature} }"""
    }
  ]
}
```

OpenSearch responds with a connector ID for the connector:

```
{
  "connector_id": "GdQn3JYBgSi1HZub0Z8b"
}
```

Register the LLM for which you created a connector in the previous step. To register the model with OpenSearch, provide the `connector_id` returned in the previous step:

```
POST /_plugins/_ml/models/_register
{
  "name": "openAI-gpt-3.5-turbo",
```

823

CHAPTER 10   AIOPS RCA

```
  "function_name": "remote",
  "description": "test model",
  "connector_id": "u3DEbIOBfUsSoeNTti-1"
}
```

OpenSearch returns a task ID for the register task and a model ID for the registered model:

```
{
  "task_id": "G9Qo3JYBgSi1HZubVJ8E",
  "status": "CREATED",
  "model_id": "HNQo3JYBgSi1HZubVp90"
}
```

To verify that the registration is complete, call the Tasks API:

```
GET /_plugins/_ml/tasks/gXDIbIOBfUsSoeNT_jAb
```

The state changes to COMPLETED in the response:

```
{
  "model_id": "HNQo3JYBgSi1HZubVp90",
  "task_type": "REGISTER_MODEL",
  "function_name": "REMOTE",
  "state": "COMPLETED",
  "worker_node": [
    "91rV9g-1QzucpDDpeH99ZQ"
  ],
  "create_time": 1747450352266,
  "last_update_time": 1747450353535,
  "is_async": false
}
```

To deploy the model, provide the model_id to the Deploy API:

```
POST /_plugins/_ml/models/gnDIbIOBfUsSoeNT_jAw/_deploy
```

OpenSearch acknowledges that the model is deployed:

```
{
  "task_id": "HdQp3JYBgSi1HZubO5_F",
  "task_type": "DEPLOY_MODEL",
  "status": "COMPLETED"
}
```

Next, create a search pipeline with a `retrieval_augmented_generation` processor:

```
PUT /_search/pipeline/rag_pipeline
{
  "response_processors": [
    {
      "retrieval_augmented_generation": {
        "tag": "openai_pipeline_demo",
        "description": "Demo pipeline Using OpenAI Connector",
        "model_id": "gnDIbIOBfUsSoeNT_jAw",
        "context_field_list": ["text"],
        "system_prompt": "You are a helpful assistant",
        "user_instructions": "Generate a concise and informative answer in less than 100
        words for the given question"
      }
    }
  ]
}
```

RAG augments the LLM's knowledge with some supplementary data.

First, create an index in which to store this data and set the default search pipeline to the pipeline created in the previous step:

```
PUT /my_rag_test_data
{
  "settings": {
    "index.search.default_pipeline" : "rag_pipeline"
  },
  "mappings": {
    "properties": {
      "text": {
        "type": "text"
      }
    }
  }
}
```

Next, ingest the supplementary data into the index:

```
POST _bulk
{"index": {"_index": "my_rag_test_data", "_id": "1"}}
{"text": "Abraham Lincoln was born on February 12, 1809, the second child of Thomas Lincoln and Nancy Hanks Lincoln, in a log cabin on Sinking Spring Farm near Hodgenville, Kentucky.
```

[2] He was a descendant of Samuel Lincoln, an Englishman who migrated from Hingham, Norfolk, to its namesake, Hingham, Massachusetts, in 1638. The family then migrated west, passing through New Jersey, Pennsylvania, and Virginia.[3] Lincoln was also a descendant of the Harrison family of Virginia; his paternal grandfather and namesake, Captain Abraham Lincoln and wife Bathsheba (née Herring) moved the family from Virginia to Jefferson County, Kentucky.[b] The captain was killed in an Indian raid in 1786.[5] His children, including eight-year-old Thomas, Abraham's father, witnessed the attack.[6][c] Thomas then worked at odd jobs in Kentucky and Tennessee before the family settled in Hardin County, Kentucky, in the early 1800s."}
{"index": {"_index": "my_rag_test_data", "_id": "2"}}
{"text": "Chart and table of population level and growth rate for the New York City metro area from 1950 to 2023. United Nations population projections are also included through the year 2035.\\nThe current metro area population of New York City in 2023 is 18,937,000, a 0.37% increase from 2022.\\nThe metro area population of New York City in 2022 was 18,867,000, a 0.23% increase from 2021.\\nThe metro area population of New York City in 2021 was 18,823,000, a 0.1% increase from 2020.\\nThe metro area population of New York City in 2020 was 18,804,000, a 0.01% decline from 2019."}

RAG retrieves documents from an index, passes them through a seq2seq model, such as an LLM, and then supplements the static LLM information with the dynamically retrieved data in context.

You'll need to create a conversation memory that will store all messages from a conversation. To make the memory easily identifiable, provide a name for the memory in the optional name field, as shown in the following example. The name parameter cannot be updated, so add the name to the conversation.

```
POST /_plugins/_ml/memory/
{
  "name": "Conversation about NYC population"
}
```

OpenSearch responds with a memory ID for the newly created memory:

```
{
  "memory_id": "HtQq3JYBgSi1HZubLp9c"
}
```

You'll use the `memory_id` to add messages to the memory.

To use the RAG pipeline, send a query to OpenSearch and provide additional parameters in the `ext.generative_qa_parameters` object.

The `generative_qa_parameters` object supports the following parameters.

CHAPTER 10 AIOPS RCA

If you ask an LLM a question about the present, it cannot provide an answer because it was trained on data from a few years ago. However, if you add current information as context, the LLM is able to generate a response. For example, you can ask the LLM about the population of the New York City metro area in 2023. You'll construct a query that includes an OpenSearch match query and an LLM query. Provide the memory_id so that the message is stored in the appropriate memory object.

```
GET /my_rag_test_data/_search
{
  "query": {
    "match": {
      "text": "What's the population of NYC metro area in 2023"
    }
  },
  "ext": {
    "generative_qa_parameters": {
      "llm_model": "gpt-3.5-turbo",
      "llm_question": "What's the population of NYC metro area in 2023",
      "memory_id": "znCqcIOBfUsSoeNTntd7",
      "context_size": 5,
      "message_size": 5,
      "timeout": 15
    }
  }
}
```

Because the context included a document containing information about the population of New York City, the LLM was able to correctly answer the question. The response contains the matching documents from the supplementary RAG data and the LLM response:

Figure 10-39 shows the RCA RAG OpenAI results.

827

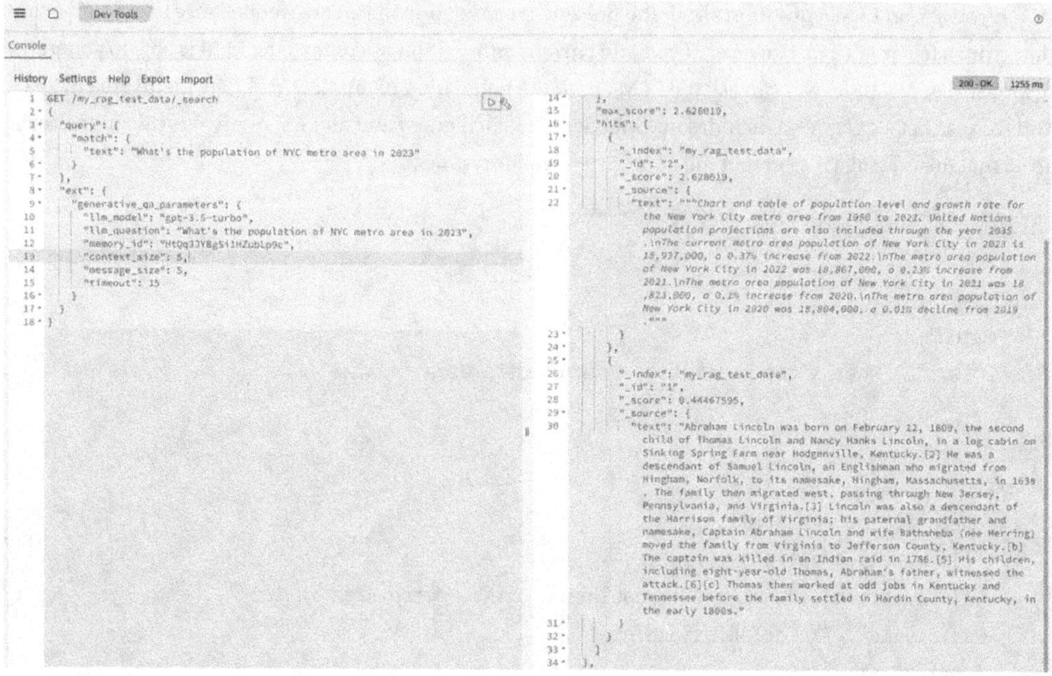

CHAPTER 10 AIOPS RCA

***Figure 10-39.** RCA RAG OpenAI results*

Using AWS Bedrock is not much different from OpenAI. It can work with a variety of models without dependencies on any particular model.

You will need a session token from AWS. You can get it with `aws sts get-session-token --serial-number arn:aws:iam::xxxxxx:mfa/xxxxxx --token-code xxxxxx`. Enter the newly generated access_key, secret_key, and session_token.

```
POST _plugins/_ml/connectors/_create
{
    "name": "Amazon Bedrock claude v3",
    "description": "Test connector for Amazon Bedrock claude v3",
    "version": 1,
    "protocol": "aws_sigv4",
    "credential": {
        "access_key": "",
        "secret_key": "",
        "session_token": ""
    },
    "parameters": {
        "region": "us-east-1",
        "service_name": "bedrock",
        "model": "anthropic.claude-3-5-sonnet-20240620-v1:0",
```

CHAPTER 10 AIOPS RCA

```
            "system_prompt": "you are a helpful assistant.",
            "temperature": 0.0,
            "top_p": 0.9,
            "max_tokens": 1000
        },
        "actions": [
            {
                "action_type": "predict",
                "method": "POST",
                "headers": {
                    "content-type": "application/json"
                },
                "url": "https://bedrock-runtime.${parameters.region}.amazonaws.com/
                model/${parameters.model}/converse",
                "request_body": "{ \"system\": [{\"text\": \"${parameters.system_prompt}\"}],
                \"messages\": ${parameters.messages} , \"inferenceConfig\": {\"temperature\":
                ${parameters.temperature}, \"topP\": ${parameters.top_p}, \"maxTokens\":
                ${parameters.max_tokens}} }"
            }
        ]
}
```

Note the connector ID; you will use it to create the model.

Create the model:

```
POST /_plugins/_ml/models/_register?deploy=true
{
    "name": "Bedrock Claude3.5 model",
    "description": "Bedrock Claude3.5 model",
    "function_name": "remote",
    "connector_id": "L9T1_JYBgSi1HZubpp8I"
}
```

Note the model ID; you will use it in the following steps.

```
POST /_plugins/_ml/models/MdT1_JYBgSi1HZub3Z-o/_deploy
```

Test the model:

```
POST /_plugins/_ml/models/MdT1_JYBgSi1HZub3Z-o/_predict
{
  "parameters": {
    "messages": [
```

```
        {
          "role": "user",
          "content": [
            {
              "text": "hello"
            }
          ]
        }
      ]
    }
```

Sample response:

```
{
  "inference_results": [
    {
      "output": [
        {
          "name": "response",
          "dataAsMap": {
            "metrics": {
              "latencyMs": 955.0
            },
            "output": {
              "message": {
                "content": [
                  {
                    "text": "Hello! How can I assist you today? Feel free to ask me any
                      questions or let me know if you need help with anything."
                  }
                ],
                "role": "assistant"
              }
            },
            "stopReason": "end_turn",
            "usage": {
              "inputTokens": 14.0,
              "outputTokens": 30.0,
              "totalTokens": 44.0
            }
```

```
        }
      }
    ],
    "status_code": 200
  }
]
}
```

Figure 10-40 shows the RCA RAG AWS Bedrock results.

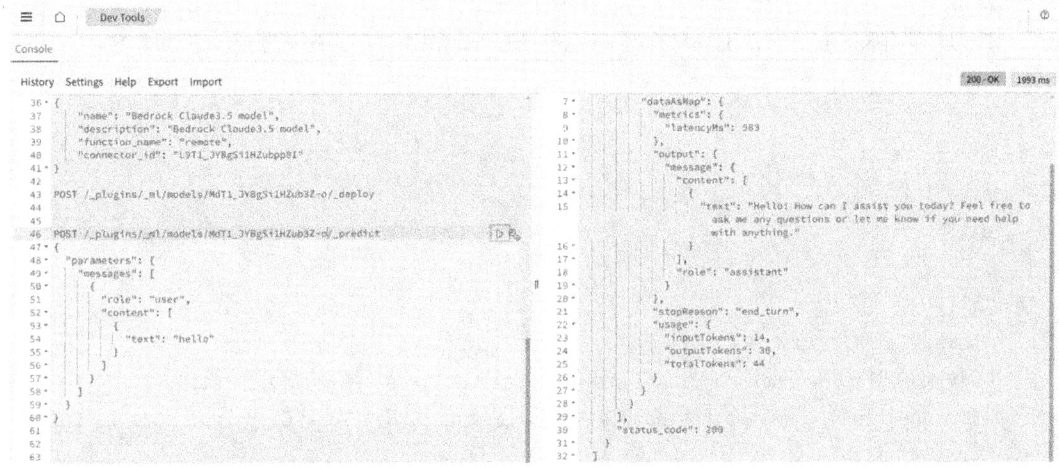

Figure 10-40. RCA RAG AWS Bedrock results

```
PUT /_search/pipeline/my-conversation-search-pipeline-claude
{
  "response_processors": [
    {
      "retrieval_augmented_generation": {
        "tag": "Demo pipeline",
        "description": "Demo pipeline Using Bedrock Claude",
        "model_id": "",
        "context_field_list": [
          "text"
        ],
        "system_prompt": "You are a helpful assistant",
        "user_instructions": "Generate a concise and informative answer in less than 100 words for the given question"
```

```
      }
    }
  ]
}
```

Basic RAG search without storing conversation history.

```
GET /qa_demo/_search?search_pipeline=my-conversation-search-pipeline-claude
{
  "query": {
    "match": {
      "text": "What's the population increase of New York City from 2021 to 2023?"
    }
  },
  "size": 1,
  "_source": [
    "text"
  ],
  "ext": {
    "generative_qa_parameters": {
      "llm_model": "bedrock-converse/anthropic.claude-3-sonnet-20240229-v1:0",
      "llm_question": "What's the population increase of New York City from 2021 to 2023?",
      "context_size": 5
    }
  }
}
```

The RCA data model is a complex table of 12 signals and entities joined together. Observability RAG and anomaly detection RAG are easy to configure using OpenSearch's built-in agents.

In this chapter, you develop three types of RAG:

- **Observability pipeline type 1:** Uses a Vector database and uses vector tools and machine learning tools.

- **Observability Pipeline Type 2:** Does not use a Vector database and stores data in the OpenSearch index. Configures a plan-execute agent similar to a LangGraph.

- **Root cause analysis pipeline:** Does not use a Vector database, but stores data in an OpenSearch index. No agent configuration.

Through a lot of testing, you should choose the optimal RAG type.

10.6.4. RAG's Advanced Features

Observability RAG primarily use traces and logs to identify and explain failures in applications and services. Infrastructure and system resources are good candidates for using anomaly detection RAG.

By using anomaly detection and applying reranking, you can improve accuracy.

As RAG system is applied to more complex service, basic RAG pipeline configurations such as semantic vector search and answer generation may not be enough to satisfy customer requirements.

This demo explains the advanced features of RAG:

- Reranking
- Guardrails
- Natural Language Processing (NLP)
- Post-processing
- LLM data management

10.6.4.1. Reranking

Reranking is a sophisticated technique used to increase the relevance of search results using LLM's advanced language understanding capabilities. A recently published paper found that the relevance of RAG is not the presence or absence of relevant information in context, but rather its order.

Simply put, reranking re-prioritizes the candidate documents generated by RAG by judging their relevance and consistency to the question. In other words, by placing documents that are more relevant to the question at the top of the context, it improves the accuracy of the answer.

Initially, a traditional information retrieval method, such as BM25 or vector similarity search, is used to retrieve a set of candidate documents or phrases. These candidate documents are then fed into the LLM, which analyzes the semantic relevance of each document to the query. The LLM reorders the documents to prioritize the most relevant documents by assigning a relevance score.

This process goes beyond simple keyword matching and greatly improves the quality of search results by understanding the context and meaning of the query and documents. Reranking is typically used as a second step after an initial quick search, ensuring that only the most relevant documents are shown to users. It can also combine results from multiple data sources, as well as be integrated into a RAG pipeline to ensure that context is ideally tailored to a specific query.

A reranking pipeline can rerank search results, providing a relevance score for each document in the search results with respect to the search query. The relevance score is calculated by a cross-encoder model.

You can query the anomaly results stored in the custom index in the previous chapter. You can use RAG to describe the anomaly in more detail. OpenSearch is currently working on an anomaly detection tool, which will be released soon. As these tools are added, it will be possible to organize a wide variety of application data into RAG.

CHAPTER 10 AIOPS RCA

You can query the anomaly results stored in the custom index in previous chapter. You can use RAG to describe the anomaly in more detail.

This demo shows you how to use the cohere-rerank model in a reranking pipeline.

Create a connector for the cohere-rerank model:

```
POST /_plugins/_ml/connectors/_create
{
    "name": "cohere-rerank",
    "description": "The connector to Cohere reanker model",
    "version": "1",
    "protocol": "http",
    "credential": {
        "cohere_key": ""
    },
    "parameters": {
        "model": "rerank-v3.5"
    },
    "actions": [
        {
            "action_type": "predict",
            "method": "POST",
            "url": "https://api.cohere.ai/v2/rerank",
            "headers": {
                "Authorization": "Bearer ${credential.cohere_key}"
            },
            "request_body": "{ \"documents\": ${parameters.documents}, \"query\": \"${parameters.query}\", \"model\": \"${parameters.model}\", \"top_n\": ${parameters.top_n} }",
            "pre_process_function": "connector.pre_process.cohere.rerank",
            "post_process_function": "connector.post_process.cohere.rerank"
        }
    ]
}
```

Use the connector ID from the response to register a cohere-rerank model:

```
POST /_plugins/_ml/models/_register?deploy=true
{
    "name": "cohere rerank model",
    "function_name": "remote",
    "description": "test rerank model",
    "connector_id": "1dTCAJcBgSi1HZub7bn2"
}
```

Note the model ID in the response; you'll use it in the following steps.

Test the model by calling the Predict API:

```
POST _plugins/_ml/models/l9TDAJcBgSi1HZubA7lt/_predict
{
  "parameters": {
    "query": "What is the capital of the United States?",
    "documents": [
      "Carson City is the capital city of the American state of Nevada.",
      "The Commonwealth of the Northern Mariana Islands is a group of islands in the Pacific Ocean. Its capital is Saipan.",
      "Washington, D.C. (also known as simply Washington or D.C., and officially as the District of Columbia) is the capital of the United States. It is a federal district.",
      "Capital punishment (the death penalty) has existed in the United States since beforethe United States was a country. As of 2017, capital punishment is legal in 30 of the 50 states."
    ],
    "top_n": 4
  }
}
```

OpenSearch responds with the inference results. Figure 10-41 shows the Observability RAG OpenAI result.

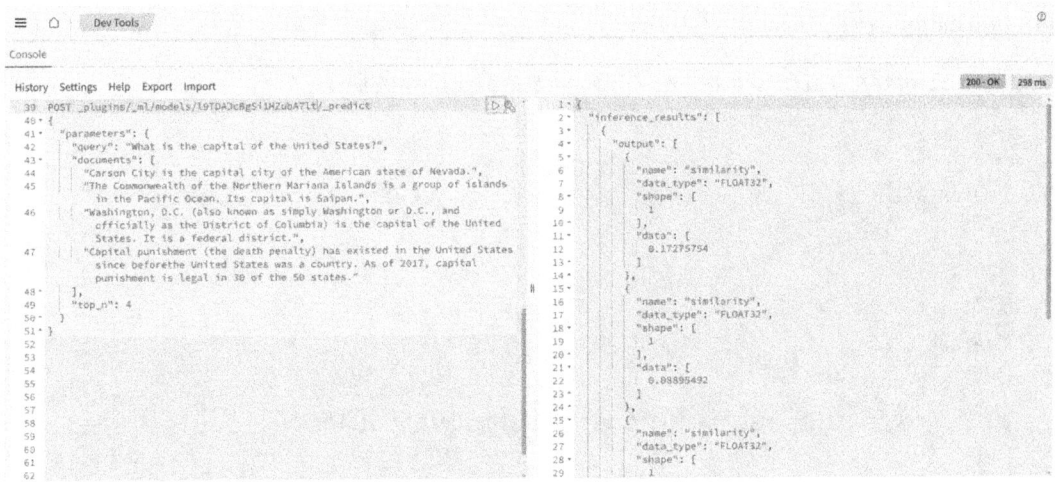

Figure 10-41. Reranking the RAG cohere result

The response contains four similarity objects. For each similarity object, the data array contains a relevance score for each document with respect to the query. The similarity objects are provided in the order of the input documents; the first object pertains to the first document. This differs from the default output of the cohere-rerank model, which orders documents by relevance score. The document order is changed in the connector.post_process.cohere.rerank post-processing function in order to make the output compatible with a reranking pipeline.

Now you will send a bulk request to ingest test data. Create a reranking pipeline with the cohere-rerank model:

```
PUT /_search/pipeline/rerank_pipeline_cohere
{
    "description": "Pipeline for reranking with Cohere Rerank model",
    "response_processors": [
        {
            "rerank": {
                "ml_opensearch": {
                    "model_id": "l9TDAJcBgSi1HZubA7lt"
                },
                "context": {
                    "document_fields": ["passage_text"]
                }
            }
        }
    ]
}
```

To limit the number of returned results, you can specify the size parameter. For example, set "size": 2 to return the top two documents:

```
GET my-test-data/_search?search_pipeline=rerank_pipeline_cohere
{
  "query": {
    "match_all": {}
  },
  "size": 4,
  "ext": {
    "rerank": {
      "query_context": {
        "query_text": "What is the capital of the United States?"
      }
    }
  }
}
```

The response contains the two most relevant documents, shown in Figure 10-42.

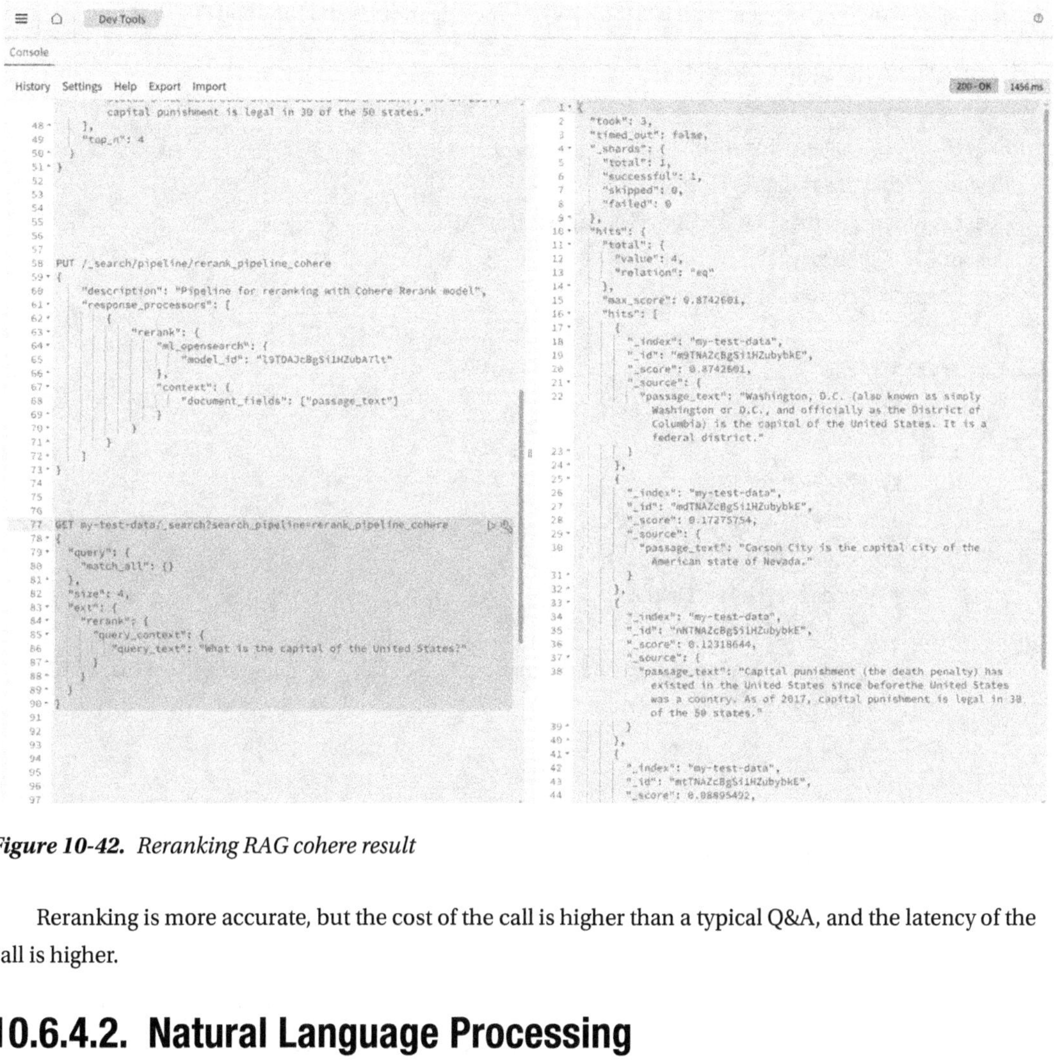

Figure 10-42. Reranking RAG cohere result

Reranking is more accurate, but the cost of the call is higher than a typical Q&A, and the latency of the call is higher.

10.6.4.2. Natural Language Processing

The data already exists in the OpenSearch index and can be utilized to configure the RAG. OpenSearch provides tools to configure the PPL, and you can configure the agent.

Consider the case where the results of an LLM are stored in an index and post-processed. Since the results are natural language text, it is necessary to convert them into a language that the system can understand. OpenSearch already provides tools to convert natural language into OpenSearch queries. You can configure the agent and the tool, as explained next.

The natural language RAG also registers two models—a PPL model and an LLM model

PPLTool can translate natural language queries (NLQ) into pipeline processing language (PPL) and execute the generated PPL queries. Before you get started, go to the OpenSearch dashboard home page and add a sample e-commerce order.

CHAPTER 10   AIOPS RCA

You need to register an agent with PPLTool. Agents include the MLModelTool and PPLTool tools.

```
POST /_plugins/_ml/agents/_register
{ {
    "name": "Demo agent for NLQ",
    "type": "conversational_flow",
    "description": "This is a test flow agent for NLQ",
    "memory": { "memory".
        "type": "conversation_index"
    },
    "app_type": "rag",
    "tools": [].
        { {
            "type": "PPLTool",
            "parameters": { "parameters".
                "model_id": "your_ppl_model_id",
                "model_type": "CLAUDE",
                "execute": True,
                "input": "{\"index\": \"${parameters.index}\", \"question\": ${parameters.question} }"
            }
        },
        { {
            "type": "MLModelTool",
            "description": "A general tool to answer any question",
            "parameters": { "parameters".
                "model_id": "your_llm_model_id",
                "prompt": "\n\nHuman:You are a professional data analysist. You will always answer question based on the given context first. If the answer is not directly shown in the context, you will analyze the data and find the answer. If you don't know the answer, just say don't know. \n\n Context:\n${parameters.PPLTool.output:-}\n\nHuman:${parameters.question}\n\nAssistant:"
            }
        }
    ]
}
```

10.6.4.3. Guardrails

User-facing RAG applications, such as chatbot, are likely to be exposed to a variety of security vulnerabilities. Responsible use of LLMs centers on mitigating prompt-level threats with guardrails. Guardrails are important safeguards to control the behavior and output of your model and make it safe. For example, guardrails can filter out harmful user input or model responses, or block malicious investment advisor user queries.

First, create a connector to the OpenAI guardrail model. Note that the OpenAI prompt instructs the model to respond only with the words accept or reject, depending on whether the input/output is acceptable. Additionally, the request contains the response_filter parameter, which specifies the field in which the guardrail model will provide the validation result:

```
POST /_plugins/_ml/connectors/_create
{
    "name": "openai",
    "description": "openai",
    "version": "1",
    "protocol": "http",
    "parameters": {
        "endpoint": "api.openai.com",
        "max_tokens": 7,
        "temperature": 0,
        "model": "gpt-3.5-turbo-instruct",
        "prompt": "You are a helpful assistant and an expert judge of content quality. Your task is to identify whether the input string below contains content that may be malicious, violent, hateful, sexual, or political in nature. Your answer should consist of a single word, either reject or accept. If the input belongs to any of these categories, please write reject. Otherwise, write accept. \\n\\nHere is the input: ${parameters.question}. \\n\\nYour answer: ",
        "response_filter": "$.choices[0].text"
    },
    "credential": {
        "openAI_key": ""
    },
    "actions": [
        {
            "action_type": "predict",
            "method": "POST",
            "url": "https://${parameters.endpoint}/v1/completions",
            "headers": {
                "Authorization": "Bearer ${credential.openAI_key}"
            },
```

CHAPTER 10   AIOPS RCA

```
            "request_body": "{ \"model\": \"${parameters.model}\", \"prompt\":
            \"${parameters.prompt}\", \"max_tokens\": ${parameters.max_tokens},
            \"temperature\": ${parameters.temperature} }"
        }
    ]
}
```

To register a model group for the OpenAI guardrail model, send the following request:

```
POST /_plugins/_ml/model_groups/_register
{
    "name": "guardrail model group",
    "description": "This is a guardrail model group."
}
```

Using the connector ID and the model group ID, register and deploy the OpenAI guardrail model:

```
POST /_plugins/_ml/models/_register?deploy=true
{
    "name": "openai guardrails model",
    "function_name": "remote",
    "model_group_id": "ntSRBZcBgSi1HZubnbnp",
    "description": "guardrails test model",
    "connector_id": "ndSRBZcBgSi1HZubJrli"
}
```

To check the status of the operation, provide the task ID to the Tasks API:

```
GET /_plugins/_ml/tasks/n9SSBZcBgSi1HZubcbnA
```

You can test the guardrail model user input validation by sending requests that do and do not contain offensive words.

This example shows sending a request that does not contain offensive words:

```
POST /_plugins/_ml/models/oNSSBZcBgSi1HZubcbnv/_predict
{
  "parameters": {
    "question": "how many indices do i have in my cluster"
  }
}
```

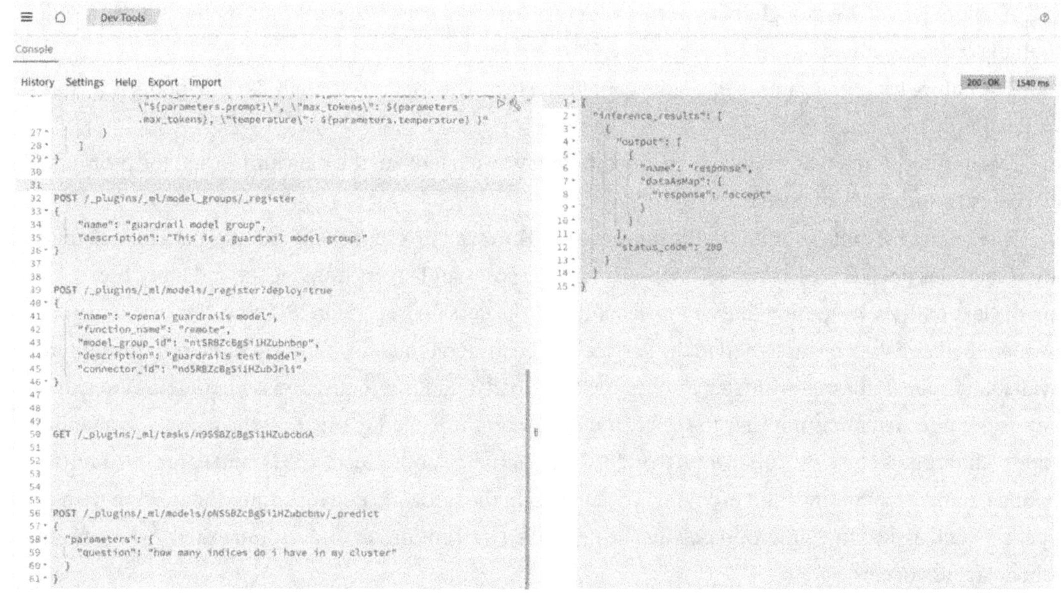

Figure 10-43. Guardrail RAG OpenAI result

10.6.4.4. RAG Data Management

Assuming that the root cause analysis data model is correctly constructed, it is necessary to understand what is causing the delay or problem when it occurs. If the list of failures is 400, the delay is likely to match one of the 400. Since it takes a significant amount of knowledge to correctly identify this, it is necessary to use AI to automate the matching of delays in the root cause analysis data model to specific failure lists.

While the root cause analysis data model is valuable enough on its own, the downside is that the data is hard to understand, so using AI as a solution to automate it is useful.

It is important to understand exactly what type of data you have and build a knowledge base.

- Table containing UUID
- Table containing number
- Table containing text
- Data containing image
- Normalized table without any joins
- Table with multiple columns joined

Given that vectors are generally less accurate, I recommend databases. You don't need to vectorize structured data to query it. Vectors are better suited for data types like images and audio.

You may not need to use a graph database if your data relationships are complex, or if your source data is not in graph type. You should minimize unnecessary transformations.

CHAPTER 10 AIOPS RCA

A failure list can be thought of as a table with text. The root cause analysis data model is a table with multiple columns joined.

The failure list is an example of a table containing text. The root cause analysis data model is a table with multiple columns joined.

Depending on the type of data, there are different ways to look up the data and enrich the prompts. This can affect the accuracy of the AI.

The failure list table contains entity information. However, in a root cause analysis data model, entities are sometimes unclear. For example, latency from CPU cores and errors from legacy and black boxes are unclear entities. Assuming that a nanosecond delay occurs on a specific CPU core, the service can be identified and the core assigned to the service can be understood only if information from the region availability zone, Kubernetes cluster, Kubernetes workload, and Kubernetes pod is identified. Due to the nature of Kubernetes, it is not easy to specify a specific core. You need to organize the regions, availability zones, Kubernetes clusters, Kubernetes workloads, Kubernetes pods, hosts, CPUs, and cores into entities to understand exactly where the problem is occurring. In the network, network equipment in the path of packets, such as switches and routers, must be organized into entities to understand exactly where problems and delays are occurring.

While it's relatively simple for SREs to manually identify delays, automating them using AI is more complex. Try to avoid using tag whenever possible, but when it's necessary, entities and tags must be set up manually. It is also useful to manually add information to the CMDB about CPU core and legacy host that are not automatically discovered by the agent. Having a clear picture of the entities that the signal represent makes root cause analysis easier. The entities of all systems required for IT operations should be clearly organized.

By evaluating the accuracy of the root cause analysis RAG and observability RAG provided in the demo, it is likely that they will surpass the capabilities of advanced SRE in the future. With the advent of cloud and managed services, AI agent-based root cause analysis will become the norm, given the difficulty for junior SREs to learn and grow with system resources.

- Feed AI uninterrupted, consistent data
- Improve AI's performance and reduce costs
- Tune AI to improve accuracy

These are expected to be in high demand in the future and are necessary engineering for AI to succeed.

10.6.4.5. Post-Processing

In the context of the overall work process, LLM is part of asking and answering questions, which requires various follow-up actions. In the RAG described so far, I haven't discussed storing the results of the LLM, understanding the stored text, and taking further actions.

It understands time series and machine learning results, allows humans to manually enter prompts, understands LLM results, and allows humans to take additional actions.

If the results of the LLM are accurate, much of the post-processing can be automated.

In Figure 10-44, there are multiple data sources, which are processed by the knowledge base, the agent, and the post-processing LLM.

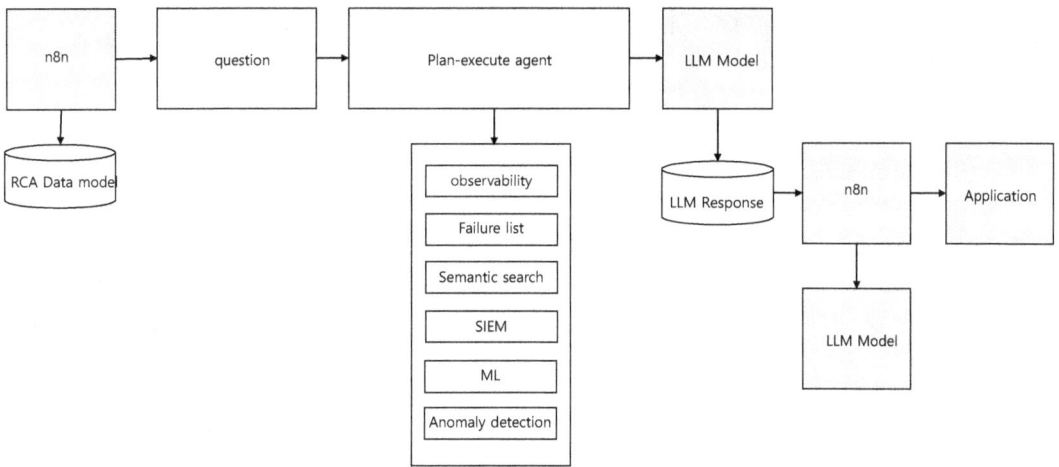

Figure 10-44. *LLM post-processing*

For example, after storing the LLM's response in the database. LangGraph and n8n reads the response. n8n calls the LLM to understand the text. n8n receives the LLM's response, reflects the results to other applications, and processes actions.

This is a simple example of post-processing in conjunction with the LangGraph and n8n and OpenSearch RAG, rather than being completed by the OpenSearch RAG.

If you have multiple agents running, n8n can schedule multiple agents. n8n does not provide agent functionality. LangGraph allows you to configure multiple agents. LangGraph and n8n have different features, so you should choose the one that suits your needs.

If data exists in an index, such as the observability RAG implemented in the plan-execute agent, it can be utilized in post-processing. Although the plan-execute agent described in this book is deployed as a single agent, it is a common AIOps process to have multiple agents working together, and the sequential processing of plan-execute agent and n8n to form a complete E2E process. It is possible to improve business processes, various guidelines, runbooks, and knowledge bases and utilize them in post-processing to increase accuracy. AIOps is not only about data, but also about processes using RAG and agents.

n8n also provides an AI agent that can connect with MCP, and in the latest version, it is possible to use MCP's tools directly through the MCP Server Trigger node. Compared to LangGraph, it is more productive, but it is difficult to configure workflows in as much detail as developing code directly in LangGraph.

Order fulfillment consists of the following four steps:

- Order creation
- Inventory lookup
- Determine price
- Determine a delivery date

When configuring LLM and the agent, consider the following

- Do you want to develop four tools within one agent?
- These are developed by splitting into four agents and processing them as LangGraph nodes.
- How do you organize a single planner LLM and multiple executor LLMs?

You need to organize your agents according to the difficulty and importance of the step.

The data and RAG described in this book are a subset of the data available, and processes can be designed to work with different RAG types and different agent.

LangGraph is suitable for implementing more complex requirements than LangChain. LangGraph can contain multiple LangChains, and it's possible to add admin interactions in mid-process. For multi-agent configurations, LangGraph is better suited than LangChain.

If you are simply developing post-processing from an application integration perspective, n8n is sufficient. For complex channel-to-agent coupling, use a LangGraph, and for simple application-to-application coupling, n8n is the way to go. In the end, you'll use different tools to develop the requirements.

10.6.5. RCA Agents
10.6.5.1. MCP

The Model Context Protocol (MCP) is a standardized communication framework that reduces the complexity of integration between AI agent and external tool. Without MCP, each tool integration would require the implementation of custom code for specific API endpoints, parameter schemas, response formats, and error handling patterns, which can result in significant technical overhead.

MCP solves this problem by providing a unified protocol layer with consistent interfaces for tool discovery, parameter validation, response formatting, and error handling. This protocol enables standardized JSON payloads and well-defined interoperability between AI applications and tool providers' server. This standardization means that agents can integrate new tool with minimal code changes because they only need to communicate with a consistent MCP interface instead of adapting to each tool's proprietary API structure.

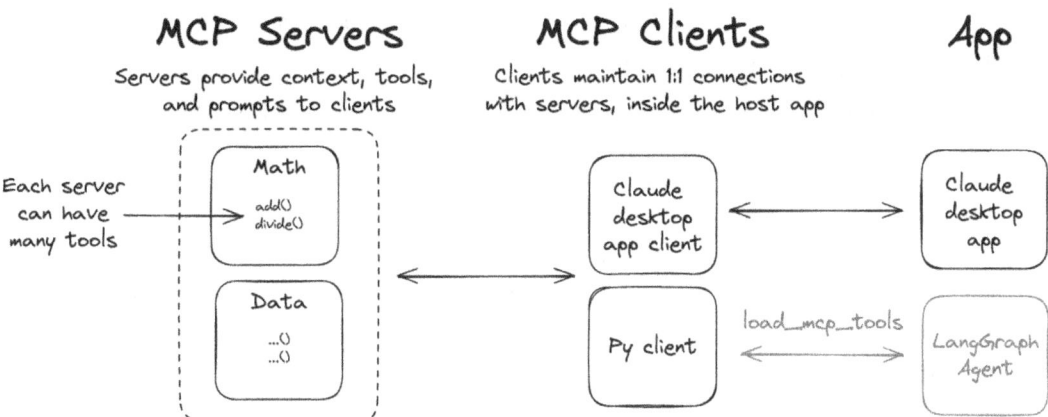

Figure 10-45. MCP processing flow

MCP acts as an intermediary layer to simplify communication and create a more scalable architecture (see Figure 10-45).

OpenSearch 3.0 provides an MCP server as part of the ML Commons plugin. The server provides MCP endpoint through a Server Sent Event (SSE) interface (/_plugins/_ml/mcp/sse) that streams the core toolset. LLM agents, such as LangChain's ReAct agent, for example, simply connect to the server, discover the tools it provides, and then invoke the tool using JSON arguments. No custom adapter code or additional REST endpoints are required.

The OpenSearch MCP Server provides agents with secure, real-time access to search data, and any index in the cluster. Product catalogs, logs, vector stores, and more, can be queried, summarized, or cross-referenced in the agent framework of your choice using the MCP Server.

Key benefits of using MCP Server include:

- **Unified data platform integration:** Provides native capabilities for AI agents to seamlessly perform search, analytics, and Vector database operations.

- **Simplified infrastructure:** Fully integrated into OpenSearch, eliminating the need to deploy, host, or maintain a separate MCP server.

- **Enterprise-grade security:** Uses OpenSearch security for authentication and provide consistent access control across tools.

- **Increased development efficiency:** Provides a standard interface to all tools, eliminating the need for custom integration code.

- **Framework flexibility:** Works with leading AI frameworks such as LangChain and Bedrock.

CHAPTER 10 AIOPS RCA

Depending on your architecture, you can configure MCP servers and clients. Although there is no technical difference, you can configure MCP in two ways:

- **Server mode:** Bind to registered tools in agents and LangGraph and invoke them.
- **Client mode:** Register an MCP server with an MCP client and call the MCP server from the MCP client.

MCP provides a way to use a variety of tools. There are many ways to pass text input from different channels to the LangGraph. First, let's look at the server mode.

Using Server Mode

For server mode, the OpenSearch MCP demo has the following setup:

```
# curl -X GET "localhost:9200/_cluster/settings?pretty"
{
  "persistent" : {
    "plugins" : {
      "ml_commons" : {
        "mcp_server_enabled" : "true"
      }
    }
  },
  "transient" : { }
}
```

Install the Python libraries for LangChain and OpenAI:

```
# python3 -m venv venv

# source venv/bin/activate

# pip install -r requirements.txt
```

When connecting to the MCP server, you must include the appropriate authentication headers based on your OpenSearch security settings. The following example shows how to add the headers to a LangChain client.

```
cred = base64.b64encode(f"{username}:{password}".encode()).decode()
headers = {
    "Content-Type": "application/json",
    "Accept-Encoding": "identity",
    "Authorization": f"Basic {cred}"
}
```

```
client = MultiServerMCPClient({
    "opensearch": {
        "url": "http://localhost:9200/_plugins/_ml/mcp/sse?append_to_base_url=true",
        "transport": "sse",
        "headers": headers
    }
})
```

The scripts included in the demo configure two tools. `ListIndexTool` and `SearchIndexTool` are available on the MCP server.

Agents can choose which tool they want to use based on the tool filter. In the demo, only `ListIndexTool` and `SearchIndexTool` are used, but you can also add `IndexMappingTool`.

Use the LangChain `initialize_agent` API. Since OpenSearch's tools are registered with the MCP server, agents in LangChain can call the tools registered with MCP.

```
async def main():
    # Create MCP client with OpenSearch connection details
    client = MultiServerMCPClient({
        "opensearch": {
            "url": f"{opensearch_server}/_plugins/_ml/mcp/sse?append_to_base_url=true",
            "transport": "sse",
            "headers": {
                "Content-Type": "application/json",
                "Accept-Encoding": "identity",
            }
        }
    })

    tools = await client.get_tools()

    agent = initialize_agent(
        tools=tools,
        llm=model,
        agent=AgentType.OPENAI_FUNCTIONS,
        agent_kwargs={
            "system_message": "You are a helpful assistant that can interact with OpenSearch
            to retrieve and process data.",
            "max_iterations": 5,
            "max_execution_time": 60,
        },
        handle_parsing_errors=True,
        verbose=True,
    )
```

CHAPTER 10   AIOPS RCA

In LangChain, you configure agents as follows:

1. `MultiServerMCPClient` configures the MCP server.
2. `initialize_agent` configures a basic LangChain agent.
3. `agent.ainvoke` runs the agent.

An agent is internally organized into several phases. They are processed in the following order: start, act, input behavior, observe, think, respond, and exit.

The `AgentExecutor` is the execution environment of an agent. By debugging by setting breakpoints in the `AgentExecutor`, you can examine the execution order of `AgentAction`, `AgentFinish`, and `AgentExecutor`, and understand how they internally start, act, observe, think, and respond. You can use debugging to understand and improve the execution of tools within the agent. To understand open source internal behavior, you can add breakpoints in your development tools and understand dependencies and variable values.

Configure the Python library as follows:

```
pip install langchain-mcp-adapters
pip install langchain-mcp-adapters langgraph "langchain[openai]"
export OPENAI_API_KEY=<your_api_key>
```

This describes `create_react_agent`. You can understand the internal structure while debugging `create_react_agent`.

The provided demo initializes the LangChain agent, discovers the available MCP tool, and asks the agent to list all the indexes in the cluster. This example uses gpt-4o, but the script is compatible with any LLM that integrates with LangChain and tool call. When it runs with a sample index from OpenSearch, the agent demonstrates intelligent tool usage. It first calls `ListIndexTool` to discover the available indexes, then uses `SearchIndexTool` on the indexes to retrieve information and display it in a structured format. This workflow demonstrates how LLMs autonomously explore OpenSearch data with the MCP tool. The output is as follows:

```
# python agent.py
Input (type 'exit' to quit): Find the most delayed flights within 24 hours

> Entering new AgentExecutor chain...
```

Here are the most delayed flights within the last 24 hours, sorted by the length of the delay (all with 360 minutes/6 hours delay):

1. **Flight Number:** Q77B7WF
   - **Origin:** Bologna Guglielmo Marconi Airport (Italy)
   - **Destination:** Lester B. Pearson International Airport (Toronto, Canada)
   - **Delay:** 360 minutes
   - **Carrier:** BeatsWest
   - **Type of Delay:** Carrier Delay

```
  - **Cancelled:** No
  - **Timestamp:** 2025-05-30T15:23:17

> Finished chain.
Result: Here are the most delayed flights within the last 24 hours, sorted by the length of
the delay (all with 360 minutes/6 hours delay):

1. **Flight Number:** Q77B7WF
   - **Origin:** Bologna Guglielmo Marconi Airport (Italy)
   - **Destination:** Lester B. Pearson International Airport (Toronto, Canada)
   - **Delay:** 360 minutes
   - **Carrier:** BeatsWest
   - **Type of Delay:** Carrier Delay
   - **Cancelled:** No
   - **Timestamp:** 2025-05-30T15:23:17
```

While it's important to understand the technical advantages of MCP, it's also important to understand how post-processing works with MCP. Assuming the information exists in the knowledge base, most of the post-processing can be defined with text alone. In the previous demo, you can use RAG and agent to configure post-processing without any additional development. With MCP, you can naturally combine ReAct and the plan-execute agent running in OpenSearch into your LangGraph workflow. Handling complex workflows with OpenSearch's agents alone is inefficient and difficult to fulfill customer requirements. LangGraph allows you to configure multiple agents using workflow. OpenSearch works as a single agent and can interact with other agents in the LangGraph. It is also possible for an administrator to intervene in the middle of a workflow and make decisions. The overall workflow can be organized as a LangGraph, and individual agents from OpenSearch, Dynatrace, and Salesforce can be interfaced through MCP. By installing DeepSeek directly without calling LLM, you can run post-processing cheaply without the cost of API calls. There are several ways to reduce the cost of API calls.

Configuring the Client Mode

The second method uses the MCP client. The OpenSearch MCP client allows OpenSearch agents to connect to external tool providers via the MCP protocol to extend their functionality. Agents are not limited to the built-in tools, but can use specialized external services such as weather forecasts, translations, document processing tools, and more.

If you're developing a Slackbot that works with an MCP server, the Slackbot is developed using the MCP Client API to communicate with the MCP server.

OpenSearch's built-in MCP server is available starting with version 3.0. To use MCP in earlier versions, you can run a standalone MCP server outside of the OpenSearch cluster. This works like this

- The agent initiates a tool call.

- This call is forwarded to the standalone MCP server.

- The MCP server makes a REST request to the OpenSearch cluster, retrieves the required data, formats the response, and returns it to the agent.

Configure Python:

```
python -m venv .venv
source .venv/bin/activate
```

Configure the Python library:

```
pip install opensearch-mcp-server-py
```

To use the SSE protocol, type the following command:

```
python -m mcp_server_opensearch --transport sse
```

Enter your OpenSearch environment variables:

```
export OPENSEARCH_URL="<your_opensearch_domain_url>"
export OPENSEARCH_USERNAME="<your_opensearch_domain_username>"
export OPENSEARCH_PASSWORD="<your_opensearch_domain_password>"
```

The following tools are currently available:

- `ListIndexTool`: Lists all indexes.
- `IndexMappingTool`: Retrieves index mapping and configuration information for an index.
- `SearchIndexTool`: Searches for an index using a query.
- `GetShardsTool`: Gets information about shards.

To run `uvx`, install `astral-uv`. The MCP servers referenced by the MCP client are listed here:

```
{
    "mcpServers": {
        "opensearch-mcp-server": {
            "command": "uvx",
            "args": ["mcp_server_opensearch"],
            "env": {
                "OPENSEARCH_URL": "<your_opensearch_domain_url>",
                "OPENSEARCH_USERNAME": "<your_opensearch_domain_username>",
                "OPENSEARCH_PASSWORD": "<your_opensearch_domain_password>",
            }
        }
    }
}
```

CHAPTER 10 AIOPS RCA

Server mode and client mode are selected based on your architecture, and agents need to communicate with channels and applications through MCP.

Developing a Custom MCP Server

There may be cases where the tools provided by the MCP server by default do not meet your requirements. In such cases, you need to develop an MCP server and develop tools using custom API.

You can develop two types of MCP servers: `stdio` and `streamable-http`.

The `stdio` MCP server looks like this:

```
# math_server.py
from mcp.server.fastmcp import FastMCP

mcp = FastMCP("Math")

@mcp.tool()
def add(a: int, b: int) -> int:
    """Add two numbers"""
    return a + b

@mcp.tool()
def multiply(a: int, b: int) -> int:
    """Multiply two numbers"""
    return a * b

if __name__ == "__main__":
    mcp.run(transport="stdio")
```

The `streamable-http` MCP server looks like this:

```
# math_server.py
...

# weather_server.py
from typing import List
from mcp.server.fastmcp import FastMCP

mcp = FastMCP("Weather")

@mcp.tool()
async def get_weather(location: str) -> str:
    """Get weather for location."""
    return "It's always sunny in New York"

if __name__ == "__main__":
    mcp.run(transport="streamable-http")
```

851

CHAPTER 10   AIOPS RCA

The two types of MCP clients are `StdioServerParameters` and `MultiServerMCPClient`.
The `MultiServerMCPClient` client looks like this:

```python
from langchain_mcp_adapters.client import MultiServerMCPClient
from langgraph.prebuilt import create_react_agent

client = MultiServerMCPClient(
    {
        "math": {
            "command": "python",
            # Make sure to update to the full absolute path to your math_server.py file
            "args": ["/path/to/math_server.py"],
            "transport": "stdio",
        },
        "weather": {
            # make sure you start your weather server on port 8000
            "url": "http://localhost:8000/mcp",
            "transport": "streamable_http",
        }
    }
)
tools = await client.get_tools()
agent = create_react_agent("openai:gpt-4.1", tools)
math_response = await agent.ainvoke({"messages": "what's (3 + 5) x 12?"})
weather_response = await agent.ainvoke({"messages": "what is the weather in nyc?"})
```

The most important tools, listed in order of priority, are

- **Knowledge base:** The knowledge base, which contains internal know-how, is the most important tool and is prioritized first.

- **Observability:** Commercial observability, including CMDB, is a critical piece of data that should be tied into the MCP.

- **Various channel history:** Data coming in from channels such as chat, Slack, and speech recognition, contains useful context.

- **Internet searches:** Real-time information such as location, weather, traffic, and currency exchange rates require Internet searches.

- **Atlassian:** Document management systems like Jira and Confluence are useful, but they're less accurate than you might think.

10.6.5.2. Workflows

This section describes how to integrate all of the root cause analysis, observability, reranking, guardrails, and MCP servers discussed so far to form a multi-agent configuration and automate root cause analysis.

Root cause analysis, AIOps dashboards provide visualization, and SREs need to intervene. Automation should be configured using AI.

There is a difference between agents and RAG as configured in OpenSearch.

- **Agents:** Contain a tool. In a LangChain, a single agent is composed of multiple tools. In a LangGraph, a single agent contains a small number of tools.

- **RAG:** Uses a knowledge base and an LLM. Agents are not required for RAG. Typically, RAG includes agents.

This requires multiple workflows and agents. Figure 10-46 organizes the workflows in a LangGraph and handles various interactions with agents in OpenSearch. MCP can simplify and standardize interactions.

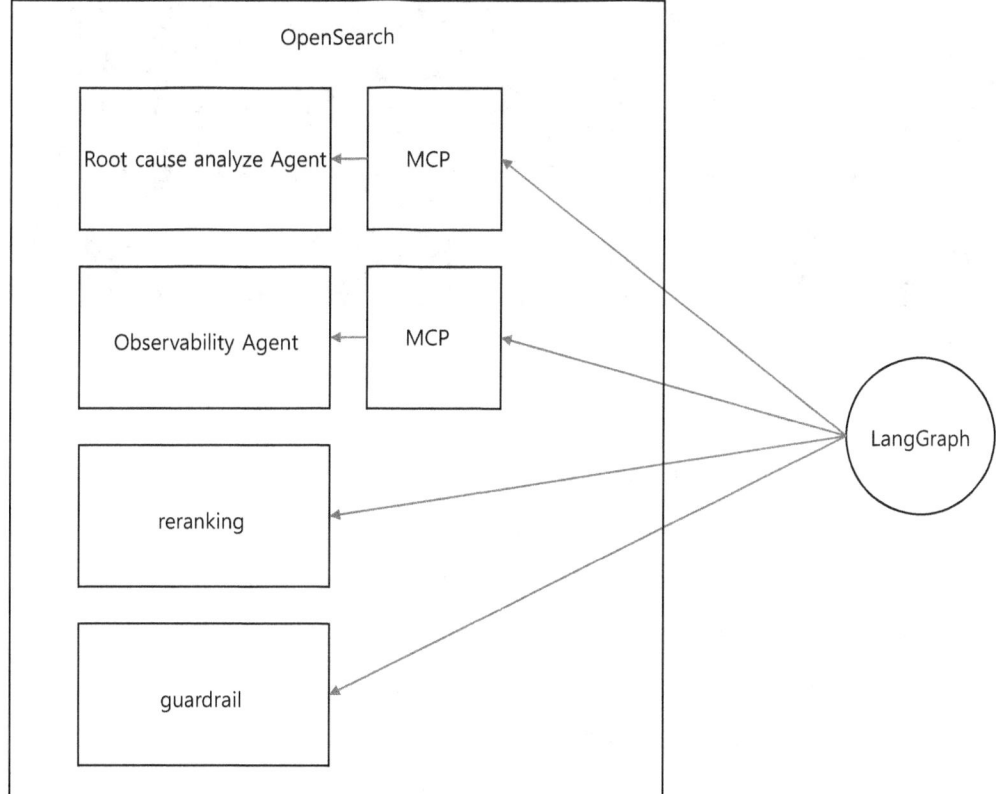

Figure 10-46. The interface between LangGraph and Agent

OpenSearch consists of ReAct, a plan-execute agent, and LangGraph, which invokes multiple agents and manages their state through MCP.

CHAPTER 10　AIOPS RCA

LangGraph provides tools for developing workflows, as shown in Figure 10-47. No labs are provided for LangGraph. I will provide a LangGraph demo with a multi-agent implementation in Git.

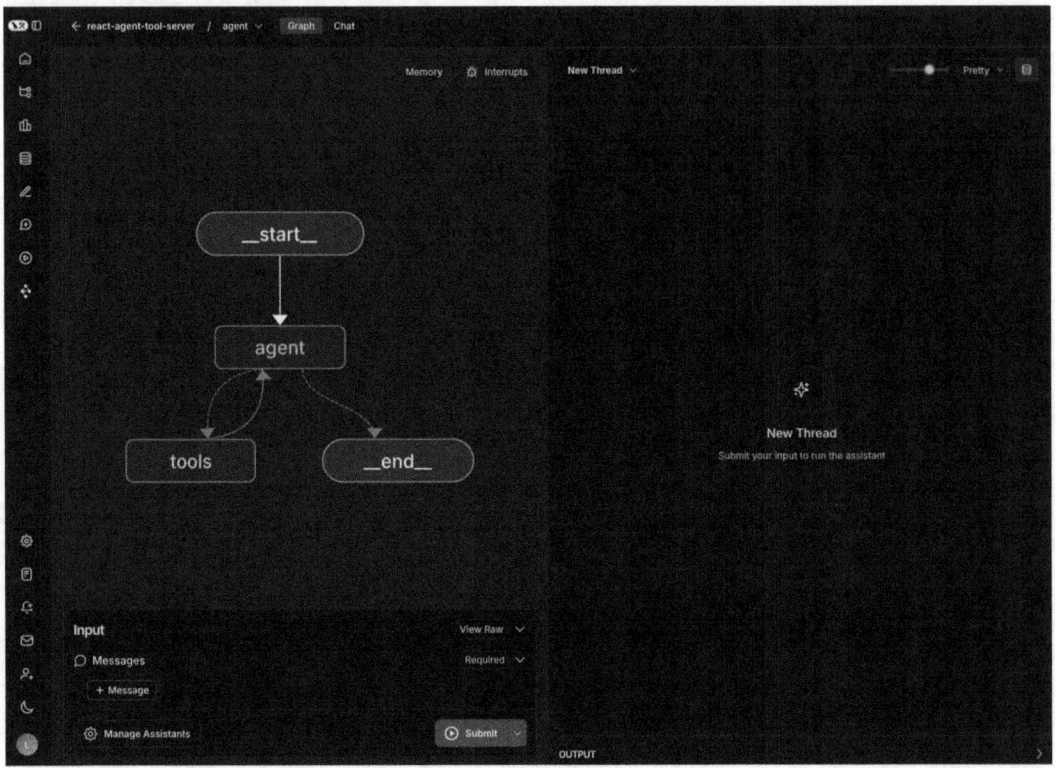

Figure 10-47. *LangGraph studio UI*

Various interfaces between LangGraph and OpenSearch are required.

- **LangChain:** Develops ReAct agents or plan-execute agent.
- **LangGraph:** Runs and manages multiple agents.
- **OpenSearch:** Provides agents, a Vector database, a knowledge base, and MCP.
- **Root Cause Analysis agent:** Consists of a ReAct agent or a plan-execute agent.
- **Observability agent:** Consists of a plan-execute agent.
- **Anomaly detection agent:** Configures a plan-execute agent.
- **Reranking agent:** After the SRE evaluates the results of the root cause analysis agent and the observability agent, it runs the reranking agent if the results are not what it expects. It is not configured as an agent.

- **Post-processing:** Configure guardrails to limit unnecessary actions. Does not consist of an agent.

- **MCP:** Associates with LangGraph using root cause analysis agents and observability agents. Reranking and guardrail use the OpenSearch API without MCP.

- **Knowledge bases:** Root cause analysis, observability, and rebanking use the knowledge base built on OpenSearch to configure RAG. Information about on-call roasters registered with Google Calendar, system admin names, application names, legacy, and black boxes are added to separate indexes. Senior engineers' know-how should be added. Multi-purpose.

- **Slack and Jira integration:** Connect with MCP server in Slack and Jira using LangGraph.

- **CMDB:** Provides various data required for IT operations such as configuration changes, resources, and services.

To improve reliability and MTTR, infrastructure engineer, first-line operators, SREs, architect, and developers collaborate with each other, but require different workflows.

The following five workflows have different characteristics and are composed of different agents. Because they have commonalities between them, this list identifies the commonalities and organizes the workflows so that they can be reused.

- **SRE's workflow:** Organized to quickly restore services to minimize customer loss.

- **Workflows for a 24x7 first-line operator:** Detects and proactively responds to anomalies to minimize outages.

- **Infrastructure, security, and network engineer's workflow:** Analyze root causes, including small delays, to improve reliability and prevent the same failures from recurring.

- **Architect's workflow:** Accurately generate a variety of reliability-related reports, including SLO and MTTR.

- **Developer's workflow:** Deploy basic deployments as well as rolling updates, BlueGreen, canary, analyze, and roll back in case of problems

RAG, MCP, and agents are more important than the technology. Optimizations for your organization and processes should be built into your workflow.

An infrastructure engineer's workflow for managing system resources is shown in Figure 10-48.

CHAPTER 10 AIOPS RCA

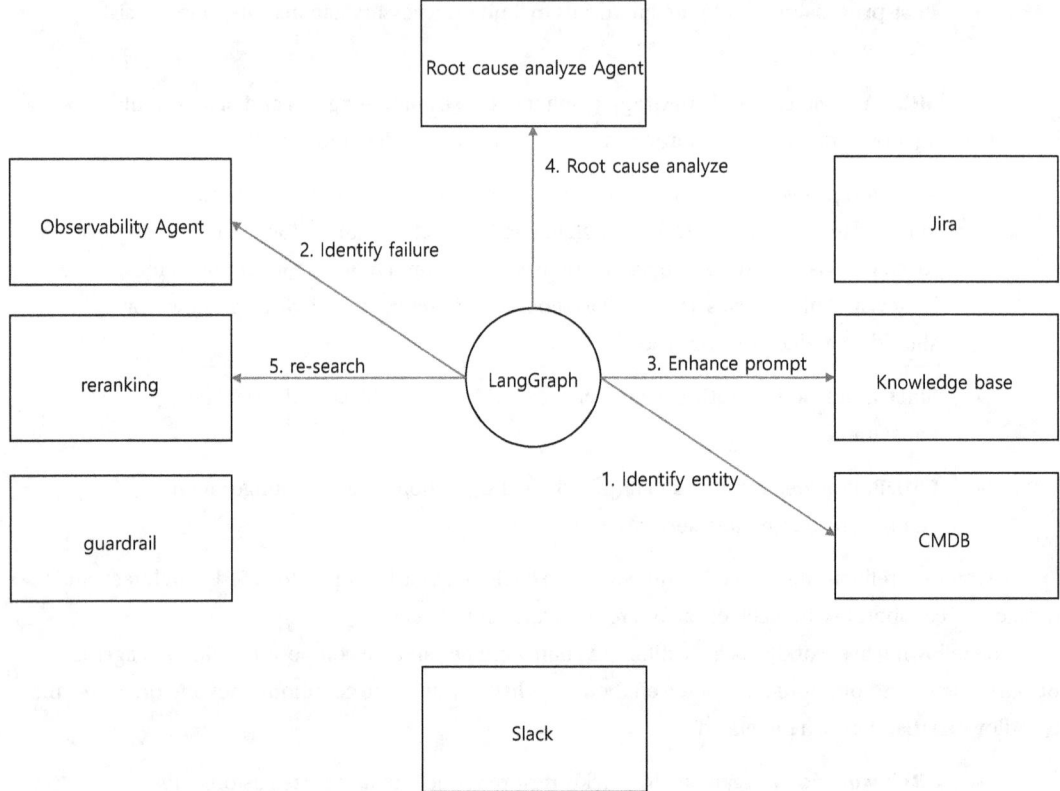

Figure 10-48. *Platform workflow*

It takes a long time to analyze failures in system resources, security, and networks. It is important to identify and analyze delays that are smaller than errors. You should use the knowledge base to augment prompts and use the root cause analysis agent. If you don't understand the cause of the failure, use reranking to research it.

Figure 10-49 shows the workflow for a first-line operator responsible for 24-hour operations.

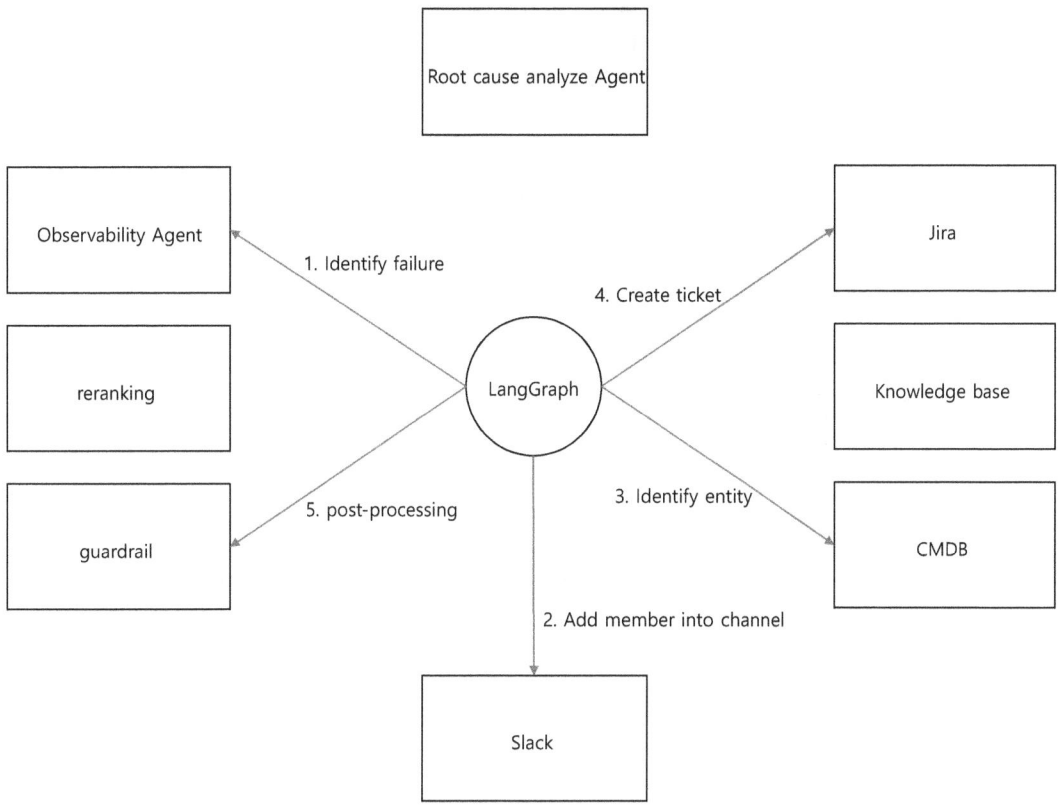

Figure 10-49. *The first line operator workflow*

It is important to use anomaly detection and observability agents to proactively identify failures in advance. The goal should not be to fix the problem, but rather to defer to second-line SRE and third-line developer. If a proactive response is required, guardrails should be applied to improve the accuracy of post-processing handling.

An SRE's workflow for responding to an outage is shown in Figure 10-50.

CHAPTER 10 AIOPS RCA

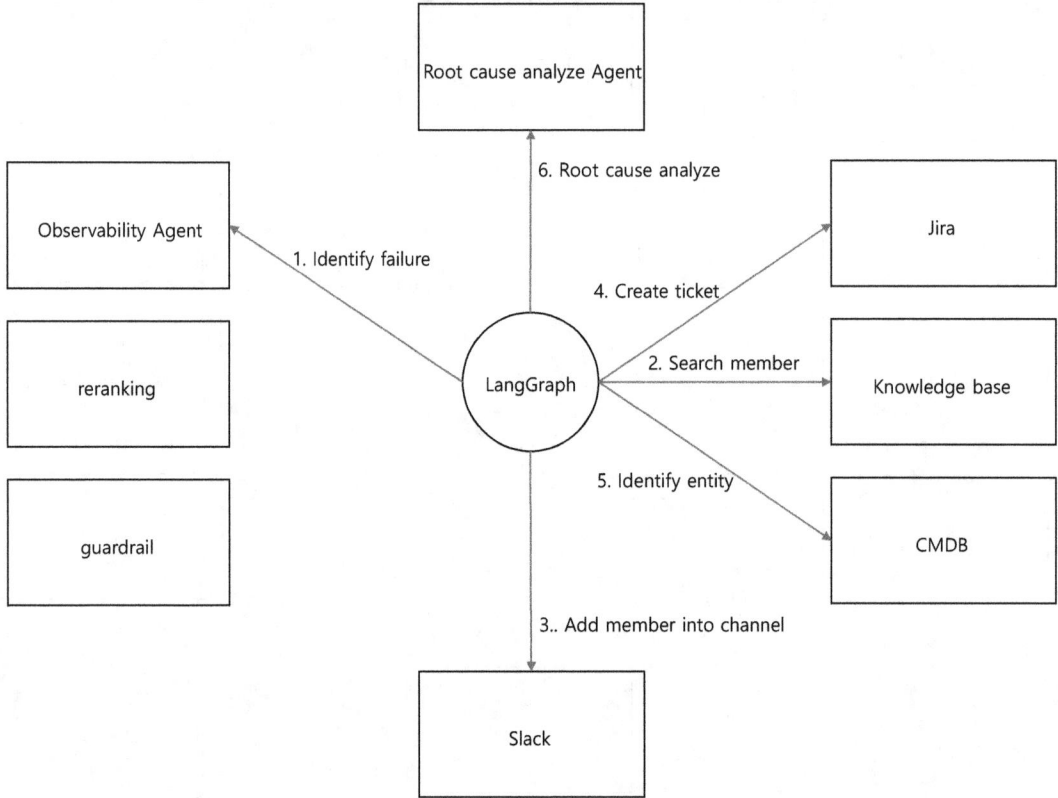

Figure 10-50. *The SRE workflow*

SREs responding to service failures in applications need to identify entities, understand whether the failure is propagating, and the negative impact on customer service. While identifying delays is important, traces and logs often output error messages directly, and error messages are clues to troubleshooting. Automate the organization and procedures to enable rapid failure response.

Figure 10-51 shows an architect's workflow for measuring SLOs and MTTR.

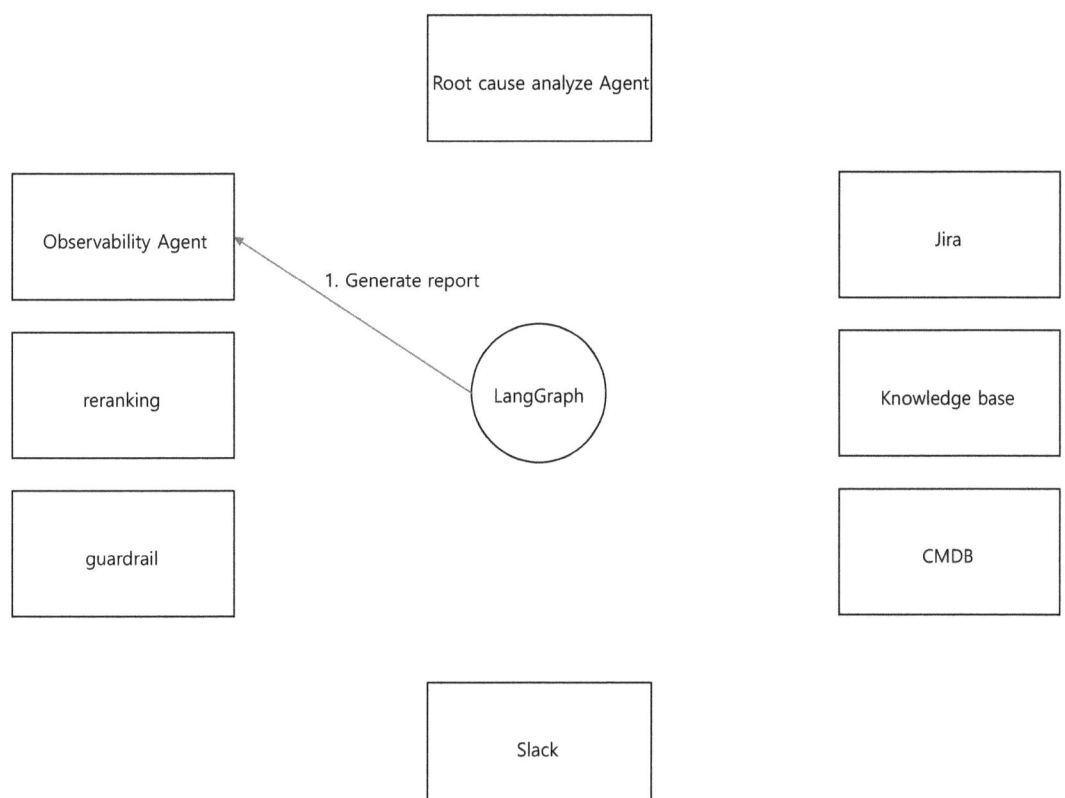

Figure 10-51. *Architect's workflow*

The architect uses the observability agent to automatically generate reports on SLOs and MTTR. Figure 10-52 shows the workflow for a developer responsible for testing and deployment.

CHAPTER 10 AIOPS RCA

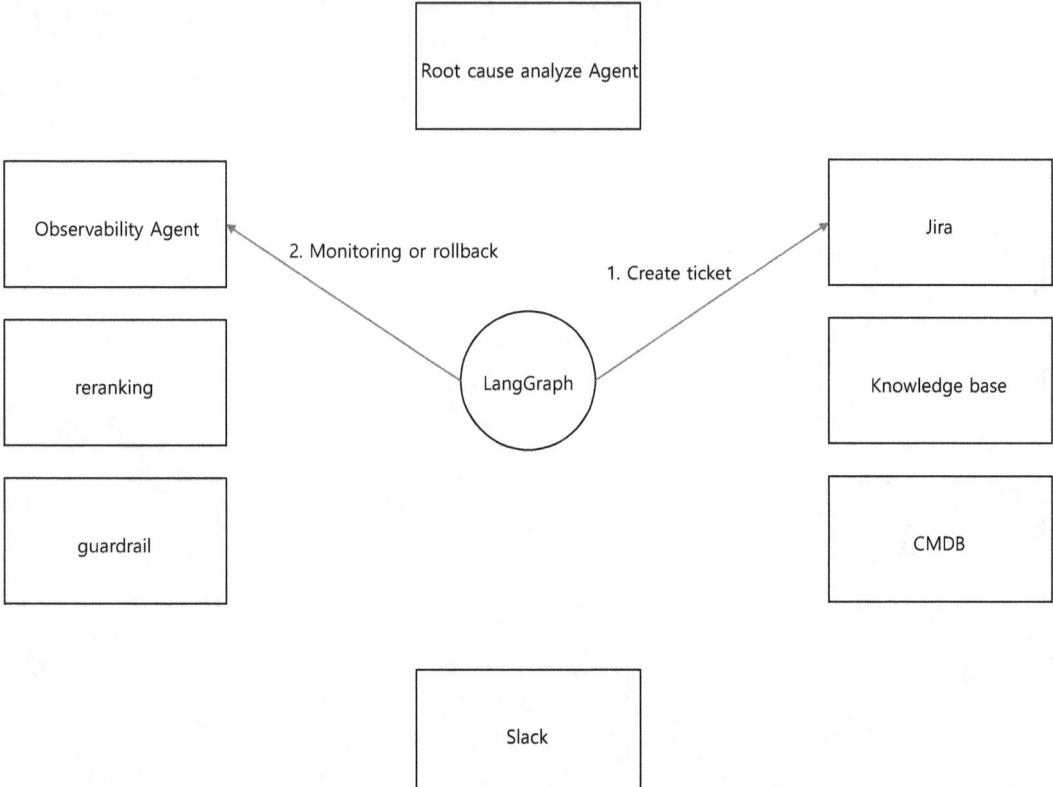

Figure 10-52. Developer's workflow

Developers automate Canary, AB, and BlueGreen deployment procedures and post-deployment monitoring. They handle rollbacks in case of problems.

The five individual workflows can be consolidated into one large workflow at the operational level, as shown in Figure 10-53.

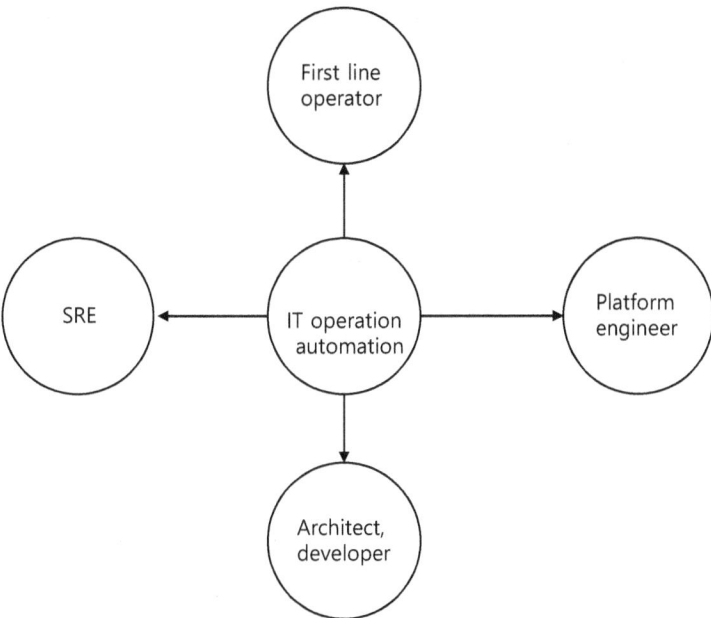

Figure 10-53. Integrate IT automation workflow

You need to create an operational strategy that integrates different organizations, people, and workflows, and automate incrementally.

If you can define the right direction, you don't need to develop a lot of agents. You should strive to improve reuse with fewer agents and keep workflows simple.

10.6.5.3. LangGraph

OpenSearch defines agents, and agents contain tools. However, LangGraph define agents, but they call tools in OpenSearch via MCP.

While LangChain can organize IT operational processes using various technologies such as RAG, agent, MCP, LLM, and knowledge bases, it is difficult to organize complex workflows using LangChain alone, which is why you need a LangGraph.

How the LangGraph calls tools is important, and the five workflows call tools from external applications. All tools are registered in the MCP. For example, if different tools are registered in the MCP, the AI can select a specific tool on its own to generate results without the need for a detailed description from the user. Automation can be achieved with workflows and MCP alone, without detailed input. Cost aside, having many tools bound to an MCP is more favorable for automation. This is why workflows and MCP in LangGraph should be linked.

For example, if you have Google Calendar, Slack, Zoom, Jira, and Confluence tools registered in MCP, you can enter "Schedule a meeting with a specific subject matter expert to discuss a specific issue" in your workflow, and the workflow will automatically perform the following steps:

1. In Slack, type "Schedule a meeting with a specific subject matter expert to discuss a specific issue" and the workflow is triggered by a webhook.

2. If you have a knowledge base with internal information from your organization, use a retriever to look it up.

3. Create an issue in Jira.

4. Search for additional relevant information in Confluence and add it to the Jira issue.

5. Search for a specific subject matter expert in Slack and Jira.

6. Read the schedule information from the subject matter expert's Google Calendar and set a date to meet.

7. Create a Zoom meeting based on the schedule information.

8. Send a Zoom invitation email to the subject matter expert on the available date.

Once the tools for Google Calendar, Slack, Zoom, Jira, Confluence, and Outlook are set up on the MCP server, you can configure third-party tools for agent in your workflow. This is why as many third-party tools as possible should be registered with the MCP server. No matter what the user's question, the agent will understand the context and intent of the user's question and will use MCP to find the appropriate tool to answer it.

I've been an IT engineer for a long time, but the pace of change is so fast these days that it's hard to predict how things will evolve and what new services will be released in the future. However, it is useful to understand how to develop MCP and workflow at this point in time.

Instead of configuring workflows inside OpenSearch, you will configure workflow and agent in LangGraph and use tools from OpenSearch and Slack. This means that the agents are configured in LangGraph, but the tools in the agents are bound to the MCP.

There are a number of ways to connect LangGraph and MCP, but this example uses three of them:

- Using `initialize_agent` in a LangGraph
- Using the `create_react_agent` of a LangGraph
- Adding MCP tools to nodes in a StateGraph

LangChain and LangGraph provide `create_react_agent`.

- LangGraph provides `create_react_agent` from `langgraph.prebuilt import create_react_agent`.
- LangChain provides `create_react_agent` from `langchain.agents import create_react_agent`.
- It's helpful to understand the existing API for LangChain and the API for LangGraph. As the API changes frequently, it can be confusing and it's important to understand the correct API usage.

The following example uses LangGraph's create_react_agent.

```python
from langchain_mcp_adapters.client import MultiServerMCPClient
from langgraph.prebuilt import create_react_agent

client = MultiServerMCPClient({
        "opensearch": {
            "url": f"{opensearch_server}/_plugins/_ml/mcp/sse?append_to_base_url=true",
            "transport": "sse",
            "headers": {
                "Content-Type": "application/json",
                "Accept-Encoding": "identity",
            }
        }
})

tools = await client.get_tools()
agent = create_react_agent("openai:gpt-4.1", tools)
```

LangGraph is similar to StateGraph, but in a different way, you can serve MCP tools from the LangGraph API server.

LangGraph requires StateGraph, so you can't configure a workflow with create_react_agent alone. You need the following API:

1. tools = await client.get_tools() gets the MCP's tools.

2. bind_tools(tools) binds the tools.

3. builder.add_node(ToolNode(tools)) adds the tools to the node.

```python
client = MultiServerMCPClient(
    {
        "math": {
            "command": "python",
            # Make sure to update to the full absolute path to your math_server.py file
            "args": ["./examples/math_server.py"],
            "transport": "stdio",
        },
        "weather": {
            # make sure you start your weather server on port 8000
            "url": "http://localhost:8000/mcp",
            "transport": "streamable_http",
        }
    }
```

```
)
tools = await client.get_tools()

def call_model(state: MessagesState):
    response = model.bind_tools(tools).invoke(state["messages"])
    return {"messages": response}

builder = StateGraph(MessagesState)
builder.add_node(call_model)
builder.add_node(ToolNode(tools))
builder.add_edge(START, "call_model")
builder.add_conditional_edges(
    "call_model",
    tools_condition,
)
builder.add_edge("tools", "call_model")
graph = builder.compile()
math_response = await graph.ainvoke({"messages": "what's (3 + 5) x 12?"})
weather_response = await graph.ainvoke({"messages": "what is the weather in nyc?"})
```

The disadvantages of a LangChain include:

- It's difficult for humans to intervene in the middle of the process, or to branch based on human choices.

- It is difficult to manage interactions between agents or organize multi-agents.

That's why I am introducing the LangGraph human-in-the-loop (HITL) (see Figure 10-54).

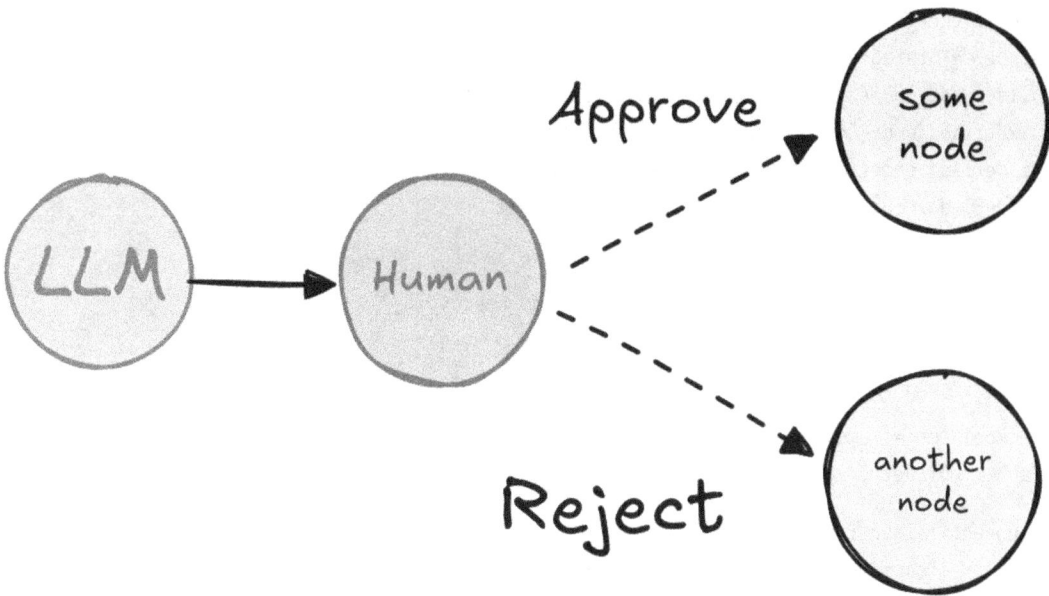

Figure 10-54. HITL

Figure 10-54 pauses the graph after an API call to review and approve the action. If the action is rejected, it prevents the graph from executing that step and allows you to perform other actions. For example, you might review the results of a root cause analysis agent and invoke a rerank if they don't meet your expectations.

```
# Human approval node
def human_approval(state: State) -> Command[Literal["approved_path", "rejected_path"]]:
    decision = interrupt({
        "question": "Do you approve the following output?",
        "llm_output": state["llm_output"]
    })

    if decision == "approve":
        return Command(goto="approved_path", update={"decision": "approved"})
    else:
        return Command(goto="rejected_path", update={"decision": "rejected"})

# Next steps after approval
def approved_node(state: State) -> State:
    print("✅ Approved path taken.")
    return state
# Alternative path after rejection
def rejected_node(state: State) -> State:
    print("❌ Rejected path taken.")
    return state
```

```
# Build the graph
builder = StateGraph(State)
builder.add_node("generate_llm_output", generate_llm_output)
builder.add_node("human_approval", human_approval)
builder.add_node("approved_path", approved_node)
builder.add_node("rejected_path", rejected_node)

builder.set_entry_point("generate_llm_output")
builder.add_edge("generate_llm_output", "human_approval")
builder.add_edge("approved_path", END)
builder.add_edge("rejected_path", END)

checkpointer = MemorySaver()
graph = builder.compile(checkpointer=checkpointer)

# Run until interrupt
config = {"configurable": {"thread_id": uuid.uuid4()}}
result = graph.invoke({}, config=config)
print(result["__interrupt__"])
# Output:
# Interrupt(value={'question': 'Do you approve the following output?', 'llm_output': 'This is the generated output.'}, ...)

# Simulate resuming with human input
# To test rejection, replace resume="approve" with resume="reject"
final_result = graph.invoke(Command(resume="approve"), config=config)
print(final_result)
```

It is important to deprecate initialize_agent and create_react_agent in LangGraph and use Supervisor, HITL, and StateGraph to configure workflows. Integration should be standardized with MCP.

LangGraph will act as a backend to integrate various agents, LLM, OpenSearch, RAG, workflows, and knowledge bases. Different channels are needed for customers and users. For example, users can enter text via speech recognition, Streamlit, or Slackbot, and the text should be fed to the corresponding LangGraph on the backend.

I've been an IT engineer for a long time, but the pace of change is so fast these days that it's hard to predict how things will evolve and what new services will be released in the future. However, it is useful to understand MCP and how to develop workflows based on LangGraph at this point.

A LangGraph workflow involves a channel and an application on the backend (see Figure 10-55). Compared to the backend, channels are more difficult and complex. Getting from the various channels to the backend is not straightforward. Using LangGraph and MCP, connecting to the application is not the hard part; most of the labor comes from connecting to the various channels and backend agent frameworks.

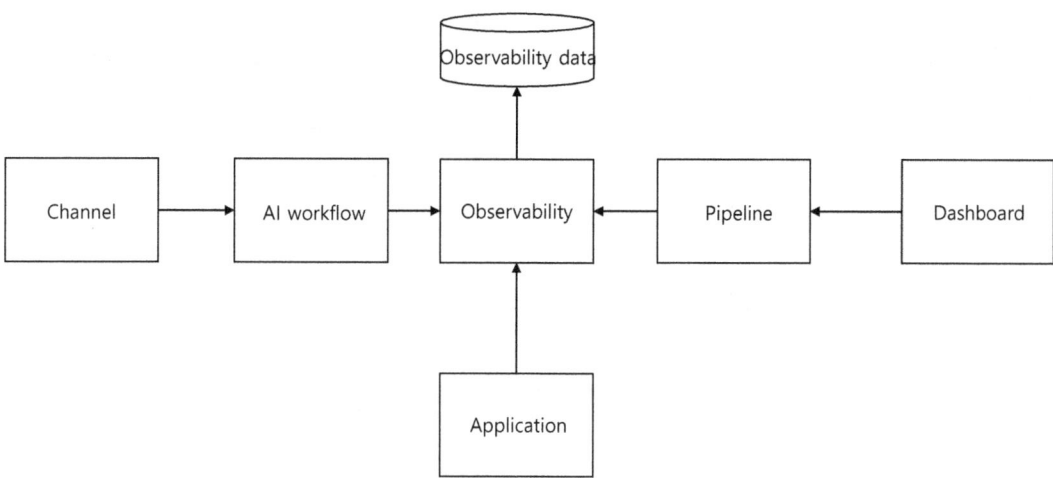

Figure 10-55. *LangGraph workflow*

While there will be better AI automation tools than LangGraph in the future, the most advanced technology at this point is using LangGraph to develop workflows, plan-execute agents, and supervisor agents.

The technology will continue to evolve, channels will be added, and frameworks will change.

Automation tools and drag-and-drop make it easy to configure workflows, but there are limitations to complex customization. LangGraph has a learning curve, but it can be implemented to fit your needs in a granular way.

For example, a workflow that triggers an event and sends it to Slack when a change occurs in a Google Sheet can be configured using only n8n. However, n8n alone is not enough to integrate agents and workflows with Streamlit, speech recognition, and Slackbots.

LangGraphs are the brains of inference, running agents, collecting and storing data from various channels.

In the following section, I detail how to integrate three channels—Streamlit, speech recognition, and Slack—with your LangGraph workflow.

10.6.5.4. Streamlit

Streamlit is universal question and answer screens. For example, you can add a Streamlit to an accounting or ordering screen and ask questions to an AI.

The screen structure of Streamlit is similar to the popular Slack. It's redundant in terms of functionality and doesn't offer as many features as Slack. Rather than adding more features to Streamlit compared to Slack, you can add features that make it easier to ask and answer questions in your existing applications.

The way Streamlit can pass text to a LangGraph is through the FastAPI.

Customize `https://github.com/JoshuaC215/agent-service-toolkit` to connect your Streamlit and LangGraph.

CHAPTER 10 AIOPS RCA

It includes a LangGraph agent, a FastAPI service that provides it, a client that interacts with the service, and a Streamlit app that uses the client to provide a chat interface. The data structures and settings are built with Pydantic.

It provides templates that make it easy to build and run your own agents using the LangGraph framework. It shows a complete setup, from agent definition to user interface, and provides a complete toolkit to help you easily get started with a LangGraph-based project.

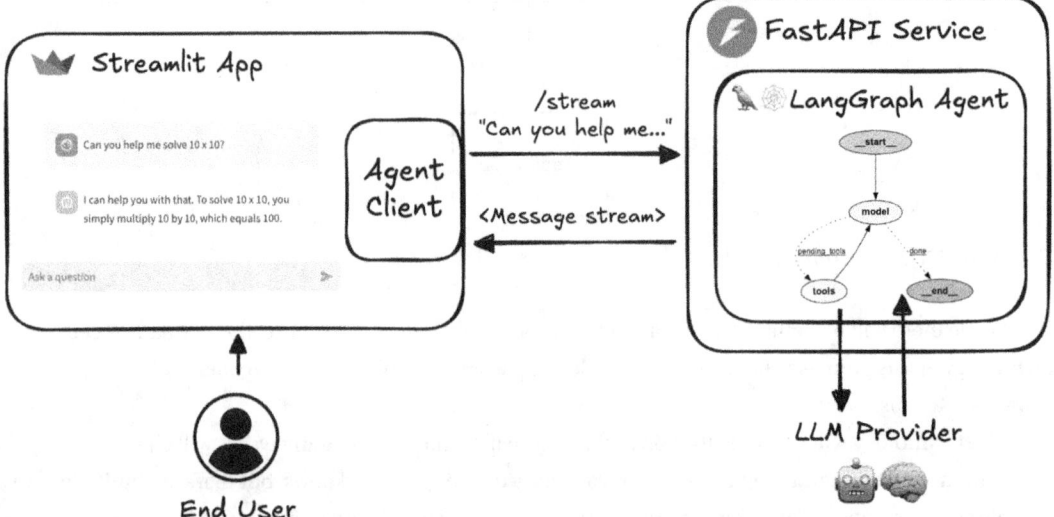

Figure 10-56. The Streamlit flow

Streamlit is the client, passing requests to the FastAPI. In the future, LangGraph may be replaced by a different backend, or other channels may be added. As technology continues to change, channels and backends like Streamlit can be linked with minimal changes.

I described a plan-do-reflect agent that separates the planner from the executor and produces good results. The plan-execute-reflect agent is one of the agent patterns. Another frequently used pattern is the supervisor pattern.

This demonstration uses the supervisor workflow. Figure 10-57 shows that when multiple agents interact with each other, the call paths become complex and unmanageable. If many unnecessary HITL is configured, automation becomes difficult because humans must intervene each time. SRE workflows can have interactions between many different agents, which can be easily managed by using supervisors.

CHAPTER 10 AIOPS RCA

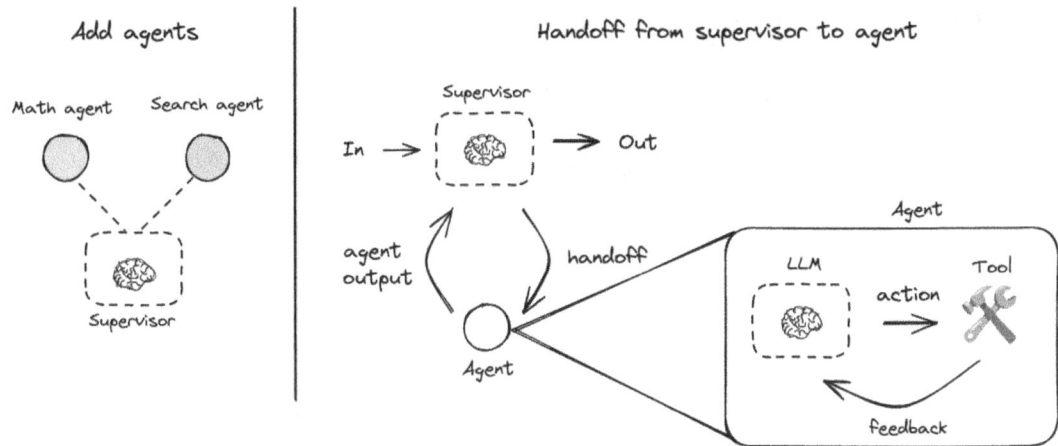

Figure 10-57. The supervisor pattern

Configure the Python library as follows:

```
pip install langgraph-supervisor
pip install langgraph-supervisor langchain-openai
export OPENAI_API_KEY=<your_api_key>
```

The following code is a supervisor workflow that works with the Streamlit provided by the framework. It is the same as a typical LangGraph supervisor.

```
def add(a: float, b: float) -> float:
    """Add two numbers."""
    return a + b

def multiply(a: float, b: float) -> float:
    """Multiply two numbers."""
    return a * b

def web_search(query: str) -> str:
    """Search the web for information."""
    return (
        "Here are the headcounts for each of the FAANG companies in 2024:\n"
        "1. **Facebook (Meta)**: 67,317 employees.\n"
        "2. **Apple**: 164,000 employees.\n"
        "3. **Amazon**: 1,551,000 employees.\n"
        "4. **Netflix**: 14,000 employees.\n"
        "5. **Google (Alphabet)**: 181,269 employees."
    )
```

869

```python
math_agent = create_react_agent(
    model=model,
    tools=[add, multiply],
    name="math_expert",
    prompt="You are a math expert. Always use one tool at a time.",
).with_config(tags=["skip_stream"])

research_agent = create_react_agent(
    model=model,
    tools=[web_search],
    name="research_expert",
    prompt="You are a world class researcher with access to web search. Do not do
    any math.",
).with_config(tags=["skip_stream"])

# Create supervisor workflow
workflow = create_supervisor(
    [research_agent, math_agent],
    model=model,
    prompt=(
        "You are a team supervisor managing a research expert and a math expert. "
        "For current events, use research_agent. "
        "For math problems, use math_agent."
    ),
    add_handoff_back_messages=False,
)

langgraph_supervisor_agent = workflow.compile(checkpointer=MemorySaver(),
store=InMemoryStore())
```

I've already described five workflows. The framework is organized so that LangGraph and Streamlit are interfaced, and it is easy to add different workflows.

The Streamlit screen, shown in Figure 10-58, allows you to select different models and workflows. It creates thread and user IDs.

CHAPTER 10 AIOPS RCA

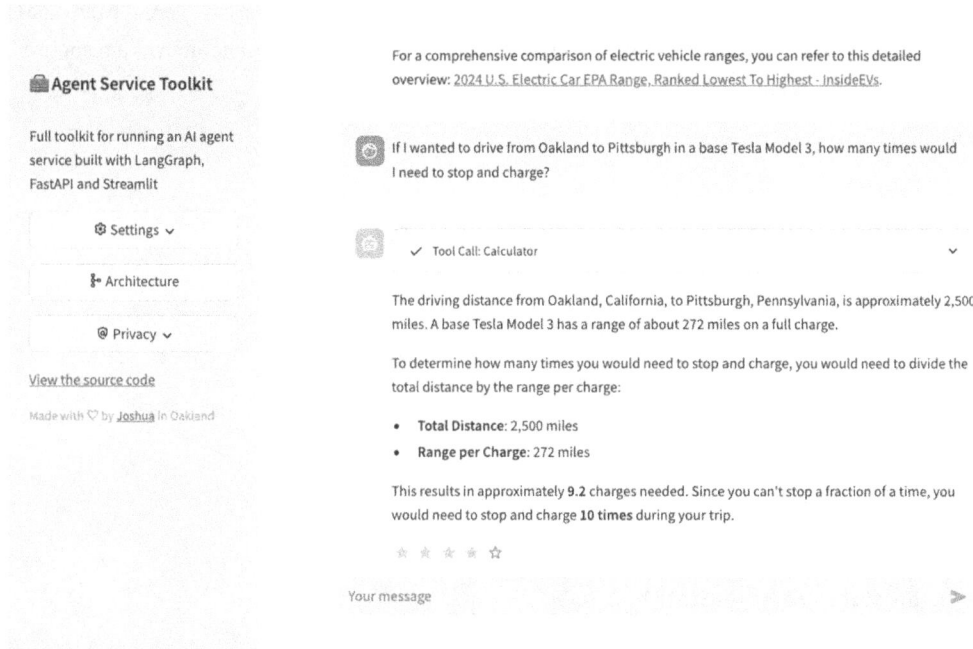

Figure 10-58. *The Streamlit user interface*

Using the LangGraph StateGraph, the workflow can be easily interfaced to the OpenSearch MCP. You used the MCP server to connect agents and various applications, and the MCP client to connect with channels.

10.6.5.5. Speech Recognition

Speech recognition is an AI agent that combines natural language processing and long-term memory to provide a more intuitive and adaptive experience. Like Twilio, it's also possible to process incoming calls directly into speech recognition. This demo doesn't use Twilio, but here's how it handles speech recognition:

- OpenAI's Whisper is used for speech-to-text conversion.
- The text is passed to LangGraph, which in turn connects with OpenSearch tools.
- ElevenLabs is used for text-to-speech.

Speech recognition is necessary for the agent to gather knowledge and learn like a human.

It's important to keep the different channels connected to the same backend LangGraph whenever possible. This is because even if the channels are different, the agents must be identical to share the same memory. If you use different agents for different channels, the user will experience a different service for each channel.

The underlying logic is the LangGraph workflow, which needs to be added to the `bind_tools` API in `task_maistro.py` to access the OpenSearch knowledge base.

871

A LangGraph requires a StateGraph, and you can configure the workflow using get_tools, bind_tools, and ToolNode. Rather than a simple question and answer, you can enrich the text generated as a response by registering the OpenSearch knowledge base as a tool.

```
client = MultiServerMCPClient({
        "opensearch": {
            "url": f"{opensearch_server}/_plugins/_ml/mcp/sse?append_to_base_url=true",
            "transport": "sse",
            "headers": {
                "Content-Type": "application/json",
                "Accept-Encoding": "identity",
            }
        }
    })

tools = await client.get_tools()

def call_model(state: MessagesState):
    response = model.bind_tools(tools).invoke(state["messages"])
    return {"messages": response}

builder = StateGraph(MessagesState)
builder.add_node(call_model)
builder.add_node(ToolNode(tools))
builder.add_edge(START, "call_model")
builder.add_conditional_edges(
    "call_model",
    tools_condition,
)
builder.add_edge("tools", "call_model")
graph = builder.compile()
```

Speech recognition is associated with the MCP server, and Slackbot is associated with the MCP client.

10.6.5.6. Slackbot

When a failure occurs, it's common to invite engineers from various departments to a Slack channel to identify the problem and discuss solutions.

Leaders invite dozens of engineers to join the discussion. The more complex the problem, and the larger the organization, the more inefficient and time-consuming the communication becomes. It's hard to find experts in the organization who can solve the problem, so I created Slackbots that are experts in a specific field and trained them on failure experiences and troubleshooting skills to improve root cause analysis. Slack is an effective communication tool and offers many features. Here's how it works:

- A Slackbot is created in Slack. Different agents are connected to different knowledge bases and have different knowledge. For example, a product owner agent, SRE agent, architect agent, and platform agent all have different expertise.

- When a failure occurs, you invite as many agents to the Slack channel as you think are needed for discussion.

- You can ask the platform agents if the SRE agent's response is correct or if they have additional comments. You can invite multiple agents to confirm or rebut a particular agent's response. For example, if the platform agent rebuts, it might be possible for the product owner agent to rebut.

- If you use multiple commercial observability, you can create a DataDog Slackbot and a Dynatrace Slackbot. You can invite both Slackbots to the channel to discuss root cause analysis.

- The human and Slackbot can collaborate, asking and answering questions together. In this way, you can have a discussion between agents to analyze the root cause.

Slack can be used to improve root cause analysis in a number of ways. You can pair it with a LangGraph workflow. Workflows and Slackbots are different.

- **Workflow method:** Receive events in Slack, process them in a workflow, and respond to Slack.

- **Slackbot method:** Configure the MCP client and add a Slackbot to the channel that corresponds to an expert. The Slackbot continuously maintains a state of past experience and knowledge.

When you create a Slack message, it sends a webhook. These are received by n8n, and can be associated with MCP and AI agents.

This Slackbot leverages the Model Context Protocol (MCP) to enhance its capabilities using external tools. It acts as an AI-powered assistant, responding to messages in channels and DM using LLM capabilities from OpenAI, Groq, and Anthropic. The bot seamlessly integrates with MCP tools like SQLite databases and web fetching, exposing them via Slack's interface. Its architecture comprises a `SlackMCPBot` core, an `LLMClient` for API communication, a server for MCP interactions, and tool representations. The bot processes messages by sending them to the LLM, executing tool calls if requested, and delivering the final interpreted response to the user, all accessible through direct messages, channel mentions, and an informative App Home tab.

Start the Slackbot as shown in Figure 10-59.

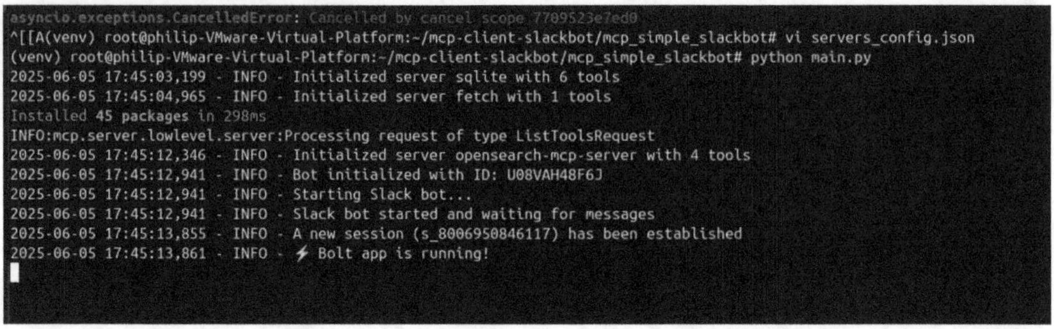

CHAPTER 10 AIOPS RCA

```
asyncio.exceptions.CancelledError: Cancelled by cancel scope 7789523e7ed0
^[[A(venv) root@philip-VMware-Virtual-Platform:~/mcp-client-slackbot/mcp_simple_slackbot# vi servers_config.json
(venv) root@philip-VMware-Virtual-Platform:~/mcp-client-slackbot/mcp_simple_slackbot# python main.py
2025-06-05 17:45:03,199 - INFO - Initialized server sqlite with 6 tools
2025-06-05 17:45:04,965 - INFO - Initialized server fetch with 1 tools
Installed 45 packages in 298ms
INFO:mcp.server.lowlevel.server:Processing request of type ListToolsRequest
2025-06-05 17:45:12,346 - INFO - Initialized server opensearch-mcp-server with 4 tools
2025-06-05 17:45:12,941 - INFO - Bot initialized with ID: U08VAH48F6J
2025-06-05 17:45:12,941 - INFO - Starting Slack bot...
2025-06-05 17:45:12,941 - INFO - Slack bot started and waiting for messages
2025-06-05 17:45:13,855 - INFO - A new session (s_8006950846117) has been established
2025-06-05 17:45:13,861 - INFO - ⚡ Bolt app is running!
```

Figure 10-59. The Slackbot log

You can create Slackbots for the SREs, architects, and platform agents, which then need to add information from the OpenSearch MCP server. When the Slackbot is asked a question, it uses MCP to get knowledge from the OpenSearch knowledge base and then answers it.

```
{
    "mcpServers": {
        "opensearch-mcp-server": {
            "command": "uvx",
            "args": ["mcp_server_opensearch"],
            "env": {
                "OPENSEARCH_URL": "<your_opensearch_domain_url>",
                "OPENSEARCH_USERNAME": "<your_opensearch_domain_username>",
                "OPENSEARCH_PASSWORD": "<your_opensearch_domain_password>",
            }
        }
    }
}
```

Currently, Slackbots are not integrated with LangGraph workflows, but in the future, Slackbots should be aligned with workflows. Slackbots require agents to be configured to share memories and experiences with Streamlit and speech recognition channels. For example, it can be problematic if Streamlit and speech recognition agents remember the cause and solution of a particular failure, but Slackbots do not. Even if you have multiple channels, the workflows and agents on the backend should be configured as one, sharing memories and experiences. They need to provide the same user experience to improve service.

If your Slackbot isn't integrated with your workflow, but instead saves conversations in Slack channels, summarizes them in a database, and queries the channel's transcript in a tool, it can be a way to share memories across different channels. There's a lot of useful information in Slack channels, so it's important to provide the ability to view and search it, and configure it to be shared across channels. See Figure 10-60.

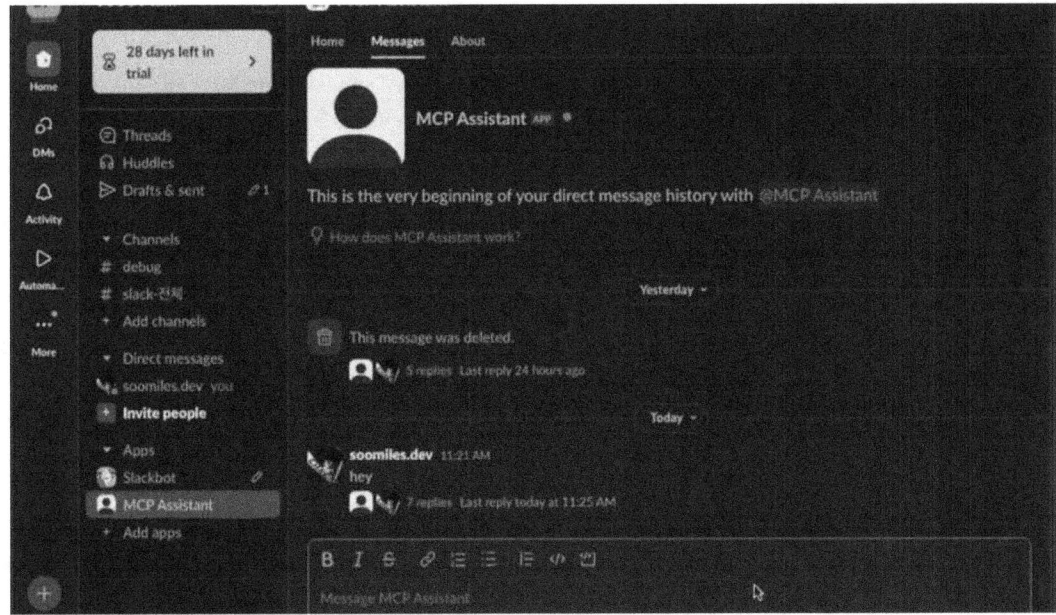

Figure 10-60. The Slackbot UI

There are several reasons to define multiple Slackbots rather than a single Slackbot.

- Queries made by a single Slackbot require frequent full scans and take a long time to process.
- Using a single Slackbot is more expensive due to full scanning.
- It's difficult to rebut or discuss between Slackbots.
- If you have separate knowledge bases within your company, it makes sense to separate your Slackbots accordingly.
- It makes sense to connect to other knowledge bases and increase expertise.

In the future, the way we develop and operate with AI agents will change—agents will be running all the time, collecting and applying a variety of information from speech recognition, Streamlit text, and Slackbots to answer questions like senior engineers.

Users can choose workflows on the Streamlit screen. However, Slack doesn't provide the ability to select a workflow from the screen, but instead requires you to select an agent implemented as a Slackbot. Streamlit is organized around workflows, while Slack is organized around agents. Streamlit and Slack need to share memory.

10.6.5.7. Workflow Automation

You can automate a variety of applications and provide automated AI services with MCP. In some cases, custom development is required, such as for LangGraph, but in simple cases, n8n can be developed quickly.

Example 1: Automating Various e-Commerce Channels and ODOO ERP

eBay, Amazon, Shopify, and ODOO ERP are popular applications in e-commerce. Shopify is the channel, where customers create orders. The orders should also be created in the backend, in the ODOO ERP. In addition to this, orders, products, customers, and inventory information needs to be linked between Shopify and ODOO ERP. AI can be used to automate the interface between the applications.

Shopify and ODOO ERP provide an MCP server, which allows you to view and manage data from Shopify and ODOO ERP via WeChat chat. When an event occurs in Shopify and ODOO ERP, you can send a message to WeChat.

Uncomplicated inter-application and MCP connections do not require a LangGraph workflow. LangGraph can develop more detailed functionality, but for non-complex requirements, n8n is all you need. n8n provides templates for connecting Shopify and ODOO ERP, so you can use them to link order, product, customer, and inventory data between Shopify and ODOO ERP. It can be implemented in a short period of time with little development effort and cost.

n8n can connect with various channels and trigger events in real-time. n8n can call LangGraph workflows. In this way, it is possible to interface n8n and LangGraph workflows.

Example 2: Twilio, MCP, and OpenAI Automation

The most frequently used channel in the service industry is the phone. Customers call and ask a variety of questions over the phone. Twilio provides AI capabilities that can respond to incoming calls with voice.

The voice is converted to text and fed to a backend AI. The backend processes internal knowledge bases, ERP, Google email, Google Calendar, SMS, inventory, and price comparisons, which are then transcribed into speech through Twilio before responding to the customer. The MCP can call on internal knowledge bases, ERP, Google Calendar, inventory, price comparisons, and any other tools it needs, meaning Twilio and the MCP must be connected.

n8n provides the ability to receive events from Twilio and connect with the MCP server on the backend. You could use a LangGraph, but if your requirements are not complex, n8n could be a good solution.

10.6.5.8. AI Observability

LangChain and LangGraph workflows contain many complex processing steps and are prone to unexpected errors and delays. Internal knowledge bases are likely to experience frequent pull-scans, and MCP connections are likely to be overloaded.

LangSmith and LangGraph Studio may have future licensing issues, and the technology does not support standards like OpenTelemetry. In many ways, it is inconsistent with the direction of observability, which is to support the full spectrum.

- Connecting applications without human intervention
- Workflows with human intervention

Both approaches require monitoring. This is because it is difficult to link applications and operate workflows without step-by-step monitoring. When introducing new technologies, it's easy to focus on development and not consider operations, which makes it difficult to respond to failures.

The concept of E2E trace applies equally to workflow and MCP operations.

OpenTelemetry focuses on tracing channels and workflows, while MCP servers and the applications that connect to them are often not traced. OpenLLMetry compensates for the limitations of OpenTelemetry. For example, it allows you to instrument LangGraph, MCP servers, and Vector databases.

While ReAct agents are relatively simple to process and therefore easy to monitor, asynchronous plan-execute agents are more complex internally.

HITL and supervisor workflows are complex and can take a long time to process.

AI applications are processed through channels, web frameworks, workflows, agents, tools, MCP clients, MCP servers, and legacy applications. In complex cases, there can be dozens of workflows.

The demo is shown next.

- OpenLLMetry
- OpenTelemetry Gen AI
- LangGraph and FastAPI manual instrumentation with OpenTelemetry

Using LangSmith and LangFuse is a good option, but it is paid, requires a license, and is not a good solution for building full-scale observability. I do not recommend using a standalone solution for AI observability. Even though you pay for them, they don't help you analyze root causes.

OpenLLMetry is a set of extensions built on top of OpenTelemetry that gives you complete observability over your LLM application. Because it uses OpenTelemetry under the hood, it can be connected to your existing observability solutions—DataDog, Honeycomb, and others.

The trace output to the Traceloop is shown in Figure 10-61.

CHAPTER 10 AIOPS RCA

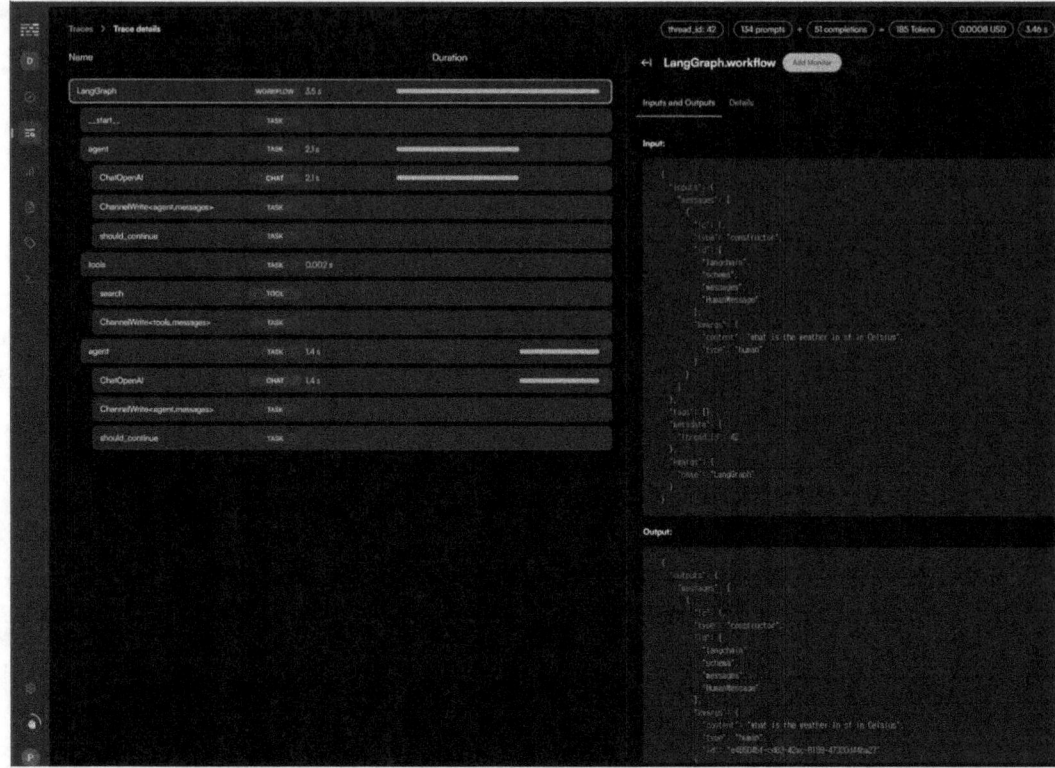

Figure 10-61. OpenLLMetry output

In the existing LangGraph source, add the following two lines

- `from traceloop.sdk import Traceloop`
- `Traceloop.init(app_name="langgraph_example")`

The full source is shown here:

```
# Define the function that calls the model
def call_model(state: MessagesState):
    messages = state["messages"]
    response = model.invoke(messages)
    # We return a list, because this will get added to the existing list
    return {"messages": [response]}

# Define a new graph
workflow = StateGraph(MessagesState)

# Define the two nodes we will cycle between
workflow.add_node("agent", call_model)
```

```python
workflow.add_node("tools", tool_node)

# Set the entrypoint as `agent`
# This means that this node is the first one called
workflow.set_entry_point("agent")

# We now add a conditional edge
workflow.add_conditional_edges(
    # First, we define the start node. We use `agent`.
    # This means these are the edges taken after the `agent` node is called.
    "agent",
    # Next, we pass in the function that will determine which node is called next.
    should_continue,
)

workflow.add_edge("tools", "agent")

# Initialize memory to persist state between graph runs
checkpointer = MemorySaver()

app = workflow.compile(checkpointer=checkpointer)

final_state = app.invoke(
    {"messages": [HumanMessage(content="what is the weather in sf in Celsius")]},
    config={"configurable": {"thread_id": 42}},
)

print(final_state["messages"][-1].content)
```

The client calls the FastAPI, which tracks the entire process of invoking the LangGraph workflow and generates spans. See Figure 10-62.

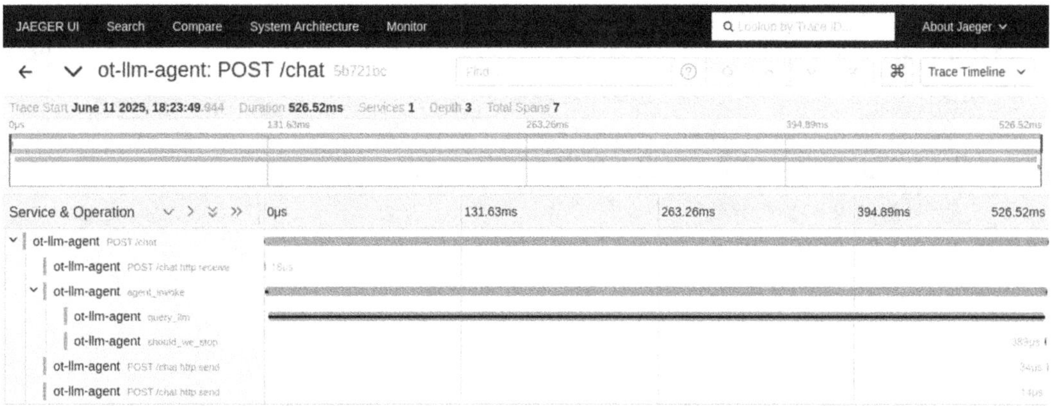

Figure 10-62. LangGraph trace output

CHAPTER 10   AIOPS RCA

The agent sources are as follows:

```python
def query_llm(state: OverallState) -> dict:
    local_client = client_large.bind_tools(tools)
    result = local_client.invoke(
        [
            SystemMessage(
                content="You are a helpful assistant. Use the wikipedia tool when
                necessary."
            )
        ]
        + state.messages
    )
    trace.get_current_span().set_attribute("query", state.messages[-1].content)
    trace.get_current_span().set_attribute("response", result.content)

    input_tokens_counter.add(
        result.usage_metadata["input_tokens"], {"model": client_large.model_name}
    )
    output_tokens_counter.add(
        result.usage_metadata["output_tokens"], {"model": client_large.model_name}
    )

    return {"messages": [result]}

@trace.get_tracer("opentelemetry.instrumentation.custom").start_as_current_span(
    "should_we_stop"
)
```

The servers that make up the FastAPI include:

```python
def chat_route(query: Query, request: Request) -> Response:
    """Handles chat requests."""
    try:
        thread_id = query.thread_id
        logger.info(f"Started processing {thread_id=}")
        message = query.message
        agent: CompiledGraph = request.state.agent

        config = {"configurable": {"thread_id": thread_id}}

        new_state = OverallState(messages=[HumanMessage(content=message)])

        final_state_dict = agent.invoke(new_state, config=config)
```

```
        final_state = OverallState(**final_state_dict)

        if not final_state.messages or not isinstance(final_state.messages, list):
            raise HTTPException(
                status_code=500, detail="Agent failed to generate a response."
            )

        response_message = final_state.messages[-1].content
        return Response(message=response_message)

    except Exception as e:
        logger.error("Processing failed")
        raise HTTPException(status_code=500, detail=f"An error occurred: {e}")
```

The Instrumentation Library is being developed within the OpenTelemetry Python Contrib under the instrumentation-genai project to automate telemetry collection for Generative AI applications. The first release is a Python library for instrumenting OpenAI client calls. This library captures spans and events, gathering essential data like model inputs, response metadata, and token usage in a structured format.

```
dotenv run -- opentelemetry-instrument python3 main.py
In realms of code where shadows play,
OpenTelemetry lights the way,
With traces woven, metrics gleam,
It captures whispers of each dream.

{
    "name": "chat gpt-4o-mini",
    "context": {
        "trace_id": "0x40584e0bf400607446aefc86a40ce04d",
        "span_id": "0x33b2cd235c684482",
        "trace_state": "[]"
    },
    "kind": "SpanKind.CLIENT",
    "parent_id": null,
    "start_time": "2025-06-10T12:13:39.175298Z",
    "end_time": "2025-06-10T12:14:00.282252Z",
    "status": {
        "status_code": "UNSET"
    },
    "attributes": {
        "gen_ai.operation.name": "chat",
        "gen_ai.system": "openai",
        "gen_ai.request.model": "gpt-4o-mini",
```

```
            "server.address": "api.openai.com",
            "gen_ai.response.model": "gpt-4o-mini-2024-07-18",
            "gen_ai.response.finish_reasons": [
                "stop"
            ],
            "gen_ai.response.id": "chatcmpl-Bgs9DOoL8Soeu44liNPIjASZNlPAw",
            "gen_ai.openai.request.service_tier": "default",
            "gen_ai.usage.input_tokens": 15,
            "gen_ai.usage.output_tokens": 152
        },
        "events": [],
        "links": [],
        "resource": {
            "attributes": {
                "telemetry.sdk.language": "python",
                "telemetry.sdk.name": "opentelemetry",
                "telemetry.sdk.version": "1.30.0",
                "service.name": "opentelemetry-python-openai",
                "telemetry.auto.version": "0.51b0"
            },
            "schema_url": ""
        }
}
```

There are seven steps to trace, as follows:

1. Trace starts in Streamlet, Speech Recognition, and Slack.
2. The channel is passed to the FastAPI server, which passes it to the RAG Vector database.
3. FastAPI starts the LangGraph workflow.
4. The LangGraph node is processed and invokes the agent.
5. The agent binds with the MCP server and invokes the tool.
6. MCP clients can call the MCP server.
7. The MCP server calls various third-party applications.

OpenTelemetry provides good support for agents, workflows, and MCP servers.

10.6.5.9. RAG Case Study

Vector embeddings and semantic search are case studies. Vector embeddings and semantic search are often required. By applying vector embeddings and semantic search, Confluence and Slack can improve the relevance of searches and serve as a RAG knowledge base. See Figure 10-63.

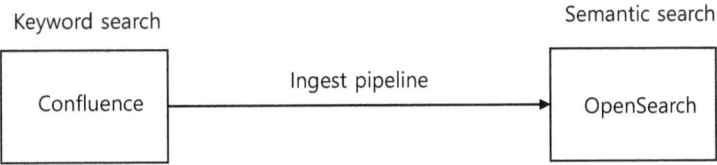

Figure 10-63. *Confluence ingest pipeline*

- **Confluence search:** Confluence is a repository of useful documents. However, it only supports keyword search, so the relevance of the search is low. You need to apply RAG to configure hybrid and semantic search. Confluence offers an OpenSearch plugin. OpenSearch uses an ingest pipeline to handle vector embedding.
- **Slack search:** After collecting Slack conversations, applying vector embeddings enables semantic search.

In this book, you configure OpenSearch in a variety of ways. It is a good example of how OpenSearch can be used to compensate for the shortcomings of Confluence, and to organize semantic search and AIOps.

10.6.5.10. The RCA Case Study

This book provides two RAGs:

- **Observability RAG:** Infers the approximate failure type based on observability errors. For example, if an error is identified in the observability index, the failure list can be inferred.
- **Root Cause Analysis RAG:** Infers 400 detailed failure lists from all incoming signals and data. When a delay is identified in the root cause analysis index, the cause of the delay can be inferred.

Root cause analysis defines different workflows:

- SRE identify error messages and MTTR.
- Platform engineers identify 95th percentile delays coming from system resources.
- First-line engineers use anomaly detection to identify outliers in various SLO, ratio, and frequency.

Different roles have different approaches and workflows.

CHAPTER 10　AIOPS RCA

With detailed error messages, logs can calculate technical as well as business failures, data consistency, and customer losses. The problem with metrics is that they are not intuitive and the values are hard to understand. This is because metrics measure rates and represent variability in data.

When errors occur, it's easy to identify the problem. Latency is harder to identify and more complex. There are many reasons for latency. For example:

- Slow loading images on the frontend, or a sudden increase in Kafka's consumer lag. CPU throttling or full garbage collection.

- Resource exhaustion caused by another service sharing physical hardware that is resource intensive.

- A DDoS attack by a malicious user, or a spike or dip in requests is evidence of a problem.

Distributed trace can detect retries, multi-threaded issues, timeouts, locks, rebalancing, cache hits, memory leaks, resource exhaustion, slow queries, incorrect resource settings, sequential processing, error handling, and more. Although tracing does not provide detailed information about system resources and only outputs service delays, it does provide many clues to speculate about failures related to system resources.

- By default, traces only span remote calls, but you should try to span threaded calls with span annotations.

- Traces do not have method calls, and profiles do, but you can use span annotations to generate spans from method calls.

You need to understand how to use distributed traces for root cause analysis. Spans in a distributed trace provide clues to understanding service delays.

- You can identify anomaly and delays in the 99th percentile of spans for an endpoint. The 99th percentile identified by the metrics provides an exemplar, but it is difficult to identify the cause of the delay. Metrics are aggregate data and are not suitable for anomaly detection and AI training data.

- With FluentBit, you can capture HTTP message bodies and generate events. Since batches also often use REST, events can help you understand what's wrong with a batch. Since the start, end, and status updates of a batch are handled by REST, it's easy to understand problems with a batch.

- You can identify system tracing through the thread number in the span attribute. By enabling system trace when needed and correlating it with distributed trace by thread number, you can get clear answers about nano second-level delays. Analyzing system resources is difficult. You should use system trace to understand the context of system resources and eBPF for additional profiles. In this way, you can correlate events, distributed traces, and system traces.

- Network span delays, 99th percentile span delays, and delays related to client resources and documents that can be caused by CDN, load balancer, and so on are difficult to answer with tracing alone. You should focus on narrowing down the problem with distributed trace. You need to understand how to use distributed traces for root cause analysis. Spans in a distributed trace provide clues to understanding service delays.

Most commercial observability handle root cause analysis like this:

- They clearly understand the failure and define its specification. They determine if an attribute exists in the data and build queries using the attributes. Once the data is collected, you can write queries that can identify any type of failure. If the attributes are lacking, add attributes if they exist in the data and refine the query to unambiguously identify the failure.

- Create and transform indexes by failure in your trace data. For example, define a query to identify incorrect resource settings, lock delays, and so on that are identifiable in the trace, and create a transformed index.

- Apply anomaly detection, 99th percentile, and histograms on the transformed index. If you have raw data, you can apply anomaly detection and generate alert with histograms and quantiles.

Metrics can further summarize availability, error rates, and more. Alerts can be sent to the summarized results as 99th percentile and histograms. Traces use a similar method. You can create an index that summarizes a portion of the trace, and through detailed analysis, you can identify the type of failure. See Figure 10-64.

CHAPTER 10 AIOPS RCA

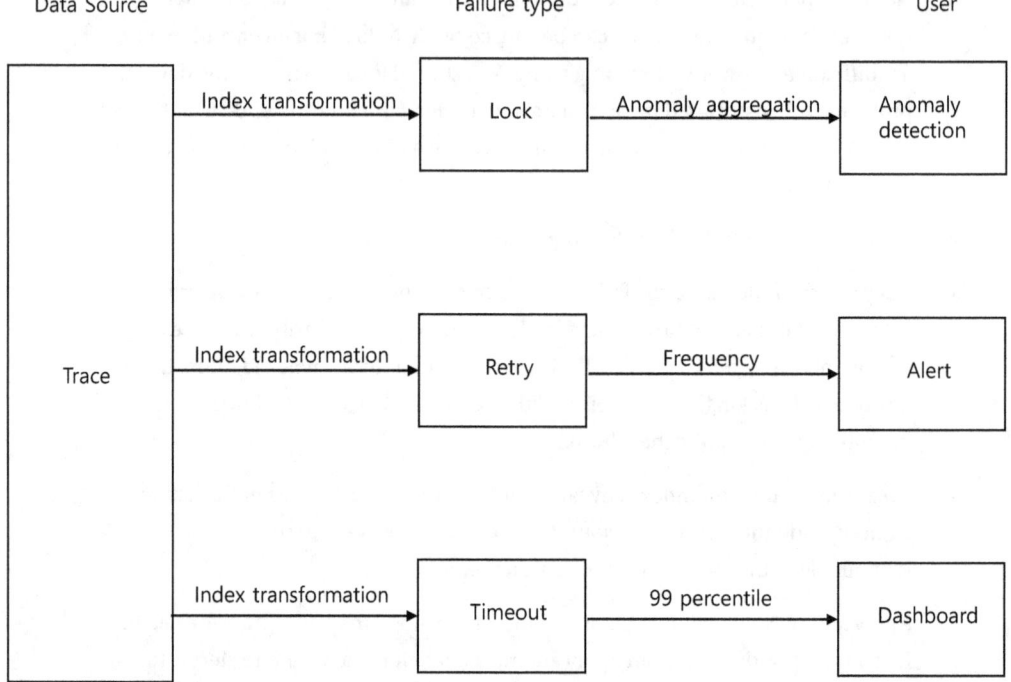

Figure 10-64. The RCA flow

The following issues were encountered during the index transform process:

- Anomaly detection does not support indexes with complex structures such as objects and nested commands. You can transform the index structure to be suitable for anomaly detection through index transform.

- Trace indexes, log indexes, and metric indexes are sometimes difficult to join. Using the OpenSearch Machine Learning Python library, you can convert them to Pandas data frames and join them easily.

- The resulting indexes from anomaly detection can be flattened and aggregated. You can get the trace and span IDs where the problem occurred.

The index transformation is shown in Figure 10-65. You can output the trace ID, span ID, and the end time.

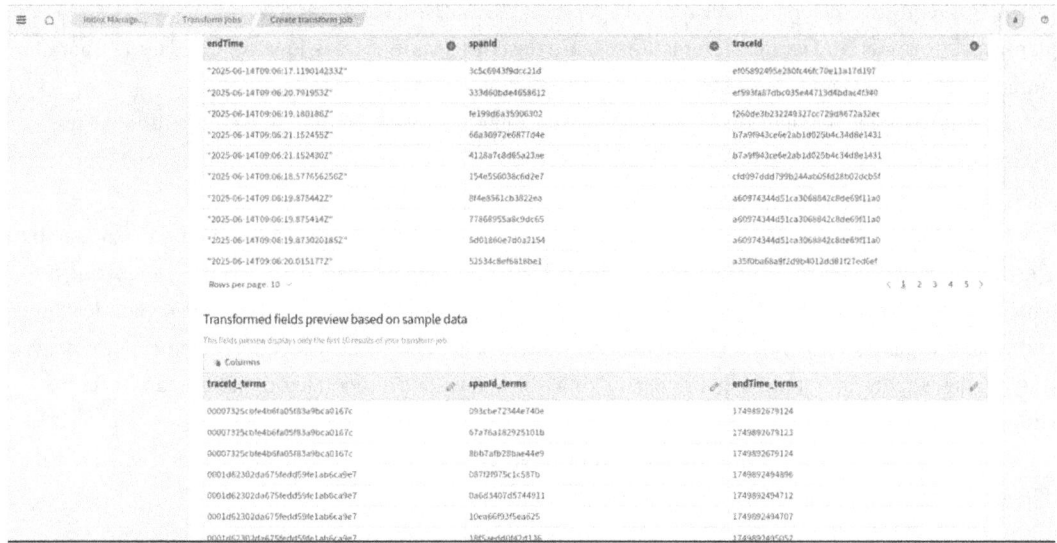

Figure 10-65. Index transform UI

Using index transformations and a Python library, you can develop a query that can identify failure types from traces. It is difficult to write a query to identify failure types using only current AI and LLM techniques. You should develop a query that can identify failure types first, and then consider automating it.

10.7. Summary

This chapter talked about IT operations as a whole, not just AI. Just as development is defined by SDLC, agile, and sprint, IT operations is one big domain. It includes data and processes, and it needs to be run effectively from an organizational and cost perspective.

I have a different take on IT operations as a whole. While a lot of money and labor is invested in developing a CMDB, the introduction of observability has a significant impact on the CMDB. Observability supports most of what is needed for IT operations, including entity, deployment, and so on, so there is overlap with the CMDB, which means there is no longer a need for redundant CMDB development. I believe the future direction is to reduce the cost and labor required for CMDB development and focus more on AI workflow for IT operations and root cause analysis.

Rather than simply introducing the technology, this book focuses on what constitutes successful observability and AIOps. A deep understanding of data and processes is required to achieve your goals, not just a technical understanding.

The more dashboards, SLO, workflows, agents, pipelines, and interfaces you have, the harder they are to maintain, and the more complex your architecture becomes. AIOps can only succeed if you have a deep understanding of your business and technology.

CHAPTER 10 AIOPS RCA

AIOps requires efficient organization of agents and RAG. Use a LangGraph workflow to organize ReAct, plan-execute agents, and various interactions. I also described various workflows required for IT operations automation, as well as advanced features such as reranking and post-processing.

LLM can provide detailed answers to root cause analysis, including individual failures and delays. However, the prompts need to be improved to provide detailed answers. By recording detailed failures in the knowledge base, you can augment the prompts and make LLM more accurate.

For AIOps to be successful, data is important, and it must be organized correctly in the Vector database. The hundreds of organized failure cases can be used as a knowledge base. But in practice, organizing this data, regardless of its technical difficulty, is a challenge. It requires collaboration between senior developers and various organizations. This book emphasizes cross-organizational collaboration beyond technology. If senior developers do not disclose important know-how, it will be difficult to organize an accurate knowledge base.

If AI is used as part of a restructuring effort in an organization, the company's approach will make it difficult to get the full cooperation of developers.

For AIOps to be successful, individuals, companies, and organizations need to be on the right track.

Most of this book is about how to correct bad data. The remaining pages briefly discuss how to automate with AI. That's because it's important to organize your data correctly. It's not uncommon for operational data to be poorly organized, resulting in joins that fail, insufficient and unclear semantics, lack of context, omissions, duplications, poorly organized relationships and structures, and breaks. There are many reasons for this: lack of development standards, developers don't follow standards, SRE misconfigure, senior developers don't share know-how. You can't use RAG, agent, and MCP to automate AI if the data isn't right. If you're an organization that's been running legacy for a long time, these issues are the same. Everyone in the organization needs to understand the technology and work together towards the same goal. In reality, this is not possible.

It used adapter to integrate many legacy applications and configure observability across the board. This chapter discussed how to use observability agent to properly collect business, application, and system data, and how to use AI agent to automate the data collected. There is a need to integrate different types of adapter and agent and manage them effectively.

If the data is organized correctly, the LLM has a better chance of success. However, the users of the LLM results also need to have a certain level of knowledge. This is because they need to be able to determine whether the LLM results are accurate or inaccurate.

Index

A

Aggregation
    anomaly detection, 604
    Druid (*see* Druid aggregations)
    machine learning, 584
    Presto (*see* Presto case study)
    Promscale, 635
AIOps, *see* Artificial intelligence for IT operations (AIOps)
Amazon Web Services (AWS), 199–202
Analyzing individual transactions
    inefficient method, 29
    limitations, 30
    parallel processing
        balance, 34
        concurrency, 34
        error messages, 35
        locks, 35, 36
        race condition, 34
        synchronization, 33, 34
    process order, 30–32
    profiles, 29, 30
    retry setting, 31
    sequential and parallel processes, 31, 32
    thread process, 31
    trace matches, 29
    transaction processing, 30
Anomaly detection
    analysis techniques, 592–604
    approaches, 572
    configuration
        detectors, 600, 601, 603
        filters, 603
        multi-feature models, 601, 602
        OpenSearch process, 599, 600
        real-time detector, 602
        visualization, 603
        window latency, 604
    features, 574
    infrastructure errors, 571
    missing data, 578
    ML (*see* Machine learning (ML))
    OpenSearch, 573
    performance latency, 572
    retransmissions, 572
API, *see* Application programming interface (API)
Application programming interface (API), 382
    anomaly detection, 594
    banking industry, 321
    correlation, 723
    EAI server, 328
    flask and exporting, 325–328
    gRPC client, 323, 324
    Kafka server, 324, 325
    server processing, 765, 766
Application Transaction Monitor Interface (ATMI), 293
Artificial intelligence for IT operations (AIOps), 393, 713, 755
    anomaly detection, 571
    architecture, 9

INDEX

Artificial intelligence for IT operations
    (AIOps) (*cont.*)
  cloud systems, 10
  commercial observability, 10
  concrete demonstration, 10
  correlation (*see* Correlation)
  dashboard, 10
  data analysts, 11
  data model (*see* Failure list data model)
  garbage collection, 716
  microservices patterns, 10
  ML (*see* Machine learning (ML))
  Nginx application
    approaches, 720
    blocking system, 717
    business process, 719
    commercial observability, 718
    compression, 717
    correlation analysis, 720
    downstream, 718
    implementation, 719
    metrics, 718
    Multiplexed IO, 716
    Non-blocking IO, 716
    parameters, 716
    process requests and
      responses, 717
    service maps and polystats, 719
    TLS encryption, 717
    upstream and connection, 717
  OpenSearch (*see* OpenSearch
    database)
  operational data
    alerts, 731, 734
    analyzing failures, 730
    anomaly detection, 729
    automation possibilities, 731
    autoscaling, 742–755
    CMDB (*see* Configuration
      management database (CMDB))
    commercial observability, 729
    cost operation, 736
    dashboards, 731, 732
    data, 729
    data analytics, 733
    data and structure, 733
    data lake, 729
    data sources, 730, 731
    data sources/visualization, 734
    deployment and rollback
      information, 730
    entities, 737
    errors, 735
    maintenance, 730
    organizations, 736
    performance, 736
    resource configurations, 731
    resources, 736
    slack implementation, 735
    time-consuming services, 733
    traditional monitoring, 733
  pipeline architecture, 432–438
  RAGs (*see* Retrieval-Augmented
    Generation (RAG))
  RUNNABLE/WAITING state, 715, 716
ATMI, *see* Application Transaction
    Monitor Interface (ATMI)
Autoscaling techniques, 742
  components, 742
  containers, 742
  custom metrics, 744
  horizontal/vertical scaling, 743
  KEDA monitors, 751–755
  Kubernetes, 743
  metric calculation and
    implementation, 744

metrics, 742
orchestration/management, 743
pod-level/node-level autoscale, 744
Prometheus adapter, 745, 746
    adapter process, 745
    configuration, 751
    discovery, 748
    metrics screen, 750
    naming, 748
    querying, 749
    working process, 746–748
replica sets, 742
standard metrics, 744
AWS, *see* Amazon Web Services (AWS)

B

Banking identification code (BIC), 308
Banking industry
    business process, 284
        advantages/disadvantages, 285
        client-side implementation, 285
        concurrency issues, 284, 285
        consistency issues, 286
        double-bookkeeping system, 288
        event sourcing, 286
        fund transfer transaction, 285
        idempotence, 289, 290
        idempotent key, 285
        payment systems, 288, 289
        reconciliation files, 287, 288
        retry/failed message queue, 288
        synchronization, 286, 287
    demo process
        advantages, 317
        API server, 320
        architecture, 319
        backoffice, 317
        commercial observability, 322
        core banking, 317
        EAI servers, 318, 321
        enterprise applications, 318
        flow processing, 318
        frontoffice/backoffice, 319
        manual/automated
            instrumentation, 320
        microservices, 317
        middleware, 316
        payment system, 318
        requests and responses, 319
        sequence, 320
    EAI server, 328
    flask and exporting server, 325–328
    gRPC client, 323, 324
    Kafka server, 324, 325
    legacy systems, 284
        account/information
            systems, 290
        batches and file transfers, 307, 308
        CASmf administration, 310
        CICS, 296–301
        core banks, 290
        DataStage, 314, 315
        E2E trace implementation, 293
        EAI server, 292, 328–330
        FileNet process, 315, 316
        integration process, 291, 292
        Korean banking, 291
        Lotus Notes, 311–313
        MDM server, 304, 305
        MQSeries, 313, 314
        Oracle ERP, 305–307
        SAP ERP, 301–303
        SWIFT networks, 308–311
        transaction processing, 291
        Tuxedo, 293–296

INDEX

Banking industry (*cont.*)
    transfer-Jaeger, 330–333
    troubleshoot problems, 284
BAPI, *see* Business Application
    Programming Interface (BAPI)
BIC, *see* Banking identification code (BIC)
Billing Revenue Management
    (BRM), 354–356
BRM, *see* Billing Revenue
    Management (BRM)
BPM, *see* Business process
    management (BPM)
BSS, *see* Business support systems (BSS)
Business Application Programming
    Interface (BAPI), 301
Business process management (BPM)
    FileNet process, 315, 316
Business support systems (BSS), 338

C

Central processing unit (CPU)
    kernel system, 480
    system traces, 477
Chaos engineering
    accidental configuration, 529
    anomaly detection, 528
    benefits, 531
    change management, 531
    definition of, 529
    demo application, 532
        application errors, 534
        configuration, 532–535
        experiments, 535
        feature flags, 533
        network faults, 533
        network policies, 532
        platform faults, 534
        retransmission status, 535
        types, 534
    experimental process, 530
    experiment creation, 531
    experiments, 529, 530
    external maintenance, 531
    failure scenarios, 528
    infrastructure, 528
    Kubernetes configuration, 535–537
    propagation and risk, 530
    real-world events, 530
    retransmission analysis
        data process, 539–541
        filtering/searching, 537
        filter packets, 537
        network state changes, 539
        SEQ and ACK numbers, 538
        tcpdump and wireshark, 537
        TCP transfers data, 538
        three-way handshake, 538
    test environment, 528
CICS, *see* Customer information control
    system (CICS)
CICS Transaction Gateways (CTGs), 299
Cilium networks
    configuration, 553
    correlation, 553
    demo application
        coreapi, 557
        distributed traces, 559
        error rate, 557
        external networks, 557
        microservices, 556
        service map, 558
        trace propagation, 558–560
    deployment, 554–556
    features, 560
    Hubble platform, 545

INDEX

ingress capabilities, 568, 569
L7 network
    architecture, 551
    benefits, 549
    Cilium networks, 550, 551
    cloud provider, 550
    connectivity and performance, 549
    connectivity problems, 552
    HTTP golden signals, 551
    infrastructure platforms, 549
    network connectivity, 549
    propagating traces, 552
    service messages, 551
    signal *vs.* noise problem, 552
    traditional network, 550
multiple clusters, 566, 567
networking/security, 543–551
network policies, 552
    failure creation, 561
    Kubernetes deployments, 562
    L3/L4 security, 563, 564
    L7 policies, 564, 565
    star application, 562
service meshes, 567, 568
CLI, *see* Command line interface (CLI)
CloudFront AWS
    agent configuration, 202
    B3 propagation, 201
    B3 Propagation flow, 199
    collector, 202
    demo process, 199
    managed services, 200
    requirements, 200
    routing requests and responses, 201
    scripts, 200
    Spring Boot, 199, 200
CLS, *see* Cumulative layout change (CLS)

CMDB, *see* Configuration management database (CMDB)
CMS, *see* Concurrent Mark Sweep (CMS)
CNI, *see* Container network interface (CNI)
Command line interface (CLI), 546
Concurrent Mark Sweep (CMS), 26
Configuration management database (CMDB)
    autoscaling, 741
    benefits, 738
    centric observability, 741
    change management, 738
    configuration items (CIs), 738
    data quality, 739
    entities, 739
    failures, 739
    hardware/software/networks, 737
    incident management, 738
    operational activities, 739
    operational architecture, 741
    operations, 738–741
    problem management, 738
    relationship, 740
Congestion
    client/server, 462, 463
    Ethernet link, 460
    inbound messages (rx), 463
    network process, 461
    outbound messages (tx), 463
    received server packets, 465
    send/receive networks, 461
    sent client packets, 464
    timestamping process, 462
    transmissions, 461
Container network interface (CNI), 543

INDEX

Coroutines
    blocking and non-blocking, 685
    callback methods, 684
    coroutines, 686, 687
    epoll, 685
    synchronous, 684
    WebFlux, 686, 687

Correlations
    API information, 723
    aggregation/filtering, 16
    businesses, applications, and infrastructures, 14
    cluster settings, 722
    dashboard, 17
    dashboards, 96
    differences, 721
    Dynatrace, 721
    distributed trace, 13
    events, 13
    event pattern, 727
    fund transfer process, 14
    Grafana, 108–116
    honeycomb/Elasticsearch, 721
    internal structure, 16
    metric algorithm, 725, 726
    metrics, 721, 723
    o11y Shop demo, 141–152
    OpenTelemetry pipeline, 722
    package installation, 724
    performance metrics, 725, 726
    Prometheus, 721
    signals, 13, 95, 96, 721
    structure and relationship, 15
    structure and relationships, 16
    suspected_metrics, 723
    system resources, 14
    technology stack, 17
    The New Stack (TNS), 117–132
    traces
        anomaly detection, 103
        distributed/system, 96–98
        error messages and counts, 104
        events, 98, 99
        flame graphs, 101
        infrastructure network, 105, 106
        logs, 99, 101, 104, 105, 107
        metrics, 102, 106, 107
        non-blocking, 97
        profiles, 100, 101
        resource level, 98
        RUM system, 102, 103
        service maps, 106
        technical benefits, 101
        visualization, 726–729

CPI, *see* Cycles per instruction (CPI)
CPU, *see* Central processing unit (CPU)
CRM, *see* Customer relationship management (CRM)
CTGs, *see* CICS Transaction Gateways (CTGs)
Cumulative layout change (CLS), 64
Customer information control system (CICS)
    access channels, 297
    client application, 298
    CTG adapter, 300
    demo application, 297, 298
    IMS databases, 296
    interfaces, 299
    legacy systems, 301
    region listeners/filesystems, 297
    socket communications, 298
    UCC server, 299
Customer relationship management (CRM), 356–359
Cycles per instruction (CPI), 468

D

Data analysis techniques
  aggregations (*see* Aggregations)
  anomaly detection
    grade and confidence, 593
    OpenSearch, 593
    perspectives, 593, 594
    results index, 594–599
    unsupervised learning, 592
  commercial observability, 609
  data utilization, 610
  indexing, 608
  logs, 609
  Promscale (*see* Promscale processes)
  root cause analysis, 610
  SQL data, 611–613
  technical dashboards, 610
Direct memory access (DMA), 387
DMA, *see* Direct memory access (DMA)
Druid, 650
Druid aggregations
  broker nodes, 656
  characteristics, 651
  clusters, 651
  component relationships, 653–655
  coordinator node, 656
  features, 651
  GROUP BY/TopN, 651
  historical nodes, 655
  index methods, 652
  observability
    components, 663
    incorrect instrumentation, 668
    log levels, 666, 667
    metrics, 664–666
    profiles, 669, 670
    remote debugging, 663
    traces, 667–669
  performance tuning
    caching, 662
    components, 659
    data analytics platforms, 656
    indexing service, 660
    multitenancy, 662
    parameters, 658
    queries, 662
    read path, 657, 661–663
    rollups, 660
    segment creation, 661
    shards and diagnose problems, 656
    system tuning, 658
    write path, 657, 659, 660
  real-time nodes, 654
  rollups, 652
  schema-less searches, 652
  segment, 654

E

EAI server, *see* Enterprise application integration (EAI) server
eBPF, *see* Extended Berkeley Packet Filter (eBPF)
ECS, *see* Elastic Common Schema (ECS)
Elastic Common Schema (ECS), 639–643
Enterprise application integration (EAI) server
  banking industry, 318
  BPM server outputs, 236
  development tool, 330
  internal structure, 235
  legacy systems, 233, 236, 328–330
  outputting process, 235
  problems, 234

Enterprise application integration (EAI) server (*cont.*)
    protocols/transformations, 234
    server processing, 768, 769
    Tuxedo method, 296
    webMethods, 236
Enterprise resource planning (ERP), 301–303, 305
ERPm, *see* Enterprise resource planning (ERP)
ETL, *see* Extract, Transform and Load (ETL)
Extended Berkeley Packet Filter (eBPF)
    BCC/bpftrace
        capabilities, 515
        filter expressions, 509
        fork() and exevc() methods, 512
        ftrace and strace, 517, 518
        funclatency, 515–517
        histogram format, 511
        histogram statistics, 506
        IO-heavy systems, 506
        kernel static instrumentation, 512–514
        latency identification, 507
        LLVM IR and LLVM libraries, 505
        OpenTelemetry extension, 511
        performance and drives, 506
        purposes/priorities, 521
        READ system call, 511
        runqlat tool, 515
        runqlen tool, 515
        strace tool, 518–521
        sys_execve() method, 512
        system utilities, 507
        tracepoint, 507–511
    bytecode instrumentation, 504
    compiled code, 504
    component, 505
    PCP solution, 521–527
    profiling methods, 504
    system traces, 504
Extract, Transform and Load (ETL), 314, 315
    failure list data model, 770, 771

F

Failure list data model
    API server processing, 765, 766
    categories, 758
    cluster failures, 763–765
    data consistency
        MDM servers, 775, 776
        orchestration server, 774
        order/payment processes, 774
        product server processing, 775
    data pipeline failures, 773, 774
    large and medium categories, 758
    legacy middleware, 758, 767
        BPM server, 769, 770
        EAI server processing, 768, 769
        ETL pipelines, 770, 771
        MFT server, 771–773
    message server, 766
    microservice development, 776, 777
    processing flow, 756
    subcategories, 757
    system resources, 759
        Java fails, 762
        Kernel failures, 761
        network failures, 759, 760
        system resources, 760
        traces, 760, 761
        ultra-low-latency applications, 761, 762
    transaction processing, 756

INDEX

FID, *see* First-input response time (FID)
Field Manipulation Language (FML)
    method, 294
FileNet process designer, 315, 316
First-input response time (FID), 64
FML method, *see* Field Manipulation
    Language (FML) method)

G

Game operation, 364
    CQRS pattern, 366, 367
    demo architecture, 367–370
    development and operation, 364
    Kubernetes operators, 365
    microservices, 365
    monolithic architecture, 366
    multiple Kubernetes clusters, 365
    observability architecture, 370
        logs, 370, 371
        metrics, 371, 372
        remote debugging, 373, 374
        traces, 372, 373
    resource provisioning, 366
Garbage collection, 26
    anomaly detection, 28
    collectors, 26
    concurrent, 27
    generational management, 26
    less memory, 28
    logs and statistics, 27
    memory leaks, 27, 28
    object creation/retention, 27
    OOM errors, 27
    optimization, 26
    paging/swapping, 27
    parameters, 26
GCP, *see* Google cloud platform (GCP)

Gen AI, *see* Generative AI (Gen AI)
Generative AI (Gen AI), 713
    OpenSearch database, 797
Google cloud platform (GCP), 203–212
Grafana
    correlations
        dashboard version, 108
        demo configuration, 112–114
        exemplars, 109
        implementation, 108
        logs-traces, 114, 115
        metrics-traces, 110–114
        Prometheus, 108–110
        requests, errors, and
            duration (RED), 110
        spanmetric metrics, 110
        tempo configuration file, 112
        trace-to-log, 115, 116
    Faro, 18
    oservability
        code description, 134, 135
        Go application, 132
        log/trace, 134
        Loki data sources, 139
        manual instrumentation, 131–134
        metric/trace, 133
        Prometheus data sources, 140
        setup process, 139–141
        system configuration, 136–139
        Tempo data sources, 140
    Pyroscope, 18
    RUM demo, 56

H

Hierarchical Navigable Small World
    (HNSW), 790
HNSW, *see* Hierarchical Navigable Small
    World (HNSW)

INDEX

Horizontal Pod Autoscaler (HPA), 742
HPA, *see* Horizontal Pod Autoscaler (HPA)

I

IDT, *see* Interrupt descriptor table (IDT)
Infrastructure observability
    application configuration, 443, 444
    application observability, 446
    approaches, 443
    aspects, 446
    Chaos, 528
    Cilium, 560–570
    containers and hypervisors, 447
    cost-effective approach, 443
    eBPF (*see* Extended Berkeley Packet Filter (eBPF))
    Linux kernel, 446
    multiple layers, 445
    networking and security, 543–551
    networks, 447
    system resources, 446
    system traces (*see* System traces)
    terminology, 444, 445
Interrupt descriptor table (IDT), 388
Interrupt service routine (ISR), 388
Inverted filesystem (IVF), 790
ISR, *see* Interrupt service routine (ISR)
IVF, *see* Inverted filesystem (IVF)

J

Java
    thread type, 53
Java applications, 252
Java Flight Recorder (JFR), 698
Java programming
    CPU profile
        contents, 681
        duration methods, 676
        garbage collection, 674
        HTTP endpoint, 679
        latency types, 677
        methods, 671
        monitoring/memory, 673
        OOM error, 675
        parameters, 672
        plans/threads/memory dumps, 679
        profiles, 677, 678
        query-specific duration, 679
        sampling, 672, 675
        synchronization block, 674
        thread dumps, 681, 682
        thread status, 674
        VisualVM, 683
        zero performance overhead, 677
        zombie threads, 673
    internal processes, 670
    JVM (*see* Java Virtual Machine (JVM))
    non-blocking, 705–711
        ExecutorService, 706
        flow process, 704
        Grafana trace, 709
        parallel scheduler, 706
        reactor components, 705
        reactor-http-epoll, 707
        reactor-http-epoll threads, 709
        reactor-http-epoll process, 708
        schedulers, 706
        scheduling, 706
        threads, 705
        trace context, 705
        WebClient, 705
        WebFlux thread profile, 707
    profiles, 670
    sampling, 671

INDEX

Spring WebFlux, 703, 704
system resources, 670
system traces, 478
thread implementation, 687
    Java threads, 688, 689
    kernel threads, 687
    lightweight processes, 688
    user threads, 688
thread state, 484
types of, 671
Java Virtual Machine (JVM)
    asynchronous/non-blocking, 25
    context switches, 683
    coroutines, 685–688
    failure list data model, 763
    garbage collection, 26–28
    internal processes, 684
    JIT compilation, 26
    memory leaks and thread issues, 24
    parallel processing and
        concurrency, 26
    parameters, 25
    system performance, 683
    threads, 25
    thread scheduling, 683
    virtual threads (*see* Virtual threads)
JFR, *see* Java Flight Recorder (JFR)
JVM, *see* Java Virtual Machine (JVM)

K

Kernel (operating system)
    BCC/bpftrace, 512–514
    Cassandra cluster, 494
    concepts, 480
    concurrency, 490
    context switches, 489, 490
    data structures, 482, 483
    development process
        device drivers, 500, 502, 503
        dynamic modules, 500
        KUtrace, 500
        modules, 500–502
        NVIDIA flow, 503, 504
        system resources/process, 499
    disk IO/CPU, 480–482
    disk problem, 494, 495
    file descriptor, 486–488
    flow/data structure, 479
    fork() method, 482
    interrupts, 490–492
        CPU processing, 491
        packet processing, 491
        post-interrupt techniques, 491
    memory, 494
    multitasking techniques, 489
    network application
        active/passive closers, 496
        application timeouts, 498
        backlog, 498
        connection pool method, 497
        connection timeout, 498
        database applications, 498
        ephemeral ports, 498
        keepalive, 497
        parameters, 497
        sending and receiving data,
            495, 496
        sockets, 497
        web service, 498
    problematic thread, 484
    race condition, 490
    RUNNABLE threads, 485
    run-queued process, 483
    scheduling, 488
    select/poll/epoll techniques, 487

Kernel (operating system) (*cont.*)
   server/file operation, 487
   stack traces, 483–485
   switches flow, 484
   synchronization, 490
   system calls, 485, 486
   task_struct/thread_info structures, 483
   timer methods, 492–494
   user-level process, 482
k-Nearest Neighbor (k-NN), 789
   OpenSearch cluster, 789–795
k-NN, *see* k-Nearest Neighbor (k-NN)
KSM, *see* Kube-state-metrics (KSM)
Kubernetes Event-Driven
      Autoscaling (KEDA)
   advantage, 753
   deployment/StatefulSets, 751
   event source, 752
   lifecycle, 752
   performance, 755
   Prometheus metrics, 753
   ScaleObject/PodToScaler, 754
   source code, 753
kube-state-metrics (KSM), 465

L

Large language model (LLM), 713,
     736, 809
   knowledge/computational
     capabilities, 786
   LangChain, 783
   OpenSearch database, 798
   plan-execute-reflect agent, 815
   retrieval-augmented generation, 782
   VectorDBTool, 812
Linux
   Chaos (*see* Chaos engineering)
   network observability, 543
LLM, *see* Large language model (LLM)
Low-level methods
   abnormal transactions/normal
     behavior, 38
   application observability, 37
   business process, 36
   distributed trace, 39
   eBPF, 40
   failures, 37
   infrastructure failures, 36
   infrastructure signals, 40
   KUtrace system trace, 39
   log files, 38
   metrics, 38
   profile data, 37
   profiles, 38
   propagation/overlapping failures, 41
     configuration conditions, 42
     CPU and IO latency, 43
     downstream problems, 41, 42
     incorrect timeout settings, 43, 44
     microservices failures, 45, 46
     non-blocking calls, 43
     SOA and microservices, 41
     TCP connection, 45
     threads, 44, 45
   system traces, 38, 40
   visualization, 39

M

Machine learning (ML)
   alerts and dashboards, 579
   algorithm, 579
   analysis techniques, 592
   configuration, 578
   data preprocessing, 736

detector creation
    analyzing populations, 588–590
    automated scripts, 589
    bucket analysis, 591, 592
    categories, 587, 588
    configurations, 585
    malicious users, 589
    patterning and data profiling, 590, 591
    ratio analysis, 585–587
    snoopers, 589
internal index, 579
intrusion detection system, 581
IT operational data, 733
IT operators, 581–585
    Aggregation analysis, 584
    detector creation, 582, 585
    feature, 582
    grade/confidence analysis, 584
    real-time view, 583
    training/testing, 582
    web log, 582
profile/events, 580
real-time and batch, 579
refrigerator, 581
time series data, 580
unsupervised learning, 580
vector embedding, 788
Managed File Transfer (MFT), 307, 308, 771–773
Master data management (MDM), 305, 306
MCP, *see* Model Context Protocol (MCP)
MDM, *see* Master data management (MDM)
MFT, *see* Managed File Transfer (MFT)
ML, *see* Machine learning (ML)
Model Context Protocol (MCP), 816

AI agent and external tool, 844
AI observability
    agent sources, 880, 881
    demo application, 877
    internal knowledge bases, 877
    LangGraph source, 878
    LangGraph workflow, 879
    Library instrumentation, 881, 882
    monitoring, 877
    OpenLLMetry output, 877, 878
    source code, 878, 879
    traces, 882
architect's workflow, 858, 859
architecture, 846
automation workflow, 861
client mode, 849–851
developer's workflow, 860
development, 851, 852
differences, 853
intermediary layer, 845
key benefits, 845
LangChain
    server mode, 846–849
LangGraph
    agent interfaces, 853
    automation, 861
    automation tools, 867
    configuring workflows, 862
    create_react_agent, 863
    disadvantages, 864
    human-in-the-loop (HITL), 864, 865
    LangChain, 862
    OpenSearch, 854, 855
    review/approval node, 865, 866
    steps, 861
    studio UI, 854
    technologies, 861

INDEX

Model Context Protocol (MCP) (*cont.*)
    workflow, 867
    workflows, 855
  line operator workflow, 857
  platform workflow, 856
  processing flow, 845
  root cause analysis, 853
  server mode, 846–849
  Slackbots
    app home tab, 873
    communication tool, 872
    definition, 875
    features, 872
    OpenSearch knowledge base, 874
    user interface (UI), 874, 875
    workflows, 873
  speech recognition
    long-term memory, 871
    OpenSearch knowledge base, 872
  SRE workflow, 857, 858
  Streamlit
    Python library, 869
    screen structure, 867
    source code, 869, 870
    supervisor pattern, 868, 869
    user interface, 871
    workflow, 868
  testing/deployment, 859
  workflow automation, 876
    e-commerce channels, 876
    Twilio, 876

N

Natural language processing (NLP), 837–839, 871
Natural language queries (NLQ), 837
Network interface card (NIC), 382
Network observability
  Cilium network policies, 543
  CNI provider, 543
  dependency, 542
  filter packets, 541
  Grafana plugin, 548, 549
  Hubble
    CLI extends, 546
    component, 545
    dashboards, 549
    degradation problems, 545
    filtering capabilities, 548
    service map, 547, 548
    status command, 545
    UI abstracts, 546–548
  IP table rules, 542
  metrics, 544
    drops, 544
    durations per seconds, 544
    requests, 544
  monitoring capabilities, 543
  traditional and Cilium methods, 542
  troubleshooting, 543
Network provisioning module
  inventory solution
    application events, 361
    events, 362–364
    interface, 362
    metasolv resources, 360, 361
  legacy system, 359
  workforce management, 363, 364
NIC, *see* Network interface card (NIC)
NLP, *see* Natural language processing (NLP)
NLQ, *see* Natural language queries (NLQ)

O

o11y Shop demo
  architecture, 141, 142
  characteristics, 142, 143
  code description, 143-146
  configuration, 141, 146-148
  Flask application, 144
  installation script, 146
  microservices, 142
  OpenSearch, 148-152
  problem, 141
  reliability/availability, 146
Observability, 7
  aggregation (*see* Aggregation)
  AIOps (*see* Artificial intelligence for IT operations (AIOps))
  analytics (*see* Data analysis techniques)
  anomaly detection, 571
  application and infrastructure, 8
  application/infrastructure level, 607, 608
  architecture, 280, 282
  bank demo, 279
  banking (*see* Banking industry)
  broad themes, 279
  categories, 17
  concurrency/consistency issues, 281
  correlations, 11
  data analysis, 9
  data utilization, 607
  debugging, 77, 78
  domains, 283
  eBPF dashboard, 18
  events
    advantages, 79
    anomalies, 85-87
    business process, 78
    data flow, 79
    deployments, 84
    fund transfer, 83
    process flow, 82, 83
    product categories, 84
    relational database, 85
    sourcing trace, 79-81
    transactions, 84
    types, 79
  failure case
    data model, 780, 781
    errors, 778-781
    operations/errors, 780
    structure, 781
  Faro, 18
  internal and external services, 281
  Java (*see* Java programming)
  KUtrace, 18
  live debugging, 393
  logging system
    commercial agents, 50
    logback library, 53-55
    MDC processing, 50
    non-blocking approach, 51
    OpenTelemetry agents, 48, 49, 51
    passing, 50
    processing order, 54
    requirements, 47
    Spring Boot processes, 48
    spring processing, 55
    trace comparison, 52, 53
    trace contexts, 49
    WebFlux, 55
  logs/metrics, 11
  long-term investment, 12
  metrics, 394
  microservices, 145

INDEX

Observability (*cont.*)
   online game, 364–374
   OpenSearch database, 18, 814–822
   OpenTelemetry (*see*
      OpenTelemetry demo)
   overview, 2, 3
   pipelines, 8
   profiles
      architecture, 70–72
      disadvantages, 71
      flame graph, 72–74
      HotROD, 75–77
      metrics and traces, 70
      multiple development
        languages, 70
      Pyroscope Helm chart, 75
      statistical/sampling profiles, 70
      thread dumps, 71
      types, 69
   profiles/traces, 12
   Promscale, 18
   Pyroscope, 18
   requirements, 283, 393
   RUM (*see* Real user monitoring (RUM))
   service-level issues, 281
   signals/solutions
      anomaly detection, 46
      configuration, 46
      constraints/issues, 46
      debugging, 47
      events, 46
      logs/traces, 46
      metric structure, 46
      profiles, 47
      real-time monitoring, 47
   technical failures, 280
   telecom (*see* Telecom processes)
   Telecom demo, 280
   traces (*see* Trace-centric approach)
   trading option, 374–392
   traditional monitoring, 4
   visualizations, 153
Online gaming process, *see* Game
     operation
OOM, *see* OutOfMemoryError (OOM)
OpenSearch
   correlation, 151
   index lookup, 151
   log search, 150
   o11y Shop demo, 148–152
   service map, 149
   service screen, 150
   trace detail, 149
OpenSearch database
   ALOps model, 797
      agents, 801
      anomaly detection, 799
      CentOS, 801
      chatbot/SIEM, 799
      cluster configuration, 802
      components, 800
      configurations, 798, 799
      connectors, 809, 810
      context pane, 807
      databases, 801
      embedding models, 799, 801–804,
        812, 813
      failures, 808
      flow agent, 811
      index creation, 806, 807
      index references, 806
      inferences, 813
      MLModelTool, 812
      parameters, 813
      pipeline creation, 805
      post-processing, 801

pretrained models, 800
principle of, 797
search/ingest/models, 799
semantic search, 799, 809
text embedding model, 811
types of, 798
vector database, 799
VectorDBTool, 812
observability
  agent framework, 816
  features, 814
  key features, 816
  memory ID/track interactions, 820
  OpenAI result, 821
  plan-execute-reflect agent, 815, 816
  solutions, 815
  time-consuming, 816
  traces/logs, 815
  workflow, 817
root cause analysis (RCA), 822–832
server mode, 846–849
Vector database
  approximate k-NN, 792
  attributes, 791
  components, 792
  documents, 792
  HNSW algorithm, 790
  IVF algorithm, 790
  k-NN plugin, 789, 790
  LangChain application, 796
  NMSLIB, FAISS, and Lucene libraries, 790
  painless scripts, 795
  process scoring scripts, 796
  representation, 792
  scoring scripts, 793
  search methods, 790
  unique attributes, 789

OpenTelemetry demo
  agents, 405
  automated instrumentation, 418, 419
  baggage context, 423, 424
  collector, 414, 415
  commercial observability, 419–421
  components, 396
  correlation configuration, 404
  dashboards, 398
  demo applications, 396
  deployment, 397
  features, 394, 395
  flag configuration, 397
  Grafana dashboard, 404
  Jaeger search, 399
  live debugging, 421–423
  Locust load testing, 398
  methods, 399
  microservices flow, 395
  observability pipelines, 396
  profiles
    catalog services, 402, 403
    correlation processes, 401
    Grafana dashboards, 401
    methods, 400
    pull/push method, 400
    Pyroscope, 399
    recommendation service, 401, 402
    tempo/pyroscope, 404–406
  Promscale kubernetes, 432–438
  recommendation service, 398
  RUM, 415–418
  SLOs app, 405–413
    approach, 405
    backend error, 408
    business-dashboards, 406
    components, 412
    configuration process, 408

OpenTelemetry demo (*cont.*)
    dashboard development, 410
    dashboards, 406, 412
    data sources, 411
    error budgets and burn
      rates, 409–411
    error messages, 407
    histograms, 409
    log dashboard, 413
    RED/USE/Google SRE, 411
    root cause analysis, 406
    technical/business errors, 408
    user's perspective, 407
    visualization, 411
    windows and alerts
      implementation, 410
    span attributes
      annotations, 429–432
      anomaly detection, 427, 428
      chaos engineering, 428
      characteristics, 425
      commercial observability, 429
      feature flags, 425–430
      getAds method, 428
      scenarios, 425
    SQL-centric data analytics, 439–441
    toggles, 397
OpenTelemetry extensions
    @Advice method, 256
    bytecode instrumentation, 253–257
    commercial agents, 253
    concepts/terminology, 252
    debugging extension
      Advice method, 263
      agents, 263
      enable option, 264
    extension demo
      automated instrumentation, 259
      bytecode conversion, 258
      cross concerns, 258, 259
      description, 257–262
      instrumentation, 262
      onEnter/onExit method, 261
      TypeInstrumentation class, 259, 260
    instrumentation, 252
    internal operation, 254
    Java applications, 252
    manual instrumentation, 253
OpenTelemetry pipeline
    correlation, 722
OpenTracing shim
    commercial observability, 196
    instrumentation, 194, 196
    manual instrumentation, 195
    migration, 194
    OpenTelemetry APIs, 195
Operational support systems (OSS),
    338, 359
Oracle, 305–307
OSS, *see* Operational support
    systems (OSS)
OutOfMemoryError (OOM), 27

P, Q

Parallel Thread Execution (PTX), 503
PCP, *see* Performance Co-Pilot (PCP)
Percentile analysis, 617
Performance Co-Pilot (PCP), 18, 39
    bpftrace scripts, 526, 527
    components, 522
    configuration, 524–526
    data sources, 522
    demo application, 525–527
    Grafana dashboard, 521
    metrics, 523

INDEX

server process, 522
stateless model, 521
Pipeline processing language (PPL), 837
PLT, *see* Procedure linkage table (PLT)
PPL, *see* Pipeline processing
  language (PPL)
Presto case study
  advantage, 636
  analytics frameworks, 638, 639
  architecture, 637
  column-oriented storage, 645
  configuration, 646–650
  data catalog, 650
  data projects, 636
  features, 636
  federated query, 637
  glue data catalog processing, 649
  hive metastore, 639
  join and aggregation processes, 645
  memory consumption, 644
  OpenTelemetry Data Model, 639
  pluggable storage design, 643
  Prometheus/Elasticsearch
    instances, 638
  query execution, 643–645
  storage, 636
  STRUCT and ARRAY types, 648
Procedure linkage table (PLT), 389
Promscale processes
  advantages, 615
  approaches, 618
  approximate percentile, 617
  commercial observability, 618
  default methods, 617
  disadvantages, 615
  features, 614, 615
  hypermethods, 617
  logs, 614

metrics, 614, 619, 620
  advantages, 619
  configuration, 620, 621
  SQL, 621–625
metrics/traces, 614
OpenTelemetry demo, 432–438
percentile_cont method, 617
percentile_agg, 617
Prometheus, 616
span count, 614
trace table
  PostgreSQL tables, 625
  span table, 627
  system configuration, 626
Propagation
  adapters, 179
  agent's process flow, 188, 189
  API server, 191
  automated instrumentation, 188
  B3 contexts, 185
  baggage, 182, 187
  baggage context
    components, 192
    development procedure, 193
    message server, 193
    transaction/request/order IDs, 193
  black box system, 237, 238
  collector settings, 187
  commercial observability, 180, 187
    agent feature, 269
    agents, 265, 272–274
    automation features, 266–272
    different traces, 274
    events, 269
    micrometer traces, 265
    problems/internal structure, 264
    pros/cons, 264
    request attributes, 268

907

INDEX

Propagation (*cont.*)
    scenarios, 273
    span entry point, 266
    standardized headers, 273
    traceparent, 272
    tracestate, 273, 274
    tracestate automation feature, 267
    tracestate demo, 274–277
  composite, 184, 185
  configuration, 186, 187
  deployment, 185, 186
  E2E traces, 179
  EAI servers, 233–237
  extension packages, 185
  format, 178
  functions, 188
  HTTP request, 183
  implementation, 179
  inbound and outbound spans, 192
  injects/extracts, 184
  JMS publisher, 189, 190
  managed services, 196
    clients/servers, 197
    CloudFront, 199–202
    different traces, 198
    internal operations, 197
    lambdas and CloudWatch logs, 197
    publishing messages, 211–217
    PubSub, 202–211
    spans, 198
    types, 196
  manual instrumentation, 188, 190, 191
  message server, 192
  microservices, 177
  observability backend, 177
  OpenTelemetry, 182, 252–264
  OpenTracing shim, 194–196
  publisher and subscriber, 178
  server frameworks
    application-specific traces, 241
    commercial observability, 245–247
    detail screen, 247
    EAI/API servers, 239
    micrometer traces, 243, 244
    middleware, 239
    policies/filters, 241
    process flow, 245
    screen configuration, 246
    SDK commercial observability, 241–243
    traces configuration, 240
    transaction, 240
    upstream and downstream fails, 245
    WebSocket demo, 247–252
  SQS span, 213
  textmap, 183, 184
  trace specification
    HTTP headers, 187
  transferring process, 177
  transferred message, 179
  upstream and downstream options, 182
  vendor protocols, 185
  W3C/composite, 182
PTX, *see* Parallel Thread Execution (PTX)
Publishers/subscribers (PubSub) services
  arc diagram, 203
  asynchronous traces, 204
  attributes, 203
  backoffice processes, 210
  client/server, 204
  environment variables, 207
  header, 204
  load balancing, 203
  manual instrumentation, 210

message and batch processing, 211
message data, 203
message server, 210
OpenTelemetry collector, 207
order key, 203
publisher span, 208
publish/receive messages, 202
REST request, 204, 208
source code, 206
subscriber span, 209
system configuration, 206
terminology, 204
traceparent, 205
trace results, 210
PubSub services, *see* Publishers/subscribers (PubSub) services

R

RAG, *see* Retrieval-Augmented Generation (RAG)
Random Cut Forest (RCF), 586
RCA, *see* Root cause analysis (RCA)
RCF, *see* Random Cut Forest (RCF)
Real user monitoring (RUM), 9, 13, 415–418
    commercial observability
        backend storage, 68
        distributed traces, 66
        events, 67
        microservices, 66
        object relationships, 67
        session records, 66
        trace configuration, 66
        web page, 67
    demo option
        correlation, 58–62
        data visualization, 62

        distributed traces, 61
        events, 58
        frontend application, 62
        set up, 58
        test scenario, 59
        trace tools, 59
    Grafana frontend/backend, 56
    instrumentation, 57
    message servers, 55
    metrics
        configuration, 64
        dashboard layout, 62
        data source, 63
        Loki configuration file, 64
        TTFB/FCP/LCP, 63
        web vitals, 63
    OpenTelemetry procedure, 57
    synthetic testing, 55
    system signal, 102, 103
    trace-centric approach, 176
    trace process flow, 56
Remote Method Call (RFC), 301
Retrieval-Augmented Generation (RAG)
    data management, 841, 842
    features, 833
    guardrail model, 839–841
    keyword search, 883
    LangChain, 783
        advantages, 783
        agents process, 785, 786
        chains, 784
        memory, 787
        models, 783
        modules, 783
        prompt templates, 784
        tools, 786, 787
    MCP (*see* Model Context Protocol (MCP))

INDEX

Retrieval-Augmented Generation
    (RAG) (*cont.*)
  natural language processing, 837–839
  observability, 814–822
  post-processing, 842–844
  reranking, 833–837
  root cause analysis
    anomaly and delays, 884
    approaches and workflows, 883
    Bedrock results, 831
    commercial observability, 885
    connector, 823
    conversational searching, 822
    definition, 883
    development, 832
    distributed trace, 884
    error messages, 884
    index creation, 825, 826
    index transform process, 886, 887
    latency, 884
    memory object, 827
    model creation, 829
    model ID, 829
    network span, 885
    observability errors, 883
    OpenAI results, 827–829
    OpenSearch, 822–832
    registration, 824
    response, 830
    retrieves data, 822
    search pipeline, 825
    storing conversation, 832
    testing model, 829
    workflow, 886
  searching data
    indexing/querying/post-
      processing, 788
    OpenSearch, 789–795
    semantic searches, 789
    technologies, 788, 789
    vector database, 788, 789
  slack conversations, 883
  system resources, 842
  types of, 782
  vector embeddings/semantic
      search, 883
    confluence ingest pipeline, 883
RFC, *see* Remote Method Call (RFC)
Root cause analysis (RCA), 1
  agents, 5
  AIOps (*see* Artificial intelligence for IT
      operations (AIOps))
  analyzing individual
      transactions, 29–36
  approaches, 5, 6
  correlation (*see* Correlations)
  data model, 731
    asset, 90
    benefits, 91
    business context, 91
    correlation, 88
    dashboards, 87
    infrastructure context, 89
    interface, 90
    kernel and system resources, 91
    kernel's methods, 89
    method level, 88
    non-instrumented traces, 88
    problems/limitations, 87
    single agent, 89
    system configuration, 91
    system resources, 89
    technical challenges, 91
  definition, 12
  degradation and issues, 6
  errors, 19

errors and failures, 1
forecasting/inference, 18
goals/description, 3, 4
horizontal/vertical line, 7, 8
individual request level, 19
infrastructure, 2
Java, 24–28
lower-level, 19
low-level methods, 36–47
observability (*see* Observability)
OpenSearch, 822–832
performance problems, 20
problem identification, 19
relationships, 13
resources settings
    cluster operation, 22
    consensus protocols, 22
    data consistency, 22
    Elasticsearch, 23
    external cloud/SaaS services, 24
    fault tolerance, 22
    management tasks, 22
    partitioning and sharding, 22
    problems and failures, 21
    Prometheus, 23
    rebalancing, 22
    replication, 22
    resource limitation, 20, 21
    threads and connection pools, 20
services and reduce costs, 1
SREs (*see* Site reliability
    engineer (SRE))
static systems, 7
system resources, 6
terminology, 1
traces, 171
troubleshooting, 4
visualizations (*see* Visualizations)

RUM, *see* Real user monitoring (RUM)

S

SAG, *see* SWIFT Alliance Gateway (SAG)
SAP, *see* System, application and
    products (SAP)
Server Sent Event (SSE), 845
Simple Queue Service (SQS)
    publisher, 211, 212
    subscribers
        architectural configurations, 213
        attributes, 217
        debug problems, 212
        links, 214–216
        message identifiers, 216, 217
        metrics, 213
        queue structures, 214
    trace context, 211
Simple Text Oriented Messaging Protocol
    (STOMP), 248
Site reliability engineer (SRE), 1, 6
    challenging role, 92
    data model, 92
    trace-centric approach, 172
Spring WebFlux, 703, 704
SQL, *see* Structured Query
    Language (SQL)
SQS, *see* Simple Queue Service (SQS)
SRE, *see* Site reliability engineer (SRE)
SSE, *see* Server Sent Event (SSE)
STOMP, *see* Simple Text Oriented
    Messaging Protocol (STOMP)
Structured Query Language (SQL)
    algorithms and visualization, 611
    anomalies (*see* Anomaly detection)
    cumulative values, 613
    metric configuration, 620, 621

INDEX

Structured Query Language (SQL) (*cont.*)
   metrics, 611
   OpenSearch, 611
   OpenTelemetry demo, 439–441
   Promscale, 611
   query demos, 621–625
   rolling calculations, 612
   seasonality, 613
   time series, 611
   time series data, 612
   trace table
      concepts, 627
      downstream graph, 633
      downstream tables, 631
      duration pie chart, 629
      duration ratio, 630
      filtered time period, 627
      Grafana Tempo, 625
      heatmap, 629
      latency histogram, 628
      service graph, 632
      slow queries, 628
      system configuration, 626
      upstream and downstream
         tables, 632
SWIFT Alliance Gateway (SAG), 309–312
System, application and products
      (SAP), 301–303
System traces
   ftrace, 471–476
   saturation
      niostat, 467
System traces
   containers and hypervisors, 450
   correlation, 449
   detailed process sequence, 451
   distributed traces, 451
   E2E configuration, 449
   errors, 450
   ftrace
      debugging information, 472
      events, 473, 475
      handler methods, 474
      method declaration, 474
      sched event, 472
      sys_enter and sys_exit events, 473
      trace kernel methods, 471
      traceshark UI, 475
   kernel (*see* Kernel (operating system))
      preemption scheduling, 488
   Kubeshark, 476
   KUtrace
      configuration file, 453–458
      congestion, 460–465
      contention, 470, 471
      context switching, 460
      distributed traces, 452, 456
      interference, 468, 469
      lock contention, 470
      page faults, 467, 468
      saturation, 465–467
      synchronizing disks, 468
      system resources, 457
      thread scheduling, 458, 459
      user/kernel space, 452
      visualization, 459
      waiting, 458–460
   logs, 449
   metrics, 449, 450
   microservices, 449
   relationship, 448
   saturation, 465
      disk utilization, 467
      iostat tool, 466
      latency, 467
      vmstat tool, 466

system traces, 479
utilities, 476–479
    CPU, 477
    Java, 478
    network, 478
    stack traces, 477
    trace technologies, 479

T

TCP, *see* Transmission Control Protocol (TCP)
Telecom processes
    architecture, 341–343
        e-commerce orders, 342
        flow process, 342
        PoNR process, 343
    cancellation/revision processes, 336
    compensation, 335
    compensation types
        components, 345, 346
        configuration, 347
        header option, 348
        order process, 347
        revision processing, 346
    distributed system, 343
        2PC, 343
        Saga patterns, 343, 344
    distributed transactions, 335
    fallout management, 351, 352
    features, 334
    master data, 350, 351
    network provisioning (*see* Network provisioning module)
    orchestrations, 334
    orchestration server
        business/technical understanding, 338
        characteristics, 338
        compensation flow, 339
        component, 338
        distributed transactions, 337
        features, 338
        fulfillment process, 349
        implementation, 335, 339
        order fulfillment/network provisioning, 340
        order processing, 340, 341
        telecom task, 337, 338
        traces propagation, 336
        wireless and wireless product, 336
    order orchestration server
        administration, 353
        application, 352
        business layer, 357
        CRM process, 356–359
        events/logs, 352
        management screen, 353
        subscription/rating/billing components, 354–356
        wireline/wireless demo, 352
    order systems, 348–350
    process revision order, 345
    product/customer, 334
    references, 344
    wireline/wireless telecom, 334
The New Stack (TNS)
    API server, 118
    chaos engineering techniques, 119
    client code, 118
    configuration, 120–122
    correlation
        custom metric, 129
        dashboard screen, 123
        demo, 122, 123
        error Search screen, 125

913

The New Stack (TNS) (*cont.*)
    exemplar screen, 124–126
    log search screen, 127
    logs-traces, 125–128
    Loki-derived field screen, 126
    metric-trace, 124–126
    trace configuration, 128
    traces-logs, 131–134
demo requirements, 116
frontend/backend/data management, 117
LB, APP, and DB, 119
logs-traces, 122
metrics/traces/logs, 117
ObserveWithExemplar method, 118
vendor dependency, 117
YAML/Helm charts, 121
Thread synchronization, 33, 34
TNS, *see* The New Stack (TNS)
Trace-centric approach
    automation and consulting services, 173
    benefits, 174
    configuration, 176
    context objects, 180–182
    development standards, 174
    exceptions/requirements, 172
    goals, 173
    instrumentation problems, 174
    logs and traces, 175
    middleware, 171, 173
    propagation (*see* Propagation)
    requests/responses, 175
    working process, 176
Trading observability, 374
Transmission Control Protocol (TCP), 382
Tuxedo method, 293–296
    adapter configuration, 296
    buffer concepts, 294
    client/server process, 295
    communication methods, 294
    components, 293
    EAI server, 296
    environment variables, 294
    features, 293
    gateway, 294

U

UDP, *see* User Datagram Protocol (UDP)
UI, *see* User interfaces (UI)
Ultra-low latency applications
    application tuning
        components, 390
        gateways, 390
        order managers, 390
        sequencers, 390, 391
    bandwidth, 387
    caches
        access/allocation, 377
        data structures and algorithms, 378
        implicit structure, 378
        performances, 377
        spatial location, 378
        temporal locality, 377
    compilers, 388
        executable and linkable format, 388
        programming language, 389
        static/dynamic linking, 389
    context switching
        blocking system, 380
        cache misses, 380
        CPU task scheduling, 379
        high-cost operations, 380
        interrupt, 379
        multitasking, 378

threads, 380
user/kernel mode, 379
CPU tuning, 391
designing process, 375
kernel/user mode
   kernel bypass latency, 383
   networking, 382
   user space rotation, 382
   zero copy, 383
locks, 380
   contention, 381
   CPU resources, 381
   deadlock scenario, 381
   priority inversion, 381
   prototype designs, 382
logging/statistical calculations, 385, 386
memory allocation, 375
   management, 376
   memory fragmentation, 376
   pool, 376
   stack limit, 376
memory mapping file
   disadvantages, 384
   I/O performance, 384
   non-persistent, 383
   OS management, 384
   parallel access, 384
   persistent, 383
   random access and lazy loading, 384
   reading and writing files, 383
memory-sharing, 391
network latency, 391
network performance, 387, 388
reduce latency, 389
system calls, 385
throughput, 387
transmit/receive (TX/RX) path, 387
User Datagram Protocol (UDP), 382
User interfaces (UI), 547

V

Virtual threads
   advantage of, 690
   EchoClient profile, 697
   Java socket server and client, 695–697
   kernel thread model, 689
   lifecycle and state changes, 690
   pin observability, 698–703
   process of, 689
   profile capabilities, 702
   Spring Boot, 694–697
   status of, 691
   traditional thread model, 690
Visualizations
   annotations, 161
   dashboard configuration, 152
   dashboard development, 161
      advantages, 166
      characteristics, 162, 166
      dashboard layout, 166
      dashboards, 168
      data source, 167
      dimensions, 164
      filters, 164, 165
      joins, lookups, and filters, 165
      monitoring goroutines, 164
      table structure, 163
   flame graph, 158, 159
   heatmaps, 156
   histograms, 156
   Polystats, 153–155
   pre-aggregation, 152
   service maps, 155, 156

INDEX

Visualizations (*cont.*)
    state timelines, 158
    stats, 160
    time series, 157
    trace chart, 160

W, X, Y, Z

WAS, *see* Web Application Server (WAS)
Web Application Server (WAS), 5, 443
WebSocket process
    clients/servers, 247
    connection, 247
    header values, 250
    manual instrumentation, 248, 251
    OpenTelemetry dependencies, 249
    routing method, 250
    server, 251, 252
    StompHeaders, 249
    STOMP protocol, 248
    subscriber, 252
    subscriber method, 251
    textmap propagation, 249
    trace flow, 248
WFM, *see* Workforce management (WFM)
Workforce management (WFM), 363, 364

GPSR Compliance
The European Union's (EU) General Product Safety Regulation (GPSR) is a set of rules that requires consumer products to be safe and our obligations to ensure this.

If you have any concerns about our products, you can contact us on

ProductSafety@springernature.com

In case Publisher is established outside the EU, the EU authorized representative is:

Springer Nature Customer Service Center GmbH
Europaplatz 3
69115 Heidelberg, Germany